JOHN FERRIS is a Fellow of the Royal Society of Canada. He is Professor of History at the University of Calgary, an Honorary Professor at the Department of International Politics of the University of Aberystwyth, and the Department of Law and Politics, Brunel University, and is an Associate Member of Nuffield College, Oxford. He has written or edited eight books and over 100 articles or chapters on diplomatic, intelligence, imperial, international, military and strategic history and strategic studies. He lives in Calgary.

BEHIND THE ENIGMA

The Authorised History of GCHQ, Britain's Secret Cyber-Intelligence Agency

JOHN FERRIS

BLOOMSBURY PUBLISHING

LONDON · OXFORD · NEW YORK · NEW DELHI · SYDNEY

BLOOMSBURY PUBLISHING
Bloomsbury Publishing Plc
50 Bedford Square, London, WC1B 3DP, UK
29 Earlsfort Terrace, Dublin 2, Ireland

BLOOMSBURY, BLOOMSBURY PUBLISHING and the Diana logo are trademarks
of Bloomsbury Publishing Plc

First published in Great Britain 2020
This edition published 2021

A catalogue record for this book is available from the British Library

ISBN: HB: 978-1-5266-0546-7; TPB: 978-1-5266-0547-4; PB: 978-1-5266-0548-1;
EBOOK: 978-1-5266-0549-8

2 4 6 8 10 9 7 5 3

Typeset by Newgen KnowledgeWorks Pvt. Ltd., Chennai, India
Printed and bound in Great Britain by CPI Group (UK) Ltd, Croydon CR0 4YY

MIX
Paper | Supporting
responsible forestry
FSC® C171272

To find out more about our authors and books visit www.bloomsbury.com
and sign up for our newsletters

Contents

Foreword

This account of GCHQ's history brilliantly brings to life many of the people and events that have shaped this critical institution over the past 100 years. It shows how far we have come, as well as the broader impact made by our predecessors in developing the technology that enables all of our lives today.

I often wonder what the men and women who founded the Government Code & Cypher School in 1919 would make of the modern GCHQ – and what would they think of the organisation we are building for the future?

I hope they would recognise their legacy. Certainly, they would see themselves reflected in the brilliant people working tirelessly, and with great integrity, to keep the country safe. I expect they would be proud to see that the values they forged in those early days still underpin everything we do. They would also be pleased that the partnerships they started to develop – with Defence, MI5 and MI6, European allies and with the Five Eyes alliance and beyond – have not only stood the test of time but have become an integral part of what GCHQ is.

In 1919 the country was dealing with the fallout of a global pandemic and, as I write this, the world is battling a similar foe. This time we face a pandemic with a society that is utterly reliant on technology and data. A new technological age, the Fourth Industrial Revolution, means the way we live, work and interact with each other has changed beyond recognition. The threats we face are different too. The current crisis has shown that the security of health systems, the cyber-resilience of businesses and the ability of every citizen to safely live their lives online are central to recovery.

As it has done throughout its history, GCHQ is evolving rapidly to adapt to this new landscape. The creation of the National Cyber Security Centre (NCSC), as part of GCHQ, to build on our long-standing cyber-security remit and to protect the digital homeland, is the latest example. Professor Ferris's narrative shows us as an organisation set up to collect and analyse intelligence and with an amazing track record of shortening wars, countering hostile states, thwarting terrorist attacks and disrupting serious criminals. Today, the reality is that GCHQ is a citizen-facing intelligence and security enterprise with a globally recognised brand and reputation. We owe all of that to our predecessors.

Of course, GCHQ is still full of brilliant people, many with strong technical backgrounds, who are working at the forefront of this new digital landscape. They are the successors to Joan Clarke, Alan Turing, Gordon Welchman and countless other unnamed pioneers whose efforts are reflected in this account. Their work, often not attributed, continues to influence the development of technologies that underpin the UK's status as a great science, technology and cyber power.

GCHQ's mission means that much of our work is carried out in secret, but for some time we have been on a path towards greater transparency. Being open about 'what' we do, even where we cannot describe exactly where we are focused, or how we deliver operations, is crucial to maintaining our licence to operate. Indeed, it underpins the world-leading ethical and legal framework that is the basis for all of our work.

And that's why this book is so essential. Many of the stories are being told for the first time. It's right that they see the light of day so we can explain our past and be open about our failures as well as successes. I hope that not only will readers be better informed about our history, they will understand the role GCHQ has played on their behalf.

Professor Ferris was given access to significant portions of our archives, and he has done a huge amount of work to piece together the most consequential moments in our history. I am most grateful for his insights and professionalism. He has worked independently, and his views are, of course, his own. For those who want to research further and form their own conclusions, we are also releasing the source material to The National Archives.

This Authorised History is just the first chapter in the story of GCHQ. With the establishment of the NCSC, and the recent opening of our superb new offices in central Manchester, we can already see how the next chapter might unfold. Whatever its final shape and location, I know that GCHQ's future success will be assured if we retain and recruit a diverse mix of minds. This history shows that when we do, anything is possible.

Jeremy Fleming, Director GCHQ
June 2020

Introduction

The archives of the Government Communications Headquarters (GCHQ) stand at the end of a corridor in the basement of 'the Doughnut', its iconic headquarters at Cheltenham. Behind a specially secured door is a long rectangular room dominated by shelves holding thousands of boxes of documents. Halfway down the room is an enclosed cage, some 5 metres wide and 10 metres long. Metal columns stretch from metalled floor to ceiling, with bars spaced every foot apart on the cage. Few staff can open the cage. Within it are tens of thousands of paper files, none copied digitally. Each file contains the positive vetting record of a member of GCHQ – their personal secrets collected from interviews with friends and families before hiring. These records are intended to remain secret forever: they are read only under restrictions and destroyed whenever anyone dies. Nothing better typifies GCHQ than this focus on privacy for people who strip secrecy from Britain's foes.

Many people regard intelligence as magic, or the hidden master of policy. Only when you know the intelligence record, they think, can you understand how and why things really happened. Such folk believe that intelligence should be completely reliable, understood, useful, and used well. Evidence has no ambiguity. You should know what you need to know and acquire complete and accurate information whenever you wish. Intelligence eliminates uncertainty. The truth and nothing but the truth can be known. It shows what should be done, and the consequences of doing so. Actions taken on knowledge have the effect one intends, and nothing else. Perfect information can be perfectly usable, because action is easy. Anything less than perfection in comprehension and action is failure, which is rare and associated with idiots.

It all sounds simple, but reality is more complex. To understand an environment and act effectively within it are hard. Intelligence provides snippets of information, always containing error and surrounded by uncertainty. Mistakes and failures are inevitable in intelligence, the only questions being: how often and significant? Intelligence rarely affects the determination of policy. Frequently, it shapes the background to decisions, how statesmen understand their environment. Often, intelligence determines the execution of policy. Sometimes, it enables decisions at the highest common denominator and effective actions. Intelligence merely is one of many inputs into a process. Before an event, the effect of intelligence is unpredictable. During one, this effect ranges widely and may be minor, betraying those who trust too much in it. The average result is balance between both sides, or superiority without significance. In a large minority of cases, however, intelligence is a winning factor.

Academics and practitioners agree that signals intelligence – Sigint, material derived from reading the content or assessing the external features of messages – is the source most likely to achieve that aim. Sigint is marked by high reliability and mixed relevance. Its reliability produces characteristics which are unique among sources, trusted by users and a gold standard against which to measure all other forms of intelligence. Sigint provides more useful intelligence on secrets, especially major ones, than any other source. Generally it provides first-rate material on second-rate matters and second-rate evidence on first-rate issues, along with a host of repetitive and minor data. Sigint works on an industrial scale, which swamps any organisation unable to handle complex problems of data processing. Anyone able to do so, however, understands basic elements of power and policy in a way inaccessible to any other source.

Sometimes Sigint strikes like lightning – more often than any other source, or all of the rest put together. The high level of certainty and relevance transforms the time needed to decide and act. Communications intelligence – Comint, material taken from reading messages – can make time stand still. It is the source which inexperienced or mediocre decision-makers most easily use well, illustrating with unique power the mentality of others and how they view issues. First-rate Comint lets even poor consumers learn and act effectively, to avoid paying the full price of experience. It makes professionals one-eyed men in a world of the blind. Sigint has been covered in secrecy, yet in past decades its importance to war and peace has become obvious, most notably through the release of Ultra, material which Anglo-American codebreakers acquired on the Axis powers during the Second World War. People gradually have learned that Sigint is linked to some of the greatest changes in human society since 1914, including the rise of computers, the internet, and of an online society where Comint affects all of us.

From 1914, Britain possessed one of the best of the world's Sigint agencies. GCHQ was marked by skill and a fanatical dedication to secrecy. It hoped to be known only to the officials for whom it worked. This aim miscarried and GCHQ learned to live in the public eye.

In 2010, GCHQ began to think of producing an authorised history, for intellectual, institutional and political reasons. The secrecy which surrounded its history hampered GCHQ's work by denying it an informed understanding of how Sigint functioned. During the Korean war, for example, Anglo-American Siginters forgot matters of tactical support they had mastered just a few years before.[1] Siginters did not know how and why their work had mattered. Armies, conversely, believed that all officers needed a critical and thorough grasp of military history. From 2000, GCHQ debated the need to reshape the balance between secrecy and openness. It recognised the public demand to know more about work done in their name, and thought itself misunderstood and under-appreciated, yet with a good story to tell. The practice of Sigint against foreigners is less grey than human intelligence (Humint) or internal security. Few citizens protest successes done on their behalf. Public trust in GCHQ remains high. Secrecy, while essential to operations, inculcates both glamour and suspicion.

Many critics of GCHQ claimed that because so much is secret, people must expect the worst, especially after the leaks made by Edward Snowden in 2013. As with its sister intelligence services, the looming approach of its centenary year encouraged GCHQ toward openness. For operational and political reasons, many aspects of GCHQ's history had to remain secret, but others did not. For years, GCHQ had released to The National Archives material on the Cold War, and was willing to release far more. Yet given the recent experience of releasing records on Sigint en masse from 1918–45, GCHQ wondered how far they would be read, or understood. GCHQ wanted a history which explained what it was and had done, and enabled interested persons to make up their own minds on the documents. In order to have credibility, such a history had to be critical and independent.

When it asked me to write that book, GCHQ had conditions. This history could not discuss diplomatic Comint after 1945, nor any technicalities of collection which remained current. British or Allied intelligence agencies with 'equities' from common work with GCHQ would discuss, and might veto, discussions on their activities. Access to primary material would end with the Cold War. Otherwise, I have written as I wished, and received more material than I originally was promised, especially on the period after 1992. This history rests on complete access to GCHQ records on many matters, and none on others. I had free access to GCHQ's internal histories, and its main records between 1945 and 1992 on policy, and those on several campaigns, such as the Falklands conflict, though not on many others. The histories vary in quality, from decent to good, are rarely redacted and offer different chronological viewpoints of developments and events from each other (and me), thus providing multiple viewpoints. I have treated the histories critically, but all have important observations. They include arguments and evidence unavailable from any source which I could view. I cite them when they offer unique evidence, which is often. The policy papers from the London Signals Intelligence Board, redacted on topics outside my remit, decline in value from 1970, though the PROD (production) files later overcome this problem. I also have seen many (but not all) files on GCHQ's internal administration, relations with Whitehall and other Sigint agencies within the Five Eyes and NATO, on its work against the USSR, and communications security. I also interviewed many members of GCHQ, mostly under 'deep background' – meaning that I could not cite them as sources or directly use their statements. GCHQ gave me little material on the techniques of cryptanalysis, and none on diplomatic communications intelligence after 1945, though I cover those topics thoroughly in the period before 1945. About 25 per cent of the book covers topics from 1890 to 1945, where the evidence already is in the public domain, because no one yet has used that material systematically, and events often are misconstrued.

Only after examining earlier experiences can the history of GCHQ after 1945 be understood. The final chapter, which assesses GCHQ between 1992 and 2019, relies primarily on material in the public domain and interviews.

GCHQ is an able organisation and, at its best, the best intelligence agency I know of as an historian. Yet the limits to intelligence matter as much as its power. Intelligence is a secondary factor for states, behind strength and strategy. No institution is perfect. This history addresses GCHQ's failures and issues which it finds uncomfortable, such as its problems in incorporating science and technology during the 1950s, and coming to terms with the internet during the 1990s. During the 1930s British codemakers performed dismally, which left Britain vulnerable during 1940. I challenge the importance of Bletchley Park and Ultra to Allied success during the Second World War, a belief which provides much of the public support behind GCHQ. After 1945 a cult of secrecy at GCHQ, the most secret servant of a state wedded to secrecy, affected the work and lives of its members. They faced traumas as cultural and political attitudes changed toward secrecy and trust in the state. GCHQ came out into the open during the 1970s and 80s through scandals such as the ABC trial and the GCHQ union ban, which shaped public views of it for a generation. Though GCHQ will 'neither confirm nor deny' the accuracy of leaks from Edward Snowden in 2013, I discuss how they affected the politics around Sigint.

Like other authorised or official historians of British intelligence, my direct access to the archives was limited, for which purpose we had research assistants. My Virgil was James Bruce, a Siginter turned historian after he retired, with whom I have worked for a decade on the history of Sigint. He provided any files I requested on topics within my remit, and all that fit it. I signed the Official Secrets Act, easing access to files that might contain material I was not supposed to see and to conduct interviews. I have no security clearance, which would have caused me problems, as GCHQ then would have had to approve again anything I wrote about Sigint. The archives are so large that had I conducted my own research, I never could have written this work. They are not a library for research, as with the Foreign and Commonwealth Office, but rather a depository for old documents that are no longer needed, reflecting GCHQ's lack of historical consciousness. GCHQ fires, forgets, and moves to the next problem. Operational units keep any records which they need for their own purposes, until they do not, when they are weeded under statute or deposited. The archives contain a complete record of 'end product': millions of its reports to consumers. Its files on major issues of policy are thorough and continuous, but documents on administrative issues often are sparse. Material on many topics are weeded once they cease to be live. Still, these records compare favourably with those held by British military services. Combined with material from other departments, they enable a broad and deep account of GCHQ's history.

Any historian writing from privileged access to records faces questions about the independence of their account. When answering such criticisms, to some degree they must rely on their reputation. In my case, the room for such criticism is diminished. Most of the material I used will be released to The National Archives after this book is published, though some files will be retained, and others redacted to varying degrees. Anyone who wants to check my interpretation soon will have the chance to do so. GCHQ's internal histories will offer a different account than mine, with more detail on administrative issues. Anyone who opposes Sigint easily can criticise me. I regard Sigint as a normal and acceptable practice of state, so long as appropriate safeguards are maintained. I have conventional views on those safeguards: at home, or when dealing with their own citizens, signals intelligence agencies must follow constitutional norms; abroad, or when dealing with foreign people or states, they can act freely, so long as they follow government policy and common sense. I regard all traffic of foreign governments (outside of the Five Eyes) and of non-state entities hostile to our countries as fair game. Foreign states have the same views towards us and apply more ruthless practices.

This book pursues two particular aims. I address the human side of GCHQ, asking who its people were, what they were like, how they did their work, what it was, and how that changed. Many of them were the eccentric geniuses of legend, but far more were ordinary men and women. This book offers the first socio-historical analysis of any intelligence service, based on empirical data. It uses internal statistical evidence to examine issues of class, gender, race, education and origin of members of GCHQ. It explains the qualities which GCHQ valued among its members, and why, and the modes of recruitment, promotion and work for people ranging from wireless operators to cryptanalysts and high-flyers. In particular, this book examines the work of the largest occupational group at GCHQ: radio operators, the people who intercepted traffic, and the role of women in British Comint between 1914 and 2019. Comint always has been women's work, but not always appreciated by men. I also attack the 'so what?' question: why did Sigint matter and to whom? That question can be answered only by examining the records of consumers and comparing the intelligence record to what happened on the ground. GCHQ mattered more to British decision-making than any other secret service. Many events are inexplicable until the Sigint record is incorporated. Half of this book assesses how Sigint affected diplomatic and military events from 1914 to today, which illustrate the many ways in which it mattered, and may do so again in the future.

This book examines the attitudes of the British public and state towards Sigint between 1840 and 2019, and the relationship between law and the act of reading people's mail. It offers the first full account of British Sigint during the First World War, where it mattered as much as between 1939 and 1945. I show how Comint affected British diplomacy between 1919 and 1939, and how problematical it was to use. During the appeasement era, Comint showed that Germany, Italy and Japan meant harm to Britain, but that material easily could be misconstrued, and was. This book shows how incompetent British communications security endangered Britain during 1940, and how it recovered from danger. It reinterprets the rise of Bletchley Park. Geniuses were central to this triumph, but many minds and bodies created Ultra, not just dons and debs dancing on the lawn at Bletchley. It honours Alan Turing's work while showing that several other people mattered as much to this success as he. I argue that Ultra mattered less during the Second World War than is commonly believed, especially since poor British communications security enabled Axis successes in Sigint and war. It also shows that Sigint continued to aid British policy, as Ultra had done, throughout the Cold War.

This book uses GCHQ records to examine how Sigint affected British policy after 1945, and why Whitehall consistently financed Sigint better than any other aspect of British national security, except the nuclear deterrent. GCHQ served Britain in crises and conflicts. It penetrated Jewish communications during the insurgency which ended the Palestine Mandate, 1945–48, but that technical success had few political gains. GCHQ, conversely, helped Britain to wreck Indonesia's attempts to destroy Malaysia during 1962–66, and so to score a triumph of counter-insurgency and counter-terrorism during the age of decolonisation. Sigint enabled British victory in the Falklands conflict, yet failed to prevent Argentine aircraft from destroying many British warships. This is the first book to show how Western Sigint fought the Cold War against the USSR. Through patient and thorough exploitation of low-grade systems, GCHQ, the National Security Agency, and GCHQ's European partners penetrated Soviet military intentions and capabilities. This work shaped events like the Hungarian revolution, the Cuban missile crisis, the Soviet invasion of Czechoslovakia, and the crises at the end of the Cold War, including in Afghanistan and Poland. Intelligence and forewarning shaped deterrence and defence against the Soviet Union. This is the first documented account of a key but secret bulwark of international stability since 1945, the Sigint relationship between the Five Eyes, Australia, Britain, Canada, New Zealand and the United States. Ironically, the existence of UKUSA damaged NATO Sigint by creating walls between the intelligence agencies of Britain, Canada and the United States, and their allies.

This is the first book, told from the inside, to discuss the entire history of any Sigint agency. It offers a broad account of how Sigint has affected states and societies since 1914. Sigint drove the development of computers and the internet. Matters which people imagine occurred only during the age of cyber, such as bulk collection of data and of private messages, were first practised in 1914. During the First World War, Britain intercepted 70 million cables, 20 million wireless messages, and a billion seamail letters of foreigners, which guided economic warfare. From 1925, Sigint agencies regularly intercepted the private messages of civilians, carried on international wireless. Later, satellite communications, involving millions of messages in 1960 and billions in 1990, became a conventional target for interception, though only tiny samples of this material could be acquired. National Sigint authorities, foreign states, and criminals at home and abroad, could intercept some communications of British civilians within the United Kingdom from 1960. That also was true of every Western country. The internet made every person on earth a potential target to hostile Comint, while millions of entities gained capabilities which once states alone had. Sigint became part of everyone's daily life. Sigint agencies changed from being just the tool of one state against another, into a sword and shield for their societies, against foreign ones.

The Origins of Modern British Sigint, 1844–1914

Comint and Empire

From 1692 to 1815, only internal subversion, or a superior hostile navy off its coasts conveying a large army, or the two in tandem, could threaten British security. Britain needed to exert power in Europe and the world and to block two particular threats: a dynastic rival, the Jacobites, supported by enemies within and without; and a coalition of sea powers. These threats could be unleashed by the secret actions of a few men. British authorities made intelligence, particularly communications intelligence – Comint – the first line of defence against them. In this era of post, the interception of private and governmental communications were intrinsically related, and of equal significance. A 'Secret Department' (or 'Secret Office') resided in the General Post Office (GPO), at Lombard Street in the financial district, miles from Whitehall, but well placed to capture traffic and provide it to consumers. It routinely read letters from the political elite in Britain through general warrants that allowed the opening of 'suspected treasonable correspondence', in order, as one law passed under the Protectorate declared, 'to discover and prevent many dangerous and wicked designs'.[1]

Everywhere in Europe, during this first great age of Comint, codebreakers in 'black chambers' had easy access to foreign diplomatic messages that were popped in the post or carried in dispatch bags which could be opened easily and surreptitiously. In an integrated, opportunistic and multilateral system of power politics, diplomatic despatches were key to strategy or survival. Minor shifts in position by many states might reshape one's position, *renversement des alliances* overturn it. Because capabilities were clear, the intentions of foreign statesmen were unusually central to strategy and difficult to determine. British statesmen penetrated this uncertainty by combining spies with the 'Decyphering Branch', about eight men strong, who worked alongside the Secret Department. The dynastic connections which followed the Glorious Revolution created Britain's first two Comint alliances, initially with Dutch codebreakers, and then with Hanoverian ones. Two families, the Bodes, Hanoverian by ancestry, and the Willes, descendants of the Bishop of Bath and Wells, dominated the Decyphering Branch during its 133 years of existence: silverbacks passing a lucrative and hereditary trade to younger males – sons, nephews and sons-in-law. Hanover led this Comint alliance, which, like the relationship between the states themselves, involved two governments that shared one monarch. These agencies transferred product and techniques, but kept secrets from each other. Monarchs did not give British ministers every solution which Hanover provided. Ministers directed the Decyphering Branch onto targets which their German confrères also covered.[2] Nonetheless, foreign secretaries regularly read all the traffic of ambassadors when negotiating with them. This advantage was doubled by Britain's tendency to negotiate not at foreign capitals, but only in London: thus, it read ambassador's reports and their master's retorts, while minimising the exposure of its own secrets – as, for example, during the negotiations to move Denmark from cooperation with France during 1801. Comint also monitored the position of the powers during the uneasy Peace of Amiens, in 1802–03.[3]

Comint was a great source for internal security, diplomacy and strategy, but not for armies and navies at war. Captured dispatches enabled ambushes which might transform campaigns, though these were windfalls which were hard to acquire systematically. A rare exception occurred between 1808 and 1813 in the Iberian Peninsula, where the Duke of Wellington developed a great system of intelligence which approached the levels normal after 1914. That system combined reconnaissance, cartography, overlapping human sources, friendly territory and a real-time and systematic ability to read enemy dispatches (mostly in plain language but sometimes encoded and available only through cryptanalysis), which were taken by guerrillas from French couriers and sold for English gold. Wellington was perhaps the first commander in history whose operations were guided systematically by Comint, though it helped him less than Ultra did his successors.[4]

Limits to signals, meanwhile, made warships hard to locate once they were beyond sight of land. Fleets were ignorant of anything beyond visual range of their furthest vessels, which, when frigates conducted reconnaissance between 1690 and 1898, was fifteen miles by day and four at night. Captured enemy dispatches could be read, as could signals when fleets converged, but these sources were weak: ignorance outweighed information at sea. The difficulty in finding enemies or forcing them to battle made the Royal Navy play for safety at sea and keep most of its warships in home waters in order to block the greatest danger – that an enemy fleet might suddenly dominate these seas. This practice weakened its sea power in war elsewhere, at some cost between 1742 and 1763, and a high one in 1783, when the concentration of Britain's fleet in Europe let the French navy provide vital aid to American revolutionaries in the Thirteen Colonies. At land and at sea, dispatches or signals were rarely encrypted. Thus, for admirals and generals, unlike diplomats, interception and cryptanalysis were disassociated.

The Napoleonic wars transformed British power and policy. Between 1815 and 1890, overwhelming at sea and on most imperial frontiers, Britain faced no internal or external threat to its survival, though problems were plentiful. Britain turned from being a European power with an overseas empire, to a world power which was based off Europe, but insulated from it. Attitudes also changed towards intelligence. After 1815, governments feared threats from the 'lower orders' at home, against which they turned to spies and the interception of mail. Postmasters regularly intercepted the mail of specific individuals and sometimes were told to 'detain and open any letters' to and from towns which were thought 'to be of a suspicious nature, and likely to convey seditious or treasonable information, or to contain money likely to be applied for the purpose of promoting seditious or other Disturbances'. From 1830, however, far fewer intercepts were ordered, and these were more specific and less political.[5] Statesmen who wished to reform politics feared internal threat less than those who resisted any change.

During the eighteenth century, the Secret Office, and the security of the state, lay at the heart of the GPO. From 1815, the GPO cared most about creating a revolution in communications for the sake of its consumers, the public. The power of the Secret Office fell as it was physically moved from proximity to mail in the new GPO building at St Martin le Grange – several hundred yards and many corridors away from the central sorting office, rather than in an office next door – while the increased tempo of delivery reduced the time available to read letters. These changes reflected a revolution in communications and a decline in the status of this office. Seemingly, no official or minister involved with security understood these developments, or cared about them. The Secret Office also provided less material to the Deciphering Branch, which now included six members, one of whom specialised in opening letters, another in 'engraving' (probably replacing any damaged parts of a seal or address) and the rest all in reading foreign languages and bad handwriting. The 'Secret Service Decipherer' and his aides gave statesmen useful material – such as dispatches from Austria and Russia during the Eastern crisis of 1839–40, when Britain deftly outmanoeuvred every other power and prevented a European-wide war centred on Turkey – but most of the content was tertiary in value, on matters such as Franco-Portuguese relations, and apparently on translations from plain language, rather than solutions of codes.[6] The 'Decipherer' received £100 for every system broken. Between 1823 and 1842, he claimed to have solved only ten codes, all from minor powers (primarily Portugal, Sardinia, Saxony and Spain). When he made one such claim, the foreign secretary, Lord Palmerston, wrote, 'we ought to be exceedingly obliged to Mr Bode for being so considerate as not to discover new cyphers oftener than he does'. Palmerston valued these reports less than one would expect of so renowned a realist statesman. They did not impress him. He and other leaders within the Foreign Office suspected the competence and honesty of members of the Deciphering Branch, because of uncertainty whether some or any of them actually could break codes, and from suspicion of the familial connections which bound – or captured – these men, at a time when Whitehall was beginning to break from patronage as its central mode of organisation. The collapse of another set of family connections caused the political break with Hanover in 1837, wrecking Britain's longest Comint alliance, which perhaps damaged the Deciphering Branch.[7]

Amidst security and reform, accident drove the fate of cryptology. In 1844, the government of Robert Peel obliged that of Austria by surreptitiously opening and copying letters to and from Italian revolutionaries living in Britain. The Secret Department, unable to read letters in Italian, sent them to the Deciphering Branch for opening, copying and translation. Austrian authorities did not see these letters, but were warned of some of the dangers which they revealed. The surveillance was competent, but the revolutionaries detected tiny cuts on the corners of letters and delays of a few hours in the delivery of mail, which then was delivered four times each day. Its chief target, Giuseppe Mazzini, passed the evidence to radical British politicians. The latter made it a weapon, by fusing public support for Italian nationalism and opposition to espionage. They combined sincerity of belief with a chance to pelt the Peelites, especially the responsible minister, Home Secretary James Graham.

The debate reflected a change in attitudes towards intercepting mail. Whigs thought the practice intolerable. Thomas Macaulay, politician and public intellectual, compared it to torture. What difference existed between a government 'breaking the seal of his letter in the Post Office' and 'employing a spy to poke his ear to the keyhole, and listen to the conversations he carried on'? Even Peel and Graham called the practice 'repulsive', however necessary.[8] Though the government won the debate, the embarrassment which ministers felt at reading other gentlemen's mail – and even worse, being caught at it – killed the Secret Department. Intercepts declined again in number and did not recover until 1914.

The government abandoned intercepts because they were no longer essential, nor were they worth the political cost. By abolishing the Secret Department, Britain also damaged its dependency, the Deciphering Branch, unintentionally. The debate scarcely addressed diplomatic intercepts. The Parliamentary Select Committee appointed to address the scandal ignored them, though it questioned the last Decipherer, William Bode, closely regarding whether his office read private letters. No one really attacked the practice, or defended it. Statesmen showed no regret in abandoning it, even when Bode emphasised that 'whatever opinions may be entertained in this country, Foreign Governments will not desist from a practice which they all follow; nor will they believe that the English Government has abandoned all control over the Post Office. The motive of State Necessity which can alone justify the practice, will accordingly still exist.'[9]

The Mazzini scandal was the occasion for the closing of a black chamber, not its cause, which really was failure to meet a revolution in communication and cryptology. Foreign Office officials held that the Deciphering Branch was 'practically useless, in consequence of the different mode of conducting official correspondence which has of late been introduced by Foreign Courts, the larger Courts especially'. That office was abolished simply because it was found to be useless. 'Before messengers were so generally employed, and while hundreds of cyphered messages were transmitted by post, there was sufficient pabulum, from the constant repetition of the same cypher, to work upon, by comparison and collation. But when cyphered dispatches became rare, and scattering, there were not adequate means of collation, and new cyphers remained consequently undiscovered.'[10]

The members of the Deciphering Branch received generous pensions to induce silence about their work. In later years, statesmen extended their dislike of intercepts from the private to the public sphere. In the key colony of India, however, internal threats, revolutionaries and independent princes made authorities intercept mail for a decade longer, and revive that practice (which was legally permissible in the subcontinent) a decade earlier than occurred in Britain.[11]

These events reflected a broader phenomenon. Around this time, most powers abandoned black chambers out of embarrassment and for technical reasons. Increasingly, states sent their dispatches by courier, railway and steamship, denying black chambers their daily bread. Spies still could steal dispatches stored in offices, as Britain did against Russia and Turkey. Codebreakers could tackle an emerging target – telegrams – but this involved new means of interception and of attack against cryptosystems, where groups of five figures represented words or phrases. Austria and Russia did so, and France after 1890. Britain did not; an odd legal barricade blocked the practice: the Telegraph Act of 1868 prevented any telegraph employee from reading or disclosing the content of any cable, except under the same warrants which ruled the post. This clause indirectly prevented British authorities from using general warrants against any telegrams, including those of foreign governments in peacetime. Only a permanent organisation with regular access to foreign messages could overcome the technical difficulties associated with codebreaking. If traffic could not be intercepted, codebreaking was impossible, nor did it seem necessary.

Victorian Intelligence and the Information Revolution

After 1832, British statesmen increasingly abandoned espionage against European states and its own subjects. Never pure cynics, even in the ancien régime, they became increasingly high-minded. Even so, few practices beyond cannibalism were beyond the pale for statesmen, subject to the principle that they were not caught publicly in the act. Statesmen had differing appetites for the fruits of espionage. Some found the taste repugnant; others deemed it a delicacy beyond compare; most sampled the dish pragmatically, according to hunger or need. Changes in attitude explain part of the turn in British espionage, but not all. Spies and Comint offered less than they had done before 1792 and the start of the French revolutionary wars. Ambassadors easily gathered information from liberal, bureaucratic and constitutional regimes. Few squabbles on the continent seemed to endanger Britain, while Europe endured its absence. Even considering the tensions and wars of 1854–71, Europe, the centre of world power, was stable. Capabilities were known. Most power in the system backed the status quo. Compared with the eighteenth century, major states had little at risk, less need for secret intelligence and more inhibitions about its collection. Most states moved from the practice, though Britain went slightly further than usual. Across Europe, statesmen were more open with each other and lied less: secrets were fewer and easier to uncover. One Victorian Foreign Secretary, John Russell, told a colleague, Lord Clarendon: 'Your very interesting letters confirm what I always thought – that a hundred spies cannot ascertain so much as an English gentleman in whom Princes and Ministers believe they can safely trust.'[12]

An information revolution further diminished the need for intelligence. Between 1830 and 1914, the rise of modes of communication using steam and electricity, and mechanical forms of data processing, transformed the foundations for intelligence, commerce and strategy. Railways and steamships knitted isolated regions, topics and domains into greater wholes, and finally into one whole. Telegraph and post transmitted messages across countries and continents with unprecedented speed and flexibility – as radio would from 1900 – increasing the volume and velocity of information. Specialist operators, including telegraphists, librarians and indexers, served communication and information management. The breadth and depth of open sources and the power of information as against intelligence expanded as never before, or since. States and firms used these developments well. Under the ancien régime, bureaucracies were secretariats which supported offices. In the age of knowledgeable states, bureaucracies transformed governments. States and unofficial organisations collected and collated increasing masses of proprietorial, secret, public and official information. They overcame the risk of drowning in data through information management: creating databases; dividing reports into parts, combining each section with elements of other papers on similar topics, and creating specialised documents which contained all relevant data, but nothing else. Bibliographies and indexes guided rapid and precise retrieval of data held in depositories.[13]

Military officers often led these processes. Military intelligence became part of elaborate and specialist staffs, who regularly collected and assessed all forms of information to guide decisions. Departments maximised the collection, processing and dissemination of an increased mass of open and official information. The value of open sources in intelligence rose, compared to that of secret ones. Specialist bureaucracies, rather than engineers or statesmen, assessed information and made plans. Technical military intelligence for strategic purposes was handled well and far better than any other matter. Superiority with it provided relative advantages – for the Prussian army in Europe, or Britain across the world. All lines led to London.

Victorians had and felt less need for secret intelligence than British regimes in the eighteenth and twentieth centuries. Open sources illuminated most of their problems, but not all, including intelligence in wartime and strategic dangers. Victorian governments collected data on these issues as a matter of course, but in unusual ways, and this shaped British intelligence until 1914. Basic information for strategic purposes was gathered through open sources and processed by permanent agencies, which ultimately became specialised ones. Britain gained more knowledge by freely available information than any state had ever done through intelligence and processed and used data better. It developed information superiority over all other states. Departments maximised the collection and collation of an increasing mass of open and official information. Open sources answered most questions, leaving just a few hard and special cases of internal or external threat. Secret intelligence was collected through a personalised process, a tradition. Victorians often created bureaus to handle clandestine tasks for a few years or decades, but these vanished when the problem did. Prime ministers, foreign secretaries, governors and generals abroad, senior officials within the Admiralty, the Foreign Office, the Home Office and the War Office, either ran these networks or collected the information themselves. They directed collection in a loose and decentralised way, often leaving sources to guide themselves. All these actors knew how to conduct espionage, but many had scruples about it, and none had to do anything they found distasteful. Intelligence was assessed by the statesmen who acted on it. This organisation was more useful for imperial security than European diplomacy, a pattern which persisted until 1914 because it suited British concerns. The approach was haphazard and its effect variable. Given the lack of permanent structures, at the beginning of crises intelligence was poor and collection makeshift, but equally, when a problem arose, everyone looked for solutions and cooperated in making them work. The performance was good enough. Sometimes it produced material of extraordinary quality, especially for Lord Salisbury, but usually its quality and influence were below the level normal at the height of the ancien regime in Europe between 1715 and 1793, or throughout the world after the outbreak of the First World War.[14]

Victorian statesmen drew an ethical distinction between spying and codebreaking. Officials and Liberal and Conservative statesmen regularly read documents which were acquired by accident or stolen from the Russian and Turkish governments. Liberal statesmen and many officials, however, loathed the idea of intercepting foreign messages. In 1884, one Foreign Secretary, Lord Granville, seemed almost to shudder at the thought that 'we had the practice and have entirely given it up'. In 1888 the India Secretary, Lord Kimberley, ordered that alleged secret correspondence between two prominent enemies of the empire, the Mahdi of Sudan and the exiled Egyptian leader Arabi Pasha, be monitored, but 'decidedly' opposed opening such letters.[15] Conversely, Salisbury and some officials were willing to intercept or to solve correspondence about subversion or espionage within the British empire, including Russian communications with and about Afghanistan and Turkey. Even they, however, did not try to intercept or to solve the encoded messages of European governments. These activities were practised sporadically and on an individual rather than a departmental basis.[16]

The Edwardian Roots of British Sigint

Between 1890 and 1902, the systems of power politics in Europe and the world became one. A series of crises in Asia and Africa – some blamed on intelligence failures, rightly and wrongly – along with uncertainty which stemmed from ignorance, triggered fears of menace in Britain. The tectonic plates of world power shifted. British strength declined while that of Germany and the United States rose. Naval competition intensified. The need to manage a balance of power pulled Britain back into Europe to keep the continent stable, divided and peaceful. The threats were real but overstated. Britain easily held its own and scored a century of successes in policy, winning naval races against all competitors and seeing off the Russian threat in Asia. Still, this tension reduced British tolerance for uncertainty and menace, and raised the demands for intelligence.

British concerns remained unlike those of any other state, overwhelmingly imperial, whether about external, internal or maritime threats. British authorities moved from but did not break with the Victorian tradition of intelligence. Yet strategic problems and intelligence needs overlapped while agencies created for one problem evolved to handle others. Intelligence grew as a group of loosely connected solutions to particular problems, defined more by personality than policy, which produced odd results. For example, codebreaking emerged in India but not England, against China but not Germany. British authorities created MI5 and MI6 to block foreign espionage in Britain and to spy in Europe, while the quasi-independent Indian government boosted its intelligence agencies abroad.[17] These authorities increasingly wished to collect intelligence through the interception of cable and wireless messages and to a lesser extent letters, so exploiting British dominance of international communications. Authorities saw these sources as forms of Comint, though they did not fully understand that concept. They were seen not as parts of one discipline practised in peace and war, but as individual offshoots of efforts to achieve other ends in war, such as censoring telegraphs. Authorities created Comint without appreciating the fact. They did not make steady progress in the area, but took a series of halting steps, some leading backwards rather than forwards. These actions usually stemmed from the initiative of middle-level officials rather than the policy of any department. If these officials left their position, departmental actions could change.

In 1898, British authorities made their greatest decision about Comint since 1844. In war, Britain must censor cables, the GPO should 'interpolate a secret listening station on the Government telephone circuits between London and Paris', while the Foreign Office must provide an 'expert in decyphering'. That department added the dampening clause, 'if the services of one can be obtained'.[18] Immediately after formulating this policy, authorities applied it to Britain's greatest war between 1858 and 1914. During the Boer war, Britain practised every possible form of signals intelligence – without knowing that it was doing so. Authorities in South Africa and a black chamber of the GPO in London intercepted letters to and from businessmen thought to be working with the Boers. The Colonial Office warned that 'to avoid unpleasantness all letters to and from foreign countries which are opened by censors should be treated carefully by experts and before being sent on or returned to sender should be closed up etc so to remove trace of opening so far as possible'. Letters 'should not be forwarded if they bear marks of having been opened'.[19] Apparently, such expertise was at hand. For the first time, British authorities censored cable traffic across the world, though most traffic passed untouched and just a few censors focused on limited targets. Censors provided 'a very considerable amount of information' about supplies shipped to Boers, which aided their interception. British officers broke codes for the first time in generations – in particular the system used by Boer commanders in South Africa and their leaders in Europe, illuminating the negotiations which ended the war. Boer field telegrams, and perhaps its traffic communicated by the flashing sunlight of heliograph, were intercepted.[20] The effect on the war was small, however, because these actions were secret and uncoordinated and affected only the short period of conventional action, not the prolonged guerrilla phase of the war, and no British authority fully understood what had been done.

Two of the personnel involved later featured in early British signals intelligence. Major Francis Anderson, a Royal Engineers officer with a reputation as a keen amateur cryptologist, worked on material intercepted in London which allegedly discussed Boer negotiations as the war ended. The results are unknown but were judged valuable enough to award Anderson a bonus of £100 (nearly £10,000 in modern terms). In Aden, Captain George Church of the Royal Garrison Artillery, appointed Chief Cable Censor at a major node on the world's cable network, practised codebreaking against it, successfully.

Over the next decade, some of these experiences were generalised into a policy. In war, Britain aimed to destroy enemy-owned cables in order to prevent any enemy from communicating, and to control messages sent on British cables. Censorship would provide Comint. Policy on this matter was coherent. Thinking globally and acting locally, interdepartmental committees integrated complex technical issues. They defined protocols, applied them across the empire, and defined a structure to embody these ideas. It needed more muscle than Whitehall realised, but the skeleton was strong.[21] Planners overgeneralised experiences from the Boer war – a time when traffic easily was controlled and targets identified – into preparations for a world war, when every message must matter but be processed in the context of them all. Planners misconstrued the mechanics of censorship because they could not conceptualise the struggle they would confront, an existential war involving every nation on earth and all of their communications. Not until overwhelmed by data could planners understand the problems of 'bulk processing' and their solutions. They misunderstood how much traffic censors must handle and how many people the task would require. Planners underrated the problem of analysis, assuming that the meaning of messages would be transparent. The War Office simply told censors that 'a careful examination of all messages passing over the wires will enable the censorship staff to collect much valuable information', which should be sent to authorities.[22] The Admiralty, viewing the wireless censorship as a Comint service, had similar views.[23] Planners saw the censorship essentially as a tool for *contre-espionnage* and military security.[24] They barely considered what became its greatest role – economic warfare – because contemporaries wished to minimise control of contraband in war. When war began, censors were overwhelmed by traffic. These failures were inevitable, but not fatal, and outweighed by the successes. Decision-makers had much to learn about censorship as the war began, but they did so fast and well because they had already learned so much.

This policy spurred preparations for Comint-inefficient ones, because cryptology and wireless were divided. Those agencies which intercepted radio traffic did not break codes, those which aimed at cryptanalysis did not intercept wireless. The only Comint agency on earth which avoided this dilemma was the *Chiffregruppe* of Austria-Hungary, where experienced codebreakers received radio traffic intercepted from a potential enemy – the Italian army – during the latter's war with Turkey in 1911–12, and generalised the lesson to all of its enemies. Again, British authorities thought that cyphers would be hard to break and did not realise how much material could be acquired so easily. Yet they understood that something must be done for Comint in war, and created the means to do so.[25] MI5, pursuing German spies, became the first regular consumer of Comint in Britain since 1844, and has followed similar practices ever since.[26]

The War Office maintained a rudimentary capacity to attack military and diplomatic codes in war. Its war plans assigned several officers to attack codes, part time, among other duties, and assumed that other officers would do so independently. The War Office published a *Manual of Cryptography*, largely authored by Anderson, which provided useful information for beginners. Officers practised codebreaking, which was studied at intelligence courses. In September 1914, two senior intelligence officers with the British Expeditionary Force (BEF), Walter Kirke and Archibald Wavell, had each practised cryptanalysis, though neither actually did so during the war. The Royal Navy, meanwhile, fumbled towards signals intelligence without quite reaching it. From the moment that warships mounted wireless, post 1900, all Royal Navy fleet manoeuvres featured Sigint, which often shaped outcomes in sensational fashions. During 1912, Paymaster Commander Charles E. Rotter, a specialist in intelligence on the Kaiserliche Marine – Imperial German Navy – began to log its radio messages. In 1914 he tried to acquire a German naval codebook through espionage, for which the Admiralty authorised a significant expenditure. When war began, the Admiralty immediately created an agency, which included Rotter, to conduct wireless intelligence and cryptanalysis. In 1906, the Indian Army created a codebreaking agency of two officers, one of them Church, which broke Russian military and consular cyphers and the diplomatic traffic of Persia and China, its material widely circulated in the Indian and British governments. This agency prepared a memorandum showing officers how to break Russian military cyphers in case of war.[27] The Indian government became the first regular British consumer of diplomatic Comint since 1844. The Foreign Office saw such material frequently, as did the Liberal Foreign Secretary, Edward Grey. One diplomat protested; most accepted the practice. During the abortive Anglo-Chinese negotiations over Tibet in 1913, for the first time in perhaps a century Comint drove British actions – penetrating the Chinese delegation so successfully that China repudiated the provisional agreement which they had signed.[28]

Britain also outstripped other powers in processing information for operational and strategic decision-making in command, control, communications, intelligence, reconnaissance and surveillance systems. These systems and their problems shaped the evolution of British intelligence during the First World War. In 1914, the BEF placed intelligence, reconnaissance and surveillance under one command. The Cavalry Corps controlled horse-borne reconnaissance, two organisations which focused on aerial reconnaissance and intercepting enemy traffic, the Royal Flying Corps, and all wireless sets. Weaknesses abounded in this system, but it helped to save the BEF.[29] Meanwhile, the Admiralty made the greatest effort of any institution to transform its command, control and communications system. Naval intelligence had followed a distinct path for millennia. Navies needed information more than intelligence and found both matters difficult to master, especially for operations in war. These problems vanished with the rise of radio. Ships at sea reported their news instantly to others far away. Admiralties could give information and orders in real time and use fleets with efficiency and economy. These developments transformed the value of intelligence for navies – suddenly, and for the first time, it mattered more at sea than on land – and sea power. All of this eased ambush and enabled counter-ambush. They bolstered the strength of functions which had been hard to practise – such as denying an enemy the use of the seas or controlled oceanic operations, including interception by fleets. Intelligence made the principles of sea power and the command of the seas a reality, rather than just words.[30]

Public and private organisations gave Britain more strength in communications than any other country, though competition rose from 1900. The Admiralty and the GPO ranked among the greatest organisations handling electronic communications equipment in the world, with significant capabilities in research and development and links to private scientific and technological experts. Cable firms and the state worked symbiotically, on even terms of trade. Each levered the other against third parties. Firms dealt with all states; but the regulatory and strategic regime of the British empire best offered profit and protection. Britain supported the interests of such firms through politics, at small financial cost. By nature more than design, their cables linked the empire and made it the centre of world communication, with the lines of and to other states often becoming offshoots of imperial links. When Britain needed new cables laid during strategic crises, firms obliged and profited. At a small cost to taxpayers, firms laid the Pacific cable, completing the 'all-Red route' – a telegraph system across the world that touched no foreign territory, making British communications uniquely invulnerable to interception among the powers. The Eastern Telegraph Company helped authorities to plan and enact cable censorship. Through the power of these submarine cables and the ability to cut foreign ones, Britain gained much at little cost in 1914.[31]

The terms of trade between firm and state differed in another mode of communication. Between 1896 and 1900, working loosely with the Admiralty and the GPO, Guglielmo Marconi developed the first workable system of wireless signals. He exploited his breakthrough ruthlessly, using litigation across the world to crush all other systems, while making customers sign monopoly contracts for long periods. The GPO, bruised by collaboration with Marconi, rejected his terms and developed its own wireless network. As the Admiralty led the world in deploying radio, it adopted these terms, buying only Marconi sets until 1912. The financial costs were small; the strategic ones were larger. This monopoly prevented the Royal Navy, the Army and the GPO from cooperating in radio before 1914.[32] It also bound the Royal Navy to a firm which delayed development of a better form of wireless – continuous wave – which other navies pursued. Continuous wave ultimately enabled far more frequencies to be used than Marconi's spark system, and to carry speech. Marconi's system hampered the Royal Navy's use of radio in battle, though the cost was low as 'spark' matched the earliest continuous wave systems, which the Royal Navy adopted from 1912. By 1914 the US Navy and the Imperial German Navy were moving towards the Royal Navy, but still the latter led the world in communications – while Marconi outweighed any rival in human, industrial and technological resources. Marconi profited during the Great War, but along with the GPO, helped to solve the problems in British wireless and Sigint. This contract served Marconi well, and Britain too, but to a lesser degree.[33]

Meanwhile, the Royal Navy developed the world's first cybernetic system of command, control, communications and intelligence. The Royal Navy sought to collect and assess all intelligence relevant to sea power; to use that material to guide informed action; trace how these actions affected the environment and the enemy, and then to act again. All of these functions were conducted in real time, within a feedback loop. Cable and wireless constantly carried intelligence from many sources across the world to the Admiralty, where the position of every merchantman and warship at sea was displayed on maps. A war room maintained direct wireless links to every fleet.[34]

These systems had mixed success. During 1914–17, speed or guile concealed surface commerce raiders, which sank some Allied merchantmen. In 1914, the German Pacific fleet, flying homeward via the southern tip of South America, sank two British cruisers at the battle of Coronel, before its annihilation at the Falkland Islands six weeks later. Yet French and Spanish commerce raiders and battle fleets abroad damaged Britain far more during wars between 1692 and 1815 than Germany managed during the Great War. The Admiralty had unprecedented power in command, control, communications and intelligence at the strategic level, and understood and managed maritime matters across the world, outstripping any rival. The Admiralty extended this system to operational levels in European waters much less successfully: sailors rushed new technology before it was fit for purpose and overestimated their ability to use it with precision and control; they solved problems of communications and data processing faster than those of intelligence and command.[35] So fine-tuned a system required strong staff and intelligence services. The naval staff, though better than often supposed, could not meet these needs.[36] Despite ample experience with intercepting radio traffic in exercises and from foreign warships, before the Great War, the Royal Navy did not develop sources fit for operations either in Sigint or aviation. The British navy underestimated the difficulties in assessing intelligence for operations and readying it for commanders. Many of these flaws were unavoidable, but together they degraded the power of the navy's system for command, control, communications, intelligence, surveillance and reconnaissance. However advanced, it could not quite use Sigint well when that practice emerged during 1914.

Cryptography

Between 1840 and 1914, British cryptography was sloppy. Britain had few diplomatic codebooks at any time and these remained in use for years on end. Any competent codebreaking agency could read most or all of the British diplomatic traffic that it intercepted. Britain's greatest security came naturally, from its dominance of communications. Through the 'safe-hand' system, the safe hands of British merchant captains carried dispatches to and from isolated outposts in Asia and the Americas, supplementing the Queen's Messengers who did so between major capitals.[37] By using British-owned cables, Britain limited any rival's ability to intercept telegrams, which, even better, rarely discussed important issues except during crises or negotiations. Able statesmen hid their intentions. Even so, every foreign power could intercept any British cable sent to its own capital. Poor security in British embassies endangered codebooks, telegrams and the more important content sent in dispatches and letters. This material, held in safes at embassies, which usually were deserted at night and where Chancery servants were local employees, was vulnerable to safecracking or bribery. During the 1890s, local Chancery servants carried British dispatches from Paris to Calais, while sealed mailbags on the *Orient Express* moved diplomatic messages between London and Istanbul.[38]

Austria-Hungary, France and Russia consistently beat Britain in diplomatic intelligence. In 1899, following the public disclosures of French espionage at the German embassy in Paris during the Dreyfus affair, the British ambassador warned that 'recent revelations have proved that there are no lengths to which the Government will not go in the endeavour to obtain possession by illicit means of secrets which may be of use to them'. French espionage no doubt also attacked the British embassy, and 'it is impossible to exercise a strict surveillance over (the) security' of cyphers and archives at night. Little was done to improve the situation.[39] Between 1892 and 1907, Russia was Britain's greatest threat, with China and Persia prime areas of contention.

During this period, Indian government telegrams routinely went to and from London via Odessa, using a decades-old codebook; a Persian employee carried British dispatches to and from Tehran via Moscow, while communications with Peking often moved in unaccompanied bags on the Trans-Siberian railway. Russia probably read most or all of these messages and Foreign Office codes. Russian intelligence constantly attacked security in the embassy at St Petersburg, which blocked many such attempts, but probably not all of them.[40] Germany was worse off: all of its rivals, save Britain, read German cryptosystems, which may explain some of the failures in Germany diplomacy in the decade leading up to 1914. Cryptanalysis gave the Franco-Russian alliance an edge against both friends and enemies. That Britain outmatched them in power politics illustrates the limits to the strength of diplomatic Comint. More power and better policy let Britain defeat rivals who were better informed, but weaker and less wise.

From 1900, the Foreign Office improved the quality of its cryptography, which outstripped that of Germany, though it was still open to codebreakers.[41] Military cryptosystems followed conventional practice. Royal Navy codebooks surpassed those of the German navy in technical terms, reflecting operational needs in the age of radio, particularly by eliminating unnecessary messages and slimming the system; though unlike the Germans they did not use superencipherment – that is, covering already encoded messages with a further layer of encipherment. For strategic communications conducted over British cables where interception by hostile entities was unlikely, the British and Indian armies used simple codebooks. To cover wireless in operations, the British Army and navy proposed an elementary substitution cipher which the Indian Army, no doubt reflecting the views of its cryptanalysts, warned could be broken 'in a few hours', and compromise every message sent on the system. The British Army rejected as too 'complicated' the Indian Army's counter-proposal that they change keys daily, through a prearranged system of 'cards'. The Royal Navy held that: 'In war, even though a code or cipher were compromised, the advantages to be gained from immediate communications with the fleets or between ships, would … more than counter balance the fact that the enemy may possibly gain some information.' Ultimately, these three services adopted the Playfair cipher as their common cryptosystem for operations. Playfair – a multi-alphabet substitution cypher, where the letters of the alphabet were changed simultaneously in several ways – was tolerably secure before 1914, but not for much longer.[42] Unfortunately, few British operators could use Playfair well. Cyphers were recognised as vulnerable, but these services intended to use them only when unavoidable because they were cumbersome to use and crippled communications. British officials minimised the complexity of codes, so weakening security against any foreign state able to intercept their traffic. When they considered the adoption of cypher machines, departments rejected any that required frequent changes of key, which was essential to security. The Admiralty thought that requirement would cause 'confusion' and 'fatal delay', while the idea of changing a key daily filled the Colonial Office 'with horror'.[43]

British cryptosystems, civil and military, proved inadequate in 1914; only France among the main powers was better prepared. British systems were constructed by ordinary officials, some being amateur cryptographers. The first case of modern practice where codebreakers advised codemakers occurred in June 1914. The British empire's leading cryptanalyst, Major Church, broke within hours a cypher machine that the Admiralty thought was invulnerable – before the eyes of naval education chief, Alfred Ewing, who would soon lead a naval Sigint agency.[44]

The Comint Revolution

Around 1900, intelligence passed a tipping point, awaiting only a trigger. This revolution stemmed from the fusion of several developments: in sources and signals systems, including some which had unprecedented reliability and real-time nature; in modes of collection, assessment and dissemination, and the integration of intelligence into planning and action; and in forms of command, control, communications and intelligence, which unified all the domains of power and tactical, operational and strategic spheres.

That trigger sprang in 1914. When it did, British admirals, diplomats, generals and statesmen had some experience with and expectations for Sigint. Rather than being a radical break with the past, the establishment of codebreaking bureaus in 1914 was the logical culmination of a long-standing trend. When war began, British authorities treated Sigint with enthusiasm, rather than embarrassment or ignorance. In differing ways, the Royal Navy and the British and Indian armies knew they would practise Sigint in war, and took steps to do so. These preparations were imperfect. In diplomatic Comint, Britain was far beneath the standards of Russia, Austria-Hungary and France, but perhaps above any other state; in military Sigint, Britain was well below the *Chiffregruppe*, but tied with France, and above Germany. The British empire ranked a poor fourth in diplomatic codebreaking, a distant second in military signals intelligence, and first in the world in command, control, communications, surveillance and reconnaissance. Britain's rank in Sigint by 1914 was better than often assumed – well ahead of Germany, and not far from France, Russia and Austria. All of these countries would soon face the test of total war.

Britain and the Birth of Signals Intelligence, 1914–18

The Emergence of Sigint

The modern age of intelligence began in 1914. Imagery – photographs taken from airborne platforms – and signals intelligence joined to the general staff system, telegraph and radio, produced greater means than ever to collect, assess and use intelligence. Armies, and doubly so navies, combined interception and cryptanalysis and applied them to war in unprecedented ways.

British Sigint was born amidst confusion and the inefficient use of scarce resources. The departments which fought the war made most of the decisions on the matter, often without consulting any other body. The Cabinet and its agencies had little role in this process, which remained decentralised and loosely coordinated. Between 1914 and 1918, Britain's veteran agency, the Indian Bureau, attacked diplomatic traffic in Asia with marginal effect on the war, though meeting the government of India's needs well. Sigint agencies sprang up like mushrooms in Australia, Africa, France and at home. During 1914, Britain started from where it had stopped in 1902, following lessons derived from the Boer war, augmented by capabilities to intercept wireless. The BEF assigned its wireless sets to intercept enemy traffic, as the Royal Navy did to intercept that of the German navy. The British Army and Royal Navy assigned officers to create Sigint bureaus and solve specific problems. Fortunately, these officers were able.

The censors scrambled for staff in August 1914, taking months to become efficient at intelligence, and so too the Sigint agencies. All but one of Britain's experienced cryptanalysts were assigned entirely to other tasks, showing the limited interest in the matter, though to make all of them codebreakers might have hastened British success in cryptanalysis by just a few months. The War Office allocated Church, its leading expert on both censorship and cryptanalysis, to handle censorship for the BEF, a clear indication of its priorities. It assigned its second-most experienced codebreaker, Anderson, to establish a codebreaking bureau. Yet Anderson's main work was also to chair the Army Sanitary Committee, a dual role that puzzled his French cryptanalytic counterparts, though reflected his background in military works.

A week into the war, the Director of the Intelligence Division (DID), H. F. Oliver, asked Ewing to attack enciphered traffic which was being transmitted between Germany and wireless stations in its overseas empire. Ewing, an amateur cryptanalyst experienced with radio and constructing codes, was qualified for the task. He and Anderson, able managers with the status and knowledge needed to acquire resources, quickly created agencies, which after many changes in nomenclature became MI1(b) and Room 40. These agencies recruited small bands of amateurs, their ranks expanding through personal contacts. The proto-Room 40 and MI1(b) initially worked together, learning from experience and each other about information processing, how to direct radio interception and to conduct cryptanalysis. A veteran of this period, and later head of British codebreaking, Alastair Denniston, disparaged this relationship, but probably it enabled some transfer of the Royal Navy's expertise with wireless and the Army's knowledge of cryptanalysis.[1] Rapidly, these groups learned their trade and how to combine interception with cryptanalysis. By November 1914, members of each group could handle simple cryptanalytical tasks, such as overcoming changes in superencipherment to known systems. MI1(b) and Room 40 then divided when each began to succeed against different German systems, which had been provided by their allies, France and Russia. By spring 1915, these agencies were competent. GCHQ stands on this foundation.

Ultimately, Sigint agencies emerged for the British Army, Royal Navy, diplomacy and blockade, which rested on the same human, technological and cryptologic base. When war began, senior intelligence officers were able and some wireless officers became excellent Siginters; however, naval and military expertise and manpower in radio were inadequate for the needs of Sigint. Two organisations which had great capabilities in telecommunications, the GPO and Marconi, solved these problems. Though each organisation aided both services, the GPO worked mostly with the Army and Marconi with the Royal Navy. With their aid, the Army quickly established radio intercept networks on the Western front, in the Middle East and in Britain, as the Royal Navy did in the North and Mediterranean seas and across the Atlantic Ocean. By November 1918, Britain possessed around 100 intercept stations. The capacity of radio surged, but a station could search only a tiny part of the electromagnetic spectrum at a time. When examining overlapping frequencies, sets miles apart howled with feedback. Switching wavelengths was laborious, while equipment was primitive and clumsy. One veteran described an early version of the rotating frame direction finder as an '8 foot square wooden frame aerial on a scaffolding pole ... rotated mainly by a motor car wheel and brute force'. To find a bearing, operators determined the point of equilibrium in the strength of signals intercepted by two aerials. They then swung the aerials, varying their physical angle, adjusting valves and condensers, judging equilibrium by ear.[2] Atmospherics, telegraph lines, cliffs or drainpipes distorted bearings.

Siginters quickly developed into the teams which continue to the present day: linguists; administrators and clerical staff; and intercept operators, codebreakers and information processors using the most modern systems for communications and data processing. Each group tackled distinct problems, such as interception, cryptanalysis, and intelligence analysis. Sigint took several forms. Britain was among the first – perhaps the first – practitioner of traffic analysis, which started on the Western front in April 1915. That discipline combined meticulous observation of the structure of communication systems with deduction, induction and extrapolation. Communication reflected command. Specific radio stations and personnel were attached to headquarters, which had conventional procedures and patterns of communication with those at lower, adjacent and higher levels of command. Direction finding and the observation of the unique key signatures of operators identified which stations worked with what headquarters. Traffic analysis reconstructed patterns of signals traffic, creating a normal base which illuminated an organisation and indications that something unusual was brewing. Much Comint did exactly the same, especially air, military and naval messages. Comint which centred on the content of messages was most common for diplomacy and blockade, and unusual for military and naval operations, except on the Eastern front, the Middle East and the Western front in 1914.

The revolution in Sigint stemmed from a collision between electronics, radio, data processing and cryptology. Britain had many experts in the first three areas, but few in the fourth. It developed power in cryptology, partly from the acquisition of German cryptosystems that the enemy continued to use. In autumn 1914, the Australian and Russian navies captured copies of the German navy's main signals books – the *Signalbuch der Kaiserlichen Marine (SKM)* and the *Handelsschiffsverkehrsbuch (HVB)*, used by warships, Zeppelins and U-boats – and gave them to Britain. A British fishing boat soon recovered a safe, thrown from a sinking German destroyer, that held a copy of the *Verkehrsbuch*, which the German navy used to communicate with naval attachés and warships abroad. Admiral William Reginald 'Blinker' Hall, DID from November 1914, later claimed to have ordered a systematic search by trawlers in that area, which is possible. Though German authorities quickly concluded that their *SKM* and *HVB* signals books might have been compromised, still they used them for several years. In spring 1915, Room 40 also received a German diplomatic codebook, Code No. 3512, which was seized by the Indian Army in Persia.[3]

In these cases, amateurs became analysts simply by translating intercepted codegroups into plaintext – for example, German words which illustrated the working of codes, signals and actions. Room 40 lurked within the enemy's command, control and communications system, exploiting poor systems and usage until 1917. Initially, German naval codebooks listed plaintext in alphabetical order and their code equivalents in numerical sequence, each progression loosely compromising the other. The *SKM*, designed for use with semaphore, was cryptographically obese and weak. It included 300,000 codegroups, most of which never were used, of three letters, to describe such orders as 'ramming speed'. If one knew two figures of a group, the third was easily guessed, from the forty figures in German Morse code. Ten thousand groups was ample for an operational codebook, which preferably would have five figures, with many books allocated to a theatre. To change a system of 300,000 phrases was difficult and was resisted by operators who were comfortable with the old one. Amateurs overcame German superencipherment systems. Compromises were infectious. The *Verkehrsbuch*, which German naval attachés used for political reports on radio circuits between Berlin and Madrid, conveyed instructions on the use of the *Satzbuch* that military attachés used for similar purposes. Many German diplomatic codebooks were 'merely keys of one archetype' (presumably one vocabulary using different codegroups on a progressive – ABC, 123 – rather than an arbitrary – MFZ, 492 – system), which could be reconstructed within hours. Thus, Code No. 13040 compromised the lot.[4] When the German navy replaced the *SKM* with a new and technically improved signals book, the *Flottenfunkspruchbuch* (*FFB*), in May 1917, Room 40 was staggered: as Admiral Hall wrote: 'we are more or less at a dead-lock'.[5] Room 40 took four months to recover its footing and never again waltzed quite so well.

The Imperial German Navy suffered from ignorance of how far its systems were captured and its traffic was intercepted. Without physical compromises, these weaknesses might not have mattered. Amateurs attacking from first principles must have been less successful than Room 40. Had the Germans been the lucky ones, they too would have found weaknesses in British systems sent by radio, which excluded diplomats and naval attachés. The Royal Navy, unlike the German navy, had reformed its signals book to account for radio, which it used far less routinely. Even so, German Sigint penetrated lower levels of Royal Navy codes and, save for Room 40, could have reached middle rungs – thus replicating much of Britain's successes, which lay in monitoring routines rather than acquiring sensational messages. In 1919, British cypher authorities believed that by breaking just one British codebook, Germany could have read a rapidly rising circle of them.[6]

Chance drove signals intelligence at sea, but not elsewhere. On the Western front in 1917–18, Allied and German forces captured scores of codebooks, but each of them covered small topics and areas, and all changed frequently. Armies outstripped the German navy in cryptography. Though the records do not adequately describe the process, Room 40, MI1(b) and I(e), British Army cryptanalysts in the field, all became skilled in reconstructing their targets: codebooks of three to five figures, sometimes superenciphered, and various forms of cypher. An arms race in cryptology began in 1914, which has never stopped.

The Emergence of Comint

Codebreakers came from many sources, including former civil servants, dons, lawyers, stockbrokers, teachers and white-collar workers – while female office staff and graduates, and war-wounded officers, often served as assistants. They were recruited through the social connections of members of codebreaking agencies, which also had links to the universities. Compared to the Royal Navy, the Army increasingly recruited Siginters through bureaucratic means, while its agencies employed more women as codebreakers and intelligence analysts. The original core of Room 40 were naval schoolteachers, who mostly left when term began, though Alastair Denniston remained – starting his thirty-year association with British Comint. Later, they were augmented by academics, particularly classicists connected to Cambridge, some with high social connections. The original core of MI1(b) included a recent Cambridge graduate and officer with the Yeomanry, George Crocker; Oliver Strachey, member of the Indian Civil Service and brother of the writer Lytton Strachey; and John Vincent Plett, an official of Marconi House, soon joined by Ian Malcolm Hay, an amateur theologian and Scottish laird. Hay joined his local battalion as captain in August 1914 and almost immediately was wounded, captured and freed in an exchange of prisoners. In mid-1915, Hay, fluent in French, German, Italian and Spanish, was assigned to MI1(b) and replaced Anderson as its head in 1916. At its peak, around half of MI1(b)'s twenty-odd codebreakers were academics, drawn particularly from Aberdeen University. They included John Fraser, a specialist in ancient Scottish philology and later professor of Celtic studies at Aberdeen and Oxford, and two outstanding linguists, Norman Jopson and James Turner. Between 1916 and 1919, Turner broke codes in French, German, Spanish, Portuguese, Swedish, Norwegian, Dutch and Turkish, and also knew Danish, Italian, Persian, Hungarian, Lithuanian, Polish, Bulgarian, Serbian, Russian, modern Greek, Arabic, Czech and Rumanian.[7]

Outsiders viewed codebreakers almost as magicians. Describing members of I(e) on the Western front ('a rummier set of fellows I never came across in all my born days'), one Marconi officer involved in wireless interception wrote:

> It was not in the smallest degree possible to teach these wonderful fellows a scrap of discipline. You had to treat them as geniuses, and to expect from them the most erratic behaviour ... I don't think that they looked upon washing or shaving as part of their day's serious work. But they were the most amazingly brilliant fellows – both as linguists and as mathematicians. As soon as a new code came along they pounced upon it like vultures on their prey, and stuffing their pipes with tobacco, and muttering the new letters over and over again as they felt in their pockets for a match, they would wrestle with that new problem until they had made it clear as daylight. Some of these codes angered them because they were so easy – problems to be solved in an hour or two. But some of them were real hard nuts to crack, and then these decipherers were in the seventh heaven.[8]

Many codebreakers were eccentric. Alfred 'Dilly' Knox of Room 40 insisted on attacking codes while in the bathtub, finding that heat and steam propelled cryptanalysis as surely as it did battleships. Other codebreakers viewed their work in more mundane terms. Gerard Clauson, a graduate in Middle Eastern languages from Oxford and prewar Inland Revenue official and working with I(e) in the Middle East, told one friend: 'I suppose [MI1(b) is] pretty tedious, but wait till you've done a clean point [sic] of nearly 11 months without a single ruddy half holiday. Mind you not for worlds would I have missed it & and not for worlds would I leave it as long as there's a show on, but even when there's nothing doing you still spend every day in the office only there's less work to do & it's all dull. At present every day you have one or two genuine pinches & feel you've earned your 30/- when you go to bed.'[9]

Cryptanalysts learned on the job, often aided by manuals of cryptography. They worked in teams, which varied by the problem. In 1918, for example, the I(e) codebreakers who attacked German codes assigned specialists to sort material, type it in standard formats, and index every occurrence of all codegroups. Unsolved messages were divided into the separate systems from which they came. They were collected and printed clearly in one numbered series, with all individual codegroups indexed, so to maximise what any eye could see at one time. Each message noted all known external features, such as the date of dispatch and the addresses of sender and recipient. When a codegroup was broken, the plaintext was incorporated onto the worksheets of all unsolved messages. 'One controlling mind' directed the 'actual solvers', sometimes against individual problems, such as groups for punctuation or numbers, or simultaneously to pursue multiple hypotheses against the meaning of one codegroup, which might break a logjam.[10] According to Hay, at its peak, MI1(b) consisted of 'about 20 solvers, and about 60 assistants, typists etc.'.[11] This small body broke important systems of virtually every neutral and enemy state in just two years from the summer of 1916, which suggests that the standards of diplomatic cryptography were low.

The Political Section of Room 40, commanding many German codes, assigned specific systems to individuals or groups of two or three officers. All were backed by a section, which switched from one system to another in response to priorities or opportunities. The section used 'labour-saving devices, such as the "pianola", a mechanical means for making troublesome group transpositions', in order to overcome 'the deficiency of staff'. The pianola presumably was some kind of punchcard tabulator system which was used to process quantitative data in bulk. In order to test cryptanalytical possibilities, codegroups were punched on cards, stacked, automatically fed into machines, filed at the far end, and analysed. The pianola attacked what Room 40 called 'hatted', or 'two-part codes', those which did not have systematic links between alphabetical groups for words, and the numerical order of code equivalents, 'the former being drawn so to say out of one hat and the latter out of another'.[12] The term 'hatted' would linger in British cryptanalytical jargon throughout the Cold War. Unlike many German naval codes, alphabetical and numerical groups had to be attacked separately, through 'trial and error by which after comparing all the contexts in which a group occurred a guess could be made which in turn might enable the same process to be repeated for a contiguous group. Given a mass of material an expert could in this way guess approximately four or five groups a day' – making a code with an eighteen-month lifespan invulnerable.

So, in 1916, the Political Section:

> set up a special staff of educated women to work machinery by which the guessing process could be accelerated. By this method the guessed groups rose at once to twenty daily and by the law of increasing returns grew mechanically to a maximum of a hundred per day by which time the cypher was approximately readable, after which they decreased. In fact, the reading of messages in such codes, which resemble those used by our Foreign Office, proved to be merely a matter of tedious drudgery for one or two experts and the staff of ladies trained by Miss Robertson.

Through these means, Code No. 64, first attacked in May 1916, became readable in the summer. When the Germans abandoned that code in winter 1916, Room 40 read 5,000 of its 10,000 groups. 'By this process some 13,000 German words have been correctly guessed from their context in about 18 months and as each word read involves an average of three guesses, this implies a missing word competition for a year and a half with an average of 70 guesses daily.'[13] On seventy guesses per day and an eight-hour shift, the pianola section tested nine hypotheses per hour. It was divided between two experts, who defined the guesses to be tested, and women who punched cards, ran the machines and processed the outcome. Together, they solved enough groups to read six German diplomatic codes, providing quick and powerful reinforcement to any attack by hand which approached the promised land – such as Code No. 10340, which carried the Zimmermann Telegram in spring 1917, when Hall wanted an accurate translation of the entire message. An experienced academic administrator led this campaign, probably the first use of data-processing machines in codebreaking. Miss Margaret Ethel Robertson, described by one colleague as 'a brilliant early graduate in Modern Languages at Cambridge', was headmistress of a leading school for girls, Christ's Hospital for Girls at Hertford, between 1893 and 1921. She is remembered there as 'formidable', which matches her portrait. During the war, Miss Robertson initially led her schoolgirls in air-raid drills, and then managed the first brute force codebreaking attacks in history, as her ladies sequentially pursued multiple hypotheses by 'grinding groups out of the hat machine'.[14]

Sigint at Sea

Signals intelligence is thought to have influenced the Great War most through actions at sea, but this matter is less well known than supposed. The evidence is largely untouched. One might expect admirals to discuss signals intelligence, and so they did; but this correspondence and the documentation from Room 40 is rarely cited.[15] Even less often is this material compared to the archive on naval operations. The Admiralty took signals intelligence extremely seriously. In 1916, Admiral John Jellicoe, commander of the Grand Fleet, was 'in mortal terror' that Germany would discover British success against its cyphers, declaring 'it would be fatal'.[16] The Admiralty also used signals intelligence to guide hundreds of attacks, yet almost always without success – most spectacularly at the battle of Jutland on 31 May 1916, most routinely against U-boats. Inexperience shaped these failures.

On 8 November 1914, Winston Churchill, the First Lord of the Admiralty, and the First Sea Lord, John Fisher, issued what often is called a charter for Room 40. In an 'Exclusively Secret' note, they told Ewing and the Chief of the War Staff that:

> An officer of the War Staff, preferably from the I.D. [Intelligence Department], should be selected to study all the decoded intercepts, not only current but past, and to compare them continually with what actually took place in order to penetrate the German mind and movements and make reports. All these intercepts are to be written in a locked book with their decodes and all other copies are to be collected and burnt. All new messages are to be entered in the book and the book is only to be handled under instructions from the C.O.S. The officer selected is for the present to do no other work. I should be obliged if Sir Alfred Ewing will associate himself continually with this work.[17]

Three months earlier, Churchill had ordered a wide-ranging and bureaucratised process of collection, analysis and dissemination of intelligence on economic warfare, because he knew that such proceedings were necessary to that task.[18] This task was different, however. Churchill and Fisher grasped at a chance that they thought was vital and feared might vanish: secrecy was intended to save the life of Comint. This fear had good cause. In October 1914, French newspapers had compromised the success of French army codebreaking, enabling the German army to improve its cryptography. During November 1914, the *Daily Mail* had reported two of MI1(b)'s solutions of German army messages, and in 1918 discussed women codebreakers on the Western front.[19]

News of Room 40's successes spread among naval officers, and further. In March 1915, citing 'a man whose own sources of information are unusual, and whose *(sic)* has just got back from England', *The New York Times* published informed accounts of the effect of British intelligence during the Scarborough Raid and the battle of Dogger Bank, which it credited to 'espionage', rather than cryptanalysis.[20] Probably this news stemmed from leaks about Sigint. Filson Young, a journalist serving as an intelligence officer for the commander of the Battlecruiser Force, David Beatty, in 1914–15, acquired broad and accurate knowledge of Room 40's activities, which he discussed in his book, *With the Battle Cruisers* (1921).[21] Meanwhile, failure to maintain secrecy led German naval cryptanalysis to shipwreck.

No one could have foreseen the nature and volume of the material which was generated by Room 40 and traffic analysis, nor the breadth and depth of analysis that was needed to make use of it. Churchill and Fisher, virgins in Sigint, and micromanagers who misunderstood staff work, expected this charter to ensure effective work by and liaison between codebreakers, analysts, operations officers and commanders. Hall received a copy of all solutions, 'to compare with information from other sources', but pledged not to let anyone else see them.[22] Instead, this system produced bottlenecks between Comint, analysis and operations, which crippled action until 1917. It lingered on for two years after Churchill and Fisher fell from office in 1915, showing that many shared their views. Meanwhile, before the battle of Jutland, the Royal Navy had only two chances to test Sigint and command in action, against the Scarborough Raid and at the battle of Dogger Bank, and misconstrued the problems which these engagements revealed. The problems of Jutland were impossible to misunderstand, and practices improved rapidly. During 1914–17, the BEF also suffered from problems in coordinating intelligence and command, and using Sigint, but frequent practice made its systems more flexible and powerful than those of the Royal Navy.

To view naval intelligence from the perspective of Room 40, from that of a source rather than a service, confuses understanding of its successes and failures. Before 1914, the Royal Navy tried to ride a revolution in command and intelligence. Through wireless, the Admiralty would collect, process and analyse information, and order admirals to action, while leaving them free to act. However, the Royal Navy's overcentralisation and focus on secrecy when formulating plans for war or battle crippled the power both of a staff and intelligence analysis. Naval plans emphasised that intelligence or reconnaissance must report whenever the German navy moved to sea. The Royal Navy failed to develop means to achieve this end. It overestimated the ease with which intelligence could be gathered for ambush, and with how signals and command would work in battle. In 1914, its command, control, communication and intelligence system suited the defence of trade against German cruisers in oceanic warfare, which was no mean feat – though the Royal Navy quickly ended that peril, without much help from intelligence. That system, however, could function in the North Sea only if every phase in the collection, analysis and use of intelligence worked well. It depended, as Beatty said in January 1915, 'on having perfect cooperation between all forces engaged, and preserving absolute secrecy about the operations beforehand'.[23] Since the means of intelligence did not emerge until after the war began, the Royal Navy could practise their integration only in battle. Thus, it won fewer battles than was possible.

Again, Sigint worked best when it had partners which were strong to compensate for its weaknesses. Initially, Royal Navy Sigint had weak partnerships. By botching the links between Comint and traffic analysis, the Admiralty wrecked the very relationship between sources which created Sigint. The Royal Navy developed seaplanes and seaplane carriers well, but given their flaws in 1914, they did not become useful until after the battle of Jutland. By 1917, the Royal Navy combined Sigint and aerial reconnaissance effectively, but until then Comint's main partner was visual reportage from warships. Comint traced intentions while eyeballs saw an enemy in sight; however, from the moment that British forces sailed to the point at which they attempted an ambush, intelligence gave them little help until they found the foe. If any one of many matters went wrong, a well-informed intention to exploit operational surprise easily could fail, or backfire. Nonetheless, the Royal Navy developed intelligence far better than the Kriegsmarine, especially – but not exclusively – Sigint. In 1914, the Kriegsmarine outstripped the British navy in air reconnaissance. Zeppelins matched Room 40 in value on many minor issues, but not major ones, with one great exception – by guiding the Hochseeflotte, the German High Seas Fleet, from a British ambush when the two fleets almost clashed on 19 August 1916. By 1916, however, the Royal Navy matched the Kriegsmarine in air reconnaissance, and then surpassed it.

During 1914–16, the Admiralty developed new sources of intelligence – including seaplanes, traffic analysis and codebreaking – but integrated them poorly. Room 40 and traffic analysis were isolated from each other and also from the specialist sections in the Naval Intelligence Division (NID), which could best have used their product. The officer in charge of analysing Comint, Captain H. H. Hope, lacked access to much material which was held within the NID. Inertia maintained this division of efforts until Ewing resigned in May 1917. From 1914 to 1916, Sigint went through the Chief of the War Staff, H. F. Oliver, to his superiors, who analysed it themselves without consulting intelligence officers. Whenever these men scented opportunity, they informed Jellicoe and Beatty.

From its base at Scapa Flow in the Orkney Islands, the Grand Fleet needed twenty-eight hours' warning to intercept an enemy force that was returning from bombarding the British coast, or to counter-ambush attempts by the High Seas Fleet to ambush British forces. The element best placed for ambush and counter-ambush, faster and eight hours forward, was the Battlecruiser Fleet at Rosyth, southeast Scotland. It served both as an independent force and as part of the Grand Fleet, but had distinct problems with signals and gunnery. Its practice of filling turrets with shell to hasten the rate of fire increased the likelihood that magazines would explode and ships sink if a turret was hit (as marked the battle of Jutland). Any of these problems could obviate success in ambush. They dogged every attempt to do so. Fluke or German caution prevented many ambushes. Confusion in British signals and command let Germans escape an abortive ambush after the Scarborough Raid of 16 December 1914, and prevented Beatty from destroying three battlecruisers at Dogger Bank on 24 January 1915, instead of just one armoured cruiser. On the day before the battle of Jutland, elementary wireless deception – conducted by leaving the call sign of the flagship ashore where it was emitted while the High Seas Fleet sailed under cover of temporary wireless silence – fooled British admirals who were accustomed to acting without consulting analysts. The Admiralty told Jellicoe that he would encounter only part of the enemy fleet, instead of the whole. A few hours before the battle, traffic analysts penetrated the ruse and suggested that the entire High Seas Fleet was at sea. However, Jellicoe was not warned. One seaplane carrier missed the battle; the other received a useful report which it could not pass to Jellicoe through the noise of spark wireless sets and the confusion surrounding tactical communication. When it encountered the enemy, the Battlecruiser Fleet was hammered, yet Beatty failed to report the situation even as he led the foe onto the Grand Fleet. Beatty and the Admiralty dealt Jellicoe a bad hand, which he played well. Jellicoe did not know that he was about to engage the High Seas Fleet until the Grand Fleet did so. German admirals were even more astonished, because their intelligence was worse than the British. Given the failure of seniors and subordinates to inform him of events, Jellicoe commanded well: the Grand Fleet hammered the Hochseeflotte but could not win the day.[24]

Jutland provided the impetus which was needed to give the Grand Fleet a good system of command, control, communications and intelligence. The fleet overcame its problems of signals, command, gunnery and tactics. When Ewing retired, Oliver moved to the Grand Fleet and Jellicoe became First Sea Lord. Room 40, meanwhile, was placed within the NID. There, Comint and traffic analysis were combined into signals intelligence, which Hall called 'the kingpin of everything',[25] and integrated with thorough analysis. Finally the Royal Navy was ready for counter-ambush, but too late. Jutland so unnerved British and German commanders that they refused to come out except under favourable circumstances. In 1917, moreover, Room 40's command over German codes wavered. German Sigint achieved its only success in the war, enabling the annihilation of two British destroyers and nine merchantmen in a convoy to Scandinavia on 17 October 1917.[26] Though the Admiralty insisted that its intelligence was sound, as commander of the Grand Fleet, Beatty – scarred by watching one-third of his battlecruisers destroyed at Jutland – declined to trust it.

Given German power in torpedoes, mines and shells, and their ability to threaten the Scandinavian convoys – to attack by surprise and at their selected moment – Beatty held that, 'the correct strategy of the Grand Fleet is no longer to endeavour to bring the enemy to action at any cost, but rather to contain him in his bases until the general situation becomes more favourable to us'.[27] However, by 1918 Room 40 had restored much of its strength – of which Hall convinced his old shipmate, Beatty. In October 1918, German admirals prepared to launch a 'death ride' of their fleet towards the Thames, to lure the Royal Navy out into a submarine trap and then to battle. Room 40 and the Grand Fleet stood ready to oblige them through a counter-ambush which avoided and exploited the enemy's ambush, but German sailors preferred mutiny to martyrdom – so sparking the collapse of the German empire.

If one gauged effect through operations alone, Room 40 would be a failure. But the reward was above the battle. At the strategic level, intelligence, security and deception were fundamental to the war at sea for both sides, their fleets standing hours from Armageddon. Simple procedures of security could achieve surprise for a fleet operation, yet twenty-four hours' warning might eliminate that edge. Victory in the war of knowledge solved the strategic dilemma which confronted the Royal Navy. It could not blockade the German coast. The German navy could bombard British towns, raid commerce, ambush squadrons, or escort an invading army at its selected moment. The only solution – frequent sweeps by battlecruisers and cruisers through the North Sea, with the battle fleet in distant support – exposed the Royal Navy to mines and torpedoes. Just before Room 40 emerged, Jellicoe and the naval staff believed that 'presumably' in any operation, the High Seas Fleet would 'leave port unobserved'. Moreover, in battle, Jellicoe must make an 'absolutely repugnant' decision not to pursue a retreating foe, if he thought it aimed to lure the Grand Fleet 'over mines and submarines', in order to avoid the 'possibility that half our battle-fleet might be disabled by under-water attack before the guns open fire at all, if a false move is made'.[28] This dilemma horrified admirals. Room 40 overcame it.

Sigint could not help the Royal Navy to achieve its greatest ambition: to ambush or counter-ambush the High Seas Fleet, which would require 'perfect coordination' or 'absolute security' – tall orders at any time. Various small problems blocked the few opportunities for such clashes, except at Jutland. Sigint, however, reduced the Royal Navy's weaknesses. The war centred on forces where Britain lacked superiority over Germany. Cruisers, destroyers, lighter warships and submarines fought daily in the North Sea, backed by the Battlecruiser Force, which also dominated efforts at ambush. Battle damage or wear from routine actions easily could drive these warships into dock for repair, and leave the rest, especially battlecruisers, weaker than the enemy and vulnerable to attack at times advantageous to the Germans. The Kriegsmarine pursued this end. It hoped that constant attacks on British coastal towns would force the Royal Navy out to sea, where mines and submarines would erode its strength. Nothing frightened Jellicoe, Beatty and their superiors more than this danger. Sigint alone could surmount it, and did so well. Sigint showed what the Germans had done or were doing every day – and planned to do on the next and where their forces stood. This knowledge of enemy dispositions and procedures was easily understood and exploited, unlike that required for an ambush. Combined with forewarning of German attacks, this material meant that Britain need not take risks nor wear machinery in pointless sweeps. Meanwhile, the capacity for counter-ambush reduced the enemy's ability to ambush, which increased Jellicoe's willingness to strike. Churchill and Fisher valued the elimination of that vulnerability even more than they did the enhanced chances for ambush. In negative terms, Beatty's caution of 1917–18 shows the operational consequences of Room 40.

This situation, combined with each side's fear that it might lose a main fleet action, the German reluctance to fight except on their own best terms and the British advantage in warships, were fundamental to the war in the North Sea, to stalemate in operations and Teutonic defeat in strategy. Full judgement of this issue requires consideration of counterfactuals. Room 40 wrecked Germany's only (however faint) chance to win the naval war – its 'whittling' strategy, aiming to provoke warships into actions against larger but hidden forces or over submarine traps – and thus denied the Kriegsmarine its best means to achieve this objective: surprise and intelligence. Sigint prevented Germany from deceiving Britain. Even more, Room 40 detected German codebreaking in its earlier stages and crippled its growth, so depriving it of the chance to match Britain in the war of knowledge.

In January 1915, Beatty noted that the enemy 'seem invariably to get notice' when his force left port: his sweeps struck nothing.[29] His fears were justified. Soon, errors by British cypher personnel, and the repetition of identical messages by high- and low-grade systems, let Germany read a naval order to merchantmen three days after it was issued, and endangered more senior systems. Fortunately, Germany imprudently reported this message by radio, which Room 40 solved.[30] Driven by Churchill, who worried that Britain might lose Room 40 or Germany create one, the Royal Navy took this danger seriously. In response, specialists, especially Paymaster Commander Edward Travis at the Grand Fleet, produced the best campaign of signals security of this war. The Kriegsmarine used a small number of systems, mostly poor, which were changed infrequently and clumsily. The Royal Navy contained infection by constructing many codes that were changed frequently and tailored to specific needs, so to hamper the enemy's ability to pool traffic against one system, and by watching for signs that any code was compromised. Travis led a large and predominantly female workforce to manage this precise and complex process of construction.[31] These acts defended major systems and their secrets, though Germans read lower-level codes which, aided by traffic analysis, betrayed the Royal Navy's routines, often indicating when squadrons left port. This success had few consequences. Germans probably read all the systems used by British merchantmen, but sank few ships as a result.[32] Room 40 is a classic case in which intelligence multiplied the power of the stronger side.

Military Sigint

Sigint was the Royal Navy's dominant source of intelligence, with aerial reconnaissance a distant second at sea – though spies accurately monitored the construction of, and battle damage to, German warships.[33] Armies had many good sources, whose value and role constantly shifted. During August–November 1914, the combination of Sigint and aerial reconnaissance proved more valuable for the British Army than every other source put together.

Siginters, working with French experts and against poor German security, gave the BEF fifty plain-language and broken messages between German corps, armies and army groups, many of them indicating how the enemy soon would use hundreds of thousands of men. These messages warned the BEF in real time of six attacks on its front, involving four or more German corps. However, they were not always used well, or were usable at all. Given the BEF's limited reserves, occasionally only 400 men could reinforce a point imperilled by 40,000 soldiers. But the battle of the Marne in September 1914 was no 'miracle' – Sigint, aerial reconnaissance and bold command drove the first mechanised attack in history, as lorries and a fleet of taxis from Paris carried thousands of French infantrymen sixty miles overnight to bolster a beleaguered French position. Sigint was also central to British survival during the 'race to the sea', which completed the continuous front from Switzerland to the English Channel – especially in mid-October 1914, when the BEF's commander, John French, was convinced to abandon an ambitious attack and stand to receive one.[34]

After the establishment of the trench line, the role of Sigint varied significantly by date and theatre: on the Western front it was useless to Britain in 1915, a failure in 1916, but valuable in 1917–18. Across the board, British, French and German performance was similar in range and equal in quality.[35] Operational circumstances determined the value of Sigint. During campaigns in Russia, Palestine and Iraq, force-to-space ratios were low, flanks often were open, and breakthrough and exploitation sometimes were possible. An army could concentrate its strength against the enemy's weakness, outmanoeuvre or destroy a defender – or place its reserves in prepared positions exactly where the foe planned to attack. Throughout these campaigns, the weight of intelligence also lay heavily in one side's favour and intelligence contributed to victories on an epic scale, just as it would in the Second World War.[36]

Conversely, between 1915 and 1917, the Western front was characterised by dense force-to-space ratios, elaborate defensive systems, and firepower which could kill but not move. Breakthrough was extremely difficult to achieve; exploitation impossible. Both sides also possessed intelligence services of high skill, which simultaneously penetrated the other's intentions and capabilities. Intelligence cancelled out much of its own effect: but not all of it. In this campaign of attrition, intelligence presided over a realm of small advantages which collectively had great impact. It affected thousands of small actions and scores of great ones, increasing one's chance for victory, and reducing its cost, for both sides at once.

Information from units was the BEF's basic source, but others dominated key niches. The Belgian resistance traced deployments of German reinforcements to the front. Artillery intelligence directed the greatest killing arm. Aircraft guided gunfire and provided the trench maps upon which planning rested. In 1916–17, I(e), British Army Sigint, played three roles. More than any other source, through interception of wireless traffic in plain language or elementary codes, I(e) reconstructed the enemy's order of battle on the front, especially for guns and aircraft – key indicators of intentions and capabilities. I(e) blunted the effect of enemy artillery, perhaps saving thousands of lives, by directing fighters onto aircraft spotting for guns, often reducing their period of observation by 10–20 per cent and warning troops to shelter from imminent bombardment. In this field, Britain led the world.[37] Finally, Sigint safeguarded surprise for British attacks, and stripped it from German ones – or not.

In 1917, the BEF held that 'the enemy cannot be surprised as to the general front of an attack on a large scale, but only to some extent as to its exact limits and as to the moment of assault.'[38] Operational surprise was impossible. Tactical surprise, regarding the time, place and nature of an attack, by a corps or below, was hard, but powerful when achieved. Defenders had precise warning of a large part, perhaps half, of the attacks launched on the Western front during 1916–17. They acquired this information through many means, but especially by intercepting emissions leaking into the ground from telephone traffic in the trenches 3,000 or more yards away. These emissions initially were intercepted by iron bars or copper plates driven into the ground – later by loops of wire – both perpendicular to the enemy's front for hundreds of yards and connected to listening sets, like telephone headsets, which Germans named 'Moritz' and Britons called 'intelligence telephones', 'IT', or 'I-Toc'. These sets were stationed as close as possible to the enemy, routinely in the trenches and sometimes in no-man's-land. Siginters formed the front line on both sides, beside and sometimes ahead of infantrymen.[39]

Like King David, I-Toc slew its tens of thousands, or more. Britain probably suffered more losses than its foe, because it developed this source later than the French and German armies. Indiscreet telephone conversations compromised the precise time and place of perhaps half or more of British attacks during the battle of the Somme.[40] This, the greatest toll of British signals insecurity in history, occurred because of failures in command, which one signals authority called 'so unnecessary as to border on the criminal'.[41] When the British Army became competent, it gained revenge. The German army blamed the 'bloody losses' of a corps attacking Wytschaete Ridge during 9 May 1917 on an intercepted call from an artillery officer to 'his observer in the front line… that the killing was to begin at 10.22". There is no doubt that this conversation … was heard by the enemy, and that in this way he may have learnt of our intention.'[42]

Successful attacks were covered by tactical surprise in some form. Thus, before the model attack of 1917, the assault on Hill 70, the Canadian Corps emphasised: 'Secrecy with regard to zero day and hour … in some recent operations the enemy was informed as to the approximate time of attack. The most probable source of information is the improper use of the telephone, and indiscreet talk by officers and men.'[43] I-Toc endangered the only possible form of surprise at the tactical level. Mastering Moritz aided the victories at Vimy Ridge and Hill 70 in ways which cannot be determined, but Canadians took seriously. On 6 August, the Canadian I-Toc security team which monitored traffic over previous weeks warned that 'a practically continuous stream of personal conversations between Battery Signallers at Battery Headquarters and OPs' leaked valuable information to the enemy. One message said: 'Well we got down there and found that the 2nd Division and 1st Division Artillery were holding it, getting ready for the big push I suppose' – 'An example of utter carelessness'. Seventy-nine copies of this report, released to maximise its effect before the attack against Hill 70 of 15 August, were circulated.[44] This effort was essential to the surprise which enabled victory.[45]

Breakthrough and mobility returned to the Western front in 1918. Both sides simultaneously won and lost the war of attrition. The offensive and defensive capabilities of most British, French and German divisions vanished, while the US Army was small and inexperienced. A few elite formations could smash enemy defences, but their powers of exploitation were miniscule. The roles which intelligence played during 1916–17 declined in value, while a new one took the centre of the stage: operational surprise, which covered the coordinated attacks of five to ten corps, or 200,000 to 400,000 soldiers.

Operational surprise required cunning manipulation or an unprepared opponent, preferably both at once. It was essential to victories in 1918.

The techniques for surprise were biased in favour of the side with the initiative, which multiplied the operational advantages that gave it that position. Typically, defenders could not locate the enemy's reserves – between 10 and 20 per cent of its forces – in rear areas. Defenders could detect preparations for major offensives, but neither invariably nor with certainty; and attackers simultaneously prepared for several attacks across the front. A defender which could detect only 80 per cent of the enemy's forces stood beside disaster; whereas one able to detect its intentions was on the road to triumph. Any defender could wreck any attack and destroy the enemy's limited strength in storm troops, if it could determine where and when the assault would come. All sources contributed to preserving or penetrating operational surprise, but traffic analysis and wireless deception stood first among equals, because of their power in determining or concealing deployments. The Germans led this competition between March and May 1918, until crushed by French successes in defensive intelligence and operations. From August, successes in surprise bolstered attacks by all of the Allies, especially Australian, British, Canadian and New Zealand forces. On the Western front in 1918, accounting for the effect of deception, traffic analysis and codebreaking, signals intelligence affected operations as much as it would in North Africa during 1940–43.

Sigint mattered even more in Palestine and Iraq during 1917. Britain read most Turkish and German messages sent by radio in those theatres, which compromised the enemy's perceptions and intentions.[46] Most of this material could not be used effectively, or attempts to do so miscarried, but still commanders sought to use it aggressively and intelligently. During the mobile phase of the war in Iraq, General Maude harmonised his two best sources of operational intelligence in a classic manner, using indications acquired through codebreaking to guide assignments for his scarce resources in aircraft reconnaissance.[47] Good Sigint guided the British attack on Gaza of 17–18 April 1917, which failed for operational reasons and bad luck. In November 1917, it enabled General Allenby to wreck the Turkish army in Palestine and seize Jerusalem. During 1918, British mastery of operational traffic in the Middle East declined, though it remained useful for Allenby's victory at the battle of Megiddo in September 1918, which broke Turkish power in Arab countries. However, codebreaking continued to achieve successes which guided British strategy more than in any other time or place of the war. Sigint traced the strategic movements of Turkish forces, including reinforcements to Palestine and Iraq, some of the debates among Turkish generals, and bitter rivalries between German and Turkish forces in the Caucasus, which contained one another rather than combined to threaten Britain. Sigint also monitored the behaviour and effect of Britain's Sharifian Arab ally.[48] This intelligence illuminated a confusing environment, where many saw a struggle for dominance in Asia. It guided the strategic assessments of the Eastern Committee, which managed Britain's war in the Middle East. This experience educated one of its members, George Curzon, who would be a key figure in shaping Sigint after 1918. From 1917 until the end of Britain's moment in the Middle East, Sigint was fundamental to its strategy and diplomacy.

Blockade and Diplomatic Comint

Through its ability to intercept or block transatlantic communications, British censorship hampered the ability of enemy states to contact foreign governments and their own agents abroad, and for enemy civilians or firms to conduct their business. Censorship could not entirely prevent these actions, but it also earmarked such communications for Comint and cryptanalysis. This process produced triumphs in economic and diplomatic warfare, which were marked by the public use of secret intelligence with surprising frequency and effect.

In particular, the maritime blockade of trade to and from Germany, whether directly or through neutrals, rested on Anglo-French sea power and control over transatlantic cables. When German cables were cut and, following international law, the United States declined to let wireless messages in secret code be sent to or from its territory, Britain and France could read the world's mail, in plain language. From 1914, they intercepted all cable and wireless messages across the Atlantic Ocean, and from December 1915, all sea mail. These advantages took time to be realised. Britain did not really begin to enforce a blockade against Germany until March 1915. Thereafter, Britain aimed to prevent Germany from importing or exporting any goods by sea, so to starve hostile populations and industries of food and raw materials, and weaken their ability and will to resist. Blockade worked in an odd fashion: it was not enforced by far-distant weatherbeaten ships; in fact, the weather beat the initial efforts. The first blockading warships were quickly withdrawn and scrapped; the second group, passenger liners equipped with guns, sailed into a wild winter in the North Atlantic, where one simply vanished. Instead, the blockade was enforced in equal parts by sailors, intelligence officers and lawyers. Few shipowners dared challenge Britain's position, instead voluntarily calling at control points. Shortly after Jutland the British removed virtually every vessel from blockade duty because they were no longer needed.[49]

Sigint was central to this power and its application to blockade, providing knowledge, evidence and means for leverage. It let Britain know when firms sought to break the blockade, which often triggered the use of other sources abroad, including detectives and consuls, to gather further information. All of this material could be given to foreign authorities in order to justify Britain's actions against one of their own. Because Sigint might be used publicly without compromising collection, it became a lubricant which let blockade strike as many enemies as possible and as few innocents. For example, censorship produced a host of data which overwhelmed blockade intelligence in 1914. During 1915, Britain's finest intelligence assessment body of the war, the War Trade Intelligence Department (WTID), solved this problem. It organised all intercepts on one index, structured around the names of individuals, sender and receivers, firms and ships, in alphabetical order. Ultimately, the index contained one million names, cross-referenced to highlight their connections. Whenever one wanted information on any name, every reference from one billion intercepts appeared on the index, which was updated constantly. Relevant files could be retrieved immediately. This – alongside the achievements of Hut 3 at Bletchley Park a generation later – was the triumph of data processing for intelligence in the age of the card index. The War Trade Intelligence Department became the central element in the blockade through the war. It processed and analysed vast quantities of Comint in real time, which was used both as secret intelligence and public evidence and enabled an elaborate machine to operate with remarkable efficiency.[50] One main consumer was the Ministry of Blockade, where several diplomats who later became permanent undersecretaries, including Robert Vansittart and Orme Sargent, worked as analysts of Comint.

The blockade was enforced by the Treasury Solicitor's Department before the Probate, Divorce and Admiralty Division of the High

Court of Justice, a British national court enforcing international law. It accepted secret intelligence (especially intercepted correspondence, above all letters) as evidence, and had tough procedures. Innocent vessels and cargoes – which could be held for months, disrupting shipping schedules and endangering firms – all wished to avoid these risks. Sigint let Britain monitor the activities of neutrals and friends, and the system through which it managed the blockade, with the optimum mixture of ease and security and so prevent treachery or punish it. Blockade was a battleaxe rather than a scalpel; it could damage relations with firms and states in a counterproductive fashion. Comint helped Britain wield it with some accuracy. The effect of the blockade is still a vexed question, but Comint was a fundamental factor on the margin, minimising the damage to Britain while maximising that to the enemy. This system was a triumph of unarmed forces, and of open sources.

Diplomatic codebreaking offered further power, because Britain was blessed with secret sources and a foolish foe. Germany committed acts of hostility against neutral countries in the Americas, passing ammunition to anyone able to intercept and read its messages. Britain's enemies rarely could intercept its traffic and thus exploit its mediocre cryptography, though its allies, including two of the world's three prewar leaders in diplomatic codebreaking, did so with cables on their territory. This vulnerability no doubt damaged Britain in alliance-bargaining. Meanwhile, British cryptanalysis against enemies and neutrals became excellent, despite initially poor relations between Room 40 and MI1(b), and bottlenecks in the distribution of intelligence. These intelligence services were remarkably uncoordinated until 1916–17, leading to redundancy and missed opportunities. By early 1916, for example, the Political Section of Room 40 read the encoded telegrams of Germany but did not realise that censorship, which was run by the Military Intelligence Division, intercepted many such messages. Only from July 1916 could the Political Section finally exploit masses of material it had been able to read months before.[51] The NID, and to a lesser degree the MID, moreover politicised Comint through selective distribution of it. They did not give the Foreign Office or senior ministers all of the material they acquired and worked to prevent Britain from supporting President Wilson's peace initiative, which they saw as impossible to achieve and damaging to British interests. Though these judgements had force, still the NID and MID subverted a policy supported by the Foreign Secretary, Edward Grey – in particular by leaking Comint to David Lloyd George, a leading minister who also opposed Grey's proposal. When Lloyd George became prime minister in December 1916, the Foreign Office and the War Office immediately gave him significant solutions of US State Department traffic pertaining to peace moves, so to guide his work against Wilson.[52]

MI1(b) was the key agency in diplomatic codebreaking, apparently mastering most of the world's systems by 1918, including fifty-two different codebooks.[53] Room 40, however, scored the greatest run. On two key issues, diplomatic intelligence gave British officials knowledge, leverage and embarrassing information to publicise. In 1916–17, MI1(b) and Room 40 provided a host of material from all key players (especially Germany and the United States) on the relationship between the belligerent and neutral states over peace moves and U-boats. British decision-makers did not understand the situation perfectly, but still they had unmatched knowledge about the secret manoeuvres of rivals and foes and the opportunity to forestall them.

By December 1916, Sigint showed that King Alfonso of Spain would not support President Wilson's peace initiative, which would fail unless supported by all of the major neutrals. If it did so, Germany would turn to unrestricted submarine warfare. Reading American telegrams and German messages which suggested that Wilson was more hostile to Britain than Germany, soured British statesmen to the president, perhaps unfairly. They believed that Wilson would pursue aims they disliked, which were to some degree hostile to Britain and manipulated by Germany, and yet so long as they remained cautious sooner or later the Germans would declare unrestricted submarine warfare and so drag the United States into the war. This knowledge sparked a cautious policy of playing for time, punctuated by public interventions such as the rejection of American mediation and the publication of the Zimmermann Telegram.[54] Hall skilfully used that telegram (in which Germany offered Mexico control over several American states should it ally with Germany) in order to affect the views of Wilson and the American people. This message was a secondary factor in this process, but it unified American opinion on entering the war.[55]

Again, in the last fourteen months of the war, solutions of Spanish, Austrian, German and United States traffic illuminated the hidden diplomatic context of sputtering efforts at separate or compromise peace; German attempts to split the Allies; Austria's attempts to flee the war, and Spanish and papal efforts to help it do so. This knowledge contributed to one key, if abortive, British action: the attempt to get Austria to leave the war. Similarly, in September 1918, when codebreaking demonstrated that Austria would request an armistice, British ministers spun the news through a public relations offensive. Comint provided a means to manage British allies – notably, whenever intelligence indicated that any state was approaching Wilson for a negotiated peace, Britain would immediately send him such material to show how open his diplomacy was and that he could not act alone. Reading communications between Wilson and his emissaries in Europe guided British success during the Allied negotiations for an armistice in the last weeks of the war.[56]

Diplomatic intelligence on Britain's enemies proved most useful against neutrals and friends. It provided powerful means to weaken Germany and to strengthen Britain. It also shaped secondary issues, such as the Anglo-German diplomatic struggle over Greece, and Latin America.

Siginters

Siginters reflected the male demographics of Britain more than did those of MI6 or MI5, because their work was corporate and technological. Regular military officers and the squirearchy populated MI5 and MI6, augmented by professionals and 'bohemians'. Regular officers were rare within Sigint agencies, though temporary ones were common. Cryptanalysts, analysts and data processors primarily were professional in origin, while intercept personnel came from the 'respectable' working class. Room 40 grew from an old boys' network among civilians, often given reserve ranks, centred on Cambridge, the City, and the professions. Military Siginters had a broader background: they were recruited from within the Army through a formal process and included many temporary personnel. Civilian volunteers dominated components of Sigint. This development reflected limits in prewar preparation for and understanding of intelligence, but even more, that authorities were right to rely on aid from civilians in wartime. Liberal democratic countries produced the greatest of Sigint capabilities, which relied on tight, thick and trusting relations between state and society. In 1914–18,

Britons thought their war was just. The talents required for Sigint existed among civilian elites, where a distinctly British web connected scientists, engineers, scholars, barristers, businessmen, technicians, men and women. Enthusiasm for wireless, automobiles, electronics, and data processing made many Britons socially acceptable for employment in civilian and military bodies, yet technically competent on Sigint. Intelligence chiefs shared these enthusiasms and were willing to solve their problems through civilian aid 'of the right sort'.

Again, Marconi and private individuals gave Britain a capacity for radio interception, matched only by France, and surpassing its foes. Marconi's engineers, the most experienced with radio in the world – especially H. J. Round and George Maurice Wright – developed wireless interception for the services.[57] (Wright's son Peter would continue the family connection with espionage, through decades of service with MI5. His memoir, *Spycatcher*, became a cause célèbre during the 1980s, and helped break the cult of secrecy around British intelligence.) The British Army, poor with wireless before 1914, and mediocre even in 1918, if equal to its French and German counterparts, became good at interception and Sigint, though senior signals officers who were inexperienced with radio slowed that development.[58] The cost is illustrated by contrast with a Dominion force with different attitudes. The Canadian Corps, otherwise modelled on British standards, drew its signals officers from every electrical engineering programme in Canada. These men, yearning to use the most advanced wireless kit and techniques, easily surpassed British performance in this field. The Canadians maintained twice as many wireless units per capita as British forces. They created an independent Sigint service which monitored plain-language transmissions by enemy and Allied forces on its flanks, so illuminating their offensives of 1918, a generation ahead of any other army.[59] So too, in 1914, the Naval Intelligence Division accepted aid offered by what it termed 'voluntary interceptors', including Richard John Baynton Hippisley – engineer and Yeomanry officer, High Sheriff of Somerset, and from a family steeped in scientific, military and political accomplishments – and Edward Russell Clarke – a barrister from Abergavenny and former student of mathematics and science at Charterhouse and Cambridge. These radio enthusiasts showed Ewing, whom Hippisley knew, that they had discovered German naval messages sent on low frequencies which Marconi sets had missed.

Thence the two groups cooperated. Hippisley, Clarke, Wright and Round established fourteen stations for naval interception in Britain, personally intercepted traffic, oversaw stations and invented and built equipment. Their sets used vacuum tubes, first the 'Round' valve, later better ones stemming from French versions of American models. These advances enabled the interception of messages which the Germans thought too low-powered to be caught, shaping the success of Sigint.[60]

The rising power of valves also drove the strength of intelligence telephones, though in this case German kit matched that of the Entente, and enabled victories over Britain. During 1917–18, each British corps on the front had two I-Toc sets, around forty in total. The Canadian Corps and the German army had perhaps twice as many sets per capita, the former due to greater interest in wireless and intelligence, the latter because they relied more heavily on this source. The corps wireless officer oversaw the location of loops, for optimum interception, which varied with the intricate peculiarities of the ground. A sergeant, usually a regular soldier, commanded each Commonwealth I-Toc set. They were manned by volunteers or conscripts, five linesmen and four wireless operators, who often were members of the GPO in peacetime. Nine 'Interpreter Operators (Wireless)' transcribed voice traffic and, along with the wireless technicians, also messages in Morse code. These men worked in three eight-hour shifts, of about six men, one-third resting for a week behind the line at any time. Linesmen routinely repaired lines across no-man's-land or carried messages to local commanders before the enemy acted on them. Intercept personnel wearing headphones hunched over listening sets, often within shellholes in no-man's-land; the better they listened, the more vulnerable they were to fire and raid. Interpreter operators were recruited just before the Somme offensive, when General Headquarters (GHQ) trawled through its personnel, the largest volunteer army ever known, for men fluent in colloquial German. Two months later, after that offensive began, many of them would have been unavailable forever.

Initially, these interpreter operators received no training. Eventually, as in other armies, they were schooled in the military slang and jargon of the enemy and trained by listening to German prisoners speaking over field telephones. These operators were drawn from professional backgrounds, including business, and others were of British and foreign origin who had acquired their German language skills by birth and experience. I-Toc employed such atypical 'Tommies' as a French wine merchant; a British commercial clerk who had spent the first eighteen months of the war interned in the Cameroons; a Bohemia-born future contract bridge champion; a Briton who had served with the German military in Africa and then as a crewman on German merchant ships plying the North Sea; a Church of Scotland minister with a PhD from Jena; and a clerk from the East End of London who had grown up in a home where Russian, English, German and Yiddish were all spoken (like nearly a fifth of the intercept force, this recruit came from a family of Russian Jews who had arrived in Britain seeking refuge from the tsar's pogroms).[61]

The best known example is Vince Schürhoff who, in mid-1916, after two years' service as an infantryman, became an interpreter operator with the Royal Engineers (Signal Service). He spent much of the next two years listening to German telephones and buzzers in frontline I-Toc stations. Schürhoff was fluent in German through his Westphalian father and a secondary education in Hildesheim. He also spoke French and some Spanish, because the family firm exported to Latin America. In his mid-twenties, well educated, a businessman and volunteer with the Kitchener armies, Schürhoff was the only British Siginter of this war known to have kept a diary of his experiences. That diary shows him to have been level-headed and enthusiastic about his intelligence work. Unlike some of his more mercurial colleagues, he also had the stoicism required for lengthy tours of duty in uncomfortable dugouts with frequent excursions around the trenches to maintain the intercept equipment. His competence was rewarded with promotion to corporal and command of stations, where he had the power and independence of a commissioned officer. I-Toc personnel were the politically least trusted group of British Siginters during the war, yet, paradoxically, left to operate with unusual freedom. Vince also used his language skills on other intelligence duties, such as prisoner interrogation and document translation. As an intelligence soldier he enjoyed greater freedom of movement behind the lines than the ordinary Tommy, which let him cultivate a network of relationships, some of them romantic, with French women. During the enemy offensive of 21 March 1918, determined to 'transmit … all information of interest and importance, at all costs', he aided a neighbouring battalion while under fire, then escaped as the position was overrun, intercept set in hand. He received the Military

Medal for this action. Despite his record of patriotism, courage, skill, and fighting his father's people, Vince's German parentage always hung over him. Just before the Armistice, for reasons which are unclear – but probably relate to his familial heritage – he was banished to a signals depot on the coast. He returned to business in 1919 and in the Second World War served with the Home Guard.[62]

Britain had approximately two hundred intercept operators, Canada twenty-five and the Australian Corps twenty, all among the first 'voice-intercept operators' in history (such communications then were impossible over radio). In 1918, many of them moved to wireless interception of Morse traffic, when operational circumstances reduced the role of field telephones in communications, and intelligence. In 1916–17, I-Toc was central to military Sigint. From 1919, its place became miniscule. Such transitions characterise Sigint.

The War Trade Intelligence Department (WTID) was the most academic of British intelligence agencies during this war, or ever before, matched only since by Bletchley Park's Hut 3. Like Bletchley Park, the WTID processed vast amounts of data, which came from the censorship of plain-language messages rather than cryptanalysis. Intelligence chiefs drove the creation of the WTID after postal censorship showed the scale of contraband and of Comint on it. Recognising their limits, they gave the work to civilians who had shown expertise in the matter. These civilians haunted clubs and high tables in search of men 'of the right sort', whose first task was to find others. Whereas Room 40 recruited primarily from Cambridge and the City, the WTID did so through Oxford and the Temple. The WTID provided the largest group of Comint analysts the world ever had known, among the best on record, with distinct sociological characteristics. In Britain between 1914 and 1918, economic warfare was the only area where civilian analysts dominated intelligence. One member of the WTID described how a 'small and amazingly harmonious body, contributing diverse experience and callings from many countries, established a free-masonry with hard-driven men in other departments'. Recruits were almost entirely 'overage or unfit', excluding anyone 'who could turn to private account any knowledge that could come to him in his official capacity'. The WTID included 'dons and barristers, men of letters and stockbrokers, solicitors and merchants', some officers with disabilities, but no civil servants. In a few days they were 'acclimatised to the universal office-equipment of trestle-tables and desk-telephones, of card indices and steel filing-cabinets, of "in" and "out" trays, of rubber stamps and "urgent" labels'.[63] In 1917, about thirty, or 7 per cent, of the WTID members worked for free. Others accepted only expenses.[64] Among them were dons from many – probably all – British universities, especially historians. Alexander Teixeira de Mattos, a Dutch national of Portuguese-Jewish descent and convert to Catholicism – famous as a translator into English of works by Danish, Flemish, Dutch, French, German and Norwegian authors – headed the 'Intelligence Section' before he became a British subject.

Women Siginters

WTID's head, Henry Penson, said that 'what was needed were copyists, filers, and really intelligent men of capacity'.[65] The WTID also included many intelligent women of capacity. Two areas where women penetrated the executive branches of Whitehall during the First World War were in departments associated with the blockade, and among intelligence agencies based in London, especially those involving data processing and Comint. These departments had no established staff, men were required for combat, while women had the skills needed for the work, and legally were paid less than men. Hence, the Treasury pressed intelligence to hire women – primarily women without children and skilled in languages or information processing. Sigint agencies offered women more chances to use their brains for their country than any other arm of the British state. Comint was women's work.

Women made up 75 per cent of the strength in postal censorship, mostly in junior capacities, though several hundred were trained to analyse commercial intelligence. One hundred of 266 officers were 'Lady Censors', a greater part of the leadership than any other British agency of this war, or the next. One of the three highest officials in that censorship was female, and tasked to manage women. Several hundred women worked in the War Trade Department, which oversaw the WTID, though its head, Lord Emmott, noted that their presence was hampered by 'unfair rates of pay'. No woman could be paid above the bottom rung of the starting salary of a man in First Division, even though she 'may have higher academic honours, greater ability and sounder judgment'.[66] Women with undergraduate or graduate degrees served as Comint translators or analysts, such as the Australian Trixie Geraldine Whitehead, previously secretary for the National Union of Women's Suffrage Societies.[67] In its quest for the finest data processors in Britain, the WTID hired the (predominantly female) indexing staff of *Encyclopaedia Britannica*, whose members, notably, were paid the same rates as men, despite regulations. By 1918, eight (or 15 per cent) of the intelligence officers of the WTID were women.[68] In November 1918, MI1(b) had thirty-four officers, eleven civilians and forty 'ladies'. In September 1919, women made sixteen of its thirty-nine staff involved in codebreaking, with another five involved in filing. About 25 per cent of the personnel of Room 40 were female, most involved in information processing, but some of them codebreakers.

By 1917, as the Army scraped manpower for the front, women of the Women's Army Auxiliary Corps (WAACs) with specialised skills took over much support work at BEF headquarters, especially in communications. Among them, GHQ Intelligence included twelve codebreakers. 'Hushwaacs' – the only female Siginters of any nation to serve at the front in this war – provided a quarter of the personnel of I(e)'s codebreaking branch. Its head and star codebreaker, Captain Oswald Hitchings (whom the Hushwaacs nicknamed 'Hitchy Koo'), had been a master at Bridlington Grammar School in peacetime. The Hushwaacs were middle or upper-middle class by origin, a few were piano or language teachers, four were married; all were speakers of German, among other languages, and all volunteers determined to serve in France. They ranged in age from twenty-two to fifty-five.

These women served with the Intelligence Corps as officers – 'Assistant administrators'. One of them was denoted as senior through a second pip, which caused bad relationships within the Hushwaacs, until she was promoted out of their ranks. Their purple shoulder straps, unique in the Army, though characteristic of the Intelligence Corps, provided an element of mystery. Some WAACs thought it signified 'gardeners', others called them 'the Secret Service Officers'. A leaked report in the *Daily Mail* named them 'the goddesses of secrets'.[69] One, Gwendoline Watkins, remembered 'surprised but proud relatives', and 'the odd sensation of being called Ma'am' and seeing 'rows of "other ranks" springing to their feet when I passed'. As the first Hushwaacs entered the headquarters at St Omer in northern France, 'some Tommies ... called out: "Have you come for Blighty? O-oh"' – a risqué question that merged the two meanings of the term 'blighty': 'wound' and 'British soldiers abroad'.

Though no WAAC was wounded or killed in action, GHQ praised their courage and discipline during the retreat of spring 1918. Some Hushwaac candidates were returned as unsuitable – having expected to work with generals, or as spies, or having rejected billets in unheated Nissen huts with sheetless beds and barely private rooms ('I should simply di-i-e,' one proclaimed). Watkins – conscious that: 'In an Army Intelligence Office we were a great experiment – and the path of pioneers is not always an easy one!' – criticised these failures for stereotypical female and upper-class behaviour. 'An affected young person, well rouged and powdered,' quailed at the thought of air raids and working after dinner. 'Rules,' said another. 'Oh I shan't keep any rules unless I choose.'[70]

Only when they arrived on station were Hushwaacs told their duties, for which none had any preparation, save linguistic knowledge, and also the characteristics required for codebreaking. One Hushwaac, Mabel Peet recalled: 'Never having seen a code message in our lives before, you can imagine the despair that filled our hearts. We were left with these awful sheets of paper for about half-an-hour … During that half-hour we exchanged impressions, and depression could not possibly reach a lower level than it reached us just then.' Originally, the Hushwaacs worked as assistants to male members of I(e), divided among its three or four 'rooms', or teams, each of which attacked a different codebook – 'or "friends" as we used to call them, known to us by absurd names such as Adolph, Gretchen, Brunhilde, etc.,' recalled Peet.

With experience Hushwaacs, denoted 'Assistant Accumulators', worked independently, decoding known systems and expanding the known parts of their vocabularies (bookbuilding), and had greater status than male non-commissioned personnel in I(e). These women developed their own jargon: the 'Secret Six', for the first to join; the 'Three Mutineers', for those who left. Hours were long, with no days off until after seven months' service, their male counterparts enjoying better treatment. Air raids broke sleep. Their WAAC superior cheerfully made them retire during one raid: 'You must think of the work; if you are all together in this Mess-room you may all be killed, but if you are in separate huts, some of you may be saved,' Watkins recalled. 'No doubt some of us who were very young took the ups and downs of life at the Office much too hardly, being ever-anxious as to the result of the experiment. At times we had, and enjoyed, considerable responsibility, rising temporarily in to the headship of our respective rooms – at other times we would be relegated to the more monotonous side of the work. Taken as a whole, the work was exacting, and at times exciting and even absorbing.' Peet recalled that the work was 'immensely interesting ... monopolising all our thoughts both waking and sleeping'. [71] Their superiors doubted the value of the experiment, thinking only two of the twelve Hushwaacs were promising, but then similar ratios ruled men. These two, Edith Watkins and Florence Hayllar, went on to work against diplomatic targets in MI1(b) and were offered positions at GC&CS after the war, though neither stayed.[72] Another Hushwaac, Mary Tiltman, became a codebreaker two years before her brother, John, began his rise to becoming Britain's greatest cryptanalyst of the twentieth century.

Sigint Alliances

Between 1914 and 1918, Britain entered many Sigint alliances. Such alliances can be transactional, involving limited exchange of product or cooperation against a cryptosystem, or else thorough, where agencies cooperate fully against all of the systems of a common foe. Anything in between is hard to achieve: walls may block, or fall, but they cannot do both things at once. These alliances of the First World War were limited to specific theatres, services and enemies, and were mostly transactional. Politics drove British actions, whether to shape an ally's policies, or to prevent it from developing inconvenient capabilities: Britain did not cooperate in Sigint with its allies in the Middle East because that might strengthen their political positions more than their military contributions warranted.

Some of these alliances were thorough, probably more so than any in existence before, and pressed by the same winds that drove the creation of Sigint. The NID and Russian naval intelligence cooperated closely against German naval codes until 1917.[73] Britain and France shared blockade and economic intelligence freely, and would have done so with the United States had the latter shown any interest in receiving it.[74] On the Western front, American, Commonwealth and French Sigint services shared techniques and kit, pooled products, and cooperated in attacks against German codes. In 1918, American Siginters had current effective access to about half of the encoded German traffic which they intercepted. Probably British and French Siginters did better because of their greater experience. These successes aided action. Against this, technical and operational failures occurred in the Mediterranean Sea. The Austro-Hungarian navy was able and had better signals security than the German navy. Austro-Hungarian submarines and many U-boats easily passed from the Adriatic into open waters and a chaotic coalition of British, French and Italian fleets. Political differences deformed Allied operations. Royal Navy command in the Mediterranean was fractured, while the Admiralty and the NID neglected the area, shaping Britain's worst performance in Sigint of the war. From October 1915 to February 1917, the greatest U-boat attacks on commerce were conducted in the Mediterranean, which inflicted 50 per cent of British mercantile losses across the world, and significant ones until October 1918. Allied navies developed decent systems for direction finding, but their liaison was poor, as was that between the Royal Navy in the Mediterranean and at home.[75]

Sigint and British Victory

Sigint was a success for Britain between 1914 and 1918, yet its limits were notable. Some of these stemmed from science and technology because Sigint was on the leading edge of the theory and practice of telecommunications. As they worked, practitioners studied electromagnetics, making discoveries which theory could not explain. Ultimately, these discoveries spurred the development of science, but in the short term such difficulties had practical consequences. How could commanders trust a source which often located the High Seas Fleet inside Hanover?[76] They tried to use Comint aggressively, but learned how to do so only through experience and error. Much of it could not be used. This was a war of lost opportunities. During the breakthrough in Iraq of March–April 1917, General Maude used Sigint to exploit victory over a broken enemy. This proved harder to do with troops mounted on mules in a wilderness than it did for mechanised forces a generation later. The Royal Navy tried to use signals intelligence to guide attacks by warships or aircraft on submarines, exactly as it would in 1940–45. Hundreds of attacks were launched; none succeeded – aircraft were too slow and their ordnance too primitive to deliver the killing blows guided by Sigint of 1943. However, some U-boats perished in minefields laid where Sigint showed that they moved.[77]

Sigint had marginally greater success in the air war, at the intersection between the learning curves of competitors who aimed to kill each other. Aeronautical and electrical engineers, pilots and wireless operators, simultaneously fought a war, researched physical phenomena and served as guinea pigs in experiments. Air warfare and Sigint emerged at the same time. As they grew together like children, so did they fight in the world's first electronic war (EW). In strategic air defence during 1915–18, Sigint provided early warning against raids by German airships and aeroplanes which, in each case after lengthy delay, led to their cost-effective defeat. Britain developed sophisticated command, control, communications and intelligence systems to handle Sigint for such issues. Some of these lessons would be applied during the interwar years, especially for strategic air defence; others remained latent, until revived in the next total war.[78]

By 1918, intelligence was using every technique that would be deployed between 1939 and 1945 – only the details were different. Around 9,500 Britons worked in Sigint (1,500 each for the Army and Royal Navy; 1,000 in the wireless and cable censorships; 5,000 for postal censorship; and 500 for the WTID). The return on that investment was remarkable. Britain won the Sigint struggle against Germany and its victories were significant. Material mastery in sea power was reinforced, so producing the easiest great war the Royal Navy has ever faced, and making the application of blockade more effective and less traumatic than usual; Sigint helped Britain evade grave dangers with the United States and instead gain American aid for free. Only on the Western front were British and German signals intelligence equal in quality. Britain led the world in Sigint which, alongside financial support, was an unsung contribution to Allied power. The French outperformed the British in military Sigint, where the Americans also did well; its allies' greatest successes in Comint may well have been against British diplomatic codes and its interests. These British (and Allied) triumphs, however, were largely cancelled out by those of Austro-Hungarian and German Sigint, which helped smaller forces to demolish a larger Russian army. In covert warfare, Britain beat Germany in the Americas, the two drew in the Middle East, and Germany subverted the tsarist state.

These successes by the Entente and Central Powers occurred at the same times, each immediately countering the other's effect before it could lead anywhere: in 1914, Tannenberg matched the Marne and the race to the sea; in 1917 the Zimmermann Telegram equalled the Russian collapse; in 1918 the two sides stood equal in Sigint on the Western front. The greatest successes of Sigint in the First World War exceed those of the Second, and its aggregate quality in 1916–18 probably matches that of 1942–45. But intelligence affected the First World War less because, at the strategic level, each side's successes largely cancelled the other out. Intelligence was harder to use for dramatic results in First World War operations than in the Second, when military forces could strike harder and faster; between 1942 and 1945, intelligence systematically reinforced one side against the other. Nonetheless, in a war where power was measured in the ability to produce hundreds of thousands of soldiers and millions of tons of steel, Sigint mattered, and more than in any previous conflict.

Whitehall's Black Chamber: British Cryptology and the Government Code & Cypher School, 1919–39

After the armistice, ministers and ministries wished to retain the advantages of espionage; in the process they created modern British intelligence. The old personalised system of secret intelligence collected material on a narrow range of issues, which went directly to leaders at the top. It was replaced by permanent, specialised and general purpose agencies, which produced intelligence on everything all of the time. That material was no longer analysed primarily by statesman, but by offices. Intelligence became bureaucratised, thus, modern.

Agencies which had grown haphazardly since 1900 were now reorganised with agent and Comint services combined into MI6 and the Government Code & Cypher School (GC&CS). The Permanent Undersecretary (PUS) of the Foreign Office controlled these services, replacing the scattered leadership of the Victorian era. The Secret Service Committee, which included the PUS, the Cabinet Secretary and the permanent secretaries to the Home Office and the Treasury – the mandarins-in-chief of Whitehall – made major decisions about the structure of intelligence agencies. The Cabinet occasionally heard about Sigint. Departments drove it.[1] The demi-official tradition about British Sigint claims that statesmen of the interwar years were indifferent to Comint, while GC&CS was starved of resources, and low in quality.[2] In fact, statesmen respected Sigint and arguably, between 1919 and 1929,

were its best users; references to Comint and squabbles over its control fill
their correspondence. Some ministers, especially Curzon and Churchill,
cared more than others, but any minister in the inner Cabinet, or of
a department concerned with external affairs, read Comint; as did
Labour ministers, contrary to myth. Nor were statesmen of the 1930s
less interested in Comint than their predecessors; they simply were
less good in its use. The Foreign Office, the military services and the
Government of India consumed Comint enthusiastically. Whitehall
maintained a large and expensive diplomatic codebreaking agency
with an innovative structure: a centralised bureau – GC&CS – linked
to military Sigint services. British cryptology achieved remarkable
successes and failures as it strode the road that would lead to Bletchley
Park. Politics drove these steps.

The Politics of Sigint

The largest units within Comint, the censorships and the WTID,
closed upon victory, leaving only the records needed to rebuild them.
This approach proved successful. In 1939, memory and history ensured
an effective base of Comint for economic warfare. Diplomatic and
military Sigint, however, became permanent organisations. During
1919, the Army and the Royal Navy intended to keep Sigint services.
They rejected a proposal from Curzon, then deputy Foreign Secretary,
that the Foreign Office should control and subsidise Comint, 'without
exception the cheapest and most reliable form of Secret Service', which,
he correctly predicted, would focus on diplomacy. He praised the 'very
wonderful achievement' of Room 40 and MI1(b), which had 'the result
today there is hardly a single Foreign Government whose messages
we are unable to read provided that we can obtain the figures of their
telegrams'.[3]

These departments agreed to combine MI1(b) and Room 40 into
one institution, GC&CS, which started on 1 November 1919, though
its predecessors never ceased work. Military and naval intelligence and
Curzon made these decisions. Only then was the newly formed Royal
Air Force (RAF) invited to participate and the Cabinet informed of
the situation. The Government of India was left to work as it wished.
GC&CS's duties, as Curzon told the Cabinet two years later, were:

The collection, deciphering and distribution of all the telegrams of
foreign Governments; and
    The construction of codes and cyphers for all British
Government Departments who require them, and the training
in their proper use of the personnel employed upon them by the
Departments.[4]

These developments triggered the greatest attack ever launched within
Whitehall against Comint. Treasury officials doubted the necessity
for GC&CS, which they sought to castrate or kill. One official, S. D.
Waterhouse, noted: 'prima facie one would suppose that the advent
of the League of Nations and the general prospect of international
peace would make these preparations for future hostilities unnecessary'.
GC&CS's supporters said the work was 'only limited by the amount of
staff that the Treasury chooses to provide. If they seriously mean to solve
every single cypher telegram they can get hold of by W/T (wireless) or
otherwise, sent to and from every country in the world, the amount of
work is clearly going to be enormous'. Waterhouse doubted 'whether it
will be worth the expense'.[5]
    Whereas intelligence authorities wanted to employ the equivalent
of dons as cryptanalysts, with salaries equal to those of civil servants
of the first class, Waterhouse instead recommended that the 'lowest
class' of codebreakers (junior assistants) come from members of the
second (or executive) class of the civil service, with 'aptitude and
liking for this sort of work', which 'requires rather a special kink in
the brain than a particularly keen intellect, and who, with their Civil
Service traditions and training would be safe repositories of these
very secret subjects'.[6] That proposal revealed ignorance of 'this sort of
work'. Still, Waterhouse raised issues which would dominate decisions
about GCHQ throughout the twentieth century: how many first-class
minds did GCHQ require, and how far could ordinary folk solve the
problems at hand? The services, the Foreign Office and their ministers,
however, broke that first attack. Treasury officials even boosted some
salaries by 15 per cent above previously agreed figures when the Director
of Naval Intelligence (DNI), Hugh Sinclair, threatened an appeal to
ministers. This high-handed success proves the government's demand
for Comint. As optimism about postwar order eroded, moreover, the

Treasury quickly changed its view. Waterhouse wrote: 'The policy of keeping the school in being is of real importance. It is far from being a war-time & emergency measure.' Salaries could not be further cut.[7] In 1919, Whitehall first made Comint a priority for spending, as that matter has remained ever since.

Of the two candidates to head GC&CS, Major Malcolm Hay seemed the obvious choice. He had run MI1(b), overseeing the management, collection and dissemination of Comint across Whitehall. He equalled the retired Alfred Ewing in status and success and worked directly with Hall on Comint.[8] Conversely, while respected, able, and senior within Room 40, the other contender, Alastair Denniston, was neither its leader nor its best cryptanalyst. Some of his colleagues, and many members of MI1(b), disliked him.[9] Politics, however, dictated the decision. Naval intelligence agencies were centralised in London, where those of the Army were smaller, commands abroad having more autonomy. The Admiralty demanded a large Comint agency in London. If Denniston did not head that agency, the Royal Navy warned, it would create one of its own. Sinclair's primary concern was to retain naval control over Comint, just recently the crown jewel of the NID. However, perhaps he also preferred the deference of Denniston to the independence of Hay, strong willed, who opposed details of the DNI's scheme for GC&CS, who would be a subordinate more expert in intelligence than himself. Lord Drogheda, a diplomat acquainted with intelligence and both candidates, thought Hay 'perhaps the cleverer of the two', but Denniston 'the better administrator'. The War Office, under Churchill – an advocate of Comint – did not want to subsidise an agency focused on diplomacy, though it maintained separate Sigint units suited to its own problems. The Director of Military Intelligence, General Bartholomew, had little experience of Hay, or Comint. Of the two candidates, Hay refused to work under and preferably not with Denniston, while the latter agreed to serve as second, naturally, given their relative status. Bartholomew used that decision as an excuse to abandon Hay and accept Sinclair's demands, soothed by the appointment of many members of MI1(b) to GC&CS.[10] Beyond hurt feelings, this outcome was insignificant. Probably Hay would have been a good head of GC&CS – as Denniston would prove to be. Hay could not have been much better because of the limits imposed on the post. That Hay was overqualified to run GC&CS illuminates British

Sigint between 1919 and 1939, and the centrality of Hugh Sinclair to its management.

These decisions combined the preferences of the Royal Navy and the Army for centralisation and decentralisation in Sigint. The navy maintained a large Comint agency focused on diplomatic traffic. GC&CS worked within the NID – though quartered separately at Watergate House on the Strand – but rarely for it. The British and Indian armies maintained smaller, but substantial, Comint agencies. In theory, Sinclair coordinated these activities and wireless interception. In practice, several departments did as they wished in Comint. GC&CS reports – nicknamed 'flimsies' because of the onion-skin paper on which they were printed – were distributed widely, too much so. In 1920, during warfare in Whitehall over policy towards the USSR, someone pursued advantage by leaking solutions of Soviet traffic to the British press. Sinclair soon warned Whitehall that this action had caused the Soviet Union to improve its cryptosystems, which threatened GC&CS's work. This warning was partly erroneous: Soviet authorities learned that their cryptosystems were compromised through captured White Russian officers, while GC&CS quickly reconstructed the new ones: yet Sinclair's warning shaped British Sigint.[11] A powerful First Lord of the Admiralty who was interested in intelligence had just retired; his successor was weaker and indifferent to espionage. Curzon, the Foreign Secretary, exploited the situation to demand Foreign Office control of GC&CS. The Admiralty, confronting budgetary pressure and GC&CS's irrelevance to current naval needs, accepted Curzon's proposal so long as the Royal Navy could withdraw naval personnel from GC&CS in wartime. The Secret Service Committee approved that transfer from 1 April 1921 for good administrative reasons: the Foreign Office was GC&CS's prime consumer and could best provide cover for its funding.[12]

The Treasury allowed this transfer to occur without penalty to anyone: it did not, as it easily might have done, exploit this transition to further reduce funding for the Admiralty, the Foreign Office, or GC&CS. Yet at precisely this time, the Treasury sought to slash expenditures generally, and particularly on intelligence. Ministers scoured every other secret service in search of inefficiencies and economies.[13] This self-restraint reveals how Whitehall valued GC&CS, which was also distinguished from other secret services because it was not human intelligence (Humint) and was an open expenditure, rather than being part of the Secret Service Vote. In 1921, the Geddes Committee swung an axe which ravaged government spending but – alone in Whitehall – amputated not one finger from GC&CS, though it did sweep codebreakers to cheaper quarters at 178 Queen's Gate, two miles from the Foreign Office. Diplomats thought this decision damaged their relations with GC&CS in many ways, which reflect the relationship between codebreakers and their consumers. This decision would harm 'the most secret and confidential aspect of Government work in any part of the world', Curzon warned the Cabinet. 'The deciphered telegrams of foreign govts. are without doubt the most valuable source of our secret information respecting their policy and actions. They provide the most accurate and, withal, intrinsically the cheapest, means of obtaining secret information that exists. But the practical use to which the information can be put is proportionate to the rapidity with which it can be made available. The minimising of delay is a matter of supreme importance.'[14]

Exile in South Kensington would cripple the interaction between codebreakers and diplomats needed to 'secure the successful and accurate interpretation' of messages. Each day, on such missions, eight members of GC&CS visited Whitehall, some occasionally entering the Foreign Office six times. Curzon wanted his subordinates regularly to give codebreakers 'cribs', information on the content of messages: he regretted that the Foreign Office could not house GC&CS, which would have further lubricated this relationship.[15] His officials, perhaps less enthusiastic about such freewheeling contact, had different concerns about liaison. Because of this exile, the PUS, Eyre Crowe, complained in 1925 that GC&CS 'suffered from lack of informed direction: it had so much material to deal with that that it was only by keeping in the closest touch with the organisation responsible for obtaining information from abroad that it could hope to make a proper selection of papers to work upon'.[16] Crowe preferred that the PUS and his private secretary liaise with SIS and GC&CS through one professional chief, and diplomats contact codebreakers through regular channels. Crowe's model prevailed without entirely solving the problems he described.

Inadvertently, this transfer hampered the coordination of Sigint. Sinclair's role, the only link between GC&CS and the services, vanished. Stripped of Sinclair's leadership – and in lodgings that were comfortable but 'rather remote from other departments', wrote Denniston, GC&CS became more autonomous and inward-looking than before.[17] The Foreign Office used GC&CS to suit itself, while any minister with access to Comint might use it to further their political position. Thus, during 1920, Churchill circulated flimsies among his colleagues to attack Lloyd George's policy towards the Soviet Union.[18] Equally, Curzon recognised the value of intelligence to foreign policy – and the Foreign Office. He used flimsies as much to monitor his subordinates and colleagues as he did to monitor foreign states – whether to rebuke an ambassador in Tokyo for exceeding his instructions, Lloyd George for private negotiations with Greeks, or to unmask a conspiracy against himself between members of his party and the French ambassador.[19] Curzon's hope to control the dissemination of flimsies could not be achieved under the Lloyd George coalition government because his colleagues appreciated the value of access to intelligence and wished to shape foreign policy. When, however, with the collapse of that coalition in October 1922, they fell and he remained, Curzon moved far in that direction, denying even the services most flimsies. Crowe further tightened distribution when the first Labour government emerged in 1924 with no minister who knew the older system. From that moment, officials not politicians controlled British codebreaking – as they generally have done ever since.

As these consequences emerged, the intelligence branches of the three services challenged Curzon's hold over GC&CS. In 1923, they argued that cryptology was uncoordinated, which damaged the strategic value of Sigint and its use to them in peace and war. Military intelligence authorities complained that it received barely 20 per cent of flimsies, while 'the services no longer have any say as to what cyphers are to be attacked, or as to what types of messages they wish special attention to be paid'. The diagnosis was correct, but not the remedy: that all-consuming departments should have equal use of the 'machinery' of GC&CS so long as this 'coincided with the agreed policy'.[20] Such a system would cause continual struggle over GC&CS, especially since no policy was agreed. Curzon preferred the existing system, which empowered him. For identical reasons, so did Denniston, who defined the interests of a British Comint agency for the first time since 1844: the system and the lack of policy gave GC&CS, and him, autonomy over its work. He hinted at the need for greater support from the services, warning that 'continuous research in peacetime' was needed to break military systems in wartime, but with GC&CS's present resources (and head), it could 'only tackle the political work'.[21] A war over cryptology, however, was avoided. The Air Ministry broke the united front by refusing to attack the Foreign Office on this issue, so to avoid its enmity on others, while cooler heads found a solution. Sinclair, having just become 'Chief of the Secret Service' ('CSS', but usually called 'C' after the first, Sir Mansfield Cumming), also became Director of GC&CS, controlling it and coordinating all agencies involved in Sigint.[22]

Soon, GC&CS and SIS were housed on separate floors of Broadway House, just off Westminster and across from the tube station at St James's Park. Social if not professional relations between these agencies were distant – in SIS jargon, GC&CS was 'the other side', bureaucrats versus buccaneers – but, as Crowe wanted, GC&CS may have become more responsive to PUS and CSS. The Foreign Office serviced GC&CS's administrative needs and paid for it. GC&CS worked primarily for the Foreign Office, but did more for the services than before. They received diplomatic Comint relevant to their work, except telegrams which might embarrass British diplomats, such as accounts of interviews with a PUS.

GC&CS routinely attacked air, army and naval attaché traffic, the operational codebooks of Italy and Japan, and the military and colonial systems of European states which had possessions in the Middle East, France and Italy.[23] Two liaison officers each from the Army and Royal Navy worked within GC&CS, serving as codebreakers and codemakers. An air section was not created until 1935, under a civilian codebreaker, Josh Cooper. From 1934, the number of military officers attached to GC&CS rose sharply. These liaison officers sometimes were mediocre, mere translators of diplomatic systems which were broken by civilians. Often GC&CS threw these officers at diplomatic targets, rather than service cryptosystems, or the officers did so voluntarily. Still, GC&CS serviced military needs fairly well. GC&CS and the British and Indian armies' Sigint agencies shared product, personnel and techniques, integrated attacks on targets, and made Asia the centre of British Comint.

Between 1924 and 1939, control over intelligence remained a powerful tool for the Foreign Office, which it used to further its policies abroad and at home. Only the PUS and the Foreign Secretary saw every GC&CS report. If they wished, the service ministers, the India Secretary and the prime minister, saw most flimsies, and a lucky few others, some solutions. No evidence supports the dubious claim that even when out of office, Churchill regularly received copies of flimsies: only a fool would give a rival such ammunition. Relevant flimsies went to intelligence authorities in the services, MI5, the Colonial Office, the India Office, and to imperial officials in Asia. During the Second World War, the range of consumers for Comint exploded, given the growth of their needs and of GC&CS's supply.

This system was the best possible at the time. It gave MI6 and GC&CS autonomy and influence. Contemporary British governments could not have placed intelligence under a non-departmental body, such as the Cabinet Office, but this arrangement had a cost: departmentalism reigned. Control over intelligence was a form of power. The obvious winner was the Foreign Office. The latter grasped hold of intelligence precisely as it restored its eminence in the formulation of foreign policy. Ultimately, the losers were the military services. In 1919–21, they surrendered their power over intelligence; in 1940–41, they would find it unprepared for war. During Britain's greatest peril since 1812, it would have to reform its intelligence services radically. This outcome, however, was not apparent when these decisions were taken in 1923, and the services caused some of these problems. That compromise met everyone's interests except those of most ministers, whose influence over cryptology declined, and to some degree, GC&CS. In 1944, Denniston wrote that GC&CS became 'an adopted child of the Foreign Office with no family rights and the poor relation of the SIS', while the Foreign Office thought 'in establishment and other general administrative matters the GC&CS was apt to be nobody's child'.[24]

In hindsight, these statements have truth. In 1923, nothing else was practicable. GC&CS was too small to stand by itself in Whitehall. The Foreign Office was the only department willing to pay for GC&CS, although none wished its death. The Treasury became more generous to GC&CS than to any other unit of the time, authorising minor additions to and unconventional practices about its personnel. In 1925, during a great drive for economy, the Treasury rejected the idea of cutting GC&CS's budget, since the services and the Foreign Office would 'legitimately' oppose any 'reduction in the field of its activities'.[25] Even when it refused petitions from GC&CS personnel for improved salaries, still the Treasury and Foreign Office considered them with respect.[26] GC&CS was autonomous internally, while its two masters would defend its interests externally until 1940 – more than Denniston's description suggest. Probably those words reflect his experiences of 1940–42 where, alone, GC&CS would have to fight for autonomy against the strongest arms of the British state, and win, while Denniston himself would fall.

Other powers with cryptanalytic agencies faced difficulties because one department ran cryptology for all of the rest, or several branches possessed competing units. Britain's centralised system avoided these problems, but caused others of its own. This system met each department's aims but complicated Britain's ability to meet changing conditions. It moved at the pace of the hindmost department, and depended on the cooperation of departments. No authority controlled Sigint. Though charged to coordinate the services in wireless interception – which British Siginters called 'Y' – and determine their targets, Sinclair's reins were loose. Inter-service rivalries dogged Y. Sinclair coordinated departments through underpowered bodies such as the Cryptography and Interception Committee and the Y Sub-Committee (consisting of Denniston and service representatives).[27] Sinclair appreciated wireless and Y. From 1925, Army Y at Chatham pioneered the interception of high-frequency circuits – which increasingly carried high-speed diplomatic communication – but lacked the personnel to write down the intercepts. Hence, SIS paid for several automatic high-speed interception recorders which transmitted traffic direct from Chatham to GC&CS, where slip readers took down the figures.[28] Sinclair pressed the services to develop Y services, but he could not command, merely persuade. He had fair success, but most failings of Sigint occurred in this area of persuasion, some of them because of him.

Many thought Sinclair too 'masterful'. He wished to control all intelligence and security services, and he did direct GC&CS. Sinclair, more than Denniston, was the true predecessor to the Director of GCHQ. He had direct contact with any member of GC&CS, and vice versa. Sinclair rated equal with the service intelligence chiefs, Denniston with the heads of their Sigint sections, who also corresponded directly with and were advised by the heads of the Air, Military and Naval sections at GC&CS. Denniston is best seen as the father of GCHQ's commercial and diplomatic sections, which would keep many of GC&CS's characteristics throughout the Cold War; his deputy,

Travis, perhaps has the same status regarding GCHQ's Cryptographic and Distribution sections. Sinclair, probably the illegitimate son of a Victorian admiral, Frederick Seymour, inherited wealth, status and naval connections.

Sinclair's commanding officers praised his qualities of tact, judgement, leadership and discretion. He had begun his career as a torpedo lieutenant, on the leading edge of sea power and technology, including electricity. By 1919, after demonstrating powers in command and organisation, with ample experience in mid-level command and staff positions, but not in intelligence, he succeeded Admiral Hall as DNI. Then, after commanding the submarine service, with a naval future before him, Sinclair became leader of Britain's foreign intelligence agencies, reporting directly to the PUS and the chiefs of service intelligence.[29] Charismatic and respected, he was the greatest intelligence chief in peacetime that Britain ever had known. His celebrated dinners attracted an eager generation of officials. He spoke straight to statesmen, once wearing his dress uniform to back a briefing of Neville Chamberlain. Sinclair was a firm but sympathetic leader of his people, acquiring resources for them and circulating their reports. Somehow, he developed monies outside the Secret Service Fund, which he used to subsidise Sigint alongside the Humint practised by MI6, including support for service Y units, covering expenses to receive cables from telegraph firms, equipment, the lease of Broadway House, and the purchase of Bletchley Park. His successor, Stewart Menzies, managed to increase those extra funds, which he used to purchase the 'bombes' that beat Enigma, and subsidise the expansion of Bletchley Park until 1942. C's slush fund probably supported GC&CS more than it did SIS. Sinclair had 'hard Tory views' on policy and peoples, including anti-communism and anti-Semitism, though these characteristics did not blind him to the perils of Nazi Germany. His personal skills contained the negative consequences of systematic problems in the intelligence system, but also concealed them.

Sinclair dominated the two leaders within GC&CS, both of whom were junior officers from subordinate branches of the Royal Navy accustomed to following their leaders. Denniston and Travis, head and deputy head, schoolmaster and Paymaster Commander, were masters of cryptographers, rather than Comint. Denniston, a member of the Scottish hockey team which won Olympic bronze in 1908, remained a keen sportsman throughout his life. He was a devoted family man, whose active social life shaped recruitment for GC&CS during 1938–41. He ably defended GC&CS at a junior level and managed his personnel and resources well. A shrewd picker of people, he raised the quality of his staff over time, through a focus on craftwork. He persuaded the Treasury to promote the best of his junior codebreakers and clerical personnel, whom he encouraged to better themselves, so freeing his strongest cryptanalysts for harder tasks. Denniston, however, was treated as a technical expert. He wanted a black chamber, not a Sigint or an intelligence service. Like the colonel of a good regiment, he saw himself as much a codebreaker, as a manager of codebreaking. Those characteristics shaped his success between 1919 and 1940, and his failure in 1941. Travis had greater experience with technology and management than any other codebreaker between 1919 and 1945, a shrewd sense of politics and the manner of a leader, which proved essential to the success of Ultra between 1939 and 1945.

Sigint Between the Wars

British Sigint fell into four parts. The main body of GC&CS attacked diplomatic and military codes, while the rest handled communications security (Comsec) and liaised with units intercepting radio traffic. The British and Indian armies and, from 1935, the Royal Navy, maintained small Comint agencies. They, the RAF, the Metropolitan Police and the Australian and Canadian navies, collected wireless intelligence and conducted traffic analysis.

Unlike the members of MI6 and MI5, British Siginters were regular civil servants or military personnel, almost all of whom received pensions. Their salaries and numbers were reported in departmental estimates and lists of officers and published openly: foreign powers, however, failed to exploit this transparency. GC&CS inherited what the civil service termed an administrative class, but what equally was a quasi-military officer class, from the wartime cryptanalytic bureaus. Its members were largely middle-aged and male, educated in the classics or modern languages, and originally academics or civil servants, usually with some military experience. Some, like Oliver Strachey, James Turner and Dilly Knox, were excellent cryptanalysts whose lives had been transformed by the practice; others were more mediocre with linguistic capabilties but no better job in view. They were joined by Ernst Fetterlein, tsarist Russia's leading cryptanalyst, who had attacked German naval cryptosystems during the First World War, working with Room 40, which he joined when the Royal Navy spirited him from Russia following the October Revolution. These people were designated senior or junior assistants (grades unique to GC&CS, though shoehorned into the conventional structure of the civil service), which reflected their presumed cryptanalytic prowess. A larger group of female clerks worked in support, clerical and information-processing roles, coming mostly from Room 40 and MI1(b). However, some women originally from the GPO sorted cable traffic, and others from the Admiralty's signal division tackled the construction of British codes and cyphers.

GC&CS began in 1919 with twenty-eight clerical and twenty-four cryptologic staff, eighteen junior and six senior assistants. Though Room 40 was the dominant institutional influence on GC&CS, half of its initial codebreakers came from MI1(b), including – not surprisingly – several leading ones: MI1(b) had better and broader experience against diplomatic targets than Room 40. MI1(b)'s strength rose from eighty-five to over one hundred between the armistice and the end of the Paris Peace Conference, where it was a hidden dimension of British policy.[30] W. F. Clarke, a veteran of Room 40 and soon to be head of GC&CS's Naval Section, noted that 'the changeover was not easy for those concerned as it is a very different matter to deal with the formal language of diplomatic telegrams after a training devoted to the telegraphese of service messages. The methods of recypherment were also very different and the staff had to learn a great deal about cryptography in its more complicated forms.'[31] Some members of GC&CS also served in the WTID, and I(e). On its initial establishment, no juniors could be hired, nor appointed to senior assistant until 1938, when the first of the latter was scheduled to retire. However, fluidity emerged at both levels. Several members soon resigned, while in 1924, Sydney Fryer, late of MI1(b), died after jumping in front of a train at Sloane Square tube station. This suicide caused Sinclair to improve working hours and conditions for codebreakers, in an attempt to counter the unique pressures of GC&CS work.

Initially, GC&CS was intended to have a Construction Section (one senior assistant, two Army and two navy officers, two assistants from civilian departments, and thirty clerks); a Secretarial Section (three or four clerks); an Intelligence Section (one navy officer, six junior assistants, and three translators); a Research Section (two senior assistants); six sections at various times called: Country, Geographical or Linguistic sections; a French and Italian Section (two junior assistants); a Central and Eastern European Section (four junior assistants); a Scandinavian Section (two junior assistants); a Spanish and South American Section (two junior assistants); a USA Section (two junior assistants); and a Far Eastern Section (one senior assistant and two junior assistants). The organisation of clerical and geographical sections soon, and often, shifted, while functional (e.g. naval) sections were added, but the basic structure remained constant. By 1927, cryptanalysts were divided into French, Slav, Middle East, Near East, Iberian and Oriental groups, and into British Code, Distribution & Reference (D&R), Naval, Type, and Cable sections.[32] By 1943, when 188 staff worked on diplomatic matters, and GC&CS no longer handled cryptography, it maintained the equivalents of the Secretarial, Research, Intelligence (now named D&R) and clerical sections, with seventeen geographical sections, and a large Commercial section.[33] Between 1921 and 1935, GC&CS had about eighty or ninety staff, including thirty codebreakers; by 1939 this had risen to around two hundred personnel, including thirty-three cryptologists. During 1919–39, between 140 and 220 men, including codebreakers, worked full time in radio interception, aided by part-time volunteers. Altogether, between 250 and 480 personnel worked full time in Sigint, with salaries totalling around £70,000 by 1925 and £100,000 by 1939. GC&CS salaries alone were £25,000 in 1921, £29,000 in 1926, and £36,000 by 1937.

By contemporary standards, this investment in cryptology was large. GC&CS had 20 to 25 per cent of the personnel of the Treasury or the Foreign Office, and equalled the strength of Room 40, or MI1(b). It was the largest and best codebreaking agency in the world, receiving more material than any other of them. GC&CS daily received under general warrant 'numerous sacks of cables which must be hastily copied and returned to the Cable Companies within 24 hours', to minimise suspicion, and also solutions of traffic from the services' codebreaking units.[34] By 1924, No. 2 Wireless Company at Sarafand in Palestine telegraphed about a hundred groups daily to Britain, and sent more by bag. Between 1929 and 1939, the Indian Army circulated 9,452 solutions in its Y/India series, some of which GC&CS reproduced as flimsies. In 1938, naval radio stations in Britain gave GC&CS 3.6 million groups, or over 90,000 encyphered messages. GC&CS 'handled' between 10,638 and 13,390 telegrams during the last three months of 1934, 1935 and 1936, suggesting that it received 44,000–52,000 telegrams in each of these years. That figure reached 100,000 by 1940.[35] Until 1938–39, GC&CS did not exploit other means of collection, such as stealing codebooks or intercepting diplomatic mail. Intelligence authorities had the GPO tap telephones of diplomats in London, but how often is unclear. Britain was reluctant to open diplomatic bags even secretly during the First World War, but began to do so in 1939 with many neutrals and Allies.

The services intercepted wireless traffic, primarily on medium frequencies, though from 1928 increasingly on high frequencies. Operators worked in shifts, mostly against known targets but with ample time allocated to 'General Search' – watching for unknown stations or links, finding frequencies as they faded, listening on headsets and transcribing messages in Morse code. GC&CS, like MI1(b) and Room 40, focused on cable, codebook, and diplomatic traffic. GC&CS retained just one wireless expert, L. H. Lambert, a magician and radio ham before the war, and leader in interception during 1914–18. He conducted experiments and interception from a station at his home, ably aided by May, his long-suffering wife. Lambert was the member of GC&CS best known to the public, albeit under a pseudonym – 'A. J. Allen', a popular raconteur of tall tales on BBC radio. Lambert was augmented by H. C. Kenworthy, a Marconi employee loaned to Scotland Yard, who aided MI5 and MI6. GC&CS relied on volunteers from the Metropolitan Police, the RAF and some private citizens, to intercept radio traffic: in 1939 they became honest Siginters. The thirty-six police volunteers, many retired naval operators, maintaining one constant watch, were nominally listed as a permanent intercept organisation of fifteen policeman, with rotating membership, under Kenworthy at Denmark Hill.[36] GC&CS personnel outside the service sections, noted Josh Cooper, 'disliked and distrusted' radio intercepts; 'it was messy pencil script, not neat typescript, and was often corrupt even when not obviously mutilated'.[37]

The Government Code & Cypher School

At the top of GC&CS stood Denniston and Travis. Denniston oversaw codebreaking – with each section head reporting individually to him – and liaison with the main consumer, the Foreign Office. Travis, not so much Denniston's second as the master of an Allied division, oversaw every other task, especially: those involving 'contact with other departments', including the Cable and Wireless, Code, D&R and Type sections; the construction of codes and how they were used; the tasks as GC&CS's 'wireless expert'; and the liaison which G. L. N. Hope and M. P. Mayo conducted with departments, and Henry Maine did with communications firms. Travis was also to 'concentrate on obtaining the maximum Intelligence value from the work performed by the G.C. & C.S., and will ensure that cryptographers are supplied with such information as they may require to assist them in their work'. As Chief Cryptographer, Oliver Strachey oversaw the execution and priorities of cryptanalysis, advising section heads on how systems should be attacked, and allocating tasks to personnel, including the 'Research Cryptographers', or seniors. Section heads liaised with each other on technical problems.[38] Most cryptologists worked in GC&CS's functional and geographic sections, which varied in size. The Russian Section included among others Fetterlein and Cooper; the Japanese Section relied on the retired British diplomats and renowned Japanese linguists Ernest Hobart-Hampden and Harold Parlett, together with Hugh Foss – who, born and raised in Kobe, was the son of the Anglican Bishop of Osaka – sometimes aided by naval or military officers, most notably the outstanding bookbreakers, John Tiltman and the Australian Eric Nave.

John Hessel Tiltman was born in 1894. At the age of thirteen, while at Charterhouse School, he was offered a place at Oxford, which he had to reject. The recent death of his father, an architect, left his family in danger of social degradation, unable to cover that cost, or to maintain Tiltman's status. His older brother, Alfred, graduated from London University and entered an apprenticeship leading to a major career in the aeronautical industry. After graduation in 1911, conversely, John became a teacher. These experiences foreshadowed the next generation of Tiltman's life – straitened personal circumstances and extraordinary talents. A hidden shyness, perhaps reflecting uncertainty about his place, underlay a firm and gentlemanly surface, a great appetite for work and an ability to put himself in other's shoes. Tiltman's personal judgements were shrewd, acerbic, but expressed only when necessary. He tolerated superficial slights, and acted vigorously when he did reply.

A series of remarkable events drove Tiltman to his career. In 1914, he joined the Army as a subaltern. He received the Military Cross for a battle in 1917 where every officer in his battalion was killed or wounded. After the armistice, at a loose end, Tiltman volunteered to join the forces intervening in the civil war in Russia, during which time he learned some Russian. On his return, Tiltman took a course in Russian organised by the Army at King's College, London. That linguistic competence led the Army to post him temporarily to GC&CS, where Fetterlein discerned his cryptanalytic promise. Fetterlein gave Tiltman, unlike anyone else at GC&CS, some training in cryptanalysis, but only against transposition cyphers. They worked together against the Russian diplomatic cypher system of 1921, a masterclass which Tiltman passed with honours. He returned the favour by helping Fetterlein's brother and son join GC&CS during the 1930s. Tiltman immediately demonstrated rare skill in cryptanalysis, above many established members of GC&CS. Hence, the Army left him at GC&CS for several years. His specialisation in intelligence limited Tiltman's opportunities at his regiment, when the Army was shedding officers, but the latter hired him as a 'Signals Computer', one of its two codebreakers. The position offered a good salary, but for years no pension. It was not regularised until 1939, almost two decades after Tiltman became a leading Siginter. Tiltman looked like a soldier, but did not like military formalities. He never was a real regimental officer, though he loved to wear the uniform of the King's Own Scottish Borderers, especially before an audience of Americans. That uniform, and the MC on his chest, gave him credibility among the soldiers with whom he dealt during most of his career, and backed the nickname which his colleagues cherished, 'The Brig'.[39]

Initially, the American Section – the largest section – included two of GC&CS's best cryptanalysts, Strachey and Knox, among others. The Naval Section fluctuated between three and five personnel between 1924 and 1931, to eleven by September 1937. Each section had a permanent core, while other cryptologists moved from one to another as priorities changed, directed by Denniston and Strachey. During the Italo-Ethiopian war, when 'the Italian Diplomatic was both wanted and exploitable', the Italian Section rose from five to twenty personnel by 'transferring parts of the Italian commitment to experienced cryptanalysts and their supporting staff taken temporarily from a variety of other tasks (French, Rumanian and Scandinavian) ... These twenty included only two or three new recruits to Sigint (ten would have been rather a hindrance).'[40] By 1938, these twenty people had dwindled to nine. This movement of personnel was limited by language difficulties. Most bookbuilders could attack traffic in French, few in Japanese. The Japanese diplomatic, military and naval sections stood apart from their confrères, and closer to each other.

One section changed its function over time. The 'Diplomatic and Commercial History' of GC&CS recalled that D&R began as a 'clearing house' to circulate flimsies to consumers, but later 'became an editing authority; reference library and indices were built up both for the editing function and for the benefit of cryptanalytical research'. This progression is true, but its dates are unclear. GC&CS initially included an intelligence office, modelled on one from Room 40, which used material from Y and other sources to aid solutions and translations. GC&CS confronted different problems, which took years to solve. Judging from the language of flimsies, D&R, interacting with the linguistic sections, quickly ensured that solutions were translated accurately and uniformly into diplomatic language. 'Diplomatic telegrams,' GC&CS held, 'were usually, if properly translated, self-evident, though they needed the checking or cross-referencing which were generally referred to as an editing.'[41] Alas, problems with translation dogged editing and the 'self-evidence' of telegrams. Aid to cryptanalytical research emerged more slowly. In 1928, as foreign cryptography began to improve, GC&CS was reorganised, particularly to improve that aid. Knox damned the existing 'distribution of information' to aid codebreakers, especially for providing 'cribs; i.e. the subject matter of the telegrams which the ambassador issues after the day's work'. While 'the supply of potential cribs from the Foreign Office is on the whole adequate and their distribution in the section fairly intelligent', reports from other departments were found to be sparse, those from open sources were badly processed, while D&R's 'policy of ruthless destruction' killed older but essential records.[42] James Turner, a respected bookbuilder who was qualified in fifteen languages, ranging from Arabic to Japanese, shared Knox's views about the intelligence available for codebreaking. Codebreakers could generate cribs about diplomatic discussions only by knowing 'what they are talking about'. This task required a 'properly equipped bureau' to serve as a 'clearing house' for information.[43]

D&R achieved these aims, probably fast. Its work was best described in 1943 by Alfred McCormack, an American observer of 'Denniston's show'. 'Like everything else that these very practical people do,' he said, 'the index is designed to serve its purpose as nearly as can be achieved with the minimum waste of effort … their primary purpose is to supply crypt people with a reference file in which they may locate quickly whatever information may be helpful to them in solution work.' The 'whole key to these British operations lies in the infinite pains they take with these files, while never losing sight of their practical objectives'. D&R, McCormack noted, 'has the most simple filing system imaginable'. Different types of records sat in distinct folders, arranged by date of issue. D&R maintained copies of each flimsy, in a master file, a spare file, and a 'Subject and Country' file, which ranked all telegrams from each state in chronological sequence. It kept standard reference books on international affairs, reports from many British departments, and clippings from *The Times* and *Daily Telegraph*. One index listed the flimsies including 19,000 names of persons, as another did on thirty-nine subjects (ranging from 'Treaties' to 'Trials'). A 'Cabinet Book' included clippings and notes about leading officials across the world. A 'Diary', written in longhand, outlined the key events in all countries every day. These indices were less developed than those of the WTID or Hut 3, because the aim was less ambitious: not to report every piece of useful intelligence from each intercept to all consumers, but rather to help bookbuilders guess groups and translators express meanings by providing easy access to multiple contexts.[44] This system sped solution through finesse rather than brute force. German diplomatic codebreakers had a more elaborate system, perhaps too much so, and seemingly no more successful: their British newspaper of record was the *Daily Mail*. American diplomatic codebreakers had a simpler system, which avoided books or diaries, and linked a much larger card index with original publications.[45]

GC&CS had a distinct social and organisational tone. Its personnel and work were interdepartmental and interdisciplinary, more than any other department in Whitehall. Outsiders viewed GC&CS as unique and made exceptions in their practices for its people. Oxbridge, especially its administrative streams, stamped the members of GC&CS far less than perhaps any other civil department, though their graduates dominated those recruits who were drawn from universities. GC&CS shared Whitehall's contradictory regard for the gentleman amateur and the expert, and emphasis on practical rather than theoretical knowledge. GC&CS also had criteria of its own. Its members regarded themselves as masters of an arcane craft, not technicians. The 'Diplomatic and Commercial History' of GC&CS noted how 'a dozen or so senior men with war experience' shared tasks offering 'opportunities for investigation and at the same time the possibility of useful intelligence', aided by junior 'apprentices' and 'such clerical assistance as was required'. GC&CS, particularly Denniston and Strachey, 'allocated the task (irrespective of country) to the man, and the assistant to the "leader" believed to have the required cryptanalytical experience'.[46] Knowledge of cryptosystems rather than languages determined who led new ventures. Self-directed cryptanalysts pursued individual projects. Tolerable and talented people jostled prima donnas and those retired on the job. The ability of individuals drove attack against states. Office politics and personality conflicts drove this small bureau, which was more like a department in a university than of a government. In so tiny an organisation, the personal was political. The desire to please some people, or to avoid their presence, shaped the organisation of work. Yet in 1939–42, despite strained personal relations Denniston and Knox cooperated, John Tiltman recalled W. H. Jeffries from retirement to salvage a failing attack on Chinese traffic, and collegiality survived disputes over policy, though barely.

Denniston oversaw this menagerie well, if too loosely. According to its Standing Orders, the Chief Cryptographer was 'responsible for the general training of the cryptographic personnel, especially of Juniors on probation'; the latter should 'spend some part of their probationary period with as many Groups as their languages and other qualifications permit', with section heads providing specific schooling.[47] In practice, these procedures were ignored, perhaps because of the departmentalism of GC&CS and the status of seniors, who treated probationers as graduate students, or property. GC&CS rejected a training regime, leaving each entrant to learn by 'devilling for an expert', if that devil wished. Its most experienced codebreaker and expert in Soviet systems,

Fetterlein, chose whom to train in cryptanalysis, or not. He rejected most officers translating Russian messages, save Tiltman who, under his tutelage, became Britain's best bookbreaker.[48] GC&CS could never have contemplated the great contemporary effort that the head of American military codebreaking, William Friedman, put into reproducing cryptographic manuals so to guide budding American cryptanalysts. Nonetheless, in 1932 Strachey produced a manual on transposition cyphers, printed in a hundred copies, which also referred students to other manuals, and he presumably produced another on substitution cyphers. He lectured on these topics to new recruits for a few hours. Only people outside the mainstream of codebreaking at GC&CS, members of the Naval and Military sections, some female members of the clerical staff, and the new personnel recruited in 1938–39, received systematic training in cryptology, ranging from three months for officers, to three days for dons. Tiltman was the senior member of GC&CS in 1940 most experienced in training virgin cryptanalysts, explaining his understanding of how to do it, when he became Chief Cryptographer.

Interwar Siginters

GC&CS recruited junior and senior assistants from a charmed circle of the wartime cryptanalytical units, military and diplomatic officers, Oxbridge, the University of London occasionally, but never the Scottish or 'provincial' universities. Only 'gentlemen' should read other gentlemen's mail. GC&CS's first personnel had impressive academic and linguistic qualifications, but Denniston believed most of them lacked the characteristics of a cryptanalyst – what the DMI termed 'cryptographic flair' and 'analytic acumen', and Op-20-G, the US Navy's codebreaking agency, called a 'cypher brain'. Travis held that 'in modern cryptography diagnosis is as important as it is in modern medicine, a matter not only of scientific approach but of experience also, and the indefinable sense of "awareness" that is called flair'.[49] Many cryptologists were originally hired simply for linguistic knowledge. Of these, Denniston thought, 'only a small percentage developed any real skills', and were GC&CS's 'backbone'.

In 1923, GC&CS regarded two senior assistants as being the cryptanalytical equivalent of six junior assistants.[50] It later claimed that members of these groups had the same value after five years' experience, which suggested that GC&CS's ability to solve codes had perhaps doubled, although its strength in personnel remained static. In 1937, the junior assistants stated that they were originally expected to handle mundane work, while their superiors formed 'a sort of aristocracy of Research Workers'; no more was this true.[51] Experience also sharpened the power of staff. By 1928, six junior assistants were upgraded to senior assistants, and the GC&CS establishment included fifteen of each. Denniston and Sinclair opposed an appeal by the remaining junior assistants of 1919 for additional pay, because they had, 'to be quite frank, reached the limit of their marketable value'.[52] By 1935 eight of its original twenty-five cryptanalysts had left, 50 per cent of the strength had joined since 1924, and GC&CS had sixteen seniors to nine juniors.

The main, and equal, sources were military liaison and retired officers, and university graduates recruited through the Civil Service Commission (CSC). To an unusual degree, GC&CS was allowed to make the CSC a post office, rather than a gatekeeper. Denniston – and during 1937–39, Travis and Tiltman – directly contacted by post or in person the placement officers or dons at universities, provided 'slightly more intimate details of the work and of the type of men we require', discussed and sometimes discouraged applicants, and monitored interviews.[53] Following conventional practice, the analysis of candidates (by the 1930s, often over twenty applicants for four positions) was objective and detailed. During the 1920s (but, apparently not the 1930s), contrary to convention, candidates met the assessment board before they sat the exams, to remove unpromising candidates from competition. GC&CS rejected unsuccessful candidates, rank-ordered acceptable ones, and offered posts by that criteria, sometimes encouraging those not offered positions to apply again. Only those offered positions learned what the work entailed. Standards were high. Joe Hooper, later a Director of GCHQ, rated fourth among seven candidates provisionally accepted in 1938.[54] Accepted candidates remained probationers for two years, to enable weeding of incompetent cryptanalysts, though none were so expelled. The women's colleges at Oxbridge usually received notice of GC&CS competitions, but sometimes were excluded, because a given post entailed service abroad during a war, or an internal candidate, in a temporary position, Miss Marie-Rose Egan (supported by all of her superiors) was certain to be offered a post, but Denniston 'could not face the prospect of having our vacancies filled 100 per cent by women'.[55] Following conventional civil service practices, 'female candidates must be unmarried or widows' and were 'required to resign their appointments upon marriage'.[56]

When recruiting among graduates, GC&CS looked at applicants with classical, linguistic or mathematical backgrounds. In many competitions, it had specific demands for expertise in languages. GC&CS hired mostly masters of difficult languages, such as Japanese or Russian, looked unsuccessfully for Arabic and Turkish linguists, and pursued all-rounders with intuition and synthetic faculties. GC&CS judged the ability of candidates by their aptitude for, rather than knowledge of, languages and mathematics, and especially their ability to solve cryptologic problems. All, Denniston thought, must be 'men of sound character, in whom we can place implicit faith ... we really require men with the type of mind of the student rather than men with administrative capabilities, for which there is very little scope'. The regulation that 'a certain degree of mathematical aptitude is of the first importance while mathematical knowledge is of no importance' suggests the true test was of analytical, logical and magical capabilities. In 1938, Denniston remarked: 'a man taking a First in any subject, thereby assuring us of intellectual ability, coupled with a taste for modern languages would be a suitable man for us ... the man with a mathematical mind is probably the most suitable, but we have several distinguished classicists who are among our most able members'.[57] That students need not understand 'recurring decimals' (numerals where the decimal representation, after a period of randomness, eventually repeats itself forever), shows that classicists and linguists were enabled to meet the upper level demanded of mathematical knowledge. The language examination consisted of 'translation and restoration or completion of a faulty passage of the language', and that in English had the same paleographical feature, alongside 'essay-writing'.[58]

Women outweighed men at GC&CS in numbers, but not status. During 1919, women made up 30 per cent of Hay's projected staff of codebreakers, all at junior levels. Denniston planned to have three female junior assistants out of eighteen, but two resigned, for reasons unknown. However, three 'lady translators' eventually were absorbed into the rank of junior assistants, after considerable turnover, probably because of low pay. Only one of the original three remained with GC&CS through to the Second World War. Helen Lunn was born in Russia, one of four daughters of an expatriate family who returned to Britain after the revolution. She joined Room 40 just before it was subsumed into GC&CS, while another sister served briefly in MI6's Middle East organisation. A third, Margaret, worked in MI6's Helsinki station before being dismissed under suspicion of espionage, only to join GC&CS in 1921! The eldest sister, Edith, a dedicated communist, married fellow activist Arnold Rothstein. The Rothsteins lived under constant MI5 surveillance, which carefully recorded Helen's visits to her sister. Nevertheless, Hugh Sinclair regarded Helen and Margaret as 'quite sound from a security standpoint'.[59] In this era, even ferocious anti-communists were surprisingly judicious when assessing the loyalties of their employees.

On its original establishment, women were 25 per cent of the GC&CS's managers, defined by personnel drawing salaries rather than wages, all clerical supervisors, with only one codebreaker.[60] Junior assistant Emily Anderson was a Presbyterian from southern Ireland, and thus outside both 'Ulster' and the professional parts of the Protestant Ascendency. Educated privately by a multilingual governess, her father was president of University College, Galway, where she became the first professor of German. In 1918, driven by a desire to serve her country and perhaps escape her parents' oversight, she trained as a Hushwaac and was then transferred to MI1(b). Hay and Denniston respected her skill and aided her career. During the interwar years, along with Agnes Driscoll and Elizabeth Friedman in the United States, Anderson was the leading female codebreaker and among the best cryptanalysts in the world. In 1927–28, Anderson, admired as a bookbuilder and taskmistress, was promoted to senior assistant and made head of the Italian Section. In order to prepare for the task, she translated Benedetto Croce's biography of Goethe, published by Methuen. A decade later, she published what remains the standard translation of the letters of Wolfgang Amadeus Mozart.

'Bluestocking' and empire-builder, Emily Anderson persuaded Denniston to give her section the services of a new entrant, William Bodsworth, originally hired for the Spanish Section, because (in the latter's words), 'as Italy was a first class Power, her need was greater'.[61] Bodsworth called this behaviour string-pulling, but the case had merit: Italy shaped British diplomacy more than Spain and the Latin American republics. Anderson's success reflects Denniston's respect for her, and the power she could wield as a senior assistant. Anderson drove the assault on Italian diplomatic traffic during 1935–38, a leading priority of that day, making her perhaps the central codebreaker in GC&CS for two years. When war began she voluntarily demoted herself as head of the Italian Section, joined the Military Section, and won an OBE for her work against military traffic at Cairo between 1940 and 1943. Tiltman complained that she bullied his officers when assigned to her, which was to say, most members of his section between 1936 and 1938. He also praised her quality and recalled with admiration the legend that, during an argument with Denniston, she said: 'You don't seem to understand, Commander Denniston, that my work starts when I leave your office.'[62] That Anderson could do so and prosper illuminates the status of women, and senior assistants, at GC&CS. Her translations of the letters of Mozart and Ludwig van Beethoven corrected lacunae and errata from earlier editions, ultimately gaining her the *Verdienstorden der Bundesrepublik Deutschland*, the Order of Merit, from the Federal Republic of Germany. The warring decorations on her chest reflect the range of her powers.[63]

GC&CS treated its female members better than was usual in contemporary Whitehall because consideration suited institutional interests, while its culture judged the quality of codebreakers frankly and by performance. Many male Siginters, including Denniston, Hay and Knox, interpreted conventional ideas of gender roles to suggest that women were as well suited to much of codebreaking as men. Patience and precision at repetitive tasks, and linguistic talent, were acknowledged feminine virtues and valuable adjuncts to cryptanalysis. Codebreaking required unusual minds, which some women clearly possessed more than most men. For a woman to become accepted as a codebreaker was harder than a man, but once inside, the standards were those of flair, not gender.

By 1938, three more women served as junior assistants, and 13 per cent of the GC&CS's codebreakers were female. Nor did women's work in cryptanalysis end with codebreakers. Denniston held that: 'Every expert cryptographer must possess at least one typist skilled in sorting, filing and analysing.'[64] Over time, some of these typists rose in status. Clarke drew the attention of Denniston and Sinclair to Miss Wendy White, who handled all information processing for the Naval Section and traffic analysis of fleet intercepts, and recovered 50 per cent of the keys of Italian cyphers. Tiltman told Denniston and the DMI that Miss Sercombe, a 'lady cryptographer', did similar work for the Military Section.[65] By 1936, White and Sercombe, what GC&CS called 'budding cryptographers ... an important adjunct to the junior and senior assistant Grades', received around £250 per year.[66] By 1939, White was treated as a veteran codebreaker, tasked with retraining returning hands – including Nigel de Grey, who had reconstructed the Zimmerman Telegram in 1917 and would drive GC&CS's reorganisation during 1940–46.

More generally, by the 1930s, as the work of the Construction Section became more routine, Denniston combined 'economy' and human resources under his control, to bolster cryptanalysis by 'providing a reasonable career to women of the clerical class' within GC&CS. He transferred 'the brighter women from the construction side', had them trained 'in the technical work involved on the other side', and encouraged improvements in their linguistic qualifications, so they could perform 'the actual technical and linguistic work in the sections'.[67] Eleven women, entitled 'clerical officers' (later 'higher clerical officers') processed information for codebreaking, recovered known keys from books and sometimes helped to build books or recover unknown keys. This human-intensive approach saved the best brains of GC&CS from servitude in the most mechanical form of codebreaking – keystripping, or detecting and removing changes in key from a known system.

The standards for clerical officers were daunting: knowledge of several languages and the capacity either for 'critical analysis' or 'to absorb the elements of the technical work rapidly even if unable to face problems themselves'. After ten years' service, their salaries entered the junior assistant level.[68] Women 'of the right sort' were also the group most easily recruited in emergencies, given assumptions about gender and class: recruits such as Sinclair's sister Evelyn and Tiltman's wife Tempe were assumed to be loyal personnel. GC&CS selected new clerical staff from an old girls' network of people known to its members, or to those of Room 40. The Foreign Office described the new support personnel recruited during GC&CS's first period of expansion, the 'Abyssinian' staff of 1935, as being 'women with a good knowledge of languages who were not looking for a career, but who were glad to help us for a limited period – some were, in fact, wives of Denniston's colleagues, others University graduates who were willing to put in a short time at an interesting job'.[69] In 1939, identical calculations drove

Denniston's recruitment of female undergraduates, vetted by old girls at the women's colleges of Oxbridge. Early in the war, Denniston pressed to have eleven female members paid above the usual women's rate of £250, because of their skills and to avoid them leaving for 'the better paid posts obtaining in other departments'.[70] During the war, a higher proportion of female clerical staff at GC&CS were educated, compared to other government departments.

Work at GC&CS ranged from the intellectual marvels of bookbreaking, mechanical work such as keystripping, the boredom of proofing codebooks, to searching through 300 key indicators to strip superencipherment from yesterday's traffic. All members of the clerical staff and Construction, Typing and Secretarial sections were female, many serving for decades, including the middle management of codemaking. By 1935, the clerical staff worked in four sections. The Construction Section prepared codebooks suited to the needs of all consumers; the Cable Section, including men and women, handled intercepted cables; the Typing Section' typed flimsies; while the 'Secretariat' managed GC&CS's records. Clarke noted that clerical staff must:

> do cheerfully any jobs assigned to them, bearing in mind that upon the proper performance of such duties depends the efficiency of the section and that indexing and transposing if done without care or interest are not only dull but even of negative value, while if done with care and intelligence are most valuable and even interesting.
>
> Even the most brilliant people in the office still do this kind of work themselves very frequently and would see that their value to the office depends on their having done much of this work in the past. Those who do this work well are learning in the only possible way the elements of an art to which there is no easy means of approach even to the most naturally gifted.[71]

These practices staggered American observers of GC&CS between 1943 and 1945. Alfred McCormack told his colleagues at Arlington Hall: 'Foreign Office officials and Cambridge professors, unlike Harvard Law School graduates, are not above putting pen to paper in order to produce good indexes.' American Siginters reported that the British adopted this approach because they believed good codebreakers must retain touch with the entire craft.[72] That the best British bookbreakers or bookbuilders frequently stripped keys by hand, which intelligent secretaries could do, was a waste of resources. That others combined such tasks reflected an optimum use of time, an egalitarian collegiality among all involved in codebreaking, and a particular sense of how to process information. The gains of this approach outweighed the losses.

GC&CS did not live in luxury, but it was adequately funded. The unfunded areas were those for which money was not asked, because no one knew it was needed. Its members carried grudges from running battles over salaries with the Foreign Office and the Treasury. The standards of performance and promotion for cryptanalysts did not fit civil service criteria. Work was secret and specialised, preventing transfer to other units. GC&CS was small and promotion hard. Denniston and Travis blocked promotion for senior assistants to administrative positions, which perhaps explains the creation of a rung of three 'chief assistants' around 1938, entitled to another £42 per year. So many senior assistants were appointed in 1919, and stayed on, that only the best juniors could rise, and then slowly. Over time, the upper half of junior assistants were promoted, leaving the rest frozen on stingy salaries. Denniston thought they received enough to attract 'the type of man needed'. Yet he feared for GC&CS's ability to recruit 'from the ranks whence come members of the Administrative class', and, implicitly, its relegation to the executive or scientific branches of the civil service, wrecking its ability to recruit from Oxbridge, and thus its status.[73] Junior assistants, the entry point for cryptanalysts to GC&CS, were selected by different criteria than entrants to the administrative class in other departments.

To maintain quality and status in Whitehall, Denniston aimed to recruit from the brightest graduates of the best colleges, although he understood that applicants would prefer the conventional civil service. In order to do so, he gilded the lily, emphasising that these positions were in the first class of the civil service, while promotion to senior assistant was normal. In fact, while initial salaries matched that of conventional assistant principals, that of 'New Scale Senior Assistant GC and CS' fell below that of principals. His concerns were understandable, but overstated. Although GC&CS's personnel wanted higher salaries than they received, theirs were better than in the government's scientific establishments, and good by the standards of the Royal Navy or the

Foreign Office. Denniston received £1,000 in 1921, when only fifteen Foreign Office personnel had higher salaries. By 1936, he and Travis were on a pay scale of £1,150–£1,450 – between that of a counsellor and an assistant undersecretary or a naval captain. Senior assistants' pay rose from £625–£800 in 1921 to £847–£1,058 by 1927 (about the pay of a first secretary or a naval commander). The salaries of chief assistants reached £1,100.[74] These personnel did not live an uncomfortable life. Codebreakers received an annual holiday of about five weeks, clerical staff of three. Excluding lunch, they worked a six-hour day, five days a week, with three hours on Saturday, rising to 6½ hours in September 1939 and to 7½ hours in February 1941. From 1937 some sections worked seven days a week. Overtime was common in other sections. Duty officers always were on call: at 2 a.m. on 26 December 1935, during the Abyssinian crisis, Denniston noted, a junior assistant of eight years' seniority viewing 'reports received', had 'to take the responsibility of assuring the naval authorities that the situation was normal and called for no special action'.[75] The Japanese Section maintained twenty-four-hour coverage before the Pacific war began, some members serving twenty-four-hour shifts.[76]

Military Sigint

Three military Comint agencies, each of four to five officers, numerically equalling the largest geographical section at GC&CS, augmented its power. No. 2 Wireless Company and the Indian Bureau dominated Comint in Asia. The fighting services regarded Sigint as a key indicator of warning of Soviet operations in the Middle East and Central Asia, or Italian ones in the Mediterranean. They also had the same hope against Japan in 1941, when the effort failed. In 1934–35, the Royal Navy established an agency on Stonecutters Island in Hong Kong, which became the inter-service Far East Combined Bureau (FECB).[77] Meanwhile, police wireless operators at Denmark Hill, London, tackled Comintern traffic, codenamed Mask. No. 2 Wireless Company and FECB depended on aid from GC&CS, but the officers of the Indian Bureau, including Tiltman and Colonel W. H. Jeffries, able as anyone at Broadway House, solved major cryptosystems themselves, and followed priorities defined by the Indian Army. No. 2 Wireless Company read the codes of Arab kings, and the military and colonial systems of France and Italy. FECB read Japanese military, naval, consular and diplomatic systems. The Indian Bureau broke the diplomatic codes of Afghanistan and China, and the military and diplomatic systems of the USSR, and took much Soviet civil governmental traffic in plain language. During the 1930s, it abandoned work on Soviet diplomatic codes, but demolished Soviet military systems and the traffic of the frontier security forces of the NKVD. It acquired far more material than military intelligence could handle or index. Tiltman's success against Russian codes in Asia no doubt aided his attack on Mask when he joined GC&CS.

From 1919 the Admiralty maintained an intercept station, which after many wanderings settled at Scarborough, while, following Procedure Y all Royal Navy vessels intercepted any foreign naval traffic received. From 1926 the War Office maintained six civilians at Chatham to intercept foreign military traffic and provide field Sigint capability at under Lionel Attwell Beale and then Marshall Ellingworth. The latter's life in communications started in 1904 as a fifteen-year-old boy telegraphist, Royal Navy. On leaving the navy in 1935, he took over the Army's only intercept site in UK at Chatham, with three receivers. By 1945, Lieutenant Colonel Ellingworth, Royal Signals, controlled about 160 Army intercept receivers in the UK. Chatham became Britain's premier intercept station. No. 4 Wireless Company at Aldershot was tasked to join any expeditionary force, as was a small RAF Y unit. From 1927, an RAF intercept station at Waddington in Lincolnshire – later moved to Cheadle, Staffordshire – intercepted all foreign air traffic, concentrating on Soviet and German systems, though turned towards Italy and Spain between 1934 and 1938. By 1939, the services had three interception stations in Britain, linked to thirteen direction-finding stations, with seventy-four receiving sets, and perhaps 350 officers and men, while GC&CS controlled two stations, with some forty personnel. Abroad, the services controlled loosely unified interception stations in Malta, the Middle East, and Hong Kong, joined by the Indian organisation.

Equally, GC&CS augmented the Comint power of the services for war. The services expected the results to be Comint agencies under their control, but instead from 1940 it was measured in Ultra and support for Y services in the field. The power rested on a combination of the services' sections within GC&CS and their Sigint components without. GC&CS had mixed views of the service liaison officers: in

1935, Travis told the Treasury that the personnel of FECB would not be of 'much use', save for paymaster officers who, like himself and Eric Nave, could be promoted for cryptanalytical work and specialise in it.[78] However, retired officers were among the best cryptanalysts at GC&CS. The RAF's interception service and the Air Section within GC&CS were excellent in quality and numerically powerful. The Army's interception system was also excellent in quality, the problem being the limits to kit and personnel, compared to the needs of a mass army. The Military Section at GC&CS, which included Tiltman and Ian Jacob, was outstanding in quality.[79] Tiltman's experience in running all aspects of Comint in India – from directing radio interception to breaking systems – and in solving encoded messages sent by wireless, made him unique among British codebreakers in 1939: well prepared for the cryptologic revolution. No. 2 Wireless Company acquired practical experience in Y. In 1940, it and Jacob quickly founded an able Comint unit in Cairo, Central Bureau Middle East (CBME). The heads of the Air and Military sections and their Y services had more experience in managing Sigint than any member of GC&CS, except Travis. In naval Comint, conversely, the Naval Section at GC&CS and Royal Navy Y were good, but Germany and Italy outclassed Britain on attack and defence. Although Royal Navy veterans dominated British Sigint, they fumbled the ball. In 1921, old hands and the Admiralty assumed that without effort, everything must be all right on the night. In 1938, they misconstrued the role of radio, codes and Comint. Nave and Tiltman broke most of the Japanese books which Britain knew between 1924 and 1939. When they were present, FECB was excellent, but otherwise often mediocre, showing how important in so small an organisation was the quality of individuals.

Codebreakers did not easily fit military structures, but organisational needs drove unconventional solutions. Before 1914, when the Indian Army's codebreakers were assessed for promotion, one favourable commentary on Major Church still noted: 'I have had no opportunity of seeing this officer on service at manoeuvres.' The senior assessor, Brigadier-General A. H. Gordon wrote:

Major Church has I think rather suffered than benefitted by being labelled as an expert in ciphers. I have therefore watched his work closely and I agree he has plenty of ability which he knows how

to use in other directions. I am quite satisfied with the work he is
doing at present, in charge of the external India sub-section, but
I do not agree that he is qualified for general staff work in amy
capacity. His previous experience has not prepared him for it. I have
had no opportunity of seeing him in the field. I have read this
report to Major Church.[80]

This conclusion was depressing, but fortunately the Indian Army was
willing to let competent specialists serve as majors for decades. After 1919,
however, military institutions were unwilling to maintain specialists at
junior ranks for long times. Britain found different solutions to these
problems, such as civilianising military Comint, while maintaining
Sigint within their signals components. Civilians, retired officers,
veterans of Room 40 and paymaster officers manned the Naval Section
of GC&CS. When the Royal Navy created a core of cryptanalysts
against Japan after 1933, it improved their emoluments, so 'to obtain
the right kind of Officers, i.e. Officers of the greatest discretion and
integrity combined with a liking and flair for cryptography, which is
rare, and, moreover, individuals ready to sacrifice their chances of senior
rank'.[81] The British and Indian armies thought that codebreakers were
unicorns, who must work as specialists, but also that all regular officers
should rotate through many positions. Convinced, correctly, that they
had 'men of genius ... who can break any cypher that can be devised by
human agency', those services created special civilian positions for those
men, without pensions but well paid, at the rate of seniors, 'signals
computers'.[82] These officers retired and joined GC&CS's Military
Section, save Jeffries, senior enough to hold a specialised position for
years. The RAF, which maintained proportionately fewer field-grade
officers than the Army or Royal Navy, would not let them specialise in
cryptanalysis, Instead, Cooper, a civilian without military experience,
but who had served at Sarafand and knew Russian, which the RAF
wanted, ran the Air Section, while its intercept operators were civilians.

Even more, cryptologic issues involved the leading edges of defence
electronics, where expertise was rare, yet just enough to overcome
ignorance among higher ranks. Officers in service Y (such as Kenworthy
and Lambert) were technically and organisationally proficient,
innovative, and long-serving. Enlisted men were keen, ready and able to
solve problems without supervision. They found prospects for promotion

by doing what they liked. Their officers looked for good men, trusted them to create and establish intercept stations without supervision, picked them for special duties, and promotion – rare behaviour for the services. In 1924, the most technologically minded and least class-bound service, the RAF, hired an ex-sergeant, Royal Engineers, William Green Swanborough, to run its intercept station. Over the next three years he gained experience with the wireless interception branch of each service. The Air Ministry emphasised the needs for 'technical knowledge and skill and trustworthiness' in his position, which also gave him 'a distinct commercial value'. It successfully boosted his career as leader of RAF Y between 1924 and 1945, as he rose to wing commander, and built a pillar of Sigint, including Britain's largest liaison relationship of the time, with Estonia.[83] So too, between 1934 and 1945, Sergeant E. W. Smith, co-designer of the standard British cypher machine, Typex, and later of its improved derivative, Mercury, backed by his colleague, O. C. Lywood, head of RAF signals between 1939 and 1945, became a leader in Comsec and Y, and wing commander.[84] During 1940, Army Y expanded by promoting the best of its other ranks to officers, rather than retraining officers from other branches of signals. The remarkable ability of members of British Y drove victories in Sigint.

Defence

In 1919, intelligence authorities, the Foreign Office and the military services concluded that during the late war their codes had been 'almost childish', as were their practices, such as sending identical messages in different systems. Many cypher personnel were trained poorly.[85] Under Travis, Britain's leading expert in signals security and cryptosystems, GC&CS was ordered to solve these problems by advising on cryptographic issues, producing codebooks and training personnel for the civil departments.

Travis had no power over the great weakness in British cryptology, the insecurity of the Foreign Office's Communications Department and in its establishments abroad, which let Italy, Japan and the USSR secretly copy British codebooks. He had no control over military practices, though much influence. Initially he achieved successes against resistance. By 1922, he led departments to superencipher their codebooks and to monitor their use. His section closely watched departmental practices and trained personnel. Each codebook received a 'life history', including every message they covered, to ease damage assessment in case of compromise.[86] Codebooks were compiled by discussions between GC&CS and the relevant department, and printed at Oxford University Press; but GC&CS created the superencipherment tables and produced them on rotoprinters in its first mechanised section.

Any cypher balanced three conflicting aims: 'brevity, clearness and security'. Security required complexity, which reduced brevity and subverted security.[87] GC&CS designed cyphers which met the specific balance of these needs for every consumer. By 1930, Travis convinced the most exposed units, the Foreign Office and the service departments to adopt an improved superencipherment system. Keys in that 'long subtractor' system routinely were 10,000 groups long, and included hundreds of 'key indicators', or points where superencipherment could start. Each start point in effect yielded a distinct superencipherment table. Plaintext words were encoded and the codegroups were written down. Then, superencipherment groups were placed below each encoded group in sequence and subtracted from them. The recipient added the superencipherment groups to each codegroup, so reproducing the encoded group, which then was returned to plaintext. Such systems were secure, varying with the 'depth on the table': that is, how often the codegroups of any long subtractor key covered messages in any codebook. The length and the volume of keys, and the number of books, yielded depth. One-time pad (OTP) figures covered each group (enciphered or plaintext) in a message only once, producing a depth of one. With each product unique, such messages were unbreakable. If an entire long subtractor key covered messages in one code twenty times, the depth was twenty. The greater the depth, the easier for codebreakers to 'recover' (or, reconstruct) a key, and to 'strip' it from the enciphered groups, so exposing the book figures. Keystripping was simple if a code was known and the depth on the table was high. The brute force of additional staff or data-processing machines easily bolstered keystripping.

Unfortunately, Travis overrated the ability of superenciphered codebooks to defend radio traffic. He underestimated developments in brute force and especially the use of wireless in war, which multiplied the power of all cryptanalysts against long subtractor systems and reduced the depth that their tables would bear. When the Royal Navy reformed its signals security between 1929 and 1932, GC&CS stated that subtractor superencipherment systems were easily used and 'provided certain very elementary rules are complied with, [are] unbreakable by ordinary cryptographic methods. No cypher is, of course, proof against loss or treacherous betrayal but unless such loss or betrayal occurs we can rest assured that any message cyphered & recyphered by the "subtractor" principle will preserve its secrecy against an enemy', if the tables changed once every fortnight.[88] These assumptions were always overoptimistic. Even worse, Travis failed to warn the Royal Navy away from elementary errors which Italian and German codebreakers exploited, such as using the Administrative Code plain, for non-confidential messages, superenciphered only for confidential ones, on keys which changed just once every six months.

These errors compromised both the codebook and the long subtractor system itself. In 1931, Denniston believed the long subtractor system would be secure and flexible; in 1944, Travis thought it had been so, though 'now we should regard it with contempt'.[89] Such views were conventional. Clarke held that a 'modern cryptographer' could solve the German key used at Jutland in 'less than a quarter of an hour', whereas the Italian key of 1935 'cannot, under the most favourable conditions, be solved in less than four or five hours', and only with 'about thirty times as much' material as had been needed in 1916. Cooper thought that 'nowadays … girl clerks!' would strip those German keys.[90] The services and the Foreign Office each had just a few secret cyphers, many used universally by all recipients across the world. That practice gave attackers ample material to break books and 'build depths': to acquire enough material to identify and strip key groups, thus exposing the book values. In 1931, GC&CS had the most exposed departments change tables only once every four months, and thought that under the worst case, any key would remain secure for a month. During 1937, it asked that tables change every three months.

By 1938, Denniston believed that the construction side of GC&CS required less attention than before. Travis received new assignments for liaison with the services. He and his senior officers focused on a Government Communication Bureau (GCB) which worked with commercial firms and the services to improve military Y, and create a signals and intercept system for GC&CS and MI6. GC&CS and its consumers failed to assess their cryptography critically. The services relied on a few books, often several years old, and changed tables just a few times annually. GC&CS said nothing about their weaknesses, nor compared them to its own offensive record. During 1936–38, experience showed that long subtractor systems, such as those of the Italian army and navy, were breakable, with effort, experience and expanded staff, because books were old and keys changed infrequently – exactly like British ones. In February 1939, Denniston viewed Italian naval cyphers as having 'a very high grade', yet GC&CS read them all. However, the Regia Marina soon introduced new books and tables.

By June 1939, Denniston wrote: 'the Italians are taking every possible step to render their book secure. Reading of them is now one of the most difficult jobs in the office.'[91] It would remain so until Italy surrendered in 1943. Reflecting several years' experience, in January 1939, Tiltman believed that with two months' work, he and a large team could read 'current messages' in new Japanese systems, which were introduced from 1 December 1938. The Imperial Japanese Army (IJA) used about a dozen books, some old, and new superenciyherment tables. Several of them were long subtractors, changing keys 10,000 groups long, every four months. By July, after five months' effort, Tiltman and perhaps a dozen codebreakers read much of the IJA traffic that Britain intercepted. These successes included notable parts of the five central books of the IJA, and 25 per cent of messages in the main cypher used in China, though important systems remained unpenetrated. Tiltman emphasised the vulnerabilities of four-figure codebooks, yet they provided perhaps 20 per cent of British military systems for major traffic. His description of attack alarmed War Office cryptographers, as they realised that it could be applied to their system. This discovery came rather late in the day, mid-August 1939.[92] So too, in 1941, when the vulnerability of British systems became clear, Tiltman created the stencil subtractor, an ingenious and simple device which enabled operators to make elaborate changes in keys for codebooks more easily than before. This stencil was fundamental to Britain's ability to salvage its systems during the war. Had his system been available in 1938, it might have spared Britain much grief: it was the easiest way to overcome Britain's cryptographic failings. This system easily could have been available, as Tiltman formulated it in 1933. Neither he nor any other leaders in GC&CS nor the services' cryptographic services pursued it, because they thought the effort unnecessary. This project made Tiltman 'quite unpopular ...

cryptanalysts weren't supposed to invent ciphers and I was told to keep off of it'.[93]

GC&CS's failure to compare its offensive experience with Britain's defensive practices shows sloppiness and incompetence in an important task. Even so, that experience generally supported GC&CS's views about acceptable depths. At most, careful consideration of that evidence might have suggested that British departments should maintain perhaps 300 per cent more books than they did, changed annually, all of five figures, and with keys altered monthly. Codes more than a year old should be presumed compromised. This experience could not truly reveal the dangers ahead, but it would have reduced the damage. The real problems were the failure of the services to follow recommended procedure, and of GC&CS to ensure that they did so, and to understand the poverty of its cryptography.

Underlying these errors were two problems. The first was a systems failure in authority for defining and enforcing Comsec within the services. This responsibility was diffuse, divided between several branches, who depended on GC&CS for technical advice and, in theory, slavishly followed it. Yet they did not actually do so, nor did GC&CS make them. Captain D. A. Wilson, a Royal Navy officer experienced with Comsec and GC&CS between 1935 and 1946, claimed that the four officers who formally were responsible for advising units on Comsec – Cooper, Denniston, Travis, and Tiltman – never had a 'collective internal discussion' on British Comsec as a whole. In fact, the situation was even worse than Wilson supposed.[94] Though Tiltman was supposed to be GC&CS's liaison with Army cryptography, neither he nor they thought that he should do anything about it. That also was true of Cooper and the RAF though, fortunately for Britain, air authorities were competent in cryptography. Only Travis and occasionally Denniston thought they were responsible for cryptography. Wilson also noted that it was hard ' "to winkle out from the School" a precise view on security'. Most 'cypher and codebreakers are not very good at explaining to a layman the real and vital aspects of a system from the defensive security angle'. GC&CS did so poorly. 'So far as the security of cyphers was concerned, GC&CS, and Travis in particular, was the fountain head. What he said went. But I do not recollect him being very precise or detailed in his advice.' Only through great effort could Wilson gain, from Foss, an (accurate) definition of acceptable depths for any key: 'one time was absolute, two almost guaranteed, three not really dangerous but that after this anything could happen, and that the use of the same part of the key five or six times was positively dangerous'. Again, Wilson held, GC&CS failed to explain how frequently basic books must be changed for security, and overemphasised the power of changes in super-encipherment tables. The 'whole problem', Wilson rightly thought, was that GC&CS thought 'intelligence gathering – breaking codes – was more glamourous and more interesting, intellectually ... than the more humdrum defensive work'.[95]

Second, GC&CS and the services believed that, in war, radio would rarely be used. The apparent widespread use of wireless silence during the Munich crisis reinforced that long-standing preconception, outweighing the evidence from Spain and China that large-scale use of radio was unavoidable in war. Sparking an explosion in brute force and use of wireless, the war suddenly demonstrated the poverty of British practices. During 1940, for example, the RAF held only one main book, which was universal (that is, used to cover all traffic across the world), five years old (and therefore vulnerable to competent cryptanalysis) and had only two tables, which changed every three months. The depth on the table was 150 – thirty times greater than Foss's definition of 'positively dangerous' levels.[96] During 1944, GC&CS insisted that keys be changed every three days on a massively larger number of books and rejected any depth greater than two: sometimes depths of one were maintained. That practice almost turned these long subtractors into one-time pads (OTP), which had a longer cryptographic shelf life.

During the 1930s, GC&CS knew that Germany and the USSR used stronger systems than Britain, but did not emulate them. It believed that British systems were equally secure in effect and simpler to use than OTP. GC&CS favoured cypher machines in principle, but offered little practical assistance in the matter, where the services' signals branches took the lead. They failed until late in the day, from execution rather than intention. From 1926, Whitehall aimed to acquire cypher machines, yet mishandled the process of research and development for a decade. British authorities saw all the flaws in contemporary cypher machines, but unlike Germany, declined to strengthen a system with problematical security but proven mechanical reliability. Instead, British authorities turned down all existing systems, because they saw their security flaws and hoped to leap to the next level. This effort failed because a system promising on paper could not be made mechanically effective: it was ingenious but impossible. This failure dampened official interest in cypher machines. Fortunately, a few dedicated men, starting on their own initiative, though increasingly supported by officials, gave Britain the means for speedy and secure communications. Officers and other ranks of the RAF's signals branch, led by Lywood, developed the backbone of British strategic communication, the Defence Teleprinter Network (DTN), and its cryptography, the Typex system. Typex was a variant of Enigma, identical for security but better for signals. Typex originally was designed to cover teletype traffic, thus becoming the world's first online cypher machine, able to convey thirty times the traffic per minute of manual ones, though almost all Typex machines were used manually offline. Typex was central to Britain's cryptographic salvation but, compared to the German military versions of Enigma, was developed late in the day. Typex was of limited value to Britain in 1939, though outstripping Enigma by 1942.[97]

Meanwhile, GC&CS and the departments grotesquely underestimated the number of personnel required to handle cryptosystems during war, and thus had far too few trained cypher operators or wireless personnel. So desperate was the RAF's position by 1938 that it ordered its Egyptian command to hire a cypher officer locally, despite an adverse report from MI5. The man was 'sacked within a fortnight after being overheard discussing the contents of a cypher telegram in a public bar!'[98] In 1939, the Indian Army of 200,000 soldiers had six trained cypher operators.[99] This problem was minor for the Foreign Office, and manageable for the Royal Navy, given their needs for communication; but between 1939 and 1945 the RAF and the British and Indian armies had to multiply the number of their radio and cypher operators by perhaps 1,000 per cent, from a tiny base of men trained in signals security – or signals, for that matter. Many old and new civilian departments which transmitted important traffic by radio faced even worse problems.

These technical misjudgements created cryptographic disaster. In 1939, as 1914, British systems were weak and operators weaker. Though the Admiralty and the Foreign Office compromised their own systems, and the services caused their failures with wireless personnel, Travis bears much of the blame for these failures, and Denniston some. They echoed throughout the period between 1945 and 1970, when Whitehall

would strip GCHQ of responsibility for cryptography. Between 1919
and 1939, British cryptanalysis had problems. Its cryptography failed.

Attack

GC&CS's purpose, Turner noted, was 'not cultivation of cryptography
as a fine art', nor preparation 'against a future contingency', but to
'deliver the goods now'.[100] GC&CS did so by processing information
for action, through cybernetic means. Radio and cable interception
provided much of the traffic of every government on earth each day.
Sorters – in 1943, McCormack described them as 'two little bird-like
old ladies' who had handled the work since 1919 – moved intercepts
to the sections. There, messages were registered in careful detail,
including notes of codebook and keys, which had had specific names or
numerals, and sent to cryptanalysts. Cryptanalysis provided one filter
for this material – the more successful, the greater the flow. Two other
filters stood between codebreaker and consumer. All solutions went
to the head of the section, who had anything they thought important
translated and sent to D&R. Under Earnshaw Smith, a veteran of the
WTID and MI1(b), D&R edited and circulated any telegram it thought
significant, and indicated recipients.[101]

Codebreakers did much cryptanalysis 'in the rough', on handwritten
worksheets, and just refined and published messages 'of sufficient
interest'. Only solutions circulated as flimsies were typed, meticulously.[102]
The reliance of British Siginters, in Y and codebreaking, on handwritten
rather than typed material, shocked Americans. It reflected social
norms – even in 1980, analysts routinely wrote reports by hand –
but greater American wealth enabled an easier and faster means of
dissemination. During the 1920s, the Japanese Section 'circulated' just
20 per cent of the material which it solved. In 1940, GC&CS circulated
only 8,000 of 70,000 telegrams read.[103] GC&CS would have liked to
circulate more messages than it did, but realised such efforts would
damage its reputation for providing worthy material. Still, GC&CS
regularly informed consumers of material they could see if they wished,
through 'summaries of telegrams decoded but not translated'. No one
accepted the offer, which indicates GC&CS understood the interests
of its consumers, however much it wished they were greater. So too,
it circulated flimsies containing excerpts from many telegrams on

specialised issues, like messages from Latin American states, or about the arms trade, rather than printing each individually.

GC&CS defined what cryptanalytical targets could be attacked, while the Foreign Office and, to a lesser extent, the services, defined which should be challenged. Compared to MI6's priorities list of the mid-1930s, GC&CS's record was mixed, though fortuitously its work and that of other services proved complementary. GC&CS offered nothing on 'Group A', the main problem with just one member, Germany – where, fortunately, MI6 and other human sources were strong – but much regarding Groups B through to F, including Italy, Japan, China, and the Middle East.[104] Some of its greatest successes occurred against the lowest groups, Afghans and Arabs, which colonial authorities rated highly.

These successes and failures had the same root. GC&CS competed against every state in the world. Some targets were hard. Resources were limited and opportunity costs tight. Against this, continuity of attack multiplied its power. Knowledge of a cypher and its superencipherment system helped one to handle changes in either matter. To attack an absolutely unknown high-grade system was more difficult. Recovering lost continuity required far more resources than maintaining it. GC&CS lacked the resources to master every possible target, while priorities were hard to define. In this process, GC&CS combined ambition and opportunism, comparing ease of assault with significance of success. Attack on one high-grade system reduced its ability to assault others. Using the experiences of the Political Section of Room 40, an average codebreaker might uncover five groups per day, or the thirty cryptanalysts at GC&CS solve 150 groups, from a high-grade book used well. GC&CS, unlike other powers, relied almost entirely on cryptanalysis, rather than stealing codebooks ('pinches'), though the last practice occurred rarely. It could have been most strengthened through more pinches, rather than machines or mathematicians. The failure to do so flowed from culture, a willingness to read all the cables and wireless messages of foreign states but not their letters, nor to burgle their offices, and from legal and organisational impediments. Such success would have required overcoming the worst relations within British intelligence, between MI5, Scotland Yard, Special Branch and MI6. These problems evaporated during war. Between 1914 and 1918, British intelligence acquired telegrams in cable offices from Tehran to

New York. During 1939–45, MI6 pinched much cryptographic material abroad, and the Royal Navy at sea, often at great risk. This preference not to pinch, moreover, ensured that in 1939, GC&CS focused on pure cryptanalysis, which shaped its openness to mathematical techniques, and its idea of what they should be – a key step down the road to Bletchley Park.

GC&CS solved far more material than these Room 40 figures indicate was possible, because of improvements in its craft and personnel, and an international poverty of Comsec. GC&CS solved within months much of the Soviet diplomatic codebook introduced in 1921. Denniston noted the 'delightful' Italian habit of enciphering translations of leading articles from the British press.[105] GC&CS frequently read foreign telegrams providing clues to the working of their cryptography, which guided its cryptanalysis. It gave consumers these reports, which GCHQ would have sent only to cryptanalysts. Generally, the cryptography of countries was weak in the 1920s, rose around 1930, and varied widely in quality at any time. Some states, especially in the Middle East, used commercial codes, designed for use by firms, or substitution cyphers, others one-time pads (OTP), where every message was superenciphered by a unique table, used just once. OTP was unbreakable, unless the tables were reused, as the USSR and Japan did between 1941 and 1945, when it became as vulnerable as any superencipherment system. The leading systems were superenciphered codebooks designed by governments, especially hatted books of up to 100,000 groups, using subtractive systems (with the vocabulary listing words in alphabetical order, and the decipher section placing groups in numerical sequence, without any links between the alphabetical and numerical values of these columns, while tables subtracted numerals from codegroups). Cypher machines became common from 1930, because they aided large organisations using radio. Properly handled, good books were more secure but slower to use than any but a few machine systems, though these happy few fused security and flexibility with unprecedented power.

Codemakers and codebreakers shared principles. The 'enemy' should be assumed as able as oneself. All traffic could be intercepted, every cypher broken. Unless 'extremely complicated … and protected by frequent changes of key, the more a cypher is used the shorter its life'. Codes could be compromised 'by the transmission of news which was public or would shortly be published, the constant use of the same group for "full stop", the repetition of name in a telegram or the sending of similar telegrams by different Departments'. Alternative and accessible accounts of a diplomatic discussion might provide cribs to a stronger system, which Turner thought 'of capital importance'. To solve two codegroups might identify two hundred: 'Therefore give us cribs.'[106] Cribs helped bookbreakers crack systems. When applied to Enigma, they illuminated 2 million words per day. More generally, experience against operators on one system enabled predictions of their practices on another, yielding cribs: words, phrases or paragraphs expected to occur in a message. Codebooks could be protected by many means: avoiding stereotyped forms, which provided clues to content; burying address groups (which marked sender and receiver) within messages, rather than at their start; and using several groups for the same word, and 'dummy' groups (without meaning) to break patterns of language. Bad operators wrecked all strengths and exacerbated each weakness.

In 1922, Travis estimated 'the life of an ordinary four-figure cipher at six weeks', a standard for assault which was above that of 1916, while, if seriously and systematically attacked, any unknown high-grade system could be solved within a year after its introduction.[107] Ten years later, perhaps reflecting the rise in power of the best systems, Denniston held that: 'It may take a couple of years to complete the breaking of a book.'[108] Working from a known book, cryptanalysts turned eight codegroups into plaintext per minute.[109] Attack involved a range of costs, and priorities, as illustrated by GC&CS's work against American systems. In early 1921, GC&CS announced that a 'very sound post-war organisation' had doubled the security of American traffic, by instituting 'a complicated cipher about a year ago which has taken some time to solve but in a month or so these messages will be legible'. This book, 'B1', had distinct superencipherment tables for different communications circuits, and many groups to be used randomly for common words, like fourteen groups for 'and'. Perhaps 20 per cent of GC&CS's cryptanalytical staff, including two of its three best codebreakers, attacked this codebook, at the cost of others.[110]

This allocation of resources reflected priorities: in 1920, Britain found American policy uncertain and important, but less so after 1932 – which is apparent through official sources from 1934 when the United States ranked on the bottom list of MI6 priorities in 'Group Z' alongside

Afghanistan.[111] Ironically, the US State Department then kept the same book in service for eight years.[112] Not surprisingly it was almost as widely read by foreign codebreakers as American officials. During 1937, Clarke held that nine months' 'concentrated work' by six people was needed 'to produce any information at all' on a well built and used naval code, 'fifteen months before routine telegrams are completely readable, longer still before good sense can be made of those of highest intelligence value'.[113] Tiltman's experiences against Japanese systems in 1939 loosely support Clarke's views, though showing that breaks came faster when more people attacked weaker codes. During 1933–35, Japanese systems became the leading priority for the Military and Naval sections, sparking the creation of FECB, and GC&CS's first use of machine cryptanalysis. Between 1935 and 1937, Italian traffic became GC&CS's top priority, absorbing 30 to 40 per cent of its cryptanalysts, because diplomatic systems were easy, while military and naval ones were hard.

In March 1935, after maintaining the same cryptography for seven years, with GC&CS reading 80 per cent of most messages, the Italian navy adopted two new codebooks, using long subtractor superencipherment, each key being 10,000 groups in length with 300 start points. Initially, these changes overwhelmed the Naval Section. From September 1935, its strength against Italy boosted from three members to seven to ten, the section made technically decent and operationally valuable breaks into these systems, which rose despite new defences. Dilly Knox, meanwhile, broke the commercial version of Enigma used by the Italian and Spanish Nationalist navies.[114] The Military Section passed its successful work against Japanese military codebooks to FECB, and its seven codebreakers and three secretaries focused on material relevant to the Spanish civil war. The section broke many Spanish military cyphers between 1936 and 1937. At the same date in 1938, two codebreakers (one part time) read Italian field cyphers in Spain. Two codebreakers and two clerical staff read constantly the high-grade book, with changing superencipherment tables, between the Italian War Office and its forces in Spain. One codebreaker attacked Spanish Nationalist naval traffic, and another the high-grade Italian military code used in Libya. Miss Sercombe, 'normally employed on book-building, indexing and registration' (organising data retrieval for traffic and the value of codegroups), independently broke keys for

Italian books used in Spain. Three secretaries handled 'key-breaking and clerical duties'.[115]

Given the power of the GC&CS and foreign cryptography, small misjudgements in priorities could have great costs. During the two great diplomatic crises of July 1923, the Lausanne conference and the French occupation of the Rhineland, Denniston noted GC&CS's priorities were 'largely guided by the events of the day': 'for the moment Turkish messages are pre-eminently important, French are of great interest and doubtless German messages would be useful if time and staff could be found to break the books'.[116] Though consumers and producers sometimes defined priorities clearly, usually this process was loose, and sometimes chaotic. During 1938, the War Office asked the Foreign Office what military intelligence it wished to receive about Italian involvement in the Spanish civil war. So to assess Italian promises and behaviour, the Foreign Office asked that Italy's reinforcements to Spain be monitored. This request, passed by the DMI to the Military Section, forced an all-out attack on every Italian military cypher. As Jacob noted: 'if any information' was required from a superenciphered code, 'all messages' in it must be tackled 'in order to get sufficient depth to extract such information', yet few signals mentioned Italian reinforcements to Spain. This task absorbed five officers and four clerks, overstraining the Military Section for months before the Munich crisis. That tertiary task overwhelmed the section because its uncoordinated superiors never directly engaged the costs and benefits of this priority. On this section's behalf, Denniston posed that question to Gladwyn Jebb, the Foreign Office's liaison with intelligence. Tiltman thought the reply not 'very definite'. The work continued.[117] The cryptanalytical cost required to monitor these reinforcements exceeded their diplomatic significance.

Opportunity costs and limited resources prevented Britain from attacking the traffic of many smaller powers which were technically vulnerable. Meanwhile, GC&CS overlooked some hard and important targets, including German systems, which became harder with time as continuity of knowledge vanished. GC&CS missed the moment when the German military first used Enigma because Germany ranked low on all priorities. During the 1930s, GC&CS allocated only one member each on a watching brief against German and Soviet systems. The Military and Naval sections assigned virtually no one to German systems. The Air Section did slightly better. Britain focused too much attention on Italian and Spanish Republican and Nationalist messages between 1936 and 1938, at the direct cost of German ones, though this would have enabled only traffic analysis and attack on low-grade systems until Enigma was solved. For much of the two years before May 1938, RAF Y attacked more Spanish Nationalist air traffic than German. The Air Section did not even attack intercepted German or Soviet traffic, though it thought progress possible with them.[118]

Hard targets demanded good cryptanalysts, perhaps without success, but GC&CS frequently accepted that demand. When attacking hard systems, characteristically, one codebreaker or a few determined whether it could be broken and, if so, how; if successful, further resources exploited the breach. That pattern was applied to German Enigma between 1934 and 1938, without success, but more so in 1939–40. The small but excellent Research Section of bookbreakers routinely broke hard systems far enough for conventional sections to complete the task. Characteristically, each geographical section (also, the Indian Bureau and No. 2 Wireless Company) had one or two excellent bookbreakers or bookbuilders, alongside several lesser members who built books and translated messages. Between 1926 and 1933, one of the largest GC&CS efforts of the interwar years failed against one of its greatest targets. Every codebreaker experienced against the USSR assaulted new and secure Soviet cryptosystems, which combined OTP, strong superenciphered books and skilled operators: notably, when human skill declined, as the Red Army deployed radio en masse to formations while the Purges raged, and during the catastrophes of 1941–42, Soviet cryptosystems became an open book. In 1929–30, Cooper spent eighteen months analysing the Red Navy's radio traffic in the Black Sea, to little avail. Ultimately, convinced that 'the most secret (Soviet) cyphers could not be broken, and that probably the second grade was also unbreakable', GC&CS abandoned the effort and its attack on Soviet traffic: the core of the Russian Section became the Air Section.[119] Between 1929 and 1935, only Tiltman succeeded, against Soviet diplomatic systems in Central Asia – good on paper but often badly used – and Mask. Ironically, from 1935, GC&CS increasingly thought Soviet military systems were breakable, but these were too low a priority for exploitation, except for the Indian Bureau. GC&CS monitored and solved the main machine systems of the era, such as Hagelin. Knox spent much time after 1934 attacking Enigma, probably GC&CS's leading target for research, with some success except against German military versions. In the year before war began, German Enigma was the leading target for GC&CS research and military Y.

Codebreaking

In different permutations, codebreakers (cryptographers in GC&CS parlance) combined penetration of eye and mind, the pedantry of grammarians, the logic of philosophers and the flair of chess grandmasters. Codebreaking joined intuition and linguistic and abstract knowledge. It had four complementary functions: the breaking of codebooks and superencipherment; bookbuilding; translation; and the mechanical process of keystripping. When discussing their needs for personnel, section heads differentiated between periods dominated by bookbreakers, bookbuilders and keystrippers. Bookbreaking, the rarest skill, required an eerie knack for recognising patterns in the figures of messages, and seeing the structure of unknown books. In 1939, for example, IJA four-figure codebooks used barely half of their full 10,000 groups. 'The (quite illogical) regular limitations of codebook groups' forced the use of stereotyped passages and eliminated defences like multiple groups for the same word, while an 'over-ingenious' method of 'indicating starting points' from a key (which allocated them by a system, and 'overloaded' some of the indicators, rather than selecting them randomly); these failures, Tiltman wrote, were 'our chief aids to solution' of high-grade IJA books.[120]

To be able to see such structural flaws required unusual vision. To break superencipherment required the return of jumbled numerals to the structure and values (known or unknown) of a codebook, by transposing columns of figures, or finding the start point of the subtractors used on each line of a message. Great bookbreakers often achieved these ends when they first scrutinised a system. They broke codes in languages they did not know, because all messages were sent in figures, exposing, for example, patterns in the Japanese *romanji* (Latin) script sent in Morse or non-Morse codes. Codebooks of this day were universal languages expressed as ten-figure groups. All natural languages were translated into them. Enciphered messages translated words twice: from a language into a cypher, often superenciphered by means which combined both linguistic and mathematical characteristics, and then into Morse or non-Morse code.

These characteristics enabled, even necessitated, binary approaches to codebreaking. When viewing messages, bookbreakers looked for patterns of figures, bookbuilders for those of language. Codes and cyphers concealed the sense of a message, but could not escape the structure of language: a grammar, a frequency of the recurrence of letters, connections between parts of speech. Books were built by attacking the relationships between code and language. While hunting the values of codegroups, visual memories compared multiple phrases which contained an unknown group in many messages. To describe books as 'readable' did not mean that every group was known, or that all messages were comprehensible, just that most groups were understood, and bookbreaking could define unknown values. Many codegroups in a five-figure codebook with 100,000 groups never would be used. To know just 5,000–10,000 groups provided a context for attack on unknown groups, which let one reconstruct most sentences. The more messages intercepted, the more stereotyped their content, and the more closely associated messages and action, the faster was bookbuilding.

Generally, military codes in war were more easily built than diplomatic ones in peace. The more experience with a book, or set of them, and the military or diplomatic actions they covered, the easier to sense meanings. Paleography, the reconstruction of dead languages from corrupt and fragmentary records, was the best professional background for bookbreaking. More generally, a classical or linguistic background aided cryptologists almost as much as a mathematical one. The latter was essential against electro-mechanical machines, which embodied mathematical relationships, and was useful for cyphers, where letters replaced others by a system, and bookbreaking. Mathematical skill, however, was insufficient for bookbreaking, and secondary for bookbuilding. Translation of diplomatic traffic required a good knowledge of a language – that of military messages a familiarity with service jargon. In 1946, GCHQ noted: 'the pure linguist was not of great use', whereas 'sound grammatical knowledge', 'current idiom' and 'power to apply knowledge as a basis for guess work', were valuable.[121]

Codebreakers hunted values down every avenue of structure or error. Bookbreaking defined the nature of codebooks and, thus, the target for attack. This work, the heart of codebreaking, was lonely, often lengthy. Tiltman once spent weeks attacking what he thought was a high-grade Japanese codebook, only to find it was a low-grade Chinese one. Bookbreaking overlapped with the first stages of bookbuilding, where codebreakers guessed the value of unknown groups, by checking their context in every telegram where they featured. Then, by generalising lessons learned from analysing messages, bookbreakers defined punctuation (indicators of sentence structure), parts of speech, groups for letters and numbers, prepositions, address groups, and some words, particularly proper nouns. Bookbuilders hunted alone, or as a team, but always under a leader. All might focus on one message with a few unsolved codegroups, each ranging freely across messages for the meanings of specific groups. By combining hypotheses and tests, this process of the probable word turned the approximate significations of codegroups into certain attributions. Cribs – anything which suggested the content of messages – breached the walls of vocabularies and aided bookbreaking when senders transmitted the same message in many systems. Guesses broke the meaning of codegroups. Guesses were educated, increasing their precision and reducing the time needed for attack, because codebreakers had experience and aids. Each section maintained its own indices and archive of uncirculated material. Denniston called the aids in D&R the 'focal point' of GC&CS.[122]

The characteristics required for bookbreaking and bookbuilding differed enough that no one mastered both faculties. Good bookbreakers often were mediocre linguists, while great bookbuilders could not break books. When breaking and building books and translating messages, codebreakers adopted two styles. Bodsworth compared the 'neat and ruthlessly methodical' approach of 'classic bookbuilders' such as Emily Anderson and James Turner, to the work of Clarke, a poor linguist with 'a particularly retentive memory for book groups … he could correct garbles in any text without reference to the code itself'.[123] Clarke broke books in his head without recording on the worksheet many values that he discovered, which slowed the progress of anyone sailing in his wake. In his own words, Clarke observed patterns, not phrases: 'the real cryptographical mind … learns book-groups and does not rely on encodes', that is, the linguistic meaning of groups.[124] Tiltman held that 'the possession of linguistic qualifications has no necessary connection with cryptographical aptitude'. No matter how able a linguist, no one entered his Military Section without passing a three-month course in

elementary cryptanalysis.[125] Understanding many languages, some of
them well, and familiar with directing mediocre linguists, Tiltman had
them translate messages with a dictionary. In 1942, he solved Britain's
shortage of Japanese translators for military messages by creating
a seven-month course which gave tolerable skills in that language
to classicists: Latin still had its uses in war. Anderson, conversely,
painstaking multi-linguist, wrote that every translator faces 'the same
problem, which consists of two processes 1) discovering the exact
meaning of what the writer was saying, 2) rendering that meaning in
lucid English, so that the reader forms in English the same idea as the
German reader of the original'.[126] When devilling for Anderson, and
improving his grasp of Italian, Bodsworth spent a year watching her
work, before beginning to build books; only in his third year did she let
him translate messages for distribution.[127]

Linguists, particularly specialists in languages difficult for
anglophones, shaped the words which formed ideas in readers' minds.
This hidden dimension of diplomatic Comint is best illustrated by the
Japanese Section, engaging a language notoriously difficult to translate
into English, which GC&CS thought the hardest of its targets. In 1945,
de Grey emphasised that 'nothing can really fill the place of the true
Japanese interpreter in the field of diplomatic correspondence where
the range of subjects treated is very wide'.[128] The 'Diplomatic and
Commercial History' of GC&CS noted that: 'To render a succession
of long, often corrupt or imperfectly recovered telegrams to and from
the Japanese ambassadors into translations up to the standards which
we maintained for European languages required a team – which was
difficult to assemble – of exceptionally well-qualified linguists; this is a
case in which "a competent linguist with a good dictionary" would not
have sufficed, no matter how successful he might have been with the
machine or the keys.'[129]

Probably this comment referred to Tiltman's methods and words.
Few members of the Japanese Section broke books, apparently because
Japanese cryptosystems initially were simple – perhaps referring to
the early 1920s, the NID later commented that 'in the early days the
difficulty with Japanese Cyphers was linguistic not cryptographic'.[130]
Tiltman, Nave and the American 'Purple replica' which broke Japanese
machine traffic handled the problem when these systems hardened. Most
members of that section were retired officials, hired for knowledge of

Japanese: their quality staggered McCormack. Many great Japanologists were British officials who had found careers in Comint. Masters of the Japanese language such as Hobart Hampden and Parlett had power in guessing the nuances of meaning hidden behind words, but questions remained. George Sansom, a renowned Japanologist and long-standing commercial attaché in Tokyo, was also a veteran of MI1(b) and founder of GC&CS's Japanese Section. In 1919, Hay credited Sansom with solving 'all existing Japanese codes and ciphers', while Denniston hoped to retain him in GC&CS. In 1939, as a consumer within the Foreign Office, Sansom doubted the accuracy of GC&CS's translations of Japanese traffic.[131] Quite how such errors, or Sansom's views of them, affected consumers is impossible to know. His ability to discuss the issue with the GC&CS's Japanese Section, and to see the solutions in that language so to check their translation, is impressive, but the problem matters. These messages, the best intelligence Britain had on relations between Italy, Germany and Japan, influenced policy. Such accuracy and influence was the measure of GC&CS's success – in peacetime.

4

Cryptanalysis and British Foreign Policy, 1919–39

Between 1 November 1919 and 31 August 1939, GC&CS provided over 75,000 flimsies. Each week, on average, it gave Whitehall seventy-four solutions of the encoded telegrams of foreign government; every week it read important systems of several great powers (sometimes all of them) and many smaller ones. No. 2 Wireless Company and the Indian Bureau, moreover, gave their consumers several thousand solutions which were not reproduced as flimsies. Between 1919 and 1930, GC&CS appears to have had near mastery of the diplomatic code systems of Japan, the United States and Italy, and strong access to those of France and, despite the myth, of the USSR. Britain also devoured the codes of secondary powers such as Spain, Brazil, Greece, Turkey, whenever it desired; the lack of success against German traffic occurred largely because Britain did not regard it as a high priority at that time – reasonably enough. During the 1930s, GC&CS's power slowly waned. This success and its decline mattered, but not in a simple manner. If GC&CS rarely illuminated the policy of major powers in central Europe between 1934 and 1939, it was little more successful at that task in the 1920s, no more so during 1923 than 1938. Central Europe consistently was the weak spot in its coverage and Asia its strong one, reflecting British interests and access to traffic; GC&CS was more useful for imperial security than European diplomacy. One cannot define GC&CS's value, without assessing how it performed its main task: diplomatic cryptanalysis.

More has been written about how Comint shapes military operations than it does diplomacy. Its role in these competitions takes different forms. Metaphorically, diplomatic intelligence affects many games of whist: victory in one game matters there, but not elsewhere. In operations, victories may have wider effects. Intelligence lets one concentrate strength against an enemy's weakness, or shelter vulnerabilities from its power. In diplomacy, intelligence provides knowledge and means for leverage; it shapes influence rather than power. Diplomatic intelligence illuminates the attitudes of states and the factions within them. It shows concealed levers and hidden hands and means to manipulate them, and how to act or to signal. It gives good news and shows the limits to bad, by increasing one's certainty that unknown and unpleasant developments are not happening. Variations, every day, in the details of access to information and its value, and in the nature of actors and problems, reshape normal diplomacy and drive crises. Minor comments in a good source determine the plausibility of major statements in an uncertain one. The reports of one party reveal the intentions of another. Knowledge may also be useless.

The point of diplomatic intelligence is to aid action by shaping one's policy or that of another party. This aim is not easy to achieve. More often than not, diplomatic intelligence provides first-rate information on third-rate issues, or knowledge which one cannot apply to policy. Actions, which in diplomacy usually are words of influence or signals of threat, may be hard to deliver as desired or with effect, and have unintended, paradoxical or counter-productive consequences. Intelligence has more direct value in cases of diplomatic bargaining, when every party must act, and on the same issues. Then, it can show the best deal you may achieve and how to get there, which cards to play, or not. Information on the bargaining strategy and tactics of other players can help one take tricks, though their value depends on the stakes. Some cases of diplomatic Comint are one-sided: yet in diplomacy, often two or more powers have excellent intelligence on each other, or on a multilateral relationship. The overall effect stems from a competition between what you gain from knowledge, compared to what your rivals do. Such competitions vary from a duel, where one thrust may yield victory, to a brawl, where instrumental action becomes hard to achieve, because of mutual interference between the parties.

Diplomatic information comes from many sources. Open or official ones usually are the most important, but the more secrecy shapes any competition, the greater the value of agents, or the ability to steal papers, to bug offices or to break codes. Their influence on diplomacy is hard to judge, especially because decision-makers often do not state how they have interpreted or acted on data, forcing one to draw inferences from the evidence. Nor is the effect of diplomacy on power easy to judge. More even than with military operations, unique features, stemming from particular political and technical circumstances, shape every instance of diplomatic intelligence. Any effort to explain and understand such cases must be complex. Diplomatic intelligence is easy neither to use, nor to understand. It is most simple as regards tactics; intelligence on another's bargaining position can shape one's own, it may be applied immediately, and its effect on action can be gauged with precision. Greater problems occur with the broader aspects of diplomatic intelligence: when it provides knowledge – lets one understand another's attitudes or policy, reveals the existence of something one did not know or confirms something in which one believed, proves statesmen are honouring their promises – or not; and when it provides leverage – indicates an opportunity and means to take the initiative or disrupt another's efforts to do so, or shows what messages one should deliver to whom so to check their manoeuvres, or those of another; and when it contributes to learning, to making people change their minds.

On major matters of policy, intelligence generally provides pieces of background information which are read in the light of complex patterns of preconception, often unconscious or unexamined, which easily can trigger fallacies of thought, such as mirror-imaging or worst-case assessments. These individual pieces of intelligence do not immediately lead statesmen to take specific actions that are carried into effect – thus allowing one to judge how information affected actions – but instead to favour policies that were never realised, or not to take certain actions at all. In diplomacy, waiting on events can be an action with consequences greater than from strokes of policy, but this effect is scarcely easy to assess. The influence of intelligence can be chaotic, varying with personality or faction; it may not help effective action.

To uncover the intentions of states is especially difficult. Governments often reach their decisions in unpredictable fashions – or, alternately, in ways that can be predicted only if one knows the aims and means of each element in their bureaucratic political processes. Statesmen frequently do not know what they will wish to do in the future; even should they think they do, they may change their minds or have their minds changed for them. Nor are all of their actions taken in order to achieve these intentions. Necessity forces leaders to march one step forward, two steps back; opportunity alters one's calculus of aims and means. Often policy – especially for the long term – is formulated and executed in a Byzantine fashion, with different departments of state (and their agents) pursuing distinct (sometimes contradictory) ends without reference to the rest. Even when all of these groups pursue the same ends, they may differ over the means. Often, central authorities fail to coordinate these bodies; even the most central of policies may be ignored or overturned at any time without notice. These problems about determining intentions are redoubled by those with the evidence on it. Intelligence rarely provides clear and unambiguous statements by the chief authorities as to what they will do on a specific topic at a given date. Instead, it provides indicators of that matter, mostly from the views of middle-level officials which one uses as a proxy for those of their masters – even though what they really are trying to do is to influence those at the top.

Between 1919 and 1939, GC&CS's central task was to provide Comint for diplomacy. Its primary consumers were diplomats, soldiers and politicians. The main task of the Foreign Office was to assess and act on information. Through the experience of blockade, its regional sections became intelligence-assessing bodies, and its personnel experienced analysts, especially of Comint. Intelligence provided as much evidence on diplomacy as any other source, including the reports of ministers. As with every element of information, intelligence was rarely read in isolation, but mostly in an alloy with material from all sources, the whole being greater than the sum of its parts. Intelligence became integral to the Foreign Office's view of most matters, and experience with it standard to the professional education of diplomats. They interpreted intelligence in particular ways, each official acting as his own analyst – a standard behaviour among diplomats of all ages. This tendency was even more pronounced when politicians with less experience used Comint.

This chapter examines four broadly representative cases where Comint shaped diplomacy. Comint, however, was often irrelevant to diplomacy, while every case of influence has unique characteristics. The diplomatic and strategic circumstances of each case and the roles of Comint, official sources and Humint within them are assessed here. The chapter considers which actors used intelligence and how Comint affected their understanding and action in normal and crisis diplomacy, bargaining and the formulation of policy. This comparison emphasises failures and limits as much as successes, and the interaction between power, perception, intelligence and action. Comint also serves as a mirror for decisions, by showing what decision-makers thought, how information affected their ideas, why they acted as they did, and what they believed their actions would achieve. The intelligence record points towards a deeper level – the ideas and attitudes that underlie statecraft. One can reconstruct the logic behind decisions only by examining the data considered by decision-makers; the intelligence record illuminates their times.

Comint and Naval Arms Limitation, 1921–36

During the interwar years, attempts to limit naval construction were central to British strategy, and intelligence. The Washington Conference of 1921–22 addressed clashes over sea power between France, Italy, and especially Britain, Japan and the United States. It featured the most famous instance of how Comint affects diplomacy. The American black chamber, under Herbert Yardley, solved telegrams outlining the lowest ratio Japan would accept in the tonnage of battleships and aircraft carriers, compared to the American and British navies. This knowledge helped American negotiators force Japan to that point, a 5:5:3 ratio, down from the 5:5:3.5 level that Tokyo preferred. Sailors on all sides thought that difference would define Japan's ability to contain the US Navy in war.

Yet the 5:5:3 ratio might have emerged anyway: the United States and Britain demanded it and had strong bargaining positions, while *The New York Times* guessed Japan's break point.[1] Yardley's organisation, moreover, had little success against British codes, essentially reading only the R code, which was designed to cover routine matters from telegraph clerks, rather than to protect important communications from cryptanalysts.[2] The United States could not read the revealing telegrams which it intercepted between the British delegation and Whitehall, as they redefined their bargaining strategy, just as the Japanese were doing – which was the condition for Yardley's success against Japan. The American proposals for arms limitation surprised everyone at the conference. Britain's chief delegate, Arthur Balfour, had to make policy as he first heard them. He accepted those proposals which, he was wise enough to see, met British needs. Balfour did well without warning, much as he would have preferred it. This lack of warning did not stem from failure of cyptanalytical skill. GC&CS easily read major American and Japanese codes – in messages it could intercept. Britain, however, intercepted only those telegrams which Tokyo and Washington forwarded to their embassies in London or Europe. The United States captured traffic sent on transcontinental and Pacific cables between Tokyo and Washington. Since Tokyo did not give its embassies in London or Europe the instructions sent to its delegation in Washington, GC&CS provided only secondary material on Japan during the conference.[3] It acquired little data on American policy, as the conference was held in the United States, which let authorities formulate policy without contacting embassies abroad. The success of American codebreaking and the limits to that of GC&CS, however, did not damage Britain. On naval bargaining, Balfour outmanoeuvred the Americans, who used intelligence on Japan in ways which suited Britain. At the Washington Conference, Britain did better without Comint than it would do at later conferences where its Comint was superb but its policy was not.

In practice, the Washington Naval Treaty left Britain stronger at sea than the United States. The American position deteriorated further as Britain and Japan built their authorised strength in restricted classes of warships, alongside many vessels in unregulated categories, especially cruisers. The United States was unwilling to spend on sea power. This development created irritation in Washington, but few warships.[4] The danger of an arms race centring on cruisers shaped international politics when hopes to remake the world on liberal internationalist lines were high, producing a naval limitation conference at Geneva in 1927. Here, Yardley's organisation gave nothing to American negotiators. GC&CS, conversely, reading American, French, Italian and Japanese traffic, gave Whitehall valuable data.[5] This success did not prevent a collapse of the conference, due to differences over policies. Britain offered to extend the 5:5:3 ratio to all categories of warships, including cruisers, but at a level of tonnage no American government could maintain. The Americans insisted that this 5:5:3 ratio rest on a basis which Congress would subsidise for the US Navy – that the Royal Navy be cut to a level which the United States could afford, rather than that which Britain would do. Although wealthier than Britain, during the interwar years the United States was less willing to build warships. The two countries also differed on the number of heavy cruisers which either should build. Japan insisted that the ratio for lighter warships must be 5:5:3.5, rather than 5:5:3.

After this failure, an arms race loomed. The Washington Naval Treaty required the naval powers to begin a massive programme of replacing battleships in 1931, which politicians among these countries feared for financial and diplomatic reasons. Thus, in 1929, new governments in Washington and London pursued naval arms limitation. Herbert Hoover, the American president, married interest to idealism, aiming to weaken British sea power while making a better world. The Labour prime minister, Ramsay MacDonald, sought to spur world disarmament, rather than to further narrow interests. He did not fear American power or aim to strengthen Britain against the United States, but instead to gain American support for moves towards liberal internationalism and disarmament in Europe. So, MacDonald accepted many of Hoover's demands. He agreed to defer the construction of new battleships until 1936, scrap many battleships and cruisers, far more than any other country, to reduce the tonnage of cruisers to the size demanded by Washington, and to let the United States build more new warships in that class, including heavy ones, than Britain.[6]

These actions damaged British sea power, but enabled a naval disarmament conference where Britain held the cryptanalytical cards. GC&CS provided a set of flimsies which were uniquely directed to the naval conference, something it never did on any other topic during the interwar years.[7] Perhaps Sinclair had GC&CS focus on these issues, which he knew would please a Labour government. The Labour Party remembered bitterly how leaked intelligence, the Zinoviev letter, had damaged it during the election of 1924.[8] Civil servants and intelligence authorities feared that a Labour government would castrate the intelligence services. GC&CS's services to Labour policy helped to block that threat, especially by helping Labour ministers defeat unofficial attempts by British naval officers to hamper the conference.[9]

As the conference occurred at London, GC&CS had unmatched opportunities to intercept traffic to and from the American, French, Italian and Japanese delegations. GC&CS mastered all of these messages, and thus the aims and means of other players. Britain monitored any diplomacy between other parties by cross-checking reports from several sources, including the cables of one, usually both, participants. In bargaining, everyone must signal its position to some degree. The Japanese, American and British civilian delegations were open with each other, in the freemasonry of liberalism, and had differences with their naval advisors. Yet each state had a bottom line to hide and Britain had an edge. It had means to discover secrets, they did not. No other state matched British cryptanalytical capacity at this conference. The United States had just abolished Yardley's bureau. Nothing suggests that French, Italian or Japanese codebreakers provided much material about the conference. Japanese naval codebreakers actually focused on reading Japanese diplomatic communications, to keep their diplomats from making undesirable concessions.[10]

The Admiralty, the Foreign Office and politicians used intelligence avidly as they faced complex political and technical issues. The debate centred on comparative tonnage in cruisers, destroyers and submarines. The United States and Britain wanted to extend the 5:5:3 ratio to all lighter warships. Japan again demanded a ratio of 5:5:3.5. The American delegation insisted on the right to build twenty-one heavy cruisers. While Britain preferred that the US Navy possess just fifteen heavy cruisers, it agreed that the United States could have eighteen of them, Britain fifteen and Japan twelve. If the United States insisted on more than eighteen heavy cruisers, however, Japan would raise its demands above twelve, forcing Britain to increase its requirements, starting a cascade that might wreck the conference. Even worse, MacDonald's pursuit of Hoover weakened his bargaining position. Britain could not block American demands which it disliked, nor seem to be manipulating Japan into opposing them. Unless these conflicts were resolved, the conference would fail. Britain worked for compromise, using the clash between Japan and the United States to play each against the other, and reduce their demands so to further liberal internationalism and British interests.

Comint helped Britain to square this circle. It confirmed the accuracy of material acquired through diplomats and provided evidence no other source could do, in real time. Comint reported debates within the Japanese and American delegations, on their negotiations and impressions of talks with Britain. GC&CS traced the conflict between American and Japanese policies, including details both sides kept from Britain, yet showed that each was truthful and fairly comprehensive when talking to British colleagues. It provided reports which the Japanese naval and civilian sides hid from each other, and sent to their superiors in Tokyo on separate cryptosystems. Britain understood the divisions between the factions in the Japanese delegation better than they did. During a tense period, when many feared the conference might collapse, GC&CS showed that an acceptable deal still could be reached with Japan. Politicians in Tokyo told the civilian delegation that when they made the best settlement they could, the government would sell it at home, and make the admirals obey. GC&CS illuminated the deal which the civilian delegation could accept, significant because their bargaining strategy was to not define a position but rather have other powers make offers, which Japan then would try to raise. GC&CS showed that the Japanese Admiralty, the Kaigunsho, would oppose any agreement which Britain or the United States could accept, hampering the freedom of their civilian colleagues, and the chances for success.[11]

Knowledge was one thing, action another. GC&CS was irrelevant to the American decision to accept eighteen heavy cruisers, but shaped Washington's offer not to start three of them until the treaty ended. This offer gave Japan a 5:5:3.5 ratio to the US Navy in heavy cruisers and the tonnage of lighter warships until 1938, while containing construction on both sides, which nicely suited Britain. Its chief negotiator, Robert Craigie, originated this alchemy, and secretly suggested it to the Japanese delegation. Craigie, acting from public evidence and Comint, monitoring the reaction to his pressure by reading the body language and the reports of his targets, pressed the other sides to negotiate. He fed them a solution which met their bottom lines, without the Americans suspecting his role. Craigie used Comint on Japan so to guide its policy in a direction which furthered Japanese, British, and probably American interests, and saved the conference.[12] This success overcame Britain's bargaining weakness and achieved its aims over cruisers and disarmament. Craigie might have achieved these ends without this success, GC&CS's main contribution to British policy during the conference, but the task would have been harder.

Meanwhile, to contain the Kaigunsho, MacDonald worked with the US Secretary of State, Henry Stimson, informing him of matters Britain knew through codebreaking, without revealing the source. Stimson had just closed Yardley's bureau on the grounds, as he later recalled, that 'gentlemen should not read each other's mail'. Now Stimson acted on the reading of gentlemen's mail, at second-hand, without knowing it. In particular, GC&CS showed that the Kaigunsho wished to work with France to wreck the conference, while the French chargé d'affaires to Tokyo, M. Doubler, was pressing Japan towards positions on submarines which might have that effect. British and American statesmen took this danger seriously. They queried the French and Japanese foreign ministers about Doubler's proposals, aiming to destroy any intrigue by showing it was known. In fact, Doubler's actions and the possibility of Franco–Japanese cooperation posed little danger – they were unauthorised by the French government and rejected by the Japanese Foreign Minister, Baron Shidehara Kijuro – but these facts were unknowable at the time. In this instance, MacDonald no doubt was grateful to GC&CS.[13]

Other issues demonstrate limits to the value of Comint on diplomacy. Japanese financial weakness was well known, but GC&CS demonstrated extreme Japanese sensitivity on that issue. The Japanese delegation was twice warned to avoid any discussions which might invoke the matter, especially because Tokyo was renegotiating major loans in London.[14] The civilian delegates and Shidehara feared that having to start the battleship replacement programme would damage the economy. If Comint showed any Japanese vulnerability to exploit, this was it, yet British and American statesmen acted cautiously. The financial embarrassment occurred in part because Japan was preparing to join the gold standard, which was a major priority for the British and American governments. This fact prevented direct pressure on the issue. Even more, to raise it openly would seem a threat, strengthening the Kaigunsho against civilians. Hence, in private discussions with Japanese civilians, British and American decision-makers referred to Japan's financial weakness in elliptical terms. Japanese civilians did not need those statements in order to understand these risks.

This card could not be played, and did not need to be. Another should not have been played at all. MacDonald and Stimson wished to counter the Kaigunsho by acting firmly in Tokyo, especially by pressing the Japanese prime minister to accept the terms on offer. The American and British ambassadors in Tokyo refused that order, fearing, correctly, that it could not remain secret and would be politically explosive. Still, the ambassadors carefully sounded out the Japanese leaders with whom they worked, especially Shidehara. GC&CS showed that even that pressure annoyed precisely those Japanese leaders whose cooperation was needed. MacDonald apologised to the head of the Japanese delegation, Wakatsuki Reijiro, for these actions, perhaps after reading a telegram in which the latter said that they 'savour of coercion' and had 'stiffened perceptibly' the 'antagonism' of his naval delegation.[15] MacDonald and Stimson reluctantly had to await Japanese decisions, but finally the three powers signed the London Naval Treaty of 1930. France and Italy, preoccupied with the balance between their own fleets, did not sign the treaty, but did not challenge it either.[16]

Another naval conference was scheduled for 1936. Between 1930 and 1936, GC&CS read the communications on this issue of the naval powers. Along with open sources, it demonstrated that American authorities hoped for major reductions in naval strength, which British ones increasingly thought suicidal, and overestimated their power over Britain. Japan, meanwhile, would demand parity in warships with Britain and the United States and withdraw from the conference (and naval arms limitation) if its demands were rejected, as would happen. Britain still hoped to avert this outcome, and to have the conference further other ends which would ease its restoration of sea power, especially by limiting the size and armament of battleships. These aims failed when Italy and Japan abandoned the conference, but Comint helped to keep British policy realistic, and effective.[17] The London Naval Treaty of 1936 enabled Britain, France and the United States to rearm without damaging relations between them, allowing the Royal Navy just enough new construction to crush the navies of Germany and Italy between 1939 and 1945.

Judging the Effect of Diplomatic Comint

In these negotiations, the effect of intelligence depended on the action it enabled. Mediocre intelligence which affected an action mattered more than excellent intelligence that did not. If action was impossible, intelligence provided mere knowledge. When action was possible, diplomatic intelligence sharpened the clarity and certainty of issues one already knew, and discovered matters one did not. Because intelligence saw things other people were hiding, it discerned unknown dangers; and distorted them. Comint redoubled that problem, because of its precision and reliability. As with Doubler's intrigues, Comint easily distorted a weak danger. Again, Comint revealed diplomatic levers with rare power, which had different effects when pulled. In 1921, Yardley showed that if one sat tight, a rival would fold.

During 1930, GC&CS made four more complex contributions. The first, playing Japan off against the United States over heavy cruisers, was obvious, but still a delicate task eased by precise knowledge. The second, using Japan's financial weakness to move its government, could be used only with caution. Little pressure was needed to make the point, with tertiary effect. GC&CS illuminated the third instance, the problem posed by the Kaigunsho, as no other source could do, yet attempts to act on that information did not work as intended and caused more trouble than they solved. Finally, knowledge of Doubler's actions caused more alarm than was warranted, and sparked actions which scotched the problem. In 1927 and 1935, excellent intelligence had little value, because diplomatic bargaining (and so, instrumental action) failed.

Care must be taken when generalising from these examples. Those negotiations were conducted between liberal governments which had few secrets, pursued common alongside national interests, agreed on basic issues and compromised on details. British leaders in 1930 could not exploit knowledge of how weak Japanese leaders thought their country was, so to push the Imperial Japanese Navy (IJN) below the 5:5:3 ratio. They accepted that ratio as legitimate. In other circumstances, such knowledge might have supported tougher bargaining by the United States in 1921 and Britain in 1930. So too, an odd form of cooperative competition between the United States and Britain shielded Stimson in 1930 – a negotiator facing a hostile foe with Britain's superiority in Comint might have suffered. Instead, when Comint enabled either state to make negotiating gains against Japan, it aided the other, unintentionally.

The value of Comint and of success in diplomatic bargaining must be placed in a strategic context – who won and lost, and how and why. Japan did better through naval arms limitation than the United

States or Britain. Japan, weaker than those powers, would have slipped in strength had rivalry continued in construction. A 5:5:3 ratio offered a far better position. Japan scrapped far fewer warships, built or building, than its rivals. Even more, unbeknownst to Britain, the United States and Japanese civilians, the tonnage of Japan's cruisers was 33 per cent heavier than the IJN officially acknowledged, because of cheating or inexperience in design when Japan built these warships. Thus, the IJN actually had a 5:5:3.8 ratio in the tonnage of lighter warships as a whole. The negotiations about relative tonnage which dominated the London Conference seem unreal, as often occurs with any set of negotiations examined in hindsight. That conference also sparked the scrapping of half of Britain's warship-building capacity, and crippled its sea power.

These events shaped Japan's relative naval power and the problems of the Royal Navy and the US Navy in 1941. Japan became master of the western Pacific, which could not have happened against serious naval rivalry. The London Naval Treaty also lit the fuse for a political explosion which blew Japan down the road to the Pacific war, turning it from a supporter of a liberal international order into an armed revisionist. Naval arms limitation was one of the major British concerns where GC&CS was most consistently successful. For Britain and naval disarmament, however, excellence in diplomatic intelligence was harnessed to mediocrity in policy.

Comint and British Policy in the Middle East, 1919–23

During 1919–23, British intelligence on the Middle East was outstanding in quality. Its consumers were able and experienced. Yet Britain failed to translate its military successes of 1917–18 into control of the Middle East as a whole. Military weakness and unrealistic aims damaged policy and risked shipwreck.[18] Britain lacked the will and power to crush Turkey, but opposed a compromise with it. That step would admit failure, and abandon much fruit from the victories of 1917–18. Authorities understood the military and diplomatic environment, but made themselves prisoners of events by waiting for something to turn up. Meanwhile, the interpretation of intelligence and the formulation of policy were crippled because no source, including Comint, could read the minds of foreign statesmen, nor overcome uncertainty about a conspiracy between enemies and their ability to move masses.

Conspiracies and Conspirators: 1919–22

Soldiers and subversion had commanded the Great War in the Middle East. Britain controlled Persia through bribes and paramilitary forces. Authorities thought that the war against Turkey involved a struggle for influence over the Muslim subjects of both empires. Islam and nationalism shaped Muslim peoples, but were mutually exclusive: the stronger one movement, the weaker the other. Britain patronised Arab nationalism to strike Turkey and to block Pan-Islamic propaganda against its Muslim subjects, especially in Egypt and India.[19] At the armistice, Britain dominated the Middle East. It hoped to make Persia a protectorate, control Palestine and Iraq and reduce Turkey to a rump. Britain and its allies, France and Italy, garrisoned Istanbul. Yet the armistice did not end the war. Local leaders and peoples resisted foreign rule. British policy drifted. Its forces shrank. Subterranean war emerged against several rivals with loose and bewildering connections – Germans, Bolsheviks, nationalists and mujahidin. These developments triggered reflexes among British officials and intelligence officers. They were used to fighting conspirators. They held that Islam and nationalism allied the Muslim masses, and could help or harm Britain. It needed to gain support by working with Muslim leaders.

Intelligence understood Britain's enemies. MI6, and security services in Egypt and India penetrated revolutionary movements, learning their plots and links to external foes. Britain mastered the cyphers of all powers which affected the Middle East, France, Greece, Italy and the USSR, and intercepted all telegraph and telephone traffic within occupied Turkey. The problem was interpretation. Britain suffered from too much and too little intelligence, and a complex foe. Its enemies were in a real conspiracy, but a dysfunctional one, resting on opportunism and ignorance. They lied to each other and enabled one another's fantasies. There was not just one fantasy, or conspiracy, but many of both. The conspiracy was dangerous in its parts, but not the whole. The real problem for the British was local leaders and peoples. Britain understood the conspiracy better than did its members, but this blessing was mixed. It understood real dangers; equally, intelligence on fantasy made Britons fantasists. Intelligence officers accurately represented the intentions of conspirators. They did not distort (as against, mistake) the facts about conspiracy, revolt, Pan-Islam and nationalism. Their interpretations were reasonable, but often wrong, sometimes strange. They had looked for the 'hooded menace' so long that it was easy to see.[20]

On these matters – the greatest concern for British intelligence between 1919 and 1923 – Comint reinforced excellent and overlapping human sources. Intelligence reduced uncertainty and error, but could not eliminate them. Comint illustrated the intentions of states: solutions of Soviet and Turkish traffic showed their alignment was close, but strained. Comint was weaker about conspiracies, which naturally were hard to disprove, while neutral evidence easily reinforced the worst cases. Solutions of Turkish nationalist traffic supported the idea of a Pan-Islamic crusade against England, by showing that Turks were 'preaching Holy War' to Arabs, which even a cynical secularist might do.[21] Intelligence was most important in shaping attitudes, where Comint could not prevent unfortunate developments.

The interpretive problem centred on the intentions and power of two rivals – Enver Pasha, the wartime leader of Turkey, exiled in Germany and the USSR, and Mustafa Kemal, the commander of Turkish Nationalist forces in Anatolia. Each man was central to any idea of the conspiracy, and power politics in the region, because Turkey was so. During 1920–21, intelligence consistently suggested that Turkish nationalists had Allied with the Bolsheviks and aimed to do so with Pan-Islamic conspirators, and Arab and Indian Muslims. However, the alignment between Muslims and Bolsheviks was opportunistic – especially by Kemal: he might join Britain against the USSR. Nor did Bolshevism attract Muslims. Still, by acting through Enver, Moscow might control nationalists in Turkey, and Muslims across the world.[22]

These views exaggerated Enver's bondage to Bolsheviks and his influence in Turkey, and the closeness of relations between Turkish nationalists and Soviets. Soviet leaders valued Kemal far above Enver. Until 1922, these parties were aligned with but not allied to each other. Still, this interpretation was fairly accurate and not unreasonable even where it was wrong. There were conspiracies. They were linked, if less systematically than Whitehall supposed. One dimension of Muslim identity, not always dominant, was fraternity. Enver had a chance to take power in Ankara, and connected Bolsheviks with Germans. He grappled with Kemal, and might have seized power had Greece defeated Turkey in 1921. The Greek failure, however, drove Enver from Turkey to Turkistan, to break with the Bolsheviks, and to die in battle against them.

Precisely as that happened, human intelligence, loosely supported by Comint, suggested that Kemal had adopted Enver's platform, becoming slave to Moscow and apostle of Pan-Islam. Even a source so good as Ultra could not have kept Britain from seeing Kemal as an echo of Enver. Kemal saw ground opening on his left and seized it. Mistrusting, manipulating and needing the USSR, he veered towards it temporarily and formed an alliance, which provided political and military support while alarming his colleagues.[23] He hid his heart from all, and expressed nationalist, jihadist and pro-Bolshevik views. Comint often revealed the views of Kemal's subordinates, but rarely his own. Kemal openly rejected British aims, pursuing objectives which Whitehall thought impossible: the 'National Pact', which would return Anatolia and Istanbul to Turkey.[24]

Interpretation abhors a vacuum. British statesmen filled the lacunae on Kemal with the best evidence they had. Thinking Kemal irrational, rather than resolute, authorities misunderstood the meaning of the rare evidence (most often from Comint) they had directly about his views, such as his intransigence during the London conference of February 1921. British diplomats in Istanbul developed a form of 'Ankara watching', routinely describing their evidence as 'facts and rumours' and the situation even on basic matters, such as whether Mustafa Kemal was 'dictator or figurehead', as 'obscure'.[25] Britain misconstrued the attitudes of Kemal and company towards the USSR: they merely used Moscow and vice versa. Turkish attitudes towards Muslims, however, were less narrow and nationalist than is commonly believed. Most nationalist leaders had Pan-Islamic sentiments. Despite his later claims to have been purely a nationalist, Kemal sympathised with Muslims under Western rule, exploited religious sentiments to strengthen Turkish influence among them and his hold at home, expressed Pan-Islamic views, and perhaps held them. Britain had reason to suspect

Pan-Islamism in Turkish nationalism. So it did. Ideas of this conspiracy shaped all British analyses of intelligence, power politics and policy in the Middle East until 1924.

During 1919–21, Britain was strong enough to stabilise its hold in Egypt, Iraq and Palestine, suppressing large revolts and finding local allies. Britain abandoned its militarily and politically untenable position in Persia. Comint had little influence on either action. The Turkish nationalists, meanwhile, raised an army and seized Anatolia – save for the Aegean coastline, which Greek forces held, and the districts across from Istanbul. Britain lacked the force to keep Kemal from seizing Istanbul. It relied on Greece to contain that threat, but could not ally with Athens without wrecking relations with France. By 1922, Greece weakened in power and resolve, while Turkey rose. Britain reluctantly accepted compromise, but Kemal rejected an Anglo-French–Italian proposal for negotiations after a conference in Paris. Throughout, Comint illuminated complex diplomatic and military issues like a searchlight. Mastery of the diplomatic codes of Greece, Turkey, France, Italy and Russia revealed their policies. It showed France abandoning British policy, Italy betraying it, Turkish intransigence and Soviet malevolence. Britain assessed the war in Anatolia by reading the highest of Greek and Turkish signals, simultaneously. Comint enabled Britain to block a Greek seizure of Istanbul in July 1922, but usually could not be acted on.[26]

Thus, Britain knew the bargaining position of all sides at the London conference of February 1921. As one official wrote: 'It is very nice of the Greeks to be so informative. I wonder if the French and Italians get their telegrams too.'[27] This knowledge was fruitless, since that conference was abortive. Comint did not enable Britain to force Turkey to negotiate, or keep France and Italy in line. It inadvertently reinforced a negative development. The main consumers of intelligence, politicians and diplomats, became emotional as their policy eroded, bitter towards France and Italy, which sold arms to Kemal, enraged at Turkey and at the Soviet Union.

In May 1922, a Foreign Office assessment of human and signals intelligence showed widespread Soviet activities among Muslim nationalists. The Bolsheviks supported the 'pan-Asiatic and pan-Islamic schemes of the Turkish Nationalists', though the two groups were mutually suspicious.[28] Curzon retorted that this information was

incomplete; much more must be happening. He told the leader of the
Conservative Party, Austen Chamberlain:

> I do not know if you have studied the Secret Service Reports
> and telegrams lately with sufficient closeness to realise that that
> combination has been growing much firmer – that Mustapha
> Kemal is tight in the grip of the Bolsheviks – that his truculence as
> regards the Paris terms arises from his reliance on their support –
> that a Secret Treaty has almost certainly been concluded between
> them; and that this is what Litvinoff meant in his allusion in the
> intercepted telegram to the 'trump card' which it was still in the
> power of the Russians to play at Genoa.[29]

The Chanak Crisis

In September 1922, something finally came up: Britain's biggest crisis of
the 1920s. Turkey annihilated Greek forces in Anatolia. British policy
collapsed. British leaders were divided over aims but united behind
the need to restore their credibility through coercion, deterrence and
prestige politics. Kemal, smelling gunpowder and victory, demanded
possession of Istanbul and European Turkey. Britain insisted that Kemal
stop short of Istanbul until a new peace conference was held which
might grant most of his demands. British authorities did not want war,
just the diplomatic leverage needed to save face. They aimed to deter
Turkey and to make France and Italy support British policy. Britain
sent forces to Turkey so to signal allies and enemies that it would fight.
When they arrived, between 1 and 15 October, Britain would have a
tenable position. Until then, the combination of local British weakness
and provocative strategy tempted Turkey to act. Explosives piled up
while sparks flew from the clash between British and Turkish policies.
Britain made threats: the problem was to have them believed. Britain
played chicken, escalating the crisis in order to improve its bargaining
position. So did the Turks.[30]

The crisis centred on Chanak, a town on the Asiatic shore of the
Dardanelles, which shaped the Royal Navy's ability to pass the straits.
When the crisis began, the British commander, Charles Harington, sent
weak British, French and Italian forces there, open to attack, to 'show
bold Allied front' as a signal and deterrent. They would warn advancing

Turks with war, but withdraw if attacked. 'Sources of our information are good enough to ensure our receiving early warning.'[31]

As the crisis heightened, French and Italian forces withdrew from Chanak. Harington reinforced it with British soldiers, believing only a signal of defiance, a show of force and even a fight, could deter the Turks. Between 20 September and 9 October, British policy centred on a military build-up and a high and precise synthesis of intelligence, force and signals. Harington tried to pass messages to advancing Turkish forces through every means. He received no reply and feared his position was deteriorating. He was willing, though not eager, to fire on Turkish units at Chanak. A demonstration of force would indicate Britain was serious, while hints of concessions would encourage Kemal to negotiate. Harington asked the Cabinet for authority to shoot so to maintain peace, but only if absolutely necessary; and thought the danger several days away.

This request shaped the most notorious aspect of the Chanak crisis. Whitehall did not understand Harington's calculations because of delays in transmitting messages multiplied by ambiguities in his reports. Through a legitimate (but inaccurate) reading of his reports and alarmist intelligence, ministers believed Chanak imperilled and Kemal about to attack. On 29 September, ministers ordered Harington to present an ultimatum to the Turks. If they did not withdraw immediately from Chanak, British forces must fire on them. Ministers did not intend to start a war, but rather to conduct diplomacy through gunfire. Only action could break Turkish belligerence. Harington, however, refused his order. Kemal had finally contacted him, announcing his intention to maintain pressure at Chanak but also to negotiate. Harington saw the prospect for a peaceful solution.

By not firing on the Turks, unintentionally Harington did so on the Lloyd George coalition government, which many Conservatives concluded, erroneously, wanted a war. The unity of Cabinet and country imploded behind Harington as he negotiated, because of the way he did it. Ironically, his first step after declining to deliver the government's ultimatum was to send one of his own. Knowing that massive Turkish forces were entering the theatre, Harington told Kemal that Turkey must immediately enter armistice talks, or face war. Over the next ten days, each side talked and threatened at the Mudanya conference. Britain showed enough power to demonstrate it could fight, and enough signals to show it would, unless its demands about process were met. Harington also indicated that Britain would largely concede Kemal's demands at a conference. Kemal accepted British terms, rather than pursue slightly more through the risk of war. Britain surrendered over content, while winning a battle over form, at a risk of provoking a world war.[32]

Comint at Chanak

The study of intelligence is essential to understanding what happened during this crisis, and why – as a lever for events and as a mirror for decisions. To enforce its will on Italy, France, the Soviet Union and Nationalist Turkey, Britain needed to know each country's intentions. Diplomats provided excellent material on Italy and France, but little on Turkey and the USSR. GC&CS and a Sigint agency under Harington, No. 3 Wireless Observation Group, easily read the diplomatic traffic of all four powers. MI6 had excellent sources on Turkish diplomats in Europe, but few in Anatolia. It trusted its sources in the USSR, whose reports were not patently false, though their veracity is unclear. Any diplomatic contact between France, Italy and Turkey could be cross-checked through two to four sources. Just one account existed of any Turco-Soviet talks, however, while their intentions were masked. The strongest combination of sources was Comint and diplomats, followed by Comint and spies. The absence of diplomatic sources crippled the value of Comint on Turkey and the USSR. Good intelligence sometimes reinforced bad assessments.[33]

Emotion drove analysis. Ministers were enraged at Kemal, their own failure, the danger, and each other. Curzon's policy was cool, but the minister was steamed by the Allies and his colleagues, whom he feared would leave 'me to fight the battle and to bear the brunt of defeat'. When the French premier, Raymond Poincaré, blamed him for the debacle in Turkey on 22 September and rejected Curzon's line, the Foreign Minister stormed from the meeting, guzzled brandy in the marbled corridors of the Quai d'Orsay, and wept about 'that horrid little man'.[34] The politics of decision-making, and the conditions of a crisis, produced systematic problems in intelligence. Though the Admiralty, the War Office, the Foreign Office and Harington had specialist officers to assess intelligence, no layer of interdepartmental assessment serviced Whitehall as a whole. Cascades of intelligence and decisions crashed together. Some authorities steered this white water through specialist assessment. Others did so by glancing at each report through the prism of memories of earlier ones, clouded by spray from the rapids. These differences in assessment did not make disaster, but it did create problems. Significantly, specialist assessment served the two men with the clearest sense of the crisis who best used intelligence to serve policy: Curzon and Harington.

Communications and politics hampered decisions. Whitehall tried to make tactical decisions; Harington made strategic ones. Every cycle of signals between London and Istanbul took a day to complete, usually more. Whitehall told Harington how to act twelve hours ahead through its reaction to a situation eighteen hours past, which led him to debate his orders, ad infinitum. The most recent or sensational reports disproportionately influenced decisions, which often had to be made immediately on the gravest of issues. Authorities in London and Istanbul reacted to the same range of political and military factors, but twelve to thirty-six hours apart, without completely informing each other of important details. Harington was the main culprit, partly because he did not know how far ministers wished to micromanage his actions. Without anyone realising it, including himself, Harington controlled power and diplomacy. When Whitehall pulled levers, nothing moved; Harington pulled levers without trying. Thus, he became Britain's chief consumer of intelligence. Even worse, Harington and Whitehall had different intelligence pictures: he was denied MI6 reports and Foreign Office and GC&CS material on French and Italian policy, but saw No. 3 Wireless Observation Group's solutions on Russia and Turkey two days before ministers did, and had more local contact with Turks. As borders vanished between high and low policy, decision-makers acted on different bases of knowledge. Thus, good evidence, well analysed, caused the machinery of state to stutter between high performance and breakdown. Fortunately, if fortuitously, Harington used intelligence well, and made Britain's decisions for war and peace. This outcome, and the unexpected way in which it occurred, defined the Chanak crisis.

British decision-makers, avid and able users of intelligence, were well informed on everything but the central problem: Kemal's ends and how far he would go to achieve them. No source solved that problem until the Mudanya negotiations, where Harington's intuition became his intelligence. He made Kemal define Turkish demands and learned how to sell British terms. Until then, intelligence suggested Kemal thought Britain an enemy rather than a problem. Belligerence and error might lead him to war.[35] The Turkish ministers in Paris and Rome mocked Britain's resolve and ability to act, leading the Cabinet to escalate the crisis, from necessity and anger.[36] The Soviet ambassador in Ankara, Semen Aralov, outlined his attempts to manipulate the Turks into hostilities with Britain, and his means to do so. The Soviet foreign ministry, the Narkomindel, advised Turkey to attack Britain.[37] MI6 reports read the Turkish nationalists from Turko-Bolshevik and pan-Islamic perspectives. MI6 perhaps distorted Soviet malevolence to Britain by picking up a disproportionate number of indications of active enmity, as against cautious hostility. Though MI6 loathed the USSR, this bias was accidental: after the Cabinet decided on an ultimatum, MI6 increasingly reported that Turco-Soviet relations were poor because its sources said so. Comint demonstrated that Soviet behaviour towards Britain was alarming, and often confirmed MI6 reports while never disproving them. Comint generally increased the plausibility of the details reported by any one agent, which were not supported by other sources, and of MI6 reports on the USSR.

This situation fuelled the most belligerent of British actions during the crisis. Britain concluded that the Soviets were encouraging Kemal to war; hence, if one occurred, the Royal Navy was ordered immediately to attack Soviet warships near Turkish waters and blockade Leningrad, so risking a world war.[38] Bad intelligence from good human sources suggested that Kemal would deliver an ultimatum and attack British forces on 30 September. On 25 September, after assessing all the intelligence at hand, MI6 warned that Kemal was the head of the 'military party' in Ankara, which wished to humiliate Britain and attack it.[39] These and other such MI6 reports drove the ultimatum of 29 September, which the Cabinet believed merely would pre-empt an imminent assault by Turkey and Russia, and force Kemal to reconsider his aims.

Comint reinforced disastrous decisions, but also helped to prevent them. Comint was Britain's leading source of information during the crisis and central to its ability to achieve its aims. Comint and official sources illuminated the positions of France and Italy in time for Britain to act. They proved those powers had betrayed Britain, hoped to gain

Turkish concessions as a result, yet also warned Kemal from attacking Britain and feared that war would wreck their interests. Whitehall applied that knowledge to send precise signals to its erstwhile allies and to force them into line. In the Allied conference at Paris on 20–22 September, Curzon used intelligence like a rapier on Poincaré. Curzon stated that, through codebreaking, Britain knew Turkish policy and its discussions with French authorities. Britain would watch French actions and hold Poincaré responsible for them. Curzon primed the pump to ensure Britain would know what was happening, by having further messages delivered and monitored. France should use 'every channel of influence' available to warn 'Kemal from precipitate action'. He did not know how nationalist agents transmitted advice, retorted Poincaré, but 'England would be better informed. The war had shown that her administrative services were much better at deciphering telegrams than the French' – showing he recognised Curzon's intention and disavowed any hostile words that might be put in his mouth. Poincaré, however, did deliver such messages, which British codebreakers monitored. This combination of signals and Sigint defined Britain's ability to shape French policy and achieve its own. French and Italian warnings perhaps swayed Kemal.[40]

Intelligence is hard to use well in crises. Harington, highly strung, ill, tired, his telegrams often drafted in the early hours, struck like a master. As chief of staff to Britain's best force on the Western front, the Second Army, he had used intelligence and Sigint in battle for three years. He had controlled an integrated collection and intelligence service, whose members had specialised in Turkish diplomacy and operations for six years, developing a strong sense not only of what messages said but what they meant. Thus, on 29 September, Aralov informed Moscow that he aimed to bribe senior nationalists, including Kemal, with valuable swords, jewels and gold cigarette cases. Harington's intelligence read this message in a counter-intuitive but accurate fashion – to indicate declining Bolshevik influence in Ankara.[41]

No. 3 Wireless Observation Group gave Harington precisely the intelligence he needed to know, with little irrelevant material. In the days before 30 September, its reports increasingly suggested that the Turks would compromise. Harington had read Kemal's mail for two years, learning how the nationalist leader thought, argued and acted. Unlike other British authorities, he respected Kemal, viewed him calmly, and rejected the conspiracy theory. 'I do not think that Mustapha Kemal wants to attack us and I feel myself that if we go quite straight now we may remove all danger of attacks from our troops,' so saving lives and 'honour' and avoiding 'another dreadful war', he wrote. 'Secret information shows Bolshevik influence at Angora is being lost and Nurredin [Pasha, a leading Turkish general] has declared Nationalists are not at war with England. I think Turks are waiting for a sign from England. If this is given they will be reasonable. Otherwise their attitude will change.'[42] Harington delivered this sign: Britain would fight if challenged, but otherwise would concede most Turkish demands at a conference. Through bold action and informed assessment of excellent intelligence, he achieved difficult aims while avoiding the obvious risks of disaster. Few generals have ever used diplomatic Comint so well, nor many diplomats.

Lausanne and Later

After the crisis, an international conference at Lausanne settled the status of Turkey. Britain, negotiating the defeat of its policy towards Turkey, had just two direct interests at stake: to keep the Mosul district, which Kemal claimed, in Iraq; and to maintain the freedom of the straits, the right to send warships from the Mediterranean to the Black seas, without Turkish interference. Britain also aimed to limit any other powers' gains from Turkey, particularly because Curzon, personalising interests, sought revenge on those states which had wrecked his policy. Britain used intelligence superiority to ensure that its rivals lost as badly as it had done, thus, ironically, helping Turkey to achieve its objectives.

Comint and diplomats identified the objectives, strategies and tactics of every other participant at Lausanne. As a member of the British delegation wrote, they had 'the position of a man who is playing Bridge and knows the cards in his adversary's hands'.[43] Comint helped Curzon block those objectives he disliked by building fleeting coalitions on one issue after another. He led every other power, including Turkey, against Soviet attempts to keep non-littoral navies from entering the Black Sea. He subverted the special French and Italian interests in Turkey, for which they had broken with Britain, by refusing them support. Britain watched the Turkish delegate at Lausanne, Ismet Inonu, press for a deal the powers could accept, while Kemal rejected compromise. This debate taught Britons the best deal they could achieve, and how to help Inonu budge Kemal. Comint enabled Curzon to reshape the politics of the Middle East by beginning the restoration of good relations with Turkey, and dividing the latter from Russia, France and Italy. Lausanne, like Chanak, restored some prestige to Britain. The Foreign Office used Comint with cunning, to retain Mosul and outmanoeuvre all comers. Many of these successes, however, served no British interest. Curzon's bullying of French leaders encouraged them to retaliate during the Rhineland crisis, and damaged a key relationship for Britain.[44]

In these events between 1919 and 1923, the emotions of decision-makers degraded the instrumentality of Comint, its interpretation and use. The inability to determine the nature of a conspiracy, or to read Kemal's mind, raised uncertainty and fear on a fundamental interpretive issue: exactly what would a Turkish nationalist victory mean for Britain and its enemies? The lack of lasting actions to influence until September 1922 constrained the value of Comint. When such actions became possible, this value leapt, though dangers grasped at its heels. The conditions of a crisis led many actors into error, but circumstances gave power to Harington. He used Comint to achieve a hard and risky policy, which let Britain define how the Turkish settlement would be negotiated, and left it powerful cards to play. British negotiators used Comint skilfully at the Lausanne conference, but in pursuit of revenge as much as national interest. As ever, failures in policy and perception limit the value even of excellent intelligence.

Comint and the Main Enemy, 1919–39

For Britain and the USSR, the Cold War began in 1917.[45] Each was central to the other's calculations of power politics, but diplomacy had an unusual role in that process. For much of the interwar years, these states did not even have formal diplomatic relations, which were frosty at best. They cooperated only by coincidence, recognised no common interests, and often saw themselves in a sort of war. Soviet leaders addressed power politics unlike liberals, combining brutal realism with revolutionary fervour. Diplomacy and subversion marched together under the Narkomindel and the Comintern. To Soviet leaders, Britain was the main enemy and target. For Britain, diplomacy with the USSR was closely linked to defence against its subversion in the

United Kingdom, the empire, or other countries. British military and diplomatic elites, and especially Conservative politicians, loathed the USSR. Liberal and Labour politicians were calmer. Though they disliked the USSR, Lloyd George and MacDonald doubted that communism could attract the people of Britain.[46]

Between 1919 and 1930, in rhetorical terms, this cold war involved the world. In reality, it centred on a revival of the 'Great Game' in Asia. A struggle between Britain, the USSR and states (or factions) in the territories between them was linked to decolonisation, as European power in Asia declined from its peak after 1919. Persia and Afghanistan became more powerful; China and Turkey collapsed, and rose again.[47] During the 1930s, however, this cold war became one of many in power politics. The international system unravelled and diplomacy was transformed. Italy, Germany, and Japan married brutal realism to revolutionary nationalism, liberal states became an endangered species, and world war began. From this basis emerged a cold war between 1945 and 1992, which did involve the entire world.

For Britain, compared to the norm of the interwar years, diplomatic Comint on the USSR was linked less to diplomats than to other forms of intelligence, especially intercepted messages, purloined documents, and agents within the Comintern and communist parties across the empire. Internal (telephone taps, letter intercepts and bugs) and external forms of Comint were merged against the USSR. During the 1920s, the strongest components of British signals and human intelligence and security focused on the USSR. After December 1920, GC&CS rarely solved Soviet diplomatic traffic in Europe; the celebrated compromises of its successes against Soviet systems during 1923 and 1927 had little impact on that power in Europe. Between 1919 and 1932, however, what concerned Britain most about the USSR was its policy in the Middle East, Afghanistan and east Asia, and its subversion against the British empire. Such material was plentiful through solutions of Soviet diplomatic systems used in Asia. Comint had triumphs but its key partner was sources of less reliability. In particular, stolen papers were Britain's central source on Soviet policy. Their authenticity is unclear. Forgeries fooled British intelligence. When compared to known facts, some stolen documents ring true, many do not, and others do not sound at all, the problem being to tell one from the other. In any case, during 1926 one diplomat noted that Britain's best source was papers from the Politburo (the political bureau and highest decision-making organ of the Soviet Communist Party) and the Sovnarkom (the Council of People's Commissars, the chief decision-making authority of the Soviet government).[48] Human sources on the USSR and its activities abroad were plentiful, with quality ranging from abysmal to excellent. Fortunately, Comint provided massive and reliable details which largely contained misapprehensions which Humint and stolen documents might otherwise have aroused.

Britain's mixed grasp of Soviet secrets produced knowledge and rage. That anger was most hot in 1919–21, but burned until 1945. Its effect was greatest on fundamental issues of strategy and diplomacy, where many statesmen declined to work with so hostile and subversive a state. This attitude most mattered in 1922 when it almost drove Britain to war with Turkey and Russia, and in the 1930s, when it hampered whatever possibility existed of cooperation with the USSR against Nazi Germany. Knowledge of Soviet intrigues so maddened Whitehall that it needlessly lost some tricks. British policies towards Turkey and China were hurt, though not fatally, because Whitehall overestimated Soviet influence and misconstrued Turkish and Chinese nationalists. This anger was not surprising. The USSR attacked British interests more than any other state had done in peacetime, and triggered old fears about links between internal and external threats. In 1926, the PUS, William Tyrell, wrote:

we are virtually at war with Russia, in spite of Russia discarding the time-honoured practice of force and substituting for it the more invidious weapon of peaceful penetration on the one hand in the internal affairs of other countries, and, on the other, the stirring up of revolution everywhere in order to prevent us from carrying on trade, and thereby undermining the commercial prosperity on which our national life depends. The two most glaring instances of recent date are the assistance afforded by Russia to the coal strike in this country, and her successful efforts in destroying our trade with China.[49]

The surprising thing is the degree of British restraint.

The central issues were British relations with the USSR – whether to have them or break them, and the significance of the Soviet threat.

Intelligence, ranging from worthless to excellent, shaped a rolling debate on these issues. The alarmist case rested on Soviet intentions and ambitions, the dispassionate one on its capabilities and limitations, both defined in political rather than military terms. In 1919–20, Comint occasionally acquired messages from Lenin, the Soviet leader, demonstrating hostility to Britain and efforts to conspire with its enemies and manipulate British politics: 'But of course all this must be done absolutely unofficially and confidentially and the most prudent diplomacy must be maintained.'[50] Rarely again did Comint provide material of such power, but flimsies, Humint reports, stolen documents, and official Soviet statements all reflected these themes. This picture of Soviet hostility was true; the response was often hysterical. That material enraged British decision-makers and left poison in Anglo–Soviet relations for the 1930s. It led officers to leak intelligence to the press so to block Lloyd George's policies towards Russia in 1920 and damage the Labour Party in the election of 1924; and British governments to publish solutions of Soviet traffic in 1923 and 1927 in the wake of the police raid of the London offices of the All-Russian Co-operative Society (ARCOS), suspected of being a front for Soviet subversion in Britain.[51] These releases damaged British cryptanalysis by showing that Soviet cryptosystems were blown.

Meanwhile, intelligence bolstered British efforts to contain Soviet actions in Asia, which were adventuristic, factionalised and driven by local agents. In this competition, Soviet intelligence was good but British better, because of Comint. These actions, and the policy behind them, were the greatest concern for British intelligence and strategy between 1920 and 1931. Initially, the balance of reports from all sources suggested that Soviets were manipulating Muslims.[52] From 1923, this balance shifted, as all sources moved in the same direction. Stolen documents indicated an aggressive policy in Asia, but mixed Soviet relations with Turkey and Persia. Comint, official and human sources traced Soviet activities well enough to confirm or deny frightening accounts, creating a more accurate and less alarming picture, if still unpleasant. Soviet influence mounted in Afghanistan and China, and to a lesser degree on Persia. Britain's image of Soviet aims rested on a combination of public rhetoric and observations of the actions of the Narkomindel and the Comintern. Despite good intelligence – and partly because of it – Whitehall misconstrued Soviet policy, which caused needless alarm. The USSR wished to work against Britain with anti-colonial nationalists and independent states, which exploited opportunity, while mistrusting both powers. Soviet actions were cautious in Turkey, pushy in Persia, and adventurist in Afghanistan and China. Britain confronted a struggle for influence, not power. As the Foreign Office fought the War Office and India Office over the response to these issues, intelligence was politicised by its primary consumers, specialist officers and officials. Yet these problems did not cause poor policy. In most particulars, intelligence aided Britain. Generally, it soothed fears.[53]

Comint was central to this process. Britain easily read Afghan, Chinese, Persian, Turkish and Soviet cryptosystems. The most spectacular traffic came from Soviet ambassadors, who hated Britain, treated diplomacy as war and sent bloodthirsty telegrams. When the security of couriers became dubious during the Afghan civil war of 1929, the Narkomindel ordered its emissary in Kabul to transmit nothing 'that might have serious consequences should it fall into the hands of others. Do not send long and extraordinarily candid dispatches but be in them – brief and exact.'[54] That minister, Leonid Stark, did not follow such advice; nor his fellows. They, and Comintern officers, exaggerated their successes and threat to Britain. These distortions were hard to cross-check. Comint most aided diplomacy where it uncovered state-to-state relations and its main partner was diplomats, while Humint mattered least. Diplomatic Comint was least useful when it addressed non-state issues, where diplomats' reportage was weak and Humint was the basic source. Then, as in Turkey during 1920–22, no matter how good its quality, Humint had to report threats and conspiracies, because they were happening, or loomed in the dark. Comint tended to reinforce, and rarely overturned, such reports, because evidence rarely refuted them. The power of revolutionary and nationalist organisations within collapsing non-Western polities, which British authorities disparaged at the best of times, was difficult to judge. Success in diplomatic Comint about the intentions of states could not overcome errors regarding the assessment of the strength of peoples and armies.

Similar problems dogged intelligence on China between 1924 and 1927, especially regarding Soviet aid to Chinese forces. Official sources were of little value on those issues, about which Humint provided some good and many misleading reports. GC&CS offered useful and unique evidence, as on the chaos within Soviet organisations, and

Soviet intrigues in north China.[55] Whitehall understood Soviet actions in China, but not how they would matter. Authorities particularly underestimated the military power and political potential of the Kuomintang, the nationalist party in south China, despite knowledge of Soviet armament of and training for its soldiers. Authorities knew the size and armament of Kuomintang armies, but doubted the competence and patriotism of Chinese forces or generals. In 1926, the Kuomintang and communists launched the Northern Expedition, which transformed Chinese politics and stunned Whitehall. Civil war between these forces quickly shattered Chinese communists, and Soviet policy. Fortuitously, Britain survived this failure of intelligence and policy better than did the USSR, but at cost, as its special political and economic position in China eroded.[56]

Elsewhere in Asia, British intelligence and policy had greater success. Increasingly, Britain was more informed and adroit than the USSR. Confronting a Soviet campaign modelled on tsarist actions in the Great Game, Britain reverted to a standard policy from that competition – masterly inactivity, which defended India on the North-West Frontier rather than beyond it, and preserved the status quo there solely through diplomacy. The Foreign Office sought to keep 'a watchful eye on future developments', minimise British interference in Afghanistan, Persia and Turkey, and systematically to contain Soviet influence through diplomacy and the strengthening of local governments.[57] Intelligence was fundamental to the formulation and execution of this strategy and to confidence it was working. Intelligence monitored Soviet intentions and actions, their internal debates, divisions, especially between Moscow and its emissaries abroad, and their successes and failures. Comint revealed Soviet paranoia about British actions and successes in Asia: for example, in 1926 and 1929, Soviet diplomats blamed risings in Iran and Afghanistan on Britain.[58] This evidence helped the Foreign Office understand the *mentalité* in Moscow, and shaped efforts not to drive its volatile rival towards hostility. Comint, the best means to penetrate the secrecy of Soviet policy, did so well, and often provided Afghan, Persian and Turkish accounts of relations with Russia. Intelligence, especially Comint, also helped the Foreign Office to defeat the War Office and the India Office, and guided effective actions by the government of India. Thus, Britain acted to calm the situation and to avoid exacerbating it.[59]

Official sources and GC&CS provided excellent material on Turkey, a country which British authorities increasingly respected, balanced well between Western states and the USSR. Soviet policy towards Turkey was cautious, as Britain understood from all secret and official sources. The USSR had more ambitious aims eastward during 1924–26. Comint illuminated Soviet aims towards Persia as the general Reza Khan seized power, their perceptions of Persian politics and reportage of Persian statements. The Narkomindel aimed to influence or dominate, but not to subvert or destroy, Persia – not far from Britain's policy.[60] In 1925, the Narkomindel told its minister to 'develop and strengthen our friendship for REZA', if possible 'pushing him to the Left', and also to support republican opposition to him. 'Your tactics may be either open or masked, as seems best to you.' In 1926, the Narkomindel warned that: 'In PERSIA more than in any other country the greatest care is necessary because each (?false) step may lead to the triumph of the British.'[61] Soviet clumsiness was having that effect. This revelation of attempts to bully Reza, followed by grudging recognition he had beaten them, and disarray in policy, showed that Moscow was not getting the best of it, nor Britain the worst. Solutions of Persian traffic supported this picture. Comint reinforced official reports and the canny calculations of the Foreign Office. Solutions of traffic between Moscow and its legation in Kabul, one leading official noted, showed 'that in their hearts they know that we are really getting the best of it, and unless something rather definite happens, there does not seem to be any reason to anticipate that their propaganda will be any more successful in Persia and Afghanistan than it has been up-to-date. (China is a different proposition…)'.[62] During Turcoman rebellions in 1926, the Soviet embassy told its consuls: 'We are against local rebellions and for a consolidated PERSIA' – one of those rare messages which refuted alarmism, the British fear that the USSR hoped to dissolve Persia.[63]

Between 1924 and 1929, the USSR pursued influence in Afghanistan, especially over its Amir, Amanullah. These activities concerned British authorities, who feared that Soviet intervention in Afghanistan threatened the security of India. Mastery of Afghan and Soviet codes, combined with diplomatic sources, enabled Britain's peak performance of masterly inactivity. Comint revealed Amanullah's erratic path, Soviet influence over him, and his hostility to Russia and Britain. It illuminated Soviet perceptions of Afghan politics and British policy.

Comint was essential during 1929–30, when Amanullah's regime collapsed and civil war raged.[64] Soviet authorities debated military intervention so to salvage a shattered position, which, the Afghan Foreign Minister declared, would force his government 'to unite whole population of AFGHANISTAN with intention of declaring Holy war against USSR and … ask ENGLAND for assistance'.[65] This intelligence helped Indian authorities to avoid alarmism and any actions that might 'scare her [Russia] into dangerous counter-action. We are convinced by far our safest course is "business as usual" as far as possible within our own borders.'[66] In 1880, such actions would have maddened British authorities; those of 1929 were sufficiently informed and confident to watch the Soviet position collapse, and subtly to help the emergence of a government favourable to Britain. Intelligence prevented alarm.

These successes were significant, compared to Soviet catastrophes in Afghanistan and China, but limited. Britain fought a strategy of imperial retreat in spheres of influence beyond its borders, trying to hold what it held, to prevent hostile governments from arising in Asia, and to limit Soviet influence on them. Intelligence and influence let Britain play the Great Game as judo: to widen divisions between the USSR and Afghanistan, Turkey and Persia, by avoiding mistakes while letting the Soviets make them, but at cost. Strong governments in Tehran, Kabul and Ankara must damage British interests as well as Soviet ones. Local states drove and won this struggle. Britain merely budged the balance of the losses which it suffered to these neighbours compared to those which the Soviets surrendered.

Around 1931, the USSR became less central to British strategy, because its activities declined in Asia, and Russia seemed secondary in Europe. Comint on the USSR also changed. Britain lost access to diplomatic codes but unmasked Comintern traffic. The importance of the loss is hard to assess. After 1920, diplomatic Comint revealed little about Soviet policy towards Britain, but much about that towards Asian states. Equal access to Soviet cryptosystems during the 1930s would have been of little value, and in any case, continued success against the systems of these states still illuminated secret actions by the USSR. Thus, during 1936, GC&CS revealed Soviet attempts for closer relations with Turkey, including a defensive alliance. The Foreign Office insistently and successfully warned Turkish diplomats away from such steps, which, they feared, would bring Turkey into the Soviet orbit, irritate Italy and

Germany, complicate Britain's position in the Mediterranean Sea and weaken its position against the Soviet Union.[67] Full access to Soviet cryptosystems, including between a Russian ambassador in London and the Narkomindel, would not have unlocked Stalin's heart, or Soviet decision-making in 1939. It would have shown hard but realistic Soviet commentary, which disparaged Britain but saw it as a lesser threat than Germany. Such material is unlikely to have swayed British thinking, whether of Prime Minister Neville Chamberlain or of generals or diplomats. Comintern traffic delineated Soviet subversion across the world, especially when combined with Humint. Mask offered the functional equivalent of Narkomindel traffic in some areas, especially Republican Spain. This success aided counter-intelligence across Britain and the empire, and British external policy in a few areas. Though Soviet intelligence outclassed British during this period, Comint on the Comintern and communist parties throughout the empire remained a strong suit.[68] They also shaped an unbalanced intelligence picture. Mask provided the largest body of evidence of any state's hostility to Britain, making Soviet machinations seem more dangerous than they were, thus perhaps reducing suspicions of Hitler and Mussolini. During the Spanish civil war, British Comint illuminated Soviet and Italian intrigues, yet those of Moscow irritated Whitehall more than did the actions of Rome.

Intelligence, Appeasement and the Road to War, 1933–39

GC&CS was less useful to foreign policy in the 1930s than the 1920s, because of changes in intelligence, actors and international systems.[69] During the 1920s, revisionist powers were weak, most states accepted the status quo, which was strong and armed, supported by most military power in the system. British leaders – liberal realists – understood the objectives of every other power. They set the pace in diplomacy, being the stronger player with the initiative in most interactions – thrusting the burden of uncertainty and the need to make the first move in bargaining onto others, who had to guess British intentions and how to influence them. Diplomacy consisted more than usually of details, which suited the strengths of GC&CS. The latter often showed Britain the cards in its opponents' hands, after it already had the advantage of picking the game – and the deck. It illuminated the current policy of other states, the views of middle-level decision-makers, and sometimes the secret intentions of statesmen. GC&CS monitored developments in challenges to the status quo. Such distant warning was an unwritten part of British strategy, which aimed to gauge dangers ten years away.

In the 1920s, able statesmen used codebreaking to guide the play of a strong hand; in the 1930s, inferior ones needed it to shape a defensive strategy. The liberal order became less cohesive, militarily weaker, atomised. The beneficiaries of the status quo declined to support it or each other. All states played a lone hand. Revisionists grew in strength and number. Britain, midway through attempts to solve every problem on earth at once through multilateral and liberal internationalist means, was caught in a confusing situation. Until 1937, it could neither achieve this policy, nor abandon it. As Britain sought to salvage that policy, it jumped to the initiative of revisionists, defending its interests against two or three states, feeling vulnerable in interactions, guessing at adversaries' aims and the means to influence them. Statesmen, thrown into uncertainty, thought every action had such unpalatable consequences that the easiest solution was to take none, or alternately, to prime the pump of better relations with Germany and Italy by paying them for the privilege of agreeing to start a bargain. A reactive power needs better intelligence than an active one – in order to understand what is happening, what to do and how, it must be right on more things. It needs to know the active power's intentions, the latter need merely know its own mind. Between 1933 and 1939, Britain needed good intelligence more than ever – precisely as GC&CS offered less than it had before.

British statesmen became more liberal and less realist; though not cowards and fools, they lost some of their elders' hard-edged realism and hard-won expertise. In intelligence, wisdom is to information as three is to one. Statesmen did not fail because intelligence was bad; they used intelligence badly because they failed as statesmen. Thus, intelligence could not help them much in a key area. Britain followed a policy of appeasement, altering some details of the international order in favour of Germany and Italy, so they would support the revised system. Britain was reluctant to match German rearmament because it feared such acts would damage its economy and drive an arms race. This policy was naive, but stemmed from both the liberal and realist streams of British statecraft.[70] Statesmen also understood that Germany was a problem and might become a threat. So to formulate and execute any policy, authorities needed to know the intentions of Hitler and Mussolini and their willingness to act on them. Statesmen had to guess at these matters and did so badly; wishful thinking, the fears they might guess wrong or bluff too far, queered their pitch. Intelligence on Germany and Italy became more politicised than any other matter of the interwar years, creating confusion, uncertainty and occasionally, chaos.

Amidst this war zone, Neville Chamberlain, megalomaniacal and obstinate, rejected reports he disliked and, hidden from colleagues and the Foreign Office, negotiated secretly with Germany, Italy and Japan.[71] The inability to be sure of the intentions of Hitler and Mussolini crippled policy and let Germans and Italians manipulate Whitehall. Britain assessed far better the aims of the revisionist state whose diplomatic traffic GC&CS still mastered – Japan.[72] Again, British policy centred on deterrence, aiming to convince foreign statesmen they dare not attack Britain. Deterrence works only if one understands how other polities act, and how their leaders view the balance between themselves and you. The limits to intelligence were part of Britain's problem during the appeasement era. An improvement in its quality would have mattered, though probably not enough to avoid another great war. Wisdom alone could have achieved that end, by creating and wielding power, and could have done so without better intelligence than Britain had.

Comint shaped a minority of British actions during the appeasement era. Thus, during the Spanish civil war, Comint helped authorities to execute a policy which, while scarcely heroic, met British interests barely.[73] The problem was limits to intelligence, and power. GC&CS provided much material upon which Britain could not act, in areas like China or the Balkans. Tapping into the international web of reports and rumours often suggested new problems or possibilities, but rarely enabled anything, with one great exception. Power and intelligence aided imperial overwatch in central and western Asia more than any other aspect of British policy. Human and official sources were excellent. Comint traced hidden actions and determined whether actors meant what they said. Intelligence from overlapping sources tracked foreign intrigues. Comint monitored Japanese actions in Afghanistan. It revealed Italian intrigues in Arabia and their discussions both with members of the Congress Party in India, and British foes on the North-West Frontier.[74] Comint illuminated relations between states in the Middle East, including two important powers. It showed Turkish wariness of Germany and Italy, and a preference to align with Britain. Radio carried the internal and international traffic of Saudi Arabia, the key independent Arab kingdom, in a region vital to British interests and vulnerable to internal agitation and external manipulation, which Britain managed through intelligence, politics and tiny forces. The Saudi monarch, Ibn Saud, shaped Arab opposition to or toleration of British hegemony. Britain read Saudi messages, alongside those of its own protectorates, Egypt, Iraq and Transjordan. Comint showed that (exactly as he said openly) Ibn Saud wished to cooperate with Britain and feared Germany, Italy and Russia. He sought to contain conspiracies against Britain and to calm Arab opinion, which, he believed, was possible only if Britain changed its Zionist policy in Palestine. Comint and human sources also achieved a rare success, as they monitored and wrecked the conspiracies directed by Arabs against Britain.[75]

All of this Arabic Comint came from an Armenian codebreaker at Sarafand, Captain Danielien, whom, GC&CS noted in 1938, knew 'Arabic and Turkish perfectly but [his] knowledge of English is poor and his translations of Arabic telegrams are now causing considerable anxiety so we have asked that the Arabic texts should also be sent back.'[76] This 'anxiety' reflected a drive for certainty in the meaning of messages, as Comint guided manoeuvres through political complexity. After negotiations with Arab states, and the Jewish Agency, Britain abandoned Zionism in 1939 and announced a policy towards Palestine which it believed Arab states and public opinion would accept. Whitehall, correctly, thought that these actions would stabilise its power in the Middle East, as external threats mounted. During 1940–42, GC&CS demonstrated Axis intrigues in the Middle East, and continued Saudi and Turkish support for Britain – a rare glimmer of hope in a bleak time, which guided British policy towards these states. The Middle East was a valuable but vulnerable area of the British empire. Comint helped the middle-level officials who managed that region do so cheaply and easily, which makes the threats they confronted seem smaller than they really were. In this instance, the mirror of Comint reflects the power of Comint.[77]

The Anti-Comintern Pact

At the highest level of power politics, the strength of cryptanalysis relative to perceptions conditioned the effect of Comint. GC&CS rarely defined the intentions of Hitler, Mussolini or Stalin – leaders who made the key decisions for their states and did not communicate them internationally. GC&CS did not break German diplomatic codes.[78] Success in this sphere would have revealed German hostility to Britain with greater breadth, reliability and, perhaps, effect than other sources. It would not have uncovered Hitler's aims, which he rarely expressed through his diplomats. Britain read all Italian diplomatic codes fairly well, but couriers carried the most important, sometimes explosive, messages as to how the Italian ambassador in London, Dino Grandi, manipulated Chamberlain, and the latter's secret diplomacy with Italy.[79] This was the only part of that diplomacy which remained hidden from the Foreign Office: GC&CS revealed private diplomacy with Japan by the Bank of England, British firms, the Treasury, the Board of Trade and Chamberlain – as MI5's sources within the German embassy in London did the prime minister's attempt to work with Hitler after Munich.[80]

Comint revealed everything about Italian policy, except the greatest things. Comint from other states mentioned the views of Hitler and Mussolini, through reports which were bitty, contradictory, far from the target, and uncertain in reliability – with one exception. Britain consistently read Japanese codes. It understood Japanese intentions well. Acting on that knowledge was hard. Only force could stop Japan, the dominant power in east Asia, as it attacked China and subverted British interests there. Given its problems in Europe, Britain could not rely on force against Japan. Unlike Germany, Britain lacked strings to pull in Tokyo. Yet this Comint had other uses. Japanese diplomats, with privileged access to German and Italian leaders, discussed their views in telegrams which Britain read, augmented by Italian traffic. Relations between Germany, Italy and Japan were also linked to a treaty. The Anti-Comintern Pact (ACP), aimed against Soviet subversion, proved a thermometer for relations between them.

During 1936, Joachim von Ribbentrop, the Nazi party's head of foreign relations, and General Oshima Hiroshi, the Japanese military attaché to Berlin, created the ACP. Their ultimate aim perhaps was a

German–Japanese alliance, but the immediate one was to simulate cooperation between Germany and Japan, so as to maximise their pressure on Britain and the USSR.[81] This bluff failed because these targets read Japanese telegrams, and knew the ACP was meaningless – at least, for the present. British authorities, including alarmists about Germany, regarded this matter as unfortunate rather than dangerous. That relationship seemed weak, perhaps embracing a few Germans and Japanese, not Germany and Japan. Though Hitler actually favoured cooperation with Japan, this assessment was reasonable. In any case, Britain carefully monitored that danger, with Comint covering the horizon. GC&CS illuminated the intentions of these states, and revealed the first indication of changes in their relationship. This knowledge mobilised other sources to search for information, where official ones rapidly matched the power of Comint. GC&CS provided early warning. That did not always yield right reading.[82]

The danger rose in September 1937, when Mussolini visited Berlin. After witnessing German military power, he decided to cooperate with Hitler, so to destabilise the Versailles order. Germany and Italy sought to keep this agreement secret.[83] GC&CS lifted the veil almost as soon as it fell, but its masters misconstrued the view. Japanese telegrams showed that Italy, seeking to join the ACP for months, soon would do so. Italy and Germany wished to turn the ACP as much against Britain as the USSR, which Japan opposed. All parties expected their cooperation to constrain Britain. The German ambassador in Japan, Eugen Ott, paraphrased the Foreign Minister, Konstantin von Neurath, as saying that, in their meeting, Hitler and Mussolini discussed 'the question of anti-communism and other matters', and reached an understanding: 'Germany recognised the special interests of Italy in the Mediterranean, while Italy recognised those of Germany in regard to Austria.' The dictators had not always seen 'eye to eye', Ott noted, but those talks 'had been of a most amiable nature and had helped to bring about a better feeling'. This report – accurate, though the fact was uncertain – suggested that Hitler and Mussolini contemplated cooperation. Italy might cease blocking German expansion in central Europe, if Germany aided Italian ambitions around the Mediterranean Sea.[84] This message was fifth-hand (Hitler to von Neurath to Ott to the Japanese Foreign Minister, Koki Hirota, to the Japanese ambassador in Rome, Maasaki Hotta).

Had Britain read the second-hand German message conveying von Neurath's message to Ott, the effect might have been greater. The report did not directly refute British preconceptions that Mussolini must fear German expansion and desire cooperation with Britain to save the status quo rather than work with Hitler to blow it up. Perhaps Mussolini did not really mean what Germans and Japanese thought that he did. British authorities knew that Japan was hostile and feared that Hitler might be; but not Mussolini. Few understood Mussolini's delusions about Italian power compared to Britain and Germany, or his hostility towards and contempt for Britain. In January 1938, however, GC&CS showed that Galeazzo Ciano, the Italian Foreign Minister and Mussolini's son-in-law, purporting to be his master's voice, warned Hotta that Japan 'would not be wise' to 'strengthen the solidarity' between Britain and the United States through its war in China. Italy could not 'help JAPAN if trouble occurred between her and the States. In the case of GREAT BRITAIN, however, ITALY was in a position to act as a check with her effective strength. In JAPAN's relations with GREAT BRITAIN he affirmed that ITALY would help her at all times with all her strength.' Britain had abandoned plans to reinforce its fleet in Asia, 'because they were afraid of Italian action in the MEDITERRANEAN'.[85]

This statement of Italy's position towards Britain and Japan was alarming, doubly so if linked to von Neurath's comment. The Foreign Secretary, Antony Eden, interpreted these statements to prove Mussolini's malevolence, and the need for firmness towards Italy. Neville Chamberlain, most ministers and officials in the service departments and the Foreign Office, rejected that policy. Comint from third parties (including some quoting Mussolini) reinforced the general view that Eden was the obstacle to friendship with Italy. This debate sparked a celebrated event in the history of appeasement. On 18 February 1938, in a meeting with the prime minister, Eden cited the comments of Ciano and von Neurath to change Chamberlain's views about Mussolini. Chamberlain called Grandi into this meeting, described von Neurath's account and, without mentioning the source, asked whether Mussolini was cooperating with Hitler. When Grandi denied that claim, Chamberlain accepted his words and denounced British intelligence. Chamberlain made Grandi his analyst of Comint on Italy, acted on his assessment, and created a triumph of policy – for Italy. Within forty-eight hours, Chamberlain drove Eden from the Cabinet. Eden, unwilling to cite a flimsy before his colleagues, could defend his position only by referring vaguely to secret sources about Italian malevolence and the value of alignment with America.[86] Chamberlain chased Italy for a year, despite Mussolini's ostentatious breaking of promises, and much Comint showing that Italy prized Germany and Japan far above Britain, which all three powers cooperated to constrain. This pursuit damaged British credibility and policy.[87] However absurd this behaviour, every Briton who read this Comint supported Chamberlain's policy, save Eden. These messages probably spurred efforts for rapprochement with Italy by indicating a danger that could be stopped rather than one already present. This, the greatest missed opportunity of intelligence in the appeasement era, was overdetermined.

Throughout 1938, Japanese telegrams illuminated slow improvements in the relationships between these three powers. Every participant fixated on minor interests except Ribbentrop, Oshima and Hitler, though the latter's role remained veiled. Initially, Germany and Italy kept a distance from Japan and its war with China. The Japanese foreign ministry, the Gaimusho, had its ambassador, Shigenori Togo, directly ask Hitler for more support on the matter, warning that 'it is absolutely necessary therefore to avoid giving a Third Power the wished-for opportunity of driving a wedge between JAPAN and GERMANY'.[88] Soon, Ribbentrop became Foreign Minister. He and Hitler publicly abandoned a decade's worth of strategic investments with China in favour of Japan, at cost, demonstrating German desire for closer relations with Tokyo. Then, Japan kept its distance. The Gaimusho focused on keeping Germany from demanding the return of its lost colonies in the Pacific.[89] It feared that Britain might cooperate with the USSR and even more, the United States, in east Asia.[90] Japanese diplomats mistrusted the German and Italian governments, but expected loose cooperation to continue between them, because it suited all of their interests. Hotta believed that by accepting Anschluss, Italy 'makes Italo-German cooperation her diplomatic axis', so boosting the value of its liaison with Japan. Togo agreed that Italy's 'trump-card' against Britain remained 'the Italo-German axis', and noted 'RIBBENTROP's frequent declarations to me in the past that the Japan–German axis will be made the basis of GERMANY's foreign policy'.[91]

These reports were worrisome and even more so other developments. By March 1938, Ribbentrop proposed to Oshima that the ACP become a 'Japanese–German offensive and defensive alliance against the Soviet'. The Gaimusho opposed that idea. It feared Ribbentrop was using 'backdoor methods' to negotiate directly with the Japanese army and the Kaigunsho via Oshima and the German naval attaché.[92] Diplomats could not control Oshima. That he became ambassador to Germany after the Munich conference was worrisome. Soon after that appointment, GC&CS provided its most alarming messages of the appeasement era. Ribbentrop told Oshima that the ACP should become a military alliance against the USSR and Britain. Ribbentrop purported to be acting on Hitler's orders, and was so. Thus, GC&CS reported Hitler's turn against Britain as soon as it could be detected, and the intended form: an alliance between Germany, Italy and Japan. The Foreign Office, uncertain how far Ribbentrop represented Hitler and trying to make the Munich agreement work, took this report seriously.[93]

Comint quickly confirmed it. Throughout January 1939, GC&CS traced German, Japanese and Italian negotiations to recast the ACP. Italy and Germany favoured a defensive and offensive alliance against any third party, including Britain and the USSR. Japanese authorities feared commitments by which Germany could force Japan into a war, an illuminating worry in itself. This Japanese reluctance annoyed Ciano and Ribbentrop, though Mussolini's position remained uncertain.[94] Then came another bombshell. In mid-January 1939, Chamberlain conducted a state visit to Rome, intended to solidify British cooperation with Italy. GC&CS demonstrated the failure of his hopes. Soon after the visit, Mussolini told the new Japanese ambassador to Italy that 'a three-Power Alliance was necessary' and 'must be concluded without delaying a single day'. France, Britain, and the United States obviously 'had come to some sort of agreement, against which we must hurry up and consolidate our front'. The aim was not war, but 'peace in the true sense', providing 'peace and time' for Germany, Italy and Japan to digest their conquests. 'If only the three Powers clung together, no other Power whatever could put an obstacle in our path.' In particular, confronted with that alliance, 'the UNITED STATES isolationist party would in a twinkling overcome those in favour of cooperation'.[95] Three days later, another Japanese telegram cited Ciano as saying that 'to show how firmly JAPAN, GERMANY AND ITALY were bound together, and to dispel all suspicions to the contrary, a very striking result could be achieved by announcing the existence of this Pact as soon as possible after the Anglo-Italian conversations in Rome'.[96]

By January 1939, GC&CS detected that Japanese cryptography was rising and sent a detachment under Tiltman to reinforce FECB in Hong Kong.[97] During February 1939, Comint slid in strength over Japanese policy towards the ACP. Japan tightened its diplomatic cryptography because of a leak in the *News Chronicle* about Japanese diplomacy, which Oshima and the Foreign Office both thought was inspired by Soviet authorities. Oshima insisted that the Gaimusho overcome its cryptographic weaknesses.[98] Ironically, its response, issuing him with the cypher machine which American codebreakers reconstructed and called Purple, made him a critical source of intelligence for the Allies during 1941–45. Occasionally, Comint aided British understanding. In March, Ciano told a Japanese diplomat that strengthening the ACP would 'make the contracting powers far stronger than the other "Group"', and justified the German annexation of the rump of Czechoslovakia for identical reasons.[99] Over the next six months, however, Britain relied mostly on open sources, which accurately showed Japanese decision-makers were debating Ribbentrop's proposal, fearing its consequences but slowly coming to accept a weaker version of it.

Comint and Strategy

This Comint, the most reliable and revealing intelligence Britain received in the months after Munich, affected British strategy in ways which cannot fully be ascertained – because the flimsies between July and December 1938 are lost, and British actions were twisted. Between October 1938 and April 1939, Whitehall transformed its strategic policy by treating Germany and Italy as threats. Intelligence, much of it bad, little of it certain, drove that process.[100] References to human intelligence fill the records, but not to Comint. Diplomatic and military officials saw it, as did Chamberlain, the Foreign Secretary, Sinclair, and the service ministers, but perhaps no one else. Comint shaped military and diplomatic decisions, but its impact often is unclear, forcing reliance on conjectural relations between intelligence and contemporaneous actions. Above all, these messages provided certain evidence which supported the trend of material from other sources, magnifying their effect. Comint suddenly demonstrated that Italy was unfriendly to

Britain. It showed that Germany, Italy and Japan aimed to strengthen their position against the liberal democracies, which posed a diplomatic problem and a strategic menace. Comint did not change Chamberlain's mind about Italy or Germany. It shaped the Foreign Office's conclusion that Hitler was hostile and must be contained, as did the more sensational and less reliable information which pressed parallel views among other decision-makers. Comint reinforced the rising willingness of all British authorities, including Chamberlain, to work with France and the United States. Probably Comint drove the sudden and otherwise puzzling identification of Italy as an enemy in early 1939 by the Foreign Office .and the fighting services, and that country's emergence as a primary target for attack in war.[101] Ribbentrop's proposal initially may have shaped the Foreign Office's increase of aid to China, so to keep Japan in the quagmire. Proof of Japanese reluctance to accept that offer, however, soon boosted cautious efforts not to antagonise Japan, which affected Britain's attempts to contain Germany. Britain limited any alignment against Germany with the USSR to Europe, excluding Asia, so not to drive Japan towards Ribbentrop's proposal.[102] Nor was Britain alone in reading Oshima's traffic. German codebreakers also did so, though this evidence was unnecessary for Hitler to see Japan's failure to accept his proposal, and so turn towards Moscow. However, knowledge, derived from reading Japanese telegrams, of the chance to drive a wedge between Japan and Germany and to break their pincers, perhaps encouraged Stalin to accept Hitler's offer, though that decision was overdetermined and rational.[103] Between 1938 and 1945, the cryptographic weaknesses of Oshima's communications affected power politics and war perhaps more than those of any other ambassador in history.

Between 1936 and 1939, GC&CS uncovered the secret relations between Italy, Japan and Germany. Intelligence on the ACP illuminated their intentions, no mean feat, given the confusion in these relations and the vagueness of the pact. The Japanese and German factions which pushed the ACP did so to alarm other powers. The pact had the opposite effect on Whitehall. It revealed the fundamental element of Axis diplomacy. Japan and Germany were discussing strategic cooperation but found action hard. There was no Axis yet. When this danger finally emerged, GC&CS penetrated it. The warning of intelligence, however, gauged danger less than one year away, too late to let Britain become militarily stronger or avoid war. It opened British eyes and led Britain to pursue a foolish policy.

Two factors limited the value of intelligence for Britain during the appeasement era. Perceptions shaped how intelligence was understood. Britain's power relative to Germany, Italy and Japan, in an atomised system of power politics, determined how it could be used. British intelligence on power politics was decent in quality. It could help people predisposed to view Hitler and Mussolini as threats, as Whitehall did Japan and the USSR, less so those who were not. As a mirror for decision-making, the Comint record on the ACP reflects how hard the preconceptions of British authorities were to shake, more so than in any other instance of the interwar years. The GC&CS showed the real relations between the Axis powers, through the words of foreign ministers, but not often directly those of Hitler and Mussolini. With so little Comint available on those issues, any distance in provenance or uncertainty in meaning provoked misinterpretation. Only unusually direct and reliable intelligence could refute basic views – anything less tended to reinforce them. Only a direct statement of aims from Hitler or Mussolini could have refuted such views, until the lessons of Munich were learned. British authorities were slow to learn from intelligence. Chamberlain could learn only from experience. The greatest problem in perceptions concerned Italy, which polluted interpretation of a greater issue, how a German–Italian alignment would unleash Hitler.

In this competition of intelligence, two rivals were better informed generally than Britain, and gained more intelligence on Britain than it did on them, though they misinterpreted evidence as badly as Chamberlain. Intelligence reinforced Mussolini's idea of British decadence and Stalin's concept of British perfidy. In Comint on European affairs, Germany, tapping the telephone lines which crossed its territory, matched Britain. This intelligence reinforced Hitler's emotional misperceptions of British power and policy.

Failure and success in intelligence had paradoxical consequences during the appeasement era. In failures of intelligence and policy, Britons stand beside Americans, French, Germans, Italians, Japanese and Russians. The greatest mistakes in intelligence were those which foreign states made about Britain. On 1 September 1939, neither Hitler nor Britain expected war with each other. The correlation between

Britain and France, seeking to bolster a fragile system and avoid war through deterrence, Germany using power politics to wreck that order and create its hegemony, Italy overrating its military capability, and the USSR believing that world war was inevitable, the only choice being when and how to enter it, produced results catastrophic for all. Excellent intelligence on every power enabled Stalin to outmanoeuvre them all in August 1939, only to find that he had outmanoeuvred himself when France fell. Intelligence successes enabled many players to take tricks, but they all lost the game. Reason, *raison d'état* and intelligence were bad guides for statesmen. They viewed events and played the game so differently, in such a dialectical, reciprocal, multilateral, atomised system, with so many actors affecting each other in such unpredictable ways, in a brawl where ideas, knowledge, policy and cause and effect were linked in an ironic fashion. Intentions were not effected, nor effects intended. Statesmen thought the state system was a machine where all one needed to create an effect was to pull a lever. In fact, the machine was baroque and broken. People thought that they knew how to get what they wanted, but failed to do so, because they did not understand the system, and the way it worked. Statesmen thought they were all playing a game with one set of rules; instead, each was playing a different game with the same pieces. Intelligence was not a tool as statesmen toiled in the machine of states – it was a broken saw whiplashing across the system.

Accident drove the outbreak of the Second World War. Yet had statesmen seen the world as it was, differences over the interests of state still would have caused another great war – though perhaps governments might have made fewer errors on the way. The Second World War started because of a systems failure; much the same would have happened had the system worked as intended. Interests and power were factors of the first order, with images and incomprehension and ideology in the second rank – and yet still the latter shaped the world in 1939–41. Ideology and image created incomprehension; intelligence could not penetrate them; its success in acquiring data mattered less than its failure to penetrate preconception, or to help intention overcome accident. Here, intelligence most affected the origins of the Second World War. A war which should have occurred by intention, did so by accident.

Conclusions

Between 1919 and 1939, Comint shaped the formulation of foreign policy. The influence shifted day to day and case to case. Comint always illuminated many secondary issues, but fewer great ones. It was weak on key matters, like German policy, stronger on politics in the Middle East than in central Europe. In January 1930, Comint penetrated two leading issues: naval arms limitation and Soviet activities in Asia; during 1938–39, it was of mixed value against a grave danger. At best, Comint provided situational awareness and certainty. Statesmen knew they were not missing a threat or an opportunity to take a trick; they understood their environment and behaved appropriately. Comint confirmed the accuracy of material in other sources. It revealed the real position of rivals and the accuracy of their statements, increasing confidence in the value of their promises, or not. Comint steadied nerves when things seemed to be going wrong. It increased knowledge of a rival's position and how to manipulate it. Comint let one know when one might try gambits, what they might be, how they were working, and when one should amend them because they were having no effect. Comint was crucial to post-mortems of events, and to learning from the actions of others. It was a tool, a balm, an insurance policy, and a sound investment. Equally often, intelligence bore no fruit, because actors were poor or action impossible. The most effective form of diplomatic intelligence – in bargaining – usually offered marginal gains on secondary issues. Individuals, as targets and actors, were fundamental to Comint. It made rational actors emotional. Consumers demanded mind readers, able to determine the intentions of individuals.

Though Comint achieves that end more often than any other source of intelligence, such successes are rare. Comint was least successful when it had to refute expectations. Few reports did so. Most Comint was neutral and fitted many explanations. British diplomacy gained from Comint, yet, as ever, its effect was subject to people, perception and power. Comint most aided the wise, alas for Britain in 1939.

Bletchley

Subtly invoked archetypes make Bletchley Park into myth. British popular culture extols eccentrics and prefers victories that stem from character rather than system. Nineteen forty is central to the myth of modern Britain, its metaphorical moment of birth. Bletchley has become associated with Britain's salvation, absorbing parts of the older myth of Fighter Command, especially the roles of wizard boffins and of immediate action based on certain intelligence. The myth is of eccentrics overcoming the odds, the enemy, and the establishment – and above all of Alan Turing: a mind martyred by his country. Yet Bletchley did not save Britain, though it did help to defeat Germany. Britain treated Turing badly, as it did many gay men and women. GCHQ did not – it was his benefactor; Turing was more appreciated at Bletchley than usual in his life. Bletchley shaped the war and the future of intelligence and data processing, Sigint and GCHQ, but in different ways than the myth suggests. Bletchley matters too much for history to be understood through myth.

This history, in turn, often is presented as a relay race, a sprint focused on breaking the Enigma electromechanical cypher machine. Enigma carried all important German military traffic at the start of the Second World War, and much of it even after 1942, when Lorenz cypher teleprinters handled the most significant material. That characterisation of a relay goes far, but not enough. It was conducted at the speed of a sprint over the length of a marathon, which involved a crisis of Sigint, a revolution in command, control, communications, intelligence, surveillance and reconnaissance, and a war of electronics in an electronic war. Sometimes the baton being passed was Enigma, sometimes not. Some legs were longer than others. They involved not just ideas, but execution. Through a string of decisions – each essential, none sufficient – the marathon ended with the emergence of an institution: Bletchley – and of a product: Ultra, intelligence generated from the highest-grade cryptosystems of the Axis powers. The relay which produced Ultra was the formative moment in the history of GCHQ, and of modern Sigint.

Decline of a Black Chamber

Despite successes during 1938, GC&CS's declining power against codebooks and failures against machine cyphers put it in danger of decadence. GC&CS's work in diplomatic intelligence during 1940 best marks its effort:

> Out of some 100,000 telegrams received, 70,000 are read and 8,000 circulated.
> Out of 120 codes, 75 are read.
> Out of 30 countries 28 are adequately covered.[1]

In fact, GC&CS read the major diplomatic systems of the United States, Italy and France, but none of Germany or the USSR, and few of Japan. GC&CS still may have led the world in diplomatic codebreaking, and neutral traffic was valuable; but during 1916–18, Britain read the diplomatic codes of all its foes, every major neutral, several of its allies' and many of its enemies' military systems. Britain was stronger in military Sigint during 1918 than 1939, especially against Germany. During 1939, British Comint agencies dominated the military and naval cryptosystems of Italy and Japan and the codes of the Red Army and some lesser powers. Power against Japanese systems, however, slipped during 1940; Britain failed against German ones until then, while key Italian naval codes were unknown.

Even more, GC&CS was unready for Ultra. Through accident or intention, institutions can be ready for revolutions. British air defence was preadapted to radar, precisely the sort of device it knew was needed and wanted. Fighter Command plugged radar into its system and found that air defence finally worked as always had been hoped.[2] GC&CS,

British intelligence and signals experts, conversely, misunderstood the revolution in cryptology and how its components – the use of radio as a standard means of communication; the mechanisation of cryptography and cryptanalysis; the practice of Sigint, unifying interception, traffic analysis and attacks on low-, medium- and high-grade systems; and the integration of Sigint with other intelligence – would fuse. Unconnected British diplomatic, economic warfare, military and naval organisations combined most of these matters in 1918. Britain commanded international communications and harvested intelligence from them. MI1(b) and Room 40 produced diplomatic Sigint by cryptanalysis; Room 40 and the Army field Sigint units produced military Sigint by combining cryptanalysis, traffic analysis and direction finding. The consumers of this Sigint fused it effectively into intelligence and operations. The War Trade Intelligence Department (WTID) was the greatest producer of Sigint and intelligence on earth, well integrated into economic blockade. With the armistice, the elements of signals intelligence split. The pre-1914 division between codebreaking and radio re-emerged; 'wireless intelligence' and 'cryptanalysis' moved into separate, though not watertight, compartments. GC&CS focused on cable and codebook, losing expertise in radio, save for the military sections. The Y services were small, if good. Less work was done against military systems than desirable, though the record was tolerable. Sigint producers lost their links with action, except with diplomatic intelligence. During 1938, no organisation integrated Sigint effectively into its operations, save the Foreign Office. Fighter Command was promising and fast improving, the Admiralty rusty, and the Army nowhere at all. All authorities underestimated how they, and other states, would use radio in war. Germany was more ready for the revolution than Britain, especially for the use of wireless in war, with military Sigint services of equal quality. Poles developed the first effective techniques against sophisticated cypher machines. Britain was less successful in the first stages of this revolution; that failure damaged its sword and shield of cryptology.

During the 1930s, British Sigint authorities, including Sinclair and Denniston, made technical misjudgements which their peers of no other country did. These errors crippled British cryptology. Deepest among them were misjudgements about signals and their security. The experts thought the publicity given to codebreaking from the last war would cripple its value for the next. An Admiralty committee on the role of radio concluded: 'in the late war, the Germans would have been infinitely better off if they had never transmitted on W/T at all. Our methods of gaining information from the enemy's intercepted signals is now an open secret to the whole world so that it is considered that W/T silence in future should be most strictly enforced until in actual contact with the enemy.' Deputy Chief of Naval Staff, and ex-member of Room 40, 'Bubbles' James, echoed these views: 'I do not believe we will ever again enjoy all the advantages of the 1914–1918 war, because people today are wiser about wireless.'[3]

Some members of GC&CS, including Denniston, considered this possibility, though others denied it. In 1938, Sinclair thought that at the start of any war, every state would change its cyphers, eliminating for some time intelligence 'by the ordinary methods of decipherment'. The Munich 'crisis appears to have shown that as soon as matters become serious, wireless silence is enforced, and that therefore this organisation of ours is useless for the purpose for which it was intended'. He questioned the value of Britain's 'very elaborate organisation' for wireless interception, which no one had developed more than he.[4] British services underestimated their need to use radio. They thought it would be an ancillary to other communications, radio silence the norm for operations, security easily maintained. They misconstrued the wireless war to come. If states used radio rarely, and defended it well, the value of signals intelligence seemed small. These attitudes caused problems for attack and defence. British actions and Polish aid let GC&CS overcome the offensive problems by 1940, but these attitudes sapped its cryptography.

GC&CS failed against the German version of Enigma; it came close – which counts in the game of horseshoes, but not the task of cryptology. It was two steps from success – misunderstanding how the system worked, and the need to attack it with machines. Why GC&CS should have failed is as hard to explain as any case of a negative, but some observations come to mind. The two groups which independently broke the most sophisticated cypher machines of 1930s vintage were a team of Poles (with no prior experience in attacking codebooks, their members selected for mathematical skill) under Marian Rejewski, and one of Americans under William Friedman and Frank Rowland, with little prior experience against codebooks, but much against cyphers (attacked letter by letter, through a greater use of abstract means than with codebooks). Each member of these teams contributed to the collective work. Until 1939, conversely, GC&CS assigned this task not to a team, but one man: Dilly Knox. When he received help in 1939, from a veteran, Tony Kendrick, and a newcomer, the mathematician Peter Twinn, Knox gave Twinn five minutes' tuition in basic cryptanalysis, told him to get on with the job, and continued to dominate it. After a week at Bletchley later in 1939, Knox gave Gordon Welchman, a mathematician recruited to attack Enigma, 'some sort of test and appeared to be, if anything, annoyed that I passed'.[5]

Before the war, Knox had broken other machine systems, including Italian and Spanish versions of commercial Enigma, through 'rodding', which combined guesses based on language, knowledge of cribs in messages, and the use of a manual tool: 'batons', which were thin cylinders of cardboard four inches long, marked with rows and columns of letters. Batons showed how letters changed in encipherment, aiding quick visual searches through alternative values. Knox believed that batons could repeat this success against German military Enigma, erroneously: only machines could slay this beast. This error shows how far he misconstrued the magnitude of the task. Knox was able in mathematics, but less so than these Poles and Americans, and he had far more – indeed, extraordinary – experience against codebooks. His mistake about German military Enigma was basic: he had not checked whether its entry plate was arranged in ordinary alphabetical order. Perhaps the assumption that German efficiency would not allow so elementary an error shaped his mistake. After a few moments explanation from Rejewski in the woods outside Warsaw during July 1939, during the first meeting of British, French and Polish codebreakers, regarding how Poles had penetrated Enigma, Knox immediately saw how to conduct the whole attack – which he had not done on his own. Rejewski noted that Knox 'grasped everything very quickly, almost quick as lightning'.[6] The mixture of technical qualities which cryptanalysts needed to attack codebooks was not optimal against cypher machines; prior experience with the former may have handicapped attack on the latter, by strengthening the wrong sets of technical muscles. GC&CS's tendency to trust the judgement of one genius also had its costs.

Other problems stemmed from organisation. By dividing their Sigint resources among self-contained and uncooperative bureaus, other states used them less efficiently than the unitary British system did – in the long run. During the 1930s, however, some foreign institutions used their resources to pursue every aspect of Sigint, which the unintended consequences of a centralised system prevented any British agency from doing. In particular, GC&CS focused resources on diplomatic traffic and away from some key military targets, especially German cryptosystems and wireless nets. Thus emerged a paradox. In 1939, Britain was mediocre in military Sigint but by 1942 rode a revolution to mastery. This failure and success stemmed from the same system, which combined centralisation and decentralisation better than any other, and learned faster than its competitors. Before 1941, GC&CS and the military Sigint services were inadequately integrated. The machine did not work, yet could be made to do so. Once this occurred, that machine did things impossible for any other system of Sigint on earth.

The Road to Bletchley Park

Like the fighting services, Sigint rearmed during the 1930s. The performance was mixed but effective. The Manchurian crisis of 1931 initiated expansion, which boomed after 1934. During 1932, when helping the service Sigint agencies 'to envisage the future', Sinclair foresaw two threats. 'The Greater Powers continue to take steps to improve their methods of enciphering, and already three or four countries have adopted methods which we know defy solution' (perhaps he meant Germany, the USSR and Britain). These developments, and cypher machines, 'may' cripple codebreaking, which might 'practically vanish away' against great powers. Developments in radio and interception technology, including high-speed and non-Morse systems, teleprinters and tape recorders, were transforming communication and interception, yet British Y already was inadequate. Personnel were keen and able but, because of 'apathy or cheese-paring methods' their kit was jury-rigged, obsolete, and dependent on financial support from SIS. 'The time has come,' wrote Sinclair, 'for the higher authorities of the various Services to consider the matter very seriously and to decide whether the intelligence obtained from cryptography may be considered of value in peace time and as essential in war, or whether it is a Service on which real economies might be effected during the economic crisis.'[7]

Denniston and Sinclair understood Britain's position well. They tackled the worst cases they could conceive, pressing the services and the Dominions to expand and adapt Y. The latter addressed these problems and coordinated their efforts fairly well. All elements in Sigint multiplied their staff and equipment. By 1935, experiences with crises, and preparations for war, illustrated basic problems and solutions in Sigint. The need for rapid communication between GC&CS, intercept stations and consumers in Britain, drove improvements in links between them, such as telephones and teleprinters, which Sinclair subsidised. This useful foundation was linked to fragile communications with Y units abroad, carried mostly by bag, with wireless transmitting tiny amounts. The relationship between GC&CS and military intelligence and Y was flawed. Kenworthy's staff officer called Y 'a happy-go-lucky hit-or-miss affair'.[8] Though Y expanded massively between 1939 and 1945, and confronted great teething problems – recruits took a year to become competent and two to become skilled – its base was sound. In 1939, British Y matched that of any other power in quality and, except for Germany, quantity, and exceeded most. Between 1942 and 1945, it led the world. Meanwhile, during 1935–38, GC&CS almost doubled its cryptanalytical staff, especially in the military sections. FECB and the Air Section filled lacunae in Comint.

From 1938, Sinclair prepared his services for war. They needed a secure locale outside London, given fears of the devastation of bombing: when holocaust did not happen, MI6 returned to better quarters, leaving the other side behind. Country houses were cheap to buy (explaining the pleasant settings of so many intelligence centres during the war), more so than buildings in provincial cities, and less likely to be bombed or noticed. Sinclair chose Bletchley Park from many options because Bletchley had good railway connections; was close to main landlines in Britain, and thus to its worldwide cable and wireless network; near to the RAF's main radio station at Leighton Buzzard, and thus to the Defence Teleprinter Network (DTN), the core of British strategic communications; and next to open territory where other radio stations could be erected. High-speed automatic recording circuits from Leighton Buzzard, enabling automatic transfer of messages from abroad, gave Bletchley typed copies of traffic.

Sinclair underestimated the power of codebreaking in war but appreciated the strategic significance of radio communication, and its problems. Britain's reign over international communications had vanished. Though it dominated cable, the latter slipped in significance, while American businesses led the rising media: radio. British cable firms and Marconi, unified under the organisation Cable & Wireless (C&W), were powerful, but no more so than the Radio Corporation of America or Telefunken. New cables were no longer built, but radio stations were: by 1935, over 20,000 of the latter worked across the globe, mostly controlled by states. The latter minimised the dispatch of key messages by radio, but that situation might change in war. Sinclair worried that American successes and policies in communications might cripple that of Britain, and GC&CS.[9] C&W and the GPO provided far less aid to Sigint than they had done during 1914–18; Siginters complained that GPO personnel damaged interception by demanding union practices.[10] GC&CS and the services had to meet their own needs for interception and communications, which they did well.

By 1937, Sinclair feared that parochial concerns would degrade the value of interception during war.[11] The Y services might focus on military traffic and abandon diplomatic collection. Though belligerents would tighten their cryptography in war, weakening the power of GC&CS for some time, neutrals might not do so, and so provide valuable information. To cover that gap, Sinclair had the Foreign Office finance the police interception station at Denmark Hill when the Home Office refused to do so any longer. To establish new stations would be difficult – 'it is extremely difficult, as I know only too well from bitter experience, to obtain W/T operators at all' – while new stations 'as things are at present, might take anything from two to three years to build and equip'.[12] By January 1938, however, Sinclair decided to construct three more intercept stations under his control, run by the Foreign Office and manned by the GPO, matching the size of any service's system. In the first taste of the problems which lack of priority inflicted upon expansion of Sigint until 1942, GC&CS found it easier to acquire brains than bricks. Only in June 1938, after gaining support from the Treasury and arranging details with the GPO and the services, did Sinclair initiate his proposal. During the Munich crisis, he maintained diplomatic coverage only by convincing C&W to intercept traffic, with inexperienced staffs, and by giving Denmark Hill three additional interception sets, intended for the new stations.[13] The Office of Works proposed to start these stations only in June 1939, and complete them twelve months later, although the GPO had men and kit at hand. Sinclair denounced this 'scandalous' delay, but in September 1939 only one of these new stations was complete, manned by crews from the GPO, C&W and Kenworthy's veterans from Denmark Hill. The others entered service in early 1940.[14]

GC&CS thought that in another war as in the last one, a few hundred people would conduct codebreaking. Since maintenance of standards was difficult when large numbers were hired in short periods, it opposed major and uncontrolled expansion, preferred quality over quantity, and trusted its own methods for recruitment (good ones, incidentally). In 1923, GC&CS held that if it were to be enlarged greatly or rapidly, 'the most that could be hoped for would be one cryptographer out of six, the remaining five drawing the same pay and being ... useless but immovable'.[15] After the Munich crisis, Denniston held 'during the precautionary period all authorities anxious to expand receive offers of service from men and women who are not employed often because they are unemployable. I am definitely opposed to taking on a staff of enthusiastic amateurs of whom one knows little or nothing and who may turn out complete failures'; expansion should come from old hands and high tables.[16] Despite his habit of hiring relatives, especially daughters, of people whose provenance he knew, Denniston better prepared his service for war than any other leader of British intelligence. Denniston filled the holes he saw through means that he knew. He aimed to double the staff doing what GC&CS already did, mostly in the diplomatic sections, no doubt assuming the services would expand their sections as they wished. He brought back an old guard from Room 40, two of whom returned from popular entertainment – de Grey, who worked for Medici Fine Art prints, which reproduced great art for discerning eyes and to bring beauty to the masses, and Frank Birch, who returned to academe from Room 40 and then forsook scholarship for the stage, becoming the definitive Widow Twankey of 1930s pantomime theatre. They shaped Bletchley, and Denniston's overthrow.

Denniston hired 'men of the professor type', either old hands with cryptanalytical experience, or linguists. So strong was this field that GC&CS turned down J. R. R. Tolkien, despite his interest in the position and mastery of languages; he turned his talents against Mordor, rather than Germany. The largest addition were dozens of recruits from the women's colleges of Oxbridge, many enrolled as 'Linguist Cryptanalysts' – junior assistants with the tasks of clerical officers, keystrippers, bookbuilders and translators, but with more room to rise. These choices were excellent. Though some of these men and women failed, most had a good-to-outstanding war. The most celebrated acquisitions were four mathematicians enlisted to assault Enigma, including Turing and Gordon Welchman, who were recruited through the greatest piece of talent-spotting in the history of cryptology. These candidates received brief codebreaking courses during 1939, including standard manual systems for all and machines for the researchers, to determine suitability for the work and to spur personal preparations in the interim.

These people lurched into the cryptological revolution in September 1939, receiving the gifts of constant German use of radio and Polish continuity of attack against Enigma – the main target which Britain had missed and most wanted to strike. Ultra would never have existed without Polish work or British exploitation. Good machine systems sent messages with unprecedented ease, volume and security, and forced a new era of cryptanalysis, which moved from the craftsman's bench to the industrial age. Codebooks were attacked through analysis by language and logic, and machines by quantity handling. Mathematical analysis chiselling the fractures of cryptosystems, reduced the number of ways to convert any letter into another to a level which the brute force of data-processing machines could defeat – if guided by cribs. Britain led the world in the movement towards machine cryptanalysis, through its unique centralised system for the collection and analysis of intelligence, high coordination between soldiers and civilians, skill in data processing and recognition of the value of knowledge in war. GC&CS succeeded through its variant of characteristics common in Whitehall – connections between state and society on matters of communications and information processing, close and collegial links with universities, scientists and firms, utilisation of centralised decision-making systems with powerful nexi for C3I, all driven by the whips of war and Winston. GC&CS and the military services quickly overcame mistakes and tapped the latent strengths of their system, yet this process was painful. A revolution occurred in deadly circumstances amidst administrative chaos. Services fought over small resources, control of organisations exploding in size and issues of establishing priorities and determining who would make them.

The Limits to Preadaptation

That revolution started from GC&CS's response to an unexpected gift. Its failure to solve Enigma on its own leads observers to conclude that GC&CS was technically reactionary, and to credit 'great men' – male mathematicians – with the conquest of Enigma. These views are wrong. Those mathematicians were essential to that triumph, but GC&CS shaped and exploited their ideas of how to attack. Nor was GC&CS technically reactionary. According to Josh Cooper, members of GC&CS routinely used 'cardboard and bootlace' tools, such as Knox's batons, as aids to attack, but not machines.[17] This statement is largely, but not entirely, true; the error is part of complicated evidence.

In 1932, Denniston told university placement officers that ability with machines was one desired quality for an appointment to junior assistant. He disavowed that priority in the next competition.[18] It never recurred before 1939. Few people linked to GC&CS had mechanical expertise, or staff and workshops to build machines. Two of them, however – Kenworthy and Beale, ex-Marconi personnel who worked on the peripheries of GC&CS – invented cryptanalytical machines, which were used against Japanese systems, but apparently no others. Judging by the timing of his invention, around 1932, Beale's system was used for a specialised but central problem, to attack the Japanese 'Red' cypher machine. GC&CS praised his machine. The War Office Directorate of Military Intelligence emphasised that it enabled 'us to get deciphers of most important Japanese telegrams (which defeated us for a long time), rapidly'.[19] In 1935, Travis, in charge of machine studies at GC&CS, asked Kenworthy to 'help as we possessed a small workshop' with 'a Japanese decoding machine on a mechanical hand operated system where a number of geared wheels were made to revolve in a certain order. This process was quite slow as the answer had to be written down for every movement of the wheels against the "key".' Whether Travis wanted help in copying the machine or improving it, is unclear, but he supported Kenworthy's proposal to record the answers 'electrically with relays ... coupled to a keyboard such as is used on a teleprinter'. The 'J' machine, perhaps an electro-mechanical variant of Beale's device, proved 'very successful' against Japanese systems.[20] During 1939, Tiltman used a 'sorter' (which sounds more like a tabulator than Kenworthy's machine) against Japanese systems, which were more powerful than before. Probably this sorter was used to attack superencipherment, where rapid comparison of multiple possibilities enabled the exploitation of the main cryptanalytical weakness of these systems, to detect the start points of keys, or to strip keys, or both. These Japanese codes were weaker in vocabularies and superencipherment than other codes GC&CS confronted, such as Italian naval systems of 1935, against which machines apparently were not used. Cooper, who worked closely with the Military Section, seemingly did not know that the latter used machines.

General issues, and matters particular to Japanese systems, explain the evidence about GC&CS's attitudes towards machine cryptanalysis before 1939. They were driven not by reactionary attitudes towards machines, though these views were mixed, but by technical choices between human as against machine-intensive approaches to cryptanalysis. Compared to other languages, few bookbreakers at GC&CS could crack Japanese systems. They had little clerical assistance, forcing bookbreakers into work which sapped their power, like keystripping. Tiltman and Jacobs, innovative officers, complained bitterly and constantly about that problem. These circumstances made machines worth developing and keeping. Clarke and the Italian Section faced similar problems but solved them by acquiring more cryptanalytical and clerical staff; and more Britons knew Italian than Japanese. Moreover, Beale and Kenworthy's machines, and Denniston's prioritisation of the matter, emerged when Japan was GC&CS's leading target, and a hard one. Beale, like Poles through the 'bomba' which they used against Enigma, created a bespoke machine, a one-off product aimed at one system; it could not be applied against any other, though the sorter might have been. With Beale's untimely death in 1933, and the failure to hire a junior with machine experience, only Kenworthy among GC&CS's satellites had the expertise to build bespoke machines, and perhaps little power or interest in the matter. His only other known, and abortive, efforts, were to build a cryptanalytical machine against Enigma in autumn 1939, and another against Lorenz cypher teleprinter systems, when GC&CS wanted them.

Few within GC&CS demanded or supplied bespoke machines before 1939. GC&CS had no reason to adopt conventional data processors, like tabulators, for codebreaking, and several not to do so. The US Navy's Op-20-G, the cryptanalytical organisation of the 1930s which most used such systems in large numbers, did so because it had few cryptanalysts but enough money to pay the high rental costs for International Business Machine (IBM) tabulators, and could detail seamen to handle the clerical work. British firms and government departments routinely used tabulators. GC&CS studied their use in cryptanalysis, though after observation, Tiltman later said: 'I didn't understand at the time its application to our work.' Travis temporarily employed one 'lady operator' with a Powers tabulating machine (similar to Hollerith devices) which, however, could not reveal the power of machine cryptanalysis. Tiltman 'did a test and I found that I could beat her in an analysis job. This was a completely unfair test, of course, because the development of machinery is not dependent on one person pounding one machine which is what happened to her. She did all the punching and everything else.'[21] Probably that test reduced GC&CS's interest in tabulators. GC&CS considered the use of machines if it saw major problems that only these could solve. Before the war, however, GC&CS pursued processes of human craftwork, like the development of D&R and the training of military and higher clerical officers, because it had more and better cryptanalysts than Op-20-G, and few tasks which absolutely required machines. Experience and additional staff mastered the systems GC&CS thought breakable. Attacks against cryptographic machines succeeded without the use of cryptanalytical ones or, as with German military Enigma, were too inconclusive to call for machine attack. Even had GC&CS wanted tabulators for cryptanalysis, its funds were insufficient to rent or buy them, especially on speculation, or to recruit, pay and train the staff needed to run these machines. GC&CS seemingly did not ask Sinclair to cover these costs. Training higher clerical officers in cryptanalysis was cheaper than having them run rented tabulators. The very success of this improved craftmanship slowed GC&CS's need to adopt machines in codebreaking.

A lack of resources, priorities and connections to people able to build machines constrained machine cryptanalysis. GC&CS understood that machines could assist cryptanalysis, but not how they could do so, nor how much. When war began, however, GC&CS quickly discovered the value of such machines, and British power in this area. War increased the demand for cryptanalytical power and the money available to rent machines, and GC&CS acquired a few tabulators from the British Tabulating Machine Company (BTM), which broke German naval attaché traffic. GC&CS realised quickly that tabulators were far faster than 'ordinary clerical labour', and recentred cryptanalysis around machines.[22] During 1940, tabulators drove successful attacks against Italian diplomatic and military codes and, in 1941, the Hagelin machine used by the Italian navy, matching the value of Ultra's take from Enigma during that period.

Diversity and Union

From 1939, the power of cryptography, the need for machines and the resources available to GC&CS, all rose, spurred by the priority placed on Enigma. After Munich, Denniston noted the GC&CS's 'best brains' were concentrated on Enigma, 'and are attacking it at its weakest spot which is the machine as used by the German Army and Air Force'.[23] He sought to bolster those brains by tapping a new source of cryptanalysts. Through the Civil Service Commission, Denniston hired a mathematician, Twinn, to aid Knox against Enigma, and recruited mathematicians specifically to attack machine systems in war. Interception of Enigma traffic became the top priority for the military Y services and attack on it the leading research priority. GC&CS split on the prospects for success. Enigma was widely seen as having 'absolute' security,[24] but some thought that it was breakable. A convoluted and partly erroneous statement by Tiltman reflects GC&CS's attitudes just before it received Polish assistance: 'The whole mechanism and usage of the military model is now thoroughly understood and it cannot be said that no progress towards solution has been made but not yet sufficient to justify real confidence in eventual success.'[25]

That success proved rapid and thorough. In 1945, one American cryptanalyst reported that: 'Daily solutions of Fish messages at GC&CS reflect a background of British mathematical genius, superb engineering ability, and solid common sense. Each of these has been a necessary factor. Each could have been overemphasised or underemphasised to the detriment of the solutions; a remarkable fact is that the fusion of the elements has been apparently in perfect proportion. The result is an outstanding contribution to cryptanalytic science.'[26] That view describes the final product of Bletchley, but not the process that created it, which was as messy as any case of making sausages. As with wireless interception during the First World War, the attack on cryptographic machines between 1939 and 1945 required work which was well past the leading edges of several areas of science and technology. This work became experiments in applied science, involving several great minds, which was exceeded only by the Manhattan Project. The combination of distinct characteristics in British academe, state and industry enabled this success. Victory could not have been predicted until it happened, because no one could have foreseen the need to weld mathematics with data-processing machines, the means to do so, nor their power when joined. GC&CS forged an alloy of machines and mathematics at the furnace of Bletchley Park. No other Sigint agency approached this success, for several reasons.

The British state applied science to strategy better than any other government. British firms and institutes were innovative and excellent in defence electronics, where the Telecommunications Research Establishment matched the size and skill of any American organisation.[27] American firms, like Bell Labs and IBM, led the world in research, design and production for telecommunications and information processing, but British ones were within reach and ahead of those in any other country, including Germany. Bell Labs had 3,600 employees: its largest British counterparts, the Research Department of Marconi and the GPO's Engineering Department, had around thirty and sixty. Yet the GPO and BTM – the leading British firm in data processing – served Allied cryptanalysis better than did IBM and Bell Labs. IBM had ten times the personnel and greater technological capacity than BTM, but did not sell its product in the British empire. IBM licensed that right to BTM: the only company in the world which was free to sell any IBM product in its territory, while also designing its own systems. One BTM employee, Arthur Humphreys, later a leader in the British computer industry, said: 'It had lots of patents and knowhow of any IBM product, and could manufacture it.' He criticised BTM for failing simply to produce IBM kit, instead designing its own, which allowed 'engineers solely to design product strategy', with mixed commercial success. Yet that criticism of BTM's business model explains why it could design machines that destroyed Enigma, and acquire the greatest order in the company's history, over £2 million for 212 bombes.[28]

Britain also led the world in people who could build cryptanalytic machines, such as the bombes and Desch systems which attacked Enigma, and the Colossi and Heath Robinsons that dissected cypher teleprinter systems like the Lorenz SZ40/42, codenamed Fish by British codebreakers. This capacity combined men able to define specifications (Turing, Welchman and Max Newman) with those who could turn ideas into effective machines (Doc Keen and Tommy Flowers) and units able to produce them (BTM and the GPO), so yielding bombes and Colossus. Few engineers could build effective cryptologic machines: they shaped success as much as did the mathematicians who developed the design parameters. Only one other group, the American team which produced the Purple replica that penetrated the major Japanese diplomatic machine, matched Britain in this area; the American Desch machine, based on bombes and guided by Turing, rested heavily on British advice.

More than in any other country, British officials combined scientists, engineers, firms and military experts in defence electronics. Bletchley led the way. It became the greatest centre of data processing power on earth. In 2020, a digitally controlled doll has more calculating power than all of these machines combined would have created, but in 1939–45 they reshaped cryptanalysis and the war.

Bletchley's Tabulating Machine Section had twelve tabulators and another hundred ancillary machines (multipliers, punches, reproducers and sorters). On average each week, its staff of 150 completed 120 jobs using 1.4 million punchcards. The variety of jobs 'covers two foolscap pages each week', including material for codemaking, and any element of cryptanalysis which could be quantified, like long subtractor systems, 'submarine tetragrams, bigram frequency counts, F/traffic, double substitution, Italian air difference tables, Birdbook index, Japanese Tama Column differences … etc. etc.'.[29] The Tabulating Machine Section also gave essential assistance in the attack on Enigma. This section had power roughly equal to its counterparts in Op-20-G and the US Army Security Agency (ASA), and second only to the 415 IBM machines in Baltimore which processed US social security data, using 3.5 million punchcards per week.[30] GC&CS could have acquired more tabulators but had all that it wanted. Conversely, GC&CS wanted more Colossi and bombes than it could get. By 1945, Bletchley had many bespoke machines, Heath Robinsons and Colossi, and 212 bombes, frequently upgraded. A new bombe reached Bletchley approximately every week from August 1941. Bletchley also controlled one Purple replica, and loosely led parts of the world's second concentration of cryptanalytic power, the Duenna and Desch machines in Op-20-G, which attacked Enigma. However, this power waned as American authorities followed Britain's lead and learned to unleash their powers in material. By 1943, the National Cash Register Company, led by Joseph Desch, produced a better bombe even than the final version, after viewing BTM's system and receiving advice from Turing. By 1945, the United States matched Britain in developing rapid analytic machines for cryptanalysis and soon surged ahead.

Germany and the United States had as many excellent mathematicians as Britain, but their Comint agencies belonged to greater organisations, which controlled the recruitment of Siginters. GC&CS, a national agency, autonomous in its field and with clear ideas about the role of mathematicians in cryptanalysis, defined its own needs in recruitment and pursued them freely. British codebreakers could acquire the aid of the renowned mathematician, Max Newman. American ones could not do so with John von Neumann, a mathematician of skill and interest in the areas which drove Ultra. American Sigint agencies recruited many officers with mathematics degrees, but few leading mathematicians who could not easily fit into their militarised structures.[31] Two key crypto-mathematicians at Bletchley, Good and Newman, were Jews – with whom Germans did not work but GC&CS did. German Comint agencies recruited as many mathematicians as Britain, including some of the world's best but got less from them, perhaps precisely because they came from the conventional groups, whom Denniston avoided.[32]

Though much of the detail is lost, Denniston exploited an old boys' network at Cambridge and Oxford, veterans both of Room 40 and academe, to identify suitable candidates for machine cryptanalysis. He deserves much credit for knowing what talent was needed, but so do his colleagues. Judging by GC&CS's past preferences, Denniston looked not for people with mathematical knowledge, but rather for those who could apply it to cryptanalysis. He and his advisors looked away from mainstream academic mathematics towards several minority groups within it: Bayesian statisticians, who accepted imprecision as inevitable, factored it into their modes of analysis, and used the results in a feedback loop to improve accuracy; applied mathematicians, who marred the purity of their art by marrying it to other matters; problem solvers rather than theorists; and mathematicians interested in machines, which were the target of attack. Though Denniston could not know it, he really was looking for computer scientists rather than mathematicians.

Characteristics within British mathematics aided his search. The continental focus on pure mathematics gained ground during the interwar years, but applied mathematics retained an unusual place in British universities, where Bayesian methods in statistics also revived. When compared to all of the mathematicians in Oxbridge, Denniston's candidates were applied scholars, not fitting easily into academe, and younger men. Twinn, Denniston's first hire as a mathematician, had become a physicist. The application of Bayesian approaches to statistics, which enhanced the power of creativity and judgement in the discipline, was the most unusual mathematical practice at Bletchley, but many mathematical cryptanalysts were not Bayesians. Though Denniston initially avoided hiring pure mathematicians, some later recruits fit that category, nor were all of the new cryptanalysts mathematicians. Success at chess, where competitors analysed patterns on a board and the behaviour of a competitor so to defeat each other in an interactive struggle, was an alternative qualification. The characteristics of chess players illuminate what Bletchley needed from mathematicians, and how diverse forms of puzzle-solving fused in this new form of cryptanalysis.

When judging how individuals shaped the creation of Colossus, the most powerful machine deployed at Bletchley, Newman noted the question of ' "Credits", of course a perennial problem'.[33] This question is important, and hard to answer. Most people would credit Turing for creating Ultra, when he simply was the most important and not the only necessary figure in that process. His near equal, Welchman, thought that 'the success of GCHQ in producing this prolific flow was largely, if not entirely, dependent on the contributions of four men: Marion Rejewski, Edward Travis, Alan Turing, and myself'.[34] In fact, perhaps a hundred people shaped the creation of Ultra, all worthy and some irreplaceable. Of them, Travis, Rejewski, Turing, Welchman, Newman, Keene and Flowers clearly were essential, but so were others to lesser degrees: Denniston hired Turing and Welchman, while Tiltman and Tutte were central to solving Colossus. Individuals also varied in significance over time. In 1939–40, Turing was the key figure but his significance slipped when Ultra became an industry. He could inspire, but not administer, and cared more to solve problems than to exploit solutions. Welchman immediately understood and improved Turing's discoveries, by conceiving the diagonal board, which dramatically increased the speed of attack and became the architect of Ultra. Later, Newman and Flowers caught Fish, where Turing was irrelevant and Welchman an impediment.

The most famous of these people was Turing, because of the tragic trajectory of his life, his intellectual originality and an eccentricity odd even among cryptanalysts. Turing, nicknamed 'the Prof', was an ardent and above-average chess player and marathoner. He had the greatest intellect at Bletchley, with a unique understanding of mathematics and cryptanalysis, and a fascination with machines – what Welchman, called 'machine-orientated thinking'.[35] During the 1930s, Turing worked in fields ranging from statistics to logic. He laid the foundations for computers and computing science, which prepared him to attack cryptanalytic machines. As soon as he saw the Polish work against Enigma, Turing understood how to penetrate its security, formulated the concept for machines which could do so, and led the mathematisation of techniques of cryptanalysis. He set a ball rolling which otherwise might never have moved. Welchman, conversely, a teacher and administrator at Sidney Sussex College, knew the mathematics students at Cambridge University well. This background shaped the expansion of personnel for Ultra and his flair for organisation at Bletchley. Welchman worked in algebraic geometry, a field entering a state of flux, and feared that: 'I did not have what it takes to work at the frontiers of mathematics. I was gloomy about my prospects at Cambridge.'[36] When Welchman left Bletchley he moved not to academe, but to operations research for firms and institutes. However, when applied to specific problems, this mathematical background shaped Welchman's triumphs at Bletchley. Welchman conceded that 'the invention of the diagonal board may have stemmed from my habit, as an algebraic geometer, of thinking in abstract multi-dimensional space'. This habit of analysing abstract spaces by algebraic means, also shaped how he grasped traffic analysis, and structured Ultra. Like Turing with cryptanalysis, Welchman was the first mind to conceive of traffic analysis, and Sigint, in mathematical terms.[37]

The Turing Test

To defeat Enigma and Fish required four sequential successes: in mathematical concept, the practice of codebreaking, the design of cryptanalytic machines, and their manufacture. No one person was expert in all of these areas, and few in any one of them. Everyone made errors because problems were new, precedents few, solutions were on the leading edges of several self-contained areas, and none could understand how large and complex Ultra would become. Both mathematicians and machinists appreciated the need for rapid and reliable data processing. They contributed as individuals and in teams. They were diverse, because so many specialists in arcane areas had to cooperate against the same targets where their faculties were transmuted in order to handle different problems. Disparate backgrounds shaped how individuals conceptualised problems, and solutions, in their collective attack on Ultra. Cryptology fascinated many of these mathematicians, such as Turing and Good, and shaped the playful attacks which dominated naval Enigma at Hut 8 during 1940–42. Many hand techniques of cryptanalysis simply were applied to machines. John Herrival translated the axiomatic principle that operators' errors might compromise keys into a new technique against Enigma: the 'Herrival tip'. Bill Tutte reconstructed the logic of the Fish systems by writing out intercepted figures in blocks, and then looking for patterns on paper, which he saw in different ways than did traditional cryptanalysts who had done precisely the same, like Tiltman.[38] Welchman and Newman, however, preferred organisational and mechanical solutions and brought brute force to their problems. Success took all kinds of form. There was work enough for all. These individuals and groups were all driven by many forms of competitive cooperation. Even those who dropped out of the competition, or took over specialist tasks, handled significant matters.

As war began, GC&CS had Knox lead Twinn and the new recruits against Enigma, and report on their work. Knox gave the mathematicians all the cryptanalytic advice they received – not much, but essential. Along with Polish work, it influenced Turing, and the start of the attack on Enigma. Knox created the loosest possible team, several individuals who worked in parallel lines, with occasional direction and liaison. He ordered Welchman to study traffic analysis on Enigma, and simply assumed that the latter would do nothing else. Instead, Welchman learned more about traffic analysis than any member of GC&CS except Tiltman, but also attacked Enigma, to Knox's irritation. Turing, as much a loner as Knox, was free to tackle naval Enigma 'because no one else was doing anything about it and I could have it to myself'.[39] A closer team emerged from confusion and success. When Turing discovered and disseminated the flaws which wrecked the security of Enigma and proposed a design for a machine to exploit them, overnight Welchman revolutionised that work through the diagonal board. These two then cooperated closely, while Bletchley engaged a BTM team under 'Doc' Keen to produce the machines which they envisaged. Keen's design and BTM's production were effective. Initially manufacturing was slow, which caused the greatest limit to the power of Ultra until 1942, but that was unavoidable. Even with British assistance, American firms built machines like bombes no better or faster. The bombes were the most complicated electro-mechanical devices yet built. Each bombe was seven feet wide, 6 foot 6 inches tall, and 2 feet deep. Each weighed one ton and held thirty-six Enigma replicas, or 108 rotors, containing ten miles of wire and one million soldered connections. At the rear, scores of cords, writhing like snakes, connected rotors. Training workers to build bombes well and rapidly took time. After eighteen months' experience, BTM produced bombes in large numbers, but until autumn 1941 they were scarce. They became plentiful just in time to help overcome the general crisis in Ultra.

Knox left this turbulent team once he realised that he could not control Turing and Welchman, because he did not understand their work. Knox, directing women – who he managed better than his male colleagues, whom he did not manage at all – then attacked valuable and productive targets where his experience was excellent – the less complex Enigma systems used by the Italian navy and the Abwehr (German military intelligence). 'Dilly's Girls' perhaps succeeded more from their own skills than his. These women too became a team – solid, self-starting and self-motivated – who finished their work after Knox's death, led by Twinn. Knox would not cooperate in a team of equals, especially one which he thought spent too much time talking rather than acting. Old cryppies thought that the mathematical cryptanalysts were too theoretical. As Birch said about naval Enigma in 1940: 'Turing and Twinn are like people waiting for a miracle, without believing in miracles ... like many brilliant people, they are not practical. They are untidy, they lose things, they can't copy out right, and they dither between theory and cribbing. Nor have they the determination of practical men.'[40]

These criticisms had truth and demonstrate problems in the first phase of the attack on Enigma, but they also reflected the infancy of mathematical cryptanalysis. Much talk was needed before actions could be useful, yet Turing and his colleagues yearned to act as fast and effectively as possible and did so with remarkable determination and speed. In 1941, when formulating the attack on a hard target – the U-boat Enigma – with four rather than three rotors, Good and Turing outlined basic elements of cryptomathematics, which later became 'tribal knowledge' at GCHQ, as one of their successors said.[41] Yet this discussion did not help the problem at hand. Only the seizures of Enigma machines from German weather ships and U-boats during 1941–42 guided a cryptanalytic attack which otherwise must fail.[42] Turing and Newman conceived the computer at Bletchley, but the baby was not born until 1948 at the University of Manchester. Bletchley's greatest legacy did nothing to win this war.

During 1939–40, the rest of the Enigma team continued its explorations, backed by Denniston and Travis, despite the doubts of the old hands. Turing and Welchman built on each other's strengths: Turing's mathematical cryptanalytic vision and Welchman's grasp of information processing. Mathematical analysis disclosed weaknesses in usage which degraded the theoretical security in the German system of Enigma to a level that was breakable, barely, if one applied machine analysis and found further cribs. From GC&CS's first study of commercial Enigma in 1927, it understood that cribs were essential to attack and methods should be found to locate them. Bletchley found cribs through the conventional means of identifying flaws in the use of systems, but even more from a heightened focus on traffic analysis. The latter identified communications links where one could guess what would be said, based on solutions of prior messages, and exploit compromises over trivial traffic in order to penetrate keys which carried critical messages. Welchman's experience with cryptanalysis and traffic analysis let him see the relationship between communications, interception and cryptography with unique power.

After a few months at Bletchley, and cooperation with the Army's intercept personnel under Ellingsworth at Chatham, Welchman understood the relationship between traffic analysis and attack on Enigma better than anyone else. He directed that interception. Welchman saw how to organise success against Enigma, by unifying traffic analysis, bombes, mathematics and cribs. Perhaps to his disappointment, Turing could no longer have naval Enigma just to himself, but he inspired the attack on Bletchley's most valued and hardest targets until enough bombes existed to enable brute force attacks. He made Hut 8 into a research group directed by a research student, rather than a professor, so producing administrative chaos until his juniors established order. Welchman exploited the most easily acquired forms of Enigma, especially Luftwaffe systems, and built the template for the whole attack. He, not Turing, replaced Knox as the head of the mathematical cryptanalysts and their liaison with the leaders of GC&CS. As bombes were being built, Welchman convinced Travis to assume that they would work and, in anticipation, to create sections for research, and for each element of the attack against and exploitation of Luftwaffe keys.[43] By May 1940, when it first achieved success, the Mechanical Section had 101 people, including ten cryptanalysts – second only to the diplomatic sections – already organised on sound lines.[44] So too, despite months of barren results, Welchman pursued the Herivel tip because it was the only possible fallback if systems based on Polish methods failed. When that happened, and operators' errors multiplied as Enigma was used in battle, the Herivel tip carried Ultra to success until more bombes arrived.

During the next year, from this base of theory, kit and staff, these cryptanalysts – inspired by their commanders, the joy of the game and the gravity of the task – learned to attack Enigma. Research into Enigma and the communications patterns which it serviced illuminated the target, its flaws and means and places to find cribs. Relying heavily on captured and pinched documents and machines, and the interrogation of prisoners, cryptanalysts developed evolving, ephemeral and labour-intensive means to further reduce German security by eliminating or accenting the importance of possible targets, before applying brute force. Turing invented brute force attacks, but he did not like or lead them, instead preferring 'Banburismus' – a practice which combined Bayesian statistics and cryptanalysis. In Banburismus, educated guesses about the starting position of rotors were represented on punchcards, which were compared by hand and eye, producing data for an analysis that combined art and mathematics to uncover cribs. Discovering and honing these manual techniques was, codebreakers noted, a 'delightful intellectual game', and the nursery of masters who led GCHQ into the 1970s.[45] Only by 1943 did these techniques and pinches become unnecessary, as the power of bombes swelled and brute force attacks became possible. Then, mathematics and machines discovered and exploited cribs, creating what Travis called 'the technique of "cribbery"' and Friedman called 'cribptology'.[46]

The mathematical cryptanalysts, especially Welchman, acquired new members through personal knowledge of people, whether mathematicians or chess players. That success in recruitment snowballed, producing a larger team with the same focused body of mathematical skills, and others essential to emerging problems. In 1940, Welchman recruited a friend, Stuart Milner-Barry, a chess player without mathematical skills, who immediately attracted Hugh Alexander, a mathematician who had applied these skills to chess and as head of research for the great retail firm John Lewis. Their work became effective and more technical than conceptual. Skills outside mathematics became essential to success, especially for management, including that of industrialised production units, which used batteries of bombes to break keys and turrets of Typex to print decrypts. Welchman oversaw the creation of this team of teams, which became standard for cryptanalysis. From late 1941, as work at Hut 8 became regularised on the lines which Welchman had established elsewhere, Turing could not function usefully in this team, which wasted his talents while he hampered their work. Instead, Turing became a crypt doctor used only for special issues, in particular working with American technical innovations and machines. Alexander managed Hut 8, which attacked German naval Enigma, as Welchman did at Hut 6, against army and Luftwaffe Enigma. Stuart Barry, his deputy, succeeded Welchman when he became chief of mechanisation at Bletchley, and directed all British and some American machine cryptanalysis every day until Germany surrendered. No one ever has dominated world cryptanalysis like Welchman, the Napoleon of crypt.

As cryptanalytic mathematicians were stretched against Enigma, a harder problem emerged. Several machines, like the Lorenz SZ40/42 cypher teleprinter, which Bletchley codenamed the Fish systems, transmitted high-level messages by teleprinter. Any attack against their strong cryptography must be purely cryptanalytic, as their workings were not physically compromised. All knowledge came from analysing their intercepted traffic, especially one crib of 4,000 characters which Tiltman found in 1941 when, like Moses, he searched for the promised land which he could see only from afar. As with Enigma, one mind, later aided by others, found the key vulnerability. Through analysis of Tiltman's crib and live traffic, Bill Tutte discovered the logic of the Fish systems, their cryptographic flaws and a 'statistical method' to exploit them. That method required comparison of massive quantities of letters in two streams of teleprinter traffic, which was beyond the capacity of any known machines. Mathematical cryptanalysts, including Turing, attacked these vulnerabilities through the techniques used against naval Enigma, with occasional success. Good noted that Peter Hilton was 'very good at adding two teleprinter letters together in his head, he could see them getting added together, he had good visualisation – which may be one reason why he is a good topologist'.[47] Ultimately, however, all leaders of the attack on Enigma failed against Fish, because they mistakenly thought that their old procedures could solve this harder system, and underestimated the need simply for brute force.

Fresh minds produced success. In 1942, Max Newman, a senior scholar from St John's College, Cambridge, joined Bletchley. No strategic organisation outside of Bletchley might have hired Turing and Welchman, but many would have welcomed Newman. Though a friend and teacher of Turing, he had no training in cryptanalysis and initially was outside the mainstream of mathematical cryptanalysts. He attacked Fish more through machines and mathematics than they did Enigma. He worked independently of them, yet had credibility across Bletchley. Newman, recommended by the eminent scientist Patrick Blackett, was recruited from the top of Cambridge, and offered his pick of opportunities. Tiltman hooked Newman towards Fish, which all agreed was Bletchley's hardest problem. Newman, whom Good thought had 'a gestalt mind – that is, the ability to see things as a whole', was an outstanding builder of teams, combining decisiveness with openness.[48] Every member of his office, inevitably named 'the Newmanry' – a research group constructed by a professor – could make suggestions in a 'Yellow Book', which were discussed by all. One of his lieutenants, Donald Michie, described the Newmanry as a 'dynamic, democratic but efficiency oriented community … a group identity certainty in which extraordinary freedom and extraordinary discipline are combined'.[49] When Newman considered Fish, he was not good at the statistical-cryptanalytic techniques used against bombes. He wanted not fun, but success. Seeing that only stronger machines could exploit Tutte's discoveries, he developed a specification for one, as Turing and Welchman had done for Enigma. As with them, Travis gave Newman command of a small team of cryptanalytic mathematicians and Wrens (from the Women's Royal Naval Service) and made this machine Bletchley's leading research and development project.[50]

Whereas Doc Keen was trusted to design and build the machine which penetrated Enigma, and did so well, that process proved harder and more politicised with Fish. Individual engineers knew only one means to build cryptanalytic machines, not all of them, and split over basic issues, like whether to transmit signals by relays or vacuum tubes. Keen mastered Hollerith machines, which conducted electricity through electromechanical relays, but not the electronic systems that succeeded them, which used valves. Hollerith machines, based on relays, could not catch Fish, and therefore neither could Keen. Instead, members of Britain's leading research units in communications, C. E. Wynn-Williams, a world authority in vacuum tubes and military electronics at the Telecommunications Research Establishment, and several engineers in the GPO's Research Department at Dollis Hill, including Tommy Flowers, produced the Heath Robinson machines. These machines, nicknamed because their mechanical complexity fitted the images of a famous cartoonist of the day – like those of Rube Goldberg in the United States – essentially ran two loops of five-holed paper tape across each other. They produced signals from two streams of teleprinter traffic which identified the vulnerabilities that Tutte had found, and aided assaults on them. The Heath Robinsons, the fastest and most complex electro-mechanical data-processing machine yet made, had some success against Fish, yet routinely broke down and were too slow for Newman's needs. He wanted a more reliable machine which worked 500 per cent faster. So to achieve this end, Flowers suggested a refined machine using 1,400 (ultimately raised to 2,400) vacuum tubes to strengthen its electronics and simplify its mechanics. Only one loop of paper tape needed to be run across the electronic system, reducing breakdowns and speeding results.

Flowers, perhaps doubted by some because of his working-class background, unprestigious degree and affiliation to a research institution less lofty than those most common in Cambridge, had conceived such a system years before in order to solve problems in telephone exchanges. Soon, it enabled early computers to work. Vacuum tubes had a mixed reputation – 'Valves? Don't like them. Nasty things. They break,' said one GPO engineer.[51] Many feared disaster from packing so many tubes into one machine. Colossus was perhaps the most valve-intensive device ever yet designed. Flowers' practical experience with valves had taught him solutions to the problems. Valves most commonly broke when devices were turned on and off, so he simply kept them running constantly, for long periods. Leading mathematical cryptanalysts and technical experts, including Wynn-Williams and Welchman, denounced the proposal, and Flowers himself. The great mathematical cryptanalysts split – Newman supporting Flowers, Welchman opposing him, and Turing irrelevant. Newman backed Flowers because he had no other choice: that machine alone could achieve the mathematician's ends and have Bletchley follow his lead. Newman and Flowers sidestepped their opponents by commissioning the work at Dollis Hill.[52] When Colossus' reliability and speed were proven, senior authorities demanded that several of them immediately be produced. The GPO did so well. Colossus worked not through the industrial-age production of Holleriths or bombes, but by several sequential and distinct steps of work by machines, 'cryptanalyst-programmers' and Wren operators. Colossus, the world's first programmable computer, pioneered many of the procedures of early computers and computer cryptanalysis, though it lacked the key component of stored programmes, or 'memory', which would be introduced with the Manchester Baby of 1948.

Craft to Industry

Power, policy and presents from Warsaw enabled Britain to act against Enigma with astonishing effect and speed during 1939–40. Britain had the human and technological resources, and the will and knowledge, needed to create the world's first mathematicised and mechanised system of cryptanalysis. Poles marked the path. Denniston prepared the expedition. His recruits delivered the goods. When Turing heard about the Polish bomba, and talked about it with the cryptanalysts who had escaped to Paris at the fall of Poland, speaking in German, their only common language, he envisaged how to make a better version – the bombe. His design inspired Welchman to develop something superior. They turned ideas into design specifications. They and Knox persuaded Travis that the approach was viable. Denniston and Travis agreed to expand GC&CS, on the assumption that these bombes would work. Stewart Menzies, the new chief of MI6 and Director of GC&CS after Sinclair's death, exploited the opportunity. With £100,000 in hand – the greatest allocation GC&CS ever had known, close to its annual budget – it approached the leading British candidate to build such a machine, BTM. Confronting the largest order in its history, approaching the company's capital value, BTM assigned the task to its chief engineer, a leading designer of tabulators, 'Doc' Keen, along with its best personnel and workshops. Within months Keen, using existing kit – including his Rolling Total Tabulator, perhaps the world's leading data-processing machine in 1940 – as a base, turned ideas into two bespoke systems; they were able, barely, to handle the problem. The combination of leading-edge mathematics and engineering transformed cryptanalysis.

Until this moment, everything fitted Denniston's ideas for the expansion of codebreaking. With the success and scale of Ultra, however, the industrial age of cryptology crushed the craftsman's bench. Everyone understood that Ultra had promise. Many problems frustrated its success. No one knew where they were going until they got there, which produced a systems failure. Until 1942, no one completely understood what was happening, or why it was not working as expected, or how to integrate every part in motion so to make the machine work smoothly. This uncertainty created other problems. GC&CS made constant and changing demands on civil and military authorities due to necessity and miscalculation. It did not need much, in absolute terms, but in this case GC&CS required priority over everyone about everything – from buildings and labour to rare commodities and dollars – without being able to tell minor bureaucrats why. Struggles over small issues produced more friction than over great ones. Until 1941, GC&CS's administrative staff was miniscule – one officer and one builder, relying on local labour. A cook, imported from London, seemed to work well, then suddenly took his own life.

GC&CS's demands contradicted normal rules of government economy and authority, annoying its administrative superiors, which ranged from MI6 to the ministries of Labour, and Works. On Trafalgar Day 1941, these problems led the four leaders in mechanical cryptanalysis – Alexander, Milner-Barry, Turing and Welchman – to warn Churchill directly that unless Bletchley's priorities were met, the attack on Enigma must erode. Immediately, Churchill ordered: 'Make sure they have all they want on extreme priority and report to me that this has been done.'[53] This decision was admirable and had some immediate effect, but was not fully followed for several months.

During 1941, for example, Bletchley confronted a crisis over labour. The Trafalgar Day memorandum decried not insufficient codebreaking machines – for which Bletchley already had the highest priority – but the lack of personnel to work them. With men conscripted, Bletchley required intelligent women in steadily rising numbers, yet its terms of employment were poor. The 'time and energy lost' in recruiting, the Naval Section complained, 'is appalling'. Bletchley could not attract the type of women needed, while applicants were unsuitable, because of 'Rates of pay – All the agencies say so – lower than anywhere else'. The National Register of Labour reported unofficially that Denniston 'liked "nice girls with good degrees"' but 'we, at B/P, were notorious and unique, we kept to Civil Service rates, but we <u>degraded</u> everybody'.[54] Bletchley demanded top-class labour, yet offered lower rates than candidates might receive elsewhere, until they proved themselves. Later, as Britain rationalised the allocation of brainpower to war, Bletchley slipped temporarily further in status. Mid-level authorities misunderstood its significance and blocked its unofficial modes of recruiting. Nor did the Trafalgar Day memorandum sweep all problems away. For months afterwards, authorities handling essential civil matters impeded the construction of buildings, which took twice as long to complete as expected, while labour always remained hard to find. As Ultra's credibility rose, however, Menzies could tell civil authorities that certain proposals were 'absolutely vital to the War effort', and demanded by Churchill and the Chiefs of Staff (COS). From mid-1942, Bletchley acquired whatever it claimed necessary. Menzies even had an expensive recreational facility built for the 'all important establishment', at 'my country place'. GC&CS was the only civilian institution in Britain able to keep able-bodied men from military conscription.[55]

The problems started from Bletchley. Had authorities known what Bletchley Park would become they would never have put it there. That Bletchley had little infrastructure seemed acceptable, for a small organisation. Sinclair and Denniston doubted that Sigint could work as well as between 1914 and 1918, but if so, Bletchley could house a larger version of Room 40. They missed practical problems from the test move to Bletchley during the Munich crisis, camouflaged as a shooting party, which emerged immediately after staff arrived in August 1939, under the cover of being a government communications headquarters.[56] This cover was successful enough to produce GCHQ's permanent name. With hundreds of MI6 and GC&CS personnel at Bletchley, and more coming, Denniston immediately warned that they could not be housed, fed, transported or function effectively. His superiors, especially Menzies, rejected these complaints as special pleading. Even Denniston misunderstood the situation, believing that once MI6 left Bletchley, a rational use of space and a few more huts should solve the problem.[57] Until 1944 the numbers of staff and the problems of handling them skyrocketed constantly. No one could prepare the surge capacity needed to handle them until the surge started. It was inconceivable in advance.[58]

We now sentimentalise Bletchley. Siginters did not. Clarke called Bletchley Park 'an ugly and inconvenient mansion … quite unsuitable for the purpose for which it was intended'.[59] Isolation, concentration and the churn of staff turnovers all drove dynamism, but issues which would have been minor in London became enormous at Bletchley – a Buckinghamshire town with few cafes, pubs or shops, or entrepreneurs willing to expand businesses to suit their new and captive market. Infrastructure had to be imported. Bletchley was not designed to handle an influx of 10,000 people. It was easy to escape only for those with cars and petrol coupons, or free to catch the 4.52 train to London on Friday afternoons (an element of control for managers). Thousands of Siginters were billeted in homes across the county, varying in comfort. Welchman's host, the publican of the Duncombe Arms, made him 'extremely comfortable'. Its billiards room became a social club for Siginters. For others, bathing involved sinks, cold water and winter. Middle-class people lived in what they thought squalor and also, complained the local MP, reflecting the irritation of his constituents, demanded 'amenities far in advance of those to which they are entitled, and at the expense of the householder (who cannot, of course, possibly provide expensive meals, unlimited hot baths, sitting rooms, central heating, personal attendance, etc)' at 21 shillings a week.[60] 'The workers' lives at B.P. consist almost entirely of work, meals, transport and billets, in invariable succession,' Travis admitted.[61]

These functions were problematical. Working conditions were uncomfortable, damaging morale and production. Bletchley's famous huts – single-storey wooden buildings with plasterboard partitions, constantly reconfigured – reflected its chaotic and explosive growth. 'Billeting and office accommodation' were GC&CS's 'two major worries', Menzies wrote.[62] From 1942, the creation of a canteen producing 30,000 meals per week, new huts and support staff, a twenty-four-hour bus service, and conveyor belts to move documents across buildings, reduced these problems. Even so, many people worked in boredom at Bletchley and were billeted in discomfort or commuted. Morale was often low, especially for the great majority of people doing routine work, knowing that better billets and jobs lay elsewhere. Many left, negating the effect of campaigns of recruitment. Bletchley included enthusiastic volunteers, but only administrative coercion filled its ranks, through the female branches of the military, such as the Women's Auxiliary Air Force (WAAF) and the Wrens. When Mrs Laughton-Mathews, Director of the WRNS, asked on visiting Bletchley why her Wrens were working with civilians, she was told: 'Because we couldn't get any more civilians.'[63] WAAFs and Wrens could also be housed in hostels, easing problems of billeting and transport.

Another set of problems stemmed from GC&CS. In 1939, it was a greying organisation, which faced block obsolescence in personnel. Most of its members had joined in 1919–20, or had been hired later while older adults. Half were on the cusp of retirement, some waiting for their pension. The best of them had successful careers during the war, most found use, but few were made to ride the revolution which transformed cryptanalysis from craftwork to industry. Most personnel were hired for linguistic proficiency and the ability to break or build books, few for management skills; GC&CS avoided such people. Few members of GC&CS (perhaps ten) were really fit for handling or managing complex work, like the attack on Enigma. Denniston was one of them, but he was unprepared to administer an organisation which swelled from 200 people in September 1939 to 10,000 in December 1944 (a tall order). Two weeks into the war, Denniston wrote: 'I shall be personally very greatly relieved when these administrative difficulties are settled as I am most anxious to take my share of the work on the increasing numbers of cryptographic problems confronting us.'[64] He yearned to join the attack on Enigma, rather than manage it. These characteristics were limitations, not weaknesses. They were not problems until GC&CS incarnated the revolution in cryptanalysis. The veterans were waning; many recruits had abilities rare and suitable to revolution. Tensions emerged as conservative civil servants, often from a pre-1918 military background, confronted hosts of wunderkinder recruited to handle new tasks. Old hands condemned new ones for unwillingness to sing 'God Save the King'. Some of the young felt their elders were not their betters. Staff with new skills were required: academics for cryptanalysis and analysis, women to operate the machines. In 1942, following the major reorganisation, Bletchley experienced a virtually complete turnover of staff. Seventy-five per cent of GC&CS's prewar personnel returned to London, along with most of Denniston's recruits of 1939, leaving perhaps fifty interwar veterans behind, and 2,000 newcomers. Despite these problems, veterans and newcomers created the best cryptanalytical organisation the world had ever known.

Individual experiences in GC&CS drove institutional developments at Bletchley. To his dismay, Denniston became a full-time manager, handling many of Sinclair's old roles regarding the services, and the explosive growth within GC&CS. Travis managed in whole or part everything at GC&CS except codebreaking, including relations with the fighting services and the production of Ultra. Most of the 75 per cent of GC&CS's staff who focused on diplomatic Comint continued that work. The rest, particularly the military sections, handled the areas of growth, which overwhelmed them to varying degrees. Expansion shattered the Naval Section, riven with personal rivalries. Its Italian, German and Japanese sub-sections split, and failed to penetrate their cryptanalytical targets, while Knox's Enigma sub-section was successful but independent. An operational intelligence section led by an officer trained by GC&CS, Commander Saunders, moved to the Admiralty. With the successes of Knox, tabulators and bombes, these sections reunited, with Birch superseding Clarke at its helm. From mid-1941, the Naval Section combined Comint, traffic analysis, Y and intelligence well, providing real-time and excellent material on tactical issues into a naval intelligence system which had recalibrated the sound model of 1918.

Conversely, the Air and Military sections were uninvolved with Enigma, shaping a vacuum in military and air Sigint which damaged Britain until 1942. During the 1930s, Cooper, Jacob and Tiltman had ample experience in attacking military systems conducted by radio, integrating attack on low- and high-grade codes, which guided their work at Bletchley and Cairo. Tiltman dominated training in GC&CS, and made the Military Section partly into a research section for attacking difficult systems. During 1939, Cooper had the Air Section cooperate with RAF Y in air defence and offence towards tactical purposes; in particular, supporting Britain's most advanced command, control, communications, intelligence, surveillance and reconnaissance system: that of Fighter Command. Jacobs led the Central Bureau Middle East (CBME) against Italian military cyphers and Abwehr hand systems, which aided Britain substantially in the desert campaign. Between 1939 and 1945, first in effect and then title, Tiltman replaced Strachey as Chief Cryptographer, and became Bletchley's fireman on everything outside Enigma. His Military Section became the core of a Research Section which, Travis wrote, gave 'sectional cryptographers a good kick off and then pass[ed] back the problem to them'.[65] Seeing an influx of newcomers, Tiltman established short and powerful systems of training in codebreaking and the Japanese language. Unlike the Air and Naval sections, however, his section ceased to link GC&CS with military Y, traffic analysis or intelligence. Tiltman was right to cover all of these jobs, but the failure to do his own inflamed a struggle for Sigint.

The Struggle for Sigint

A final set of problems combined organisation, politics and the ideas of institutions. During the 1930s, the armed services imagined that in war, the Military, Air and Naval sections would leave GC&CS and join them, fusing with their Y units. Three organisations would conduct Sigint separately while GC&CS researched hard systems for them all. GC&CS doubted but did not challenge this idea. Denniston feared that service plans for Sigint in a major war were of 'a somewhat hazy nature', and posed the 'danger of decentralisation'. GC&CS preferred to coordinate all interception, rather than divide it by services, to maintain the unity of GC&CS, and to expand on that basis.[66] As the prospect of war rose in 1938–39, these issues were complicated because, more than before, the services emphasised conventional Y, which they named WT/I (wireless intelligence), while the Air, Military and Naval sections had outside masters, which naturally challenged decisions made at Bletchley. The Air Section tested decentralisation by sending elements to work with RAF Y at Cheadle, while cooperating with GC&CS. The Admiralty and the NID demanded a Comint unit for the Mediterranean Fleet. Ultimately, when war began, the services left their sections at GC&CS while maintaining control over their own Y units and gaining forward Comint in varying ways. The Air Section worked with Cheadle, fusing Y and low-grade Comint. Part of the Naval Section went to the Admiralty to handle operational intelligence, but soon returned to Bletchley. The Mediterranean Fleet received a tiny Comint section. The RAF and Army Sigint sections in the Middle East coalesced loosely in the Combined Bureau Middle East around Cairo.

Tension soon escalated over these issues. Small Army and RAF Y and Comint sections joined the BEF, which Denniston feared might absorb the work of the Military Section, as the RAF had done the Air Section and, incidentally, cripple attack on Enigma. The fall of France eliminated that danger, while causing others. When Italy joined the war, British Army and air commanders in Egypt demanded that the Italian subsections of the Air and Military sections and their scarce machines move to Cairo. GC&CS correctly opposed this campaign, but less rightly resisted expansion of CBME. Meanwhile, the three services intelligence branches in Egypt refused to cooperate in Sigint. Denniston denounced a 'tragic farce', which Jacobs thought was producing 'disaster'. Ultimately, on the advice of Denniston and Menzies, the Chiefs of Staff made the services coordinate their cryptography in Egypt, where GC&CS sent half of the Italian Air and Military Sections.[67] CBME became a major Sigint centre, with initially mixed but increasingly strong connections to Y, traffic analysis and General Staff Intelligence at GHQ Middle East, well led and trusted. While superficially better integrated, Far East Combined Bureau (FECB) was even more fractured between its service elements and by the convoluted command system at Singapore.[68]

Control over Y was reconfigured in 1940, just before Ultra emerged and the war became one for national survival. At that time, the services overrated the relative significance of WTI, while no one could know how Ultra would develop. The DNI, John Godfrey, who understood Sigint better than any other director of intelligence and as well as anyone, drove this reorganisation. He did so by lobbying Lord Hankey, whom the Cabinet had tasked with recommending improvements in the intelligence system. Godfrey convinced all parties to accept his proposals, including the two men whom this restructuring weakened, Denniston and Menzies. Godfrey doubted 'if we are ever likely to be able to regain the priceless source of information which was available to us during the late war. The Germans are thoroughly on their guard, and have developed a technique which is difficult, if not impossible, to break.' The 'only really bright spot, in fact, was the "Y-side", in particular the intercepted signals and call-signs, which the Admiralty found of the greatest possible use', even though, in hindsight, this product was fragmentary. Godfrey pursued political and managerial ends, in particular aiming surreptitiously and successfully to maintain naval power over Y. Work at Bletchley, he noted, was a full-time task for Denniston, because 'the fruits of cryptography are of such supreme importance and the evolution of the particular technique imposed by modern conditions, so intricate'. Equally, Y required specialist management. The services must control their own services, yet coordinate them with each other and GC&CS.[69] Godfrey's proposal reduced the power of Menzies over Y, compared to that which Sinclair had held. Menzies, lacking a background in Sigint or the Royal Navy, remained head of the 'Main Committee' for Y, including the directors of intelligence, but it rarely met. A leading serviceman, working half-time, whom Godfrey attempted to ensure always was an admiral, replaced Denniston as chair of what became the main executive body, the Y Committee. That committee included Denniston and the heads of the service Y branches.[70]

This system was unstable. As Britain created its first truly inter-service agency around Bletchley Park, the services jostled each other. Differences emerged over what civilians and service personnel should do, or even who they were: one officer and one civilian might both have been students in 1939, and do identical work, at radical differences in pay. The system also rested on subterranean differences, which no one fully recognised, between naval and Army approaches to Sigint. Military intelligence had a unique position, reflecting its experiences of 1914–18 and 1939–41. It believed traffic analysis was a great source, while theatre commanders must control large Sigint resources. The NID preferred centralised Sigint, so long as this gave the Royal Navy the resources it needed. Leaders at Bletchley preferred centralised Comint and, outside the Air and Naval sections, underrated traffic analysis. Unconsciously, experience with Room 40 drove senior figures at GC&CS to work with the NID against the MID. Meanwhile, the RAF and Royal Navy achieved their own ends in Sigint while shifting the burden of intercepting Enigma onto the Army. During 1939, all military Y services intercepted German traffic, but the Army's section at Chatham dominated work against Enigma. Experience in penetrating the well-run Soviet system of wireless traffic prepared it for the German one. Unlike RAF Y, when war started Army Y had no other immediate task to serve. It enthusiastically worked against Enigma, rather than for MI8, the War Office's Sigint command. Gradually, MI8 became an excellent traffic analysis organisation against both the German army and Luftwaffe. The Army's two assets in Y did not work together, or with the Military Section, and carried burdens for other organisations, especially the RAF.

When war began, conversely, the Royal Navy focused on German naval Enigma, directly meeting its service's needs. The RAF integrated its excellent Y service into its air defence system. When pressed to intercept Enigma, and enable Chatham to serve the Army, the RAF created a new, inexperienced, unit, which GC&CS refused to trust, correctly – the emerging technique of 'cribbery', fundamental to the attack on Enigma, required first-rate Y. Thus, the RAF subordinated attack on Enigma to giving Fighter Command tactical intelligence. Denniston could gain even this mixed blessing only by warning the head of RAF Y, Wing Commander Blandy, that the 'research party' believed that with the arrival of the 'super bombe' designed by Turing around Christmas 1939, they could receive the present of reading Luftwaffe Enigma. However, he doubted that the War Office would let military Y at Chatham continue intercepting this traffic: 'I think that if Chatham starts searching for military traffic in field cyphers they will find it, that Tiltman will then break the Army field cyphers; and that by the time the G.A.F. [German air force] point-to-point problem is ripe for attack, Chatham will be more or less fully occupied on programmes that produce traffic of interest to the War Office.'[71] If the RAF did not establish an effective system, the elements of Army Sigint would handle their own tasks and move away from work against Enigma.

This situation demonstrates the limits to Denniston's ability to manage Ultra and Y, and why gains against Enigma were possible only at the Army's cost. From September 1939, Army Y focused on Enigma traffic and remained frozen in this situation for thirty months. In September 1941, 97 of the 155 sets intercepting Enigma traffic were Army, and 122 of 206 (59.2 per cent) five months later; yet only 38.8 per cent of 'enemy tasks covered' were German army. During much of this period Ultra offered little to the Army in active theatres. The Army might have gained more in the short term had it completely controlled its Sigint resources, including Tiltman, and focused on the desert campaign. Its attempts to break from this situation provoked contempt at Bletchley; Denniston held that the Army aimed 'to dissipate what cryptographic strength we possess and to create cryptographic sections in positions where it is extremely doubtful if they will be able to produce results'.[72] On the issue of ruthless priorities, he was correct, except about CBME, but wrong to dismiss the Army's case. So many things had to be put right in British cryptology that some were bound to go wrong. Moreover, CBME proved essential to the Eighth Army, which by summer 1941 integrated Comint, Sigint and intelligence well, creating the system the British Army would follow until 1945.[73] That situation drove GC&CS to annoy the Army and it to challenge Bletchley. Army intelligence and Y also had worse liaison with Bletchley than the other services: the Military Section ceased to work with them while MI8 was kept distant from Ultra. Unfairly, but unsurprisingly, GC&CS's resistance to the establishment of CBME and the technical difficulty of penetrating the Enigma links of the German army, led the British Army to think Bletchley was ignoring its needs. Had Bletchley deliberately wished to alienate the Army, it could have done little more.

By early 1941, MI8 and military intelligence in the Middle East condemned the system around Sigint, with some justice. The Army received little help from GC&CS or Y. GC&CS controlled the Army's intercept sets. It refused to house the traffic analysis section of MI8 at Bletchley, even though it did so for the air and naval equivalents, and all acknowledged that traffic analysis and cryptanalysis needed close coordination. GC&CS and MI8 mistrusted each other, driven by personality conflicts and different opinions of traffic analysis. Personalities drove institutional friction in Sigint during 1939–41. The two heads of MI8 during this period, Colonels Butler and Nichols, and the RAF's intelligence liaison in Hut 3, Wing Commander Humphrey, were proud and able men who thought they were being impeded and exploited. Denniston damned Army policy towards Sigint. Tiltman dismissed the Army's culture of uniform and rank and rated its needs below those of GC&CS. Thus, the DMI demanded greater service control over Y and GC&CS and insisted that this should be directed through the Joint Intelligence Committee (JIC), the inter-service intelligence organisation which was starting to organise intelligence assessments. Menzies resisted this onslaught on his empire. The NID and Air Intelligence rejected this proposal, because neither shared the MID's problems. Godfrey thought the idea unsound. The system met the needs of RAF intelligence and Y, and gave it the comfortable swing vote between the Army and Royal Navy. The MID's proposal might well threaten RAF interests. As the dust cleared, service ownership of Y organisations and the need to coordinate them was recognised, as was the independence of GC&CS and its duty to meet military requirements. Nothing changed but names. The Main Committee became the Y Board. Members of the services' intelligence branches also joined the Y Committee. A cryptanalytical committee, with representation from GC&CS and the services, was established, with little power.

The DMI and MI8 remained disgruntled and, from September 1941, constantly challenged the Sigint system, which also failed. The Y Committee was underpowered, its chairmen ineffective. The pieces of the machine did not fit together, producing friction and breakage. Organisations used their resources to further poorly coordinated expansion and actions. Interception was inadequately integrated. The emergence of Ultra created a crisis in Y, where every success caused problems. The initial difficulty was too few wireless operators. Not until 1940 did Britain begin to create new Y units, which could not become useful until 1941. Not until 1941 did it expand its dismal base in wireless and Typex operators and sets for Sigint communications abroad. Resources in personnel and material were too small for immediate needs, yet exploding in size. This expansion raised problems with labour at Bletchley and Sigint communications.

Throughout 1941, Siginters constantly played catch up with transmission of intercepts taken in the Middle East to Britain, and solutions sent from Bletchley to Cairo. Initially, all Ultra for Middle East commands was sent personally to Jacobs, who distributed it himself to a few consumers without denoting the source. This system collapsed as Ultra became successful. By summer 1941, Britain found a solution to the problem. Special Liaison Units (SLUs) – RAF units using Typex – communicated intercepts and solutions, while Special Communications Units (SCUs), run mostly by Army officers, received Ultra and carried it personally to all consumers, who knew the source and read but could not keep messages. This system worked well for the small number of solutions, enabling Ultra to aid British commanders in the Middle East, but failed regarding the huge number of intercepts. In autumn 1941, the Crusader battle in the desert was central to Churchill's strategy of crushing Italy. Before and during Crusader, messages intercepted in Egypt from crucial Enigma circuits took two to five days to reach Bletchley by wireless. Sometimes cypher clerks required another few days to strip the Typex code from the Enigma message it covered. Intercepts taken from lesser links took a month to reach Bletchley. In order to clear the backlog, authorities ultimately destroyed, untouched, a million intercepted messages – one month's work of interception in the Middle East.[74] Problems in coordination degraded the development of technique and units and the selection of attacks. The Y services and GC&CS fought each other on these issues, vital to all, and to Sigint and intelligence.

Sigint and Intelligence

This system for Sigint emerged suddenly and haphazardly. No one knew how it would work and everyone had different ideas of how it should. All agreed that GC&CS should break codes and Y intercept traffic, and military intelligence analyse data. How far GC&CS should conduct intelligence, which bodies should analyse Comint and Sigint and control Sigint, and how to join Comint and intelligence, remained unclear. This confusion stemmed from Sinclair's system, and its collapse when he died, uncertainty about the theory and practice of Sigint and the different doctrines of the services, GC&CS and SIS. These doctrines involved ingrained but often unconscious ideas that divided cryptanalysis from both Y and intelligence. They were expressed in words with uncertain meanings. In particular, the term 'operational intelligence', Denniston noted, could mean either material from Y without cryptanalysis, or else 'intelligence concerning enemy craft from any source'.[75] Neither definition quite fits our modern interpretation that operational intelligence fuses material from all sources to support operations, as against tactics and strategy. Nor did anyone conceptualise the central problem at hand: how to make Sigint into intelligence, by combining Comint with Y, and squeezing meaning from the mixture through firm and penetrating analysis.

Clarke held that service intelligence saw GC&CS 'as mere crossword puzzle solvers and not as the experienced intelligence officers which years of training had made them'. He was right about the services, but not quite about Siginters.[76] Some members of GC&CS knew how to combine and analyse Comint and Sigint. They did not understand intelligence more broadly, which none of them had practised, or how to combine intelligence with Comint, nor coordinate this fusion with military actions. Any solution of Enigma produced masses of material at the speed of typewriters, overwhelming an organisation used to processing solutions slowly and steadily, by hand. Years of serving the Foreign Office had turned GC&CS away from practices which were conventional in Sigint during 1918, like passing hot material immediately while combining and analysing fragments. Analysis was something diplomats did, not codebreakers. During 1938–39, GC&CS recognised that military Comint needed the help of intelligence. The military sections created small equivalents of D&R, usually consisting of one officer, where intelligence aided cryptanalysis by identifying units, combining Comint and Sigint, studying radio frequencies and call signs, and learning how systems were used on links. This idea was sound, but covered only small topics, such as Italian forces in Spain. It also missed essential matters, like fusing Comint and Sigint and exploiting their product through intelligence, by assessing current and distant problems. GC&CS wanted this process to provide 'items of foreign military intelligence obtained mainly from a study of foreign message traffic and their stations', combining Comint and Sigint, on matters like order of battle and command links, but this hope miscarried.[77]

Denniston was reluctant to claim a role in intelligence for GC&CS, which he wished to remain a black chamber. When, days into the war, Saunders, head of the operational intelligence section at the NID, pressed on GC&CS's prerogatives, Denniston retorted that GC&CS handled 'all matters cryptographic', while Saunders assessed Comint and Y within the Admiralty's Operational Intelligence Centre.[78] Denniston opposed any efforts to build forward Comint organisations. He complained that the Army ignored the advice of Tiltman, 'their only real advisor on cryptography': yet to the services, Tiltman was a retired captain, promoted temporarily to colonel, who had gone native (missing, from the perspective of military intelligence); Clarke was a veteran of Room 40 with similar characteristics and a difficult personality, irritating the Admiralty since 1920; and Cooper an eccentric civilian (here, the RAF's prior refusal to have any of its officers specialise in Comint damaged its understanding of the matter, and ability to use it).[79] Naturally, the services relied on the best experts from their own ranks, some of whom, including the heads of service Y, were able, but their liaison even with the military sections of GC&CS was poor. When the services sought to overcome this problem by assigning military intelligence officers to GC&CS and giving them control over the military and air personnel there, they made it worse. These officers challenged GC&CS over issues they did not understand. Everyone misconstrued elements of the equation. Welchman, who best understood it, grossly underestimated the value of traffic analysis. In 1941, he regarded an expansion of Army Y and MI8 as a 'danger' to Ultra.[80] Despite his mistakes, after the initial experience with Ultra, and the military debacles of spring 1940, Saunders grasped the need to combine Comint and intelligence better than anyone else and drove GC&CS to start that process, which key figures like Birch, Cooper and de Grey resisted.[81]

GC&CS had no idea how to do so. De Grey, tasked to fuse Comint and intelligence, created a small inter-service bureau, Hut 3. By 1941, it and he understood that task well. De Grey held that Bletchley Park must 'produce intelligence', and through 'civilians (not in fancy dress but owing allegiance to G.C. & C.S. and trained in its methods of work) ... first-class brains, more accustomed to the compiling and weighing of evidence, men of imagination and judgment'.[82] He did not explain how to make the services trust such men above those in their fancy dress. So too, Menzies tried to have a 'Standing Advisory Committee' of military intelligence officers and key Bletchley hands improve GC&CS's production. This effort failed.[83] The Royal Navy and the Naval Section solved part of their problem because the Admiralty had complete control over naval and naval intelligence resources, used them well, and fought a single service war. Even so, they merely solved tactical problems: by 1942, Hut 3 far surpassed the Naval Section's analysis of broader issues. When the Air Section independently conducted effective Comint research into the Luftwaffe, Air Intelligence rejected these reports, partly because Cooper's staff were civilians.[84] Until 1942, all efforts to solve broader problems failed. Everyone knew that something must be done. No one knew what or how. None remembered the only previous body to combine Sigint and intelligence, or to conduct Comint research, the WTID. What it did in six months during 1915, took thirty at Bletchley during 1940–42. Not until its third year did Hut 3 match the WTID's power in its first year, but then quickly surpass it. The WTID solved an equally complex problem far faster because it was led by experts in information processing, given a task they wanted to execute, which no one else was handling or had any claims for expertise, did not duplicate work done by other units, and was backed by all relevant authorities. WTID did what military intelligence wanted done: they supported it.

None of these factors existed in 1940–41; many were opposite. Among the leaders at Bletchley Park, only Welchman and Travis understood information processing. Welchman focused on production, rightly – it was essential to success. Travis's expertise aided the development of Ultra, but not the combining of Comint and intelligence. GC&CS mishandled intelligence analysis. Hut 3's personnel, mostly civilian academics given temporary military rank, were called not intelligence officers but 'emenders', tasked to translate solutions accurately, no easy job given the jargon and corruptions at hand. They were untrained in intelligence analysis or information processing, but increasingly learned these skills and combined Comint and intelligence better than anyone else did. That fact and its significance were unrecognised; even more, it involved Comint research on military matters, which the services claimed as their own field. In January 1942, Hut 3, divided into four watches each supervised by a watchkeeper, was 33 per cent below its authorised strength of forty personnel. It attempted to disseminate Ultra to appropriate authorities, but faced friction everywhere. Its connections to the leaders of Bletchley and consumers outside were convoluted and weak.

Comint analysis and its relationship to intelligence became politicised, on all sides. The two strongest analytical units, Naval Section and Hut 3, barely cooperated. GC&CS thrust control over Hut 3 onto the military intelligence officials seconded to Bletchley. This move reduced the services' ability to criticise GC&CS, but that troika, chaired by Saunders, defined their work as operational intelligence, and did what they knew. These officers, sometimes justifiably, saw mistakes by Hut

3 and criticised them. Ultimately they overrode the watchkeepers and confused their work, competed with and annoyed their own services by producing appreciations instead of reports, while intriguing against each other and GC&CS. Birch and Tiltman loathed their opposite numbers in Hut 3, Saunders and Major Curtis. Saunders competed with the Naval Section in assessing Ultra for the Royal Navy. In Tiltman's absence from the work, Curtis became the main analyst of Comint for the Army at Bletchley. Humphrey, an able analyst and linguist, challenged Hut 3 and the Air Section. The sections at GC&CS reported material to military bodies in a bewildering variety of ways, confusing consumers. The services did not understand this intelligence problem because they did not know what Comint really could give them.

A Crisis in Comint

During 1940–41, these problems slowed the development of Sigint and its use, but not fatally. Progress occurred, slowly and in part invisibly. Problems were obvious. The production of Ultra required acquisition of bombes and experience in using them. Success was small until 1941, from which it steadily rose. Just enough labour was found to exploit the rising numbers of machines. Things were easier to produce than ideas of what to do with them. Bletchley's success in production, combined with failures in analysis and dissemination, drove a crisis in the management of Comint.

During 1914–18, the War Office, the Admiralty and the Foreign Office had squabbled over their one common property in intelligence: MI1(c). These squabbles were restrained because each consumer could develop the services it wished. Control over strategic resources was decentralised, while intelligence resources were ample. In 1939, there was far more common property in intelligence, for which resources were scarce and tightly controlled by the state; Sigint needed top priority for its needs, all of which were scarce, some among the scarcest in Britain. These resources could be used well only if rationally coordinated. Every intelligence agency found the turn from routine to wartime traumatic. Coordination and control were in chaos; agencies exploded in size, their command systems imploded under the weight, old leaders died or were fired. Between May 1940 and March 1941, MI5 had two external reviews and three sets of leadership. It was damned for incompetence, its data retrieval system (or 'Registry') in danger of collapse, its old leadership purged, their replacements failures: its third head in a year, David Petrie, condemned the service for 'want of control and direction from above', 'muddle and inefficiency'.[85] The same could have been said of SIS and the GC&CS – and was. In fact, these agencies simultaneously failed and succeeded in unprecedented ways, through the 'double-cross' system of controlled agents, Ultra and deception. Where MI5 and MI6 confronted crises, GC&CS experienced a revolution, which negated its strengths and turned its limitations to weaknesses. Except for the high level of cryptanalytic skill, GC&CS's inheritance from diplomatic codebreaking was of little value in developing Ultra during 1940, or in a political battle over military Comint and Sigint. GC&CS was mediocre in coordinating Y and codebreaking and, like every other cryptanalytic agency on earth, unprepared to handle mechanised and industrialised Sigint.

Suddenly, from the summer of 1940, the services and Churchill rose to dominance in decision-making, while all other actors shrank. These changes affected no unit more than GC&CS. Its old consumers and protectors, the Foreign Office and MI6, could not help it against the military. The services' intelligence branches became its main consumer, and masters. Their Sigint units became its main partners, and competitors. In 1938–41, the Y services exploded in size. They considered what they had done in 1914–18, and might do again. This strengthening strained their relationships with GC&CS. Naval officers partly trained in cryptanalysis challenged GC&CS. MI8 understood Y well, though military Siginters overestimated its power during this Comint intensive war. MI8 saw Bletchley's failures and promise and thought it could do better. This view was wrong, but not unreasonable. Meanwhile, the military intelligence services expected GC&CS to produce self-evident pieces of Comint which they would analyse, as did any commanders who thought about the matter. Ultra provided such traffic, but also masses of material useful only if researched by specialists in Comint. The military intelligence services were reluctant to trust Bletchley with producing intelligence, though slowly they did so in 1941.

The death of Sinclair and the rise of Ultra in 1939, and the perils of 1940, disrupted the position of GC&CS and the fragile system for Sigint. Menzies, the new C, politically weaker than Sinclair and unschooled in Sigint, focused on saving MI6, his own agency, and one in crisis. During 1940–41, as he confronted unprecedented difficulties, Menzies also unintentionally created problems with Ultra. For security's sake, he told consumers that Ultra emanated from a spy, codenamed Boniface. This cover damaged the impact of Ultra and rapidly became threadbare. Even worse, MI6 delivered Ultra direct to the services' analytical sections, rather than having GC&CS do so through the air, military and naval Y services, which crippled the central links in Sigint. The producers of air and military Sigint were isolated from their consumers as, to a lesser degree, air and military Sigint were from their intelligence superiors. In 1941, MI6 gave this function of liaison to the military officers attached to Hut 3, which led them to send independent appreciations to their intelligence branches, bypassing authorities at GC&CS and the Y services. MI8 was denied full knowledge of Ultra while being asked to sacrifice itself for Bletchley. Following its own doctrine that to let any source know the reports of another risked conscious or unconscious duplication of reportage, MI6 also tried to keep Y material from the military sections and Hut 3, though the Air Section and Cheadle always overcame this barrier, as did the Naval Section and the NID from spring 1941. For a year MI6 unknowingly damaged the integration of Sigint, when a sophisticated merger was possible and necessary. Menzies, however, made up for these problems by simultaneously speeding the development of Ultra through one great and unsung contribution: using his non-audited funds to subsidise the purchase of bombes and expansion at Bletchley until 1941, eliminating the delays likely with regular channels.

Without Ultra, Britain might have followed a conventional pattern in Comint, with GC&CS servicing the Foreign Office, while the military services formed their own agencies. Instead, the success of Ultra, promising triumph for military intelligence but not initially delivering it, forced a political battle over Sigint as a whole. Menzies bolstered his beleaguered empire by giving snippets of Ultra to Churchill, but neither he nor the Foreign Office could protect GC&CS from the services. GC&CS had to do several things at once that it never had done before: to fight the greatest beasts in Whitehall, to prevent the services from dominating Sigint and to direct their Y services. The central means to feed Ultra, cribbery, which aimed to find and exploit places where cribs might be found, required control over Y so to understand German communications links, find cribs and then exploit them. GC&CS sought to make the Y services sacrifice immediate gains for their masters so to maximise the power of Ultra a year ahead. GC&CS had to convince Whitehall to make its needs a top priority. GC&CS and the services accused each other of failures. Each was right. Everyone failed on major issues – unavoidably. Every organisation had crying needs, few could be met. Every good decision must have bad consequences. The situation negated a strength of the British system, the ability to concentrate and to switch resources in a centralised fashion; this aim could be achieved only by inflicting an equal and opposite weakness elsewhere.

These problems and prospects caused mutual and heated suspicions. Military intelligence was driven to unprecedented involvement in cryptanalysis at Bletchley, where they met GC&CS's strengths, weaknesses and staff. GC&CS confronted extraordinary technical problems, which an outsider might think it was mishandling. Riding a revolution in cryptology was hard. Leadership was lacking. Conventional views of Denniston are defined by his failure in 1941, while the authors of the most influential private and public accounts, Birch, Clarke and de Grey, disliked him. Even Denniston's successes were turned against him. With some exaggeration, Alexander wrote that when war began, 'probably only two people' thought that naval Enigma 'could be broken': Birch, 'because it had to be broken', and Turing, 'because it would be so interesting to break it'.[86] Denniston sometimes doubted the prospect of breaking naval Enigma, which his foes later held against him. When Birch took over the German Naval Section, he claimed to have been warned that: 'All German codes were unbreakable' and 'it wasn't worth while putting pundits onto them'. He told Denniston: 'Defeatism at the beginning of the war to my mind, played a large part in delaying the breaking of codes.'[87] Granted, GC&CS's attack against Enigma failed until August 1939, but that was not Denniston's personal failure, and it was he who put 'pundits' on the trail. Denniston was retired in 1945 without an honour – shabby treatment for a good and faithful servant.

These critiques are right in part, but incomplete. Denniston brought GC&CS to the industrial age of cryptology but could not master it. He was ill, inexperienced with bureaucratic battles conducted with such intensity and at such high levels, and temperamentally unsuited to them for precisely the reasons Sinclair had appointed him. He continued to manage directly every cryptanalytical element of GC&CS. Their expansion overwhelmed him, causing fudge, impotence, micromanagement and stalemate. He managed interdepartmental relations at a time of crisis. Denniston, responsible for challenging the services, too easily could seem the scapegoat for every problem, whether between departments or personalities. Yet some of the solutions to these problems emerged during his tenure, as his successor later recognised: 'many of the plans of the old regime have come to fruition during the past year', while in 1941 Bletchley gave 'good service both in volume and rapidity of service'.[88] Denniston is accused, rightly, of failing to grip problems when the system was loose and exploding, while he attempted to direct it more than anyone ever had done. Yet, he had little expertise in the technical issues at hand and did not handle them well. His subordinates managing work at the coalface saw his failures with problems and solutions, like Birch and de Grey with intelligence, and Welchman with C3ISR and machines. C and the services often heard of dissension within GC&CS. The Trafalgar Day note showed outsiders, including a prime minister concerned with Comint, that key technical officers within GC&CS mistrusted their masters, Denniston and Menzies, which suggested the latter were failing their brief.

These officers could not take their masters' place, only find help from outside to gain a new one. These Young Turks had just one Old Turk in mind: Travis. By 1939, GC&CS had failed more in the areas overseen by Travis than Denniston. Yet this was not obvious at the time: Travis managed many areas, mostly well. Denniston was a teacher, Travis a paymaster – the civil managerial branch of the Royal Navy. No leader in any other codebreaking agency matched Travis's qualifications in management. He was the only senior Comint officer anywhere experienced in a combatant command at war, the Grand Fleet. Denniston thought of codes, Travis of communications. He understood chains of command and how to move them and through them. He had longer experience with machine systems, Comsec for wireless traffic, communications, managing clerical staff and working with civilian and especially military services, than any other officer in GC&CS and probably in the world. Travis handled every function outside of cryptanalysis that mattered in the crisis. From 1938, Denniston and Sinclair thrust every new administrative task regarding Sigint onto Travis. In effect he became as much the deputy to Sinclair and Menzies, as to Denniston. Travis was delegated the management of Ultra from the start. Although underestimating the task like everyone else, he understood its functional divisions well, and effectively managed the men involved, including Turing and Welchman.[89] Travis substituted for Denniston when he was ill or on a liaison mission to Washington, showing skill in administration and politics and an understanding of the cryptologic revolution.

A series of murky battles ensued – sometimes (erroneously) called a coup. Accounts of this topic tend to be personalised and to miss key individuals. Personal politics bloomed in Bletchley, but greater forces drove decisions about it. No one present liked the position, but few old hands, certainly not Cooper, Knox, and Tiltman, moved to overthrow Denniston. The Young Turks and the old guard owed no loyalty to Denniston, or the system of GC&CS, and wanted changes. How coordinated or active they were is unclear, as is Travis's role: perhaps he discussed the problems with Menzies, which was his duty, while remembering that kingmakers rarely become king. Probably de Grey and Birch, perhaps Clarke, briefed Godfrey, the only director of service intelligence to visit Bletchley regularly. Curtis, Humphreys and Saunders lobbied for increased power against each other and GC&CS.

Yet the key changes occurred at a higher level. Increasingly, Britain centralised strategy and resources, pursuing highest common denominator decisions through a rational process of competitive cooperation. Offensive action alone could win the war. That the Royal Navy could not do: Churchill gave it enough resources not to lose, nothing further. The Army and the RAF got more. The institutions which drove the Sigint system during 1940–41, the Admiralty and the NID, waned. Army Y, MI8, and the general staff increasingly outweighed their Royal Navy equivalents in resources and influence in strategy. The other rising player, the RAF, switched to back the Army on Sigint, which forced the hands of Menzies and Godfrey. Above all, events caused a seismic shift in the unstable system of Sigint. As the war escalated, Britain suffered hard times. Desperate battles revealed the power and weaknesses of the Sigint system. Ultra appeared both essential and failing. Something seemed rotten in the state of Sigint and the top dogs caught the scent. On 23 December 1941, the Chiefs of Staff ordered the JIC to investigate, reform and expand Sigint. In political terms, the DMI finally beat Godfrey and Menzies over the organisation of Sigint.

So to stop the rot and save himself, in December 1941 Menzies let the directors of intelligence reform Ultra, Y and Bletchley. He finally worked with rather than resisted the MID. Menzies and the DMI seconded the deputy DMI, William van Cutsem, a veteran consumer of Ultra, to suggest how Bletchley could better provide intelligence. After three weeks observing Bletchley, and speaking to many people, van Cutsem produced intelligent proposals to help GC&CS and the services overcome their central problems. These proposals streamlined departmental responsibilities, simplified and centralised lines of command, settled relations between civilians and servicemen, and, without compromising its characteristics, made Bletchley Park formally part of the military system with authority over service resources. The head of GC&CS must have authority to manage all activities at Bletchley Park, aided by adequate staff. Sigint must centre on GC&CS. Bletchley Park and MI8, and thus Comint and traffic analysis, should be integrated. Van Cutsem packaged these proposals in ways the services could accept, by what Travis called 'a nice and tidy paper organisation'.[90] The fiction that officers manned Hut 3 let the services accept the judgement of civilians in fancy dress analysing Comint. Tiltman and Cooper should control all Army and air personnel at Bletchley, including many MI8 personnel, under the titular authority of DMI and Air Intelligence. MI8 must have free access to all Ultra, but treat it securely. Nichols of MI8 would join the management board at Bletchley Park, where a centralised traffic analysis organisation should be established – the origin of SIXTA, the great traffic analysis unit which carried Ultra through hard times ahead. Curtis, Humphreys and Saunders must leave Hut 3 – Curtis expelled from the garden, Humphreys remaining to serve under Cooper as an intelligence officer (he quickly escaped to other pastures), and Saunders to become an administrator, where he was useful. Emenders must be treated as intelligence officers and given military training in the matter. Civilians (perhaps with temporary commissions) should man Hut 3 and be a central producer of Comint and intelligence. They should send Ultra (which, internally, Bletchley called 'Source') straight to the services and commanders without disguising it as 'Boniface'. A Royal Navy component should join every watch at Hut 3.[91]

Menzies adopted these ideas because he saw their value and they appeased the MID.[92] Meanwhile, responding to the COS, Menzies let Godfrey reorganise Sigint. Denniston and Menzies had used the Trafalgar Day note diffidently. Clarke complained that 'the Prime Minister has given us a very big gun but no one uses it'.[93] On 27 December, the first working day after the COS's order, Godfrey drew the gun. In a meeting with senior staff at GC&CS, Godfrey enunciated a new policy for Y, which overturned his old one. This new policy surrendered some power from the NID and the Royal Navy, though still keeping its present Sigint assets at Bletchley and beyond self-contained, not surprisingly. Ultra was achieving its peak value against the U-boats, which the Admiralty (perhaps rightly) thought halved the loss of mercantile tonnage. Godfrey defined Churchill's order to 'make sure they have all they want on extreme priority' as granting GC&CS power over every department in Britain, particularly the services' Sigint agencies. 'Departmental barriers', emanating from mid-level civil and military officials ignorant of Ultra, had blocked Bletchley from receiving 'highest priority in personnel and material'. This 'very limited service' required 'absolute priority' over the labour and kit which were required to launch a massive expansion in Ultra, Y, and Sigint communications. Y must be tightly centralised, placed on an 'inter-service basis' and controlled by the COS collectively, not the services individually.[94] Supported by Churchill and the COS, these ambitious aims soon were achieved. No longer did difficulties with bricks and labour cripple Bletchley.

Menzies had careerist and professional reasons to change leadership at GC&CS. No director of intelligence supported Denniston. He had opposed the DMI too often. Godfrey thought him incompetent. By jettisoning Denniston, Godfrey and Menzies could find a scapegoat for the failings of the system they had created. During January–March 1942, Menzies and the military intelligence services forced a settlement on their common property, which achieved the optimum outcome. Two experienced intelligence and staff officers, Godfrey and van Cutsem, rewired Sigint. GC&CS and service Y were driven into closer cooperation and given greater resources. GC&CS was divided. Bletchley was militarised: civilian Siginters received power over service Sigint resources, while being absorbed as an autonomous unit into military decision-making. The service representatives left Hut 3. The diplomatic codebreakers, the only part of prewar British intelligence to avoid crisis, went to offices in Berkeley Street. Under Denniston, they had a good war, outmatching any other diplomatic Comint agency in the world. Under Travis, the rest remained at Bletchley, where they made a legend.

The Problem of the Trinity

Travis took command at Bletchley just as it approached maturity. Sigint was balanced; its base was so big that to solve one problem no longer created another equally large. The machine worked with increasing power and precision. Danger and experience drove the components of Sigint to cooperate and their masters to give them autonomy and attention. Travis pledged to meet the needs of the services, if they met his. All kept their word. Travis inherited certainty, resources, lessons and authority. He pursued effective aims, which increasingly were integrated, one step at a time, such as centralising control over wireless interception, developing the infrastructure that Bletchley needed to function and overseeing the integration and expansion of Ultra and Y. He created a chain of command, delegating authority to proven veterans, including managers of the machine sections and wireless interception. These men ceased being craftsmen and instead became managers of an industrial Comint system based on creativity in thought and discipline in power.

No other intelligence organisation on earth expanded and adapted like GC&CS between 1939 and 1945. GC&CS's weak administrative structure of 1939 hampered its evolution, but any firmer one would have impeded adaptation to a specific and complex problem on an intelligence and strategic niche. Whereas GC&CS was like a department within a school, Bletchley was a university and a factory. At its peak, Bletchley had 10,000 members – 76 per cent of them women – working in continuous eight-hour shifts, night and day. They processed information through batteries of machines in serried bays, beside the world's greatest concentration of research laboratories in information processing. Genius was freed. Training, self-criticism and improvement were institutionalised. Industrialisation and specialisation drove Bletchley. Bureaucratisation did not stop it. As Travis wrote in 1943, given 'the peculiarities of the work and the quicksands upon which it is founded … this apparently loosely knit organism has a resilience and strength which the muscle-bound can never achieve. A more formal machine could never adjust itself so readily to the ever-changing needs.'[95] This organism lived by a credo, what Travis called 'a brief statement of our aims and beliefs … we believe that we should try to read every enemy signal, neglecting none however apparently unimportant; we believe in the unholy trinity of Interception, Cryptography and Intelligence; we believe that communications have been the secret of the German success in this war and might be ours'.[96]

This informality and effect staggered American visitors to Bletchley. William Friedman, a leader within the US Signals Intelligence Service (US Army SIS), was 'much impressed with amount of checking and double checking enforced in Easy [Enigma] operations to ensure that absolutely nothing is overlooked and that every possible fragment which can be used as basis for crib is not passed up. Indeed my impression is that the science pursued at Park is not cryptanalysis but cribtology or cribtography, a field in which we can learn a great deal from them.' Moreover, 'these people have almost a mania for preventing intelligence from falling into watertight compartments'.[97]

These visitors reflected another development: a Sigint alliance. Between 1919 and 1939, British Siginters had two liaison relationships. With mutual reservations, GC&CS and Section D of the French army's Service des Renseignements discussed German and Soviet systems, while RAF Y and Estonia cooperated thoroughly on traffic analysis against Soviet systems. In 1939, GC&CS entered a thorough alliance with France and Poland against Germany. They cooperated as well as Anglo-American Sigint later did. When Poland and France fell, and their Siginters stayed silent, even in Auschwitz, Britain became the sole beneficiary of their work. Almost immediately, while the United States was still neutral, GC&CS and its two American counterparts, Op-20-G and the Signals Intelligence Service, cooperated against Germany and Japan. This cooperation intensified when the United States entered the war. Rivalry, as much between these American agencies as the two countries, marked this relationship, but it centred on thorough competitive cooperation. Britain and the United States pooled resources and formulated strategy through the Joint Chiefs of Staff machine. Sigint evolved within this framework. Britain was senior in this Sigint relationship, but American agencies fast became big and good. They were willing to learn, Britain to teach, both to cooperate, in everything from interception programmes to the development of cryptanalytical machines and techniques of cribbery. Ultra's triumph of 1944 exemplifies this integration. Solutions of messages from the Japanese ambassador and naval attaché in Berlin illuminated German strategy and defences, which shaped planning for the invasion of Normandy. British Y intercepted and Berkeley Street, using a reconstructed analogue of the 'Purple machine' provided by the US Signals Intelligence Service, broke Japanese traffic which reported Hitler's words. Britain and the United States, the only heavyweights in Sigint, flattened their opponents. Britain led Sigint in Europe, as the United States did against Japan, though each gave support in the other theatre. Sigint support ranked second only to the Indian Army as a British imperial contribution to Allied victory in the Asia–Pacific war; a significant one, though below the American contribution in Europe. Australian Sigint, under American control, almost equalled the power of Britain against Japan.

American Y units in the European theatre did not become efficient until late 1943, and few reached the highest levels of quality, but United States resources boosted interception, Y and Sigint communications. World-leading American radio equipment strengthened British Sigint. Anglo-American forces intercepted almost all Axis radio transmissions. American forces adopted SLUs and SCUs, and the Allies produced the cryptographic and wireless kit and personnel needed to make the system work across the world. Ultimately, forty SCUs served in Europe and the Middle East. During 1943–45, the US Navy Naval Computing Machine Laboratory (NCML), ultimately holding 121 of Desche's bombes, led the assault on U-boat systems, while Op-20-G matched the Naval Section in analysis of Comint. By 1945, the NCML may have equalled the brute force of Bletchley's bombes. British aid in cribbery multiplied the NCML's force, some 45 per cent of which, under Bletchley's guidance, was applied to targets beyond U-boats. That aid freed Bletchley Park to attack other targets, the core of its work during 1943–45. Their joint and integrated effort created Ultra's contribution to the Allied victory in Europe.

Despite the importance of Colossus and tabulators, British cryptanalytical power centred on bombe machines assaulting Enigma. Part of this power can be counted. In September 1941, Hut 6 (which

attacked all non-naval Enigma traffic) received 32,000 intercepts, rising
to 82,000 by November 1942. In December 1942, with 19,069 'bombe
hours', it broke 272 Enigma keys of the Luftwaffe, 106 of the Army, 32
of the SS and 29 of railways. On average, Luftwaffe Enigma keys were
broken in 28 bombe hours, SS in 41 and German Army in 94.[98] The
initial staff for the first bombe in March 1940 was 3; by May 1945, 263
men and 1,676 Wrens ran 210 bombes. The first bombe took a week to
finish one menu, or 336 wheel orders, against U-boat traffic; by 1944,
6 four-wheel machines completed one menu against four-rotor U-boat
systems (which multiplied wheel orders by 26, from 336 to 8736) in
24 minutes, on average. Bletchley Park's brute force in bombe power
per machine had risen about 1,456 per cent times, while the number
of machines went from 1 to 211. Unquantifiable (but more important)
improvements in cribbery multiplied this success:

Year	Number of Bombes	Jobs Done	Jobs Up
1940	2(as of 31.12.40)	180	178
1941	16(as of 31.12.41)	1344	844
1942	49(as of 31.12.42)	5772	3685
1943	99(as of 31.12.43)	14,965	9064
1944	192(as of 31.12.44)	15,302	8444
1940–45		36,004	20,414[99]

Here, the term 'Jobs Done' means attacks on specific Enigma keys, and
'Jobs Up' (a term coined by Travis after he witnessed the first victory) meant
'successful solutions'. These figures show that the crisis at Bletchley occurred
when it first handled a small expansion in personnel and output, whereas
it handily absorbed a tenfold rise in both matters during 1942–44. Bombes
slowly grew in number until 1942, after which production continually and
sharply rose. Successful attacks steadily increased between 1941 and 1944,
when a plateau emerged. Hut 3 received the greatest number of Enigma
Teile (messages) per day during late spring 1944 – 3,000, compared to 800
in 1940, while the great days of fishing were 1944–45.[100]

   Bletchley attacked hard and moving targets. Its success leads us to
underestimate the problem. German cryptography was good. It looks
bad only because Bletchley was brilliant. German cryptographers
steadily improved their defences, especially for U-boat Enigma in 1942
and generally during 1944–45. This strengthening partly explains why

in 1944, despite having twice as many bombes (and better ones) than in 1943, Bletchley Park broke fewer keys, which says nothing about the value of the intelligence produced. In spring 1942, six three-wheel bombes required seventeen days of work to break one day's key for four-rotor U-boat Enigma, guided by exceptional opportunities for cribbery. Though priorities became easier to achieve, heartburn never ceased. An ambitious set-piece assault, guided by reason, intuition and cryptanalytical generalship, alone enabled success. Welchman explained one version of this problem of the trinity in January 1943:

> the exploitation of 'E' [Enigma] traffic is a single and indivisible
> problem of increasing complexity. The G.A.F [German Air Force]
> keys are connected by key repeats, so that the breaking of any one
> of them may prove a valuable stepping-stone towards the breaking
> of others. All the Mediterranean Army keys have been connected
> by reencodement, and it has always been necessary to concentrate
> equally on all of them, because any one of them might prove to
> be the best starting point. The other Army keys also show signs of
> reencodements, though not on the same scale ... Further it is not even
> possible to regard Army and Air keys as two separate problems. The
> Mediterranean Army keys have often been broken by reencodements
> from Air keys ... Finally, a watch is continually kept on every scrap
> of 'E' traffic for carelessness in the form of cillies [easily guessed keys];
> any key may be suddenly and unexpectedly broken by this means, and
> an isolated break of this nature may well lead to further breaks of the
> same key or of other keys by cribs or reencodements.
>
> Thus the 'E' cryptographers in Hut 6 are faced with some sixty keys
> which are so linked together that they constitute one single problem ...
> As more keys are broken and as the cover on the broken keys improves,
> more cribs and possible reencodement routes are discovered, and
> consequently more sets are needed to exploit new chances of breaking.
> At the same time more frequencies are found to be passing traffic of
> high intelligence value and still more sets are required to cover them
> adequately. Thus greater success implies a greater number of sets.
>
> The whole object of Hut 6 is to provide intelligence, so the
> rival claims of two frequencies for interception or of two keys for
> bombe time must be decided ultimately by the relative intelligence
> values. But, since unbroken 'E' traffic is of no value, the needs

of the cryptographers must come first, and ... these needs are
extensive. For, apart from the fact that the breaking of any key
for intelligence purposes may depend on the breaking of other
keys which are not so important, the regular breaking of a key
of high intelligence value nearly always depends on months of
preparatory work. Further, owing to the unpredictable nature of
the whole problem, this preparatory work has often been done
without any definite knowledge of its coming importance. In
fact, in order to satisfy the needs of intelligence in the future, the
cryptographers must study and attempt to break every single key,
however unimportant it may appear to be at the time. Ideally
the cryptographers need complete cover on all traffic so that no
chances of breaking are missed, and as soon as cribs or regular
reencodement routes are discovered, they need additional cover
to ensure as far as possible that attempts at breaking do not fail
through one wrong letter in an intercepted text. This cryptographic
ideal is certainly not within sight, and strict economy has to
be exercised in the use of sets for purposes that are not directly
connected with the most important intelligence requirements. The
same applies also to the use of bombes.

    With such a large field to cover ... the identification of crib
messages, the discovery of reencodement routes, the planning of
an interception policy, the control of the sets, and the ability of the
intercept operators to pick up a required frequency quickly, demand
a sound knowledge of the German W/T networks. In fact, 'E'
cryptography cannot be separated from the study of W/T ...[101]

Britain finally had the resources and expertise needed to support
Ultra and conventional Y. Each aided the other. By 1942, the Y units
created in 1940–41 became large and efficient, increasingly excellent.
Intelligence authorities, GC&CS and the COS, considered how many
more of them Britain needed, compared to other requirements. The
COS made Y a top priority, from human and industrial resources fully
stretched for war. These units became useful during 1943 and first rate
by 1944. The leaders of Y knew their trade, trained personnel, organised
units well and developed powerful techniques. They and their American
counterparts met the expanding needs of armies and air forces against
Germany. Y was the second greatest source of Allied intelligence after

Ultra. Traffic analysis enabled Ultra. It unravelled Germany's order
of battle, guided operations and unleashed air attack on targets of
opportunity.

This trinity produced truth in mass. Information overload struck
the weakest part of Bletchley's system in 1941: the analysis of Comint.
However, Travis made a businessman turned temporary RAF officer,
Eric Jones, its head – a great choice. Despite their poor reputation in
theories of management, many British businessmen of this period were
able, decisive and good information processers. As a manager of Comint
analysis and analysts, Jones was an inspiring perfectionist who drove
and led his people. He emphasised rapid analysis and focused research,
giving consumers any information of conceivable value to them through
accurate and concise messages; and minimising errors, admitting those
which happened, and learning from them. He made his watchkeepers
Comint managers and editors, and every watch and section a team. His
staff of 581 at maximum – packed close in eight-hour shifts – fell equally
between data processors, educated women, and analysts, generally male
academics, especially students of history and literature. They were the
largest and strongest analytic unit in the world, scholars dedicated to
enabling a higher form of war. Compared to the WTID, Hut 3 was
almost twice the size, serviced every aspect of war against the enemy,
received more material, analysed a greater range of topics and processed
a greater number of fragments. As the Hut 3 history noted: 'it was often
upon the trivial or boring small items, when accumulated, that some
of the most important long-term pieces of intelligence were built up
… much of the red-hot tactical Intelligence could have been jettisoned
without irreparable harm, but the long-term things, nearly always less
spectacular, often individually very trivial, were yet indispensable, and
unique in the history of intelligence'.[102]

Hut 3 organised all intercepts on card indices for air and Army
matters, and several specialised ones, structured around the names of
individuals, formations, weapons and issues like morale, in alphabetical
order. Ultimately, the indices contained perhaps a million cards, cross-
referenced in microscopic detail to highlight connections. Sections
analysed issues such as cover names, railways and German Y. Jones and
his section chiefs built the contacts in Whitehall needed to learn Allied
strategy and plans and the wants and needs of consumers, reinforced
because intelligence appreciations referring to Ultra passed over SLU

channels, which Hut 3 received. Hut 3 advised Hut 6 on which keys provided the greatest intelligence and the best allocation of bombe time. The DMI and Air Intelligence applied this material to strategy and let Hut 3 decide what reports commanders abroad should receive. Commanders often received German messages just hours after the enemy did.

Acting on Intelligence

In 1941, British forces acted on Ultra in many ways. Fighter and Coastal Commands and headquarters in Egypt integrated Ultra and Y, but no others in the RAF. Eighth Army handled Ultra and Y well, but not the armies in Britain. Admirals used Y, Ultra and intelligence in manners ranging from admirable (in the Operational Intelligence Centre and Western Approaches Command) to infantile (Admiral Tom Phillips, commanding Force Z off Malaya on 9 December 1941, made little effort to collect intelligence and interpreted it himself, without consulting FECB). The JIC and strategic planners gained from Ultra, but intelligence and strategy were not well integrated. Between January 1942 and summer 1943, Ultra rose in prestige and power. Huts 6 and 8 (which attacked naval Enigma) and the NCML provided Comint in quantity. Hut 3 analysed Ultra, and SLUs and SCUs disseminated reports, in real time, enabling an elaborate machine to operate efficiently. Through education and experience, Commonwealth and American staffs and commanders learned to apply Sigint to actions ranging from instantaneous air strikes, to planning and conducting operations. Finally, they did so better than Germany. Under General Bernard Montgomery, the British Eighth Army combined good Sigint, planning, command and forces. American and British forces in Operation Torch failed that test in December 1942, but passed it in operations from mid-1943. The Royal Navy, the Royal Canadian Navy and the US Navy used Sigint effectively against German submarines and surface warships. Increasingly, all forms of intelligence aided the RAF and the USAAF, especially for strikes against ground targets, though not until 1944 did Sigint guide or aid their strategic bombing forces. Above all, intelligence and staff officers in London used Sigint to devise sound strategic plans.

Bletchley claimed proudly that Churchill once said: 'better lose a battle than lose the source'.[103] Contrary to myth, caution rarely impeded action. When using Ultra, commanders were told:

The two main principles to be observed are:-
 That it is never worth risking the source for a momentary tactical advantage, and,
 That steps must always be taken, when an endeavour is to be made to anticipate enemy action, to cover our fore-knowledge of events by aerial or other reconnaissance.[104]

Ultra rarely provided 'momentary' tactical advantages. At tactical levels, cover almost always could be simulated. Above them, action hardly ever could compromise Ultra. In only two major cases where the tactical and strategic spheres overlapped did Britain not act on Ultra so to save the source, with revealing and ironic consequences. In May–June 1941, acting on Ultra and seeking to aid it by seizing Enigma settings, the RN captured two German weather ships, but also coincidentally sank two other German warships. Authorities, fearing that these successes might compromise Ultra, became more cautious in using it to harvest intelligence, but not for battles. In 1943, British authorities initially refused to attack U-boat supply submarines, whereas the US Navy did. British admirals changed their tune when the American slaughter of German supply submarines, called *milch cows*, showed how mighty a fortress Germans thought their Enigma. Allied forces used Ultra so far as they were able. The problem was action, not limits on it.

Ralph Bennett, veteran and historian of Hut 3, wrote of many Ultras: its nature and value shifted by time and topic.[105] In 1940–41, both Ultra and Y were weak. Ultra played to its weak suit, tactical and operational intelligence, for forces largely on the defensive. Even so, strategic intelligence emerged – against the U-boats and Axis maritime logistics. From 1942, as the Anglo-American alliance assaulted enemies on the defensive, the new system of Sigint penetrated Germany in complementary ways: Fish, which produced material from the highest of levels by penetrating traffic on Lorenz teleprinters; Enigma, for strategic and operational intelligence; and Y, on tactical and operational issues.[106] Hut 3 correctly assessed: 'The Value of Ultra – accurately handled' for 1942–45:

Our role in Intelligence is strategic rather than tactical, and our value is therefore far higher in a pre-offensive planning period than during a battle. This does not mean that our tactical products are not valuable to our consumers and much appreciated by them: they are, since they confirm or deny intelligence from other sources and frequently fill in gaps. But whereas ours is outstandingly the best strategic source – it is, indeed, worth far more than all the others put together – it is only one of many tactical sources, and at that probably not the best of them, if only because it is inevitably less current than on-the-spot sources.[107]

Y, of course, was the best of these tactical sources.

Only by the summer of 1942 was Ultra ready to serve the offensive war the Allies must fight in Europe, right on time. The earlier failures mattered little as Britain could not have exploited success decisively. When Ultra became successful, the Commonwealth and the United States finally were ready to act on it. The question was, what power had the trinity in a world at war?

6

Ultra and the Second World War, 1939–45

GC&CS's most famous product is Ultra – high-grade Anglo-American Comint against Germany, Italy and Japan during the Second World War. This chapter analyses how GC&CS affected the war and British power and victory.[1] It challenges the common view of Ultra. Operations are often treated purely as a function of cryptology. The story is told uncritically, from the perspective of Allied sword against Axis shield, at Ultra's peak. Intelligence, however, shapes actions, but does not make them. It affects events in complex ways. The intelligence war was a competition involving Axis successes and Allied failures. Axis intelligence ranged from incompetent to good, but was mostly mediocre.[2] Allied services were poor to great, but mostly good. Initially, the states superior in intelligence and material misused these advantages. American, British and Soviet forces were often too poor to exploit the advantages provided by intelligence. Before 1942, intelligence worked marginally for the Axis by multiplying the value of their large and good forces. From 1942, the balance of intelligence and power turned simultaneously and systematically towards the Allies. The effect was one-sided for a long time. Intelligence did little to cause Axis defeat, but much to shape Allied victory.[3]

Ideology, perceptions, military rationality and open information drove decisions about strategy more than did secret intelligence. In operations, intelligence routinely served as force multiplier and tiebreaker. It supported firepower which, unlike in the First World War, could both kill and move, enabling decisive actions. Every source mattered, including prisoners, agents and one's troops, but the leading sources combined technology and organisation. During 1914–18, limits to aircraft and cameras made imagery and aerial reconnaissance sources of tactical intelligence. During 1939–45, they served operational and strategic intelligence: one aircraft provided 10,000 images from 1,000 miles away, in real time; a new source, radar, routinely acquired targets for strike warfare.[4] In the Second World War, Sigint– above all, Comint – was the best source, perhaps more than any other conflict in history. Sigint mattered most by reading operational communications, though traffic analysis and target acquisition in strike warfare also mattered. The states which first integrated the components of Sigint, combining traffic analysis with cryptanalysis against systems with low–, medium– and high-grade security and applied them to war, had an edge; so too, those nations which best handled the task.

The quality of intelligence services changed as they switched from power politics to war. Those of Italy, Japan and the USSR slipped because their strengths – such as stealing codebooks from embassies – worked better in peace than war. Three other powers surged as they acquired intelligence through technology. Germany led with imagery and air reconnaissance, though Britain and then the United States rapidly passed it; no other country was in the race. Regarding radar, Britain held the lead, pulling the United States to its level, which the latter soon exceeded, Germans hot on their heels, all others far behind. Sigint had more complex stories. Japanese navy (IJN) signals security was poor, that of the army (IJA) good. Both were weak in Sigint. Soviets were poor on defence and attack, Italians decent. American military forces were mediocre in signals intelligence and security, though the US Navy used data-processing machines well against IJN cryptosystems, while their army counterparts broke sophisticated Japanese code machines. Britain initially was weak in signals and security, but improved rapidly. During 1939, Germany led the powers in signals and security. Its military treated radio as a normal means to communicate, used flexibly and securely through the Enigma machine – a good system which Germany handled badly.[5] They gathered Sigint from enemy radio nets, though on easy cryptosystems and away from hard ones. These characteristics caused failure after 1941; until then, Germany won the wireless war.

Axis Swords, British Shield

Britain's shield failed its signals. When war began, Britain's system for overseeing military cryptography collapsed. GC&CS could not monitor the matter, guide improvements, or produce effective cryptosystems. All lessons were learned by individual organisations through experience, at cost. Not until 1942 did GC&CS and consumers effectively cooperate over Comsec, though then they quickly led the world. Initially, Whitehall assumed that strategic communications would move on British cables, secure from interception and cryptanalysis, while radio carried little traffic. These cryptographic calculations collapsed in 1940–41. The capacity of British cables to Asia fell when Italy cut those in the Mediterranean; when Japan wrecked them in the Pacific, it rested on one cable around South Africa, 'rather wonky ... and not to be relied on'.[6] By 1942, just the transatlantic components of Britain's cable network survived. Meanwhile, the needs for strategic communications exploded. Britain could meet them only by expanding, and hastily, its radio services. In May 1941, the Army's teleprinter section in Cairo transmitted 20,000–25,000 groups per day, 400 per cent more than nine months before. By November 1942, it carried 62,000 groups per day, sustaining adequate liaison for 'practically all' traffic. In 1927 the services assumed that during war they would send 110,000 cypher groups by all means, mostly cable, to and from Britain each day. Between 1943 and 1945, the wireless stations in the Air Ministry and the War Office each handled ten times this load, 1.11 million groups per day.[7]

This enhanced volume of traffic solved communications problems but magnified cryptographic ones. Typex was forged late in the day. Britain had no cypher machines suitable for field service and ready for production until 1938, or widely distributed before 1941. It relied on one high-grade system – superenciphered codes – which Axis experts broke. In 1940, the nadir of modern British cryptology, GC&CS discovered that many British superenciphered systems were compromised, and feared (erroneously) that the same was true with Typex, since the Germans had captured a machine (without its rotors) at Dunkirk. Whitehall recognised its cryptographic peril and buttressed that shield. It multiplied its orders for Typex machines and bolstered their internal security. Until mid-1942, however, Typex could defend Britain's central communications, but not all of its important ones. Given the ratio between the increase in radio traffic and cypher machines, Typex covered only the same proportion of traffic as in 1940 – the quantity of important traffic which it could not defend rose, most notably in the Mediterranean and Middle East. Whitehall lacked the high-grade facilities needed even for the crucial link between London and its embassy in Washington.[8] By 1941 Britain had brought one-time pads into service, providing absolute security for a few messages. German codebreakers could not break the superencipherment of Tiltman's 'stencil subtractor frame' without having a copy of the codebook being protected.

Problems of testing, of production, of distribution across seas haunted by U-boats, all delayed the introduction of these new systems. The SS Frame, while ready for trial by April 1941, was not adopted until March 1942, nor applied until June 1943.[9] By spring 1941, Britain understood how to repair the cryptographic errors of a generation. Time was needed to do so. Until then, communication to and between British commands in the Middle East and south Asia was the most exposed of any strategic traffic on earth.

Superenciphered codebooks carried far more intercommand traffic than they had in 1940, including communications to and from Army headquarters in Abysinnia, Crete and Greece; non-operational traffic between all commands in the Middle East (and sometimes between Cairo and London); and all signals between higher formations before and during operations. These systems were improved, but their security hung on a knife edge. In 1940, the RAF's main codebook, five years old, had only two universal sets of keys, which were used by every unit and formation in the world. Tables changed once every three months; by 1941, authorities concluded that security required such changes every two days. During May 1941 on Crete, the enemy captured a 'complete set of S.(ignal) and C.(ipher) Publications' – including copies of all save a few RAF keys. In 1941, Britain could defend the security of its current level of radio communications only through the use of superencipherment systems which were cryptanalytically vulnerable – by codebooks often known to be in the enemy's hands. The War Office could not replace its main codebook, 'W', until fourteen months after the enemy was known to be reading it. The integrity of these systems cracked.[10] New systems must be distributed to overseas commands, slowing the ability to use them and risking physical compromise. The German seizure of Royal Navy codebooks carried on SS *Automedon*,

The earliest known end-product reports from British Sigint, from interception work done at Simla station in the Himalayan foothills of northern India in 1907.

The famous 'Room 40 Charter', initialled by Winston Churchill as First Lord of the Admiralty in November 1914. This is as close to a founding document as modern British Sigint has.

In the charter, Sir Alfred Ewing, Director of Naval Education and an enthusiast for radio and codes, was asked to create a naval codebreaking bureau 'to penetrate the German mind and movements'. This became Room 40, which he led from 1914 to 1916.

Brigadier-General Francis Anderson, an experienced army codebreaker, was also chair of the Army Sanitary Committee – a dual role that puzzled his French cryptanalytic counterparts but reflected his background in military engineering works. He set up the first War Office cryptanalytic bureau in August 1914, leading it until 1916.

In October 1914, the Royal Navy's nascent Sigint operation in Room 40 of the Admiralty received a boost when Russian authorities passed it a copy of the main German naval code book, captured from the German cruiser the *Magdeburg*, which ran aground in the Baltic in August.

The Director of Naval Intelligence in the First World War, William Reginald 'Blinker' Hall, and a caricature of Hall greeting his staff in the Intelligence Office, by G P Mackeson of Room 40. It was Hall who, recognising the significance of the 1917 Zimmermann telegram, concocted the ploy to approach the Americans, leading to their entry into the war on the Allied side.

The first aerial bombing raids on Britain were carried out in 1915 by German airships, such as this Zeppelin pictured flying over a German dreadnought battleship. British Sigint stations could intercept coded radio transmissions made by the airships, tracking their location and enabling advance warning to be given to defence forces. Pictured is a decrypt of one such airship (L9) signal, handwritten by the duty cryptanalyst Alastair Denniston, and a remarkable chart showing the tracking and defence system at work over the North Sea in 1916 – in some regards, a prototype for the famous Fighter Command defence system of 1940.

An example of the vital 'Interpreter Operator' role of the First World War, Vince Schürhoff was fluent in German through his Westphalian father, also spoke French and Spanish, and spent 1916–18 in the frontline IToc stations as a Royal Engineer (Signal Service), listening to German field telephone conversations. He won the Military Medal in 1918.

Major Malcolm Vivian Hay replaced Anderson as head of the War Office's Sigint bureau MI1(b) in late 1916. Like other military men who entered intelligence, he had been wounded in action, in his case during the retreat from Mons in 1914.

A 1918 front line map overprinted with German communications networks. Updated weekly, these graphics gave customers an easily understood summary of German dispositions and command structures.

A leading cryptanalyst in Room 40, Alastair Denniston was the successful candidate to head the new Government Code and Cypher School (GC&CS), which was formed under Admiralty control on 1 November 1919. He would remain a key figure in British Sigint until the end of the Second World War. In 1908 he won a medal playing hockey for Scotland at the Olympic Games.

William Green Swanborough – 'Swannie', seen here in the rank of Flight Lieutenant in 1937 – was instrumental in the establishment of RAF 'Y' Service wireless intercept between 1924 and 1945. Before that he spent time as an Army intercept operator in Afghanistan and superintendent of Port Sudan wireless station.

A wireless interception set in Kabul, Afghanistan, in 1921.

A rare image of running repairs to aerials in Kabul.

— TIRED OF IT —

РУССКИЙ
УНИВЕРСАЛЬНЫЙ
ТЕЛЕГРАФНЫЙ
КОД.

ИЗДАНИЕ
Редакционно-Издательской Междуведомственной
Комиссии.
Сбор объявлений произвела „Двигатель".

The All-Russian Co-Operative Society (ARCOS) was the body responsible for the orchestration of Anglo-Soviet trade in the early days of Communist Russia. In 1927, its London offices were raided, the British government accusing the USSR of using the organisation as a front for espionage and subversion. Diplomatic and trade relations were suspended as a result, as pictured in this contemporary sketch by Charles Sykes. This Russian telegraphic code book is believed to have been captured during the raid and sent to GC&CS.

The iconic Bletchley Park, wartime home of GC&CS.

Skating on the frozen pond at Bletchley Park.

Alan Turing was recruited to Bletchley Park and put to work on German naval Enigma. At Bletchley he devised the bombe – an electromechanical device to recover Enigma settings – and worked on secure speech systems. Later he would be instrumental in developing theories of computing.

A German army Enigma machine in action. Standing over his cipher operators in the back of a Sonderkraftfahrzeug 251 half-track is the famous German general Heinz Guderian, on the offensive in France, May 1940. Enigma was generally used to protect operational-level comms.

Sir Edward 'Jumbo' Travis, originally a paymaster officer in the Royal Navy, became one of the giants of British Sigint, leading GC&CS from 1942 to 1946, and then as Director GCHQ until 1952. His abilities took GC&CS into an age of industralised Sigint necessary to overcome the challenge posed by complex Axis cryptography and the demands of the fighting services for intelligence.

The ciphering branch of the Foreign Office Communications Department, hard at work in the famous Locarno Suite in 1941.

Bombe machines were manufactured by the British Tabulating Machine Company at Letchworth in Hertfordshire. These are bombes in the process of assembly on the factory floor.

The 'Morrison Wall': a graphic representation of traffic flow on German target networks.

Sturgeon, the British codename for a type of enciphered teleprinter traffic generated by the Siemens Geheimschreiber machine during the Second World War. Very large, very secure and very complex, it was one type of teleprinter traffic intercepted by the Allies under the codename FISH.

and passed to Japan, gave edges to Axis navies.[11] Given the scale of compromises and the enemy's use of mechanised procedures for cryptanalysis, older superenciphered codebooks – the systems most frequently used for important traffic – were frighteningly vulnerable. The results were worst in Britain's two most active theatres against the European Axis powers: in the Mediterranean, and in the war at sea.

By 1938, the German naval cryptanalysts of the B-Dienst, or 'Observation Service', had solved most of the Auxiliary Code, which covered traffic by minor warships, and one of the Royal Navy's two main code systems, the four-year-old and five-figure Administrative Code, which was used for the movement and deployments of warships in European waters. This success taught B-Dienst how to attack the long subtractor superencipherment system as a whole. This success stemmed from poor security: the Royal Navy used the Administrative Code plain, for non-confidential messages, but superenciphered it for confidential ones on tables changed only once every four to six months. (The Administrative Code and Naval Cypher each had four universal sets of tables, for different hierarchies, and one for China gunboats.) Copies of both systems were captured during the Norwegian campaign; the Royal Navy abandoned them on 20 August 1940.

B-Dienst solved the first version of the replacement for the Administrative Code within two months of introduction and read it currently for half its period of use. B-Dienst also mastered the second version, introduced in June 1942, and found the third a tougher but still profitable target. From December 1943, when stencil subtractors were added to the system, German success vanished. More seriously, by 1938, B-Dienst had broken the five-year-old four-figure Naval Cypher and its long subtractor system. It maintained access from September 1941 to June 1943, despite changes in the book during August 1940 and October 1941. B-Dienst read between 30 and 50 per cent of traffic – including all of the important material in the Norwegian campaign – and sometimes up to 80 per cent of traffic (though only in the less important 'Captain's Tables', never the 'Admiral's Tables'). When added to German penetration of codes used by the mercantile marine, the successors to the Auxiliary Code, this intelligence especially aided the U-boat campaign.[12] During the war at sea between 1939 and 1942, Germany gained as much from cryptanalysis as Britain did.

Meanwhile, from spring 1941 until November 1942, with increasing difficulty, German cryptanalysts read superenciphered traffic on a four-figure RAF codebook used in the Mediterranean area, with an average time lag of two to four weeks. They broke one superenciphered Army codebook (a variant of 'W') used between Whitehall and Egypt between 'at least' August 1941 and January 1942, and infrequently thereafter, sometimes solving messages with a time lag of one week. These successes, and those against the local version of the 'Interdepartmental Cypher', did not violate operational or strategic planning, but did reveal the RAF and Army's order of battle in the Mediterranean theatre. German operations profited from its success against Royal Navy systems, against American military attaché traffic from Cairo and plain-language transmissions of the British Army. Italian cryptanalysts matched German success against the Eighth Army. They had fair success against the same RAF four-figure codebook as the Germans and middle-level naval systems, especially when both books and superenciphering tables were old. The latter occasionally provided useful intelligence during operations or forewarning that a convoy would enter the Mediterranean, or a submarine sail, but never compromised intentions.[13] Nonetheless, the Axis gained as much from signals intelligence in the Mediterranean theatre as Britain did until May 1942.

As often in the history of cryptology, however, God chose to be an Englishman. Precisely as Germany shattered this old cryptographic shield, a new one emerged. After June 1941, the superencipherment systems of the Army and the RAF were increasingly relegated to non-operational traffic (mostly administrative) and to subordinate headquarters and higher formations. This process was complete by the start of 1942, containing German cryptanalysts at the middle of the cryptographic pyramid and steadily pressing them down. Even in 1941, Typex and OTP, systems which the enemy never penetrated, carried all important traffic on intercommand links: by mid-1942 they covered all of that within the Mediterranean and Middle Eastern theatres. From summer 1941, British forces in the Middle East improved all cryptosystems, especially superenciphered codes. A centre produced books and tables for local formations. By June 1942, the RAF always had two high-grade books in use at any time with four separate 'series of tables', each table changed several times per month. Such steps restored integrity even to Britain's superencipherment systems – the Germans lost access to the codebooks from the Middle East which they had exploited in 1941, and to naval traffic in 1943. Thereafter, they broke into only one other such system, the variant of Cypher 'W' used by Home Forces in Britain.[14] Parallel improvements occurred in American cryptosystems, which in 1940 were worse than British ones, but equal by 1944. In 1938, GC&CS gave its consumers 286 codebooks and tables: it issued 78,000 in 1943.[15] The low-grade systems of the Western Allies, however, remained vulnerable, with operational significance. In 1944, traffic control communications during advances, which revealed the location of formations advancing behind the front, were transmitted on low-grade codes which Germany read easily. For such reasons, German intelligence officers in Italy told Allied interrogators that before battles Sigint produced little intelligence, but 70 per cent of it during engagements.[16] This differential reflects the poverty of German cryptanalysis.

After 1942, redundancy in British cryptography crippled German cryptanalysts everywhere they turned: OTP, several kinds of Typex machines, rotors routinely upgraded, different circuits using unique and frequently changed settings and dozens of superenciphered codebooks with tables changed at blinding speed. By 1940, British cryptography and communications confronted deadly dangers; by 1942 they smashed them, their triumph parallel and complementary to that of Bletchley Park. This position was redeemed only by the presiding graces of modern British cryptology: luck, skill and a willingness to accept the possibility that its cyphers might have been compromised. This success also stemmed from the earlier failures – the delay in Typex's development. Between mid-1940 and the spring of 1941, few Typex machines were distributed, precisely as the GC&CS began to break Enigma and learn the technical weaknesses in Germany's use of the system. Radical modifications still could easily be incorporated even in the Typex machines which already were out, whereas when Germany began to appreciate the problems with Enigma, so many were in service that a systematic solution was hard to apply. That Britain applied its lessons from the attack to the defence is an unsung story from the wireless war. In cryptology as in war, that side wins which makes fewest mistakes. Between 1939 and 1941, Germany, Italy and Britain raced to make the most. German and Italian codebreakers won. The astonishing thing is how poorly Axis cryptanalysts exploited their opportunities.

The British cryptographic record defines the level of incompetence of Axis cryptanalysis.

The Turning Point

In 1939–41, Axis intelligence stood at its peak – a high one. German air and army intelligence supported blitzkrieg by providing easily acquirable intelligence for immediate airstrike or attack. Assisted by security and deception which masked intentions, they outweighed Britain and France in 1940 in all areas ranging from collection to assessment, and Russia during 1941–42.[17] Germany and Italy matched British intelligence in the desert war. Erwin Rommel's great days as a general coincided precisely with those of his Comint. When it declined, so did he, and other German generals. Axis commanders relied as heavily on intelligence as Allied ones – they just realised the fact, and nurtured the source, much less. In mobile operations, the interception of radio messages in plain-language or low-grade systems multiplied German success against Britons until 1942, Americans in 1943, and Soviets before 1944. Probably, Sigint affected no aspect of the war more than German operations against the Soviet Union.[18] German naval agencies matched their Allied competitors until 1943, as its air ones did until 1944. Above all, in 1941, deception, intelligence and security helped Germany and Japan to start wars with surprise attacks against the USSR, Britain and the United States, though the main problem was intelligence failure by defenders, rather than success by attackers.[19] Each strike matched the effect of Ultra in Europe, or the Pacific. The Axis destroyed, at low cost, 50 per cent of the soldiers and 90 per cent of the tanks and aircraft which the USSR fielded in 1941, and 20 per cent of the warship tonnage of Britain and the United States. These strikes gave Germany and Japan valuable resources, the initiative for a year and boosted their slim chances for victory, though they made greater intelligence failures in 1941 than their enemies.

In 1939–41, intelligence was a low secondary strength for the Axis. From 1942, it became a high secondary strength for the Western Allies. Measurement of the effect entails adding Allied rise to Axis decline. Britain and the United States organised Sigint and imagery with unprecedented effect, enabling power in the collection and assessment of evidence, and the rapid and secure distribution of material to commanders. Typex and its American counterpart, Sigaba, remained unbroken. The United States, Britain and the Commonwealth applied more brains and resources to intelligence than the Axis, because they had more of them, and greater respect for its value. British and American Sigint services expanded by 3,000 per cent in numbers between 1939 and 1945 and pursued new forms of organisation and technique; Italian and Japanese stagnated, and German services were good, but faced excellent enemies. In 1940, German Sigint personnel outnumbered British, though the tide turned fast. At its peak, 30,000 Germans worked in signals intelligence, more than in every such organisation on earth during 1918. The British and Americans had 35,000 each, with far better cryptanalysts and mathematicians and perhaps a hundred times the power of Germany in data-processing machines applied to cryptanalysis. Until 1942, B-Dienst, the best German cryptanalytical agency, did not own any data-processing machines and could only borrow time on them from other bureaus. Only then did it form a Hollerith section, much smaller than that at Bletchley, though used well. Other German codebreaking agencies which had Hollerith machines used them to attack low-grade Western systems, which sought to preserve the secrecy of traffic only for twenty-four hours.[20] Ultra attacked the hardest shells, because they shielded the richest meat.

Ultra and Its Enemies

In intelligence, the Western Allies multiplied each other's strengths. German and Axis agencies divided them. They competed not only against the enemy, but each other. They could not transfer best practices, nor pool their power, acquire the resources their rivals did, or understand the need to do so. They failed to exploit the weaknesses in British cryptography during 1941, and then slid behind all their enemies. Only the weakest Axis powers – the non-fascist ones, Hungary and Finland – cooperated in intelligence like Britain, the United States, Canada and Australia did.[21] The Western Allies' cooperation in intelligence was imperfect, but better than anything ever known before.[22] They worked to expand the common pool, honed by cooperative competition in the pursuit of common tasks. British services worked better with American ones than German agencies (or for that matter, the US Army and Navy) did with each other. Cooperation with the USSR was low, simply because the Soviet Union rejected Western overtures for a large and equal trade.[23] Successes by American and Commonwealth intelligence aided the actions of all their national forces. The Western Allies developed unprecedented power in strategic sources of intelligence, where the Germans were poor. German imagery never provided strategic intelligence against the Western Allies. Its coverage of the USSR never passed the Urals and collapsed in 1943. German spies against Britain, the USSR and the United States were controlled by its enemies. The payoff was most particular in Sigint. The Germans failed to attack high-grade American or British cryptographic machines because the task was hard, resources scarce, and only massive and centralised cryptanalysis could break them. This, the divided German system could not provide. One German cryptanalyst called a unified system 'a monster organisation'. Britons named it Bletchley.[24]

Nor did superiority with intelligence end at collection. For every belligerent, strategic assessments and decisions were made by rational bureaucracy joined to charismatic leadership. British and American leaders made errors in such areas, especially regarding Japan in 1941. At worst, they were as bad as anyone, but better on average and unmatched at best. Churchill always read Ultra optimistically, which drove both his strategy and his demands that commanders act aggressively. Intelligence often spurred him towards odd proposals. These problems were mitigated because he had unique experience with the use of Comint, including against dangerous foes in wartime; his military advisors were tough and smart, while great collection provided good evidence which was analysed well. Churchill had strong opinions, but could change them. Few of his bad ideas were executed, and Ultra drove perhaps only one mistaken engagement – the Battleaxe operation of June 1941. Though impelled by Ultra, Churchill's sacking of two Army commanders in the Middle East, Archibald Wavell and Claude Auchinleck, was justifiable in terms of military performance. The dynamic relationship between Churchill, commanders and Ultra, generally drove and guided the machine well. By making Ultra an arbitrator of truth, Churchill let his subordinatess counter by referring to evidence and reason. Anyone with a better case countered him, with few hard feelings. He made his subordinates consider intelligence and used Ultra to spur action. He was harnessed to an open and highest common denominator system of strategic decision-making.[25]

Here, Britain outclassed all other belligerents because it was the only one to exploit the experiences of the Great War. Working through cooperative competition, rational bureaucracies combined the best of British and American approaches. In Europe, Britain handled the collection and analysis of intelligence and its use in planning, and both states drove strategy and action. The Anglo-American alliance took a lead in assessing comparative power and advantage, correlated strategy and operations, and intelligence with actions – with the USSR far behind, followed by Italy and Germany, with Japan lagging. The most powerful of states formulated and executed strategy in the most rational of fashions and used intelligence best. Weaker ones did so less well, increasing the rate of their rout. Anglo-American strategists treated intelligence as essential to action: they emphasised the source best suited to provide these gains – Sigint – and accepted the need for specialised assessment and a rational process of decision-making; good consumers even of mediocre material, their fare was often excellent. Anglo-American operational commanders varied in quality, but across the board used intelligence as well and gained more from it than did those of any other nationality.[26]

Stalin and Hitler used intelligence in ways poorly suited to war. Neither wished to hear contrary analyses from subordinates, merely echoes of their own minds. Both wanted intelligence to provide just facts, which they filtered through ideology, preconception and the belief that their will created reality. Stalin and Hitler, overconfident micromanagers, were mediocre consumers of good intelligence, let alone the mixed bag which they received. They dominated intelligence analysis and strategic decisions in their states, crippling the capabilities of their subordinates. Within Germany, collection and assessment were divided between institutions which cooperated poorly. An idiosyncratic mode of military logic drove Hitler's decisions. He cared little about intelligence. Hitler rarely mentioned Sigint as a source for his decisions, despite the quality of the material available to him, though he often discussed human sources. He saw as much Comint each day as Churchill did, but it was inferior in quality – more about diplomacy than strategy.[27] When Hitler received material to match Ultra, he never praised the product or strengthened the producers. Hitler used Comint effectively when it was self-evident, addressing immediate concerns; he could judge its accuracy himself, as by pre-empting the Allied incursion into Norway of 1940 – one of the greatest actions impelled by intelligence during this war, though also reflecting many open signs of Allied intentions, and the only one involving the Führer. When he used intelligence after 1941, however, the sources mostly were weak and controlled by Germany's foes.[28]

Hitler's generals and admirals were better consumers of intelligence, many of them good. The Führer precluded intelligence from aiding theatre-level strategy, or producing illumination through deduction drawn from fragments – the areas where Ultra most aided his enemies. He also capped its value in operations. Intelligence was useful only where Hitler's lieutenants had autonomy – that is, in operations; here it reinforced their greatest area of superiority – in mobile warfare. Such autonomy was common before 1943. Intelligence aided planning for the campaign in France during 1940 and the first phase of campaigns against the Soviet Union in the summers of 1941 and 1942. When possessing the initiative in operations, German fighting services used intelligence effectively but less so when on the defensive, especially regarding strategic matters. Nor did Germany emphasise the improvement of intelligence, even when its quality was eroding. It expected little, and increasingly got it. It underestimated the power of Comint and overestimated that of spies. The more desperate the situation, the more Germany trusted agents controlled by enemies or forged by intelligence entrepreneurs. German intelligence became a delivery system for disinformation to its leaders. Anglo-American leaders used intelligence better than those in other states, but their superiority was insistence on the best.

The sequence of British success against German services using Enigma was broadly similar, although the dates at which success began varied. First came a period of limited and often fragmentary access to Enigma keys, coupled with major problems in assessing such material; then a cryptanalytical breakthrough, producing high-level material continually and currently. Finally came a long period of mature exploitation, when analysts determined the main lines of the enemy's organisation, drew powerful conclusions about its operational intentions and capabilities, and mastered such fundamental matters as the enemy's order of battle. Ultra was the greatest source of intelligence during this war, but it was never perfect. It took words straight from the enemy's mouth, but rarely were they straightforward. Its value differed with time and theatre. Ultra became more successful and useful over time, but its history was replete with reversals of fortune. The Allies never read every important enemy message, or even most of them. Ultra was not the best source on everything, nor were technical achievements in cryptanalysis and battlefield success linked in a simple way. During the desert campaign, Ultra could have been most useful when it was technically primitive rather than mature, because of the conditions which governed operations.

When Ultra was primitive, force-to-space ratios were low, as were both sides' strengths; hence, victories with decisive consequences were possible. Intelligence helped Rommel to achieve some of them. Once Ultra became mature from 1942, large and good armies were locked in prolonged and high-intensity struggles of attrition on narrow fronts, as during the First World War, though more fluid. Even so, intelligence budged the balance of attrition towards the Allies. The quality of Allied intelligence, and its superiority over the Axis, provided much certainty to Anglo-American assessment and planning and let them use their forces with remarkable precision against an enemy which increasingly was ignorant, uncertain and outgunned. When they held the initiative, the weaknesses in Axis intelligence were irrelevant and their strengths in tactical collection counted. On the defensive, their strengths became irrelevant and their weaknesses a danger. As Nazi power declined, Germany's chances for success hinged on deploying elite forces to sectors the enemy would attack, where, with their weaker brethren, they might stop breakthrough and force foes into costly and one-sided battles of attrition towards strategic stalemate. This aim required Germany to guess where and when the enemy would attack. It did not do so. Instead, from autumn 1942, Germany suffered a steady run of operational and strategic surprise at the hands of the Western Allies, and to a lesser extent the Soviets. German intelligence failed precisely when Nazi strategy most needed it to succeed; though, given the material odds, Germany might have lost even had it possessed an Ultra and the Allies had not.

Sigint and Strike Warfare

Target acquisition for strike warfare involves attack by weapons upon objects that their users cannot see, guided by C3ISR systems which locate targets and guide fire. These technical and tactical matters drive power and strategy. In 1917, British Sigint constantly located U-boats, prompting air or surface strikes which failed because units were slow and their ordnance weak. By 1943, intelligence on U-boats was little better but Allied forces more deadly. In 1944, air forces could hit any reported target more or less immediately, but not accurately; in 2003, during the Iraq war, aircraft launched instant, precise and devastating strikes based on information acquired ten minutes earlier by headquarters 10,000 miles away. When strike warfare first emerged, between 1914 and 1918, command, control, communications and intelligence was stronger than the weapons it supported: artillery, with limited range, accuracy and power, attacking the hardest targets in the world – trenches and turrets – in exchanges against enemies with equal capabilities. In strategic terms, this outcome was indecisive: it simply sharpened the process of attrition by both sides at once.

Twenty years on, this process caused revolutions in operations, as able strike forces and their first masters, such as Air Chief Marshal Hugh Dowding and Admiral Karl Dönitz, exploited the opportunities enabled by C3I, guided by fusions of Comint, Elint (intelligence derived from electronic emissions), traffic analysis, radar, artillery intelligence and imagery. Several of these new partners overcame the problems with tactical intelligence which had dogged Sigint at sea during the First World War. For example, Ultra revealed the last major German effort to block the Murmansk convoys at the battle of the North Cape on 26 December 1943, and guided the Royal Navy's deployments; shipborne radar tracked the battleship *Scharnhorst* and, with the help of star shells, enabled its destruction.[29] Tactical and technological developments, manifested strike by strike, transformed the role of intelligence and air power for war, first aiding the Luftwaffe and then American and Commonwealth forces.[30] Collectively, they transformed tactical combat at air and sea, and thus air power and sea power. Sometimes, intelligence became target acquisition, and operations, strike warfare. Key forms of Sigint performed like artillery intelligence, defining targets for aircraft to attack. Aircraft delivered distant and one-sided blows of unprecedented weight and precision, reshaping the power of armies or navies and the ways in which they struck. These processes were fundamental to how American and Commonwealth forces fought and to how Sigint shaped the war.

Anglo-American armies relied on strike by aircraft and guns, the quick and massive application of firepower, close support against soldiers and the interdiction of soft and distant targets central to enemy power such as units on the move, logistics, communications and transport. Aircraft matched armour, artillery or infantry, as arms in land warfare.[31] This, the single greatest area of Anglo-American superiority over the German army, forced it to fight as the Allies wished, rather than as the Germans did. At sea, the effect was revolutionary. Aircraft, based on ships and shore, became first-rate naval forces, gradually superseding guns and armour. To strike first might win a battle and ambush or counter-ambush decide a campaign. Comint, backed by radar and traffic analysis working through radio, aircraft, aircraft carriers and submarines, created new forms of maritime war, centred on distant and precise attack against soft targets, thin hulls or decks rather than armoured turrets.[32] During 1942–43, centimetric radar and high-frequency direction finding (HFDF) overcame the greatest Allied naval weaknesses by breaking the superiority in night fighting which underpinned IJN operations and U-boat attacks on convoys.

Intelligence transformed strategic air war in an asymmetric fashion. The bomber could get through only at cost. Traffic analysis and radar gave strategic air defence forewarning of assault and guided concentrations of force against all attackers, which fought blind. This power was first deployed by Dowding in the battle of Britain, to orchestrate an optimal campaign of ambushes where defenders smashed larger numbers of attackers, enabling Britain to check German strategy. Over the skies of Germany, fighters contained bombers attacking at day and night in a cost-effective fashion, until overwhelmed by interceptors.[33] German intelligence, especially Sigint for strategic air defence, was excellent. That battle also involved the first mature struggle of Elint and electronic warfare, where Britain suffered its worst intelligence defeat of the war. British bombers used an airborne radar system, H2S, to determine their position over Germany. German fighters homed in on H2S, destroying 1,000 Lancaster bombers during 1943–45, their task eased by the reluctance of British authorities to believe such detection was possible.

Intelligence for strategic air offensives was harder to gather, and successful in only one case. Anglo-American air forces integrated all forms of intelligence, especially imagery and Ultra, into command and bomb damage assessment. By monitoring the impact of raids, the campaign and the enemy's economy, intelligence boosted the effect and efficiency of complex operations, and the destruction of German forces and resources, moving the ratio of costs in strategic air warfare towards the attacker's favour during 1944–45.[34] Given the huge resources which the Western Allies allocated to strategic air warfare, intelligence on it affected the war as much as that for Anglo-American armies. In technical terms, British intelligence was slightly better than German in the area. Yet strategic air defence was the greatest success for German intelligence against Britain, and in the latter's central offensive effort, because power tilted so heavily against the attacker that intelligence could not redress the balance, only force. This one German success in intelligence countered Allied triumphs in many other fields.

Sigint at Sea, 1940–43

The nearest-run intelligence competition of the war was fought on the Atlantic and Arctic oceans and the Mediterranean and North seas. These operations centred on raids, ambushes and counter-ambushes by warships, submarines and aircraft. Britain was more exposed to attack than its enemies and on the defensive – though the empire struck back on the Norwegian coast and the central Mediterranean.[35] For Britain, Germany and Italy, Comint and traffic analysis were the main sources, aided by aircraft reconnaissance, imagery, the Norwegian resistance, HFDF and radar. All three navies had good intelligence. None understood how good its enemies were until the battle was over – their sources worked without wrecking each other. Intelligence aided both sides simultaneously in a one-sided struggle between navies. The Royal Navy outweighed its Italian and German enemies in strength, and also received American and Canadian aid. Intelligence was a tiebreaker in individual engagements, but across the board it aided both sides equally, which most helped the stronger navy. Squadrons, not fleets, dominated operations. Many ambushes failed. Chance shaped engagements. The balance of intelligence shifted constantly, no one having a prolonged advantage until 1943. Each side launched ambushes or counter-ambushes, with individually indecisive results, which cumulatively damaged all three navies and improved Britain's relative position. Even at the nadir of the Royal Navy's strength in January 1942, it remained far stronger than the German and Italian navies, whose surface fleets were listing. The entry cost to victory was high. Britain could take it. Rarely since 1690 has the Royal Navy wrecked its enemies so thoroughly and rapidly as in European waters between 1939 and 1943.

Every British victory at sea stemmed to some degree from intelligence, sometimes because of fluke, as with the sinking of the battleship *Bismarck* in 1941, but mostly through system.[36] In March 1941, Bletchley gave the Royal Navy little more help at the battle of Cape Matapan than Room 40 did at Jutland, yet improved naval technology and luck enabled better results. Scattered reports from Luftwaffe Enigma and, in its major success at sea, from the women of Knox's Enigma group – a Regia Marina message stating 'Today is D-3' – suggested that on 28 March 1941 Italian warships would attack British convoys south of Crete. The NID assessed this complex evidence well, though the commander of the Mediterranean Fleet, Admiral Andrew Cunningham, bet 'ten shillings that we would see nothing of the enemy'.[37] Sigint offered nothing else on the battle; without its aid, however, ambush would have been impossible and a convoy perhaps lost just before Germans attacked Allied forces in Greece. Aircraft and radar overcame Britain's bane in tactical intelligence at Jutland, by guiding the Royal Navy onto Italian forces. Though Ultra did not define Italian strength, any such operation must be large, especially since the Luftwaffe across the eastern Mediterranean was charged to assist it.

Cunningham threw all that he had – an aircraft carrier, three battleships, seven cruisers and seventeen destroyers – to ambush what proved to be an Italian battleship, eight cruisers and seventeen destroyers. The Italian commander had more confidence than intelligence, in all senses of the word. He mistakenly believed that battle damage had immobilised two of the Mediterranean Fleet's three battleships and its only carrier. Italian air reconnaissance reported that at 1900, 27 March, two battleships and one carrier still were in Alexandria harbour (Cunningham sailed after dark, to gain security). Thus, Italy would have numerical superiority even in the worst case, if ambush failed and battle ensued. While at sea, Admiral Angelo Iachino ignored Sigint which hinted that large British forces were out. When a seaplane sighted Royal Navy warships, which had been tasked to lure Italians towards ambush, Iachino did precisely what Cunningham hoped he would do. Fluke framed the battle. With great luck, Italians might have sunk some British warships. Slightly worse Italian decisions could have destroyed their own fleet. One better decision might have prevented 66 per cent of their losses. In the event,

British carrier aircraft crippled the modern Italian battleship, *Vittorio Veneto*, and a cruiser, *Pola*. Iachino sent two cruisers to tow *Pola* home, demonstrating his ignorance of peril, which perhaps the presence of a British aircraft carrier might have demonstrated. Radar and searchlights guided three British battleships to sink three heavy cruisers, including *Pola*, and two destroyers, through five minutes of point-blank gunfire.[38] *Vittorio Veneto*, and other Italian warships, fled just fast enough to escape. Cunningham rescued most Italian survivors but, aware that attack by the Luftwaffe loomed, informed the Regia Marina by radio where the rest were swimming, and sailed safely to Alexandria. In return, the Royal Navy lost one aircraft and three aircrew.

Intelligence also aided Britain systematically with the strikes on the Italian navy at Taranto in 1940, ambushes of convoys in the Mediterranean Sea during 1941–43, the sinking of *Scharnhorst* in 1943, and in air actions against German convoys off the Norwegian coast during 1944–45.[39] These successes hastened Britain's aim to break its enemies rapidly. Axis signals intelligence agencies, especially B-Dienst, won the wireless war for much of 1940–42, but not enough to win these campaigns as a whole. They backed aggressive German operations, sustained an Italian strategy of avoiding risk and keeping their fleet in being, shaped the destruction of more British than Axis surface warships, and multiplied the power of U-boats. Yet, at a strategic level, these successes were minor, even counter-productive. Pursuit of these objectives wrecked the German navy and smothered the Italian one. German forces came out too often. Britain made it hard for the Italians to stay in. The land, sea and air campaigns of the Mediterranean overlapped: if Rommel penned British forces in Egypt, Britain's ability to aid Malta declined, and the Regia Marina faced less pressure to come out. Effective forces in Malta forced Italians out into ambushes enabled by Ultra, so threatening Rommel's logistics and his ability to contain his foes, ad infinitum.

Axis navies won victories but could not exploit them. Britain could afford to lose battleships. Simple sources of intelligence enabled Italian minelayers and frogmen to cripple the Royal Navy during late 1941. This victory, combined with attacks by 1,000 German (about 33 per cent of the Luftwaffe's strength) and 2,000 Italian aircraft, drove the RAF and Royal Navy from Malta, temporarily, so saving the Afrika Korps from strangulation. Neither German nor Italian forces exploited that victory. Within nine months the RAF and Royal Navy, superior in power and intelligence, surged back to Malta, wielding a razor against Axis arteries. They wrecked Italian warships and sank supplies to Rommel, shaping defeat at El Alamein. Allied forces surged east and west towards Tunisia and an Axis garrison 250,000-men strong, driving the Italian navy and Axis merchantmen into catastrophic losses for convoys: Axis merchantmen died alongside their protectors. American and Commonwealth air forces crushed those of Germany and Italy.

Similarly, B-Dienst enabled Hitler to pre-empt an Allied attack on Norway in 1940. This action beat Allied strategy but broke the German surface navy, which lost half its strength sunk and more crippled − heavier losses than those of Britain, which could better absorb them. Advance warning from Comint, and tactical guidance from radar, traffic analysis and air reconnaissance, gave Germany an edge against the Arctic convoys to Murmansk. They enabled German forces to hammer and occasionally to annihilate a convoy, or even halt them, but these battles consumed what remained of its surface navy, at disproportionate cost and to little effect. Intelligence successes lured Germans into operational failures.[40]

The same story marked the central instance of intelligence in European waters. Allied intelligence veterans thought their finest hour was the battle of the Atlantic, as do many scholars. This claim has truth but misses two points.[41] German intelligence matched that of the Allies, while this campaign was won more by strategic, economic, and administrative matters than battles. The campaign never neared its strategic objective − to sink so much shipping as to stall the Allies. It merely inflicted a cost-efficient but minor drain on Allied resources, at some cost to German ones.[42] German strategic air defence, and Sigint for it, damaged the Allies far more than B-Dienst and U-boats. The U-boat was beaten by its limits and Allied power, in which process Ultra and B-Dienst played low secondary roles, largely because each constrained the other. In this campaign (and the British and American submarine campaigns in the Mediterranean and the Pacific) intelligence worked as it did in the battles of Britain and Germany. The British and German navies centralised intelligence and command, and disseminated orders to forces across the Atlantic by radio, yielding chances to enemy cryptanalysis and traffic analysis. U-boats also reported daily by radio. As with aircraft in the London Air Defence Area in 1918, Germany distributed U-boats on search lines, covering arbitrary and limited areas, and intended to prevent convoys from slipping past without sighting. U-boats sped on the surface rather than crawled beneath. They attacked convoys with concentrated forces – wolf packs – on the surface at night. Against this threat, the Allies allocated few warships and aircraft until 1943. Any wolf pack overwhelmed escorts and sank many merchant ships, yet U-boats were few and the ocean large. U-boats ambushed twice as many convoys when B-Dienst was effective and Ultra was not, than vice versa.[43]

The U-boats killed 14,000,000 tons of Allied shipping, mostly between mid-1940 and mid-1943. B-Dienst bolstered German attacks during 1940 and 1942 by letting Dönitz orchestrate an optimal campaign of ambushes across the Atlantic Ocean. In 1941, Ultra saved perhaps 3 million tons of shipping and cargo – a useful gain – by enabling admirals to reroute convoys away from U-boats. By 1943, so many submarines were at sea that evasion was impossible and convoy battles unavoidable. A symbiotic combination of Ultra, radar, traffic analysis and HFDF, enabled an additional 20 destroyers and 200 aircraft to wreck this danger with ease and efficiency. The tininess of these forces demonstrates the limits to U-boats and the significance of Sigint and its fellow sources. Ultra achieved a rare success in any battle of attrition – gauging whether one is winning or losing – by monitoring the desperate communications of Dönitz. He ordered submarines into hopeless actions which his captains claimed to be executing, when in fact they avoided action. His captains lied to him, and he called them cowards. They simply were realists. Ultra and traffic analysis enabled counter-ambush through strike warfare. Aircraft killed U-boats moving on the surface or forced them underwater, out of battle. Destroyers joined convoys known to be in peril, matching wolf packs in strength. Radar and HFDF located submarines as they attacked convoys and guided escorts against them. Britain deliberately sailed convoys at U-boats, to draw them into battle. Ironically, for B-Dienst to locate convoys now helped the Allies to sink U-boats.[44] That victory was inevitable – if at greater cost – once the Allies decided to achieve it, while escorts remained a costly necessity until the end of the war. Under these western waters, as on them, Britain won the war handily and speedily because its sea power was greater, while Ultra contained its competition – that was all it had to do. When Ultra crushed its competitors, German and Italian navies already lay dead in the water.

Ultra and the Mediterranean Strategy

Sigint most affected British strategy and operations as the war flowed from the Mediterranean in 1940 to the Rhine in 1945. Britain's decision of 1940 to fight on transformed the war. Immediately, it left British forces in an awkward position – powerful for defence at home, weak for attack abroad. The Royal Navy and the RAF were great forces, but the small and mediocre British Army needed to expand dramatically to engage any continental foe. The Mediterranean Sea was not the best locale for a British offensive strategy, but it was the only one. The first great success of Ultra was to aid this destruction of Axis air, ground and sea forces in the Mediterranean campaign, which precipitated the collapse of Italy and forced Germany into a three-front war.[45]

Between 1940 and 1942, a competition between the power and intelligence of Allies and Axis drove the Mediterranean campaign. Britain sent a large fleet and small though growing air and Army forces to Egypt. Sigint helped them all to crush Italian forces. Initially, Sigint at sea relied on low-level codes and traffic analysis, but during 1941–42 it profited from success against the Italian naval Enigma, C 38m Hagelin machines, and Kriegsmarine and Luftwaffe traffic. The Regia Marina's book codes, its main systems, remained invulnerable. Ironically, because Germany criticised these systems as insecure, Italy adopted the C 38m to cover traffic about convoys and operational issues, which became their greatest cryptographic vulnerability.[46] British aircraft reconnaissance slowly but steadily rose in value. Italian naval Sigint provided useful background but little operational material, though Axis aerial reconnaissance was able.

The Regia Marina numerically matched the Royal Navy in the theatre, but was not as good or as confident. In 1940, it routinely declined to attack smaller Royal Navy forces in the central Mediterranean. The Royal Navy, more aggressive, used any intelligence to enable attack. Aircraft imagery guided the strike at Taranto on 11 November 1940, which sank or disabled half of Italy's battleships. Ultra enabled victory at Cape Matapan. These disasters so weakened and frightened the Regia Marina that its major warships rarely entered any danger zone. When the commander of the Italian battle fleet, Admiral Iachino, engaged heavily outnumbered Royal Navy surface forces convoying supplies to Malta on 17 December 1941 and 22 March 1942, they escaped disaster because of the caution he learned from Matapan, though the convoy missions failed.[47] Yet in strategic terms, honours were even: the Royal Navy could not safely enter the central Mediterranean until the Army seized Libya, which would enable forward air support. That aim proved impossible to achieve. Instead, throughout 1941, campaigns of attrition and ambush dominated a stalemate at sea. German U-boats and aircraft crippled or sank many large British warships. Small British air and naval units (Force K, with four cruisers and four destroyers) at Malta, relying on Ultra, ravaged Italian convoys to North Africa, until simple intelligence guided Italian successes. Italian minelayers mined routes used by British warships, which wrecked Force K in December 1941, and with it the offensive value of Ultra in the theatre. Italian frogmen sank two British battleships in Alexandria harbour. From then until August 1942, the Royal Navy could not threaten Axis logistics across the central Mediterranean, nor save Malta, which the Axis could have taken, had they wanted.

Meanwhile, Sigint drove campaigns in northeastern Africa. When Italy entered the war in June 1940, both sides had primitive Comsec and relied heavily on plain language for operational communications. British forces were aggressive and willing to act on Sigint, while Italian ones were not. The Central Bureau Middle East (CBME) and the Air and Military sections at GC&CS quickly built on prewar successes. In the last three months of 1940, Bletchley provided 2,600 solutions of Italian army traffic in Libya, and CBME around 8,000. CBME broke so many lower-grade codes that it had to ration their exploitation, while plain-language Italian traffic was useful, especially during battles.[48] The Commander in Chief, Middle East, General Archibald Wavell, experienced with intelligence and operations as a senior staff officer in the Middle East during 1917–18, relied on Sigint for a daring plan to demolish Italian power in Africa. Italian air and army traffic betrayed their order of battle in Libya and Ethiopia – their intentions, defences, plans, and disastrous logistics. In Ethiopia, Britain read the daily reports from the Italian viceroy to Rome, and Italian military plans and appreciations before they reached their intended recipients. Other sources were also useful. Intelligence drove small African, Australian, British, Indian and South African forces – with just two trained divisions and a few hundred aircraft and tanks – into precise and devastating attacks. In Libya, Sigint delineated Italian dispositions into isolated camps. Tanks penetrated weak spots in these defences – located by air and physical reconnaissance – and crushed their occupants. As Italian forces ran west along the coast, British armour drove through the interior and trapped and destroyed them at the battle of Beda Fomm. At tiny cost, Britain wrecked and captured an Italian army five times larger than British forces in Libya (of 140,000 men) and three times greater in Ethiopia (of 370,000 men). RAF commanders held that ' "Y" information forms our most important source and is of direct operational use to us'. Military intelligence in Cairo doubted that 'any commander in the field had been better served by his intelligence' than the commander in East Africa.[49] The latter, Alan Cunningham, agreed: 'there can seldom in the history of war have been a campaign in which the Commander was so continuously served with accurate information of the enemy's movements and dispositions. The bulk of this information was received from "Y" sources.'[50]

In the spring of 1941, Britain could have driven Italy out of Africa and raided its homeland, for whatever that might have been worth, but Germany sent small army and large air forces to check that prospect. This changed the balance of power and intelligence in the Mediterranean. Small and improvised forces, with many tactical flaws, achieved these British successes. Plain language carried tactical communications, while Comsec for operational signals was poor. Italian Sigint was competent, but commanders did not act on knowledge.[51] This fragile system worked only because of Italian passivity and ineptitude. It failed against German forces in the desert campaign. British inferiority had many roots: weakness in training a mass army and organising formations, misjudgements about mechanised warfare, mediocre generals and anti-tank weaponry, terrain better suited to mobile than to set-piece battle. German forces were good and Italian forces became better than is generally stated.[52] The problem was not that individual British generals were worse than German ones, but that their system was. British commanders did not fail because they underrated the value of intelligence: they overrated its value and regarded it as their trump card. Initially, however, Rommel's Sigint outstripped British.

The Afrika Korps – tough, aggressive, well officered, better suited to mobile operations in the desert than British forces – was perfectly formed to exploit the British system of signals, security and command. Its commander, Erwin Rommel, was not the leading German general of the war, nor their greatest user of intelligence (though the best ones, such as Erich von Manstein, might have done little better in his shoes). Still, like Dönitz at sea, Rommel illuminates what able German commanders with good intelligence could do against American and Commonwealth forces armed with Ultra. Rommel's real strength was his men, rather than himself, though he was an excellent tactician, trainer of troops and leader. A good general, but no Hannibal, he tended to disrupt his own command system, which often left him leading battalions, while staff officers commanded the Afrika Korps.[33] He moved rapidly and sought to exploit every opening which fortune offered him. Always optimistic in interpretation, Rommel often acted hastily on incomplete and misinterpreted fragments of information. This behaviour was shaped by his formative moment as a soldier. Whenever he scented confusion in enemy command, he no longer saw the desert but the Alps, around Caporetto in 1917, where his aggression and initiative as a battalion commander had taken 9,000 prisoners from a routed Italian army. For Rommel, nothing was easier than to imagine an army on the verge of collapse, nothing more natural than to gamble everything he had for the highest of stakes.

This daring led him to remarkable success against inferior enemies. This recklessness also led him to ruin against able ones. The easiest thing for intelligence to do was to prompt Rommel to attack. The hardest thing was to get him to think. Hot and hard intelligence was essential to his victories in three corps-level actions against enemies of equal strength – British forces in June 1941 and January 1942, and American ones in February 1943 at Kasserine Pass. Rommel, however, used good but ambiguous intelligence badly, before and during two army-level battles against numerically equal British enemies, in the Crusader and Gazala battles. His performance was mediocre at corps, army and army group levels when he confronted defenders of equal numbers or attackers of greater strength but with better intelligence – as happened at El Alamein and Alam al Halfa in Egypt, Medinnine in Tunisia, and Normandy. Rommel used intelligence well when he could play to his strengths – fluid operations at corps level – but not when he had to work to his weaknesses, set-piece battles at army or army group level. To have outstanding intelligence, better than his enemies, was a major advantage for him. Good intelligence, equal to his enemies, was not. Any inferiority was a handicap. Rommel gained much from intelligence in small actions, less in major ones. He depended on intelligence, but did not use it very well.

Fortunately, for him, until July 1942, Rommel was as well served by intelligence – and sometimes had as much superiority over his enemies – as any other commander in this war. His excellent Sigint unit, Strategical Intercept Company 621 under Captain Alfred Seebohm, had served him during the battle of France, which created mutual comprehension and confidence. This force, focused on plain-language traffic and low-level traffic analysis, matched British Sigint in the desert. It easily traced British strength, movements, condition and intentions, providing most German intelligence before October 1941 and much of it until July 1942.⁵⁴ Attacks on War Office codebook 'W' also consistently provided useful material throughout this period. For Rommel, this material equalled Ultra. He used hard and hot information well, but not ambivalent material requiring thoughtful analysis. You always can tell a pilot, but not much – so with Rommel. Given information which stated unambiguously what an enemy intended or was able to do, and in time to act, Rommel struck like a snake. Seebohm gave him precisely this, which enabled three stunning and sequential victories in 1941. Between 31 March and 8 April, Rommel destroyed a numerically superior British division by surprise, but also became mired in a messy and mishandled siege of Commonwealth forces at the port of Tobruk. On 15 May, and then 15–17 June, in Operation Battleaxe, he hammered first a division and then a corps, as they attempted to relieve Tobruk. Seebohm penetrated British intentions and dispositions. Rommel struck their weaknesses hard and fast, crippling but not annihilating them. Seebohm gave Rommel nine hours' warning of the start of Battleaxe, perfect knowledge of British perceptions, concerns, dispositions, confusion and lack of supplies and confidence. These defeats caught British attention. Intelligence authorities were 'scandalised' to conclude that 'in the recent operations, in CYRENAICA, the enemy's command directed his operations largely from information given in clear by our units'.⁵⁵ British forces radically improved their signals security and intelligence. These improvements let British commanders catch

Rommel by surprise with their Crusader offensive in October 1941, to maintain parity with his intelligence during that battle and helped to achieve victory. Thereafter, Britain contained Seebohm's unit before battles, but he remained valuable during them.[56]

Another excellent source soon joined Seebohm. Between January and June 1942 the American military attaché in Egypt, Colonel Bonner Fellers, reported in detail about British capabilities, intentions, operations and forces, on which he was well informed. He reported to Washington by the best cryptographic system American diplomats had: the Black Code. Alas, Italian and German codebreakers read it. Within a narrower sphere, Axis solutions of Bonner Feller's reports matched the value of those which Magic provided on General Oshima Hiroshi from Berlin. Bonner Feller's reports were among the best Axis sources of this war. However, the British hid much of their intentions, plans and dispositions from him, on which he had to guess – not particularly well, but still from a better basis than anything else the Axis had. He never heard of Ultra, which otherwise he might have inadvertently compromised. Rommel trusted what he called the 'Good Source', or his 'little fellers'.[57] Bonner Fellers provided not just data but estimates – professional, well informed, and fairly accurate, if always too pessimistic about British weaknesses. They influenced no one more than Rommel, who in effect had an American intelligence advisor on his staff and followed his advice closely. Between January and June 1942, these three forms of German Sigint aided each other and matched all British ones. The 'Good Source' was best before operations and Seebohm during them; the 'W' codebook useful at all times.

Stormy Weather

By autumn 1941, Britain's forces matched Rommel's in Sigint and signals security. Both planned major offensives by armies of 110,000–120,000 men. The British had slightly more infantry, and 40 per cent more aircraft and armour, than their foes. Rommel's intelligence for these purposes was inadequate, whereas British was excellent. Ultra did everything which intelligence could do for a battle. Sigint exploited general Kriegsmarine and Luftwaffe systems, as well as special Luftwaffe Enigma keys used in Libya, Italian army and air force systems, Y and middle-grade German codes, and, intermittently, German army

Enigma. British authorities used Sigint well for strategy, but not for operations. Despite impatience for an offensive, Churchill accepted Auchinleck's arguments that British forces needed more training, and that Ultra would warn when battle was nigh. Ultra soothed the friction of command and gave British forces an extra month of time for training, which was valuable, though inadequate for the task ahead.

On 17 November 1941, Britain launched the Crusader offensive, seemingly with perfect intelligence. It caught Rommel entirely by surprise with regards to time and strength. Panzer Group Afrika noted the movement to the front of many forces, but missed two key formations – the New Zealand Division and the Seventh Armoured Division – and failed to realise an attack was looming. Despite this gross failure of intelligence, its forces were well placed against that threat. The Italians missed details of British efforts but appreciated that an attack was imminent and deployed their mechanised forces effectively against it.[58] British commanders understood the enemies' order of battle, an essential but technically hard task. They attacked on the last day possible before Rommel struck the isolated and vulnerable garrison of Tobruk, pre-empting his plans almost perfectly. Commanders understood the enemy's numerical strength in tanks and anti-tank guns with 99 per cent accuracy. Unfortunately, they did not realise how good those weapons were and how they would be used to ravage Commonwealth forces – in particular, that German anti-tank guns could crush any British tank at medium range. Ultra was better at order of battle than capabilities; at numbers than value.

Even worse, the British were good at intelligence and bad at operations. Planning for the attack by Alan Cunningham, commander of the Eighth Army, was amateurish. Five days into the battle, an army divided into five disconnected parts disintegrated. Rommel simply had to mop them up so to destroy the Eighth Army and then take Alexandria. However, he threw victory away from hubris. He interpreted intercepts of fragmented messages from Commonwealth officers to mean that Caporetto was close. Instead of smashing the fragments before him, he drove deep into their rear, achieving nothing, while determined Commonwealth command and forces recovered and ravaged his base. British officers kept their nerve and, in confusing circumstances, re-knitted their command. Engineers refitted hundreds of immobilised British tanks and destroyed hundreds of Axis ones, settling who really had won the armoured battle.

Auchinleck relieved Cunningham and took personal command. A broad picture of German capabilities and intentions reinforced certainty about strategy. Aware from Ultra that Rommel's logistics were fragile, Auchinleck adopted an attritional strategy, fighting a scrum which wrecked Axis forces, though the Eighth Army failed to exploit Sigint on the field in order to rush for victory, much as it tried. Commonwealth infantry divisions performed well and wrecked Rommel's plans. British armour won few engagements, even when acting on Sigint. German and Italian forces fought combined-arms battles, while British armour acted on their own, weakening all parts of the army. Only when put in its place as part of the Army by autumn 1942, could British armour do its duty. The Axis lost 340 tanks and 275 aircraft, virtually all they had, and 38,000 men killed or captured – 33 per cent of their strength. The Commonwealth lost 17,700 men killed or captured, 280 tanks and 300 aircraft.[59]

This victory was significant, but not decisive, In December 1941, for the only time in the war, all of the Axis powers attacked Britain simultaneously. Churchill's hopes for Crusader faded, as Britain scrambled for survival across three continents. By January 1942, with Force K wrecked, Axis reinforcements reached Libya freely. The outbreak of the Pacific war disrupted British support to Egypt. Exploiting reinforcements, and intelligence drawn equally from Bonner Fellers and Seebohm, Rommel hammered back a scattered British division. British commanders assumed such operations were impossible, and intelligence, though broad and good, provided nothing to shake that conviction. In May–June 1942, Rommel scored a last triumph in the Gazala campaign, involving armies of around 100,000 men each, neither of which used intelligence effectively. Ultra followed enemy order of battle and reinforcements fairly well, but could not penetrate Rommel's intentions, which caught Britain by surprise, though it knew an attack was looming. Their defensive system was well suited to containing an attack, but not to take the initiative. British command was weak. Seebohm provided little material, British security kept key matters from Bonner Fellers, while the Germans interpreted his reports too enthusiastically. Bonner Fellers underestimated British armoured strength in the theatre; hence, the Germans missed 400 tanks which reached the front during the battle and hundreds more which stalled their advance afterwards. These included Grant tanks, which ravaged

Panzers. Above all, Bonner Fellers insisted that that the British would remain weak until June, and collapse if the Axis made Egypt their leading priority. These reports reinforced Rommel's hopes and shaped his plans, although he knew the assumption about Axis priorities was wrong.[60]

Rommel used this intelligence exactly as the British had with Ultra before Crusader: to illuminate enemy strength and reinforcements for comparison with knowledge about his own forces. He expected to build power faster than the British and to attack at his maximum relative strength. Whereas British calculations of these issues in the autumn of 1941 were good, Rommel's assessment of May 1941 was wrong because he trusted Bonner Fellers. Like the British at Crusader, he linked intelligence to a foolish plan. Rommel launched the Gazala offensive with great hopes, a gross underestimate of the quantity and quality of British tanks before him, and a misunderstanding of their dispositions. The 'Good Source' and Rommel led his forces almost to annihilation. Rommel launched a deep inland hook which he claimed would reach the sea and destroy the Eighth Army in three days. Instead, the Afrika Corps crashed part-way into British defences and then stalled – almost surrounded and isolated from its supplies, and the Italians. Though succoured by the Italian army, Italian signals intelligence and Seebohm, Rommel escaped disaster only because his forces were good and British command bad.

Had the Eighth Army been well trained and led, it would have crushed Rommel's force rapidly. It was not and did not. British commanders had a winning hand, but no idea how to play it.[61] Unlike Rommel, they could not use the intelligence they received. Ultra and other sources, however, guided devastating RAF attacks on Axis forces and logistics, which foreshadowed the rise of a great Allied strength on the battlefield.[62] Bonner Fellers led Rommel into an intelligence failure, which produced an operational triumph, just as the success of Ultra before Crusader led the British first to disaster, and then to a near-run victory. Rommel's chief of intelligence, F. W. von Mellenthin, noted the paradoxical nature of intelligence in Gazala. 'Perhaps, fortunately, we underestimated the British strength, for had we known the full facts even Rommel might have baulked at an attack on such a superior enemy.'[63] During several furious weeks, Axis forces gradually dismantled the Eighth Army, killing or capturing half its personnel and wrecking most of its tanks. German and Italian losses were far smaller. Again, Rommel set off down the road to Alexandria, and failed to get there.

Tsunami

By June 1942, Ultra had uncovered the compromise of the Black Code. When Churchill personally gave the evidence to an embarrassed Roosevelt, the Americans withdrew Bonner Fellers from Cairo, ending the 'little fellers', and dramatically increased supplies to British forces in Egypt. Ultimately, Bonner Fellers gave the British more armour than he cost them and led the enemy into error. In its last days, as Tobruk fell, the 'Good Source' bolstered Rommel's decision to drive all-out on Alexandria, rather than to build his base and occupy Malta. Bonner Feller's belief that one last blow would break Britain reinforced Rommel's over-optimism. Again, both men were wrong; but this failure was irrecoverable. In June 1942, Auchinleck took command, his resolution overcoming disaster. His command was inept, but he threw so many forces into a narrow front at El Alamein, especially first-rate Australian and New Zealand formations, that the Axis advance stalled.

Major and overlapping changes to intelligence and power shifted the balance in the Mediterranean, permanently. The 'Good Source' died, and Australians captured Strategical Intercept Company 621 when Rommel threw them into a collapsing front line. With other sources on his intelligence menu running thin, Rommel turned from relying on excellent sources to a new diet, one which peddled British deception – the British-controlled agent 'Cheese'. After months of cold relations with his Abwehr controllers, on 2 July 1942 they sent Cheese the following radio message: 'Be very active these days. Good information will be well rewarded. From now onwards we are going to listen in every day for your signals.' Both sets of masters appreciated the taste of his response: Security Intelligence Middle East, which managed deception in the region, noted that Rommel 'insisted that the full text' of messages from Cheese 'be relayed to him as soon as they were received' by Abwehr station Athens. This information was obtained by 'Ice', slang for 'Illicit Services Oliver Strachey' (ISOS) – GC&CS solutions of the codebooks of the Abwehr intercepts.'[64] ISOS and Knox's team attacking Abwehr Enigma – 'Illicit Services Knox' (ISK) – rapidly joined GC&CS's key assets. GHQ Middle East had sources it knew the enemy trusted, to monitor what it expected to happen and thought was happening, real battles to fight, and useful lies to spread. Through Cheese, GHQ passed reports which blinded Rommel between July and October 1942, shaping the bizarre overconfidence which doomed Panzerarmee Afrika. As he entered this mousetrap, Rommel's decisions deteriorated. Rommel was the first victim of the power of British deception and intelligence; more would follow.

Ultra became better than before, and German intelligence incompetent, but the real change lay in forces and command. The main causes for this victory were bad German decisions and good British ones, and the RAF and Commonwealth armies – for whom deception, intelligence and security were force multipliers. Finally, the British Army was well trained and equipped, and could be led to victory. It matched Germany's army in quality. The RAF outweighed the Luftwaffe. Finally, Ultra had effective forces to multiply and British generals to use it. The Eighth Army received more and better American armour and British anti-tank weapons, eliminating its greatest weaknesses, and of British aircraft, strengthening its greatest area of superiority. The RAF and Royal Navy surged back to Malta. Rommel exposed all of the weaknesses of his forces and negated many of their strengths. German and Italian forces were marooned at El Alamein. Their supplies moved across the Mediterranean and then 1,000 miles overland by truck, exposed to air and naval attacks which were honed by Ultra, traffic analysis and aerial reconnaissance. Axis armies were driven into high-intensity set-piece battles on thick and narrow fronts which could not be turned. These circumstances suited Axis strengths less, and British ones better, than any other in the desert.

From August 1942 the Eighth Army was commanded by a general who could exploit these edges and exceed Rommel at set-piece battles. This story usually is told through warring cults of heroes, which distorts events. Montgomery – sometimes slow and unnecessarily cautious – was no Hannibal, but he was competent: an underrated military virtue, except when you need it. Few commanders of the war better knew how to combine intelligence and operational power. He knew what his forces could do and made them do it. He was an excellent trainer and motivator of men, with an uncanny ability to read an enemy and a battle. He predicted Rommel's battle plan through instinct, soon confirmed by Ultra, and developed and executed a means to stop it. When

Rommel attacked at Alam al Halfa on 30 August 1942, Montgomery saw him off with a whiff of grapeshot.[65] Montgomery made German and Italian forces stand and fight like Englishmen: in the months before El Alamein, Montgomery trained his men to fight in their style of 1918, which they could achieve, made them all operate as an army, and prepared a plan to crush an enemy. In hindsight, Montgomery's victory seems inevitable: but at the time, Rommel expected to win. He was out-thought and outfought.

Ultra served Montgomery well in these preparations. Sigint guided air and naval attacks on Axis logistics, which gutted its strength. It precisely tracked Axis deployments and strengths, especially in tanks, their desperate logistical weaknesses and betrayed their operations. It showed Rommel's preconceptions by monitoring the mousetrap: baiting the cheese, reading the Abwehr's reports on it to Rommel and his requests to them for information, and his orders to subordinates and debates with superiors. Sigint let deception precisely deform Rommel's thoughts and actions. Few commanders have ever been so whipped in intelligence as Rommel was before El Alamein, though this was not the greatest area of British superiority. Rommel, certain that danger was distant and underestimating his foe, was in Germany, leaving his army badly placed for battle, caught completely by surprise and soon destroyed. When Rommel returned two days after the attack began, immediately he knew that his forces were doomed, something he had not considered possible before he left. Intelligence and intuition had enabled Montgomery to read the battle and – precisely as he told all of his officers – after a dogfight of twelve days the enemy collapsed. The Axis lost 54,000 men killed and captured and almost all of its armour and guns. Montgomery, however, failed to mop up 60,000 Germans and Italians as they fled defeat, which Ultra showed was possible. He preferred to cross the desert without any risk of ambush, the only thing which might prevent victory.[66]

Ultra and the Strategy of Overthrow

Until mid-1942, Britain was not quite strong enough in the Mediterranean to exploit the value of Ultra, which could not quite multiply this power enough to execute Churchill's strategy, primarily because the British Army was unable to defeat the Germans in the desert, even when they outnumbered the foe by more than two to one. However, British production of good weapons and units and Allied strategic decisions then revived his strategy with greater effect than before. Germany could have countered this transformation of intelligence and power only by transferring great forces to the theatre, as it was stretched thin in an effort to crush the USSR. Initially, few were sent. In November 1942, Rommel's forces collapsed, while Operation Torch – the boldest assault of the war and Germany's greatest intelligence failure – brought Anglo-American forces across the Atlantic to Africa and tripled Allied strength in the Mediterranean.[67] American air forces rapidly matched British ones in quality, though its ground forces required a year to do so and to shake out their weaknesses. Germany could not match this escalation, even by allocating 25 per cent of the Luftwaffe's squadrons to the theatre, where they failed – too weak to save Tunisia, and so large as to cripple Stalingrad. The disastrous decision to reinforce Tunisia forced Italian sailors and Axis aircrew to fight courageously but hopelessly in ruinous circumstances. Axis losses of 250,000 men killed and captured, 450 tanks, 1,000 artillery and anti-tank guns, and 2,500 aircraft (and most of their aircrew) destroyed were heavy – even by the standards of the Eastern front, and far above Allied ones.[68] This victory justified all the costs of Churchill's Mediterranean strategy and opened a new phase of the war. Germany confronted threats to the south and west and the possible loss of its main ally: for the Allies, desperate scrabbling in strategy and inconclusive battles were done. Superior Allied forces built on one victory after another. German offensives could not disrupt Allied strategy. Underlying this transformation of power was another in intelligence. Ultra let the Allies attack Germany with remarkable precision, success and surprise, while supporting a deception campaign which exploited the poverty in German strategic intelligence and compromised its decisions.

Ultra's second great contribution to the war was to help the Allies pin great German forces in southern and Western Europe during 1943–45 and shatter them at surprisingly small cost. By illuminating German intentions and capabilities, Ultra served the two key Allied strategic decisions of the period: first to drive Italy from the war and stretch Germany thin through the Mediterranean strategy; second, to smash Germany head-on by invading France. In 1942, the Eighth Army had 100,000 combatants; in 1944, millions of Allied combatants, over half of them American, fought in France and Italy. They outnumbered German soldiers, sucked eastward to maelstrom. After D-Day, American commanders matched British ones as consumers of Ultra. It enabled the Allies to detect and wreck German attacks, with important exceptions – including Kasserine Pass and the battle of the Bulge. Such attacks were rare. German forces remained good and fought defensively, exploiting the value of firepower and narrow force-to-space ratios. Anglo-American forces could not conduct mobile war until after winning set-piece battles, most notably when breaking out from Normandy, Rome and across the Rhine. In such battles, intelligence played roles varying between those of 1917 and 1918, while aiding artillery and air forces to strike with greater power. For planning before battles, continual access to German operational and logistical traffic gave the Allies an excellent and certain grasp of enemy capabilities, perceptions and intentions, despite constant gaps. Knowledge, above all from Ultra, with lower-grade Sigint matching any other source, let Western generals use their resources efficiently and effectively, and better than any before. It sped the operations which drove the Axis from Africa and then aided the success of Allied forces in the most complex and risky form of military operations. Amphibious operations hit the enemy like thunderbolts at weak points and caught them by surprise, transforming the front, because German intelligence was incompetent and its command manipulated by British deception.[69]

The problem for both sides was the amphibious assault on Fortress Europe. The Allies chose their beaches along a 1,500-mile front using strategic criteria, assisted by intelligence – especially Sigint – on enemy expectations and power. Victory was not foredoomed. Germany had sizable military power and could stall defeat by breaking the Allied cover. This did not occur because intelligence services suited to a sprint gasped in a marathon. Germany, thrown on the defensive, needed to know Allied strategic capabilities and intentions. These needs were ill met. Beyond the communications of neutral diplomats, only one German source really provided strategic intelligence. The Luftwaffe's Sigint agency, the Forschungsamt, intercepted radio-telephone calls between British and American officials. It broke the A-3 scrambler system which covered these messages until mid-1943, and some even after the 'Sigsaly' speech encipherment system was developed. Allied intelligence, aware that the A-3 was easily breakable, warned all users to take care with it and monitored communications. The Forschungsamt gleaned mere fragments of economic and political data from such conversations, yet these were the best strategic intelligence Germany had. Above all, on 28 July 1943, Hitler and Oberkommando der Wehrmacht grimly noted that Churchill and Roosevelt had mentioned a possible 'forthcoming armistice with Italy'. In principle, this compromise was unfortunate, but the effect was miniscule.[70] Mussolini had just been overthrown. Germany, mistrusting other Italian leaders, was already preparing to seize Italy, where they deployed large forces. This intercept, just one of many reliable indicators of this danger, had little effect on these preparations or the war. Germany easily took Italy in September 1943 because its government, and its negotiations with the Allies, were incompetent.

German imagery and signals intelligence failed at strategic intelligence; this threw OKW and Hitler onto the unchecked word of the Abwehr, a corrupt and inefficient service, and so to agents under Allied control. MI6 later held that the Abwehr 'gradually became a conspiracy to conceal the success of Allied deception', because of a broader context. The Abwehr failed, but so did every branch of German intelligence, while British deception and codebreaking succeeded.[71] With Britain able to build credibility for controlled agents and the enemy unable to see the truth, Germany could not grasp Allied intentions. British lies mailed through the Abwehr blinded Hitler and the OKW before the attacks on Sicily and Normandy.

The Allies could return to the continent only through great seaborne assaults – a hard operation of war – and against a strong foe with time to prepare stronger defences. Strategic success depended on the tactical situation at the sharp edge; even against weak positions, attackers faced agonising slogs or were pinned in their beachheads for months, as at Salerno, Omaha Beach and Anzio. In every amphibious assault, the attackers might have easily suffered heavier casualties or been sealed off before they broke out – as at Anzio. Such failures might have triggered the key weakness of Allied forces: the politicisation of Anglo-American field command, which produced crises at Anzio and Normandy. Every amphibious assault of 1943–44 would have been tested had the Germans focused more defensive resources on the right beaches, or had 20,000 soldiers more on the spot, or another 50,000 within two days' marching. Hitler had this power. With better knowledge of Allied intentions, Germany easily could have quadrupled its strength at Sicily in July 1943 or Normandy in June 1944. The war would have taken a different course had the Normandy beachhead been sealed off – five miles deep and fifteen wide – had the Allies abandoned their attack on Sicily, or every seaborne assault cost twice the lives it did. Intelligence and deception prevented such possibilities; instead, the Allies struck the least well defended of useful sites, where deception kept the enemy weak. Intelligence and deception sheltered Allied weak spots from enemy pressure and eliminated much of the risk of seaborne assault. They let attackers evade the enemy's defences and forced Germany to improvise a response from a poor position. Intelligence and deception made these operations look easy, when they rank among the greatest and most risky in the history of war.

A symbiotic relationship between counter-intelligence, Comint and deception enabled that manipulation. Each element was essential to that outcome. When war began, Germany, with few agents in the British empire, threw masses of untrained spies against its foe, hoping some would stick. Britain captured these agents and used them to pass masses of messages to German leaders, which occasionally reached Hitler, all tailored to ease Allied attacks.[72] Mastery over German cryptosystems showed what the enemy expected and how it reacted to misdirection. In July 1942, A Force, under Dudley Clarke, which ran deception in the Mediterranean theatre, received copies of the communications between Rommel, the Abwehr station in Athens and the controlled agent Cheese, which were carried on Abwehr cryptosystems. Until the spring of 1943, however, Clarke did not know about Ultra, nor Bletchley about him. When GC&CS discovered his work, acting on its own initiative, it made Clarke and his fellow deceivers into specialist consumers. From spring 1943, GC&CS, MI6, the NID and the MID gave the deceivers monthly reports drawn from Ultra entitled: 'German Appreciations of Allied Intelligence', with analysis illustrated by intercepts.[73] One report, noting German concern with an Allied threat to the Aegean and the Balkans, shaped the cover for the invasion of Sicily, Operation Mincemeat.

The British understood the threats which concerned Germany and reinforced them, so to cover intentions to strike elsewhere. Deception failed as often as it succeeded, but failure cost little and success recouped dividends. When deception worked, it was the most precise and devastating form through which Ultra damaged its enemy. Before the invasion of Sicily in 1943, and Normandy in 1944, Britain deceived Hitler into thinking that the Allies would attack elsewhere. In both cases, again, Rommel was caught by surprise in Germany when his forces were attacked and returned only to realise the battle already was lost. During May 1944, when Allied forces broke German defences in southern Italy and forced Germany to run for the north, Allied security and deception worked almost exactly as intended, crippling the enemy's defences. After capturing German intelligence records, Allied headquarters in Italy held that the enemy was 'almost entirely blinded by the fog of war, misled as to where the main weight of our attack was to fall, he had placed his reserves where we wanted them'.[74] Intelligence and deception were fundamental to Allied success in those campaigns. Without these edges, the Germans might have deployed their forces in France or Italy so as to pin the Allies far longer in their beachheads, or else to force postponement of attacks. Either outcome would have degraded the strategy of overthrow.

Ultra and Overlord

In Operation Overlord, intelligence was excellent and influential. This case shows the best that can be expected from intelligence, its limits, and how far decision-makers must act in the face of uncertainty, error and ignorance. Intelligence for Overlord conventionally is viewed as precise and powerful, accurate and certain, despite some errors.[75] In fact, success, failure and irrelevance overlapped. Commanders and planners at several headquarters made key decisions purely from military rationality, with intelligence irrelevant – such as the plan to strike Normandy, and then to double the frontage and strength of the attack. Intelligence was secondary when Overlord initially was formulated, though it became central when that plan was refined and applied between April and June 1944. Allied commanders and planners, able and experienced, debated all issues thoroughly and well, and incorporated intelligence into planning, through competition. As Montgomery's intelligence chief Edgar 'Bill' Williams told one colleague: 'there is real value in an agreed text. If we are to be wrong, let's all be wrong together. At least then our Commanders will not have had divided counsel.'[76] Most decisions emerged through arguments between mid-level military bureaucrats, who were confronting a situation up to twelve months away. They argued over predictions as much as assessments; all strove for accuracy, each understood its limits. They thought less about Germany's current strength in France than how it would meet amphibious attack, its power relative to Allied forces in recent battles, its uncommitted forces across Europe and their speed of deployment. Enemy intentions and capabilities were not distinct matters, but fused – what Germany would do was what it could do. If the enemy guessed right, its forces already deployed against invasion in the west could defeat, or deter, Overlord.

Allied planners used whatever intelligence they had. Its limits demonstrate that no service ever can be perfect. GC&CS used its resources almost perfectly against a myriad of tasks, fortunately, since other sources were crippled. Tactical intelligence on German dispositions was almost non-existent, while fear of tipping the Allied hand hampered photo-reconnaissance. Simple order of battle was hard to follow, as German formations shuffled in and out of theatre. At any time, Ultra was excellent on the identification, numbers and locations of formations in, entering or leaving the theatre, and almost perfect in the weeks before D-Day. So too, the best source available to Ultra was problematical. Magic captured reports by Japanese authorities who inspected the defences of France in 1943–44, such as General Ōshima Hiroshi, the Japanese ambassador, and Admiral Kojima Hideo, the naval attaché to Germany. Their reports ranked high within the intelligence available for planning in Overlord, but also reflected a Japanese overestimate of Nazi power and German efforts at disinformation. Oshima and Kojima overstated German capabilities in the west, tempered by professionalism in observation, which discounted German lies. The more they relied on what they were told, as against what they saw, the less accurate became their comments. British intelligence found treasure in these reports, while throwing out the trash, by comparing them to material from all other sources, including Ultra.[77]

Between the time plans were made and executed, much might change. Most key points did not lie simply in the sphere of intelligence – such as how good the enemy would be and how it would prepare its defences and counter-attack. This created a dynamic tension in planning between worst-case and better-case assessments. Some worst-case estimates were so pessimistic that, if taken seriously, the invasion must be abandoned. Just before the invasion, the Joint Intelligence Committee (JIC) and Eisenhower's headquarters, Supreme Headquarters Allied Expeditionary Forces (SHAEF), held that Germany 'may possibly' have 3,000 tanks in France – 159 per cent above the true figure.[78] In his celebrated briefing of Allied generals at St Paul's School in west London, on 15 May 1944 – treated as the touchstone for expectations before 6 June 1944 – Montgomery made points which he knew were misleading but that fitted the worst-case assessments of SHAEF and the JIC. He held that Germany had ten Panzer and twelve infantry assault divisions in France, which would launch a 'full-blooded counter attack' on the bridgehead between D+6 and D+8.[79] His actual planning rated German strength at a far smaller – and accurate – level of twelve assault and Panzer divisions. Bill Williams's last estimate of the German armour which Allied forces would engage on D-Day – 280 tanks and assault guns – was inaccurate only by 10 per cent. In practice, worst-case planning was for the record, while better-case assessments drove planning. Commanders and planners recognised that they were applying worst-case logic and tried to minimise its impact, and to calculate how Germany (not the Allies) would act. These efforts were successful.[80]

Intelligence revealed German expectations, understanding and intentions. It showed the enemy was behaving as Overlord assumed, how the Allied deception plan, Fortitude South, was working, and the weakness of enemy intelligence. Ultra and Magic showed that German generals and Hitler exaggerated Allied forces in Britain by 200 per cent and the initial strength of a seaborne assault by 400 per cent; remained fixed on the Pas de Calais, 175 miles north of the Normandy peninsula; but during May paid increasing attention to Normandy and strengthened the garrison there. Only a few more divisions would preclude Overlord. That Germany came so close to seeing the real danger and to blocking it proves not the failure of Fortitude, but its success. Almost half of the German forces in the west – good and mediocre – were badly placed for the attack on Normandy, while the formations there were just too weak to crush or contain the invasion. All that Germany needed to defeat an Allied attack on Normandy was superiority in intelligence. They were inferior, for which Ultra deserves much credit.

Error and uncertainty surrounded issues such as the capabilities of all German armoured and infantry divisions, which generally were overestimated; while Allied commands split over assessment. Intelligence, however, was correct on most major matters and trusted by the key actors: Montgomery and his staff at 21 Army Group. Williams's predictions were imperfect but close enough to work. Since these errors were not systematic, many cancelled each other out. Others shaped matters which did not matter – so too often the successes.

Success was greatest at the strategic level, on issues such as the number of enemy formations in France (especially, Normandy) and their locations. Intelligence was fundamental for knowledge and psychological certainty. It overcame divisions over planning. Many key issues, however, were uncertain, such as the number of enemy tanks (as against armoured divisions) in France, where estimates varied widely. This failure stemmed from limits in Ultra, which did worse in tank counting than in 1941. Changes in how German formations reported their tank strengths stymied Bletchley until D-Day itself. Allied assessments overstated the efficiency of German divisions in France, the speed and scale with which Germans could reinforce Normandy, and their command system – though none could safely have predicted that the latter would perform so poorly as it did. Worst-case logic spurred effective action. It led Allied commanders to focus on jamming the German machine through every means possible, including air strikes, special forces, the French resistance, and speed of assault. Fortitude was ordered to shape German actions long after Overlord opened, and did so. These means achieved their end; they might have worked less well without the spur of such fear and uncertainty. Those errors cost little because they drove effective counteraction and their significance was small. Twenty-first Army Group made the fewest mistakes among Allied commands and acted on its own views. The greatest area of failure lay at the tactical level, especially regarding the details of German strength and defences at Normandy, as at Omaha Beach and Caen, and how the bocage, the chequerboard of hedged farmland in the interior, would affect battles. These failures in assessment mattered little: neither would have successes. The problem was the enemy, not intelligence about it. Once forces were ashore, attrition could not be avoided, through a high-intensity clash between large and good armies on narrow fronts, where intelligence aided the Allies, though not dramatically. Intelligence did all that could be hoped. The rest was up to the men.

British Sigint and the Pacific War

British success against Japanese cryptosystems slipped during 1939. When the United States gave GC&CS a Purple analogue in 1941, its exploitation absorbed all the energies of the Japanese Section. GC&CS ceased to attack Japanese military or naval targets, leaving them to FECB and the Americans. Britain mastered Japanese diplomatic traffic but not IJN and army codes. In 1941, Britain's best source on the IJN was traffic analysis, where it suffered from weak units, technical problems and Japanese superiority in intelligence. FECB's weekly assessments of the Pacific theatre and Japanese intentions were cabled to its consumers, including the military attaché in Tokyo, via the Interdepartmental Cypher, which Japanese codebreakers read.[81] Though in 1945 Japanese authorities destroyed evidence on their use of these assessments, making any case speculative, this issue may have been Britain's greatest cryptographic failure of modern history. Probably knowledge of British preconceptions aided Japan's campaign of security and deception to cover the start of the Pacific war. Japanese signals security and deception were good. British Comint and human intelligence picked up reports which fed those preconceptions, just as Britain deceived Germany. In any case, FECB and British commanders misconstrued Japanese intentions. They thought Japan probably would not strike Britain and the United States until mid-1942, and would attack Thailand, but not Malaya, in December 1941. These errors affected American assessments, and its exposure to a surprise attack at Pearl Harbor. The outbreak of the Pacific war was the first test of the Anglo-American intelligence alliance: it failed. The Japanese attack on Thailand and Malaya of 8 December 1941 surprised Britain, paralysed its reactions and spurred Japanese victory.[82] The commander of the Royal Navy's Force Z at Singapore, Admiral Tom Phillips, ignored intelligence when he sailed out to a disaster, in which Japanese Sigint played a minor part. Sigint did little to help Britain avoid the fall of Singapore – its greatest intelligence failure of the twentieth century and a proximate cause for the fall of the British empire. Yet the real problem was power, not knowledge. Japan was so much stronger than Britain in this region that it would have taken Singapore sooner or later even had British intelligence been better, though perhaps with less British humiliation.

This attack splintered the British empire in Asia. Its fragments never re-knitted. Between 1942 and 1945, Britain contributed more to victory against Japan through Sigint than any other means, except the Fourteenth Army in Burma. British Sigint was successful, but no imperial force could use it with effect. Sigint aided RAF and Royal Navy elements in India and the Indian Ocean, but their actions were marginal to the war. Sigint would have guided Britain's reconquest of Singapore, but Japan surrendered before it was launched.[83] The African, British and above all Indian, soldiers of the Fourteenth Army reconquered Burma through superior command, skill and power, with little help from Ultra. Australian Sigint and soldiers worked under American command in the New Guinea campaign, matching the United States' contribution in those areas.[84] British Siginters in India broke the IJA's code for maritime movement, which boosted a major action: the Allied submarine campaign against Japanese merchantmen. Berkeley Street exploited Magic better than American codebreakers. It and the Ministry of Economic Warfare produced economic intelligence on the Japanese empire which won American admiration. GC&CS aided American codebreakers against Japan significantly, and offered even more, but the latter resisted its help; they did not think it necessary. American authorities minimised British participation in the campaign for political reasons: to prevent their ally from restoring its power in Asia, while boosting their own.

Conclusion

Cryptology was that part of power where Britain most led the world during the Second World War. Yet as a whole, sword and shield together, Sigint did little to help Britain block defeat in 1939–42; it worked marginally to Germany's benefit in the west, and massively on the Eastern front. The weaknesses in Enigma had little to do with why Germany failed to win the Second World War, though much to do with the pace of its defeat. When Britain stood on the defensive, Ultra did well. Better armies and generals could have enabled Ultra to do more; Britain would have gained dramatically from improved signals security. Once the Western Allies took the initiative, however, Ultra worked in a one-sided way. Ultra augmented British influence over the formulation of Anglo-American strategy in Europe, and Allied power in its execution. Without Ultra, probably Britain could not have imposed the Mediterranean strategy on the United States in 1942–43. Sigint aided Germany by blunting one great Allied endeavour – the Combined Bomber Offensive – and to a lesser degree by boosting the U-boat campaign. Ultra, conversely, nudged bold Allied strategies in the Mediterranean and Europe. It gave accurate and trusted estimates of the enemy's intentions and capabilities that enabled surprise attacks which transformed power across continents. The only comparable campaigns were the American triumphs in the Pacific war, which Sigint also supported.

The relative value of Ultra can be gauged only through comparison with the effect of manpower and industry, other forms of organisation, with the quality of military institutions and of commanders. The Western Allies won the war primarily because of command and power – the quality of forces and commanders and the scale of resources – and secondarily, because of intelligence. Ultra provided mastery in the war of knowledge, which significantly multiplied Allied power and command. It let Allied commanders use their resources efficiently and win faster and more cheaply than otherwise would have been possible. Yet once the tide had turned, Allied power was so much greater that probably the Allies would have won without Ultra, though at much greater cost.

Allied victory had many causes. To judge how any of them shaped a prolonged war of attrition is hard, especially one which worked in such complex ways as intelligence. The thought that: 'we could shorten the duration of the war by months, at a saving of thousands of lives a day', haunted Hut 3.[85] The effect of Ultra is a matter for speculation, counterfactual logic and an attempt to winnow the effect of one cause from a complex process. The best-known effort is the 'conservative estimate' by F. H. Hinsley, a leading analyst during the war, and chief editor of the official history of British intelligence, that Ultra saved the Allies three to four years of war and huge expenditures in lives and resources. His case focuses on the superiority of Ultra to its German equivalent, its centrality to the battle of the Atlantic, and of the latter to the war. This case overestimates Ultra's contribution to the U-boat campaign and of the latter to the war, and overlooks Axis successes in intelligence. Germany might even have won its intelligence war against the Allies, if the USSR is included in the toll. Hinsley defines the value of Allied intelligence by adding its victories and ignoring its defeats – and the successes of the enemy.[86] Ultra significantly multiplied Western power against Germany, but the Soviet Army also shaped German defeat. Counting the results from all clashes between swords and shields between 1939 and 1945, one might conclude that victory in intelligence, especially Ultra, shaved several months from the war in Europe, and saved the lives of tens or hundreds of thousands of Western Allied soldiers. That impact would rise if one counted only the effect of Ultra, and disregarded the damage caused by poor Allied Comsec. General Dwight Eisenhower held that Ultra had 'priceless value to me. It has saved thousands of British and American lives and, in no small way, contributed to the speed with which the enemy was routed and eventually forced to surrender.'[87] The question: 'How many divisions had Bletchley Park?' cannot be answered definitively – but British statesmen asked it when they considered the future of GCHQ in 1945.

Cheltenham: GCHQ, Britain and Whitehall, 1945–92

Strategy and Power

In 1938, Britain was the world's central power in an atomised political system. By 1945 it was a world power, secondary only to the United States and the USSR, but greater than any other.[1] Over the coming decades, which spanned the Cold War and decolonisation, Britain abandoned an empire that cost more than it offered and became one of the strongest second-tier states – an island off mainland Europe but with residual power and interests remaining elsewhere. Meanwhile, Britain's old means for security, especially sea power, declined in value and strength. By contrast, hydrogen weapons guaranteed Britain's destruction in a nuclear war. Therefore, when handling top-tier nations Britain worked from a position of weakness or parity, yet still remained superior to most states. Economic problems produced crises which shook its society and policies. Britain worked within a loose coalition of Western nations, led by the United States, with which it pursued and achieved a 'special relationship', albeit threadbare in patches. That coalition simplified British security: nuclear destruction would involve everyone, while no great power directly threatened Britain on her own. At the peak of imperial overstretch, Britain seemed in endless decline, but it remained formidable. In the decades after 1980, British economic competitiveness and its power in the world revived somewhat.

Britain created intelligence and strategy via elaborate and integrated bureaucracies, which were generally better coordinated than in other countries.[2] In time of peace, intelligence mattered more than ever before for Britain – and GCHQ was its most important and successful strategic institution, for several reasons. GCHQ was a 'cheap date': small investments produced a return which constantly justified the cost. GCHQ gave Britain comparative advantages within the Western coalition, which enabled political leadership and strategic profit, doubly so when utilised against non-Western states. Intelligence, especially UKUSA – the Sigint relationship between the Five Eyes: Australia, Britain, Canada, New Zealand and the United States – drove the special relationship. GCHQ was the most economical and cost-effective area of state activity where Britain could maintain credibility with the United States. American interests spurred Britain to make GCHQ its highest strategic priority.

Cryptology and Intelligence

GCHQ's history spans two ages of Sigint during the period from 1914 until the present day. That span stands on five pillars: the births of the age of military radio in 1914; of mechanised cryptanalysis in 1940; of computerised cryptanalysis from 1955; of satellite communication and interception by 1970; and of the internet by 1996. Two of these pillars, those of 1914 and 1996, marked the start of new ages of Sigint. Across this period, modes of communication changed constantly and some elements of attack died or were transformed, but not all of them. By 1916, for example, Siginters had mastered important techniques, such as gathering intelligence on the external characteristics of messages, rather than their content. This technique – traffic analysis (T/A) – first developed against radio communications on the Western front, remained the main source for military intelligence on the Warsaw Pact until 1992, and became even more important when applied to the bulk collection of internet communications carried on telephone lines. GCHQ witnessed that span of time through the movement of generations, groups of people with similar experiences and mentalities which were unlike those of their predecessors and successors. Between 1919 and 1939 the first practitioners of Sigint led and staffed GC&CS. Siginters from the Second World War dominated GCHQ's leadership until 1978. Recruits from 1970 onwards led GCHQ into the internet age. Only after 2015 did most members of GCHQ's staff have no experience from the radio age.

Over this century of Sigint, GCHQ as an organisation took many forms. Its social and institutional history involves more than just intelligence. After 1945, GCHQ, like MI5 and MI6, was an intelligence agency, with collectors, analysts, linguists, data processors and clericals, but with far greater technologically based sections. Unlike its sister bureaus, but like imagery agencies, GCHQ collected and produced material on an industrial scale and in several fields at once. It created information on an assembly line. More than in MI6's complex business of Humint, every part of GCHQ's Sigint machine had to cooperate for any element to work. GCHQ was a factory, linked to a university, where scientists studied and technicians applied the leading edge of communications and computing. GCHQ owned Whitehall's first concentration of computers, which ranked among the largest outside the United States. GCHQ was no more like MI6 than it was the Atomic Energy Research Establishment at Harwell or the Mechanical Department of the GPO (which was a world leader in communications research). By 2020, GCHQ, responsible for cyber offence and defence, was a diplomatic tool, an intelligence bureau and an executive agency.

Many things drove that evolution, but one above all. One explanation for institutional development – 'path dependency' – holds that ephemeral conditions shape how organisations solve new problems.[3] Once started down a path, only rare circumstances drive them to switch to another. GC&CS was the first Comint agency to leave the road travelled by other Comint agencies and to move towards Ultra. That movement shaped GCHQ's footsteps after 1945, though not in a simple way. Many observers assume that after 1945 Sigint followed the model of Bletchley, focusing on cryptanalysis against high-grade systems. In fact, while an ideal type for intelligence gained from content analysis, Ultra is not a universal model. During 1940–45, cryptanalysis and traffic analysis were integrated, with Ultra the master. After 1945, Britain deployed the model of Ultra wherever possible, but it rarely worked against the Soviet Union, where T/A became the main source. Instead, GCHQ's path in the Cold War started from two places. GC&CS was the root of commercial and diplomatic codebreaking. The rest of GCHQ combined Bletchley's enterprising spirit with a workmanlike approach to traffic analysis, an element that key cryptanalysts such as Tiltman and Welchman despised. Bletchley showed how to organise Sigint organisations, which are inherently complex and fragile, in changing circumstances. Traffic analysis became the forge for a blade against the USSR. This path was easy to follow because in 1945 GCHQ was already on it.

Initially, experience from the Second World War drove GCHQ. Indeed, for a decade after 1945, GCHQ hoped to replicate Bletchley by rapidly providing Comint from the high-grade systems of its main enemy – previously the Axis, now the Soviet Union. That hope faded and different successes drove GCHQ down other paths where work emphasised the analysis of the metadata of signals, traffic analysis and exploitation of low- and middle-grade systems, leavened by high-grade cryptanalytic research and diplomatic and operational Comint. Hut 6 had disparaged the role of T/A during the war; in contrast, from 1960 Siginters attacking Soviet traffic doubted the value of codebreaking. Like all Anglo-American strategic agencies, GCHQ expected the next war to be like the last. Plans for expansion in wartime, which represented lessons learned from the experience of Bletchley, shaped its organisation right after the war. GCHQ lived off wartime kit and expertise until 1954–58, when the ground shifted all round, threatening to swallow it. These changes forced reconfiguration, recapitalisation, re-equipment and many crises – especially because Britain could no longer purchase, nor produce, all of the equipment needed to master Sigint.

Decisions around 1956–57 by the COS and the JIC about defence and intelligence led GCHQ to redefine its aims and organisation. Many argued that Britain would be wrecked in a major war. It could fight only one war at a time and just with the forces at hand. Expansion in war would be impossible and victory improbable. Thus, deterrence was the only rational strategy for Britain, which intelligence, diplomacy and force must combine to sustain.[4] In 1956, GCHQ and the US National Security Agency (NSA) had unified war plans. For the next decade, GCHQ wrestled with changes in these plans, while NSA could not define one.[5] That they cooperated fully despite this gap shows the insignificance of the topic in the nuclear era. When the agencies finally discussed war plans again in the mid-1960s, the differences were stark. NSA expected some part of American Sigint to survive a nuclear exchange under a service agency which could attack enemy systems. GCHQ expected annihilation. Its remnants, and those of the BBC's monitoring system, would provide basic information from plain-language traffic for whatever national command they could find. NSA intended to move one British liaison officer to the American Sigint command[6] – they might have controlled whatever survived of British Sigint.

After 1945, the topography of cryptology was transformed. Every country had Sigint agencies, which were stronger than ever. In 1938, the world probably had around 20,000 Siginters; by 1988, perhaps 500,000. Far more traffic was intercepted than ever before, both state and private. Communications relied decreasingly on cables and moved to wireless systems of various sorts. Decolonisation tripled the number of state targets for attack. New states, and the USSR and China, had poor landline systems and relied heavily on radio. This opened new opportunities for interception, especially of 'civil' traffic, which produced intelligence on foreign administrative and economic affairs. From 1914, Siginters intercepted private traffic carried by wireless which later were termed 'international leased carrier', or ILC. After 1945, such messages were increasingly common, opening opportunities to Siginters. In 1929, GC&CS intercepted perhaps, at a guess, around 10,000 ILC messages sent by wireless; by 1980, GCHQ captured tens of millions via communications satellites (Comsat).[7] Only powerful and sophisticated data-processing systems could sift through the irrelevant 99.9 per cent of ILC and civil messages in order to uncover the gold.

Much radio interception worked as it had during 1945, but from 1970, satellite intercept systems captured and processed traffic automatically. Computers transformed cryptanalysis. If properly used, many cryptosystems were unbreakable, yet at the same time many leading states were mediocre in cryptography. In 1968, some states still used systems that were little advanced from Enigma, which was vulnerable to techniques from Bletchley, but they did not much interest GCHQ. The story that Britain deliberately flogged copies of the Enigma to foreign countries is false. At the same time, the discovery of 'Tempest' – the leakage of electronic emissions from machines, which could be intercepted hundreds of yards away, threatening cryptography – created dangers at home and opportunities abroad.

Politics and Path Dependency

Ephemeral circumstances had consequences when Whitehall discussed how to organise intelligence after the Second World War. In 1919, military intelligence and the Foreign Office had dominated such discussions. Each department controlled its own property and played a lone hand. Interdepartmental discussions were few and tended to occur only on issues such as linking the security services of all colonies or restructuring political policing in Britain. They led nowhere, save in Sigint. The heads of the intelligence agencies usually had little voice in these matters. During 1943–45, conversely, the Cabinet Office and the Foreign Office dominated discussions, especially those officials involved in the intelligence machinery such as Victor Cavendish-Bentinck and Denis Capel-Dunn from the JIC, and Peter Loxley, the Foreign Office liaison with the intelligence services. Untimely death in an aircraft accident (Capel-Dunn and Loxley) and retirement eliminated these officials just as their advice was adopted. Their recommendations were debated widely. The military intelligence services were left to handle their own problems, but addressed the main settlement, which required cooperation between all parties. MI6, MI5 and JIC were the central topics of debate, in which they participated;[8] GC&CS was mentioned far less and did not speak in that debate, since the chief of MI6, Menzies, represented it. Yet GC&CS shaped these discussions because everyone thought it the intelligence success of the war. Key decisions were made before anyone realised Britain's failures of Comsec in 1939–43, which later led Whitehall to strip GCHQ of responsibility for that matter. In this debate, MI5's wartime performance was attacked more than was fair. The Foreign Office and military intelligence scoured MI6 to ensure its competence before releasing it from receivership. GC&CS simply received praise and trust. The question of which organisation should take credit for Ultra also shaped debate. C tried to borrow GC&CS's record to support MI6, unsuccessfully. MI5 denounced that effort. Others wanted to see what Ultra and MI6 had actually done in order to guide decisions about their future.[9]

Authorities rejected radical ideas, such as merging MI5 and MI6 (which they also had opposed after the First World War), and made the system of 1944 the basis for the future. The JIC, under the COS, was chaired by a Foreign Office official and staffed by officers from the services' intelligence branches. It provided interdepartmental assessments from all sources for all consumers. MI5 handled security at home and within the empire, as MI6 did human intelligence abroad; they overlapped on counter-intelligence. GCHQ, under the Foreign Office but responsible to the COS, dominated Sigint, and loosely coordinated the services' branches in these areas. All of these agencies would be larger and better organised than in 1939, and intelligence and policy far more integrated. These judgements sought to derive principles from the organisation of intelligence since 1918, which no one fully understood. As the leading civil servant Norman Brook noted, in war ministers become interested in intelligence: 'In more settled times, however, it has been recognised that the organisation of the Secret Services is a matter best dealt with by senior officials reporting direct to the Prime Minister.'[10] Brook overrated the role of the prime minister in the interwar system, and underrated that of the Foreign Secretary, something which the Foreign Office did not forget. Still, everyone agreed that Britain needed intelligence more than ever before, against all targets. The USSR was far and away the major target. No one anticipated how big it would become, or how rapidly. All thought that intelligence had been starved before the war and organised erratically: these problems must be solved. Intelligence, and especially GCHQ, must receive more resources, yet these would naturally be scarce. Cavendish-Bentinck and Capel-Dunn expressed the aim: 'to ensure that our Intelligence Service after the war is the most efficient possible' and 'as economical as can be without sacrifice of efficiency'.[11]

Authorities knew that what C called 'that key-stone – finance', and public support for it, would drive success in intelligence. Both aims could be achieved, especially if after the war Churchill and military leaders publicly praised the value of intelligence to victory. Cavendish-Bentinck saw:

> no reason why public opinion at the end of this German war should not be receptive to a statement of what we lost by the starving of the Secret Service between the two wars, of the immense additional expenditure that was made necessary during the war largely because of the 'pennywise, pound foolish' policy, and of the debt that we owe to those services in achieving victory ... if H.M.G. will make it clear that Secret Intelligence no less than aeroplanes and guns is necessary if we are to avoid a repetition of 1939–45, they will find no real difficulty in obtaining and continuing to obtain those funds.[12]

C wanted such a statement to stress 'the vital necessity for maintaining an adequate informational organisation as a minimum insurance requirement. The word "Insurance" seems to me all important, as Departments must be made to realise that even if the Secret Service is giving no ostensible return, it is maintaining an organisation of specialists, who can be augmented directly the amber light goes up.'[13] These hopes miscarried because Whitehall decided to hide its intelligence successes. This concealment of past success also heightened the need for secrecy over future work and to hide expenditures plausibly. Anything which legitimately could move on open votes should go there, minimising the call on secret funds, which inadvertently prevented anyone, including the Treasury, from understanding the real cost of Sigint. This discussion was incomplete, because Menzies concealed his slush fund, a second source of unaudited monies which he had developed, and thus his hidden ability to reinforce any area he chose.

These circumstances shaped discussions about the future of GCHQ.[14] Everyone agreed that GCHQ must stand at the top of British intelligence priorities, which themselves were at the pinnacle of British strategic ones. The Bland Committee, which assessed MI6 in 1944, held that: 'Both before, and still more during, the war, the G.C. and C.S. has performed its work brilliantly, and, broadly speaking, all that is necessary is that nothing should be done after the war that would in any way weaken its ability to deliver such goods as may still be available ... no time, labour or money should be spared to permit the G.C. and C.S. to read everything that is readable.' The committee warned of 'the probability that cryptography was a wasting asset', because 'it seems unthinkable that we shall ever be able to read more traffic than we can read now'. When assessing the entire 'intelligence machine' for JIC, Cavendish-Bentinck and Capel-Dunn held that during the war, GC&CS was 'beyond price'. Though Britain might fail 'in future to retain this great advantage over our competitors in the same field, we have no doubt that it is of high importance that research in cryptography in peace time should be energetically pursued'.[15] Military intelligence insisted that GCHQ outweighed MI6. The Directorate of Military Intelligence (DMI) thought 'it essential that no effort should be spared to keep [GC&CS] a live and up-to-date organisation'. Air Intelligence agreed that: 'Intelligence from Most Secret Sources has proved to be more valuable than any other and although it is liable to sudden cessation at any time I consider this should be exploited as fully as may be practicable for as long as may be possible. I feel very strongly that no financial obstacle should be put in the way of the development of this source and that "War Station" activities should be supported on as high a level as personnel and finances will permit. The normal RAF "Y" service should also be maintained at a high standard of proficiency.'[16]

No one could predict what GCHQ might do in the future, including Siginters. John Tiltman, 'did not know what future there would be for GC&CS but he could not help thinking that the difficulties of the work might become insuperable when the governments of the world realised the mistakes that they had made during the war'.[17] Few expected another Bletchley, but none could deny its possibility or utility. All agreed that GCHQ needed great help. Its expenditures would be carried, disguised, on open votes, which must be greater than before 1939, though no one quite understood what that meant. Furthermore, no one knew how GCHQ, presently under C, the Foreign Office and the COS, should be housed after the war. Diplomats thought that MI6 must be under the control of the Foreign Office, but that – given its significance to the services – the same did not necessarily apply to GC&CS, 'though it is undoubtedly a convenient arrangement'. They assumed that GCHQ probably would stay under the Foreign Office, which would handle its administration. Diplomats wanted C to control GCHQ personally, distinct from MI6. The JIC rather than the Sigint Board should control Sigint policy: 'a single high-level organisation should deal with the policy directing this specialised branch of intelligence as well as all other work in the intelligence field'.[18] The politics of this proposal were obvious. Diplomats had fair influence over JIC, but none on the Sigint Board. Service personnel did not really address these issues until the war was done.

During 1944–45, GC&CS had considered its postwar structure. Three young Turks, Welchman, Hinsley and Edward Crankshaw, proposed that Britain create a 'Foreign Intelligence Office' – cybernetic, based around Sigint, but combining all sources. This proposal sank, but it displayed views about Sigint which were conventional at Bletchley, that is, that Sigint must be centralised, unified, flexible, large and industrialised; service Sigint must be integrated with and under GC&CS; the Army's old practice of WTI was obsolete; traffic analysis was handmaid to mechanised cryptanalysis; and both of them must be integrated with intelligence and interception on an assembly line. GC&CS required great resources, capabilities for engineering, machine-making, administration, planning, and control over Sigint. The plans produced by two committees, which included most of the heavyweights at Bletchley and the leaders of the Radio Security Service (RSS), RAF and Army Y (but, significantly, without naval representation), reflected these assumptions. Tiltman's committee on 'Cryptanalysis and Traffic Analysis' noted that cryptanalysis might decline in success. Still, it was GC&CS's main function, both against easy systems and any which might matter in war, no matter how hard the task. In 1945, GCHQ required at least 500 staff for cryptanalysis, traffic analysis and signals security. Beyond that, a 'T/A Centre' of 15–20 officers should monitor technical developments in communication and ensure that interception met the needs of cryptanalysis and intelligence. Cryptanalytic personnel should oversee cryptography and signals security. Josh Cooper's committee on 'Collection of Raw Material' wanted an inter-service office, linked to the cryptanalytic and intelligence sections at the Sigint centre, to control all radio interception including that of the services. That task would require 900 'teams', that is: the number of people required to run one intercept position on a 24/7 basis. These estimates proved far too low for cryptanalysis and traffic analysis, and unreachable for teams, but they reflect the best guesses of the leaders of British Sigint at the time.[19]

Travis presented these proposals to the directors of service Y and the Sigint Board in 1945. In essence, Britain must learn its lessons from the war. Sigint should be centralised, unified and large. Interception, traffic analysis, cryptanalysis and intelligence must be integrated. Policy for Sigint should be made by the Sigint Board, which would be responsible to the COS. The Sigint Board, chaired by C, should include a Foreign Office representative, the Director of GC&CS, and the directors of the intelligence and signals branches of the services. C and the Sigint Board would control GCHQ, which would be responsible to both the Foreign Office and the COS. GC&CS would coordinate all Sigint activities, including those of the services. The heads of service Y would be based at GC&CS. It would have four branches, each with a deputy director: technical (including interception and machine development); cryptanalysis and traffic analysis; intelligence; and cryptography.[20]

The tangled relationship between every element involved in Sigint, especially the services, and the Royal Navy's efforts to maintain independence in the field, drove the response to these proposals. Royal Navy officers, out of the mainstream at Bletchley, had no part in preparing GC&CS's plans. Army and RAF Y criticised the plans constructively, but accepted their logic, and claimed credit for them. The Royal Navy demanded a return to the Sigint structure of 1939, better coordinated but no more integrated. The Sigint Board and GC&CS should handle the tasks proposed by Travis, but with less authority and resources. The Admiralty wished to strip C of power over Sigint, which, parenthetically, would reduce the power of the Foreign Office. Each service Sigint branch should be independent, with the Foreign Office controlling GC&CS. Travis resisted these proposals, as did every other element in Sigint. When the Sigint Board and COS discussed these issues, the Royal Navy abandoned its attack, perhaps realising its isolation.

Travis's proposals were generally accepted, though not all of its details. For example, the directors of service Sigint remained with their ministries, which ultimately marginalised them and strengthened GCHQ. Meanwhile, GCHQ decided to make traffic analysis a fifth branch and redefined its proposals for personnel.[21] The COS approved a strength of 260 civilian officers and 750 support staff, and 125 military personnel at GCHQ. The three services and the Foreign Office would each provide 200 teams for radio interception. GCHQ actually controlled the Foreign Office branch, later called Government Communications Radio Branch (GCRB). This aggregate strength of 503 officers and 5,972 other ranks (of whom 2,100 were civilians) was 1,000 per cent greater than that of 1938, only 25 per cent that of 1944, but far more than actually existed in reality. All of these proposals would be reconsidered in August 1946. The Foreign Office and the service departments would split authority over GCHQ, and also divide its expenses four ways, equally. GCHQ and the JIC were among the first elements of the British state to be centralised and non-departmentalised. The Sigint Board and the COS rejected JIC oversight of Sigint policy, which involved not merely intelligence, but resources and management. Only then, with reluctance, did the Foreign Office join the Sigint Board, where it was weak compared to the services.[22]

During 1945, GC&CS's strengths – its successful attack on German and Japanese cryptosystems – became obsolescent. It had to bolster hitherto weak areas which became new and pressing priorities, such as work against the USSR. Its strength plummeted, but losses were manageable among those with skills suited to a new age. Intercept operators fell sharply in number, but Britain kept more experienced junior and senior Sigint leaders than any other power. The core of GC&CS's Diplomatic Section stayed on, though many, including Denniston, retired. Several of GCHQ's best people, including Turing, Newman and Welchman, left, as did F. H. Hinsley. Yet others stayed: leading youngsters, Bill Bonsall and Joe Hooper; the rising star, Eric Jones; great machine cryptanalysts and cryptomathematicians such as Gerry Morgan and Hugh Alexander; the two masters from GC&CS, Cooper and Tiltman; and a skilful chief in Travis, who exploited opportunity, GC&CS's independence and tradition of timely innovation, knowledge of his people, and the room to promote juniors. Travis moved his best people to key positions as they emerged. For instance, Jones went on to negotiate UKUSA in Washington. Tiltman became Chief Cryptographer at a time when the practice of cryptanalysis was in flux. Aided by Nigel de Grey, and supported by Menzies, Travis restructured GCHQ and maximised GCHQ's interests against every other party. He maintained the Sigint alliance with the United States, and budged it marginally in Britain's favour.

GCHQ provided intelligence that Whitehall wanted, by moving resources from old tasks to new. As the war ended, underemployed interceptors systematically searched the electromagnetic spectrum for unknown signals, nicknamed 'Exotics', probably focusing their energy on Soviet systems, which had been ignored since 1941.[23] GCHQ had a huge capital of diplomatic systems, especially because since 1943 it had capped its help to minor allies in cryptography in order to ease British attack on them after the war. As Peter Loxley noted in 1943: 'I have consulted the various Departments concerned here to see whether any of them considered that we ought to take steps to induce any of our Allies to improve their cyphers. All concerned are agreed, however, that we should not try to improve Allied diplomatic cypher security to a point where we are no longer able to read their cyphers ourselves.'[24] By late 1944, Cavendish-Bentinck thought: 'it does not matter much whether the enemy read Allied Diplomatic cyphers, whilst it is of importance that we should continue to read them. We have taught our Allies enough – and probably too much – about the secrets of secure cyphers. I hope that we shall not henceforth try to improve their service cyphers unless this is absolutely essential.'[25] GCHQ mastered new targets, using old machines and mathematics. It began an attack on Soviet systems. Between 1946 and 1948, it produced Britain's best intelligence, which consumers rated equal to Ultra.

Travis's success provoked challenge. At the war's end, unexpected financial pressure forced the services to reconsider their priorities. One, but only one of them, responded by seeking to cut Sigint. In 1946, the Royal Navy had no obvious enemies which it expected to fight, so it needed Sigint less than the other services. No foreign navy threatened Britain. Instinctively independent, the Royal Navy stood outside the Sigint system of 1942, where all worked for one, and one for all. Reducing naval intercept personnel would have been the Royal Navy's prerogative before 1939; but in 1946, the Sigint Board controlled them. Airmen, diplomats, soldiers and Edward Bridges, Permanent Secretary to the Treasury and Cabinet Secretary, rejected its efforts to reduce these personnel, which must increase their own burden or weaken the overall effort. In order to achieve small savings, the Royal Navy had to attack GCHQ and Whitehall's consensus about its value. In early 1946, the Admiralty told the COS that the Sigint system was 'very luxuriously' staffed. Siginters should pursue 'utmost economy, particularly in manpower, both service and civilian', and meet only 'the essential minimum requirements of signal intelligence in peacetime'. No one supported the Royal Navy's aims, but all agreed to audit Sigint earlier than had been intended. Menzies recommended that a senior officer investigate the issue and announced his faith in present Sigint policy.[26] For the Admiralty to attack GCHQ might seem one-sided, but then so thought Goliath when first he saw David. Without understanding the contest, the Admiralty attacked Whitehall on an issue where naval interests seemed small and wider British ones large, at a time when GCHQ's prestige was peaking and that of the Royal Navy sinking.

The Sigint Board ordered an expert to assess British Sigint, especially its need for staff. Air Chief Marshal Douglas Evill, originally a naval officer, had worked with the Army, RAF and Royal Navy. His technical and technological background, and experience with Ultra and senior staff appointments, helped him to understand and to illuminate the issues at stake. Evill conducted an exemplary enquiry, and an empirical one: he addressed facts which were recognised by both consumers and producers from ample and recent experience. His judgements were pragmatic, without speculation, trusted, and suited to circumstances.

Later assessors, conversely, confronted more open-ended and uncertain circumstances and unleashed hares about bureaucratic reorganisation which confused the reception of their reports. Evill visited every section of GCHQ, and an intercept station from each of the four branches. He asked probing questions of every party. He mastered his topic, perhaps better than any other outside examiner of GCHQ.[27] He was empowered to suggest additions or reductions in resourcing, In fact, Evill cemented GCHQ and British intelligence. He did what Whitehall had not done in 1945: he examined GCHQ's resources, ambitions and achievements in detail, and compared them to British policy aims and power. GCHQ's successes against Soviet civil messages and cryptosystems impressed him. He told the COS that 'the general lines of Sigint Organisation are sound and economical', and 'necessary'. To bring Sigint to its authorised level was the priority, but when that was achieved, further expansion might be necessary. He rejected half of the Sigint Board's requests for new staff, but recommended an increase of about 400 personnel, mostly for Sigint communications, and also forty more each for Russian cryptanalysis and civil text. The Sigint Board and the COS accepted Evill's recommendations, which would define British Sigint policy for a generation.[28] These remarkable events show the rise in power of GCHQ. The Royal Navy lost its special place in Sigint and had to allocate its scarce manpower to the demands of other services and the Foreign Office, without daring to appeal to the Cabinet. Officials and officers made these fundamental decisions on Sigint without consulting the Cabinet, though undoubtedly the prime minister and some of his colleagues approved them.

Autonomy on a Margin

Between 1919 and 1939, GC&CS had achieved autonomy because its work was arcane and self-contained. GC&CS lost autonomy between 1940 and 1942 because it required large resources and mattered to many parties. These circumstances remained after 1945, yet GCHQ again achieved autonomy, as it escaped or absorbed its old masters, MI6 and the service Sigint services, and faced new ones, the powers of Whitehall.

Evill missed only one trick. He recognised the 'need for an authority under the Sigint Board for the day to day execution of its policy over the whole range of the Sigint Organisation and for the detailed processes of coordination and development'. Under the 1945 arrangement, Menzies had these responsibilities, loosely assisted by the Junior Board, or what Evill called, using wartime parlance, 'the D.D.'s "Y"'. Evill suggested that this Junior Board should continue to exercise those powers, and 'to give each D.D. 'Y' a collective responsibility for the general efficiency of Sigint as a whole'.[29] That aim failed, as DDs Y instead declined rapidly in status and expertise. GCHQ took over that function. The Sigint Charter of 1946 maintained the status and membership of the Sigint Board. It also delegated execution of policies, 'in particular also for planning, coordination and matters affecting general operational efficiency' to a 'Junior Sigint Board', chaired by the Director, GCHQ, including the DDs Y and a Foreign Office representative, and others as desired.[30] Soon, the Sigint Board was called the London Signals Intelligence Committee (LSIC) and the Junior Board, the London Signals Intelligence Board (LSIB).

This development did not happen through sleight of hand, but by accident: no one intended the consequences. GCHQ did not create the outcome but naturally exploited it. It took these circumstances for granted – they continued the autonomy it had restored by 1943. The evolution of that autonomy was obscured outside GCHQ, which saw this transformation more clearly than its partners. The complexity of hiding Sigint expenditures even let GCHQ evade Treasury control over its spending. One official later thought Sigint 'an administrative mess … When it comes to money, the situation is even more chaotic. The GCHQ Vote is spread amongst the Foreign Office and the Service Departments, and concealed under various heads'. Another noted 'the basic illogicity (*sic*) of the whole situation in regard to GCHQ which cannot be removed because of the security considerations'.[31] The continuity of honorific control at high levels – C, the Foreign Office, and the Sigint Board – camouflaged the reality: GCHQ controlled itself, and British Sigint. GCHQ became independent from 1946, when it had its own administration, reported directly to the Treasury, and its leaders were drawn only from professional Siginters.[32] GCHQ remained among Britain's top priorities for security, alongside nuclear forces. Compared to its diplomatic and strategic policies, British policy towards GCHQ was remarkably consistent, despite an odd mode of formulation.

GCHQ balanced between various bodies, whose roles fluctuated over time. The military was GCHQ's largest consumer and among its main directors. As the individual services declined in power, the Ministry of Defence (MOD) rose in importance, and the COS stood stable. The services retained power over Sigint, but not within it. In 1945, their authorities on matters of Sigint were veterans and often technical leaders. Soon, they left the field to GCHQ. It told them what to do, while they controlled the means of doing so. GCHQ increasingly commandeered their resources. In 1945, the services provided 90 per cent of intercept operators, but thereafter GCHQ as well as each service maintained large and numerically equal units. From 1957, the services knew that the imminent end of National Service would strip their Sigint branches of key manpower. They required uniformed elements to cover the need for Sigint in military circumstances. Their civilian branches were essential to the national effort but could not grow to meet any service's needs, except at the cost of servicemen. Having these elements join the Government Communications Radio Branch (GCRB) would leave GCHQ responsible for strategic interception, but degrade the services' power over Sigint. GCHQ thought that unification would enable economy and efficiency, but was unwilling to annoy the services over the matter, which, as Hooper said, would damage 'the amity, unity and so the efficiency of the Sigint structure'.[33] These agencies debated those issues but declined hard decisions, until the last National Servicemen left and budgetary pressures heightened. In 1960, the government asked General Gerald Templer, eminent soldier and intelligence officer, to investigate military intelligence in order to 'effect economies' and 'avoid duplication'. He recommended the unification of the civilian branches under GCRB, while leaving each service with small uniformed branches for work on military tasks in dangerous places. This sensible recommendation was executed speedily.[34] The services continued to pay for their old civilian branches, which GCHQ now controlled, while it also had more authority than the military over their uniformed elements.

GCHQ and the Foreign Office had thick, but thinning, relations. During 1945, especially through its influence over the JIC and MI6, the Foreign Office nearly matched the military in dominating GCHQ. That position eroded, particularly when the Cabinet Office took command of the JIC from the COS in 1957, but the Foreign Office remained a force in Sigint. Diplomatic codebreakers at GCHQ serviced the intelligence needs of diplomats. The latter certainly shaped

GCHQ's priorities, second only to the MOD and NSA. Further, the Foreign Office handled human relations and finances with the Treasury for GCHQ, until its incompetence enraged both parties. The Treasury official in charge of intelligence expenditure, John Winnifrith, told GCHQ it was 'utterly intolerable that the Foreign Office administrative machine should be taking your problems so light-heartedly'.[35] In 1947–48, GCHQ acquired those roles. Though the Foreign Office took pride in being the parent of GCHQ, it was essentially just a post office. Until the Single Intelligence Vote was created, the Foreign Office handled GCHQ's public accounting – to the anguish of officials who did not know what GCHQ did and disliked taking responsibility for the 75 per cent of its expenditure which was provided by the armed services. The outcome was secretly to divide responsibility for expenditure of the hidden Sigint budget and to inform the Cabinet Secretary and Treasury (but not Parliament) who was responsible for what. The Foreign Office had the last voice in appointing the GCHQ Director, after consulting other departments, but lost that status to the Cabinet Office in 1981.

The power of politicians over intelligence varied with each Cabinet. The prime minister, and anyone they nominated, and the Defence Secretary and the Foreign Secretary, were as central as they wished to be. Attlee, Eden and Thatcher seem to have been more interested in Sigint than other prime ministers. When Churchill again became prime minister in 1951, GCHQ bid for his support to hire fourteen scientists and engineers for the project to attack Soviet high-grade systems, with some success. Churchill minuted: 'Proceed as proposed' – but otherwise did little on the matter, save to back Eden's support for GCHQ.[36] Meanwhile, the key position on control over GC&CS of the interwar years vanished. From 1942, Menzies helped GCHQ as much as he could, but Travis ran it. Menzies' successor as C, Major General Sir John Sinclair, remained Director General of Sigint in name, without any role in Sigint. His successors lost even that status. From 1952, the Director of GCHQ affected Whitehall as much as C did. GCHQ and MI6, however, remained sister services, with closer relationships than either had with MI5. That relationship bolstered both sisters against all of their suitors.

As C's power over intelligence declined, that of the Cabinet Office rose. Edward Bridges, the Treasury's liaison with the intelligence services during the interwar years, cared about cryptanalysis and cryptography. The Cabinet Secretary matched and then exceeded the Permanent Undersecretary of the Foreign Office (PUS) as the overseer of the intelligence services, both augmented by a new institution. The Permanent Secretaries' Subcommittee on the Intelligence Services (PSIS) – combining the permanent undersecretaries of the Home Office, Foreign Office, the MOD, and the Treasury, plus the Cabinet Secretary – assessed the budgets and programmes of the intelligence services, twice each year, later raised to quarterly reviews. PSIS stemmed from a review of British intelligence which Attlee commissioned from the Cabinet Secretary and from Norman Brook, a veteran on these topics. Brook held that Britain must better coordinate the resources and work of the intelligence services. PSIS 'would become a source of authority and direction for the various intelligence organisations, and an instrument on which the prime minister of the day would come to rely for advice on intelligence matters'. In particular, PSIS aimed 'to estimate the total sum which should, as a matter of policy, be devoted to intelligence and to decide the proper distribution of this expenditure between the various agencies'.[37] Taken literally, this statement suggested that PSIS's main purpose was to manage GCHQ. It took twenty years to do so. By October 1964, PSIS formally replaced the COS and the PUS of the Foreign Office as the final authority in Sigint. No Cabinet, and few prime ministers, shaped these developments.

As intelligence-related budgets exploded, the Treasury became more involved than before with intelligence, especially GCHQ. Initially, the Treasury had little idea of intelligence spending, which came in secret from many sources. It did not begin to control Sigint expenditure until in 1951 PSIS made departments reveal their true spending on the topic. The 'Cost of Sigint' (COSIG) astonished authorities, though they decided to live with it.[38] For the next decade, the Treasury restrained GCHQ expenditure loosely, through negotiations between them and the COS over 'Measures to Improve' in Sigint, but the Exchequer controlled COSIG less than it did any other element of government. GCHQ collated expenditures from the departments and presented the whole to PSIS. The Treasury investigated all issues of finance, which were difficult for outsiders to follow. Conventional control was weak, as information was dispersed among MOD and FCO files. Only from 1959 was a Sigint Finance Committee established, with Treasury representation, to integrate issues of costs into the basis of all Sigint planning.[39] GCHQ was a secret organisation with high national priority which no outsider thought they understood. All accepted that GCHQ could not always follow conventional rules, while its demands might need to be taken on faith. If GCHQ appealed any verdict by the Treasury, the only court of appeal was PSIS, which outweighed both parties, and might place security over economy.

Yet the Treasury saw little sign for concern until 1961, when Templer's report showed how ramshackle liaison was within British Sigint, and its modes for financial control. Treasury experts wished to challenge 'one fundamental point ... there is no clear assessment of the requirements, and of the order of priority between requirements (and consequently the deployment of finance) by which Intelligence Departments' activities should be guided. There is some machinery for considering these aspects, but it is not as clearly dominant as perhaps it ought to be', which made the task of PSIS 'really extremely difficult'. A more senior Treasury official, and soon to be Cabinet Secretary, Burke Trend, stopped this campaign by retorting that Sigint priorities were handled 'regularly and reasonably efficiently'.[40] The Exchequer, however, acted on these suspicions from 1962, in a decade-long campaign to control GCHQ. That so long was taken to achieve this end demonstrates the power of GCHQ's position.

The development of PSIS illuminates GCHQ's place in Whitehall. Only the top officials involved with intelligence, in concert and served by a staff, could oversee GCHQ. Beneath them, power and responsibility took strange forms. The dignified and efficient parts of state were divided. From 1945, a Sigint Board, later called the LSIB and the 'Senior Board', augmented by the LSIC, the 'Junior Board', oversaw GCHQ. Both boards had representatives from every agency which worked with GCHQ, especially military ones. The Senior Board met rarely. It left direction to the Junior Board, which the Director of GCHQ dominated. GCHQ determined its own direction, unless any of its many masters objected to the course or cost. The structure for control was ethereal, because of the gaps between GCHQ, these boards and departments, PSIS and the JIC – not to mention the 'glamour', priority and secrecy surrounding the topic. If any of its masters challenged GCHQ's direction, they would be heard, but usually their challenges were checked; often they were divided. The court of last appeal for disagreements was not the Cabinet, nor prime minister. Instead, the decision was depoliticised. Top officials agreed to accept the advice of eminent external authorities, who received free access to GCHQ. Even powerful organisations which suffered from this advice, such as the Royal Navy and the Treasury, accepted their defeats. Between 1946 and 1990, two such committees met under Evill and Professor Stuart Hampshire. That no further examination occurred until 1992 (under the industrialist Roger Hurn) demonstrates the stability of policy towards GCHQ. That these authorities moved from being an air marshal, to a don, to an industrialist, reflects changes in British attitudes towards expertise on strategic issues.

Masters and Commanders

The political history of GCHQ during the Cold War was bookended by two efforts to remake it from without, unsuccessfully in 1952, successfully in 1995. During 1946, the COS approved a Sigint Charter which specified that deputy directors and directors of GCHQ must be civil servants.[41] This regulation aimed to prevent the services from making these posts a perk for senior officers as they retired. Instead, Siginters should fill these posts, making GCHQ autonomous and professional.

The first test of these aims came with Travis's retirement in 1952. Given GC&CS's habits in hiring before 1940, and its sudden and recent rise to eminence, no internal GCHQ candidate had the seniority which Whitehall demanded for such a post. The only internal candidate, Eric Jones, was born in 1907 to a middling family of businessmen from Lancashire. 'Contrary to my father's wishes but with his consent,' Jones declined to attend university. He wished to apply his intelligence elsewhere. A quick learner and autodidact, Jones showed creativity, independence and prowess on paths outside Whitehall: in business, diplomacy, politics, information processing and management.[42] He entered the family firm at fifteen, as a junior. A dynamic force in the declining textile industry, at the age of eighteen Jones joined a different firm and later founded another in Manchester, becoming its governing director at the age of twenty-six. He became a fixture of the Conservative Party in Manchester. By 1939, the Conservative Central Office had groomed him as a parliamentary candidate under 'a scheme to attract a limited number of younger men by paying their expenses'.

Jones did not abandon that ambition until 1946, when he became a permanent civil servant. He entered the RAF's German intelligence branch in 1940 as a volunteer, without knowing German. By 1941, as squadron leader, he headed the section 'which was chief user of GCHQ products'. Upon joining GC&CS in 1942, Wing Commander (soon to be Group Captain) Jones made Hut 3 the world's centre for intelligence. After 1945, he organised two of GCHQ's main divisions, Intelligence and Traffic Analysis, negotiated UKUSA, and became the first Senior United Kingdom Liaison Officer (SUKLO) in Washington, and Travis's right hand.[43] His contribution to GCHQ rivals that of Tiltman or Turing. Outsiders did not understand the difficulty of the problems Jones solved. But his colleagues did, and supported his candidature strongly.

In their last contributions to GCHQ, Travis and Menzies championed Jones as Director. They aimed to give the intelligence services autonomy and to keep top jobs for experts. Only a veteran, they claimed, could manage GCHQ. While that claim was debatable, other arguments were unshakeable. To appoint an outsider and leave Jones as deputy Director would paralyse promotions for all promising personnel in GCHQ, damage morale and create a precedent which might become the norm. The making of this decision illustrates the peculiar position of GCHQ in Whitehall. Two meetings of the Sigint Board rejected the recommendation of Menzies and Travis, forcing a competition and stalemate. Half the members confessed incomprehension, and almost all uncertainty, about the issues and individuals involved. The three service directors of Signals abstained from voting. The military intelligence chiefs were divided, admitted ignorance and let others dominate the decision, unlike the cases of 1919 and 1942. Travis annoyed members by raising the needs of a 'Specialist Department' and the regulations of the Sigint Charter, which many were willing to abandon. These men disliked being responsible for a selection which they could not shape. That situation needed to change, one way or another. Without Menzies' support, Travis would have lost this battle and GCHQ its hopes for autonomy. Among civilians at the top, however, Travis's recommendation carried weight, more than Menzies.

Deference to C, and personal quirks, gained Jones support from Percy Sillitoe – head of MI5 and another outsider in the intelligence services embittered by experiences with his social superiors; the ACAS

(I) from Jones's home service; and from General Kenneth Strong of the Joint Intelligence Bureau (JIB), one of GCHQ's main consumers, who undoubtedly knew Jones. Several other members of the Sigint Board preferred to appoint an outsider for some time, groom Jones for the task, and, if he proved his mettle, make him Director. The outsider, Charles Daniel, was an admiral with expertise in management, industry, technology, wireless and science, but not intelligence or Sigint. As Controller of the Navy, he oversaw great construction projects. As Commandant of the Imperial Defence College, he showed intellect. That authorities ranked Jones equal with Daniel shows Whitehall's respect for the Siginter, and GCHQ's opinion in its field. The DMI preferred Daniel but would accept Jones. The DNI and Dr Bertie Blount, the Director of Scientific Intelligence, preferred Daniel, but not vociferously.[44]

Judgements of individuals and expectations for leadership drove the Foreign Office to a remarkably personalised analysis. Its liaison officer with the intelligence services, Patrick Reilly, knew GCHQ well, perhaps better than anyone else in Whitehall. Diplomats felt caste bias against Jones. No department of comparable size was led by a northerner with a background in business and not Oxbridge or Whitehall. Jones was at the extreme end of the diversity that Whitehall could accept for leadership in 1952. GCHQ's expansion was a key job, which Daniel could manage. Jones, forty-five years old, seemed young for the post, which he could hold for ten to fifteen years.

Were Jones appointed, Clive Loehnis might become his successor. Loehnis met Whitehall's social expectations for leadership, but diplomats questioned his qualifications and those of Menzies' successor, John Sinclair. Reilly held that Loehnis does 'not carry the guns for the Director's post'; Permanent Undersecretary William Strang wrote: 'I agree.' though: 'He has his points.'[45] Reilly saw promise in the younger generation at GCHQ, above all Hooper. 'The proposed team – General Sinclair, Jones, Loehnis, Cooper and Hooper, is not as strong a one as we should have during the next three critical years,' Reilly held, especially for the key task of 'breaking the Russian cyphers'. A team led by Daniel would be better. Jones could cover Daniel's inexperience in Sigint, while developing breadth. By appointing Daniel for three years, Jones then could rule for a decade, groom Hooper for success and bypass Loehnis.[46] Reilly's position was not unfriendly to Jones, or GCHQ. Daniel's supporters wanted well for GCHQ.

The Foreign Office prepared to present this case to the COS and the Secretary of State, Anthony Eden. Unexpectedly, scientists working for the government, especially the MOD, entered the fray. Frederick Brundrett and Henry Tizard treated the directorship of GCHQ as a scientific post and sought to control the perk. Menzies distrusted them, rightly. Brundrett and GCHQ clashed frequently on control of Elint. Brundrett also misconstrued GCHQ and Sigint. He told Reilly that although GCHQ has done 'extremely good work, it bears certain marks of amateurism. It has been built up ad hoc by people who work by rule of thumb and have not an adequate conception of the fundamental scientific approach to their problems and of the way in which scientists work.' Travis, Brundrett thought, had a 'somewhat bureaucratic conception of organisation'. He refused to recognise the need to pay scientists above civil service rates. Thus 'the Universities did not think that G.C.H.Q. was a good employer for scientists and it was therefore hard for them to get the right kind of recruit'.[47] These comments had force. GCHQ's grasp of science and scientists was flawed, but Brundrett's critique personalised a systemic problem. Though GCHQ found employing scientists difficult, and organised them inefficiently, Jones was the prime advocate of improving the situation – they were central to his plan to crack Soviet systems through cryptomathematics and 'electronic cypher-breaking machinery'.[48] And no one who gave Turing, Welchman and Newman the resources they needed to break Enigma and Fish and build machines to exploit the fractures – as Travis did, on faith – could be regarded as bureaucratic. The government, not Travis, constrained GCHQ's ability to hire above civil service rates. Daniel, Brundrett concluded, could put GCHQ on the right lines, after which Jones, 'within his limitations, an admirable person', should take command.[49] Brundrett expected Professor Max Newman, the academic most involved with GCHQ, to support these views.

To contextualise these arguments, on 11 January 1952, Reilly suggested that Strang consult Tizard, Brundrett, the great atomic physicist John Cockcroft, and Newman – 'the most eminent academic authority with a knowledge of G.C.H.Q.'. Before British scientists lined up to shape this appointment, they were outflanked: on the same day, Newman and Turing, visiting GCHQ to assess its attack on Soviet cyphers, authorised Travis to present the following echo of the Trafalgar Day memorandum:

> Even with their background of work with us during the war, and that of Turing during one vacation since, they would need weeks of study here before they could feel competent to express a definite opinion on our plans; others, without that background, would need an even longer period of study; no opinion formed without weeks of solid study would be of any solid value; from their personal knowledge of the personnel primarily involved (Alexander, Morgan, Cooper and Good) and from what they saw and heard today, <u>they have no impression that our plans are in any way radically wrong</u>…[50]

C sent this report straight to Strang, who saw the need to take command. Strang consulted only one scientist, Newman, who gutted Brundrett:

> Speaking from his wartime experience, [Newman] would not have said that G.C.H.Q. was in any sense an amateurish organisation. It was an organisation with a limited objective and the scientists that it employed in the higher reaches were people with a special skill rather than people with a broad scientific capacity. People like Messrs. Alexander, Morgan and Good were probably unequalled in the world in this field. He had been struck during his service in G.C.H.Q. with the way in which these highly skilled people had been allowed to pursue their own researches without disturbance or frustration. He himself had been allowed six months to solve a problem of which he had in fact succeeded in finding the solution … this intelligent and deft handling of staff must be put to the credit of Sir E. Travis himself. The highly skilled staff of G.C.H.Q. were rather queer people who would react badly if driven or pestered.

Newman declined to offer an opinion about Jones or Daniel, whom he did not know.

The Foreign Office produced the evidence and its preference for Daniel to two senior officials who understood intelligence. Brook, another grammar school boy, though with a degree, backed Jones. Bridges supported Daniel. The COS backed the sailor and rejected autonomy for GCHQ. A 'fresh brain without preconceived ideas' might help GCHQ down its new path. The COS, like MOD scientists, favoured radical but unspecified changes in GCHQ and expressed concern about its ability to manage expansion. Finally, Strang told Eden that the directorship of GCHQ was a 'big job … Sigint is our best source of intelligence about the Soviet Union and Satellites. In war it would again of course be vital. We are not at present reading any Russian cyphers, but we have plans for a big Anglo-American research programme which should give us a fair chance of success in peace, and a good chance fairly early in a war. Our share involves a considerable increase in the size and cost of G.C.H.Q. Success depends on very fast calculating machines and requires high priority for scientists and equipment in the field of electronics, where the competition is fierce.' Jones, 'who is nearly 45, has ability, strength of character, a good personality, great power of work, and a successful record at G.C.H.Q. during the war, and since. He is a good organiser and administrator. He has come on well since he became Deputy Director early in 1950, and has of late shown up well when in full charge of the organisation during Sir E. Travis's frequent absences. He is not however of outstanding intellectual distinction and he is a little limited in background and outlook'. Daniel had greater ability, broader experience and 'would be more likely' to get GCHQ help from universities, strengthen its scientific credentials, and boost Jones's abilities. 'In a time of severe competition, Sir C. Daniel's standing and experience would be valuable in fighting G.C.H.Q.'s battles in Whitehall.'[51]

Eden rejected Strang's advice. He respected Travis's opinion. 'A retired Admiral needs to be exceptional to justify such a choice,' yet the candidates were matched in quality. Noting GCHQ's 'highly specialised character', Eden supported 'the principle that its senior posts should be filled if possible from its regular staff'.[52] This Eden doctrine, which ruled throughout the Cold War, met GCHQ's demands for autonomy. Whereas the appointments of Denniston, Travis and Jones were contested throughout Whitehall, later ones were quieter affairs, if not always pleasant. Only internal candidates became Director. The key to success was professional respect and the eye of the incumbent. GCHQ was sufficiently small that candidates were few in number and known commodities. They competed more in the middle ranks of GCHQ than at the top. GCHQ and its masters continued a pattern of succession planning, under which a Director defined one or two officers to his superiors as potential successors and gave them senior responsibilities to prove their quality. If an internal candidate impressed the outside authority – the Foreign Secretary or the Cabinet Secretary – they would win without competition: even Loehnis, despite the reservations about him. Loehnis's immediate successors, Hooper and Bonsall, were excellent choices who had been marked for advancement since 1945. Those until the end of the Cold War were solid choices. Peter Marychurch and John Adye, however, emerged as leading contenders for promotion to Director just a few years before their appointment, while from 1980 Cabinet secretaries managed leadership in GCHQ more firmly than anyone had done since Sinclair.

Jones was an outstanding appointment. Daniel is unlikely to have been better, or equal, or to have created a different organisation. He might have solved the problem with engineers and scientists several years faster than Jones did. Still, Jones did so, and acquired the resources that GCHQ needed for expansion. He found the staple market for Sigint, and oversaw the means to collect, process and disseminate it. Jones created an organisation which carried GCHQ through the Cold War. He rationalised GCHQ's employment of scientists by following the advice of those at the MOD. Jones's promotion also let Loehnis, Cooper and Hooper each advance a step in GCHQ and receive greater experience. Yet the critiques about Jones's limits had force. His record was broad in Sigint, narrow in government, which was central to GCHQ. During the debate, C 'wondered if enough weight had been given to the management of a technical and complex Organisation some 4,000 strong, and relatively too much weight to an authoritative voice in Whitehall. Surely the latter function was the duty of the Director-General.'⁵³ Yet John Sinclair was a weak advocate for his own service, let alone for GCHQ. As C and the Foreign Office lost their roles in managing GCHQ's relations with other departments, the directors had to develop weight in Whitehall. Daniel would have had more weight than Jones and maintained greater ties with Whitehall, perhaps to permanent effect. Instead, the appointment of Jones, the nature of GCHQ's successes and consumers, and the move to Cheltenham, made GCHQ an insular organisation. Far more than for most government units of its size, directors were selected for technical competence above political skills. GCHQ was not the only geographically isolated and high-technology government agency in Britain: so too was the Atomic Energy Research Establishment at Harwell. Unlike Harwell, however, GCHQ was not just a research centre producing high-technology products but an intelligence body serving the centre of the state. GCHQ could do so from Cheltenham because it had consumers who knew what they wanted and were happy to take whatever GCHQ offered. These consumers were big and their need persisted for decades. GCHQ did not need wide-ranging pursuit of new customers or relationships. Nonetheless, GCHQ became insulated and isolated from Whitehall and Britain. It knew foreign politics better than those of its own country. These characteristics drove many of the problems of the 1970s and 1980s, which shaped how GCHQ became public.

The Directors

The directors of GCHQ came mostly from professional families. Jones, however, stemmed from a business family and Marychurch from the clerical class. Of the first four directors, Loehnis and Travis were educated as officers within the Royal Navy, Jones finished a good grammar school but never entered university, and Denniston studied at universities in Bonn and Paris. After them, all directors save Marychurch received the standard education of the British elite, in good schools and British universities, mostly Cambridge and Oxford. The directors between 1919 and 1995 fall into patterns. Usually two of them came from one generation which were distinguishable from predecessors or successors. The first two directors, Denniston and Travis, were born to professional families in 1881 and 1888, at the peak of British power. They served during its afternoon, as civilian and quasi-civilian officers in the classic imperial institution, the Royal Navy. Their earliest experience with Sigint came in 1914, when it first emerged in Britain. Aged thirty-eight and thirty respectively, they became Director and deputy Director in 1919. In 1942, Denniston kept his position but under a different description, while Travis became head of Bletchley Park, and later Denniston's superior. They spent the interwar years running a small specialised institution and took GC&CS into the ages of Ultra, UKUSA and British decline. Their superiors, with responsibility for Sigint, had gentry and military backgrounds. Admiral Hugh Sinclair, born in 1873 and educated in the Royal Navy, started work in intelligence only after a successful naval career. Menzies was born in 1890 and schooled at Eton, after which he joined the Life Guards. Severe wounds in 1915 turned him from his regiment towards security intelligence, and ultimately to MI6.

After Travis, directors served between five and seven years. Of the first three directors appointed after Travis, Jones was forty-five years, Hooper forty-one, and Loehnis fifty-eight – after which the normal age for appointment became the middle to late fifties. Jones and Loehnis, born in 1907 and 1902 respectively, came of age when Britain remained the world's greatest power, albeit declining. Their backgrounds were unconventional for success in Whitehall. One was a businessman without a degree, the other a signals officer who left the Royal Navy for a few years to pursue a technical career. Each man encountered Sigint via Ultra in 1941, which reshaped their lives. Jones became Director in 1952, Loehnis in 1960. Jones had an unusual grasp of strategy for Sigint, where he was a manager more than a practitioner. Loehnis was a calculating bureaucratic tactician who, with a distinctive writing hand and light blue ink, spent much time editing documents intended for authorities outside GCHQ. His 'fancy waistcoats' maximised the elegance of sentences and the power of arguments. He would spend two days of the week at GCHQ's London office in Palmer Street, Victoria, and managed relations with Whitehall more than any other Director between 1919 and 1995. Jones and Loehnis carried GCHQ to success for a generation. They would occasionally race each other in their cars from Palmer Street to Cheltenham, down the old A40: Loehnis's slowest record time for completion was thirty-two days, which were spent in hospital after a road accident.

Then followed two directors whose social and educational bases followed normal patterns for success in Whitehall and for whom Ultra was the decisive influence. They spent their professional lives working up the rungs at GCHQ, and, far more than any director since Travis, were professional Siginters. Leonard 'Joe' Hooper, born in 1914, joined GC&CS in 1938 and became Director in 1965. Bill Bonsall, born in 1917, joined Sigint in 1940 and became Director in 1973. They understood the details of Sigint as a whole perhaps better than any of their predecessors, but also lacked the political skills of Loehnis or Travis, reflecting the personal characteristics favoured by selection processes at GC&CS.

Hooper, the dominant figure of his generation at GCHQ, a master of detail and management, steered British Sigint through a turbulent decade. Bonsall perceived the direction of developments with unusual acuity and power. Neither was politically powerful within Whitehall, but each built great relationships with fellow professionals at NSA.

Then came two officers too young to serve in the war or with Ultra, but whose academic or military education provided skills in unusual languages. After National Service they joined GCHQ, and climbed its ranks, as their country declined to a European power. Brian Tovey, born in 1926, and educated at Oxford and SOAS, joined GCHQ in 1950. After stellar successes in managing Comint during the Konfrontasi ('confrontation') with Indonesia, and against Soviet forces during the Czechoslovak crisis, he became Director in 1978. Tovey – able, energetic, impulsive and, as one of his daughter's wrote: a man of 'romantic idealism' – was politically the boldest leader GCHQ had known, willing to challenge superiors head-on.[54] Peter Marychurch, born in 1927, joined GCHQ in 1948, at the bottom end of the executive grades after realising that he would not be admitted to the Russian language programme in Cambridge. He failed to consider the possibility of another subject, which perhaps reflects his non-elite background. He demonstrated remarkable skill in technical tasks, including counter-clandestine work. His career moved slowly but boomed once he reached middle leadership, aided by Tovey. He became Director in 1983. John Adye, a man with a sharp mind and tongue, and political shrewdness, was born in 1939 to a gentry family and joined GCHQ in 1962. After success in many key posts he became Director in 1989. When he retired, Whitehall intervened in the succession and selected directors by different criteria.[55]

Rise and Stagnation

From 1947 to 1970, GCHQ experienced continual but steady growth. Its demands were constrained, slightly on the low side of justifiable, but it built firmly and well. Jones inherited strong foundations on which he raised a tower. From 1948 to 1953, GCHQ's manpower rose 50 per cent above the level proposed by Evill. From 1953–4 to 1962–3, spending on Sigint rose well above the rate of inflation, from £9.75 million to £21 million and on GCHQ from £4.75 million to £7.75 million, mostly on salaries.[56]

Jones favoured economical and efficient units, which contained spending on a cheese-paring basis and monitored costs and income, in order to pursue priorities and profit. Jones's policy made GCHQ remarkably efficient and among the most culturally 'northern' of British state departments, but also potentially exposed to shipwreck whenever it was not treated as a high priority. During 1950–52, when preparing a bid for increased staff to attack high-grade Soviet systems, Jones scraped together economies, including a temporary 1 per cent reduction in all areas, which were returned when he succeeded. In accepting GCHQ's case to deploy 204 new personnel against high-grade Soviet systems, PSIS made it Britain's top priority in defence spending.[57] In 1958, after consolidating all gains, Jones asked his subordinates to answer three questions about GCHQ's performance: 'are we failing where, with substantial additional resources, we would be liable to succeed against … e.g. advance warning? Even if we are not failing … now, are we in serious danger of failing in the future if we do not invest substantially now? Are we contributing a fair share to the UKUSA partnership … ?' His answers were yes, yes and no. He told LSIB that hitherto he had restrained demands for greater resources, 'because I believe it better that GCHQ should have too few rather than too many people and therefore have to allocate resources with the greatest care and economy', but expansion was needed again.[58] From 1959–60 to 1962–3, procurement of equipment needed to rise from £1.5 million to £2.51 million and 400 new staff were required, including 46 cryptanalysts and 120 production staff against the USSR.

When Britain faded as an independent power, less likely to pursue narrow ends single-handedly and more in need of American support, the demands of NSA became central to the case for GCHQ and its value to Britain. For the first time, Jones brought UKUSA explicitly into the reckoning of GCHQ's needs. At some point UKUSA might:

> appear to the US to be one-sided in the UK's favour. Just where
> this point might lie is impossible to determine, but the value of this
> partnership to this country is so great that every effort should be
> made to avoid even approaching it … a failure on the UK's part in
> general to keep pace with developments, and in particular to retain
> its skill in solving new problems, would undermine the good will
> … the UK remains better at exploring and developing new lines of

Sigint, and one of my principal anxieties is that UK resources are now so stretched that new possibilities cannot be probed as often and as deeply as they should be.[59]

LSIB and the COS supported this proposal. By 1961, that increase was largely achieved, although the Treasury cut GCHQ's base budget by £1 million to £20 million in 1962–3, and blocked the hiring of 100 new staff. Further battles were obvious.[60] Sigint confronted radical changes, while American aid to purchase kit would soon end. GCHQ had grown more since 1945 than any component of British power outside nuclear forces: where would this end?

Both GCHQ and the service Sigint agencies proposed major programmes for expansion. When assessing military Sigint in 1960, Templer noted that the service intelligence units all regarded GCHQ as having 'prime importance' and 'the enormous extent to which the services rely upon G.C.H.Q. for essential intelligence'. GCHQ was 'the most productive and, in some cases, the only, agency', able to garner intelligence on the USSR. Its tasks would probably become 'more difficult' and its call for resources would rise. He stressed GCHQ's 'vital importance' without assessing its 'priority... in competition with other claimants upon scarce national resources'.[61] In 1962, Loehnis warned Whitehall that GCHQ resources were stagnating, while calls for its product, and the difficulties in attacking foreign communication and Comsec systems, rose steadily. Success required 'a greater investment of money and of scientific and engineering resources' and more 'mechanisation of data-handling' and 'computer resources to assist cryptanalysis on major problems'; otherwise, UKUSA would be 'undermined'. For some time, GCHQ's older skills could hold its own, but 'if the UK is to continue to play an effective role in the production of Sigint and to remain a full Sigint partner of the U.S., a sizable and increasingly expensive effort is required particularly in the engineering field'.[62]

The Treasury preferred to cap GCHQ's budget at around £20 million. This, the first battle between GCHQ and the Treasury over Sigint, was marked by shrewd politics in Cheltenham, led by Loehnis and executed by his deputy, Hooper, and an uncertainty in the Exchequer, which did not understand the technical issues and knew its limits.[63] Rarely has the Treasury been routed so thoroughly as it was by GCHQ over the

'Hampshire Report'. In order to illuminate these conflicting issues, PSIS had asked one man to assess GCHQ's policies and spending: Stuart Hampshire, Grote Professor of the Philosophy of Mind and Logic at University College, London, later Warden of Wadham College, Oxford.

Stuart Hampshire had a great record of wartime service with the Radio Security Service (RSS), as a senior analyst of high-level traffic of the German SS (Schutzstaffel), combined with a personal scandal. His affair with and later marriage to Renée Ayers, wife of the philosopher A. J. Ayers, shook their conjugal and academic dovecotes in London and Oxford. Hampshire knew leading members of the Humint and Sigint communities, including the Cambridge Five. He had a razor-sharp mind, experience in Sigint and intelligence analysis and no commitment to the existing system. GCHQ knew Hampshire well; in contrast, when he was appointed, the Treasury did not even know he once had been a Siginter. Whereas Evill worked without staff, Hampshire had one aide: a GCHQ official. No other department had anyone worth offering, which symbolised GCHQ's advantages in this battle. PSIS asked Hampshire to assess the 'requirements for the whole Sigint organisation' until 1970, 'the technical developments and the political, strategic and economic factors which are likely to affect its operations', 'the working of the UKUSA agreement', GCHQ's 'future scope and policy' and 'any changes needed to ensure [its] effective implementation and control'. [64] Hampshire was briefed by PSIS, the Treasury, GCHQ and its consumers. In turn, he made them answer probing questions.

Much of his work lay with NSA, which all saw as central to British policy. The Treasury pressed Hampshire to consider whether UKUSA and compatibility with American Sigint would force greater spending that Britain needed or could afford. GCHQ briefed Hampshire about the significance of UKUSA to British security and NSA about Hampshire's centrality to GCHQ's future. Hampshire spent a week at Fort Meade, Maryland, where the Director of NSA (DIRNSA), General Blake, had his deputy, Lou Tordella, devote his services as chaperone and directed senior NSA staff 'to ensure an outstanding job'. The SUKLO wrote that:

> The whole programme went off without a hitch, and the visit was
> highly successful and valuable. Professor Hampshire was surprised

and pleased that he was able to acquire so much concentrated and pertinent information in such a relatively short visit. I am sure that, in addition, he was surprised by the friendliness of the US side and the general air of intimate and informal co-operation. The main result of the visit is that he has returned with the conviction that the maintenance in being of the UKUSA Agreement is of the first importance to this country and is a practicable proposition, at least within the time-frame of his review [the 1960s].[65]

These American views would inform Hampshire's analysis, and British policy for a generation.

Hampshire offered a better case for GCHQ than it could do, or Whitehall might conceive, because of his broader and dispassionate mode of analysis, combined with experience in attacking traffic and assessing Ultra at the highest level. His commentary reflects how an intelligent, informed and tolerably objective person viewed British Sigint at the time – indeed, it is perhaps the clearest statement on record of the contemporary value of GCHQ. Sigint, he wrote, 'is a continuous source, which at all times provides "hard" information, however fragmentary and incomplete it may be'. Its 'very nature ... enables its reliability to be assessed absolutely and, for this reason, in peace as formerly in war, Sigint is almost uniquely valuable as a check upon the reliability of other secret sources, which may carry no guarantee of reliability with them'. Writing just after the Cuban missile crisis and crises in Kuwait, Lebanon and Yemen had dragged Britain towards war, Hampshire noted that GCHQ had provided the 'solid core of the current, timely intelligence, not derived from open and official sources', which the JIC, COS and ministers had used to formulate policy regarding the USSR and in the Middle East.[66]

Changes in communications and Comsec increasingly hampered Sigint, which required 'keeping up to date a more or less complete picture of the communications of target countries; without the complete picture, it is usually impossible to identify and select the transmission which will yield, under analysis, useful intelligence'. To identify 'new networks is of prime intelligence importance', while 'the early identification of new types of transmission greatly increases the chances of analysing them effectively, and of extracting a flow of intelligence from them. GCHQ has owed some of its most conspicuous recent successes, e.g.

the identification of the network associated with the Soviet Strategic Rocket Forces, to its general search among unclassified transmissions. General Search for the new and unusual must be ineffective, if an overall picture of established target communications is not at all times immediately available.' Yet 'there is a built-in tendency, arising from the nature of the material itself, for an ever-increasing effort to be required in order to maintain an equal flow of useful intelligence, even if all other factors are disregarded ... where Sigint is concerned, one will generally have to increase the investment if a constant intelligence dividend is to be maintained. There may be breakthroughs and windfalls, particularly in cryptanalysis, which may for a time modify this iron law. But those who are best able to judge do not doubt that, in the long run, the law holds.'[67]

Discussions at Fort Meade drove Hampshire's assessment of the state of UKUSA in 1962, which probably did reflect NSA's real views:

> The U.S.–U.K. partnership has so far retained its vitality and intimacy, largely unaffected by vicissitudes in relations between the U.S. and Britain in other spheres, for one very simple reason: that both sides can be seen to have greatly benefitted from it, and to be still benefitting from it now. The production of Sigint (and perhaps of intelligence generally) depends for its success on an unusual combination of skills shared among a group of men, who work closely together over a long period of time in confined conditions, and who acquire a kind of professional enthusiasm. This enthusiasm, or professional spirit, is neither that of a serving officer nor that of an academic researcher, but rather is a peculiar amalgam of the two. Continuity in personnel and close interworking in a tight organisation are of the essence of the work.[68]

NSA recognised GCHQ's past contributions, and its present unique value: 'GCHQ has been particularly successful in the identification of new networks and new types of data transmission including those used by Russian and Chinese targets of interest. In Elint, GCHQ invented the method of reducing Soviet Telemetry transmissions to analogue readout form, and has led the way in the discovery of Soviet missile control systems and new radars in ships and aircraft and ground defence.' H division:

has been so far consistently in the lead in cryptanalysis, and has made a much more than equal contribution to the relationship. GCHQ has generally kept the initiative in diagnosis and analysis. GCHQ also has introduced new cryptanalytic techniques ... and developed, sometimes on behalf of NSA, original programmes, and special-purpose designs, for computers. Thirdly, GCHQ has applied original methods of research, not only to such technical problems as the Soviet callsign system, but also to the analysis of military and naval exercises, of the order of production of Soviet missiles and ships, of the characteristics of new types of aircraft, and of the organisation and deployment of parts of the Soviet Air Force.[69]

These successes, Hampshire presciently noted, stemmed 'in part' from 'the very same fact which is already, and may increasingly become, a source of some embarrassment and difficulty; namely, the comparative smallness and compactness' of GCHQ and 'the British Sigint effort as a whole, when compared with the U.S'.[70]

American authorities would treat 'the demand for reliable secret intelligence of all kinds to be immediately available in Washington ... as one of the first priorities in the Cold War'. Its cost would be 'counted negligible within the total costs of the Cold War. That there should be no possibility of a failure in intelligence at a moment of crisis, and that no expense should be spared to ensure early warning of any threat, whether of total or limited war, will be a first principle of U.S. policy in the foreseeable future.' NSA wished GCHQ to remain a viable partner. American service Siginters were unsentimental and would pursue and achieve independent power in all areas of Sigint, unless GCHQ hastened its pace. If GCHQ passed this test, Britain would remain fundamental to American security. If it declined, so would Britain. In 1962, US Sigint already outspent British by fifteen to one in money, seven to one in manpower, and ten to one on a leading American priority.

'The choice of greatly increased expenditure on technical equipment to maintain joint working within the UKUSA partnership, or of abandoning joint working in many areas, is now well recognised as a choice confronting British Sigint by NSA no less than GCHQ,' noted Hampshire. In particular, investments in computers were unavoidable. 'NSA estimates that speeds of computer operations, and analytical capability, have increased by a factor of one million in the last ten years, and that the speed of operations increases as the square of the increase in financial investment.' This approach enabled states 'to keep abreast of Foreign Comsec', but at cost. The human and machine resources used in the attack on non-Soviet cyphers (including Middle Eastern systems) have more than doubled since 1958', and probably needed to do so again in the next four years, 'if vulnerable cyphers are to be exploited with the same success in 1966 as in 1962'.[71]

Hampshire linked these technical issues to grand strategy better than Whitehall had ever done. Britain's ability to protect its national interests, and international peace and stability, 'largely depends, and will increasingly depend, on its residual ability to influence the policy of the Western alliance at its principal source in Washington, and, to a lesser degree, in NATO. Unless Britain shared the same sources of intelligence with the U.S.A., the remainder of this influence, which is increasingly threatened by the disproportion in military effectiveness between the two powers, will steadily diminish toward zero'. The special relationship was eroding fast outside intelligence, but could survive for the next decade, if GCHQ kept its place within UKUSA. 'Because Britain still has something of proven worth to contribute – an equal professional competence,' GCHQ enabled other British authorities to enter high levels of American military and diplomatic decision-making. Shared Sigint let Britain influence American decision-making in ways which otherwise were impossible, and which might support 'the primary British interest ... the prevention of nuclear war'. In words written just after the Cuban missile crisis, Hampshire noted: 'I have not received clear evidence that fear of surprise, so strong in U.S. thinking since Pearl Harbor, has in fact ever led to, or been associated with, any serious misinterpretation of Sigint evidence in the U.S.A. But the mere possibility of such misinterpretation, remote as it may be, surely justifies the retention of independent evaluation by U.K. experts who have the professional respect of their colleagues in Washington. Here at least duplication, the possibility of a double check, is not wasteful.'

Hampshire's recommendations were independent and informed. They generally met GCHQ's interests, but he challenged those of every actor at some point and of all actors at a few of them. Current projected expenses might double the cost of Sigint in five years, which was impossible. Rationalisation was necessary. UKUSA, Hampshire emphasised, was central to British Sigint and security. During the 1960s, Britain needed to spend much more to sustain Sigint and UKUSA. In 1962, GCHQ's budget was 1.2 per cent that of the MOD and would probably reach 2 per cent by 1970. The costs of research and development and new kit, especially computers, simply 'must be met', and specialists, especially scientists, found. Britain had to boost its areas of comparative advantage. It should develop its already great powers in cryptanalysis and traffic analysis. A base on remaining fragments of empire could enable coverage of new targets, especially in Africa. A custom-built Sigint ship could cover traffic across the world with flexibility and power. The USSR and Middle East should remain GCHQ's main targets. If necessary to achieve these aims, Britain could reduce airborne collection, tactical Sigint in Germany, Elint, telemetry and counter-clandestine programmes: Hampshire's RSS experience gave him authority here. More than anyone outside GCHQ, Hampshire sensed the weakness of control over Sigint. In order to achieve that end, a 'committee of four' – the Cabinet Secretary, the Permanent Undersecretary of the MOD, the CDS and the chair of the JIC – should replace PSIS, and the London Signals Intelligence Committee (LSIC) must become their agent. The London Signals Intelligence Board (LSIB), meanwhile, should be abolished. The MOD should become responsible for COSIG, which should be formulated on a five-year basis. This well-intentioned but badly informed proposal sparked an internecine struggle between the powers of Whitehall and failed utterly when the COS, LSIC and, discreetly, GCHQ, revolted against PSIS's attempts to adopt it.[72] Inadvertently, if temporarily, this process extended GCHQ's autonomy and the weakness of central control by sparking PSIS to agree that 'only' Cheltenham could recommend Sigint expenditure. GCHQ and the Treasury had common interests in containing proposals for increases in service Sigint.

The COS, LSIB and PSIS accepted most of these recommendations, which were honoured until 1967, though to a diminishing extent afterwards. The Treasury learned how to negotiate with and over GCHQ, and restrained growth, while the losing units cramped expansion by preventing Hampshire's recommendations for economies. The Hampshire Report occurred at virtually the last time that major increases for expenditure on British Sigint were possible during the middle Cold War, aided by Whitehall's willingness to link his proposal to a seven-year programme. Between 1963 and 1970, COSIG rose by perhaps 30 per cent, excluding inflation, and reached 1.5 per cent of the MOD budget. The Hampshire Report enabled the acquisition of much equipment and some specialists, though GCHQ could not hire all the scientists authorised. The report marked the end of a string of victories. It was most effective in solidifying the idea that one of GCHQ's central roles was to satisfy American needs and generating the 'Tordella doctrine', which guides policy within and about GCHQ to the present day. That doctrine held that Britain must maintain breadth and depth in Sigint and offer something meaningful in every major area of UKUSA activity, while preserving its originality. Reflecting the language of the day, Tordella said, in short: 'Do your own thing.'[73]

High Tide

GCHQ procured and allocated resources like a military rather than an intelligence institution – the RAF, say, rather than MI6 – but with more unity. Conflicts between entrenched and independent interests such as airmen and submariners drove policies for the services, but not at Cheltenham. GCHQ's leaders agreed even on the greatest of conflicts, such as radio grades. The department tried to think five to ten years ahead. In order to reinforce priorities, GCHQ exploited every chance to acquire new resources, which it shifted between tasks and sections every day. GCHQ strengthened its core, while leaving areas to decline as they waned, because empire eroded and technology changed. Growth or reduction in bases or staff did not mean the same for GCHQ as an institution. Cuts in personnel might signal success, while shabby buildings could reflect sound management. GCHQ did well in Whitehall because its heart was strong – as were its leaders, each with different styles. Loehnis outmanoeuvred opponents, while Hooper and Bonsall managed and massaged favourable conditions.

Jones and Loehnis managed growth, while Hooper and Bonsall managed austerity. The underlying trends which Loehnis emphasised in 1962 continued to rise, while GCHQ's response sputtered. Hooper exploited the Hampshire Report to enable expansion in select areas, also subsidised by maintaining GCHQ's budget and gradually transferring funds between areas. He reduced staffing costs and increased the acquisition of machines by, say, switching personnel from J

(Eastern bloc) to K (rest of the world) divisions, or the savings from retirements for new kit. Success was gradual: over five years, personnel costs as a share of GCHQ's expenditure fell by 2 per cent and the procurement of machinery rose by 2 per cent. By reallocating power to attacks in the rest of the world, Hooper boosted GCHQ's ability to produce unique Comint, while still working against the Eastern bloc. Driven by economy and compatibility with the United States, GCHQ was a lean, muscular and cost-efficient organisation pursuing the best means to stay so. Thus, the United States could build collection platforms beyond Britain's reach. Britain possessed excellent processing and analytical capacities and, unlike the United States, also held technically useful and politically secure real estate, which could support these platforms. Combining these strengths enabled the intercept stations at Bude in Cornwall and in Hong Kong to make significant contributions throughout the Cold War.

GCHQ disliked the need to sell itself, but after 1970, for the first time, it actively built political support by publicising its work to consumers. 'Trumpet blowers' – secret but widespread papers – showed how Comint aided British policy.[74] Officials in GCHQ visited London for interdepartmental meetings; those in Whitehall rarely returned the favour. LSIB meetings generally occurred in Whitehall to ease attendance. GCHQ's offices at Palmer Street were too small to host major meetings and lay outside the Whitehall village. So GCHQ organised day trips for mid-level consumers, in order to show its stuff and let customers meet the producers. Meetings in Cheltenham posed administrative and transport challenges. On one typical date in February 1975, for example, GCHQ officers collected from Cheltenham Spa station many visitors from the LSIB and LSIC who had departed Paddington at 0630, chatting their way to the Cotswolds. After tea, coffee and biscuits, the day began at 0945 with briefings on Soviet command and control, aircraft, exercises and intentions. After beer and tea at lunch, in a canteen somewhat beneath the better standards of London clubland, attendees heard about 'the Sigint attack on Diplomatic and other international messages: this will end at 1540 to enable to those who wish to do so to catch the train leaving Cheltenham at 1613 and arriving at Paddington at 1855'. Those who stayed on for briefings on the Soviet navy and current problems had to then be chauffeured south to the railway station at Swindon, where they caught the train arriving at Paddington for 1940.[75] All could be at home by 2300, for a weekend's rest, after a productive day in the provinces.

For the decade following the Hampshire Report, GCHQ's case was strong and opposition was weak. The power of its old protectors – the services and the Foreign Office – declined, though they remained allies. In that decade of reform, optimism and inflation, GCHQ faced just one threat, which was both half-hearted and weak. The Treasury did not really seek to constrain spending on Sigint until 1962; after that failed attack and the rebuke of the Hampshire Report, its power generally slipped in Whitehall and only revived slowly. The Treasury aimed to contain all spending, including that on GCHQ, but was not an enemy of Sigint – it merely followed the priorities of state. Few politicians knew of GCHQ or its role, and none of its size and expense. The best-informed politicians, including prime ministers, supported GCHQ in general, if vaguely. The key officials in decision-making – who, incidentally, were also members of the PSIS – especially the Cabinet secretaries, had to formulate strategies in general as well as for the intelligence services. They favoured control of expenditure and investment in priorities, and understood issues of security and intelligence well. GCHQ was the department involved in national strategy which provided the greatest return on investment: its annual costs were small, not much more than maintaining a division, or constructing a nuclear submarine. And despite their focus on social reform, the Labour governments of Harold Wilson spent much money on defence, with GCHQ a top priority.

Cheltenham's successes in the crises over Hungary, Czechoslovakia and Cuba, in Konfrontasi in Malaysia, and in impressing the Americans, resounded across Whitehall. Initially GCHQ was helped not hindered by trends in political power over intelligence – the rise of centralised control over budgets and policy, through the creation of PSIS and an intelligence coordinator with advisory authority, and in the rising strength of the Cabinet Secretary. That official between 1963 and 1973, Burke Trend, cut his teeth managing intelligence expenditure as a junior Treasury official. He held that Britain must 'make our way in the world by influence rather than power', which fitted intelligence and GCHQ nicely. Trend hoped to contain the cost of new technology, including computers, but loved the romance of espionage.[76] He accepted GCHQ's case and admired its work. In 1967, Trend thought 'the existing machinery for gathering intelligence was broadly satisfactory'; there was 'not much wrong with the agencies which collect intelligence – i.e. mainly MI6 and GCHQ. They are held on a tight financial leash; they are directed with considerable professional competence; and they are as well staffed and equipped for their functions as money and circumstances allow.'[77] This judgement was sound: GCHQ had enough bone and muscle to handle priorities, and little fat.

GCHQ sought to maintain that status by pursuing a 'deliberate policy to reduce Sigint expenditure in order to free more funds for what may broadly be termed "capital investment": research and development, equipment procurement', rebuilding select stations and creating new ones.[78] 'Within the overall aim of maintaining a balanced and flexible effort able to meet the requirements of the future,' GCHQ emphasised, 'the four particular aims of current Sigint policy remain: a reduction in the proportion of expenditure on manpower, particularly at intercept stations; maintenance of an adequate interception effort in the 1980s when a large number of civilian radio operators reach retiring age; the allocation of an increased proportion of Sigint funds to long-term development, especially in research and development and equipment procurement; and the maintenance and development of our close interworking with the US Sigint organisation.'[79] GCHQ's problems were complex, and so were its solutions. For example, in order to subsidise other areas and meet the 'probability that, in ten to twenty years, a smaller interception force, and one probably somewhat different in composition, should suffice to meet the foreseeable requirements', GCHQ reduced GCRO 'through natural wastage and deliberate under-recruitment' by forty to fifty personnel per year. Yet GCHQ still recruited heavily in these grades, which remained a leading area of new employment, in order to maintain current coverage and avoid the collapse of that workforce when its older members reached retirement age in an age clump around 1985.[80]

These aims were hard to balance. Sometimes, annual expenditures were embarrassingly large, particularly when it came to computers, where GCHQ was Whitehall's pioneer. As politicians warmed their hands beside the white heat of technology and computers became common, they accepted GCHQ's claims that its 'increased cryptanalytic success' required the insurance of a second mainframe computer in case of 'a lengthy breakdown, particularly in a crisis situation'.[81] Yet decision-makers could not really understand just how complex and costly the procurement of kit would become until broader experience produced emotional understanding. GCHQ achieved no striking success for national interests between Konfrontasi and the Falklands conflict, denying it the easiest way to justify that need, yet lesser events boosted its case. Decolonisation destabilised order across the world and inspired many wars of the British succession. Soviet power expanded across the globe, where its warships prowled and potential allies called. The 'progressive build-up of Soviet power and influence in the Middle East ... has produced new high priority targets', GCHQ noted in 1971, as had tensions between Israel and Arab states.[82] Wars between developing nations challenged British interests and the balance between East and West, exacerbated by the Sino-Soviet split. Consumers demanded increasing amounts of Sigint on military and diplomatic issues, from more countries than ever.

Consumers also grew in number; between 1951 and 1963, British consumers cleared to receive forms of Comint rose from 1,683 to 15,859, in thirty-three departments, including the Ministry of Agriculture and Fisheries, and Customs and Excise.[83] Sigint serviced fishery patrols, and wars on drugs. Consumers rarely abandoned old requirements when new ones emerged. Success against new modes of communication and cryptography required costly investments in emerging forms of interception and cryptanalysis. The US cut its Sigint resources and made Britain share the burden. GCHQ claimed that its actions enhanced 'the profile of the UK's Sigint reputation in the US', and gained the 'privilege ... virtually free of cost' of joining the Pentagon's worldwide communication system. As ammunition, GCHQ also used comments by intelligence coordinators about 'excellent Sigint coverage', or: 'Sigint once more proved its indispensable value in the judgement of military events.'[84] These claims were credible, and weighty, in the circumstances.

PSIS sharpened its tools for financial control, wishing to prune rather than amputate. The Sigint Finance Committee, chaired by the Treasury, with representatives from every department in the field, scrutinised programmes.[85] Techniques of cost analysis, borrowed from the Pentagon and Whitehall, showed Sigint spending against specific targets and what Britain's investment in GCHQ bought.[86] GCHQ warned that this approach was misguided because many of its 'activities were conducted in support of other forms of intelligence-gathering and much of their effect was unaffected by changes in intelligence priorities. We were a long way from being able to apply cost-effectiveness in intelligence.'[87] It generally outlined Sigint spending, though with less detail than other units did. The Treasury rarely pursued greater precision. Intelligence coordinator Dick White, the only person ever to direct both MI5 and MI6, and among Britain's greatest practitioners of Humint, advised PSIS on how to handle the agencies. Still, Sigint remained mysterious. PSIS controlled GCHQ spending less than any other department, debating details it did not understand, about an institution which it respected.[88]

Between 1960 and 1975, economic and fiscal problems across Britain, together with changes in the priority both of security among government priorities and of categories within defence spending, drove policy over GCHQ. Questions emerged such as: how should GCHQ change to meet alterations in national policy, and: how far was UKUSA a British interest? Old demands for product remained while new ones arose. Resources were stable or stagnant. GCHQ handled this problem through careful economies, once more, aiming to switch spending from pay to kit, or J to K. This process was slow and limited at the time and hard to judge in retrospect. Inflation hampers any calculation of the value of budgets, which increasingly rose in nominal terms. The cost of much equipment, especially computers, swelled above the general level of inflation, which also spurred salary increases in unpredictable ways. The decline in the exchange rate of sterling raised costs for anything purchased abroad. When assessing GCHQ's success or failure during this period, fiscal figures are less useful indicators than the amounts and characteristics of the personnel and kit that remained or was gained. By those criteria, GCHQ's strength in personnel stayed stable, their quality was refreshed well enough, while adequate amounts of improved kit were procured. Even cuts are hard to assess, because GCHQ planned them to finance reinvestment. Simply because GCHQ was cut does not mean that it lost, so long as resources were redeployed. In particular, the striking number of closures of interception stations at home and abroad essentially eliminated inefficient and costly bases while coverage remained fairly constant.

During the decade after 1963, the pressure for economy caused more efficiency than damage. In 1963, PSIS pressed GCHQ to reduce its annual spending for 1964–5 to 1969–70 by £1 million,[89] thus eliminating many of the gains from the Hampshire Report. This proposal was a warning shot, focused on projected expenditures rather than a signal for slaughter. To execute it would require major reductions in GCHQ, or the abandonment either of airborne collection or the building of a 'Sigint ship'. That ship would offer mobile means to intercept traffic at a time when Britain was unsure how far it could retain intercept bases abroad after decolonisation. Ultimately, the idea was abandoned and the ship never built, because it was an easy economy, without institutional support; during 1967–68, the Israeli attack on the American Sigint ship *Liberty* and the North Korean seizure of USS *Pueblo* showed that such vessels were vulnerable; while Britain retained enough bases abroad to meet needs for interception.[90] Though GCHQ and PSIS doubted the cost-effectiveness of airborne interception, the RAF and MOD defended the programme, which produced useful intelligence. In response to PSIS, GCHQ focused on protecting new programmes and kit, above all on establishing principles for the procurement of computers. 'It was essential to maintain compatibility of inputs and outputs, and be able to exchange programmes with the US, so that the UK could not automatically choose the cheapest computer if it did not meet these requirements.' Though no one could predict the cost, computers would be expensive. GCHQ needed to buy the best computers regularly and 'establish the principle that it should be at UK expense'.[91]

In 1963, LSIC simply promised to think about cuts in Sigint. By 1964, it accepted PSIS's proposal, without actually cutting anything – save paper – in the future.[92] By 1965, PSIS floated and then sank radical ideas. The MOD demanded economies on any areas it subsidised, a scrutiny of the military value of Sigint and offloading costs onto NSA. The MOD became a minor problem for GCHQ, as well as a major ally. PSIS deflected these proposals, which risked Sigint expenditure and policy. When someone suggested that UKUSA should be reexamined 'at the highest political level', PSIS replied: 'we were advised that the result might be awkward questions regarding the value of our present contribution and the possibility of other Powers being brought into the partnership'. PSIS merely asked GCHQ to assess the costs and benefits of its military and diplomatic work, how much of it was needed for British rather than American interests, and whether NSA would provide further financial aid.[93] GCHQ retorted that such aid was impossible, while to request it would be dangerous. UKUSA was so vital a national interest that Britain needed to pay to aid its ally and that expense was cost-efficient. NSA provided 60 per cent of Sigint end product available to Britain, with the rest being primarily British, but also Australian and Canadian.⁹⁴ PSIS accepted this view.

The pressure slowed the completion of some projects, but not their cancellation.⁹⁵ The personnel increases recommended by the Hampshire Report mostly prevented attrition in technical areas, rather than aiding the 'direct reinforcement of Sigint production', because GCHQ could not attract all of the skilled staff it wished to hire.⁹⁶ GCHQ could not even use all of the funds offered from the Hampshire Report. Still, GCHQ hastened the acquisition of a new mainframe computer and an unexpected pay rise for the radio grade.⁹⁷ Its balance of cuts and reinvestment impressed PSIS and LSIB, but pressure remained. In 1968, after the Czechoslovak crisis, PSIS asked Dick White to propose cuts in Sigint spending between 1969 and 1974, of £2 million, £5 million or £7 million. White ostentatiously acted unlike Hampshire had done. He consulted all departments involved in the work, but not NSA. His tone was rhetorically neutral. Still, Hampshire and White, extraordinary and different men, had similar views of GCHQ. White held that 'any major reduction of the Sigint product would be the most serious setback the intelligence community could experience', but given Britain's 'economic circumstances ... it is essential to judge intelligence expenditure against the test of the UK's national interests'. White's experience, his access to GCHQ's self-studies of its budget, and his independent study of cost-efficiency reports, gave him an unprecedented power to assess its value and cost effectiveness. He rejected, rightly, GCHQ's claims that its strength had declined significantly, but accepted the core of its case. GCHQ recently had scored successes across Africa and Asia, including perhaps a 'decisive effect' during Konfrontasi. 'By what means,' White asked, 'this swift and flexible employment of Sigint coverage has proved at a time when resources increased only very modestly before beginning to decline. The answer is by robbing Peter (the Soviet area) to pay Paul (East of Suez).' Work against the USSR had not dropped 'below an acceptable level' only because of 'ruthless pruning of unprofitable work, greater mechanisation and, above all, offloading of more Soviet tasks on to the shoulders of NSA'. GCHQ had made 'its valuable contribution to the handling of successive emergencies of direct British interests mainly because of the UK–USA relationship, whose value is thus underlined by the history of the last five years'. Yet this policy of robbery had to end.

GCHQ should work more against the USSR, without cuts elsewhere. White supported all the core elements of GCHQ's case, especially on computers. He proposed an £7 million cut of projected expenditures between 1969 and 1974, perhaps aimed to inoculate GCHQ from further pressure for some years – sinking the Sigint ship before it floated, and escalating economies within GCHQ. Hooper supported that proposal. LSIC and PSIS accepted it as meeting needs for economies in Sigint for several years, which let GCHQ trade paper cuts for institutional growth.[98]

In 1966–67, for example, 20.3 per cent of GCHQ expenditure covered supporting elements; 33.9 per cent addressed targets in the USSR, 5.6 per cent those in other Warsaw Pact targets, and 12.9 per cent Elint against the Warsaw Pact; 1.9 per cent went on to 'security intelligence', 9.8 per cent to China, 3.1 per cent to Indonesia, 8.9 per cent to the Middle East and North Africa, 3.2 per cent to 'International Trade and Finance', and 5.9 per cent to 'General Search'.[99] Later, expenditure remained constant on support and grew against Soviet targets, together absorbing 75 to 80 per cent of GCHQ's budget. Spending on the rest of the world declined slightly but varied by target. In 1966, Indonesia was a notable target, but not Argentina – but vice versa in 1982 because of actions by those states. Normally, the Middle East received more attention than in 1966–67, and China less, reflecting conscious British priorities. GCHQ protected General Search as offering its best means to find new fields – but strength there stagnated, except for a massive expansion via Comsat interception, where that practice was essential to exploiting the source.

Decline

GCHQ handled these problems well, until the swinging mood in London turned sour. From 1970, this cautious policy was increasingly besieged. Economic, political and social stasis forced governments to cut defence spending and to ask whether Britain should remain a leading military power. If GCHQ's budget was linked to that for defence as a whole, it would have to decline when the latter did. GCHQ's small cost and the breadth of its work had sheltered it from earlier defence reviews. Between 1960 and 1964, National Service ended and service budgets declined by 10 per cent; in contrast GCHQ estimates rose by

10 per cent and it absorbed the service Sigint units for free. The retreat from Asia to Europe around 1970 damaged the Army and Royal Navy, but let GCHQ concentrate its strength in the key theatre. When the Defence Review of 1975 savaged British defence policy at home and in NATO, GCHQ could not escape harm. Intelligence services of the first class could aid a country striving for high second-class status, but not one with smaller ambitions at a time when leaders tended to think that high defence spending led to low economic performance. As blood flowed, old friends would not protect GCHQ against their own vital interests, and rational masters questioned its case. GCHQ became less autonomous as its masters found common interests concerning Sigint. PSIS became the efficient power over GCHQ and the Cabinet Secretary its master, the first replacement for Sinclair.

PSIS asked GCHQ to assess the impact of budgetary cuts in constant pounds between 1975 and 1983 by 5 per cent, 10 per cent and 15 per cent. GCHQ honestly described the impact of a 10 per cent cut eight years down the line. GCHQ's own planned cuts, including the closure of bases in Malta and Singapore, would reduce its planned expenditures by 10 per cent by 1983. Any further reductions would require the 'complete closure' of another major station abroad, such as Hong Kong, or would cripple UKUSA and British work against the USSR or in the Middle East. GCHQ's cuts would meet the government's demands, but unless those funds were shifted elsewhere, its proposed expansions would fail and its status erode quickly. In a reflection of the mood in Whitehall, the Cabinet's intelligence coordinator, Joe Hooper, accepted this case. 'On the basis of present planning,' the intelligence agencies could 'achieve a reduction of 10 per cent or better by 1983/84 without damage to their programmes or intelligence relationships.' They also should expect 'some pressure from their patrons to seek some further economy measures', which 'might best be deal with on a case-by-case basis'.[100] By that time, of course, times might change, and so too the agencies' power, either way. PSIS agreed that GCHQ needed to cut its 1975–76 estimates by 10 per cent in constant pounds by 1983–84, which allowed some chance of expansion through further efficiencies. GCHQ defeated another proposal for a further 3.5 or 5 per cent cut in its 1977–78 estimates, with little opposition.[101]

GCHQ's strength was defined as the minimum needed to have the United States maintain the special relationship in intelligence and, indirectly, with Britain as a whole. Constraining GCHQ's expenses, while guessing how America would respond, became central to policy about Sigint, causing uncertainty for GCHQ and Whitehall. GCHQ agreed to cut, while warning of the consequences. Proposed expansions were abandoned or extended, general capabilities reduced, and unique capabilities abandoned. Those closures crippled Britain's ability to collect traffic in parts of the world which featured increasingly in power politics. The cynical might regard this act as a means to annoy American authorities and acquire their aid against PSIS. Yet to meet the proposed reduction, GCHQ needed to take steps which would annoy Americans anyway, and the alternatives were more irritating.

This outcome shocked GCHQ more than it harmed it. The services faced immediate damage and the loss of 11 per cent of their budgets in constant pounds by 1981.[102] GCHQ lost 10 per cent of its proposed expenditures, phased gradually, in early years including only matters it knew were already gone. GCHQ could not reject cuts, which might alienate its friends, yet its policy also projected them, to subsidise expansion elsewhere. Given such an expansion, GCHQ could cut fat, meet PSIS's demands, and pursue its old policy of 'saving manpower through increased automation and productivity'.[103] If not, over years, deferred expenditures would snowball, endangering key acquisitions.

GCHQ confronted threats unprecedented since 1946. Its only rival at the top of defence priorities – the nuclear deterrent – escaped cuts. The deterrent gained the Chevaline upgrading of the Polaris ballistic missile system, soon famed for operational mediocrity and cost overruns, yet deemed a national capability – a status that GCHQ lost: it was treated like every other branch of defence, not as a privileged body. That degradation transformed old strengths into vulnerabilities. That GCHQ was squeezed so hard for such small savings reflected changes in broader attitudes. Officials did not understand how GCHQ worked or why it mattered, unless they were reminded by some striking success. Compared to the armed services, GCHQ's budget was tiny and its policy more efficient and economical. More lean than the services, GCHQ could not easily sidestep the government's policy of austerity in defence by financing major priorities through scraping together internal economies – because it had always done so anyway. GCHQ could expand only by openly challenging that policy. The government's demands on defence and PSIS's on intelligence were serious and reasoned; leading politicians and civil servants desired a fundamental change in policy; and Treasury control over expenditure rose, though it never mastered Sigint as it did other areas of defence. Together, PSIS and the Treasury attacked GCHQ's central fiscal means to enable organisational adaptation, by closing old areas and reallocating funds to emerging priorities.

GCHQ responded by biding its time and preparing the ground. While it cut, GCHQ noted the need to spend, especially on equipment, citing as justification the slow rewarming of the Cold War. GCHQ explained to consumers the success of its attacks on new Soviet targets, such as command and control systems, naval aircraft, nuclear delivery systems and deployments abroad, and continued its moderate procurement of computers and its cooperation with American ventures. GCHQ mostly aided the military – a body under siege and with many priorities to pursue, yet its chief consumer and one with little aid to offer in the short term. GCHQ also monitored diplomatic developments in the Middle East and supported British policy 'including the promotion of the UK's trading position and the protection of the UK economy' during 1976, the year of the International Monetary Fund (IMF) crisis which, after Suez, was the most embarrassing moment for British policy between 1940 and 2020.[104] GCHQ's arguments were accurate, but generally beyond the comprehension of its consumers. The arcane nature of its work, which had often been useful to its political power, now hampered it.

GCHQ's secrecy prevented its masters from understanding how efficient and economical it was. Old arguments which once had carried weight – like the claim that Britain carried only 10 per cent of the cost of UKUSA but received most of its benefits – became questioned. One MOD official 'pointed out the problems of trying to defend GCHQ from the false accusations that UKUSA was the trump card GCHQ brought out when under financial pressure, and nothing more substantial'.[105] Underneath these open discussions lay hidden the old struggle for status. Would GCHQ be treated like other elements of defence and be subject to normal restraints, or again become a priority: its judgement unquestioned, allowed to sidestep constraints, and able to act autonomously? GCHQ's leaders yearned to return to a status they thought normal. Its masters wished to keep it in the status of a normal organisation which they felt they had finally established. Their definitions of normal differed.

Rise Again

Ultimately, between 1975 and 1981, GCHQ maintained its core capabilities and staved off the PSIS target in an attritional daily struggle over base budgets and new requirements. However, managing decline wore down the directorate, making it wary of pursuing ambitions which could not be achieved.

In 1976, Bonsall told PSIS that although the first year of cuts would not cause 'any immediate loss of intelligence in high priority tasks, they would restrict further flexibility for example in the ability to meet the unforeseen requirement and developments, and did diminish the UK Sigint weight in the eye of our US partners'. By 1977, he noted ominous signs on the horizon. American Sigint withheld material from GCHQ when 'the control over the relevant Sigint source had not rested entirely with NSA'. Hooper told the JIC about 'the potential areas for US withholding and the consequent effects for the UK'.[106] By 1978, Bonsall's warnings were immediate. NSA 'valued the UK contribution very highly and could not replace it from their own or other resources'. NSA tolerated Britain's reduced contribution, but less so other American Sigint agencies.[107] GCHQ's contribution to Britain and the UKUSA was substantial, yet failing with emerging areas and needs. Reductions in expenditure were 'already leading to the expected loss of intelligence', and 'serious worries will therefore remain over meeting future intelligence requirements and in making an adequate contribution in US eyes'. Yet, 'despite increasing complexity Sigint will continue to be a major source of high priority intelligence'. About 75 per cent of GCHQ's budget covered personnel and 19 per cent handled maintenance for bases and existing kit, leaving little for new equipment. Only big and new investments could overcome the rising communications and cryptographic capabilities of targets, especially the Warsaw Pact. 'Whereas in the past equipment was less complex, tended to last longer, and be cheaper to replace, current intercept, communications and analysis requirements are more complex more highly specialised, cost more to replace and have shorter lives ... Although it becomes increasingly expensive (and requires skilled manpower) to keep just sufficiently ahead of our targets, cryptanalysis is still one of our most important activities and pays dividends to the UK both directly and in the context of the US relationship.' Without great and immediate expenditure, GCHQ's heart would fail: it faced 'the urgent replacement due to age of a specialised cryptanalytic computing capability'. GCHQ needed to procure another mainframe computer by 1982, and 'invest substantially in other parts of automation, notably improved remote access, data storage and interconnections between computers'.[108]

In 1979, facing a new government – and Cabinet Secretary in Robert Armstrong and prime minister in Margaret Thatcher – the Siginters struck back. A new Director, Brian Tovey, sought to break out from the 10 per cent cut which bound all other elements of the military except for nuclear forces. To do so he began to blow his department's trumpet much more than his predecessors had done. He revived a generation-dead tradition of presenting annual reports on 'the state of Sigint', so GCHQ could present a 'stocktaking' to LSIB.[109] 'The present level of success in Sigint – as high as most GCHQ staff could remember' stemmed from 'previous wise decisions'. More of them were needed now, 'to enable GCHQ to meet national requirements to the standard that had come to be expected over the past thirty years', and 'to make a fair and valid contribution to the totality of the UKUSA Sigint effort', where America spent ten times more than Britain. 'It was only by continued close collaboration with the US that UK national requirements for Sigint could be met.' American investment in kit, and British access to it, ensured 'a service of intelligence that is substantially better (in terms of coverage, depth and timeliness) than it was ten years ago'. Without major investments now, GCHQ's power would erode fast. However, with just a few million more pounds per year, it would hold its own.

In January 1979, these arguments impressed LSIB, which let Tovey make proposals on those lines. The PSIS secretariat, however, unenthusiastic and confronting a change in Cabinet Secretary, rejected it – significant testimony to the decline in GCHQ's status. Yet several months later the proposals went forward, after a line-by-line review by LSIB.[110] PSIS accepted these proposals as 'a basis for planning' for future – but not present – programmes. Though most departments emphasised the value of Sigint to their work, in 1980 LSIB would not accept the details of Tovey's proposals unless ministers expressly ruled 'whether or not intelligence was to be regarded as a special case separate from Defence in the context of the government's policy of reducing public expenditure'.[111] Until 1982, ministers did not do so. That is, the civil servants addressing defence and intelligence agreed that GCHQ had a case, but not one they could judge. Without higher authority, they refused to breach policies towards general and military expenditure which had been maintained by two Labour governments and a new Conservative one. This position also aimed to hush Tovey, who turned his trumpet towards a more appreciative listener: Margaret Thatcher.

That a few million pounds – the price of a new mainframe computer in one year – caused of all this angst shows how central these issues seemed, and how far GCHQ had fallen in Whitehall. Ministers and officials, depressed and obsessed by Britain's parochial problems, were factionalised. Domestic policy and personal experience drove their reception to GCHQ's arguments, not technical prowess or strategic value. Tovey's emphasis on aiding service Sigint in times of tension and war heightened military support for Sigint, but had little effect on civilian officials. A new defence review loomed; if GCHQ could break old restraints, so other institutions might do likewise, and then where would matters end? GCHQ's successes – essentially technical, for one department at a time – were what Britain paid for and expected to receive. Its demands involved issues that people did not understand, such as computers, and challenged policies which civil servants favoured.

Perhaps for these reasons, GCHQ's arguments impressed Mrs Thatcher. No doubt after careful arrangement, on 10 April 1980 she became the first prime minister to visit GCHQ. Thatcher received an intense and hands-on day-long tour, suited to a micromanager, policy wonk and scientist. This briefing might have been among the most important of her career, aiding her understanding of intelligence and her effective use of Sigint two years later in the Falklands conflict. Thatcher was shown 'the range of Sigint production processes, from the interception of raw material to the finished end-product issued to meet consumer requirements, and the value of Sigint research and development which helps GCHQ to carry out those responsibilities'. She heard of UKUSA's interception capabilities, witnessed cryptanalysis by hand, machine and computer, and saw K and J divisions and JOC in action, including 'a presentation of Sigint on the Afghanistan crisis, a subject of current high priority and interest'. Z briefed her on the dissemination of Sigint, and V on Elint, their areas of specialisation. So did the Chief Scientist, Ralph Benjamin, on research and development, no doubt emphasising the need for new equipment. 'I found very rapidly that she had a very quick and active mind,' Benjamin noted. 'As soon as one told her something, she would try to jump ahead and decide in her own mind to what it led. Unfortunately, not having the relevant background, she was likely to jump to the wrong conclusion. It was then very hard to shift her from that. However, if one provided her with information and ideas sufficiently rapidly that she could only just keep up, this was a very effective and fruitful way of communicating.'[112] Thatcher thanked GCHQ for 'an extremely interesting programme. The insight which I was able to acquire from your interesting and fascinating work will be of permanent value to me.' She praised the 'importance' of GCHQ and UKUSA, and 'the sense of enthusiasm and dedication conveyed' by all she met.[113] The official photographs of Thatcher's visit reflect a gleam in her eye, and even more in those of GCHQ officials, including a dapper and confident Brian Tovey.

To impress the prime minister was good for GCHQ, but bore no immediate fruit. For several years, Tovey's campaigning met with mixed success. GCHQ procured a new mainframe and other computers, meeting its leading priority for expansion.[114] It became more efficient and effective for consumers, particularly the military. GCHQ's success against the Soviets mattered more as the Cold War heated up. Top decision-makers understood its needs. When PSIS treated GCHQ more favourably from 1982, it understood the consequences, rather than having to learn them. Yet PSIS took long to be persuaded and found Tovey's constant challenges annoying. Friction marked Tovey's relationship with the Cabinet Secretary Robert Armstrong. Tovey challenged planned cuts – such as having each department surrender 0.5 per cent of its base budget annually to the Treasury – which would wreck the means used by every Director since Jones to rebuild GCHQ. That reduction would damage GCHQ far more than was true for larger, or fatter, organisations, as much as would the general 10 per cent cut. It would eat any internal economies by GCHQ, when the chances for major breakthroughs against targets were unlikely. Tovey's challenge sparked a striking reply from Armstrong:

Sir Antony Duff: I append a draft reply, from the banks of the Ouse. RA 15.ii.81

Dear Brian,
    I know that it's tough, and enough must seem never enough, but your annual rent is a half a per cent as assessed by

Yours ever
T Duff

PS In case this may seem terse, I'm sending some doggerel verse,
composed by your friends; it may not make amends, but can hardly
make matters much worse.

The Story of the PSIS half per cent
or
Tovey's Nightmare

Director dear, we greatly fear
You have not understood
The doctrine pure you must endure.
Now make it plain we should.

The Chairman's smile cannot beguile
Nor mask the horrid truth,
And Douglas Wass, the Treasury boss,
Will back the Rayner-sooth.

There's no HQ of such virtue,
So all-efficient
That it cannot sustain a cut
Of one more half per cent.

And there's no end. Each year we'll send
For one more half per cent,
And every year, Director dear,
We'll say: 'Sound management!

That's all we ask! Be that your task!'
– For so will run our letter –
'A well-run ship, with ne'er a slip,
Can always be run better.'

But take this consolation,
That every time we ask,

A little less the ensuing mess,
And easier your task.

The smaller will the total bill
Become, the more we've cleft;
The smaller slash the annual bash
Will make in what is left.

So run your show the best you know,
And let your mind be bent
On this our theme, your nightmare dream:
Each year a half per cent.

This tension shaped Tovey's early retirement in 1983, after he scored GCHQ's greatest success since Ultra and then was moved on, leading him eventually to become an authority on the Florentine scholar, banker and artist, Filippo Baldinucci. Until then Tovey took ground.

In 1979, PSIS authorised GCHQ to acquire a new mainframe computer through internal economies. GCHQ marginally improved its funding, sidestepping the cuts. The 1981 Defence Review crippled the Royal Navy and damaged the other services, but GCHQ survived with little harm, remaining above every other conventional element of defence though still behind the deterrent. GCHQ's leadership in honing military Sigint for warning, crisis and war prepared it well for that review's focus on capabilities in Europe. Then, the Falklands conflict broke the logjam. Thatcher stood with her back against the wall, alongside civil servants, especially Armstrong. GCHQ saved them all, as they knew. Whitehall rediscovered GCHQ's value in hard times. This success drove Thatcher to trust her judgement and that of her friends more than ever before, and drove other decision-makers to meet GCHQ's demands. GCHQ's analysis of Soviet reactions to NATO's 'Able Archer' exercise of 1983 drove Britain's road out of the Cold War. As governments sought to restore British credibility, GCHQ's requests seemed cheap compared to boosting conventional forces, or subsidising Chevaline or replacing it with Trident.

Tovey took care not to crow in his report on 'The State of Sigint 1982'. To assess his department's contribution to victory in the Falklands conflict would be 'premature', he wrote. Mistakes had been made, lessons must be learned, but GCHQ's performance had been 'remarkably good'. Instead, Tovey used the success to aid stocktaking: 'The Falklands crisis has demonstrated very clearly that there is great value in a flexible Sigint capability which can support military operations anywhere in the world; and that the UK's Sigint organisation has maintained that capability at a reasonable level.' Events in the South Atlantic reinforced the weight of the dry detail about GCHQ's contribution to British intelligence on diplomatic and military affairs elsewhere in the world.[115] GCHQ's success received a spectacular reward: a 33 per cent increase in its budget for 1983–84 and 1984–85, with new spending focused on computers, data-processing systems and collection from satellites.[116] That level of expenditure continued until 1989 and the waning of the Cold War. GCHQ's fiscal position surpassed its best hopes of the early 1970s. It managed the damage of a decade of retrenchment and again became the government's top priority and most autonomous institution, though it never fully restored its autonomy of the 1950s.

GCHQ's resurgence had limits. In particular, during the 1980s, GCHQ sought to procure a British-designed and built Sigint satellite, Zircon. Ralph Benjamin, a German Jew who had emigrated to Britain as a boy during the 1930s, originated that policy. A brilliant researcher and manager of research into computers, electronics and satellites, Benjamin became a leading defence scientist and, between 1971 and 1982, Chief Scientist at GCHQ and, more broadly, the entire intelligence community.[117] He oversaw research and development for all of GCHQ's equipment during an era of radical change. His unconstrained thinking inspired a generation of young technologists. Benjamin believed that GCHQ could no longer achieve its aims through incremental reform, but only through revolution. Though his broader programme succeeded, Zircon did not. Instead, its public disclosure marked a scandal. Zircon also became GCHQ's most costly and embarrassing failure in acquiring high-technology equipment – among Britain's worst of the Cold War. It was comparable to the collapse of the Blue Streak and Skybolt missile programmes which forced Britain to abandon an independent national nuclear deterrent programme after 1960 and enter a junior partnership with the United States.

The fall of Zircon showed that Britain could not practise independently the full range of Sigint activities. Still, it remained more significant there than with nuclear weapons because GCHQ invested in other advanced collection capabilities: NSA welcomed GCHQ's commitment and valued the quality of GCHQ's analysis.

Coming in from the Cold War

By 1975, GCHQ was a good organisation but less dynamic and innovative than in 1950. Its Five Eyes partners, particularly NSA, were stronger than before. GCHQ's resources had grown, but mostly had been committed to fixed investments. It had relatively fewer resources available to exploit new circumstances, those which had established GCHQ's staple roles in Sigint during the 1950s. New developments involved expensive modes of interception and analysis which might produce greater dividends than old investments or supersede them. GCHQ could not easily handle these developments, which occurred in areas where Britain was comparatively weak or dependent on the United States. Fiscal and political crises eroded Britain's ability to pursue even leading priorities. At the same time, all British strategic institutions faced tough priorities. GCHQ did better than any other, always being a first priority, if sometimes joint-first with others.

Collecting and analysing massive amounts of high-frequency radio traffic from the military forces of the Warsaw Pact kept GCHQ at the top table of Whitehall and the Five Eyes until the end of the Cold War. Then, however, GCHQ was dangerously overspecialised in an evolutionary niche, moving towards monoculture. Its greatest consumer, the MOD Defence Intelligence Service (DIS), was drowning and threatened to drag GCHQ down with it, while its masters placed GCHQ in anticipatory receivership. Fortunately, its native ability, and the transformation of ideas that started in the Benjamin era, helped GCHQ to surmount a change in ecology and a revolution in politics, targets, techniques and priorities. GCHQ was preadapted to enter the second age of Sigint, and would do so with success.

UKUSA and the International Politics of Sigint, 1941–92

The Path Dependency of Politics

From 1945, the web of relationships between the intelligence bureaus of states grew to match those between their military and diplomatic agencies. Bilateral and multilateral intelligence alliances became a hidden dimension of international politics. They bound each camp of the Cold War. The alliances of the Western camp still bind their members today. This chapter addresses the evolution of these alliances, from the perspective of GCHQ.

UKUSA dominates that view.[1] This alliance between the 'second parties', the Sigint agencies of the Five Eyes – Australia, Canada, New Zealand, Britain and the United States – is unique in history. UKUSA involves wholehearted cooperation between departments of state, in the most secret work of states. The technicalities of the task force a distinct form of international politics. These departments cooperate more with their colleagues across national borders than with other agencies of their own governments. Through competitive cooperation, despite political strains, GCHQ and NSA work with and trust each other, and share more secrets than either does with MI6, the CIA or their national diplomatic and armed services respectively. Their operations are often fused technically, making it hard to determine where GCHQ ends and NSA begins. For decades, the command of GCHQ, the Australian Defence Signals Directorate (DSD) and New Zealand Government Communications Security Bureau (GCSB) were integrated. According to General Michael Hayden, ex-Director of the CIA and NSA, recollecting the days after 9/11, were Fort Meade and a fallback headquarters to be paralysed, GCHQ would command all American Sigint.[2] The opposite would occur were Cheltenham incapacitated. Throughout the Cold War, such ideas permeated war plans for these agencies. GCHQ has tasked American units abroad. In 2000, GCHQ facilitated American Sigint efforts in many areas when computer problems swept NSA. In 2007, when floods swept Cheltenham, GCHQ almost gave NSA control of British Sigint. GCHQ and NSA trust each other's loyalty and competence, elements of their systems are integrated, while no other national bureaus could handle the task.

UKUSA emerged because sub-institutions in several countries concluded that they could achieve their aims only by cooperating intimately with each other, which their masters let them do. These decisions rested on a fusion between trust, respect, sentiment, calculation and need. UKUSA, an agreement (but not a treaty) and a relationship between Sigint agencies, lies at the heart of loose alliances between the military and intelligence sub-institutions of several anglophone countries. Many matters shaped those relationships, but none alone enabled them. These relationships rest on common interests, culture, language, law and assumptions about politics and propriety. Those factors also shaped the limits for cooperation with 'third parties' – the Sigint agencies of any other state. The power of UKUSA also drove the structure of Sigint relationships among Western countries. Because UKUSA was a thorough alliance, its members' relationships with third parties had to be transactional.[3]

The written and unwritten alliances within the Five Eyes, which often were produced directly at subnational levels rather than at the conventional state-to-state level, have underpinned Western power and strategy across the globe for generations. During 1942–45, cooperation between American and Commonwealth air forces, armies and navies was tight, as they fought side by side. The cooperation was closest in strategic bombing. British and Dominion service personnel were fused in the aircrew of Bomber Command, which attacked the same targets as the USAAF, at different times of the day and night.[4] Cooperation was weakest at sea in the Pacific Ocean. In 1944–45, the US Navy attempted to stop British sailors even from operating there. Attitudes changed when officers on dry American warships discovered that British ones came armed with alcohol.[5] After 1945, the cooperation between these American and Commonwealth services declined, then revived as friends proved scarce but useful during the Cold War.

This process took many forms. Initially, the Atomic Energy Act of 1946 prevented American cooperation in nuclear weapons with any foreign power. Britain's greatest defence priority between 1945 and 1965 was to develop V-bombers, and later nuclear-powered submarines, both equipped with atomic weapons.[6] These programmes achieved their objectives: to symbolise Britain's status as a world power and warn off the USSR. They also gained Britain far more access to American nuclear technology than any other nation, but as a dependent. Between 1945 and 1992, conventional British armed services were powerful, Commonwealth ones smaller but good, and all linked to American forces. Until 1970, Britain was a real, albeit declining, partner to the United States in stabilising the world. American leaders valued Britain as an ally more than any other country – American human intelligence and security agencies cooperated more with their British and Commonwealth counterparts than those of any other countries – but reservations remained and the British position waned. In 1946, American authorities closed their wartime human intelligence agency, the Office of Strategic Services (OSS), partly because they feared that MI6 controlled it.[7] Yet they authorised UKUSA, despite knowing that it would give GCHQ almost every cryptanalytic secret of the United States. A fundamental difference between the CIA and NSA was and is the latter's belief that it must work wholeheartedly with its British counterpart. Within this hand, GCHQ was Britain's strongest card. It remained closer in power and more essential to the work of its American partner than any other British institution. GCHQ, with a budget varying between 1 and 2 per cent of the expenditure of the MOD, bought Britain disproportionate knowledge and influence in Washington, compared to the other 98–99 per cent. In contrast, Britain had to spend more to acquire less cooperation and influence in nuclear matters or conventional forces.

The Emergence of UKUSA

UKUSA stems from a mixture of accident, necessity, the state of intelligence liaison in 1940, and the collective and individual psychology of Siginters. Uncoordinated interactions between many individuals set Anglo-American Siginters down paths they still follow today. Had one of many American or British officers behaved differently, especially in 1940–42, these paths might have been diverged, but by 1945, their directions were parallel and set.

Between 1919 and 1939, intelligence officers and military attachés drove British liaison relations. MI6 had many of them, GC&CS few. British officials gave American ones much material and received some in return; relations between their intelligence personnel were distant, however: none existed in Sigint. American attachés liaised with many naval and military intelligence services abroad: British no more than French or German, and few with secret intelligence agencies. In fact, American Siginters had no liaison relationships at all. They often rated Britain as their second target after Japan, but rarely attacked its codes, and with little success. GC&CS routinely read American traffic, which provided reportage on third parties, but rarely illuminated American aims.[8] During 1939–41, if Whitehall wanted to understand American policy, it asked statesmen in Washington, not codebreakers. After the United States entered the war in December 1941, Britain ceased attacking its codes.

War transformed these practices. British, French and Polish codebreakers thoroughly attacked Enigma. Axis Siginters made transactional alliances. After France fell, Whitehall sought to show American leaders that Britain was powerful and Americans should help it to survive. In particular, Britain provided, for free, leading-edge technologies, such as radar and cavity magnetrons, which showed American authorities British superiority in applied military science. Combined with American industry, each device transformed Allied power as much as Ultra did.[9] A liaison arrangement emerged between British intelligence and Roosevelt's advisor in the area, William Donovan. Roosevelt and his admirals and generals decided that limited American aid would enable Britain to survive and prevent the nightmare of isolation in a world dominated by Nazi Germany. From July 1940, Washington sent teams of experts to Britain, first to test this conclusion and then to discuss cooperation.[10]

The idea of extending this cooperation to Sigint was obvious, but the process took an odd and often undocumented form. Since detailed notes were not often taken at the time, many key events can be reconstructed only through use of interviews taken decades afterwards.[11] In September 1940, entirely on his own initiative, General George Strong, a senior American observer in London, asked his British contacts whether Britain would discuss cryptanalytical issues. When some unknown Britons evinced interest in the matter, Strong asked his masters whether the United States would 'exchange full information on German, Italian and Japanese code and cryptographic information' and make a 'continuous exchange of important intercept'.[12] No responsible British authority had made such a proposal, which split the American services. The US Navy spearheaded military support for Britain, but opposed any exchange on cryptanalysis, since that might facilitate British attacks on American systems. In contrast, the War Department, the MID, and the American codebreakers in the US Army's Signal Intelligence Service (US Army SIS), especially William Friedman, ignorant of German and Italian cryptosystems, regarded this exchange as being 'absolutely essential to National Defense'.[13] Neither knew much about GC&CS, but US Army SIS was predisposed to respect and the US Navy's Office of Chief of Naval Operations (OpNav) 20th Division of the Office of Naval Communications, G Section/Communications Security (Op-20-G) to fear it. Churchill and the COS, and Roosevelt and senior American commanders, agreed that their Siginters should discuss the matter. Though no one understood it at the time, politically this arrangement favoured GC&CS. British Siginters had more experience with liaison and closer ties to their superiors than American ones did, a stronger technical hand, and were better integrated. Menzies, doubting American security and the value of its help, convinced Churchill that GC&CS should not reveal its attack on Enigma.[14] American counsels were equally divided: Op-20-G questioned cooperation, while US Army SIS wanted it more than any other of the agencies involved.

On 8 February 1941, two army and two US Navy (USN) codebreakers began a visit to GC&CS, under Lieutenant Robert Weeks (USN) and Lieutenant Abraham Sinkov. After crossing the Atlantic by battleship and British waters by a cruiser to London, Tiltman escorted them by car to Bletchley. They arrived just before midnight, exhausted and grubby, to exchange toasts of sherry with Denniston, Tiltman and Travis, and then retired to 'really elegant living' in a local country house.[15] The next day, as Britain had done with radar, US Army SIS broke the ice through a gift: it described its success against Magic and gave GC&CS a Purple analogue – one of only four that it possessed, and the main item which American Sigint had to offer Britain – without bargaining over it. Why US Army SIS did so is undocumented. Perhaps US Army SIS, knowing that it did not know what to bargain for, sought to prove its prowess to people it respected from afar, and so encourage reciprocity. In any case, this gift was essential to cooperation. In coming weeks, thorough discussion of every detail of the work of these agencies – with the exception of Enigma – showed GC&CS that American Siginters were decent, but well behind British ones everywhere except in attacking Purple. GC&CS gave much to the Americans, collectively matching the value of the Purple analogue: work against Japanese military and Italian diplomatic codebooks, interception kit, and technical expertise. Yet senior figures at Bletchley feared that to inform the Americans of bombes might imperil their project, and dared not challenge Menzies or Churchill on the issue.[16]

The only explanation for their change in heart, and a convincing one, comes from an interview with Tiltman conducted decades later. Like the Trafalgar Day memorandum, it reflects how middle-level British Siginters of the time dared take key matters straight to the top, if their leaders would not, and Denniston's diffidence in doing so. Tiltman, masterful and admired by his colleagues, grasped the psychological position. He had more experience in liaison than anyone else at Bletchley, especially with the American visitors. Familiar with Japanese codes and machine attack, he better understood and appreciated the cryptanalytic quality needed to produce Purple. Tiltman told Denniston that in order to create an effective alliance, GC&CS must reveal its work against Enigma to the American officers. Denniston let Tiltman make that pitch to Menzies, who, after consulting Churchill, agreed – so long as these officers pledged to tell only their immediate supervisors about Enigma. American, British, Finnish, French and Polish Siginters of this period were willing to trust national secrets to each other, on a gentleman's word. Tiltman was party to all of these arrangements. In contrast, the fascist powers' arrangements were very limited in frequency, scope and depth. The Soviets took without giving. Naturally, these American officers did not wish to sign on to something they had not seen. 'You know, this is something you can't go away without, or the whole thing will break down,' said Tiltman. '... Sometimes we have to make decisions without authority.' Sinkov replied: 'I can see saying that to my General' – but the four Americans signed on. They saw the bombe machine but not its product, Ultra. Welchman gave them all the technical assistance they wished to construct bombes of their own, though the cryptanalytic and mathematical skill which guided this force could not be transferred so simply.[17]

The Sinkov mission is often seen as a failure, because commentators do not realise how much material Britain gave it on their attack against Enigma. In fact, by casting Purple upon the waters, American cryptanalysts returned to Washington laden with more gifts than they had brought with them. Soon after these men returned, Denniston followed them across the Atlantic, met the leaders of US Army SIS and Op-20-G, and began a process which took GC&CS years to complete: that of understanding the psychology and politics of American Sigint. With a combination of reservation and regard, both sides agreed to pool their work and product in both thorough and transactional ways. American Siginters would lead a combined attack on Magic and Japanese book systems. GC&CS alone would assault Enigma. US Army SIS, however, would construct bombes of its own, as GC&CS had enabled them to do.

Getting to Know You

The Anglo-American Comint alliance of 1941–45 was the closest yet known. It involved liaison between isolated communities of specialists, which suddenly discovered they had partners. In Sigint, as everywhere, centralised, tried-and-tested British systems of organisation confronted ramshackle American ones, which for the first time handled issues of grand strategy.[18] GC&CS and Op-20-G developed good, but limited, working arrangements, marked by both frankness and friction. That GC&CS's naval personnel were largely civilians, while Op-20-G's remained resolutely naval, caused distance.[19] GC&CS's relations with US Army SIS were wholehearted, but complex. GC&CS fully aided US Army SIS's diplomatic codebreakers and Army Y, but not its development of independent means to attack Enigma. The convoluted organisation of MID and US Army SIS, driven by personality, frustrated GC&CS. It tried to aid the position of William Friedman, whom GC&CS correctly thought the best American Siginter, and who was well disposed towards Britain. Unfortunately, his friendship with Tiltman and Denniston contributed towards other American officials marginalising Friedman during 1942–43, a process which was exacerbated by his health problems.²⁰ All participants carefully met the letter of their obligations and accepted criticisms from others if they did not. Cooperative competition drove a rational, open and highest-common–denominator system of decision-making. Personal relations involving trust and respect between Siginters emerged, especially as each side sent liaison officers to one another and integrees into work units – but suspicion, conflict and jealousy were natural, and essential to the outcome. Americans suspected British wiles, Britons questioned American maturity.²¹ NSA internal history notes that American divisions 'scandalised' GC&CS, which found the Americans 'disorganised and frustrating at times, but they could still play one off against another to achieve their objectives'.²² This comment is true, yet unavoidable, just as Americans exploited the varying degrees of access agreed by SSA and Op-20-G with Britain to gain more from GC&CS than they gave. Only when Siginters worked through these matters and developed autonomy could a partnership emerge. Ultimately, conflicts between these partners produced greater confidence and cooperation among them.

During 1941–42, GC&CS did not give all of its cryptologic techniques and product to American agencies. It had not promised to do so. GC&CS gave Americans as much as they could handle and more than the latter returned. If asked, it would have met most of their requests for more material, outside Enigma, including the single largest lacunae: Italian diplomatic and military cryptosystems. Though disorganisation within each bureau complicated the process, GC&CS aimed merely to conceal progress against the diplomatic cyphers of Middle Eastern and Balkan states, which Americans did not request. US Army SIS and Op-20-G did not send liaison officers to Britain – except for two US Navy officers whom Bletchley trained in bombes – although GC&CS asked them to do so and other US military agencies sent similar such personnel to Britain. American Sigint-specific agencies had no tradition of liaison, nor independence: military and naval intelligence controlled these agencies, which were treated purely as technical producers of Comint. GC&CS, meanwhile, was freewheeling: it had become the first Sigint agency on earth to achieve autonomy, and was to become the leading priority for Anglo-American strategic resources, alongside the Manhattan Project.

American Siginters did not understand their partner. Consequently, dissatisfaction grew among American intelligence officials about the exchange, and the 'back-door' methods by which British liaison officers worked with divided authorities in the United States.[23] Yet these methods were simply those of competent liaison, which American officers from other branches practised in British institutions. GC&CS liaison officers tried to avoid irritating their hosts while they struggled to understand the convoluted American system of Sigint. In the process, unavoidably, they exploited and shaped their partners, who remained divided, though they did cooperate more with each other over time.

In Washington during the spring of 1942, Tiltman pursued a thorough technical interchange with both services. He was tactful, met only military and naval officers and Siginters, and learned the ground. He warned Travis not to press for matters unlikely to emerge, such as unifying US services' Sigint. Technical relations between these services were sound; further pressure might backfire. For example, 'the dislike of Jews prevalent in the U.S. Navy is a factor to be considered, as nearly all the leading army cryptographers are Jews', reported Tiltman.[24] One wonders how far this factor, compared to the lack of anti-Semitism at senior levels within GC&CS, shaped the relations of all these agencies with US Army SIS in this formative period. Conversely, Tiltman's successors, Captain Edward Hastings and Major Geoffrey Stevens, contacted all American agencies involved in Sigint. That practice, natural for officers from a unified system, annoyed American officers who wished that FBI and the Coast Guard had no cryptanalytic units. Hastings approached Coast Guard Sigint, for 'purely crypt. liaison', because it was under the US Navy. This action annoyed Strong, now head of the MID.[25] That liaison had practical motives, and not necessarily ulterior ones. Privately, Stevens held that: 'They are hopelessly overorganised in many ways,' and disorganised in others. Senior officers did not know what their subordinates did. 'For this reason it is necessary for me to get to know well the man who actually does the job. There are an awful lot of these and I do my best by attending their parties and giving parties for them to get to know them well enough so that they will tell me their troubles as I wander in to pass the time of day.'[26]

Still, these experiences produced annoyance. Stevens told Denniston: 'Sometimes I think they are just a lot of kids playing at "Offices". You must have noticed yourself how very many childish qualities the American male has: his taste in women, motor-cars and drink, his demonstrative patriotism, his bullying assertion of his Rights, his complete pig-selfishness in public matters and his incredible friendliness and generosity when he likes you – Hell! Anyone would think I didn't like them. But perhaps it is as well that I am fond of children.'[27] So too, standing beside a urinal in Arlington Hall, Virginia, on Boxing Day 1942, Colonel Carter Clarke from US Army SIS damned the 'bloody British' and described Hastings, who was confrontational in arguments, with 'extreme' profanity.[28] Noticeably, these explosions occurred offstage: in meetings, manners were restrained, on all sides.

This situation led superiors to prefer an inferior policy, which would have weakened Sigint. By October 1942, the US War Department began to limit the access of liaison officers.[29] Meanwhile, Menzies aimed 'to cut out gradually all liaison officers and for Denniston and Travis to deal direct with their opposite numbers'.[30]

Tension emerged in Anglo-American Sigint precisely as it did in wider strategy, rising from mid-1942 until early 1945, then suddenly subsiding.[31] Unlike other areas, in Sigint Britain remained the stronger party. Frustrated American Siginters watched colleagues in other fields expand their positions, while they could not. This status caused irritation which concealed the nub of the matter: though Americans wished it otherwise, British Sigint was superior. British Siginters initially responded firmly, sometimes with condescension, but adopted measured tones as they came to like and understand their partners. Crossed wires among cryptanalytical and intelligence organisations caused confusion and irritation. MID did not know the details of the cooperation between GC&CS, US Army SIS and Op-20-G. In 1942, it accused GC&CS of withholding material which Britain had actually already given US Army SIS and American commanders. These false accusations annoyed GC&CS. Tiltman's chilly refutation of them showed anger at how they impugned its standards as gentlemen.[32]

Yet Siginters also confronted real political and technical differences. Without liaison officers or integrees in Britain, American Siginters did not realise how far and fast British Sigint was leaving them behind, and how difficult independent attack on Enigma would be. GC&CS wished to monopolise the attack against Enigma in order to maximise security for the work. It rightly feared American sloppiness in security. Op-20-G and the SSA wished to enter the field in order to practise the state of the art against the biggest game in town. Politically, GC&CS's monopoly against Enigma gave it, and Britain, power in the Anglo-American alliance. Though GC&CS freely gave Ultra to the SSA, Op-20-G and American commands, Bletchley controlled the process. An independent position against Enigma would give the SSA or Op-20-G more power, both against GC&CS and each other. The SSA and Op-20-G each feared that they would decline or die after the war, or only one of them would survive. Many of their actions against Bletchley were really aimed at each other. Ultimately, British Siginters in the United States knew American Sigint better than any American did; despite their complaints about GC&CS, until 1944 the SSA and Op-20-G worked better with it than they did with each other.

Ultimately, the MID and SSA abandoned their demand to attack Enigma independently. Though they acquired bombes based on Bletchley's model and powerful data-processing systems, they could not intercept enough Enigma traffic to sustain an attack. Probably Bletchley's willingness to make concessions to Op-20-G on this issue, but not the SSA, embittered the latter. Op-20-G broke that monopoly because it knew American assistance was possible and necessary against U-boat Enigma. It could intercept Enigma traffic and attack it with Desch machines. Fortunately, Tiltman convinced Travis to help Op-20-G do so, manifested in the Holden Agreement of October 1942.[33] Subsequently, Turing improved the Desch machines dramatically.[34] In cryptanalysis, American brute force rose faster than British, but they did not know how to use it to full effect; Americans had the hardware but not the software. Bletchley and Op-20-G then integrated their efforts, which soothed their concerns about each other. GC&CS praised Op-20-G's efforts and urged their increase.[35] Meanwhile, Sigint cooperation in the Pacific was far more complex. The US Army and US Navy, General Douglas MacArthur and Australia, GC&CS and its outstation in Ceylon, and the Indian government all maintained different cryptanalytic organisations, which did not fully cooperate with each other until the BRUSA agreement of January 1944. In 1944–45, Op-20-G sought to limit GC&CS's attacks on Japanese naval traffic, reflecting the desire in Washington to monopolise the Pacific war. Then, they embraced British aid, which reinforced them almost as much as Op-20-G had aided attack on Enigma.

Friendships and Frictions

During 1943, in a bruising debate between Strong and Travis, power shaped the Anglo-American Sigint relationship perhaps more brutally than at any other time. MID and GC&CS then signed the BRUSA (British–United States) agreement, which gave each a victory.[36] BRUSA regulated procedures for the exchange, security and dissemination of Sigint, especially Ultra, which were then enforced across Allied commands. Each side adopted the same procedures to communicate and disseminate Sigint. Informal 'back-door' methods were institutionalised. The SSA and Op-20-G liaison officers and integrees entered GC&CS.

Immediately, and for the first time, American Siginters understood how much they had to learn from GC&CS, and how much more agile, innovative and powerful it was than they. They were '*absolutely amazed* by what British have here – beyond all imaginings'. Friedman credited Bletchley's success to its staff, 'dons, professors, and highest type businessmen who are accustomed to getting much done in a very quiet way without fuss and feathers'.[37] Telford Taylor, a civilian lawyer and leader in MID, noted that two 'elderly' and 'practically palsied' British ex-civil servants produced as much from one secondary Japanese system, J-20, 'as the twenty young men doing it at Arlington'.[38]

Increasingly, Americans liked and admired British Siginters. Both sides shared all technical developments freely. Arrangements between GC&CS and Op-20-G were similar, though without the obligation to share technical developments. These arrangements enabled American Siginters to gain more from Britain – which also had more to offer – than GC&CS could gain from them. This was a significant step down the road to UKUSA, reducing American suspicions of Britain and increasing their respect for it.

Both sides knew their Sigint alliance might not survive the war and acted to insure themselves against that risk. In 1943, Telford Taylor formulated its strategy towards Sigint over the long term. MID had considered 'a complete breach of relations' with GC&CS, but feared its superiors might reject that approach. GC&CS had greater access to Churchill, who cared about the issue, than American Siginters had with Roosevelt, who did not. The US Joint Chiefs of Staff would support winners over whiners, and the War Department would not fight the COS on the issue. MID had to lick its wounds and look to the future, so 'securing the most advantageous (from our standpoint) basis for British–American collaboration … <u>The long term interest of the United States requires the greatest possible self-sufficiency in the field of signal intelligence</u>.'[39] The MID could best achieve these aims by stationing integrees at Bletchley Park, so getting a 'foothold' in all techniques of mechanised attack and by acquiring every diplomatic system the British cryptanalytical effort at Berkeley Street had mastered. As the war ended, Taylor continued, 'diplomatic signal intelligence will be a premium. And the closer the end of the war appears to be, the less eager the British will be to share their diplomatic secrets with us. When the parting of the ways comes, as it probably will, the United States must be in in full command of the art as it then stands.' When his superior, Colonel Carter Clarke, head of Special Branch MIS, presented this proposal to Strong, Clarke wrote that these ways 'most assuredly will' part.[40] Then, SSA would possess cryptanalytic skills equalling Britain, and outweighing Op-20-G.

Both sides also considered attack and defence against each other's systems. Until the American Sigaba machine became effective in middle 1943, Typex was the only high-grade cypher system available for combined operations. American agencies received original Typex messages in volume. Soon, Whitehall believed that this practice might compromise Typex. These unparaphrased messages would be perfect cribs, if Americans intercepted Typex traffic, especially because they held six Typex machines with special rotors for high-level communications.[41] By 1943, diplomatic differences between Britain and the United States were rising. Whitehall believed that American codebreakers would attack and break Typex traffic. Edward Bridges, the Cabinet Secretary, told Churchill that the 'greatly increased efficiency' of American cryptanalysts, 'which has been built up with the help of our own cryptographers, who have passed on all our methods and skill', combined with the passing of unparaphrased traffic and 'numberless Plain Language "cribs" to our cypher traffic', had compromised Typex. Britain initiated a series of messages, codenamed 'Guard', for the small category of messages which American authorities were intended '*never*' to know had even been sent. Guard would separate the sheep from the goats: Typex would cover most traffic against enemy attack, but signals about issues where major British and American interests clashed would receive 'absolute security' against American assault. Against enemies, the compromise of any important traffic was a problem. Against friends, only the most important messages required protection.[42]

Churchill accepted this proposal, with revealing reservations:

> I wonder however whether it would not be as well for me to suggest to the President a self-denying ordinance by which on a gentleman's agreement both the British and American Governments would refrain from trying to penetrate each other's cyphers. This would enable the existing easy circulation of messages to proceed without prejudice to the 'GUARD' arrangements.
>
> I have not authorised the decoding of an American message since they came into the war with us, and I told the President so. I have little doubt that they would say the same.[43]

High authorities rejected these sentiments. Bridges doubted that any such arrangement would have 'a very lasting validity in technical circles'. After talking with Travis, Menzies held 'there could never be a satisfactory gentleman's agreement, as even if orders were issued on the highest level, the temptation to have a peek would be more than some experts could resist'.[44] 'Absolute security' rested on a new cypher machine, Rockex II, which was designed primarily to block American attack. It was a creature of the mid-Atlantic, inspired by American technology, invented by a Canadian professor of communication engineering, Benjamin de Forest Bayly, and developed by leading British engineers, scientists and mathematicians, including R. J. Griffith, Turing, and Welchman.[45] The production of Rockex II barely met British requirements. Two Rockex IIs stood on the London–Washington circuit in February 1945, with more on the way. One member of the Foreign Office Communications Department wrote: 'Keep them up to it! These machines may just save our bacon if peace were to break out suddenly.'[46]

These precautions were wise. Op-20-G studied Typex to determine whether attack was possible, but concluded that it was not. Given Op-20-G's advantages, this conclusion demonstrates that the agency was less good in attack than it liked to claim – or else Typex was better in defence than Americans wished to pretend.[47] American authorities never gave Britain access to Sigaba machines or unparaphased messages from it in order to minimise temptation and vulnerability.[48] Op-20-G had an 'N.B. designation' ('No British') for Sigint material it did not wish to share.[49] Conversely, GC&CS never attacked Sigaba. The Foreign Office deprecated the idea of espionage against the United States after the war. One of the rare exponents of doing so, and a Foreign Office expert in intelligence, Gladwyn Jebb, agreed that 'with America everything is common property anyhow!' Another diplomatic expert in intelligence, Sir Nevile Bland, summarised the conventional view: he had the 'strongest disinclination for "working" the U.S.A. I don't believe there is anything there which we could not find out by legitimate methods, or by investigations, in the case of commerce & finance, *at* the other end; and the result of detection would be utterly calamitous.'[50]

Anglo-American discord reached a peak in 1944. Official and public American opinion of British intentions and capabilities was negative, largely over divisions about the shape of the postwar world. By 1945, that shape was setting: leaders in London and Washington thought their vital interests rarely clashed and often overlapped, and the immediate stakes of differences between them were smaller. Each looked more benevolently at the other than when they had seen themselves as rivals. Both accepted that Britain was strong, but the United States stronger. The world was chaotic; the USSR was powerful and unpredictable; atomic weapons existed, and friends were few. Britain and the United States remained aligned after the war, but wartime links eroded between their military and intelligence organisations. Whether the United States would maintain commitments to Europe, or Britain, was unclear. Only in Sigint did the Anglo-American strategic relationship continue unbroken.

UKUSA had many causes. In 1945, Britain was the junior partner in atomic weapons, which were public knowledge. But American politicians broke that relationship with Britain; they might have done so with UKUSA, had they known about it. British and American Siginters rightly feared that danger, which drove their attempts to conceal the union. By 1945, their secret cooperation in Sigint was thorough, rivalries had declined and the more they worked together the easier the work. Each side believed it could trust the other's competence and loyalty. BRUSA built trust. American officers at Bletchley learned everything it did. The SSA demanded copies of every system and solution held by Berkeley Street: GC&CS happily agreed to provide them, but the Foreign Office was more reluctant. Naturally, British diplomats did not wish to help the State Department in areas Britain thought its own. When the

SSA demanded that the Foreign Office provide material which it denied some British consumers, such as foreign reports of discussions with the Foreign Secretary, a telling compromise solved the problem: GC&CS enabled American Siginters to break diplomatic codes and gave integrees access to almost all flimsies, and explained why certain categories were retained. The SSA and MID did not pass some of these messages to the State Department. The Foreign Office simply trusted their word on the matter, as Menzies had done regarding bombes a few years before.[51]

The success of American Sigint raised the status of its agencies, which became more autonomous, respected and increasingly masters of their own fates – though far less so than GC&CS. During 1943–44, the SSA and G-2 considered cooperation with GC&CS after the war and discussed the topic with it. Telford Taylor wrote: 'It is not intended, of course, that full collaboration on the intelligence or technical levels be put on a binding treaty basis. Relations between America and Britain in this highly confidential field must be determined anew as circumstances and personalities change. But the present seems an unusually favourable moment to bring about full collaboration, and its establishment should serve as a powerful deterrent towards any 'separatist' tendencies which might subsequently arise.'[52] The trust between the SSA – primarily civilians – and GC&CS was the key element in UKUSA. Denniston, Tiltman and Travis built friendships with leading American cryptanalysts, as did many of their subordinates. American Siginters were smitten with Patricia Bartley, recruited by Emily Anderson at the start of the war, who led the attack on German diplomatic codes – codenamed Floradora – thereby gaining praise from the Foreign Secretary, Antony Eden. Op-20-G's suspicions of Britain declined. Intelligence, especially Sigint, was the area of statecraft where Americans believed that Britain equalled or outweighed them and from which they could most gain and learn.

As the war ended, senior American Siginters considered GC&CS carefully. The two US agencies were now coordinated in an Army–Navy Communications Intelligence Board (ANCIB; renamed STANCIB when the State Department joined, and ultimately USCIB). ANCIB agreed 'that advantage should be taken of the present opportunity to obtain all possible information from the British', including systems, technique and machines. The SSA and Op-20-G needed to 'present a united front towards them'. Top personnel emphasised the collection and coordination of all reports from GC&CS and of American officers there. This process demonstrated British prowess, superiority and willingness to honour a one-sided part of the Sigint agreement. The American attachment of attachés to GC&CS stemmed from suspicion, but ironically boosted trust. American Siginters also pursued a net assessment of the cryptanalytic capabilities of every state against the United States, with 'England' the first priority and 'Russia' the second. In this study, 'an intelligence approach rather than a cryptanalytic approach is intended, looking to the future rather than to the past'. Friedman noted: 'it was important to know how good other countries were at cryptography in order that we shall be able to know what we may be up against'.[53] Though this study was not completed, American actions reveal respect for British prowess. One root of UKUSA was an American wish not to slip unknowingly behind British Sigint; another, to benefit from GCHQ's power against Russia.

Towards a Gentleman's Agreement

In May 1945, as the European war ended, GCHQ made Eric Jones its liaison officer in Washington, to gather information and shape attitudes without creating complaints of intrigue. This appointment of a man admired by all who knew of Ultra, skilled in liaison, but whose office had closed, showed GCHQ's concern with cementing relations with Op-20-G and the SSA, which in September was named the US Army Security Agency (ASA). GCHQ informally asked these agencies whether they wished to cooperate against Soviet cryptosystems. Equally informally, ANCIB proposed complete cooperation on all parts of the Soviet target, technical, product and intelligence, including 'collateral', material from non-Sigint sources, and all-source analysis. It asked GCHQ to suggest means to achieve these ends. That cooperation began just before Japan surrendered, and included other targets, even before any Sigint agencies contacted their superiors on the matter or the UKUSA agreement was signed.[54]

For personal and technical reasons, GCHQ and its American counterparts wanted to continue their relationship, and their governments were willing to let them do so without supervision. A technical arrangement between these agencies was possible, but a treaty between states was not. Since these governments wished to keep those agencies secret, any arrangement between them must likewise be secret. The more people outside the Sigint agencies who knew of the cooperation, the less the secrecy. British and American Siginters believed their work was fundamental and required great resources, which were deteriorating as the war came to an end. Thus they confronted a collapse in strength, as well as new problems – primarily Russian. Continued cooperation would let each aid the other, especially against the greatest uncertainty they confronted: the USSR. Division would weaken their efforts and create a new threat, each other. Cooperation against Soviet systems could create a new Ultra, as the old one passed into history.

Just before the Japanese surrender, GCHQ asked the Foreign Office and the COS for permission to maintain the wartime Sigint relationship with the US. These bodies approved the proposal, which fitted their hopes for relations with Washington, in an informal and unrecorded manner. Presumably they informed the prime minister, Clement Attlee, through similar means: he knew of the matter, as did some ministers. Authorities freed Travis to negotiate one of the greatest British diplomatic agreements not to have been defined by a diplomat. The only comparable example – the technical discussions between the British and French general staffs between 1905 and 1914 – were rather more narrow and less successful than UKUSA. Meanwhile, ANCIB approached its chiefs on the matter in a more formal fashion. On 12 September 1945, the US Chiefs of Staff and the State Department told President Harry Truman that this cooperation was essential to American national security, given 'the disturbed conditions of the world and the necessity of keeping informed of the technical developments and possible hostile intentions of foreign nations'.[55] Here, American strategists coined the classic claim that the greatest danger to their security was a surprise attack – 'another Pearl Harbor' – this time with nuclear weapons. Intelligence, particularly cooperation with GCHQ against the USSR, was essential to prevent this danger. Immediately, Truman supported their recommendation and authorised ANCIB to negotiate with Britain on the matter, 'to continue collaboration in the field of communication intelligence between the United States Army and Navy and the British, and to extend, modify or discontinue this collaboration, as determined to be in the best interests of the United States'.[56] The past and future of Sigint was already on his mind: Truman had just issued an executive order forbidding the release of any 'Information regarding the past or present status, technique or procedure, degree of success attained, or any specific results of any cryptanalytic unit'.[57] Truman, like Attlee, approved Anglo-American negotiations on Comint, but deliberately disinterested himself from the process and outcome.

GCHQ had the initiative on the negotiations and determined the details of its brief. This enabled a technical rather than a political offer – GCHQ declined to address anything beyond Sigint, although ANCIB had raised the exchange of collateral intelligence – but the connections were obvious. GCHQ's proposal was a simple means to test American intentions, perhaps the most important one conducted just after the war. The secrecy surrounding Sigint has hidden its significance. This action determined that Britain and the United States saw strategic cooperation as a vital need, centred on Sigint. Knowing the strategic logic behind Truman's decision would have eased weary minds in Whitehall, but Britain lacked that advantage. While Jones increasingly reported on American intentions for complete cooperation – or 'joint ownership' – in Sigint, GCHQ understood that American counsels were divided, while some American Siginters, especially naval ones, were dubious about Britain.[58] Dangers abounded in an arrangement where Americans could work with British codebreakers, monitor their techniques, maximise their success against the Soviets, and end the arrangement at will – all of which in fact US Navy intelligence was considering.

From years of experience as the most autonomous agency in the Anglo-American relationship, GCHQ knew what its masters and partners would tolerate. Travis asked Hinsley to draft a proposal, which senior Siginters and the Sigint Board amended. Under it, Britain and the United States should enter a formal Sigint alliance between equals, rather than an informal arrangement, which would involve a complete and thorough exchange on all targets, not just the Soviet Union. Siginters would sign it, not states. Parity was unavoidable – sweetening the pot for Americans, but insured Britain if American capacities rose. It also implicitly boosted GCHQ's immediate bargaining position against any American preferences for transactional or informal arrangements, such as Op-20-G would have, and the experiences of the past year where Britain had given American Siginters far more than they had provided in return. Britain was superior in Sigint; Americans would not admit the fact, but cooperation against the USSR would remind them of it. This alliance would follow GCHQ's wartime practices with ASA, rather than with Op-20-G, which obviously would split the American services. Relations with any other countries, 'third parties', would be restrained, with one exception: Britain would cooperate with its Dominions, which would not be 'third parties'. The United States could approach any Dominion on Sigint only through Britain. Security procedures for Sigint would follow those presently in force but would be more restrictive. Both sides would exchange liaison officers and integrees, coordinate interception and cryptanalysis, and share all of the product. Neither would attack the other's traffic. Each would maintain its own cryptosystems.[59] Either could end the arrangement at will. GCHQ gambled that its partner would never call triple talaq: 'I divorce you, I divorce you, I divorce you.'

During October 1945, Travis and Hinsley (briefly backed by Tiltman, present to coordinate attack on Soviet systems) joined Jones in Washington to negotiate with ANCIB. The British delegation consisted purely of Siginters. The ASA and the MID cooperated within the US Army's delegation. Admiral Joseph Redman, until recently Director of Naval Communications and in charge of naval Sigint, dominated the US Navy delegation, where Op-20-G had little power. These discussions rested on common interests and agreement on most issues, coloured by an element of mutual suspicion. Any minor irritant caused problems which Jones and well-disposed Americans finessed. In the first meeting of American and British Sigint authorities on 15 October, Travis argued that 'the most desirable type of collaboration to be achieved [was] a partnership ... the field of communication intelligence is not readily adaptable to the separation of its several branches and ... any cooperative effort will be severely weakened by any limitations to full collaboration. He recommended that complete partnership with mutual access to all branches of communication intelligence and on all tasks be accepted as a basic principle for cooperation.' The parties might, however, define a specific task (such as Palestine or the Panama Canal) as a 'national' one, and exclude the other from it: 'if there were to be any reservations, they would be "open reservations", subject to the knowledge and agreement of both parties'. After a long discussion of all aspects of Sigint, ANCIB agreed that GCHQ and American Siginters should consider a draft, to be prepared by Hinsley, 'based upon complete U.S.–British collaboration', and 'complete coordination'.[60]

The agencies interpreted the adjective 'complete' in different ways. Despite their constant injunctions to maintain a 'united front', American Siginters had key differences. GCHQ and the ASA agreed on most matters and often worked against the US Navy. GCHQ and the US Navy, conversely, clashed on three matters where British proposals challenged Op-20-G's established positions. First, could Americans contact Canada directly on Sigint? GCHQ, a virgin in transatlantic politics, just said no, assuming the mother country could speak for Canada. Instead, the SSA, Op-20-G and Canadian authorities all wished to be able to contact each other directly. When Travis visited Ottawa, he hinted that Canada either must let GCHQ speak for it or leave the imperial home of Sigint. He learned that this ultimatum would drive Canadians reluctantly to pursue the best relations possible with the United States. That error compromised GCHQ's immediate claims to speak for the other Dominions and shaped the odd and delayed ways in which they became second parties over the next decade.[61] Second, the US Navy agreed that all current material – intercepts, end product, T/A, techniques and kit – should be shared, with one reservation: 'We might have a technique which could not be relevant to a current problem and might even apply to one of our own cyphers. It would not be in the national interest to turn over such a technique to anyone else.' Thus, the US Navy insisted, acting 'as a free agent', either side could secretly deny the other any technical advances it wished. Admiral Redman emphasised: 'we are trying to keep the implementation of the agreement on a current basis because we cannot be sure when the agreement will end ... a total exchange would be proper only if there were a treaty of alliance between the two countries ... any exchange would be governed by what we conceive our national interests to be'. Third, the US Navy also thought 'the present liaison arrangements should be curtailed', whereas GCHQ wanted them to grow. On the latter two issues, the ASA shared GCHQ's views, because both had learned from the same experiences. These differences in attitudes show the odd interaction between technique and realpolitik in Sigint. The surprise is not that the US Navy held these views, but that the ASA and GCHQ rejected them.[62]

Travis and the British COS considered breaking negotiations over these points, or formally raising them with the American COS. Ultimately, however, British authorities concluded that, once both sides worked together, suspicions would vanish and cooperation grow. GCHQ found creative compromises to the disputed points, which gave the ASA the casting vote on all issues in dispute. Thus, Americans could contact Canada directly on Sigint, so long as they consulted GCHQ in advance. Experience in Ottawa led Travis, correctly, to realise that US Navy cooperation with Canada 'won't amount to a row of beans'.[63] Jones influenced American Siginters to change the wording of their position on exchange. ANCIB agreed that any signatory could withhold from the other any technical advance it desired, so long as it openly described that matter, and aimed to 'limit such exceptions to the absolute minimum'. This conclusion paralleled the treatment of 'national' issues.

During February–March 1946, discussions in London put technical flesh on principles. On 5 March 1946, American and British Siginters signed 'The British–U.S. Communication Intelligence Agreement', BRUSA, which soon was called UKUSA, a secret agreement between subnational elements, authorised by their states.[64] With the UKUSA agreement, as in the Anglo-American Sigint relationship of 1941–45, negotiations raised tensions, which agreements and action ended.

UKUSA: Secrets and Rules

The UKUSA agreement is a formal arrangement, but not a national treaty. It is deniable, non-binding, and open to instant abolition. In the strictest sense, UKUSA is merely a memorandum of understanding between two national interdepartmental intelligence coordinating groups, from which broader multinational arrangements have emerged. It was the most secret of modern alliances. Twenty-five years after being signed, its existence remained unknown. Only in 2010 were the documents about the agreement put into the public domain. This public record ends around 1961, when the UKUSA agreement ceased being updated in formal terms. Once its existence became known, as often with Sigint, the secrecy surrounding the agreement created hysteria. Critics routinely claimed that the agreement enabled the members of UKUSA to sidestep domestic internal law, for example, by having second parties acquire messages of their citizens without a judicial warrant. These claims are false. The agreement says nothing on the matter, because no one even conceived of the possibility, which all would have denounced. Such behaviour was and is illegal under the national laws of each signatory, and risked the political survival of Sigint in them all. The signatories addressed only state-to-state relations, ignoring anything involving private parties, foreign or national. Members of UKUSA did inadvertently intercept traffic from International Leased Carriers, ILC, which included messages from their own civilians, but this interception was inadvertent and arguably not even illegal, and nor did Siginters care about such messages. They focused on weeding out most traffic from ILC in order to find the small number from foreign states, or those involving espionage. So too, since 2005, when intercepting internet traffic, Five Eyes Siginters have touched metadata – the anonymised envelopes of messages – but their procedures aimed to weed communications from UKUSA citizens with the intention of discarding rather than reading them. In order to do that, a ministerial and judicial warrant may be required to do so, depending on the partner.

Secrecy was central to UKUSA. British and American leaders feared that public revelations of their close relations might destroy them, by causing unpredictable public reactions. One senior GCHQ officer, Colonel Marr-Johnson, warned that UKUSA was acceptable as an agreement but illegal as a treaty. Dynamite might explode if the American press 'blew the gaff'. American authorities repeatedly emphasised this danger.[65] These concerns reinforced autonomy and secrecy for Siginters. Officials in Britain sheltered politicians from intimacy with the process (but not the product) of Comint. American authorities feared that their public disliked intelligence organisations in peacetime. That idea shaped the closure of the wartime OSS. In August 1945, ANCIB wanted any Anglo-American Sigint agreement to 'be determined finally at a governmental level'.[66] When UKUSA neared completion in 1946, however, the Chairman of the Joint Chiefs of Staff (CJCS), Admiral William Leahy, refused to let STANCIB approach Truman on key questions, such as bringing the FBI within UKUSA. 'STANCIB had full authority to effect the agreement without any further reference to him or the President ... Admiral Leahy does not wish to commit the President in this whole matter any further than he is now committed because of the excellent ammunition all such dealings would furnish to the opposition were the facts to be made public at some later period during his tenure of office.'[67] Leahy's view reflected the politics of the congressional inquiry into the December 1941 attack on Pearl Harbor, within which Republican senators used the release of Magic to build a conspiracy theory involving Roosevelt and the Democratic Party.[68] To avoid further such political attacks, US Navy cryptologic and intelligence authorities warned GCHQ in 1946 that UKUSA must be kept secret. GCHQ knew that UKUSA was anomalous by American standards, and avoided compromising its partners. These political calculations help to explain why Truman was not informed of 'Venona' – a counterintelligence programme of interception aimed at unearthing Soviet spies in Western governments – until after the trial of American federal official Alger Hiss, although the president saw more orthodox forms of Comint.

Regulations were intrinsic to UKUSA. The original UKUSA agreement required complete exchange of all collection, product, knowledge and techniques, 'except when specifically excluded from the agreement at the request of either party and with the agreement of the other'. Both parties aimed 'to limit such exceptions to the absolute minimum and to exercise no restriction other than those reported and mutually agreed upon'. The existence of UKUSA must be hidden from the public and all third parties. American and British Sigint authorities must agree on relations with any third party before they began. Security was central. 'The value of Communication Intelligence in war and peace cannot be over-estimated; conservation of the source is of supreme importance ... It is essential that all references to its existence either direct or indirect be avoided,' except to those who needed to know it to perform their duties. 'The time limit for the safeguarding of Communication Intelligence never expires.' Even if some Comint was compromised and publicly discussed, anyone who ever had been indoctrinated must maintain 'complete and absolute silence', forever.[69]

The agreement defined rules governing the dissemination of Sigint, later called 'Instructions and Regulations Concerning the Security of Signal Intelligence', or IRSIG. Knowledge of Sigint should be restricted to codeword-classified documents, made available only to 'indoctrinated' recipients, whose numbers would be kept 'to an absolute minimum'. Sigint was categorised in ways best defined in 1953: Category 1, low-level traffic analysis and plain-language traffic, rated 'Confidential'; Category 2, middle-grade traffic analysis and cryptanalysis, rated 'Secret'; and Category 3, 'COMINT for which the protection of source or content is the overriding consideration', usually derived from cryptanalysis, rated 'Top Secret'. In peacetime, these categorisations must be 'rigidly upheld'. In war, some Sigint might be downgraded, to ease 'action-on' by commanders, and sanitised distribution to the hoi polloi. No commander should use Comint without balancing the military gains against the prospect of compromising the source. They must always conceal the existence of Sigint. No parties would release Comint to any agency or individual which might use it for commercial ends, a bugbear stemming from American fears of British wiles. Either side could end the agreement at any moment. The parties would cooperate in attack and establish safe and effective Sigint communication channels. They would exchange liaison officers, with free access to all offices save those 'which contain unexchangeable information'.[70]

Cooperation began immediately over issues controlled by cryptanalytic agencies, but more slowly when American service Sigint did so, particularly with regard to the coordination of interception. GCHQ and American Sigint exchanged all material on cryptanalytic tasks and worked together, especially against Soviet systems. By November 1946, UKUSA was attacking 109 'units': the attaché, diplomatic, military or naval systems of any country. Of these units, Britain exclusively assaulted twenty and American agencies thirty. They jointly attacked fifty-one. Ottawa attacked two units exclusively and worked with Americans against five. Without the Australians knowing it, Washington and Melbourne jointly assaulted one unit, linked by GCHQ. A Wren secretary in the British offices at Washington aided liaison.[71] By 1950, cooperation was normal in Sigint, but not integration: both sides remained free to shift their resources as they saw fit. Areas of 'unexchangeable information' remained small, purely on national matters, with none in technical areas.

Between 1948 and 1961, the UKUSA agreement was revised several times, mostly on technical matters, but also to admit Australia and New Zealand as second parties.[72] These negotiations involved more American than British representatives, but Britons had disproportionate influence because their American counterparts were divided.[73] By 1961, the UKUSA agreement had become archaic: circumstances had changed so much since 1945 that any further revision might force fundamental decisions. GCHQ and many American players had to agree on every detail in order to alter the agreement one jot. That process consumed time and effort and involved the American service Sigint agencies. The latter might challenge an arrangement satisfactory to GCHQ and NSA, the only agencies which really cared about these changes. In 1958, Jones warned: 'There may always be one or two in Washington who think that the Comint basic agreement goes rather too far, and to start rewriting it for any such purpose as incorporating Elint might open doors to such ideas being made more vocal.'[74] Instead, GCHQ and NSA simply acted as though they had an agreement on Elint. Few outsiders knew what was in UKUSA, except through IRSIGs, which adequately covered security and 'action-on'. The UKUSA agreement already provided all that NSA and GCHQ needed in terms of technical rules to govern outside agencies. Everything else they could negotiate between themselves, case by case, through what ultimately became called the 'NSA/GCHQ Memoranda of Understandings'. Thus, GCHQ and NSA agreed that New Commonwealth countries would not become second parties, a politically significant point.[75] Archaic principles which could be ignored or finessed suited GCHQ and NSA more than drawing attention to them. They ceased updating UKUSA because it had already achieved its aim: a working relationship based on a kind of Comint common law. General principles, understood through experience, were applied to specific cases and enforced on outside agencies through IRSIGs.[76] The UKUSA agreement became the equivalent of a Masonic handshake. Its members relied on trust between themselves, and rules and secrecy in their relations with all outsiders.

UKUSA in Practice

UKUSA, as a form of words, has not changed since 1961. UKUSA, as a body of practices, follows principles defined before 1945, which vary in application case by case. UKUSA is not a matter of form, defined by a treaty. It is a relationship between organisations which follow parallel paths and share ideas and behaviours, expressed through formal and informal arrangements. This fusion centres on British and American paths, reinforced by Australian, Canadian and New Zealand ones.

In 1945, GC&CS and its American partners were heavyweights. During coming decades, American Sigint developed into several heavyweights which cooperated loosely. British Sigint remained a heavyweight, but one more agile, balanced and independent than its colleagues. Compared to other Sigint agencies, of course, American and British Sigint were both agile superheavyweights. Increasingly between 1946 and 1960, GCHQ controlled all British Sigint, which was more coordinated than American. Not until 1970 was American Sigint as integrated as British was in 1945. Even in 2020, the DIRNSA did not control all American Sigint, which was large, diffuse and bureaucratic. Liaison and turf wars ate resources. Cooperative competition and combining talents was hard. NSA was greater than GCHQ, but less independent.

GCHQ and NSA were embedded in different structures. In the United States, the State Department was weaker and the military far stronger over Sigint than were their British equivalents. PSIS directed GCHQ, whereas the Department of Defense (DOD) directed NSA. Presidents commanded Comint more than any but a few prime ministers, particularly Attlee and Thatcher. GCHQ had better relations with British authorities than NSA did with American ones. At some point, all directors of both agencies were forced into transatlantic collusion, working with each other against some national obstacle. UKUSA gave NSA much power but less autonomy, and multiplied both factors for GCHQ, which sat equipoised between the MOD, the Foreign Office, the Cabinet Office, the Treasury, and NSA. UKUSA let GCHQ give consumers far more material than it generated itself, which most helped the Foreign Office. UKUSA gave GCHQ a tool in Whitehall and an ally in Washington. GCHQ gave NSA an ally in American intelligence, especially Sigint: GCHQ was NSA's best friend, sometimes its only one. NSA's weakness in Washington reinforced the value of GCHQ. GCHQ had many of the buccaneering characteristics of CIA and blocked rapier thrusts aimed at the back of NSA.

Since 1946 – indeed, 1942 – GCHQ has been part of two national decision-making systems, not just one. American intelligence officers generally thought GCHQ was a unique ally. It was more productive than other British intelligence agencies, and trustworthy, unlike other foreign services with strong regional capabilities. American Siginters brought GCHQ into their system, where it became a middleman – they often preferred to work with it, rather than with each other. An able and trusted foreigner offered more and threatened less than many national rivals. This reflex drove the uncoordinated actions of Americans for over fifty years. Thus, to varying degrees between 1948 and 1992,

GCHQ influenced the targeting of American Sigint assets in Europe. In the initial Anglo-American war planning for Sigint, GCHQ was the European base for UKUSA, steering American resources there. Later, it retained that position both formally and informally. NSA sometimes found this situation irritating because it gave Cheltenham advantages, but never found it alarming. In return, GCHQ used this power to aid NSA, and American Sigint, by ordering their largest concentration of units of different agencies as Fort Meade would have wanted. In doing so, GCHQ solved a fundamental problem of command and control in American Sigint, perhaps better than any national US agency could have done.[77]

In 1948, conversely, USAF created a Sigint agency, the Air Force Security Service (AFSS), from elements of the ASA. For its sister services to train this unit would suggest subordination, nor could they provide the training needed. The ASA was weak. The USAF was battling the US Navy, which had a strong Sigint service.[78] The USAF and US Navy had conducted fusion during the Pacific war, but Cheadle provided far better service, as USAF leaders remembered.[79] When AFSS was established, its members knew nothing of fusion. The USAF asked GCHQ to send four experts to train its Siginters for several months in Texas. Instead, GCHQ sent the master of fusion, Bill Bonsall, to do so, and later trained many USAF Siginters in Britain. These Siginters adopted many British procedures, soon became able, and built their system on that foundation.[80] GCHQ and NSA did not entirely like the outcome. AFSS rapidly became the largest and most independent element of American Sigint, twice the size of Britain's. AFSS provided the intelligence which guided Strategic Air Command (SAC) – the core of American power and one of the greatest consumers of Sigint – during the 1950s and 1960s. For this reason, GCHQ's criticisms of alarmist USAF Sigint reports during several crises were disquieting.[81] AFSS duplicated much of the work of NSA because SAC demanded direct service from an agency under its own control. With this support, AFSS routinely ignored direct orders from NSA. Only after 1965, when SAC lost its centrality to American strategy and its independence, did AFSS accept NSA's authority.[82]

GCHQ also had to work thoroughly with other American agencies without alienating NSA. For instance, it was responsible for Elint; initially, NSA was not, while American agencies handled the topic in a chaotic fashion. GCHQ always addressed Elint with the responsible American agencies. GCHQ used its status as middleman to strengthen Western intelligence, and itself.[83]

Two instances reflect the ambiguities of the situation. During 1954–56, GCHQ and MI6 established Operation Regal, the 'Berlin Tunnel', which tapped Eastern bloc communications that were carried on telephone trunk lines in East Berlin. For eleven months – until compromised by the traitor within MI6, George Blake – Regal taped hundreds of thousands of hours of military and administrative messages, often significant in nature. Centres in London and Washington translated the take. The London centre, the Main Processing Unit (MPU), was staffed by expatriate eastern Europeans, who could translate vernacular German and Russian. NSA had little involvement in the project, to its annoyance, whereas via MI6, GCHQ received whatever information it wished.[84] After the Berlin Tunnel closed, MI6 expected to shut MPU quickly, after it had finished translating its tapes. Meanwhile, British Sigint discovered how to acquire and exploit the voice transmissions of the Soviet army in Germany. This material, in technical and idiomatic language, overwhelmed GCHQ. It suggested that MI6 transfer 33 per cent of MPU's personnel (thirty Russian translators and eight typists) for a trial attack to determine the material's value, and perhaps start a permanent organisation. MI6, GCHQ and NSA ran and subsidised the new organisation. For several decades, the London Processing Group attacked transmissions which were intercepted from many sources. NSA paid for the kit and 70 per cent of the personnel, which reached 127. The Treasury covered the remainder, above GCHQ's normal budget.[85] Thus, GCHQ worked with MI6, improved NSA's position, and increased Treasury funding for Sigint. This initiative pleased everyone and provided an intelligence coup, with long-term consequences.

UKUSA worked differently in cryptanalysis and cryptography. GCHQ and NSA were involved with cryptography, but neither fully controlled it. In Britain, CESC controlled cryptography between 1953 and 1970, with GCHQ doing so during 1945–53 and after 1970. In the United States, specialised branches of the military services controlled cryptography. Relations over cryptography caused fractures within UKUSA. During the Second World War, American institutions denied Britain access to their best cryptographic kit. This tradition continued after the war, when CESC felt vulnerable to the American services on these issues. It was willing to give Americans complete access to British cryptosystems in order to gain partial access to American ones. Differences over cryptography also complicated American and British cryptologic policy towards the North Atlantic Treaty Organisation (NATO).

Hands Across the Water

UKUSA drove the reorganisation of American Sigint by shaping a debate within Washington over national issues. UKUSA emerged precisely as debate began over that topic, driven by the politics of military reform, recognition that American Sigint was ramshackle and wasteful, and a desire never to repeat the intelligence failure of Pearl Harbor – doubly so after they seemingly were repeated at the outbreak of the Korean war.[86] GCHQ, both unavoidably and deliberately, shaped this debate, though Americans forgot that GC&CS had shaped the failures before Pearl Harbor. GCHQ inspired those American Siginters who favoured a centralised service. Op-20-G, which opposed this idea, recognised that influence, and tried to counter it by accenting GCHQ's weaknesses. GCHQ pressed American authorities to reform Sigint, and advised on that issue, as the service agencies became increasingly aligned.[87] Allegedly these agencies were unified: first, in 1949, under the Armed Forces Security Agency (AFSA), and then in 1952, under NSA. Actually, these steps increased the divisions within American Sigint, by removing civilian cryptanalysts from the services and placing them within another agency, precisely as USAF created one of its own. Thus four agencies jostled for power, instead of two.

GCHQ was a friend to all during this period, simply by following UKUSA. It influenced the targeting of USAF and US Army Sigint in Europe, and trained their staffs, when no American agency would cooperate with another. GCHQ helped AFSA and NSA slowly to strengthen American Sigint. A trip to Cheltenham inspired General Ralph Canine, whose career as the first DIRNSA centred on hammering the service Sigint agencies with one hand, while working the rapiers against CIA with the other. He sought to translate British practices and principles to American conditions. The first generation of leaders at NSA, including Canine and Louis Tordella, become Anglophiles in personal terms, and admirers of GCHQ. As NSA's internal history notes, American Siginters viewed GCHQ with 'a certain awe'.[88] After retirement, Canine told NSA historians that GCHQ: 'do twice as much as we do with one third the number of the people, because ... They have a say in their requirements, which we never have had ... It'd be cheaper to hire (B per cent four spies) and drop them some place. Didn't make much difference. They could be answering requirements just as well as we could because we weren't ... didn't ... couldn't possibly answer most of those requirements ... And I found out that Eric [Jones] could answer a good many of my requirements without any further buildup of his outfit except that I gave him a [Univac] 1103 computer'.[89] Canine was guided by a 'Master Requirements list' which, one American committee concluded, was 'about the size of the Washington phone directory, and about as specific'. Since 'consumers wanted COMINT to tell them everything, without narrowing the target further, NSA simply specified its own requirements', which might make the cryptologic community isolated 'from its customers and insensitive to them'.[90]

After his first meeting with the incoming NSA Director, General Samford, the SUKLO, Peter Palmer, wrote: 'Respect of GCHQ. This is so high that the only comment is an embarrassed blush.'[91] GCHQ helped to solidify the base of American Sigint just before the latter began its great expansion of the 1950s. Otherwise, it would have been far weaker during the Cold War. More than any other British institution, GCHQ realised Harold Macmillan's aphorism, that Britain would play Greece to the American Rome. Until 1955, American Siginters requested or accepted British tutelage in many areas. For another decade, they thought British Siginters qualitatively superior, unit for unit. GCHQ shaped NSA into being an organisation with which it could work, for convenience, and to strengthen an ally. That process made the agencies complementary and their paths congruent. Later American and British efforts maintained this relationship.

Since American Sigint essentially had no experience with liaison until Ultra, its contact with Britain was formative. The path for American Sigint included liaison with its British equivalent, starting from a particular point for both sides. American Sigint ingrained cooperation with Britain, especially through personal relationships between the civilians in the ASA and GC&CS, and NSA and GCHQ. These civilians, teams of problem-solvers attacking cryptosystems through cybernetic means and assembly-line processes, had more in common with each other than they did with members of their own national agencies. British civilians reinforced American ones, who lived within a system directed by the military. These civilians were each other's peer group, the only people on earth like each other. They also liked each other, sharing experiences which were continually refreshed.

Personal ties between old hands across the Atlantic, and their influence on new recruits, carried UKUSA through to 1975. Legends from Bletchley, such as Jones, Hooper and Bonsall, led GCHQ. Conel Hugh O'Donel Alexander, master of Hut 8, ran H division, and with it Britain's relationship with NSA in the highest reaches of cryptanalysis. Tiltman served as UKLO in Washington, retired there, and then joined NSA. The leading figure in the early history of NSA, its deputy DIRNSA between 1958 and 1974, Lou Tordella, prized GCHQ. As a civilian mathematician at Op-20-G, he attacked Enigma, witnessing Bletchley's power and originality. He saw the same in the early years of UKUSA, as GCHQ ravaged Soviet civil and machine traffic. At AFSA and NSA, Tordella worked behind the scenes with Britons to reconfigure American Sigint. He shared their enthusiasm for cryptanalysis by maths, machines and computers. As American Sigint expanded during the 1950s, Tordella held: 'If we can't have quality, let us go for quantity.' In the interim, implicitly, GCHQ would handle quality control.[92]

Tordella was an Anglophile. When his career ended, he was awarded an honorary KBE which he could never wear publicly. Tordella fostered the special relationship in Sigint, because he knew how much it aided NSA. In particular, he shaped the Hampshire Report, which incorporated a victory for GCHQ. The 'Tordella doctrine', as GCHQ dubbed his words, emerged just after GCHQ's – and in particular its Scarborough outstation's – successes with traffic about intercontinental ballistic missiles (ICBMs), and Soviet merchantmen shaped the Cuban missile crisis, but when Britain's decline was clear. The doctrine aimed to maintain GCHQ's place at the top table, and in order to aid NSA in all emerging areas of Sigint,[93] GCHQ understood the risks of this doctrine which, as Millward said, might 'make us spread resources too thinly'.[94] Yet, as Tovey said, Tordella's 'single greatest contribution to UKUSA' was:

his recognition that UKUSA would only survive if the UK and US *both* maintained *some* level of involvement in *all* the major technical areas (using 'technical' in its broadest sense). He was emphatically averse to the heresy – which cropped up occasionally then and still does – that the UK should, in effect, stick to the comparatively easy, cheap and old-fashioned aspects of Sigint, feed its results to the US, and in return be the beneficiary of US concentration on high-technology Sigint. I think that Tordella's insistence that the UK must – albeit often in a smaller way – keep up with the high-technology side of Sigint and 'share the heat and burden of the day' saved us from going down the primrose path to becoming a Third rather than a Second party. Hence, for my money, you <u>cannot</u> praise Tordella too highly.[95]

That aim has been achieved ever since, though it eroded during the 1980s, and rose afterwards.

NSA was the greatest partner of GCHQ, and vice versa, to a smaller extent. The American service Sigint agencies cared less for UKUSA. Their transactional attitudes mattered as they did, being great in 1956, minor after 1968. UKUSA involved diplomacy, subnational and secret from superiors, precisely as the latter wanted it to be, which increased the autonomy of GCHQ and NSA. Records of that relationship remain among the greatest secrets for both agencies. SUKLOs with close connections to DIRNSAs provide many of the most revealing comments cited by this history. This relationship involved constant conversations between many personnel in Cheltenham and Fort Meade and talks with liaison officers, rarely recorded, and, less often, visits by senior authorities. Above all, on 12 September 2001, the heads of GCHQ, MI5 and MI6 crossed the Atlantic on the only aircraft allowed into the United States just after 9/11, to coordinate work directly with their opposite numbers. Many key discussions were never disclosed outside Fort Meade and Cheltenham, nor recorded even there. The only records about discussions between directors of GCHQ and NSA are those they wrote down, which often they did not.

DIRNSAs rarely visited Cheltenham, outside Canine's seminal excursion. When visiting Britain, they met GCHQ in London. GCHQ directors sometimes visited incoming DIRNSAs at Fort Meade, individuals they did not know, who often were inexperienced with

Sigint, or with UKUSA. These missions, supported by SUKLOs and American friends at lower levels, aimed to build personal connections, gauge DIRNSAs and the state of UKUSA. Two of them changed GCHQ's views about UKUSA and British policy.

In May 1956, the Treasury wished GCHQ to reduce its establishment through attrition, like all British departments. Jones thought that to reject this request 'would be wrong ... certain to fail', and damage relations with the Treasury. Hence, he proposed a 5 per cent cut, or 200 posts from 4,000 staff.[96] After the Suez crisis, in order to soothe relations and meet the incoming DIRNSA, General Samford, Jones visited the Fort. This visit, and the experience of Suez, led Jones to refuse the cuts he had earlier promised, for new and important reasons. Samford favoured close cooperation, while NSA was more like GCHQ than a military organisation. This offered great room for cooperation between GCHQ and NSA. Jones also warned London Signals Intelligence Committee (LSIC) that: 'some people in the United States ... might use the cut to harm relations between GCHQ and NSA'. LSIC and the Foreign Office supported his view, which the Treasury accepted without rancour.[97] From that moment, the political value of UKUSA rose from centrality to primacy in Whitehall's calculations about GCHQ.

So too, in 1965, Hooper visited Meade to meet the new DIRNSA, General Marshall Carter, and to conduct 'preliminary soundings' about PSIS's hopes to gain American subsidies for GCHQ. Hooper acted with care. He did not disclose PSIS's hope, or every factor which drove British decisions. He clearly told NSA (and more cautiously, the United States Communications Intelligence Board and the American Sigint community) how British efforts might change in coming years, while times were tight. NSA, 'guardedly sympathetic', accepted Hooper's logic, though emphasising that GCHQ must 'retain its individual ability to follow developments in Sigint techniques, particularly with regard to the Soviet task'. NSA favoured projects which shaped British actions, such as the Sigint ship. Hooper concluded: 'The U.S. continue to value the UK's contribution, in spite of our smaller resources. They will assist us when opportunities occur in which they can see advantages to themselves, but not otherwise. We cannot expect them to respond to positive requests for assistance solely in order to contain or reduce our own expenditure or resources. They will gladly discuss with us means of achieving greater interdependence, but will wish us to retain independent capabilities in areas where independent judgment and skill can contribute to the partnership as a whole for that is one of our major values to them.' NSA would work with British strengths, but not substitute for British weaknesses. LSIB and PSIS accepted these conclusions, which cemented the Tordella doctrine within British policy on Sigint.[98]

At lower levels, American and British Siginters worked the same targets, as diplomats (liaison officers) – and skilled migrant labourers (integrees within units). Both were selected to impress through highly competitive processes, as these positions were coveted: they stitched the Five Eyes together. As Abraham Sinkov said, these arrangements offered: 'quite an effective interchange of techniques, solutions, general cryptanalytic effort, as well as close interworking on the policy level'. The position of SUSLO was 'one of the most desirable assignments within the Agency. It was truly a plum', because it was 'a very effective and interesting position', and in London, 'a delightful city'.[99]

Ideally, integrees were technical leaders in their field, whether analytic or cryptanalytic, able to draw resources in from home to help their new units. Otherwise, their presence would embarrass their home agency. Successful integrees spread technical advances across the community and multiplied its power. Liaison officers provided knowledge and influence in ways varying by person. Those from GCHQ and NSA attracted respect from every agency. Officers from the smaller Five Eyes had to work harder to attract attention, and sometimes shared information on how to do so with each other. As a rule, albeit with many exceptions, SUKLOs tended to be elder statesmen, with wisdom and connections to offer, while SUSLOs were rising stars. All Five Eyes agencies sent able youngsters to build experience and contacts. They followed a 'no poaching' policy, to minimise irritation on any side.

Liaison officers learned a partner's needs and interests, how to aid or influence it, and emerging areas of mutual interest. They collected information through many means, such as official meetings and more informal sources. In the 1960s, liaison officers at NSA worked by walking the halls. In 2020, walking the halls at GCHQ was impossible, given its open-plan and hot-desking arrangements, but the internal blogs of analysts and others identified information or people worth contacting. Changes in generation and gender composition – the distinction between old boys with memories of Bletchley in 1954, to matters after 2000, when many liaison and Sigint officers were women born after 1970 – shaped this process. Liaison officers translated frank complaints from and about allies into solutions for problems, or early warning of unhappiness. They learned local practices, often exposing themselves to criticism at home for having gone native. Liaison officers and integrees worked through specific personal relations, which might accidentally provide misleading material. These interlocutors did not know many key technical or political matters – in 1968, when asking a SUKLO to assess NSA opinion about a crucial issue of allocating resources for GCHQ, Milward asked for 'a central view', not that merely of individuals – but still much more than anyone outside these agencies.[100] They ran the risk that after returning home, colleagues might view them not as having new insights and skills, but rather as finally earning their pay after a long vacation.

Integrees and liaison officers were common throughout the military forces of the Five Eyes, but only NORAD, the integrated North American Air Defence system of Canada and the United States, matched their role in Sigint.[101] Every year, scores of cross-appointments in Sigint offered adventure for all, romance for some, and promotion for high-flyers, cementing ties at the top. In one legendary moment, an American integree at Cheltenham and a British one at Fort Meade conducted negotiations between GCHQ and NSA on behalf of their adopted services; in another, every member of a Sigint conference between Australia, Britain, Canada and the United States held a British passport. Personal relations lay behind the links on organisational charts, where the keynotes were regard and respect.

British and American Siginters had many opinions about each other, each unique but all generalisable. Until 1960, British Siginters regarded Americans as promising but professionally inferior. In 1958, when Abraham Sinkov asked GCHQ for help in improving American reports, one SUKLO, Peter Palmer, privately regretted that British assessments of American work were too rude to be shared. 'Unfortunately, phrases such as "leaven the American lump" make this impossible, even with such a friend as Sinkov. Our friends here do not have to be handled with delicacy; only with common courtesy.'[102] From 1960, however, British Siginters understood their own and American strengths and weaknesses and the need to work with NSA. Though elements of indifference or hostility always remained, American Siginters viewed British ones with a certain awe, declining towards respect. Between 1970 and 1980, veterans of the greatest generation of cryptology from the 1930s to mid-1950s retired, replaced by people who entered the field from the later 1950s. Generational changes in two institutions, and nations, shaped these relations in a period when British decline was clear. In 1952, the peak of the Anglo-American alliance, Britain had more credibility than it had in 1976, though its military and cryptologic capabilities remained high, however terrible its political stasis. The 1970s, however, were also traumatic for American self-regard, and the personal relations of Sigint were firm. Never did the chain break. Though perhaps eroding during the 1980s, ties revived after the Cold War, reinforced by generations of mutual support between institutions with common interests, problems and solutions.

Strong forces in favour of isolation from national institutions at GCHQ, and weak ones within NSA, drove the two Sigint institutions together. At Cheltenham, GCHQ was physically distant from consumers. Workers could more easily communicate with colleagues at Fort Meade than consumers in London. NSA became second only to the MOD among GCHQ's consumers, and the most dynamic of them. Sigint passed automatically to US diplomatic and military consumers. Cooperation between GCHQ and NSA involved greater dynamism and discrimination, especially for joint programmes. Though integrated within the DOD, NSA was distanced from politicians and diplomats, who rarely wished to spend two hours driving back and forth on the beltway from central Washington.

Two Eyes

One Director of the CIA, Admiral Stansfield Turner, referred to NSA and GCHQ as 'Siamese twins'.[103] Though unusual, this description catches something of their symbiotic relationship. NSA and GCHQ shaped each other through competitive cooperation and co-dependency. Each developed complementary strengths, tending not to develop muscles the other already had. In 1946, GCHQ led technically almost everywhere. As American Sigint exceeded British in size, taking the lead in technology and increasingly technique, GCHQ emphasised areas of relative advantage, where its quality added value and provided profit. From the start, some British practices were distinct from American ones, stemming usually from differences in restraint and resources.

GCHQ focused far more than NSA on the cost-efficiency of every step, because it had fewer resources and needed to squeeze every drop. Americans translated and distributed far more solutions than GCHQ. GCHQ accepted delays in analysis in order to provide more coherent reports. American authorities demanded immediate reportage, a need which their Siginters met. Each approach had advantages, but many Americans preferred GCHQ reports. Its consumers were widespread through Washington.[104] In 1957, after his retirement Canine told Palmer, reportage 'is our weakest spot. We have never put enough into it and have hardly started improving. Consumers have said to me "Just let us have these GCHQ reports which are finished intelligence documents and NSA need not bother with reporting."' Canine's successor, General Samford, told Palmer that: 'NSA would be well advised to follow GCHQ's methods in both reporting and consumer relations.'[105]

From 1960, GCHQ was only about 33 per cent the size of NSA, and British Sigint 20 per cent that of American, but the organisations were still comparable. Americans were divided into four groups, none so well integrated as British Sigint. British quality was higher in important areas of analysis, cryptanalysis, interception, languages and reportage. Each system had different strengths and weaknesses, assumptions and analytical approaches, but together their alliance was effective. Because it had such resources, American Sigint was both powerful and wasteful. Because it never had quite enough, British Sigint was resourceful and efficient. NSA drove hardware and GCHQ matched it in software; effectively, they were the world's only schools of higher education on Sigint. But whereas GCHQ could be likened to a university, NSA is a military college – both important models when addressing strategic and intelligence issues; each changing constantly in spirit and structure, but always mutually exclusive. Engineers, lawyers and military officers had and have greater influence within NSA than GCHQ. During the Cold War, American power in management and technology transformed the nature of Sigint, particularly in the development of computers, satellites, the mechanisation of interception, C3ISR and C4ISR, and the internet. Each of these achievements was difficult. Collectively, they rank among the greatest triumphs in the history of technology, though few understand that fact. British Sigint was at number two. GCHQ – resourceful, well informed, agile and entrepreneurial – tried harder. It exploited its status as middleman between all agencies in the intelligence and military relationships of UKUSA, its comparative advantage as an actor, and its technical edges in action. Confronting many competitors in many niches, partner to the most disruptive player in Sigint, GCHQ had to evolve more constantly than any other agency. GCHQ learned generally how to adapt better than anyone else, including American Sigint – the dominant predator on the central plain of the practice. Pioneering technology drove American adaptations; pioneering search and analysis drove those of GCHQ.

That NSA financially supported GCHQ operations is often taken as a sign of British weakness.[106] In fact, it reflected strengths and weaknesses – or limits – on both sides. In joint ventures, the capitalised partner routinely funds the entrepreneur to complete an opportunity the latter has discovered, for mutual profit. This Sigint relationship is unusual only because the venture capitalist trusts the pioneer, time and again, to provide an unusual return on investment. Presumably results have been profitable. Success required both scout and financier. One retired Director of GCHQ, David Omand, joked when he told BBC News: 'We have the brains. They have the money. It's a collaboration that's worked very well.'[107] Actually, GCHQ also has money and NSA certainly has brains. The joke shows something, but not everything, about the relationship between the relative advantages of partners. If GCHQ discovered a problem and a solution suited to its strengths, for NSA to duplicate the work would be costly and inefficient: why not license the work to a trusted expert? The greater matter occurred when NSA had brains, GCHQ no money, and Americans got something for Britain, wholesale, because minor profits in one deal mattered less than keeping a partner for future ones. The essence of the relationship was not when NSA reinforced British strengths, but its weaknesses. Britain often returned the favour.

GCHQ and NSA strengthened each other across the board, which paid dividends to both sides. From 1946 to 1964 and 1996 to 2020, GCHQ and NSA helped each other fairly equally. From 1964 to 1995, NSA gave and GCHQ took more. NSA helped GCHQ to handle fundamental changes in targets, technology and techniques. In the late 1950s, NSA ensured that its main partner remained in the front rank, by helping GCHQ to acquire its first supercomputers. In return, GCHQ bolstered NSA's highest Sigint priorities. Meanwhile, GCHQ convinced PSIS that Britain must finance the computerisation of cryptanalysis itself. In

1963, through the Hampshire Report, Tordella told Whitehall what it had to enable GCHQ to do for Britain to remain a partner in Sigint. Five years later, GCHQ returned the favour by defending NSA against an all-agency American commission under Frederick Easton which was investigating Sigint. Tordella feared the committee, which he likened to 'playing Russian roulette with three or four of the chambers loaded'. When the committee visited London, NSA provided GCHQ with advice on how to help it. GCHQ provided a powerful reception, which supported NSA's case, while also admitting doubts on key areas, such as the value of the continued attack on high-grade systems.[108]

The balance of strength between American and British Sigint did not follow a linear progression, but fluctuated constantly. During 1952–96, as a rule, British Sigint declined relatively compared to American, but it rose around 1970, and especially after 1996. From 2000 to 2020, the relative position of British Sigint perhaps approached that of 1960. This balance was driven by changes in the budgets and personnel of agencies, the quality of Siginters, the nature of their skillsets, and modes of communication and interception. GCHQ's position was strongest with some specific technologies and weakest when interception required massive new investments. Later, Britain's centrality in advanced technologies restored much of its power.

During the reductions in Sigint of 1945–47, GCHQ fell less than its American partners and recovered faster and more steadily, thereby providing a firmer basis for expansion. Among American agencies, US Navy Sigint recovered best from this slump. After VJ Day in August 1945, the ASA collapsed; USAF Sigint began only in 1948. Both then exploded in size. Until 1952, British Sigint was better and bigger than American. In 1962, it was smaller but still better, and not far below all of the American agencies collectively in power and quality.[109] In 1955, GCHQ provided around 30 per cent of the end product available to NSA, and more in many key categories.[110]

During the 1950s, GCHQ contributed disproportionately to new developments in Sigint. British Sigint was well-placed to monitor Soviet targets in Central Asia and the Atlantic, and its lead in a key area of collection enabled pioneering work against telemetry – the science of measuring objects at a distance and transmitting the results by radio. Conversely, in some areas British Sigint missed key target developments that emerged by surprise, and thus lost a major role. After that, hard work merely maintained their position against targets already being prosecuted. In order to remain relevant during the Cold War, GCHQ had to outpace both the USSR and NSA in leading edges of military development. It did so surprisingly often.

Between 1952 and 1962, GCHQ received support from consumers and the Treasury. It doubled in terms of personnel and power, but at the same time American Sigint increased sevenfold, rising steadily in quality and quantity. A widening gap in capabilities began to emerge. In 1963, American Sigint outspent British by 1,500 per cent, had 700 per cent of its staffing levels and aimed to expand another 25 per cent by 1969.[111] Meanwhile, the British empire vanished and governments reduced military spending. Every service slashed cherished ambitions. The retreat to Europe challenged GCHQ's position in the world, and it faced unparalleled criticism. The MOD and the Treasury scoured Sigint for economies. Against this, PSIS rose in power over GCHQ, as did GCHQ's value in keeping Britain alliance-worthy, when the country ceased to be a world power and entered the European Economic Community (EEC). The diplomatic need to restrain GCHQ's decline minimised it. Whether the American card was the ace of trumps or deuce of spades drove debates about GCHQ.

The end of empire reduced the real estate available for interception, but Britain had retained ample areas for antenna farms. The decline of Britain eased that of GCHQ, by reducing the range of languages which it had to cover, or emergency calls on resources. From 1950, GCHQ focused overwhelmingly on the USSR, which thereafter absorbed 60–75 per cent of its resources.[112] The end of empire furthered that focus. American and Australian Sigint covered secondary targets which GCHQ abandoned in Asia and Africa, often from real estate under British ownership, while providing the traffic to Whitehall. That real estate became increasingly valuable as third parties expelled American Sigint stations. During the 1960s, GCHQ made economies and lost assets. Teams and analysts declined in number. It could meet new commitments only by sacrificing old ones, and then only slowly, on the margins. The shifts from focus on the Soviet military target around 1964, and back to it after 1968, caused disruptions across GCHQ, especially in J division, which attacked Eastern bloc targets. The rise of task-sharing with American Sigint pinned proportionately more of GCHQ's resources to defined targets, hampering its ability to shift them freely. Yet in the long term, GCHQ kept the fruits of its economies, enabling new investments and efficiencies, especially in areas pioneered by NSA: for example, trading reductions in manpower to acquire funding for computers and mechanised interception and reportage. GCHQ remained numerically constant, even as it dropped certain lines of work. Sigint and nuclear forces were the only instruments of British external policy to leave the 1960s stronger than they entered it.

Even so, danger loomed. During the 1950s, GCHQ's successes stemmed from the ability to find new possibilities and pioneer new modes of attack on them; in qualitative uniqueness and ability, and capacity to surprise. GCHQ searched for problems and found solutions to them, saving American Sigint the trouble of finding or addressing them. GCHQ preferred to minimise commitments to fixed tasks because its resources were constrained, largely committed to the USSR, and much material was needed for search. The stagnation in resources of the 1960s and the rise of task-sharing hampered these powers, though GCHQ remained powerful in analysis and languages. By 1960, GCHQ's leaders conventionally understood the dangers. One head of J Division noted: 'As Sigint techniques increase in cost with increasing sophistication of the target and mechanisation of all kinds there is a distinct threat that J division will be priced out of the UKUSA market.' The head of S division, John Somerville, warned: 'of the GCHQ role in a UKUSA relationship in which US capabilities are expanding rapidly in all directions. Have we the resources to make a definite impact? What are our biggest assets today as partners in UKUSA? What fields of activity should we choose in order to ensure that five years from now our value as a partner has not diminished in US eyes? Can we concentrate on activities where the value of original ideas to cash costs is high?'[113]

The directorate debated where to find such ratios, and whether GCHQ could exploit them. Hooper favoured task-sharing against the USSR, but expected 'independent, fast UK work to pay off better for UKUSA than integration' in the rest of the world, especially in Africa and the Middle East. J division should be squeezed to feed K. Milward retorted that GCHQ must 'beware of white elephants in the K area', where GCHQ already was 'skimming the cream', while few resources could be squeezed from J division. The head of K complained that 'task sharing arrangements produce short-term gratitude and long-term millstones round our necks'. GCHQ should 'beef up' its intelligence and 'freshness of inspiration'. Alexander sourly warned that rationalisation of work against Soviet targets might irritate some NSA analysts, who viewed 'any attempt at objectivity as an anti-American activity'. The head of S held that GCHQ must 'keep alive the impression that we manage to find something new in whatever we look at'. The head of V, wrote: 'the more we can be opportunistic and the less tied down the more likely we are to play the role of a joker or wild card in NSA's hand and hence to turn out to be really valuable to them in important but unexpected ways'.[114] Hooper's line prevailed, but K gained and J lost little: GCHQ had few disposable resources in the short term.

Many GCHQ comments like these regarding its qualitative differences with US Siginters sound like whistling past the graveyard or the GCHQ history's suggestion that problems 'requiring patience and individual insight are more suited to the British than to the American genius', but they do reflect faith in their own areas of superiority.[115] One head of the CIA, William Colby, told a British ambassador that he regarded GCHQ as far better than NSA, which also assessed GCHQ in flattering terms.[116] Then the slide reversed and GCHQ's relative position rose. Between 1970 and 1979, American Sigint collapsed, reducing the gap in capabilities. The DOD cut American Sigint personnel and expenditure by 44 per cent, and threatened more, some self-contained – as in Vietnam – others not. Though the American service Sigint agencies absorbed most of these cuts, NSA's manpower fell by 14 per cent in the 1970s. Simply by standing still, British Sigint almost doubled in personnel compared to its US counterpart.[117] NSA was ordered to cooperate more with second and third parties in order to rationalise work and eliminate duplication, just at a time when many third parties in Asia and Africa ceased cooperating with American Sigint. GCHQ, far and away the party best suited to help NSA, gained from this opportunity, though it also caused problems. NSA wanted interdependence – combined programmes where GCHQ guaranteed specific 'fractions' of collection, analysis and reporting. GCHQ accepted the need for more guarantees, but wanted greater flexibility than the Americans wished: 'the best form of cooperation varies from problem to problem and from time to time and is a matter for decision on the merits of the case and not on some abstract principle'. Otherwise, no resources would remain for agility and originality.[118] GCHQ largely won this battle, though it made further commitments to fixed projects. American Siginters often thought that GCHQ hogged the interesting and prestigious assignments, while leaving them drudges. Interdependence also meant a redefinition of relations between second and third parties, where the United States might change UKUSA unilaterally, to Britain's detriment. The more its resources declined, the more GCHQ stuck to the letter of UKUSA. The details of interdependence produced irritation and suspicion among American and British authorities, but ultimately Britain controlled the big assets, and influenced more.

In 1946, Britain and the United States coordinated parallel but independent systems. From 1965 to 1992, they retained independent programmes and created integrated ones. The latter were especially common against the USSR, though arguably each partner over-insured itself in order to retain autonomy on the central intelligence target. American engineering, ingenuity and money drove new developments in UKUSA, especially in advanced collection techniques against sophisticated targets. Following technological developments and military demands for rapid reportage, American Sigint became faster and more centralised, concentrating on machines more than people. Often reluctantly, GCHQ followed American practices, which challenged some of its own – particularly the preference for thorough and careful consideration over speed of delivery, and the amount of technical detail attached to intercept reports, which balanced precision in intelligence with security for a source. Ultimately, GCHQ's synthesis of old and new made British Sigint more efficient and powerful, just as American Sigint did, in different ways. These differences strengthened UKUSA.

GCHQ could not independently deploy some advanced collection technologies, but had much to offer elsewhere through interdependence. NSA collected more material than it could analyse. GCHQ solved that problem through its excellent analytical and linguistic resources, which processed material from many sources for the alliance. At NSA's request, GCHQ created a body of 'British-born' linguists, distinct from the London Processing Group, to process plain-language traffic from many sources.[119] NSA helped GCHQ to develop automatic means of interception. Alongside other Five Eyes members, Britain aided the US in developing a capability to intercept Soviet military traffic worldwide. Together, GCHQ and NSA established some of the biggest Sigint innovations of the 1970s. While it suffered from financial limits, NSA was developing a capability to intercept traffic from advanced technologies being developed by adversaries. GCHQ believed that satellites would soon carry most ILC and that basing a satellite interception centre in Britain was essential to its position in Sigint during the next generation. GCHQ shaped a programme that focussed on target communications on several satellites, in keeping with its constant preference to pursue multiple opportunities through the same means. GCHQ solved NSA's problem of gold drain, by eliminating its need to spend abroad. GCHQ provided the necessary land, buildings and support staff, and arranged to move intercepts automatically for processing at GCHQ and NSA. GCHQ and NSA coordinated their sharing of databases better than American agencies did their pioneering Community On-line Intelligence System, defined in 1965.[120]

During the 1970s, without trying to nag, NSA complained often that GCHQ needed more resources to be taken seriously. Instead, GCHQ's relative position slowly began to erode again. PSIS insisted that GCHQ reduce its real expenditure by 10 per cent between 1976 and 1981 and, along with the MOD, pressed GCHQ into the embarrassing position of asking NSA for more financial aid.[121] By 1982, GCHQ calculated the Sigint balance between Britain and the United States at; 1:4 in manpower; 1:1,000 in capital expenditure on advanced collection techniques; 1:5 in general purpose and 1:7 in special purpose computers; and 1:3.6 in 'totally exchangeable' end product.[122] From 1982, GCHQ's strength rose again, but it merely matched the surge in American Sigint and could not fully maintain the 'Tordella doctrine'. That phrase, perhaps largely unknown in NSA, drove discussions among British Siginters. Stocktaking about the relationship – often obsessive – characterised GCHQ. Britain failed to deploy a Sigint satellite, though Margeret Thatcher vowed that 'we will strain every sinew' to do so.[123]

Despite its relative decline, until 1992, British Sigint remained formidable: weaker than American and Soviet, but far surpassing any other service in the world. Americans appreciated GCHQ's value even at its weakest and assessed its relative strengths roughly as British Siginters did because its people were excellent and its organisation was superior. In 1979, GCHQ noted that the United States valued British Sigint because 'the UK is still disposed to take a "world view" of Sigint, not limiting itself to a narrow range of targets, but contributing in varying degree towards the common effort in virtually all areas. Last but not least, the US attaches considerable value to the technical expertise, in both collection and analysis, which the UK has traditionally brought to bear on a wide range of shared Sigint problems.'[124]

After retirement, speaking to NSA historians, one DIRNSA, Marshall Carter, said: 'we are fortunate in having a very close relationship with the British'. NSA outweighed GCHQ, but 'without them we were helpless in a large number of areas and we needed them ... We were all in bed together. This was truly a joint operation between the U.S. and the British and the magnitude of effort isn't something we could measure by number of people or amount of money ... I consider the British as co-equal in our efforts without any analysis of comparative value in input or output'.[125] Even more, Carter held, 'I have much greater faith in British security of GCHQ activities than I did in the proliferation of people that we had to keep informed of our activities.'[126] NSA internal history noted that in the 1970s: 'With the British, collaboration remained almost total. The key decisions that kept the two countries closely tied related generally to advances into new technological realms. At each bend in the road, NSA made a conscious decision to remain engaged ... Each country lived with the foibles of the other.'[127] In 1985, NSA held that: 'Each country makes unique contributions, and while the U.S. has moved far ahead in total resources committed and in technology development, the contribution of the UK continues to be of great value ... The value of this relationship is high and allows for a much fuller Sigint effort than is possible with only U.S. resources.'[128]

The ending of the Cold War eliminated one of the forces which sustained UKUSA, but Britain and the United States still cooperated to pursue common ends. Meanwhile, the change from an overwhelming focus on Soviets freed up GCHQ's resources. Through luck, leadership and agility, GCHQ transferred these resources to other tasks, which paid dividends when it entered the new age of Sigint before NSA did, enabling it once again to serve as scout and entrepreneur, with disposable resources and ingenuity at hand. As NSA charted a new world of Sigint, its assessment of GCHQ was high. 'The U.S.–U.K. Cryptologic Relationship will continue to be broad and deep well into the 21st Century.' In a big statement, NSA wrote: 'The cryptomathematics exchange with GCHQ is the heart of our INFOSEC relationship. GCHQ is our only peer in the field of cryptomathematics and virtually all of our advances within the field of cryptography have occurred as a result of our mutual sharing. We enjoy a mutually beneficial exchange at the highest technical level in the design and evaluation of cryptoalgorithms.' Other NSA officers wrote that: 'The UKUSA relationship has been of inestimable value to NSA and cannot be abandoned.' GCHQ provided 'a strong analytic workforce, with a capability for independent interpretation of events; an especially competent cryptanalytic workforce; savings in US resources by analytic divisions of labour; the pooling of resources on key technical projects during austere financial periods ... and, perhaps most important, a record of supporting the US as an ally in confronting world problems'. As ever, Americans complained of British attempts to manipulate them through the use of liaison officers and integrees, but NSA clearly respected the relationship.[129]

Three Eyes

During the radio age, Dominion Sigint agencies worked in niches. Lacking breadth and flexibility, they could not easily switch targets and might be swamped if GCHQ and NSA changed priorities. Their significance varied with that of the niche. During the Cold War, collectively the Dominions contributed about 30 per cent of the intercept and analytical capacity of GCHQ. Around 1970, for example, GCHQ had 9,000 Siginters, Canada 2,000, Australia 1,100 and New Zealand 60. This contribution mattered operationally and helped sustain UKUSA. The roles of these agencies were driven by the rise of the United States, the decline of Britain, British efforts to maintain influence over Dominion forces and to integrate their commands, and the impact of diplomacy and internal politics in Canberra, Ottawa and Wellington. Commonwealth Siginters respected GCHQ and felt more at home with it than NSA. For each of them, however, the United States was the major partner and national interests surpassed sentiment. Each agency had a distinct part in UKUSA.

GCHQ's initial conception for postwar Sigint assumed that it would direct Dominion services and conduct all high-grade cryptanalysis. Dominion cryptanalysts might be attached to GCHQ, which would disseminate whatever product it believed their governments should receive. Immediately after the UKUSA agreement was signed, Britain pursued these aims through an abortive conference, which attempted to coordinate the work of all the Dominions and Britain. These assumptions sank on the rock of politics. The Dominions would not accept British rule, while the Americans would not let the Dominions into UKUSA automatically: only by 1948 did USCIB and LSIB agree on how to handle this situation. GCHQ could handle this imbroglio only by negotiating individually with each Dominion, and the United States, one after another.[130]

By 1918, Canada led the world in parts of Sigint. In 1919, that strength vanished because it had no institutions able to continue the work. Instead, the Canadian navy supported the Royal Navy's Sigint system by intercepting American and Japanese traffic.[131] Between 1939 and 1945, under British tutelage, Canada became a secondary power in Sigint. Its military services developed Y and received Ultra, which officers used at an army level, and in commanding the northwest quadrant during the battle of the Atlantic. A 'Discrimination Unit', under Colonel Ed Drake, loosely coordinated service Y. GC&CS trained a civil agency, the Examination Unit, which aimed to build influence by developing capabilities in niche areas where foreign consumers had interests which their National Services did not meet. This practice foreshadowed an unspoken assumption within UKUSA that members must add to the pot in order to take from it. Canadian diplomats and officers became veterans in Sigint.[132] By 1942, GC&CS regarded the diplomat Lester Pearson as a partner in Sigint.[133] Pearson and the British Labour politician Roy Jenkins were the wartime officers involved in Sigint who reached the highest political offices after 1945. Strength in Sigint and competence in its use is part of the Pearsonian tradition of Canadian foreign policy. GC&CS realised that Canadian civil Siginters felt 'rather younger brothered', but could not overcome that feeling, which stemmed more from Canadian sensitivity than British condescension.[134] Canadians were offended by GC&CS's suggestion that they attack plain-language Japanese commercial traffic, which in fact would have interested consumers more than the targets they did pursue, successfully: Japanese army codes in China. Canadians wished to prove their mettle in cryptanalysis. Britain helped them to do so, but with friction on both sides.

At the end of the war, civil and military authorities in Ottawa merged their Sigint agencies into the Communications Branch, National Research Council (CBNRC), under Drake, augmented by some members of GCHQ. CBNRC was governed by a Communications

Research Council, with a civil and military membership modelled on LSIC. Canadian authorities concluded that they must maintain independent Sigint capabilities and cooperate with allies. They thought and acted like authorities in Washington and London, with two exceptions. They did not intend Sigint to suit narrow interests so much as to build influence by giving friends useful and unique material. They aimed to achieve independence and influence, and to attack major targets, at the smallest possible cost, preferably tiny.[135] Though Canada did not affect American and British decisions over UKUSA, its presence shaped them. From the start, Canada was treated differently from any other element of the Commonwealth, dealing independently with Britain and the United States. Unlike Australia and New Zealand, Canada entered UKUSA without British aid: Canada was already part of the Anglo-American Sigint relationship – a channel of Sigint communications ran through Ontario, it rebuilt an intercept capability quickly, while Americans wanted Canadian cooperation to defend North America.

Between 1919 and 1939 Australia cooperated with Britain in Sigint more than any other Dominion. The Royal Australian Navy (RAN) worked closely with the Royal Navy in intercepting Japanese traffic. By 1938, Australian authorities tried to develop an independent capability in Sigint and cooperated with the Far East Combined Bureau (FECB).[136] By 1942, as Japan drove south, the Australian Chiefs of Staff analysed Ultra as well as their American and British counterparts did. Australian commanders used Sigint effectively, at a corps level, in the New Guinea campaign. Their Sigint capabilities became large, joined with American personnel in Central Bureau Brisbane and Fleet Radio Unit Melbourne. These agencies, more integrated than any others in this war, were fundamental to General Douglas MacArthur's intelligence, his successes of 1944–45, and his autonomy in command. Of course, he gave Australia and intelligence little credit for their role in his achievements.[137]

At the end of the war, MacArthur's system of intelligence vanished, without lasting influence. Unlike Canada, Australia was outside the Anglo-American Sigint system. It agreed to combine its wartime Sigint agencies into a Defence Signals Bureau and to create a unified system with Britain and New Zealand, but rebuilt its strength slowly. Weak and conflicting forces drove Australian decisions on Sigint. Intelligence and military authorities had tolerable relations with Britain, fewer with the United States, but wished to cooperate with both nations. Their political masters were less enthusiastic.[138] The Labor government was naive about the USSR and communist penetration of Australian offices.[139] Australia developed an unfortunate reputation for insecurity: its security was worse than Britain or America's, but less so than seemed at the time. Though Venona ultimately revealed as many American or British traitors, its early reports disproportionately caught Australians, including many who served the government or the Labor Party. American and British security officials saw traitors at work, and thought more were at hand. In 1947, USCIB hinted that it might end UKUSA if GCHQ gave Australia any material on traffic analysis or cryptanalysis against the Soviet Union. During 1948, American authorities regarded Australian security as disastrous, eventually rejecting cooperation with Canberra on any classified topic, let alone Sigint, even threatening (though not acting on the threats) to break many ties with Britain if it cooperated with Australia.[140]

Britain first tried to pre-empt and then solve these problems in order to maintain Australian strategic cooperation – their joint ventures were central to British nuclear weapons programmes – and Commonwealth unity. Its efforts were complicated by Venona's centrality to events, and prickly American security officers and Australian politicians. Discussions had to be handled through Comint channels. They involved people who were not cleared for the highest categories of intelligence. The service intelligence chiefs understood the Venona connection, because they were members of LSIB. The service chiefs were not and had to be specially briefed on the problem and solutions. British authorities sought to end the difficulty by pulling strings, which were yanked from their hands. Percy Sillitoe, head of MI5, and a senior aide, Roger Hollis, visited Australia to alert the authorities there to a serious leakage of UK classified material to the Soviets. They outlined the problem to the Australian Defence and Foreign permanent undersecretaries, John Dedman and Herbert Evatt, but could not reveal the source of the accusation. As the US insisted on protecting the true source (Venona), Sillitoe had to claim that it came from a defector, but Evatt evolved an alternative theory which exculpated Australia. Although the British prime minister, Attlee, vouched personally for Sillitoe, the Australian prime minister, Ben Chifley, treated him flippantly. Chifley telephoned

Francis Shedden, the Secretary to the Australian Department of Defence: 'There is a fellow here with a bloody silly name – Sillitoe. As far as I can make out he is the chief bloody spy – you had better have a look at him and find out what he wants.' Sillitoe was heard, and the Australian government rejected the accusations.[141]

Whitehall found another solution. Britain would reform Australian security and vouch for it in Washington. Attlee would tell Chifley verbally that Comint to and from entities in Canberra demonstrated Australian insecurity. Until that threat ended, the United States would not cooperate with Australia on defence matters. Chifley could so inform Dedman and Evatt. These Australians must pledge not to mention the source to anyone else and to act on the material. Sillitoe and Hollis convinced Australian officials and politicians that Australia could solve its security problem only by creating a local version of MI5, the Australian Security Intelligence Organisation (ASIO). Then Whitehall approached the Americans with their solution. A diplomatic campaign in Washington, gathering support from senior authorities such as the Secretary of State George Marshall, drove American security officials to accept this proposal reluctantly. These officials mistrusted Australian Labor leaders, above all Evatt. They loathed the idea of giving such men material from Venona, which risked the source. To minimise that risk, American security insisted that their involvement not be mentioned. These views had force, however tinted by political views.[142]

Chifley and Dedman were approached as Britain suggested, but probably not Evatt. If so, British authorities and key Australian colleagues distrusted Evatt, who never knew the proof of communist penetration of the Labor Party. Chifley and Dedman pledged to eliminate the threat. In order to support that effort, American security gave relevant Venona to MI5 officers who were attached to ASIO, which acted aggressively at second-hand to eliminate the threat. However, American security still rejected any intelligence and security cooperation with Australia. Attlee pressed Truman to intervene: 'The intermingling of American and British knowledge in all these fields is so great that to be certain of denying American classified knowledge to the Australians, we should have to deny them the greater part of our own reports. We should thus be placed in a disagreeable dilemma of having to choose between cutting off relations with the United States in defence questions or cutting off relations with Australia.'[143]

Ironically, Attlee could not discuss the issue in detail with Truman, who was not cleared to read Venona. Even a visit to Washington in April 1949 from Shedden, respected architect of ASIO and enemy to Evatt, failed to sway American security. Only the election of a conservative government under Robert Menzies achieved that end, by persuading Americans that Australians could be loyal.

A plague fell upon all of their houses. For a decade, Venona convinced American and British security services that the Australian Labor Party could not be trusted – with reason. American pressure drove ASIO, guided by MI5, to investigate communist penetration of the Labor Party.[144] Thus, foreign allies and ASIO interfered in internal Australian politics. Yet that communist penetration was major. Evatt, Labor's leader from 1951 to 1960, denied its existence and tried to protect men who truly were traitors. The Petrov affair, involving the defection of two Soviet intelligence officers in Canberra during 1954, sparked a political transformation in Australia. Evatt publicly claimed that Menzies had engineered the Petrov defections and forged documents simply in order to defeat the Labor Party in an election. Evatt justified this claim to Parliament by announcing that the Soviet Foreign Minister had just informed him that, of course, the USSR did not spy on Australia. This odd response shattered Labor's position for a generation, convinced many Australians that Evatt was a menace, poisoned politics, and fuelled a feud between his party and ASIO. Echoes of these attitudes affected events the next time Labor was in power. Comint shaped this tragedy, which drove Australia's role in UKUSA.[145]

By helping to guide Australia from receivership, Britain integrated Australian, British and New Zealand Sigint into an independent Commonwealth capability in Asia. This approach helped all parties. By 1954, NSA had reopened an intelligence exchange with Australia, but with restrictions on what would be exchanged. With British assistance, DSD became large and competent. Australian Siginters worked alongside British and New Zealand ones at Hong Kong and Singapore. DSD directed these organisations, in liaison with GCHQ. A GCHQ officer became deputy Director of DSD, an influential position for a generation. For Britain, this cooperation bolstered an important area, which for Australia was a key border. Australian Siginters and soldiers supported British and American wars in southeast Asia during the 1960s, for what all thought were common purposes.[146]

Around 1970, DSD confronted a perfect storm which caused common purpose and effort to collapse. Britain's withdrawal from east of Suez involved slashing its strength at the Sigint stations in Hong Kong and Singapore. American Sigint declined in southeast Asia. Foreign help for DSD vanished. The election of a Labor government under Gough Whitlam broke decades of conservative domination of politics, and exposed a generational gap in Australian attitudes towards intelligence and its allies. Whitlam had no commitment to existing Australian policies or knowledge of them. Scandals involving Australian intelligence, especially ASIO, shaped his troubled tenure. When a public broadcaster referred to DSD and the Singapore base, Whitlam publicly announced that DSD conducted Sigint. This, the first such statement by any leader in the Five Eyes, challenged all of their cover stories for Sigint. It raised hackles at the highest levels in Britain, the United States and Singapore – where the Sigint station was abandoned. These Sigint issues had no role in the collapse of Whitlam's government, but intelligence and mistrust over it did.[147]

All of these political issues delayed Australia's ability to combine aims and means in Sigint. From 1980, however, Australia adopted a mature strategy and an independent role in UKUSA. Its Siginters took responsibility for the Indonesian target, which was a national priority, and cooperated with GCHQ at Hong Kong. Australian leaders found DSD useful to its strategic policy, which became sophisticated as the Cold War waned. It was central to Australia's status as a self-reliant regional power.

New Zealand entered UKUSA as a matter of course, or courtesy, as an old Dominion. A contradiction between security, internal politics and allies drove its role. A military Sigint unit, too small to stand alone, was created to show UKUSA that New Zealand was alliance-worthy, and to give it something to ally with. By 1977, this organisation had become the Government Communications Security Bureau (GCSB). That New Zealand took these steps, given the need to ration resources for its military, illustrates how the Five Eyes valued Sigint. During the Cold War, New Zealand provided around five stations, bolstering a Commonwealth connection in a weak area for UKUSA in southeast Asia and the southwest Pacific. Its Sigint was good, yet no one in Wellington understood the matter well enough to define a policy for it. GCSB's role as an alliance-maker also conflicted with New Zealand's ostentatious independence from Allies. In 1974, when New Zealand recalibrated its Sigint, it sent a mission to consult every UKUSA partner except Australia. After 1985, when seeking to prevent French nuclear tests in the South Pacific, New Zealand banned any warship which would not deny that it carried nuclear weapons from entering its ports. The United States sent a signal to other states considering such action, cutting New Zealand from any American assistance for a generation. New Zealand was mostly, but not entirely, expelled from UKUSA until 2006, when normal ties renewed. That step probably damaged New Zealand's ability to reduce French nuclear tests in the South Pacific. By 2010, New Zealand Sigint became astute, seeking to exploit unofficial affection within the Five Eyes, and to find niche areas which would interest its partners. New Zealand was the member of the Five Eyes least able to integrate Sigint into national strategy. Its leaders received much material, but how useful it proved is unclear.[148]

The politics of decolonisation led Britain itself to limit UKUSA. Until 1939, Britain treated South Africa like other Dominions. During the war, however, they cooperated little in Sigint. After the war, Britain rejected such cooperation, because mutual mistrust and the rising political dominance of Boers wrecked relations with South Africa. The last prime minister of South Africa trusted by Britain, Jan Smuts, warned that given the likelihood that the Nationalist Party would take power, his country should not enter any Commonwealth Sigint relationship.[149] In 1946, meanwhile, British authorities realised they could not maintain Sigint facilities in India without giving Indian authorities the product, which they would not do.

UKUSA: Crises and Friction

Cases of friction illustrate how UKUSA normally works and how it changes under pressure. This section examines and generalises three such cases.

The Suez Crisis, 1956

In 1956, the withdrawal of British forces from Egypt freed that country to act independently. The Egyptian leader, Colonel Abdel Nasser, immediately challenged Britain's remaining interests in Egypt, particularly its control over the Suez Canal and British power in the

Middle East. The politics of decolonisation crippled British responses. It had the military power to overthrow Nasser, but no politically acceptable excuse to do so. The United States sympathised with Britain, but refused to condone military action against Nasser, even when he asked the Soviet Union for aid. Ultimately, to escape this dilemma, the British prime minister, Eden, joined a secret alliance: Israel would attack Egypt, leading Britain and France to intervene on the excuse of protecting the Suez Canal, but truly to overthrow Nasser. Eden hid these actions from most of his subordinates, as well as the United States. America pressed Britain to abandon this policy just after it had wrecked Egyptian armed forces. Nasser triumphed, and Britain's status as a great power vanished.[150]

GCHQ and NSA continued technical cooperation during the Suez crisis as the political clash – the worst crisis in Anglo-American relations since 1945 – took place above their heads. They had no other choice. The crisis overlapped with the Soviet invasion of Hungary, where UKUSA had to cooperate. Still, relations were shaken in ways which illuminate UKUSA and GCHQ's role in it. The controversies included the general one: Washington's confusion and anger over the actions of Britain, France and Israel, which it quickly recognised somehow were colluding, while the Hungarian crisis raged during the last week of a presidential election campaign. These emotions fuelled a small problem which for a short period became major: unintentionally and briefly, Britain withheld small amounts of material from US Sigint because of the way British Siginters in Cyprus distributed end product. When GCHQ perceived these problems, it ended them. Without the Americans' suspicion, neither of these problems would have mattered much.

The greater problem, for operations and UKUSA, was British cooperation with France. For its security, Britain needed to help France improve its cryptological strength and use intelligence effectively in the field.[151] In planning before the invasion of Egypt, Britain controlled intelligence, avoided cooperation in Sigint, but could not stop French efforts. France sent a Sigint unit to Cyprus, under Capitaine Fabre, to gather intelligence for the operation (and no doubt to observe British capabilities). Britain kept Fabre's unit from contacting more than a few liaison personnel, who thought his men good, especially against Arab voice targets – perhaps reflecting the linguistic talents of pieds noirs from French-ruled Algeria. Initially, Britain placed them in drafty tents at a bad intercept site and with useless targets. Later it provided better accommodation, partly as a means to avoid any cooperation with them. Britain ignored the work of Fabre's men, who left Cyprus when British and French forces withdrew from Egypt.

This sabotage of cooperation with French Sigint angered France without appeasing the Americans. During the summer of 1956, GCHQ knew that any cooperation with France would irritate US Sigint authorities, but sought to control and finesse the problem. After sounding out Canine, the head of NSA, LSIB told USCIB that, in war, Britain would downgrade the lowest levels of Sigint (plain-language intercepts and call sign identifications) to Category 1, which would be available to all headquarters under its command, including French ones. Material from Arab military codes would drop to Category 2 and be used as background for assessments, but never be seen by Frenchmen. USCIB tolerated these changes, until war began and suspicion grew, exacerbated by the fact that GCHQ was acting at all.

These military operations surprised GCHQ; it had only four days' warning of war, and that unofficially, derived from drawing inferences about secret preparations to cut cables to Egypt. By conspiring against his own government, Eden castrated its capabilities. During the campaign, GCHQ received no briefings on operations, which it followed only through 'a black-market service' through the Admiralty.[152]

Days into the war, GCHQ, confused and embarrassed, faced a dilemma which it had hoped to avoid but could not redress. It merely could let NSA know that GCHQ had not violated UKUSA, and given nothing to France. The SUKLO, Palmer, noted that had GCHQ not informed USCIB of what it intended to do, or given France anything, 'NSA could not have protected us against the wrath of certain USCIB members.'[153] A member of NSA said: ' "Although a SUEZ unlikely to recur, cooperation of that sort, where both UKUSA partners not involved, could well lead to foundering of whole UKUSA agreement." No further comment.' This view, Palmer reported, was 'coloured by desperation and frustration produced by the emotional deadlock over categorisation in USCIB. It is possible they reflect the attitude voiced by some USCIB members!'[154]

Fortunately for GCHQ, the crisis was brief. However calamitous for Britain's status as a power, Suez amounted to just a short spat with the

United States. American statesmen understood Britain, or thought they did. Eisenhower blamed British misbehaviour on Eden, not Britain. He and US Secretary of State John Foster Dulles perhaps felt some responsibility for British misfortunes, and rightly so. American and British authorities, nowhere more than at Cheltenham and Fort Meade, wanted to forget Suez. GCHQ sent NSA honest assessments of their successes and failures during the Hungarian and Suez crises, admitted its failures of liaison, yet truthfully denied that it had violated policy with France. NSA replied with equal detail and honesty. To withhold material was 'of utmost importance. Any impression that GCHQ is screening COMINT before passing it to the US should be avoided.'[155] GCHQ drew greater lessons: above all that it needed NSA far more than vice versa. GCHQ needed to follow IRSIG carefully. It must never expose NSA unnecessarily to criticism from American Siginters or decision-makers. UKUSA could not survive another Suez; no longer was it an alliance between equals, though NSA did not realise this fact for years. The impact of this knowledge did not become clear until the last decade of the Cold War.

Exchange during the Middle Cold War
National restrictions on exchanges, whether NOFORN (No Foreigner) and UKEO (UK Eyes Only), remained, especially for Americans, but more in national than technical areas. Concern about exchange of product continued, but the system worked, despite many complexities. In 1964–65, for example, during Konfrontasi in Indonesia, British forces operated discreetly across the Indonesian border with Malaysia. Britain so informed the Five Eyes, but worried that material sent through diplomatic channels to a few decision-makers might be leaked to a worldwide audience. When Indonesians killed two Gurkhas on one mission, the Anglo-Australian Sigint organisation in Singapore solved an Indonesian signal on the issue. Local British political authorities attempted to prevent its circulation to the Five Eyes until Whitehall informed their governments. This request upset the Australian Sigint commander in Singapore, and GCHQ, which had complex relations with DSD regarding 'action-on' in Konfrontasi.[156] The Foreign Office replied that such material should be distributed normally, through Sigint channels. 'The idea that SIGINT available to us might be withheld

from our SIGINT partners is, of course, behaviour of the very worst kind in GCHQ's eyes.'[157] Bonsall emphasised:

> it is one of the facts of life that Comint is organised on an
> international basis and that it is not realistic to think in terms
> of withholding the product from the partners in it. It is a basic
> concept of this co-operation that the work is shared out between
> the partners to their mutual advantage, and this concept rests
> in turn on confidence that each partner's contribution will not
> only not be withheld, but also will not even be delayed. This
> contribution may take any or all of a number of forms, such as
> raw intercept, cryptographic recoveries and the final reported item.
> In spite of great temptations to the contrary, the Americans have
> continued to co-operate with us on this basis in their exchanges
> with us, to the very great benefit of the United Kingdom. It is
> therefore of the greatest importance to avoid any action which
> might lead the Americans to think that the British were being at all
> selective in their release of Comint to the U.S. ...
>
> Our co-operation in Sigint is based on the fact that, by and large
> and subject only to considerations of cost, each partner could if he
> wished, and if he had to, produce for himself the Sigint for which
> he relies upon the other. Ceasing to co-operate in Sigint would
> not therefore deprive the partner of the possibility of obtaining
> the results – particularly as applied to the Americans, who are
> much nearer in self-sufficiency in Sigint than we are. Indeed, they
> duplicate so much of our work that one must always reckon with
> the possibility that they will be producing for themselves any item
> reported by the British Sigint organisation.[158]

For its part, NSA has cooperated loyally with GCHQ. In 1973, the National Security Advisor, Henry Kissinger, tried to stop supplying some intelligence to Britain because it refused to support American policy over Israel as he wished. NSA, protected by the DOD, rejected this order, which would have wrecked American Sigint collection in Europe and the Middle East for some time, and cited UKUSA as a binding agreement, which it is not.[159]

Yet even in the best of times, differences over national interests shade the Sigint relationship. During the Falklands conflict of 1982, some American authorities supported Argentina and Whitehall feared that they might leak information to it. Some information on British military policy – but not Sigint – was kept from NSA because of these fears. The SUKLO also emphasised that GCHQ needed to work harder to convince American authorities that they should place British needs above their own.[160]

Personalities and Friction

As DIRNSA from 1985 to 1988, William Odom kept a diary. The frankness of his views is remarkable, even more so NSA's decision to declassify them. Odom condemned GCHQ for not carrying its share of the weight of UKUSA and for demanding too much authority. He purported to prefer a particular third-party partner to GCHQ, which was a serious challenge to the tenets of UKUSA. 'The British clearly can't accept happily their own loss of pre-eminence in this business while the Third Party is moving ahead rapidly,' wrote Odom. Those criticisms reflected bad relations with GCHQ Director Peter Marychurch, whom Odom characterised in scathing terms. Among European Sigint leaders:

> Peter Marychurch, my UK counterpart, is the least attractive of the
> lot. A tense, nervous, slightly insecure civil servant, he has as his main
> task to stay fully entangled with the US system, to try and act as
> our equivalent in Europe, to stand between us and other Europeans
> if possible. He and his immediate subordinates hold, in my view,
> a vastly inflated view of their own competence and talents. Their
> system, under the Foreign Office, has poor ties to the MOD and
> therefore cares little about intel support to military operations …
>
> The potential for conflict with Marychurch also abounds in
> our bilateral ties – resources, security, 3rd Party rules, etc. The big
> question for me is what geographic access in the UK will cost for
> the rest of the century. This is really about all we are getting and can
> get for this excessively entangled bilateral connection.
>
> Socially I no longer find the British amusing, merely a pain in
> the ass. Marychurch and Johnson [J. A. Johnson, a leading GCHQ
> officer] must take me for an ordinary American with no education
> to speak of. They didn't have a good grasp either of current strategic

affairs or history. They are semi-educated newspaper readers, not intel analysts worthy of nat'l level posts.[161]

Notably, these 'newspaper readers' were the first Western analysts to understand how the Soviet reaction to NATO's 'Able Archer' exercises of 1983 reflected fear and alarm among Soviet decision-makers.[162]

The relationship between Odom and Marychurch shows how far personality shaped UKUSA, but also how it did not. The scale of this case of friction is unique. The leaders of GCHQ and NSA usually cooperate. They share unique responsibilities where each can help the other, and perhaps no one else may do so. With the exception of Marychurch and Odom, who were not fond of each other, these leaders have respected or liked one another. The problem was what Marychurch and Odom did, and who they were. Both were provincial outsiders, rising through different means. Odom, a very American American from an educated but unwealthy family, used West Point military academy to receive an education. He became a soldier-scholar, with a PhD in strategic studies. Marychurch was a very English Englishman, in manner a civilian generalist in the Whitehall mould, less so in reality. He entered GCHQ as a clerical officer after National Service, with a lower-middle-class background but no degree, after realising that Cambridge would not admit him to study Russian. That failure caused personal insecurity, which his critics sensed. His rise to the top of GCHQ despite these problems shows ability. Marychurch's talent lay in listening to, working with, organising and motivating people. Odom, like most DIRNSAs, had no background in Sigint, but he was a seasoned analyst, a contrarian and conservative intellectual with forceful and informed opinions on the Soviet military, which was the primary intelligence target in an era when analysts were divided. Differences with Marychurch on that issue probably sparked and perhaps justified Odom's contempt of his analytical expertise. Given the strength of his views, arguably Odom would have been better as a policymaker than an intelligence officer. Given his accomplishments, Odom revealed a surprising sensitivity to British manners, which suggests insecurity on his part. Had Odom really felt and been what he claimed, he easily could have cut Marychurch down to size. Instead, he did so only in his diary.

As a military intelligence officer, Odom favoured forward Sigint support for combat forces, where perhaps he recognised NATO's disastrous disorganisation. Marychurch maintained the preference for strategic work which characterised GCHQ and NSA. Also, Odom was DIRNSA during the height of NSA's success against the Soviets, and the nadir of British aid, when American Sigint most outstripped its ally. Perhaps that fact drove Marychurch to defend old ways, thereby annoying Odom. By Odom's testimony, Marychurch fought his corner, successfully. After retirement, each man had successful careers. Odom became a leading strategic commentator, while Marychurch was a significant figure in British musical education.

Diaries rarely tell the whole truth. Often they let authors blow off steam privately rather than publicly. Odom's journal criticised almost everyone he met, within NSA as much as GCHQ. After his first year as DIRNSA, the sneers at GCHQ and UKUSA declined in number and force, while the foreign Siginters with whom he most worked came from 'this excessively entangled bilateral connection'. Odom's personal views had no institutional effect; not well-liked by people at NSA, he did not affect its attitudes or practices. Old hands from NSA and GCHQ recollect that during his tenure their relations changed little. That was fortunate for the United States, given all the help GCHQ has provided since.

Lessons Learned

Within UKUSA, only a sustained personal effort can overcome the inertia of institutional change. Only a president or prime minister could end UKUSA on a whim. Anyone else would have to work at it. UKUSA drives GCHQ and NSA to cooperate despite divisions between their states, with an odd impact on realpolitik. GCHQ hampered British policy on Suez by rejecting cooperation with France. Though this degree of dissonance was unique in the history of UKUSA, it recurs to varying degrees whenever London or Washington do not agree on foreign policy, as has often happened since 1945. The relationship works best when its members face common threats, against which joint programmes are helpful, as in the Cold War and after 9/11. The relationship erodes when common interests and threats decline, or divisions arise, as with American concerns about British involvement in Europe around 1970 and 1990. In the former case, GCHQ felt it necessary to persuade Whitehall why closer Sigint cooperation with European partners was unwise: it would give Britain little while wrecking UKUSA. Whitehall was easily convinced on the matter: the Cabinet Secretary, Burke Trend, called GCHQ's paper 'a first-class piece of work'.[163]

UKUSA assumes that Britain and the United States do not fight over fundamental issues. When they do so, UKUSA cannot function. Were they to do so often, UKUSA would collapse – so too, if any member of the Five Eyes used Sigint collected on third parties in order to support a policy against each other on major issues. This prospect is most common in negotiations over issues of trade, which have been too small to hamper the partnership, so far. During the Suez crisis, GCHQ provided some of its material to Australia and Canada. The UKLO in Melbourne believed that this Comint shaped Australian decisions to support Britain on Suez.[164] One may wonder how Comint affected the different ways in which Canada and the United States split from Britain during that crisis.

Barring fundamental diplomatic divisions, GCHQ and NSA control their relationship, complicated by tension between technical cooperation and political differences. During the 1950s and 1960s, decolonisation forced Britain to work with third parties without alienating the United States, hampering its ability to use Sigint. The United States had similar problems, though also more freedom to act in parallel cases, like South Vietnam, which it probably aided in Sigint more than Britain did France in 1956. Where Britain confronted an independent problem and the United States chose to support it, UKUSA reinforced American decisions – a favour returned when the United States needed help, as in the Cuban missile crisis. American Sigint has been generous towards its partners, and never rapacious. Given the degree of integration between the Five Eyes, to drive any partner from the pot causes problems for all. The freemasonry of Siginters eases political divisions between the Five Eyes. New Zealand's GCSB retained a toehold within UKUSA after 1985, though was expelled from every other anglophone strategic relationship. In 2003, the United States cut military cooperation over Canada's opposition to the invasion of Iraq, but not with the Canadian Security Establishment (CSE).

Enemies and Third Parties

Two groups in Sigint shaped the world as much as UKUSA. The Eastern bloc, a formidable foe, was probably weaker than UKUSA in pure cryptanalysis but equal in cryptography. Though geography limited Soviet interception largely to Eurasia, the collection of microwave traffic from embassies abroad and the large intercept station at Lourdes in Cuba extended that reach. Slowly, over decades, the USSR imposed its excellent cryptography on its allies in the Warsaw Pact. The USSR, and some of its allies, had good Sigint services, which had transactional relations. Bloc Sigint overwhelmed many members of NATO, while its Humint wrecked American and British success against Soviet cryptosystems in 1948, which degraded UKUSA Comint throughout the Cold War. Via the American Walker–Whitworth family of spies, Soviet Humint ravaged US Navy cryptosystems. That success weakened Western navies between 1968 and 1985 and would have mattered in war. Western Humint, especially MI6, beat the bloc as much as it was beaten, but these successes did not shape Sigint. All told, Eastern bloc Sigint may have outweighed that of NATO and UKUSA during the Cold War.

What UKUSA termed third parties – all other countries with which any of the Five Eyes partners cooperates – were usually weak in Sigint. The few exceptions had strong bargaining positions with UKUSA. The rest maintained weak to mediocre capabilities against their neighbours; their focus was on home security rather than a global intelligence capability. Third parties mattered to UKUSA less as threats than as bases for interception and as sources of linguistic capabilities. Every relationship between second and third parties had a different form. The UKUSA agreement and national interest limited what could be done with third parties. If the latter asked too much, relations ended. Such relations were transactional. The closest of them involved sharing programmes of interception, the lowest categories of Sigint and cryptographic advice. They involved no assistance in cryptanalysis nor guarantees against attack on their systems. Against this, all third parties had interests and independence: they could end relationships when they wished. Third parties in the third world found these arrangements profitable. They loaned the temporary use of territory for American or British aid in relationships they could end at will.[165]

The interests of American and British Sigint conflicted most over third parties. The United States had more money and kit to offer than Britain, even when parties preferred to work with GCHQ. American Sigint defined relations with third parties more flexibly than Britain and needed them more for interception, which Britain could more easily find in its empire. From 1970, the United States found that reliance on third parties in the third world left it diplomatically vulnerable to local demands or regime changes.[166]

UKUSA's greatest foreign relationships were in NATO, the core of Western security. American and British Sigint had distinct relations with these allies. American Sigint took a harder line over cooperation in the 1950s and 1960s, as did the British during the 1970s and 1980s, but generally their views overlapped. Each feared insecurity among their allies: any help the latter received might easily be compromised.[167] UKUSA aided its allies in military Comsec in order to reduce their vulnerability to the Warsaw Pact; and in military Sigint with some limitations. Cooperation on Category 2 attacks against Warsaw Pact systems, such as encrypted call signs, was limited to allies who had discovered the basics themselves.[168] No NATO Siginters were helped past these levels. At the same time, none were impeded from advancing – though none did, even after 1970 when interdependence offered them greater opportunities to improve in Sigint. NATO allies had niche capabilities, given limits to their geography, quality or resources. Some countries had excellent intercept capabilities, but others were mediocre and insecure. Although Siginters from some NATO allies were allowed to visit GCHQ in the 1960s, others were not, for fear of leaks to the Warsaw Pact. These precautions were wise.[169]

Until 1970, NATO had a ramshackle, irrational system of Sigint. By the mid-1950s, all third parties were circulating their Sigint to their national forces, which were pooled in Special Handling Detachments (SHDs) at international commands. These reports were often inaccurate while, initially, UKUSA material remained hidden. Thus, NATO commands did not receive the Sigint needed to correct errors. CANUKUS (Canada–United Kingdom–United States) officers received UKUSA material, which they could not discuss with commanders or staff, except cleared members of a Five Eyes country.[170] Throughout NATO's history, American or British officers handled most senior commands, with one exception: the main ground forces on the central front. Between 1952 and 1956 Field Marshal Juin, the French commander of the Central Army Group, was denied UKUSA Sigint, which his American and British staff received; so too, German generals commanding Allied Forces Central Europe during the 1970s and 1980s.[171] In theory, during crisis or war, these CANUKUS officers would release much of this material to commands, directly or sanitised. In practice, American, British and French experiences during the Hungarian and Suez crises and those of NSA, GCHQ and BND, the German intelligence service which controlled Humint and Sigint, during the Czechoslovak crisis, show how before and during the start of a war, UKUSA would have weakened NATO Sigint and its political, strategic and operational decisions. In 1968, just after the Soviet occupation of Czechoslovakia, BND estimated that between twenty-seven and thirty Soviet divisions had moved from western Russia to East Germany. GCHQ calculated that number as seven. BND's conclusions caused panic in Supreme Allied Command Europe (SACEUR), which feared an imminent Soviet attack on NATO or Yugoslavia. GCHQ soon helped calm SACEUR but, unable to use its best evidence, needed months of patient persuasion to have BND overcome its overestimates.[172]

American commanders in NATO frequently complained that this system was militarily absurd.[173] It improved after 1970 when UKUSA began to help NATO more. Cooperation over Category 2 Sigint, a central source on Soviet forces, aided the Sigint agencies of NATO third parties and incorporated UKUSA reports into international commands. Parallel but distinct Sigint lines of reportage linked intelligence and command, the international system and the CANUKUS one. They intersected at NATO commands, where the streams flowed together well under Five Eyes commanders, much less so in the few under third party control.[174] Both systems were tested regularly in exercises; relations between NATO Siginters became stronger. Still, one may wonder how well this complex and fragile system would have worked in an emergency; it would probably have collapsed in war.

The interaction between UKUSA and NATO had perverse consequences for Western Sigint. The third parties of NATO knew that its Anglophone members had a special relationship. This knowledge drove them to collude against UKUSA.[175] For any third party to get military intelligence on the Soviet Union was hard. This discouraged them from undertaking such tasks and turned them elsewhere. The targets most easy to attack and offering the most valuable material were the diplomatic or commercial systems of their allies. At least one third party exploited such systems enthusiastically, as perhaps others did as well.[176] Non-UKUSA members of NATO used much of their cryptanalytic resources against each other. Even in the 1980s, their Sigint system was mediocre and perhaps worse than that of the Warsaw Pact.

The NSA–GCHQ relationship under UKUSA was and is the central thread in the quilt of the Five Eyes. For the United States, UKUSA reinforced its Sigint collection and analytical capabilities. For Britain, UKUSA did the same but also reinforced the special relationship and influence in Washington at low cost. For the other three Eyes, these political calculations were even more important. After the Cold War, intelligence relations between Western states became more thorough. Other Western states knew of the Five Eyes arrangement and often tried to manipulate it, but also lived with it. Seemingly one of the biggest questions in the field is why some third party partners never became a member of the Five Eyes. The answer is simple, and revealing: the lack of complete trust and common purpose and the fact that to enter UKUSA now would be a public process, not secret. Probably, if UKUSA did not exist today, it could not now be created out of the blue either. How long it will survive is a fundamental question to its members and to power politics across the globe.

'We Want to Be Cheltonians': The Department

GCHQ managed Sigint well, but less so Siginters, who included analytic, clerical, cryptanalytic, intercept, scientific and technical personnel. In April 1945, Britain had 30,000 Siginters, 10,500 of them at Bletchley Park. By September 1946, that strength was down to 5,932 military and 1,168 civilians. British Sigint then expanded steadily to around 11,500 by 1965.[1] It remained numerically constant until 1992, as more people entered and retired.

In 1946, GCHQ moved to Eastcote, Bletchley's largest bombe outstation, in northwest London. Eastcote had tolerable tube services, but transport was slow and costly for staff thrown across London. It was too small to host all of GCHQ. A public pathway split the site's two buildings. The construction of double fences and an overhead footbridge complicated arrangements. Between 1950 and 1954, GCHQ relocated to Cheltenham, a move which illustrates many institutional interests. Whitehall deliberately decentralised postwar government facilities from London to the provinces in order to promote economic growth. GCHQ was too big to be based in London, but the scattering of its parts caused inefficiency. Cheltenham was linked well to national and international signals communications, though rail and road transport links were mediocre. The government already owned large buildings there. MI5 and MI6 would have resisted such a move, in order to maintain contact with consumers. GCHQ and its consumers ignored that issue. GC&CS worked well from Bletchley, Eastcote was already outside the Whitehall village and Cheltenham felt scarcely further away. End product was signalled routinely to consumers as fast as it had been from London. The Templer Report of 1960 considered a return to London by GCHQ, but rejected the idea because of cost, while GCHQ and military analysts 'are always in direct touch' and met frequently, whether in Cheltenham or the capital city. Indeed, Templer thought the danger was not isolation, but that 'an over-enthusiastic [analyst] may make misguided demands upon a consumer'.[2]

GCHQ's move to Cheltenham shaped both parties. Approximately fifty prewar members of GC&CS moved to Eastcote. Most of them, and many veterans of Bletchley, preferred retirement over relocating to the Cotswolds. Support staff stayed behind as did the cryptographic mission, separated from GCHQ and called the LCSA. To enable the move, the government subsidised the construction of council houses for members of GCHQ, which initially angered Cheltonians.

Attitudes soon changed. As often with British industry, GCHQ offered livelihoods to locals. Gloucestershire was already a centre of technology, in particular aircraft manufacture. GCHQ steered the local economy even further away from the rural and agricultural and strengthened the already high cultural status of Cheltenham. GCHQ became a major employer; locals, often trained through apprenticeship programmes, provided much of GCHQ's support staff. Their unwillingness to relocate solved the chronic problems which had been caused by GCHQ's combination of high standards and low salaries, though GCHQ still placed advertisements 'in the national and local newspapers and in trade, hobby and Armed Forces magazines for a variety of specialist and non-specialist staff. Under 'Female Vacancies', the *Gloucestershire Echo* noted, 'young women of good education to be trained in the operation of punched card, electronic and computing equipment for statistical purposes'.[4] A distinct local variant emerged for security procedures. Local applicants for posts were tested en masse in the restaurant at the Oakley site on a Saturday afternoon.[5] Boys, with parents alongside, faced positive vetting interviews in their family kitchens. Inspectors, often retired local policemen, would make their decision after popping out for an hour to visit the referees, neighbours, or church folk up the road. Rural families debated solemnly whether children should take jobs at Cheltenham that involved a twenty-minute bus ride, each way. The location also aided retention of higher staff with families, for whom movement would cause disruption. So said the saw, if you stayed in Cheltenham for three years, GCHQ had you for life.

F.O. STAFF "WANT TO BE CHELTONIANS"

APART from their confidential work, there is to be nothing insular about the Foreign Office staff who have come, and are yet to come, from London to Cheltenham to take over Government Communications Headquarters, which have been established in the town:

"We want to be Cheltonians," is the way the feeling of the staff was summed up by a senior officer, interviewed by the "Echo."

A third of the move has now taken place, and it is expected to be completed in October, six month ahead of schedule. This means that work will take place in "crushed" conditions pending the take-over of the huge new buildings —including the four-storey largest-in-the-town administration block at Oakley Farm.

The new buildings will probably be occupied section by section until the autumn of next year, when it is expected that the last workmen will leave the site after their high-speed, high-priority operations, which for a time kept a small army on day and night (by floodlight) shifts.

The new buildings at Ben-hall, including a large work-shop and technical building, have been completed and are already in use.

The reason for the speeding-up of the transfer and the temporary acceptance of cramped conditions is the very human one of keeping families together. As the 560 houses built by the Town Council for the Foreign Office at Hester's Way have become available, so they have been occupied, even if this has meant occupation by wives and their children while husbands have gone on working in London.

LOCAL RECRUITING

Naturally, a considerable number of temporary staff who have strong ties with London have decided not to make the move, and, in order that these losses should be made good, new staff with a variety of qualifications is being recruited in and around Cheltenham.

Response so far has been good, but it is pointed out that there is room for plenty more.

"We have vacancies for men and women in a wide range of employment," said the spokesman. "This is a permanent transfer, and the work has the benefit of a degree of permanency. It may be an additional attraction to some to know that temporary staff are eligible to sit for examinations for entry into the permanent Civil Service."

The coming of G.C.H.Q. may well mean Civil Service careers for a big proportion of young Cheltenham people, "for," the "Echo" was told, "we do offer very good and interesting careers to children from the grammar schools and technical schools and colleges."

Asked how members of the staff were taking to Cheltenham, the spokesman replied that the great majority were delighted with their new surroundings.

"It is a wrench for people who have their roots in London suddenly to be moved into a new place, and, naturally, the first reaction of people on being told about this sort of thing is not to welcome it. Nevertheless, people who are coming here are forgetting that and are settling down very happily. They love the town, and are happy in the houses that the Town Council has built for us."

Figure 9.1
Gloucestershire Echo[3]

The move also reinforced internal trends within GCHQ towards isolation and autonomy. GCHQ's London office, in a drab 1950s Ministry of Works office building on Palmer Street, was small. It was

Figure 9.2

In 1952, GCHQ moved to two government-owned sites in Cheltenham: Oakley and Benhall, each roughly forty-six acres in size, together forming an L-shaped area half a mile long and about 150 metres wide at the bottom and middle of this aerial photograph, expanding to 300 metres in Oakley at the top. Initially, Oakley was a small campus containing many large and well-built single-storey buildings of wartime government style. Benhall had a few labs and engineering buildings, but mostly was open space available for development. That space originally was intended for radio intercept facilities, but fortuitously was free to house computer facilities decades later when that need arose, so precluding a major problem. From 1970, GCHQ at Cheltenham was like a medium-sized and crowded military base, surrounded by a chain-link fence crowned by barbed wire.

Oakley and Benhall had some 245,000 square feet of building space in 1952, and GCHQ thought that it might need to develop another 100,000. The need for expansion proved far greater, because GCHQ and Sigint developed in ways no one predicted. The Cheltenham site was intended to house all GCHQ personnel, which never occurred. As the size and duties of staff changed, however, new buildings were added, many of them multi-storey. C Block was built in the 1950s, followed by M, L and Q Blocks and, in the 1970s, by F and G Blocks and F Annex, to house computers. Modular buildings, car parks, incinerators and power installations were squeezed into empty spaces. Incineration of old papers was a major function at GCHQ, serviced by one large and several smaller buildings. Increasingly, buildings of wartime vintage were modified to accommodate changes in machines, technology and work.

Staff reached the main entrance at Oakley by foot, bike, bus or car. As they advanced through the security gate uphill, they moved sequentially past offices servicing administration, languages, operations and management and, finally, engineering, computers and cryptography, after the Communications-Electronics Security Group (CESG) moved to Cheltenham in the 1970s. A Block housed human resources, finance and services, with the canteen adjacent. B Block handled training and languages, while C, D, E and L Blocks serviced intelligence and cryptanalysis. The directorate and communications were in C Block, later augmented by M Block. F Block, F Annex and G Block covered computer operations.

That everyone who controlled British Sigint worked at Cheltenham, and could quickly and conveniently meet, provided power in normal operations and crises, but the physical location of their offices and buildings still affected the organisation and culture of GCHQ. Staff used the terms 'Oakley', 'Benhall' and 'across town' as shorthand to represent different elements of GCHQ. Divisions emerged between staff working primarily with machines, technology and science, and those handling administration and intelligence, but also in different ways between offices in both sites. Personnel at one site might never enter certain buildings there, while frequently visiting offices 'across town'. When walking across the site, especially when it was raining, staff regularly cut through buildings where movement was unrestricted, but physical security restricted access to some buildings and offices. Culturally, staff accepted that one did not visit places where one had no business. Outside working hours, offices were sterile, all papers secured, classified maps secured or hidden behind lockable shutters, and waste locked away. GCHQ became divided into a series of small and self-contained compartments, with a byzantine nature, well suited to the needs of Sigint during the Cold War, but not to the age of cyber.

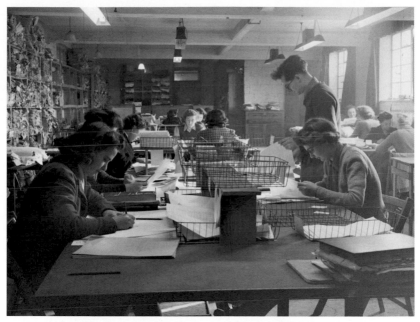

The Hut 6 registration room, one of the busiest offices at Bletchley.

Seventy-six per cent of the workforce at Bletchley were women. A large proportion of bombe machines were operated and maintained by members of the Women's Royal Naval Service (WRNS, or Wrens). These are at Eastcote, GCHQ's outstation in north-west London.

Colossus, a complex valve-based machine and the world's first electronic computer. Ten machines were built, providing vital intelligence in the closing years of the war. ERNIE – the random-number generator for the Premium Bonds – would be a civilian development of Colossus.

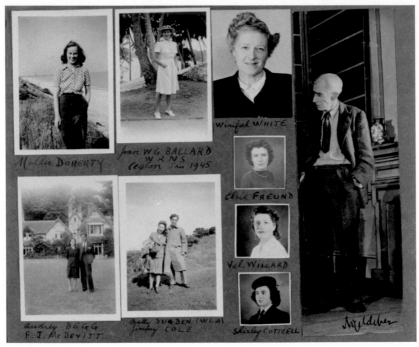

Mollie DOHERTY
Joan W G BALLARD
W R N S
Ceylon Jan 1945
Winifred WHITE
Elsie FREUND
Val. WILLARD
Shirley COTTRELL
audrey BEGG
F. J. McDEVITT
Betty SUGDEN (WLA)
Jimmy COLE

Eric George de Carteret worked at Bletchley Park, Eastcote and Cheltenham, first in the Army and then as a GCHQ civilian, retiring in 1967. He was an enthusiastic amateur photographer, and collected photographs of his colleagues. Some were snaps he took himself, some were copies of formal photographs (weddings or amateur dramatics performances) and in many cases people gave him copies of their own formal ID photographs. He wrote in names for virtually everyone in the album.

Celebrations at Bletchley Park on VE Day in May 1945.

Three GCHQ Directors (Travis, Jones and Loehnis) at lunch at Eastcote, late 1940s, with the eccentric Josh Cooper (sixth from right) and others, including Gerry Morgan (standing on the left) and the bearded Hugh Foss.

Soldiers and civilians try to rescue victims trapped in the debris of the King David Hotel, Jersualem, on 24 July 1946, following the explosion of a bomb in the basement two days earlier.

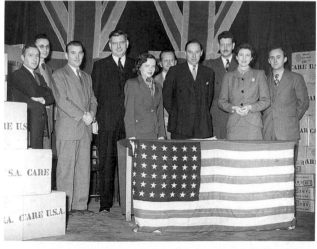

As a gesture of friendship in 1949, Christmas food parcels were collected and donated to junior GCHQ workers by staff at the US Armed Forces Security Agency, the predecessor of the National Security Agency, at a time when rationing continued to bite in the UK.

The 'FO' comes to Cheltenham…
A front-page mention in the
Gloucestershire Echo for the unavowed
department's move west in 1949.

Sir Eric Jones KCMG CB CBE,
GCHQ Director April 1952–May 1960.

Early programming, on some sort of plug board, in the 1950s or 1960s.

The Central Processing Unit, early 1960s, whose job it was to convert data recorded on magnetic tapes by the intercept stations into a form suitable for running on GCHQ's computers. Note the manual checking of tape.

State-of-the-art computing, 1960s-style. The CDC 1604 computer, a large American computer with eight magnetic-tape units for input and output, and slow-speed paper-tape reader and punch. The core store was 32,768 words of 48 bits each. The tapes could be read or written on at a speed of 150 inches per second.

GCHQ scientific officers managing a tropospheric scatter experiment in Australia in the late 1950s.

'The Brig' John Tiltman, behind, with Josh Cooper and leading US cryptanalyst William Friedmann in the 1960s.

Sir Clive Loehnis KCMG, GCHQ Director June 1960–December 1964.

A patrol of the 1st Battalion, Queen's Own Highlanders (Seaforths and Camerons), searches for rebels in the jungle of Brunei during Konfrontasi in Indonesia. Successful CLARET operations were guided by Sigint.

Sir Leonard Hooper KCMG CBE, GCHQ Director January 1965–October 1973.

Modified Elint and Comint collection aircraft of the RAF's 51 Squadron, based at RAF Wyton, included the English Electric Canberra B6 and de Havilland Comet R2, seen here in the 1960s. They were flown on dangerous missions to test Warsaw Pact defences and collect information on communications arising in response.

The ACARA Linear Array at CSOS Cheadle, Staffordshire, in 1966. It was at Cheadle that 'Swannie' of RAF Y fame set the record of thirty-seven years as officer in charge of one intercept station, from 1927 to his retirement in 1964.

Sir Arthur Bonsall KCMG CBE, GCHQ Director November 1973–June 1978.

The original front cover of the seminal (but secret) 1970 paper by James Ellis describing the concept that would become known as Public Key Cryptography: a principle that lies at the heart of all secure transactions on the internet. In 2010 the Institute of Electrical and Electronics Engineers (IEEE) recognised the pioneering secret work done at GCHQ by Ellis, Clifford Cocks and Malcolm Williamson.

Scarborough, on the North Yorkshire coast, is the location of the world's oldest continually operating Sigint site. It began as a Royal Navy wireless telegraphy station as early as 1912 and became an intercept site two years later. This is a view of the site's bunkers, huts and aerials in the 1960s.

Banks of ALVIS machines in a communications centre in 1972. Designed in-house, ALVIS became the workhorse for secure communications for over thirty years and was used nationally, with NATO and with other foreign powers.

not an embassy to Whitehall, though directors attending JIC meetings did work there for parts of two days a week. GCHQ staff demanded a cost-of-living bonus and aid in finding flats before moving to London. They preferred postings to Fort Meade. Few Siginters knew ministers or politicians. For officials to visit GCHQ was difficult, though from 1970 GCHQ organised regular day trips down the old A40, to show Whitehall what its money bought. Not until GCHQ had been in Cheltenham for thirty years did a prime minister visit – Margaret Thatcher in 1980.

GCHQ was a self-contained unit. Transfer to other departments was hard. Once rising in GCHQ, one had no other place to go. Until 1964, GCHQ worked with the service Sigint organisations and then absorbed them. British Sigint was half military and half civilian in constituency in 1952. From 1965, it became a civilian agency in Cheltenham, with outstations manned mostly by civilians (many ex-services) and some service personnel.

GCHQ was divided into many distinct groups, some large, such as the radio grades, others involving a few specialists with rare skills. In the later Cold War, these groups included: experimental officers, translators, aerial riggers, kebuns (Malaysian gardeners), confidential clerks, reprographic assistants, storekeepers, cypher clerks, librarians, photographers, hostel wardens, linguists, fitters, officer keepers, radio officers, transcribers, electricians, tracers, porters, communications and cypher officers, gatemen, duplicator operators, photoprinters, vetting officers, cleaners, telegraphists, gardeners, shorthand typists, nurses, overseers, data processors, scientific officers, technical officers, scientific and technical officers, watchmen, graduate engineers, radio technicians, slip readers, craftsmen, telecomms mechanics, handymen, traffic handlers, clerical officers, cypher operators, drivers, craft apprentices, messengers, security officers, typists, draftsmen, security guards, house maids, labourers, instrument makers, machinists' assistants, executive officers and telephonists. Many of these groups were further divided into trainees, highers, seniors, principals, and other modifiers.

Each group or office had its own distinct subculture. H, the cryptanalytic division, was a centre of idiosyncrasy at GCHQ, only some of it affected, which reflected the external impact of the internal means by which cryppies attacked problems. One cryptanalyst recalled Hugh Alexander 'turning up one day with his knuckles covered in blood so we asked him what had happened and he said, "I was thinking about your Ruritanian cipher problem and I cycled down a flight of steps."[6] K division – like GC&CS, a confederacy of linguistic sections – worked through craftwork, on short assembly lines. J division fused different occupations into a great assembly line against Soviet military traffic. K division relied far more on Comint and text, and, reflecting its targets, was technically more conservative than J, which, confronting bigger and harder tasks, was 'ever anxious for new tools, and exciting to work for', one cryppie recalled.[7] Intercept operators worked in shifts, each man married to a machine. This all-male workforce, working class by origin and comprising many ex-servicemen, combined a blokey culture within a disciplined structure. Clerical, data processing and communications staff, mostly women, worked in pools. One graduate of GCHQ's typing school in 1990 recalled 'being slapped on the wrists with a ruler for looking at the keyboard. And having to raise our hand if we needed to use the toilet.'[8] Female computer operators in Cheltenham had great space and independence, however, as did women in outstations. Most clerical sections were segregated by gender, following social norms rather than official dictation, though men and women served together in the larger interception stations within Britain, and within H, J and K divisions. To monitor and manage cryptosystems – the painstaking creation, use and destruction of systems, keys and enciphered messages – absorbed as many personnel, almost all female, as worked in attack, though many of them managed crypto material within other departments, not GCHQ. Groups worked in different offices or stations, isolated from each other, but cross-posting was common.

In 1945, able Siginters had good chances for promotion in a booming field. Anyone who stayed through the moves from Bletchley to Eastcote and Cheltenham was well placed, like Maureen Jones, daughter of a Welsh railwayman. At the bottom of Bletchley as an unestablished junior clerical assistant during 1945, in 1983 she was the most senior woman at GCHQ. As head of Intelligence Production for the Rest of the World, and the first female senior principal in GCHQ, she received GCHQ's one OBE for its triumph during the Falklands conflict. Though the limits to higher positions slowed movement, GCHQ's expansion between 1945 and 1960 offered room for promotion or cross-posting. By 1965, however, these chances were like those generally in the military or civil services, with a slight wrinkle. Siginters were hired in chronological and occupational blocks for much of the interwar years, the 1950s and the 2000s. Block hiring hampered areas where continued recruitment was desirable; it slowed GCHQ's ability to expand in emerging areas. When such areas boomed, personnel already in place rose fast, while those who followed faced the danger of block hiring. Consequently, during the Cold War, promotion was difficult in the largest groups at GCHQ, the radio grades. While functionally appropriate in key areas such as codebreaking and radio interception, this matter damaged labour relations across the department.

GC&CS had a flat structure, with three bands. Movement between clerical staff and junior assistants was impossible in name, though common in functional terms at the lowest level of cryptanalysis. Movement between clerical groups was possible, though abnormal. It was slow between junior and senior assistants, who, along with many clerical staff, were hired for expertise in one area: cryptanalysis. Military Siginters also handled interception and traffic analysis. Many personnel served in the same positions for decades. Promotion from senior assistant was impossible. GC&CS's procedures for recruitment were haphazard. In retrospect, Denniston thought: 'The pre-war G.C. & C.S. must be considered lucky in its recruitment to its various sections in not having to record a higher percentage of failures. But the method adopted was too haphazard to provide a sufficient safeguard against the dangers that beset secret organisations, i.e. that failures have either to be dismissed with considerable knowledge of the work and its results, or to be retained as a dead-weight on the establishment.'[9] For Bletchley, priorities were high and criteria simple – creative anarchy in organisation, small numbers of people with esoteric skills, machine fodder in masses, and intense compartmentalisation between every section of an assembly line.

GCHQ needed a large base of clerical and industrial staff, and a few specialists of many sorts, more than GC&CS had done. GCHQ had a small central administration, and barely enough competent managers to handle the work. Units reported to an internal directorate of leaders, which worked through meetings and round-robin minutes, extended to divisions on policy issues. The directorate and divisional heads considered problems in collegial, collective and frank ways. A. R. V. Cooper, one of the two renowned Cooper brothers and a divisional head, noted: 'the Society of Friends that our department is' – though not always.[10] In internal documents, people were identified impersonally by their position, for example: 'K34', but personal relationships were close. GCHQ was famed for its quality in a crisis situation, but with ample time to pore over data and for all to state their piece, reaching consensus could involve long-winded and hair-splitting debates. Yet that process never prevented action.

Consensus was preferred and respected, with the Director always having the final word. He often formulated it after assigning a problem to one person, whose solution was criticised by the directorate and divisions. Faith in government, experts, scientists, social scientists, committees, working parties, the reaching of a highest common denominator through reasoned argument and competitive cooperation, marked decisions within GCHQ, and of Whitehall about it. A system of patronage linked generations, exemplified by Travis's mentoring of Jones and his of Hooper in turn, but also was conventional at lower levels. Clubs, choirs and sports linked people across GCHQ, in house leagues, across Cheltenham, Gloucestershire, regionally or nationally. Alexander, head of H and a celebrated chess player, conducted exhibition matches against all-comers, several often simultaneously. Outstations had sports facilities including cricket pitches and golf courses. Hooper was a fixture at rugby matches, gauging juniors by watching them on the pitch. The local press reported many of these events. The easiest way to monitor GCHQ was by a subscription to the *Gloucestershire Echo*, which identified senior leaders, many staff members, and hinted at the existence of UKUSA. GCHQ was small enough that every senior leader knew each other and all of their major details.

GCHQ's initial organisation of five 'groups' (Technical, Traffic Analysis and Task Control, Cryptographic (i.e. Cryptanalysis), Intelligence, and Cypher Security) followed Bletchley's model. It was well suited to manage a single task, which was intended to be attack on and penetration of high-priority cryptosystems. That assault failed, however, while new successes involved every department: fusion, and attack on national targets, whether military, civil or diplomatic. From 1946 an unwieldy structure of committees arose to coordinate the work of groups in interception, traffic analysis, fusion or cryptanalysis, against every target. Jones looked for solutions from Hooper, who had just attended the Imperial Defence College: the first Siginter to receive higher education in policy and strategy, which reflected GCHQ's rising status.

In 1954, GCHQ was divided into several divisions, including: smaller ones to handle specialised functions such as training, machines, cryptanalysis, the steering of interception, reporting and planning; and two bigger ones to control all aspects of Sigint against the Soviet target (J), and the rest of the world (K). This restructuring carried GCHQ through the Cold War, albeit with many revisions.[11] In particular, during the 1960s, divisions were created to drive key issues, such as Policy and Planning, and Machines, and by the 1970s, Computers (X). These divisions were integrated into higher committees which coordinated the elements involved in greater matters such as Task Assessment, Production, Research and Administration, and enforced priorities and efficiencies on these tasks. Informally, members of different departments were fused into semi-permanent task forces. One cryptanalyst recalled spending the 1980s in 'what I might call Greater H, a cross-organisational grouping of H, parts of L [Comsec], some of the application programming parts of X [Computers] and a tiny bit of G that did operational research. This entity had a strong identity and culture, clearly identifiable for those of us within it, but was perhaps invisible to those who were not.'[12] These practices prepared GCHQ for the sudden reorganisations required in crises.

Recruitment and Retention

During 1944–45, authorities recognised that a bigger GC&CS needed a unique structure, which did not utterly violate all standard procedures. The Bland Committee on the intelligence services noted the nub of one problem: how to reward both technical and administrative competence, which rarely resided in the same mind; but raised another issue. Since 'the training and gifts of cryptographers are of a very special nature ... it is a mistake to think that the ultimate future of a young cryptographer ought to be "promotion" to the Headship of the Department, and ... its head and/or its establishment officer may have to be sought elsewhere'.[13] Yet to do so might sap professional autonomy, and quality. To combine expertise over many administrative and technical issues, and to sustain general promotion and specialised careers, would be hard. Although the Foreign Office administered GCHQ, Whitehall agreed that Siginters and the Treasury must define these matters directly. Negotiations over the structure of GCHQ occurred in a rush at the war's end. They were complicated because GCHQ did not know establishments; nor the Treasury Sigint: for example, it admitted Alexander, Britain's greatest organiser of cryptanalysts, as an administrative officer, only after intense pressure.[14] In hindsight, the discussions focused too much on the needs of codebreakers – the scarcest and highest-status element of Sigint, but one where GCHQ was strong in 1945 – against those with other essential skills, who were far larger in number.

Conditions for clerical positions were defined easily but not for officers. GCHQ preferred a system to find 'the right kind of people', modelled on cryptanalysts. It requested relatively more 'senior posts' than usual in departments, and unique flexibility for early retirement, enabling older minds to leave cryptanalysis and young ones to enter. 'Unless we have these senior posts we have no flow of proper promotions and the good people will not come into the organisation … Cryptography and work connected with it is at least a mental adventure and the Permanent Civil Service can hardly be described as an adventurous career.'[15] Later experience demonstrated that older minds remained adventurous in cryptanalysis. The Treasury rejected that stricture and structure, but treated GCHQ flexibly, by its standards. It agreed that GCHQ required 200 'first-class minds' – that is: officers in the administrative class of the civil service. This figure was below that of the 260 just authorised by the Chiefs of Staff. It also included fifty-seven members of a B grade – unique in Whitehall and sitting above the executive and below the administrative grades – which was intended to reward specialists for staying in place. These 200 personnel covered all leadership and Sigint tasks at GCHQ. They joined at higher rates and initially advanced faster than civil servants in normal units, but mid-career that status stalled. Opportunities for the A grade, the top fifty-seven officers, to reach the highest levels of the civil service were less than elsewhere, and impossible in the B grade. The same was true for many appointments, especially engineers, in the executive grades. Though initially called 'cadets', the AIVs were Whitehall's standard administrative trainees, while BIVs were what later would be called 'DSs', or Departmental Specialists, focused on techniques of Sigint. Initially, personnel admitted to the A or B class joined a common level, the cadet class, without knowing which stream they would enter.[16]

Only motivated people would take an administrative position at GCHQ, compared to other departments; yet for decades GCHQ could not motivate them in advance by describing its work. Until 1982, candidates without prior experience in Sigint did not know what work GCHQ did, until they reached Cheltenham, signed the Official Secrets Act, were briefed, and allowed to stay or go. The need for positive vetting further slowed appointments, leading applicants with multiple offers – often the best candidates – to go elsewhere. The Civil Service Commission (CSC) always described GCHQ to applicants as a 'Department of the Foreign Office' – presumably in order to counter the impression that it was an entirely technical unit – and offered optimistic calculations of salary and career prospects. In 1950, the CSC described GCHQ's work as being 'very varied and although mainly specialist requiring high-class linguists, mathematicians and scientists, it also covers most aspects of the work of a medium-sized Government Department'.[17] From 1965, the CSC described GCHQ's work as 'specialised, but in its own particular field it is wide in scope, complex and varied, and by no means exclusively technical in nature. It should appeal to graduates who are seeking work which is both interesting and mentally extending. The range of activity is that normally to be found in any medium-sized Government Department and includes, for example, individual and team work, committee work, and contact with the Services and with other Government Departments.'[18] By 1963, GCHQ believed that this problem of secrecy had declined, at least for B-class appointments, because after 'several years intensive effort, we have gained the active co-operation of most University Appointments Boards' (UABs), where some members were indoctrinated into its work.[19] A generation later, however, GCHQ worried that this effort still impeded the acquisition of key personnel. Since 'we use the obvious but deceptive description "problem solvers", when actually GCHQ wanted "able all-rounders", focused on intelligence in mind and work, there is a danger of over-stating the H-type research nature of the work precisely because it is our most distinctive feature and of forgetting that many of our middle and senior managers are likely to be increasingly concerned with planning and running sophisticated, computer-based operational systems'.[20]

The initial system failed. Beyond veteran Siginters, few AIVs joined GCHQ: not one between 1955 and 1959. Problems of promotion surrounded the B grade, which Hooper (AD2) called 'the professional Sigint class at GCHQ ... upon whom (together with the mathematicians and scientists) depends the future success or failure of British Sigint'.[21] With retirement of the wartime generation in sight, institutional succession had to be solidified. During 1959–63, GCHQ and the Treasury renewed the battle over rankings. GCHQ accepted the figure of 200 first-class minds – budged 10 per cent higher, despite the department's trebling in size, because the executive class (Cs, or executive officers, EOs) solved problems that no one expected in 1946, when their capabilities were unknown. The Treasury agreed that mid-level posts often required 'qualities of executive management, of a high order and a very specialised kind'. It would not count these factors towards numbers in the A class, or general increases in ranks or salaries, but undoubtedly they affected its decisions. In 1963, the Treasury authorised an improvement in strength. GCHQ turned that offer into a greater number of senior positions for members of the A, B and C classes, boosting the promotion prospects for the best of each cadre. GCHQ aimed to have 220 first-class minds – 150 Bs, 30 As, and 40 scientists – and to hire one A, four Bs and one scientist per year; so, at first, to fill the establishment, and then to replace retirements.[22] That rate of replacement roughly occurred, though success fluctuated in practice. From 1967, the new class of 'language specialists' – of 200 translators and intelligence analysts – ultimately added scores more graduates to GCHQ, while also regrouping some people already at hand.

Executive officers (EOs) gained access to many more senior positions in administrative or technical areas, reflecting their ability and initiative. B officers, renamed Departmental Specialists, dominated all the technical areas for GCHQ, especially those involving science and cryptanalysis. They headed H, V, J and K, the codebreaking, Elint, Soviet, and rest of the world sections, and most senior positions in all technical branches. GCHQ doubled the number of senior DS positions but concentrated them on cryptanalysis. The chances for promotion in other DS positions were mediocre, sometimes 'very bad'.[23] GCHQ concluded, correctly, that those involved would accept the outcome. GCHQ focused its new resources on replacing the A class with a class of 'Government Communications Cadets' (GCCs, later called government communication trainee, GCTs, then graduate management trainees, GMTs), as fast climbers. GCTs were hired for administration and leadership positions. Over their first four years, GCTs received a broad introduction to GCHQ through six to nine jobs, including 'starred posts' open only to them, such as 'Current Intelligence Coordination' in J and K divisions. GCTs always served in H division, practised intelligence reporting, and handled a cadet 'project' – a special problem requiring individual judgement. After managing a small section, meeting their boards, which determined their initial promotion either to principal or SEO (senior executive officer), then being given a larger unit to run, they were on their own, confronting the press of people for a narrowing number of senior slots, though from a superior position.

The first generation of AIVs generally made division heads, but not GCTs entering after 1973. The GCT class finally attracted the number of administrators which GCHQ required and provided the means to produce intelligence. Few GCTs became Director. Increasingly, however, GCTs provided most divisional heads and members of the directorate. By 1979, the officer class at GCHQ included 725 EOs and HEOs (higher executive officers), and 295 ex-GCTs, as well as linguist specialists.[24]

GCTs overwhelmingly dominated the senior membership, the assistant secretaries and senior principals of the core departments of Sigint and intelligence production, H, J, K and V, and provided 35 per cent of their middle leaders, principals and senior executive officers. GCTs provided 75 per cent of the thirty-two senior officers in GCHQ as a whole, and 33 per cent of its middle leaders. The lower half of GCTs ranked equal with the upper 25 per cent of executive officers, who dominated the middle leadership. The leading 10 per cent of personnel recruited as executive officers reached the ranks of approximately the upper 50 per cent of GCTs, some entered the directorate, and one became Director.[25]

After Avowal

During the 1960s, GCHQ solved its enrolment problems. From 1975, however, far more graduates applied to GCHQ than ever had before, from new disciplines such as sociology and new institutions such as polytechnics. GCHQ rejected unprecedented numbers and proportions of applicants, raising questions about supply, and reconsidered its own demands. As Hugh Denham, head of H, wrote: 'in the next two decades the practice of SIGINT will change faster and more fundamentally

than it did in the 50's and 60's *[sic]* and even more than it did in the
70's *[sic]*, because 'of computerised intercept stations, computerised
electrical forwarding, computerised handling, processing and storage
at HQ and computerised preparation and distribution of end-product.
These developments may call for a different type – or more precisely
a different mix of types – from what our present practice requires.'[26]
GCHQ considered whether the divisions between old specialisations
and categories, such as 'a. high-flying administrators (the A class)
b. high-powered researchers (the DS class) c. non-specialist, medium-
level researchers and managers (the old Executive class)', remained valid.
Researchers were now required to understand 'resource management'.
GCHQ needed to overcome the 'psychological gap' between the
administrators in A block and the 'operational' areas of Oakley.[27]

During 1979–80, GCHQ painstakingly addressed these issues. Its
conclusions seem sound, however traditionalist the tone. The most elitist
of comments damned polytechnics, yet advocated internal promotions
for non-graduates. A senior member of K division wrote: 'there has
been a steady decline in cadet quality over the past 30 years. Can we
put our hands on our hearts and say we have recruited anybody recently
whose calibre even remotely matches that of, for example, the late
Hugh Alexander or the Cooper brothers? ... individuals are at the heart
of the matter ... our reputation with NSA quite certainly, and with our
London customers and paymasters probably, rests upon the brilliance
of about a dozen individuals throughout GCHQ ... With our budget
about a tenth of NSA's, they would hardly consider us a serious partner
otherwise.' The 'cadet recruitment procedure', he continued, 'should
be unashamedly elitist and concentrate on the top end of the market,
even if this means we get only one or two people a year. I suggest that
the default be made up by internal promotion to GCHQ of those who
joined as EO or equivalent'. The ' "worse-than-average" ex-cadets soon
get overhauled by the best of the ex-EOs', while 'we've seen the people
working for a couple of years and know that they're more or less what
we want'.[28]

GCHQ concluded that its offers to graduates were mediocre
compared to other departments or businesses. Graduates were
more focused than before on careers, salaries and the private sector.
GCCs and GCTs came from eighteen universities, about 30 per
cent from Oxbridge, but rarely the newer red-brick universities or

polytechnics. Excluding mathematics for the codebreakers of H, no academic disciplines predicted success for applicants, but some, such as archaeology, history, engineering and PPE, produced more good candidates than others, such as psychology and politics. It was thought that GCHQ should reform, rather than transform, its recruitment practices. It needed to improve the 'development' of internal candidates for promotion. GCHQ should emphasise the schools and disciplines which produced useful graduates, without ignoring the rest. 'We need to sell the Cadet scheme very hard at the top end of the under-graduate market. So long as we can show that we are fair towards all candidates (including internal candidates) we should not be ashamed to have what many deride as an elitist form of entry ... Status is still of importance to many of the better undergraduates; in recent years we may have tended to undersell ourselves in the pursuit of egalitarianism.'[29]

In order to help UABs and the Civil Service Commission understand the characteristics needed by candidates, GCHQ defined more precise indicators than its previous overused terms, 'puzzle-solving' and 'brightness'. This redefinition illustrated GCHQ's evolving self-image and a more sophisticated assessment of its requirements for personnel. More than any other major element of Whitehall, GCHQ emphasised mind over character, though ability to work in teams was mandatory and qualities of leadership desirable. Divisions expressed different views, which illustrates the range of the department's needs: S emphasised 'curiosity, ability to absorb complicated data (including very technical data), discarding misleading and "wild" data, formulating hypotheses, selection of the most likely, testing them for accuracy, further refining them and if possible proving them, taking account of previous occurrences, and experience elsewhere'; while K preferred 'a lively and curious mind, taking an interest in everything that's going on both on the international scene and locally within GCHQ; the ability to react and adapt instantaneously to a constantly changing situation; and a general willingness to learn enough of a new speciality, be it Arabic, statistics, computing or signals theory, at least to be able to converse sensibly with, or explain a problem to, experts in these areas ... "an intelligence nose" ... we are after people of the same intellectual calibre as CSCB [Civil Service Commission Board] Entrants to the main Admin class, but with a slight technical bent (i.e. not so narrowly technical as to warrant a career in the technicality)'.[30]

GCHQ gave UABs and selection panels a 'GCT profile'. There was no 'single stereotype of ability or formal qualification. Different types of work and, ultimately, different types of career at GCHQ ensure that there will be a mix of successful candidates.' Generally, candidates needed 'qualities of penetration, judgment, originality, independence and persistence', and 'some aptitude for what might be called puzzle-solving ... an interest in solving problems for their own sake, and a bias towards the quantitative, objective, impersonal aspects of a problem'. Candidates required 'a broad capacity to learn "new tricks", and to absorb complex information and to appreciate difficult processes or techniques ... an ability to get on with people and to lead is important. The individual should be prepared to work within a team.' The profile advocated two ideal types of GCT, though rare persons embodied both. One would show 'exceptional ability in the puzzle-solving field ... and should be capable of undertaking original research with persistence and dedication. His or her work will comprise difficult intellectual problems, often involving detailed systems analysis and modern data processing techniques.' The other type would be 'less specialised in ability, while still being of an analytic and numerate cast of mind. His or her strong points will be comprehension of data, insight, deduction, selection and good judgment. A lively curiosity and interest in current affairs (especially foreign affairs and defence) are useful assets. This type of GCT will be expected to write clear and accurate reports and to express himself or herself convincingly in argument and discussion.'[31]

After avowal, GCHQ could also explain itself better to applicants. In 1983, GCHQ's brochures were well pitched to graduates, including photographs of young staff at work and play, its modern offices and stocks of high-end kit. The brochures matched those of any contemporary department, but differentiated GCHQ from them. They told candidates how to contact GCHQ's graduate appointments office. They described explicitly the value of arts, engineering, mathematics and sciences graduates, and GCHQ's linguistic, administrative and policy-making, and engineering, mathematical and scientific streams. These brochures emphasised the charms of Cheltenham – 'one of the pleasantest parts of England' – and its ease of access to the rest of Britain, the quality of GCHQ's sports facilities, alongside the intellectual challenges of the work and its 'creative multi-disciplinary environment'. Although brochures did not explicitly describe Comint among GCHQ's tasks, the point was clear. GCHQ, 'one of the larger Government research organisations', addressed all aspects of communications, emphasising their 'practical use' and 'security'. Its 'main tasks – communication and data-handling projects', were beyond 'the range of those normally encountered elsewhere'. They required 'graduates with sufficiently broad and up-to-date knowledge and sufficient originality of mind to be able to break new ground', while retaining 'a good sense of what is practical'. Linguists and mathematicians learned what elements in their fields were desirable, and computer scientists what kit they could work, or play, with. Abstract algebra, linear algebra, error correcting codes, combinatorial analysis, organisation, Fourier analysis, numerical analysis and information theory – each of these were valued, but above all statistics and probability theory. Attack 'on communications analysis in general requires tackling concrete problems', though some mathematical posts emphasised theory. All candidates would face 'challenging problems with scope for imagination as well as mathematical penetration'. Scientists would confront 'challenges that require thinking along lines outside normal scientific disciplines', develop equipment 'from the applied research stage to the production of the final engineered models', and work closely with consumers and contractors. Managing these programmes, engineers were told, would be taxing but exhilarating.[32]

The Department

GCHQ faced many of the same problems as GC&CS had done regarding promotion and skilled practitioners. As at Bletchley, high standards and low salaries for clerical personnel crippled recruitment and retention. Initially, GCHQ assumed that women, even university graduates, would fill its substantial number of unestablished clerical positions because they would not expect permanent careers and appreciated the marriage bonus offered by the civil service. By 1946, however, GCHQ told the Treasury: 'we cannot recruit, or if we recruit, we cannot hold girls of the requisite quality on the [unestablished] Grade II clerk rate'.[33] GCHQ trained female clerical staff so well that they could easily find better jobs in London, and paid them so little that they preferred to do so. The move to Cheltenham, and access to staff who wished to stay put, ultimately solved that problem, but other issues remained. As one administrator noted: 'We cannot offer public fame or great riches, or indeed a career pinnacle as high as the Civil Service proper; we must therefore sell the job on the positive advantages, which I see as:

a. Supremely, the fascination and importance of the work itself – the mix of technical and administrative qualities;

b. The work environment – very much between the strict rigidity of factory production and the airy-fairyness of most University research departments;

c. The pleasant, stable location – and possibility of overseas tours for those who would like them;

d. The opportunity for the best people of becoming a big fish in a not too big pond.[34]

Proportionate to other government departments, GCHQ needed more first-class minds, from a wider range of areas, including some where candidates were scarce. GCHQ never acquired all of the first-class minds it wished. The figure of 200 assumed a wider organisation of 1,000. As GCHQ reached 4,000 people, did it require 800 administrative officers – more than the Treasury had? Learning from experience in 1919–20, reinforced by Treasury warnings not to hire in large blocks, and with experienced hands already holding most A and B positions, GCHQ avoided mass hirings in 1945–48. This left it ample room to expand and minimised the collection of dead wood at its start. Confident that its establishment was secure, GCHQ was picky in its selection. Combined with its low attractiveness, initially its recruitment was mixed. GCHQ offered AIV entry to people who, having already served in Sigint, whether during the war or for National Service, were known quantities who knew and liked the work. These entry routes produced a large fraction of GCHQ's leadership during the middle Cold War. GCHQ used the old boys' network at universities to find others. GCHQ officers served on CSC panels in order to identify 'near misses' – potential candidates who had not quite reached the status of administrative officers, but who might be right for Cheltenham, especially in the B grades. The situation improved gradually, boosted by broader social changes. The rise in the number of universities put more graduates on the market, many with 'exotic' skills which fitted the needs of GCHQ, such as linguists and scientists. The government's decision in 1949 to allow women to remain civil servants after marriage perhaps reduced problems of retention.

As GCHQ became an increasingly conventional department, it moved to the mean in civil service practices. Hut 3 was the world's leader in information processing for intelligence, but GC&CS had had no expertise in basic administration. Its administrators were brought up to Whitehall standards, ranging from accounting to 'organisation and management', and 'operational research'. Training systems were established for personnel of all ranks, though learning through on-the-job training remained the norm. Underneath this conventional exterior, GCHQ's structure was unique among British departments or firms. And while GCHQ was a factory designed to produce information, not every part of that assembly line required broad or deep skills. The latter could not often be acquired at school or university; graduates could not fill every slot requiring intelligence and initiative – nor would the Treasury have financed that cost. Furthermore, often these positions could not be predicted in advance. Yet so long as GCHQ had enough geniuses and a sound basic system, many means existed to staff the factory. GCHQ's self-image and recruitment practices were unashamedly elitist. Collectively, Siginters were proud of their best individuals as their champions. During the Second World War, few had known 'the Prof'; all prized their association with Turing. Yet GCHQ could not attract all of the elites it needed. Instead, GCHQ used well the elites it could hire and found replacements for those it could not through a process of substitution, which emerged via agency from below more than by policy from above.

Though GCHQ quadrupled in strength between 1946 and 1956, its requirements for first-class minds rose by just 10 per cent. The best executive–class officers handled technical management within units and much of the work assigned to the A class, and competed with them for senior positions. Below, GCHQ was almost equally divided between work units which were regimented and self-contained, whether radio interception or typing pools, or flexible and open-ended. This system helped the able and ambitious to advance. GCHQ offered formal apprenticeships to school leavers and without realising or intending the effect informally served as an apprenticeship itself. In Britain throughout the Cold War, few school leavers received post-secondary education, even after the expansion of that sector during the 1960s. Their employers emphasised on-the-job training, augmented by short courses for specialist topics. Regularly, shrewd school leavers entered business or government and rose to middle or senior management. The largest entry to GCHQ every year were school leavers, most from local backgrounds in and around Gloucestershire, who joined the clerical ranks. The hardest-working group in the Sigint business – the 'Apprentices' Committee' – focused on individuals and matched each departments' needs for skills in hundreds of frequently shifting areas with appropriate technical training for all incoming staff and from the best sources across Britain.[35] Bright entrants, pushed by agency and pulled by the patronage of friends and superiors, tackled advanced work, especially in areas where graduates were few or academic programmes scarce, and where their practical skills and experience met needs – as in the early days of IT.

These young people enabled GCHQ to meet many new developments fast and effectively, whereas trying to do so through graduates took more time and cost. Such practices enabled ambitious members of non-elite classes to rise more than they ever thought possible, and for the 'factory' to function efficiently and economically. GCHQ formalised such opportunities through regular 'limited competition(s) among permanent officers serving at GCHQ in the Executive, Departmental Executive or C class for appointment to the A and Departmental Specialist Classes of GCHQ'. A university degree was 'desirable but not essential' for these posts. Candidates without degrees needed to demonstrate equal 'standard of education and ability': each could apply in both streams, increasing the likely numbers of promotions in each competition. GCHQ extended this approach to technical signals officers, involving the most sophisticated forms of electronics and interception, such as radio telemetry, where GCHQ aimed to demonstrate quality. Military signals officers with science or engineering degrees were preferred, but 'exceptionally other candidates with suitable experience may be considered'. Such limited competitions sopped up the A and DS positions which graduates would not cover. GCHQ's willingness to employ school leavers for such positions indicated their quality and its flexibility.[36]

More men than women exploited these opportunities. Most women at GCHQ who were not university graduates worked in regimented units, with less room to move flexibly, and often had reason to leave GCHQ's employ earlier than others. Given expectations of gender roles, especially in a largely socially conservative part of the country, women took primary responsibility for family commitments. GCHQ became socially more traditional than was usual for Whitehall between 1960 and 1990 because its staff did not change as much as elsewhere. This was due to its provincial location; the large portion of older working class people in its ranks; its difficulties in hiring new personnel from metropolitan areas; and the paucity of new recruits between 1965 and 1985. Photographs of members of GCHQ at work during the 1950s and 1960s show civilian uniforms – men in jackets and ties, even when operating radio sets, pipe-smoking de rigueur; women in tailored clothing of good material, often more distinct than the men, their hair cut in simple yet individual styles. Both women and men followed conservative patterns of dress, looking much alike, though leaders, such as Loehnis, dressed almost raffishly, reflecting the style of the day and a right to distinction. By the late 1960s, styles had changed with greater disposable income especially among the lower classes and changing generational attitudes in terms of display, as the generation of wartime and postwar rationing was replaced by their children. Gradually, men's dress became more casual. Younger women adopted far more distinctive styles and, after 1975, began to wear trousers, and then jeans, to work – anathema a decade earlier.

By contemporary British standards – among white men of all classes – GCHQ's personnel were diverse, especially in higher positions, but only average among women. A 'four British grandparents' rule, originally aimed primarily at Europeans and enacted for security purposes, blocked admission to non-white applicants, though a few did enter. Here GCHQ followed Foreign Office policy for personnel, and until around 1980 adopted a de facto colour bar. Given the use of the Civil Service Commission for executive and administrative grades, and the population of Cheltenham at clerical level, probably few non-white staff would have applied, but racism would likely have constrained the chances of any who did apply. That rule was eventually abolished. Non-white colonial subjects were not employed in Sigint, except in Hong Kong and Singapore.

Specialists

GCHQ's main source for specialists was the universities, through the Civil Service Commission. Though Oxbridge remained the preferred background, openings were advertised at every university. In the postwar period, more working-class people entered university than ever before, broadening the social pool for GCHQ's candidates. Robert Churchhouse, for example, a cryptanalyst and computer systems analyst at GCHQ, 1952–63, and later a key outside advisor and recruiter for candidates from universities, came from an impoverished working-class family in Manchester. Propelled by education in Catholic private schools, he reached Manchester University, where he was taught by Good, Newman and Turing. (When asked what they had done during the war, they replied 'nothing very interesting'.) Then Churchhouse's career became more conventional – a PhD in number theory at Trinity Hall, Cambridge, and recruitment to GCHQ through National Service.[37]

From 1949, women received the same opportunities and, in 1955, pay as men in the civil service. Recruitment and retention were not easy. In order to keep them in place, specialists had to be rewarded. GCHQ's salary structure did so, albeit barely. Once in GCHQ, many specialists looked for a way up, or out. In 1970, for example, both the scientific and administrative streams accepted Dr David Pepper, a graduate in theoretical physics from Oxford, as a GCC. He thought that if he entered the scientific stream he would be competing with mathematicians on their territory, as he wasn't one.[38] So, he entered the general stream, which swept him to several stints of higher Sigint management under the watchful eyes of Marychurch, Adye and Omand, and finally to appointment as Director. GCHQ's size and need to administer itself made management a normal career. For promotion, specialists must cease to practise their speciality, or even, eventually, to manage members of it.

In retrospect, Chief Scientist Ralph Benjamin said: 'GCHQ was always heavily over-subscribed by applicants for appointments. That applied above all to mathematicians. It was well known that the most challenging work in the country for that profession was at GCHQ.'[39] That statement was true from 1970, though not before, and the problems and solutions varied by specialisation. Solving difficult problems – especially by employing leading-edge kit and techniques which were years ahead of those fielded by civilian institutions – offered a delicious mixture of secrecy and superiority in return. It enabled one to be the hidden master, though with the potential for annoyance when a public academic later rediscovered something one had already found in secret but could not publish. When asked whether he was irritated that his work on public-key cryptography remained hidden until decades after the concept was discovered independently elsewhere, Benjamin replied, 'GCHQ gives recognition largely internally. People are very happy who they are working for.'[40] Once within GCHQ, this type of reward attracted specialists of every persuasion, especially those with the scarcest of talents. Cryptanalysts received a rare chance to solve the sorts of problems they longed to attack. As one legendary codebreaker, Paul 'Bunk' Whitehouse, said: 'I cannot imagine anyone paying us to do this work, it is so much fun.'[41] A contemporary cryptanalyst describes cryptanalysis as producing 'lightbulb moments like no other work I've ever done'.[42]

Mathematical cryptanalysts at GCHQ and NSA, exploiting both open work and secret studies, were five to ten years ahead of their civilian colleagues – for example, on public-key cryptography (PKC). James Ellis, a mathematician and computer scientist with a physics degree from Cambridge and experience at the Post Office Research Station at Dollis Hill, joined the Communications-Electronics Security Group (CESG) in 1952. One colleague, Richard Walton, recalled: 'He was a rather quirky worker, and he didn't really fit into the day to day business of CESG. But in terms of coming up with new ideas he was quite exceptional. You had to sort through some rubbish sometimes, but he was very innovative and always willing to challenge the orthodoxy. We would be in real trouble if everyone in GCHQ was like him, but equally we need some people with his flair and originality.'[43] Ellis drove many important cryptographic developments, above all his identification of the concept of PKC, which he lacked the mathematical expertise to realise. Two younger colleagues, both of whom had left PhD programmes in Oxbridge and joined GCHQ, found means to realise this concept. Clifford Cocks, who took a silver medal at the International Mathematical Olympiad in 1968, and later retired as Chief Mathematician at GCHQ, devised the public-key encryption system now known as RSA. Malcolm Williamson, who competed on the British team in the same Olympiad, winning a gold medal, devised a method of public key exchange which allows two parties to obtain a common secret key while communicating only in public. This is now known as the Diffie-Hellman key exchange after the academic researchers who independently found it.

Mathematical authorities at GCHQ, and Churchhouse from the University of Cardiff, confirmed the power of these ideas. GCHQ, however, had little use for PKC, and perhaps feared that to publicise it might cause some targets to heighten their security. This discovery remained classified for years and was used only for Sigint communications. It had little practical use until the invention of the World Wide Web. Now, however, PKC is the basis for all secure transactions on the internet and an unspoken part of the life of billions of people. GCHQ was the secret seedbed for scientific advances which did not become public until rediscovered years later. The discoverers of these results also were independent and original scholars, reflecting how the security around Sigint affects the working of science. As Ellis wrote in 1987: 'Cryptography is a most unusual science. Most professional scientists aim to be the first to publish their work, because it is through dissemination that the work realises its value. In contrast, the fullest value of cryptography is realised by minimising the information available to potential adversaries. Thus professional cryptographers normally work in closed communities to provide sufficient professional interaction to ensure quality while maintaining secrecy from outsiders. Revelation of these secrets is normally only sanctioned in the interests of historical accuracy after it has been demonstrated clearly that no further benefit can be obtained from continued secrecy.'[44]

From the outbreak of the Second World War, knowledge of mathematics replaced that of language as the core of cryptanalysis, though, as ever, success occurred through problem-solving rather than grasp of theory. Until the internet, civilian competition was weak except for the few appointments in universities, at a time when GCHQ salaries were adequate. GCHQ profited from the loose division of pure mathematics into 'two cultures', as the Cambridge mathematician W. T. Gowers wrote: 'the distinction between mathematicians who regard their central aim as being to solve problems, and those who are more concerned with building and understanding theories'.[45] Theorists tended to dominate university mathematics departments, leaving problem-solvers to pursue opportunities elsewhere. Many successful cryppies entered GCHQ after a few years in a PhD programme had demonstrated that theory-building was not for them. If one lived in one's mind, Cheltenham was as good a place to be as any. Cryppies were happy to find GCHQ. It opened their minds and changed their lives.

At universities, GCHQ looked for cryptanalysts exclusively among mathematicians. It understood the emergence of a new study, mathematical cryptanalysis, better than civilian mathematicians initially did. Even when the field was established, GCHQ remained among its greatest finishing schools. In the mid-1950s, H division could not recruit all the mathematical cryptanalysts that it wished to find, partly because the field was only just emerging. Alexander thought that if university mathematicians understood how interesting the field was, they would recommend more students to GCHQ.[46] Secrecy slowed the start and broke the continuity expected in an open field of mathematics, preventing masters from enlightening their students. Despite being taught by those pioneers of mathematical cryptanalysis at Manchester, Churchhouse had no education in the field, until he began to practise it. When he returned to civilian life, he could guide his students in a recognised field.

Ultimately, the old boys' network, friends and ex-colleagues in the mathematics departments at Oxbridge, enabled low-profile talent spotting. Though CSC advertisements usually just mentioned the need for high-quality mathematicians, that lure – and guidance from professors and fellow students already in place – caught sufficient attention in a rich, if narrow, pool. Many candidates were attracted when they heard that Alexander headed the organisation, because they admired his prowess at chess. This approach excluded much other talent from consideration, and tended towards self-reinforcement, selecting individuals of a certain cast of mind and, to some degree, social background. Cryptanalysts were a smaller proportion of GCHQ than they had been at GC&CS, especially before 1939, because so many more people in supporting functions were required. Few cryptanalysts were needed in the first place, wastage was low, and supply was augmented by putting graduates and school leavers from other areas of GCHQ through tours of H division to find people with cryptanalytic flair. Anyone who had the aptitude and inclination found themselves conscripted into cryptanalysis – usually for life – thereby giving the profession diversity by not necessarily being made up of graduates, nor mathematicians, nor Oxbridge-educated, nor even just men.

Recruiting and retaining scientists and engineers posed a greater problem. In 1944–45, key members of Bletchley promoted a machine culture.[47] They focused on a dying breed – mechanical engineers with academic training, but who were driven primarily by practical experience. That influence waned after the war, when a confusing environment emerged. As data-processing machines moved from mechanical to electrical, academic training trumped hands-on expertise. Scientific knowledge was necessary to understand and exploit developments in Comint and computers, yet GCHQ worked beyond academic departments on the leading edge of these activities and the secret spheres that stood further beyond. GCHQ's leaders were not sure what to do with engineering and scientific graduates, nor how to find them. These graduates generally knew nothing of GCHQ. By 1950, Jones was trying to attract them by working through Tizard, who promised help but did not deliver it. However, when Tizard's successor, Williams, insisted that GCHQ create a scientific department, Jones moved fast, despite uncertainty and division among his colleagues. The concentration of scientists in one locale, and the appointment of a senior scientist to manage their recruitment, work and careers, was necessary and helpful, doubly so when engineers received their own division. Still, engineering and scientific entrants were hard to recruit. In 1961, Loehnis expressed 'grave anxiety' over the situation. Five or six senior positions were unfilled, as were 20 per cent of the general positions. Templer warned Whitehall that this situation was 'urgent'.[48]

In Sigint, the supply and demand of engineers and scientists did not mesh, outside competition was great, salaries were low, and wastage high – even though personnel received opportunities to work on the cutting edge, ahead of any non-classified equivalent. GCHQ could not recruit them directly, but only through the Royal Navy Scientific Service, which sometimes was uncooperative. Unlike with mathematicians, GCHQ had to work hard to define its value to engineers and scientists. In 1972, via the CSC, it advertised positions for 'Graduate Electrical Engineers' – in hindsight, among the best postgraduate positions available at the time in an emerging area. This offer reflected GCHQ understanding of the work, and how to handle it:

> The role of the Government Communications Headquarters is to carry out research, development and production in the field of communications on behalf of Her Majesty's Government. It has built up a research and development capability of unique scope and depth and engineers work on problems not found in other organisations, playing a part in producing devices that are in advance of those developed elsewhere. The activities involve all types of communication systems, from closed circuit television and telephone through microwave and satellite systems, to high frequency and very long range radio communications. Throughout the work on this range of systems there is an emphasis on their practical use and particularly on their security.
>
> Graduate Electrical Engineers will be given carefully planned and directed training and experience designed to enable them to undertake full professional engineering duties. They range from the initial interpretation of a non-technical statement of requirement through the management of design and development of the resulting contracts, installation, maintenance and logistic support, to the overall supervision of large projects or functional areas of engineering activity. The training and experience will cover the requirements of the Institution of Electrical Engineers and/ or The Institute of Electrical and Radio Engineers for attaining corporate membership. Some of the training may be given at other government departments or by industrial contractors. A senior engineer will act as tutor and direct the training programme.[49]

Eleven years later, in 1983, after public avowal, GCHQ felt far less need to give engineering applicants detail about their work than it had in 1972, though still more than it did other specialists.[50] GCHQ constantly had fewer engineers and scientists than its establishment strengthened and, for purposes of recruitment and retention, offered them better terms than it did cryptanalysts and linguists. Despite the struggle, from 1970 GCHQ acquired enough staff to solve the problem, augmented by its rare access to work from the world's leaders, American firms and NSA.

Linguists

Machine and computer attack reduced the role of linguists in cryptanalysis. 'Crypt-linguists', combining cryptanalytic and linguistic abilities, remained in K division, in teams whose members were linguists but not cryptanalysts. A situation which Denniston had condemned in 1923 became useful after 1960, because cryptanalysis had changed. Linguists, meanwhile, were needed far more than before as interceptors and translators. The number of intercepts rose exponentially from text by cable or wireless, but especially in voice, taken live or by tape. Much of this work, in through the ear and out through the fingers on the keyboard, was extremely boring and tiring. Many types of linguists were needed, which government departments described by different ranges of terms, such as 'limited', 'simple', 'educated' and 'bilingual'.[51] For Siginters, these types included first class, or interpreters, able to translate voice or text instantaneously and precisely; second class, able to translate complicated messages accurately, given time and dictionaries; and elementary or 'applied', able to capture military voice messages using limited and stereotyped vocabularies. 'Applied Language Training' was the only form of language education specific to Sigint.

GCHQ found linguists through variants of traditional means. Between 1800 and 1945, British universities and colonial governments had created language and area studies schools for the education of imperial officials. Whereas the military trained officers in foreign languages and cultures to create and acquire interpreters and intelligence officers, including personnel employed on Sigint, the Foreign Office expected applicants to acquire languages at their own cost. Language schools aimed to create small numbers of first- or second-class linguists, with one exception: every British officer of the Indian Army had to know one Asian language well; many knew several. That officer corps required 2,500–3,000 first-class linguists at any time, and over a hundred new ones every year. The Indian Army was probably the greatest consumer of Asian linguists in the Western world.

Initially, British Sigint followed and exploited these models, relying on the universities and military systems. In 1940, however, new demand for linguists swamped British Sigint; few organisations in Britain, or the world, had ever needed so many linguists as GC&CS. Its internal priorities, and those of the government, gave GC&CS thousands of linguists, many university trained, especially women. Tiltman overcame the main lacunae by creating a course which converted hundreds of classicists into functional Japanese linguists within forty-four weeks, rather than the three years recommended by academics. Professors, focused on the fine points of poetry in foreign languages, often overrated the linguistic requirements for Sigint. GCHQ viewed languages with ruthless functionality, as tools to handle tasks.

Until 1961, National Service enabled great days for linguists and GCHQ. It propelled social mobility, enabling young working-class men to rise and departments to tap new pools of talent. The services, flush with money and able manpower, needed linguists as interpreters and intelligence officers, especially for Sigint. They handled that work for GCHQ, without needing its direct involvement. Across the Five Eyes, strategic departments drove language and area studies programmes at universities. In Britain, the needs were overwhelmingly in Russian, with about 5 per cent each in Arabic and Mandarin. Whitehall underwrote the greatest Chinese and Russian area studies schools in Britain which, focused on the highest end of studies, aided talent-spotting. In 1963, the professors of Chinese languages at Oxford and Cambridge, David Hawkes and Denis Twitchett, were both ex-Siginters. The armed services also created excellent language schools, for training at all levels from elementary to advanced, against the tongues of the targets of the Cold War.

From the end of the European war in May 1945, GCHQ began with many excellent civilian linguists – though not in the main emerging areas of Russian or other eastern European languages, nor in Mandarin, and especially not in voice. Military Siginters overcame these weaknesses and enabled GCHQ to locate and attract new candidates. The dissolution of empire released officers with rare expertise in African and Asian languages, looking for new careers. From 1959, however, conditions began to change. The end of National Service eliminated manpower and funding for linguists. As military budgets tightened, some service schools closed and pressure mounted to reduce costs in language training. The service education branches and language schools began to defend parochial interests. Likewise, each department had distinct and legitimate needs for languages and parochial interests, preventing an overall rationalisation of effort. The decline of the services' Sigint bodies forced greater GCHQ involvement in policy concerning languages.

The abandonment of preparation for prolonged war reduced the requirement for first- and second-class linguists, almost by half around 1960. Requirements for voice interception rose, as did recognition that operators with small vocabularies could meet much of this need.[52]

Linguists employed as interpreters in NATO were easily found. Service schools still met needs for intelligence officers in what were called 'hard' languages – primarily Arabic, Mandarin and Russian. As demand changed and then declined, problems emerged with supply, especially the split between clashing interests. British language schools, civilian and service, were excellent but, like those of other countries, did not play well together. Government consumers of linguists wanted universities to meet their needs. Language departments wanted governments to subsidise students who would be taught languages in a way that reflected their departmental academic or literary focus. Such graduates were essential for interpreters, required by the Foreign Office, GCHQ and the services, but not for the largest classes needed in Sigint, where, of every hundred linguists, probably fifty were elementary, forty-five second class, and five first class.

Led by A. K. V. Cooper, head of K and a renowned Chinese linguist, during the 1960s GCHQ shaped this environment to meet its linguistic ends. Cooper analysed in detail all aspects of language instruction, consumers and producers of languages, and GCHQ's need for linguists. Some of his efforts were ambitious but abortive. For years, he led GCHQ to pursue command of the British national effort in languages, coordinating all producers and consumers – every university language department and the government units which used them. The universities rejected his proposal that Britain focus its linguistic resources on 'instruction', driven by consumers, rather than 'education', defined by educators, and likewise rejected his effort to coordinate a national programme in Chinese studies for all universities in Britain.[53] Cooper, however, did establish a central, independent and inexpensive position for GCHQ in government policy and resources for languages. After visiting Hong Kong, he concluded that in order to handle their jobs, many intercept operators needed only a twelve-week course, rather than the standard forty-four (later raised to fifty-two)-week one. This step eased the supply of a scarce source of expertise which was chronically hampering GCHQ.

Amidst changes and cuts, often focused on the details of instruction or moves involving just two students or instructors, GCHQ improved the working of the service schools and generally of languages in Sigint.[54] A new source was found. Templer thought that women were 'particularly suitable for Sigint work which is on the whole more attractive to women and for which women have a special aptitude'. He hoped that his reforms would entice 'substantial numbers of women graduates from the red brick universities' to enter GCHQ, which proved true, if less pronounced than he hoped.[55] A new 'linguist specialist' class, fusing area and language studies, for 'specialisation in the recovery of knowledge from cryptic material in foreign languages', created intelligence analysts and culturally aware translators. One linguist stated that: 'Members of the LAS class ought to be the sort of people who learn languages for the fun of it.'[56] Applicants were told that, initially, they would work within a team, but as they rose were 'likely to assume increasing responsibility for the administration and the technical direction of the work'. They required 'linguistic ability of a high order. Candidates should be interested in the everyday use of language rather than in literature, and they should possess or be capable of acquiring a thorough knowledge of one or more modern foreign languages both written and spoken ... the Commissioners will look for evidence of capacity to learn difficult languages. Versatility, breadth of interest, and an analytical approach are important qualities.'[57] GCHQ's brochure of 1983 repeated these points, with even more emphasis on the prospect that linguists should contemplate a broad career in administration: 'Versatility, breadth of mind and an interest in world affairs will help linguists to accumulate the necessary background information to enable them to appreciate readily the content and significance of a variety of technical and semi-technical material.'[58] Self-study would give crypt-linguists the background 'Distribution and Requirements' had provided codebreakers at GC&CS.

This linguist specialist class of 200 staff, with a career progression parallel to the A and DS classes, made up the main part of GCHQ's addition of graduates in the 1960s. Initially, as Nicholl, the head of K, complained in 1968, it 'brought us disappointingly few recruits from outside the Sigint world'.[59] This class took years to be filled, more through redirection of internal resources than new recruitments, but at least it outpaced attrition, and boosted GCHQ's power in languages and analysis.

For languages within Sigint, problems with supply and demand never ended, though GCHQ always managed to meet minimal requirements, and sometimes did better. Snapshots show the varying demands and supplies for languages during the Cold War. In 1960, primarily for purposes of Sigint, the three services planned to train thirty-two officers and twenty-three other ranks annually to interpreter status, and 120 other ranks to elementary status. Almost 80 per cent of the posts involved Russian.[60] In 1967, GCHQ believed that it needed to hire twenty-five new linguists, sixteen for Russian, three African, one Turkish, four Arabic and one Chinese;[61] K division thought that annual requirements for Mandarin added up to two new interpreters, twelve graduates of the forty-four-week course, and sixteen from the twelve-week programme;[62] and to reallocate one or two Arabists from military Sigint posts was hard, while temporarily increasing their training from one to six per year was a major investment. Between 1967 and 1971, British-born Russian linguists, perhaps numbering forty, filled 45 per cent of the bottom linguist specialist rung in J division. Yet during the 1970s, J division faced chronic shortages of executive and clerical staff with basic or O level equivalent Russian, to handle the most elementary processes – such as log-reading, needed to move the linguistic assembly line along. It acquired barely half the seventeen to twenty-one personnel per year with O level equivalents calculated as necessary to meet needs and cover attrition and provide flexibility for these personnel to handle other tasks.[63] By 1982, this problem had declined in force, while another rose, 'with the massive influx' of voice material which became accessible through the Natural Language databases. J division had only thirty-five of the fifty-one translators required from the executive class, with wastage rates at about 25 per cent over the previous four years.[64]

Voice posed particular problems of supply and demand. In 1956, GCHQ told the CSC that over the next three years it needed to hire 'about 25 people with a near-perfect knowledge of certain foreign languages. The ability must include a thorough grasp of the present-day colloquial languages and an ability to reconstruct conversations which might be conducted at high speed, imperfectly heard, and containing specialised jargon. Most of these recruits would be needed for Russian, though a few would be required for other East European languages, and for Arabic.' The CSC replied that 'even if modern language graduates of sufficient linguistic proficiency could be found, they were unlikely to find the type of work or the career prospects of the post attractive'. It suggested that GCHQ look to existing 'bi-lingual candidates' and concluded that it 'may decide that they do not really want such a high degree of proficiency for what one suspects may be menial linguistic work'.[65] Later, service schools and Cooper concluded that specialised training could produce competent voice operators in 12–44 weeks. GCHQ found voice linguists from three sources. Graduates from universities or service schools handled the most sensitive and important translation tasks. Non-academic bilingual resources addressed less secret but linguistically complicated material. From 1958 until 1976, the London Processing Group (LPG), a large body of eastern European emigrés, mostly Poles, drove UKUSA's exploitation of plain-language traffic from Eastern bloc countries. When the supply of elderly Poles declined, GCHQ independently found new British recruits, which it fed in through the CSC.[66] A dozen Eurasian and ethnic Chinese linguists intercepted voice from Hong Kong, despite the de facto colour bar, proving GCHQ's difficulties in procuring competent personnel. Finally, military schools taught lance corporals from the Intelligence Corps – men already committed to a career – elementary military German, Mandarin or Russian, to allow them to successfully intercept rather than translate voice traffic. GCHQ adopted the same process to train personnel for elementary processing in J division: 'We take whomever we get, and do the best we can with them – and with a fair degree of success.'[67] Like Denniston's conversion of clericals to cryptanalysts, training lower-grade personnel to handle sophisticated problems helped sidestep financial limitations. 'Lifers', often from relatively humble backgrounds, reached a better position than they might have elsewhere, and simplified GCHQ's search for expensive applicants and also its training needs.

The main sources for translators were the universities, augmented by service schools. GCHQ, like the services, usually dodged special programmes organised by the universities because of cost, but was happy to hire regular graduates. University graduates who entered GCHQ did not know that they were becoming Siginters, but already were some way towards accepting that status. They knew they were entering a Joint Technical Languages Service (JTLS), co-located with GCHQ, which valued their linguistic expertise more than other government departments. They were eschewing the main areas of employment in their field – teaching and business – and moving to Cheltenham. Though pay and conditions were tolerable, linguists could easily enter other fields at GCHQ. Wastage – flowing elsewhere within as well as out of GCHQ – was high over a ten-year period, including perhaps 30 per cent of Russian linguists and 60 per cent of those from other languages. This loss of scarce skills seems high, but perhaps was inevitable. Most translation tasks were numbingly repetitive while, inevitably, some candidates failed the high demands of the 'linguist specialist' class.

Overall, GCHQ consumed a small part of British graduates in languages. The best of them received fascinating opportunities – to know hidden things, to become the world's authority on some issues, however secret, and to shape high policy. GCHQ squeezed the linguistic value from the rest and then discharged them, while giving these people alternative, and often satisfying, opportunities. Linguists provided most of the graduates who were redeployable to other areas of GCHQ, and were needed there. They offered an area studies background well suited to analysis and personalities perhaps better suited to administration than those of other specialists. Along with the executive class, they were the valuable reserve army of the redeployed in boosting GCHQ's administrative capacity.

Comint and Technology

GCHQ is a high-technology and machine-intensive institution. At any time, its range of equipment includes obsolescent material – kept because it works and is cheap – up to the most advanced and expensive machines of the day, which alone can solve essential problems. People and kit have baroque relationships, which change constantly and often in radical, sudden and unexpected ways. From 1940 all the way to 2020, GCHQ's most consistent form of technology was five-hole punched tape, through which data was entered into machine-readable or digitised form, while computers drove the greatest changes in technology and organisation. Yet during the shorter period of the Cold War, the rise and fall of typewriters – seemingly mundane equipment – transformed work and gender roles across GCHQ more than any other piece of kit.

Radio and punchcards dominated the first age of Sigint. Different forms of paper drove data processing and machine and computer cryptanalysis. Around 1965, an ICL 1904 computer 'with about the processing power of a digital watch [of *c*.1995 vintage] ... occupied most of F Block. If you wanted to run a programme you produced your own punch cards or wrote it out and sent it to the punch room to be produced, then you carried them up the hill to F Block – woe betide you if you dropped them on the way! Three days later – or the next day if it was a really high priority – you'd get the answer back but most crypt was faster by hand.' A decade later, computer cryptanalysts, 'sent jobs across town by van on decks of punched cards, getting the results back 24 hours later. We prepared the cards on card punches, huge machines themselves, the size of desks. Alternately you could write your code up on pre-printed FORTRAN coding sheets, and have them punched up by professional typists.'[68] Later, analysts tore work off remote terminals and studied them at their desks, while others examined their problems online, with more waiting their turn. During the Falklands conflict, paper reprographic systems posed key limits on GCHQ. The team assaulting Argentine traffic could print material only by gaining night-time access to one photocopier, while the British fleet had but three Sigint printers, one with each of the main shipborne parties.

Throughout the Cold War, the British services had many successes and failures with research and development and procurement of equipment. This record was slightly better than that of most Western states, but still unimpressive. The problem was not one of resources, where Britain still had blessings, but one of overambition: British services, engineers and firms tried to compete with those of every other nation in all areas of military significance. As a result, Britain produced much good and some world-leading kit, but pursued too many programmes, most having few orders, which generally served to heighten unit costs. Financial and technological resources were spread thin, making projects more expensive, prone to delay, and often inferior in cost-effectiveness to the best equipment produced elsewhere. Britain survived the worst cases only by relying on American generosity, at some political cost.

GCHQ had the same mixed record as the services, though for different reasons and with a sharper learning curve. It confronted new problems in conducting and financing research, development and procurement on several leading edges of technology – especially with communication and computers. Before 1939, British data-processing and communications firms and technology were excellent. Individuals and firms built effective material at small cost, for the tiny numbers required. Given its priority, Bletchley easily procured world-leading kit in quantities. From 1945, Britain's power in communication systems and technology declined, though it remained formidable. Britain lost many of the advantages of cost and technology which underpinned the acquisition of equipment. Sigint involved large amounts of material from the most advanced technology in several fields. More than in most components of force, the cost of Sigint exploded, especially with the need to acquire Rapid Analytical Machines (RAMs), computers, and collection platforms; and likewise in procuring American kit which Britain had to buy with dollars, which were a scarce commodity.

How Computers Came to Cheltenham

In 1945, GCHQ led the world in data processing and pioneered the development of computers and mathematical cryptanalysis. Over the next decade, British academics and firms were a powerful presence in computing. From the University of Manchester, Newman and Turing liaised with GCHQ, especially their colleagues who managed cryptanalysis, Dr Gerry Morgan and Alexander. Jack Good, a leader at Bletchley and in mathematical cryptanalysis, rejoined GCHQ from Manchester from 1948 to 1959, while Turing worked at Cheltenham for several weeks.

GCHQ watched the development of computers more than any other institution in Whitehall, where they were merely means for accounting. It gave staff remarkably advanced lectures on the present state and trends with computers, which perhaps two or three universities in the world could have matched.[69] Despite its experience with research and development and procurement, however, GCHQ failed to develop RAMs and computers well for cryptanalytic purposes. For the first time, GCHQ pursued a general and long-term programme of research and development, but one which it did not control. Fairly quickly and for many reasons it lost the people, such as Gordon Welchman and Tommy Flowers, who had driven these programmes during the war, and lost its status as Britain's leading priority in technology. Symbolically, the GPO disassembled eight of the ten Colossi in 1945, not as is often assumed to ensure secrecy – that was provided just by people not talking – but to reuse the parts for civilian equipment. GCHQ retained four Robinsons and two Colossi, their circuitry reconfigured, along with its best tabulators, in order to attack Soviet teleprinter traffic.

GCHQ liaised with computing and data-processing firms, but not on cryptanalytic machines. Contrary to its plans of 1945, GCHQ did not link cryptanalysts and engineers, nor establish its own research and development or manufacturing capacity for cryptanalytic machines. However, it built some small ones, and bought an early commercial computer, the Ferranti Mark I*, codenamed Cleopatra, which attacked specialist problems until 1958. Neither Peter Twinn, head of the Machine Section, nor Tiltman, the Chief Cryptographer, advocated more ambitious programmes; GCHQ already had colossal power, guided by the world's best machine cryptanalysts, and handled all of the problems it needed to attack until 1948. GCHQ perceived the technical problems within Britain's computing effort better than any other government agency – matched only by a few researchers, mostly veterans of Bletchley – but made no effort to solve them.

These failures stemmed from disorganisation over science and technology within GCHQ, with the Machine Section being its Cinderella.[70] Initially, GCHQ left the GPO to handle research and development and production for the matter, which was outside the latter's mainstream, and tasked the services research elements and its own Government Communications Research Establishment to develop Sigint equipment. Later, the Royal Navy Scientific Service and the Defence Research Policy Staff of the MOD joined this process, but did no better. Several sections of GCHQ each had a few scientists to advise on special problems, such as radio equipment or computers. Because GCHQ did not know what the efficient use of science or scientists could provide, its senior members did not know what it was missing, with one exception – Gerry Morgan. In 1955, he proposed that GCHQ create a scientific branch, to oversee research and development and corral the scientists spread across departments. GCHQ's leadership rejected this position. Each department wished to control the scientists it employed, but all requested advice from the MOD's Scientific Advisor, E. C. Williams. He offered a blistering, and prescient, critique:

1. From the outside, it seems extraordinary that an organisation as large and as important as GCHQ should not have a Research and Development Division; and, equally importantly, should not have scientific participation at all levels in the formation of policy.

2. The future contribution to intelligence-gathering by GCHQ will depend essentially upon scientific and technical cleverness. That being so, the root problem is to ensure the continuance and expansion of scientific assistance to GCHQ whether internally or from outside.

3. The environment in which scientists work, or to which they supply assistance, is of dominating importance. It is necessary that scientists should believe, and be manifestly shown, that any organisation in which they work, or to which they supply assistance, is so arranged that the scientists' views and methods of thought receive proper attention at all levels of policy-making.

4. There is thus no choice but to set up a Research and Development Division at GCHQ, responsible for all Sigint research and development whether carried on inside GCHQ or outside, and taking its proper share in the formulation of Directorate policy.[71]

GCHQ Director Jones immediately accepted Williams's advice, unilaterally overturning the views of his own directorate. He made Morgan head of M division, with control over all engineering and scientific staff in GCHQ. Josh Cooper – personally respected and the senior officer most experienced at coordinating technology and Sigint – became the member of the directorate responsible for overseeing the issue, perhaps to assuage relations between Morgan and the rest of GCHQ. M division started with a staff of 225, including 10 per cent of GCHQ's 'first-class minds', virtually all the relevant B-grade personnel, twenty professional scientists and nine engineers. It quickly unified and strengthened GCHQ's scientific resources, pursued a rationalised programme of research and development and operational research, and enabled GCHQ to enter the scientific age of cryptanalysis as it dawned. From 1956, GCHQ quickly developed the means to pursue a rational policy towards engineering and science, though hiring personnel proved hard.

RAMs and computers involved some of the most complex programmes of research and development and manufacture in the world. RAMs were far more powerful for specialised tasks than general-purpose computers, but often had only one application, which might vanish. General-purpose machines avoided that problem and produced the greatest return in the long term, as many expected, but were weak in the short term. Success in developing cryptanalytic machines required the pursuit of many devices at once. GCHQ could have done so only had it handled its resources very well. Instead, its management was mediocre. GCHQ did not understand the problem or its mistakes until they had occurred. American Sigint handled these issues somewhat better, though mostly because it had greater resources. It pursued new RAMs after the war, partly to match GCHQ. The key difference was that US Sigint had resources enough to cover all bets: to run several programmes simultaneously, fail in many, and win through one success. A vibrant American industry – supported by American Sigint, and driven by the behemoth IBM and many other big beasts – developed undisputed superiority in computer technology and capacity. Sigint orders sustained strong firms, and created competitive cooperation. By 1956, NSA had created a new norm for cryptanalysis and was learning how to handle it.[72]

GCHQ failed in the key component of cryptanalysis, where its partner succeeded. In 1957, Morgan, who understood this situation better than anyone else, feared that, given the growing discrepancy between the American and British computing industries, 'the co-operation and collaboration which [GCHQ] enjoy with the Americans would tend to cease, presumably much in the same way that it had ceased in the field of nuclear energy'.[73] Contrary to these fears, NSA helped GCHQ to solve this problem, in order to maintain their partnership. NSA was generous but not altruistic. By comparison, the British Atomic Energy Research Establishment at Harwell was in a junior position to its American counterpart because the United States needed no help from Britain with atomic weapons. Conversely, during the 1950s, British Sigint still outstripped American; GCHQ had given NSA far more help than it had received up to this point. GCHQ's efforts bolstered NSA's highest Sigint priorities and reinforced its reputation in cryptanalysis. When opportunity knocked, NSA gave its cryptanalytic advances to GCHQ, wholesale.

The Birth of Computerised Cryptanalysis in Britain

In 1955, the United States government established the Mutual Weapons Development Program (MWDP) which subsidised allies to develop military capabilities. NSA realised that it could gain by helping GCHQ to bid on these opportunities, which the latter did, successfully. Through three three-year programmes between 1955 and 1965, codenamed HUSH I, II and III, MWDP subsidised GCHQ to acquire staff, advanced computers and intercept and Elint kit. MWDP perhaps doubled GCHQ's expenditure on leading-edge material during that decade. HUSH I equalled, in financial terms, 10 per cent of one year's cost of British Sigint.[74] For free, this programme enabled NSA to increase the cryptanalytic power of UKUSA, salvage a partner, and let GCHQ enter the new age of cryptanalysis, just as it began. Important targets were adopting cryptosystems which computerised cryptanalysis alone could attack. This case, NSA's first great financial contribution to British Sigint, did not entirely please Whitehall. The Treasury feared, rightly, that soon Britain would have to pay to continue the project. The British ambassador to Paris and old intelligence hand Gladwyn Jebb, said: 'I hope you know what you are doing, Jones; we surely don't want to be tied to the Americans' apron-strings!'[75] Later, the services sought to seize some of the funds for their own Sigint services, provoking a spanking from Solly Zuckerman, the Scientific Advisor to the MOD. MWDP funds were being provided, Zuckerman opined, because American authorities had 'an unbounded admiration of the British Sigint effort and output': to quarrel 'about the division of the loot' would 'not only be stupid but ungracious'.[76]

In 1958, GCHQ received its first advanced computer, a 1103A UNIVAC Remington Rand, which it codenamed Effigy. Ninety-five per cent of its time was allocated to attacking high-priority cryptosystems and five per cent to 'the stock-in-trade of present-day Sigint production'. Through this five per cent, GCHQ quickly solved a system which had defied NSA's computerised cryptanalysis.[77] However, the limits to its capacity were clear. In 1961, GCHQ used its independent computing power to break one set of cryptosystems, only by risking continuity against a different set. MWDP provided another advanced computer by 1960, the CDC 1604, precisely as American military consumers received it. Annually, between 1960 and 1964,

GCHQ purchased one CDC miniature computer to work with the CDC 1604. From 1963, at the rate of one every two years and then faster, it began to acquire new state-of-the-art computers, especially from IBM, such as the ICT 1301 and IBM 1410, and then IBM 360s and 370s.[78] When MWDP funds ended, NSA let GCHQ purchase with sterling cutting-edge American computers and to control their use. In the later 1960s, GCHQ bought the IBM 360 and 370 systems and a British ICL 4–70. This process strengthened GCHQ's power when it was needed and reinforced its ability to upgrade systems and combine seemingly incompatible ones.

GCHQ quickly acquired hardware and software at the state of the commercial art, becoming the largest and most sophisticated user outside the United States. From 1960, GCHQ procured and used computers well, partly because experienced and technically qualified managers handled the task, unlike any other British department of the day, while Whitehall let it act independently. Especially under the dirigiste and technocratic Wilson governments, which inadvertently delayed Whitehall's adoption of computers by years, authorities made departments purchase British-designed and manufactured systems unless they cost 25 per cent more than foreign competitors, or enter single-vendor contracts. Sometimes, especially on minor systems, Whitehall made GCHQ do the same. In the later 1960s, GCHQ brought a British ICL 4-70 computer with so many technical flaws that GCHQ cryptanalysts refused to use it. The machine became a glorified Hollerith system for other Sigint purposes, after GCHQ engineers improved its performance and reliability.[79] Normally, however, Whitehall let GCHQ pursue a distinct strategy – to buy the best American computers and train a workforce to use them. Throughout the Cold War, IBM Britain was GCHQ's major contractor. IBM offered the best kit – purchasable with pounds, sidestepping the problem of foreign exchange – which was also compatible with NSA's equipment. GCHQ resisted purchasing British-built computers, which were inferior to American ones. Its relations with British firms were frosty. That isolation marked Whitehall's mistakes concerning computing and the British industry's slide from world leadership to receivership between 1945 and 1990.

GCHQ and the British Computing Industry

Since 1830, the British state has worked closely with communications and data-processing firms, to their mutual benefit, with one terrible exception: the computing industry. During the Cold War, many British defence electronics firms did well, aided by Whitehall, including GCHQ and CESG. In computing, GCHQ and British academics and software engineers punched well above their weight, but manufacturers failed, and fell. That collapse stemmed from special circumstances: the weaknesses of British firms and the power and ferocity of their competitors. In 1945, IBM was far richer, stronger and better organised than any British competitor. IBM and other American firms hungered for expansion in computers, where the American market, driven by government spending, exceeded that of the rest of the world for generations. British computer firms were led less ably than the most successful of British manufacturers in high-technology areas or defence technology, like Plessey, Marconi and Vickers, though they had some associations with those businesses. British state orders for computers never could have matched American ones, but the government's policy towards them was myopic. Siginters were a minor factor in this failure, but a useful mirror for it.

Former Bletchley hands were central to Whitehall's first attempts to formulate policy in the area. Their involvement reflects their unique expertise in the area and Whitehall's inability to understand it. When Stuart Milner-Barry, the only mandarin of the time to understand data processing, took over computer policy for the Treasury in 1956, he consulted widely, including Gordon Welchman (whose 'long shots have in the past had an uncanny knack of coming off') and GCHQ. Milner-Barry thought GCHQ personnel were good engineers but naive policymakers. They 'are generating considerable heat amongst themselves about the lack of effective direction of computer effort in the U.K'. They understood the technical problems of the British computer industry better than any other authorities in Britain, but not economics, innovation or serendipity. Their solutions were naively technocratic: a national effort in computing, with 'a powerful central government research and development organisation' to guide firms, including what hardware to manufacture, and each firm to construct only one type of kit.[80] Experience of life only within a command economy, featuring centralised control of resources, shaped GCHQ's thinking about science, industry, and research and development during the 1950s. These ideas quickly improved. Meanwhile, France and Japan adopted better statist policies, which worked well for them, and Britain moved in the same direction.

Ex-Bletchley hands saw the problem, but not any solutions. When Milner-Barry left his post, GCHQ was cut from decisions and government authorities turned to the magic of managerial solutions. By 1968, Whitehall saw that Britain's computing industry was failing; it tried to counter this decline by unifying the many firms building computers into International Computers Limited, ICL. Only when Whitehall again brought GCHQ into its decisions did it really understand the problems.

GCHQ knew where computers and their industries would evolve over the next generation, better than any but a few academics, and mastered the technological, organisational, policy and financial elements of the problem. In 1971, for Whitehall as a whole, GCHQ assessed ICL's next generation of computers. Its team included five seasoned specialists, scientists and senior administrators (the only ones in Britain expert in the field), including Churchhouse – once a mathematical cryptanalyst and systems analyst at GCHQ, and its expert in British-made computers, and now Professor of Mathematics at Bristol University. Given ICL's chaotic history during the 1960s, Churchhouse and other members of the team understood ICL's weaknesses better than it did. GCHQ pledged 'that no unfairness' would occur during the examination because of its superiority in knowledge over ICL. It concluded that the British computer industry could thrive only if ICL's management was purged and technically competent leaders assigned. After this investigation, Whitehall gutted ICL's management and the apologias of its allies in government, though British policy in the area remained poor.[81]

During the first two generations of the computer age, the government's lack of technical expertise damaged policy decisions towards computers, as did divisions between undercapitalised and poorly managed firms. No one could have matched the United States and IBM in this area, but Britain also fell astern of France, Germany and Japan, which started behind it. Secrecy prevented GCHQ from helping Britain as much as it could have done with computers. When asked to advise Whitehall, GCHQ helped it finally to understand its environment, but whether better integration of GCHQ into decision-making would have helped is uncertain.

The Rise of Computerised Cryptanalysis in Britain

By 1967, GCHQ upgraded its databases to enable, within a year or so, 'a disc store with a capacity of some 200 million characters' or 200 megabytes, which was large for the day. Remote-access stations, each costing £11,000 per unit, let many users access this data simultaneously.[82] Between 1970 and 1977, GCHQ doubled its number of supercomputers and its data storage and physical floor space (from 3,600 to 6,200 megabytes, and 11,400 to 26,000 square feet). By 1977, GCHQ had four supercomputers, a 'brand new' CDC 7600 (Pole Star), an IBM 370/165 and 370/168 (Twin Star), and an old war horse, an IBM 360/85. Normally the latter three machines were integrated, using the same peripherals – as all four could be, in need, operated by only one controller. They worked as parallel systems. Normally, Pole Star handled cryptanalysis and the others processed data for J – the core of its work: ILC traffic, support for speech research and miscellaneous tasks.[83] A Univac 1108 and twenty-one Honeywell 316 and 516 machines ran one of the world's largest and most advanced computer control systems at Bude. GCHQ constantly patched the hardware and software for the Univac 1108, 'to the point where the original structure is no longer visible, and many programs have been completely rewritten or have disappeared'.[84] This system carried GCHQ to triumph in the Falklands conflict. GCHQ also routinely applied microcomputers to smaller tasks, such as station control. In 1981, seven Hewlett-Packard microcomputers were on hand and seven on order for tasks such as call sign conversion.[85]

The success of this effort is hard to define. As one cryppie recalled: 'The 70s and 80s were wonderful times for machine cryptanalysis. Within the UKUSA community, the science of cryptanalysis was very advanced, and there were rich pickings to be had,' especially when 'ignorant clients' bought 'laughable machines', which sometimes replaced systems GCHQ could not break. 'Those happy days are, I fear, long gone. If there is a lesson from all that, it is that Siginters must make hay while the sun shines.'[86] The sheer number of solutions by K Division, driven by the computerised cryptanalytic system Hectra, is impressive. In 1979, K issued 11,000 reports of its own, and reissued 33,000 from NSA.[87]

That success, GCHQ rightly claimed, stemmed from 'the policy of automation and software development over previous years and the need to continue to invest in this area. The power of Pole Star and Tri Star and the capability of Hectra and existing crypt programmes enabled H division (but only just) to maintain the flood of timely decrypts that provided the foundation of K's reporting.' So too, with its computerised distribution system, New Moon, and data retrieval systems. The computer branch 'X considers foresight in long term planning the key to effective computer support. The basis of our success in MARGAY [operations in the Falklands] lies in the HECTRA and HIGH KICK initiative of the 1970s, the persistence in developing the systems over a long period, and allowance for growth potential. Likewise our current plans for computer acquisition and new systems under development will lay the foundations for future success.'[88] These plans succeeded in the 1980s, but by 1990, GCHQ had fallen behind universities and leading-edge firms in addressing the new world of personal computers and the internet. New recruits were struck by GCHQ's backwardness in computers, though it recovered quickly, and faster than NSA.

The Royal Navy always travels first class, wrote the Edwardian admiral Jacky Fisher – and so did NSA. GCHQ moved by coach. Characteristically, between 1956 and 1980, GCHQ was well behind NSA in power of supercomputers; it had fewer of them and they were further behind the state of the art. After 1982 that power rose steadily. Access to NSA computer cryptanalysis became normal, though from the start GCHQ pursued an independent path. GCHQ could adopt or adapt American systems, or develop its own. In attacking its own specialised tasks, it matched NSA, and equalled any other advanced users, with remarkable cost efficiency. This economical policy avoided the waste inherent in NSA's tendency to solve problems by throwing money at them, and its love for the most recent systems – which lumbered Fort Meade with lemons, such as the Cray X-MP. GCHQ's need to improve old or mediocre systems strengthened its powers in creating cryptanalytic software and its limits in brute force drove it to search for cheap short cuts and reinforcements. Probably, moreover, it exploited the frustration of British software engineers at the incoherent policy of computer firms.

The opportunities at Cheltenham would have attracted any programmer who knew of them and whose characteristics easily fitted GCHQ. As Jerry Poulden, the head of computerised cryptanalysis at GCHQ, wrote in 1971: 'The ingredients for success' in software development 'are that most basic of resources, brainpower, and the necessary collections of hardware on which the programmes can be developed and proved … Like many other creative work, software is ultimately a highly individual job; and many programmers of distinction are introverted.'[89] The introduction of computers forced changes on GCHQ. It altered workspaces, recruited different personnel, and placed computer staff on a three-shift-per-day basis, so as not to waste the power of the machines. This ruffled staff, perhaps because it forced women who staffed computers into unaccustomed work patterns, which disrupted their family responsibilities.

By 1965, GCHQ was among the world's best users of computers, tied with many American government organisations, and well behind perhaps only the US Social Security Administration, NSA and IBM. Computers colonised the largest space at Oakley, F Block Annexe, but this was not enough. Between 1973 and 1977, GCHQ restructured its holdings in Cheltenham to create a specialised building, G Block, where computers were based alongside F Block Annexe. Before the digital age, computers were capital-intensive systems, requiring complex forms of labour-intensive handling. Ultimately, the move from cryptanalysis using electromechanical machines and RAMs to electronic computers, drove a structural shift in personnel and organisation from mechanical engineers, inventors and workshops, towards electrical engineers, computer scientists, mathematicians, universities and factories. By 1981, one computer officer at GCHQ noted that 'the high demand on scarce programming resources' was the real bottleneck for computer projects and for cryptology.[90]

Just Who Are These Guys, Anyway?
A Historical-Sociological Analysis of GCHQ, 1939–89

Women at GCHQ

Often when thinking of women at GCHQ, people imagine the 'debs' of Bletchley Park, glamorous young women breaking codes after a night spent dancing with dons on the lawn. That image is a myth. The real history of women in British Sigint is unknown, and mostly forgotten once it was lived.

This story involves two sudden expansions in wartime and two long periods of service in peacetime. It includes elite and working-class women, codebreakers and clerical staff. The tale is not simple, nor one simply of progress: some women had more senior roles in Sigint between 1915 to 1945 than any did during the Cold War. The relationship between women and Sigint was driven by female agency – what tens of thousands of women wanted and took from that work; by the institutional interests of GCHQ, and the attitudes of its leaders; and by official, unofficial and unconscious ideas, and social norms, about class, and the place and powers of women, which members of all genders either shared or disputed. Female wants and work shaped the structure and success of British Sigint.

In the two world wars, female Siginters contributed more to British power than any women other than munitions workers. Between 1915 and 1918, women provided half the Britons working in Sigint, most notably in economic and diplomatic Comint, with scores in military Sigint. Perhaps the most senior woman yet in the history of British Sigint was among the top four personnel of the postal censorship, appointed to supervise women, in this primarily female-dominated agency, where many junior and middle managers also were women. Most female Siginters worked in data processing, but many served as translators and analysts. In age, they varied from eighteen to fifty years of age, mostly in their twenties, in class from elite to respectable working class, all selected for their education and intelligence. Institutions chose many older women for their supervisory or specialist skills. Though few veterans left accounts of their experiences, women seem to have enjoyed the work, which combined adventure, patriotism and pay, yet also happily retired at war's end. Probably, GC&CS hired most of the female Siginters who wished to remain in the field. Most women who were offered codebreaking positions at GC&CS in 1919 rejected the offers, while enough stayed on to cover clerical ranks.

The experiences of MI1(b) and Room 40 secured a place for women in British Sigint after 1918. Around 66 per cent of GC&CS personnel were female, though only about 40 per cent of those in Sigint as a whole. Gender norms dictated membership in its largest areas. Clerical and codemaking positions were deemed women's work but not radio interception, although men and women were employed in all of them. Women were integrated with men into the main work at GC&CS. Though males held almost all middle positions and all senior ones, women were accepted in its highest function, as codebreakers. They received more status in the tasks of officers than perhaps any other part of Whitehall, far above the Foreign Office. GC&CS was indifferent to the arguments which denied women a role in diplomacy.[1] To a department which prized eccentricity, what could be more appropriate than to employ female officers?

That GC&CS was less attractive to graduates of elite universities than most government departments made female candidates more attractive to it, likewise veterans with physical disabilities. GC&CS accepted diversity more than any other unit in Whitehall because that alone could provide the brainpower needed. Since GC&CS could not recruit enough codebreakers to meet its needs, it encouraged perhaps a dozen women in clerical tasks to learn that trade, enter and rise in it, so bypassing barriers of class and gender. Though one should not over-extrapolate from a single case, the interwar experience of Emily Anderson demonstrates that women codebreakers could command junior males, including military officers. All evidence suggests respect for women as cryptanalysts. GC&CS was a good place for bright and ambitious women because they faced relatively little resistance and received some support. GC&CS's attitudes towards codebreaking downgraded some characteristics traditionally tied to men, such as leadership, and emphasised others commonly associated with women, such as patience and attention to detail. Once at work, men and women were judged by the same standards regarding codebreaking ability, and seemingly with fairness – more so than any other institution or profession in Britain did with its chief task, save possibly teaching.

Institutional interests drove these actions, but Denniston and his fellows were progressive regarding the roles of women. In 1939, young female graduates provided over 60 per cent of the personnel recruited to boost the codebreaking ranks of GC&CS during wartime, with the best of them expected to rise. This structure dominated the civil part of GC&CS at Berkeley Street, where women provided much of the lower element of codebreakers, and some of the higher one. When mentioning specific female codebreakers, GC&CS officials used their first name (say 'Emily'), but called new recruits individually ('Miss Anderson') and, generically, 'girls'. Dilly Knox selected women for his Enigma section in part because he felt less challenged by them than men, while he could have his pick of the female crop. Still, he led them to glory, or vice versa, and gave them credit, which rebounded on himself. He described Margaret Rock, a graduate in mathematics with years of practical experience using statistics who was employed as a junior administrative assistant, as being 'entirely in the wrong grade. She is actually 4th or 5th best of the whole Enigma staff and quite as useful as some of the "professors". I recommend that she should be put on the highest possible salary for anyone of her seniority.'[2] Rock's independent success as a codebreaker confirmed Knox's opinion. Other women defeated manual systems and, long afterwards, remembered help and recognition from male superiors. Patricia Bartley's superiors supported her when a male codebreaker grasped at credit for her success against Floradora, the leading German diplomatic system and the acme of Berkeley Street's success. At Combined Bureau Middle East (CBME),

Emily Anderson and Marie Rose Egan ravaged Italian cryptosystems, an underrated triumph stemming from female prowess.

Women had less success in cryptanalysis by machines and mathematics, where an informal network of mathematicians drove recruitment. Joan Clarke joined through this route, became skilful, was appointed deputy head of Hut 8 and, alongside Anderson, Bartley and Rock, became the ranking female British Siginter of the war. Few other women were recruited through this means, though they were easier to acquire than men, reflecting their miniscule presence in British mathematics. Other than Clarke, no women rated at the top of machine codebreaking, far fewer than those in manual areas. Few worked in the field at all, and those who did were primarily women in the Machine Room, some with degrees in maths and law, who generated bombe menus for Enigma attacks. The switch from manual to machine attack increased the gulf between the creative side of codebreaking and the routine, replacing steps such as bookbuilding and cypher-stripping, which required and engendered skill, with the more automatic input of menus and monitoring of machines. Comint required more women than ever before, yet trapped them in routine work. The machines, like those in cotton mills, required a large labour force; the hazards here were not loss of limbs, but of minds through boredom. The switch to mathematicised and mechanised means of cryptanalysis also changed the skill sets which cryptanalysts required, and those who had them. Old hands working with manual systems encouraged female cryptanalysts more than young mathematicians did. The Enigma section trusted Clarke and assigned the most routine parts of cryptanalysis to educated women. Male cryptanalysts in the Fish section, where mathematical intuition remained more crucial to codebreaking than with Enigma, disparaged the role of women because, in effect, most members of the Women's Royal Naval Service did not know higher mathematics or Bayesian methods. The machine cryptanalysts declined to train the few Wrens with degrees in mathematics because, Newman said, 'women wouldn't like to do any intellectual work'.[3] Donald Michie held that women processed data in catching Fish, but: 'I do not know of instantiation-decisions being made by Wrens ... We usually used a term like "duty officer" for the decision-maker in charge, reserving "operator"' for Wrens.[4] Turing 'jocularly' called Wrens 'slaves'.[5]

A snapshot of Bletchley's personnel at any hour might include some male administrators and codebreakers, slightly higher numbers of male analysts and an equal number of female ones, with the other 75 per cent being women handling data processing and communication. All people in leadership posts were men and most support staff female. By 1945, about 25 per cent of British Siginters were women, perhaps 8,000 of them. Thousands of women handled translation and analysis in the postal censorship (though its value to Sigint sank compared to that in the First World War) and hundreds in Hut 3. Bletchley could not have worked without thousands of female bombe, clerical and communications staff, and intercept operators – though in combat zones most of the latter, and almost all Siginters, were male. Initially, men doubted the value of female help. When considering sources of personnel for wartime, Nobby Clarke noted: 'Whether it will be possible to employ women on night watches I cannot say, I personally see no objection to it in the present state of society. If capable women can be so employed it would save a great deal of trouble in the search for personnel as they would be readily available from the Universities.' In March 1941, eight Wrens were assigned to bombes 'as an experiment, as it was doubted if girls could do the work'.[6] So rapidly did this development occur that by 1944 one memorandum from Bletchley noted: 'We are particularly vulnerable to panic during a raid due to dense concentrations of very junior female staff having no male supervision at night.' In fact, when the bombe outstation at Eastcote was bombed at 0035 on 19 February 1944, male firefighters arrived only to find Wrens already attacking the blaze. 'Together the men and girls soon had the fire under control.'[7]

Women did much labour that was normally seen as men's work, and were praised for it, despite sexist shadings. This was especially true of Y, the leading area where women and men did the same work and females were placed equal with males, or better. When discussing the interception of civil wireless messages – one of the most advanced and difficult forms of interception – H. C. Kenworthy, Britain's leader in the field, emphasised how Cara Bell, a seventeen-year-old 'whose aptitude for this type of work amounted to something approaching brilliance', had taken the lead in identifying new lines of traffic, which placed her amongst the best operators in the world. Female staff generally outpaced males, Kenworthy thought. He had female interceptors train delinquent men at outstations in analysis and reporting, an extraordinary act for the time.[8] The GC&CS history noted that in Hut 3:

One of the specialist Watches (at the very end, two) was entirely composed of women, who, though never found to reach the standard of No. 1's or No. 2's on the Main Watch, always showed a special talent and readiness for dealing with matters at first sight trivial or dull, which by the frailty of human nature, were habitually pushed on to them … A good Indexer could help the Advisor or Watchkeeper far more than by merely turning up the card asked for. Often she knew the Index contained information that he did not know to exist. She was in fact a first-class Indexer only if she also was an Intelligence Officer. Many Indexers graduated to the Watch or to specialist sections throughout the Hut.[9]

The greatest criticisms against women occurred on grounds of class and education, not simply gender: for example, de Grey expressed the view that teleprinter and Typex staff 'were the lowest form of life generally not up to school certificate standard', taken by all students in secondary schools at sixteen.[10]

These women are the only female British Siginters whose voices survive publicly, from comments made decades later. We know more of their experiences than we do those of non-elite men at Bletchley. In retrospect, these women expressed pride in being a cog in the machine and recognition that they were cheap and forced labour. They were almost all unmarried and young, generally between eighteen and twenty-one years of age, a few debs (rarer at Bletchley than at MI6 or MI5), some upper-middle class, but mostly from the lower-middle and respectable working classes, and disproportionately from provincial towns. Women could remain at work if they married, but not if they became mothers. Many, especially middle-class women, were undergraduates or graduates of university or secretarial colleges, which led them into advanced offices, usually in a junior capacity. Others had a good education, or a Higher School Certificate, but most from the services women's branches had indifferent schooling. Old girls' networks caught some of these women as individuals, especially those who entered codebreaking, where ability and personal relations drove opportunities and experiences. Emily Anderson, billeted with Patricia Bartley's family and discerning her qualities, led the latter into GC&CS, where her brains, beauty and vivacity swept senior Siginters off their feet. The fact of being one of Welchman's students when he needed help brought Clarke into Ultra, where her interests, personality and lack of stereotypical femininity brought her, alone, into the male society of mathematical cryptanalysts.

Most of these women, however – motivated by adventure, ambition and patriotism, and attracted by the smart uniform, hopes of going to sea, or maybe growing up and escaping parental control or conscription into the Land Army – chose to join the female branches of the services. They volunteered to become conscript labour for industrial tasks, often in the face of opposition from parents. After her mother kept her from training as a nurse, while her boyfriend taught her Morse code, and seeing 'an advert in a magazine "Join the girls in blue"', Margaret Porter joined the Women's Auxiliary Air Force (WAAF). 'I liked the uniform,' she recalled, but not conscription to munitions work.[11]

Servicewomen entered Sigint almost accidentally, because, when tested, their aptitudes suited those that GC&CS sought. Each service tackled different targets: Wrens worked the bombes, the affectionately nicknamed 'teleprincesses' of the WAAF handled communications. The women involved in postal censorship, codebreaking, Hut 3 and Y received opportunities to use their brains for their country, which motivated hard and able work. Wrens were caught in a gilded cage of domestic drudgery. Most women worked in all-female units, under female supervision but male leadership. In order to reach any supervisory or specialised position, women needed support from some senior male in want of an 'aide', whom he (rather than the institution) selected on individual grounds. When Joan Kidman's colleagues complained to Peter Freeborn of her Stakhanovite performance on Hollerith machines, immediately he made her their supervisor.[12] These women had opportunities they never expected, doing war work and men's work in uniform, mixing with peers from other classes and regions at work and in barracks, amidst a concentration of older male authorities, dons and officers and male prejudice. Yvonne Jones recollected how during their 'invasion of the all male territory' at Chicksands, women operators initially had to share the bath hut with the men, only to find 'that some of the knot holes had been tampered with and unwittingly we had been entertaining the troops!'[13]

Margaret Arbury's mother 'thoroughly' opposed her 'intention to join the ATS so I was actually 19 before I braved her wrath and took the plunge'. She had 'a romantic notion' of 'wearing the rather dashing yellow gauntlet gloves' used by drivers of Army lorries. Tests demonstrating no aptitude for mechanical matters but 'brilliant' ones for Morse, dashed that hope. Quartered in a requisitioned hotel on the Isle of Man, Arbury spent six months on the technicalities of Morse and German wireless procedures, and practising interception. In October 1943, she moved to Forest Moor, a Y station outside Harrogate, still under construction and with 'primitive' conditions, which later improved marginally. Billeted in a requisitioned school, personnel moved to and from Forest Moor by lorry, usually crowded and uncomfortable. Each watch had 200 operators on rotating shifts, changing worktime every day. Each watch had a 'distinctive personality', created by women working together for months on end: Arbury's watch always sang a 'signature tune' as their lorries approached the station. Each operator monitored one set of headphones, faced generic problems such as boredom at quiet times and overload on busy shifts, noting every message they heard ('nothing was ever repeated for us – we had to hear it correctly the first time or lose it'), following targets despite changes in call signs or frequencies. Female non-commissioned officers handled all the technical and organisational issues necessary for operators to work. Further promotion was rare, though Aileen Clayton, a Y operator since 1940, became an intelligence officer in 1942. Operators virtually lived within specific German networks which became like family: 'In a strange way we all grew close to our own groups as we got to know them very well.'[14] Clayton recalls vomiting outside her building after hearing the death cries of a German pilot whose radio-telephone traffic she regularly intercepted calling for his mother as his aircraft crashed in flames.[15]

When the war came to a close, so did the biggest Sigint units employing women, postal censorship, specialised Y units, and the bombes. These veterans were not offered employment in Sigint, nor does anything suggest that they wanted it. Most female Siginters joined for the duration. Once the war was won, like male conscripts, they wanted to build new lives, together. Shared work in Sigint sparked many marriages, where neither spouse could tell the other what they had done in the war, for thirty years to come. Women within other parts of GCHQ had the same opportunities to remain as men did. Probably most women who wanted a place there found one, because GCHQ's demand exceeded the supply. GCHQ became a large permanent organisation, with many specialised parts, and greater needs for management and leadership. It moved to the norm for government departments and away from its old peculiarities, including progressive attitudes toward the employment of women, and towards more conventional views about the characteristics of females as workers and leaders. GCHQ had relatively less need for women in skilled areas than before, and a greater supply of men. Female candidates were few in areas where GCHQ most needed reinforcements, like scientists. Skill with languages or work in keystripping once opened the door for women as codebreakers; it closed with the emphasis on machines and mathematics. As the institution changed, so did its interests: a combination of unarticulated social and institutional attitudes, and official views, shaped developments. Women's experience of work illuminates all of these processes.

From 1946, outside the Foreign Office women no longer were made to retire from the civil service on marriage. Later changes in regulations gave women and men equal pay and opportunities in the civil service. These changes in form affected practice, but did not create equality in effect, especially because most males and females expected women to meet family responsibilities and subordinate a career to them. When, in 1971, the Civil Service Department reformed procedures to help women's careers, it emphasised 'that domestic responsibilities normally fall on the women in the family'.[16] In 1970, a GCHQ brochure directed towards graduates wrote: 'We regret, of course, that women have a natural tendency to spend only a few years with us, but they make a useful contribution during that period.'[17]

Like their peers across Britain, GCHQ's management held latent sexist views about the capabilities of women as workers, and especially as leaders. These views, unchallenged because they lay unconscious among insulated generations of men, most clearly surfaced around the flashpoint of night shifts. After leading K division to triumph during the Falklands conflict, its divisional head thought the fact that 'there are too many young women in K' caused its difficulties in maintaining shiftwork during the crisis.[18] This comment was widely circulated among the middle and senior leadership of GCHQ; all were male, and none challenged it. As hundreds of contemporary photographs show, GCHQ was a resolutely male organisation, with women present but concentrated in small pockets. Members of GCHQ took these circumstances for granted.

A slice of GCHQ's personnel at any hour might include some male and fewer female administrators, and significantly more male analysts and an equal number of female ones. Staff at overseas outstations were overwhelmingly male, but in British ones, women (with some male supervisors and specialists) ran communications, photocopying, printing, and traffic handling. They processed all material from ILC and traffic analysis for transmission to GCHQ, which usually involved copying data from one medium to another. Conventionally, these female tasks were managed in one room, distinct from other work areas, in the data-processing and communications nub of the station, sometimes called a 'Comms and ILC Processing Area'.[19] Support staff at Cheltenham were equally divided between genders. Women dominated communications and data processing – that is, filing, indexing and retrieval and running Hollerith machines – as they had done before and during the war. Probably most female Siginters who stayed on after 1945 were in these fields, later reinforced by female members of the service Siginters during unification. Women were the majority of new recruits in these areas.

Only in administration, communications and the main Sigint and intelligence areas did men and women work side by side, though men held most middle and all senior management positions there. Work in the specialised parts of GCHQ's middle and lower levels was differentiated by gender, according to social norms and educational practices. The effect was most clear with radio intercept operators, the largest group at GCHQ. Some women who had been wireless enthusiasts during the interwar years were blocked from professional work in the area. Thousands did yeowomen's work in Y during the war. By 1945, men knew that women could intercept wireless just as well as they could. GCHQ tried to have the services solve their staffing problems at intercept sections by employing women, yet refused to do so itself.[20] Then, GCHQ incorporated these military sections, which were almost all male. After 1945, new recruitment in the area was low. Women did not see wireless as their work – though against much opposition some females entered that career as civilians after 1945. Many males would have resisted females entering this area of men's work, but seemingly few if any tried, until the late 1980s when mass retirements forced a change in attitudes and employment. This almost instinctual decision blocked women from key areas of promotion.

Typing, conversely, remained women's work. At GCHQ, as at most large organisations, typing pools were organised like regiments of redcoats because the work involved a scarce and significant resource and required discipline, hard training, precise skills and constant recruitment to cover high wastage. The importance of typing at GCHQ rose steadily, especially as it became the means to make data manually enterable and readable by machine, through punchcards and punched tape. Given the number of women who retired from clerical positions each year, typing unlocked more entry-level positions at GCHQ than perhaps any other, yet also locked those entrants into watertight compartments. To advance from typing to anywhere other than administration, or sideways to computing or Hollerith machines, was difficult. So too in the other areas stamped by women, communications and data processing. Within these units, older women could not easily tell younger ones how to get ahead. Women lacked mentors of either gender, at any level, which was the greatest impediment to their rise in ranks. Male school-leaver entrants were not employed as typists or clerical staff but rather in general or technical services – often wandering throughout the institution – and were provided with mentors and space to progress. So too, women were not part of the system of National Service, which was a major source of recruitment for Sigint, including in languages, an area where they were recognised as particularly skilful. These consequences were important, but unintended. The key means of reinforcing comradeship at all levels of GCHQ – such as sports and the pub – tended to exclude women. Ironically, from 1960 the ability to type became key to promotion for intercept operators, something which they resisted. Meanwhile, computer operators were initially female because it seemed to be clerical work involving typing, though the maintenance personnel, programmers and experts were men. From 1980, when IT boomed, opening room for advancement, most computer practitioners were men, but many women, especially graduates, also would find places there.

Women at GC&CS were typically unmarried and childless. Though some female members of GCHQ also had that status, most were married with children. Women in Britain thought the civil service was a good employer, and for many females GCHQ ranked among the best. GCHQ met the interests of women who were not pursuing a permanent career: a job after completing school, which they could leave when they had a family, and perhaps rejoin later, which many did. This bargain resonated in socially conservative Gloucestershire. It hampered women in junior ranks who might have wished to rise, but underwrote the social base of GCHQ. A constant flow of young women, on low pay scales, filled clerical ranks. Hiring spouses of employees at GCHQ simplified security when expansion beckoned, while the concentration at Cheltenham obviated the problems of mobility which complicated women's promotions in the civil service. Spouses, moreover, often influenced a partner's decision-making, including the bodies for which they worked. When the armed services abandoned conscription, they found that wives, dissatisfied with salaries and conditions, pressed husbands with scarce and valuable technical skills into early retirement. To prevent this disruption, the services improved these matters for lower ranks, at costs in other areas.[21] At GCHQ and its outstations, the opposite was found: the existence of spouses and families were stabilising for personnel, perhaps easing demands for pay rises.

Anonymised human resources statistics illuminate, with unparalleled power, the status of women as leaders at GCHQ. Indeed, without these, this task could not be undertaken: it was not a topic which the institution assessed then, or later, while female veterans have never been free to discuss the issue. Institutional peculiarities affect interpretation of this data. Within H, and to a lesser degree K, many positions were handled by just one person, often for long periods, or a career. A deep performer in such a field might have more value, and be more valued, than a generalist who was promoted for reasons of breadth. Many cryppies and analysts did not want to be managers, or were poor at such tasks. This situation complicated the rewards for expertise in a system where promotion drove pay and status. Though women were often thought to rise more quickly in 'soft' areas of Sigint (such as HR) than 'hard' ones (like cryptanalysis), GCHQ's experience was slightly different. Its insularity kept outside middle managers away and drove GCHQ to rely on home-grown talent at a time when men dominated lower management and thus the selection pool. When that insularity declined from 1995, women became much more common in middle management for HR and finance at GCHQ, as they already were across Whitehall. Equally, before 2000, perhaps the most powerful women at GCHQ were the personal assistants to directors and divisional heads, and the divisional administration officers. These positions were pinnacles to a career, equal perhaps to regimental sergeant majors – important figures, as wise officers know, and foolish ones discover.

In 1970, across GCHQ, all divisional heads were men and few women were branch or section heads. In administrative divisions, women headed all sections dominated by females, such as typing and libraries. Men headed all other aspects of HR: administrative, executive and scientific staff, recruitment, reporting, promotions, training and relations with unions. In finance, men held all the main positions – forecasts, audit, procurement and construction; women managed only the administration of pay. Women had more status in intelligence-producing organisations, however. In divisions H, J, K and V, men and women attacked problems as teams, side by side, in different ways. J and K stemmed straight from GC&CS, though their members analysed intelligence much more than their predecessors had done. V applied normal modes of Sigint analysis to Elint, but demanded expertise in science, where, at Cheltenham as across Whitehall, women were companions, rather than doctors. Women were marginalised in mathematics, and thus also among the cryppies of H division. Virulent sexism infected the British computing industry, though unlike it, senior male leaders at GCHQ actually understood such matters well, which the institution treated effectively.[22]

Between 1946 and 1960, a few women were among the analytic branches of H, J, and K, where many were support personnel. From 1960, women, generally in junior slots and coming from local secondary schools, provided around 50 per cent of the personnel in J and K, including those in production sections. During 1970, in J division, men headed every branch, but one woman was an assistant branch head. In J and K, women ran several sections of between ten and twenty analysts, as many did smaller groups of linguists. Women had no role, even junior management, in V, but they had more leadership roles in the highest-status division, H, than almost anywhere else at GCHQ. By 1990, women had acquired marginally more leadership roles in support services, but rose in the middle management of intelligence departments. In both J and K, one woman was a group head, overseeing two or more branches, on the border of upper management. In V, the 'hardest' of the hard scientific intelligence divisions, one woman ran the largest analytic group, while another led another major group. In H, women entered the top layers of management, though cryptomathematics remained a male game.

This increase of women's power in functional areas paralleled changes in grade. Between 1965 and 1990, women rose from being 10 per cent to 25 per cent of the executive class. They consistently held perhaps 20 per cent of the posts in the administrative class, but were scarcer in its upper grades. By 1972, women held 15 per cent of SEO positions, that is, junior manager or section heads, in H, J and K, though none ranked higher. Soon, women made up 19 per cent of SEOs, and 6–7 per cent of principals and senior civil servants (SCSs), branch and division heads, in H, J, K and V. After 1988, women held 20–25 per cent of SEO positions and around 13 per cent of principal positions, though they varied between 3 and 8 per cent of SCSs. Surprisingly similar patterns emerged in E division, handling establishments, where women were plentiful, despite the belief that women Siginters rise faster and further in 'soft' areas than in operational ones. Perhaps this discrepancy arises less in middle levels of management than in higher ones. From 1976, women were SEOs in H and X divisions, overseeing computerised cryptanalysis – the most advanced and scientific areas of Comint – though promotions to higher grades were few in number.

At GCHQ, women were underrepresented in management, but not wildly so in middle levels. This status was above the average in Whitehall, especially at the FCO and MOD, and even more so than in analytic units such as the Joint Intelligence Committee (JIC) and Defence Intelligence Staff (DIS).[23] Still, the numbers of GCHQ women as SEOs, principals and SCSs stalled after 1976. The amount of female SCSs veered yearly, reflecting how retirements and promotions affect a small body of people, sometimes at 0 per cent, never exceeding 8 per cent. Unlike Emily Anderson, no woman broke that glass ceiling. None had an independent command, such as running an intercept station, because none had experience with radio. No woman became a division head until 1995, or joined the directorate until 2006. Instead, the old boys promoted the best men they knew. At GCHQ – a self-contained and relatively small bureau with few senior positions based in Cheltenham – women could not easily move across ministries, which helped females in central departments reach senior ranks. For this reason, but also because of sexist attitudes and socially accepted roles for family responsibilities, even in divisions at GCHQ where men and women did the same work, males were two or three times more likely to become middle managers than were females, who never gained senior positions. Yet these female analysts and cryptanalysts mattered as much to GCHQ as had female codebreakers at GC&CS, whether in 1919–39, or 1940–45, because their new role in analysis bolstered its expertise. No other women in Whitehall affected British power as they did, or did so much to drive the work of their department.

The experience of women at NSA was comparable to those of GCHQ, including a reliance on heavy employment from the local area, but women mattered in middle management earlier than at Cheltenham, and rose higher. In the 1960s, women often represented NSA in discussions with GCHQ; British ones featured as spouses at parties. NSA had its first deputy DIRNSA, Ann Caracristi, in 1980–82, and its second, Barbara McNamara, during 1997–2000 – before any woman in GCHQ headed a division. These developments say less about GCHQ than NSA, which was more progressive towards women than any other security agency in the world. The key issues were female agency, institutional needs, the attitudes of leaders, and the effect of mentoring. In 1945, women were fairly equal as leaders in British and US Sigint. Several of these American women stayed permanently in Sigint, but only two Britons, Joan Clarke and Margaret Rock, did so. With so few women involved, differences in personality and ambition mattered. The most successful American women were driven, compared to their fellow nationals or the comparatively diffident Clarke and Rock. Two strong codebreakers from Bletchley, Mavis Batey and Jane Fawcett, retired, raised families, and then had great public careers in heritage preservation. For any female Siginter of that era, motherhood almost always ended hopes of high rank, and certainly hampered it. The leading woman at GCHQ from that time, Maureen Jones, was tough, able, ambitious and unmarried, but without remarkable technical skills.

Women had more room to rise in American Sigint, which was characteristically less mature and settled than GCHQ, yet booming and ultimately destined to be larger. In 1946, the US Army Security Agency (ASA) had fewer good codebreakers than GCHQ, and needed more. It recruited among just-retired veterans. Several of the strongest returnees, reflecting personal interests and comparative prospects in cryptanalysis and civilian employment, were women. Caracristi and others built reputations to match any man, but their careers stalled.

Then, just as at GC&CS, but not GCHQ, patronage by male leaders – DIRNSAs drawn from military professions not notably progressive towards women – helped females to break glass ceilings. As the first DIRNSA, General Ralph Canine inherited an agency where all senior leaders were male officers. He emphasised the promotion of able civilians. Perhaps reflecting his reading of the quality of his male and female subordinates, he insisted that women be considered for senior positions, even though any such appointment would prevent that of a man. These decisions were fair and wise: those women had strong careers and became a notable minority of the middle to senior officials at NSA during the period 1960–80. Caracristi emphasised how 'glass ceilings' and 'glass walls' still blocked women in NSA from senior positions and key areas, especially those involving operations rather than softer issues of administration. She attacked that problem by mentoring younger staff, male and female. More generally, after a lawsuit broke NSA's resistance, from 1976 every promotion board had at least one female member: GCHQ did not adopt that practice until decades later. Caracristi, Juanita Moody and Polly Budenbach were promoted because of their ability, but for some years together, as a 'showcase' for NSA. By 1960, each led major cryptanalytic teams tackling the hardest targets, the equivalent of major middle-level sections of H or J at GCHQ. Soon, Caracristi was promoted individually. From 1975, one DIRNSA, Lew Allen, made her Director of Organisation within the key A division, Research and Operations, and another, Bobby Rae Inman, promoted her over several senior men to be deputy DIRNSA.[24] Meanwhile, Budenbach became deputy Director of G division, and several other women rose higher at NSA than GCHQ. Their success reflects what GCHQ lost, without knowing it.

British or Not?

From 1914, questions of loyalty, security, ethnicity and 'Britishness' affected the employment of British Siginters. When hiring foreigners with essential skills, Sigint agencies were pragmatic, though concerned about security, reasonably and not. Deciding when and whether immigrants to Britain, or their children, were British, and should be treated as such, was a more complicated and emotional matter. During the Great War, the concerns were over Britons with a parent from an enemy state, primarily Germans, and recent Russian Jewish immigrants and non-Britons who were employed for their linguistic skills. Members of IToc – the field telephone interception stations – with one German parent were trusted operationally, yet watched as security risks – even when, like Vince Schürhoff, they held a Military Medal for courage under fire.[25] So were non-British members of the Postal Censorship Department, which stopped all letters in a few languages – for example: 'Judeo-Chaldean', because it could not ascertain the honesty of the only censors able to read them.[26] A few British Jews, and scores of Jewish immigrants from Allied countries, well below their proportion of the population as a whole, were recruited into Sigint, but none from enemy states.

Army codebreakers in the Middle East hired several members of non-Muslim minorities from the Ottoman empire. As one army Siginter recalled: 'This cosmopolitan workforce included Hazan (Smyrna Jew), Papazaglou (Cairene Greek), Danielien (Cairene Armenian) ... Utidjean (Cretan Armenian) and Chavooshian (a chemist from Brighton believe it or not).'[27] Many of these men remained with Army Sigint until 1923, performing sterling work and trusted by soldiers who often had unpleasant views about race; however, for security reasons, GC&CS denied them knowledge of its work against foreign systems. After the war, the Army tried to keep two of these men as codebreakers. One, Hazan, through complex means requiring the king's approval, became a commissioned officer in the British Army. Soon after the monarchical magic was exercised, he cashed several cheques that he could not honour and vanished to Paris, and from British Sigint. The other of these Siginters, Shemavon Danielien, served with No. 2 Wireless Company at Sarafand. He was initially rated as a Signal Computer and paid well, then made second lieutenant and served as a 'civil assistant under the War Office', retiring in 1950.[28] As Britain's expert in Arabic, Persian and Turkish codes, Danielien ranked alongside the major members of GC&CS. Civil service regulations insisted that any appointee be a 'natural-born' British subject whose father had the same status, but let departments make special exceptions for foreigners who had served Britain in the First World War.[29] Danielien presumably received this dispensation, as did the Russian Jewish refugee Ernest Fetterlein, despite some initial 'objection' to his employment.[30] Seemingly no other member of British Sigint between the wars was a foreigner, and none Jewish.

During the Second World War, GC&CS regarded the children of white immigrants to Britain from before 1914 as Britons. In particular, GCHQ recruited many Jews, including Sigint veterans from the Great War or their relatives, some of whom stayed on afterwards. A larger proportion of British Jews served in Sigint than their share of the population, including many leaders and mathematical cryptanalysts, such as Jack Good and Max Newman, because after forty to sixty years' residence they were regarded as British, and had linguistic and educational skills essential to Sigint.[31] GCHQ showed no signs of anti-Semitism, being among the more progressive group of British security organisations. Denniston and Menzies trusted individual British Jews to work loyally against the messages of Jewish terrorists in Palestine and, supported by MI5, defended these men against charges of disloyalty which were conveyed by the Foreign Office.[32]

Soon after the State of Israel was founded in 1948, however, Whitehall began to consider whether its own intelligence and security agencies should employ British Jews, concerned that they might have dual loyalties. These suspicions, fed by the recent war between British and Jewish intelligence agencies in Palestine, were checked by fear of the political consequences. The professional head of the Foreign Office, William Strang, wished to avoid a 'witch-hunt' against Jews in Whitehall. Incompetent and provocative actions by Israeli intelligence exacerbated these concerns. In 1950, Britain discovered that the Israeli embassy in London was running a British Jew, Cyril Wybrow, as a spy within the Joint Intelligence Bureau. In 1954, during the 'Lavon affair', Israeli military intelligence had Egyptian Jews bomb buildings in Egypt in order to entangle British and Egyptian forces. As a result, until 1980, British intelligence and security services generally did not employ British Jews.[33] How far GCHQ followed that policy is unclear. Probably it never rejected any Jewish entrant with scarce skills. Perhaps it refused those less blessed, though in 1956 Jews were not listed among the ethnic groups banned from GCHQ positions. With one exception, stemming from personal rather than ethnic considerations, GCHQ did not discriminate against Jewish members who already were on their staff. Ernest Ettinghausen, brother of the professional head of the Israeli foreign ministry, Walter Eytan (himself an old Bletchley hand) was involuntarily removed from codebreaking work, and instead assigned to civil service positions in London, culminating in his appointment as "Controller of Stamps". Though this followed a proposal that Ettinghausen be 'tactfully moved', he would have preferred to stay with GCHQ.[34] Naty Doniach held a key position at the Joint Technical Language Service for twenty-five years, while Jack Good served at the heart of GCHQ's cryptanalytic effort throughout the 1950s. By 1971, when Ralph Benjamin became Chief Scientist, GCHQ ignored Jewishness when considering any entrant, and may always have done so.

Meanwhile, during the Second World War, some other ranks in the Sigint units of the Indian Army were Indians. From 1945, GCHQ hired hundreds of foreigners – eastern Europeans in the London Processing Group, and Chinese in Hong Kong – after the directorate and LSIB thoroughly considered the security implications. These people could not receive conventional positive vetting, but were regarded as trustworthy because of personal experiences with communism. They worked in translating or radio intercept teams which were segregated from other personnel and also from the most secret elements of Sigint.

After 1945, GCHQ confronted a new issue: non-white immigrants to Britain and their children. They had the same rights for employment in the civil service as any British passport holder, but departments dealing with security were reluctant to employ them. Under open statute, these departments already were legally allowed not to hire communists or people with 'character defects', a category which could include anything from homosexuality to alcoholism. In 1956, the Foreign Office recommended that such departments be legally allowed to refuse any person who, as an individual and through both parents, had not always been a citizen of the Republic of Ireland or 'a British subject'. Whereas MI5 and MI6 controlled their own recruitment, GCHQ worked through public sources, and preferred tougher definitions than the Foreign Office allowed. GCHQ wished to avoid employing any citizen of Ireland, anyone married to someone who was or ever had been an alien, and any 'coloured' person, that is, anyone 'either or both of whose parents is not of old Dominion white stock ... There will obviously be cases – Anglo-Indian for example – where we can't be positive one way or the other on the basis of a visual inspection of the candidate combined with an educated guess whether his parents' names and addresses provide any clue. I do not think we can possibly use the more searching interrogation of the Positive Vetting stage for this purpose: obviously we cannot risk a candidate connecting G.C.H.Q.'s refusal to have him with his coloured ancestry.' The Civil Service

Commission agreed not to send GCHQ any candidate for the clerical or executive classes whose 'appearance' or details of parentage raised any 'suspicion' of being 'coloured'.[35] In any case, GCHQ's representatives on committees could themselves veto any applicants for the A and B grades, or in scientific or technical areas. GCHQ imposed the same 'racial requirement' on military Siginters, which staff associations criticised as 'a colour bar'. The few 'Anglo-Asian' Sigint personnel already in the RAF were withdrawn to Britain, but continued that work there. Military Siginters who later married Chinese women in Hong Kong were returned to Britain and mostly transferred to the Meteorological Service, though some stayed in Sigint. Those who married German women continued to conduct Sigint in Germany or Britain.[36]

Parts of GCHQ's position reflected genuine concerns over security, as regards non-British passport holders, and perhaps the idea that some non-white Britons might be susceptible to calls based on colonial nationalism. Nonetheless, the core concern was racist: a mistrust of the loyalty and competence of 'coloured' candidates perhaps more than had ever been true of Britons with German or Jewish connections. GCHQ was more willing to bend its rules for Chinese intercept operators in Hong Kong and eastern European linguists in London – who could be insulated from its normal work – than it was for non-white people in Britain, who would (if employed) work within its mainstream and be treated as British. GCHQ's personnel had little personal experience in working with Caribbean, Chinese or south Asian peoples, and stereotypes drove some of their views. GCHQ, moreover, requested extra-legal means to sidestep the regulations of the CSC in order to avoid embarrassment arising from any candidate suspecting that skin colour had caused their rejection, and relied on personal scrutiny rather than positive vetting. Even more, when assessing applicants in the A and B grades and scientific or technical areas, GCHQ's representatives would look for the faintest of signs of 'colour', that is, non-Britishness. Perhaps such scrutiny explains how it assessed less well-documented areas, such as 'character defects'.

In our time, such views are outrageous, especially since GCHQ emphasises the need for diversity in its workforce, but they require context. All British government departments of the era held such views when considering the employment of non-white immigrants. In the United States, until 1945 Op-20-G would not employ Jews, though the

ASA did so in great numbers. After 1945, Jews were more prominent in American than British Sigint, but Americans far more aggressively removed homosexuals from their ranks. Americans confronted a greater issue than Britain with non-white citizens, but addressed it earlier. For moral and political reasons, in 1948 President Truman insisted that the military end segregation, which it did for institutional reasons: the military needed black manpower. US Sigint, an element of the American military, had institutional interests of its own. It was short of personnel trained in higher forms of data processing, matters which black colleges taught well, thereby providing a valuable pool of personnel. In the 1950s, black and white American Siginters worked in segregated work units, with African Americans assigned the more routine tasks. Still, African American officers led their segregated shifts and provided a path for promotion; from the 1960s they became integrated. In 1956, none of these elements was true of GCHQ: it saw no institutional reason to hire non-white subjects, while all organisations involved in security had similar attitudes. From 1965, however, debate on the role of non-white Britons became a live political issue, which drove changes in attitudes and practices. By the 1980s, black, Asian and minority ethnic (BAME) Britons slowly entered departments involved in security, including GCHQ. The process remains painful and incomplete.

Character Defects?

Institutional interests drove these decisions on recruitment. Between 1946 and 1951, GCHQ frequently had Newman and Turing, a Jew and a known homosexual, assess its greatest secrets. Compared to most British government departments involved in security, GCHQ was generally more liberal, especially regarding issues of class, though not colour. GCHQ's responses to what contemporaries called 'character defects', also varied. The evidence on these issues is good on policy, but not on people. Policy aimed to keep members of 'suspect' groups from entering GCHQ, which, if successful, left no evidence. The Foreign Office handled dismissals from GCHQ, on which records are sparse. How many people fell in categories regarded as suspect, whether communists, homosexuals or alcoholics, is unknown. Before 1945, the security screening of civil servants was perfunctory, and some members of Bletchley Park were known to be homosexuals, or to have communist inclinations. Many GCHQ staff were hired before security procedures were well developed and though questioned at five-year intervals later, could be dismissed only with proof. GCHQ had few non-secret jobs. Thus, security officials noted, it faced 'particularly acute' problems with cases involving 'grounds of character defects alone, when there are insufficient grounds for making a disciplinary charge', like people in financial difficulties or living a 'very shady existence', or 'suspected homosexuals about whom there is no direct evidence on which to base a charge'. GCHQ could not transfer such suspects to non-secret work, but only dismiss them, which again required proof. That was hard to find.[37] Although all new entrants were positively vetted, investigators seemingly did not pursue the possibility of homosexuality as thoroughly as they did communist inclinations, in an age where gay people routinely and successfully shielded that status.

Under the main technique for security, positive vetting, investigators gathered evidence about prospective entrants, and those already in service, and interviewed these individuals and others who knew them.[38] This process was competent, but weak against people who concealed their behaviour or beliefs. Moreover, GCHQ and the British security services were reluctant to violate the privacy and rights of Britons, or to dismiss people through the 'purge process'. In 1955, the highest committee on security heard of 'an extreme case', described in the terminology of the time as involving 'a woman in a cypher section who had lived in the same house as Communists before her marriage, had had an illegitimate child by a negro, had married a man who was suspected of being a Communist, was suspected of being a Communist herself, and had lived with Communists while her husband was abroad' – yet the Foreign Office was 'advised not to invoke the purge procedure, because a strong enough case could not be made out'. Fortunately for the authorities, she retired voluntarily.[39]

In another 'borderline' case within GCHQ, a 'Miss W/Mrs. O' took the *Daily Worker* to her office, discussed its contents with her colleagues and said that she 'did not approve' of GCHQ's work. She had many contacts with communists, 'boarded out' her illegitimate child with communist foster parents, and married an African man who was suspected of being a communist. She was open with superiors about her actions and a 'very thorough investigation' concluded that neither she nor her husband were communists. Dick White, the Director of

MI5, 'thought the evidence against her was thin for action under the Purge Procedure'. GCHQ 'worried lest purge action, whether it be successful or not, might embitter her and so, in the ultimate, increase the risks involved in her association with Communists'. Instead, it hoped that Mrs O might voluntarily resign, which eventually she did.[40] Admittedly, these cases occurred when the security system was in its early days; probably later cases were simpler, but the process rarely was simple.

These security principles were directed primarily against communists, and kept them from GCHQ, but not so other types of 'character defect'. If GCHQ had no alcoholics, spendthrifts or 'shady characters', then it was unique among British institutions. GCHQ wished not to employ homosexuals, but realised that this task would be hard to achieve. Departments concerned with security did not conduct witch-hunts against gays, but they did act when behaviour was obvious.[41] More than in virtually any other government department, GCHQ's institutional interests protected staff with scarce talents, which shielded some gay people directly, and reinforced the emphasis on individual rights to privacy and tolerance of eccentric behaviour that generally restrained investigations. An internal study of homosexual staff fired for security reasons in units under the Foreign Office includes no member of GCHQ. This evidence suggests, though does not prove, that personnel from the highest levels at Cheltenham – the A, B and EO administrative classes – were not caught in this trap.[42]

Still, some people were fired from GCHQ because of their sexuality, with personally tragic consequences. GCHQ could not have protected Turing when he was tried for homosexuality in 1952: it had no authority on this matter, though Hugh Alexander offered the greatest evidence in his defence. Yet Turing was not the only victim of these attitudes, which probably most affected members of GCHQ without scarce skills. In 2016, GCHQ apologised publicly to 'Ian', an RAF Siginter who, in 1969, had been dismissed summarily after seven years of exemplary service on these grounds. 'Ian' found another job within the government, but lost a career which he loved and in which he had served his country well.[43] Later, however, official attitudes towards gays within GCHQ changed. In 1981, when revising security rules across Whitehall, the Security Commission demanded a bar against homosexuality for the Foreign Office and military services, but eliminated that stricture for 'officers employed by GCHQ for specialist work which will not involve their ever being posted outside England and Wales'.[44] This decision recognised that gay people offered skills needed by GCHQ, and perhaps reduced that restraint in the entire institution. Quickly, GCHQ became more liberal regarding homosexuals than any other British government department involved in security, and a model for those pursuing reforms in other departments.[45]

Outstations

GCHQ had civilian and military outstations in Britain, and established joint military–civilian stations after the war at its largest overseas garrisons: Cyprus, Germany and Hong Kong, and at more transient locations abroad. Perhaps 25 per cent of its personnel, and all members of the service Sigint organisations, served in such stations at any time. This system evolved through several rationalisations of stations which existed in 1945. Cost and changes in strategy, targets and technology all drove rationalisation. Stations survived through natural selection and politics. The development of new interception kit, expensive and powerful, constantly reshaped their value. Fewer and bigger stations, with less staff and better machines, acquired more intelligence material. While stations closed after 1945, coverage grew. Many stations were sacrificed to feed the satellite interception station at Bude, rightly so. Decolonisation drove good stations in India and Sri Lanka to Singapore and Mauritius, and then, Hong Kong apart, entirely from Asia. These stations and that at Singapore closed after 1971, as Britain abandoned its position east of Suez and concentrated on other targets and means of collection. Larger stations were more cost-efficient than small ones, but Whitehall maintained, without modernising, tiny stations of marginal value within Britain – often in poor areas, years after better ones shut – in order to promote regional development. Between 1965 and 1979, economy and efficiency combined to close these bases and consolidate others, while bigger stations were modernised for the first time since 1945.

Every station shared characteristics and each had unique ones. Generally, types of kit and targets remained constant for a decade or more. Until the military and GCHQ interception services were unified in 1964, those of the Army, RAF and Royal Navy focused on their Soviet opposite numbers. Thereafter, J, K and V assigned tasks to all stations, but the ex-service ones (Cheadle and Scarborough) and the remaining Army and RAF stations monitored their opposite numbers, as did those on warships. Stations, closed compounds with fences and security which were rudimentary by modern standards, usually had one large building with outbuildings. All had external antennae or antenna farms (thirty-two at Flowerdown, Hampshire), workshops, maintenance and T/A sections, Comcentres and 'set rooms' for interceptors. Between 1951 and 1955, Army Siginters at Langeleben in West Germany worked from lorries, played in a 'wild-west atmosphere' and lived in tents on the snows of Saxony beside the Soviet Third Shock Army. The Siginters' latrines were boards on barrels, which were emptied once per week, within corrugated iron shacks.[46] Elsewhere, the physical infrastructure of 1940s vintage lingered for decades. In 1971, just before a major renovation, staff at Flowerdown worked in 'a large barn-like structure visibly aged', though 'warm and clean'. Some unlucky men lived in rooms that were condemned as soon as they moved on.[47] By the 1970s, stations (including Langeleben) had become more spacious and pleasant, designed to enable expansion in order to accommodate new equipment.

The largest stations, drawn from the best British intercept organisations of 1945, had great continuity in personnel and organisation. Old hands from prewar days led and staffed Cheadle until 1970. During the 1960s, a large building was erected there, with spacious rooms, modern kit, and a 200-acre 'aerial "farm"'. Each set room specialised in one area of interception, with staff rotating through them all. In 1973, its 400 personnel included twenty-six traffic handlers; five positions intercepting ILC; three engaging 'German Communist' traffic; while twenty-six operators and thirty-two traffic analysts attacked Soviet air defence traffic.[48] Scarborough is the oldest continually operated Sigint station in the world. Its location in Yorkshire was one key to its survival, the other being its excellent location against naval traffic. Until a new building opened in 1974, Scarborough had 'about the poorest' working conditions of any station – being cramped, cold, damp and stuffy. Rainwater seeped into a building, built half underground and covered with earth. In the 1950s, staff worked on chairs and desks resting on concrete slabs. In 1981, Scarborough had 538 personnel – 421 radio grades, 47 technical grades, 30 cypher grades, 6 traffic handlers, and the remainder administrative and industrial personnel.[49] Culmhead in Somerset, a continuation of the GCHQ station at Knockholt in Kent, primarily attacked non-Morse radio traffic. By 1975, '20 different operator skills [were] performed in the set rooms and TA sections', the greatest range in CSOS. It had the most skilled intercept staff at GCHQ and the most advanced kit. Each shift had two duty officers, as one alone could not control the work.[50]

Outstation staff worked in a disciplined and quasi-military environment, but of a technical sort, more like the RAF than the Guards. Smaller units often had just one officer, living for years among operators who worked almost without supervision. Their working relations were not hierarchical. The Army's Sigint units, too small to offer a career for officers and too specialised for cross-postings with normal signals units for officers below colonel, followed Second World War practices, and promoted their most able non-commissioned officers to junior- and field-grade posts.[51] Major stations had more buildings, staff, specialised subdivisions, bureaucracy and direction of operators, but still supervision was constrained, and willing cooperation was necessary and normal. Staff in British stations served together for decades on end, those abroad for several years. Most stations operated two eight-hour shifts, but larger ones maintained twenty-four-hour coverage. An overtime culture ruled stations, paying staff to reduce their time at home. According to legend, operators often died not long after retirement, perhaps not always entirely to their wives' regret.

No matter how mechanised, interception was tedious and required hard and honest graft. As one National Service operator, Chris Rundle, noted:

> If there was little going on during a night shift, I would read
> Tolstoy's *Anna Karenina* in Russian, in preparation for my future
> university studies. At the same time I would be searching the
> airwaves, going up and down the bandwidths – 'knobbing' as we
> called it ... I remember once tuning in to a concert of classical music
> from Leipzig, a place which seemed impossibly far away the other
> side of the frontier. The air in the operations room was fetid. There
> was no natural light, and one could not wait to get out at the end
> [of] one's shift. But in its own way the work was absorbing: we were
> listening to real Russians talking just the other side of the frontier.[52]

Failure by individuals to do their work was hard to detect and to discipline. Some National Servicemen reported poor relations with officers, rejection of the regulations that operators not read books while intercepting, and occasional skiving rather than reporting.[53] Friction was frequent at GCRO. Success required esprit de corps, which was generally at hand. Army operators recollected: 'We all shared the pleasure, no, glory of getting the keys first and I took it as a gross personal insult if anyone beat us'; 'All the watches were a team and worked together as such.'[54] To minimise boredom among operators, GCHQ provided 'a variety of cover on stations in order to raise the level of job satisfaction', and rotated personnel through tasks.[55] This need also drove the organised sports and activities, social and welfare clubs, and wives' associations, found at all stations. Interception was the area where GCHQ received the greatest return on its investment in mateship.

Between 1945 and 1996, few women served in stations abroad – most in Jerusalem, where many wartime traditions continued. Wives and families lived in quarters in the great overseas garrisons where GCHQ had stations. At stations in Britain, staff frequently owned homes and joined the local community after decades of life among them. When stations closed, Siginters often retired and stayed put, while the cost of housing and quality of schools concerned staff who might move between stations. In stations abroad, staff and families lived in government-owned homes within British communities; they shared distinct cultural characteristics, including the experience of constant movement across the globe and domestic upheaval, isolated from the local population. In Cyprus, Germany and Malta, service Siginters resided within British military communities. While many civilians lived within those bases, Siginters abroad might at times live outside. They faced danger from guerrillas in Cyprus and Singapore: several Siginters were murdered in Palestine. So too, during the 1970s, security was tight around CSOS Gilnahirk, in Ulster – whose mission was to elicit agent traffic to and from the UK – to the extent that one radio operator explained his reluctance to be reassigned to England because 'I hear you have a law and order problem over there.'[56] In Malta during 1972, failed negotiations over a post-colonial settlement forced a large station into a rush evacuation, in which Royal Marines formed a security perimeter. Families fitted their belongings into twelve crates each, and left hastily.

All sensitive material was burned 'in a 24 hour holocaust known by those who stoked it as the Great Fire of Dingli', yet coverage continued until the base was evacuated, and was picked up immediately after by evacuees aboard HMS *Bulwark*.[57]

Some stations abroad, such as Masirah in the Indian Ocean, were hardship posts, hot, cramped and dirty. Others less so. Because civil service regulations said that foreign service allowance 'should be sufficient in amount to enable staff concerned to maintain an appropriate standard of living, having regard to the climate of the overseas station and the habit of the local community', Siginters found paradise in Singapore, importing cars and memorising the prices of drink in bars.[58] Every station had a distinct history.

Thus, Ascension Island, between Africa and South America, had been an intercept base in both world wars. It reopened in 1962, when having an intercept site in the southern Atlantic became a higher priority for UKUSA. Interception was excellent and an uninhabited island eliminated political problems. A support staff was imported from St Helena. By 1966, after small military teams established a beachhead, the GCRO manned a new and expensive station, costing £2.5 million. It stood at the edge of GCHQ's operational aspirations and financial capabilities. The base closed in 1978. It reopened and closed twice during the next six years, after stalwart service during the Falklands conflict.[59] Personnel from the BBC and NASA served on the island. American personnel lived on their own base there. Britons lived in a village, with shops, school, power plant, hospital and local administration. They suffered from boredom, and scarce and costly supplies of fresh food. Eggs, one officer noted, fall 'into the same category as a gold brick, and if any prospective visitors wish to procure instant popularity the production of fresh eggs is the key'. Personnel responded by organising frenetically active sports, diving and fishing clubs, which seemingly absorbed the spare time of all British men on the island. At age eleven, British children moved to boarding schools, or their families left the island. British families lived in eighty bungalows and single men in suites at the senior mess. In 1971, twenty-seven men, fifteen of them unaccompanied, worked at CSOS Ascension, a spacious building at the village edge. They stood two eight-hour watches, each man handling fifteen hours' overtime per week, an additional two days' service. Each shift managed fourteen positions, mostly for Morse, but including one for non-Morse wireless and a few for voice. Each position was multipurpose, including several receiving sets able to switch immediately from covering the ether to a few frequencies. The ample take pressed T/A and communications to their limits. All staff rotated through the four-man T/A section, to minimise boredom.

Strife and Strikes

GCHQ avoided block hiring for graduates and officers, but not for personnel below that level. For years after 1954, the move to Cheltenham forced the hiring of many support staff. Those taken first had good prospects for promotion, but a demographic bulge soon emerged. On the basis of retiring after thirty-five to forty years' service, or sixty and sixty-five years of age, retirements would rise sharply from 1990. Promotions became harder in Cheltenham, but room remained for the ambitious, especially at starting and middle levels. Merging four groups of radio operators into the Government Communications Radio Bureau (GCRB), however, with different grades and pay, caused worse conditions at all levels. All these groups hired significantly between 1939 and 1950, creating gridlock for decades, and cascading retirements from 1979. In April 1969, 1,420 of 2,760 radio operators were between forty-three and forty-nine years old, born between 1920 and 1926.[60] The situation was just slightly less dire among cypher operators. Opportunities for promotion were scarce among the largest grade at GCHQ and another but smaller body, between them involving about 30 per cent of its total personnel. Cypher and radio operators had a flat structure, each operator working alone, with few supervisors. In 1970, just sixteen radio operators could be promoted. The youngest of a hundred candidates had served twenty-two years as an operator, without promotion since 1948! Meanwhile, twenty new operators (soon rising to fifty) had to be hired each year, to counter the effect of block retirement fifteen years away.[61]

The integration of the four services eliminated some of their scarce higher ranks. Executive-grade personnel absorbed other slots (especially those involving coveted day shifts) at the ex-service outstations, which the radio grades might once have claimed – or so they thought. Radio and cypher grades, with roughly the same technical skills as executive officers, though rarely the educational or personal ones, believed they deserved greater pay because their working conditions (including night shifts) were harder: tedious, dirty and precise. In the mid-1960s, operators received excellent pay settlements because of night duties, and the skill required to follow wandering signals – one part of GCHQ's superiority over its American partners and a source of status at Cheltenham. As an experienced analyst from J wrote:

> The main quality I have admired in the operators (nearly all unknown and unsung so far as I was concerned) who produced 'my' traffic for me has been their sheer ability to find the target. Admittedly we sent out callsigns and frequencies, but honestly it seems to make remarkably little difference whether the original information we have is full or sketchy in the extreme – operators will find the task and of course (why 'of course'? It is certainly not something we have a right to expect it seems to me) they bridge the gap at times of callsign and frequency changes, develop new associated notations, find the missing night outstation continuity and so on, all often without guidance from the Centre ... being an operator is still a very human activity and not so easily automated as some may think. For instance we are still a long way from computerised recognition of national characteristics in Morse transmission, so far as I know [a reference to the odd procedures of many signallers in developing nations].[62]

Each intercept operator, an independent craftsman, handled the whole process of listening, recording and reporting on one machine. The value of these skills declined with the end of the valve era, though they still worked against important targets. Rising areas of interception involved techniques which reduced the independence of operators, and some older men found this hard to handle. From 1965, NSA began to industrialise interception, in part because its operators lacked the individual skills of British ones. Rightly, GCHQ felt the need to keep pace, through systems such as Embledon and Grouper. Increasingly, operators worked under central control, linked closely to others. Each monitored several sets through a console, where computers tracked fluctuations in signals and guided interception, with the take typed straight to a teleprinter and sent directly to GCHQ, or automatically processed, without human hand. Grouper proved better than humans in tracing wandering signals.[63] These procedures reduced the autonomy of operators in finding, recording and reporting signals. They turned craftsmen into clerks: the automation of collection, for instance, offered opportunities for some radio operators, but only if they learned to use keyboards and computers, and in many cases learned touch typing – an advanced and, at that time, traditionally female skill. Many operators disliked and resisted any form of typing.

Technical changes in collection by individuals and at stations raised fundamental questions of skill and value, while the closing of stations to rationalise interception disrupted lives. Staff having to move might lose friends, and perhaps money, if forced to sell homes on a falling market. Staff moving to Scarborough in 1972 were warned of housing shortages, prices 'bounding skywards', and uncertainty about schools.[64] These changes were unavoidable; GCHQ tried to treat personnel fairly, and the radio grades were used to changes in procedures: they were not Luddites. Still, these actions challenged the status and interests of operators, who became irritated about their conditions and 'the Admeanies' or 'Admini', as they nicknamed their superiors.[65] GCHQ gave men from declining industries, such as radio operators from the merchant marine, a haven in which to live off old expertise. Civilian demand was scarce for men with these skills, especially those set in their ways, nor was there much call for their skills in other government departments. Both sides were stuck with each other.

Once GCHQ controlled itself, in 1947 it adopted the Whitley Council system to manage industrial relations, which was standard across government. Representatives of management (the 'official side') and labour (the 'staff side') compromised and negotiated over pay and workplace conditions. The official side consulted and listened. The staff side balanced operational requirements with its members' interests.[66] National union officials, sometimes members of the British Communist Party in the early days of the Whitley Committee in GCHQ, received limited access to GCHQ in order to conduct their business. The official side, including the most senior members of GCHQ, consulted the staff side over all changes involving the workplace, where the latter had real influence, but did so often from a lofty position. When staff opposed the closure of Hawklaw naval intercept station in Scotland because their families had roots and would suffer if made to sell their homes all at once, Director Eric Jones advised this response: 'If people wanted a settled life in one locality for fifty years or so they should not join GCRB.'⁶⁷ That attitude perhaps was acceptable in 1958, for civilian employees of state, but not for much longer.

Between 1967 and 1981, a weakening economy and rising expectations for pay created new problems between management and staff across Britain. Inflation swamped everyone. It drove competition for pay increases in a society where wages with comparative groups defined assumptions about the proper size of one's own. Over two years, inflation might devalue everyone's pay by 40 per cent, and wage increases of 35 per cent become normal. Strong but divided unions, shop-floor militants, weak governments and social trends, including a decline in deference, accelerated the pressures.

These problems were harder for GCHQ than most firms or government departments. At a national level, both sides weakened Whitleyism, but for GCHQ strikes augmented consultation between staff and 'officials'. Senior management faced issues at which they were weak, such as liaising with unions, and which went against the grain of their characteristics, such as the need for secrecy and inexperience at dealing with the public sphere. Inflation particularly affected GCHQ. For a unit of its size, it had an unusually large number of distinct grades – about forty. Each grade sought to maintain or enhance its position against all others. That aim was complicated because Whitehall linked the pay of every grade to that of different civilian groups with comparable jobs, which received distinct increases. Any wage increase in Britain or Whitehall might cascade across grades within GCHQ. To improve the conditions of any group would annoy others.

For radio operators, grades alone determined their status. Any pay increases threatened an organisation with a stagnant budget, which sought to reduce costs of personnel in order to subsidise other expenditures. Several unions fought each other for members, escalating problems without aiding solutions. Jones may have brought the Association of Government Supervisors and Radio Operators (AGSRO) into GCHQ, in order to counter the presence of an overmighty body, the Civil Service Union (CSU).⁶⁸ If so, this act backfired. GCHQ officials thought AGSRO a 'poaching union', and CSU weak in leadership and organisation.⁶⁹ Both unions raised high expectations for settlements and avoided responsibility when these failed to materialise. When labour troubles first struck GCHQ, no one knew the rules of the game, which caused confusion between management, unions and the shop floor – or, more precisely, the hundreds of shop floors in an atomised agency, with fifty buildings on two sites at Cheltenham, and twenty outstations across the UK. When GCHQ assessed work stoppages, it noted that each station had 'a hard core of militants'.[70] These men were scarcely revolutionaries, simply hard men annoyed at their position – many of them ex-serviceman who once had loathed unions. GCHQ's management assessed the issue with alarmism, but acted with appeasement. Many ex-service Siginters, romanticising their previous leadership, saw GCHQ as interlopers. What were then termed Spanish practices – inefficient and costly working systems – were perhaps augmented by a slight sense of demoralisation: anecdotes often mention night-shift operators arriving with sleeping bags.

For over a decade, crises involving the greatest labour actions in the history of Sigint blindsided GCHQ. The first trouble occurred between 29 August and 3 September 1969, when all GCRO operators worked to rule. This action was not a strike. Some work continued, though much coverage was lost, and three of those days were holidays, which reduced the impact. Still, GCHQ did not need cryptanalysis to read this signal. The crisis emerged when, during a wage arbitration, the head of E division (human resources) openly denied agency (and therefore value) to operators in interception. He said that GCHQ controlled their actions, by which he meant to compare GCHQ to the brain and its operators to the fingers. His comments had much truth but enraged operators. Those in Hong Kong refused to meet a delegation from E, if the head of the division was among them.

In order to escape the dilemma, Joe Hooper took command of the issue. He reacted cautiously, avoiding escalation, pressing the Civil Service Department to compromise, and aiding the union. He brought union leaders to his flat for Sunday lunch and talks, and then won their case, overturning the arbitration they disliked and gaining them more money. Operators saw their director defend them. When the Labour minister handling negotiations suggested that the government risk a temporary breakdown of work at GCHQ, Hooper was horrified: no damage to Sigint could be risked.[71] US elements had just warned NSA that British delays in forwarding semi-processed material and end product 'reinforces the requirement for independent, totally US-controlled cover, processing and reporting of high interest Soviet military activity'.

Tordella, seeing this demand as a political move during a period of cuts, told GCHQ he could manage the issue, but regretted it.[72] This signal too was in plain language: problems with labour might trigger bigger ones with UKUSA. Whenever British labour problems cost coverage for the Americans, GCHQ winced, for professional and political reasons. The Sigint veteran Michael Herman recounted his 'feelings of sadness and shame ... when a Cold War 24-hour surveillance unit' under his control 'closed down for a night watch as part of a departmental pay dispute', passing the work to NSA. He was grateful that NSA tolerated GCHQ's reduction in production during the three-day weeks of 1973.[73] Through careful management, GCHQ and NSA kept the worst cases of labour unrest in Britain from affecting American service Sigint. NSA forgave GCHQ, but could not forget.

GCHQ concluded that most operators disliked the go-slow, but would follow their unions into another one. This group was a barrel of gunpowder within GCHQ. Problems linked to salary and promotion were 'indeed intractable and likely to persist' until 1985. Operators would have to take what they could get, like it or not. One so-called 'propagandist' retorted that 'the Radio class is the whipping boy of the Department'. Their unions condemned GCHQ for 'an anti-Radio class philosophy'.[74] GCHQ responded by trying to improve the morale and solidarity of all personnel, especially the radio operators. A newsletter, Contact, promoted Hooper's hope that staff would bridge 'the gap between stations and the centre', and become 'more aware of the needs, problems and interests of their colleagues'.[75] Its NSA equivalent focused more on technique and kit, as did the in-house magazines of the British armed services. GCHQ sought to pre-empt problems through constant negotiations with the unions.

During 1972–73, the major crises centred on cypher operators, spurred when personnel doing identical work at MOD received far greater pay increases, which, ultimately, GCHQ staff also acquired. GCHQ leaders sympathised with these actions, which twice caused 'virtual paralysis in the transmission of Sigint data and reports'. Again, GCHQ worked for compromise and aided the union. In February 1973, GCHQ feared that a projected civil service strike might force the closure of its computer centre – that is, of cryptanalysis. Hooper's beer and sandwiches approach to industrial relations fitted contemporary British society, and failed for the same reason – events. Work stoppages, great and small, sputtered throughout 1970s Britain, peaking when 2,000 GCHQ personnel struck during national days of action on 23 February and 11 June 1979. These events crippled 'all but the barest element of computer processing' for six weeks, damaging 'some current and all longer-term studies'.

Ultimately, pay rises and appeasement did enough to keep the sparks from lighting the gunpowder barrel. Radio and cypher operators controlled two bottlenecks in Sigint, namely collection and communication. Militarised, militant and – more than any other element at GCHQ – unified by identical conditions and forms of work, these grades were better placed to exploit work to rule. During the 1970s, the pay of radio and cypher operators, which had been equivalent to clerical officers, rose to become equivalent to that of executive officers. GCHQ ignored the latter's protests, as they lacked the muscle to redress. After the union ban, critics condemned GCHQ for always having bad labour relations, with a 'pathological' desire to destroy the union presence, which it viewed as 'the enemy within'.[76] In fact, GCHQ was a well-managed organisation doing its best in difficult circumstances, which staff generally appreciated. In *Contact*, the staff sides at stations regularly reported decent to good relations with their management. *Contact* magazine distributed accounts, such as this one from Wincombe station in Wiltshire across GCHQ: 'Staff committee work at the moment is very much concerned with DO's paper on the problems of the Radio Classes and with the Director's recent letter on the disposition of GCRO stations. The conclusions of the Director's letter have unfortunate implications for us, and we and others need to do a great deal on the problems that arise from them. Indeed, our very future as Radio Officers, our prospects and movements are cause for concern.'[77]

Meanwhile, GCHQ encouraged newcomers to join unions. It canvassed the staff side's views on any issue affecting personnel, and accepted the legitimacy of their arguments, even when these complicated key issues, such as the acquisition of linguists to work on Soviet targets.[78] More than in most units, at GCHQ members of both 'sides' were on first-name terms and interacted informally, often over a pint, in Cheltenham, let alone at small stations. GCHQ had better experiences with labour unrest than most government departments during the 1970s. Unlike the national trade union leadership, most union members at GCHQ were reluctant to exploit their ability to damage UKUSA as a bargaining tactic. However reluctantly, the radio grades accepted great changes in their conditions and status.

The Union Ban

These characteristics changed when Margaret Thatcher came to power in 1979. At immense cost, her government wrung inflation from the economy and power from the unions. It broke old practices of labour relations across the civil service. National unions, and the Council of Civil Service Unions, responded with days of action during 1980, which disrupted GCHQ like all departments. The following year, however, the unions launched selective strikes in areas where they expected impact: airports, tax offices and civilian support agencies of the military. GCHQ no longer confronted only home-grown problems, driven by local conditions and pay; it also faced political ones, launched by outsiders for strategic reasons.

GCHQ once complained that national unions misunderstood its work: but when they grasped it, things became worse – GCHQ became a primary target for the civil service unions. The unions saw that to pull forty-five men from Bude scarcely bothered their members or the country, but shook the government more than if they placed 100,000 people on the streets. Union leaders justified these actions with startlingly syndicalist boasts, which they soon found embarrassing, claiming they could cripple Britain's nuclear deterrent and Western defences against the USSR: 'Our ultimate success depends upon the extent to which ... defence readiness is hampered ... by this and further action.' For several weeks, the unions placed Bude on a 'permanent strike', or so they claimed: the results were rather less damaging. Director Brian Tovey rightly thought the unions regarded GCHQ 'as a damned good place to hit'. And so the unions promised: 'We are going to hit this department as hard as we can.'[79] On 9 March 1981, 2,500 members of GCHQ went on strike. Smaller actions followed over the next month. Many of these strikes threatened national security, NATO and UKUSA, during a bad patch in the Cold War. Later, the leaders of the civil service unions, and members of GCHQ who resisted the union ban, regarded this behaviour as mistaken. A better term might be suicidal.

These actions threatened GCHQ and its workforce. With unprecedented force and detail, Tovey warned station staff that the stoppages had caused MOD to feel 'a serious loss of confidence in the Sigint organisation, and more especially in the GCRO'. Such concerns might damage GCHQ's budget and 'the numbers of staff we could usefully employ ... for the time being, any new Sigint interception projects that are of vital importance to the Armed Services will have to be undertaken by the <u>Service</u> element of the Sigint organisation' only. NSA too 'is losing confidence in British Sigint, and more particularly in the GCRO ... not only I but the whole of GCHQ have been placed in an embarrassing and indeed humiliating position as a result of the action taken by those relatively few staff who, by their recourse to industrial action' caused DIRNSA to ask that GCRO not handle certain joint issues.[80]

Culturally, for Tovey and other leaders to express public shame for GCHQ's failures, and admit that others should not depend on it, was unusual behaviour, both honest and political. Siginters understood the meaning of this clear signal, which perhaps served to reduce subsequent industrial action. Personnel frequently refused orders to strike, even in the militant and disciplined GCRO. In H, 'plenty of people were not union members and so came into work anyway, some union members refused to go on strike, and one or two came into work anyway, unpaid, whilst on strike, wearing a big "I am on strike" button'.[81] Even so, Mike Verrion, the head of staff side, warned the CSU, 'about the risks to continued employment if, as a result of what could be construed as a politically motivated strike, the supply dies up even for a short time'. In order to preserve GCHQ, and the unions' place there, 'great care should be taken in the application of industrial action. Careful thought should indicate how the best interests of the membership will be served, and that may not be industrial action. Nailing one's colours to the mast or taking part in a kamikaze-like strike is of no use if, after the ship goes down, there are no life boats around.'[82]

Things could not go on as they were, but to change them was difficult. Tough decision-makers in GCHQ and PSIS wavered over the solution for five years. During 1979–80, GCHQ explored the possibility of a no-strike agreement with union locals and the previous head of staff side, Jack Hart, and later the leader of the hold-outs against the union ban. These discussions offered 'little or no chance of successfully negotiating safeguards to avoid disruption on the basis then under consideration by GCHQ management'. Whitehall let GCHQ make that approach, while blocking similar ones by any other unit, for concern over graver issues. The unions 'are well aware that the areas of greatest concern to us are precisely those where their power to put pressure on the Government is at its greatest'.[83] Ironically, this pursuit of a no-strike deal at GCHQ might have provoked more disruption there, as happened when the CSD privately tried to have the unions cease disrupting GCHQ in 1981.

After the unrest of 1980, GCHQ concluded that it was 'the sole intelligence organisation in the Western world which suffers from a substantial vulnerability to labour disputes'. These disputes could damage British performance and its interests 'unpredictably and in a way that GCHQ management could not fully control. Furthermore GCHQ's reliability in the eyes of its allies, principally NSA, was brought seriously into question.' The DIRNSA 'has hitherto attempted to conceal from the wider U.S. community the level of damage sustained as a result of industrial action within GCHQ, but has warned unofficially that his position in this respect must be open to review.' The DIRNSA could not hide the sudden absence of GCHQ's product from the many American agencies which normally received it, because Britain contributed so much to Americans through interdependence. Critics of the union ban demonise American authorities and present British ones as lickspittles. UKUSA was 'a master–servant arrangement of convenience'.[84] In fact, what is astonishing about this time are NSA's restraint and Whitehall's reluctance to tackle the union problem.

GCHQ and PSIS agreed that GCHQ needed to be insulated from national union decisions on industrial action, but could not agree how to do so. They skirted the obvious solution: banning strikes and national unions at GCHQ. By mid-1981, however, after further slowdowns, Tovey warned that 'the psychological impact on NSA was very great. We regularly note, for example, that the possibility of future Industrial Action in GCHQ is being taken into account in a wide range of NSA plans. At some point, unless we set our house in order, we shall cease to be regarded as a reliable and worthwhile partner, with the consequent risk that we shall then be excluded from major new and vital developments in the supply of high-grade Sigint', against the backdrop of a rising NSA.[85] NSA did not demand that GCHQ solve this problem, but could not hide its growing reservations, more in sorrow than anger, about further cooperation. In an unauthorised statement, the retired Tovey later publicly said: 'We do not interfere with each other but, having said that, the Americans could not be unconcerned if a major partner fell down on the job. We noticed a reluctance to enter into work-sharing and we read this as a message. It was the beginning of a reluctant feeling that "Oh Lord, we don't know if we can rely on the Brits."[86] When DIRNSA Admiral Bobby Inman learned of the intention to ban the unions, he replied: 'That's marvellous.' Tovey addressed these issues through private discussions with DIRNSAs, which eliminates an important part of the record.

Tovey concluded that the problem could be solved only by banning GCHQ personnel from joining unions and creating a 'house union', which, he claimed, many labour leaders at GCHQ had urged him to pursue. That statement is difficult to judge but, notably, most of these people later accepted the union ban. After careful assessment, GCHQ concluded that most staff would accept the idea, and created a basket of sticks and carrots to achieve that aim. Gradually, during 1981–83, Whitehall accepted the argument, which was linked to other issues, especially the official avowal that GCHQ was a Sigint agency. Though in hindsight the danger of union disruption of GCHQ was ebbing, no one viewing the record of the past fifteen years could have thought so at the time.

The Cabinet Secretary, Robert Armstrong, thought that without de-unionisation, 'the disruption experienced in recent years will be repeated'. He and Thatcher pressed the idea after her government won a landslide election in 1983.[87] Peter Marychurch succeeded Tovey in part because he had prepared the details of the ban, and could be trusted to make it work. Armstrong presented the decision to union leaders on 25 January 1984. Members of GCHQ could no longer belong to any union, except the GCHQ Staff Association. In return for surrendering those rights, every member of GCHQ staff would receive a taxable one-time bonus of £1,000, which would not count towards retirement pay. Anyone who wished to keep the rights would be helped to find a comparable government position elsewhere, or receive a redundancy package.

The ban shocked union leaders, doubly so when they considered how their past actions and words justified it. Quickly, they offered what GCHQ had wanted in 1979: a no-disruption agreement. So long

From: P H Marychurch - Director

Government Communications Headquarters
Oakley Cheltenham Glos GL52 5AJ
Telephone Cheltenham 21491 ext

D/8489DQ/1501/29A

25 January 1984

To all members of staff

The purpose of this letter is to tell you of an important development which will affect us all in GCHQ. Our future work will depend on its success.

2.   Ministers have recently decided that because GCHQ must be able to work in secrecy and to provide a service on which the Government and our allies can confidently rely at all times, it should be freed as far as possible from the dangers of its operations being discussed publicly (for example at industrial tribunals), and from the risks of industrial action. For this purpose, certificates have been signed by the Foreign and Commonwealth Secretary excepting GCHQ staff from provisions of the Employment Protection Acts. This is further explained in GN 100/84, a copy of which is enclosed.

3.   The general effect is to limit (as in other British security and intelligence services) the right of the staff to have recourse to an industrial tribunal, and their rights in connection with union membership and activities. Other conditions of service relating to pay, allowances, etc will remain unchanged as explained in the GN. But in recognition of the fact that staff are being deprived of certain rights previously enjoyed, Ministers have agreed that a financial payment of £1,000 (to full-time staff) will be appropriate for those who remain at GCHQ. Part-time staff will receive a pro-rata payment. This also is explained in the GN which I urge you to read carefully.

4.   E Division is ready to provide any further information and advice which you may need but, as the GN explains, you have the opportunity to seek a transfer elsewhere if you do not wish to remain in GCHQ. Many of you will I know wish to consult your families before making up your mind, and I urge you to do so, drawing on this letter and the accompanying GN which are both unclassified. You must of course not reveal any classified information.

5.   In making their decision Ministers recognised the critical importance of the work of GCHQ. The value of that work depends on the dedication, loyalty and professionalism of individual members of staff: I hope that all of you who are affected by the changes will wish to stay with GCHQ, so that we can continue to provide the high level of service which is of such vital importance to the country.

6.   When you have made your decision, please fill in and return to the Establishment and Personnel Officer the attached option form. This should be done as soon as possible, and not later than 1 March 1984.

P H MARYCHURCH
Director

Figure 10.1
Marychurch letter to staff

as GCHQ members could join unions, the latter would not threaten its operations through industrial action. This issue merits delicate judgement. Armstrong, Marychurch and Tovey were right to insist on banning the unions rather than negotiating with them first. A ban was a precondition for negotiations: otherwise, the unions would not have talked, but rather agitated or struck. A no-disruption offer would require ratification from the membership, and militants, of several unions. Such an outcome was not certain, but it was possible: a very similar arrangement has worked since 1997.

This was the best solution to the problem and probably the option most preferred by GCHQ staff. Later, Marychurch and Tovey supported this solution, though the former opposed the idea in 1984. Armstrong thought that the union leaders were 'desperate about it. They would go to almost any lengths to keep their foot in the door.' He recommended serious consideration of their offer for a no-strike agreement which, he thought, met 97 per cent of Whitehall's aims and would commit future Labour governments. So did many other officials and ministers, to no avail. [88] At GCHQ both management and union leaders thought that support for the unions wavered and then fell and rose for the idea of a staff association. Marychurch feared, rightly, that to change tack would create confusion and threaten success. If GCHQ abandoned the ban for a no-strike agreement, which the unions then rejected, his position would be dire. Mrs Thatcher's closest advisors warned that compromise on GCHQ would weaken her political credibility. She regarded union leaders as fools and traitors – unfairly, as regards the civil service unions. She rejected any compromise on labour issues, as clashes loomed with the national miners' union. This action was calculated and aimed more at allies and neutrals in her government than her enemies, or GCHQ itself.[89] Thatcher's intransigence won the miners' strike, but damaged GCHQ. Like the unions before her, she made GCHQ a pawn in her game.

GCHQ banned unions, but their members abandoned them. Union and management relations at GCHQ had strains. The union ban triggered none of them. Initial concern about the ban was high, but opposition eroded fast. The hold-outs were few, and mostly not from the classes which had been most unhappy in the past. These people were respected by their peers, motivated by principle and independence, were strong believers in the value of Sigint, and often middle-aged graduates. The hound did not sound for many reasons. Staff at GCHQ were intelligent, pragmatic, professional, loyal to the department and each other, and trained to read signals. The union ban was a hard signal to misread. Half of GCHQ was not unionised. Union members did not see the union actions between 1979 and 1981 as defending their interests, but instead as damaging them and GCHQ. The unions sapped their own credibility.

Feelings on all sides were mixed in complex ways. The actions of 1981 angered many union members. Many at GCHQ disliked both the unions and the ban. The challenge to their dignity angered them, that to the unions less so. Many who signed Option A regretted the need. Yet most local union leaders did so. The AGSRO and CSU branches at Cheadle led their members unanimously to sign Option A. One activist said he knew the game was up when no local member would meet his eyes in a meeting at a pub.[90] Thatcher broke the cycle of inflation which drove labour unrest at GCHQ; few staff at GCHQ or outstations hated her, and £1,000 was real money for most people. These bonuses sparked a boom in the Cheltenham economy and family holidays abroad. To refuse the ban meant disrupting one's life. Many members of GCHQ did not want to leave Cheltenham or, especially in the radio grades, could not easily find jobs elsewhere. The looming surge of retirements also reduced militancy and boosted a reflex simply to serve out one's time. Intercept operators perhaps feared that authorities would happily see their numbers fall. Despite its failings, management and almost all staff regarded this outcome as the best one possible, however coercive.

Before the ban was announced, GCHQ calculated that to lose 100 staff would have a negligible impact, 500 would be difficult but manageable, and 1,000 serious. The Foreign Secretary, Geoffrey Howe, publicly stated that the government would reconsider the ban if enough members of GCHQ refused the offer. Thus, union members knew they could break the ban. The unions fought the ban hard, with access to GCHQ staff. Yet just 130 staff refused to sign Option A. After retirements and movements, only thirteen were dismissed, on hard terms. Those who chose to become martyrs, did so: everyone else received a generous redundancy package. The union ban drove valuable people to retire prematurely, but not many, and none who were essential. Doubts about their own loyalty angered many among those who stayed. Morale declined, damaging an organisation driven by self-direction, but not by much, nor in a simple way. Personnel still pursued problems which interested them. Retirements made promotion more possible than it had been for decades. Skiving continued on some shifts, but was eradicated on others. The GCHQ Staff Association acquired as many members as all the unions had held previously. Thatcher boasted: 'I saw to it that they did a damn sight better with the staff association than they had ever done with a Trade Union.'[91] Her government gave GCHQ and its staff more money than any had done since 1955, which increased morale across the department. The GCHQ protesters became demoralised, as they waited outside the wire.

Externally, in terms of perception the ban harmed GCHQ. It was hard to justify even to those who knew the story. The government's unwillingness to discuss the damage to intelligence operations caused by union actions damaged that case. The annual march of the trade unions at Cheltenham became an icon for commemorations over the corpse of Whiteyism. GCHQ became a party political matter as it never had been before, precisely as it became a publicly avowed agency. Whenever a Labour government took power, it would seek to overturn the union ban, as the new Labour Foreign Minister, Robin Cook, told GCHQ's leaders on the second day after he took office in 1997. The outcome proved simple. The remaining hold-outs paraded into GCHQ, and were welcomed. Only two or three could be reinstated. New negotiations between GCHQ and the unions solved the old problems. Within one, the Public and Commercial Services Union (PCS), a Government Communications Group (GCG) was formed and received negotiating power with GCHQ. All unions agreed they never could abandon their members' right to strike, but, equally, agreed that they would not disrupt GCHQ's work. The 1984 union ban was a tragedy for some members of GCHQ, but beneficial to most, and an incident to the institution.

Intercept to End Product: the Collection, Processing and Dissemination of Sigint, 1945–92

Seen as a snapshot, Sigint looks like a thing; but really it is a process with many moving parts. This chapter assesses change and continuity within these parts and the whole during the Cold War. Siginters, working on the leading edge of communications and data processing, are sensitive to any developments in either area. Change characterises Sigint, but revolutions are rare.

The years between 1939 and 1992 were the heart of the first age of Sigint. Until 1992, computers essentially supported cryptanalysis, rather than transformed organisation. Computing power rose steadily, as did collection by and against satellites, through automated systems. The roomfuls of data-processing machines employed to shatter Enigma vanished, but other systems rose to tackle different targets. Otherwise, until 1992, GCHQ essentially used variants of the equipment, approach and structure which had characterised British Sigint in 1945. Teams of operators still intercepted voice and HF and VHF Morse. To some extent data processing still rested on card indexes and punchcards, and on teams working in typing pools and communication centres. GCHQ was a machine to produce information, driven by a flow of paper instead of steam. Overwhelmingly, its personnel worked in labour-intensive tasks of interception, involving some skilled craftwork and data processing, and always the pristine copying, recopying and movement of paper. This system was agile for the time, but obese from the perspective of digitisation. The fat melted away only in the white heat of a second age of Sigint, which stemmed from decades of technological and organisational innovation.

After 1975, GCHQ (and NSA) began to perceive remarkable changes in Sigint, which signalled the transition towards the beginning of the second age. The technology for collection and computing changed exponentially, while analytical practices began to transform:

> The way in which our research work is now conducted is different from what it was 20 years ago or more ... In the past it was more common for the various processes to be conducted in isolation from each other. Both inclination and technology (or the lack of it) encouraged the idea of the pure researcher, working alone, in a small well-insulated unit. Things have changed; in particular improvements in technology offer the researcher's material to flow uninterruptedly from the point of origin to the customers, and to be readily available for manipulation and consultation by all who require it. An increasing amount of our experts' attention is now devoted to the study not just of the data itself, but of the way in which the data flows and can be stored and accessed. This inevitably means a much greater emphasis on interaction between various parts of the organisation, and a considerably greater emphasis on management: the complex organisation of diverse people and operations becomes as important and as demanding a task as the organisation or manipulation by a single individual or a given set of data.[1]

During the 1980s, GCHQ and NSA were on the leading edge of the information age; they were sensitive to changes in it, and adapted well to these challenges, better than almost any other commercial or state agency in the world. This boosted UKUSA's immediate power against adversaries, yet slowed its response to further developments. The revolution which GCHQ and NSA dimly foresaw around 1980 arrived in an unanticipated form after 1990. The end of the Cold War, the rise of personal computers and communications devices such as smartphones and the World Wide Web – and their combined effect on assessment, communication, consumers, organisation, resources and targets – transformed every basis of Sigint at once. GCHQ and NSA found these changes hard to manage.

Forms of Collection

Between 1945 and 1992, means of communication and interception constantly shifted. Voice, captured by ear, hand or tape recorders, matched text in significance. Oceanic telegraphs, once central to communications, declined. After 2000, new submarine fibre-optic cables restored that position. This material was provided under warrant to GCHQ. Despite predictions that Morse was dead, HF and VHF dominated military signals. Antenna farms – aerials concentrated in good locations for interception – best collected such transmissions, which were shielded by complex shifts in frequencies. Only interception and data-processing systems of unprecedented sophistication could handle the flood of traffic from satellites. Sigint caught far more material than ever before, but proportionately far less of the whole than GC&CS had done between 1919 and 1945. Knowing which channels carried the best material at any moment – an extension of the old practice of long-range technical search – exploded in significance and absorbed more staff. Learning the timings and frequencies for messages on Morse, or keywords or telephone numbers for traffic on satellites, improved the take more than merely expanding the power of interception. In these areas, GCHQ was strong.

During the heroic age of interception, operators wearing headphones would sit hunched over clumsy sets, hunting wavering frequencies, scribbling messages by pencil. GC&CS and stations assigned broad tasks to intercept operators who, over the space of a shift, must cover a net or several frequencies. Individual skill and autonomy remained high, driven by knowledge of the nets which operators penetrated. Increasingly after 1945, technological and organisational developments changed working conditions. From 1955, the Racal RA-17 receiver eliminated frequency drift and improved interception at high frequencies. Good RA-17 operators managed more sets and monitored more frequencies than before. Operators controlled usually two or four sets, guided by GCHQ, station staff and computers. They monitored Morse on many frequencies, but heard only two at a time (one in each ear) and recorded their transmissions. Targets routinely worked to known schedules. Once an operator knew that they should take a five-minute sample from 12345Khz at 1700, and switch to another frequency ten minutes later, the efficiency and power of interception and centralised control rose. While the autonomy of operators fell, experience of living within a network focused their accuracy. GCHQ operators remained masters of that skill.

Craftmanship was crucial, yet industrialisation boosted interception. From 1970, positions in all major stations had many RA-17 sets, tuning aids, links to computers, and VDUs to ease data processing. Racal Store-4 reel-to-reel tape recorders augmented human transcription for voice. Microcomputers, mostly Honeywell 316s, linked GCHQ to stations and guided their work. Catfish – 'a computer-controlled, spectrum-surveillance system' – shaped search at Cheadle. At an RAF station, an 'Intercept Controller', a senior NCO, directed 'RIFIFI-aided search positions manned by experienced operators'. Computers controlled the work of 340 RA-17s sets at Scarborough. At Culmhead in Somerset, computers directed one channel-watching system and also the attack on ILC, probably to weed unwanted traffic and maximise desired collection. These systems required human agency, but cut their cost. At Scarborough, sixty operators intercepted Morse in 1955, down to just thirty-two in 1981, while the number of traffic handlers at Culmhead fell from seventy-five to forty.[2] Throughout the 1970s, all stations increasingly adopted automated systems. Grouper directed interception and strengthened centralised power: on each station, a controller with broad and instantaneous access to data guided six operators, minute by minute. Through Embledon, operators typed manual reports onto computers, which produced a hard copy and signals tape, which enabled automatic distribution of content to consumers, without recopying. Through 'Tasking by Objectives', GCHQ and stations directed the work of operators. Some intercepted Morse flowed automatically to headquarters.

By 1974, GCHQ had moved technology and data processing a generation further through Carboy, the satellite collection facility at Bude. Two hundred feet from the Atlantic Ocean and 400 feet above sea level, the station at Bude probably had better intercept capability than any other UK antenna farm had ever had. Bude collected more material than every other GCHQ station put together – though most of it unwanted, which posed unprecedented problems of filtering and discarding, the first quantum leap in that area since 1915. Bude, the first entirely computer-controlled station, had huge spaces and numbers of machines, but few people. 'Based on the maximum use of computers and a minimum use of manpower', Bude was designed around antennae and machines, not humans and desks. Computers outnumbered operations staff. The 'System' was 'a real-time, computer-controlled, receiving, dechannelling, recording, demultiplexing, message processing system, with facilities for data forwarding'. 'Vast arrays of electronic hardware seem to stretch as far as the eye can see. Some are arranged in rows with guardsman-like precision, others stand alone. In pairs or in more complex groupings, computers, monitors, demodulators, recorders, teleprinters, control consoles, tape-decks, card readers, discs, drums, VDUs, oscilloscopes, illuminated status titles gleam their reds, greens, embers and whites from every cranny. Only the Daleks are missing. Or are they?'

Each shift had just eight operators, to keep the system working as the doctor ordered. 'The process can be impressively independent and frighteningly efficient. It can also, on occasion, be infuriatingly perverse,' Bude's leaders noted. Twenty-two computers controlled 'interception and processing ... data processing and the routine control of antenna steerage, receiver tuning, base-band demultiplexing and dechanneller and recorder allocation'. Two parabolic dishes, 97 feet in diameter and fully steerable, intercepted traffic from two satellites simultaneously. Each satellite carried a 'mind-boggling' number of channels.[3]

Not all signals involved words. At the battle of the Tsushima Straits in 1905, Japanese warships followed Russian fleet movements by gauging the strength of their wireless signals. Elint, which examines non-communications signals from electronic emissions, is therefore among the first forms of Sigint. Through the same means, before the battle of Coronel in 1914, the German navy understood that the British warships ahead of them were divided, and were able to destroy half of them. For decades thereafter, Elint aided traffic analysis, but was not seen as an independent topic.

In 1940–45, however, Elint, often referred to during the Second World War as 'noise', captured and analysed the emissions of electronic equipment, including radar. It became central to tactical air intelligence and to electronic warfare (EW). After 1945, Elint was essential to Sigint and EW, and to Siginters and military services. Its highly technical development was an American triumph.[4] Elint gave air forces and navies tactical intelligence and situational awareness; it enabled EW, while boosting operational assessments for Siginters. Both Sigint and military intelligence needed Elint, and sought to control it. These competing needs placed Elint under continual judgements of Solomon, with less happy results for the baby than in the Bible. Analysis of radar was essential to Elint, yet in the United States measurement and signatures intelligence (Masint), under military intelligence, controlled much radar intelligence (Radint). Telemetry on nuclear targets was initially classified as Elint, but later moved to Masint. American and British politics on these matters affected GCHQ. It managed Elint, telemetry and some Radint within Britain, though the services controlled Radint and EW. NSA, CIA and the American services shared responsibility for Elint, often bickering over it. These divisions damaged Elint and its relationship with Sigint. Neither GCHQ nor NSA used Elint as well as it deserved, yet the source remained strong and valuable.

During the Cold War, Comint, Elint, Masint and traffic analysis were fused, and Sigint was central to national intelligence. Through pencils and typewriters, tape recorders and ear, hand or computers, Siginters provided staggering quantities of material that required many forms of analysis – which were always technical and usually expensive. Elint was taped, reproduced in many ways and sent rapidly to analysts. In 1955, intercepted Elint was projected onto a cathode ray tube and filmed. People using oscilloscopes, vibralisers, filters and cameras analysed these images of the shape, size and nature of signals, reporting their results through graphics and text. In 2000, radar pulse analysis automatically handled this machine- and operator-intensive process. Codebreakers did not touch most Sigint, yet they received more material than ever before.

The Story of H

For a generation, leaders from Bletchley – above all the head of H, Hugh Alexander – drove cryptanalysis at GCHQ down a twisting path. During 1946–48, GCHQ penetrated high-grade Soviet systems, until the Soviets ceased using them, or sending significant communications, on radio. High-grade traffic still moved on landline, however, while a new Soviet machine, codenamed Albatross, carried radio traffic. Siginters failed to shoot that bird, but assumed any future war would be prolonged. In that case these vulnerable systems would be used over radio and, like Albatross, might eventually be read. The authorities regarded preparations for another Ultra as a top priority. Siginters attacked Albatross in force, even after they realised that war would not happen as conceived. Alexander took a 'gloomy view' of the prospects for success, but his superiors did not. Josh Cooper wrote: 'I am convinced that until we can get back to the "main cypher" of the main enemy we are just not producing the article which was marketed so successfully in the war.' Jones made that attack GCHQ's leading priority, which PSIS also did for British defence.[5] Though this work failed, it spurred developments in cryptanalysis and gained computers for GCHQ. Its power in cryptanalysis boosted that effort, whereas American Siginters relied on their unique strength in brute force. As at Bletchley, these approaches were complementary. Each side taught the other.

Between 1952 and 1964, H division was tied into a joint attack against high-grade Soviet cryptosystems, which began as a unique contribution, demonstrated its skills to Americans on a daily basis, and became a loss leader to showcase British prowess. Whitehall initially loved this venture, but enthusiasm dimmed when results failed to materialise. GCHQ hoped to reduce the effort it spent on the attack, which tied scarce resources to failure and prevented satisfaction elsewhere. Divisions J and K controlled cryptanalysis in their own areas, while H was divided from GCHQ. Even directors knew little of H. In 1964, Hooper accused Alexander of not letting the 'wind of priority change to blow sufficiently strong through H'. In fact, without informing anyone else, Alexander used new recruits to shift bits of H quietly from the Soviet target onto others.[6] H gave unique and valuable material to K and NSA, through new targets and techniques. Targets used a range of manual, electro-mechanical and increasingly electronic systems. Some well-used manual systems were unbreakable; many electronic ones collapsed. Much codebreaking was done with 'squared paper and a set of coloured pencils', with GCHQ punching far above its weight, but computers moved from aiding cryptanalysis to embodying it. In 1962, H used over '6,500 hours of computer time ... on crypt problems ... Increased programming resources and increased computer time are the steps chiefly needed to improve our overall cryptanalytic capacity.'[7] By

1971, GCHQ ran its 'first automated crypt production line'.[8] Thereafter, cryptanalysis turned on the relationship between codebreakers and computer hardware and software: cryppies and coders became two, then one.

Siginters followed civilian trends, where users shared ideas and addressed problems through customised computer operating systems, languages and software. GCHQ produced material on an industrial scale and immaculately recopied across myriad media – this duplication occurring often ten times between interception and dissemination. Corrupt ciphertext impeded the performance of computerised cryptanalysis even more than that processed by people. One seasoned cryppie wrote: 'Crypt success is very dependent on having clean, that is garble-free and dit-free, cipher, and most important of all, no dropped or gained characters.' In the radio age, a ' "best copy", that is a composite with the best possible chance of being right in each character position, or failing that, a "least bad copy" ', was created.[9] Intercepted ciphertext was translated from its original figure groups to bigraphs in computer language, and stored on magnetic tapes – originally reel-to-reel, later cartridges. Initially the tapes were disorganised because no one foresaw the scale to be stored; soon, however, they were well indexed for data-retrieval purposes. Messages selected for attack were copied in batches onto punchcards and fed into computers. Machine-readable content was transferred electronically onto 'disc packs' (hard drives) and interrogated through code in a special language – IMP – which was 'written by cryptanalysts for cryptanalysts, and a more gloriously flamboyant and dangerous language there never was'.[10] After interrogation, disc packs were flushed and content from new punchcards entered.

GCHQ performed distinctive cryptanalysis on American computer systems. Hectra – 'Handling and Editing of Cipher TRaffic Automatically' – and Theta – 'Telecipher Handling and Editing of Traffic Automatically' – attacked different sorts of cryptosystems through a supervisory computer model. 'With about the CPU power of a modern digital watch, and 50 simultaneous users,' Hectra used Pole Star, a supervisory CDC 7600 computer, to run cryptanalytic routines against databases stored on the two IBM machines of Twin Star. When combined, Pole Star and Twin Star were called Tri Star. The 'huge hash tables' of these databases held traffic and metadata, like a record of what processing had already been conducted against specific messages. Hectra and Theta prepared cypher text for cryptanalysis, and decided how to attack hundreds of target systems – cryptosystems which were translated to binary form. Trigraphs were written in Idasys, also called Folklore, an operating system written by the Institute for Defense Analyses, a leading research organisation of the American government, and developed by NSA. Idasys was far better than any civilian operating system of the 1970s, or the early versions of MS-DOS and Mac OS which revolutionised home and business computing during the 1980s. Even in 1995, Folklore handled cryptanalysis better than commercially available systems. Folklore let software designers develop programmes on screen, without using punchcards, and gave multiple consumers simultaneous, simple and interactive access to data.[11] Four thousand new messages were loaded onto these British databases each day. Hectra and Theta absorbed all the X and H personnel assigned to computer cryptanalysis and produced much unique material which its American and British consumers valued.

This success stemmed from the quality of British cryptanalysis, and of Anglo-American software more than hardware. CDC 7600 was a supercomputer, but dwarfed by Cray-1. The databases on Twin Star easily could have been stronger. H and X divisions wished to acquire more modern computers, yet their masters had other priorities. Tri Star served its purpose well against any system it could break, despite a limited surge capacity. Before the Falklands conflict, one disc pack, which never exceeded 70 per cent of its capacity, serviced Hectra. As the Falklands conflict began, and more traffic was taken, problems emerged. A 'Hectra black hole' blocked some transmissions on magnetic tape between Pole Star and Tri Star.[12] Torrential rains at Cheltenham temporarily paralysed one IBM computer on 21 May 1982. Two disc packs – one purely for Argentine traffic – began to be used for Hectra, which broke 'hideously' as it moved past 70 per cent capacity. Twenty-four hours of work restored that database. Ultimately, two disc packs handled Argentine traffic, at maximum surge, perhaps producing 300 per cent more messages daily than before the crisis, though Hectra abandoned some of its usual work. GCHQ thought these systems had saved the day, though 'barely'. Hectra 'is not easily or quickly adaptable to changing circumstances'. Twin Star was 'capacious, physically robust, capable of a 168 hour work week but inflexible; Pole Star powerful, simple, versatile, suited to interactive (analyst-computer working) robust software, not conditioned to a full 168 hour week'.[13]

Immediately, GCHQ moved to improve that situation. As the Falklands conflict progressed, GCHQ tested a uniquely British system which it had commissioned: Hyberg. This 'crypt computing' system emphasised 'performance at the expense of programmability' and had great success. Whitehall let GCHQ purchase a Cray-1, which joined the Tri Star configuration after the war ended, though IMP worked poorly on it. GCHQ aimed to develop a new cryptanalytic programme, Ramsay, with more flexibility than Hectra.[14]

By the end of the Cold War, GCHQ's computer hardware was state of the art, finally, and its cryptanalytic firepower among the greatest on earth, just as a tsunami swept Sigint.

Codebreakers

Postwar cryptanalysts looked for non-random patterns – as Tiltman had done, but through a different lens. That lens was ground during 1941–44, when three acts of genius opened a new age of codebreaking: Bill Tutte, Max Newman and Tommy Flowers caught Fish with 'the Brig's' hook and gutted it. Tiltman found two enciphered versions of the same 1,000-group message while scanning hundreds of thousands of groups in the Lorenz SZ40 system (codenamed Tunny by Allied codebreakers), and broke it. By filleting Tiltman's catch, Tutte reconstructed the logic and structure of a machine that he never saw, and defined the characteristics which another machine would need in order to be able to break it. Flowers used his unorthodox knowledge of data processing to create Colossus, the world's first computer, and killer of Fish. Cryptanalysis thus became mathematicised and computerised, fusing the work of cryptanalysts, hardware engineers and computer programmers. Good code broke good codes.

One head of H during the late Cold War wrote that his predecessor had said: '"Don't worry about running H, it will run itself." He didn't mean it literally of course, but there is a grain of truth there. I think he meant it of the crypt part … which … is staffed by gifted and committed people who understand the mission in their bones, know most of the strategy without having to have it written down for them, and can work out for themselves what they need to do.' Hugh Alexander once said that, in cryptanalysis: ' "It is hard to find a middle ground between the deep slough of overpowering detail and the high plateau of vacuous generality." In other words, even to find out what is going on, let alone to manage it, one has to dive down into detail from time to time.' One cryptanalyst paraphrased the novelist L. P. Hartley: ' "H is a foreign country; they do things differently there." And in H I believe they mostly do things better there, but getting anybody else to even recognise it as a theoretical possibility that a bunch of geeks doing things differently just might be doing them better is an uphill struggle with many more failures than successes.' This head concentrated not 'on managing H but trying to manage the rest of GCHQ to enable H to do its business, in an age when increasingly the rest of GCHQ was quite rightly no longer content to let H run its own business behind high walls' – as Alexander had done. H could no longer be a foreign country: 'In the internet age … it has to integrate or die, but integrating might kill it.'[15]

This head of cryptanalysis thought that H was brilliant for 'the world of off-line ciphers', but not for 'an age where encryption is embedded in the communications protocols', part of the base rather than the superstructure. H's success turned on 'agility … one needs both the right business processes and the right technical architecture ... most of the engineers didn't, perhaps couldn't or wouldn't, understand why agility was needed, so explaining how to do it was a poor place to start. The general feeling was that H changed its operational software so often because they were a bunch of amateurs, incompetent at configuration control, and that they needed to do things properly.' The cryptanalyst replied:

> We do data processing, but our data is prepared by someone who does not want us to process it … whose only purpose in life is to prevent us from processing it. That is fundamentally different from the paradigm of all other data processing organisations, so all best practice in data processing that depends upon the notion of having control over the format of the data is suspect for us. We cannot for example put up a website saying, 'If you want your traffic to be intercepted by GCHQ, please enter it into this form.' This is roughly what most data processors do, and so the format of their data changes when they choose to change it. Our data format, on the other hand, changes when any target anywhere chooses to

change their formats for whatever reason, and they generally won't tell us in advance. When this happens we have to respond. Our software met our specification half an hour ago, but now it doesn't, and we are all out of business until we can find out what the new spec is, and bring the software up to spec.[16]

A contemporary cryppie believes that, characteristically, his folk 'over-engineer' attacks on fleeting targets, which they analyse in depth, while codemakers practise 'precision engineering', against all threats which they can imagine twenty years off. Compared to mathematicians and computer scientists, cryptanalysts focus 'not on a theory approach but problem solving, especially mathematical problem solving capacity'. Hackers, tactical and technical, fish for any catch of the day. Cryppies hunt the biggest catches, including great white whales; they 'always find solutions on the very edge of the cryptanalytical power available', combining brute force and a razor edge.[17]

Different but complementary styles of cryptanalysis enhanced the capacity of UKUSA. American cryptanalysts played to their trump suit – brute force. British ones made a virtue of limitations in force, by honing their razor. As a contemporary cryptanalysts says: 'Often operating under a bit more constraint, they looked to getting the idea right before building large computers, and spent a bit more time on the blackboard before hitting the keyboard.' The 'cryptanalytical mindset is most strongly applied early in the problem'. It 'added the greatest value' by attacking the combined weaknesses of hardware, software, encryption and humans, rather than each element alone, or by preferring one target always above the others. These combined weaknesses and opportunities fluctuated constantly, causing a fundamental characteristic of computerised cryptanalysis. Over-engineered assaults are the best way to defeat individual targets, at the risk of general waste. Any change in a target may void the value of an entire mode of assault, and force the development of another, requiring heavy costs in programmers.

In order to achieve these aims, H gave cryppies both direction and freedom. Analysts or requirements 'steered' work, as did the influence of generic problems, such as internet security. During the early Cold War, one cryppie recalled that half of the eight young cryppies in 'H-R' – the cryptanalytic research branch – were in:

a room close to Jack [Good]'s, working directly for him, while the others would be 'farmed out' for a year or two to various other sections where it was thought that a bit of mathematical thinking might help solve some of their problems. This was a 'Good' arrangement ... One of the pleasant things about working at GCHQ at that time was the lack of formality and the disregard of the official working hours. There was of course the 'need to know' restriction on exchanging information, but – at least for us mathematicians – there was a great deal of freedom. We worked the hours we felt like, often got in late and sometimes worked all night. It was not unlike a university atmosphere. Lots of people brought their dogs into their offices. Not many people had cars then, most people cycled or walked to work, or used one of the many buses that came to the offices from different parts of town. And we all worked in small offices, usually for one, two or four people; though there were some rooms with as many as sixteen people of various skills working together on a single problem. But the idea of 'Open Plan' working for everyone would have appalled us.[18]

After 2000, H divided cryppies into several teams; each tackled part of every problem at hand, so all could be covered. Every team might be assigned 'one big technology' which linked many other problems. Since you 'don't control where you have the success, individual problem solvers were best set several different problems at once, a wide range of problems in a wide range of difficulties'. Some cryppies worked quietly until they were close to solutions; others conferred from the start. Once assigned tasks, individuals worked at their own pace, but H nudged them to cover their tasks, and reassigned any which were missed.[19]

Modes of Analysis

According to the doctrine of intelligence, Siginters should produce intelligence, but not assess it. Only specialist agencies with access to all sources can assess intelligence well. Consumers should receive intelligence only after experts have assessed it, not directly from producers. Across UKUSA, other agencies try to keep Siginters from assessing intelligence, or sending it directly to consumers, because Sigint can be an overmighty subject and the one most likely to violate this doctrine. If so, Sigint agencies might castrate analytic ones, while providing worse service. That dogma has some truth. The technical virtuosity required for success in Sigint does not suit the highest forms of analysis. GCHQ products lack the breadth of the best analyses of the Joint Intelligence Committee (JIC), though Siginters are part of the team which writes them. Most GCHQ end-product reports are based on a single transmission, with commentary limited to the elucidation of detail or Elint, delivered to consumers for analysis or action. GCHQ fires and forgets: it solves a problem, reports the solution, and turns to the next. Yet analysis necessarily enters its work, in varying ways, and Sigint does not work simply as doctrine dictates.

By 1944, experience with Sigint in war led Victor Cavendish-Bentinck and Denis Capel-Dunn to emphasise that: 'The experienced cryptographer can make useful deductions from the cyphering characteristics of the traffic with which he deals, just as R.S.S. [Radio Security Service] have developed a remarkable skill in analysis of signalling characteristics.'[20] Since 1945, Sigint has been the source which most escapes oversight by all-source analysts and reaches consumers directly.

Analysis affects every phase of Sigint. Usually, Comint requires translation from one language to another. At GCHQ during the Cold War, linguists fell into two streams, each with different practices. Those with few colleagues were craftsmen, translators and analysts, tackling every message with little oversight or support. When many linguists attacked one language, they worked on an assembly line, each translating messages only in specific areas. Russian linguists worked mostly on an assembly line with voice intercept from tapes. One group processed basic logs of stereotyped messages, largely to aid traffic analysts. Another translated material into English, but transcribed all major passages into Russian, which Russian language analysts treated without time pressure. Even compiled reports, which reproduced the gist of several messages under one heading, were precis, rather than analyses.

These forms of translation largely were mechanical, but others were not. Most K linguists covering the rest of the world were linguistic reporters using language as a tool, who translated Sigint and open source material from text. These personnel often had to report quickly and faced constant crises, working twelve-hour shifts for days on end.

In K division, 'an international crisis is always looming'. Because K confronted a multiplicity of languages, linguistic flexibility was 'highly prized', even involving just log readers with a 'cross-Branch smattering'.[21] Some 'multilinguists' could work in seven languages, even twenty with the aid of a dictionary. Meanwhile, some research analysts provided high-grade translation and intelligence analysis. Thorough knowledge of an area, and intelligent analysis, underpinned many translations of diplomatic messages, especially the most obscure or important ones. Often – indeed, generally whenever Sigint most mattered – key messages went straight to consumers without analysis by any intelligence personnel because their meaning was self-evident, or the consumer did not care about the views of analysts. When the MOD's Defence Intelligence Staff (DIS) and the JIC addressed Sigint, sanitised or otherwise, they analysed it more broadly than GCHQ did. GCHQ provided little analysis for Comint, but unlike the case with Ultra, neither did anyone else, except consumers. The Comint which GCHQ produced most aided consumers in areas where JIC had little role – pre-eminently diplomacy and military operations.

Furthermore: often, only great analysis by Siginters can create information fit for conventional analysts. Without it, two major sources of the Cold War, Elint and telemetry, would have failed. So too, UKUSA's main work against the Warsaw Pact rested on fusion, when high-grade Comint failed, but several low-grade systems together provided useful intelligence. Nor was this a single oddity – it is characteristic of Sigint as a whole. Similar practices occurred on the Western front during 1917–18, for identical reasons. Fusion forced an industrial scale of collection, assessment and reportage. Every piece of traffic analysis received almost as much attention as messages in Ultra had done, which required expanded analytic staff among producers and consumers. Fusion required as many human resources as Ultra, for a product that was not as good, though still fit for purpose. Every day, tens of thousands of operators monitored communications networks that they knew like their own families for any sign of change or danger. Traffic analysis reports on major Soviet exercises – some of the best military intelligence of the Cold War, revealing how Warsaw Pact forces planned to fight – might involve eighteen months' work, thousands of hours of analysis and reach 200 closely typed pages in length. No other means or agency could achieve this end. Appreciations turned on agonising analysis and comparison of detail in hosts, like generating datasets from fragments, or considering whether words were used in plural or singular forms. This work reflected the paucity of intelligence on key questions, and the great expanse of time and effort available for analysis, because usually decisions need not be immediate. Under fusion, the bittiness of evidence increased the power of Siginters in analysis. They were the key observers and explorers, the only ones able to understand and explain the data. Conventional intelligence could not use these sources, until Siginters had done their work first. That task fused analytical and clerical tasks. It was assigned to junior staff who developed the requisite skills in several distinct analytic areas of Comint, Elint, fusion and telemetry. These Siginters were largely men and women without degrees, compared to the male officers and graduates who staffed assessment at DIS and the JIC. However technical, this was still a form of intelligence analysis, and among the most important of the Cold War, alongside the target folders which guided planning for nuclear attacks. Even more, this form of intelligence analysis was international: GCHQ and American Sigint agencies exchanged work at this level and argued about conclusions, which shaped debates at higher levels within their countries. There is more to analysis than is dreamt of in intelligence philosophy.

Consumers and Consumption

The JIC dominates understanding of intelligence analysis in Britain during the Cold War, which inadvertently cripples comprehension of the role which GCHQ, and Sigint, played in that process. During 1943–45, GC&CS's main consumers were the Foreign Office, the intelligence branches of the services and field commanders, which most acted on Sigint. The JIC ranked below these bodies as a consumer, because it affected action less. After 1945, the JIC quickly became Britain's central analytic agency, but just one of equals as a consumer of Sigint. During crises of the Cold War, GCHQ's main consumers were commanders, diplomats and ministers, who received its material directly, with little analysis by any agency. Normally, the JIC was the main assessment agency for strategic issues, where its performance was good, and Sigint ranked among its central resources. However, GCHQ's strengths and the JIC's needs did not mesh well. For most of the Cold War,

GCHQ's successes in Comint were primarily in diplomatic, operational and technical areas, and thus more useful to the Foreign Office or commanders in the field than to the JIC. GCHQ's Comint and Sigint successes against Soviet targets were more essential and useful to DIS, the JIB and military consumers, than the JIC. The Russia Committee of the Foreign Office, not the JIC, was the main consumer of GCHQ Comint against Eastern bloc targets, and most aiding strategy between 1947 and 1953. GCHQ served many masters, not one.

Much GCHQ product was similar to that given by other agencies and was treated in the same way. Most reports from diplomatic Comint, MI6, ambassadors or attachés might address hosts of different matters and be best understood by an area expert who combined all of their material side by side. Perhaps more than any other source, Comint started new lines of investigation, but rarely did it provide most of the key material on important diplomatic issues. The FCO's functional and geographical areas handled the work the JIC did in other matters – every official his or her own analyst. Conversely, in areas where GCHQ had a firm grip and consumers a constant demand – such as military traffic in war and peace – Sigint reports were unique. They swamped all other sources by combining an industrial scale of production with a craftsman's attention to detail. GCHQ was the main engine for DIS and the JIB, and perhaps the most important one for the JIC.

GCHQ automatically exchanged most end product with the Five Eyes. Its liaison elements inside its policy division had strong relations with a few British consumers. Distribution was formalised, with new consumers from the regular departments added and old ones deleted as required. GCHQ did not search constantly for consumers – who would not have been aware of what they were missing – outside a charmed circle. Though much of this barrier was the intentional consequence of secrecy, some was unfortunate. In the United States, senior consumers sometimes reached deep down into NSA to grasp material. Such practices were unnecessary in the smaller and less bureaucratic British system.

Within Britain, during crises or war, Sigint passed straight to commanders, diplomats and ministers without intervention by analysts. Normally, however, the main consumers of Sigint were the JIB, DIS, JIC, the Foreign Office, MI5 and MI6, select commanders and, on matters of finance, trade and economic policy, the Bank of England and civil departments such as the Board of Trade and the Treasury. Many of these consumers received single-source products from GCHQ and other agencies, which they assessed themselves. Consumers received GCHQ reports in secure areas or within locked pouches, signalling their significance. Most recipients assessed such Comint themselves, alongside other reports, except when using Sigint which was sanitised by DIS or the JIC. In 1962, GCHQ complained 'that the UK machinery is not so well geared to handle intelligence which is non-military in character (and the concern of more than one Department) as that which is military'. Its consumers refused to address the question, presumably because they preferred that situation.[22] In economics, finance and security, no one could compete with the experts, nor were they encouraged to try, though politicians and other officials sometimes tried to do so on matters of diplomacy, intelligence and trade. In 1979, however, GCHQ noted that Sigint provided 'the most prolific source of intelligence on international trade and financial subjects of concern to the Economic Departments'.[23]

Normally, Sigint was given to DIS, the JIB and the JIC and processed into multisource assessments, which were distributed to other consumers, with Sigint sanitised where possible. Sanitised Sigint routinely provided 70–80 per cent of the useful intelligence of Western analyses of the era, including JIB and JIC reports. Decision-makers were affected by Sigint without knowing it. The JIB and DIS, the main consumers for Signit's central products – strategic intelligence, especially on the USSR – circulated it in reports across Whitehall at appropriate levels of classification or sanitisation. Assessment was routinised. Current Intelligence Groups met as required and drafted reports for the weekly meetings of the JIC. Their members, drawn from every intelligence agency, the MOD and Foreign Office, tried to create solid and relevant reports which also reflected the work and interests of their organisations. On Tuesdays, a '4 o'clock', chaired by DR (Director of Requirements) and including representatives from across GCHQ, prepared GCHQ's response to these drafts. It emphasised all references to GCHQ material, and any challenges to its views. On Wednesdays, the Director visited his London office. He received 'stop press' signals in the afternoon and, if necessary, 'stop stop press' material via secure telephone just before he left for the meeting at 9.30 a.m. on Thursdays. Afterwards, he signalled GCHQ about the meeting, its atmospherics and the results of any dispute of interpretation and then returned to Cheltenham. On Friday, another '4 o'clock' looked back at the intelligence week and prepared GCHQ for the following week's cycle of analysis.

End Product and Its Effect

Throughout most of its history, GCHQ's performance is best judged by the quantity and quality of end product – each a distinct numbered report in a Sigint series. At its peak during the Cold War in 1978, GCHQ issued nearly 50,000 original end-product reports per year, and reissued perhaps twice as many end-product reports from the other Five Eyes. GCHQ yielded much unique and valuable material – proportionate to its size, perhaps more than American Sigint did, though the latter disseminated far more end product. Every form of end product had different characteristics and consequences.

Comint was less effective as a source between the great powers than it had been during the interwar years, because forms of defence rose in power. Otherwise, diplomatic codebreaking had two main forms. The first was attack by strong states on weak ones. This material was useful in itself, while secondary states with weak cryptography but informed ministers inadvertently illuminated the policy of every great power to all others. So too, smaller states developed powerful regional faculties through cryptanalysis, which boosted their diplomacy against their neighbours: diplomatic Comint perhaps aided their governments more than it did most great powers. The second form was more peculiar. The rival Cold War coalitions were stable. The Sigint struggle between them focused on strategic matters; some material, available through simple means such as plain-language intercepts, was easier to acquire than high diplomatic intelligence across the great divide. Generally, Comint provided great situational awareness, but it perhaps most aided the actions of its consumers by illuminating the bargaining positions of others. Within these coalitions, diplomatic codebreaking shaped minor rivalries and alliance management by the powers most responsible for and informed about such matters, where states have no friends, merely rivals.

GCHQ followed these patterns. The classified evidence available to this history, while fragmentary, suggests that GCHQ maintained high and steady success against other states, which pleased consumers. 'Now that the flood of Suez telegrams has subsided after the negotiations before the Suez crisis,' wrote Joe Hooper in 1956, thanking H, K and W – the sections responsible for codebreaking, translation and communications – for their product, and especially for 'overtime and weekend working'.[24] The Foreign Secretary, Selwyn Lloyd, wrote: 'Since the tension in the Middle East began to grow and especially since Nasser's seizure of the Suez Canal, I have observed the volume of traffic relating to all of the countries in the Middle East area. I am writing to let you know how valuable we have found this material and how much I appreciate the hard work and skill involved in its production.'[25] All leaks after 2000 – whether from Katharine Gun, Clare Short, or Edward Snowden – suggest that GCHQ's success in diplomatic Comint during the internet age has reached the highest levels in history, providing much first-rate material on first-rate issues.

GCHQ affected the formulation of British policy in a peripheral way, but often fundamentally shaped its execution. All consumers happily received material from GCHQ, yet key targets remained invulnerable, while Comint alone does not produce success in diplomacy. One Director General of Intelligence noted: 'When ministers and senior officials find fault with our intelligence, it is nearly always because we have failed to give them advance warning of an intention. This is of course one of the most difficult tasks with which intelligence is faced, and one where the limitations on our resources are most severe.'[26]

In any case Hooper, then intelligence coordinator for the Cabinet, drafted a memorandum to tell ministers: 'What Intelligence can and cannot do'. He warned that: 'Only when the top-grade systems of a target country are being intercepted and read currently can Sigint be expected to provide positive evidence of the country's intentions, political or military.' At best, such a performance would 'inevitably take time'. It was impossible against states with good cryptosystems, especially the Warsaw Pact, China and some Western countries. Given 'continuous coverage' for long periods of time, penetration of medium- and low-grade systems and fusion could spot abnormal developments for a few targets at once. MI6 and MI5 could produce useful intelligence only if given time to build networks 'in the right place at the required time to cover a particular target', though when MI6 'has a technical operation in being ... it can however provide hard and reliable evidence in very short time'. Some open and military sources worked more flexibly, but 'an intelligence requirement which has not been foreseen well in advance can therefore generally not be met or at least not rapidly'.[27] Other intelligence chiefs thought Hooper's views overly defensive and pessimistic; his final draft was less so than the first:

1. Intelligence gathering operations are limited by the extent to which they exist and can be brought to bear on required targets at the required time. In an unforeseen situation the intelligence requirements can only be met if collection resources are available on the spot or in the immediate area and can quickly be brought to bear. When new collection resources have to be created there is inevitably a lag-time before intelligence flows. To be met quickly a requirement has to be foreseen.

2. Thus there is a distinction between long-term and foreseen intelligence requirements and short-term unforeseen requirements which call for immediate intelligence coverage. In the former case, such as the standing requirement for intelligence on the various forces or threats to British interests posed by the Soviet Bloc, it is possible to deploy intelligence resources in advance in such a way as to maximise the chances of obtaining the required information. In the latter cases which cannot be foreseen until (at best) shortly before the event or after its occurrence, intelligence depends on the fortuitous existence of collection resources in being in the area. With the present or foreseeable scale of our intelligence resources (including those of our intelligence collaborators) it is impossible to cover all areas of the world where a sudden need for information may arise, and whether or not we can meet that need depends on the positioning of our resources at the relevant time. They are normally deployed against foreseen and high-priority requirements.

3. There is a further distinction, even in the case of long-term and high priority targets, between what intelligence can provide on the capabilities of foreign Governments and their intentions. With reasoned deployment of our resources and in consultation with our intelligence collaborators, we can expect to cover our long-term targets in such a way as continuously to observe their normal behaviour and activities and thus be in a position to assess the probabilities of their courses of action in particular

circumstances at particular times. But it is rare for intelligence to provide hard information on foreign intentions. When a foreign power intends a particular course of action, especially military action, it will normally seek to disguise its intentions; there may and often will be pointers to the intention but we cannot be sure of correctly assessing it, the more so as the final decisions may not be taken until the last possible moment. What pointers we receive from one source of intelligence will moreover normally need to be corroborated by another before we can be sure of our assessment. When the target for intelligence is not under continuous coverage in advance the possibility of assessing even a probable intention is virtually nil.[28]

Britain's 'long-term intelligence targets – for example: the Soviet bloc and developments in the critical Near East area – are covered as fully and continuously as is possible within the limits of our financial and human resources', augmented by assistance from allies. Nonetheless, many possible targets were uncovered, and neither Sigint nor any source could prevent major forms of surprise.

Hooper was writing just before computerised cryptanalysis boosted GCHQ's power against diplomatic Comint, but these views – from Britain's most experienced Siginter of the early and middle Cold War period – provide context for the case studies in the following chapters.

GCHQ vs the Main Enemy: Signals Intelligence and the Cold War, 1945–92

In the popular imagination, Cold War intelligence centred on a struggle between spies from the West and spies from the East (where the KGB reigned supreme). In fact, military intelligence dominated that struggle in which Sigint was the best Western source. Berlin, the iconic heart of Cold War espionage, mattered more as a bastion for Western military intelligence against the Soviet Union – where it exploited a 'Sigint bonanza' – than it did as a battleground for Humint.[1] Its epicentre was not Checkpoint Charlie, as honoured in fiction, but military installations such as RAF Gatow, on the western border of West Berlin. This struggle was GCHQ's main task between 1946 and 1992.

This history shows, for the first time, how Western Sigint fought that war. It shows how, through patient and thorough exploitation of low-grade systems, GCHQ, NSA and their European partners penetrated Soviet military intentions and capabilities. It explains why this success mattered in the great crises of the Cold War: GCHQ's role during the Cuban missile crisis of 1962, where the intercept station at Scarborough caught the crucial news that Soviet merchant vessels carrying nuclear warheads had turned back to Russia; its failure during the Hungarian crisis of 1956; its success during the Czechoslovak crisis of 1968, and its dogged work through the decades, until the Soviet bloc collapsed. GCHQ shaped a stand-off in intelligence with the 'main enemy', which aided Western victory.

The Echo of Ultra, 1945–53

As the Cold War emerged, British and American leaders yearned to repeat a form of Ultra, but rarely found one. Anglo-American Comint reached its peak of success against high-grade Soviet traffic between 1945 and 1953; after that, Soviet espionage quickly compromised some of these forms, and its communications security contained them all. Ultimately, this drove UKUSA to rely on lesser sources.

The first success, which Americans named Venona and Britons Bride, penetrated Soviet espionage traffic. During 1942–43, Soviet authorities accidentally produced and then reused duplicates of one-time pads, which, like any reused key material, then became vulnerable. American cryptanalysts discovered this weakness and provided product and techniques to GCHQ, which later cooperated in the attack. In 1948, a Soviet agent in MI6, Harold 'Kim' Philby, betrayed the existence of Venona without damaging it: the compromised one-time pads had not been used for years. Venona revealed how Soviet espionage worked, as well as details of its agents and actions. It drove Western security and counter-intelligence until 1960 but arguably mattered little elsewhere.[2]

The second attack, against the machine cyphers of the Red Army, followed Ultra, aided by German reports on Soviet systems. After VE Day, the Colossus machines under Gerry Morgan – Bletchley's specialist in Hagelin systems and the best machine cryptanalyst to remain with GCHQ – were turned against Soviet crypto machines. The landline circuits of the Red Army, which carried most of its major traffic, remained untouchable, but UKUSA succeeded against entities which relied on radio and would reflect signs of Soviet aggression.

Seemingly little of this material survives and the quality is controversial. This penetration produced a flood of communications which reflected the routine working of Soviet forces, initially perhaps often from what would have been the middle levels of Ultra, but mainly from lower ones. The KGB later concluded that this work gave US intelligence 'important data concerning the stationing of the USSR's armed forces, the productive capacity of various branches of industry, and work in the field of atomic energy in the USSR'.[3] This statement may be true, but equally could have been said about the plain-language civil text which UKUSA acquired from 1946. This KGB account appears to have conflated all material which UKUSA received at the time from civil text, cryptanalysis and traffic analysis. Later UKUSA accounts were most impressed by cryptanalytic proof of broad and deep Soviet demobilisation in manpower and industry, which was unavailable from any other sources. This material enabled inferences on central issues, such as whether the USSR was preparing for war, or perhaps its policy towards crises in China and Persia. This material would have been a good source until 1992, though no better than the Comint which UKUSA later acquired from low and middle sources. Moreover, during 1947–48, UKUSA traffic analysis on Soviet forces across Eurasia appears to have provided material which matched that taken from cryptanalysis on a few frontiers.[4] Together they determined the Soviet order of battle in the early Cold War, a foundational success for intelligence. In any case, a Soviet spy within the ASA, William Weisband, compromised this success, which wrecked a live and valuable source, though this action may simply have hastened an inevitable process. On 'Black Friday' – which, contrary to its name, stretched over several months – the Soviets ceased using these machines for radio traffic and sent military traffic in the USSR by landline only. Until 1951, UKUSA still gained from attacking old traffic which had not earlier been high priority, but remained grist for the mill (such as the training of junior gunners or cypher operators, or the activities of aircraft and merchantmen).[5] Later, the Soviets adopted a new crypto machine for radio traffic, which was well used and well designed. Thus, from 1948, high-level Soviet cryptosystems became a hard target.

Thirdly, between 1946 and 1953, UKUSA read some internal and diplomatic traffic of the states in eastern Europe.[6] The significance of this success, some of which has been released to The National Archives – reflected in reports of issues such as the activities of Bulgarian, Czech and Rumanian security, and the strength of the Yugoslav air force – is hard to trace.[7] Probably that material was most useful in illuminating the details of how communist power solidified in the states of eastern Europe, and perhaps in dimly reflecting the diplomacy of the last Stalinist era.

Beyond these efforts, UKUSA acquired Comint by attacking plain-language traffic. From 1930, many Soviet institutions, in a huge and undeveloped territory, used radio for traffic which landlines would have carried elsewhere. GC&CS, like German Sigint, understood that fact, yet lacked the resources to exploit this civil text. That material was a leading target during GC&CS's search for 'Exotic' signals during 1944–45. From 1945, GCHQ attacked this traffic systematically and convinced American Sigint to do the same. Between 1946 and 1956, US Siginters alone intercepted around 78.8 million items of Russian civil text, of which 6–7 per cent were retained as intelligence, 1 per cent was fully translated, and the rest discarded as irrelevant. GCHQ had roughly similar experiences. Techniques echoing those of the War Trade Intelligence Department (WTID) enabled the elimination of irrelevant messages and the intensive exploitation of the rest. When, in 1946, leading American cryptanalysts like Louis Tordella first saw the techniques that the WTID had coined in 1915, they were staggered by their power and sophistication. Decades later, Tordella thought that civil text was 'the biggest intelligence success' of Western Sigint during the early Cold War and 'made a terrific contribution to the knowledge that the West had of what was going on in Russia'.[8] The take from Morse, teleprinter and radio telephony was scattered but widespread: immense detail about the work of one factory, or scientific installation, or mid-level official, usually in isolation from others.[9] Civil text provided a thousand points of light amidst darkness. Carefully judged, it offered much useful material about Soviet capabilities and the general social, economic and administrative conditions of the USSR, but little on intentions.

Meanwhile, between 1949 and 1956, British and American intelligence built tunnels from which they tapped plain-language telephone and teleprinter traffic on the cables used by Soviet headquarters in Berlin and Vienna. Until compromised by accident and espionage, these taps provided masses of material, which took years to process. Monitoring one hour of tapped telephone calls required one hour of translator time, at least. The Berlin Tunnel alone yielded 67,000 hours of telephone communications of East German (GDR) and Soviet officials. During the 1950s, plain-language Comint gave analysts a cornucopia of intelligence, far greater in quantity and probably in value than anything produced by cryptanalysis. The Russian-language translators of UKUSA could barely handle the load. Throughout the Cold War, surreptitiously tapping Soviet communications links which used plain language rated among UKUSA's best sources against the USSR. It provided more significant material from top-level discussions and about strategic issues than perhaps was acquired through any other means, including cryptanalysis. As one NSA official, Oliver Kirby, later said: 'Plain language turned out to be the greatest, continuous thing that we ever invented. Few of us around here really ever want to admit to that. But it was.'[10]

During the early Cold War, British consumers hoped to assess their enemies with precision and accuracy. The Foreign Office, for example, analysed all information on politics within the emerging Eastern bloc through the 'Fortnightly Summary of Soviet Intentions', usually called the 'Crystal Gazer'. In 1949, the Foreign Office told C that: 'The "Crystal Gazer" started off as a top secret document of very limited distribution for the use of officials in the Office and a few chosen officials from other Government Departments. It seems to have proved valuable and like all good things its fame has spread abroad and everyone now wishes to have a sight of it. You are aware it is based on material drawn from all sources, including S.I.S. and Sigint.'[11]

Given 'our preoccupation with a possible leakage to the Russians', the Foreign Office emphasised the need to sanitise Sigint for non-indoctrinated readers of the Crystal Gazer. 'It is no use swimming against the tide and this sort of information must be made available to Ministers as well as senior officials. It is quite understandable that Ministers need not or ought not to be indoctrinated for the sole purpose of reading "crystal gazers".'[12] Much attention went to solving this problem of sanitisation, which reflected the belief that Comint would illuminate Soviet intentions. This view proved optimistic. Though sanitisation hampers any historical analysis, Comint seemingly entered only perhaps 33 per cent of Crystal Gazers, usually on peripheral matters, and most often in references to the attitudes of states outside the Eastern bloc. Neither Venona, the attack on Soviet military traffic, or civil text would have provided much material fit for crystal gazing. That from eastern European states would have been more useful, but rarely appeared. Crystal Gazers remained a useful compilation, but little aided by Comint.

Decision-makers were unhappy with their material on the USSR, even when Comint worked at its peak. In 1948, the Chiefs of Staff (COS) considered 'Intelligence Requirements for "Cold War" Planning'. It thought the problem difficult and success inadequate. 'The collection of intelligence about Russia presented a most difficult problem and every effort was being made to increase and improve the sources from which it was obtained.' The COS emphasised 'the vital importance of obtaining information on all kinds of Russian activities. Without such information our defence policy, and indeed our foreign policy, could not be expected to be successful. Adequate financial provision on a long term basis for the organisations responsible for obtaining overt and covert information was therefore essential.'[13]

Underneath these concerns lay a recognition of some successes. The COS noted good and improving intelligence in two areas where Sigint was productive, without describing GCHQ as a source: 'our knowledge of Russian tactical moves in Germany and of industrial activity. It had been learned that Russian divisions recently taking part in manoeuvres in the Frontier Area had been withdrawn.' Kenneth Strong, head of the Joint Intelligence Bureau (JIB), emphasised that the JIB, 'was carefully watching Russian industrial activities as these might be expected to give us a good indication of Russian intentions. Up to the present there had been no sign of any adjustments being made in Russian economy to bring it to a wartime tempo ... He thought that Russia was industrially capable of mounting a short war lasting possibly two or three months. He did not believe Russian industry was at present capable of supporting a major war of long duration.' Though Strong referred only to material from open sources, civil text was significant in this area, and no doubt shaped his judgement on an important issue. C offered a 'detailed review of the present conditions and said that as a result of measures now being taken there was every prospect of an improvement in obtaining low and medium grade intelligence from both Russia and the Satellite countries'.[14] This comment probably referred to Sigint alongside spies, and reflected real developments in GCHQ's capabilities against the main enemy.

In 1948, the broad concerns for British intelligence were signs of immediate attack and the need for detailed material on Soviet military and economic capabilities. The JIC defined a set of 'Sigint Intelligence Requirements', aimed 'to guide the Sigint Board in allocating its resources', though recognising that 'technical issues will influence the final allocation of priorities'. These requirements fell into five groups of priorities, which reflected their significance as components of Soviet power and threat. The first was Soviet nuclear, biological and chemical weapons, scientific research and weapons development, strategic bombers and air defence forces, and 'guided weapons' (missiles). The second priority was the aggregate economic, industrial and demographic resources available for military forces and the development of the conventional forces most dangerous as offensive tools – and therefore indicative of preparations for aggression – in the form of submarines, air forces and airborne troops; espionage, counter-espionage services, high politics and Soviet intentions and activities in Austria, Germany and Greece. The third priority included all other aspects of Soviet conventional forces and weapons; and science and technology and its ability to influence events in Europe and Asia. The fourth addressed Soviet military activities in eastern Europe and among Muslim countries; the fifth assessed Soviet satellite countries in eastern Europe, Soviet activities in east Asia, and other issues including Zionism.[15]

In later years, some of these political concerns waned, others rose. Low priorities on this list were no doubt higher on those of other entities, such as the Foreign Office. These JIC priorities did not mention what everyone would have thought essential – warning of imminent attack – because all took it for granted as a priority, while few thought the danger likely, at present. The JIC underrated the value of matters upon which GCHQ later focused during the Cold War – for instance the order of battle and activities of Soviet forces or indicators of military mobilisation for war. Debate smouldered about the relative allocation of Sigint resources to the Soviet task. In 1956, Jones asked the JIC to let GCHQ turn its resources away from targets suited to 'hot war' – such as order of battle – towards others which better reflected 'Cold War' problems, such as Soviet military industries. He received some support from the JIB, but the armed services rejected this proposal.[16] As events proved, hot war indicators proved essential to Cold War intelligence.

Nonetheless, these JIC desiderata of 1948 reflected concerns which continued until 1992. GCHQ's main targets were the Soviet Union's intentions for war and its ability to wage one, especially Soviet forces linked to a conventional or nuclear offensive. In 1948, GCHQ provided material for all of these priorities – more than any other British source did, and perhaps more than all of them put together – mostly from civil text, which illuminated general conditions in the USSR. GCHQ provided a broad knowledge of Soviet capabilities, which reinforced the conclusion that the Cold War would not 'go hot' imminently. Still, British consumers wanted more from GCHQ; however, from 1948, the power of high-level Comint on these issues began to slide. By 1952, the JIC noted that Soviet security 'had a high level of efficiency and we obtain little information directly revealing the policy and intentions of the Soviet leaders ... we are unlikely to obtain direct information of Soviet intentions from secret sources, including Sigint'.[17] Decision-makers had to act with greater uncertainty than they liked, but got used to it. Anglo-American leaders abandoned hopes for a new Ultra: without good and sure material on Soviet intentions, they turned to Moscow-watching, which left much uncertainty within strategy. GCHQ could not answer directly many of the key questions posed by consumers, but this challenge drove it to improve what it could deliver. Its successes without high-grade Comint yielded more than seemed possible in 1948. Low- and medium-grade Sigint on Soviet military deployments in Europe became a proxy for Soviet capabilities in the short and medium term, and almost (but not quite) for its intentions.

British Sigint and NATO Strategy

This intelligence sufficed to support both Britain and NATO's strategy until 1992. Through NATO, Britain balanced its relations with enemies, friends and rivals across the industrialised world. In the long term, NATO followed a rational strategy by maintaining political cohesion and a military deterrent against Soviet attack. Victory, however, lay far down a twisted path. GCHQ worked within the context of alliance politics throughout. National and technical issues were difficult enough, but GCHQ also shaped debates between and within every member of NATO, most of which remained ignorant of UKUSA's work. The influence of GCHQ could not be controlled by Britain alone. GCHQ's chief consumer was Whitehall, but almost equally American administrations and, in more distant, complex and indirect ways, other NATO allies. The interests and policies of these states did not coincide. Until 1968, Britain and Western Europe were far more exposed to destruction from nuclear war than the United States, and remained more vulnerable to conventional attack until 1992. These circumstances drove differences in strategy, which shaped GCHQ's place as a provider of intelligence. It also gave GCHQ a role in supporting diplomacy – which neither it, government ministers or the Foreign Office fully understood – to keep Britain at the top table of all discussions over strategy within NATO. GCHQ's success in this endeavour occurred as much by accident as intention.

Until the 1960s, American policy overshadowed NATO's efforts to formulate military strategy. While NATO planned for conventional conflict, the United States adopted an 'air atomic' strategy which assumed that a nuclear war could be won in a meaningful way. National leaders aimed to deter the Soviet Union from starting World War Three but, in order to do so, the USAF needed to be able to win it, and the USSR to recognise and understand the fact. Since air defence was impossible, USAF Strategic Air Command (SAC) needed to be able to destroy Soviet delivery systems, initially just bombers, before they struck. This strategy assumed that immediate surprise was always possible and was the Soviet aim.

These assumptions stemmed from the experiences of Anglo-American airmen with intelligence – Ultra and Cheadle – during the Second World War, which led them to focus on Sigint as a source. By 1952, the USAF had approached GCHQ to train its air intelligence personnel and multiplied the number of its Siginters. The RAF also expanded its Sigint resources. The status of its intelligence soon satisfied SAC, primarily because it thought itself overwhelmingly stronger than its Soviet adversaries. Still, mistakes were inevitable, and any would have unpleasant consequences. These operational issues were distinct from the questions of a 'bomber' and 'missile' gap – alarmist views of Soviet production of these weapons which roiled American policy through the 1950s. Different views on these matters centred on how many bombers and nuclear missiles the USSR was developing and when they would reach service, rather than which forces were deployed at any time. Notably, GCHQ provided more accurate material on these issues than did most American intelligence agencies, which helped Britain to ameliorate alarmism in Washington. Even so, only great and prolonged effort achieved these aims, which reflects the ambiguity of the intelligence, and the power of preconceptions.[18]

For over a decade, much of UKUSA's effort focused on tracking signs of war from Soviet nuclear forces, locating them and enabling their destruction. In this process, UKUSA Sigint informed a policy outside Britain's control and one which might trigger a war that would destroy Britain. British authorities accepted that sort of danger as being an unavoidable byproduct of keeping and constraining an American ally which was necessary to win the peace, but few British officials understood how GCHQ shaped the process. GCHQ's role in the Cuban missile crisis was not an anomaly, but rather an illustration of that during the air atomic era as a whole. In any movement towards war, much intelligence would be British, but all command would be American, though GCHQ's reporting offered a means to moderate the risk by providing evidence to shape that strategy. Between GCHQ and Prime Minister Harold Macmillan's relationship with President Kennedy, Britain influenced the key decisions of that crisis, but did not make them.

From 1961, however, American strategy adopted the ideas of 'mutually assured destruction', and 'flexible response'. The central purpose of nuclear forces became deterrence, because their unrestricted use meant mutual suicide. Both sides had large numbers of nuclear weapons, which remained the greatest target of intelligence. Western strategists, however, emphasised conventional forces and thought that war might be prolonged. With both sides increasingly reliant on reserves based outside Europe, Western strategists needed more warning of war in order to fight one. These changes in strategic circumstances and attitudes transformed the role of military intelligence and Sigint. NATO no longer planned an offensive to break a Soviet attack as it began. Its stance was defensive, but preparation for conventional war became more serious than before. The elimination of the hair trigger eased problems of intelligence and analysis. More time was available to think and act, and also to exploit a broader and more interactive base of sources. UKUSA and Allied Sigint both grew in power and ability, because their work was more important and difficult than before. Satellite imagery expanded even more in strength, offering overwhelming amounts of data, too much for analysts to handle at the time. American, British and French liaison missions (such as BRIXMIS – the British Commanders-in-Chief Mission to the Group of Soviet Forces in Germany) in Berlin travelled with fewer constraints than the Soviets would have liked in the GDR, providing physical observation.

These changes complicated the politics of intelligence and decision-making. American presidents and their advisors made the key decisions, but the European members of NATO rose in power. NATO, while politically cohesive, was incoherent on many military matters, because national interests conflicted frequently, especially between the United

States and its European allies, including Britain. Following the Berlin crisis of 1961, the United States aimed to have its European allies increase their forces, to make a conventional war possible. Precisely to avoid that fate, they refused to do so, which in turn increased the likelihood that any conflict would become nuclear. Many states contributed to NATO decisions on strategy, especially as it approached any threshold to war. Each might trip another up. NATO command was convoluted and fragile, and elements of its strategy were often intended just to camouflage disagreements. No one really thought that war was imminent or could stay conventional for long if one began. Some warning was necessary to mobilise reinforcements, while strategy required accepted and accurate facts. Yet intelligence which convinced one group might not do so with another. The criteria for 'Indicators & Warnings' (I&Ws) and warning periods were therefore often arbitrary; none could cover all cases and organisations within NATO, and its individual members differed over them.

The politics of NATO Sigint drove GCHQ to be independent, able and persuasive. GCHQ, like Britain as a whole, emphasised its relationship with the United States as its best means to influence NATO policy, while using its European allies to influence Washington. Britain used its almost primary role in intelligence to strengthen its far-more-than-secondary position as a power. This process was messy and easy to miss, because the evidence remains closed. In order to be politically effective, GCHQ had to provide accurate intelligence which would aid NATO policy. American, British and Canadian authorities could see the evidence unvarnished; Europeans heard just an echo of it. Intelligence could not end uncertainty, but GCHQ could increase certainty, and hope, at national levels of decision-making and at the top of NATO commands.

Sanitisation and Strategy

Only sanitised Sigint could be used for all-source assessments sent outside indoctrinated circles, including key headquarters such as the British Army of the Rhine (BAOR), Fleet Command and Strike Command. During the 1960s, 350 copies of the annual estimates of United States Army Headquarters, Europe were distributed to American planners and commanders.[19] Sanitised appreciations aimed to preserve as many key facts as possible, and to avoid any error and needless specificity, which might make readers wonder whence such knowledge came. A yearly assessment need not say that a unit arrived on 11:32, 7 March 1965: 'March' would do. In sanitised reports, Sigint was not described as such, but silently checked other sources, steered all-source assessments, prevented error and added truth.

Sanitisation led 'unwashed' consumers to underestimate the centrality of Sigint to intelligence, which caused shock in the hour when first they were baptised and finally could see. It also enabled the UKUSA officers who controlled the machinery of force down to unit level, but saw nothing above Secret intelligence, to plan and act in ways congruent with top-secret material. This process best balanced the value and security of Sigint, and eliminated the impact of erroneous material from other sources within UKUSA. Commands outside UKUSA received none of these gains and suffered other losses. Even after the Sigint reforms around 1978, these commands did not receive such material thoroughly or directly, but just through cleared CANUKUS personnel. Probably non-UKUSA commands learned what they needed to know, which would matter most during crises. Category 2 material, moreover – the meat and potatoes of military Sigint – was traded to individual NATO countries. They could interpret that material themselves, and disseminate it to their national forces, though without the context available to UKUSA. It rarely gave allies any Category 3 material – the steak and lobster of military Sigint – and only if it was vital to understanding, and then by taking precautions to prevent them from guessing the source and thus UKUSA's power. UKUSA commands without access to top secret material were still better informed than any non-UKUSA ones with their own national Sigint.

None of this would help NATO in a conventional war, which it increasingly emphasised. From 1980, for the first time in twenty-five years, Britain systematically honed Sigint for conventional operations during 'tension and war between NATO and the Warsaw Pact'. GCHQ, backed by service opinion, drove these proposals, which were congruent to and necessary for NATO's adoption of Air/Land Battle, in which long-range air interdiction and mobile defence would stall any assault by the Warsaw Pact. GCHQ's proposals emphasised that Sigint must maximise warning of attack, strengthen all services just before war broke out, and survive if war started. Operations needed to be dynamic, not defensive. Warning and collection could no longer be passive and isolated: they needed to be integrated with operational preparations just before war. These proposals would redefine the strategic and tactical use of Sigint and their relationship with Elint and electronic warfare (EW). They would force major expenses and changes in Sigint and command, sanitisation and strategy, and relations within UKUSA, and with third parties in NATO.[20]

These proposals were enacted – slowly, incompletely, but significantly – over the next decade. For the first time in a generation, the British military boosted its Sigint forces. RAF Siginters moved from Digby, Lincolnshire, to Germany, augmenting Sigint in the forward area. BAOR received the 14th Signals Regiment for EW in war, the Royal Navy boosted its shipboard Sigint, which was integrated with data links on the 'Outboard' system, while the Royal Marines created their first Sigint unit. The only test of these developments occurred just as they began, in the Falklands conflict. Supporting forces that were inexperienced with these practices and out of area, GCHQ reduced sanitisation to the lowest possible level consistent with IRSIG, yet still the integration of Sigint with tactics was poor. Probably British forces would have used Sigint better in war against the Warsaw Pact, and abandoned sanitisation even more, but how far cannot be known.

Meanwhile, UKUSA became more flexible in circulating Sigint, especially Category 2, to NATO. The heads and officers of NATO Sigint agencies met often, lubricating their relations, institutionally and personally. The 'Wintex' command post exercises schooled theatre and national leaders across NATO in crises and the start of a war with the Warsaw Pact in real time. These exercises helped authorities to test their machinery for decision-making, and their own mettle. They also helped authorities in UKUSA, though not third parties, to overcome some of the problems caused by sanitisation and to understand how Sigint would work during crisis and war. From 1981, Britain integrated Sigint into the British parts of Wintex. One group within GCHQ generated thousands of imaginary reports to reflect the material which Sigint should provide in circumstances like the exercise scenarios. This material was released realistically within GCHQ and to decision-makers, including the JIC, MOD, commanders and politicians. All participants received an opportunity to learn interactively. GCHQ personnel analysed all of this exercise information for consumers, interpreting 'Indicators & Warnings' for Whitehall in the early stages of the crisis, and later guiding BAOR, RAF Germany and the fleet. Authorities peppered GCHQ with questions like: 'We are getting reports of BACKFIRE bombers deploying to CUBA? Can you confirm this please?' The exercise also practised personnel in passing sanitised Sigint to other NATO forces.[21]

Formal and Informal Estimates

In order to plan forces, deployments, and war, strategists required an idea of the warning they could expect of Soviet attack. As the COS wrote: 'All Global war planning must to a greater or lesser degree depend upon agreed assumptions about the warning likely to be available.'[22] Alas, several problems dogged the use of 'warning periods'. The JIC and COS concluded that basic 'differences of opinion … based on opinions as to the lines on which the Soviets might think, rather than on concrete evidence', must hamper any assessment of war with the USSR.[23] Kenneth Strong, for the JIB, saw 'scarcely any evidence as to how their leaders think or would act in given circumstances'.[24] Soviet attack might take many forms. 'No single period of warning … can be assumed as valid to cover the different possible methods of attack with which NATO may be faced and which would be applicable to all types of force throughout the NATO commands.' Soviet planners 'might well catalogue targets in a different manner' than British ones might expect. The COS rejected attempts to have NATO define more thorough and longer periods of warning, because these might reduce the incentive of its allies to maintain their forces, though Whitehall privately made such calculations for precisely that purpose. British strategists used arbitrary rules of thumb about warning periods, which governed forces in different ways. Many of its nuclear and conventional units must always be ready for surprise attack, without warning. All other conventional forces, including BAOR and RAF Germany, the crown jewels of Britain's commitment to NATO, should be mobilised within seven days, but many of their support elements might not be ready for a month.[25] All of its allies followed similar procedures, often with less attention to forces able to fight without warning of attack.

Ideally, estimates compare problems and intelligence and then guide actions. At worst, they become parts of checklists for planning, or compromises to conceal chasms between views. Formal estimates always reflect a political relationship between the interests of organisations, and differ from informal ones – what decision-makers really expect. Routinely, informal estimates cause leaders to disregard expertise without engaging it – to unfortunate effect. NATO followed the first part of this pattern, but not the second. Warning periods always involve forms of worst- (or worse-) case planning. In this instance, they reflected real but remote dangers. Soviet conventional or nuclear forces might attack by surprise from their standing position, while full mobilisation would increase their superiority in numbers over NATO. Soviet leaders controlled these decisions; Western intelligence and statesmen had to guess about them, which they did through a range of assessments.

From 1954, British strategic decision-makers simultaneously assumed warning periods ranging from 0 to 4 hours against a bolt from the blue – provided only by radar detection of enemy aircraft as they struck – to perhaps seven (and, implicitly, even twenty-eight) days if the Soviets mobilised in order to increase the weight of attack. American forces in Europe adopted a similar formula of 0 to 4 hours, to four to nine days.[26] These formulae were partly political, aimed at making NATO allies increase their conventional strength. Had NATO leaders really believed these formal estimates of warning periods, they would have had to maintain far larger forces, on a hair-trigger basis, which would have alarmed the Warsaw Pact, which exaggerated Western aggression and power. These warning periods also contradicted the possibility of reinforcing forces in Europe, which underlay American, British and Canadian planning for war, especially after 1970. Here, as often, NATO planning aimed simply to complete a paper record. NATO was politically cohesive, but operationally fragmented. National forces and commanders were poorly coordinated, while modes for mobilisation of forces were optimistic. Throughout NATO's history, especially during the Berlin crises between 1958 and 1962, the United States wished its allies would strengthen their conventional forces so that a non-nuclear war might be fought in Europe. For precisely that reason, they refused to do so.

Judged strictly, NATO's warning periods failed to achieve their ends, being both vague and ignored, which should have crippled its capabilities for deterrence and defence. That outcome did not happen because of the way that politicians treated the problem, and intelligence, especially Sigint, filled the gap. NATO leaders ignored these formal warning periods. Informally, they thought that war was possible, but not imminent, nor likely to occur suddenly. In 1959–61, the JIC agreed that 'we have virtually no chance of intercepting either the policy decision to go to war or the operational orders for the attack', yet also did 'not expect an attack whilst there is no exceptional political tension'.[27] Political developments, which they could detect, probably would precede steps towards danger. NATO responded tolerably well to such signs, as in the Berlin crises. Hydrogen weapons would explode when shots were fired, eliminating victory, but also deterring war. These informal estimates enabled NATO members to cap their conventional forces and states of readiness, and reduced the chance that uncertainty and fear about ever-imminent danger would paralyse decisions, or provoke the Warsaw Pact into undesired escalations.

These steps also increased the Warsaw Pact's chances for victory in war, if it was lucky (and NATO blind), but Western eyes were sharp. These challenges with warning periods caused intelligence providers, especially GCHQ, to adopt roles which no one fully understood at the time. I&W emerged to increase the real likelihood of detecting signs of Soviet preparation for war, days or months before they started one. Good models of I&W were successful in measuring changes in danger. Even when overly schematic and bureaucratised, they aided assessments and actions with a timeframe of weeks or months. Most sets of I&W were formulated through debate between institutions and intelligence services. Siginters devised their own sets, based on experience and technical factors which no outsider could understand or challenge. These models had to be trusted on faith alone, or else all hope be abandoned. Given Sigint's centrality to intelligence, these were the dominant elements of I&W, though they were never discussed or authorised by superiors, or by the JIC – just taken on trust.

These Sigint models covered periods ranging from hours, to months, but usually days and weeks. Siginters had to provide the best real warnings possible, based on their own sets of I&W, rather than fit the artificial deadlines of warning periods, which were arbitrary. The questions were, 'Will World War Three start today? Or in a week, or a month, from now?' Siginters steadily improved their answers, thereby reshaping the balance of deterrence and defence. Sigint was one of the few sources both of illumination for warning and of encouragement for the decision-makers confronting that bleak picture. The daily empirical success of Siginters thus built the confidence of NATO leaders in the stability of the military balance, and their ability to understand it. That confidence served to reduce the effect of fear and uncertainty in planning, and stabilised one side of the Cold War. Nor was it unreasonable. This defensive effort could have no deterrent effect, because neither side could know in advance how it would work. One hidden problem in deterrence during the Cold War was that neither side could know how far its intelligence, and that of its foe, would shape the balance of certainty and uncertainty which guided actions. Perhaps a sense of that ignorance reinforced caution for both sides.

Strategic Forces

Relations between American and British airmen and Siginters in 1945 drove their cooperation in nuclear intelligence until 1992. During the Combined Bomber Offensive, British and American air forces quarrelled but cooperated. In particular, the USAAF, weak in intelligence, relied on British Sigint and photographic interpretation.[28] After 1945, both air forces aimed to win an air atomic war, through atomic bombs delivered by bombers.[29] They made that an UKUSA of their own, exchanging all aerial photographs, including those each had seized from the Luftwaffe. Their relationship was looser than the UKUSA in Sigint. The McMahon Act limited American ability to work in atomic weapons with any foreign state, the core of air atomic power, until Britain independently built its own weapons. The USAF outweighed the RAF in size, and hoped not to depend on British intelligence. Yet by 1952, after years of effort, the USAF remained weak in collection and analysis.[30] It went backwards, while the RAF and GCHQ honed their craft and power. They outweighed their American counterparts in intelligence, while British aircraft, especially the English Electric Canberra bomber, matched American ones as platforms for aerial photography and Sigint.

Knowing its inadequacies and respecting British prowess, the USAF intensified cooperation in intelligence. Each boosted the other, with effects that lingered through the Cold War. British Sigint was central to American intelligence for nuclear war between 1950 and 1962, and important until 1992.

For years, the RAF conducted hair-raising overflights of eastern Europe and the western USSR. They provided useful imagery of most major LRAF bases at a time when this knowledge was essential and available through no other means.[31] By 1956, Lockheed U-2s succeeded Canberras as deep intruders, yet British crews still flew U-2 missions under the Union Jack. President Eisenhower and the USAF happily let allies share the risks and rewards of this game.[32]

Sigint probably gave SAC and Bomber Command the intelligence they needed to blunt enemy forces and defeat the USSR during the air atomic age. Certainly, it built their confidence in the likelihood of that prospect. Yet the process and outcome were never simple. The division between NSA and the Air Force Security Service hampered the quality of American airborne Sigint, which was shaky throughout the 1950s.

Between 1960 and 1966, the air-atomic age ended. Ballistic missiles replaced bombers as the main delivery component of nuclear strength, with the aim of deterrence through mutually assured destruction, rather than victory. GCHQ carried some strengths into this new age. Soviet strategic forces remained a preeminent target. When American satellites became the main platform to collect imagery from inside the USSR, and significant to Sigint, Britain continued to receive and analyse the data. It also was fundamental to the one area where Sigint flights on the Soviet periphery remained vital.

From 1960 to 1990, pairs of modified Canberras and de Havilland Comets, formidable aircraft for the task, flew low and fast over the Baltic Sea towards Soviet airspace. Suddenly, one climbed sharply while the other loitered to watch the fun. The Soviets scrambled their air defence, using radars and plain-language commands freely, thereby exposing sensors, command and communications systems and, often, their incompetence. These missions revealed not just local matters, but far better than any other means tested the working of the PVO, the air defence shield around the USSR. They aided planning for the air strikes which remained central to Western strategy, whether nuclear or conventional in composition, especially under the concept of Air–Land Battle. Not surprisingly, the Foreign Office insisted on approving each of these politically risky missions beforehand. When, in 1989, it challenged all of them as being unnecessarily provocative, the end of the Cold War, and of that particular age of Sigint, was at hand.

Meanwhile, Sigint built power against another Soviet delivery system. By 1955, an AN/FPS-17 radar system was installed at an American base in Turkey. It initially aimed just to trace Soviet missile launches from their bases in Kapustin Yar, in Central Asia, but soon collected data which could betray key intelligence on Soviet nuclear power, if analysed well.[33] GCHQ and the best analytical agency of the era, the JIB, showed how to do so, by unifying an effort which was divided between far larger American agencies. British Siginters, in Cyprus and elsewhere, collected Sigint from these tests at Kapustin Yar, as did the advanced British radar systems, Chaplain, Sandra and Zinnia.[34] Soviet telemetry signals were transmitted on multichannel radio systems, which inadvertently hindered encryption and helped attack.[35] Whereas the Soviets never appreciated that technical weakness, GCHQ discovered and exploited it. British authorities created telemetry intelligence by combining radar, Elint and Sigint in an excruciating analysis of an unknown problem, with two parts. In order to acquire data from signals, and then intelligence from the data, British authorities tapped their best civilian and governmental scientists, including world authorities at Jodrell Bank Observatory such as Sir Bernard Lovell. After a ten-man cell in GCHQ solved the signals problem, Air Intelligence and the JIB tackled the difficulties with data. They differed over their significance and the process. RAF intelligence thought that its 'opinion, experience and judgment' mattered most, and more than the method of scientists. The JIB credited the success to the method and organisation of its group of scientists, who also integrated assessment of nuclear missiles, warheads, and sites.[36] The Templer Report, which assessed these issues and evidence thoroughly, firmly supported the JIB and rejected the RAF's position.[37] Probably the JIB mattered more than Air Intelligence, but no matter the truth, all of these Sigint attacks required craftsmanship, experience and flair. Once Britain succeeded, for decades it kept that preeminent place on fundamental issues regarding nuclear intelligence for UKUSA, at a small cost in personnel or money. Against this, NSA and the USAF separately processed Sigint; NSA had no role against Elint, while Lockheed Missile Systems Division and the Stanford Research Institute analysed radar intelligence. These American organisations were excellent, but none had full access to all the relevant material. Difficult tasks, with high priorities, overwhelmed them, as did their rivalries. Nothing else in the record of Cold War intelligence better illustrated the virtues of Britain's small but unified Sigint and intelligence systems, compared to a larger but diffuse American effort.

GCHQ also survived another characteristic American problem: lack of security. On 21 October 1957, the periodical *Aviation News* exposed every American element of the programme, but none of the British ones. Robert Cutler, Eisenhower's Special Assistant for National Security Affairs, called this action 'treason'. Fortunately, it inflicted little damage.[38] The Soviets failed to overcome the problem because missile tests were necessarily exposed to radar and needed communications links, and the Soviets misunderstood the vulnerability of their multichannel radio systems. *Aviation News* did not compromise GCHQ's mode of attack, which worked effectively for another two decades, boosted by additional muscle from American radar. Telemetry matched imagery as a source on Soviet ballistic missiles, becoming the foundation upon which UKUSA built its intelligence against Soviet nuclear capabilities, and stood to watch the horizon for signs of war. Between 1974 and 1977, however, what GCHQ called 'traditional missile telemetry analysis' declined in value. Though Strategic Arms Limitation Talks (SALT) prevented the encipherment of missile telemetry, that of associated traffic – especially from satellite communications (Satcom) and spacecraft – became enciphered, which, GCHQ warned, 'affects exploitation for warning and indicator purposes'.[39] Meanwhile, signals became increasing complex. Against this, the expansion of the Soviet enterprise – the need for range control, security, and chase aircraft, among other things – increased the number of targets to attack. As ever in Sigint, any chain of security is as strong as its weakest link. Until 1992, GCHQ remained a useful partner to NSA in telemetry, though the latter waned in value as a source.

Sigint and imagery were the two great sources of Western intelligence on Soviet nuclear capabilities during the Cold War. Even combined, their power had great limits. Between 1955 and 1962, Western military institutions grossly overrated Soviet strength in bombers and missiles, as the US later underestimated the construction of Soviet nuclear forces. These failures primarily reflect the power of institutional perceptions and self-interest in analysis, but also the limits to the intelligence at hand. Imagery and Sigint counted deployed forces fairly well, but were weak in predicting their rates of expansion and their strength in the years ahead. GCHQ and the JIC were better at assessing these issues than most other intelligence organisations, partly because they had less self-interest in the issues than American agencies.[40] Again, UKUSA leaders such as Eisenhower often hoped that Sigint could reliably warn of Soviet nuclear attack; these hopes drove the creation of Criticomm, a fast-moving C3I system which aimed to warn a president within ten minutes of danger being discerned.[41] Their subordinates downplayed some of these hopes. After the Czech crisis of 1968, the British Minister of Defence, Denis Healey, asked 'whether it would be possible to deduce, from the patterns of Soviet exercise activity (and especially Strategic Strike exercises) what would be the main targets of the Soviet nuclear delivery systems in war. DIS Colonel thought not, and pointed out gently that no nation would be so foolish as to disclose its targeting plans in this way.' For GCHQ, Tovey wrote: 'I agree entirely with DIS on this point; we can deduce a great deal from LRAF/SNF [Long Range Air Force/Soviet Nuclear Forces] behaviour, both in exercises and at other times, but would not expect precise targeting data to emerge.'[42]

These caveats were powerful in general; yet in practice, Sigint and imagery provided powerful and precise warning intelligence on nuclear matters, every day. LRAF, SNF and PVO would take part in any dangerous Soviet activity, and reveal major intentions. GCHQ remained active against all of these targets throughout the Cold War, to aid war-fighting, but especially deterrence. GCHQ consistently contained alarmism on nuclear issues throughout the Cold War, especially during crises.

Economic and Technological Intelligence

Economic and technological prowess were fundamental to the Cold War, and to net estimates of Western and Soviet power. Intelligence on these matters was unbalanced. Western states publicly provided accurate economic statistics and open access to many leading matters of technology. They were also more exposed to espionage than communist states. The latter could gain most of the knowledge they needed through subscriptions to statistical digests, and periodicals such as *Aviation News*. They also collected technological material through an admirably effective campaign of espionage, the most successful branch of Eastern bloc intelligence activity during the Cold War. Meanwhile, especially before the Khrushchev thaw, the USSR hid basic data on all of these issues, while its public statistics were always incomplete and of dubious accuracy. Only good collection and analysis of intelligence could penetrate that shield. The best intelligence possible could not match the adversary in attack or defence, but merely staunch the bleeding. The USSR sought to blind the West to Soviet strengths and weaknesses, causing confusion and uncertainty, while stealing as much Western technology as possible. Western states aimed to minimise confusion and uncertainty, illuminate the struggle to determine and counter emerging threats, and guide offensive actions, such as controls over technology exports to the Eastern bloc, which contained these dangers in a cost-effective fashion.

These issues have received less attention than they merit, while much of the evidence about intelligence remains secret. Neither of the two histories of the leading British analytic organisation, the JIB, had much access to GCHQ records.[43] These problems obscure a central element of the Cold War. Soviet intelligence on technology was excellent in collection, decent when analysing technical issues, but incompetent on broader ones. Western intelligence on economic, scientific and technological matters behind the Iron Curtain was far from perfect, yet better than supposed. The key was excellent analysis of volumes of fragmentary data, building on a British method stemming straight from the War Trade Intelligence Department (WTID) in 1915. Western intelligence always had enough good sources, varying in significance by time and issue, to sustain such analysis. From 1956, imagery and open sources dominated that process. Sigint was overwhelmingly the primary source during 1946–56, when the task began; accurate evidence was fundamental and hard to find. Interception of civil text provided accurate intelligence, and a trusted means to judge the quality of other sources, including official Soviet statistics, which prepared analysts well for the moment when Sigint waned on the matter. British consumers expected GCHQ to analyse this kind of material, which its Commercial Section had done capably with economic intelligence since 1938. GCHQ and its main consumer, the JIB, simply continued work which their predecessors had done in economic warfare during 1939–45.

Between 1946 and 1956, GCHQ published probably several hundred thousand summaries and translations of civil text messages which, cross-indexed with each other and sometimes with reliable material from other sources, entered thousands of Sigint assessments. These messages had little value until they were collated, processed and analysed by experts both in Sigint and economic intelligence. GCHQ, sometimes aided by experts from other military or technical organisations, maximised the power of one source, while the JIB and military analytic units assessed material from all of them. These Sigint reports reproduced every relevant message, either verbatim or summarised. Their data was analysed painstakingly in diagrams, tables and text for the purposes of understanding and presentation. Reports illuminated many industrial, technological and military–economic issues, but were too fragmentary to do so with the Soviet economy as a whole. They included material on shortages of labour or raw materials, such as oil or coke, at factories or across the country; or on the links between Soviet establishments and the 'personalities' (names and work of individuals) within them. During the famine of 1946–47, civil text tracked grain requisitions across the USSR, demonstrating the scale of the catastrophe, and the state's ability to meet its needs, if not those of a million dead.[44] Civil text aided assessment of Soviet aircraft capacity, by tracing the work of aircraft plants, the Soviet electronic industry, and the provision of kit to the air forces. It provided many otherwise unavailable facts on key issues, such as political dissidence within the USSR, serial estimates of Soviet aircraft production, the capacity of munitions factories, specific areas of technology, including atomic research, and the poor quality of manufactured kit.[45] Civil text illustrated the confusion and friction within a command economy spread across Eurasia and the shoddy workmanship of manufactured goods in many emerging areas of technology, which was important to know and also reinforced underestimates of Soviet quality at its best.

From 1956, Comint on most economic issues vanished. During 1968, amidst a major rationalisation of analytic resources, GCHQ 'drastically' reduced its section addressing these matters, which 'had lost their importance', while 'the material was progressively becoming poorer'.[46] Still, from 1975, Sigint significantly penetrated Soviet defence economics by tracking raw material allocations, food production and new weapons, including warships, but especially those using communications at high altitudes, such as aircraft and ballistic and cruise missiles. Sigint was particularly useful in identifying research and development programmes, and the testing of prototypes. In 1979–83, GCHQ monitored the development of anti-tank guided weapons, the construction of major warships, submarine navigation and fire control systems, airborne anti-submarine kit and Soviet spacecraft.[47] Sigint bolstered a defensive campaign of economic warfare in peacetime, which contained Soviet strengths in intelligence and security and exposed its weaknesses in economics and technology. This was the area where Eastern bloc intelligence most beat Western, but to little avail. Western analysts misconstrued the Soviet economy, but overall their errors were too small to matter. Intelligence and the tighter security it led to impeded the Soviet acquisition of Western technology, despite the power of Eastern bloc espionage. Ignorance of its own economic position compared to Western states crippled Soviet understanding of and the ability to wage the Cold War. Ultimately, and ironically, lack of true data on their own economies led Eastern bloc authorities to rely on published CIA estimates of their economies. As usual in the history of intelligence, wisdom was to data as three is to one.

The Early Cold War: Challenge and Response

British Sigint against the USSR developed several layers between 1945 and 1970. In 1945, organisations hitherto focused on Germany immediately turned to attack similar targets in the Soviet Union, reflecting the realism of Siginters. GCHQ stations across the world followed Soviet targets. Cheadle continued to collect intelligence for defensive and offensive strategic air warfare, until air defence became impossible and the V-bombers declined in value. Then, converted to civilian status, Cheadle and other air-focused stations covered all Soviet Air Force traffic in western Russia, providing deep coverage beyond East Germany.[48] Scarborough, originally a Royal Navy base but converted to civilian status, remained Britain's main naval Sigint station, covering naval and mercantile traffic of the Warsaw Pact; and the alliance between the USSR and its satellites in eastern Europe in the Baltic Sea and the Atlantic Ocean. The station's reporting went to GCHQ and the Royal Navy, continuing old traditions of naval Sigint. Scarborough also loosely controlled the East Atlantic Direction-Finding network of NATO.[49] Culmhead, inheritor of the old GC&CS stations, used the most advanced techniques to attack the hardest targets in the Warsaw Pact.[50]

Surface warships collected Sigint, as did submarines, through intrusive missions deep in Soviet waters, among them some of the most sensitive and courageous acts of intelligence-gathering during the Cold War.[51] Radio Proving Flights, or 'ferret' flights, tested Soviet air defences, especially over the Baltic Sea. Bases in West Germany – mostly Army but also RAF, reflecting the traditions of field Y – focused on targets within East Germany. Western Sigint in Berlin was most visibly based at Teufelsberg, an 80-metre mound of rubble constructed after 1945, and more discreetly at RAF Gatow. Located in the heart of the Group of Soviet Forces Germany (GSFG), the greatest conventional formation in the world, Gatow was ideally placed to collect Sigint, especially voice, in 'a Sigint gold mine, a window into the heart of the Communist Bloc military system'.[52] The Army and the RAF concentrated much of their effort in Berlin, because Sigint would matter greatly in any period before war. Any units based there, however, would probably be lost when war began, and have only a degraded value in defence elsewhere even if successfully withdrawn in time of war. Elaborate plans for this process were drawn up at the peak of the Berlin crisis in 1959–61, but otherwise ignored.[53] Parochial concerns multiplied these strategic contradictions: Britain's reluctance to base units in Germany, which cost more than at home, and the physical limits to Gatow itself. The Army kept a large detachment at Gatow, for voice collection, but held most of its capabilities at Langeleben, balanced to provide intelligence in peace and war and to serve BAOR. The RAF concentrated its forward efforts at Gatow. It rated Sigint in deterrence, or in any period leading to war, above any aid for defence during battle or the needs of RAF Germany. These hard choices each met the needs of their masters and Britain.

GSFG stood on a peninsula assaulted by Siginters from three sides, simultaneously the most exposed and significant territory of the Cold War. UKUSA had great Sigint capabilities against enemy units in East Germany, its leading priority for conventional forces. They were reinforced by Sigint from third parties, and an interactive and inter-Allied combination of other sources. Through Allied arrangements in 1945–46, American, British and French ground and air forces were legally allowed to monitor East German and Soviet forces in the GDR. A few soldiers in Commanders-in-Chief Missions, including BRIXMIS and its American, French and Soviet counterparts, travelled in each other's zones. American, British and French military aircraft also collected imagery when using three twenty-mile-wide air routes from West Germany to West Berlin. These American and French flights collected some Sigint, but not British ones.[54] This was one of the few means for France to gather Sigint on Soviet forces in Germany, while the United States picked up everything it could. Britain had better and cheaper means to acquire Sigint. Meanwhile, under the guise of maintaining aircrew proficiency, personnel (nicknamed 'Biggles' and 'Algy', after famous fictional British aviators) in RAF Chipmunks based at Gatow conducted low-level air missions across the GDR, including imagery taken from hand-held cameras through open windows in freezing weather.[55] Through Chipmunks and BRIXMIS, Britain maintained greater air and ground reconnaissance capabilities than its allies were allowed. Each source could corroborate anything reported by another. Ideally, BRIXMIS and Chipmunks would shadow a Soviet exercise, and Sigint monitor all traffic to and from it. Chipmunk personnel were trained on BRIXMIS missions before flying, to ensure knowledge of the ground and kit. The Allied air and ground missions interacted loosely, but were insulated from Sigint – in theory. During 1978, one incoming head of 26 SU, Tony Cunnane, was introduced to BRIXMIS and its American and French counterparts by his predecessor. Next morning, Cunnane was ordered onto the first flight west to meet the senior RAF intelligence officer in Germany, who warned him never to repeat the exercise.[56] Reports from these air and ground sources flowed back to UKUSA intelligence authorities in Germany, who integrated the information to help guide future missions. Siginters independently added to that pot, and took from it, to guide their own activity.

American and British Sigint sought to monitor all Soviet targets, certainly the most central of them, with the aim of identifying every anomaly, and warning their masters of any signs of danger. Ultimately Siginters achieved these ends by living within the net of Soviet signals by monitoring the same command links for decades and developing anthropological skills based on a finely granulated attention to detail. This skill and success were not easy to achieve.

GCHQ and Crises in the Early Cold War

During the autumn of 1956, GCHQ confronted two unexpected crises at once – its greatest challenge of the Cold War. Throughout 1956, Egypt subverted and aimed to overthrow Britain's position in the Middle East. In particular, Egypt nationalised the Suez Canal, which Britain and France owned. British forces planned for war, which GCHQ supported by penetrating diplomatic and military systems of the Middle East, especially Egyptian ones. GCHQ also prepared against an Israeli attack on Britain's Arab allies, which might have the potential to involve Britain in war, by aiming to provide 'a reasonable chance of detecting signs of aggressive intentions and of making a rapid change-over to a wartime degree of exploitation', without damaging collection on Russia.[57] Force alone could stop Nasser's threat to vital British interests, but only with difficulty, which Eden's government multiplied. Trapped in the world politics of anti-imperialism, and leading a state uncertain whether it was or was not a great power, Eden declined to use force directly. Instead, he did so through a conspiracy with France and Israel, which Britain hid from its allies and officials. Israel would attack Egyptian forces in Sinai, without provocation, and drive for the Suez Canal. Britain and France would use this event to justify occupation of the Canal Zone, and Egypt. Even a determined and able government would have found this plan hard to execute. Britain lacked such a government.[58] Even worse, Eden launched the conspiracy without fully consulting his strategic advisors or intelligence agencies, which crippled Britain's ability to execute his aims. As GCHQ noted right after the crisis: 'We were alerted 4 days before HMG's ultimatum … and, one day before, by gaining unofficial knowledge … but the public news was the first that GCHQ officially gained about HMG's intentions. (MI6 clearly knew a little more)… Even after operations had started we had to rely for briefing about operational plans on a black-market service from Admiralty. An official service from the Ministry of Defence would have been preferable but, in the event, perhaps less efficient.'[59]

That four days of warning and 'black-market service' enabled GCHQ to focus its resources against Egypt during the intervention of 1–7 November. GCHQ effectively aided an operation on which it was barely briefed and created means to deliver its product to decision-makers, including Eden.[60] The effect was futile. Good intelligence could not save incompetent policy.

Suez was a big crisis, yet precisely as GCHQ improvised its way through it, a greater one emerged in Europe. During October 1956, political unrest in Hungary sparked a revolution, and a Soviet onslaught during 1–11 November. These events coincided with the Suez crisis, increasingly bad Anglo-American relations, the last days of an American presidential election, and great tensions between the USSR and Poland, where popular anti-Soviet unrest was manifest. The Hungarian crisis surprised everyone. This sudden and large use of force raised the issue of where the Soviets would stop and tested the rules for order in Europe. Soviet panic proved contagious. The DIRNSA, General Canine, thought 'drastic changes' were needed in American decision-making. 'Worst thing in a crisis is a jittery G2 [military intelligence] and that we have had.'[61] Sigint did not predict the crisis and could not have done so, but the Five Eyes response was confused and mediocre, for political and organisational reasons. Britain and the United States were unready for such a crisis; NSA was a new organisation with fragile control over US Sigint agencies and uncertain contacts with American headquarters. After the crisis, NSA commented that it 'received very little information on U.S. plans, intentions, and operations during the crisis', with 'painfully obvious' damage to its work.[62] American Sigint was confused in structure and had never confronted a crisis of this nature and magnitude. Whitehall and GCHQ had more experience of such matters, but lacked procedures or preparations to handle the crisis. GCHQ, concentrated on war in the Middle East, was not a twenty-four-hour organisation. British Sigint was uncoordinated: GCHQ did not control army Sigint in Europe, while the latter was technically mixed in quality and reported to Army headquarters, which could not direct these units, or even know that they should.

UKUSA was even more uncoordinated. British Siginters believed that they were good, while their American colleagues often were not. US Siginters made alarmist – and alarming – claims, which British Siginters rejected. One of GCHQ's aims became to minimise alarmism in American reporting and among American consumers. One senior British Army Sigint officer 'thought US military reports in the crisis were "rubbish"', and disregarded by NORTHAG, the British headquarters which commanded NATO in northern Germany – a frightening commentary.[63] Sigint communications were clogged perhaps more than ever during the Cold War. For the first time, amidst crisis, UKUSA confronted the unintended consequences of its standard operating procedures for reporting and dissemination. US Siginters transmitted only spot reports, but did so immediately, which at this stage NSA could not properly collate. Their widespread and instantaneous dissemination spread alarm and error as reports ricocheted across the Five Eyes: as

Francis Raven, a leading NSA official told Palmer: 'Basic problem is U.S. consumer demand for everything from everywhere to everyone at top priority.'[64]

These problems were serious, doubly so because leaders in Britain, NATO and the United States feared extreme Soviet actions: military intervention in Poland, the dispatch of 'volunteers' to Egypt, and possibly more. Here, GCHQ played its greatest role of the Cold War, and a unique one, which combined a professional focus on accuracy with an openly political campaign to contain alarmism across UKUSA. That aim was easy to achieve in Whitehall, where intelligence and military authorities accepted GCHQ's evidence calmly. The JIC, for example, held that Soviet mobilisation against Poland was small in scale, indicating 'that the Russians are placing themselves in a state of complete readiness to strike at once if any trouble should develop in POLAND, but there is no evidence that they are preparing to strike now'.[65] GCHQ's aim was much harder in Washington, where events in Suez caused American authorities and Siginters to suspect British motives, precisely at the peak of the Hungarian crisis. Americans were particularly sensitive to British manipulation, precisely as GCHQ manipulated them more than at any other moment of the Cold War. Though Suez blindsided GCHQ, Americans were right to wonder whether it was lying to them over the Middle East; and if so, why not in Europe too? Here, fortunately, the personal trust between Director Jones and DIRNSA Canine, and the latter's friendship with the SUKLO, Palmer, reduced tensions.

GCHQ focused all of its resources on quality control, addressing the fears of Soviet intentions and correcting mistakes among American Siginters which might cause errors in action. Internally, GCHQ established a large section to study 'Russian intentions' and report on them daily. GCHQ's judgements rested on positive and negative intelligence about matters which changed and remained the same. They were expressed in detailed reports and broad appreciations, despite the supposed ban on that practice. For example, GCHQ told NSA:

1. ...Latest Sigint information as of 1600 8/11 gives no indication of Soviet preparation for global war or of intention to intervene with force in the Middle East. Soviet Air, Naval and Merchant Shipping activity appears normal, subject to Hungarian situation.

The only other communications activity which appear at all unusual is in the Group of Soviet Forces in Germany where cumulative evidence from 30 October to 8 November suggests a general state of readiness. The evidence is that military practice traffic has virtually disappeared from the main networks of the Mech Armies in GSFG since 4 November; that there has been a silence on certain links from HQ to Armies from about 1350 on 6 November; and that there was on 7 November (Soviet holiday) a small amount of fighter code in an Air Army in Germany which is unusual during a holiday.

2. With present intercept resources it is virtually certain that Sigint would detect Soviet preparations for global war or any large scale preparation to intervene in force in the Middle East. The scale of Sigint resources and their state of alert is such that negative evidence in these contexts is considered reliable.

3. Sigint could not however be guaranteed to detect small-scale Soviet moves in connection with the Middle East situation. The movement of technicians, small supplies or small amounts of aircraft to the Arab countries would not necessarily be detected by Sigint, though there is a reasonable chance that aircraft movements would be observed.[66]

GCHQ traced the Soviet suppression of the Hungarian revolution in detail, as Soviet forces abandoned signals security in combat. This material illuminated current events and, later, underwrote exhaustive analyses of the operations and command and control of all Soviet formations involved in this campaign, from divisions to army groups, airborne to air forces – all priceless information for any military officer considering how their enemy would actually fight.[67] GCHQ contained fears of Soviet mobilisation against Poland or Egypt, Turkish accounts of Soviet air mobilisation in the Caucasus and Black Sea, and reports of LRAF flights to the Arctic Ocean, which would have been an alarming signal.[68] It compiled original evidence that the LRAF was about to begin flights in the Arctic, but offered a counter-intuitive reading of that evidence: 'It is however considered most unlikely that such a movement (which would almost certainly be detected) of LRAF aircraft would be connected with present international situation.' GCHQ defined the LRAF's real states of alert, which were high but not warlike. That a

Soviet atomic test was proceeding normally suggested a similar pattern.[69] J division 'is keeping an eye on Kapustin Yar range to see if any evidence of weapons being transferred westward', and found none.[70] Despite constant harassment and tension, GCHQ was remarkably calm and stoical. It rarely issued alerts to military Sigint units, which it thought able to understand their situation without direction.[71]

The Cuban missile crisis occurred because American intelligence, at almost the last moment possible to act, detected a covert Soviet attempt to deploy medium-range ballistic missiles (MRBM) to Cuba, which would have weakened the United States in political and strategic terms. Had this action been discovered earlier, the United States could easily have blocked it without crisis; weeks later, it would have been a fait accompli. The American problem combined a lack of intelligence, the power of Soviet security and the weight of preconception. The seeming unlikelihood of the Soviet action kept suspicions which bubbled deep in the bowels of many agencies from reaching the brain of all-source analysis. *Maskirovka* security and deception covered the loading of missiles and warheads onto merchantmen in Soviet ports, the middle passage to Cuba, and their conveyance to bases.[72] Soviet ships' crews were denied knowledge of their cargoes. When they approached Cuba, their captains, alongside their KGB minders, opened written orders telling them their next actions. No wireless signals mentioned their task. This *maskirovka*, basic but competent, failed in the end, but prevented GCHQ or NSA from sounding an alarm that Siginters yearned to ring earlier.

Experience of the Hungarian crisis taught GCHQ that Soviet mercantile shipping was 'an entity to be watched as an indicator (positive or negative) of war', through 'the sudden increase in cypher traffic to and from ships, orders to ships concerning dangerous areas, re-routing of tankers and other ships and the apparent decrease in the numbers of positions reports sent in the clear'.[73] Siginters routinely covered Soviet mercantile traffic by reading open reports from Lloyd's of London and newspapers, foreign port officials and plain-language messages, and noting the use of cypher. In the months before the crisis broke, a sharp rise in Soviet shipping to Cuba caught the attention of Siginters. Every report emphasised that Sigint had no idea of the cargoes. Any unusual reports were marked 'Priority', and distributed to the JIC, the Foreign Office, DIRNSA, and sometimes MI6 and

American and British naval intelligence, along with usual consumers. On 20 July, for example, GCHQ's outstation at Scarborough noted that two Soviet passenger and cargo ships, ostensibly bound for Vladivostok, had mentioned positions which 'would normally indicate' they 'were possibly en route Cuba', and that they had received enciphered messages which might suggest 'that their voyages are other than routine'.[74] Ultimately, these two vessels did not sail to Cuba; many Soviet merchantmen leaving the Baltic turned north towards Murmansk, where they loaded 'military associated cargoes to Cuba' (which many sources also reported was occurring). GCHQ monitored an unusual 'large-scale communications exercise' between all Soviet merchantmen at sea and their controllers in the USSR, and an unusual wireless transmitter on board a Soviet tanker on a 'routine' trip to Cuba.[75] Probably GCHQ and NSA read all messages to and from Soviet merchantmen bound for Cuba. None seemed alarming, even in hindsight, while Soviet conventional and nuclear forces worldwide avoided abnormal behaviour. When collated, the Sigint evidence simply showed that the USSR was shipping some conventional weapons to Cuba, and aiding the development of its military and air defences. Soviet Comsec blocked UKUSA from offering any evidence, and also restrained potential fear.

Instead, the crisis broke just before Soviet actions were complete, in the explosive circumstances of an American Congressional election. By early October 1962, other sources provided enough evidence to raise suspicions: some emigré reports about Soviet deployments in Cuba proved accurate while buried within a spoilheap of rumour; imagery suggested that some of the deck cargo on some Soviet merchantmen fitted the profile of the standard Soviet medium bomber of the day, the Ilyushin IL-28; while Soviet surface-to-air missile (SAM) sites on Cuba were deployed like those found around Soviet ICBM bases. Contrary to popular legend, John McCone, head of the CIA, was not the only intelligence chief worried about Soviet shipments to Cuba: the US Defence Intelligence Agency, GCHQ and NSA had equal concerns, as did junior officials in many agencies. McCone and the Pentagon, however, could bring another source to bear. On 14 October, a U-2 spyplane caught the first proof that Soviet missiles were on Cuba, setting UKUSA, and the crisis, into motion. NSA and GCHQ promulgated Sigint alerts on 23 October.

GCHQ's normal work in monitoring Soviet nuclear forces and conventional formations in Europe illuminated matters which were fundamental to the crisis. So too, Scarborough's daily toil in following Soviet mercantile traffic proved fundamental to watching merchantmen carrying nuclear warheads to Cuba, until they gradually turned about, and the sudden flurry of urgent enciphered messages from Moscow to its transport ships after President Kennedy announced a pacific blockade of Cuba – the moment when the fever broke.[76]

GCHQ spoke with credibility and intimacy to its American counterparts. They appreciated its performance. GCHQ worked well because it needed only to service its standard links to British forces and NSA. However, the chaotic command system of American forces during the crisis would have determined the impact of this intelligence, had war occurred. In particular, Sigint would have provided excellent intelligence to guide NATO nuclear strikes. Had war broken out, however, the US Secretary for Defense, Robert McNamara, planned to abandon plans for that campaign and improvise his way to victory, as he later did so well in Vietnam.[77]

GCHQ and the Middle Cold War

By 1964, when GCHQ absorbed the individual service Sigint organisations, it had become the sole national organisation responsible for Sigint on the Warsaw Pact. Its military and intelligence consumers also became more unified as the MOD grew in power over the services. Some problems declined, while others rose.

Warsaw Pact manoeuvres became large and constant. Exercises produced more traffic, along with uncertainty and 'noise'. The Pact did not intend exercises to pose an intelligence problem for NATO, but they had that effect. The actions of exercises were hard to distinguish from those which marked the start of a crisis. As the MOD's Defence Intelligence Service (DIS) noted in 1968:

> It will always be difficult to make a timely, correct and definite
> interpretation of the significance of Russian activities. Individual
> indicators could have alternative explanations, for example: as
> reflecting a military exercise. A combination would clearly be
> of more significance; indeed it might only be by shrewd study

of a number of concurrent indicators, some of them small in themselves, that we could hope to arrive at a true interpretation of Soviet activities. Such a combination could be interpreted as indicating that an attack was being planned. But if each side was alerted and reacting to the other's successive moves, it might well be wrong to deduce warning of impending attack from the enemy's preparations, which might only be designed to intimidate, or to demonstrate to the West that the Union could not be intimidated. Indeed, the precautionary measures could reach a stage at which the Soviet Union was fully mobilised but had no intention of initiating general war.[78]

Errors of analysis might expose NATO to surprise attack, or spur the USSR to start one. Only hard and able work could prevent these dangers. The 'generally increased and more realist Soviet Armed Forces' activity', J division warned, caused an 'atmosphere of high activity and greater realism', which produced welcome 'stimulation', but added 'strains and stresses on an already over-stretched Division'.[79] That stress became the norm. Twenty-one major exercises occurred in 1967. From 1970, Warsaw Pact manoeuvres occurred almost every day.

UKUSA's reliance on traffic analysis would have appalled Bletchley. Historically, traffic analysis was a good source, especially for order of battle, but weaker about enemy intentions and vulnerable to signals deception. It worked best, as with 'Sixta' at Bletchley, when combined with good Comint. That component was absent against the USSR, which had demonstrated competence in signals deception. In 1945, Soviet *maskirovka*, including wireless deception, matched the Western Allies' in operations, though not in strategy.[80] Western analysts misunderstood Soviet quality in that sphere at this time. Excessive secrecy over the historical record damaged UKUSA's general understanding of wireless deception while, misled by the conspiracy theories of the KGB defector Anatoly Golitsyn, some intelligence officers and politicians distorted *maskirovka*'s general power to deceive Western strategy.[81] Soviet security was good, but its deception less so. Mediocre executions of field *maskirovka* could too easily be mistaken for a KGB masterplan. Elementary *maskirovka* covered the Soviet deployments to Cuba before the missile crisis.[82] A few Siginters thought they observed Soviet wireless deception during the Czech crisis of 1968.[83] The JIC accepted

GCHQ's view that wireless deception had not occurred, but demanded a 'record' – that is, justification – of its views.[84] The intelligence coordinator, the admired veteran Dick White, still insisted that 'the KGB's Disinformation Section was well capable of carrying out a first-class deception operation through secret agents'.[85]

In its post-mortems of that crisis, DIS, anticipating consumers' questions, asked whether wireless silence would handicap predictions, 'since almost all of our current intelligence comes from Sigint sources'. If so, that danger could cripple every assessment of Soviet preparations for attack and diminish the power of Sigint, thereby multiplying the effect of fear, uncertainty and alarmism on Western strategy. DIS concluded that the danger was small: the Soviets could not avoid using radio, while wireless silence would betray that something unusual was afoot. GCHQ wished to refute this danger in even firmer terms. Any 'evidence' of large-scale wireless deception 'would clearly be a discovery of considerable importance'. GCHQ searched for signs of it in vain. The evidence was 'blatantly incompatible' with that idea, as 'the behaviour of the General Staff communications provided the clearest possible indicator of what was really happening'.[86] Britain 'must put this whole business of "radio silence" in context. Frankly – so far as the Soviet Army is concerned – we have no real evidence of any attempts to put such a concept into practice.' Whether because of that practice or 'more likely' through 'technical SIGINT difficulties not primarily of the Russians' own making, moves of one or two Divisions into the Forward Area could go undetected by us until a few days after arrival ... We must honestly confess to some degree of doubt about our ability to discern, or at least, to identify as such, Rear Service exercises, mobilisation measures, and the like.' Still, Sigint observations, especially of General Staff traffic, would detect 'any major reinforcement of the Forward Area', that is, of more than a few divisions.[87]

As with Cuba in 1962, Soviet secrecy on political matters aided tactical surprise for the invasion of Czechoslovakia. Again, signals deception did not aid that outcome, which Soviet signals insecurity compromised, this time damaging *maskirovka* as a whole. GCHQ's critique helped to inoculate Western strategy from Golitsyn's conspiracy theories, which infected only Western Humint. A foe able in wireless deception might have fooled UKUSA. The Soviets were not that foe – their wireless operators were sloppy and their command and communications cumbersome, though NATO was no exemplar. Soviet signals insecurity also crippled its ability to conduct wireless deception. UKUSA, meanwhile, developed traffic analysis of unparalleled skill and experience in the radio age, which, from 1955, probably could have contained *maskirovka*.

UKUSA's central task was to be an intelligence tripwire: to calculate order of battle and thus infer capabilities and intentions. Any sign that Warsaw Pact forces were improving their ability to attack sounded a warning. Little sound was needed for NATO states to adopt their only possible response, which was to reinforce their cover, and stand for war. UKUSA's ability to follow enemy movements, and crucially to know when it lost track of any formation, eliminated the danger of a surprise attack followed up by a secret mobilisation, which many other sources would be able to monitor too. The narrow space of the Central Front also denied the Soviets the bewildering range of alternative prospects which best aids deception.

Still, the Soviets could launch a conventional or nuclear strike without any background of political tension, or military mobilisation. In that case, they might conceal concentrations of standing forces at select points, if they were skilled or lucky enough to execute the efforts. Any systematic efforts at wireless silence to cover any other eventuality would backfire, however, by drawing attention to deception, especially if applied for the first time by inexperienced practitioners. *Maskirovka* might marginally have reinforced Soviet tactical surprise at the start of a war, but little else, and equally, might have eliminated it altogether. We shall never know, fortunately.

The Test of Czechoslovakia

During the Cold War, the Soviet Union often considered whether it must forcibly prevent the defection of an ally: with Yugoslavia in 1948, Hungary in 1956, Czechoslovakia in 1968, Afghanistan in 1979, and Poland in 1980–84. Ultimately, the USSR invaded three of these countries. For observers in Britain and the USA, the military concentrations needed to achieve these ends might enable the USSR to pursue greater ambitions. These examples demonstrated the problems in predicting any Soviet attack on NATO. They, and the Soviet efforts to intimidate NATO into abandoning West Berlin between 1958 and

1962, ranked among the Five Eyes' greatest challenges of the Cold War. These challenges also gave GCHQ and NSA opportunities to measure and improve their skill.

During the 1960s, American Sigint rose sharply in quality and quantity. GCHQ's analytic capabilities were great, and matched those of NSA. But during the Czechoslovak crisis of 1968, American Sigint provided most of the relevant coverage while transitional problems reduced British power. GCHQ relied on semi-processed American material, which it could challenge only carefully: 'this process inevitably involves a certain element of inspired guesswork and is barely a substitute for an adequate study of one's own intercept'. Also, J division was part-way through the process of changing from a reliance on hand logs of intercepts to automatic semi-processed material. 'Analysis thus tended to have the worst of both worlds, having lost both the facility and the habit of studying raw logs, but being unable to take full advantage of the machinable semi-processed material by which logs had been replaced.'[88] These problems reduced GCHQ's characteristic strengths. GCHQ made a 'significant contribution' in 'interpretation', through 'presenting in a reasonably digestible form (the daily ARU-H reports) what otherwise would have been a mass of paper well beyond our customers' power of assimilation'.[89] Fifty ARU-Hs, which compiled and analysed reports received over one to three days, were released between 11 August and 24 September 1968, more than one per day.[90] Hooper, Director of GCHQ, later praised its 'rapid and readable end-product' despite the 'steady drain of manpower and teamage' in recent years, but this statement perhaps gilded the lily.[91]

The crisis demonstrated UKUSA's power in determining order of battle, and its weakness over intentions and the politics of policy.[92] Sigint demonstrated that the Soviets could overwhelm Czechoslovakia, but did not penetrate the intentions on either side, except to show that Czech military traffic was 'deliberately passive and non-provocative'. In order to overawe a major ally on the frontier with NATO, the USSR had to transform its command and deployments. These actions gave NATO ample time to prepare as it wished. From 7–9 May, a major and unexpected Command Post Exercise occurred. GSFG command links were extended to the GDR–Czech border, to where the 20th Guards Army advanced from Berlin. On 10 May, Soviet airborne and general staff command links escalated in unusual ways. GDR officials discussed the movement of Soviet troops towards the Czech border. A GDR soldier warned his wife that he soon would leave East Germany. From 11 to 30 May, Soviet troops advanced from one of their two main feeders into central Europe, the Carpathian Military District, towards Czechoslovakia, as did Soviet and Polish aircraft. In June, manoeuvres mobilised the Warsaw Pact against Czechoslovakia, and left Soviet forces in the country. Around 7 July, exercises and command links produced a 'distinctly suspicious appearance', though GCHQ recognised that many actions that the press thought dangerous stemmed simply from logistical exercises. Then, tension declined.[93] The military standstill suggested that the crisis had abated, reinforced by the withdrawal of Soviet forces from the country after exercises, and public negotiations between Czechoslovakia and the Warsaw Pact. Beneath this surface calm lay agitation within the capitals of the Warsaw Pact, and a decision to solve this problem by force.[94] These states hid signs of this agitation, which no Western source penetrated.

GCHQ showed that Soviet forces could strike from out of the blue, but it did not predict an invasion and ended its emergency staffing. Soviet movements had been aimed to lull suspicions in Prague, and also did so with NATO and GCHQ. On 20–21 August, forces from the Warsaw Pact struck Czechoslovakia with tactical surprise and quickly subdued the country. Over the next tense month, GCHQ watched the movements of all Warsaw Pact forces and allayed fears that the USSR would strike elsewhere. Analysis of this traffic honed GCHQ's baseline for assessing the nature and intentions of Warsaw Pact redeployments and preparations for major attack, which may have guided its acute reading of Soviet movements during the Polish crisis of 1980–81.

This performance, Tovey noted, produced an 'almost euphoric adulation of SIGINT … at the height of the crisis', replaced by a 'rather more sober appraisal' when other sources emerged and analysis of the event as a whole become possible.[95] He thought this change was good for GCHQ, as it also was for judging the performance of intelligence against the main enemy. Czechoslovakia was a success for Sigint, but not a triumph; had this mobilisation been directed westward, NATO would have had ample time to counter-mobilise its full strength. It would have confronted only the smallest and unavoidable forms of tactical surprise, at a time when it would already have suspected danger, and been able to assess Soviet intentions, if only from diplomatic contacts. DIS credited

Sigint with providing 90 per cent of its material.[96] Military attaché and press reports delivered the rest. GCHQ enabled its consumers to understand Soviet capabilities and its ability to act as and when it wished, though Cheltenham could not precisely predict the attack. As Tovey said: 'until AFABF aircraft were actually flying over Poland en route to Czechoslovakia none of us could point to any firm SIGINT indication of imminent invasion. Even then there could have been other indications, right up to the time when the aircraft approached the Czech frontier.'[97] These errors, and uncertainties, demonstrated what the best traffic analysis on earth could not deliver, which an Ultra might have done.

This mixed success led GCHQ and DIS to reconsider how well they could detect a Soviet attack on NATO. During the lull in the crisis, DIS concluded that experience confirmed their pre-existing views. In November 1966, the JIC had concluded that the Warsaw Pact could launch a surprise attack from a standstill, but if it deployed the LRAF and naval air forces, NATO would have forty-eight hours' warning – four to nine days if the enemy entirely abandoned 'strategic surprise'. Military movements might be exercises, defence against expected NATO actions, or 'measures intended to intimidate the West or the prelude to Soviet attack'. Yet GCHQ had traced every indicator which the JIC emphasised: the extension of GSFG communications, westward movements of Soviet forces, staff and logistics exercises and troop concentrations. 'Our experience here,' DIS wrote:

> shows that we were able to detect the military warning indicators
> of the move of Soviet troops in the Carpathian Military District
> on to the Polish/Czech border. This warning was received very
> shortly after the troops had started to move and therefore should
> strengthen our confidence that similar indicators would be detected
> if such large scale movement appropriate to an attack on NATO
> should begin ... we were able to detect air deployments very soon
> after they had occurred. All this information should enable us to
> build up an accurate intelligence picture of Soviet deployments
> from Western Russia in sufficient time to be able to warn NATO.[98]

That confidence waned after the surprise Soviet move on 21 August. DIS concluded that it could not predict intentions purely by military preparations divorced from political ones. The Warsaw Pact could launch a successful surprise attack from a standstill, while NATO could expect three to eight days' warning if the Soviets mobilised in order to multiply their 'weight of attack ... In either case the Russians could achieve tactical surprise in terms of the moment of attack.' Meanwhile, Soviet power was strengthened by its constant improvements in Comsec and communications.[99] GCHQ was even more disconcerted, reflecting its discovery of unexpected technical problems. As Tovey wrote:

> Immediately before the invasion we were faced with the apparent contradiction of a situation of seemingly lowered political tension accompanied by a military posture indicating immediate readiness for intervention. Therefore, when the Russians assessed (unknown to us) that they were not going to achieve their aims as a result of the Cierna–Bratislava discussions, they were able to achieve tactical surprise by their political decision to intervene ... the lesson for the future is clear. A period in which both the political and military indicators are 'red' can be followed, as they were in this instance, by a situation in which the political situation shows itself as 'green' while the military situation obstinately remains at 'red' – in such circumstances in future we cannot (as we and our consumers have tended to do in the past) gloss over the military indicators by, for example, attributing them to exercise activity or the like, but must continue to take them very much to heart.[100]

Ultimately, GCHQ concluded that the problem was just marginally worse than before: GCHQ could provide the three to eight days' warning which DIS wanted of major movements, say of several divisions from several Military Districts, but not necessarily just one division from a single Military District.[101] To do so would require greater resources and heightened procedures, every day.

GCHQ set out to provide just that. For years beforehand, GCHQ had readjusted its resources, reducing J division and Siginters in Europe marginally, so that K division could go forth and multiply. GCHQ wished to avoid becoming mired in tasks involving Cold War Europe, which had inexhaustible calls for resources, in order to maximise its chances for original work elsewhere. Partly as a result, in 1968, British Sigint did not collect much material relevant to the greatest crisis in Europe for a decade. GCHQ's reliance on semi-processed American material undercut its claims for 'that independent British contribution which is a primary justification of J division's existence'. It had sufficient resources to handle the crisis, but only barely. As Tovey wrote: 'the Soviet invasion, including the manner of its preparation and the way it was actually carried out, can leave us in no doubt that the situation confronting J division today is fundamentally different from that of a year ago. What we cannot do, therefore, is to revert simply to the policy and procedures which were in vogue before the crisis supervened.'[102] Equally significant were revelations about morale within GCHQ:

> Virtually all staff, irrespective of level, obviously derived a sense of stimulus and satisfaction from the realisation that J Division's product was now at the forefront of Whitehall's thinking; these considerations far outweighed any inconvenience in the working of extended hours. Similarly, the almost neurotic belief that 'nobody really cares about the Soviet bloc anymore', the chilling sensation that there was no point in producing intelligence quickly ('the Americans will get it out first anyhow') – these undesirable if understandable concomitants of the reduction of J manpower over the past few years evaporated over night as the Czech crisis gained pace.[103]

The Czech crisis exposed GCHQ's limits as a worldwide organisation, just as Indonesian Konfrontasi did in 1964–65. Afterwards, GCHQ stopped its reductions of J division and military Sigint in Europe, which threatened 'the maintenance and development of that sound technical understanding of the Soviet problem in depth on which all our work, whether in crisis reporting, routine reporting, or long-term studies, ultimately depends'.[104] It steadily boosted the capabilities of J division.[105] These steps significantly increased GCHQ's capabilities in Europe, while diminishing those elsewhere. The end of empire and the Czechoslovak crisis led GCHQ to reverse its strategy of the previous decade, and to concentrate its resources in Western Europe, thereby maintaining a flagship position in the greatest theatre, while declining elsewhere across the world. This policy was telling, yet mirrored the main trends in British strategic policy. It also achieved its end.

Living in the Force: the High Cold War

GCHQ produced intelligence on an industrial scale, which its consumers processed in the same way. Together, they drove a flood of data through the mill of analysis to produce Sigint, the most powerful form of military intelligence during the Cold War. GCHQ assessed British material and everything it received from second and third parties.

Assessment always had a political dimension. Multiple and overlapping consumers were driven by different interest and concerns. 'For Distribution to Sigint Producers Only', GCHQ issued 'Technical Supplements' on matters such as the frequencies and call signs of signals entities.[106] Another great set of consumers were British intelligence assessment bodies, of which the JIC was not the largest. In the early Cold War, the JIB was GCHQ's main consumer for strategic intelligence, especially on economic issues. The JIB's successor, the more military-focused DIS, became the main consumer for GCHQ's material on the main enemy. Many DIS reports were sanitised Sigint. None directly contradicted the Sigint record; most were confirmed by it, in various ways, and some stemmed from the source. The structural problems which dogged British analysis – bad liaison between DIS and the JIC, or officers swamped with responsibilities – were largely absent in assessing the Soviet problem in the Cold War, because Britain created analytic capabilities fit to handle it. Even on peripheral issues such as Soviet relations with, say, Afghanistan, GCHQ and DIS analysts constantly addressed intelligence and demanded and provided constant warning about minor matters.

More than in wartime, military consumers were usually staff and analysts rather than commanders. The security procedures within Sigint – the distinctions between Categories 2 and 3, or of Special Compartmented Intelligence (SCIs) and their British equivalents, Very Restricted Knowledge (VRK), differentiated military consumers into different groups. Reading folders kept Sigint distinct from everything else: analysts across the desk from each other might have different categories of access. Security procedures blocked these reports from NATO third parties, who received sanitised versions or none at all. From 1970, UKUSA gave much Category 2 material to NATO third parties, in sanitised forms, as 'NATO Secret'. Security also limited the combination of Sigint and non-Sigint sources for any consumer. Every year, GCHQ produced a few finely granulated assessments which compared the Sigint record with other sources. It lacked the analysts to do so often, while DIS and the BAOR lacked the staff and the clearances needed for the purpose. Security restrictions limited their distribution. BRIXMIS never received a copy of an excellent 1981 report on Soviet armoured tactics, for which its personnel provided key material.[107]

GCHQ was not supposed to offer appreciations unless consumers requested them, but in military intelligence it could encourage such queries, or convey the answers unasked. Most military Sigint reports were factual narratives, but many were organised analytically – appreciations in all but name. GCHQ presented data in powerful and sophisticated graphic forms. Analysts loved nothing more than to squeeze yet another drop of data from a report and to represent it in even more complicated graphs. Regular reports addressed specific issues at the same level of analysis, categorisation and audience. Individual specialists, or dozens of them, produced special reports, each tailored to distinct readerships. Some special reports, reflecting secrecy or narrowness, had tiny distributions. Others were downgraded from Category 3 to 2 by removing individual items of Comint from the text, which, against the Warsaw Pact, rarely damaged comprehension. This step allowed wide distribution among anglophone military commands and enabled the technically most qualified officers to consider the best evidence on enemy practices alongside that from other sources. One such report, 'was intended to convey, in a timely manner, short items of original and noteworthy information' about narrow matters; others provided broad and detailed accounts of everything known about great topics.[108] Many special reports were Sigint analyses of the order of battle of Warsaw Pact forces, intelligence fundamental to assessing their numbers and organisation, though inadequate to define capabilities.[109] Other GCHQ reports illuminated capabilities insofar as they could be judged outside war.

GCHQ did not give consumers the raw intercepts which it received, nor did it show how the sausages were made within the factory of analysis: they were generally incomprehensible to outsiders. Daily and weekly summaries were hard enough to follow; spot reports were even worse. GCHQ issued two genres of weekly reports – one detailed, the other a synopsis – on matters such as 'Soviet Air Force and Air Defence',

'Eurcom Activity' and 'Soviet Bloc Political and Military Activity Abroad', within GCHQ and to NSA and major British intelligence and military agencies. GCHQ provided detailed observations and notes on abnormalities. It had enough analysts to handle the work, as could specialists in other departments. Britain allocated enough resources in collection and analysis to squeeze juice from low-level sources and to make rye whiskey from strong but crude ones.

GCHQ and Crises during the Later Cold War

Between 1976 and 1985 the Cold War intensified. Both sides became more fearful, angry and confrontational. Western countries thought their position across the world was challenged and that hard responses were necessary. Soviet leaders feared decline, the loss of allies and, perhaps, a pre-emptive strike by NATO. Crises and exercises were constant. The old problems remained: how to discern the unusual detail taken from a host of routine reports and to determine whether an exercise marked the opening of a crisis. GCHQ's track record on these matters was good – powerful in technique and effective on policy, yet limited by its inability to determine Soviet intentions directly. Those mixed characteristics marked its performance during two great crises which set the end game of the later Cold War, when the USSR invaded Afghanistan, but not Poland.

GCHQ monitored Soviet intentions through their reflections within links for command, control and communications, especially airborne warning and control aircraft (AWACS) or those platforms 'associated' with specific commanders, and of Soviet organisations central to emergencies, such as nuclear or airborne forces.[110] Two of these links shaped GCHQ's work during the Afghan crisis, though in both cases past practices changed.

During 1979, the communist regime of Afghanistan imploded. Soviet leaders, fearing that the Afghan dictator, Hafizullah Amin, might betray them and align with the United States, decided to overthrow him with 700 special forces and paratroopers, occupy the country with 50,000 soldiers, and reform the regime. This issue is usually seen as an intelligence failure for Western countries.[111] In fact, the USSR – grossly distorting Amin's ties with the United States and underestimating the difficulty of controlling Afghanistan – made far greater errors of intelligence. The role of intelligence during the invasion of Afghanistan was diametrically opposite from that in the Cuban missile crisis.

Throughout 1979, GCHQ looked for signs of Soviet aggression by searching the signals of those forces which would support it. Originally, this issue was on the periphery of British concerns, but GCHQ and DIS had enough analysts to handle it well, probably just a few in each case. GCHQ's professional performance aimed to avoid alarmism while pinpointing danger. GCHQ was preadapted to assess events in Afghanistan, where open sources revealed crises between Soviets and their clients. For one thing, Amin's murder of his rivals was a hard signal to miss. GCHQ associated changes in communications between Soviet headquarters and their offices in Kabul with 'unrest in Afghanistan'. This attention exploded in September 1979 when Amin overthrew his rivals. Painstaking review of every Soviet communication with its offices in Kabul and airborne forces showed anomalies: codeword messages from the airborne command in Moscow to formations in Asia 'of a type not seen before', their meaning unknown, but probably taken 'from a list which includes codewords raising and lowering readiness status'. Yet there was 'no repeat no evidence of preparations on the Soviet side for intervention ... no repeat no evidence of any state of heightened readiness on the part of Soviet forces such as might have been expected if there was an intention to intervene militarily'. By October, everything returned to routine, including minor abnormalities. Just before December, anomalies slowly swelled again. GCHQ noted a 'slight increase' in enciphered text and voice between general staff Moscow and stations in the Military Districts of Turkestan, Central Asia and Transbaikal. Its 'significance ... is not known, but the fact that the communications have involved probably the Military Districts Head Quarters and have not been continuous suggests that it is not exercise related'.[112]

This traffic turned to a flood, as the USSR positioned itself to pre-empt a problem abroad rather than react to it. Increasing numbers of transport aircraft landed at the Soviet airbase at Bagram, near Kabul, while airborne forces across Russia flocked to Central Asia. On 12 December 1979, GCHQ warned that these developments might be 'related to events' in Afghanistan or Iran. Quickly, the target became more precise. The Soviet invasion did not surprise GCHQ, though it did Amin, who experienced the KGB's favourite form of overkill: poison followed by gunshots.[113] In coming years, GCHQ monitored the Soviet campaign in Afghanistan, its failure, and major political developments, like truces with and attacks upon the resistance leader Achmed Shah Masoud, in the Panjshir valley – first-rate information on a major theatre of the late Cold War. [114]

GCHQ viewed its own performance as a success, rightly. It warned accurately, without alarmism, that the USSR was creating capabilities to enter Afghanistan. GCHQ revealed Soviet intentions and gave a week's warning that intervention was imminent. This was all the information Whitehall needed to know, on an issue where Britain had major concerns but no plans to act. It also illuminated an issue that concerned the United States rather more, though NSA probably drew parallel conclusions from the same evidence and cared more about it because its consumers did so.

The limits to such intelligence emerged a year later in Iran, a country with which the USSR had mixed relations. In August 1980, military exercises in Transcaucasia and Turkestan, adjacent to Iran, led GCHQ to give consumers a special report with a rare warning, a 'Summary and GCHQ Comment'. 'Live play' by air and ground forces in these areas was low. Soviet signals followed routine hours, but they

> are in their scope and capability much in excess of what would be
> required for exercises involving a single front, and are clearly being
> practised to control both the Transcaucasus and Turkestan fronts ...
> the evidence at present is insufficient to suggest that any assault on
> Iran is imminent. On past experience a build up of ground forces
> and transport aircraft in the border areas would be expected: none
> has so far been seen, in many areas e.g. Eastern Europe normal
> training appears to be in full swing. But CPX [Command Post
> Exercise] in the Transcausasus in July, together with the capacity
> of the Communications being exercise[d] from Baku, suggest that
> the Russians are setting themselves to acquire the competence to
> conduct an operation against Iran in the future if they chose to
> do so.[115]

Throughout autumn 1980, GCHQ followed these developments, which waned and then vanished.[116] GCHQ tracked changing Soviet capabilities, which suggested concern over conflict with Iran, yet could not indicate what these actions actually meant. Ultimately, they led nowhere, and may just have reflected the faintest form of Soviet contingency planning. These reports reflected GCHQ's close attention to any signs of Soviet aggression, aided British policy, and encouraged analysts to think about possibilities.

They also show how other developments affected British analyses of Soviet actions in Poland during 1980. Sigint showed that explosives were piling up, and then had been decommissioned without exploding, but remained in place and could easily be rearmed. Were the Warsaw Pact to attack Warsaw, it would need massive forces, which would force redeployments of divisions and the development of new systems of command, control and communications. Such actions would surely echo elsewhere. On 22 August, ten days after the crisis became obvious, GCHQ gave its consumers an unusual report, which prepared them for an unexpected development. GCHQ offered two pages of commentary about the situation in Poland based on open sources, for context, followed by a long record of all relevant Sigint, including material which might have been noted before, but was now being applied to this situation. Then, during September 1980, GCHQ detected the creation of a Comsat link between the general staff in Moscow, subscribers in western Russia and an unidentified 'high-level authority in the Warsaw area'. The latter, perhaps 'a communications centre for a General Staff operations group acting as a theatre level authority', was little used, 'which suggests that the network is in the early stages of setting up and is not being used for actual command and control purposes'. The 'precise nature' of this system 'is as yet unclear', but it may 'represent the initial testing of communications facilities required for contingency operations. No Sigint reflections of troop deployments have been noted.'[117] In the coming months, GCHQ carefully monitored this system, which became linked first to the general staff's command train and finally to the headquarters of the Soviet Northern Group of Forces at Legnica, the USSR's main base for influence throughout the Polish crisis. By December 1980, GCHQ noted, this system remained in being, but quiet: a latent rather than a live capability. So it stayed for years.

Almost certainly, GCHQ had caught the Soviet command, control and communications system which was being developed for an invasion of Poland, just as it was being established. Such new links often emerged within the Warsaw Pact. This news was useful, but otherwise GCHQ's surveys of Sigint offered little on the crisis. For example: 'The recently announced closure of the Polish/GDR border to persons not possessing a visa has been widely discussed by staff in many WBKs (*Wohnungsbaukombinant*, the state construction enterprises in each state of East Germany, which combined political and paramilitary activities) and an apparently directed sounding out of local opinion has produced an almost universal favourable reaction. Such a reaction seems to be due at least equally to the stopping of Polish shopping trips to buy consumer goods in GDR as to any condemnation of political events in Poland.'[118] In 1981, GCHQ noted that: 'Fears of strikes occurring in the GDR are increasing. Any hints of such troubles will be dealt with severely as official opinion towards Poland remains hard-line,' while the 'combined forces (WP) HF (Warsaw Pact High Frequency) comms network in the GDR' continued in being, and the Polish general staff developed a military communications link seemingly intended to sidestep problems posed by the Solidarity movement.[119] Sigint lacked the precision to follow such events in Poland, but, fortunately, other sources carried this burden.

At the Cold War's End

GCHQ and NSA played many parts in the struggle with the main enemy. Any conclusion about their effect requires an averaging out of many loosely connected cases. British and American Sigint had three main tasks: to trace the Eastern bloc order of battle, warn of war, and help to fight one. Its performance for the first task was excellent, for the second tolerable, outweighing any other source, but only weak for the last. Overall that record is imperfect, but good, and better than conventionally understood. The failures of Western intelligence, and its debates over the biggest of uncertainties such as the bomber and missile gaps, and the Soviet economy, do not demonstrate incompetence, but rather the irreducible problems in interpretation which remained after a good attempt at a hard pitch. These debates reflect UKUSA's success in containing confusion and uncertainty.

Still, their limits left ample room for uncertainty and error on military matters, especially given the confused politics of Sigint and decision-making within NATO. These dangers were contained because Western statesmen doubted that Soviet counterparts would risk mutual extermination, while intelligence remained sufficiently credible and powerful to warn of real threats, stop the distortion of imaginary ones, and to indicate that war was not quite at hand, even in the worst moments of the Berlin and Cuban crises.

Sigint was one part of a global competition against able enemies in many areas. Soviet Humint crippled UKUSA Sigint. Western Humint never returned the favour against the Warsaw Pact, though Western Sigint hurt Soviet spies. The Eastern bloc won the Humint struggle against UKUSA, though not by much after 1960, partly because of a renaissance in the power of MI5 and MI6. Britain is often seen as being uniquely vulnerable to penetration by foreign espionage during the Cold War, in part because British writers export the *vice anglais* into the history of espionage, searching for any excuse to flagellate themselves. In fact, Warsaw Pact Humint penetrated Britain far less than it did France, Germany and the United States.[120] American Sigint lost more to spies and traitors than did GCHQ. The Soviets and their allies, good in many areas of Sigint, struck UKUSA directly and indirectly. UKUSA regarded Soviet Sigint with respect but not the cryptosystems of its NATO allies. The USSR gained from material on members of NATO, even if it could not penetrate UKUSA. Knowledge of Soviet successes in Comint is sparse, but the KGB told its masters that it devoured the communications of foreign embassies in Moscow, including those from NATO countries.[121] While these claims perhaps were exaggerated, no doubt the USSR exploited the weak security in NATO embassies, including those of Britain and the USA, and intercepted plain-language traffic in foreign capitals, especially that carried by microwave. The huge forces of Warsaw Pact military Sigint undoubtedly picked up much of the same material acquired by the UKUSA system, but probably mined it less well.

One cannot yet determine the relative quality of both sides in this struggle, nor who won it. Yet these questions of quality and victory are secondary in significance. In the struggle with the Warsaw Pact, NATO wanted Soviet Sigint to be decent or good, because that status helped to achieve its strategic aim: deterrence. For the enemy to know that NATO was politically unified, militarily formidable, but not preparing an offensive war, was good. Soviet leaders found those points hard to believe. Since so many NATO decisions were made openly, espionage declined in value as a source against them. Yet Soviet espionage wormed deep into the secrets of NATO, which still never neared defeat in the Cold War, and won it. Equally, the secrecy around decisions within the Pact maximised the value of high-level penetration by any Western source. By eliminating this danger, the greatest Soviet victories in intelligence during the Cold War were defensive in effect, not offensive.

NATO did not need intelligence to answer the biggest questions of the Cold War: how would its political cohesion and economic health compare to that of the Warsaw Pact? Who was winning this struggle of attrition? NATO did need intelligence to address the military aspects of these issues, but these were secondary in importance, unless the Cold War turned hot. Here, GCHQ and NSA sustained confidence in London and Washington, which flowed to other NATO capitals, that at any given time the Warsaw Pact was unlikely to launch a surprise attack while such an assault could be predicted. Better intelligence on Soviet intentions would have helped achieve this outcome, but proved unnecessary to it. UKUSA reinforced the many factors which enabled the members of NATO to pursue a reasoned policy with calm, especially by capping uncertainty and alarm. UKUSA was thus an unsung element in the success of deterrence. Without UKUSA, NATO would have done less well, but probably still have won the Cold War. UKUSA was a useful secondary factor behind Western victory in the Cold War, yet two weaknesses remained: UKUSA could not have predicted a Soviet surprise attack launched from a standing position, which would have boosted an already powerful stance, while the NATO Sigint system would have collapsed in a hot war, without providing a force multiplier. The factors which helped NATO to win the Cold War might not have done so in a hot one.

Comint and the End of Empire, 1945–82: Palestine, Konfrontasi and the Falkland Islands

In 1930, Britain was the foremost power on earth. Its prestige and power deterred threat. It could guarantee commitments across the globe without having to defend them physically, a resort which rarely happened more than one case at a time. After 1945, British power shrank steadily towards that of a great secondary power. It faced a succession of economic problems, imperial overstretch and commitments across the world which were beyond its strength to maintain; political challenges within its colonies, and painful decolonisation. Britain made concessions to its colonies, including the granting of independence while pursuing a hegemonic status over them, in order to try to preserve its status as a global power. After the Suez crisis of 1956, British elites increasingly came to see world power as impossible to maintain, and the attempts to do so as damaging their country. Britain abandoned inconvenient colonies on the best terms possible and retained some possessions, such as Gibraltar, Hong Kong and the Falkland Islands, where conflict with neighbours remained a possibility.

Decolonisation was accompanied by armed struggles between Britain, challengers within colonies and imperial neighbours. Britain's decline in power and prestige increased the number of these challenges, including those from protectorates which it had lost, such as Egypt. Deterrence became harder to maintain and wars more difficult to win. Britain had to defend many colonies against challenge, often by force, and sometimes several at once. The conventional armies of non-Western countries improved. Between 1815 and 1939, Britain's ability to deny modern weapons to its subjects and imperial neighbours had let small home and colonial forces manage large enemies. This edge ended from 1955, as rival states offered Britain's imperial neighbours significant supplies of modern arms. By 1960, only major British forces could protect clients like Kuwait from powers such as Iraq. Yet sustained commitments hampered the handling of other problems, in particular economic ones. This contradiction drove Britain to abandon empire, though a degree of world power remained.

This chapter studies three instances of this phenomenon, and how Comint affected it: in the Palestine Mandate, 1945–48, the confrontation with Indonesia, 1962–66, and the Falklands conflict of 1982. This history has complete access to the record of military Comint in these cases and to many secret British policy records, but none to the diplomatic and civil traffic of the key players or of other states. It does, however, make use of such material where it is in the public domain. This account of how Sigint affected these cases is accurate as far as it goes, but necessarily incomplete. It will note how documents which are withheld might affect these stories when they are released.

These cases and others, such as the Suez crisis of 1956, share characteristics. Britain confronted the international politics of anti-colonialism and challengers driven by differing fusions of mass politics, nationalism, religious conviction and revolutionary ardour. Increasingly, international opinion saw empires as fundamentally bad, their cases as inferior to nationalist ones when these clashed, and the first use of conventional force as automatically wrong. Britain's enemies adopted practices such as terrorism or covert action, which challenged older ideas of the legal use of force and harassed Britain. Response through the deployment of conventional arms was delegitimised, unless managed carefully. When the British embassy in Jakarta was ransacked in 1963, Prime Minister Harold Macmillan told the Cabinet: 'Palmerston no good anymore.' The need to avoid looking 'Neo-Colonialist' dogged British policy in Asia throughout the 1960s.[1] All of these cases involved threats to British prestige and power and struggles of political attrition short or long in duration. Britain militarily outmatched its challengers: the problem was how to make this superiority serve politics. The balance of intelligence affected that of power. A second-rate power possessing first-rate Sigint confronted third- or fourth-rate powers possessing usually poor Comint and Comsec.

These cases have commonalities but also differences. For Britain, the Falklands conflict was a political and strategic crisis involving the fate of states. The other issues were major but secondary. One of these case studies involved action aimed at preventing decolonisation, another to manage it, the last to survive the process. In Palestine, Britain's foe fought to live; in the other instances, imperial neighbours threatened British interests for reasons of internal politics and to achieve limited diplomatic ends. In the event, Jewish success enabled the State of Israel; Indonesian and Argentine failure wrecked their regimes. The attitudes of the United States, Britain's chief partner for strategy and intelligence, varied in each case, and so too the value of other sources of intelligence and the balance between them.

One case featured major conventional operations. Two involved guerrillas, terrorists, counter-insurgency and counter-terrorism, where Britain's enemies found it rational to murder civilians, British personnel or their families. Broadly, these cases illuminate the relationship between force, politics and Comint during the age of decolonisation and the Cold War. They also illustrate the technical side of Sigint mobilisation, communications and their relationship to command. Sigint was so good that it enabled much more to be done than could be acted on in political or operational terms. The limit was political – what Britain was willing and able to do with its power and intelligence. Even in the Falklands conflict, Britain held its military hand, fearing that to use British power fully would impede victory.

Sigint and the End of the Palestine Mandate, 1944–48

The Anglo-Zionist Divorce

Between 1944 and 1948, GCHQ worked well on the Palestine question, but power and politics limited its effect.[2] British authorities misconstrued how their power compared to that of the Yishuv – the Jewish population of Palestine – and their Arab counterparts. Authorities assumed that the Yishuv needed British support to swim in an Arab sea. It must know that fact and follow Britain. The Yishuv had different views, and many of them at that. Most Palestinian Jews would have followed Britain had it accepted their demands, but since Whitehall could not do so,

Jews chose to survive through their own strength, which was greater than they originally knew. Zionist propaganda painted Britain as anti-Semitic; Britain was the only state of the time which was willing to protect Jews on its terms, which Zionists rejected. Conflict flashed over how to replace the Mandate, the borders between Jewish and Arab populations in Palestine, and emigration. After the Nazi holocaust, 600,000 Jewish survivors needed a new home – old ones were no more. They happily would have gone to Canada or stayed in France, but no Western state wanted them. Gentiles found Palestine the simplest solution to the Jewish problem, which they threw at Britain and the Arabs. US President Harry Truman was a Zionist from conviction and calculation: he knew Americans favoured Jewish immigration to Palestine but not to the United States.

Holocaust survivors needed succour: the Yishuv alone offered it. Only by letting them into Palestine and expanding the area of Jewish settlement would the Yishuv support Britain. British intelligence, military and political authorities thought, rightly, that to do so would wreck British politics among Arab countries.[3] As British power in India evaporated, the Middle East rose in importance as a base for influence.[4] The Anglo-Zionist alliance foundered on the rock of immigration. Without the prospect of almost doubling the Jewish population of Palestine, the Yishuv would probably have continued to shelter behind Britain. An existential issue for the Yishuv clashed with a great British interest – a clash that caused a revolution in Anglo-Zionist relations, which no one understood. Each side stumbled as they entered a new game, where no one knew the rules, the moves, the next step, or the final one. Neither side understood the true balance of power between them.

Britain had lost control of Palestine. It could be restored only by conquest, which Britain could not stomach. In 1937, the leading Arab politician in Palestine, the Grand Mufti of Jerusalem Amin al-Husseini, led an Arab revolt against Britain. A tough colonial policeman, Charles Tegart, broke Arab power, almost as much as did their internecine feuding. By neutering one community in Palestine, Britain destroyed the opportunity to balance between them. Meanwhile, in order to withstand threats from Arabs and Germans, Britain strengthened the Yishuv. The Jewish Agency, a state within a state, administered the Yishuv. It had a large army, the Haganah, which was poor compared to the British and Transjordanian ones, but better than other Arab forces.

Britain trained the Palmach, the competent core of Haganah, and Jewish intelligence services. Haganah hid within the Jewish Settlement Police, a British-subsidised paramilitary force formed to protect kibbutzim, which included at its peak 3,000 permanent and 16,000 temporary personnel. Britain trained the core of Palmach, expected it to prepare others in order to resist potential German occupation of Palestine, and helped it to build a fallback wireless network to aid resistance. Britain gave battlefield experience to the Jewish Brigade of 5,000 Palestinian Jews, drawn from Haganah and Palmach, as were some members of the Special Operations Executive (SOE) who served in the Balkans. British intelligence at its peak trained those of two peoples, Americans and Israelis; both students took firsts.

Many British military intelligence officers were Zionists; consequently, British experts on the Yishuv were not employed during the Palestine campaign. They helped Jews develop military and intelligence organisations and, during 1944–48, were kept from service against the Yishuv, probably because their loyalties seemed uncertain. Meanwhile, the fascist terrorist group Lehi, which Britons called the Stern gang, assassinated the experts on the Yishuv within the Criminal Intelligence Department (CID), the political police force in Palestine. Imperial police forces, managed by a few British officials, who kept their files in their heads, were particularly vulnerable to assassination. In 1945, British intelligence relied on advice about problems and solutions in Palestine from the intelligence services of the Jewish Agency more than from the CID. With the best of British understatement, MI5's authority on the Middle East, A. J. Kellar, called this position 'embarrassing'.[5]

British politicians assumed that Jews and Arabs would recognise their wisdom and accept their solutions as being the best compromise for all; soldiers thought their bayonets could shape politics like scalpels. Both were hubristic. Britain could control Palestine only through one of the largest commitments ever made in peacetime across its empire. It lacked the will and power to rule Palestine purely by force, against four simultaneous threats. The Yishuv and its central institutions, the Jewish Agency and Haganah, resisted British policy by all means short of war. After a ceasefire between both sides during 1940–44, the Revisionist Zionist movement, Irgun zvai Leumi, also sought to overthrow British rule by violence. It demanded treatment as a legitimate belligerent. When Britain treated Irgun's actions as criminal, and executed some of its members, Irgun hanged captured British soldiers. Lehi murdered any British policeman, soldier or official it could find whose back was turned. Thus any British action was vulnerable to one or another of these threats: non-cooperation by the Yishuv and Haganah, armed resistance by Irgun (and some elements of Haganah) and terrorism by Lehi, and sometimes also by Irgun. Ultimately, the Yishuv beat Britain because it was more determined, powerful and ruthless. Meanwhile, Arab power and resistance to both Britons and Jews grew. Militants on both sides rejected compromise and pressed for maximal aims, taking them towards war. For Britain to appease one side would enrage the other. Alan Cunningham, the High Commissioner of Palestine, saw powder keg and sparks: the reviving power among Arabs of a 'war criminal', the Mufti, who had allied with Germany during the war, and 'the unbalanced emotionalism' of the Yishuv which its leaders 'constantly whipped up'.[6] He warned that 'temporary expedients in the absence of an imposed solution' would only 'lead us deeper into the mire'.[7] Yet Britain could neither avoid expedients nor impose solutions. In 1948, when it realised that Jewish and Arab populations would not accept its rule – nor its rules – Britain abandoned Palestine, leaving these peoples to fight each other.

An Intelligence Struggle

Fundamentally, superiority in intelligence could not have overcome these weaknesses. Quite apart from that fact, it also did not exist. Jews beat Britain in Humint, which was central to campaigns of subversion and terrorism. Britain was superior in Comint against a competent foe. Haganah Sigint monitored Coast Guard radio nets, which helped it to aid ships carrying emigrants towards the Palestine coast. Jewish operators ran the civil telephone network of Palestine. In February 1945, Kellar found that Jews 'entirely manned' military and secretariat switchboards at the King David Hotel in Jerusalem, the centre of British administration in Palestine. 'Police monitoring was operated by Jewish personnel with every possibility that the latter doctored what they handed in.' Jewish cleaners freely entered offices where official documents could easily be stolen.[8] Haganah's intelligence service, Shai, devoured the messages of Arabs and rival Jewish organisations alike. Jewish superiority in Sigint and Humint aided them against Arabs during the Mandate, as well as after it. Shai also acquired much intelligence from the British military and occasionally the CID, but the latter threat was contained through British use of veiled language and scrambler telephones.

When British and Jewish forces worked together against the Mufti, the Zionist leader Moshe Shertok warned Tegart that the King David Hotel was insecure. 'There should be a sort of "Holy of Holies" in the CID where information would only be seen by British personnel.'[9] Britain duly created a tabernacle for Sigint between 1944 and 1948. Through elaborate protocols, Comint personnel hid the receipt of communications to the 'OATS block', sometimes called the 'SIME (Security Intelligence Middle East) unit' and 'L.S.S.L.U.', the title for the Sigint communications unit in Jerusalem. The term 'FOG unit' meant both the 'OATS block' or just its members indoctrinated in FOG, within 'the FOG cage'. Similar protocols covered the dissemination of intelligence to indoctrinated – 'Oated' or 'Fogged' – personnel. Sigint Liaison Unit links carried all Comint traffic between Jerusalem, Cairo, Cyprus and London. Direction-finding reports from Cyprus were routed through No. 2 Wireless Regiment at Sarafand and then to the Oats block via a secret, dedicated and rarely used telephone, 'led into FOG Unit by BUTTERCUP Section'. The phrase, 'I have a message for you' was followed by a verbal dictation of Typex groups, which simply covered bearings.[10]

Between 1939 and 1945, Britain developed capabilities against Jewish traffic, driven by the combined threats of Haganah, Irgun and Lehi. The Radio Security Service (RSS) monitored communications within Britain and the empire, searching for signs of subversion and espionage. Its branch in Egypt, the Middle East Radio Security (MERS) group, followed all Haganah and Palmach radio networks within Palestine. The latter used simple procedures and cyphers, subdivided into just a few different superencipherment systems, which changed infrequently. Jewish soldiers and politicians signalled rather more than necessary. A commercial codebook, *Bentley's Second Phrase Code* (1929), which used simple superencipherment, covered Jewish Agency traffic on cable.[11] Codebreakers found that these systems were easy meat.

Reading the meaning of traffic proved harder than breaking it. The greater problems were linguistic and political, reflecting the complex relations between British Gentiles and Jews about Palestine. Few British subjects except Jews understood modern Hebrew. Only those with Zionist affiliations really understood the colloquial language, which raised questions of loyalty. Until 1945, Britain and Zionism had been allies. GC&CS could trust British Jews to work against Irgun and Lehi, as the Yishuv's intelligence authorities did, but some went further. In 1943–44, at Berkeley Street, ISPAL (Illicit Signals Palestine) attacked traffic from the Yishuv. Initially, Haganah cable and radio traffic – codenamed Ispal I and, from 1944, Isoats – was the main target, while that of the Jewish Agency – first called Ispal II and later Istria – was a secondary one. Ispal I/Isoats provided military intelligence, with Ispal II/Istria tracing the political and diplomatic activities of the Jewish Agency. By November 1945, Isoats 37,220 was produced and Istria 110.[12] Ultimately, around 50,000 Isoats and 5,000 Fog messages were published, and an unknown number of Istria and Buttercup ones.

In 1944, an academic at London's School of Oriental and African Studies (SOAS), James Heyworth-Dunn, warned that one of ISPAL's members, Bernard Lewis, later a renowned scholar, was a Zionist, and thus untrustworthy to handle ISPAL messages. That the Foreign Office liaison officer to the intelligence services raised this issue, and the head of MI6 and GCHQ replied to it, shows its significance and complexity. Menzies wrote:

> LEWIS has been engaged on his present work with us in ISPAL II for a year or more, and it is clear that if he had been responsible for any leakage, this would have been reflected in the material itself. It would clearly be preferable not to employ a Jew on this particular work, but the language difficulties make it virtually impossible to employ anyone else. DENNISTON is entirely satisfied of LEWIS's reliability and I understand that KELLAR of MI5 who has lately worked with LEWIS on ISPAL II shares this favourable opinion of him.
>
> Heyworth DUNN himself must be regarded as a very tainted source of information. He has an Egyptian wife and is known to be violently anti-Semitic.[13]

When MI5's Director of Counter-Espionage, Guy Liddell, asked Denniston if Lewis and his colleague Samuel Stalbow would 'read back some Hebrew reports for us relating to the activities of Shertok and others, Denniston was quite prepared that they should do this work, and regarded them as 100 per cent reliable'.[14] Stalbow, born in

Hackney in 1916 to a Jewish family of eastern European origin which ran firms in the rag trade, became an artillery captain in 1943 and was seconded to Berkeley Street. Lewis and Stalbow translated material on the Jewish Agency for Britain without feeling that they were betraying 'their' side. Neither Lewis, Stalbow, nor any of the many Jews who worked at Bletchley, such as Walter Ettinghausen (later, Walter Eytan, the professional head of the Israeli foreign ministry), betrayed their trust, though experience in Hut 3 perhaps inspired Israeli diplomatic Comsec. His brother, Ernest, another Bletchley veteran, ran GCHQ's library until 1956, when he was made to resign, and returned to the brighter lights of London. Postwar, Siginters showed no signs of anti-Semitism towards their colleagues, whom they treated as exactly that (though the same was not always true at Bletchey Park). British intelligence trusted these British Jews with Yishuv traffic more than they did Englishmen in Palestine with Jewish 'mistresses' or wives.

However, the divorce between Britain and Zionism caused ruptures in many unions of dual loyalties. From 1945, intelligence and military authorities eased Jews from work with Palestine. To make them work against their kin raised questions of fairness and security. New recruits attacked Jewish codes in a unit directed by Captain Hastings, the Deputy Director for diplomatic intelligence (DD 2, and later DD 3). When Berkeley Street operations moved to Eastcote in 1946, the unit took an office at Chesterfield Street in London, isolated from other elements of GCHQ. Though no hard evidence survives, probably one or two members of the Commercial Section stayed to handle cryptanalysis. Stalbow remained the core of its translating effort through 1945, perhaps longer, while Lewis returned to academe.[15] The records suggest a churn in personnel, which cannot be traced in detail. Probably new entrants were Englishmen who knew biblical Hebrew and/or Arabic, which eased entry to modern Hebrew, though causing occasional misidentifications. Until 1948, Siginters and their consumers found translation from Hebrew a real test, eased because the Jewish Agency sent much of its traffic in English. Their targets and procedures were unique; the unit attacked commercial codes for diplomatic purposes. In 1944, Hastings's unit had peculiar communications characteristics.[16] It retained them and an SLU structure – even when GCHQ generally abandoned these practices – simply because they worked and the task was urgent. Like RSS, but generally unlike GCHQ, the unit intercepted the messages of British subjects for purposes of security and counter-terrorism. In the special circumstances of Palestine, GCHQ was granted a special warrant to intercept and read the traffic of British subjects. Initially, MERS and No. 2 Wireless Company in Sarafand intercepted radio traffic. In 1946, however, MERS shifted to Cyprus; its personnel were slowly replaced during that year and it was replaced by a direction-finding station in Egypt.

Material was signalled from Palestine to London, where codebreakers broke, translated and returned it by wireless and Typex. When Comint was first introduced for operational purposes, processing 'special messages' took eight to twenty-four hours, and normal ones three to four days. Soldiers thought the 'operational value of these messages would increase tremendously' if major messages were returned within eight hours, and average ones within twenty-four.[17] Soon, this process worked with blinding speed: priority messages intercepted in Palestine were read and returned from Britain within four hours, routine ones in sixteen to thirty-one hours.[18]

In 1944, the Foreign Office had rated among its three intelligence priorities in the Middle East the 'prime importance' of obtaining 'reliable secret intelligence about Zionist activities', especially 'the Jewish Agency's contacts with foreign Governments', and its 'efforts (if any) to establish good relations with the Arabs'.[19] Ispal was carefully restricted. Only four diplomats, 'all permanents' and 'the Departmental lady', received it. From 1945, as the system became mature, the Defence Security Officer (DSO) disseminated material to consumers and summarised every 1,000 messages for all major ones, including the Secretary of State at the Colonial Office. Officials noted that DD 3 'are daily telephoning Colonial Office with most important' Oats messages. Key authorities in London read Oats and Istria.[20] The DSO reported that General Barker, the General Officer Commanding Palestine, said: 'We are entirely dependent for our only absolutely reliable information' on Oats.[21] Comint channels carried messages on high policy, such as those entered in the 'TOP SECRET NIGHTCAP' series, which were destroyed when the task to which they referred ended. Their loss affects the record.[22]

In 1944, the main consumer of Comint was a cell at SIME in Cairo, a quasi-autonomous British military agency which ultimately was incorporated within MI5. In 1945, the SIME cell was placed under the

DSO, a military intelligence position which was just becoming MI5's station chief in Jerusalem. Though Comint was his central source, the DSO had others, along with many tasks. Quickly, Comint became a source for operations as well as counter-intelligence. So much material was produced that SIME asked to receive only parts of it.[23] Even so, in June 1946, Kellar claimed that SIME 'is almost entirely concentrated on Jewish affairs. Arab matters are sadly neglected.'[24] An attempt to maximise security intelligence against Jews may have damaged that against Arabs. By 1947, as Director General of GCHQ, C made the DSO, Gyles Isham, his personal representative for Sigint in the Middle East. MI5 and MI6 also had an unusually harmonious relationship in Palestine. The DSO had remarkable, perhaps unique, powers for any authority in British intelligence. He was the main analyst of Comint and Humint, including material from the CID and military intelligence; he advised British political and military authorities on matters of intelligence, security and counter-terrorism, and directed British warships and aircraft to intercept immigrants' ships.

Just a few people ran this system. The unit in London had perhaps five cryptanalysts and translators, a small and highly specialised group with limited surge capacity. In Palestine, nine cypher and wireless operators handled all Comint traffic in and out. Probably similar numbers served in London. The MERS party had thirty-five personnel when it reached Cyprus. In April 1947, probably a representative date, the 'SIME party' in the DSO's office had ten members indoctrinated in Fog: four officers, a corporal and 'five women', who processed data and analysed intelligence. These officers, three of the women and five other Sigint personnel were indoctrinated in the broader Comint category, 'Cream'.[25] The Fog unit consisted of an officer and two to three women. The former oversaw intelligence production and the latter handled intelligence, 'case work', a combination of data retrieval and intelligence and, during 1947–48, probably aided bookbuilding of new Haganah systems. The other two to three secretaries managed the Registry of Comint traffic, the less secret Comint material, and other secret material.[26] These women were trained MI5 secretaries, or the wives of British servicemen in Palestine. J. C. Robertson, an inspector from MI5 visiting around April 1947, had reservations about the quality of the DSO's personnel, but not the DSO himself, Colonel Magan: 'In this atmosphere of continuous monotony (interrupted only occasionally by real danger), it is much to the credit of Magan that the morale of his staff, especially among the women, is so high' – probably referring to their response to the terrorist bombing of the King David Hotel on 22 July 1946. In particular, Robertson noted:

> The FOG Unit is in a class apart from the rest of the office. Captain Burbidge, who is responsible for its organisation, is a first-class intelligence officer whom Magan has praised very highly. He receives useful assistance from Mrs. Sales and Miss Ann Clerk (who however left for Singapore just before my return to the U.K.). The FOG records and situation map are a model of precision and clarity. This assists materially in maintaining the prestige of the D.S.O., since the most important part of the service he provides is derived from CREAM. It is in the 'FOG cage' that the daily G.O.C.'s meeting is held.[27]

The FOG unit created an efficient Registry of traffic and a card index system listing proper names of people, units, ships and places. It was the main source for a 'Black List' which traced the loyalties of Palestinian Jews, in order to guide British authorities working with them.

Security against Jewish espionage in Jerusalem drove these processes. When Britain first considered sending ISPAL to Jerusalem in 1943, Liddell warned the Director of Military Intelligence (DMI) that 'it was extremely important to ensure that the material was properly handled at the other end. We knew that most offices in Palestine were penetrated.' In 1944, the DMI and C refused to send ISPAL to the DSO Jerusalem, Henry Hunloke, until he was 'completely white-washed' from allegations of having a 'Jewish mistress'.[28] The DSO hid Comint from most British personnel. Only top civil and military authorities and key staff members were indoctrinated. In April 1947, these included the High Commissioner, the Chief Secretary of the Mandate government and the general officer commanding (GOC) Palestine and five of their staff officers, the air officer commanding (AOC) Levant and two RAF officers, three officers in the Palestine Police, and the naval liaison officer (NLO).[29] Some of them had ample experience with Sigint, especially the High Commissioner, Cunningham, who had been a major recipient of Ultra in 1941.

Comint was concealed from most analysts, including those working with other sources on issues which Comint affected and who received it in sanitised forms. The monitoring of individuals shows how any mistake or misfortune complicated indoctrination and confused intelligence. Lieutenant Hodge from the Royal Navy's Mediterranean Fleet hinted about Comint to his brethren and was admonished. To transfer an indoctrinated officer from Jerusalem to the cage at SIME might raise suspicions in Lieutenant Roberts, who worked on illegal immigration, but was not indoctrinated. 'There have, as you know, been signs from time to time of his suspicion that he has been excluded from some available intelligence on shipping. He has also shown some curiosity on occasion about the function of the cage.'[30] To make matters even more confusing, Roberts actually had been indoctrinated in FOG several months prior, which the DSO might not have known.[31] When captured documents referred to Mossad wireless nets, a Palestine police officer, John Briance, and a government official, G. G. Grimwood – neither indoctrinated – suggested that they be monitored. The DSO's office mounted elaborate discussions to convince them that the idea had been tested, but proved impossible to execute.[32] In November 1947, without warning, the NLO brought Commander Stannard, communications officer for C-in-C Mediterranean, to visit the assistant DSO, Captain Wright. Hastings himself had indoctrinated Stannard, of which Wright had not been informed. Stannard aimed to ensure that the Royal Navy received adequate Comint to handle illegal immigration, but did not know that the NLO was initiated. The NLO later informed Stannard that his relations with the DSO's office were good. Wright declined to address the issue until Stannard 'revealed so much knowledge of FOG set-up and officers employed in it that I decided to take him at face value'. Wright implored that he 'not be placed in this invidious and insecure position again owing to failure to keep us informed of changes in initiates' list'.[33]

Comint in Palestine

GCHQ acquired diplomatic Comint on Palestine from Arab and European states, which shaped the key international dimension of British policy, but it is unavailable to this history. Comint provided many thousands of reports between 1944 and 1948, through four means. By telephone taps in Palestine, run through an office technically linked to the SIME cell, Buttercup, penetrated Arab politics, especially the revival of jihadist and nationalist resistance, and gained some information on the Yishuv. From 1945 British personnel managed much of Buttercup, though probably some operators remained Jewish. Via Isoats, Istria and Fog, GCHQ attacked the codes of Haganah and Palmach, the Jewish Agency, and Mossad Le'aliyah Bet, which ran illegal emigration to Palestine (not to be confused with the later intelligence service Mossad). Isoats traced in detail the order of battle and personalities of Haganah and Palmach, and their policies and preparations. It monitored constant concerns – whether Haganah was preparing an insurrection, or supporting sabotage. Isoats probably inspired many or most of the arms raids on kibbutzim, which met with mixed success. It constantly provided guidance for plans by British military authorities to seize important targets, such as Kol Israel, Haganah's radio propaganda station, and Palmach headquarters.[34]

Isfog replaced Isoats as a codename in February 1947, and divided its work almost equally against Haganah and Mossad Le'aliyah Bet – for intelligence on military and emigration matters. Istria illuminated the complex politics within the Yishuv and the work of the Jewish Agency, especially its manoeuvres abroad. The Yishuv was an amalgam of peoples from many countries, marked by political traditions, including conspiratorial and revolutionary ones, from central and eastern Europe. The Jewish Agency was not a party, movement or government; it represented the Zionist movement and world Jewry to the British Mandate, especially on issues of immigration and security, and was elected from all Jewish parties in Palestine. Secretly, it was led by conspirators who controlled an army which its executive funded, often without understanding that fact. British authorities found these matters even harder to understand.

The sheer mass of sources and reportage obscured the useful material on the leaders who most drove the Yishuv, including David Ben-Gurion and Moshe Shertok. Reports were easy to misconstrue. Thus, Lehi's assassination of Lord Moyne, British Resident Minister in the Middle East, on 6 November 1944, drove Haganah to help Britain stop Jewish attacks on its officials. In December 1944, Liddell noted, Istria showed that: 'SNAKE has given the Palestine Police over 500 names and addresses of terrorists and dumps of arms.

The police have already made over 250 arrests. There is no doubt, I think, that the more moderate elements in the Zionist Movement are afraid that the actions of the extremists may jeopardise the whole future of Zionism.'[35] These points were true, but not the whole truth. Haganah aimed to protect Jewish interests, if possible with – but if necessary, against – Britain. It guided British intelligence to arrest its rivals in the Yishuv, Irgun, and the murderers of Lord Moyne. Otherwise, Haganah detained some members of Irgun and most of Lehi in its secret prisons, preventing them from terrorism and British punishment – albeit momentarily: Haganah released them all when it turned against Britain in autumn 1945.

British Comint never touched Irgun and Lehi, which did not use radio. It could not overcome what Cunningham thought the greatest limit of intelligence: 'the lack of information available regarding the terrorist organisations and individuals and the small success we have had in tracking them down', which he blamed on the Jewish Agency and CID.[36] Initially, soldiers, Cunningham and the DSO mistrusted CID, partly for reasons of class and ethnicity. Kellar called its head, Arthur Giles, 'a difficult personality ... Of Cypriot origin and married to a Maltese, he suffers from a noticeable inferiority complex and is unnecessarily sensitive to any suspected slight.'[37] These attitudes had one unfortunate consequence. CID did not receive access to Isoats or Istria until 1946, damaging its revival and the union of Comint and Humint. Even in 1947, the two bureaus worked at some distance, if in the same direction. Still, MI5's inspector Robertson regarded CID as a 'high-grade intelligence organisation' and respected 'the extent and power of the C.I.D., and ... the calibre of its senior officers', including Giles.[38]

By 1946, CID covered the Yishuv well, with two sources at high levels in the Jewish Agency, and others beneath. Combined with Buttercup, Oats and Istria, Britain briefly had good and multisource material on politics in Palestine, enabling each to augment or check the other. Oats, Isham noted, showed 'the Hagana source at CID HAIFA sometimes misleads them'.[39] This material illuminated the views and actions of Britain's main challengers, Ben-Gurion, Haganah and the Mufti. The news was gloomy. Perhaps for that reason, British authorities misinterpreted it. Comint provided much neutral evidence, which supported all interpretations without challenging prevailing views. It illuminated bureaucracies, but not the conspirators who nudged them from the shadows. These limits, combined with the weight of preconceptions about Jewish dependence on Britain, led British authorities to error. Even more than usual, authorities exaggerated the significance of reports supporting their preconceptions, and resisted those that challenged them. In particular, from autumn 1945, Haganah, Lehi and Irgun loosely cooperated in sabotage against Britain, which revealed the radicalisation and resolution of the mainstream leaders of the Yishuv. Isoats and the CID each accurately noted this cooperation, but their masters were slow to appreciate its significance.[40] British authorities thought the Jewish Agency should, and could, abolish Haganah and suppress Irgun and Lehi. They overestimated Jewish leaders such as Chaim Weizmann, who favoured cooperation and compromise with Britain, and underrated their hostility to British policy. Authorities misunderstood the power of Ben-Gurion, though they knew he was predominant.

As hostilities intensified, on 18 June 1946 an indoctrinated member of DSO's staff, Owen Chadwick, was among five British officers kidnapped by Irgun in Jerusalem. SIME doubted that Irgun knew of his role, but if so, 'we must expect third degree and consequent danger to OATS material, personnel and installations. Request closest scrutiny all messages for indications uneasiness or possible change to use OATS for GALVESTON purposes.' SIME concluded that Haganah had not known of this act in advance, minimising the danger to Oats, but since it 'probably' knew Chadwick worked with the DSO, it 'may therefore attempt [to] arrange interrogation'. Irgun, 'through [a] series of cut-outs', told British authorities that the officers were being treated well, and would remain so, if a sentence of death passed on two of its members was not carried out. Then, Chadwick managed to escape, returning 'cheerful but dirty'. He reported that the real target of the kidnappers was General Barker, whom Irgun was 'determined repeat determined to "get"'. Chadwick had been well treated, fed with white bread and propaganda, and had escaped when his guards fell asleep, fleeing to safety on a bus with Irgun gunmen in hot pursuit.[41] Chadwick was immediately moved to MI5 in London while, pressed by Haganah, Irgun released the other kidnapped officers. This episode was a foretaste of tragedies in store for British personnel in Palestine.

Operation Agatha

During 1945–46, officials experienced a frustrating stalemate, what MI5 called 'the practice of a well-nigh intolerable restraint to preserve conditions in which a just and lasting settlement might be found'.[42] Arabs and Jews were atomised. Each atom had a veto, every action a perverse consequence. Delicate calculations tripped over each other, especially as Britain negotiated with the United States to solve the problem of Palestine. The extraordinary complications of the internal and international politics of Palestine deterred action. Holding Palestine had heavy diplomatic, financial and military costs for Britain. The Colonial Office, the Foreign Office and the Army split over policy in Palestine, which further impeded action. So did faith that conferences between British and American authorities, or Arab and Jewish ones, could somehow end the political stalemate.

The difficulties of action, and in using intelligence, were illustrated in the summer of 1946. British authorities finally understood the cooperation between Haganah, Irgun and Lehi, the political and military power of the Yishuv, and its refusal to accept British terms. Attacks on British personnel and installations escalated, enraging Britons and eroding their will to hold on. Comint and human sources showed that Ben-Gurion and Haganah aimed to challenge British policy in cooperation with Irgun and Lehi – through confrontation, and perhaps insurrection.[43] Yet Moishe Sneh, the head of Haganah and of its most militant section, warned Ben-Gurion of its 'catastrophic financial position', suggesting Haganah's power was fragile.[44]

British authorities sought to break the stalemate through the precise use of force. Guided by intelligence from Comint and the CID, Operation Agatha aimed to arrest the Jewish politicians who opposed British policy, paralyse Haganah, intimidate all players, and force Arabs and Jews to accept British terms.[45] Authorities understood that this effort was a gamble against the odds. Cunningham warned the Colonial Secretary, George Hall:

> with all the force I can that BEN-GURION and SHERTOK should be detained if the operation is to have more than a limited success.

(2) We have unimpeachable evidence that they direct the Hagana as witness ISOATS message 37793 which I have just seen from BEN-GURION to the Chief of Staff HAGANA and SHERTOK.

(3) To allow them to remain at large will leave leaders who are in position to sway YISHUV against us and to coordinate the broken armies in a manner that no one else can.[46]

Ironically, Isoats 37,793 may have been Ben-Gurion's order of 25 June that Sneh and Shertok force Irgun to release the kidnapped British officers, without giving it any concessions.[47] Cunningham's message effectively admitted defeat before Agatha even began, because Ben-Gurion was already out of British hands, in France.

Britain's efforts under Operation Agatha failed mainly due to its limits in intelligence, power and ruthlessness – but only barely. Shai Comint compromised Britain's first attempt to move. Knowing action was imminent, some Jewish leaders hid their papers. On 29 June 1946, with tactical surprise, British authorities arrested half of Palmach and many Jewish politicians whom they wished to detain, including Shertok and hardliners such as Rabbi Abba Hillel Silver, head of the Zionist Organisation of America. However, several key targets were missed, especially Sneh, the head of Palmach, Yigal Allon, and some unit commanders. Haganah's chain of command survived intact, but its relations with politicians and control over units were disrupted. Documents seized from Jewish leaders, including Sneh, and from Haganah and Palmach headquarters, shed light on the Jewish Agency's support for stealing arms and sabotage, which enlightened and shocked British authorities. Borrowing words from Cunningham, the Colonial Secretary described Haganah espionage against Britain as 'a vast system for the theft of Top Secret' documents, which 'could have been obtained only by means of a wide-spread system of corruption and espionage'.[48] These seizures stunned Shai, surprised by British intelligence superiority for the only time in the Palestine troubles. If British authorities could launch one bolt from the blue, why not another – especially given the intelligence they just had gained.

Until Agatha, Jewish leaders outside Irgun and Lehi did not know how they would react if Britain forced them to submit. Agatha made them ask: what did they want? Dare they break with Britain? Agatha also exposed the conspiracies of Ben-Gurion and his lieutenants. Many, perhaps most, moderate leaders, and possibly the majority in the Yishuv, wanted to restrain Ben-Gurion and negotiate the best deal possible with Britain. The leader of Irgun, Menachem Begin, later conceded that 'defeatism raised its deadly head. People began to question our ability to fight the British regime'. This drove him to escalate the crisis.[49] Britain's inability to penetrate Irgun proved fatal to many of its servicemen and officials, and its policy.

British authorities thought they had succeeded in killing a conspiracy. They overestimated the effect of Operation Agatha and over-interpreted the evidence behind it, including Comint. Sneh signalled Ben-Gurion (and, unknowingly, Britain):

> The internal situation is steadily deteriorating. Hayyim is gathering a collection of personal friends and has passed an ultimatum that all activities must cease. Hayyim has invited Shaw to his house to have a cup of tea. Nobody knows who is the Executive. The detainees are kept silent as are Rcksch and Yemin. I am excommunicated and banned by the Jerusalem Executive. Let me have a clear answer as to what I am to do and please give me specific instructions.[50]

That message inspired British authorities. Cunningham signalled Hall that this 'deterioration ... refers to the position of the more extreme Jews, and the advocates and perpetrators of violence, and not to the more stable elements represented by Weizmann, nor the Government's position. Connection of Ben-Gurion with extreme elements is sufficiently clear from this message.'[51] The DSO's office agreed that Sneh's message showed a weakening of the extremists, a rise of moderates and confusion in Jewish politics, though Ben-Gurion had power to play in a Zionist conference convening in Paris.[52] Isham noted Weizmann's 'present self-assurance and particularly conviction that [he] could control more extremist members of Agency'.[53] Yet the situation was volatile: certainly some Jews would retaliate, the only questions being who, when and where. On 3 July 1946, Sigint showed that Haganah communications and command were broken. 'Morale. Impression from traffic is that organisations are stunned and PALMACH temporarily disrupted.' Remaining commanders could 'do high-level planning', which units might be unable to execute. However, 'violent reaction' against British forces or to free detainees was inevitable.[54] 'All overt sources suggest violent reaction will not be long delayed but its most likely forms are (a) mob violence and (b) IRGUN operations.'[55] On 8 July, Isham reported that Palmach and Haganah were reorganising slowly, and 'there is nothing in OATS traffic to show that Hagana realise Army operations resulted from interception of their W/T traffic and breaking of their ciphers'. However, 'Hagana, like British authorities, suspect right wing terrorist reaction forthcoming.'[56] Both were right.

Attlee and Irgun

The Cabinet hoped to exploit Operation Agatha by doing 'everything possible' to 'strengthen the hand of Dr Weizmann and his associates'.[57] They all overrated their power. Britain quickly pledged to release most detainees, including Palmach members, in order to enable negotiations with the Jewish Agency as a whole and representatives of the Palestinian Arabs at a new conference in London. That aim immediately stalled, as the collision of atoms produced an explosion. On 22 July, exploiting dismal British security, Irgun terrorists bombed the King David Hotel at a time when they knew it would be most crowded. Through incompetence or cynicism, Irgun provided warnings which could never reach British authorities in time. Later, Irgun tried to blame the victims for having murdered them.

Haganah's role in this action remains uncertain. Decisions were made by a few conspirators, who purposely did not record them well. Then, driven by subsequent conflicts between Irgun and Haganah, they offered conflicting accounts of what they had said and done at the time. The evidence is contradictory. Agatha incapacitated Haganah's body, but not its will. Haganah had previously destroyed British government property, but attempted to avoid killing Britons. It also tried to prevent Irgun and Lehi from doing so until autumn 1945, when it loosely cooperated with them in actions where the latter spilled blood. After Agatha, Sneh – wishing to retaliate but lacking the means – asked Irgun to attack the King David Hotel, allegedly at a time when it would be most empty, but still with the aim of killing Britons. Then, according to Haganah accounts, Sneh asked Irgun to abandon the attack and give time for civilian resistance to grow instead. If so, Irgun rejected this advice, which would have served to strengthen its rivals, Haganah and Ben-Gurion. Irgun thus used its strengths to achieve its aims, simultaneously attacking both its British and Jewish rivals. Haganah and Ben-Gurion then disassociated themselves from terrorism, while still exploiting it.

Irgun killed ninety-one people at the King David Hotel, including British clerical staff and officials, and civilians of many nationalities. Among them were eleven of the thirteen clerks and the cypher operator who handled OATS from the DSO's office. This strike was a human tragedy for British Comint, however it missed its centre of power. The Registry of Comint traffic was a 'total loss': a number of other papers were destroyed, but most of them, above all the card index and the reports, and all intelligence personnel, survived unscathed. Fluke drove this outcome.[58] On the day of the bombing on 22 July, the leading British intelligence authorities in the Mandate, Giles and Isham, had driven to Beirut to investigate stories that Irgun aimed to bomb the British legation there. The traitor in SIS, Kim Philby, distorted and disseminated these stories so to confuse British intelligence. Accidentally, he spared it harm.[59]

By bombing the King David Hotel, Begin created a victory – for Ben-Gurion. This act finalised and embittered the Anglo-Zionist divorce. Not surprisingly, British intelligence failed to report precisely what the conspirators had done. Two top CID agents – its best one in the Jewish Agency, 'Circus', and another 'independent high-grade' source – stated that Haganah knew of the attack in advance, and did not stop it. Isoats 38,465, sent thirty minutes before the explosion, 'shows that Haganah may have been anticipating a large scale curfew'. Many sources warned that Haganah and Irgun had cooperated in the affair, but offered alarmist and perhaps inaccurate details. Begin and Sneh had drawn lots on who would conduct the bombing. Haganah, Irgun, and Lehi would soon assault many other British installations.[60]

The hotel bombing aroused horror and anger in the Yishuv, first against the perpetrators, then the occupiers. Intelligence and outrage sparked a British crackdown. Operation Shark, enforcing harsh martial law through troops on the street, served to bolster the civilian resistance which was Haganah's strength and Ben-Gurion's hope. Operation Agatha evaporated, and terrorism triumphed. Yet a more tepid British response also would probably have sapped its position. Isham reported that the Yishuv was unified against Britain, awaiting decisions from the Zionist conference in Paris. 'Moderate Jewish elements here unlikely exert any influence.' Haganah would cease restraining Irgun and Lehi, which would strike, while Palmach perhaps would 'go over to sabotage and Hagana cause crowd nuisance'. 'Consider possible H.M.G.'s actions may strengthen hand of BEN-GURION, SILVER and SNEH. Impossible forecast exact shape of events to come.'[61] When Dr Arie Altman, leader of the Revisionist Zionist movement, the political parent of Irgun, asked, 'What did I think the Jews should do now?' Isham replied, 'Stamp out terrorism. He said terrorism is futile if the British Government have really got a policy. But some people argue that they have not got one and bombs may make them think quickly.'[62] That comment cut to the quick. Britain could handle Jewish resistance, if it wished to rule by force, but lacked the stamina to do so. It could not find Jewish terrorists, would not match their attacks on civilians, and could not stop the Yishuv's turn against Britain.

In September 1946, Circus reported that since Operation Agatha, a struggle between moderates and hardliners had dominated politics in the Yishuv. 'BEN-GURION and his clique' had outmanoeuvred Weizmann and his allies, and seized power over the Yishuv, by playing 'Haganah and the youth of the country against the moderate elements'. Ben-Gurion 'always' supported 'exaggerated reports of British brutality during searches of Jewish colonies, etc ... and has steadily built up that feeling of enmity and hatred towards the British'. Thus, he and his friends could 'call any Jewish leader willing to cooperate with Gt. Britain, a Quisling. Threats were also issued against the Moderates' who 'were without any power in the Yishuv'. At Paris, Ben-Gurion overrode moderate views, claiming that he represented the Yishuv.[63] He was right. Jewish parties boycotted the British conference intended to exploit Agatha, meaning that Britain freed most of the opponents it had captured in Agatha for nothing. Shortly, Britain started down the slippery slope to failure when it accepted that Palestine had to be partitioned and the United Nations (UN) given responsibility for the matter.

By October 1946, the DSO in Jersualem concluded that Haganah was assassinating specific police officers for alleged misdeeds, showing the personalisation of the campaign and the superiority of Jewish intelligence.[64] In 1929, when handling subversion in Bengal, Tegart had emphasised that his men could succeed only if they thought themselves on top of the terrorists.[65] That sense of confidence did not exist in

Palestine during 1946. Even worse, Britain inadvertently boosted Jewish intelligence by wrecking its own. In August 1946, Britain published a White Paper which included intelligence that showed the links between the Jewish Agency and Haganah, and the latter with Irgun and Lehi. At its core were eight messages from Oats and Istria, which the paper implied were just part of Britain's collection. MI5 briefed ministers not to say anything more than the White Paper about the source of these messages, 'which was prepared with the most scrupulous attention to the protection of our sources of information and further comment is liable to destroy those sources' – but the damage was done.[66] After all, some Jews could read English.

Operation Agatha became politicised in Britain and the United States, where Whitehall was negotiating for support over Palestine and a loan. The Attlee government correctly regarded these negotiations as important. Much of the Labour Party opposed official policy, supported Zionism and condemned Agatha. Its leaders felt personal betrayal and irritation at having been fooled by Zionists. Naively, they thought that to prove that the Jewish Agency controlled Haganah and cooperated with terrorists would be enough to embarrass it into cooperation and justify Agatha to Parliament and the world. British officials in Palestine, Whitehall and within the Cabinet believed that to publish this material might even 'ruin the Jewish Agency in its present form', and thus Zionism.[67] Attlee, stung by criticism, justified Operation Agatha to Parliament by noting that 'some' but not all leaders of the Jewish Agency directed Haganah, which was linked to terrorists. When challenged to prove the point, he promised to do so after papers seized from the Agency were inspected. Later, he agreed to provide the material which had inspired Agatha, rather than anything gathered through it.

When asked in turn what evidence was available for the purpose, Cunningham erroneously replied that Attlee had overstated anything sent to him from Palestine. Comint alone proved these points, yet to publish it would be a disaster.

> The compromising of these sources will result in the loss of all incontrovertible information available to us about the illegal activities of the Jews. These sources are within the sphere of activities of the Chiefs of Staff with whom the matter would require to be discussed. I would most strongly urge that the security of

this information be not compromised unless overriding political considerations render this absolutely unavoidable. I hope means may be devised that if the information has to be utilised its source may be disguised. If in spite of all objections it is found politically necessary to use this information I feel it is essential that an intelligence officer from this country should proceed home to discuss possibility of providing cover.[68]

Hall retorted: regarding the 'vital necessity for producing as convincing a statement of evidence as possible. We shall have to consider disclosure of evidence from top secret sources if such a statement cannot be based on other sources.'[69] Hall told Attlee that the Cabinet 'faced the difficult choice between declining to reveal documentary evidence in support of the statement we have made or "blowing" our sources', which would 'have a most disadvantageous [effect] on immediate military operations', and 'wider repercussions, in view of the use made of similar means of interception in other spheres'.[70] Cunningham attempted to solve this dilemma by formulating a case without involving Comint, but it was weak, if one excluded material seized during Agatha. Lord Jowitt, the Lord Chancellor, who assessed the evidence for the Cabinet, noted that documents seized through Agatha were useless as a means of justifying it. 'We must, as it seems to me, give some strong and clear indication that we had knowledge before acting which compelled us to act; or at least strong grounds for suspicion which have now been confirmed.'[71]

Authorities in Jerusalem sought desperately to save Comint. Barker warned 'that if he is required to deal with internal security situation in future and armed violence of HAGANA and PALMACH he will be virtually without necessary operational intelligence should CREAM sources be divulged. This will involve him in possible mistakes which may have serious political consequences.' Comint enabled Agatha to seize the 'right' targets. 'Without OATS he would have had to risk more wrongful arrests and possible failure of operations owing to the lack of intelligence. Owing to his knowledge he was able to avoid casualties. This might not have been possible without his CREAM sources.' Meanwhile, Haganah and Palmach were reorganising; without Comint, future operations might involve casualties. 'We may be ignorant of the operational set-up of the Jews and be with the same difficulties as confront us when dealing with IZL and STERN group who we are unable to neutralise owing to lack of precise intelligence.' Cunningham, Isham, Shaw and the DMI shared these prophetic views.[72]

Reluctantly, Cunningham accepted publication of Comint, as did C and MI5.[73] MI5 preferred that the paper be based 'on evidence not derived from wireless interception. If this source of intelligence were destroyed, the General Officer Commanding in Palestine would be deprived of information without which recent operations would have been impossible, and future operations would have to be carried out in the dark and with much greater risk of casualties.' Attlee retorted that 'his undertaking was to produce the evidence on which action was authorised and therefore any post hoc evidence secured from examination of Jewish Agency documents was only of value as confirmatory. By revealing our interception of wireless traffic we were not revealing our methods of breaking cyphers. The task would be to overcome a change of cypher on the part of the Zionists, which was no novel problem.' The powerful minister, and Labour Leader of the House of Commons, Herbert Morrison, added: 'The Parliamentary statement on the complicity of the Zionist leaders must sweep public opinion both here and in the United States and might have a salutary effect on those whose contributions to the Zionist cause had been misappropriated by the leaders to finance violence in Palestine. A revelation of the extent of our knowledge might shake the nerves of the organisers of these activities.'[74]

Given two chances to make an effective White Paper without Sigint, MI5 could not do so. MI5 also perhaps preferred to use Sigint because the only other good evidence would endanger the CID's sources within the Yishuv, who 'must be protected, since disclosure would imperil the lives of those on whose testimony some of the evidence is based'.[75] This position was humane and rational. Other authorities failed both these tests. Admittedly after the terrorist outrage of 22 July, the Chief Secretary's Office in Palestine advocated publishing portions of a CID report, even though if the source's '"high treason" were divulged, he would not be likely to survive for long'.[76] British officials were willing to risk burning all of their intelligence to bolster this propaganda. Despite the unfortunate consequences of releasing Comint to justify Operation Agatha, in the spring of 1947 Whitehall considered burning what remained of Britain Sigint capabilities to provide evidence to the UN Commission. Fortunately it abandoned that effort.[77]

After the Fall

Attlee achieved what Irgun could not: decapitating British Comint in Palestine. When Britain had compromised its grasp of foreign cryptosystems to score political points in the 1920s, the causes were trivial; not so in 1946, however much legalism and party considerations distorted ministers' minds. The publication of Istria and Oats reduced unofficial American and British public attacks on British policy, and angered moderate political leaders in the Yishuv, suddenly aware of how Ben-Gurion had gulled them.

This action had some political gains, but greater cryptanalytical costs. The Jewish Agency quickly adopted better cryptosystems and ended the operators' errors which had helped to compromise the old ones. It retained Bentley's codebook, but adopted a better, though still simple, subtractor system, and changed it frequently. Britain found it unbreakable.[78] Jewish leaders avoided discussions by cable and wireless and moved to the cumbersome yet secure method of face-to-face meetings. Haganah's wireless operators improved, probably through training by veterans of the Jewish Brigade and SOE.

From 15 September 1946, months after the White Paper was published, two GCHQ successes against Haganah traffic collapsed. Haganah and Palmach units adopted new cyphers on 1 November which proved time-consuming to break, and massively increased the number of distinct superencipherment systems in use, and their rate of change. These units transmitted less material by wireless, while codewords covered proper nouns.[79] Britain's difficulty in overcoming simple improvements in cryptography reveals this Palestine-based unit's isolation from the mainstream of GCHQ (though Tiltman offered assistance) and the increasing indifference towards its work by Whitehall. Had this traffic remained a high priority, it would have been broken.

Britain lost its best source during a critical period, but Comint had always missed key matters, while other sources continued to provide insight. CID and Buttercup remained excellent on politics in Palestine. Abroad, liaison relations with foreign services, and British and foreign intercepts of cables and telephone calls by Jewish leaders, provided many useful fragments on Zionist politics.[80] From autumn 1946, Britain lost this battle of intelligence, but as ever, the key problems were weaknesses in policy and power. The Attlee compromise cost Britain precision, power, thoroughness and certainty, in two areas. Istria and Isoats alone had penetrated the conspirators around Ben-Gurion. That capability was wrecked. Its loss also eliminated a useful means of validatory checks on CID information, which came from people in direct or indirect contact with that inner circle. Isoats alone had illuminated the policy and intentions of Haganah and Palmach, and, better than any other source, the activities of Irgun and Lehi. That power withered, but did not quite die.

Thus, by late 1946, British Comint in Palestine faced disaster. It read no current Jewish military traffic, nor did it know where Haganah's headquarters were. Britain was exposed to Palmach, the 'prime threat to security after terrorists', and also vulnerable to the greatest danger: full mobilisation by Haganah 'in event unfavourable turn Palestine situation' (i.e. if Britain turned decisively against the Yishuv). The need to suppress both bodies 'may arise at any moment'.[81] Precisely as the Jewish threat rose, intelligence on it declined, eroding the value and raising the cost of the use of force. Improved direction-finding soon tracked some Haganah headquarters. Perhaps exploiting the poor practices of specific operators, British codebreakers cracked the cryptosystems of Haganah's northern Galilee district, and occasionally those of other groups, such as Unit 2 of Palmach, one of its four battalions, in Negev. The Galilee traffic may include a series of messages entitled 'DAN', perhaps referring to Dan settlement in the area, traditionally associated with the eponymous Hebrew tribe.

Isoats once covered all of Palestine, from Dan to Bersheeba. In 1947, it covered only those towns. Still, this intelligence from the ends of the Mandate enabled the British to draw cautious, but accurate and useful, inferences that Haganah and Irgun were feuding, Palmach was not conducting terrorism and perhaps trying to impede it, while insurrection was not imminent.[82] From current and back traffic, analysts steadily reconstructed internal codewords and book values, group by weary group. By June 1947, Comint enabled a detailed order of battle for Haganah and Palmach, and operational intelligence, albeit more speculative than certain.[83] As usual when attacking back traffic after current accesses had vanished, success declined on major issues, but rose against minor tasks, such as comparing the card index to names in a CID report or the Jewish press. The *Palestine Post* became a major source. Britain monitored 'typical Palmach punitive expedition[s]' against Arabs, or assassinations of Hungarians or Germans interned in Palestine and suspected of involvement in the Holocaust.[84] As Comint ceased to indicate major issues, the DSO abandoned the 1,000-message summaries, and focused on consumers' requirements in Palestine, rather than London.[85] From October 1947, the DSO again derived significant intelligence from Haganah traffic. The latter's reports 'on Arab activities which might affect the Yishuv' were often dubious or alarmist, but sparked military preparations in Galilee.[86] Even so, only in December 1947 – after Britain ended the Mandate, and war began between Jews and Arabs, forcing Haganah into long and often emergency communications – did Britain again routinely penetrate Haganah communications.[87]

GCHQ's greatest success in Palestine during 1945–48 – and its only one after September 1946 – was against 'illegal' emigration, carried over what it called the Diaspora network, from across Europe to Tel Aviv. Military authorities wished to 'attempt intercept every ship no matter what size carrying illegal immigrants to PALESTINE', though, SIME noted, 'need not be unduly disturbed however if small ship succeeds in running gauntlet as this provides degree of cover for OATS'.[88] In this campaign many British intelligence sources overlapped. Comint – as Oats and later Fog – assisted by other intelligence sources, accurately tracked the preparation of every shipment of immigrants. Fog, and Y, especially MERS, tracked ships through European waters. Inefficiencies in collection and reportage by the direction-finding station at Abu Sukir in Egypt, however, compromised coverage on the important southern approach to Palestine.[89] 'It is vital repeat absolutely vital that we receive bearings on ships as soon as you can despatch them,' the DSO warned the intercept organisation in Cyprus – which was efficient but badly placed to pick up traffic from the southern approach. 'RAF aircraft hours here is extremely critical and there is a limited number of search days each month. Most careful calculations have therefore to be made in order to avoid running out of aircraft during searches,' including time for maintenance and stand-downs.[90] Firm but factual admonishments spurred improvements of interception in Egypt and Cyprus.

Good camouflage and signals security covered the identity of immigrant ships in the waters between Egypt and Cyprus, from which they could lunge towards Palestine. Without Fog, many or most of these ships might have reached their destination, reshaping the politics of the Mandate.[91] However, Fog – camouflaged as 'reliable intelligence' to hide the involvement of Comint from British personnel (the DSO once noted 'complete absence overt information to serve as cover for search is most embarrassing') – guided reconnaissance aircraft and warships to locations well suited to intercepting these inbound vessels.[92] Almost all of these ships were stopped and their passengers interned in Cyprus. In this, Comint best aided an aim of British policy for Palestine and pleased its consumers. Internment of refugees in Palestine would have overwhelmed the police, at barely 50 per cent of their authorised strength.[93] Control of immigration was a powerful card for Britain to play with Jews and Arabs. Intelligence and military authorities agreed, as one head of SIME wrote: 'Occasion of any PALESTINE disturbance will almost certainly be illegal immigration.'[94] Cunningham feared that an inability to control incoming migrant ships 'would unquestionably produce an immediate and hysterical Jewish reaction' and Arab counter-reaction, wrecking any hope for negotiations.[95] Comint helped to avoid that risk, and to press Ben-Gurion; yet control of immigration remained a public relations disaster for Britain and an unpleasant practice.

In Palestine, GCHQ was one of Britain's two main sources, matched by CID. All forms of Comint strengthened Britain's policy, but could not save one so weak as this. Ultimately, Comint sustained a stalemate but could not end it. Even if British authorities had understood the truth, which only a combination of Comint and CID at their best could have provided, they would have been reluctant to believe it. The truth simply would have made Britain surrender faster than it did.

Konfrontasi: Living Dangerously

The Suez crisis of 1956 shook British power over its colonies and its will to hold them and encouraged all local competitors to challenge it at once. Against this, over the next decade, Britain sought to preserve its economic interests within and influence over these colonies via indirect rule: by giving independence to the best-disposed of local leaders while maintaining regional hegemony through an effective but affordable military presence in the Indian Ocean. In particular, Britain sought to combine all of its colonies and protectorates in southeast Asia (Singapore; and Sabah, Sarawak and Brunei, on the northern coast of Borneo) with the already independent state of Malaya. This 'Malaysia' would give strategic depth to a base in Singapore, which might enable a cheap but strong presence to sustain Britain's friends in east Africa, the Persian Gulf and southeast Asia.[96] To fuse such a federation around a Muslim and Malay state was not easy. Most people in Sabah and Sarawak, neither Muslim nor Malay, were no more attracted to Malaysia than Indonesia, and indifferent to either. Some preferred Indonesia to Malaysia. Brunei was an independent principality, Singapore a Chinese city. Politicians in all these regions pursued competing interests. None were puppets, although Britain influenced them all.

Indonesia exacerbated these problems. Its nationalist and irredentist leaders had won independence through war. They believed in their own power and Western weakness. Their chief, 'Achmad' Sukarno (born Kusno Sosrodihardjo), wanted to lead African and Asian states to overthrow a Western-dominated order and to have Indonesia match the USSR and China as a revolutionary power. However unrealistic, these ambitions drove his actions. Sukarno also pursued revolution at home, aiming to weaken the political positions of the strongest factions outside his control – Muslims and the military – by working with the Indonesian Communist Party, the Partai Komunis Indonesia (PKI). The PKI became the strongest political force in Indonesia, organised but unarmed. Sukarno's policies created political and economic crisis in Indonesia. All of these forces drove Indonesia to challenge Britain.[97] Sukarno and his generals viewed Malaysia as a creature of neo-colonialism, which bolstered imperialism in Asia. For Sukarno, confrontation – Konfrontasi – with Britain simultaneously served prestige politics and his internal and external aims. It diverted his army towards shared aims abroad and away from differences at home, turning their guns at Britain rather than the PKI – or himself. Sukarno proclaimed Konfrontasi 'a year of living dangerously'. He was more prophetic than he knew.

Through politics and force, Indonesia sought to splinter Malaysia and to control Sabah, Sarawak and Brunei. Though it borrowed from Maoist and Vietnamese theory and practice, Indonesian strategy was innovative. An unconventional campaign aimed to pin large British forces in perpetual check, erode Britain's patience and to multiply political divisions in Malaysia. To prove Indonesia's power and shake local nerve, terrorists, moving by ship or parachute, attacked targets in Singapore and Malaya across the 550-mile long Straits of Malacca, augmented by black radio broadcasts, propaganda letters sent to individuals and the pasting of posters or slogans on walls. Soldiers infiltrated the 1,000-mile frontier between Indonesia, Sabah and Sarawak, terrain dominated by hill and jungle. A few lateral roads approached both sides of the frontier, where they became trails. Indonesian volunteers, regular forces and local supporters pursued indigenous political influence, attacked Commonwealth and Malaysian positions, and pursued 'liberated zones' where armed men might build popular support and subvert Malaysia. The purpose of military activity in zones inside Malaysia was to carry out sabotage and illegal political activities in order to radicalise politically peoples and leaders.[98] These zones were located in areas where the local population was thought to be hostile to Malaysia, generally among Chinese settlers. British authorities regarded liberated zones as their greatest danger; Indonesia's failure to create them drove its defeat. Indonesia could escalate these practices at will, but fear of British conventional power capped its actions at the level of systematic infiltration. These Indonesian raids usually involved forces of ten to a hundred men. During 1963, Indonesia committed some 2,000 irregulars to the frontier with northern Borneo, which reached 12,000 irregular and regular personnel by 1965.[99]

This pocket version of the Suez crisis divided British authorities. Calculations were delicate. Authorities wanted to defeat Indonesia's policy without alienating it. Politicians did not want to lose a contest over prestige, but wobbled over the details of policy. They paid much to avoid defeat, yet considered compromise about Malaysia and wanted good relations with Indonesia, especially on economic issues. Conservative governments took a harder line than their Labour successor, but valued sales to Indonesia; Harold Wilson's government, while more open to compromise, refused to be bullied.[100] Meanwhile, British military leaders confronted a threat at the peak of imperial overstretch, in a time of economic and military crisis, which threatened their strategic effort to manage decline. Containing Konfrontasi required a military commitment approaching that to NATO, 56,000 soldiers and large naval and air forces, with no end in sight. In order to break Konfrontasi, during 1964–65 military leaders advocated major acts of retaliation, including covert raids on Sumatra, and open maritime and air war. Indonesian authorities feared them, but British politicians rejected these ideas.[101] Britain's allies – Australia, New Zealand and the United States – wished it well but kept aloof. Too much cooperation with Malaysia might make Sukarno confront their own interests too, like American firms in Indonesia, or the Australian protectorate of Papua New Guinea.

Sukarno was right to think that a prolonged war of political attrition would damage Britain, but wrong about its power and policy. Britain defeated every level of Konfrontasi, if sometimes at frustrating cost. It let Malaysian leaders take their own political decisions, demonstrating their independence, which also undermined British policy. British diplomats defeated Indonesia in international fora, building legitimacy for Malaysia and driving Sukarno to stupid responses. Britain won the battle of infiltration and deterred Indonesia from escalating, while showing the power and capability to do so itself. British and Malaysian police and regular forces defended Singapore and Malaya and the interior of Sabah and Sarawak. The Australian and British special air services (SAS), and Australian, British and Gurkha infantry dominated war on the frontiers, supported by artillery and mortars. Helicopters aided logistics, mobility and medical evacuation. In order to break infiltration, from 1964 Britain secretly authorised its forces to operate up to 3,000 yards, and then 10,000 yards, within Indonesian territory on Borneo, sometimes informally extended to 20,000 yards, thereby enabling ambushes on the lateral roads to the front and attacks against forward Indonesian positions. These British operations, codenamed Claret, were politically risky and tactically difficult. For Indonesia to capture any Commonwealth prisoners or bodies in its territory would prove that Britain was doing something that it publicly denied was happening. To kill fifty Indonesian soldiers but leave two Commonwealth casualties behind might lose a battle. The few soldiers available for these operations – in a vast and difficult area, with astonishingly low force-to-space ratios – could easily be worn out by the need to return casualties or by employment in blind searches, through rough country, always vulnerable to accident or counter-ambush.[102]

Under these circumstances one would expect a hard and long campaign of counterinsurgency, but this was not such a case. Britain confronted an irregular war, not a guerrilla one: constant small raids across a frontier by conventional units or 'volunteers'. In conceptual terms, the campaign was more like strategic air defence than counter-insurgency – which explains its success. Indonesian forces stood or moved behind the frontier and the Straits of Malacca, or raided across it, with no secure insurgency base within Malaysia. They could be ambushed where they stood or moved, especially through the able use of intelligence. A shot of Comint served to fortify the Claret.

Sigint Preparation of the Battlefield

The first step towards Konfrontasi surprised Britain. The Brunei revolt of December 1962 shook its colonial structure, briefly, in part from misjudgements by MI5's outpost, Security Intelligence Far East (SIFE) and poor coordination between intelligence and security agencies. Brunei police officers anticipated the revolt and prepared for it. Indeed, their arrests of revolutionaries precipitated the revolt. Meanwhile, SIFE and Special Branch in Borneo denied the danger, which kept military reinforcements from being deployed to Brunei before the revolt, and confused their response to a rising by 4,000 rebels.[103] This failure enraged both the Malaysian prime minister, Tunku Abdul Rahman, whose warnings had been ignored, and British political authorities in Singapore.[104]

GCHQ's local representative, the Government Communications Officer (Singapore), (GCO(S)), Harold Fletcher, asked it and the Australian Defence Signals Bureau (DSB) to 'examine their conscience' self-critically. They must test their competence and prepare for politics. Fletcher, warning that 'a storm might eventually brew' over the intelligence failure at Brunei, gathered 'evidence of Sigint's prescience and alertness while subject still fresh, in case witch hunt develops'.[105] Comint cleared their conscience: it had uncovered Indonesian contacts with politicians in Brunei but not evidence for the coming revolt, which no one expected it to have done. Fletcher held that 'all consumers are satisfied that Sigint has done and is doing all it can'.[106] He soon noted 'the almost childlike faith in the miraculous powers of Sigint in these parts'.[107] DSB warned that 'the stakes are large for Malaysia and for Sigint and want to be sure that we are all "on net" to produce fullest intelligence for consumers'.[108] Throughout Konfrontasi, Siginters remained sensitive to their reputation among intelligence consumers. For GCHQ, this crisis was a test of the Hampshire Report's recommendation to increase spending and of the Treasury's counter-attack. Its success in this theatre paid dividends elsewhere.

How far Indonesia inspired the Brunei revolt was unclear. The Far East Sector Heads of intelligence in London saw 'no evidence of direct Indonesian involvement'.[109] Apparently, Sigint could not answer the question. British authorities, however, expected Indonesia to act against Malaysia as it had just done successfully against the Dutch in New Guinea: through confrontation, combining constant pinprick raids, cooperation with local rebels, the creation of liberated zones and vehement diplomacy and propaganda. Unlike the case of Suez, GCHQ had time to plan a measured response to the threat. Australia and Britain could work on Indonesian communication systems, because of Indonesia's reliance on radio for communications with scattered forces. From Australian stations, DSB dominated this coverage, its main mission under UKUSA. Civil links were not covered, but DSB held that military nets would carry all 'worthwhile intelligence', while 'anything of any importance or value' would pass through Jakarta.[110] 'It is Ninety per cent probable that indications of Indonesian intentions would be available from present strategic intercept (since policy messages are habitually referred to Jakarta on currently exploitable links),' though neither this coverage nor additional tactical intercept might give 'exact areas of e.g. planned operations'.[111] Britain and Australia realigned collection from existing resources, sacrificing coverage of other southeast Asian military targets. Diplomats in Jakarta also provided strategic intelligence on Indonesia, but Comint dominated collection on Konfrontasi. Though Indonesia had decent human sources, the Commonwealth outweighed it in intelligence.

Despite the differences between Australian and British policies over Malaysia, DSB oversaw operations there, including control of targets, which it had to justify to a senior partner with changing demands. DSB told Fletcher: 'It is essential that we know of "wind-changes" or of approaching high/low pressures which may affect winds of consumer requirements.' DSB's normal processing of Indonesian traffic assumed a two- to seven-day time lag in translation and distribution; for consumers to demand reports in four to twenty-four hours would cripple other efforts.[112]

That problem soon emerged, as DSB adopted a seven-day-a-week effort against urgent messages.[113] For UKF 200 during Konfrontasi, 'urgency' became the 'prime consideration', forcing more ' "T" (translation of individual message) reporting' as against ' "C" (collated or round-up) reporting', and thus the dissemination of more messages, often minor in nature.[114] The GCO(S)s, Fletcher (1962–64) and Brian Tovey (1964–66), commanded British Sigint resources in Malaysia, as well as Australian ones, subject to decisions in Australia. They dealt separately with DSB and GCHQ, while connecting the two. GCHQ worked closely with the services in London, as the GCO(S)s – based in a two-room office within British headquarters at Phoenix Park – did with local British commanders. Britain, Tovey noted, was so reliant on Comint that GCHQ communications channels carried key British military communications, especially during periods when Indonesia escalated its actions.[115] SK2's large Comcen, of fourteen British and fourteen Australian personnel, including several women, handled these swollen signals well. NSA was not much involved. The Commonwealth could handle its own problems, while Americans had more than enough of their own in the region.

Konfrontasi marked GCHQ's last hurrah of the radio age. Its resources were stretched to their maximum: there was no fat left, as GCHQ insisted to PSIS, but thankfully enough bone and muscle remained to sustain it and to find new operators and train linguists. GCHQ was not just an intelligence agency, but an executive one, with microscopic control over the resources needed to create intelligence across the world, which it did with informality, professionalism, self-criticism, and a focus on problem-solving. Communications with officers abroad were frank, and fast, including details about individual operators and pieces of kit. Errors were admitted by apology, and acknowledged without elimination. GCHQ negotiated directly with sister agencies in the Five Eyes, and British military services. Its few administrators minuted incoming messages by hand with ballpoint pen and passed them to others with advice or queries, to streamline and speed up decisions. Pneumatic Lamson tubes moved information by paper within GCHQ in seconds, not much slower than the speed of email. Signals carried messages across the globe from desk to desk in hours. Messages were divided into letters, and especially cables in categories of Flash, Operational Immediate, Priority and Routine. The need to transmit so much material so urgently crushed signals and cypher resources on Comint links between London and Singapore, and Singapore and Borneo; yet still they moved.

During Konfrontasi, as Brian Tovey later noted: 'Basic principle was to retain normal peacetime Sigint structure and to modify this only to extent dictated by genuine operational necessity.'[116] In 1963, that structure was sound. The main problem was the provision of too many 'innocuous' messages to consumers, and too few synthetic or compilation reports, due to the lack of 'good C Report writers'.[117] Fletcher thought 'the coverage of main lines ... is just about the maximum that can be done, and is very efficient'.[118]

The challenge was tactical Y in Borneo, especially against low-frequency traffic which could not easily be intercepted outside the island. This need required the formation of a new unit, which DSB estimated would require five teams, and GCHQ four, about the number of intercept operators in UKF 200 or 121 Signals Squadron.[119] The great administrative and political problems involved in creating units of twenty to forty men reflect the limits to GCHQ's resources, confronting financial pressure at home and growing problems abroad, and the undeveloped state of Borneo at the time. GCHQ faced global limits on interceptors, and of personnel able to read Indonesian languages, and above all, to understand voice. It could reinforce UKF 200 only by cannibalising units handling important missions against the USSR and China, and by retraining two local British interpreters of Malay in the related Indonesian language. It hoped that DSD would solve the problem by providing a tactical unit. DSD would have done so but, to GCHQ's annoyance, could not until the Australian government chose to confront Sukarno openly. Nonetheless, Australian Siginters offered much technical assistance. In 1963, the services assembled 14 men with experience in the Malay or Indonesian languages for training as Morse and voice operators, for service in Singapore.[120] UKF 200 temporarily based a forward team in Borneo, which was withdrawn when a team and a half of nine British intercept operators and analysts from Germany – later doubling in size and augmented by an Australian interpreter of Indonesian – moved there.[121] By June 1964, as Konfrontasi intensified, GCHQ sent twenty civilian wireless operators to Singapore, replacing 121 Australian Signals Squadron. The latter moved to Borneo, providing the bulk of the Indonesian linguists there. Two British and Australian tactical units, each around twenty-men strong and based in Labuan and Kuching, handled the task, using substantial amounts of kit like amplifiers and tape recorders to maximise voice interception. To find even three more cypher operators for Singapore to cover traffic to London was hard, yet just about possible.

Two problems emerged on Borneo. If unusual languages carried Indonesian voice, new translators needed to be found. Initially, British authorities thought Indonesians might use Dayak, the language of the majority population of northern Borneo, for voice. Britain could cover it only by recruiting Dayaks from the paramilitary Sarawak Rangers, and training them in interception. While this problem did not emerge, during 1965–66 some Indonesian operators used Javanese, which Britain covered by retraining four local interpreters.[122] More ominous was the question of what Comint could enable. The UKLO in Melbourne noted that Sigint might fail to track 'in advance exact areas, or even timing of operations ... though the build up of forces (and their location) and the fact that something was planned usually became very clear'.[123] Commonwealth forces improved on this performance, because they had more intelligence and power than the Dutch, and better opportunities for offensive rather than defensive action.

Scattered across wide territory, Indonesian forces signalled mostly by radio via voice and Morse, augmented by field telephones. Some traffic went in plain language, and operators were generally inefficient. They used fixed call-signs, frequencies and skeds, simplifying interception, and communicated primarily during office hours, enabling SK2 to focus on those periods and minimise personnel for other shifts.[124] Comint was the dominant British tactical and operational source during Konfrontasi, married to eyeballs on the ground for tactical purposes. The tertiary sources – aerial or photo reconnaissance, agents, prisoners and the local population – determined some enemy positions and penetrations, and provided cover for Comint. Simultaneously, Comint removed the errors of these sources, and revealed their truths. The most fruitful communications links were within Indonesian units on Borneo, and between the authorities in Jakarta and Indonesian Special Services (which combined political subversion units and commandos) and military commanders in Borneo and Sumatra. In organisational terms, Special Services was highly personalised, while the army was hyper-bureaucratic. Both worked via micromanagement, handling subordinates through an odd combination of detailed orders and political exhortation. Comint mastered the intentions, plans, operations and after-action assessments of Indonesian Special Services and army battalions on the front. Those Comint successes wrecked enemy operations, and eased British fears that action might compromise intelligence sources. A massive quantity of details about the Indonesian army, often from logistical and administrative traffic, and occasional revelations of plans and intentions, exposed any planned escalation of its strength or operations in Borneo.

These reports illuminated Indonesian attacks, but less so its underlying policy. Comint defined the convoluted Indonesian chain of command, and the role of each link in Konfrontasi. It enabled sophisticated British analysis of Indonesian decision-making, which allowed Britain to avoid elementary errors, but not to overcome more significant ones. In particular, Comint revealed that Special Services, the most aggressive Indonesian agency, reported directly to Sukarno.[125] This knowledge perhaps led British analysts to overstate the significance of Special Services as an indicator of Indonesian policy, and to oversimplify the latter's nature. In fact, Indonesian policy was formulated in a chaotic and personalised fashion. The head of Special Services, Colonel Magenda, and his deputy, Colonel Rujito, were belligerent partly in order to maintain their status in Jakarta. They had bad relations with every conventional arm. Military Comint revealed those ruptures and hinted at disputes in Jakarta over the execution of policy. However, it rarely penetrated the plans of top leaders, but did so just enough to show that the latter supported Konfrontasi with Britain, and its escalation, precisely as other secret, official or public sources suggested. Diplomatic Comint probably provided more material in this sphere.

Comint and Claret

Konfrontasi escalated the more that Malaysia integrated. From April 1963, Indonesian forces, mostly Special Services, began shallow incursions – codenamed in their messages as 'A' operations – into Borneo. They failed to prevent integration or to build liberated zones. By early 1964, Comint was able to show that Indonesia aimed to intensify the pressure, by combining force, subversion and a diplomatic effort to delegitimise Malaysia across Asia. Several organisations prepared independently to launch deeper penetrations across Malaysia. They strove to destabilise all of its parts and to build liberated zones, which would demonstrate opposition to Malaysia and subvert it during national elections and international conferences. Special Services moved to Sumatra, to begin a campaign of terrorism in Malaya and Singapore, working with the Indonesian Air Force, Marines, Navy, and allied Chinese and Malay political parties. Two Indonesian army battalions reinforced the strength of 3,500 volunteers and irregulars in Borneo. Comint illuminated the strength of a number of smaller units, and then showed that 5,000 to 10,000 volunteers would reach Borneo with plans to attack on specific dates.[126]

The slow development of Indonesian actions let Commonwealth forces prepare an effective counter. They did not want to move faster and further than necessary. Too eager action might antagonise decision-makers in Canberra and Washington, who hoped for a diplomatic solution. Any action required the development of elementary infrastructure. Merely to build or rent houses for Siginters and to find locations to deploy aerials – and to do so while achieving effect, security, and plausible cover – proved to be daunting tasks. Comint followed these developments. This period of operational warning enabled a military and Sigint build-up which eventually provided a tactical triumph.

By January 1964, GCHQ and the Australian Defence Signals Division (DSD), the renamed DSB, recognised that Indonesian actions made an escalation of their own effort 'inescapable'. Thirty-one Australian and British teams covered 'high-level links from which intentions and O.B. [order of battle] can normally be recovered', plus tactical links in Borneo. The rise in Indonesian forces and ambitions created more links and traffic to monitor, needing another five intercept teams in general and three in Borneo, expanded Sigint communications, and requiring a reorganisation of processing and distribution.[127] As the crisis grew in mid-1964, experience guided recalibration of effort.[128] A card index enabled intelligence to exploit every name of individuals or units mentioned in an Indonesian message. It enabled astonishing granularity of commentary, which was printed neatly in black pen on printed messages. Comint penetrated Indonesian efforts at deception – including its public claims to be withdrawing forces from Borneo – as part of international efforts to end the crisis.[129] Instead, as Indonesians purported to negotiate a ceasefire to Konfrontasi, they prepared to intensify the war of nerves. They aimed to send large forces into Borneo for just a few days, in order to evacuate them immediately in front of international observers, purporting to come from long-standing liberated zones.[130]

This material drove Australia to back Britain in Borneo and Whitehall to increase intelligence and military resources there. Commonwealth forces deployed four brigades in Borneo, reaching 17,000 soldiers, controlled by a Joint Force Headquarters (JFHQ) under DOBOPS (Director of Borneo Operations), Generals William Walker (1963–65) and George Lea (1965–67). In 1964, DSD reported the 'unanimous opinion of all intelligence authorities … that without Comint, Australia would have been in dark concerning Indonesian planning and implementation of "A" operations against Malaysia'. Stations should be thanked for their 'excellent service of timely voluminous and meaningful Sigint'. Via the GCO(S), 'the intelligence community of Singapore' echoed this praise.[131] The C-in-C Far East pressed MOD to support GCHQ's expansion in Malaysia, given 'how dependent we are on Sigint for the successful prosecution of operations'.[132] Statesmen in Canberra and London frequently read Comint, which illuminated issues about which they cared.

Relevant staffs and commanders in London, and in Malaysia down to brigade level, were indoctrinated to receive Comint. In Singapore, conventional practices continued. Comint was disseminated rapidly to consumers during the day, but between 2015 and 0730 hours they had to visit UKF 200 to see any emergency messages.[133] On Borneo, the aims were speedy and thorough dissemination, which did not always follow standard practices. Initially, one-time pad-encrypted messages sent by radio, and cleared officers conveying top secret material by hand, carried Comint to DOBOPS. It was handled and transmitted by his intelligence chief, who also served as an SLO. Intercepts from local sources were returned to Singapore by Top Secret bag. In June 1964, a more orthodox organisation emerged. A 'secure Comint cell' was established at JFHQ. Raw and finished Sigint was carried between it and Singapore on two radio lines, serviced by cypher machines.[134] An officer at JFHQ, GS (Int) (S), received Comint and disseminated it to DOBOPS and his senior intelligence officer, who verbally briefed British brigade commanders. Many lower ranks involved in moving Comint at JFHQ also were indoctrinated.

GCHQ considered limited cooperation on Sigint with Malaysian officers, but rejected the idea. JICFE was authorised to brief them with sanitised material from Comint.[135] Otherwise, Britain aimed to keep knowledge of Comint from Malaysian officers, who commanded many forces in Malaya, one of the brigades in Borneo, a fleet, the police and especially Special Branch. Walker thought 'half' the intelligence 'value' of a policeman 'is lost if he has not access to club's material'.[136] That comment was an understatement. Indonesian messages routinely discussed their collaborators in Sarawak and Singapore, often including names and addresses and negotiations with dissident politicians and parties within Malaysia. This material enabled any competent security organisation, like Malaysian ones, to disrupt or control internal subversives working with an external enemy. Comint shaped an important but hidden dimension of Konfrontasi – political warfare, defensive and offensive – on both sides at once. It explains Indonesian failure in that campaign.

So to assist these Malaysian forces, and to gain corroborating material from them, Britain indoctrinated a few 'expats' – retired British officers serving as deputies within Malaysian organisations – to ensure their quality while Malaysian officers gained experience. Since this process was unusual under the rules of UKUSA, GCHQ asked NSA to present it to the United States Communications Intelligence Board. GCHQ emphasised that only a few men, previously indoctrinated, would be involved. USCIB approved the request albeit, as SUKLO soon discovered, with major reservations, especially about the numbers of expats. To raise the number would anger the US services and embarrass NSA, which privately tolerated a rise from six to eight expats, and later 10, without informing USCIB. Hooper, emphasising 'we must be very careful not to abuse General Blake's confidence or trust!', insisted on authorising every additional indoctrination.[137] Keeping the number of indoctrinated expats to ten men remained a headache.

Expats were briefed orally by visiting intelligence officers. They never saw end product and rarely saw appreciations based on Comint, which they could read but not retain. This process enabled Comint loosely to guide and to gain cooperation from Malaysian organisations.[138] Claude Fenner, the Inspector General of Police of Malaysia, was authorised in an emergency to give material from Comint described as such to the Tunku. If their Malaysian superior officers questioned proposals based on Comint, expats were to reply that they rested on intelligence which British authorities thought reliable, leaving the impression that they stemmed from MI6. Expats could not be vetted normally. Their past police or military service was usually sufficient to solve the problem. Britain also found means to send Comint during emergencies direct to the officer commanding the British battalion under Malaysian command in Borneo. He received Comint only if it could be used 'in such a way as to not arouse suspicion on the part either of the enemy or the Malaysian Bde Cmd and his staff'. He was briefed verbally, either from DOBOPs or his chief intelligence officer, who also 'indicates how it can be safely used (info not given unless safely usable)'.[139] In return, the Tunku probably had better human intelligence on Indonesia than Britain did, but did not share it, save when it suited his interests.

GCHQ wished to prevent Commonwealth and Malaysian military units from practising Sigint for fear this would compromise its work. It briefed the British Chief Signals Officer of the Malaysian Army to keep his men quietly from the practice.[140] When DOBOPS authorised the SAS to tap an Indonesian field telephone line across the border, Tovey sternly warned him from repeating the action.[141] GCHQ insisted that Comint be concealed from the personnel who acted on it: battalion, company and platoon officers, section or patrol leaders. The army accomplished this well: soldiers did not understand how Comint guided them; in fact, many thought intelligence better served the Indonesians than their own side. The dissemination of Comint to these levels was effective, though deliberately imperfect. Orders followed principles such as: 'translate SIGINT into operational orders. It is better to say to a Bn Cmd "Watch your left flank" than "We think an attack on your left flank is imminent".'

[If] compelled to make an intelligence statement to Bn Cmds ... the information MUST be suitably generalised. Thus, to say 'A very good source shows that the enemy is planning to mount recce patrols against the following places (X, Y and Z)' is WRONG; to say 'We are inclined to think that the enemy may be planning to deploy patrols in the general area Q' (this area would incorporate the particular places X, Y and Z) is MUCH BETTER ... The invention of spurious sources (JAMES BOND etc) is to be avoided and should NEVER be done without consulting GCO through GCO (Int) (S) ... The use of collateral (ground sources etc.) – being guided by Sigint in selecting the 'right' collateral item – is by far the BEST method whenever possible ... any action taken by our forces as a result of SIGINT information should be so carried out as NOT to arouse enemy suspicion of our extraordinary percipience. One good way of achieving this effect is to 'generalise' such action: for example, to bring down mortar fire on <u>one</u> jungle trail (known from SIGINT as a likely enemy approach/withdrawal route) is RISKY; to mortar several jungle-trails (<u>one</u> of which is known as a good likely target from SIGINT) is MUCH SAFER.[142]

Reconsidering Konfrontasi

Tovey emphasised that Comint provided 'impetus and direction to search for relevant ground source intelligence on which military action could then be taken', especially by police and Special Branch.[143] This camouflaging of Comint distorts official documents on Konfrontasi, and previous accounts of it, through no fault of the authors. Some of them, such as Nick van der Bijl, David Easter and Jeffrey Grey, used the Sigint records they found in open documents well.[144] Any reference in records to accurate foreknowledge of Indonesian intentions almost certainly stems from Comint, as do all physical interceptions of their forces. GCHQ's records force a reconsideration of a campaign where Britain had military advantages, problems and opportunities.

Regular and irregular Indonesian forces and commanders were largely mediocre. Malaysian units were inexperienced, though Indonesians respected their security services. Gurkha and other Commonwealth forces were excellent and also outnumbered their foes. They followed doctrines and trained for jungle warfare and the 'hearts and minds' school of counter-insurgency, which suited this campaign. Indonesian forces conceded that Commonwealth counter-insurgency denied them any local support save among the Chinese population in Sarawak and ensured toleration of Malaysian rule through most of that country.

Commonwealth forces could crush any enemy attack they might predict and any Indonesian unit found on the frontier. Surprise was therefore essential to Indonesian success. The more it happened, the greater their effect, and vice versa. Walker, a veteran of the Burma campaign of 1944–45 and the Malayan emergency, was a master of jungle operations, counter-insurgency and the use of intelligence. So was his successor, Lea, commander of 22 SAS during the Malayan emergency. Translating operational knowledge into tactical success was easy against maritime and air insertions on Malaya, but harder in Borneo. Movement was slow. Ambushers advanced perhaps 1,000 yards per day. One snapped twig might lose the element of surprise for a company. Routine movements were tough and tedious, punctuated by

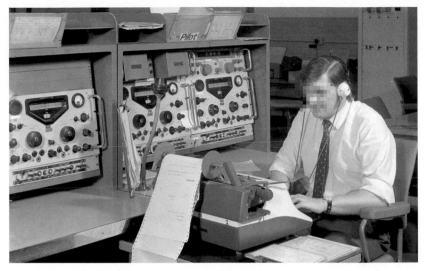

A typical radio set position in the 1970s. The RACAL RA17 radio receiver was the mainstay of UK Sigint from the 1950s to the 1980s. Its design combined extraordinary frequency stability for a valve set together with high sensitivity and selectivity.

GCHQ's internal staff magazine, *Contact*, provided one means of reaching staff across a disparate set of sites and locations. It often featured cartoons relating to the unusual working environment that Siginters found themselves in.

Margaret Thatcher became the first Prime Minister to visit GCHQ when she attended briefings at Oakley in Cheltenham in April 1980. She came away seized by the case for expansion and investment put forward by Brian Tovey, Director from 1978 to 1983.

HMS *Endurance*, the Royal Navy's polar-research ship, played a leading role in the Falklands conflict in 1982. She carried a small intercept capability that fed crucial intelligence back to decision-makers in the UK.

Devised by CESG as part of GCHQ, the BRAHMS secure speech phone was used to provide encrypted voice comms over landlines. The decision of the Cabinet meeting that changed the rules of engagement for British forces off the Falklands – which would lead to the sinking of the Argentine cruiser *Belgrano* by HMS *Conqueror* – was communicated from Chequers to the MOD on this equipment.

Sir Peter Marychurch KCMG, GCHQ Director October 1983–June 1989.

National and local press – as well as staff, Whitehall and intelligence partners – followed the GCHQ union-ban story closely in 1984.

One of the main NATO Sigint collection sites during the Cold War was Teufelsberg, situated on a man-made hill, seen here in the 1980s. Note the RAF Chipmunk trainer aircraft, which collected aerial intelligence on Soviet forces to be fused with Sigint and other sources.

The methods that GCHQ has been able to employ to attract recruits have evolved over the decades. This is a colour brochure for the Joint Technical Language School from 1989, advertising the work but also the benefits of a life and career in the civil service outside London.

Her Majesty Queen Elizabeth II has been receiving GCHQ's intelligence reports for longer than anyone else in the world. In 1995 she paid her first visit to GCHQ at Oakley as the guest of Director John Adye, pictured. This souvenir programme was created for staff.

Sir David Omand GCB, GCHQ Director
July 1996–December 1997.

Sir Kevin Tebbit KCB CMG,
GCHQ Director January–July 1998.

GCHQ's site at Morwenstow near Bude, on
the north Cornish coast.

Bude's A6 dish, known locally as 'Ocean
Breeze', stowed against the Atlantic elements.

GCHQ's old headquarters site at Benhall was knocked down in stages, the last block demolished only once staff had moved into the 'Doughnut', at the time the largest construction project in Europe, and formally opened by Her Majesty Queen Elizabeth II in 2004.

Sir Francis Richards KCMG CVO DL, GCHQ Director August 1998–March 2003.

Sir David Pepper KCMG, GCHQ Director April 2003–June 2008.

Sir Iain Lobban KCMG CB, GCHQ Director July 2008–October 2014.

Robert Hannigan CMG, GCHQ Director
November 2014–April 2017.

In 2014, to commemorate the centenary
of the outbreak of the First World War,
GCHQ joined forces with the Royal British
Legion to launch its annual Poppy Appeal
in Gloucestershire. Over 1,400 staff, civilian
and military, worked together to create a
giant poppy in the centre of the Doughnut.

Land Securities Group

In October 2016 the National
Cyber Security Centre was set up
as part of GCHQ. In February
2017 Her Majesty Queen
Elizabeth II opened the NCSC's
headquarters at Nova South in
London.

On 17 May 2015 GCHQ illuminated its Cheltenham
headquarters with the colours of the rainbow to mark
International Day against Homophobia, Transphobia
and Biphobia.

Jeremy Fleming, Director GCHQ at the time of its centenary in 2019.

On 31 October 2018 GCHQ launched its Instagram account with this photograph – two years after becoming the first UK intelligence agency to join Twitter – to give people a chance to see behind the scenes at the organisation.

Her Majesty Queen Elizabeth II unveils a commemorative plaque on 14 February 2019, during GCHQ's centenary year, to mark the first home of GC&CS at Watergate House.

His Royal Highness The Prince of Wales and Jeremy Fleming, Director GCHQ, watch a special flypast by the Royal Air Force Aerobatic Team – the Red Arrows – over GCHQ's Cheltenham Headquarters on 12 July 2019 to mark its centenary year.

fear, stink, and occasional action, mostly involving a few men across metres and minutes.

During the first phase of Konfrontasi, in Borneo during 1963, several attacks by Chinese or Malay volunteers overseen by Indonesian Special Services surprised small police or military posts. Oddly enough, large Commonwealth forces were always in the vicinity. They quickly destroyed or expelled these infiltrators – killing far more men than they lost – and denied them local support. Probably Comint inspired these deployments by showing that attacks were imminent in specific areas, without precisely indicating where and when, as with the Dutch experience a few years before.

In 1964, Comint helped to wreck two campaigns with precision. Special Services and the Indonesian air force, marines and navy undertook the maritime or airborne insertion of volunteers and irregulars from Sumatra to Malaya, while the Indonesian Army raided Borneo with regulars and irregulars. These efforts required surprise for success – all were vulnerable to interception or pre-emption. In Borneo, Britain poured Claret, maximising its strengths by using a blend of Comint and seasoned soldiers offensively against the crust of Indonesian forces on the Borneo frontier. Sukarno's means to threaten Britain became hostages to fortune. Indonesian attacks declined; regularly ambushed, their forces on the frontier began to move over to the defensive and towards demoralisation. Commonwealth mortars and artillery hit men moving to forward positions and aided ambushes. Indonesian units were ordered to halt every British incursion, while being careful to avoid enemy tricks; indeed.[145]

Britain wrecked attacks on Malaya and Singapore in one of the best-recorded campaigns of counter-terrorism. Indonesian Special Services ordered infiltrators to build liberated zones in Malaya and terrorists to strike Kuala Lumpur and Singapore. It did not foment the race riots between Chinese and Malay peoples which shook Singapore during 1964, but immediately strove to exploit and deepen divisions between the two communities.[146] Infiltrators, acting as though disaffected members of the population, should target both economic targets and the authority of the government of Malaysia itself.[147] Instead, during 1964, British forces intercepted Indonesian forces in international waters or airspace. Warships blocked infiltrations, capturing forty-one sampans running guns and carrying infiltrators, and deterred many more. The RAF intercepted aircraft, causing some to crash in the Straits of Malacca and killing their cargo of parachutists, and others to abort missions. The few infiltrators who landed were surrounded immediately by Commonwealth and Malaysian forces and crushed. Malaysian security caught ships at sea and infiltrators at customs posts and wrecked subversive 'reception committees' which were expected to guide infiltrators to safety.

As its efforts and allies failed, Indonesian Special Services looked desperately for further friends, such as triads from Hong Kong. It strove to contact the Malayan Communist Party, crushed in the Malayan emergency and now becalmed in southern Thailand.[148] Infiltrators tasked with disposing of enemy leaders were able to conscript anyone they came across who might be useful, though, in the event of doubts about their loyalty, the conscripts might be killed.[149] Recriminations arose from the rot. The Indonesian navy refused to support Indonesian Special Services.[150] The latter believed that criticism of their lack of success 'might be motivated by enemies within' or rivals in Jakarta who were, consciously or unconsciously, obstructing 'A' operations.[151]

Comint drove the greatest Indonesian defeats in this campaign, as when a hundred Indonesian soldiers and infiltrators landing at Pontian in Malaya were captured in August 1964, and when the British frigate HMS *Ajax* seized sixty-one infiltrators on Christmas Eve 1964.[152] Indonesia's only intelligence on these disasters were reports from the BBC, Malaysian newspapers, or the few survivors who returned. Morale among infiltrators-to-be crashed. One Indonesian Special Services officer noted that his men were affected by Radio Malaysia broadcasting an interrogation of a captured Indonesian Lieutenant Sutikno.[153] Sutikno's messages, believed by some Indonesian officers to be a shameful betrayal, became central to Malaysian propaganda.

By January 1965, realising that every raid of recent months had failed, Special Services abandoned large ones. It returned to small attacks, which faded to nothing.[154] Comint let Commonwealth and Malaysian forces crush all major operations, but not all small ones, including the murder of three civilians at MacDonald House in Singapore on 10 March 1965. These attacks, while personal tragedies, were politically irrelevant. They did not affect Indonesian aims to split Singapore from Malaysia – not that this trend needed reinforcement. The difficulty of attacking Singapore and Malaya, and the disasters that Indonesians tolerated before abandoning their efforts to do so, show the significance which they placed on these targets, and of British success against them.

Meanwhile, focused by Comint, Commonwealth and Malaysian forces punctured all Indonesian-liberated zones like balloons. Indonesians preferred that large forces establish such zones, but also sought to do so through small bodies which tried to regularise supplies and intelligence before embarking on combat.[155] Special Services and the army routinely reported that local populations refused to cooperate with them due to fear of Britain and opposition to Indonesia. For example, one Indonesian raid failed because it could not find a target. At least some of the local population was suspected of active help to 'the enemy' while among the rest there was no willingness to provide any support at all.[156] Britain's tactical ability to destroy pockets of men and wreck small operations crippled Indonesian strategy.

These failures weakened Sukarno and his allies in Jakarta and intimidated his generals and admirals. During the Sunda Straits incident of September 1964, a small Royal Navy force deliberately crossed international waters bisecting Indonesia to symbolise the country's vulnerability. Indonesian forces issued a war alert and considered the danger of hostilities.[157] One provincial military command warned that Britain might launch Gulf of Tonkin-like raids without declaring war.[158] Special Services insisted that its operations must not give Britain a pretext for war. Tovey later noted that Comint revealed Indonesian reluctance to risk escalation.[159] When the British read communications between Sukarno and his ambassadors about Britain, the JIC noted: 'Our recent actions impressed them far more than any word could have done.'[160] The deputy Chief of the Defence Staff, Vice Admiral Norman Denning, said that 'the principal Indonesian fear in recent weeks had been that we might mount an attack upon them and Sukarno was known to have asked his attachés in Western Capitals to report on our intentions'. Yet Sukarno still might escalate the crisis. Denning recommended diplomatic means to press Sukarno towards de-escalation, which the Foreign Office thought unlikely. The interdepartmental 'Joint Confrontation Department' noted 'the large number of peace feelers being put out by the Indonesians in almost every quarter of the globe', yet warned that 'we must retain the military deterrent which had in itself been the cause of these peace feelers, which were really nothing more than probes to detect cracks in the deterrent. None had apparently been detected so far and it was therefore a nice question of judgement as to whether it would be desirable to increase this deterrent at this particular moment, and run the risk of being considered provocative. It was primarily a question of timing.'[161] The British Ambassador to Indonesia, Andrew Gilchrist, agreed that Indonesian leaders, 'now visualised as a distinct possibility offensive action by the United Kingdom if there were a repetition of Indonesian operations such as the recent air drops into Malaya', but still 'would continue covert subversive and infiltration activities, which cost them comparatively little, since they believed that in the longer term the United Kingdom would wish to liquidate their expensive commitments in the Far East'. Britain had no means to avoid a long stalemate. British military and political authorities accepted this hard logic.[162]

Britain and Malaysia outmanoeuvred Sukarno in diplomacy, overcoming the international politics of anti-colonialism and delegitimising Konfrontasi in Asian and international politics. Yet still Indonesia escalated. Sukarno ordered Special Services to increase the level of confrontation effort in Malaysia and Singapore, and the army to do likewise in Borneo.[163] Between October 1964 and January 1965, Comint noted a national intensification of Konfrontasi, the intentions to send 16,000 volunteers and three brigades (12,000 soldiers) to Borneo, and the actual deployment of formations and units. These forces practised airborne and amphibious assaults and developed the infrastructure necessary for major attacks. Special Services and the army warned units that British forces might attack them and raised the prospect of direct contact, though generally emphasising the need to avoid that threshold. Major conferences in Borneo and Jakarta discussed how to use these forces.[164] Operations by Special Services reached their peak while the army seemed to be readying itself for unprecedented actions. They pursued liberated zones both in Malaya and Sarawak. Commonwealth intelligence foresaw a crisis. DSD concluded that: 'Though Indonesian intentions have frequently run ahead of their capacity for fulfilment, there is body of opinion that present build-up will cause logistic problems forcing either early attack or withdrawal of forces. All evidence points to intention to attack in some form. We therefore have to cover next six months period on assumption that we shall have short (we hope) limited war within that period.'[165]

Tovey warned that current Indonesian strength against north Borneo equalled three to four battalions, or 2,000 men. Indonesia planned to add another twelve to fourteen battalions, to 12,000 men. Precise Indonesian intentions were unknown, but this expansion would let them 'increase the scale and depth of their cross-border incursions', create a 'psychological weapon against Malaysia and her allies', and even to launch a major incursion into Borneo.[166]

These British expectations reflected Sukarno's hopes. In an unpredictable turn, however, the Indonesian army refused to act fully on them. It feared British power and the danger of war, especially as Britain escalated its actions. Instead, Comint showed that, rather than exploiting enemy losses on Claret operations for propaganda purposes, Indonesian units rarely mentioned Claret attacks, and reported imaginary actions in which British units had been annihilated.[167] Indonesian forces buried Gurkha dead outside their own military cemeteries without military honours. In February 1965, Britain authorised attacks up to 10,000 yards across the Indonesian border, and reinforced Walker's command. These developments had consequences for Sigint. Tovey reported that when he and Director DSD visited Borneo, 'with a singular but none the less refreshing lack of inhibitions, Commander West Brigade, GSO 1 (Int), DOBOPS and COMLANDBOR all referred to the vital need for Sigint, both before and after the event in the context of their greatly expanded scope for cross-border operations'.[168] Tovey held that: 'the struggle in BORNEO is being very largely fought (and so far contained) on the basis of the sound, rapid intelligence which SIGINT alone provides. Unless SIGINT can provide an efficient service, of the same kind as it is providing now, on the vastly larger complex of communications targets presented by the build-up of Indonesian forces troops in KALIMANTAN, the military consequences – and indeed the political implications – could be extremely serious.'[169]

Commonwealth Sigint on Borneo had ten Morse and two voice positions. They needed to immediately receive four more Morse and one voice position. If Indonesian forces developed more sophisticated command and control for a force approaching a division in size, another four Morse stations would be needed.[170] DOBOPS would provide weekly reports to commanders and Siginters at Singapore on Claret and Comint, including Indonesian reactions to attack. He would warn of every proposed mission, so DSD and UKF 200 could provide 'any relevant intelligence on the strength, dispositions, etc. of enemy forces in the target area ... without delay ... at suitable precedence to DOBOPS/JFHQ'.[171] These actions enabled the Commonwealth successes of 1965, which wrecked Indonesian forces on the frontier, broke their nerve and deterred attacks on Malaya. British intimidation of Indonesia shaped the revolution which occurred in Jakarta in autumn 1965. Against this, the prospect that Singapore and Brunei might join Malaysia collapsed.

The Wilson government reacted rationally to these developments. It understood that Britain's initial strategic aims were impossible, yet defined victory of a sort. 'Our long-term aim is a reasonably non-aligned, stable and viable Indonesia, with which Malaysia and Singapore can live peacefully. Any tolerable approximation to this ideal requires an end to confrontation, other than by surrender.'[172] Britain achieved this end. After negotiations in 1966, Indonesia abandoned Konfrontasi and recognised Malaysia. In turn, Britain withdrew from Borneo. Tovey warned that Britain could not rebuild its Sigint capabilities there easily, or at all.[173] Britain promised to defend Malaya from attack, but not necessarily Borneo, where elections would determine if the population wished to join Malaysia. Britain took a calculated gamble, which accepted an outside prospect that Malaysia might collapse. Indonesian intentions and actions were unpredictable. As DOBOPS intelligence noted, 'all Indonesians tend to allow their emotions to overcome their reason', while 'the Eastern mind' worked unlike the Western one.[174] The JICFE held that Indonesia wished 'to disrupt Malaysia, or at least to bring its government into a state of subservience to Indonesian wishes, using chiefly political and subversive means'. Indonesians dreamed of conquering north Borneo, but probably in vain. The JIC in London varied from believing Indonesia does 'not intend to indulge in external adventures for a long time to come', to holding:

> that the Indonesians have called off military operations for the moment; that they are more likely to use propaganda and bribery than sabotage or attacks on security forces in order to influence the forthcoming elections; and that as long as the present Indonesian Government remains in control and their economic difficulties persist, they are unlikely to use military force on a large scale either in a direct attack or as the last phase of a long term plan to separate the Borneo territories from Malaysia.[175]

Tovey called Konfrontasi, a 'classic example of safe but effective use of Sigint', with 'superb service' in processing, 'efficient welding' with other sources, and 'admirable caution and readiness to abide strictly by our action-on rules in use of our material'.[176] Examples from the campaign illustrate this fusion, which did not entirely follow Tovey's formulation. During 1964–65, Special Services supported local Chinese communists to infiltrate the western corner of Sarawak, where much of the population was Chinese and communist organisation was powerful. This combination continued into 1966, even though the Indonesian army was slaughtering the largely Chinese PKI in Java. Indonesia pressed Malaysia militarily as the two states negotiated an end to Konfrontasi and communists hoped to establish a liberated zone. In February 1966, guided by intelligence, 600 Commonwealth and Gurkha soldiers waited in depth along the Serian Road, in the Tebedu region, where Indonesians planned to pass three platoons in sequence. When the first echelon was crushed, Indonesia abandoned its plan and formulated another. In later months, human intelligence, especially Special Branch, reported an imminent incursion to Bau district. Sigint identified the time, extent and range of these operations, their armament, approach routes and orders. That military authorities in Jakarta planned these operations showed their political significance. DOBOPS analysed this evidence well. Deployment of forces to the anticipated approach routes faced no 'action-on' problem; Humint provided adequate plausible cover. Even more, the commander of West Brigade noted, his men lived in an atmosphere of war. 'No one here is the least suspicious if I make plans against their use anywhere on my front. I have even been accused recently by Police and my COs of being smug about this threat.' Eight hundred Commonwealth soldiers covered every expected approach route in depth. Thirty-six infiltrators in two groups crossed the border on 4 June, almost exactly to the day and within the area DOBOPS expected. One group, claiming to have been hit on the frontier, and perhaps struck by mortars or artillery, withdrew immediately. Between 15 and 24 June, Australians thrice ambushed the other group. Most were killed and captured, the rest chivvied back to Indonesia. Many Chinese civilians, perhaps communist cadres, were arrested alongside infiltrators.[177]

Comint has driven few campaigns so much as Konfrontasi. Lea held that without Comint he would have needed another twenty to thirty battalions to succeed in Borneo – triple the size of his command, which would have been impossible for Britain to provide.[178] Comint increased certainty about enemy operations and its immediate to medium-term intentions. This knowledge let Britain deploy its forces effectively, especially by pre-empting the Indonesian expansions in Borneo during 1964 and 1965. By monitoring the state of readiness and movements of Indonesian ships and aircraft – just like the British Grand Fleet had with the German fleet in the First World War – Comint eased the wear on the RAF and Royal Navy. In tactical terms, Comint increased the ratio of successful contacts and reduced risk and wasted effort. Tiny forces acted surgically on the basis of accurate Sigint, inflicting massively one-sided damage, stalling any enemy successes and crippling the morale of Indonesian units and commanders. This, the most remarkable success of Claret, feels strikingly modern – like the use of unmanned aerial vehicles (UAVs) and special forces against mobile insurgents over the past decade.

Yet Comint had its limits. It could not reveal Indonesian strategic intentions, which turned on a political struggle. Comint could not reveal Sukarno's intentions directly, though it did so in effect by following military orders or his messages with ambassadors. No intelligence source could penetrate the convoluted high politics in Jakarta, especially when British actions contributed to a revolution there. As the JIC Far East noted: 'Even the more practicable Indonesian plans have an element of fantasy: they normally plan for operations on a lavish scale, but only a small proportion are actually put into effect.'[179] Konfrontasi was more bluster than force: a puppet show. The Commonwealth build-up of 1965 rested on a worst-case idea of Indonesian intentions, though British actions frightened the Indonesian army into rejecting its orders. British authorities did not understand what the Indonesian army intended in 1966. They always overestimated the unity of Indonesian decision-makers and the coherence of their strategy.

Any interpretation of the evidence, including orders to conduct 'terrorism', is conjectural to some degree. Translations can be tested only against the original messages in Indonesian archives, which may not be possible for decades, if ever. IRSIG prevented thorough documentation on how Comint was interpreted. Enough evidence remains to solve that general problem, but some matters are still unclear. Indonesian officials certainly feared internal security problems and thought Britain or Malaysia manipulated them that way. These states may have done so, perhaps guided by Comint, which showed that Indonesia was feeling the strain. Indonesian operational reports were generally factual and honest. They reported Indonesian casualties with detail, which aided battle damage assessment for Britain. When compared with the reports from their own units, British commanders understood the attritional exchange well, unlike Americans in Vietnam. Reports often mentioned the morale of attackers in positive and negative terms, and suggested problems among the Chinese and Malay allies which Indonesians sought to move across the frontier. However, some Indonesian reports from the front lines, and many which commanders in Borneo sent to Jakarta or to their subordinates, reported imaginary actions or distorted British losses in real ones. They rated Commonwealth forces as mediocre, with poor morale. British analysts and commanders had to guess why such reports were issued and whether they were believed. Perhaps Indonesian authorities exaggerated their actions? Did they feel that lies alone could maintain the morale of their subordinates, and the trust of their superiors? In a prolonged struggle of political and military attrition, these questions mattered. Comint could not answer them.

So What?

The Labour Minister for Defence during Konfrontasi, Denis Healey, rightly called it 'a textbook demonstration of how to apply economy of force, under political guidance for political ends'.[180] In particular, 'the CLARET operations were highly successful from all points of view. They were indeed most carefully planned and reflect the greatest credit on all those who carried them out both on the staff and in the field'. John Grandy, Commander-in-Chief Far East between 1965 and 1967, thought 'the whole 900 mile border area was totally and completely dominated by our forces and that Indonesia had a very great fear of the border. All operations were proceeded by meticulous and most careful planning, training and practice. Hazardous operations in appalling conditions of terrain, jungle and climate were successfully carried through not only by SAS specialists but by many line British regiments and Marines Commandos, as well as Gurkhas. These operations provided a tremendous fillip to morale and there were countless examples of heroism, tenacity, courage, and fine junior leadership.'[181]

This campaign was marvellous, and myth-making. Healey and Walker held that Britain conducted counterinsurgency far better than did the United States in the Vietnam war, which would have gained (and perhaps won) by adopting British practices.[182] Indeed, here, as in the Malayan emergency, British intelligence and counterinsurgency were excellent, and better than American practices in Vietnam. However, the North Vietnamese Army was stronger and better than the Indonesian one. It would have smashed efforts based on these British models and force levels, and would have turned low-level insurgency into high-intensity battle. Nor could Claret have been poured in Vietnam. NSA provided little help to American attacks (larger, but less precise and successful than those of Claret) on the Ho Chi Minh trail – the supply conduit from North to South Vietnam, via Laos and Cambodia.[183] Superiority in Comint would have strengthened these attacks, but not enough to win the war.

Again, Healey, Walker and other authorities held that Claret sparked the collapse of Sukarno and Konfrontasi. These claims have some truth, but require perspective. During 1964–65, Claret and British diplomacy stalled Indonesia in a losing position, which it dared not escalate. Britain's escalations of summer 1964 and spring 1965 intimidated the Indonesian army. The latter also began negotiations for compromise with Malaysian leaders, which both sides hid from Sukarno and Britain.[184] The PKI used the stalemate to challenge the army, and demand arms for a militia under its control. These developments ratcheted the strains which wrecked Sukarno's regime: they drove him to the PKI, and the latter to demands which frightened the generals, who would strike only if struck. When the generals did strike, they killed hundreds of thousands of PKI members and civilians, abetted to some degree by Britain and the United States, though this game was bound to end in blood, no matter who won the throne.

Yet the effect of any penultimate cause on an event is easy to overestimate. For Britain and Indonesia, Konfrontasi simply intensified strains which stemmed from other matters, rather than created new ones. An incompetent coup on 1 October 1965 by some communist leaders and officers triggered the implosion. Had the coup not happened or been competent, Sukarno might have won the internal struggle and thus his external one. In prolonged wars of attrition, victory goes to he who lasts the final quarter of an hour. During 1965, as Britain contained

Konfrontasi, relations between Singapore and Malaya collapsed, and with them the strategic value of Malaysia to Britain. Singapore could no longer be a cheap and secure base. When Singapore left Malaysia in August 1965, Sukarno proclaimed victory; he might have secured one had his regime lasted another year. Britain considered abandoning its policy towards Indonesia, constrained only by the need not to lose prestige, nor to antagonise Australia, New Zealand and the United States. Six weeks later, the tables turned, and blood was spilled.

The battlefield successes of Comint and Claret shaped the near-run power politics of Konfrontasi. They ensured that strains intensified on Indonesia more than Britain, by calming British fears, and raising those in Jakarta. Comint and Claret bought time to contain the contradictions between American and British policy, and British politicians and generals; and to lead elements within the PKI and military to believe they must strike the generals; and to drive Sukarno against his soldiers and the United States, while unifying the latter. Konfrontasi was a case of the dog which did not bark in the night: something which mattered less than it might have done. Comint and Claret silenced the dog.

For Britain, Konfrontasi was a tactical triumph with mixed strategic results: a failure, but not a disaster, for its power, and a success for decolonisation. The real confrontation was not between Britain and Indonesia but, rather, factions in 'Indonesia' and 'Malaysia', imagined countries struggling to be born. 'Malaysia' won because the Tunku outmanoeuvred his rivals abroad. A subalterns' revolt against Britain and Sukarno drove the outcome. Comint and Claret enabled Britain secretly, and cheaply, to defeat Indonesian policy without alienating Indonesia, but not to achieve the victory it pursued. Malaysia could be created only through a shotgun marriage between Malaya and four brides. Two blushed, and two refused the veil. Differences between politicians and peoples, not Konfrontasi, pushed Singapore and Brunei away from Malaysia and drove a stake into the heart of British strategy. Indonesian generals and Malaysian leaders outflanked Britain and Sukarno through secret negotiations. They could find a modus vivendi, so long as both their masters were eliminated.

These defections led Britain to conclude that a cheap and secure presence at Singapore was untenable. That conclusion shaped the abandonment of Britain's greatest aim in the campaign: the maintenance of its position east of Suez and its status as a world power, though economic, political and military trends really drove that outcome. When imperialism became philanthropy, Britain counted its change. Defeat in Konfrontasi helped the generals to seize Indonesia, but not the adjacent ex-colonies of Britain, which secured Britain's secondary aim: a peaceful and stable transfer of power. The consequence of Konfrontasi is the success of Brunei, Malaysia, Singapore and Papua New Guinea. That this last battle of the British empire in Asia was a brilliant victory obscures its significance. Failure at Suez hastened the end of empire perhaps by a year. Victory in Konfrontasi lengthened it by not one day.

Sigint and the Falklands Conflict

Origins and Impulse

The Falklands conflict was the last British imperial campaign and the first battle in a new age of Sigint. For both Argentina and Britain, the Falkland Islands were a minor issue involving major principles. Argentina claimed sovereignty over the islands. Britain maintained that 1,820 anglophone islanders had rights to national self-determination. The resulting war began by fluke, and was dominated by it. Margaret Thatcher's government bungled its policy towards the matter, partly because the Argentine junta also did so. In 1981, Britain told Argentina that only if the Falklands population accepted rule by Buenos Aires – which all thought unlikely – could Britain accept that outcome. The JIC concluded that Argentina might respond by invading the islands. Argentine armed forces were large and competent; 'Fortress Falklands', a British garrison able to withstand them, was almost impossible to maintain, given other British commitments.[185]

During early 1982, the junta publicly demanded that it gain sovereignty over the islands. Whitehall dithered and increased the problem by planning to slash the British sea power assets which defended the islands. Nor did the JIC raise Argentina's low place on its priorities. These decisions tempted fate, and disaster. In April 1982, the Argentine junta seized the Falkland Islands impulsively, to score a victory which would stabilise its political position at home. The junta assumed that Britain could not and would not retaliate. That assumption would have been true within a few months, had Britain carried out its plans to sell the ships which became essential to victory. In 1982, however,

Britain still had the power needed to retake the islands, and a prime minister determined and desperate enough to use it. Failure to retake the Falklands would wreck Britain's status as a power and Thatcher's as a politician.[186]

In simple terms, had the Falkland Islands been a hundred miles closer to the South American mainland, they would have become Las Malvinas. Britain would have lost the war and probably not even attempted it in the first place. In contrast, had the islands been a hundred miles further offshore, Britain could have won almost bloodlessly. One-sided superiority in Sigint was fundamental to British success in this war, which was a more close-run thing in general than most realise. Without Sigint, Britain might have lost, though many other factors also might have caused defeat. Argentina might have won the war had its air forces possessed twenty Exocet anti-ship missiles instead of five – and trained with them; or primed their iron bombs to detonate properly during attacks on Royal Navy ships at San Carlos Sound – instead of failing to explode or passing through ships before they did. The main causes of British victory were the quality of British forces and, once the conflict started, of its military and political leaders.

Argentina had no rational plans for war against Britain in 1982. Though its air force was decent in quality, it had never prepared to fight warships. Its initial attacks were its first tests in the area. Argentine air force and navy aircraft lacked the infrastructure needed to attack warships effectively, having few air tankers to extend the range of attacking aircraft, or reconnaissance platforms to guide them onto targets. This inexperience caused the bad priming of bombs which lost the fruits of self-sacrifice at San Carlos Sound. The Argentine army was poor and those on the Falklands among the worst. They were unready for battle, raw recruits missing massive amounts of necessary kit. The Argentine navy, its warships half obsolete, half modern, was also unprepared for war. A few weeks at sea in a South Atlantic autumn eroded its quality, as mechanical failures sent one warship after another back to port for repairs. Perhaps these failures of their own led Argentine admirals to underestimate how a well-prepared navy could handle such conditions.

The Argentine admirals wanted war. They pursued aggressive, ambitious and unachievable plans. British strategists too were stunned; they had thought little about to how to fight such a war, for which Britain had decided no longer to prepare. In the event, Britain conducted a campaign at the extreme level of possibility, which only one other country – the United States –, could have mounted, though more easily.

Britain sent Task Force 317 (TF 317) south in several echelons. Two nuclear and four conventionally powered submarines took the lead, followed by eight destroyers, fifteen frigates and two aircraft carriers, *Hermes* and *Invincible*. This Carrier Battle Group had few escorts, which also had to defend other valuable units. It was unusually vulnerable to all forms of assault in ways which British planners both understood and misconstrued. Behind them, amphibious groups carried two brigades on transports, accompanied by landing assault ships and flotillas of supply and auxiliary vessels. In blue water, this fleet would have overwhelmed the Argentine navy. In green and brown water it was vulnerable to airstrikes. British authorities anticipated '25 per cent battle attrition of naval, and maritime air forces', including ten Sea Harrier fighter aircraft, twenty-two to twenty-seven other aircraft, an aircraft carrier, a nuclear submarine, four destroyers and frigates, and eight support vessels. Of these losses, the carrier, two surface warships and five support vessels nominally could be repaired.[187]

These academic and worse-case calculations were accurate about aircraft, but overstated the losses to warships and misunderstood the menace. Britain preserved its greatest assets, the carriers, by minimising their exposure to attack – and so reducing their use to the minimum necessary for victory. Submarines achieved their missions without loss. However, any warships exposed to aircraft suffered greater losses than expected. Argentine aircraft and warships had ship-killing weapons; British warships had weaknesses. Air and naval data links unified the sensor feeds from all parts of a unit – say, every radar on all ships in TF 317 – and gave each part the same overall sensor picture. No Western force had used data links in war, and much remained uncertain about their working. RAF and Royal Navy officers were inexperienced with data links; their failures to marry data links and properly organised radar to defensive weaponry aided Argentine air strikes. The RAF quickly overcame its mistakes by refitting platforms based in Britain, but warships deployed thousands of miles from home had to suffer until war was done. Inexperience with data links shaped the destruction of the Type 42 destroyer, HMS *Sheffield*, on 4 May 1982. In order to protect flotillas at sea, the Royal Navy made individual ships serve as radar pickets, acquiring data for the whole force, while advertising themselves to Argentine detection. Failures to coordinate radar collection to guide surface-to-air missiles crippled British anti-aircraft defence.[188]

Ethnocentrism affected assessments and estimates, albeit marginally. Tovey, by now Director of GCHQ, removed the phrase 'typically Latin' from one JIC assessment.[189] Nonetheless, British intelligence analysed Argentine capabilities well, if anything overstating them, save in one area: air attack at sea. That failure occurred because of divided responsibilities in green water, a tendency to overrate British capabilities in defence electronics and data links, and the focus on the threat posed by Argentine surface and submarine forces. Some British observers viewed Argentine air forces using a car-racing analogy: good drivers and mediocre pit crews. As a widely disseminated analysis noted in 1970: 'In general flying skill is of a good standard. Airmanship, however, could certainly be better if a high degree of self-discipline could be imposed. Patriotism, national spirit and bravery are undoubtedly marked in most officers and NCOs,' and concluding: 'The standard of training is relatively high both on the ground and in the air.'[190] The RAF assessed the Argentine air force well on issues of strength, quality of personnel, surge capacity, sortie rates and ability to handle attrition. It gained from the willingness of the French air force to let Harriers practise dogfights against Mirage fighters, learning lessons for free. French authorities also prevented the export of a key weapon to Argentine air forces, the Exocet anti-ship missile. The RAF, however, did not ask what would happen when Argentine aircraft struck British warships, other than to raise two key points: Argentine aircraft had not prepared for such actions; their quality here was unclear.[191]

Not unreasonably, the Royal Navy focused on blue water operations more than green. It thought the two modern Argentine submarines could endanger its carriers and nuclear-powered attack submarines (SSNs), as its four veteran ones also might do. British surface vessels were prepared for older Soviet missiles, but not the Exocet missiles based on Argentine (and British) aircraft and warships.[192] The Royal Navy boosted defences against Exocets for HMS *Illustrious*, the carrier under completion, the only platform it could materially upgrade and strengthen for war.[193] British planners understood that they were unprepared against Exocets, but misconstrued their menace. Exocet missiles, whether mounted on Super Etendard aircraft flying from aircraft carriers, or on surface warships, were dangerous, but electronic countermeasures (ECM) such as chaff could (and did) degrade their power. British planners addressed well how these technical and tactical issues would work in a fleet battle scenario. The one threat which the naval staff did not examine in detail was that which most inflicted harm during the war: opportunistic raids from land-based aircraft, whether Super Etendard or older Skyhawk, Dagger and Mirage aircraft, in green water close to shore. These older aircraft could be 'dealt with adequately' unless they were operating within 350 miles of their bases – as, unfortunately, occurred during the British landings.

These technical and interservice issues were multiplied because the military intelligence chief, the Deputy Chief of the Defence Staff (Intelligence) – DCDS (I) – was a soldier. General James Glover said that Argentine air forces 'have only an outside chance of inflicting severe damage' on the Task Force 317.[194] The naval staff thought Argentine radar 'generally poor', while that on the Task Force was good, though it 'may suffer from jamming'. It was 'well balanced' in anti-aircraft capability – 'Provided the Task Force is not too widely scattered, it has a very adequate AA defence capability.'

TF 317, alas, was extraordinarily scattered. The threat of Argentine aircraft was 'negligible' 700 nautical miles from any air base, but 'much greater' at 300 miles.[195] The RAF and Royal Navy each misunderstood tactical and technical capabilities in an area where neither service was the sole authority – how land-based Argentine aircraft and weapons systems would fare against British warships. They continued to underrate that danger until HMS Sheffield was sunk. Even when planning the invasion two days later, the worst-case view was that Britain might lose two or three warships.[196] Instead, Britain lost four warships – with many more crippled and only prevented from destruction by Argentine inexperience – along with several assault and supply ships.

TF 317 avoided the worst consequences of this situation by keeping its carriers far east of the islands, save when launching an attack. Had Argentina crippled one of the carriers before the British landing, the counter-invasion probably would have failed. Only the twenty Sea Harrier 'jump jets' initially carried by the British fleet (joined by eight more by mid-May) could defend it and the amphibious force and, along with fourteen other RAF Harriers, hope to achieve air superiority. The Argentine air force and navy had 130 fighters and bombers able to attack the fleet from the mainland and operate over the Falklands, and a dozen less effective Pucará ground-attack aircraft based on the islands. These aircraft were badly maintained, ground crew made errors, and aircrew could operate for just a few minutes over targets – yet every ship in TF 317 was at risk within their reach. To get men and supplies ashore and forwards was a difficult task for the British. After these perils had been surmounted, invading ground forces must cross arduous terrain and defeat an enemy numerically equal and dug in, albeit an enemy correctly presumed to be inferior in quality. As Glover said, 'aggressive attrition' could wreck 'the crucial and most vulnerable element in the Argentine defence': the morale of untrained conscripts, marooned far from home.[197] This best part of British analysis was the key to its desperate victory.

GCHQ records, and its history of the Falklands conflict, frequently mention diplomatic intelligence, though often in vague terms – such as 'a message which reflected the Junta's thinking on future UK action' which had fifty words redacted.[198] The GCHQ history of the Falklands conflict frequently mentions diplomatic intelligence, especially about British efforts to block arms shipments to Argentina. Politicians and diplomats carefully followed intelligence reports as a key part of the broad war effort.[199] Initially, this Comint overwhelmed the FCO which, GCHQ thought, 'were not equipped to deal with such volumes'. By May, the FCO received 'about 1,100 items of SIGINT a week on the Falklands crisis'.[200]

Diplomacy was central to this war. To enable TF 317 to sail, and to keep that support as war began, Britain needed to convince other states that Argentina was in the wrong. Unprovoked Argentine aggression alone let Britain overcome the politics of anti-imperialism and achieve these ends. That the local population wanted rescue affected public views in the Five Eyes, but nowhere else. UN Security Council Resolution 502 demanded that Argentina evacuate the Falkland Islands and negotiate with Britain over their status, while avoiding hostilities. Britain, invoking Article 51 of the UN Charter, then dispatched the Task Force in self-defence. Yet this diplomatic success was fragile and became eroded once the Argentine cruiser *General Belgrano* was sunk and Argentina finally took diplomacy seriously. The JIC warned that 'intelligence was needed on the positions, secret and public, of foreign governments. In this context, public positions might be the more important.' GCHQ produced 'evidence that Argentineans are keen to present a more favourable image in W. European nations', while 'the Argentines were considering whether to call a meeting of the Security Council'.²⁰¹

The more militarily successful Britain was, the more even its friends wanted it to negotiate on unfavourable terms. That diplomatic tension drove the need for speed in operations felt by the War Cabinet and all senior commanders, especially two politically desperate actors: Prime Minister Thatcher and the Royal Navy. Diplomatic Comint mattered as much as its military counterpart to Thatcher's strategy, and more tempered her will. As the Foreign Secretary, Francis Pym, wrote to GCHQ: 'Timely intelligence has been of the essence during the past few weeks, and I have been deeply impressed by the speed and efficiency with which you have responded to the demands placed upon you to provide us with comprehensive signals intelligence coverage of all aspects of the dispute ... The overall contribution you have made to our efforts ... has been very substantial indeed, and I know the Prime Minister shares my gratitude.'²⁰²

But in diplomatic terms, even Britain's allies were lukewarm. Without the personal support of a few statesmen, particularly François Mitterrand, Ronald Reagan and Caspar Weinberger, their countries might have offered Britain little help. Many American agencies kept their distance from Britain, save those which mattered: those under the military, particularly the US Navy. American agencies cultivated good relations with Argentina as part of its struggle for influence in Latin America, especially against Cuba and Nicaragua. Aid to Britain would wreck those relations, and damage those in Latin America. GCHQ was reluctant to press NSA for support, not wishing to cause 'political embarrassment', or make it refuse a request because of politics in Washington.

Wrong-footing to War

The invasion, as Britain's able ambassador to the UN, Anthony Parsons, said, wrong-footed Britain. Argentina held the islands – it could lose them only by leaving, voluntarily or otherwise; Britain could win only by making Argentines leave through threat or violence. Miscomprehension shaped actions. Each side pursued credibility; neither had it at the outbreak of war. The COS did not understand how much force was needed to retake the islands – in part because that was not Britain's initial aim – and barely reached a minimum strength for success. Britain had to build credibility and take belligerent actions, which would both strengthen and weaken its diplomatic position. Soon after the crisis began, Defence Secretary John Nott said: 'Our submarines were now committed to the blockade. We should soon have to consider whether it was right to allow Argentinean naval vessels to leave port. [The American Secretary of State] Mr. Haig commented that if Argentinean ships did leave port, and nothing happened, British credibility would suffer. He had already received some information suggesting that the Argentinians did not believe that we meant to fight.'[203] In addition, Thatcher was warned that Argentine counsels were divided: 'The Navy were looking for a fight. The Air Force did not want a war. The Army were somewhere in between.'[204] Sigint shaped some of the interminable debates, such as whether Argentine submarines had entered the Exclusion Zone.[205]

Though war was the most likely outcome, Britain preferred a negotiated settlement, on humanitarian and realist grounds. In the first week after invasion, military planning centred on re-establishing posture and presence. A beachhead in the Falklands would strengthen Britain's hand in the negotiations which external pressure would surely make Argentina entertain. These attitudes changed only when Thatcher decided that if Argentine forces did not withdraw, Britain must force them out. Yet the Iron Lady was no desiccated calculating machine: after *Sheffield* and *Belgrano* were sunk, Thatcher wept for the dead, whose ends she had shaped. She deplored, she said, the:

> most awful waste of young life if we really have to go and take those
> islands … We have more respect for young life than they do. But
> the resolve will still be there but I just feel that absolutely everything
> should be done to make it absolutely clear that in the end it is they
> who have no respect for young life … and they have to matter.
> And in the end they'll fight for ideals … I will do everything before
> the final decision has to be taken to see if we can uphold the rule
> of international law and the liberty and justice in which I believe
> passionately for our people to see if we can stop a final battle.[206]

Spooked by memories of Suez, civil servants and admirals warned of Britain's tenuous diplomatic and military position. Frank Cooper (PUS to the Minister of Defence) emphasised that unconsidered actions, perhaps involving a few deaths among Falkland civilians, 'might create such a backlash that Ministers might feel unable subsequently to authorise a landing ... the worst outcome would be for Ministers to have to stop the operation after it had started but before it was completed'. Armstrong warned of an even worse case: for Britain 'to be held responsible for the failure of diplomatic efforts to get a ceasefire and withdrawal agreement now and then not to be able to repossess the Falkland Islands: to end up either in a stalemate with continuing casualties and attrition ("Gallipoli") or in a withdrawal'. The First Sea Lord and Chief of the Naval Staff (CNS), Admiral Henry Leach; Admiral John Fieldhouse, Commander-in-Chief Fleet; and General Edwin Bramall, the Chief of the General Staff, also feared stalemate.[207]

Intelligence built certainty against fear. Antony Duff, the coordinator of the intelligence services for the Cabinet, told GCHQ: 'At this time, with the prospect of diplomatic negotiations continuing for at least a week or two, it is particularly important to obtain every scrap of intelligence we can about the advice, counsel and information being given to the Argentine government. In collection terms this means, I think ... issuing a very large proportion of relevant traffic ...'[208] Britain bent further in diplomacy than Argentina, accepting forms of words which could place the islands under temporary international control and might eventually give Argentina sovereignty over them, against the inhabitants' will. Ultimately, neither side would abandon its case in advance. Argentine diplomacy was mendacious, aimed to hamper British operations, and stubborn – it would only accept a settlement which guaranteed its sovereignty over the islands, rapidly. This diplomatic intransigence legitimised warlike British actions. British diplomats at the top of their game prevented Argentina from wrong-footing Britain again, as their countries waltzed to war.

GCHQ and the Outbreak of the Falklands Conflict

During 1976–77, Argentina had challenged Britain's claims to the Falkland Islands. The Labour government had responded with firm diplomacy, silently backed by deploying a nuclear-powered attack submarine and a ten-man GCHQ team to the area. This combination of force and intelligence trumped any likely Argentine attack, but Argentina did not know of their presence, and folded in the face of

British determination, rather than through deterrence. After these events, GCHQ declined to leave a permanent presence on the islands, which would have been difficult and expensive to deploy and maintain, and vulnerable to capture in case of invasion.[209] It also would not have shaped the outbreak of war in 1982 at all.

Before the 1982 crisis, the JIC had placed the Falkland Islands in 'Priority 4', the lowest group of intelligence priorities, alongside Brunei and below Belize, Gibraltar or Hong Kong. Among these dependencies, the Falklands were the least defended; indeed, defenceless. In 1981, the MOD's Defence Intelligence Staff (DIS) tried to place the islands in Priority 2, without noticeable effect on what the DCDS(I) later described as a 'complacent' level of collection and analysis effort.[210] These decisions were wrong, so too was GCHQ's belief that it would predict hostility in time to deter Argentine action. The 1982 crisis astonished GCHQ. Because of delays in receiving routine messages about the Falklands, it misconstrued the first signal received on the issue, on 20 March, from the only Royal Navy vessel in the South Atlantic.[211] HMS *Endurance*, with a small but unique Sigint capability, helped monitor the crisis from start to finish.[212] Just after the invasion, Tovey 'exploded' on hearing that *Endurance* would return for refuelling to Ascension Island. Glover, 'very apologetic', offered to find alternatives, the JIC adopted a 'no gap' policy, and a refuelling vessel was sent to *Endurance*.[213] For several weeks, unsupported by other British forces, it hid among icebergs from Argentine warships while intercepting unique elements of their traffic and sending it home. When, as war waned, Whitehall wished to withdraw *Endurance*, morale crashed among its crew, until GCHQ sent them well-deserved thanks for their work, and let them finish it.[214]

The crisis began on 19 March. Scrap-metal dealers from Buenos Aires, ostensibly searching for salvage but in truth looking to undermine British rule in the Falkland Islands, visited one of its uninhabited dependencies, South Georgia Island. There they raised an Argentine flag. For the next fortnight, matters escalated in a complex fashion. An Argentine vessel reached that island and withdrew most of the civilians. Secretly it left a dozen men behind, as Britain discovered through observation and Comint. British authorities accepted that they must tolerate Argentine force against islands associated with the Falklands, having allowed an Argentine presence on Southern Thule since 1977. Following a decade-old reflex regarding the Falklands, and fashionable ideas about rationality and 'escalation ladders' during crises, Britain reacted cautiously in order to avoid provocation and to buy time. Whitehall thought that crisis loomed, but it was months away – likely after a slow and rational process of escalation, focused first on negotiations, then on economic and diplomatic coercion from Argentina, but possibly reaching war within the year. Whitehall disassociated the flashpoint of South Georgia Island from the Falkland Islands. It overestimated the rationality of the Argentine junta and the pace of the unfolding crisis. Thatcher later said: 'It seemed utterly ridiculous to contemplate an invasion of the Falklands then.'[215] British diplomatic, military and political decision-makers were capable, and took good note of signals, but they fell victim to a classic failure of intelligence. Authorities saw what they expected to see, interpreting intelligence and actions within a schematic framework of how they thought a competitor must move. They overthought the game and misunderstood their rival. Whitehall thought the Argentines were climbing a ladder. The Argentines preferred to dance the tango.

Several factors bolstered these preconceptions until late in the day. Whitehall generally did not assess outbreaks of war well – except regarding the Warsaw Pact where its performance was decent. British authorities, ethnocentric and overly rational, projected their logic onto foreigners. In particular, reflecting the impact of nuclear deterrence, and the politics which impeded British use of force during decolonisation, authorities believed that states would start wars only with reluctance and when risks were low. They forgot their experiences with Hitler, Mussolini, Nasser and Sukarno when analysing the assessments and actions of foreigners. If authorities saw a threat, they assessed evidence on it well. If not, they were slow to see danger or to change preconceptions. The JIC buried evidence of specific threats in broad discussions of many issues, and monitored them badly. Outside priority areas, no JIC officer and few DIS officers were assigned to assess all the cumulative evidence on emerging problems. Only a startling piece of intelligence, or an alert analyst, could shake this complacency. A senior Siginter, Doug Nicoll, warned the JIC of these flaws, just as it repeated them in the Falklands crisis.[216] This failure was an extreme example of general problems.

Few people handled intelligence on the Falkland Islands, which slowed its processing and impact. Busy people not already focused on the area found the reportage hard to follow. Everyone was busy, nobody specialised. Most Argentine signals were opaque or minor, and many were garbled – incomprehensible until corrected days later. DIS, charged with basic analysis, had no specialist on the Falklands and only two officers tasked to handle Latin America, meaning one person at a time.[217] Ministers and senior officials were swamped with other important matters, including renegotiating the terms of Britain's nuclear deterrent with the United States. Often they were out of Britain and rarely in direct touch, hampering the personal liaison which dominated decision-making under Thatcher. Meanwhile, Argentine counsels remained divided. Their decision to invade the Falklands was impulsive and irrational, driven by factional rivalry and internal politics. The signals acquired by GCHQ reflected these ambiguities. British decision-makers reacted well to the first public statements which clearly contradicted their assumptions – but these were late in the day. Had Argentine leaders followed more conventional modes of aggression, nuclear-powered submarines might have reached the Falklands before the invasion, perhaps enabling it to be deterred.

GCHQ provided Whitehall's first and best warnings of Argentine intentions, and of changes in them, though diplomats provided useful and parallel analyses. GCHQ monitored Argentine signals, initially without concern. Naval exercises explained Argentine actions. On 25 March, however, GCHQ distributed a day-old message from the Argentine naval commander, Admiral Jorge Anaya. He reported that Britain wanted the scrap merchants removed from South Georgia, but that Britain recognised that to do so via force and HMS *Endurance* might inflame the Argentine public. Argentina agreed to withdraw them, but secretly intended to leave some civilians behind 'on the South Georgias. The MFA's objective is to exert pressure for an urgent meeting (on) the Falklands Group.' That message, GCHQ's only reflection of Argentine intentions before the invasion, suggested that Argentina would intensify pressure on South Georgia Island to break the diplomatic stalemate over the Falkland Islands. An Argentine naval message distributed alongside it described in detail British forces across the South Atlantic and Caribbean Sea, concluding: 'If there is any information, I shall give a daily routine 20 hours, update or when possible.'[218]

Scenting a crisis, GCHQ's Latin American codebreakers and traffic analysts immediately adopted twenty-four-hour shift work in order to solve and distribute signals quickly. This surge in procedure reduced the time required to process intercepts, from an average of forty-eight hours down to eighteen. It also led to frustratingly incomplete record-keeping about the times when GCHQ reports were distributed, which hampers analysis of how Sigint affected British actions on 31 March. Between 26 and 30 March, GCHQ reported Argentine naval preparations and assessments of British forces across the Atlantic. These messages could be explained as part of pressure on South Georgia Island. Quite which authorities saw what GCHQ reports, and precisely when, is impossible to know. Thus, the Anaya message immediately prompted analyses by DIS and the Foreign Office, but took days to reach the top. Thatcher probably saw only the most important of reports – as did the two ministers most involved with intelligence. Nott and Foreign Secretary Lord Carrington were caught with pressing and complex concerns, and were often travelling away from Britain. Nott's staff overlooked the evidence until it became unambiguous; so too did military and diplomatic subordinates. Referring to the Anaya signal, Fieldhouse later said, 'there was a rather more sensitive [message], it was a code word signal which I did not see at the time, and arguably need not have done, and I think that it had a strictly limited distribution and was somewhat later'.[219]

Each worrying GCHQ report caused authorities to think that Argentina had advanced one step up the escalatory ladder, until suddenly it leapt almost to the top. The signals showed Whitehall that a crisis was at hand, but reinforced the usual reflex to avoid provocation. By 24 March, Carrington told Thatcher that further negotiations over the Falkland Islands were 'unlikely'. A GCHQ solution of diplomatic traffic indicated 'that the Argentines may be prepared to take early actions to withdraw Argentine services to the islands' – that is, Argentina would take the first step on its escalatory ladder, to cut the commercial and air links which connected the islands with the world; and then follow each schematic stage of confrontation in sequence.[220] In the face of this danger, Carrington advocated only cautious and preparatory action. By 26 March, probably reflecting the Anaya message of two days prior, the Foreign Office told ministers that negotiations on the issue would be fraught, probably impossible. The MOD warned that to deter Argentina, possessing 'some of the most efficient armed forces in South America', would be expensive. To reconquer the Falkland Islands would be difficult or impossible. Thatcher underlined a minute written on this paper: 'Very gloomy.'²²¹

On Sunday 28 March, politicians suddenly took alarm. The cumulative effect of reports, perhaps including the Anaya message, led Thatcher to telephone Carrington at home and warn that the Argentine junta aimed to provoke a 'confrontation' over South Georgia Island. Around 7 a.m. on Monday 29 March, as Carrington and Thatcher met to fly from RAF Northolt, they concluded that Argentina would attempt to seize the island. In order to start building a negotiating position, they immediately asked Nott to send a nuclear-powered attack submarine to the region. He sent two, while Carrington asked for a third. The Royal Navy rejected that request, which would disrupt prior commitments to NATO. These submarines would not reach the theatre for two weeks. By 30 March, the MOD and FCO saw 'at present no sign' that Argentina intended to invade the Falkland Islands. The JIC doubted that it would do so imminently.²²² None thought an emergency was at hand. The naval attaché in Buenos Aires warned that a small Argentine invasion of East Falkland Island was possible, and asked GCHQ for any indicators of that issue. GCHQ could not confirm that danger, because no evidence supported it.²²³ A matter of hours later, GCHQ was able to show that Argentine forces were bound for Port Stanley, the capital of the Falkland Islands.

The central intelligence at this point – Anaya's message – was high-level, self-evident and reflected Argentine views – but of the previous week. Carrington, Nott and Thatcher thought their actions were prudent and timely. DIS and the JIC felt no need for new estimates. Events were moving as the last estimate predicted. Unfortunately, the junta changed its mind. Again, GCHQ was the first to detect the truth. At some time on 30 March, GCHQ distributed an Argentine order that the Type 209 diesel-electric submarine *Santa Fe* sail with remarkable caution, launch a 'reconnaissance of the beach and/or disembarkation (word garbled)', and then move twenty miles east of the San Felipe (or Pembroke) lighthouse, just off Port Stanley. Obviously, the beach being reconnoitred was in the Falkland Islands.²²⁴ This remarkable message might not have arrived until late evening on 30 March, but it would have been on a DIS desk at 0900, 31 March, alongside another one: the Argentine aircraft carrier, *Veinticinco de Mayo*, would receive special meteorological reports. On this basis, an alert DIS officer might have called the alarm several hours faster than actually occurred, though taking that action would not have changed the situation. No doubt desks were already inundated with paper. The 'beach reconnaissance' message did not mention Pembroke lighthouse: perhaps no one enquired where San Felipe was.

No one raised an alarm until late in the afternoon of 31 March, when GCHQ began a drumroll of alarming messages, collectively showing that Argentine warships would concentrate around Port Stanley on 2 April. The precise nature and sequence of reportage and analysis cannot be reconstructed. Only one, or perhaps two, messages, along with the 'beach reconnaissance' and the meteorological reports, can certainly be shown to have triggered the alarm. At 1436, GCHQ distributed a message showing that an Argentine auxiliary vessel was to take 'a position south of the Falkland Islands' and, at 1738, that 2 Marine Infantry Brigade would soon land somewhere. In the evening, but too late to shape British decisions, a cacophony of messages demonstrated that Argentina would invade the Falklands, and suggested details of the time and organisation of attack. Several messages on 31 March which cannot be timed also made that point; possibly some of these also shaped the first DIS warning, though probably not, so finely poised is the evidence.

That defence intelligence warning and key GCHQ reports reached military and diplomatic consumers just after 1800 on Wednesday 31 March. These messages, too obvious to need analysis, and strong enough to overcome the prospect of error, had among the most instantaneous and electric effects of any reports GCHQ has ever issued. While Nott was preparing a speech for the House of Commons on Britain's nuclear deterrent, aided by his Private Secretary, David Omand, DIS delivered two (or, just perhaps, three) reports from GCHQ about the Falklands, one of which was the 'beach reconnaissance' message.[225] The two men immediately recognised its meaning. They rushed to Mrs Thatcher's office at the House of Commons, followed by a stampede of ministers, officials and messengers carrying leather pouches with GCHQ reports, to discuss what she called 'this appalling piece of information'.[226]

All British calculations to date had been wrong. Argentina would seize the Falklands immediately. British authorities attempted to deter the threat, by raising the issue at the UN and asking President Reagan to warn off the leader of the Argentine junta, General Galtieri, but it was too late to matter. Britain was confronted with a choice between humiliation or war. As Thatcher recalled: 'That night no one could tell me whether we could retake the Falklands – no one. We did not know – we did not know.'[227] Nott and the DIS believed that Argentina had achieved a fait accompli to which Britain could not even respond. Ministers knew that inaction would create humiliation at home and abroad. Then, the First Sea Lord, Admiral Henry Leach – in full uniform – arrived in Thatcher's office unbidden, after having been detained and almost arrested by security in Parliament. He told Thatcher that Britain could send a large force to the islands quickly – and must do so, or suffer a decline in status. His assessment, drawn from instinct not intelligence – and Thatcher's nerve, spurred by outrage – drove another Reconquista.

GCHQ and the Falklands Conflict

Many decision-makers blamed Britain's inability to forestall invasion, in the words of Rear Admiral D. W. Brown, Assistant Chief of the Defence Staff (Operations), on 'an intelligence failure of the first order'. Beetham said, 'here we were badly let down'.[228] They were wrong. This was a failure of policy: neither to make the Falklands Islands population join Argentina, nor to deploy a permanent garrison able to deter attack and enable help to arrive. Neither approach was palatable before the invasion. Instead, Britain adopted a magical policy which assumed perfection both in operations and intelligence – the ability always to predict Argentine intentions in time to deploy a deterrent from the North Atlantic. Any mistake in timing could wreck this delicate hair-trigger policy. Britain made many mistakes, all of them minor. JIC's failures merely exemplified those of policy and decision-makers. On the other hand, GCHQ's performance during the crisis suggests that it would have enabled an effective response to anything but an impulsive action by Argentina, especially since ministers considered redeployment of sizable forces to the islands from the moment that they knew a crisis had opened. Only by 30 March did intelligence suggest imminent action against the Falkland Islands. Argentine authorities made that decision at 1915, 26 March. GCHQ detected that intention just days later, when Britain already was dispatching a deterrent. Conversely, even had Britain dispatched nuclear-powered attack submarines right after receiving the first *Endurance* signal, they could not have reached Stanley by 2 April. This gap was the fatal error in British assessment, foolhardy in so many ways. GCHQ performed well, and many other authorities tolerably, during the crisis. They could not save an incompetent policy.

GCHQ adjusted to these events with speed, turning *Titanic* on a tuppence, a practice in which it specialises. Before the crisis, 'good housekeeping' ensured that it was abreast of all major Argentine systems, which two linguists and traffic analysts kept on a 'care and maintenance' basis alongside other duties.[229] GCHQ did its job about Argentina better than any institution in Britain. Soon after Stanley fell, GCHQ circulated floods of deciphered Argentine traffic from high-frequency Morse, mainly naval, with less from the army and little from the air force. That pattern reflects the nature of Argentine communications which Britain could intercept, more than British success in cryptanalysis, with exceptions. Britain intercepted but could not break the communications between the garrison commander at Stanley, General Menendez, and his commanders at home. Though Argentine commands on the mainland signalled by landline, radio carried significant operational and strategic messages to forces in the Falklands, and at sea. Many of these messages – especially those of the Argentine Navy – unnecessarily addressed war plans and intentions. During the first month of the crisis, Argentine communications security was dismal. Argentine forces did not think about security until disaster struck, and then could not improve it. For Britain, the take matched Ultra at its best. Solutions were fast: during much of the crisis, on average the time between interception of encrypted traffic and dispatch to TF 317 of translated solutions was just three to eight hours.[230] As the Task Force advanced, its Sigint components intercepted voice from the islands, where, again, Argentine commanders and personnel were indiscreet. The naval Siginters received some keys to Argentine systems, but probably focused on direction-finding Argentine stations, where no other sources existed; on Argentine submarines, which were seen as a particular threat; and electronic warfare.[231]

During the campaign, DIS synthesised and distributed material under its own name. Much of it was sanitised Sigint, which decision-makers did not know. They relied more on GCHQ than they knew, which multiplies the force of their praise for it. This material reached three classes of consumer: politicians and officials; diplomats; and military and naval officers. Thatcher took her key decision – to make Argentina leave the islands through compulsion or war – without considering intelligence. Thereafter, Comint shaped the War Cabinet's diplomacy, its demands for speed in operations and its self-confidence in strategy. Politicians praised GCHQ's performance. Though most of its product came sanitised by the DIS, Carrington, Nott, Pym and Thatcher received much GCHQ material direct. Diplomats acted in the context of Comint, guided by a special series of daily highlights which the FCO had GCHQ prepare. Sigint drove the plans and actions of staff officers, military intelligence and commanders. Much Comint also went straight to SAS headquarters at Hereford, to guide its missions, which were strategic and independent, intended to cripple Argentine air power and to aid deception – successfully in both cases. GCHQ, however, provided little help for SAS attacks against Argentine aircraft on the mainland.[232]

The political significance of the crisis was obvious within GCHQ and Whitehall. Tovey noted that the special JIC meeting of 4 April was drafting a 'full blown JIC note. Its purpose is to defend ministers and indeed the intelligence community, against far-fetched accusations of "an intelligence failure"'.[233] Tovey and his colleagues thought they deserved no blame, though Z noted that questions concerning the low priority the JIC had attached to the Falkland Islands 'may be asked by those not well-disposed to it'.[234] When Thatcher established the Nicoll committee to assess British intelligence before the invasion, Tovey warned that 'repeated investigations into the efficiency of our intelligence arrangements were liable to be construed as insulting and could be highly damaging to morale'. Nicoll should 'confine himself as far as possible to looking at our end-product and to refrain from lengthy interrogations of staff who are already very hard pressed ... I have no doubt we shall emerge from this investigation with our credit if anything enhanced.'[235]

Partly for this reason, GCHQ maintained close touch with consumers, to determine their needs and to meet them. As consumers suddenly witnessed its success in achieving that aim they replied effusively. A witness of the War Cabinet meeting on 29 April told Tovey that 'all those present from the Prime Minister downwards spoke in glowing terms of the value of the Sigint contribution'. Others praised GCHQ to Tovey's face. Glover, the DCDS (I) described GCHQ as 'a service beyond all possible praise'. He had been an ardent fan of GCHQ for some time.

> But even I was amazed by the speed and remarkable efficiency with which you honed in on the Argentine target when the crisis broke. From a standing start you developed an operation whose breadth, relevance and immediacy was extraordinarily impressive. Certainly it provided me with the material I needed to brief both the Chiefs of Staff, and John Nott. And I believe that the intelligence you provided formed the base line for some of the most difficult decisions taken during the campaign. Without it we would have been blind and without it the outcome might have been very different. Such, if I might say so, is the measure of GCHQ's achievements ... Day in, day out, night in, night out, queries and requests were invariably received – often no doubt by tired men (and women), with wonderful patience and understanding.[236]

The Director General Intelligence, head of the DIS, thought Sigint was 'virtually the only hard operational intelligence that we have'. The Chief of the Defence Staff, Admiral Terence Lewin, called it '500 per cent marvellous'. Tovey noted: 'Anything I can add is liable to verge on the superfluous but this much I can say: in over thirty years' service in GCHQ I have never known us do a more thoroughly professional job or receive more well-earned compliments from those whom we serve.'[237] The Commander-in-Chief Fleet, Admiral John Fieldhouse, praised 'the tremendous value of Sigint' as a 'revelation', and recognised GCHQ's 'tremendous service' and 'priceless information'.[238]

Crisis and Recalibration

As the crisis began, Thatcher opened the vaults. GCHQ, like the fighting services, abandoned cash limits, spending whatever victory required.[239] On 5–6 April, it moved to 'get its own house in order' in order to handle 'future intercept'. GCHQ created a fusion centre, which combined sub-units from its codebreaking, intelligence and Elint sections to attack the new target: H74X, K25X and V2X. GCHQ expanded its personnel and considered how and where they should work. Z liaison must attach personnel to intelligence bodies in London and support 'an action-on component'. K might handle 'additional crisis-related in-depth analysis (up to now the main effort has been on decrypts)'; outside of periodical summaries of messages, however, this recommendation was not exercised. GCHQ must build 'some knowledge of a technical base of Argentine communications – there is little knowledge either in UK or U.S.'. Cheltenham calculated how to liaise with allies and third parties.[240] J division outlined GCHQ's technical aims:

> Our interests are two-fold. First is the need to fill out the strategic intelligence picture, both now and for the crisis period two–three weeks hence. Second (and in a way more pressing) is to provide a technical base of Comint and Elint target data on which the Navy can start to plan their tactical Sigint efforts afloat. On this they are starting almost from scratch on this target. A third consideration is that we can easily saturate transcription and processing resources if we adopted a mass vacuum cleaner approach. It all points to an intelligent and discriminating search and development effort, and this takes time, of which (despite the apparently leisurely pace of the Fleet) we may not have too much.[241]

Since this was one crisis in a minor area, resources could be borrowed from others, especially J. Ultimately, K25X, V2X and H74X had around a hundred Siginters and Elinters, and perhaps as many typists and messengers. They would 'handle' around 5,900 Comint and 900 Elint reports during the war, with other sections perhaps producing as much diplomatic intelligence.[242] GCHQ, pressed to its limits, might not have done so well during a greater crisis. The head of K division praised H's 'usual outstanding cooperation', and prior success against Argentine systems.[243] Yet H barely handled the strain, and only did so by abandoning computer and cryptanalytic work against other targets. GCHQ's product then overwhelmed the FCO. Spanish linguists were in short supply, above all in TF 317, which may have cost ships and lives. K division's experience with crisis management spurred success, alongside problems. K noted that: 'Starting from almost virtually nowhere, we built up a very creditable effort which provided a very good quick comprehensive service which received bouquets from all directions.' However, in Cheltenham's version of Maoist self-criticism, he noted, regarding himself: 'K Management ... was too slow to realise that this was, in important respects, much more like a J than a K crisis (requiring fusion and short/medium-term analysis, T/A etc, with backup overseeing distribution, clearing up loose ends, etc). We started with things K traditionally does well (quick textual reporting, essentially without (and without need of) comment or fusion), and only came to others later if at all.'[244]

As the card index and computerised ages of cryptology collided, GCHQ faced technical and organisational problems in every atom of its organisation simultaneously. A nine-to-five agency focused on eastern Europe and the Warsaw Pact – in which translators and analysts wrote reports by hand, passed them to typing pools or the Comcentre, usually for transmission within days – now confronted a war in the South Atlantic and the urgent need for speed and mass. Immediately, GCHQ communications warned: 'An Achilles Heel is signals output.' Normally, every day, the Comcentre – manned by five shifts each of thirty-eight officers and operators – rapidly transmitted large volumes of traffic, some marked 'Flash' for immediate signalling. However, the duty signals officer had to read all manuscript messages to assess legibility and action-on. The simultaneous receipt of nineteen handwritten messages in crisis overwhelmed him.

Soon, however, such loads became routine and manageable because GCHQ already had the knowledge and resources to strengthen its surge capacity, while ensuring the accuracy of every character in any message. Shifts of several officers took over action-on. Material moved through a tough system of priorities. The Comcentre rejected any manuscript reports, except on emergency issues. An improvised section of touch-typists on twenty-four-hour shifts, using IBM Selectric typewriters, put handwritten messages onto special forms, returning them to translators to ensure accuracy, and if necessary retyping them. The Comcentre fed these forms physically into an Optical Character Recognition mechanism, producing punched tape to be put into teleprinters, which obviated the need for further typing or encipherment.[245]

The sections attacking Argentine traffic boomed in size and moved to twenty-four-hour shifts. Initially swamped by reports, the newly created Elint section V2X first adopted two eight-hour shifts, and then three on 18 April, when acquisition reached maturity and the Task Force entered dangerous waters. V2X developed an 'Elint/EW data base', which automatically identified and collated all reports on every source of emission. Cryptanalysts spent much time 'answering a deluge of questions from an assortment of LONDON customers'. They mastered changes in cryptosystems, new computer programmes for cryptanalysis, and frequent 'hardware/software faults', one caused by torrential rain in Cheltenham. On 28–29 April, as fleets clashed in the South Atlantic, the Hectra decryption programme crashed, eliminating Comint; heroic efforts created an entirely new database, focused purely on the Falklands, within eight hours.[246]

A secondment of most Spanish linguists in GCHQ, originally over twenty but perhaps rising past thirty, handled the explosion in Comint. Intercept operators and traffic analysts switched from other targets, and learned new ones. They reconstructed Argentine radio networks, determined the most valuable and vulnerable links, and attacked them. Locations were represented on a paper map – not very different to those paper plots used by the London Air Defence Area in 1917–18 – yet this was the first Sigint war fought without card indices. No index existed when the crisis began. Material was entered on an electronic database. This 'data-base interrogation system known as FINDERS KEEPERS' – by implication more powerful than any GCHQ had used before and perhaps its first – enabled analysts to enter search terms for given periods into perhaps the first widespread production-branch IT collaboration system used by GCHQ. The Time Sharing Option (TSO) enabled multiple users to interrogate the Sigint database. 'This helped greatly to save time when answering customer queries, and remained in use for some years after the crisis was over.'[247]

Production was automatic and industrialised. At the time, Michael Herman, head of J and V at various stages of the war, wrote that:

> crisis analysis and reporting is a difficult, worrying and exhausting
> activity. Part of the key to doing it well is the right balance
> between seeking perfection (which we must strive towards …), and
> recognising that we can never achieve it. We must guard against
> mistakes but they are going to happen; the important thing is to
> learn from them and not be rattled; the only inadmissible error is
> to play safe and do nothing … it seems to pay to spend a lot of time
> getting the paper handling and record keeping routing as good as
> possible, simply to reduce the chances of error when people are
> keeping watches and are tired and under stress.[248]

Later, Herman recollected that Siginters had 'no real idea of priorities' for consumers, who never defined them. 'You have a certain amount of material, you whizz it through to [RN Headquarters] Northwood as fast as you can' without spending time on analysis, which personnel had no time to do. Codebreakers followed the principle of 'doing the plain things well as the priority, not trying to be too clever'. GCHQ 'rediscovered' the methods of Bletchley's Hut 8, producing verbatim translations of text and sending them straight to consumers, with the usual annotations as in any textual report. 'K Division product was largely though not entirely a decrypt reporter.'[249]

Morale – a 'Falklands Spirit' – was high. At GCHQ, as across the country as a whole, people thought this a 'good' war, where Britain rescued Britons from aggression. When Herman 'asked an elderly lady in V why she was still sorting signals late after normal closing', she replied, 'I'm doing it for my son – he's in the Task Force.'[250] Another veteran remembers a cryppie running into the codebreaking office, H74X, during the early hours, bicycle clips on trousers, to test an idea that arrived in his sleep. That spirit eased organisational frictions. Initially, night shifts were established in H offices, because cryptanalysts could not walk down the Oakley hill constantly with solutions. Instead, linguists crawled up and down at dusk and dawn from their offices, working aids in hand. Messengers carried incoming signals up the hill. The 'crisis crypt/reporting party' was based in Spur 9 of C Annexe, an H space, 'because of the proximity of machines for H usage and the convenience for K reporters'. Pole Star terminals were added to enable the use of Hectra. Spur 9, initially without secure links outside the building, was soon connected with SUKLO Washington by STS, Northwood and the National Security Operations Center (NSOC) at NSA by Brahms. H74X, K25X and the T/A and map-plotting staff shared an open-plan office. Because of inadequate space, the Elint office, V2X, and a reading room stood across the hall.[251] Even that small split damaged liaison, preventing Elint from being automatically displayed on the map serviced by T/A and Comint, but rather first on a separate map of its own. Since Spur 9 was outside the pneumatic tube system, messengers ferried signals between the shift party and the W Comcentre. Basic kit stood in offices working on a nine-to-five basis. Triumph occurred when the night shift gained access to the library and a photocopier in KHQ, the main intelligence office. Typists and messengers also adopted twenty-four-hour shifts. Initially, eleven personnel from H division worked the shifts, soon reaching thirty after volunteers were trained 'in the systems pertinent to the crisis'. The intelligence section, K25X, had five shifts each of four people, some temporarily seconded from J, which also handled ancillary tasks. Eight sailors were seconded as transcribers and analysts.

The T/A party, initially four, reached six. Its work was aided by material seized from the Argentine submarine *Santa Fe*, captured when Britain retook South Georgia Island on 25 April. After a missile launched from a Wasp helicopter carried by HMS *Endurance* penetrated its conning tower, the crew raced to beach the *Santa Fe*, which lay ashore for a day. Its cryptosystems were ditched at sea but British forces captured many 'valuable documents', including recent operational messages and technical and procedural signals matters, valuable at a time when the Argentine navy's 'call signs were [*sic*] not understood'.[252] As Royal Navy officers noted sniffily, the boat was 'in poor condition before attack, dirty, scruffy, haphazardly stowed'.[253]

An around-the-clock effort between intercept and cryptanalytic units, and military headquarters, caused surges in new forms of traffic, and changes in processes and communications. GCHQ filtered transmission of irrelevant Comint and Elint to Northwood, which did the same for TF 317. Northwood communicated with TF 317 via a tight bottleneck of off-line cypher systems and narrow bandwidths. At one point, GCHQ feared that TF 317 might receive just 600–1,000 groups an hour, though that level rose enough to enable effective operational and intelligence communications.[254] Fortunately, when testing the shipborne intercept/DF system Outboard in 1981, HMS *Hermes* received an RN INTEL set, a dedicated Comint channel on the ship's Satcom system, which, the Fleet Comint officer said, 'is like having Christmas every day'.[255] Every other British vessel except *Hermes*, however, transmitted intercepted Argentine material back to GCHQ through extraordinarily cumbersome procedures, further slowed by the focus on radio silence. Improperly transmitted traffic produced a 'black hole' with Hectra.[256]

Intercepts from high-frequency stations moved through normal channels to GCHQ. There, H division attacked the traffic and sent messages to analysts, which were worked on and forwarded to consumers. Each message was recopied and resent at every link. Comint and T/A reports at GCHQ were written by hand, typewritten, proofed and walked down the hill to the Comcentre, where they were sent to Northwood, which retyped the messages it sent to the fleet by satellite. Northwood, suddenly GCHQ's main consumer, received and assessed all political and military intelligence, becoming the operational interface between the JIC and military operations. Northwood directly gave TF 317 all tactical material, including 'positional info. What where whither when of Arg naval forces', while sanitising all strategic and political intelligence.[257] Intercepts from the Task Force were returned by satellite to Northwood, sent to GCHQ, and returned as intelligence. Midway through the war, GCHQ adopted the computerised system, New Moon, by which dedicated typists released reports from K to customers including Northwood, overcoming bottlenecks at the Comcentre by enabling the elimination of one repetition of reportage. New Moon sped the delivery of messages by some ninety minutes, and eased the overload, especially for priority items.[258] GCHQ officers deployed to Northwood – GCO (N) – worked shifts to liaise between these organisations and handled the key questions of 'action-on': another twenty-four-hour rota of officers at K handled queries from Whitehall. Task Force commander Admiral Sandy Woodward and selected officers on *Hermes* and *Fearless* received Comint up to Category 3, selected by Northwood and signalled over Comint channels.[259]

Meanwhile, the Task Force received a capability to pick up signals in-theatre. The Royal Navy provided three sets of printer equipment and five 'Chandos packages' – Sigint suites, with two HF and two VHF receivers and an Elint position. *Hermes*, *Fearless* and *Coventry* were the main platforms, *Sheffield* and *Endurance* secondary ones. *Hermes* carried five communications technicians, two interpreters, a Chandos suite and an intercept equipment tailored to a specific Argentine system, plus a teleprinter facility to send and receive Sigint information securely. *Fearless* and *Coventry* each carried four communication technicians, one interpreter and a Chandos set.

Sigint proved a jinx for ships. *Coventry*, *Sheffield* and the supply ship *Atlantic Conveyor* were all sunk carrying GCHQ kit. In fact, Argentine forces destroyed 20 per cent of the Sigint equipment sent to TF 317, without killing any personnel.[260] The Task Force had sixteen naval Siginters, including four RAF Spanish linguists, ten army Siginters, aided by RAF linguists. Unfortunately, many of these linguists were rusty, or worse. Few could handle tactical voice communications – astonishingly, given the services' focus on the medium. Even worse, perhaps, the eight best RAF translators, originally assigned to Gibraltar by the Chief of the Air Staff (CAS) despite protests from RAF Sigint authorities, reached TF 317 only on 25 May.[261] Collectively, these personnel provided useful material for the fleet, but little material for land forces, or against air forces.

Approaching a New Age of Sigint

GCHQ was the first codebreaking agency to confront a seismic shift in public attitudes towards secrecy in war. During a parliamentary debate after the Argentine invasion, Ted Rowlands, the Labour spokesman for Foreign Affairs, said:

> I have great difficulty in understanding how the intelligence failed. Our intelligence in Argentina was extremely good. That is why we took action in 1977. We found out that certain attitudes and approaches were being formed. I cannot believe that the quality of our intelligence has changed. Last night the Secretary of State for Defence asked 'How can we read the mind of the enemy?' I shall make a disclosure. As well as trying to read the mind of the enemy, we have been reading its telegrams for many years. I am sure that many sources are available to the Government, and I do not understand how they failed to anticipate some of the dangers that suddenly loomed on the horizon.[262]

What Rowlands called 'a very personal emotional statement' shattered prior standards of discretion about Comint by politicians.[263] Rowlands' loathing of the government's failures to deter Argentine aggression – which he believed a Labour government had managed successfully during the crisis of 1976–77 – dovetailed with the Labour Party's partisan assault on the Iron Lady. He compromised British intelligence at a time when war was likely: perhaps not the best moment to remind foreign states, especially one's enemy, to mind their codes and cyphers.

Rowlands' statement might be expected to alarm Argentine diplomatic and military authorities, yet he was not publicly admonished for the act. Meanwhile, during the campaign, the press published accurate accounts of military planning. The problem was not so much leaks as reporters adding facts one by one, and using their presence in the MOD to squeeze confirmation. Retired officers, commenting on television and in the press, analysed issues precisely as the MOD did; some of that speculation was bound to be accurate. Leading British and American newspapers published several stories which either revealed GCHQ's capabilities against Argentine cryptosystems, hinted at them, or even cited its reports. The veteran A. R. V. Cooper called these actions 'putting good copy before the national interest, which is irresponsible at best and treasonable at worst'.[264] The British Defence Staff Washington emphasised, 'how Americans in positions of responsibility speak with the most remarkable freedom to press enquiries even on sensitive subjects. Thus investigative reporting on intelligence activities and cooperation is not likely to be damped down.'[265] Nor did this occur in Britain. Robert Armstrong feared that articles in the *Sunday Times* on 18 April 1982 'enable the Argentines to speculate knowledgably about our intentions and possibly to take deceptive measures themselves. In so far as methods are concerned the damage to our capabilities, though possibly not immediate, is likely to be widespread and long lasting.' These stories included material that must have come from officials, whom he asked 'to deal with all questions on intelligence matters in the only approved manner: that is, by refusing to comment'.[266] The Chief of the Defence Staff (CDS), Terence Lewin, told the Chiefs of Staff: 'If DCDS (I) is to give us a worthwhile intelligence brief, he must continue to quote from intercepts,' which must not be leaked.[267] Some members of the MOD accused Defence Secretary Nott of leaking material when he briefed backbenchers, though Lewin exonerated him.[268] Whitehall pressed media outlets to avoid 'speculation about future operational plans and interception of Argentine communications'.[269] Neither effort met with success.

GCHQ believed that Argentina could easily change its procedures in order to block penetration. Argentina 'applied greatly increased protective COMSEC procedures' which caused 'some delay in our ability to exploit their traffic', yet these changes failed to achieve that end. On 22 April, H division reported that 'difficult' problems affected some material, but 'there was no specific move by AR to change their procedures in reaction to press reports etc'. In any case, a new age dawned in the relationship between Sigint, state and society. Journalists had broad access to Comint from many officials. They and politicians felt free to discuss it in war and were not stopped from doing so, despite the risk to lives. Crypto went public amidst a war. And there it has stayed ever since.

Nor was this the only change in the practices of Sigint. During 1982, that art stood at the dawn of a revolution which converted C3I (command, control, communications and intelligence) into C4ISR (command, control, communications, computers, intelligence, surveillance and reconnaissance), and enabled the second age of Sigint. Britain was the first nation to enter this new world in warfare, largely through aid from the United States which was far further ahead in technical terms. New forms of fusion between sensors and Sigint from across the world, and within warships, reshaped combinations of intelligence, electronic counter measures (ECM), electronic warfare (EW) and operations. Data link systems gave every ship within a fleet the material from all sensors on every other one, and let national intelligence agencies automatically service fleets at sea. In 1982, however, Royal Navy equipment could not exploit most of the latter opportunities, nor all of the former ones. Consideration was given to the use of a pioneering concept and system, Special Support Activity (SSA), which gave commanders 'precisely tailored real time intelligence support to a tactical operation', through powerful modes of data retrieval and display, and 'careful' and centralised selection and synthesis of reports, transmitted through special kit and personnel. This would 'ensure that the intelligence support to the Task Force Commander was not only timely but was adequately packaged and tailored to meet his needs, and that as early as possible the controlling headquarters should somehow simultaneously be able to "see" the information that was available to the task force, given particularly the close control that was likely to be exercised by London over this operation'.[270]

GCHQ longed to use SSA but decided not to, because of its lack of experience with it, inadequate time to install the system on TF 317 and train personnel, and fears that SSA would swamp the Royal Navy's C3I, which 'are not accustomed to full service of relatively raw Sigint'.[271] This calculation was correct: the Royal Navy could not use SSA during 1982. Had it tried, any attempt to suddenly incorporate such a new system in communication, organisation and command would have degraded intelligence, which worked well enough in any case. In 1982, a C3I system more like that of 1916 perhaps worked better than the

1982 versions of C4ISR could have done. As K division noted, a crisis was not 'the time to create (or even use in hot blood for the first time) new channels of command and consultation ... we need to use the existing channels with which people are familiar, with reinforcement if necessary'.[272]

During the war, consumers were positive about Elint, but less so afterwards.[273] Thus, perhaps referring to occasional pieces of Elint suggesting that Argentine submarines might be out at sea, Glover held that 'on balance ELINT was for the DIS something of a mixed blessing, producing almost as many spurious reports as it did reliable ones'.[274] Fieldhouse thought Elint 'relatively minor' as a source compared to Comint.[275] These criticisms have force, but the critics still placed Elint second as a source, overshadowed only by Comint, which Herman described as being of 'marvellous value'. He emphasised how V, handling 'tactical real-time Elint' for the first time, conducted 'a tremendous feat of improvisation' that achieved 'colossal success'. Elint provided much valuable material on Argentina, without 'detailed steerage and feedback; and no one is going to be able to write thank-you letters. In the fog of war we are never going to know in advance what are the vital items. We just have to proceed largely on a basis of reporting everything that we think may be useful, as quickly and accurately as possible, in the conviction that it may be quite vital to someone.'[276] This approach was defensible. None was better at the time, but for consumers encountering Elint for the first time it may have been confusing.

These developments in Elint favoured Britain, but also gave Argentina its greatest intelligence successes against Britain, and significant ones at that. By tracking the feed from British satellite communications to TF 317, the Argentine air force guided its sole long-range reconnaissance asset, a Boeing 707 aircraft without Sigint capability, to follow the Royal Navy south. That knowledge was unactionable, though the Task Force monitored the menace of ambush posed by submarines. The Argentines abandoned these missions after abortive attacks by Harriers. More significantly, by detecting the take-offs and landings of Harriers, Argentine radars at Port Stanley located *Hermes* and *Invincible*. Thus, Argentine aircraft, either land- or sea-based, could theoretically hit British carriers even 700 miles from the mainland. Britain understood this vulnerability, which forced caution on carriers and restricted the time Harriers could spend on missions – so making Argentine airstrikes easier on British warships to the westward. These radars also provided the only early warning of airborne Harriers to Argentine aircraft attacking around the islands. British V-bombers – based on Ascension Island and flying 'Black Buck' missions over distances of 7,000 miles, which required refuelling eleven different times – sought to destroy this radar system with missiles homing in on radar signals, but failed. The Argentines detected these flights, probably through Elint or traffic analysis, understood their aim, and simply closed down their radar during the period of operations, which aided Britain marginally. This radar system, Argentina's greatest strength in intelligence, cramped British sea power as much as Argentine warships.

The General Belgrano

Initially, Comint was almost the only source on the Falklands crisis, and remained the main one for operations. Eventually, other sources provided key material. GCHQ guided SSNs onto Argentine warships, which they shadowed through sonar and observation. RAF imagery and Sigint flights around the islands occasionally covered most areas. Harriers provided tactical intelligence. The SAS and Special Boat Squadron – good consumers of Sigint and Britain's best national source for intelligence collection after Sigint – provided superb material from the islands, including around Port Stanley.

The British campaign had two phases: southward deployment of warships and aircraft, mostly based at or supplied through Ascension Island; and invasion of the Falkland Islands by ground forces, aided by aircraft and warships. The Royal Navy headquarters at Northwood and its adjunct, the RAF's 18 Air Group, commanded all warships and aircraft assigned to the fleet. In order to use intelligence effectively, the navy and RAF had to cooperate – which historically they had often found difficult – and to pass reports and orders forward over thin communications links. Fortunately, long experience at Northwood and friendship between commanders eased relations between the two services; their standard procedures for reporting forward met operational needs, and signals proved able to carry that material. Military customers received masses of Sigint, which aided war at sea, and invasion of an island – but not its conquest.

Meanwhile, Britain warned that it would sink any Argentine warship within an Exclusion Zone, 200 miles in radius, around the Falkland Islands. Initially, British military intelligence thought the Argentine navy competent but since 'many ships, particularly the aircraft carrier, have serviceability problems', it would behave cautiously. 'National pride' would drive the navy to keep a 'substantial' fleet at sea, on the 'pretext' of defending the mainland, but it would avoid the Exclusion Zone and, implicitly, conflict with British adversaries.[277] Though some later assessments admitted that the Argentine navy might fight, most concluded, in Glover's words, 'they would be unlikely to risk their surface fleet in a match which they must reckon they must lose'.[278] National chauvinism affected these assessments; Sigint corrected this view, and showed that Argentine forces, especially the navy, grossly overestimated their position. They misconstrued British professionalism and determination and their own capabilities. Argentine forces did not believe that Britain could retake the Falklands. The Argentine navy told commanders that the international political situation was 'becoming complicated', yet 'the British force is neither ready nor trained for crossing the South Atlantic'; while Thatcher's opponents 'are still reacting strongly'. Even if 'an armed clash occurred, the balance would weigh in our favour'. Argentine naval officers reported an 'extremely effective' performance in their first ever naval/air exercise, which somehow they imagined would translate to success in war, and outlined their tactical preparations in detail. After a visit to the Falklands, the Argentine air force commander found morale of 'all personnel ... of great comfort'.[279] Argentine commanders misunderstood how a good fleet could handle the South Atlantic, and how the Royal Marines might conduct amphibious assault. The Argentine army thought that its defences were good, but they collapsed immediately when hit. Only as TF 317 neared the islands did the Argentines begin to exhibit alarm and understand the true military balance. Once the shooting started, Argentine forces rapidly improved the quality of their system for intelligence and operations, especially in the air, but too late to matter.

GCHQ also showed that the Argentine navy aimed to fight aggressively, if naively. The Royal Navy grasped enemy intentions and deployments perfectly, and its capabilities just well enough. It used knowledge effectively against an enemy inferior in power and intelligence, yet still dangerous. This pre-landings phase perhaps led

British admirals to overestimate their invulnerability and the power of their intelligence – both matters that would be shaken with the loss of HMS *Sheffield*.

By 22 April, GCHQ thought 'as yet there was no indication of the AR battle plan or indeed their intentions'.[280] The situation quickly changed. Solutions of Argentine naval traffic illustrated that it aimed to fight the Royal Navy. None suggested any intention for compromise or to avoid action.[281] GCHQ also penetrated the Argentine plan of attack. Argentine forces fell into three groups: the aged aircraft carrier *Veinticinco de Mayo* and three destroyers to the north; a body of three corvettes; and the *General Belgrano* and two destroyers to the south. A fourth loose collection of spy ships disguised as fishing vessels, including the *Narwal*, sailed to the east of the islands to locate the Task Force. Destroyers and corvettes carried Exocet missiles, able to sink a carrier. When Argentine warships moved to meet the Royal Navy on 24 April, their orders were alarming: to advance on the Exclusion Zone without entering it, in 'a "wait and see" attitude' to threaten the navy, 'assess the situation before the decision to use force' and 'to make it difficult for the opponent to act by dividing his effort by means of a threat from different directions'. They should prepare an ambush. Warships must maintain tight communications and full fuel loads, 'the concept being to use them to the maximum of their ability with the minimum of forewarning'. Argentine forces should 'operate as a dissuasive element in the region'. However, 'if an escalation of the situation leads to a generalised conflict', warships and land-based aviation must 'intercept and/or neutralise' the Task Force through 'the mission of force as a whole, by acting in as coordinated a way as possible with the other groups' – a coordinated assault by land- and sea-based aircraft, followed closely by warships carrying Exocet missiles, from many vectors at once.[282]

Between 28 April and 2 May, just before the attack on *Belgrano*, GCHQ gave its consumers interceptions of increasingly warlike Argentine orders. On 29 April, the Argentine naval command told commanders: 'The lack of progress in the diplomatic negotiations does not permit any expectation of immediate change in the existing situation' while 'a continuation of British offensive action is foreseeable'. Argentine ships would penetrate the Exclusion Zone in order to test British responses, following its prior offensive plans, 'use of arms without restriction'. On 1 May, the Argentine command gave all warships 'freedom of action', and ordered 'commencement of offensive operations'. *Veinticinco de Mayo* would 'deploy by night to a favourable position in order to launch a daytime air attack on units detected' through its own air reconnaissance. 'This movement will be carried out during the night, keeping one's distance from the enemy in order to minimise risks of a night air attack, in order to subsequently initiate an attack at first light.' The corvette group would assault 'units damaged by the air attack and any other dispersed units'. The *Belgrano* group would hit British warships with missiles. 'Attacks should only be made on targets when conditions are favourable, taking into account the threat from the air.' Every Argentine warship must launch an early reconnaissance and unleash 'a massive attack on the surface units before they withdraw'.[283] These plans were academic, but not unachievable. If they worked, Argentina would win the war, and Britain cease to be a reckonable power.

As the fleets closed, this knowledge of Argentine plans alarmed as well as assisted the Royal Navy. Intelligence focused on finding 'the Argentinean Aircraft Carrier Group' so British SSNs could locate and, if necessary, destroy it.[284] Although GCHQ and Royal Navy submarines frequently tracked *Veinticinco de Mayo*, often its position, course and speed were unknown. The combination of its speed, the range of its aircraft, and the guidance of Neptune tracking aircraft endangered British carriers. On 27–28 April, the CNS Admiral Leach warned Chiefs of Staff that *Veinticinco de Mayo* had mounted five Super Etendard aircraft with Exocet missiles. 'The 500 nautical miles operating range of Super Etendards would, once they were embarked, make it very difficult to determine when the threat would materialise; it was therefore essential to neutralise that threat from the outset. The safety of our own ships required the ability for immediate pre-emptive action once attack was threatened.' *Veinticinco de Mayo* had to be destroyed whenever possible at sea, or warned of this potential fate if it left port.[285]

Leach marginally overstated the danger. Argentine Neptune aircraft did guide the attack on *Sheffield*, but then became unoperational, replaced by C-130 Hercules with unsatisfactory performance. Limited catapult capability had prevented the placing of Super Etendards on *Veinticinco de Mayo*, which were replaced by seven A-4Q Skyhawks with half the range and less punch. Against this, the Royal Navy was not yet aware of how detectable it was at range. Harriers had to fly combat air patrols to protect the fleet. The Argentine radars at Port Stanley regularly located British carriers by picking up the aircraft operating from them, though perhaps their reports were poorly integrated with Argentine naval intelligence. Yet if these radars found the Task Force 200 miles to the east, while *Veinticinco de Mayo* was 200 miles offshore, its aircraft might strike British carriers within ninety minutes. One lucky hit could deliver Argentine victory.

Leach was correct to claim that *Veinticinco de Mayo* gave Argentina a small but real chance of victory. He understood the danger of underestimating an enemy: Leach had served in the Royal Navy's Force Z during 1941, where his father had died on the new battleship, HMS *Prince of Wales*, sunk by Japanese bombers. His warning clears the Royal Navy from any charge of underestimating the foe: its errors of assessment, however great, were on the complex interaction between several untested weapons systems.

The Chiefs of Staff split over Leach's demands, but the War Cabinet authorised it, driven by Comint and a sense of danger. This debate and Sigint both shaped British decisions during the abortive Argentine ambush of 30 April–2 May. Early on 2 May, the Royal Navy lost contact with *Veinticinco de Mayo*, which Woodward feared had penetrated the submarine screen. He was right – it had. Following its orders precisely, the *Veinticinco de Mayo* prepared a Skyhawk strike on British carriers, which weather conditions prevented. When detected by a Harrier, the Argentine carrier withdrew temporarily towards the mainland. Meanwhile, to the south, the British SSN HMS *Conqueror* had the *General Belgrano* in sight, but believed it might easily lose her. Like the northern half of the pincer, the *Belgrano* was withdrawing temporarily, albeit in order to strike again. Given the risk, and after consulting the War Cabinet, Fieldhouse ordered *Conqueror* to sink *Belgrano*, which it did with two Second World War-vintage Mark 8 torpedoes. Tragically, while *Conqueror* was ordered to withdraw, and did so, *Belgrano*'s destroyer escorts not unreasonably assumed that *Conqueror* was still nearby and could sink any vessels attempting rescue. The escorts thus refused to try, which magnified the loss of life from *Belgrano*. Probably they could have rescued most if not all of those who died.

These reports justified the attack on the *Belgrano*, a classic counter-ambush of an ambush. Good Sigint well used, however, had perverse consequences. Without wider knowledge of this source, the attack seemed fishy – anyone hostile to British policy could claim it stank. Britain had warned that it would attack any Argentine warship threatening its forces, and also any entering the Exclusion Zone. *Belgrano* entered that zone to ambush the Task Force, commanding destroyers mounting Exocet missiles, but was sunk outside that zone as it withdrew to prepare another attack. That fact complicated public understanding of events. Britain had overemphasised the issue of the Exclusion Zone compared to that of the general threat posed by the Argentine fleet wherever it might be. Indeed, on 27–28 April, General Bramall rejected a pre-emptive strike on *Veinticinco de Mayo* at sea without prior, specific and public warning that it would be sunk on sight. On 1 May, the Foreign Secretary, Francis Pym, warned that such an immediate public warning would 'immeasurably' strengthen such an action'.[286] Civilians and opinion-formers across the world also underrated the Argentine navy, and therefore the warlike necessity of British action. The action could easily be presented as an unnecessary and unprovoked assault, with nefarious motives – to scupper a compromise pursued by Peru. Yet any such military action must necessarily disrupt diplomacy, since these spheres intersected. Both sides made diplomacy an adjunct to war, and display of force a tool of policy. Many people sought to mediate; the Peruvian proposal arrived after the fleet engagement began, and Britain took it more seriously than Argentina did. Any British response to danger must seem bad when based on intelligence it could not report without losing the source.

The British government declined to justify this act by publishing Sigint – it understood very well the centrality of the source. Indeed, the first official statement on the topic was intended precisely to draw attention away from the role of Sigint in the sinking of the *Belgrano*.[287] Nott claimed that it was sunk while advancing to attack Task Force 317, and because that act had been detected. Unfortunately, because the MOD did not know what had happened, Nott's statement was erroneous. After the war, these errors became public, through leaks by the civil servant Clive Ponting. He knew about the role of Sigint in the sinking of the *Belgrano*, but did not leak material on it, presumably to protect the source. Together, these actions enabled conspiracy theories to flourish, crippling understanding of these issues for thirty years, until Lawrence Freedman published parts of the Sigint record in his official history of the Falklands conflict.

This action was justifiable but eroded support abroad, except in the key quarter: Washington. After the *Belgrano* was sunk, Alexander Haig said that if any further British attacks occurred, 'US opinion, and for that matter Western opinion more generally, might become less favourable toward [the UK]. People might say we were overreacting.' Nicholas Henderson, the British ambassador, retorted that, 'according to information he [Haig] would have seen, the Argentineans had ordered three frigates to attack the *Hermes* and the carrier had been given instructions to attack British ships. It could not therefore be said that the Argentineans were behaving peacefully and that it was only us who were prepared for continued action.'[288]

GCHQ Comint prevented members of the Reagan administration from trying to use the sinking of the *Belgrano* to discredit Britain, or micromanage its policy – rather, the reverse. Similarly, GCHQ Sigint sapped Haig's attempts to convince Whitehall of 'a degree of Soviet involvement and/or interest' above that accepted by American or British analysts, or his 'claims to have evidence (known to no one else) of the emergence of a 'moderate centre' in Argentine politics'.[289]

To San Carlos Sound
The sinking of the *General Belgrano* transformed the war. Thereafter, the Argentine navy specialised in study of the mainland shore. The Royal Navy stood off the Falklands, guarding against attack and preparing for amphibious assault. GCHQ shaped its success in both areas. Yet until the end of the war, the MOD feared that the Argentine navy might come out and somehow win. On 11 May, the CDS was informed: 'Argentine Appreciation?? Time beginning to run out to attack UK amphibious/ logistic group before it RVs with main task force – must commence attacks shortly?'[290] This risk was overstated, but not impossible. By any conventional standard, TF 317 had far too few aircraft and surface warships to defend two carriers or an amphibious assault from Argentine air and submarine attack, let alone these three tasks at once. GCHQ simplified the problem. As Fieldhouse wrote after the war:

Exploitation at the strategic level was of the utmost value to me
personally and to the Task Group Commanders, revealing the
changing political and military attitudes of the Junta and of senior
Argentine commanders, their frustrations, dwindling morale,
internal dissent and most importantly their will to fight. It revealed
a very different story to that being broadcast to the world from
Buenos Aires, and gave a vital insight into the likely intentions of
the forces they commanded. It was also invaluable in our assessment
of the Argentine ORBAT and of the effectiveness of their efforts to
buy more military equipment. With the benefit of this wide ranging
information, I and my subordinate commanders were able to plan
with increased confidence ... At the tactical level, COMINT on
slow moving targets such as ships and of the Argentine Fleet and
Submarine Broadcasts, in particular, allowed CTG 317.8 [task force
commander] to conserve assets, bias his disposition towards AAW
(anti-aircraft warfare), rather than ASW (anti-submarine warfare) at
a vital time, and was a highly important compensator for his lack of
surveillance assets. It also was a key factor in the dispositions of our
submarines.[291]

In other words, GCHQ guided the posture of TF 317 and overcame
its lack of warships and aircraft. It prevented waste of TF 317's scarce
escorts, and heightened the certainty that British SSNs would kill
enemy warships which attempted to sail. At the end of the war, the
Task Force's commander, Sandy Woodward, valued Sigint as equivalent
to two SSNs and six frigates – almost 20 per cent of his fleet – without
which invasion would have failed.[292] Meanwhile, Sigint guided the
destruction of Argentine assets at sea, especially Elint surveillance ships
such as *Narwal*, which might aid air strikes. Northwood constantly
had specific requests for GCHQ. For example, on 14 May, during
an SAS raid against Pebble Island which might have caused a major
reaction, Northwood tasked GCHQ 'for signs of air attack being
prepared/launched at first light assumption that *Hermes* etc are still in
same area. Note that details of Skyhawk attack were noted in material
from this source.' Two weeks later, Northwood asked GCHQ to study
'patterns of activity' of the Argentine radars at Stanley, to determine

the best 'time frame' for a Black Buck attack.[293] GCHQ derived its own priorities – for example, making submarine broadcasts 'flash priority'.[294]

Military planners emphasised the need to collect 'tactical intelligence' for invasion.[295] 'It goes without saying, also, that intelligence on Argentinean equipment, strength, activity and disposition of forces will be a high priority requirement for the commander of the Task Force in planning his options ... especially ... in preparing for the insertion of Special Forces.'[296] Planners assumed that SAS, SBS or aerial reconnaissance would meet this need. Though they provided useful material, the best source was Comint. It captured all elements of the Argentine order of battle on the islands and it provided an excellent grasp of Argentine perceptions, including its rank-ordered views of likely British actions and the danger they posed.[297] Panicked by a growing sense of their own vulnerability, Argentine commanders on the Falklands demanded help.[298] The Argentine air force would intervene, but not the navy. Argentine forces were absent from San Carlos Sound (where military logic suggested Britain should land), and were instead divided into immobile pockets, unable to effectively counter-attack or cooperate.

Any sign of special forces or RAF raids on mainland airbases alarmed Argentina.[299] Here Comint may have shaped action and effect. Britain considered but abandoned an elaborate global deception plan aimed at passing material to Argentine intelligence in order to draw aircraft and warships away from the Falklands.[300] Still, it sought to divert forces from the target, through leaks to diplomats or journalists. This campaign shaped press reports and SAS actions, suggesting that Britain might attack other parts of the islands, or the northern or southern edges of the Argentine mainland, and mentioning every possible target save San Carlos Sound. In particular, during the nine days before the counter-invasion, actions by helicopter, special forces, electronic emissions and the 'leak[ing of] spoof area of operations to locals' in Port Stanley built the credibility of a 'spoof beach'. On D-Day, 'dummy para drop and radar echo multiplication to simulate helo assault' occurred there.

As ever, judging the effect of deception is hard because it works by reinforcing perceptions rather than creating them. In this case, perhaps the best judgement is that deception was effective, but unnecessary. Comint, aided by the SAS and SBS, shaped the selection of the target by showing that few Argentine forces stood at San Carlos Sound, or were likely to move there. As in the fight against Nazi Germany during 1943–44, Comint enabled Britain to monitor the effect of this campaign, and learn enemy intentions. On 16 May, GCU Northwood noted: 'Mention of San Carlos in 3/AA/98444 caused problems today. MGRM [Major General Royal Marines, the commander of the land element, Jeremy Moore] believes that although something has aroused ARG suspicions there does not appear to be evidence of detection of patrols. 2. Pending discussions, planned insertions/extractions were postponed in the Ajax and San Carlos areas but decision has been taken to go ahead with plan laid down. Useful info contained in above report will obviously be now be taken into account.'[301]

More broadly, Comint showed that Argentine commanders had no idea where Britain would land. It also noted that many Mirage aircraft, a large part of a declining fleet, were committed to territories too far away to interfere in the Falklands theatre. Most or all of this deployment, however, reflected an effort by the Argentine air force to conserve and salvage its scarce assets, paralleled by the Argentine navy's concern with Chilean forces and concentration around Tierra del Fuego. Though Chile was a rival, this focus conveniently saved the Argentine fleet from destruction and left the air force to defend the Falklands. As the British embassy in Chile noted: 'everything has to be seen against background that as a traditionally peacetime force, each of armed forces has regarded the others as rivals for slice of annual budgetary financial cake in order to keep up amount of men equipment and thus share of influence of balance in military/political power play. Each service is thus desperate to avoid loss of equipment in current conflict knowing how difficult it may subsequently be to regain former position of influence for lack of ability to resupply, and each is ready to launch accusations at any moment of being forced to lose e.g. aircraft or ships so to benefit the other.'[302]

On 20 May, GCU Northwood reported:

1. H Hour was formally announced as 210630Z. Support vessels will start moving into Falkland Sound from 202359Z onwards and various direct actions by SAS/SBS already on Falklands will take place over next 24 hours to create confusion/diversions. Main amphibious landing will take place from 211130Z onwards in the San Carlos area.

2. For the first few hours after the landing it will be important still to disguise from the Args the scale of the operation. It has been agreed that key personnel may be told the full story but that they should be asked to treat the release of any information in the same manner as embarked press, i.e. that initial reports should indicate another series of softening-up landings (like Pebble Island) with suggestions that what started as a raid is developing into a major assault when it has become obvious.

3. As far as tasking is concerned main priorities are:

A. Any Elint indications of impending air attack (this I believe will be confined to detections of Neptune and poss C130 surveillance activity) which may be used to direct attack A/C onto Blue targets.

B. Any Comint reflections of A/C movements real or intended into or within the operational area.

C. Any Comint or Elint reflections of movements of major surface or submarine forces.[303]

As Britain landed men and kit, Sigint could not help against air attack which, after the sinking of HMS *Sheffield*, GCHQ called 'our single biggest intelligence gap'.[304] Glover later noted: 'Air to air, air to ground and Air Force command communications remained a closed book.'[305] Planners knew that invasion would cost ships and lives; Britain could not stop air attack, merely try to contain damage and beat the threat slowly. Argentine aircraft did not need elaborate communications to attack targets in a known location, but as ever, stereotyped signals accompanied air strikes, and opened opportunities for Sigint. GCHQ worked fast, but any problem with processing hampered its use for tactical purposes.

On 8 June 1982, GCHQ produced much material about the Argentine attack on British landing ships *Sir Galahad* and *Sir Tristram* offloading infantry at Bluff Cove near Port Stanley, which was processed far faster than was usual for Ultra, yet still too late to save fifty-one British lives.[306] Errors by Siginters and about Sigint shaped this failure. Siginters on TF 317, inexperienced against the danger, took time to pick up indications of attack. A Flash message from Rio Grande naval base in Tierra del

Fuego to Port Stanley preceded many attacks, which even unread still enabled warning of their time, though not place. Such information could have enabled concentrations of Sea Harriers to loiter over targets, but still perhaps not have saved even one ship. On 9 May, Siginters at GCHQ and TF 317 discovered this pattern, but failed to exploit it, or cooperate against this threat.[307] This discovery and its exploitation might have been made faster had superior officers outside the Sigint chain of command not seized Sigint resources for other purposes. The Chief of Air Staff, against warnings from his Siginters, sent a tactical Sigint unit elsewhere, with seemingly its best Spanish speakers, while RAF Sigint linguists later were landed to be interpreters during the interrogation of prisoners.[308] The failure with voice interception was astonishing, given Britain's focus on the medium against the Warsaw Pact. A greater number of experienced traffic analysts, or voice interceptors, might have discovered more radio indicators of air attack, which could have minimised unnecessary deployments, maximised concentrations and saved warships.

British sensors could not easily detect Argentine aircraft skimming the sea, climbing for an updated radar fix and then diving again to run against warships. This tactic prevented Britain from concentrating aircraft for defence, instead forcing constant combat air patrols by just a few Sea Harriers at the extreme edge of their operating radius. Instead, the Royal Navy saved supply and landing ships by standing on Calvary. Warships sited at the mouth of San Carlos Sound, and radar pickets covering flotillas further out, attracted Argentine attack, sacrificing themselves to save others while enabling attrition by Sea Harriers and anti-aircraft missiles. Argentina sank or damaged warships and the supply ship *Atlantic Conveyor* – carrying much kit essential to supporting the land operations, such as heavy-lift helicopters and GCHQ material for the army section – but still British forces moved. The desperate expedient of unloading troops from the requisitioned P&O liner *Canberra* directly in San Carlos Sound succeeded – as did its flight away – yet it risked annihilation had Argentine forces attacked the ship, as they later did other British forces in Bluff Cove.

If slightly better, or luckier, Argentina could have crippled British forces as they landed, like a Gallipoli. Instead, Argentina scored tactical successes without strategic effect. Rather like Admiral Beatty, as battlecruisers blew up before his eyes at Jutland sixty-six years prior, when Argentine aircraft hammered his surface fleet, Admiral Woodward wrote: 'There is something wrong with our ships again.' A few days after the landing, Woodward pulled the carriers back to sea, crippling British air defences at San Carlos Sound. 'Convoys will be run in and out by night' only, Woodward commanded, limiting transshipment to a few hours per day, so slowing the logistical build-up needed to advance, and feeding the vicious circle.[309]

Soon, on 27 May, Fieldhouse reminded his subordinates that even American support for Britain was wobbling. Despite 'world wide calls for ceasefire and a degree of uncertainty in her own team, PM has held out resolutely for victory not ceasefire. The one thing which could undermine her position and could lead to complete about-turn in public opinion in UK, which at present strongly supports her, is catastrophe at sea with large loss of life.'[310] His fears illustrate how commanders balanced tactical, strategic, diplomatic and political concerns during this near-run battle.

To Port Stanley

Once forces were ashore, Comint instantly became less useful. High-level Argentine assessments still drove Whitehall's confidence and demands for speed in attack and concerns for its carriers. Just after the invasion, GCU Northwood noted: 'Northwood assesses threat of Argentine air attack on Blue Force carriers, particularly *Hermes*, to be probable during 23 May. This based on CDR Falklands (Arg) insistence and poss indications of planning for such an attack (Comint).'[311] On 1 June, intercepts of Argentine naval orders for operations around the islands, combined with ambivalent material from traffic analysis that the modern submarine *San Luis* was at sea, caused a temporary 'furore in London'.[312] This lack of certainty and accuracy about the location of one Argentine submarine reflects how intelligence on them minimised waste. GCHQ perfectly determined enemy losses and sometimes illuminated enemy morale. Argentine commanders grossly overstated British aircraft losses, and often underestimated Harrier strength by 100 to 300 per cent.[313]

Traffic showing that the Argentine navy preferred port to combat no doubt pleased Admirals Fieldhouse and Woodward. The British assault at Goose Green on 28–29 May stunned Argentine officers, who reported receiving 'intense naval and mortar fire' and a 'rapid (British) advance in the face of all supporting fire and deterrent, and even deployed whilst receiving (possibly recoilless) rifle fire, automatic fire and under air attack'. They overestimated the British forces by 300 per cent, as three battalions, who 'attacked through the weakest position'.

Hours after Goose Green fell, the Argentine air commander in Port Stanley praised the British airmen, sailors, squaddies, marines and special forces who bled for their victory. Britain maintained 'absolute supremacy at sea, with all the operational and logistical consequences which this implies'. British 'absolute air superiority ... allows him to develop air and helicopter transport operations with absolute freedom of action' and to erode Argentine power. At Goose Green, 'the enemy demonstrated great mobility through [the use of] helicopters, overwhelming fire power and anti-air [fire power] through the use of portable missiles, acting in exact coordination with supporting naval fire, employing it as back-up and relief for the troops engaged in the front line'. These advantages in material and training 'became decisive' in the battle, and 'represent the most important differences with our own troops' capabilities'. Argentine forces 'offered strenuous resistance', but were badly trained and led. Their defence relied utterly on air support, which Harriers wrecked. Britain had 'unsurpassable conditions to extend the occupation of the islands ... When the enemy decides to operate again against our positions, he will find a defence lacking in mobility and with relatively less fire power and training, which ... will previously have been softened up by intense naval, fire and air support ... a modification of this situation is not anticipated because of the total absence of our own naval resources. This message is top secret.'[314] Northwood received the commander's missive, headlined 'Commander Falklands Group Laments the Inferiority of the Argentine Forces', at about the same time that authorities in Buenos Aires did.

GCHQ's success was reflected in MOD and FCO requests for material they understood it could not provide, based on the likelihood that the regime would collapse: 'We could do with more on the Argentine internal situation, the impact of our landing on the Junta's standing/ popular support, the reported tensions between the Argentine navy and air force and other potential indicators of Argentine will to continue fighting or to negotiate. But those needs are already recognised and for obvious reasons we cannot expect a great deal in those directions.'[315]

Yet Sigint gave little help to land forces at the kill, because disorganisation distorted supply, demand and command. Initially, when the Falklands crisis began, the JIC and DIS made errors aplenty. DIS complained of a twenty-four-hour delay in receiving one Elint report from a partner organisation. GCHQ investigated and found that claim to be a 'complete mare's nest': DIS had 'had the info but did not know it exclam'.[316] Despite infighting and crossed wires, ultimately JIC and DIS handled the problems well for their consumers in Whitehall.[317]

The difficulties lay elsewhere. The Falklands conflict occurred just after Britain changed its military command system, by boosting the power of the Chief of the Defence Staff over the Chiefs of Staff. The CDS, Admiral Lewin, was in New Zealand when the crisis broke. By the time he returned, he claimed 'things were almost out of control'.[318] He found a way to exercise his power as the government's chief military advisor. Beneath the strategic level, command and intelligence followed traditional patterns which, as an old salt, perhaps Lewin found natural. Established modes of command and intelligence, designed for the different circumstances of NATO, were unsuited to this crisis. When the JIC proposed to create 'a JIC Military Working Group to produce rapid tactical assessments of military-related int', Lewin rejected 'any additional machinery which might slow down the existing service to the Chiefs of Staff', from DIS and GCHQ.[319] Northwood dominated operations, more than even the Royal Navy at its peak had done. Only Northwood could integrate British operations with the War Cabinet's strategy. Lewin and Fieldhouse were friends, from a fraternity of submariners more experienced in intelligence than any other British sailors or any decision-makers, save a few diplomats; they were accustomed to acting independently, striking silently, and explaining afterwards. Worried by leaks, and the dangers confronting Task Force 317, they restricted the amount of operationally sensitive information given to the MOD to the minimum needed to support operations. Consequently, senior levels of Whitehall understood the intentions of Argentine forces better than their own.

This approach short-circuited normal strategic decision-making in Whitehall, which was designed for NATO matters. However, although the usual middlemen were shut out, the proper chain of command was maintained in an undocumented fashion. Every evening during the key moments of the campaign, Nott, Thatcher and their private secretaries drove to Northwood to be briefed by Fieldhouse and Lewin on the logistical and operational circumstances and dangers. They carried this knowledge to decisions by the War Cabinet.[320] This approach may have been better suited to circumstances than the standard British model; it certainly fitted Thatcher's preference for small and flexible groups for decision-making. The arrangement shaped loyalties towards Prime Minister Thatcher – and facilitated an understanding of her fragile political position – leading Lewin and Fieldhouse to press ground commanders on the Falklands to win quickly once they landed.

Northwood received all relevant Comint and Elint straight from GCHQ, rather than through DIS. GCHQ swung into action to support the Royal Navy as it had in 1940, tailoring its production to military needs. Even officers who disparaged intelligence during the crisis praised that support. Glover, the DCDS (I) said: 'SIGINT was the fundamental ingredient of almost all our assessment effort, and COMINT and ELINT provided as much as ninety per cent of all our raw intelligence. It was this input that enabled us to keep S of S [Secretaries of State], CDS and the Chiefs of Staff well briefed, not only on the interplay (at UN headquarters) in NEW YORK, but also on the tactical intentions of the Argentine Service commanders, the relationships between them, their individual grip on their units, and even on the strategy of the Junta itself.'[321] British land forces praised GCHQ for its 'very great assistance ... This most excellent service has been our greatest single source of reliable intelligence, indeed for much of the time our only one,' which gave General Bramall 'accurate and timely briefing[s] which [have] been vital to the host of decisions he has had to make'.[322] Unfortunately, the system created to give intelligence about Argentina to Northwood and TF 317 rode roughshod over standard modes of dissemination to organisations outside that chain of command. As RAF intelligence complained: 'the "need to know" principle was applied so vigorously that it became counter-productive and divisive', failing 'to keep essential personnel informed of future intentions'. If 'a non-standard command and control system is to be established in time of tension or war, than the peacetime structure must be modified to mirror that system', backed by 'a fusion centre where all source intelligence could be analysed and properly distributed to all concerned'.[323]

Nor did that standard system work. By 1982, British military intelligence had shrunk to two good organisations: for forces in NATO, and GCHQ. Britain fought in an area where it was unprepared and intelligence was fragile, inflexible and weak. Every element of British intelligence failed in the Falklands conflict, except those which could be refocused on crisis diplomacy or the South Atlantic, above all GCHQ and Northwood. These organisations had capacity enough to enable victory at sea, but nowhere else, where many problems combined. Once ashore, the key nodes of command were at levels which were not supposed to receive Sigint. Command was loose – almost tribal – over elite formations such as the Royal Marines Commandos and the Parachute Regiment, who preferred to fight as separate brigades or battalions. In the first week after landing a Royal Marines general commanded his brigade and, allegedly, two paratroop battalions one hundred miles away, who pursued a plan he thought pointless. Days before the assault on Stanley, the Royal Marines Major General Jeremy Moore took command while a third brigade of Guards and Gurkhas entered the fray. Furthermore, planning was initially dominated by Royal Marines officers, used to seizing and securing bridgeheads rather than driving deep and fast. This produced the seeming stalemate in the week after the British landing which alarmed Northwood and Thatcher. These improvised arrangements did not make for effective command. Soldiers won this war, not generals, which in turn undermined the value of Siginters.

By 1982, beyond forces committed against the USSR, military Sigint was decadent. Neither GCHQ nor the MOD controlled these resources: they were the small and separate property of each service, without senior and experienced leaders, or 'an identifiable MOD co-ordinating authority'.[324] GCHQ and the services issued conflicting orders to military Sigint. Siginters on board Task Force 317 did not cooperate between them, weakening their already limited capabilities; they did not even know others were present, until they met accidentally. At the last minute, the Royal Navy appointed a 'Force Comint Officer' to the fleet, without any experience in the field. He did not even visit GCHQ before he sailed. Not one Sigint unit in TF 317 accepted his command.[325]

Once landed, fighting units had little sense of what Sigint could offer. For example, 3 Commando Brigade headquarters was inexperienced and incompetent regarding any form of intelligence, let alone Sigint. As the Army Sigint commander, Major Thorp, reported: 'having a person with experience of our product collocated at the Bde HQ int cell would have made a big difference'. Noting that another brigade and perhaps a divisional headquarters soon would reach the island, Thorp asked: 'Please advise soonest chain of command for this det and to whom we should provide our product. This information essential to plan future intentions.'[326] This question never received an adequate reply.

Comint confirmed the planning assumptions for the land campaign and every order or appreciation from Northwood until the kill. In particular, high-level Argentine assessments drove Whitehall's confidence and demands for speed in attack. On 14 May, Fieldhouse told Woodward and the ground commander, Royal Marines Brigadier Julian Thompson, that 'a relatively calm overview of the last few days of battle' indicated 'despite some severe pain we are winning and furthermore clearly hold the initiative. Increasing signs of desperation from your local enemy all serve to confirm.' Britain must 'take full and early advantage of this situation before the international call for ceasefire becomes unbearable' and strike for Stanley.[327] Royal Marines General Jeremy Moore, land commander at Northwood, emphasised that 'the enemy possesses neither will nor means to mount effective offensive ground operations, and that rapid and powerful action will bring about speedy resolution of overall situation'.[328] Thompson must 'push forward from the bridgehead area, so far as the maintenance of security allows'.[329]

That situation was far from pleasant. Thompson's forces faced harrowing air attack, with only two helicopters to support the advance in a large area vulnerable to counter-attacks. Following Royal Marines doctrine designed to seize Norwegian fjords during war with Warsaw Pact countries, Thompson wanted to secure bridgeheads, not drive deep and fast. His focus on building supplies, security, air superiority and certainty – reinforced by intelligence on the enemy – before launching an open-ended attack, produced the seeming stalemate which alarmed Northwood and Thatcher. 'Info aval here on en determination is thin but performance so far and questioning of PW tends to show that he must be expected to fight.'[330] Thompson had 'so far seen no sign of imminent enemy collapse and therefore consider we must plan on defeating him in the conventional sense', while being ready to exploit 'any signs of collapse which might appear'.[331] Northwood replied with estimates, drawn from Comint, that few Argentine aircraft could attack his forces, but had no intelligence to shake his strategy.[332]

Whitehall's confidence in Thompson was shaken, unfairly. However cautious, he faced an unpleasant variant of a difficult task – amphibious assault against defended positions. Judging enemy willpower is hard, while he and Northwood had divergent intelligence pictures, one drawn from Sigint and the other from battle. When Moore superseded Thompson as commander on the islands, he asked his own successor at Northwood, Richard Trant, 'to do all you can to keep instant strategists off my back'.[333] Moore knew the Sigint record to 26 May. For the first time since the landing, a general combined both Sigint and local knowledge. Yet after the first major engagement on land, a stunning British victory, Moore still adopted Thompsonian views. 'The final defeat of the enemy is dependent on his will to fight. At Darwin/Goose Green our intelligence assessments underestimated both his strength and the fervour with which the more fanatical core fought. We must be prepared for this to occur again at Port Stanley leading to a protracted battle.'[334] Moore and Thompson both overated the enemy – a Victorian general would have estimated the odds better. This mistake stemmed from experience in preparing for difficult operations against a serious foe, and had no cost, save a few days in time.

Siginters had little to offer on land and failed to cooperate with each other and their customers. Partly because of the loss of kit on *Atlantic Conveyor*, military Sigint units failed to advance, or to aid the new consumer. The Royal Marines' Sigint unit, just established, collapsed in its first use. The beach swallowed its vehicles. Its RAF linguists were conscripted to interrogate Argentine prisoners, which Royal Marines officers thought more valuable than Sigint, which produced useful material. GCHQ insisted that Thorp exercise control 'with particular emphasis on restricting' the distribution even of sanitised Comint to the brigades on the islands. When Thorp followed these instructions, an Army officer who knew his function physically assaulted him. Thorp then disobeyed his orders by briefing straight from Sigint Colonel 'H' Jones – soon to lead 2 Para's assault at Goose Green – with the objective of protecting the base at San Carlos Sound while the main force assaulted Port Stanley. Thorp claimed, plausibly, that he reversed an incompetent briefing to Jones by 3 Commando Brigade. In any case, Sigint provided excellent material about Argentine forces at Goose Green. Jones was among the British deaths for a victory in which 600 British paratroopers killed or captured 1,000 Argentine soldiers and broke their nerve across the islands.[335] Other superiors ignored Thorp and his intelligence that Argentine forces might counter-attack British positions in San Carlos Sound. He provided no intelligence for the assault on Stanley. The main source became tactical intelligence from troops, who also jury-rigged Sigint of their own.[336] An indoctrinated officer, Major Dawkins, was attached to the staff of General Moore to handle Comint, but he received little from the source.

In terms of its direct contribution to battle on the Falkland Islands, British Sigint failed. On 13–14 June, Argentine air forces at Stanley reported: 'Their strategy is clear and they are probably planning to move in late evening or tomorrow morning. Their fire power has complete dominance over ours.' Argentine forces would collapse 'in 24 to 48 hours'.[337] British forces could observe these same facts themselves. Fortunately, intelligence was unnecessary for the victory on land. The men proved themselves enough.

Professional Deformations

Comint and Comsec were GCHQ's stock-in-trade, honed against excellent adversaries. As a result, GCHQ was predisposed to overrate Argentine Comint. However, reinforced by an assessment that Argentine Comint was effective only against internal opponents, GCHQ correctly told the JIC 'that the Argentinians would not be able to break British cyphers provided that these were properly used'.[338] Argentine practices, however, initially rudimentary, improved rapidly. Their national effort produced decent traffic analysis by 14 June. GCHQ easily traced this rise.[339] GCHQ's conclusions about Argentine Comint were alarmist, but its actions were reasonable; it devoted no more effort to the Argentine threat than was justified, and perhaps contained its growth. However, this exaggeration shaped a greater issue: GCHQ's effort to follow IRSIG.

Siginters and their consumers had little experience with Sigint in war. They followed rules written by those who had done so: folk memories of what was supposed to happen confronted startling instances of Comsec incompetence. RAF security noted 'the extremely amateur attempt to "make safe" an operational topic through open reference to *Jane's Fighting Ships* is a classic and appalling breach of security'.[340] Actors wished to use intelligence that addressed their problems, which, in the Falklands conflict, were among the greatest they had known. Given the nature of this crisis, the power of GCHQ and its use by the FCO, non-codeword diplomatic telegrams often mentioned material generated from Comint – even worse, exclusively from that source. GCHQ could not prevent this spread of knowledge, but did contain action taken on it. In particular, diplomats wanted to act on intelligence to stop Argentine arms purchases, say, by warning foreign governments off actions they were known to be considering. One diplomat complained that 'over-strict adherence to the letter of the rule book may prevent ... tactical advantage of fresh COMINT reports that is their only real value'.[341] GCHQ retorted that warning foreigners 'we were reading their international commercial traffic' was dangerous, let alone hinting at compromises of their diplomatic cyphers.[342] It controlled such actions, often small in significance and liable to compromise the source, but sometimes imperative. Britain might have gained from burning its coverage of diplomatic and commercial targets in order to stop the sale of ten Exocet anti-ship missiles, though that dilemma never emerged.

GCHQ never challenged how senior commanders acted on Sigint. Why not? Victory was at stake, few actions could really endanger the source, while imagery could be used plausibly to cover British actions. GCHQ authorised Fieldhouse to use Sigint as he wished, so long as the source was not mentioned outside Comint channels or in orders. Its material for Northwood aimed for 'packaging and tailoring ... in best Savile Row style – neat smart and pertinent'.[343] Much friction, however, arose from efforts to provide Sigint to staff officers, or to give predictive intelligence – where enemy ships might move, or the strength of enemy garrisons two days away – to the commanders of ships or battalions, who often acted independently, far from superior officers. To pass predictive intelligence from Category 3 Comint to recipients outside Sigint channels, such as junior commanders – when by definition 'there is no real cover (real or notional)' – only endangered the source.[344] GCHQ resisted this pressure, particularly after the Ted Rowlands compromise led Argentina to improve its cryptosystems. Junior officers had less need for Comint than senior ones, and standard procedures to sanitise information seemed sufficient.

Still, this friction caused pain. On 23 April, Fieldhouse informed many ships that 'intercepts' showed *Santa Fe* was near South Georgia. GCHQ had just shown that Argentine forces anticipated a British attack in the area.[345] This timely warning to a command 1,000 miles away from TF 317 that was about to attack the island shocked GCHQ, primarily because the submarine was named. The liaison officer at Northwood, GCO (N), reported this event secretly to Z in a teleconference, because 'it is totally informal with only the one paper record which I can destroy, whereas a formal signal is kept here on file and our STS phone is in the middle of the working area surrounded by all ranks, etc'. GCHQ representatives fought to keep Fieldhouse 'on the even keel of asking permission for action, taking advice on rules etc, but our success was not total'. Z replied: 'Only you [GCO(N)] at NORTHWOOD have power to take codeword off. The RN has to accept that or get a hell of a rocket from enormous height. If you can give evidence of flagrant abuse we can and will take up the cudgels but I guess that it's mainly a case of creeping sin which is harder to stop.'[346]

In signals copied to DGI and DCDS (I), GCHQ soon reminded Fieldhouse of the rules, and its flexibility with them. He promised to behave well, and to have Woodward do so: but a war was on. GCHQ tolerated this situation, concluding that 'whilst the matter had not been handled correctly, no harm had been done to Sigint', especially after documents captured from the *Santa Fe* showed Argentine confusion and ignorance.[347] Still, it warned Fieldhouse that if Argentina concluded:

the UK is intercepting important traffic (which we are) they can easily stop us doing so by some quite simple procedural changes ... GCHQ has given to authorities at Northwood blanket authorisation for action-on (if downgrading to secret level) only for actual or past locations of Argentinean or Soviet military units. All other requests for action-on must be taken in consultation with GCHQ and we have posted GCHQ officers to Northwood with delegated authority to take action-on decisions to make this as swift and efficient a process as possible. These officers are under strict instructions to report after the fact to GCHQ, all cases where action-on has been taken, including those cases where Sigint security rules have been breached by action being taken without prior consultation with GCHQ.[348]

As the war became hot, GCHQ authorised the downgrading of Category 2 Comint to secret levels, but not of 3, which Fieldhouse and Woodward received in floods. Ultimately, Siginters met military needs, enabling the use of actionable Sigint without compromising security. GCHQ was more concerned with its rules on secure handling and Comsec than absolutely required, but only at miniscule cost.

The Falklands conflict was the first of a series of cases, which continue today, where GCHQ aided expeditionary forces which suddenly fought in unexpected areas. To get national level or tactical Sigint to forces of divisional strength or below in size proved hard in Kuwait in 1991, Bosnia in 1992, and Iraq and Afghanistan after 2001. GCHQ was good at sudden crises, but better at set pieces. GCHQ worked best where it had more time for preparation and to work with larger forces. Time and experience was needed to deliver Sigint to small forces, as the mixed records of the cases of Konfrontasi and the Falklands conflict illuminate; even so, GCHQ's performance in these cases was excellent, and it handled these emergencies better than its enemies.

Secrecy, Translucency and Oversight, 1830–2019

Comsec and Communications-Electronic Security, 1945–92

In 1939, British – and American – Comsec was mediocre. Hostile Sigint agencies compromised many British systems. Only Ultra ensured British and American victory in the wireless war, which demonstrates the poverty of their cryptography. Allied forces did not understand their failures until after Germany surrendered and Axis Siginters outlined their successes. These failures affected British policy only years after the war. GCHQ always believed that Sigint and Comsec should be unified. Many Comsec authorities countered that if so, as before 1939, the needs for attack would always overwhelm those for defence. In 1945, GCHQ planned to control cryptography which, it claimed, needed to be combined with cryptanalysis. Initially, no one challenged GCHQ's view, since Britain had moved to the top of the world in Comsec and cypher machines.[1] However, by 1952, no new online systems had been completed since the war's end.

The most ambitious of the crypto projects pursued by GCHQ – designed by cryptanalytic machine experts such as Pat Bayley and Welchman – failed partly because GCHQ managed them poorly. GCHQ's work with all forms of technical research and development hit its nadir perhaps due to a failure to appreciate the significance and complexity of these matters, leaving other institutions to lead them.[2] GCHQ was led by the man most responsible for the prewar failures in cryptography, Travis. Its personnel had little or no responsibility for Britain's best crypto machines – for example Typex, Typex Mercury, 5 UCO (Secretype) and Rockex II – which outsiders designed and other institutions, such as the Army, RAF and SIS, carried through initial development. GCHQ worked with only one of these developments, the later stages of Rockex II.[3] GCHQ's great success in Comsec kit – Tiltman's Stencil Subtractor Frame – was not a machine. Experts in Comsec, especially in the military services, and some civil servants, particularly Edward Bridges, who had handled policy towards cypher machines for fifteen years, discerned a connection between past and present failures. In 1953, they concluded that the Comsec elements of GCHQ had to become independent, in what ultimately was named the Communications-Electronics Security Department (CESD). That GCHQ did not challenge this approach, nor anyone else, shows that its competence in cryptography was questioned. In any case, GCHQ had work enough elsewhere to absorb its attention.[4]

Though the leaders of CESD reflected signs of empire-building and an allergic reaction to cooperation with GCHQ, this division was justified. CESD and GCHQ maintained the necessary links between Comsec and cryptanalysis. CESD did better in developing cypher machines than GC&CS and GCHQ had done. CESD unified the efforts of the technical teams working on cypher machines in many units and brought them into one. It established sound means for research and development and production based on the models of military work with signals. CESD bequeathed good systems which saw British cryptography through to 1980, though few prototypes entered standard use. Mistakes were made and recovery from major ones was slow and hard. CESD had to work with every technical research group in Whitehall that handled signals security, which sometimes overwhelmed it. Ultimately, CESD died as a separate organisation because the need was no longer clear, partly because of its own success, while the costs were obvious – not financial, but human. The greatest limit for British Sigint was in procuring scientists and technicians. CESD needed far more of them per capita than GCHQ – indeed, absolutely almost as many as Cheltenham required – yet found them even harder to hire because it was a small and isolated unit and essentially military in character. CESD's solution to these shortages – to hire retired officers – solved problems of quantity and quality only in the short term, and perhaps reinforced the unwillingness of young scientists to join CESD. The fighting services refused to cooperate as CESD needed them to, as they moved away from leadership in Sigint and the expertise of retired personnel became obsolete. Though no one fully appreciated the fact, CESD fell behind in technical areas involving cryptography.

GCHQ had greater skills than any other government organisation for the new age of digitisation.[5] GCHQ became competent in managing research and development and production for technical equipment, and in acquiring scientists and technicians. CESD leaders served far longer than those of GCHQ, because they ran a technical unit, where leaders were few. By 1969, when Captain Stannard, RN, the second head of CESD, died, seventy-three of its complement of 310 were vacant (including 30 per cent of its research and development staff) with no likelihood of improvement in sight. GCHQ's complement of scientists, conversely, at last was complete.[6] No one questioned the quality of CESD's work, but all doubted its viability as an independent institution. After an investigation led by the intelligence coordinator Dick White, Whitehall abolished CESD as an independent unit and returned it to GCHQ as a distinct division named the Communications-Electronics Security Group (CESG).[7] The abolition of CESD was as justifiable as its creation had been. CESG remained quasi-independent until two decades after the Cold War ended, with enough resources to handle its task.

The experiences of CESD and CESG provide a useful mirror for GCHQ. Politically, CESD was weaker compared to American organisations than GCHQ. The United States service Sigint agencies controlled cryptography, where NSA was weak, the opposite situation to Sigint. CESD bargained from an inferior political and technical position with its American counterparts. It defended core British interests in cryptography, but had little effect on American decisions or modes of decision-making. This weakness particularly shaped 'equities' – the need to balance the conflicting interests of security and intelligence such as the classic question affecting all decisions about cryptography with third parties: would spreading awareness of a Comsec vulnerability reduce Siginters' capability to exploit it? American Siginters were unwilling to let any ally, including Britain, near their best cryptographic equipment. American and British Comsec authorities routinely bickered, and sometimes fought, over the level of aid they should give NATO. In 1962, shortly before aiding GCHQ during the Hampshire Report, Tordella warned that if Britain were to challenge American policy over marketing cypher machines to NATO it would cause 'quite serious strain in U.K./U.S. dealings'.[8] UKUSA also hampered British firms from exploiting fully the possibilities for sales of cryptographic machines to Commonwealth countries, where substantial interest existed.[9] Whether independent, or subordinate, CESD and CESG also distanced GCHQ from some outside organisations. They worked better with British industry than GCHQ did. CESD ensured that British defence electronics firms benefitted as much from contracts for cypher machines as any other Western country and financed technological and commercial developments, whereas GCHQ did little to help the British computer industry.

New problems emerged in Comsec. Between 1945 and 1980, the use of telephones rose more than any other form of communication, yet speech security initially was primitive. Creating secure speech systems became essential, and difficult. Consumers disliked the first generation of speech encryption kit, the American Sigsaly, which they said made them sound like Donald Duck.[10] Those factors, and clumsy protocols, caused irritations among consumers throughout the Cold War. The first decade of British work in the field failed because direction was weak. In 1958, high-level telephone conversations between Eisenhower and Harold Macmillan were covered only by scrambler systems, which provided no security.[11] Then, however, Britain regularly developed sound secure speech systems, moving from Pickwick in 1958 to Brent in the mid-1990s. Brent machines became the most familiar cryptographic items in Whitehall. Thousands of copies sat on official desks in the UK and its establishments abroad.

The discovery around 1956 of the phenomenon of Tempest, which enabled emissions from electronic equipment to be intercepted from hundreds of yards away, threatened any electronic system of cryptography by compromising layers of encryption. Overcoming Tempest imposed a huge burden on machine design to minimise radiation, and an even greater cost for physical infrastructure – such as shielded rooms – in locales where they were based. No crypto machine designed before Tempest was prepared to handle it, which crippled many of them – particularly the standard system for the Foreign Office, Rockex II. The problem was both the machine and the many areas where it was deployed, Eastern bloc and third-world countries where Soviet intelligence might intercept traffic from British embassies. Earlier versions of Rockex II could not be used securely for teleprinter traffic except on circuits where remarkably shielded areas protected both points – as on the most important links, like London to Moscow.[12] A later version of Rockex II, Mk IV-BID/08/07, produced in small numbers, was 'Tempest compliant', as were later online machines like Noreen. In any case, for a decade, suddenly British diplomatic systems returned almost to the stone age. Rockex II was used in manual format in a stripped-down version, which eliminated its main value – rapid one-time pad security for teleprinter traffic – and exposed its weak point: the reliance on expensive and fragile one-time tape. Diplomats returned to books, covered by manual one-time pads.[13] These problems were smaller for military Comsec, where machines were not used in vulnerable areas. Typex Mercury and 5 UCO were used for top secret traffic until 1965. By the 1980s, further problems emerged for Comsec with digitisation and then with the advent of personal computers – where encryption increasingly was baked into the body of the cake, rather than being added on later as a layer of icing.

More than perhaps any other Western country except the United States, Britain produced good and cost-effective cypher machines during the Cold War. Its best kit outmatched anything produced by European members of NATO. CESD and British industry developed better and cheaper cypher machines than any of these competitors. In a cut-throat battle of the 1960s, NATO adopted the British system, Alvis, to cover high-level communications. This success helped the British economy, exports in defence electronics and Western cryptography.[14] Yet many CESD programmes failed. Its problem was standard for the British defence industrial sector: the pursuit of too many prototypes simultaneously, overstretched the limited strength in engineers, increased costs and extended the time for completion. The loss of time led to missed opportunities and exposed programmes to continual upgrades while still under design, which produced further delays or made machines obsolete before completion. In the 1960s, it took seven years to move cryptographic machines from a statement of requirements to production – assuming they ever reached that stage.[15] Soon, seven years was seen as a remarkably fast time to finish that process.

The system worked as it was supposed to on many good British cryptosystems, such as Alvis. Yet almost equally often, only emergencies or a high priority could provide enough pressure to overcome the problem of time. Small teams, with able leadership, which pursued unorthodox solutions to problems best exploited such opportunities. Problems and solutions varied, however, and not every unorthodox approach succeeded; just as not every orthodox one failed. In every success, skilled and visionary technicians treated these projects as their main work, and controlled research and development up to the moment of production, rather than passing the project over to others halfway through. These characteristics marked the development of about half of the best British cryptosystems of the twentieth century, such as Typex, Rockex II and 5 UCO between 1934 and 1945. Experienced signals personnel independently pursued innovative approaches, which their institutions backed as soon as the first signs emerged of success. So too, in the later 1950s, when military authorities demanded immediate secure speech, CESD rapidly converted a prototype scrambler telephone system, Pickwick, into a good system for secure speech. Pickwick was then applied across British commands, overcoming a decade of CESD's failure to produce such a system.[16]

Some of these characteristics continued after the Cold War. Between 1988 and 1995, CESG developed Brent, 'the first UK desktop High Grade fully Tempest-approved secure telephone', designed to be user-friendly, with 'true-to-person speech quality'. CESG did so by giving a small team control over design and development to the production stage, rather than passing the system over to a civilian contractor when development began, so to control events, minimise bureaucratisation and exploit advanced commercial practices. The team rejected older procedures, and '1950s to 1970s ironmongery'. Instead, they combined the aims of state security with the convenience of the best civilian kit, substituting public key cryptography for old labour-intensive means. Brent pleased a generation of Whitehall users and became a commercial success. A few years later, however, while attempting to follow this model, CESG handled another secure speech system, Pippa, as clumsily as any other project in the history of British cryptosystems.[17] These patterns of success and failure are not British, but universal. Designing effective cryptosystems is hard. Protecting them is even harder.

CESD and CESG produced equipment for defensive purposes and manuals on how to use it, not intelligence. CESG handled distinct customers, on the long timescales that characterised procurement rather than on the short ones for the consumption of intelligence; its successes were seldom dramatic or even knowable. Furthermore it was remote from GCHQ, geographically from Cheltenham and psychologically from Oakley or Benhall. Comsec was outside the mainstream of GCHQ, but close enough to enable technical cooperation and the exchange of knowledge and people. Cryptosystems were developed rationally and avoided the errors of the interwar period. The wastage, and the number of failed or abandoned projects, fell within the normal range for British defence electronics. The successes kept Britain at the upper end of a competitive market in encryption. One cannot know the success of British Comsec until the records of the other side are released. The success of the Walker family of spies in penetrating US Navy cryptosystems demonstrates the costs of slips in Comsec, and the range of enemies it confronts.

The Contradictions of Secrecy

For Siginters, secrecy was more than just a means for security; it was almost an aim in itself: part of their being – membership in a cult involving honour and doctrine. When their secrecy was violated, Siginters felt disgust, like Malcolm Kennedy when the US Congressional committee on Pearl Harbor released Magic, and Tiltman when Frederick Winterbotham published *The Ultra Secret*.[18] Even in 2020, Siginters feel disquiet when they see the name GCHQ, in press headlines.

Whitehall had equally intense views on the secrecy of Sigint, but focused on security. All of Whitehall was secret, but GCHQ was its quintessence. Whitehall oversaw GCHQ in a unique and unorthodox fashion, treating it both as a normal department and a secret service. MI5 and MI6 were open secrets; Whitehall sought to keep GCHQ a real secret. GCHQ reported to the Foreign Secretary and acted only on principles approved and monitored by LSIC and PSIS, while the Treasury audited its finances, loosely. Whitehall felt that any closer management might endanger GCHQ's work or political neutrality and expose politicians to embarrassment. One Foreign Secretary, Austen Chamberlain, expressed this traditional view in 1924: 'It is of the essence of a secret service that it must be secret, and if you once begin disclosure … there is no longer any Secret Service and … you must do without it.'[19]

For secret services, secrecy was paramount, and parliamentary control impossible. This situation was tolerable constitutionally, because Britons could trust honourable men to guard the guardians. For anyone who knew the facts, these arguments about GCHQ had force and those arrangements arguably were proper. Whitehall, however, kept these facts from the public, where from 1960 faith eroded in honourable men. Since GCHQ was an unavowed institution, any of its actions, if known, must raise suspicion, as would the secrecy around it. Since GCHQ was a large department, which interacted openly with tens of thousands of people, such suspicions were hard to avoid. GCHQ knew that material already in the public domain would reveal its existence and work and believed that the story of Ultra, and hence its existence, would become public. Changes in public and official attitudes towards privacy, secrecy and security soon exacerbated these contradictions in the secrecy around Sigint. They emerged particularly in law and history.

Between 1844 and 1914, officials and politicians disliked intercepting communications outside of war, and thought the British public had similar views. During the Great War, it was noted how censors working in postal censorship felt 'an involuntary and deep-seated disgust when (they) first broke the seal of an unknown person's correspondence, a natural sentiment which indicates how profound was the confidence men had in the posts and how inconsistent with liberty and with good faith it appeared to invade the rights of private correspondence which ought to be held peculiarly sacred'.[20] Yet such experiences taught Whitehall that Sigint – and secrecy about it – was essential in peacetime. These ends required the legal ability to intercept diplomatic cables in times of peace, which did not exist in Britain. Intelligence authorities, fearing public opposition to that power, handled it gingerly.[21] Section Four of the Official Secrets Act (1920) ordered cable and wireless operators to give the government, under the warrant of any Secretary of State, 'all telegrams, or of telegrams of any specified class or description, or of telegrams sent from or addressed to any specified person or place, sent or received to or from any place out of the United Kingdom'.[22] This section openly changed prior practice, yet received little public criticism, unlike other clauses in the legislation, which suggests that experiences with censorship and war had changed public attitudes towards the interception of communications. In any case, this section was moderate, compared to the censorship regime between 1914 and 1919, and seemed simply to extend agreed rules for postal censorship to telegrams.

In fact, bulk intercept became more common with telegrams than post. Under a rolling warrant, automatically renewed each year, cable companies give GC&CS drop copies of the telegrams of all foreign governments which passed through British territory. Any further intercepts required a special warrant, which might be substantial. The Home Office warrant during the General Strike of 1926, for example, covered 'all telegrams into and out of Great Britain containing messages directed to impeding necessary action, or to procuring undesirable action in the present emergency ... one of the main objects ... is to prevent the transmission of messages directing payment of large sums of money to persons and bodies acting in defiance of Emergency provisions'.[23] Companies could not scrutinise every cable entering or leaving Britain on such a broad range of issues, which emphasised communists and some trade unionists: they simply would have examined the telegrams of specific individuals or organisations named on a list, or those sent to and from specific addresses. Though contemporaries would have considered this warrant, and the rolling one, to be general warrants, in modern terms they warranted bulk collection.

For thirty-five years, that rolling warrant regulated the collection of telegrams, which fell in significance. Procedures were taken for granted as experiences in a second total war reinforced those from the first. By 1955, however, legal authorities in the Foreign Office questioned this approach, because the Official Secrets Act aimed to prevent espionage, not to collect intelligence on foreign states.[24] No one had raised this objection before, or acted on it, but it signalled changing attitudes towards law and Sigint. The Vienna Convention on Diplomatic Relations of 1961, and the British Diplomatic Privileges Act of 1964, raised questions about the legality of intercepting foreign traffic, though these instruments legitimately could be read to mean that diplomatic messages might be copied so long as they were delivered.

Nonetheless, changes in attitudes, and technology, and the sting of scandals, made legal issues matter to GCHQ. Public debates emerged over the danger of the interception of telephone conversations – forms of industrial or personal espionage which were often called 'eavesdropping'. Though these fears overstated the danger, foreign states, and criminals at home and abroad, became able to intercept communications within Britain – as could, of course, British authorities. Several scandals drew public attention to the issue. In 1956, for example, authorities publicly used telephone taps against a criminal, Billy Hill, in a successful effort to disbar his barrister, Patrick Marrinan. A decade later, Chapman Pincher, a journalist with the *Daily Express*, disclosed the rolling warrant, while naming the MOD (rather than GCHQ) as the recipient. That Pincher failed to discover GCHQ's role reflects the effect of security procedures around it. This story provoked the D-notice affair, a major scandal in British politics during the 1960s.[25]

Though these scandals, with the exception of the D-notice affair, were unrelated to GCHQ, they sometimes produced public statements or legal rulings which affected its work. Matters involving Sigint were discussed openly in the press. Through backstairs work, GCHQ kept itself and Sigint from these public discussions, even over the D-notice affair, which quickly turned to personal scandal and abuse. GCHQ representatives met the Birkett and Radcliffe committees, which examined these two scandals, and explained GCHQ's involvement in these issues or how they might damage British security. These committees kept GCHQ from their reports and safe from their proposed legislation.[26] The Birkett Committee of 1957, which examined the Hill case and more broadly 'the interception of communications', did not even mention GCHQ or the interception of foreign communications, Instead, in sections nominally dedicated to MI5, but extendable to GCHQ, the committee stated obliquely that 'the problems of national security are such that no reasonable weapon should be taken from the hands of those whose duty it is to watch over all subversive activities in the safeguarding of British interests … the methods of interception hitherto employed are necessary, and have been productive of important results which could not have been obtained in any other way'.[27] In particular, the committee approved the interception of communications between a British subject in Britain and any entity based abroad. Viscount Radcliffe originally aimed to discuss interception practices thoroughly, but first requested briefings from the intelligence agencies. After hearing the accounts of GCHQ, JIC, MI5 and MI6, the Radcliffe Committee instead focused on D-notices rather than drop copies, though it gave the government a 'Confidential Annexe' on Sigint.[28]

These issues caused GCHQ and the government to consider more thoroughly than ever since 1920 the legality of their practices of interception, and to institute regular reviews which continue to the present day. After both the Birkett and Radcliffe reports, the prime minister of the day chaired a committee of senior ministers and civil servants which reviewed all practices for interception of communications. These committees tightened procedures without transforming them, while extending practices to cover emerging forms of communication, such as trunk telexes. GCHQ asked the Foreign Office's approval for any changes in practices. It never touched British-to-British communications, unless this accidentally occurred through interception of ILC or Comsat traffic.[29] Due to pressure from the prime minister at the time, Harold Wilson, any foreign communications which mentioned MPs, or the accidental harvesting of their own messages, were treated with special discretion as 'UK Governmental' – which was the same category covering similar practices regarding ministers. When the D-notice affair demonstrated confusion over the practices of interception, Whitehall issued new general warrants in 1969, which thereafter were renewed every six months, and only after an explicit revaluation of their work. The privatisation of the GPO raised questions about whether the government could collect correspondence through warrants, which ministers and officials maintained through brilliant obfuscation. The Post Office Bill of 1969 ordered the private company to obey ministerial orders, 'to secure that a particular thing that it or a subsidiary of its is doing is no longer done or that a particular thing that it has power to do, but is not being done either by it or a subsidiary of its, is so done'. Such orders must remain secret – if anyone could understand their meaning.[30]

The government acted to ensure that Sigint worked legally, yet secretly, with one gap. When capturing ILC and Comsat traffic in international space, GCHQ unavoidably caught the traffic of British people. It simply discarded this traffic unless a special warrant covered the person or content. The dictates of the Birkett Committee, and of two prime ministerial committees, supported this approach, but legally questions might be raised. The issue seemed minor, given GCHQ's focus on military and diplomatic traffic, but its significance swelled after 1990, with the end of the Cold War and the reduction in high-frequency radio, and the rise of the internet.

Meanwhile, history compromised secrecy. Between the wars, British intelligence attempted to prevent any publications about British Sigint, with mixed success. Admiral Sinclair, Denniston and the Cabinet Secretary, Maurice Hankey, held that Britain must hide the existence of the GC&CS so not to have other governments raise their cryptographic standards or alarm the British public. Yet the publication of Soviet telegrams of 1920–23 and 1927 showed everyone these facts, while details of the GC&CS's personnel were published with the Naval Estimates until 1922, and the Foreign Office Vote until 1941.[31]

In 1920, the NID and MID kept Marconi from publishing a monograph about its role in military wireless and Sigint during the Great War. 'Most civilised countries must have realised that we did possess a highly organised Wireless Intelligence and a Cryptographic Bureau, but practically no information has ever been available to them as to the pitch of perfection that these organisations reached, and it is most desirable that this information should still remain unavailable'. So to maintain advantages over any enemy, 'it is most desirable that as little information as possible should be made public either as to the organisations employed, or the nature or method of handling of the information obtained'.[32] Yet the NID and MID simultaneously let the Marconi officer H. J. Round, Britain's leading expert in wireless interception, publish a long technical report on that matter through the Institute for Electrical Engineers, including some discussion of the role of direction-finding against submarines and Zeppelins, and at the battle of Jutland. Conventional scientific considerations motivated Round. He thought that through interception, 'the most amazing developments have taken place, in which I think we may safely say more knowledge has been obtained than in all the years before, since wireless was first thought of', although 'we have all been working under the difficulty that the ordinary safety valve of the scientific man – the ability to show off his stunts and gadgets to an admiring audience is absent due to war secrecy'.[33] In 1921, moreover, several writers who had served in Sigint – Ferdinand Tuohy, Filson Young, and Stephen McKenna – published accurate accounts of Room 40, military wireless intelligence and the WTID. Many veterans, including Churchill and Ewing, later wrote of their experiences with Sigint, without efforts to suppress them. Such publications inspired naval Sigint in Italy, Germany and the United States. From 1932, however, with the trial of Compton MacKenzie over his memoirs as an MI6 officer in Greece during 1916–17, attitudes stiffened towards histories of intelligence. Admiral Hall was soon prevented from publishing a ghostwritten memoir.

Those attitudes escalated after 1945, and prevented any publication to match the most significant of the interwar years. Even so, many official and unofficial histories referred obliquely and sometimes directly to Sigint during the Second World War, enough to point towards truths. GCHQ believed that sufficient evidence was available in the public domain to confirm that it was a Sigint agency.[34] It also thought that public knowledge of Ultra and the breaking of Enigma was just a matter of time.[35] By 1966, the pioneering historian of Sigint, David Kahn, almost discovered the Ultra secret as he researched *The Codebreakers*. GCHQ and NSA regarded Kahn as among the greatest security threats they had yet faced. When he visited Cheltenham in an abortive attempt to interview Hugh Alexander, GCHQ announced uneasily that 'Kahn is at the gate' – as one internal GCHQ history noted, whether Genghis or David was unclear. GCHQ thought that Kahn would discover and describe Ultra. He did not quite seize that prize, although he mentioned that British Sigint centred on Bletchley Park, employed over 30,000 people by 1944, and asked what they might have been doing. In order to ease publication, and perhaps for reasons of patriotism, Kahn and his publishers also agreed not to use much material he had collected about the work of GCHQ and NSA after 1945, which demonstrated the vulnerability of their cover stories.

Soon after these histories, the Polish and French veterans Marian Rejewski and Colonel Bertrand openly described how they and GC&CS had broken Enigma during 1939–40. GCHQ knew that the rest of the story would come out, especially after Britain put its archives open to historical scrutiny and on a thirty-year basis. GCHQ and the JIC discussed these issues every few months between 1966 and 1973, and also the commissioning of an official history of British intelligence during the Second World War. GCHQ prevented writers of the late 1960s, such as Donald McLachlan, from mentioning Ultra, and blocked Patrick Seale from exploiting his privileged access to Denniston's papers. GCHQ, however, decided that it would not oppose the next author who tried simply to publish the story. That the book in question had significant errors eased this decision. During 1974, in *The Ultra Secret*, Winterbotham, who commanded comint communications between 1940 and 1945, released the first general account of Ultra. Even so, 'a basic GCHQ aim' remained 'of discouraging further attempts by private individuals, following Frederick Winterbotham's example, to fill gaps in the public history on intelligence subjects, particularly any such attempts which might include information on methods and techniques'. GCHQ hoped to further this aim by announcing that it would publish an official history of the matter, while discouraging competent authors from tackling the topic.[36] The next question obviously would be: what happened to GC&CS at the end of the war? For GCHQ, history was not dead; it was not even known.

Coming Out: Scandal and Avowal

GCHQ managed these challenges quietly and well, behind the scenes. This very success left it unprepared for a public competition over secrecy and openness, which opened suddenly between Whitehall and forces that GCHQ had never faced before: public critics, and a decline in deference towards and trust in government. GCHQ, the most secret agency of a government marked by secrecy, was most exposed to these forces. As this struggle opened, no one knew the rules. It reflected and shaped subliminal changes in public attitudes. The particular way that scandals exploded shaped the relationship between contradictory trends which echo today about the value of intelligence and security against those of privacy and secrecy.

Until 1970, outside Gloucestershire, GCHQ was simply an entry in government directories. GCHQ was not only secret, but anonymous. Between 1945 and 1975, GCHQ appeared in *Hansard* only on lists of departments. *The Times* mentioned GCHQ on just ten occasions: nine were 'situations vacant', while the last repeated the revelations of a former NSA employee about UKUSA and GCHQ, originally published in *Ramparts* magazine across the water. After thirty years of happy obscurity, journalists and events gave GCHQ fifteen years of unsought publicity. Chapman Pincher revealed elements of intelligence, though his work later became peculiar, sometimes conspiratorial. Revelations about GCHQ moved from anti-establishment magazines to the quality press. In 1976, *Time Out* published two articles by Duncan

Campbell and Mark Hosenball, each at the start of outstanding careers as journalists. These articles, well researched and generally accurate, provided the best snapshot of GCHQ on the public record. As GCHQ already knew, much evidence about it was public, including material which Campbell and Hosenball overlooked. Whitehall, believing that politically motivated adversaries were assaulting Western intelligence, launched a heavy-handed counter-attack. Though it was bound to use the Official Secrets Act, the flimsiness of which no one understood, to ignore Campbell would have served the cult of secrecy better. Together, in ways which suited neither of their aims, Whitehall and its opponents drove Britain down a road of scandal, which ultimately made GCHQ a public and trusted institution.

Whitehall deported Hosenball, an American citizen, as a threat to national security, but Campbell remained to torment mandarins for decades. Campbell, an able and courageous man of the left, whose mother had served in Sigint during the Second World War, denounced British foreign and defence policy, and Sigint, as illegal, immoral and unnecessary. 'Why do I keep going?' he wrote in retrospect. 'Because from the beginning, my investigations revealed a once-unimaginable scope of governmental surveillance, collusion, and concealment by the British and U.S. governments – practices that were always as much about domestic spying during times of peace as they were about keeping citizens safe from supposed foreign enemies, thus giving the British government the potential power to become ... a virtual "police state".'[37] His *Time Out* articles led a former Royal Signals NCO, John Berry, to offer further details about GCHQ. Berry and Campbell were arrested, alongside another *Time Out* journalist, Crispin Aubrey. Their subsequent trial under the Official Secrets Act – inevitably the 'ABC trial' after the names of the defendants – generated more publicity than the original article. Although the three were convicted on minor charges, this was a Pyrrhic victory for the government. The Official Secrets Act was discredited, and GCHQ became a target for many journalists and for the three stalwarts of the left-liberal press, the *Guardian*, the *New Statesman*, and the *Observer*. Campbell and the *New Statesman* together published many attacks on British intelligence and security policy.

The ABC affair, GCHQ's equivalent of the Lady Chatterley trial, revealed how old hands misunderstood new attitudes, though the lessons were not learned for another fifteen years until an Australian court embarrassed Robert Armstrong, the Cabinet Secretary, over efforts to censor *Spycatcher*, the memoir of retired MI5 officer Peter Wright. The establishment could no longer manage the press. The Official Secrets Act could no longer block disclosures about intelligence. The press no longer would police itself or be policed. Any evidence about GCHQ attracted attention, like a drop of blood amidst sharks. Anything secret must be scandalous, or bad. The mere existence of secrecy sparked conspiracy theories, which overwhelmed public understanding of intelligence for a generation. With so little evidence in the public domain, any real or alleged fact could be made to fit any case. GCHQ, which really was fixated on the threat from the Eastern bloc, could be described as an agent of 1984. Scandals stemmed simply from reporting basic facts, which often were innocuous. Accounts of GCHQ's successes could not be reported. GCHQ could not defend itself publicly against attacks. Any defence of its actions had to be made by others and taken on trust, which was where the problem began in the first place.

Several scandals struck GCHQ between 1982 and 1986. The first was the trial of Geoffrey Prime, the greatest traitor in the history of GCHQ. During the 1960s, Prime had trained as a Russian linguist with the RAF, and then entered the London Processing Group and GCHQ. Shortly before leaving the RAF, Prime sold himself to the Soviets because of 'a misplaced idealistic view of Soviet socialism which was compounded by basic psychological problems within myself'. He remained undetected throughout his career in GCHQ. His treachery was discovered only in 1982, after he retired, following his arrest for sexual assaults on young girls around Cheltenham.[38] The Prime case, which combined a favourite recipe on Fleet Street – sexual deviance and treachery – attracted sensational press interest. The Security Commission publicly condemned GCHQ and recommended that polygraphs be used for security vetting. This proposal was never adopted, partly because the prime minister, Thatcher, thought it useless, but it drew further unfavourable attention to GCHQ. Simultaneously, the quality newspapers, including teams of the best investigative reporters in Britain, published material which threatened security and victory during the Falklands conflict without being challenged by the Official Secrets Act.

These actions described the details of Sigint during a live crisis more than ever before anywhere, and inflicted far greater damage to British security than Campbell ever did – though they also gave the British public its best view of GCHQ's prowess during the Cold War. Two years later, in 1984, the government banned trade unions at GCHQ, which became a major issue in partisan politics. Annually, for the next twelve years, Labour politicians and trade unionists marched down the streets of Cheltenham, wielding banners and umbrellas. In 1986, Campbell, commissioned by the BBC to develop a six-part TV series entitled *Secret Society*, scored his greatest coup. He revealed the project to develop a British Sigint satellite, Zircon, and that its cost had been concealed from Parliament. The BBC was persuaded not to broadcast the episode on the grounds of national security. The *Observer* publicised this action. Injunctions and/or Special Branch raids struck Campbell, his researchers, the *New Statesman*, and the BBC. Attempts to show the episode to MPs within the House of Commons were thwarted, but samizdat copies were shown elsewhere in the UK. The Attorney General accepted that prosecutions would be inflammatory and probably unsuccessful: government overreaction generated far more publicity for GCHQ than unfavourable journalism. Once ignored, the Zircon affair faded from the headlines. Only the chattering classes cared about scandals over Sigint, and then not much.

GCHQ was not the only part of the secret establishment that was dragged into the open during this period, but it suffered the hardest blows. MI5 had always endured suspicion. GCHQ moved suddenly from anonymity to becoming a favourite target for suspicion on the left of British politics and the media. These events killed the cult of secrecy. From 1975, for administrative and political convenience, GCHQ quietly aimed to move from secrecy towards 'status', or a more conventional position as a department. These aims were enacted slowly. After the Prime case, in 1982 Thatcher avowed that GCHQ was an intelligence agency. The Intelligence Services Act of 1994 gave GCHQ statutory existence, alongside MI5 and MI6. Later, Britain borrowed the idea of parliamentary oversight of agencies from American practices. GCHQ led rather than resisted these developments, in order to disarm attacks based on its secrecy. No one knew, however, what would result. GCHQ did not intend to have its current activities made as public as they are in 2020.

The unexpected driver became the effect of history and myth on public attitudes. With the disclosure of Ultra, some veterans wrote memoirs and historians worked with records and interviews. The multi-volume official history of *British Intelligence in the Second World War* described wartime Sigint in detail. A few academics began to study the history of British intelligence because it was an important and unknown topic. First, without fanfare, and later through the Waldegrave Initiative, authorities declassified most Sigint records before September 1945. Enthusiasts tackled British Sigint during the Second World War. Aided by a substantial donation from British lotteries, they rebuilt Bletchley from a series of dilapidated buildings into a sort of shrine, a locale for pilgrimage, with relics such as working versions of Colossus. These enthusiasts struck a public chord. To the astonishment of Cheltenham, and without much encouragement from it, Bletchley – and by extension, GCHQ – came to symbolise British virtues and survival during its darkest hour. Soon, the cult of Bletchley, its saints and a martyr, protected GCHQ more than the cult of secrecy ever had done.

GCHQ and the Second Age of Sigint, 1990–2020

Coming in from the Cold War

The late Cold War was a marvellous time for GCHQ. Its work was honoured by those who knew of it. GCHQ solved long-standing structural problems, acquired more resources and power, and became an avowed organisation. Despite failing to develop a purely British Sigint satellite in Zircon, GCHQ realised that bold innovation was necessary, which prepared it for the period of transformational change as the Cold War waned.

By 1989, indications abounded that the Cold War was ending. The Foreign Office questioned the need for even routine Radio Proving Flights against the Warsaw Pact, implying that their political risks outweighed their intelligence gains.[1] GCHQ noted increasing signs of erosion within the Warsaw Pact and unprecedented civil unrest in the USSR.[2] The London Signals Intelligence Board (LSIB) linked Sigint closely with military operations. By 1991, however, it expected service Sigint units to evacuate Germany and decline.[3] For the intelligence services which had enabled victory, the consequences were bitter sweet. Many agencies specialised in narrow topics, which soon no one might support or fund. GCHQ ranked high among them. The Soviet threat absorbed most of GCHQ's effort. Ecological change exposed GCHQ – overdeveloped in one niche of Sigint – to disaster, like its greatest consumer. DIS was trapped in specialised analysis of minutiae. It demanded full servicing of its needs – Sigint alone could enable the work and careers of specialists in, say, tugs for the Baltic Fleet. Another danger was that DIS might grip GCHQ like a drowning man. Siginters, however, were agile and suited to many ecosystems, if only they could swim there.

The Director, John Adye, sidestepped disaster through an astute version of GCHQ's standard strategy of the Cold War. Victory was won, but any troops left on the field might die; so he withdrew as many as possible. He abandoned some tasks so to preserve the whole by shifting resources from the Warsaw Pact to broader matters, keeping bodies for trade. That effort began in 1990. It became a flood after the abortive coup in Moscow of 1991 showed the Russian threat was disintegrating. J division moved most of its resources to K, ultimately 90 per cent of them, while still servicing DIS demands. If GCHQ's masters were willing, it might provide great economies in resources, especially intercept operators and stations, to trade for the funding needed to serve new missions, could they be found.

This strategy reduced risk, but could not evade the Treasury's desire for a peace dividend. GCHQ faced demands for cuts like those imposed on all departments involved in hard power – which ultimately ranged between 20 per cent for the services as a whole to 50 per cent for organisations focused on the Warsaw Pact. This fate was avoided through a national, but secret, process, involving external reviews, backstairs manoeuvres, leading civil servants, the membership of GCHQ and a succession of directors able in different ways. This process unfolded through serendipity, without a master plan, or a Svengali. Several groups tackled parts of a problem, without knowing what it was, or the solution would be. As they acted, targets and threats evolved, and changes in communications and computer systems opened a new age of Sigint. No one understood where these developments would lead, until they got there. Only the terrorist outrages of 9/11 and 7/7 crystallised that understanding in Cheltenham, and in NSA.

In 1994, Whitehall began a series of defence reviews. Michael Quinlan, a retired permanent undersecretary from the MOD famed for understanding the theory and practice of strategy, assessed intelligence needs. He and his staff, Treasury and joint intelligence officials, considered all aspects of intelligence. They interrogated GCHQ and its consumers, visited NSA, DGSE (Direction générale de la sécurité extérieure) and BND, and read much Sigint product. Quinlan, grasping what intelligence had done for Britain during the Cold War and might do again, distilled several principles to guide policy. Defining the resources required for intelligence and Sigint rested 'more on judgment than on measurement and calculation; no formula existed … Even with the benefit of hindsight … it was not possible to assess the absolute value of secret intelligence since the difference between "with intelligence" and "without" would be hypothetical and unquantifiable, especially in those circumstances where the benefit was an unwelcome event averted.'[4]

Secret intelligence aimed to 'offset gaps, uncertainties or distortions in overt information in order to advance national interests', especially 'by enabling national forces to prevail in conflict, with minimum loss'. The end of the Cold War reduced 'the direct military threat', but produced 'a world more complex and interdependent, less certain and less stable, with a wider and shifting range of conflict risk'. These circumstances increased the value of secret intelligence, especially Sigint, with its ability 'to build up patterns of understanding over time, especially in military and security fields, and the wide range of targets that were amenable to attack'. The nature of targets and power between attack and defence shifted constantly: 'careful cost/benefit analysis would be needed and … there would remain constant pressure for innovation and investment to maintain capability'. GCHQ's costs had risen since 1984, but it was efficient and economical. Any 'significant' reduction in its budget would cause 'an unacceptable reduction in the provision of intelligence … GCHQ's current level of capability must be maintained'. GCHQ 'provided a national asset of high standard', whose 'capabilities should be maintained at broadly planned levels of cost'. However, its work against Russia should be examined, while an 'outsider, experienced in the high technology private sector', might assess the room for economies and efficiencies.[5] Prime Minister John Major, who proved a friend to GCHQ – critical but judicious – endorsed Quinlan's 1994 report.

These comments whetted the Treasury's appetite for economies and GCHQ's desire to survive. Whitehall had Roger Hurn, chair of Smith's Industries – an industrialist with a national reputation, connections to Cheltenham and a love for hunting, high technology and institutional change – assess GCHQ. All departments hoped he might lean their way, and schemed to shape his terms of reference, and panels of advisors.

GCHQ loaned Hurn a team, led by David Pepper, a rising star, who had executed Adye's strategy, aided by MOD and Treasury officials. Hurn, inexperienced in intelligence, but not in business and industrial management, was a fast learner with some *idees fixes*. He saw how GCHQ functioned as no outsider had done since Evill or Hampshire. Hurn's focus on the idea of charging consumers for intelligence wasted much space, but at this stage he understood the relationship between high technology and institutions well. Hurn illuminated other issues with a power which impressed Pepper. Hurn assessed processes, how value was added in intelligence, and visited the shop floor. He asked units why they worked as they did. Personnel often could answer only that they always had done so, and then rethought their work.

Hurn reported that: 'GCHQ is a very high quality, well-funded organisation employing a large number of talented and committed high quality people, most of whom stay with the organisation for all of their careers. They are justifiably proud of their record and place in the nation's intelligence community. In short, GCHQ is undoubtedly a centre of excellence which responds impressively to the many new challenges it faces in requirements, targets and technology.' Civil service bureaucracy marred GCHQ less than most departments, he found, though every unit still should 'delayer' one level of management. The focus on Russia must end immediately, and planned reductions of staff be completed rapidly. The formulation of policy on all matters, such as intelligence production and human resources, should be more centralised, but its execution more decentralised. He offered proposals which guided GCHQ for a generation. GCHQ officials must work in other departments, and vice versa, to emphasise contacts between consumers and producers. Palmer Street must become a permanent embassy in London to reduce GCHQ's isolation within Whitehall, and a few outsiders should become permanent members of the directorate to reduce the impact of 'inbreeding'. Above all, GCHQ must continue its ongoing 'shifts in behaviour and organisational culture, there is no simple prescription to achieve these things but without them the changes will be piecemeal and will fail to achieve their full effect. This is the biggest part of the challenge for GCHQ's management.'[6]

Much of Hurn's conclusion was implicit, and perhaps expressed verbally to his consumers. GCHQ was a great national asset which must reform to handle changes in consumers, targets, techniques and technology. With DIS and the Soviet threat both waning, GCHQ must find new tasks and consumers. Its strategy for change was broadly right, but must accelerate. Reinvention was necessary, though Hurn did not prescribe its forms. GCHQ's proposed economies were of the right size but he did not mention (or oppose) expansion or recommend any budget for GCHQ. The organisation which had won the Cold War was too slow and hierarchical to handle emerging tasks and needed outside leadership to do so.

This report convinced the civil servants responsible for Sigint. Even the Treasury switched its focus from economy to efficiency. Through a process which is not entirely clear, GCHQ kept most of its share of the peace dividend to reinvent itself – under new management. Again, GCHQ and the deterrent were Britain's priorities in defence. During the Defence Reviews of 1994–95, 50 per cent of the forces under BAOR and RAF Germany were disbanded. Collectively, the services lost 18 per cent of their personnel. DIS became a ghost. Military Siginters declined by 33 per cent in size, precisely as demands for them in conflicts grew. In Germany, No. 26 RAF SU and 13 Signals Regiment were disbanded, though some elements moved to other units; 14 Signals Regiment transferred to Wales, where its aid to the local economy helped it live. Military Sigint bodies in Britain were unified. GCHQ lost many civilian personnel, but reallocated those savings to new tasks, which paid dividends. GCHQ's manpower was cut; and some of the savings from this were reinvested in GCHQ's advanced collection capabilities. Intercept organisations focused on HF radio traffic in Europe were traded for the means to acquire all kinds of traffic across the globe. GCHQ achieved its greatest priority of the late Cold War, rebuilding its collection infrastructure for the digital age, at a price it could pay.

Reinvention

Privately, Hurn recommended that Britain exploit Adye's looming retirement to appoint a director from outside GCHQ. If GCHQ was a national asset, then its control must be nationalised. Prime Minister Major, the Foreign Secretary, the Cabinet Secretary and the Permanent Secretary of the Treasury agreed on this recommendation and a candidate: David Omand, a leading civil servant in the MOD – whose first civil service job, helpfully, had been in GCHQ – and a member of the advisory board on Hurn's report. Whitehall thought well enough of GCHQ to send three high-flyers there in a row. These actions upset a seventy-six-year-old tradition of appointing Sigint leaders from within, and began five years of outside instruction, while people and attitudes changed in Cheltenham.

Omand had joined GCHQ as a cadet but soon moved to the normal civil service, an unusual step at that time. He knew how GCHQ and Whitehall worked and how defence was managed. Omand was a mathematician, Fortran programmer and early adopter, but learned through experience. Clearly, the age of radio interception was ending, while the internet enabled some new era of communication and information. GCHQ could economise further on radio interception, meeting MOD demands with legacy systems, while investing in sources suited to the digital age and new consumers. Omand sought to make GCHQ a 'consumer facing organisation', which cultivated new customers across Whitehall, such as counter-proliferation and counter-narcotics units. GCHQ must give decision-makers 'value added intelligence' through agility and speed, unlike the industrial line production for DIS during the Cold War. The office at Palmer Street was staffed by an undersecretary and a team ordered to act 'more like SIS' – to identify potential consumers, determine their needs and meet them. Whereas DIS had known exactly what it wanted, new consumers might not know what they needed or could receive.

Knowledge of GCHQ, and a feline sense of opportunity, drove the formulation and execution of Omand's campaign. By 1990, reflecting its targets and consumers, GCHQ was a civilianised version of military models, more than at any other time in its history. Omand sidestepped these structures. He gave many employees his email address. If they raised important issues, he visited them directly rather than going through channels, which shocked his subordinates. GCHQ's leaders debated the case for change in informal meetings at Omand's flat in Cheltenham, rather than through directorate meetings with memoranda. Siginters were characterised by analytical ability and preference to work as a team. The leadership group was small, unified and knew each other well. This empirical approach produced consensus and detailed processes and systems for reform. NSA took years more to achieve similar ends because its leadership was larger and scattered across a continent – rather than concentrated at Cheltenham – and embedded within military organisations, where theories of an RMA, imposed top down, drove efforts at reform. When NSA did move, however, the speed and effect were extraordinary.

These developments changed lives. A generation of individuals, many groomed for promotion in a patronage-driven system, were frozen from the highest levels of GCHQ. The value of old technical skills diminished and those of new ones multiplied. Basic competence with PCs and the internet became essential for success, which opened new opportunities below. However, old hands worked loyally, including some who had seen the directorship in their future and now saw it slip from their grasp. All could see that GCHQ had escaped a worse fate and was proceeding on rational lines. The time needed to continue legacy systems and to inaugurate new ones enabled a phased pattern of retirements and dignity to all. Not until after 7/7 did the last of the old hands retire. For younger staff, these decisions were liberating. The old system and the obsolescence of its approach to computers and the internet frustrated many who joined after 1989. Young staff received the chance they wished – to play with the best kit and to match the successes of their parents and grandparents since 1940.

Reform involved re-education. GCHQ did so by hiring a private agency, ITS, which helped firms manage change. The firm educated, first, the upper 200 members of GCHQ, and ultimately the top 30 per cent of them – every manager and worker on any creative coalface. Through this programme, 'Lead 21', several outsiders regularly met small groups of Siginters who were drawn from different parts of GCHQ. These presenters received unparalleled access into Britain's most secret agencies, an indicative change in its own right. They addressed issues such as organisation and psychology, using devices including the Myers-Briggs personality assessments, which illustrated how different groups of people perceived circumstances and acted on them. Despite much academic criticism, these assessments often cause reflection among non-specialists. This approach challenged all the old conditioning of Siginters. They tended to be introspective. They were not encouraged to reflect on their work, but just to do it, generally in self-contained groups, without talking much to others. They had no collective experience of education in their profession or nature. Suddenly, large groups of Siginters went through the same collective psychological experience, talking openly about themselves and their work with others, and discussing, explicitly, issues such as introversion and extraversion, sensing and intuition, thinking and feeling, judging and perceiving, and emotional intelligence. Veterans of Lead 21 and ITS remember the experience as illuminating, causing them to criticise concepts which they had internalised without thought and to change their attitudes and behaviour. Throughout this process, the personal views of people were canvassed on a variety of matters. Many requests were made, not all of which could be honoured, but enough to satisfy people. This process marked the morale and attitudes of an entire generation at GCHQ, overcoming the shock of change and loss of colleagues, and leading people to move happily in new directions.

Success created problems of its own. The technical and cultural transformation at GCHQ caught Whitehall's attention. After eighteen months at GCHQ, Omand became Permanent Undersecretary at the Home Office, which ministers wanted an outsider to reform. He invited Pepper to lead the modernisation programme within the Home Office, including big PFI projects for IT and accommodation. This move aimed to give Pepper experience outside GCHQ, so to make him an effective director there, but it also took the two leading proponents of reform from Cheltenham. Kevin Tebbit, a senior Foreign Office official, replaced Omand. He calmed nerves which were palpitating over transformation, but after only a few months became Permanent Undersecretary at the MOD. In January 1998, after a year of three directors, he was succeeded by Francis Richards, a former military officer turned diplomat. Richards had no hands-on experience of intelligence, but much in an unusual number of other areas, where his hands had always proven safe. He understood consumers, leadership and management. He inherited a reform just beginning and sketchy in many details. Rather than abandon it and pursue a programme named after himself, Richards honed the one he was with. He stayed for five years, long enough to establish the Omand–Richards reforms, and for GCHQ to reinvent itself. When Richards retired, Pepper replaced him, beginning a twelve-year period where GCHQ's directors were Siginters, yet with an understanding of Whitehall which matched that of Cheltenham.

GCHQ adapted itself to the second age of Sigint just as it emerged, but not without error. The construction project that would become 'the Doughnut' – making this most secret of agencies iconic across the earth – illustrates how that process combined success and failure. In 1996, GCHQ launched the initiative 'Sinews' – Sigint's new systems – to define and hone the procedures needed to live in the digital world. This project was pioneering but complicated because the engineers and computer scientists in Benhall were physically and psychologically distinct from the directorate, cryptanalysts, analysts and linguists in other buildings. To coordinate their work, or even converse about it, was difficult. The convoluted organisational and physical structure of GCHQ was well suited to the radio age and the Cold War, but not to answer new questions, let alone to execute solutions or ride a revolution.

Digital technology was hard to introduce in the warren of GCHQ's old, often dilapidated, offices. GCHQ needed new accommodations, which its capital budget could not start, let alone complete. Opportunity emerged when the Treasury asked departments to surrender their capital budgets in favour of public–private partnerships, where private investors would finance the construction of buildings, to be repaid over decades. Omand convinced the Treasury that an ambitious partnership, aiming to bring all of the scattered parts of GCHQ into one building, would heighten its efficiency and effect. An open plan would help Siginters transform their culture to meet a digital environment. The project, for several years the largest construction site in Europe, met that aim, and proved a key to reinvention. It also was far more expensive than predicted: partly because GCHQ lacked the experience needed to manage large programmes, as it ceased to be simply an intelligence agency but also became an executive arm of state, but mostly because Siginters underestimated the scale of change that processing the global packet switched networks of the internet would demand of GCHQ.

As Pepper said, in the early 1990s, GCHQ's information technology:

> was essentially composed of a number of stand-alone systems, large systems but they were not interconnected and they were not networked because at that stage networking was not the way IT was organised ... we began gradually to introduce networking to our systems for two reasons: one, because that was the way technology was going, but also because we faced a change of circumstances in that we had an IT system which had evolved during the Cold War when we had very large, monolithic, essentially static targets and we were able to operate in effect with stove-piped IT systems. During

the early 1990s the Cold War ended; we were faced with a much more volatile and varied set of targets and it became necessary to make our systems much more flexible and to make the way we used them more flexible.[7]

By 1995, 'there were a lot of networking connections between the systems'. Engineers and cryptanalysts patched together powerful, but disconnected, networks of computers and specialised systems, relying on individual memory rather than documented configuration control. No one recognised 'quite the extent and the full implications of the transition we were going through, the totally new IT world that we were moving into'. Technical personnel did not realise that dismantling each system and reconstructing them in the new building would be difficult. They did so only after a study, involving 150 man years, assessed how all of their networks could handle 'Y2K', the bug which many feared might wreck all computer systems on midnight, 1 January 2000. Engineers, now grasping the greater problem, mapped all the processes needed to install their capabilities in the Doughnut. These unforeseen factors caused a cost overrun, and eventually a much greater cost was incurred than originally announced. Richards had to plead for more resources, which were granted, after an independent report was published. Its author, General Sir Edmund Burton, an experienced manager of major projects, immediately became a non-executive director. The Treasury covered £216 million of this overrun, demonstrating that Whitehall was impressed by GCHQ's work. GCHQ was left responsible for the rest. Ultimately, the NAP costs were underestimated in error but were corrected before the programme was approved, after an encounter with the Public Accounts Committee. Omand, rightly, stated that the Doughnut more than paid its way, but these cost overruns demonstrate elementary flaws in GCHQ's understanding of Sigint in a new age, even as it adapted to them.[8]

Meanwhile, military Sigint paid a heavy peace dividend, for a peace that never came. The cuts in military Sigint temporarily stopped recruitment. Some personnel retired, others retrained in new technologies and languages. Royal Navy Siginters, integrated into communications, command, control and intelligence systems on warships, were least affected, but still faced problems with targets and languages, when operations began in the Balkans during 1996. Army and RAF Sigint units shrank, but their personnel, forced into successive expeditions, served in war zones more than ever since 1945. In a slow and halting fashion, at some cost, these campaigns retaught GCHQ and the services lessons about Sigint they had known well in 1945, but had since forgotten. GCHQ and the military were badly coordinated when wars began in the former Yugoslavia – 'not our finest hour', Adye sighed.[9] During the 1991 Gulf War, Sigint was 'an invaluable source', but many of its problems in tactical use from the Falklands conflict recurred.[10] Siginters bickered over 'jointery' – the need for people with many cap badges to cooperate seamlessly – and over what practices were electronic warfare or Sigint, for either the services or GCHQ to fund and control. GCHQ was tough about funding service Siginters. They usually cost more than civilians but possessed skills the latter lacked and, unlike them, could operate in combat zones. Slowly, however, GCHQ and the MOD improved their coordination and the dissemination of Sigint to commanders. Government Communications Officers (GCOs) already in the MOD, and static commands to coordinate supply and demand in Sigint, became normal in expeditionary headquarters. The Transportable Cryptologic Support Group, borrowing American terminology but following British practices of 1945, gave commanders tailored feeds of Sigint. Though this group originally was intended to support a theatre-level headquarters, its first use was three echelons of command below. It supported a battle group in the Balkans, whose commander praised its 'outstanding source of high-grade intelligence and endless cups of tea'.[11] The MOD established a senior military advisor at Cheltenham, to bring operational experience into Sigint planning for military operations.

GCHQ faced dangers during the 1990s. The end of the Cold War threatened its resources, while the rise of the digital age particularly imperilled Sigint agencies. GCHQ surmounted these challenges rather well. GCHQ transformed itself to fit the digital age because of its small size, unity, its institutional culture of teamwork and agility in action, and reasoned and empirical debate. Unlike many organisations which tried but failed to transform, GCHQ ignored theories of an 'information age', or revolutions in business or military affairs, but focused on real problems and solutions. GCHQ's early exposure to practical issues drove its rapid adaptation to them – transformation was not about theories, but tasks. GCHQ was able to reinvest the peace dividend into new forms of Sigint and to exploit government fashions of economy to finance its reconfiguration. As it shed some of the largest elements of its staff, such as intercept operators and clerical personnel, it received ample opportunity to hire youngsters with different skills. GCHQ developed the kit, personnel and organisation suited to the new targets and threats of the digital age. These developments eliminated GCHQ's main technical weakness of the Cold War – its inability to meet the costs of emerging forms of interception – and returned it to the top table, at an affordable price. GCHQ ceased to decline compared to NSA: for several years after 1995, GCHQ rose sharply in relative quality. It was also the first institution in the world to enter the second age of Sigint. That age had many roots and was driven by unintended and unexpected consequences.

On the Cyber Commons

Between 1945 and 1989, Siginters attacked two communications targets. They aimed to collect as much material as possible from military radio networks protected by specialised personnel and cryptography, and small amounts of traffic – mostly of states, but sometimes foreign individuals or entities – on civilian communications systems, including cable, microwave and satellites. The end of the Cold War accelerated changes in technology that had affected the collection and processing of Sigint for decades. HF radio, and the large conventional sites that collected it, became marginal to communications and Sigint, though Siginters maintained capabilities in these areas, as they did against manual codes – just in case. Satellites, and land and maritime cables, became the mainstays for state and civilian communication and Sigint. GCHQ's targets, whether diplomats, spies or terrorists, no longer used distinct and unique communications systems, but rather civilian ones. Their traffic could not be intercepted unless one also touched that of civilians, including one's own people, because the source and destination of messages could be identified only by checking external features. That characteristic had been true since ILC emerged on radio during the 1920s, swelled through use on satellites and after 1990 became universal across all modes of communication.

Civilian systems also changed. Before the digital age, few countries could intercept any traffic outside of their borders at a time when postal and telegraph services created the first world-wide information commons. Liberal states, above all Britain, were masters of these media. They did not intercept the communications of foreigners because they valued privacy and liberty for themselves and others. Necessity drove Britain to censor all internal and international cable and postal communications during the First and Second World Wars, but these practices ended with those conflicts. Even then, it acquired only private data moving across the waves, not that resting in drawers. Strong boundaries between nations, and media, marked civil communications. The only exception was ILC which, nonetheless, after 1960, became one of its main types, through satellite communication. Different means were needed to garner information resting in drawers, and moving by cable, or post or telephone. Rarely could private parties attack others, or states. The limits of technology and the power of governments kept individuals from intercepting the traffic of other parties. State censorship of information became hard in liberal countries and easy in totalitarian ones. Even when the bars to collection were raised – in fact, precisely for that reason – private material threatened information overload far more than did the traffic of foreign states simply because it was so voluminous and its importance was so difficult to gauge. The problem became one of data storage and retrieval – as letters had to be copied and telephone calls transcribed manually, and their myriad details indexed and filed.

Regular attacks on civilian systems and private messages, outside of war or within one's own state, emerged through a halting process, which was linked to the legal and technical characteristics of telephone and wireless traffic, especially from foreign countries. Radio telephones emerged around 1930. Their traffic easily was intercepted, with effective modes of security for states arriving only in 1942–43. Private shields remained weak. From 1960, private messages were transmitted in large volumes by satellite or wireless media and were easy for all states (liberal or otherwise) to intercept, unlike cable, line telephone or post. Many states began systematically to intercept foreign messages of this sort, especially commercial traffic such as telexes, which gradually expanded to include telephone calls. This expansion was enabled by the absence of legal restraints and the end of taboos about violating individual privacy, coupled with the rise of radical pragmatism. States mired in decades of hot and cold wars learned the value of Comint. Liberals viewed the traffic of foreign states as fair game, and the privacy of foreign individuals as collateral damage. Totalitarian states became even more cynical than before. These processes were driven by the presence of Comint institutions that wanted to exploit all modes of data collection. Even so, the best Sigint agencies on earth could attack only tiny samples of the material carried on Comsat, and never the postal systems of foreign states. No attacker could read every document scattered through millions of drawers – which provided some security to states and far more to individuals.

Increasingly from 1990, communications and information were digitised and joined into one system: the internet. Anyone on the internet was connected to everyone. The internet was jury-rigged, rather than designed, but its prevailing characteristics placed disclosure and surveillance above security or privacy. Electronic mail, dispatched by telephone lines, carried voice and print messages. Data at rest and in motion became unified and digitised, simple to acquire, store, retrieve, analyse – and to intercept. All could be attacked by the same cryptanalytical means. Once state and individual archives went online, documents were exposed to attack, just like email. This step increased the power of sampling. If one could detect a current threat and access its computer, its data-processing system would provide its past records. The rise of mobile wireless devices increased the amount of private communications susceptible to interception. Communications, carried online and through wireless telephones by signals that crossed national boundaries promiscuously, linked to any data stored on computers connected to the internet, became open to interception by all-comers at once – not merely to states with sole control over cables or postal services. This material could be copied as easily as electrons, although retrieval and analysis remained frustrating. Prevalent modes of communications were a cryptanalyst's dream: unprecedented numbers of communications junkies, actively drawing attention to themselves and exposing their secrets with abysmal security. A novel threat emerged: that of a nuclear strike on data. One could not merely read the documents in someone's archive, but write them.

The internet also enabled the rise of an anarchic international order. 'Cyberspace' is not a metaphor, realm or place, but rather a part of many things and of the connections between them – a commons of communication and information. As on other commons, such as markets or the seas, a struggle between many players, states and others defines the practices within overlapping competitions between state and non-state actors. These practices alter with changes to conditions, interests, power and time. They always are in dispute. Those practices which emerged over cyber involved as many actors and interests as ever on any commons: intelligence and security for states, and privacy and surveillance for individuals across the world. A social market emerged on the cyber commons centred on the ability of people to communicate and for messages to be intercepted. This market was marked by the self-interest, cooperation, warfare, intelligence-gathering, deception and security characteristics of the individuals, states and pirates that abound on every commons. In order to maximise their gains from this social market, people simplified the processing of information. They paid for that end with privacy, thus easing piracy. Privacy and surveillance are problematic concepts, as attitudes towards them vary by culture and time. There may have been no more privacy or less surveillance in villages than there is in the global village. Bourgeois forms of privacy and respectability aimed to contain surveillance, which limited one's opportunities on the signals market. Given the mass of other people, one best could find individuals, attract their attention or pursue comparative and mutual advantage, by combining openness with the constant transmission of, and search for, broad and narrow signals. People commodified others, and themselves. Voting with their digits, they assigned privacy a low price, if sometimes pretending that its value was higher. Their modes of communication transformed the relations between their reputations and themselves. New needs to communicate outweighed old modes of privacy, which produced a society based on signals and surveillance, with individuals being simultaneously subject and object.

These developments eased the interception and transmission of signals and dissolved established borders between states and societies, internal and external relations, war and peace, civil and military, security and insecurity, and sovereign and non-state actors. Once Sigint agencies could distinguish between traffic intercepted at home and abroad, it let liberal states combine civil liberties and cryptanalysis. That status no longer was true when messages surged automatically between servers at home and abroad and Sigint agencies had an unparalleled ability to read the mail of private people, as against foreign states. Once, states fought only each other, and alone controlled the highest levels of violence (part of the problem with terrorists was their claim to act like states, and their efforts to do so). Now, non-state actors used the same techniques of Comint as governments and applied them against foreign states, or people. Citizens were threatened by attack from their fellows, foreign governments, firms and criminals. States could not easily protect their people against these threats, and thus failed a fundamental condition of sovereignty.

Privacy and surveillance, intelligence and security, and old distinctions between states and individuals, and their competitions, were transformed. The greatest change was not in the ability of states to attack each other, or their own people, though these capabilities did rise. It was the ability of states to monitor foreign civilians, and above all of private parties to read anyone's mail or memoranda – private or governmental, home or abroad. As ever, states lacked the resources to read all of the traffic they could intercept, but they no longer were the only power on these seas. Individuals were more open to attack from pirates and foreign governments than on any other commons. Pirates attacked from desks, not decks. Individuals relied for security on whatever encryption their computers or cell phones possessed. For most civilians, these levels were higher than possible in the analogue age, but not for states. Cryptanalysts easily broke the basic encryption in most commercial kit. Good encryption, including high-end commercial cryptography, required trained personnel using specialist procedures and cryptosystems. For perhaps the first time in history, anyone could acquire cryptography proof against the best of codebreakers. A few civilians did so, but the overwhelming majority did not, while even many state entities slipped in security. Pirates had unprecedented power, precision and range. States attacked the communications of foreign individuals and corporations far more than ever before in peacetime and faced greater challenges in defending their citizens.

Changes in the characteristics of communication spilling across national borders also affected how liberal states intercepted any traffic of their citizens, home or abroad, or foreign messages passing through their space. In the analogue age, lawyers and Siginters could differentiate between traffic transmitted at home and abroad, and illegal and lawful interception. In the digital age, domestic traffic moved abroad, and foreign messages through one's home. Messages between offices in Cheltenham might pass, say, through Beijing; traffic between Russian intelligence in Moscow and Petersburg move via London. Foreign targets might best be attacked by intercepting communications passing through your home, even though the legal position might be different. Domestic traffic would be acquired through legally acceptable interception abroad. Bulk collection of any internet traffic must include one's citizens, in the first instance. To do otherwise would be to abandon Comint, which one's rivals would not. Yet any analysis of such material, whether intercepted at home or abroad, must touch the envelopes, the metadata, of their citizens' mail without warrant. These procedures were legal, but felt unpleasant.

Cyber Intelligence, Terrorism and Strife

No commons can survive without security. They all feature competing forms of securitisation. The cyber commons was securitised from its birth and then militarised by actors across the earth. The 'weary giants of flesh and steel' never left that commons free from realpolitik, as one internet libertarian prophesied.[12] However, even its practitioners did not fully understand the degree of that militarisation until a decade after it began. The public, even civilian technical experts, took rather longer to appreciate its existence.

GCHQ entered this commons when it was terra incognita, as old practices of Sigint were dying and new ones began. People learned from experience with no idea of the outcome. During the 1990s, GCHQ translated the practices of Sigint from one age to another; it was among the first and biggest institutions to combine technical skills from both sides of the divide, to learn how to attack and defend the new target systems on the cyber commons – the internet, individual computers and cryptosystems. GCHQ hired 'hackers', a different group to cryppies in both technical prowess and intellectual background. Its hackers came from the ethical rather than the malicious branch of that tribe. Together, they created cyber intelligence, a practice distinct from Sigint or Comint. Hackers – whom the Five Eyes termed Computer Network Operators (CNO) – opened doors themselves, or brought cryppies there to do so. Cryptanalysis struck the cryptosystems embedded in computers. Computer network operators carried that success to the heart of computers, then vanished, leaving no signs of their passing – merely hidden payloads to enable later re-entry, or viruses to spread insecurity or chaos across networks. Operators pursued general tasks which earlier auxiliaries to Sigint had handled through human means in unique cases, such as acquiring access to traffic or cryptosystems opportunistically through black bag jobs or suborning telegraph clerks. These tasks simplified the work of cryptanalysis, often to dramatic effect. CNO was divided into several categories, such as: CNE (computer network exploitation) or 'cyber intelligence'; computer network attack (CNA), to incapacitate computers or corrupt the data they contain; and CND, computer network defence, against both threats. CNO became an ally to cryptanalysis, rather than an auxiliary, both working interactively against targets. It was a technical and universal discipline, with the exploitation of human frailty one of its categories, rather than an individual opportunity.

Cyber intelligence became central to GCHQ's repertoire, but was used essentially against traditional targets, until powerful acts of terrorism and long wars in Afghanistan and Iraq drove escalations of that effort. These acts included 9/11 – the largest terrorist attack in history, when on 11 September 2001, hijacked airliners struck buildings in Manhattan and Washington, killing 2,996 people – and 7/7: 7 July 2005, when one of the largest terrorist assaults ever on British soil resulted in the deaths of fifty-two civilians. The Five Eyes confronted loosely organised but persistent foes, mainly groups of Salafi-jihadist terrorists. They had to block attacks by – or kill – motivated individuals. Cyber intelligence became their main source, ahead of Humint and Imint (imagery intelligence).

For GCHQ, the only parallel experiences in these areas were fights against guerrillas or terrorists. Experiences such as Konfrontasi and Palestine demonstrated that success was rewarding, but hard to achieve against adversaries with good Comsec. Siginters had to provide detailed and live intelligence on specific people to other agencies, such as MI5, or to forces in a position to attack enemies, such as deployed aircraft. Intelligence might involve the names of people in Britain who communicated with terrorist recruiters abroad, or, say, the location of Taliban insurgents preparing to ambush British soldiers near the Kajaki dam in Helmand province on 3 September 2008. Such material must be found amidst billions of messages each day crossing civilian systems. Attack and defence also involved third parties, which faced threats from common foes, and had sources of intelligence unavailable to UKUSA. Greater cooperation was necessary with such countries against terrorism than fitted the classic model of relations between the Five Eyes and third parties. States might attack each other's cryptosystems, but cooperate against terrorists.

Achieving any of these objectives was hard. Other issues made it harder. In particular, terrorism is a danger which is easily overrated. Events combining low probability and high costs are difficult to calculate and counter, particularly when the danger is a hidden enemy which might suddenly strike close to home. Terrorists exploit media and attack emotions in order to drag fear and rage onto the scales of calculation. They build an emotional bomb among electorates, which any outrage might detonate at any time. Counter-terrorist personnel often feel personal responsibility for any failure. Treating terrorism as war, and making the prevention of every possible act of terrorism the criterion for competence, distorts all balances between intelligence, security and other objectives. Terrorism, like the cyber commons, dissolved old boundaries: between war and peace, uniformed and non-uniformed belligerents, foreign foes and traitors, and the idea of home and abroad. Like a black hole, terrorism sucked in intelligence agencies. They were pushed to allocate greater attention to terrorism than the danger was probably worth, compared to other enduring interests of state or society. After 7/7, GCHQ made counter-terrorism one of its major concerns for the allocation of resources, but still developed the most rapid and precise means possible to gather Sigint on a host of individuals posing known threats, and to try to detect as-yet unknown ones.

Support for counter-insurgency during wars reinforced that trend. It followed patterns from conventional operations, like Iraq in 2003, where air forces coordinated command and intelligence with unprecedented skill, multiplying all forms of rapid, precise and long-distance weapons. Strikes rose even more in power for special forces or UAVs against insurgents, whether individuals or small groups, in Iraq and Afghanistan. Intelligence and precision weapons enabled exact attacks, by the standards of air power or counter-insurgency, often the equivalent of snipers firing at known individuals. As ever, when force is used near civilians, innocents die – the only question being, how many? Excellent imagery and human and signals intelligence helped to define targets, to execute strikes, and to minimise civilian casualties. Siginters became more entangled in battle than ever before. The decline in service Siginters and the rise of military precision strikes threw civilian officials into kill chains. Military Siginters wanted to be there, but civilians psychologically preferred some means to distance themselves from decisions for death. GCHQ no longer was just an intelligence organisation, but part of executive agencies for the use of force. It was the executive authority for the burgeoning areas of CNA and CND.

Britain's enemies had many targets. GCHQ could not keep every threat at bay. Some would bite Britain. At best, GCHQ could maintain a favourable balance of order on the border and bite back harder; which it did. British civilians and soldiers died. Cybercriminals, some associated with foreign states, pillaged the accounts of private citizens, or stole technology from UKUSA firms. Other states or pirates might match UKUSA in hacking, but none could touch its power in cryptanalysis, cyber intelligence, or bulk collection. GCHQ also minimised interference with the lives of their own people, and civilians in other countries too.

States remained the major target, struck through tailored attacks. Government and public opinion, however, understanding the problems only through their manifestation in murder, drove GCHQ to protect British civilian and military lives from terrorists, insurgents and pirates. Had GCHQ and UKUSA not beaten these threats they would have failed their duty and been reviled. Internal and external threats fused. GCHQ acted as it rarely had before: more like policemen within Britain than soldiers abroad. Such acts stretched its legal mandate against external threats, yet if it did not take the work, who else had the technical capabilities for it? How else could GCHQ prevent agents based abroad from stealing secrets from firms in Glasgow, inspiring terrorism by British subjects in Bradford, or subverting elections across the country?

In order to man British frontiers on the cyber commons, GCHQ adopted a new and unique form of bulk collection. The old warrant to collect diplomatic telegrams worked entirely through cable addresses and caught them all. The WTID and Siginters working against Russian civil text attacked unencrypted traffic. They read every message they intercepted, discarded 95 per cent of them based on a quick scrutiny of content, and analysed the rest. All of these Siginters aimed to intercept 100 per cent of the traffic sent. Workers against ILC, especially satellites, took tiny samples of traffic. They treated plain-language traffic as the

WTID had done, and then used traffic analysis to determine the addressees of encrypted ILC messages and cryptanalysis to attack those which from external features seemed interesting. Traffic analysis was useful essentially to guide cryptanalysis. After 1990, against internet traffic passing through cables or wireless, GCHQ took even tinier samples than that from ILC. If all the world's internet traffic was a billiards table, GCHQ sopped up a beer mat's worth of messages and processed through traffic analysis only a full stop, with far less than that amount attacked and read.

All of this material had some encryption, elementary at lower levels, but often hard at upper ones. As a practice, traffic analysis turned systematically from assessing the external features of signals between HF radio sets, to the IP addresses of computers within networks. This transformation required operators with different skill sets, though they retained the creative and painstaking ability to analyse the external features of communications which drove GCHQ's successes in fusion during the Cold War. This traffic analysis illuminated potential threats or problems long before any content was read, and was the main part of success against bulk traffic. Cryptanalysis provided just the icing on the cake. The metadata of IP addresses was anonymised, stripping all personal details, which simplified Sigint and GCHQ's legal position. Traffic analysis determined which IP addresses communicated with those already under suspicion, so identifying further suspects. Cryptanalysis attacked only messages from suspect addresses. If these addresses involved non-Five Eyes citizens working from non-UKUSA addresses, the decision to attack was purely technical, made by analysts and cryptanalysts. If they touched a Five Eyes citizen, location or address, warrants were needed to justify attacks on the content of messages.

As Iain Lobban, the Director of GCHQ, said in 2013

If you think of the internet as an enormous hay field, what we are trying to do is to collect hay from those parts of the field that we can get access to and which might be lucrative in terms of containing the needles or the fragments of the needles that we might be interested in, that might help our mission. When we gather that haystack, and remember it is not a haystack from the whole field, it is a haystack from a tiny proportion of that field, we are very, very well aware that within that haystack there is going to be plenty of hay which is innocent communications from innocent people, not just British, foreign people as well. And so we design our queries against that data, to draw out the needles and we do not intrude upon, if you like, the surrounding hay. We can only look at the content of communications where there are very specific legal thresholds and requirements which have been met. So that is the reality. We don't want to delve into innocent e-mails and phonecalls … If I have that haystack, I am looking for needles and fragments of needles. That is what my queries pull out. I do not look at the surrounding hay. It may have been intercepted. A small portion of that may apply to British citizens. We will not look at it without a specific authorisation.[13]

The overwhelming number of potential targets, compared to the tiny resources for traffic analysis, cryptanalysis and languages, drove this process. GCHQ lacked the means to attack any message which did not have high priority. Every day it could assess the metadata of billions of messages, yet perhaps touched just tens of thousands of them, and read a small proportion of the traffic of hundreds of new targets. The latter, however, enabled many successes. GCHQ devised efficient means to sample massive quantities of traffic; to hold, examine and, where relevant, retain traffic; and then to flush its databases and repeat the process. As it later wrote: 'GCHQ uses its bulk powers to access the internet at scale so as then to dissect it with surgical precision. By drawing out fragments of intelligence … and fitting them together like a jigsaw,' GCHQ could 'discover new threats', provide 'unique intelligence about the plans and intentions of current targets', and 'protect the UK against cyber-attack from our most savvy adversaries and to track them down in the vast morass of the internet'.[14]

In 2009, 'complex analysis' of bulk data led GCHQ to identify several different terrorists in Britain working with leaders abroad, who were arrested before they struck. During the war in Afghanistan, GCHQ enabled the rescue of kidnapped British nationals without loss of their lives, and the disruption of attacks on its base at Camp Bastion. GCHQ's work in analysis of bulk collection was essential to the work of MI5 and MI6 against threats.[15] These gains were smaller than those acquired through GCHQ's work in war against Germany or Argentina, but they secured Britain's border on the cyber commons and saved British lives.

From Secrecy to Translucency

These developments drove GCHQ into new relationships with some elements of society. GCHQ moved cautiously into the open, especially after 9/11 and 7/7. Restrained by an instinctive focus on secrecy, still GCHQ built contacts with the press, some academics and many firms worried about cybersecurity and cybercrime. It offered assistance, at arm's length, mostly through loans of equipment, to the Bletchley Park Trust, which fostered the memory of British Sigint during the Second World War. GCHQ expanded cooperation with other ministries, which saw its value in aiding Britain against threats which the public thought were existential. GCHQ built good relations with parliamentary oversight authorities, whom it treated with respect. GCHQ became much more open within Whitehall, yet remained weak in areas where other ministries liaised with the public. In particular, its offices for press and public relations and law were tiny, essentially servicing contacts in Cheltenham.

GCHQ did not openly address the operational and legal elements of bulk collection because it did not know how to do so, rather than having anything to hide. Since 1815, British agencies have followed the law about intercepting the communications of British subjects. The few documentable instances of illegal actions are illuminating. During 1914–15, Admiral Hall illegally used powers against suspects which he did not have the right to apply. He and General Cockerill went to the edge of the law, and perhaps just past it, in intercepting letters for blockade – though that mail was foreign, not British, and authorities quickly authorised these actions.[16] Between 1919 and 1936, MI5 routinely and, so it claimed, inadvertently, violated the law when acquiring warrants for telephone tapping, which its Director arranged straight with the GPO, without approval by a Secretary of State.[17] An official in 1930s India illegally intercepted a rival's telegrams for political reasons.[18]

More actions than these probably occurred, but nothing suggests that British authorities often or routinely illegally intercepted private communications. The greater issue, legal but inappropriate monitoring, is a matter of opinion as much as fact. MI5 bugged Communist Party offices in King Street for decades and intercepted the correspondence of left-wing agitators more than that of right-wing ones. Political inclinations shape how far one thinks those actions were legitimate, or not, but certainly they were legal. More broadly, these actions show how the ability to intercept messages increased the power of states against political dissidence during the twentieth century, where Britain fell within the more restrained group of liberal states. GCHQ and MI5 were certainly not like the Stasi, if less restricted than British agencies had been between 1844 and 1914. These agencies did not create the surveillance state in Britain; this stemmed from surveillance capitalism, from private firms deploying CCTV and commercial monitoring of internet data.

Law prevented GCHQ from monitoring the messages of British subjects, which it did in only three cases. First, as in Palestine, when security services required Sigint against internal armed opposition, but could not collect it, GCHQ was warranted to do so, legally. Second, GC&CS executed lawful warrants to intercept telegrams of political agitators and collected them because its work with diplomatic traffic provided the necessary connections with cable companies, which no other department had. In 1925, GC&CS told the Treasury that the number of telegrams to and from Britain which were checked 'depends on the number of Bolshies whom the SOS, in the public interest, decides to keep his eyes on'.[19] These numbers expanded dramatically during and after the General Strike, under a general warrant from the Home Office. This action, incidentally, shows that the warrant for cable intercepts did not cover British civilians, which otherwise would have been unnecessary.[20] Finally, after 1928, GCHQ intercepted civilian wireless traffic on the ether: all of the take was legal and some of it valuable. Sometimes, GC&CS captured messages from British civilians, whether communicating between Britain and another country, or between two foreign states. GC&CS could not know that British subjects were involved until an analyst saw that fact, when they read the message and discarded it. That action contained the potential illegality of the action, which no one really considered. Legal and operational needs supported each other. The interception of ILC aimed to capture espionage or diplomatic traffic. A warrant would already cover any Britons suspected of espionage; GC&CS lacked the personnel to waste time on anyone else. Its procedures for handling bulk traffic always began with purging anything but material on a few topics.

Ample experience since 1928 coloured GCHQ's response to bulk collection and British civilian communications in the digital age. Yet it no longer collected such material from the ether, but often from a legally different space: British subjects in British territory. GCHQ used such material only after anonymising metadata, which hid the identity of British subjects. Little intercepted material was touched. Content was not read without a special warrant. GCHQ believed these procedures were legal. Its personnel knew they were not behaving badly, but rather saving British lives. GCHQ explained these practices and their legal and operational rationale to its ministerial masters, and to the parliamentary oversight committee, which approved them. Yet these practices were unknown to the public, and their possibility buried amongst a host of details in the relevant legislation, the Intelligence Services Act of 1994, and the Regulation of Investigatory Powers Act of 2000 (RIPA). The law for the interception of British traffic was obsolete, and GCHQ alone could not modernise it. Only a government effort could do so, and no one particularly wished to handle the task. GCHQ believed that its work was essential and legal. GCHQ did not consider how the public would react if suddenly, without explanation, it learned of these practices. GCHQ assumed that such an event could not happen, because it could control any movement away from secrecy.

This belief contradicted the record of recent decades and proved optimistic. In 2013, Edward Snowden, a contractor and systems administrator at NSA, copied reams of records about the working of UKUSA, and leaked them to journalists and activists, though GCHQ and NSA neither confirmed nor denied their authenticity. Suddenly, the public and technical specialists confronted the reality of militarisation and Comint on the cyber commons, and were genuinely shocked. Initially, the disclosures were incomprehensible. As every case of traffic analysis against metadata (and sometimes, merely the number of messages collected and anonymised) was taken to mean the reading of mail, people assumed that the Five Eyes read infinitely more messages than was true – confusing the 'full stop' for the 'beer mat' and sometimes even the 'billiards table'. The *Guardian* wrote that authorities had powers 'beyond what Orwell could have imagined'. Privacy International complained that 'while the Stasi had files on one in three East Germans', GCHQ 'intercepted and stored' the 'communications of almost everybody in the UK'.[21]

These disclosures were one-sided and naive. Critics assumed that just a few Western countries conducted Comint on the cyber commons, unlike nice states such as China and Russia, which swore on their word as gentlemen that they never would consider doing such a thing. Critics held that these practices aimed solely to monitor UK and US citizens' lives, ignoring matters such as war, terrorism, cybercrime and hostile state activity. Critics of Sigint – competent or incompetent, principled or hostile – drove the disclosures. A classic press campaign, like Lord Beaverbrook's 'Empire Crusade', aimed to sell newspapers. Internet libertarians, viewing state intelligence and secrecy as evil, purported to defend freedom from the slavery caused by pursuit of security.

These comments had some force, but more melodrama. They ignored the problems of competitions on common ground, and the existence of enemies. The metaphors used to describe this situation – 1984 or the panopticon – were one-dimensional. They considered only peoples being attacked by their own state – not those assaulted by foreign governments or exploited by criminals. Nor was the question simply the gaze of the state. People used this panopticon for their own purposes – to attract attention and display what they wanted to show, rather than to tremble before the unblinking eye. In Western countries, most people would not be assaulted by their own states: more would be attacked by foreign governments and private parties. Fewer people might fear Big Brother than need his help, or want it.

This crisis stunned GCHQ, still more a Cheltonian than a national institution. It did not know what material would be published and lacked a press office with a remit to counter criticism at a national level, though it rapidly developed one. Its representatives could not at the outset clearly explain the legal or technical issues in public, nor how GCHQ had saved British lives. However, GCHQ's record and myth saved it. Leading Conservative and Labour politicians agreed that GCHQ had properly informed them of its actions. The technicalities involved, and the constant drip of information, confused and bored the public. Quickly, evidence emerged that every competent state conducted Sigint, while cybercriminals and terrorists planned to exploit or attack British subjects. The enemies of Sigint overplayed their hands by making statements which obviously they could not substantiate, and which were untrue – such as that bulk collection had not reduced terrorist attacks, or by inflating the number of messages of British citizens which GCHQ read. The debate turned on myths. Critics insinuated that GCHQ was Big Brother or Sauron. Civilians could not easily imagine Bletchley's heirs as Orcs. British people thought they faced existential threats, against which they viewed GCHQ as Gandalf and themselves as Hobbits in need of help. Slowly, the debate became informed and public. Balanced reports by objective experts undercut alarmism.

In 2015 and 2016 the British government commissioned David Anderson, QC to assess the legal and operational aspects of bulk collection Although few knew the fact, Anderson's report followed older genres: the assessments of British intelligence by Evill and Quinlan, and of GCHQ by Evill, Hampshire and Hurn. Their reports were written for mandarins familiar with Sigint product but concerned with cost-effectiveness and value. Anderson wrote for the public, both the knowledgeable and those who did not know what GCHQ did, but all of whom cared about issues of defence, freedom and terrorism. Anderson said nothing about cost or cost-effectiveness. He focused far more than earlier reports had done on the technicalities of collection, and on correlating operational and legal issues. His mandate was unique, public rather than secret. The major political parties cooperated in a bipartisan fashion, on an issue which they understood was complex in many technical areas, was important and required solution. They depoliticised the issue – unusually difficult for politicians of those years to do – in order to ensure the best technical balance between liberty and security.

A wise man must handle this assessment task. Anderson, a leading barrister on matters of national security and civil liberties, and the Independent Reviewer of Terrorism Legislation, was already responsible to the Home Secretary and Parliament. Unlike previous investigations of the intelligence services, departments did not provide his staff. He selected them from outsiders, including leaders in civil liberties and national security law such as Cathryn McGahey, QC; in Sigint collection and security, Dr Bob Nowill, with senior experience from British Telecom and GCHQ; and Gordon Meldrum, a consumer of secret intelligence on organised crime. They, and he, were cleared to see anything relevant to his brief, including material never before viewed by anyone outside the intelligence agencies. Anderson canvassed widely among critics of Sigint, and his staff applied those critiques to the agencies' cases. His position was unique among external assessors of intelligence. He could demand documents from the intelligence agencies, and have them offer their best sixty cases on the issue, for his staff to interrogate in detail. They could check the arguments of critics against the reality of intelligence, and of practitioners against other possibilities, to determine how far bulk collection was useful and necessary. Anderson could publish a sanitised version of the evidence, and a critique of it, to Parliament and the public.

Anderson treated all parties with respect and praised their aims. The sincerity and competence of British intelligence officers, especially from GCHQ, impressed him and his staff. Anderson largely rejected the critics' challenges to the necessity of these procedures or their proposed alternatives and kindly demolished their supposed value or practicability. Many of these critics' proposals were forms of unilateral digital disarmament, which would prevent bulk collection and Sigint more widely, and for Britain but not for anyone else. Britain would walk naked across the cyber commons, where everyone else remained armoured.

Anderson concluded that the agencies had not abused their powers in bulk collection and justified its necessity and utility: bulk collection was essential for British security, and GCHQ had handled it well:

> Much of its work involves analysis based on a fragment of
> information which forms the crucial lead, or seed, for further work.
> GCHQ's tradecraft lies in the application of lead-specific analysis
> to bring together potentially relevant data from diverse data stores
> in order to prove or disprove a theory or hypothesis … significant
> analysis of data may be required before any actual name can be
> identified. This tradecraft requires very high volumes of queries
> to be run against communications data as results are dynamically
> tested, refined and further refined. GCHQ runs several thousand
> such communications data queries every day. One of the benefits
> of this targeted approach to data mining is that individuals who
> are innocent or peripheral to an investigation are never looked at,
> minimising the need for intrusion into their communications.[22]

Nonetheless, Anderson proposed a stricter version of GCHQ's procedures, with much more oversight. 'RIPA, obscure since its inception, has been patched up so many times as to make it incomprehensible to all but a tiny band of initiates. A multitude of alternative powers, some of them without statutory safeguards, confuse the picture further. This state of affairs is undemocratic, unnecessary and – in the long run – intolerable.' Instead, 'a comprehensive and comprehensible new law should be drafted from scratch, replacing the multitude of current powers and providing for clear limits and safeguards on any intrusive power that it may be necessary for public authorities to use'.[23] That process must be public and transparent.

In coming years, the issue received much attention from press and Parliament, perhaps more than any other case of intelligence in British history. Anderson's views did not please opponents, who labelled the new law the 'Snooper's Charter', yet even they recognised that their opposition had little public support.[24] Debate turned from the public to the legal sphere, which continued into 2020, on minor issues not involving the intelligence agencies.

GCHQ's relationship with the public, and secrecy, changed more between 2013 and 2020 than ever before in its history. Long before 2013, GCHQ staff knew that their actions on the internet might infringe upon the liberties and privacy of fellow citizens, and themselves. They turned from temptation, guided by an institutional 'Ethical Framework', an 'ethics officer' to hear complaints, and protection for whistle-blowers. After the Snowden disclosures, GCHQ staff internalised the idea of 'a democratic license to operate', as it was named by an independent team of hard-headed and eminent figures whom the government put in place to review the recommendations of Anderson's committee.[25] During the crisis of 2013–15, its level of secrecy exposed GCHQ to accusations of bad behaviour. Iain Lobban did not 'think "secret" means "sinister"', but critics did.[26] Secrecy gave glamour to GCHQ, and inculcated conspiracy theories. This level of secrecy weakened GCHQ's ability to handle public attacks, or to explain its actions; so it took a difficult decision. GCHQ entered the public sphere, discarding the cult of secrecy while looking to maintain operational security.

This decision has transformed public discourse. The more material that has been released about British intelligence, the weaker conspiracy theories about it have become, even when the grounds for criticism have risen. Critics who attacked GCHQ for secrecy lost their best card, the ability to raise suspicion about everything it did, and saw it gain new ones. GCHQ took several steps, each political and principled, aimed to explain itself to the public, consider criticism, and gain informed consent for its actions.

GCHQ behaved like other departments. It increased its press office and engaged with national periodicals. Journalists received tours through the Doughnut, which civilians found attractive, and spoke to analysts, sparking newspaper articles and television programmes. Directors became public figures, discussing their profession, aided by one retired colleague, Omand. Some other Siginters were cleared to speak openly, though most remained bound by old constraints. Support from friendly outsiders, especially the royal family, was gratefully accepted. GCHQ expanded its legal staff, from one part-timer in 1980 to thirty-two full-time personnel by 2020, to handle public debates about law. As critics challenged GCHQ through legal means, it had to explain its views. By forcing Siginters and critics to argue openly, this system aided an elevated public debate, on both sides, and a highest common denominator of liberty and security. GCHQ commissioned an independent account of its history, so readers could understand its roles, failures and successes, and judge its value as they could other civilian and strategic departments. It is in your hands.

The National Cyber Security Centre and the Cyber Commons

GCHQ's greatest challenge lay in adjusting to the cyber commons and the needs of a new consumer – society – alongside its traditional customer in the state. Comsec, a secondary task for GCHQ during the Cold War, handled by a subsidiary element – the Communications-Electronics Security Group (CESG) – became its most public and perhaps greatest job. The new technical world threatened CESG more than any other part of GCHQ. While the skills of radio operators, Russian linguists and traffic analysts of the Warsaw Pact waned in value, legacy requirements and age demographics let careers end gracefully. Senior GCHQ personnel carried principles from their work into new areas. The old skills of linguists and analysts remained useful. Cryppies and CDOs cooperated. The principles of traffic analysis were basic against bulk traffic, even if analysts changed.

CESG had less to bequeath and more to learn. It had focused on setting standards and designing equipment for the Cold War, above all machines to protect communications by radio and cable and, to a lesser degree, telephones. CESG produced technical pamphlets, designs for equipment and masses of ephemeral 'keymat' – the punched tapes, plug settings and other media that provided key settings for cypher devices. As CESG's military consumers declined, so did need for that product, which gradually became obsolete, though some remained useful in 2020. CESG had little expertise with computers and cybersecurity, while its consumers in government were slower to adopt new equipment than firms and individuals – which suddenly it was expected to serve. Traditional Comsec and cybersecurity involved specialised kit and skills, which proved mutually exclusive. The characteristics which suited CESG's long twilight struggle – precision engineering, controlled pursuit of projects to serve for generations, reliance on firms (closely and expertly supervised) to produce designs and equipment – did not suit this revolution. Union between generations proved impossible, compared to the combination of cryppies and CDOs. Nowhere else in GCHQ did the gap between the expertise of old hands, and new, matter more than with CESG.

For a generation after the Cold War ended, CESG approached cybersecurity as it had done Comsec. Like most departments and firms, CESG was slow to understand cybersecurity, seeing it as a problem for IT departments, not as a transformation in work. Businesses with technical expertise would provide advice and equipment about IT. Alas, these firms were often more expensive than they were useful. CESG lacked the expertise to control the quality of their work, or understand it. Most of GCHQ understood that it must change, or die. CESG did not, nor did its masters, until they suddenly demanded that it lead a revolution. CESG embodies what might have happened to GCHQ as a whole, without the Omand–Richards reforms.

The growing need to police the cyber commons posed organisational problems for Siginters. Cybercrime endangered large firms and countries with significant financial sectors, such as Britain. States struggled to organise Sigint and Comsec as they confronted new relationships with military organisations and internal ones. Should Siginters, or soldiers, command Computer Network Attack, where digital and kinetic means combined? Should Siginters or policemen handle cybercrime? These questions raised complex issues of organisation and law. Everywhere, the internal structures of countries drove answers. Some smaller states, especially Israel and Singapore, coordinated cybersecurity years before Britain and the United States, where many agencies confronted larger and more complex versions of these issues.

From 2007, when it stood below American or Israeli standards, a confluence of events pressed Britain to pursue a coherent policy for cybersecurity. Politicians, driven by their own observations, not advice from GCHQ or departments, thought cybersecurity was a great problem which required solution. They treated the issue in a non-partisan fashion, not constantly overturning each other's work. As prime minister, Gordon Brown had Britain define a strategy for cybersecurity. The government produced stirring statements: 'Just as in the 19th century we had to secure the seas for our national safety and prosperity, and in the 20th century we had to secure the air, in the 21st century we also have to secure our advantage in cyber space;' basic principles, especially the need to coordinate state and private actors, but few practical changes. A small central unit monitored developments on the cyber commons. Another at GCHQ handled threats. GCHQ quietly advised firms about cybersecurity. Still, fifteen departments acted as they pleased in the field.[27]

The Conservative–Liberal Democrat coalition of 2010–15 built on Brown's work. Its leading members, including the prime minister, David Cameron, made cybersecurity a national priority. As Robert Hannigan, Director of GCHQ, wrote, ministers sought to make Britain:

> 'the safest place to live and do business online' … It is, of course,
> a relative ambition and does not imply that the UK can be 100
> per cent safe. It was based on the key assessment that the UK
> could harden its defences to the point that cybercrime would be
> displaced elsewhere to easier targets. While this may sound cynical, it
> assumed that an international raising of the baseline would make all
> economies harder targets and encourage others to up their game. The
> long-term bet was that good resilience and security would become
> a market differentiator for UK business and attractive for inward
> investors.[28]

Cybersecurity was a leading priority, among Britain's four 'Tier 1 threats', in a tough national security strategy, which slaughtered many sacred cows.[29] The government defined clear criteria for success on the strategy bridge between policy and action, including coordination between departments, and with private firms. A £650 million programme over four years funded cybersecurity well.[30] GCHQ seized almost 60 per cent of that budget, and responsibility for 'the most sophisticated nation state attacks'. The Computer Emergency Response Team, an open body under the Cabinet Office, handled most assaults on firms.[31]

Directors of GCHQ recognised that the danger existed and must be solved, and offered rewards. They did not understand the technicalities of cybersecurity, but drove subordinates to address them. This sudden shift in demands exposed the generation gap. The older members of CESG were reluctant to handle non-state consumers and relied on IT firms they knew for guidance. The younger generation disliked those producers and procedures and thought many of these firms alarmist and expensive. They wished to revolutionise Comsec to fit the cyber commons, and to lead a national effort in cybersecurity. GCHQ's leaders let old hands at CESG handle its traditional roles, while others controlled policy for cybersecurity. Ciaran Martin, an official with wide experience in Whitehall, including intelligence, but not at GCHQ, became manager of cybersecurity and Comsec at Cheltenham. He worked with the radicals to handle cybersecurity, where they followed original ideas, and studied American and Israeli models.

Between 2011 and 2015, GCHQ worked closely with government agencies and firms, and established offices to assess cyber threats. As Hannigan wrote, assessing threats and risks on the cyber commons:

> is particularly difficult not just because it is a relatively new field but because it requires in-depth technical understanding alongside assessment of other sources ... ministers who had a framework for judging the seriousness of a terrorist threat or incident had no framework against which to measure cyber threats. The figures were always large, because all figures on the internet are, and no one knows what 100 per cent is: internet data is hard to measure and not static. Traditional assessment bodies, notably the venerable UK Joint Intelligence Committee, simply did not have access to the right technical skills to make useful assessments or even to second-guess those made by others.[32]

Even more, policy faltered because 'no one has asked the obvious question of the right experts. Particularly in the UK civil service, which tends to favour generalism over deep and long expertise, there simply were not individuals who could give creative technical advice, or indeed assess suggestions made by others.'[33] Some of these criticisms could also have been applied to GCHQ, at the time.

These successes were dissipated because agencies gave conflicting advice to firms, which could not handle the burden thrust on them. GCHQ gave intelligence, and fought foes on the cyber commons, but firms mostly received advice, not aid, and could not be chivvied into line. State defence for firms was dislocated. Hacking attacks became high grade, sometimes linked to foreign state Sigint agencies. The Bank of England warned that this chaos damaged Britain's economy and softened security enough to attract cyber criminals. The national policy based on coordination had reached its limits. Leadership was needed. After the election of 2015, the Conservative government demanded a national strategy, guided by one public centre for cybersecurity, and led by GCHQ. 'When a cyber incident happened there were lots of departments represented at the table, but most of the questions gravitated to GCHQ,' Cameron told Hannigan. GCHQ, said the Chancellor of the Exchequer, George Osborne, 'is rightly known as equal to the best in the world ... It is the point of deep expertise for the UK government. It has an unmatched understanding of the internet and of how to keep information safe.'[34]

Other departments resisted the loss of authority in cybersecurity, until MI5 did so, breaking the logjam. Only law enforcement agencies, responsible for tackling forms of cybercrime, remained independent, though working closely with GCHQ. Many within GCHQ disliked becoming public and taking responsibility for cybersecurity. Senior ministers overcame these reservations and assigned those responsibilities to the 'National Cyber Security Centre, a part of GCHQ'. That body had a unique name, and structure. Its leaders came from the reformed CESG. Martin was the first head of the NCSC, with Ian Levy its Technical Director or, as he said, the government's 'chief cyber security geek'.[35] Five of its leaders were avowed, able to speak and be named openly, more than in the rest of GCHQ. By spring 2019, the NCSC had 740 staff. It had elements within the Doughnut, alongside world leaders in cyber intelligence and CNO, and offices in London, beside private citizens. The NCSC was within the Government Security Zone, outside the Whitehall village, yet close to ministers. During emergencies, the NCSC and GCHQ gave Whitehall real-time knowledge of cyber threats and struck them down where possible as they rose. The NCSC combined two compartments: one working with open cybersecurity communities; the other with secret agencies. Like Bletchley, the NCSC was freewheeling, with many parts. Once the Khyber Rifles defended far-flung British frontiers: now the Cyber Rifles did so, in the far, mid and near space. The NCSC became inspector general for cybersecurity

with firms; the mobiliser of civilian resources for that purpose; agony
aunt for those suffering digital heartaches; and missionary for social and
educational change in the nation.

Once the NCSC was created, it quickly took command of British
policy for cyber security, aiming to defend Britain's society and economy.
As Martin said: 'We want this digital revolution to succeed. Our job is
to help make the digital economy and digital Government work, by
making it safer' against 'the three main motivations for systematic cyber
attack ... One is power: the traditional "statecraft" just playing out in
the digital age. Countries and rogue actors seeking to gain advantage by
stealing secrets, or by pre-positioning for a destructive attack in a time
of tension. Another one's money: anything from the sophisticated theft
of intellectual property to the simple theft of cash from a bank account.
Another is propaganda.' Hostile states included 'great powers, using
cyber attacks to spy, gain major commercial and economic advantage
or to pre-position for destructive attack'. Smaller states exploited 'the
relatively immature rules of the road in cyberspace to tweak the nose
of those they see as bigger powers in a way they would and could never
contemplate by traditional military means'. Some criminals 'operate
under the protection or tolerance of uncooperative states, and this is
something new about cyber because it makes it much harder to bring
them to justice because they don't need to set foot in our jurisdictions
or those of our allies to harm us. Some of these gangs are extraordinarily
sophisticated. We've seen some of the most MBA-grade management
information systems that tell them, in great detail, which lines of attack
are profitable and which are not. But not all that much of the crime we
see is MBA-grade and too much of it gets through.' The 'world's major
terrorist groups have the intent, but not the capability, to launch a
destructive cyber attack. Now, that might change.' Meanwhile, Britain
must contain 'the horrific misuse of the Internet by terrorists across the
globe for the purposes of propaganda and radicalisation'.[36]

The NCSC worked with GCHQ and military cyber forces against
attacks by hackers and nation states, including regular forays across the
cyber commons to find threats and disable or ambush them. It also
followed a deeper strategy, aimed 'to make the UK safer in cyberspace
... put right some of the security flaws built into the internet', and
'change the economic equation for cyber criminals and alter the attacker-
defender landscape'. The government moved 'from blaming users and

expecting individuals to bear all the strain of security'.[37] Levy formulated this strategy, the Active Cyber Defence programme, which the NCSC published openly. He emphasised 'a common complaint from industry to governments about cyber security. It's generally that governments tell them they're not doing enough and must do more, often without really understanding the real-world impacts or commercial implications of their demands. Well, our strategy is to use government as a guinea pig for all the measures we want to see done at national scale. We'll be eating our own dog food to prove the efficacy (or otherwise) of the measures we're asking for, and to prove they scale sensibly before asking anyone to implement anything.'[38]

The NCSC challenged fundamental principles of the internet, by making security rather than surveillance its base. Working with private firms, the NCSC tackled technical weaknesses within the internet, such as improving standards for email or infrastructure protocols by which internet providers routed messages. The NCSC would 'drive the UK software ecosystem to be better', by warning British entities that communicated with government websites of vulnerabilities in their software. Levy also attacked firms whose sales pitch 'basically says "you lot are too stupid to understand this and only I can possibly help you – buy my magic amulet and you'll be fine." It's medieval witchcraft, it's genuinely medieval witchcraft.'[39] The NCSC also would 'go looking for badness and take it down', disabling websites across the internet which attacked British targets. 'We're still going to do things to demotivate our adversaries in ways that only GCHQ can do.' That statement was 'euphemistic by design'. Levy warned: 'All of this will evolve. Some of it will work: some won't. We'll have to respond to adversaries as they respond to our defences. That's probably the new normal though ... It's time to stop talking about what the winged ninja cyber monkeys can do and start countering in an automatic way the stuff we see at massive scale that causes real damage to citizens and businesses alike every day.'[40]

This programme involved many actions which might arouse suspicion of government censorship or surveillance. The NCSC countered that danger by establishing a reputation 'as a trustworthy and transparent organisation', and publicised means for anyone to opt out of its proposals. The public, even seasoned critics of GCHQ, knew that the problem was great and must be solved. They viewed NCSC as a bobby on the beat, rather than a secret policeman. Openness created trust that Siginters worked for the security of the nation, rather than subverting its liberties. The NCSC warnings of threats – and weekly and yearly estimates of security problems, with different versions for technical specialists, businesses, and individuals and families – became a common feature in British media, and reached many audiences. They were an open equivalent of the reports which GCHQ and JIC published throughout the Cold War. NCSC was the first organisation to provide national intelligence assessments to plain folk regularly, providing, for example, 'evidence of Russian pre-positioning on some of our critical sectors, along with detailed technical guidance to business on how to get rid of it from our networks'.[41] Though most of these reports came from open sources, some involved the NCSC's own work. No doubt old practices of sanitisation covered the dissemination of material from more secret sources. That the NCSC and GCHQ both released far more material about their work than ever before, including that against states, was another sign of differences between the first and second ages of Sigint.

Underlying this strategy was a campaign to prepare Britons for life on the cyber commons. Inspired by Israeli models and a desire to increase diversity in business, government and GCHQ, the NCSC spread knowledge of cybersecurity. It expanded GCHQ's traditional recruitment in Cheltenham, to help schools across Britain offer courses in computer science, and universities to develop cybersecurity programmes. 'Cyberists,' the NCSC told candidates, 'are intrigued by unexplored technology. Dedicated to fulfilling a bigger role in society. Keen to protect friends, families, communities and commerce. Determined to make an impact. Eager to learn and never let up. They are our new generation of cyber security experts. As technology enhances more and more of our daily life, cyberists will be the ones who'll safeguard it from all manner of threats. Cyber security roles are constantly evolving, consistently challenging and crammed with potential. They could be anybody – and they could come from anywhere. To help find them, support them and train them, we've created CyberFirst.'[42]

Through CyberFirst Bursaries, hundreds of schoolchildren spent summers working in cybersecurity with firms or government. CyberFirst Degree Apprenticeships let undergraduates 'earn while they learn, ready for a job at GCHQ'. The NCSC particularly addressed schoolgirls through special bursaries and courses: the 'CyberFirst Girls

Competition provides a fun but challenging environment to inspire the next generation of young women to consider a career in cyber security'. Over 800 schools entered that programme in 2019, from Jersey to the Orkneys. The leading ten teams conducted a well-publicised contest in London.[43] GCHQ developed outreach programmes of its own, which combined the glamour of past accomplishments with emerging challenges. GCHQ teams attended national meetings in Science, Technology, Engineering and Mathematics (STEM) disciplines, including of 80,000 students at the Big Bang UK Young Scientists and Engineers Fair. Boys and girls handled Enigma machines, played interactive games on computers made by apprentices at GCHQ, and solved puzzles with cypher wheels, pencils and paper. Earnest adolescents discussed cryptography and careers with Siginters. GCHQ became the school of the cyber nation.

Conclusion

GCHQ began as a secret intelligence organisation, as the first age of Sigint opened. Until 2000, it remained an intelligence agency, marked by the highest levels of secrecy. No other Sigint agency pioneered more advances. Only one, NSA, matched or exceeded GCHQ's level of quality. GCHQ had failures, and Sigint had limits, but it ranked among Britain's most cost-effective investments in power and was a great force multiplier. GCHQ helped to keep Britain a great secondary power until 1992, and to maintain the 'special relationship' with the United States. After the Cold War ended, GCHQ rose in power and quality again.

By 2020, GCHQ was one of the great agencies in the second age of Sigint – but no longer secret, nor simply an intelligence bureau. The NCSC was a public body, shaping discourse across Britain, and guiding individuals and firms; while almost on a routine basis GCHQ was in the news. Both gave the public intelligence estimates. GCHQ was the behemoth among British intelligence agencies, and increasingly a fighting service as well. Jeremy Fleming, the incumbent Director, said that GCHQ had 'responsibility for a major national risk for the first time in our hundred-year history'.[1] It also supported the agencies which handled every other risk. Between 1914 and 2019, states across the advanced world moved from units based on brute force, like infantry divisions, towards those stemming from C4ISR. GCHQ was at the vanguard of this trend, as one crude indicator shows: in 1938, Britain had 200,000 sailors to 1,000 Siginters, a ratio of 200 to one; in 2020, the ratio was more like seven to one. Until 2000, GCHQ supported only actions conducted by other state bodies, mostly military and law enforcement. Afterwards, GCHQ supported many consumers, private ones matching the military in moment, and acted independently on its own product. Its budget rose commensurately. During the Cold War, GCHQ's estimates moved slowly towards 2 per cent of that of the MOD. In 2018, the Single Intelligence Vote, spent mostly on GCHQ, was £2.2 billion, or 7.7 per cent the size of that of the MOD.[2] GCHQ was better funded than core elements of British conventional forces, such as armoured units or the Royal Marines.

GCHQ was not merely public, but also popular. Walter Bagehot emphasised that 'mystery' was the 'life' of the monarchy, which must avoid daily politics so to preserve reverence 'from all combatants' – 'We must not let daylight in upon the magic.' For GCHQ, daylight fell upon magic without destroying reverence or power. GCHQ's public reputation was high. Bletchley Park became a metaphor for British genius, and one of its finest hours – reinforced by memories of sections such as Room 40. Television programmes, popular fiction and films were set at Bletchley almost as often as 221B Baker Street. Journalists and other outsiders were allowed to watch GCHQ analysts track terrorists and drug-trafficking networks, and report on their observations. Leaders of GCHQ and the NCSC became perhaps the most public civil servants in Britain, with a remarkable ability to speak their minds. They were seen as genuine and objective experts on technical issues which few understood, but many needed to know. Controversy continued, but media accounts were far more positive, or neutral, than negative – even among old critics. The *Guardian* found good words for GCHQ.

These developments, of course, were subject to change. Since 1914, any major development in communications and data-processing systems, in power and geopolitics, or social and political mores within polities, has affected Sigint – in some cases transformed it. They would do so again. Lesser things were already changing. GCHQ's expansion occurred mostly outside Cheltenham. While the Doughnut remained its headquarters, large elements of GCHQ emerged or grew in London, Manchester and Scarborough. Changes in locale always altered GCHQ, which surely would happen again. The importance of being Cheltonian would decline, its staff would become more national, and their diversity would rise. The expansion in GCHQ's importance also eroded other ambitions. As one old condition of GCHQ changed – its tight finances – so did its internal autonomy. GCHQ was the first of the intelligence agencies to bring Non-Executive Directors on to the Management Board. Directors were once again drawn from across Whitehall. Would this pattern become normal, with all it entailed for management of GCHQ, and promotion within it? Would greater movement in mid-career between GCHQ and other departments become normal for Siginters and civil servants from elsewhere? If so, might GCHQ's qualities of agility, creativity and technical mastery erode, or perhaps find themselves exported across other sections of the British state?

Politicians openly discussed the value of Sigint, which was described as central to British policy. These discussions were phrased in national terms, with less attention to the Cold War arguments that GCHQ did the most to maintain intelligence relations with the United States. A generational time bomb emerged under UKUSA. Common threats of terrorism, and China and Russia, provided grounds for cooperation, while Americans appreciated the resurgence of GCHQ. Yet the ties provided by cooperation against an existential threat eroded, while new generations in its member states were culturally cooler towards each other. UKUSA, the pillar for Sigint between the Five Eyes for generations, was more shaky than before. It might vanish; if so, all of its members would weaken. That UKUSA might vanish, however, was less surprising than the fact that this improbable alliance had lasted so well for so long.

Meanwhile, changes in technology and targets, such as terrorism, NATO's wars in Asia, bulk collection and the focus on non-state actors, transformed the relationship between second and third parties. Each needed some access to each other's databases and to Comint derived from cryptanalysis. These practices could not easily be placed within UKUSA's old 'Categories'. Whether UKUSA eroded, or cooperated more with Sigint agencies from other Western states, one thing was clear. GCHQ would remain a powerful sword and shield for Britain, and its people, as it had been from its start.

Appendix

GCHQ by the Numbers, 1960–95

Analysing statistics, and drawing inferences from them, illuminates GCHQ as a social organisation, particularly its normal folk. The figures in question come from HR records for GCHQ personnel, taken from snapshots in 1965, 1975, 1985 and 1995. 'Scampi', the database of that era, recorded basic personal information – such as previous employment and education, posts, promotions and training at GCHQ. Scampi was an electronic system but flat, without analytic functionality – like material entered in file cards. Over time, its structure gained extra elements, the significance of others was forgotten, and data entry conventions changed. My research assistant, James (Jock) Bruce, anonymised these figures and converted them to a format which modern IT could search and analyse. He checked this data with a sample of witting individuals, to ascertain the accuracy of Scampi data after conversion.

Jock Bruce then combined these raw figures and organised them into data fields. All material on educational background, for example, was converted into terms such as 'local school leavers' or 'polytechnic graduates'. Career data was gathered into functional fields, such as 'clerical' or 'intercept', to avoid difficulties caused by changes in unit designations. The term 'generalist' describes the standard positions in civil service departments, whereas 'specialist' denotes occupations exclusive to GCHQ, or those requiring particular qualifications, such as engineers, scientists or technicians. This data remains classified. Jock Bruce then turned it into several graphs and charts, published in this book, which illustrate basic issues about GCHQ as a whole: the average age on entry of its members between 1960 and 1995; and the gender, age, and entry as generalists and specialists of entrants into various divisions of GCHQ. Charts and graphs illustrate women's positions in leadership roles at GCHQ between 1972 and 1994. Jock Bruce is the basic analyst of this data, though we discussed his findings at length, and compared them with qualitative evidence on these matters. The two sources generally pointed in similar directions, but the statistical evidence raised nuances and questions which shaped interpretation at many important points, such as career advancement by non-elite members of GCHQ, and the status of women in leadership roles.

This material illustrates social and demographic dynamics inside GCHQ, but with reservations. The outcomes might vary marginally with different snapshots, say 1963, 1973, 1983 and 1993. Since, with Department Specialists (DSs) and some other areas, few people were involved, small changes in absolute numbers may distort their representation as percentiles. The year 1995 had a small intake, and our figures end before their careers did, which prevents complete comparison between these sets of data. The crude terms used in the analysis, such as 'military service' or 'local school leavers', cover many backgrounds – for instance for the latter: the appropriately named Crypt Grammar School in Gloucester; St George's School, Hong Kong; the Army Apprentices College, Harrogate; the Royal School of Needlework, and one alumnus from both the RAF School of Wireless and the Goethe Institute. These figures also exclude the backgrounds of entrants to the service Sigint agencies, which recruited even fewer personnel, almost all male, through military channels – some of whom later entered GCHQ under our category of 'ex-servicemen'.

The number of entrants to GCHQ each year was small, and variable. Absorbing the civilian units from service Sigint created 768 entrants in 1965. The 138 entrants in 1995 reflect the planned rundown of GCHQ personnel. On average, GCHQ, with around 8,000 staff, enrolled about 375 entrants annually, enough to maintain that strength, or to run it down to achieve rationalisation. Superiors and the Apprentice Committee could manage the training of individual Departmental Specialists, and technical specialists, in detail. GCHQ's enrolments aimed to give areas the desired strength five to twenty years ahead. Most notably, a careful rundown tried to reduce the radio grades by 50 per cent between 1970 and 1990. Afterwards, that decline became terminal.

The average age for entrants was surprisingly high, since many were school leavers: around twenty-six years for women and thirty for men.

These averages reflect the large number of males entering GCHQ after military service, and of women returning to work after raising families. The radio grades and communications and cypher officers were almost exclusively male for most of this period, and almost all originally uniformed or civilian members of the services. Otherwise, at GCHQ the two largest sources for male entrants were local school leavers and retired military personnel, with graduates far behind. For women entrants, local school leavers were far and away the dominant source, with graduates also far behind. The groups were perhaps almost different castes. Male entrants usually stayed for life. The proportion of women at GCHQ remained much smaller than their share of entrants, reflecting higher rates of retirement, for which GCHQ planned. The proportion of women among GCHQ personnel declined steadily between 1955 to 1973, from 23 per cent to 18 per cent, but then rose steadily to 28 per cent by 1995. Although the absorption and retirement of members of the services' intercept organisations boosted this decline and fall, still, by 1995, women were a notably larger part of GCHQ than in 1955, or 1973. GCHQ's leaders were civilians, and Siginters, but below that it had a civilianised military atmosphere. Older men with military experience, aided by younger civilian males, dominated collection and technical issues. Females, divided equally between young and fairly transient clerical staff, and older career women, handled administration. Only in intelligence and analysis did men and women normally work side by side.

The smallest group of entrants for both sexes, between 0.5 per cent and 1.5 per per cent, were in the departmental specialist class, where wastage was high. Most entrants, marginally more women than men, resigned or never reached the administrative class. Those who remained had quite a clear run for senior positions. Had Oxbridge graduates recognised how open this field was, they might have found it more attractive.

As the DS scheme sputtered, GCHQ boosted recruitment into the executive class by almost 200 per cent, by directly reducing the prior numbers of personnel taken into the clerical classes. In particular, during each of 1965, 1975 and 1985, around ten male entrants into the executive class were scientists or engineers, a sharply rising percentage of that class, especially if it really represented yearly practices. Male entrants into the clerical classes also increasingly had technical skills, which reinforced this means to augment GCHQ's power among scientists and engineers. GCHQ had non-elite men and women handle middle to senior leadership roles and tasks, and particularly reduce its perennial problems with lack of engineers, scientists and linguists. A large proportion of men, rising from 28 per cent in 1965, to 44–45 per cent in 1975 and 1985, entered the executive class. Most of them, 42 per cent in 1975 and 1985, and 66 per cent in 1965, were in the radio grades. (In 1965 neither radio grades nor communications and cypher operators were rated as 'executive class', but both soon achieved this status under a system of 'unified grading'.) Other entrants to the executive class varied in occupation, every year. In 1965, they primarily were vetting officers, recruited from retired local policemen. In 1975 and 1985, most male entrants to the executive class were university or polytechnic graduates, with the rest being ex-military. Of these graduates, 10 per cent entered as generalists, or executive officers, 30 per cent had science and engineering backgrounds, and 15 per cent, declining to 8 per cent in 1985, were linguists. The clerical class remained almost tied with the executive class as the largest category for male entrants, though falling from 55 per cent in 1965, to 33 per cent in 1975, and 40 per cent in 1985. Men entered equally as general assistants, or in science and engineering grades. Entrants mostly were local school leavers, many with technical degrees from colleges. The rest had military experience, especially communications and cypher personnel.

Far fewer women than men entered the executive class – 5 per cent of female entrants in 1965, rising to 14–16 per cent in 1975 and 1985. This discrepancy was fundamental to the lack of advancement for women, compared to men, in middle management across GCHQ. It may explain most of this difference between genders in advancement. These women were hired primarily as generalists or linguists, in proportions varying each year. From 1975, they overwhelmingly were graduates. Far more than men, women entered the executive class as linguists and generalists, and less often as specialists, scientists or engineers. The largest group of women entered in the clerical class, 90 per cent in 1965, falling to 66–69 per cent in 1975 and 1985. Half of them were recent school leavers, but about 10 per cent were older than thirty-five. In 1965, about 66 per cent of these women entered essentially in secretarial roles, as clerical assistant or clerical officers, or typing staff. About 20 per cent were in technical branches, as laboratory assistants or drafting technicians, and about 15 per cent as CCOs at outstations. Later, almost all female entrants in the clerical class were clerical assistants or officers, with an average age of twenty-two. The lack of substantial further recruitment of women in technical branches or

CCOs suggests that once recruited into these areas, women stayed rather than retired, even after motherhood. Needs in those areas did not decline and males did not take them over. That women selected taxing technical careers suggests more investment in them. CCOs characteristically worked in small provincial towns where other jobs and women with the requisite skills were scarce, and a steady career suited both them and GCHQ.

About 20 per cent of male entrants annually were in the industrial classes, like labour and drivers, declining to 12 per cent in 1995; 5 per cent, rising to 18 per cent, of women entered the industrial classes, as caterers and cleaners, perhaps also being older.

Promotion within a class offered money and status, especially if moving from executive officer to senior principal in the executive class, and even more so, advancement between classes. These advantages drove the ambitious, like many young males originally enrolled in the lowest ranks of the clerical class. In these snapshots, advancement within and between classes was not different between men or women in any given area, but likelier among those who joined young and stayed on, which was more true of men than women, and also in the areas dominated by males. In the largest male groups, however – radio and communication grades – promotion even just within class was almost impossible, and little better within the largest female clerical grades. Advancement within grades, and between clerical and executive classes, was easiest for people classed with scientific and engineering skills, which, however, generalists might acquire, especially in the early days of IT. About 30–35 per cent of clerical entrants in these areas reached the executive classes before retirement, fewer in other areas. C or E grades were not promoted to DS in any of these sample years, although this occurred rarely at other times.

These socio-historical figures describe a dead body. The GCHQ of 2020 is a different beast. Since 1992, two major occupational groups, the radio grades and secretarial branches, have died; military and ex-military personnel fell in significance, while graduates became the core of the organisation. Yet matters which seemingly illustrate change actually show continuity. That 35 per cent of GCHQ's staff in 2018 are female, compared to 28 per cent in 1995, stems partly from the passing of all male groups, such as the radio grades. The rise in their proportionate share between 1995 and 2019 is no greater than between 1973 and 1995. Women are not much larger a proportion of GCHQ in 2019 than in 1992, though they have achieved higher ranks.

1965

Intake by role, 1965

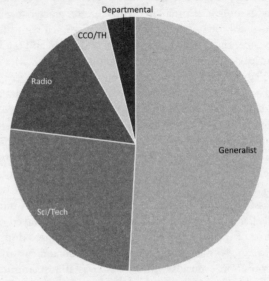

Intake by band, 1965

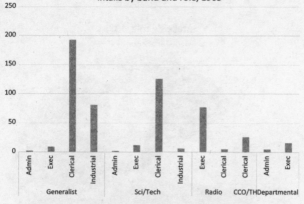

Intake by band and role, 1965

Gender-split intake by role, 1965

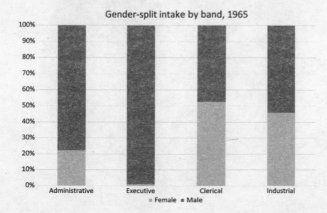

Gender-split intake by band, 1965

1975

Intake by role, 1975

Intake by band, 1975

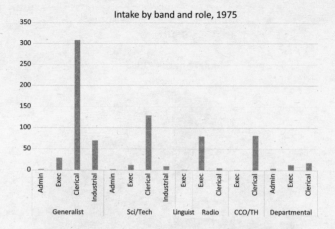

Intake by band and role, 1975

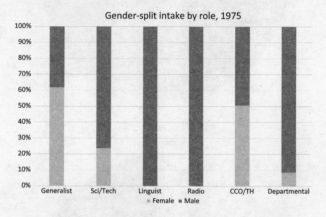

Gender-split intake by role, 1975

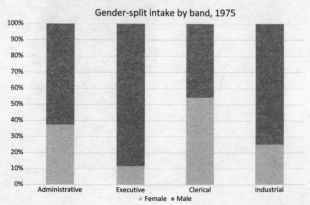

Gender-split intake by band, 1975

1985

Intake by role, 1985

CCO/TH
Departmental
Radio
Linguist
Generalist
Sci/Tech

Intake by band, 1985

Administrative
Industrial
Executive
Clerical

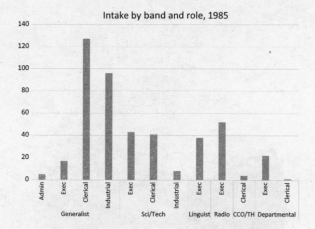

Intake by band and role, 1985

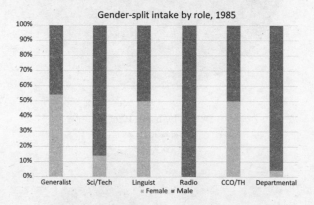

Gender-split intake by role, 1985

Female Male

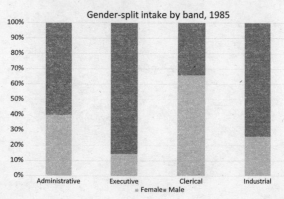

Gender-split intake by band, 1985

Female Male

1995

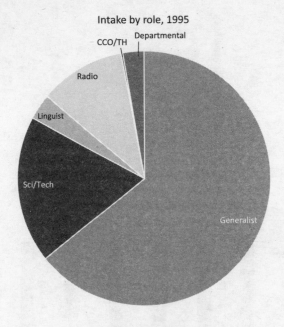

Intake by role, 1995

Departmental
CCO/TH
Radio
Linguist
Sci/Tech
Generalist

Intake by band, 1995

Administrative
Industrial
Executive
Clerical

Intake by band and role, 1995

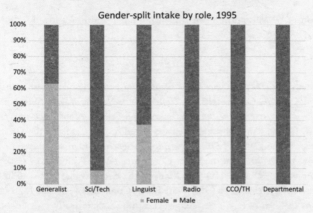

Gender-split intake by role, 1995

Gender-split intake by band, 1995

Notes

INTRODUCTION

1   Report of UK/Australian Sigint Mission to Japan and Korea (April to July 1953), 1.7.53, SS/1940.

CHAPTER 1

1   Kenneth Ellis, *The Post Office in the Eighteenth Century* (London, 1958), Chapter 6; David Kahn, *The Codebreakers, The Comprehensive History of Secret Communications from Ancient Times to the Internet* (Simon and Schuster, 1996), pp. 170–74, 187–88; W. Gibson, 'An Eighteenth-Century Paradox: The Career of the Decipherer-Bishop, Edward Willes', *British Journal for Eighteenth-Century Studies*, 12 (1989), pp. 69–76; 'Report from the Select Committee on the Post Office Together with the Appendix', 5.8.1844, HD 3/15. Many of these reports may be found in the SP 107 series, cf. Jeremy Black (ed.), 'State Papers Confidential', in *State Papers Online, Eighteenth Century, 1714–1782*, Cengage Learning 2018, https://www.gale.com/intl/essays/jeremy-black-state-papers-confidential

2   Neil Kent, 'The Hanoverian Connection: British Intelligence and Counterintelligence as Recorded by Spymaster Thomas Pelham-Holles, 1st Duke of Newcastle, Against the Jacobites', *Journal of Intelligence and Terrorism Studies*, 2016, 1; Jeremy Black, 'British Intelligence and the Mid-eighteenth-century Crisis', *Intelligence and National Security*, 2 (1987), pp. 209–16, and 'Eighteenth-century Intercepted Dispatches', *Journal of the Society of Archivists*, 11 (1990), pp. 138–43.

3   Bernstorff to Reventhow, 16.6.1801, marked 'Decyphered', *passim*, Comte de Marcov to Alexander II, 11.3.03, Add. MSS 38237, Liverpool Papers, British Library.

4 Mark Urban, *The Man Who Broke Napoleon's Codes: The Story of George Scovell* (Faber, London, 2001); Huw J. Davies, *Spying for Wellington, British Military Intelligence in the Peninsular War* (University of Oklahoma Press, 2018).

5 Home Office to General Post Office, 7.4.1818, *passim*, HO 79/3; cf. HO 32/20, HO 151/7; Emialiana P. Noether, ' "Morally Wrong" or "Politically right"? Espionage in Her Majesty's Post Office, 1844–45', *Canadian Journal of History*, 22 (1987), pp. 73–91; F. B. Smith, 'British Post Office Espionage 1844', *Historical Studies*, 14/54, (1970), pp. 189–203.

6 There is no complete collection of solutions after 1815, but these statements fit the material surviving in the substantial collections of drafts by the Deciphering Branch in the W. A. MacKinnon bequest and the Willes Papers, Add. MS. 32353–32309 and 45518–23, British Library, and those scattered through the papers of recipient, like an Under Secretary at the Foreign Office between 1824–28, Lord Howard de Walden, cf. FO 360/3–5 (e.g. Baron de Mareshal to Metternich, 28.9.25, FO 360/3).

7 Bode to Backhouse, 25.10.28, *passim*, minute by Palmerston, 22.1.31, HD 3/3; Backhouse to Addington, 21.11.43, HD 3/22; cf. HF 3/11, 15, 16, 17, 35.

8 House of Commons Debates (HCD), 24.6.1844, Vol. 75, cc. 1264–305; HCD 18.2.1845, Vol. 77, col. 698. For context, cf. Bernard Porter, *Plots and Paranoia: A History of Political Espionage in Britain, 1790–1900* (London, Unwin Hyman, 1989) and David Vincent, *The Culture of Secrecy: Britain, 1832–1998* (OUP, 1998).

9 Bode to Aberdeen, 21.12.44, *passim*, HD 3/14.

10 Memorandum by Addington, 'Office of Secret Service Decipherer Messrs. Willes and Lovell', 7.8.1844, *passim*, HD 3/16; 'Mem sic on Mr. L. H. Lovell's letter of 5 Jan sic 1846', HD 3/22; HD 3/35, *passim*.

11 John Ferris, 'Before Room 40: The British Empire and Signals Intelligence, 1989–1914', *The Journal of Strategic Studies*, Vol. 12, Number 4, December 1989.

12 Herbert Maxwell, *The Life and Letters of George William Frederick Fourth Earl of Clarendon, Vol. II* (London, Edwin Arnold, 1913), p. 282.

13 Max Jones, '"Measuring the World": Exploration, Empire and the Reform of the Royal Geographical Society, c. 1873–1892', in Martin Daunton (ed.), *The Organisation of Knowledge in Victorian Britain*, OUP, 2005).

14 Ferris, J. R., 'British Intelligence and the Old World Order', in Greg Kennedy (ed.) *Imperial Defence, The Old World Order, 1856–1956* (Routledge Press, 2008), pp.176–96; John Ferris, *Intelligence and Strategy, Selected Essays* (Routledge, 2005), pp. 8–44; William Beaver, *Under Every Leaf, How Britain Played the Greater Game from Afghanistan to Africa* (Biteback Publishing, 2012).

15 Minute by Granville, nd but c. April 1884, FO 83/909; Godley to Burne, 18.2.1885, *passim*, L/PS/8/1.

16 John Ferris, 'Before Room 40: The British Empire and Signals Intelligence, 1989–1914', *The Journal of Strategic Studies*, Vol. 12, Number 4, December 1989.

17 Christopher Andrew, *The Defence of the Realm, The Authorised History of MI5* (Allen Lane, 2009); Keith Jeffery, *MI6: The History of the Secret Intelligence Service, 1909–1949* (Bloomsbury, 2011); Richard Poppelwell, *Intelligence and Imperial Defence, British Intelligence and the Defence of the Indian Empire, 1904–1924* (Routledge, 1995).

18 'Censorship of Submarine Cables in Time of War', 2.10.1898, CAB 17/92; cf. David Paul Nickles, *Under the Wire: How the Telegraph Changed Diplomacy* (Harvard University Press, 2003).

19 High Commissioner for South Africa to Governor, Natal, telegram No. 2, 24.2.1900, DO 119/513; War Office to Kitchener, 6.7.01, WO 108/306; Milner to Colonial Office, 16.5.00, FO 2/441.

20 Ferris, 'Before Room 40'.

21 Report of Censorship of Cable and Wireless Committee, 7.7.1908, CAB 17/92; Admiralty Intelligence Division, 8.11, 'Regulations for the Censorship of Radio-Telegraphy in Time of War', FO 371/ 1283, 38965; Memoranda by General Staff, 1906 and 1907, A 1039, 'Censorship of Submarine Cables in Times of War', and Second Meeting, 'Censorship of Submarine Cables', 26.10.10, L/MIL 7/13581.

22 Memorandum by War Office, ibid., ADM 1/7576; War Office, A 1039, 'Censorship of Submarines Cables in Time of War', 1906 and 1907 versions, L/MIL 7/13581.

23 Admiralty Intelligence Division, 8.11. 1911, 'Regulations for the Censorship of Radio-Telegraphy in Time of War', FO 371/ 1283, 38965.

24 War Office to Foreign Office, 21.2.06, FO 371/165, 6428.

25 First meeting of the Censorship of Cables Committee, 11.7.10, CAB 17/92.

26 Andrew, *Defence*, pp. 37–48.

27 Ferris, 'Before Room 40'.

28 Government of India to Foreign Office, 6.3.13, *passim,* FO 228/2579; cf. FO 228/ 2581–86, L/PS/11/47, L/PS/10/393.

29 For the background, cf. Thomas G. Fergusson, *British Military Intelligence, The Development of a Modern Intelligence Organisation* (Arms & Armour Press, 1984), pp. 166–236, and Jim Beach, *Haig's Intelligence, GHQ and the German Army, 1916–1918* (CUP, 2015), pp. 1–23.

30 John Ferris, 'Intelligence, Information and the Leverage of Seapower', Daniel Moran and James A. Russell (eds), *Maritime Strategy and Global Order, Resources, Security,* (George Washington University Press, Washington D.C., 2016).

31 Daniel Headrick, *The Invisible Weapon: Telecommunications and International Relations, 1851–1945* (OUP, 1991); Daniel R. Headrick and Pascal Griset,

'Submarine Telegraph Cables, Business and Politics, 1838–1939', *Business History Review*, 75/3, autumn 2001, pp. 543–78; Peter Hugill, *Global Communications since 1844: Geopolitics and Technology* (Johns Hopkins University Press, 1999).

32 Minute by MacDonogh, 11.2.14, WO 32/7048; meeting of Committee on Imperial Wireless Telegraphy, 17.1.12, WO 32/7045.

33 Elizabeth Bruton, 'Beyond Marconi; The Roles of the Admiralty, the Post Office and the Institution of Electrical Engineers in the invention and development of wireless communication up to 2008', University of Leeds PhD diss. 2013); cf. ADM 1/9204, ADM 1/29126.

34 Nicholas Lambert, 'Strategic Command and Control for Maneuver Warfare: Creation of the Royal Navy's "War Room" System, 1905–1915', *The Journal of Military History*, 69/2, April 2005, pp. 361–410.

35 Andrew Gordon, *The Rules of the Game, Jutland and British Naval Command* (John Murray, 2005).

36 Nicholas Black, *The British Naval Staff in the First World War* (Boydell, 2009), pp.1–74.

37 Memorandum by Spring-Rice, 19.2.1898, FO 83/1651.

38 Currie to Rosebery, 28.8.1893, Algernon Thomas (GPO) to 'Eric' (Chief Clerk's Office), 5.4.1894, FO 83/1424.

39 Monson to Sanderson, 18.12.1899, FO 83/1760.

40 Arthur Hardinge to Sanderson, 30.9.1901, FO 83/1883; Langley to Jordan, 6.4.12, FO 350/1.

41 Minute by Currie, 18.2.90, HD 3/80.

42 War Office to India Office, 14.11.11, 14.10.12, L/MIL 7/10223.

43 Ferris, *Intelligence and Strategy*, pp. 139–40.

44 Ferris, 'Before Room 40'; Nicholas Hiley, 'The Strategic Origins of Room 40', *Intelligence and National Security*, 2/3, December 1987.

CHAPTER 2

1 Undated and unsigned memorandum on the origins of Room 40, by Denniston, Denniston Papers, DENN 1/3, Churchill College, Cambridge.

2 Unsigned and undated memorandum, presumably by Sir Ronald Nesbitt Hawes, 'An Intelligence Section of the First World War', Intelligence Corps Museum, Accession No. 198.

3 Undated and unsigned memorandum on the origins of Room 40, by Denniston, Denniston Papers, DENN 1/3.

4 Undated memorandum, *c.* 1918, George Young, 'Political Branch of Room 40', ADM 223/773.

5 Hall to 'My dear Commander in Chief' (Beatty), 'Personal and Secret', 18.5.17, ADM 223/768.

6 Report of Cypher Conference, 27.2.19, ADM 1/8637.

7 Alice Ivy Hay, *Valiant for Truth, Ian Hay of Seaforth* (London, Spearman, 1971). https://archive.is/20120722130348/http://www.archiveshub.ac.uk/news/0508fraser.html

8 Ferris, *British Army and Signals Intelligence*, pp. 10–11.

9 Clauson to Crocker, 9.10.1917. Clauson papers, Imperial War Museum.

10 Ferris, *British Army and Signals Intelligence*, pp. 241–95.

11 Hay, *Valiant*, p. 78.

12 Young, 'Political Branch of Room 40'.

13 Ibid.

14 Ibid. Walter Bruford,' "Room Forty" in the 1914–1918 War', 23.2.77, BRUF Misc 20, Churchill College Cambridge; Elizabeth Tucker, 'Some Anniversaries and Ceremonies at Christ's Hospital, Hertford', Dr Doris Jones-Bakers (ed.), *Hertfordshire in History*, University of Hertfordshire Press, 2004, p. 296.

15 The works which use the material from Room 40, most thoroughly, Patrick Beesley, *Room 40, British Naval Intelligence, 1914–1918* (London, 1982), and Paul Gannon, *Inside Room 40: The Codebreakers of World War One* (Hersham: Ian Allen, 2010) do not tackle naval records generated from outside the NID. The Room 40 tradition focuses on the NID more than the Royal Navy. Norman Friedman, *Fighting the Great War at Sea: Strategy, Tactics and Technology* (Seaforth Publishing, Barnsley, 2014), pp. 89–97, places Sigint within the context of contemporary seapower.

16 Jellicoe to Beatty, 1.4.16, Beatty Papers, 13/22, National Maritime Museum.

17 W. F. Clarke, *History of Room 40*, 1914–1919, Chapter Two, pp. 1–4, HW 3/3.

18 William Carless Davis, *History of the Blockade Emergency Departments* (1920), p. 8, MUN 5/113.

19 Entry, 5.11.14, M05b war diary, ADM 223/767.

20 'English Spy System Said to Excel German', *New York Times*, 3.3.15, p. 3.

21 Filson Young, *With the Battle Cruisers* (1921).

22 W. F. Clarke, *History of Room 40*, 1914–1919, Chapter Two, p. 1–4, HW 3/3.

23 Battlecruiser Force to Grand Fleet, NO SE, 20.1.15, ADM 137/1938.

24 Gustav Kleikamp, 'Der Einfluss der Funkaufklarung auf die Seekriegfuhrung in der Nordsee 1914–1918', Gehiem MDiv. 352, Dientschrift Nr. 13, Leitung der Fuhrergehilfenausbildung der Marine (Berlin, 1934); Keith W. Bird and Jason Hines, 'In the Shadow of Ultra: A Reappraisal of German Naval Communications Intelligence in the First World War', *The Northern Mariner*, XVIII/2 (Spring 2018), pp. 97–117; Hilmar-Detlaf Bruckner, 'Germany's First Cryptanalysis on the Western Front: Decrypting British and French Naval Ciphers in World War

One', *Cryptologia*, 29/1, 9 2005), pp. 1–22; Martin Samuels, 'Ludwig Foppl: A Bavarian Cryptanalyst on the Western Front', *Cryptologia*, 40/4, pp. 355–73.

25 Unsigned letter (but Hall by internal evidence) to Sturdee, 25.5,17, ADM 223/768.

26 Gustav Kleikamp, 'Der Einfluss der Funkaufklarung auf die Seekriegfuhrung in der Nordsee 1914–1918', Gehiem MDiv. 352, Dientschrift Nr. 13, Leitung der Fuhrergehilfenausbildung der Marine (Berlin, 1934).

27 Grand Fleet to Admiralty, No. 50/H.F. 0022, 9.1.18, ADM 116/1349.

28 'Conference on Board "Iron Duke", 17 September', Grand Fleet to Admiralty, No. 339/H.F. 0034, 30.10.14, No. 411.H.F. 0034, 12.11.14, passim, ADM 137/995.

29 Battlecruiser Squadron to Grand Fleet, 20.1.15, ADM 137/1936.

30 Admiralty Committee Report, 4.2.15, ADM 1/8411.

31 Commander in Chief Grand Fleet to Captains, Grand Fleet, 'Grand Fleet Code 1914', 10.10.14, ADM 137/472; Commander in Chief Grand Fleet to Admiralty, No. 2840/HF 008, 16.12.15, *passim*, ADM 137/1896; Commander in Chief Grand Fleet to Admiralty, 31.1.17, *passim*, ADM 137/1895.

32 Bird and Hines, 'Shadow of Ultra'.

33 Jeffery, *MI6*, pp. 84–5; cf. ADM 223/267.

34 John Ferris, 'The British Army and Signals Intelligence in the Field during the First World War', INS 3/4, 1988, pp. 32–5.

35 Sophie de Lastours, *La France gagne la guerre des codes secrets 1914–18* (Paris, Tallandier, 1998) and Douglas Porch, *The French Secret Services, from the Dreyfus Affair to the Gulf War* (London, MacMillan, 1996), are useful studies. John R. Schindler, 'A Hopeless Struggle: Austro-Hungarian Cryptology during World War 1', *Cryptologia*, 24/4 (2000), pp. 1–10, is excellent. The longest account of German military sigint, Wilhelm F. Flicke, *War Secrets in the Ether, Vol. One* (Aegean Park Press, Laguna Hills, Ca., 1977), pp. 1–78, must be used with extreme caution. Yves Gylden, *The Contribution of the Cryptographic Bureaus in the Great War* (Aegean Park Press, 1978: original, Swedish and French, 1931), compiles useful material about signals intelligence from the German army's official histories, and also those of Britain and France.

36 Ferris, 'Signals Intelligence in the Field', pp. 32–44.

37 Ferris, *British Army*, pp. 14–16, 85–114; Ferdinand Tuohy, *The Crater of Mars* (London, 1929), pp. 132–48.

38 Memorandum OAD 314, Kiggell, CGS, GHQ, to Third Army, 17.2.17, AWM 51/52, Australian War Memorial, Canberra.

39 Jim Beach and James Bruce, 'British Signals Intelligence in the Trenches, 1915–1918: part one, listening sets', and 'British Signals Intelligence in the Trenches, 1915–1918: part two, interpreter operators', *Journal of Intelligence History*, 19/1, January 2020, pp. 1–23, and pp. 24–50.

40 Ferris, *Signals intelligence*, pp.13–14, 25–54.

41 R. E. Priestley, *The Signal Service in the European War of 1914–1918 (France)* (Chatham, 1920), p. 236.

42 FAIS No. 890, 21.6.17, WO 157/76.

43 Canadian Corps Operations Orders No. 156, 11.7.27, No. 140, 28.7.17, WO 95/1050.

44 2nd Canadian Division, 6.8.17, 'Report on Conversations Picked up by Wireless Intelligence in 2nd. Canadian Division Sector', RG 9/III/C–5/4438, National Archives of Canada.

45 CCIS No. 117, 24.7.17, WO 95/1050, John Ferris, 'Seeing over the hill: the Canadian Corps, intelligence, and the battle of Hill 70, July–August 1917', INS, 32/2, April 2017, pp. 351–64.

46 J. R. Ferris (ed.) *The British Army and Signals Intelligence During the First World War* (Army Records Society, 1992, pp. 297–316). The best accounts of intelligence in these campaigns are Polly Mohs, *British Intelligence and the Arab Revolt: The First Modern Intelligence War* (Routledge, 2008) and Yigal Sheffy, *British Intelligence in the Palestine Campaign, 1914–1918* (Frank Cass, 1997).

47 Ibid. and WO 95/4966.

48 EC 850–51 (GHQ Salonica to DMI, two telegrams, 17.7.18), CAB 27/29; EC 1071, 'The Turco-German Advance into the Caucasus', General Staff, 7.8.18, CAB 7/30.

49 John Ferris, 'Pragmatic Hegemony and British economic warfare, 1900–1918', in Greg Kennedy (ed.), *Britain's War at Sea, 1914–1918: The War They Thought and the War They Fought* (Praeger, 2016).

50 John Ferris, 'The War Trade Intelligence Department and British Economic Warfare during the First World War', in T. G. Otte (ed.), *British World Policy and the Projection of Power, 1830–1960* (CUP, 2019).

51 Undated memorandum, *c.* 1918, George Young, 'Political Branch of Room 40', ADM 223/773.

52 Hardinge to Lloyd George, 14.12.16, 15.12.16, F/3/2, Robertson to Lloyd George, 14.12.16, F/44/3, Lloyd George Papers, House of Lords Record Office.

53 'Note on the division of responsibility between the War Office and the G.C. & C.S. in the event of war', 21.7.32, HW 62/19. Peter Freeman, 'MI1(b) and the Origins of British Diplomatic Cryptanalysis', INS, 22/2, 2007, pp. 206–28; James Bruce, '"A Shadowy Entity": MI1(b) and British Communications Intelligence, 1914–1922', INS, 32/3, 2017, pp. 313–32.

54 Daniel Richard Larsen, Ph.D diss., 'British Intelligence and American Neutrality during the First World War', Cambridge University, 2013.

55 Ibid. and Thomas Boghardt, *The Zimmerman Telegram: Intelligence, Diplomacy and America's Entry into the First World War* (Annapolis: Naval Institute Press, 2012).

56 Washington to Vienna 22.2.17, Vienna to Washington 27.2.17 (Austro-Hungarian decrypts), HW 7/17; cf. HW 7/22; Bullitt Lowry, *Armistice 1918* (Kent State University Press, 1996), pp. 83–4, 126.

57 Captain H. J. Round, 'Direction and Position Finding', *The Journal of the Institution of Electrical Engineer,* Vol. 5 8 (1920).

58 Brian Hall, *British Army Communications on the Western Front, 1914–1918* (CUP 2017).

59 Major W. Arthur Steel, 'Wireless Telegraphy in the Canadian Corps in France', Chapters One–Eleven, *Canadian Defence Quarterly* (Vols 6–9, 1928–31).

60 Undated and untitled memorandum by Denniston on the origins of Room 40, Denniston papers, 1 /2 and 1/3; Ann Powell, 'In Memory of Edward Russell-Clarke', n.d., https://historypoints.org/index.php?page=in-memory-of-edward-russell-clarke; Elizabeth Bruton, 'Hippisley Hut: Wireless Interception at the Outbreak of World War One', 29.3.2015, http://blogs.mhs.ox.ac.uk/innovatingincombat/tag/world-war-one/

61 Beach and Bruce, 'British Signals Intelligence in the Trenches, 1915–1918: part two', *Journal of Intelligence History,* 19/1, January 2020, pp. 24–50.

62 Jim Beach (ed.), *The Diary of Corporal Vince Schürhoff, 1914–1918* (Army Records Society, 2015).

63 Stephen McKenna, *While I Remember* (Thornton Butterworth, London, 1921), pp. 163–65.

64 'Origin and Development of the War Trade Intelligence Department', 'A', by Penson, undated. c/.11.17, BT 61/12/7; Ferris, 'The War Trade Intelligence Department, in Otte (ed.), *British World Policy,* pp. 24–45.

65 Meeting at Trade Clearing House, 11.3.16, ADM 137/2735.

66 Memorandum by Emmott, 27.3.19. CAB 15/6/4

67 Tamson Pietsch, blog, 24.1.17, 'Trixie Whitehead: Intelligence and the First World War', http://expertnation.org/trixie-whitehead-intelligence-and-the-first-world-war/

68 Memorandum by Emmott, 27 March 1919, CAB 15/6/4. 'History of Postal Censorship', pp. 321, 329, 330, DEFE 1/131.

69 Jim Beach, 'The HushWAACS – The secret ladies of St. Omer, September 2017', https://www.gchq.gov.uk/information/hush-waacs

70 Memorandum by G. E. G. Watkins, 'Memoirs of a HushWaac in France', undated, MCN 944, National Army Museum.

71 M. D. Peel, *The Story of the Hush-Waacs* (Newcastle-under-Lyme: Mandley & Unett, 1921).

72 Memorandum by Brooke-Hunt, 'Nominal Roll of M.I.1.b.', 2.8.19', HW 3/35 'History of the Cryptographic and Wireless Intelligence Organisations'; unsigned, *c.* 1.23, HW 3/39.

73 Ivo Juurvee, 'Birth of Russian SIGINT in World War One on the Baltic Sea', INS, 32/3, 1917, pp. 300–12; Admiralty to Foreign Office, 'Urgent and Secret', 7.9.14, *passim,* FO 371/2095.

74 Betsy Smoot, 'Impermanent Alliances: cryptologic cooperation between the United States, Britain and France on the western front, 1917–1918', INS, 32/3, 2017, pp. 365–77.

75 Mediterranean Station W/T Orders, 8.11.16, ADM 137/1603; Commander in Chief Mediterranean Fleet to Admiralty, 14.1.16, *passim*, ADM 137/2171; Commander in Chief Mediterranean Fleet to Adriatic Force, 5.12.17, ADM 137/2125; cf. ADM 116/429.

76 Captain H. J. Round, 'Direction and Position Finding', *The Journal of the Institution of Electrical Engineers*, Vol. 5 8 (1920), p. 238, *passim;* Round to Royal Commission for Awards to Inventors, 20.12.26, War Office to same, 5.1.28, T 173/428.

77 Robert M. Grant, U Boat Hunters: Codebreakers, Divers and the Defeat of the B-Boats, 1914–1918 (Annapolis: Naval Institute Press, 2003); cf. ADM 1/8512.

78 J. R. Ferris, "Airbandit":C3 I and Strategic Air Defence During the First Battle of Britain, 1915–1918' in Michael Dockrill and David French, (eds), *Strategy and Intelligence, British Policy During the First World War* (Hambledon, 1996).

CHAPTER 3

1 John Ferris, 'British Intelligence and the Old World Order', in Greg Kennedy (ed.) *Imperial Defence, The Old World Order, 1856–1956* (Routledge Press, 2008), pp.176–96.; J. R. Ferris. "'Now that the Milk is Spilt": Appeasement and the Archive on Intelligence', in B. J. C. McKercher and Michael Roi, (eds), *Appeasement Reappraised* (special issue, *Diplomacy & Statecraft*, 2008).

2 Beesley, Room 40, p. 304; W. F. Clarke, 'The Years Between', Chapter Three, W. F. Clarke Papers, Churchill College, Cambridge.

3 Curzon to Austen Chamberlain, 25.3.19, T 1/12517; conference of ministers, 29.4.29, *passim*, ADM 1/8637.

4 C.P. 3105, July 1921, Lord Curzon Papers, F. 112/302, India Office Records Library.

5 Minute by Waterhouse, 9.5.19, T 1/12517/13418.

6 Ibid.

7 Ibid., 13.12.19, T 1/12517/13418.

8 Bruce, 'Shadowy Entity',; Hay, *Valiant for Truth*.

9 Clarke, 'The Years Between', Chapter Three.

10 Record of Conference held at the Admiralty on 5 August, 1919, HW 3/35.

11 Andrew, *Secret Service*, pp. 262–74; Richard H. Ullman, *Anglo-Soviet Relations, Vol. III, The Anglo-Soviet Accord*, Chapter Nine (Princeton, 1972); minute by Sinclair, March 1921, Lloyd George Papers, F/25/1.

12 Curzon to Lee, 25.4/21, ADM 8637.

13 'Report of the Committee Appointed by the Cabinet on March 22nd', 27.7.21, 15/B/10, *passim*, KV 4/157.

14 C.P. 3105, July 1921, Lord Curzon Papers, F. 112/302, India Office Records Library.

15 Ibid.

16 Meeting of the Secret Service Committee, 2.3.25, FO 1093/68.

17 Alastair Denniston, 'The Code and Cypher School between the Wars', *INS*, 1/1, January 1986, pp. 48–70.

18 Ullman, *Anglo-Soviet Relations*.

19 Curzon to Lloyd George, 5.10.22, F. 112/224 B, Curzon to Baldwin, 9.11.23, F.112/320, Curzon Papers.

20 Report of the Inter-Service Directorate Committee, 9.4.23, AIR 2/246.

21 Undated memorandum by the GC&CS, July 1923, AIR/2/246.

22 Curzon to Hoare, 20.12.23, AIR 2/246; cf. WO 32/4897

23 'History of the Cryptographic and Wireless Intelligence Organisations', unsigned, *c*. 1.23, HW 3/39.

24 Denniston, 'Code and Cypher School'; Draft memorandum by Loxley, 4.11.44, FO 1093/195.

25 Undated, unsigned memorandum by the Treasury's Finance Branch, probably December 1925, T 160/239.

26 Howard Smith to Denniston, 7.5.37, HW 3/64.

27 For records of these meetings, cf. AIR 2/246 and WO 106/5392.

28 Draft 'History of Sigint Communications', p. 28, HW 3/91.

29 H. F. P. Sinclair's Service Record, ADM 196/43. p. 368. I am indebted to Jock Bruce for his unpublished study of Sinclair's personal background, 'The Secret Admiral: Notes on the Life of Admiral Hugh Sinclair'.

30 'Note on the division of responsibility between the War Office and the G.C. & C.S. in the event of war', 21.7.32, HW 62/19.

31 'History of Naval Section, 1919–1941, Introduction', by W. F. Clarke, undated but *c*. 1946, HW 3/16.

32 'Inter-Departmental Conference', 8.5.1919, T 1/12517, 'G.C. & C.S. Standing Orders', 1.12.27, HW 62/19.

33 Memorandum by McCormack, 'Berkeley Street', n.d., c 5.43, RG 457/1119, NARA, College Park.

34 Curzon papers, Vol. 302.

35 Foreign Office to Treasury, 13.1. 37, FO 366/978, X. 7105.

36 Memorandum by Kenworthy, 3.5.32, 'Y Station New Scotland Yard', HW 3/81; Minute by Howard Smith, 7.10.37, HW 3/80.

37 'J. E. S. Cooper, 'Air Sections GC and CS and the Approach to the War, 1935–39', June 1975, HW 3/83.

38 'G. C. & C. S. Standing Orders', 1.12.27, HW 62/19.

39 John Tiltman, *DNB*; Peter Freeman and Ralph Erskine, 'Brigadier John Tiltman: One of Britain's Finest Cryptologists', *Cryptologia*, 27/4 (2003), pp. 289–318.

40 'Diplomatic & Commercial History', n.d. *c.* 1946.

41 Ibid.

42 Memorandum by Knox, 1928, HW 3/1.

43 Memorandum by Turner, 1928, HW 3/1.

44 Memorandum by McCormack, 'Berkeley Street', n.d., c 5.43, RG 457/1119, NARA, College Park.

45 Memorandum by Armed Forces Security Agency, 'The Significance of the Archive as an Aid to Cryptanalysis and a Source of Information (Lecture Delivered to the 5th Chi-Meeting, 7.3.1945', RG 457/1313; Memorandum by Aurell, 'Intelligence and Information Section', 1.6.43, RG 457/1009.

46 Diplomatic & Commercial History.

47 Memorandum by McCormack, 'Berkeley Street', n.d., c 5.43, RG 457/1119, NARA.

48 NSA Oral History, Interview with John Tiltman, 11.12.78, 05–7B, https://www.nsa.gov/Portals/70/documents/news-features/declassified-documents/oral-history-interviews/nsa-OH-05-78-tiltman.pdf

49 Memorandum by Travis, 18.2.43, HW 14/67.

50 Undated memorandum by the GC&CS, July 1923, AIR/2/246.

51 Unsigned memorandum by Junior Assistants, 22.1.37, HW 3/64.

52 GC&CS to Chief Clerk's Department, 4.10.27, HW 62/19.

53 Denniston to Creswell, 7.7.38, HW 72/9.

54 Ibid.

55 Denniston to Wilson, 16.5.38, HW 72/9.

56 For regulations for applicants to the GC&CS, cf. FO 366/815, X 8536, FO 366/846, X 3567, CSC/30.

57 Denniston to Guy, 25.2.38, HW 72/9.

58 For regulations for applicants to the GC&CS, cf. FO 366/815, X 8536, FO 366/846, X 3567, CSC/30.

59 Minute by 'B.' (Major Joseph Ball), 19.3.26, KV 2/2317.

60 Denniston to DNI, n.d., *passim,* HW 3/35.

61 Memorandum by Bodsworth, 'Naval Section, 1927–1939', HW 3/1.

62 NSA Oral Interview with John Tiltman, 06–78, 13.12.78, https://www.nsa.gov/Portals/70/documents/news-features/declassified-documents/oral-history-interviews/nsa-OH-06-78-tiltman.pdf

63 Cf. Jacqui, Uí Chionna's forthcoming, *Secrets and Sonatas: The Lives of Emily Anderson.*

64 Denniston Papers. 1/3.

65 Clarke to Denniston, 24.3.31, HW 3/1; Memorandum by Military Section, 14.6.38, HW62/21.

66 Wilson to Wright, 4.1.40, FO 366/2378.

67 Denniston to Robinson, 27.4.36, HW 3/57.

68 'Clerical Staff as authorised by T. L. E. 4278/4 of 7th December 1936', HW 3/39.

69 Robinson to Foyle, 31.7.37, FO 366/1000.

70 Denniston to Wilson, 24.11.39, FO 366/2378.

71 Memorandum by Clarke, 21.10. 35, HW 3/1.

72 Memorandum by McCormack, 'Berkeley Street', n.d., c 5.43, RG 457/1119, NARA.

73 Denniston to Howard Smith, 2.1.36, FO 366/978, X 185.

74 Ferris, 'Whitehall's Black Chamber', pp. 62–3, 89–90.

75 Robinson to Foyle, 31.7.37, FO 366/1000.

76 'G.C. & C.S. Standing Orders', 1.12.27, HW 62/19; Malcolm Kennedy Diary, entries 12 February 1941, 6 December 1941, Sheffield University Library.

77 John Ferris, 'Consistent with an Intention: The Far East Combined Bureau and the Outbreak of the Pacific War, 1940–1941', INS, 27/1, 2012, pp. 5–26; Richard Aldrich, *Intelligence and the War Against Japan: Britain, America and the Politics of Secret Service* (CUP, 2000) pp. 25–45.

78 Minute by Parker, 1 February 1935, T 162/972, E 17426/3.

79 Peter King, 'The Military Career of Freddie Jacob OBE', (Bletchley Park Trust, 2017).

80 Military Secretary's Division, Simla, 'Annual Reports for 1911 on the officers of the British Service serving on the Headquarters of the British Army in India', 2.5.1912, Major G. R. M. Church RA, L/MIL 7/17047.

81 Minute by Dickens, 26.10.33, ADM 116/3114.

82 Memorandum by Jacob, 20.4.26, L/MIL 7/12541. The Indian Army called codebreakers, 'signals computers'. During 1939–45, British Siginters described military personnel trained to decode known systems as 'computers'.

83 Richards to Waterfield, 15.6.28, *passim,* T 162/974/4.

84 Ferris, *Strategy and Intelligence*, pp. 150, 178, 354–5.

85 Report of Cypher Conference, 27.2.19, ADM 1/8637.

86 Foreign Office Circular, 30.1.21, FO 513/1; cf. HW 3/39.

87 'Report of Cypher Conference', 27.2.19, ADM 1/8637.

88 Memorandum by Wright,14.3.29, for DNI, ADM 116/2445; memorandum, undated but circa 1932, 'Battle Code', ADM 116/2978.

89 Minute by Denniston, 19.3.31, HW 3/52; minute by Travis, 12.6.44, FO 850/134.

90 Memorandum by Clarke, 16.9.35, HW 3/1; Cooper to Denniston, 24.4.38, HW 62/21.

91 Denniston to Director, 6.2.39, Denniston to Titterton, 23.6.39, HW 62/21.

92 Memorandum by Tiltman, 3.1.39, Military Section, G.C. and C.S., Progress Report, 15th July, 1939, Tiltman to Page, 16.8.39, HW 62/21.

93 NSA Oral History Interviews, John Tiltman, 13.12.78, 06–78, https://www.nsa.gov/news-features/declassified-documents/oral-history-interviews/

94 Wilson to Davenport, 24.9.79, transcribed by Peter Freeman, original lost.

95 Ibid.

96 'Security of R.A.F. Signal Communications', n.d., and no author cited, but
    c. December 1944 by internal evidence, AIR 20/1531,

97 John Ferris, 'The British Enigma: Britain, Signals Security, and Cypher
    Machines, 1906–1953', Ferris, *Strategy and Intelligence*, pp. 138–80.

98 Southey to Lywood, 17.1.39, AIR 2/1255.

99 Indian War Department, undated draft chapter, 'General Staff and Analogous
    Matters, 1939–1944', L/R/5/278.

100 Memorandum by Turner, 1928, HW 3/1.

101 Memorandum by Alfred McCormack, 'Berkeley Street', n.d., *c.* 6.43, RG 0457/
    1119.

102 Undated memorandum by the GC&CS, July 1923, AIR/2/246.

103 Undated and unsigned memorandum on diplomatic cryptanalysis in 1940,
    31.1.41, HW 14/11.

104 'Order of Priority of Foreign Countries from S.I.S. Point of View', n.d., *c.* 1935
    by internal evidence, *passim*, WO 32/5392.

105 Denniston, 'Code and Cypher School'.

106 Memorandum by Turner, 1928, HW 3/1.

107 Second meeting of Colonial Office Code and Cypher Committee, 3.1.1922, CO
    537/625; Inter-Service Directorate Report, op.cit. AIR 2/246.

108 Unsigned memorandum, but probably by Denniston, 29.4.32, HW 62/19.

109 Air Section, Report on Experiment into Decentralisation, 26 March, 1938, to 1
    April 1938, HW 62/21.

110 Unsigned, undated 'Memorandum', *c.* 1921 by internal evidence,
    HW 3/39.

111 'Order of Priority of Foreign Countries from S.I.S. Point of View', n.d., *c.* 1935
    by internal evidence, *passim*, WO 32/5392.

112 Ralph E. Weber, *United States Diplomatic Codes and Ciphers, 1775–1938* (Chicago,
    Precedent Publishing, 1979); Daniel Larsen, 'British Codebreaking and American
    Diplomatic Telegrams, 1914–15', INS, 32/2, 2017, pp. 256–63.

113 Memorandum by Clarke, 'Naval Section, Government Code and Cipher
    School', 4.8.37, HW 3/1.

114 Head to Naval Section of Head of GC&CS, 20.1.36, *passim,* HW 3/1.

115 Unsigned, undated, memorandum, but by Jacob and 1938 by internal evidence,
    'Nominal role of officers of the Military Section of the G.C.& C.S. and a
    summary of the work carried out by each officer during the past year', HW 3/88.

116 Undated memorandum by the GC&CS, July 1923, AIR/2/246.

117 Memorandum by Jacob, 14.6.38, Denniston to Jebb, 17,6.38, *passim,* HW 62/21

118 Cooper to Buss, 13.1.38, Air Section, Report for Second and Third Quarters,
    1937, 12.1.38, unsigned memorandum, 'German Air Force', 27.4.38, HW 62/21

119 Coordination of Interception Committee, meeting 7.11.34, HW 42/1.

120 Military Section, G.C. and C.S., Progress Report, 15.7.1939, Tiltman to Page, 16.8.39, HW 62/21.

121 'Directorate-level Overview of GCCS at Bletchley Park with Recommendations for GCHQ in the Future', 1946, HW 3/87.

122 Memorandum by Denniston, AGD 1124, 11.10.44, HW 3/169.

123 Memorandum by Bodsworth, 'Naval Section, 1927–1939', HW 3/1.

124 W. F. Clarke, 'History of Naval Section, 1919–1941, Chapter VI, War, 1939–1941', HW 3/16.

125 G.C. and C.S. Military Section, Monthly Report, No. 1, 1.7.38, HW 62/21.

126 'Emily Anderson and Beethoven's Letters', *The Beethoven Newsletter,* 1/3, Winter 1986, pp. 48–49.

127 Memorandum by Bodsworth, 'Naval Section, 1927–1939', HW 3/1.

128 de Grey to Cavendish-Bentinck, 30.6.45, FO 1093/480.

129 'Diplomatic and Commercial History'.

130 'Mediterranean O.I.C. War Communications', N.I.D. 00714/39, by DNI and D.S.D., 7.39, HW 62/12.

131 Hay to DNI, 11.5.19, HW 3/35; Denniston to Jebb, 18.11.39, FO 1093/106.

CHAPTER 4

1 The standard account of Yardley, his bureau, and its role during 1921–22 is David Kahn, *The Reader of Gentlemen's Mail, The Story of Herbert O. Yardley* (Yale University Press, 2004). Useful studies of naval arms limitation between the wars, and of the Washington Conference, are Emily O. Goldman, *Sunken Treaties: Naval Arms Control between the Wars* (HIA Book Collection, 1994), and Erik Goldstein and John Maurer (eds), *The Washington Conference, 1921–1922: Naval Rivalry, East Asian Stability and the Road to Pearl Harbor* (Routledge, 1994).

2 Director, Naval Communications, to Secretary of the Navy, 21 January 1931, Secret, 'Report on decrypting activities in various branches of the Government', file 'Earliest Naval Comint', and Herbert Yardley Papers, Box 1 / 2, David Kahn Collection, National Cryptologic Museum, Fort Meade.

3 Notes on docket F/1/23, February 1922, FO 371/8042.

4 John Ferris, '"It is our Business in the Navy to Command the Seas": The Last Decade of British Maritime Supremacy, 1919–1929', in Keith Neilson and Greg Kennedy, *Far Flung Lines, Maritime Essays in Honour of Donald Schurman* (Frank Cass, 1996).

5 Tadeshi Kurumatsu, 'The Geneva Naval Conference of 1927: The British Preparation for the Conference, December 1926 to June 1927', *The Journal of Strategic Studies*, 19/1, March 1996, pp. 104–21; Richard Fanning, *Peace and Disarmament: Naval Rivalry and Arms Control, 1922–23* (University Press of Kentucky, 1995).

6 John Ferris, 'British Intelligence and the London Naval Conference, 1919–1930', in Chris Bell and John Maurer, *Crossroads of War and Peace, The London Naval Conference, 1930* (Naval Institute Press, 2014).

7 'London Naval Conference' file, HW 12/126.

8 Gillian Bennett, *The Zinoviev Letter: The Conspiracy That Never Dies* (2018).

9 Ben Pimlott (ed.), *The Political Diary of Hugh Dalton, 1918–1940, 1945–60* (Jonathan Cape, London, 1986), pp. 69–72, 80–81; NC 278, 27.3.30, HW 12/126.

10 Sadeo Asada, 'From Washington to London: The Imperial Japanese Navy and the Politics of Naval Limitation, 1921–1930', *Diplomacy & Statecraft*, 4/3, September 1993, p. 177.

11 Asada, 'Washington to London', pp. 147–91; NC 135, 25.2.30, *passim*, HW 12/126.

12 NC 102, 15.2.30, NC 188, 11.3.30, HW 12/126.

13 NC 112, 18.2.30, NC 247, 22.3.30, HW 12/126; Ferris, 'London Naval Conference'.

14 NC 132, 24.2.30, HW 12/126.

15 NC 299, 31.3.30, HW 12/126.

16 Ferris, 'London Naval Conference'.

17 Minute by Smith, 10.1.36, FO 371/19804, A 279.

18 The best accounts of diplomacy and strategy in the Middle East between 1918–23 are, Zara Steiner, *The Lights that Failed: European International History, 1919–1933* (OUP, 2005), pp. 80–130; David Fromkin, *A peace to end all peace: The fall of the Ottoman Empire and the creation of the modern Middle East* (H. Holt, New York, 2001); Paul C. Helmreich: *From Paris to Sevres: The Partition of the Ottoman Empire at the Paris Peace Conference of 1920* (Ohio State University Press, Columbus, 1974), and Sean McMeekin, *The Ottoman End-Game, War, Revolution and the Making of the Modern Middle East, 1908–1923* (Penguin, 2016). Strong accounts of British policy are, John Darwin, *Britain, Egypt and the Middle East: Imperial policy in the aftermath of war, 1918–1922* (St Martin's Press, New York, 1981); John Fisher, *Curzon and British Policy in the Middle East, 1916–1919* (HIA Book Collection, 1999); and Keith Jeffery, *The British Army and the Crisis of Empire, 1918–1922* (Manchester, Manchester University Press, 1984).

19 John Ferris, 'The Internationalism of Islam: British Perceptions of a Muslim Menace, 1840–1951', *Intelligence and National Security* (24/1, February 2009), pp. 57–77.

20 John Ferris, 'The British empire vs. the "CUP-Jew-German-Bolshevik Combination", 1919–1923', in Greg Kennedy (ed.), *The British Way in Warfare: Power and the International System* (Ashgate, 2010); John Fisher, 'The Interdepartmental Committee on Eastern Unrest and British Responses to Bolshevik and other Intrigues against the British Empire during the 1920s', *Journal of Asian History*, 34/1, 2000; Andrew Orr, "We Call You Now to Holy War": Mustafa Kemal, Communism and Germany in French Intelligence

Nightmares, 1919–1923', *Journal of Military History*, October 2011, Vol. 75 Issue 4, pp. 1095–1123; A. L. Macfie, 'British Intelligence and the Causes of Unrest in Mesopotamia, 1919–21', and 'British Views of the Turkish Nationalist Movement, 1919–22', *Middle Eastern Studies*, 35/1 (1.99) and 38/3 (7.02).

21 War Office to GOC Baghdad, 87609 21.1.21, 15.11, High Commissioner Cairo to Minister Jeddah, 8.2.21, FO 141/433/3.

22 Minute by D. G. Osbourne, 23.9.20, FO 371/4946, E 11702.

23 Bulant Gokay, *A Clash of Empires: Turkey between Russian Bolshevism and British Imperialism, 1918–1923* (I. B. Tauris, London, 1997).

24 Documents on British Foreign Policy (DBFP) xvii, pp. 301, 714; minute by Churchill, 9.12.20, WO 32/5743; minute by Curzon, 10.2.21, FO 371/6265, E 1478.

25 DBFP xvii, pp. 45, 47, 224–27, 242–43, 424

26 Memorandum by Harington, CR/BFT/58410/C.H.H., 'British Forces In Turkey, C-in-C's Dispatch, Period 1920–1923', WO 32/5743.

27 Minute by Osbourne, n.d., March 1921, FO 371/6466, E 2919.

28 Memorandum by Leeper, 19.5.22, 'Anti-British Activities of the Soviet Government', minute by Curzon, 30.5.22, FO 371/8193.

29 Curzon to Austen Chamberlain, 13.5.22, AC 23/6, Austen Chamberlain Papers. Maxim Litvonov was the second-ranking official in the Soviet foreign ministry; the Genoa conference was an abortive effort to settle political and economic problems in Europe.

30 John Ferris, '"Far too dangerous a gamble"?: British Intelligence and Policy during the Chanak Crisis, September–October 1922', *Diplomacy & Statecraft*, 14/2, June 2003, pp. 139–84.

31 DBFP, xviii, p. 25.

32 Ferris, 'Gamble'.

33 Ibid.

34 Curzon to Hardinge, 16.9.22, FO 800/157;

35 S.I.S. No. 887, 22.9.22. Military Intelligence I.C. (i.e. M.I.I.C.) HC/3918, 19.9.22, WO 106/1504; SIS 'Eastern Summary' No. 865, 13.9.22, FO 371/7891.

36 Harington to WO telegram. No. 2509, 29.9.22, FO 371/7897; Harington to WO, No. 2462, 26.9.22, FO 371/7895; Harington to WO, telegram No. 2460, 27.9.22, FO 371/7896.

37 Rumbold to FO, No. 474, 'Private and Secret', 28.9.22, WO 106/1441,

38 Admiralty to Commander in Chief, Mediterranean Fleet, telegram No. 929, 19.9.22, WO 106/1503; Admiralty to Commander in Chief Atlantic Fleet, 24.9.22, 'Appreciation of the Situation in the Near East, a.m., Sunday, 24.9.22, ADM 137/1778.

39 S.I.S. No. 877, 18.9.22, WO 106/1503; Note of telephone message between Tyrell and Curzon, 6.40 p.m. 22.9.22, FO 800/157; record of telephone conversation

between Lloyd George and Hankey, 4.30 p.m., 22.9.22, Cab 21/241; S.I.S. No. 892, 25.9.22, WO 106/1507; SIS CXG.433, 23.9.22, FO 371/7893

40 DBFP, Vol. XVIII, Nos 41–43, 48, 49.

41 Harington to War Office, No. 2516, 29.9.22, FO 371/7897.

42 Harington to WO, telegram No. 2506, 28.9.22, FO 371/7899; Harington to WO telegrams No. 2493, 29.9.22, WO 106/1441; Harington to W.O., telegrams No. 1222, 27.9.22, No. 1223, 28.9.22, No. 2485, 28.9.22, FO 371/7896.

43 Keith Jeffery and Alan Sharp, 'Lord Curzon and the Use of Secret Intelligence at the Lausanne Conference, 1922–1923', in Christopher Andrew and Jeremy Noakes (eds), *Intelligence and International Relations, 1914–45* (Exeter Studies in History, No. 15, Exeter, 1987), pp.103–26.

44 Sevtap Dimirci, *The Lausanne Conference: The Evolution of Turkish and British Diplomatic Strategies, 1922–23* (PhD diss., London School of Economics, 1998) is the best account of the conference. For British policy there, cf; Erik Goldstein, 'The British "Official Mind" and the Lausanne Conference', *Diplomacy & Statecraft*, 14/2, June 2003, pp. 185–206, and for intelligence, Keith Jeffery and Alan Sharp, 'Lord Curzon and the Use of Secret Intelligence at the Lausanne Conference, 1922–1923', in Christopher Andrew and Jeremy Noakes (eds), *Intelligence and International Relations, 1914–45* (Exeter Studies in History, No. 15, Exeter, 1987), pp.103–26.

45 T. G. Otte, "A Very Internicene Policy": Anglo-Russian Cold Wars before the Cold War', in Christopher Baxter, Michael L. Dockrill and Keith Hamilton, *Britain in Global Politics, From Gladstone to Churchill* (Springer, 2013), pp. 17–49; and Keith Neilson, *Britain, Russia and the Collapse of the Versailles Order, 1919–1939* (CUP, 2006).

46 Neilson, *Versailles Order* is the best account; for an alternative view, cf. Gabriel Goredetsky, *The Precarious Truce: Anglo-Soviet Relations, 1924–1927* (CUP, 1977).

47 Timothy Edward O'Connor, *Diplomacy & Revolution: G. V. Chicherin & Soviet Foreign Affairs, 1918–1930.* 1987); Samuel J. Hirst, 'Transnational Anti-Imperialism and the National Forces: Soviet Diplomacy and Turkey, 1920–1923', *Comparative Studies of South Asia, Africa and the Middle East* 33/2 (2013), pp. 214–26; and Ben Fowkes and Bulant Gokay (eds), special issue of *Journal of Communist Studies and Transition Politics*, 25/1, 2009, 'Unholy Alliance: Muslims and Communists'.

48 Minute by Strang, 13.1.26, FO 371/11775, N 32; Jeffery, *MI 6*, pp. 183–96.

49 Minute by Tyrrell, 4.12.26, FO 371/11787, N 4881.

50 GC&CS No. 003934, 20.8.20, HW 12/13.

51 Andrew, *Defence*, pp. 139–59; Jeffery, *MI6*, pp. 176–209; and Victor Madeira, *Britannia and the Bear: The Anglo-Russian Intelligence Wars, 1917–1929* (Boydell & Brewer, 2014).

52 Ferris, 'CUP-Jew-German-Bolshevik Combination'.

53 Fisher, 'Inter-Departmental Committee on Eastern Unrest'.

54 No. 34377, 8.4.29, HW 12/117.

55 No. 23652, 26.8.26, No. 023660, 27.8.26, No. 023661, 27.8.26, and No. 023663, 27.8.26, HW 12/85.

56 E. S. K. Fung, *The Diplomacy of Imperial Retreat: Britain's South China Policy, 1924–1931* (Oxford, 1991); Bruce A. Elleman, *Diplomacy and Deception: The Secret History of Sino-Soviet Relations, 1917–1927*; M. E. Sharpe, 1997; Alexander Pantsov, *The Bolsheviks and the Chinese Revolution, 1919–1929* (Richmond, 2000); Michael Share, 'Clash of Worlds: The Comintern, British Hong Kong, and Chinese Nationalism, 1921–1929, *Europe-Asia Studies*, 57/4, June 2005, pp. 601–24; and Michael Weiner, 'Comintern in East Asia, 1919–39', in Kevin McDermott and Jeremy Agnew, *The Comintern: A History of International Communism from Lenin to Stalin* (Palgrave Macmillan, 1996), pp. 158–90.

57 Minutes by O'Malley, 2.1.25, Wellesley, 3.1.25, and Austen Chamberlain, 3.1.25, FO 371/10984, N 16.

58 No. 34384, 9.2.24, HW 12/117; No. 24005, 27.9.26, HW 12/86; No. 34315, 4.4.29, HW 12/117; cf. Hasan Ali Karasar, 'Chicherin on the delimitation of Turkestan: native Bolsheviks versus Soviet foreign policy. Seven letters from the Russian archives on razmezhevanie', *Central Asian Survey* (2002), 21 (2), pp. 199–209; Anna di Briago, 'Moscow, The Comintern and the War Scare, 1926–28', in Silvio Pons and Andrea Romano, *Russia in the Age of Wars* (Milano: Feltrinelli, 2000), pp. 83–102.

59 John Ferris, 'Counter-Insurgency and Empire: The British Experience with Afghanistan and the North-West Frontier', Scott Gates and Ray Kaushlik (eds), *Counter-Insurgency in Afghanistan* (Routledge, 2014); and Brandon Marsh, *Ramparts of Empire, British Imperialism and India's Afghan Frontier, 1918–1948* (Palgrave Macmillan, 2014)

60 Stephanie Cronin, *The Army and the Creation of the Pahlavi State in Iran: 1910–1926* (New York and London: Tauris Academic Series, 1997) and Houshang Sabahi, *British Policy in Persia, 1918–1925* (Taylor & Francis, 1990).

61 No. 22197, No. 22242, 26.1.26, HW 12/78; No. 23271, 8.7.26, HW 12/86; Nos 24034, XXX, 023891, 16.9.26, No. 23994, 25.9.26, HW 12/84.

62 Minute by Gregory, 19.8.25, FO 371/10841, E 4803.

63 No. 24005, 27.9.26, HW 12/86

64 Leon B. Poullada, *Reform and Rebellion in Afghanistan, 1919–1929* (Ithaca, NY, Cornell University Press, 1973); Ludwig W. Adamec, *Afghanistan's Foreign Affairs to the Mid Twentieth Century: Relations with the USSR, Germany and Britain* (University of Arizona Press, Tucson, 1074).

65 No. 34443, HW 12/117; Nos 35132, 34998, HW 12/119; No. 023721, 31.8.26, HW 12/85; 34315, 4.4.29, HW 12/117

66 Telegram from Viceroy to India Office, 14.2.29, *passim*, FO 371/13992, N 1037; cf. FO 371/13995, FO 371/14003.

67 Minute by Craigie, 5.10.36, *passim*, FO 371/20094, E 5280

68 This material may be found in the HW 17 series. The best, if brief, account is Andrew, *Defence*, pp. 171–3.

69 'Image and Accident: Intelligence and the Origins of the Second World War, 1933–1941', in John Ferris, *Intelligence and Strategy, Selected Essays* (2005); Neilson, *Versailles Order*, pp. 41–2, and Zara Steiner, *The Triumph of the Dark, European International History, 1933–1939* (OUP, 2011), pp. 1–9, 1036–58.

70 The literature on appeasement is overwhelmingly large. The articles in a special issue of *Diplomacy & Statecraft*, 19/3, 2008, especially Sidney Aster, 'Appeasement: Before and After Revisionism', pp. 443–80, present a balanced account of the topic, with good bibliographies.

71 Though most commentators on Chamberlain's statesmanship remain negative (cf. John Ruggiero, *Hitler's Enabler: Neville Chamberlain and the origins of the Second World War* (Santa Barbara Ca., ABC-Clio, 2015), and Steiner, *Triumph*, pp. 610–59), he has some supporters (cf. John Charmley, *Chamberlain and the Lost Peace* (Chicago: Ivor Dee, 1990). For balanced overviews, cf. R. A. C. Parker, *Chamberlain and Appeasement: British Policy and the Coming of the Second World War* (London, 1993) and David Hucker, 'The Unending Debate: Appeasement, Chamberlain and the Origins of the Second World War', INS, 23/4, 2008, pp. 536–51.

72 Antony Best, *Britain, Japan and Pearl Harbor: Avoiding War in East Asia, 1936–1941* (1995) remains excellent, although published before the release of flimsies in the HW 12 series.

73 No account incorporates the Comint record; Jill Edwards, *The British Government and the Spanish Civil War, 1936–1939* (London, 1979), remains the best study.

74 No. 067433, 14.1.1937; No. 067440, 15.1.1937; No. 067442, 15.1.1937, HW 12/211; Foreign Office to India Office, 'Most Secret', 29.1.1937, Walton (India Office) to Metcalfe (Government of India), 1.2.1937, Foreign Office to India Office, 'Most Secret', 4.5.1937, L PS/12/225, India Office Record Library, British Library.

75 Stephen Wagner, *Statecraft by Stealth, Secret Intelligence and British Rule in Palestine* (Cornell University Press, 2019), Chapter 9.

76 Untitled and unsigned Memorandum, 24.11.38, HW 62/21.

77 Wagner, *Statecraft*.

78 John Ferris, 'Vansittart, Intelligence and Appeasement' and 'Image and Accident: Intelligence and the Origins of the Second World War, 1933–1941', in John Ferris, *Intelligence and Strategy, Selected Essays* (2005).

79 W. C. Mills, 'The Chamberlain–Grandi Conversations of July–August 1937 and the Appeasement of Italy', and 'Sir Joseph Ball, Adrian Dingli, and Neville

Chamberlain's "Secret Channel" to Italy, 1937–40', in *International History Review*, 19/3 (1997), pp. 594–619, and 24/2 (2002), pp. 278–317.

80 GC&CS No. 070481, 1.1.38, No. 070552, 9.2.38, HW 12/224; No. 070729, 8.3.38, No. 070754, 11.3.38, HW 12/225; Andrew, *Defence*, pp. 195–209; Bruce Strang, 'Sir Alexander Cadogan and the Steward–Hesse Affair: Assessments of British Cabinet Politics and Future British Policy, 1938' (forthcoming, *International History Review*).

81 Carl Boyd, 'The Role of Hiroshi Oshima in the Preparation of the Anti-Comintern Pact', *Journal of Asian History*, 11, 1 (1977): pp. 49–71; J. W. M. Chapman, 'A Dance on Eggs: Intelligence and the "Anti-Comintern"', *Journal of Contemporary History*, 22/2, 1987, pp. 333–72; John Fox, *Germany and the Far Eastern Crisis, 1931–1938: A Study in Diplomacy and Ideology* (Oxford, 1982); Wolfgang Michalka, 'From the Anti-Comintern Pact to the Euro-Asiatic Bloc: Ribbentrop's Alternative Concept of Hitler's Foreign Policy Programme', in Koch H. W. (ed.) *Aspects of the Third Reich* (Palgrave, London, 1985; Tajima Nobuo, 'The Berlin–Tokyo Axis Reconsidered: from the Anti-Comintern Pact to the Plot to Assassinate Stalin', in Christian W. Spang and Rolf-Harald Wippich (eds), *Japanese German Relations, 1985–1945, War Diplomacy and Public Opinion* (Routledge, London, 1999), pp. 161–80; Ōhata Tokushirō, 'The Japanese–Soviet Confrontation, 1935–1939', in James Morley (ed.), *Deterrent Diplomacy: Japan, Germany and the USSR, 1935–40, Selections from The Road to the Pacific War* (Columbia University Press, 1976); Neilson, *Versailles, Order*, pp. 191–95.

82 Ferris, *Intelligence and Strategy*, pp. 55–87, 134–5.

83 Gerhard Weinberg, *The Foreign Policy of Hitler's Germany, Vol. II, Starting World War Two* (Chicago, The University of Chicago Press, 1980), pp. 282–83; Steiner.

84 No. 069514, HW 12/220.

85 GC&CS No. 070335, 12.1.38, HW 12/223.

86 Mills, 'Chamberlain-Grandi Conversations', H. Matthew Heffler, "In the Way": Intelligence, Eden and British Foreign Policy Towards Italy, 1937–1938', *Intelligence and National Security*, 33/6, 2018, pp. 875–93.

87 Reynolds M. Salerno, *Vital Crossroads. Mediterranean Origins of the Second World War, 1935–1940* (Ithaca, NY, Cornell University Press, 2002), pp. 73–107.

88 GC&CS No. 070335, 12.1.38, No. 070383, 20.1.38, HW 12/223; GC&CS No. 070505, 4.2.38, HW 12/224.

89 GC&CS No. 070755, 11.3.38, HW 12/225.

90 GC&CS No. 070539, 8.2.38, HW 12/224.

91 GC&CS No. 070690, 3.3.38, No. 070830, 19.3.38, HW 12.225; GC&CS No. 071392, 12.5.38, No. 071337, 19.5.38, HW 12/227.

92 GC&CS No. 070829, 19.3.38, No. 070861, 23.3.38, HW 12/225; No. 071026, 6.4.38, HW 12/226; No. 071295, 12.5.38, HW 12/227.

93 Dilks, 'Flashes of Intelligence', pp. 154–8; memorandum by Sargant, 19.11.38, FO 371/21639, C14209.

94 CG&CS No. 073458, 26.1.39, HW 12/235

95 GC&CS No. 073447, 073467, 25.1.39, HW 12/235.

96 GC&CS No. 073585, 28.1.39, HW 12/235.

97 Memorandum by Tiltman, 3.1.39, HW 62/21.

98 GC&CS No. 073729, 20.2.39, HW 12/236

99 GC&CS No. 073921, 9.3.39, HW 12/237; GC&CS, No. 074271, 11.4.71, HW 12/238.

100 Dilks, 'Flashes'; Andrew, *Defence*, pp. 201–8; Andrew, *Secret Service*, pp. 262–9, 537–41; Jeffery, *MI6*, pp. 303–12; Ferris, *Intelligence and Strategy*, pp. 45–137; Steiner, *Triumph*, pp. 671–1058, integrates the intelligence record as it then was known.

101 Lawrence Pratt, *East of Malta, West of Suez, Britain's Mediterranean Crisis, 1936–1939* (CUP, 1975); Christopher Bell, *The Royal Navy, Seapower and Strategy Between the Wars* (Stanford University Press, 2000) pp. 117–25.

102 Neilson, *Versailles Order*, pp. 260–70

103 Hiroaki Kuromiya and Andrzej Peplonski, 'Kozo Izumi and the Soviet Breach of Imperial Japanese Diplomatic Codes', INS, 28/6, 2013, pp. 769–84.

CHAPTER 5

1 Undated and unsigned memorandum on diplomatic cryptanalysis in 1940, 31.1.41, HW 14/11.

2 John Ferris, 'Achieving Air Ascendancy: Challenge and Response in British Strategic Air Defence, 1915–1940', in Sebastian Cox and Peter Gray (eds), *Airpower History: Turning Points from Kitty Hawk to Kosovo,* (London, 2002, Routledge).

3 Report of Admiralty Committee on W/T Organization, ADM 1/8740/69.

4 Meeting of Wireless Interception Committee, 28.4.38, HW 42/1; Minute by Hugh Sinclair, 17.10.38, HW 3/1; Memorandum by Godfrey, 12.47, ADM 223/284.

5 Gordon Welchman, *The Hut Six Story, Breaking the Enigma Codes,* 2nd revised edition (New York, William Morrow and Co., 1997).

6 Stephen Budiansky, *Battle of Wits: The Complete Story of Codebreaking in World War Two* (London, Viking, 2000), pp. 98–102.

7 29.4.32, untitled and unsigned memorandum, but by Sinclair, according to internal evidence, HW 62/19.

8 'History of C.M.Y. Section and The Development of Civil (International) W/T Interception during the War, 1939–1945', HW 3/162.

9 Sinclair to Dill, C/8794, 13.3.34, 'Memorandum on United States Communications Merger, Proposals and Effect', HW 62/19.

10 Minute by Travis to Dennison, 28.12.39, HW 3/81.

11 Sinclair to Walton, WO 208/5063.

12 Ibid.

13 Maine to Wilshaw, 28.9.38, DOC/CW/1/516, Telegraph Museum, Porthcurno.

14 Minute by Howard Smith, 1.5.37, HW 3/79; Sinclair to Howard Smith, 30.9.37, HW 3/80; Sinclair to Jebb, 21.1.39, FO 1093/105.

15 Memorandum by GC&CS, undated, c. July 1923, AIR 2/246.

16 Denniston to Sinclair, 21.10.38, HW 3/1.

17 J. E. S. Cooper, 'Air Sections GC and CS and the Approach to the War, 1935–39', June 1975, HW 3/83.

18 Denniston to Peters, 26.4.32, HW 72/9.

19 Memorandum by Temperley, DDMO&I, 3.1.33, HW 62/19

20 Undated memorandum by Kenworthy, HW 3/81; Nigel de Grey, draft 'Allied Sigint Policy and Organisation', c. 1946, Chapter 3, p. 29, HW 43/75.

21 NSA Oral History Interviews, John Tiltman, 13.12.78, 06–78, https://www.nsa.gov/news-features/declassified-documents/oral-history-interviews/

22 Tiltman to Menzies, 11.8.40, HW 14/6.

23 Denniston to Sinclair, 21.10.38, HW 3/1.

24 Memorandum by Saunders, 15.2.39, 'Position regarding "Y" Interception of German Naval and Naval Air Traffic'; memorandum by Bodsworth, undated, 'Naval section 1927–1939', HW 3/1; undated memoir by Kenworthy, 'Chapter VI', HW 3/81.

25 Minute by Tiltman, 'Military Section G.C. and C.S., Progress Report: 15th July 1939', HW 62/21.

26 Albert W. Small, 'Special Fish Report', RG 457/ 1417.

27 David Edgerton, *Warfare State, Britain 1920–1970* (CUP, 2006); Paul Kennedy, *Engineers of Victory, The Problem Solvers Who Turned the Tide in the Second World War* (Random House, 2013).

28 'An Interview with Arthur L. C. Humphreys, OH 23, Conducted by Erwin Tomash on 28 February 1981, Los Angeles, CA', Charles Babbage Institute, Center for the History of Information Processing, University of Minnesota.

29 De G, 'Allied Sigint Policy and Organisation', Part 2, pp.148–49, HW 43/77; Memorandum by Travis, 18.2.43, HW 14/67.

30 Eames, Charles and Ray, *A Computer Perspective: Background to the Computer Age* (Harvard University Press, Mass, 1973).

31 Chris Christenson, 'US Navy Cryptologic Mathematicians during World War Two', *Cryptologia,* 35/3, 2011, pp. 267–76.

32 Frode Weierud and Sandy Zabell, 'German mathematicians and cryptology in World War II', *Cryptologia,* 44/2, June 2019, pp. 97–117.

33 Untitled notes by Newman, for Newman to Rendle, undated, but c. 1976, f. 32, Max Newman Papers, St John's College, Cambridge, Box 3.

34 Joel Greenberg (ed.), Gordon Welchman, 'Ultra Revisited, A Tale of Two Contributors', INS, March 2017, 32/3. The best accounts of the attack on Enigma are, Nigel de Grey, draft 'Allied Sigint Policy and Organisation', *c.* 1946, HW 43/75–77; Andrew Hodges, *Alan Turing: The Enigma* (Princeton University Press, 1983); Gordon Welchman, *The Hut Six Story, Breaking the Enigma Codes*, 2nd revised edition (New York, William Morrow and Co., 1997); Gordon Welchman, 'From Polish Bomba to British Bombe: The Birth of Uktra', INS, 1/1 (1986), pp. 70–111; Ralph Erskine and Michael Smith (eds), *The Bletchley Park Codebreakers: How Ultra Shortened the War and Led to the Birth of the Computer* (Biteback Publishing 2011); H. H. Hinsley and Allen Stripp (eds), *Codebreakers: The Inside Story of Bletchley Park* (OUP, 2001); Joel Greenberg, *Gordon Welchman: Bletchley Park's Architect of Ultra Intelligence* (Frontline Books, 2014); Hinsley. Et.al, Vol. Three, Part II, pp. 945–61, and R. A. Ratcliff, *Delusions of Intelligence, Enigma, Ultra and the End of Secure Ciphers* (Cambridge, CUP, 2006).

35 Joel Greenberg (ed.), Gordon Welchman, 'Ultra Revisited, A Tale of Two Contributors', INS, March 2017, 32/3.

36 Ibid.

37 Ibid.

38 Tutte, 'FISH and I', pp. 11, https://uwaterloo.ca/combinatorics-and-optimization/sites/ca.combinatorics-and-optimization/files/uploads/files/corr98-39.pdf

39 A. P. Mahon, 'The History of Hut Eight, 1939–1945', p. 14, HW 25/2

40 Ibid., p. 23.

41 Interview with DS, 2.10.18.

42 David Kahn, *Seizing the Enigma, the Race to Break the German U-Boat Codes, 1939–45* (Houghton Mifflin Harcourt, 1991).

43 Memorandum, unsigned, but Travis by internal evidence. 18.11.39, HW 14/2.

44 Unsigned and untitled memorandum, 20.5.40, on GC&CS structure, HW 14/5.

45 Mahon, 'The History of Hut Eight', p. 20.

46 Memorandum by Travis, 18.2.43, HW 14/67.

47 John A. N. Lee and Golde Holtzman, '50 Years After Breaking the Codes: Interviews with Two of the Bletchley Park Scientists', *IEEE Annals of the History of Computing*, 1995, 17/1, p. 37.

48 I. J. Good, 'Early Work on Computers at Bletchley', *Annals of the History of Computing* 1/1, July 1979, p. 43.

49 Lee and Holtzman, '50 Years', *IEEE Annals of the History of Computing*, 1995, 17/1, p. 39

50 The best accounts of the attack on FISH are, Jack Good, Donald Michie and Geoffrey Timms (1945), 'General Report on Tunny, with Emphasis on Statistical Methods', HW 25/4 and 25/5; B. J. Copeland, *Colossus, The secrets of Bletchley's code-breaking computers* (OUP, 2010).

51 Allen W. M. Coombes, 'The Making of Colossus', *Annals of the History of Computing*, 5/3, 7/83, p. 253.

52 Tommy Flowers, 'The Design of Colossus', *Annals of the History of Computing*, 5/3, 7/83, pp. 239–52.

53 Hinsley et al., *British Intelligence*, Vol. Two, Appendix Three, pp. 655–7.

54 Memorandum by Head of Naval Section, 28.3.41, excerpt from 'Rates of Pay for Women', HW 50/18.

55 Menzies to Brittain, 15.10.42, CAB 301/74; Menzies to Waley, 25.8.42, CAB 301/ 74.

56 De Grey. 'Sigint Policy and Organisation', p. 24, Chapter One, HW 43/75.

57 'Housing of the Commercial Section', 29.9.39, unsigned but Denniston by internal evidence, HW 14/1.

58 W. F. Clarke, 'B.P. Reminiscences', HW 3/16.

59 Ibid.

60 Whiteley to Churchill, 22.12.39, FO 1093/307.

61 Memorandum by Travis, 18.2.43, HW 14/67.

62 Menzies to Brittain, 10.6.42, CAB 301/74.

63 Welchman, *Hut Six Story*, pp. 146–7.

64 Denniston to Director, 16.9.39, HW 14/1.

65 Memorandum by Travis, 18.2.43, HW 14/67.

66 10.6.32, 'Memorandum by the G.C. and C.S.', 13.6.32, 'Memorandum on Wireless Interception in the Event of a National Emergency', HW 62/19.

67 Unsigned note, but Denniston to Menzies by internal evidence, 23.10.40, HW 14/7; Jacob to Arcedeckne-Butler, 28.11.40, HW 14/8.

68 John Ferris, 'FECB'.

69 Godfrey to Hankey, 2.2.40, FO 1093/193.

70 Memorandum by Hankey 11.3.40, 'The Secret Services, Inquiry by the Minister Without Portfolio, First Report', FO 1093/193.

71 Denniston to Blandy, 4.11.39, HW 14/2.

72 Unsigned memorandum, 1.3.40, 'Interception of Enigma Traffic'; Denniston to Menzies, 29.4.40, HW 14/4; 'The History of Military Sigint', pp.193, 206, 214A, 215 A, HW 3/92.

73 John Ferris, 'The "Usual Source": Signals Intelligence and Planning for the Eighth Army "Crusader" Offensive, 1941', in Alvarez, *Allied and Axis Signals Intelligence*, pp. 84–118.

74 Hinsley et al., *British Intelligence*, Vol. Two, p. 22.

75 Denniston to Menzies, 6.2.39, HW 62/21.

76 Clarke, 'History of Naval Section, Chapter IV, Wars and Rumours of Wars, 1944–37', HW 3/16.

77 HW 62/21.

78 Denniston to Saunders, 27.10.39, HW 14/1

79 Denniston to Menzies, 29.4.40, HW 14/4.

80 'The History of Military Sigint', pp.75–76, HW 3/92.

81 Memorandum by Saunders, 'Proposals for G.C.C.S', 15.5.40. *passim,* HW 14/5.

82 Appendix A, Memorandum by de Grey, 17.2.41, HW 3/158.

83 Memorandum by Menzies, 'Special Section, G.C. & C.S', 12.6.40, HW 14/5.

84 Arthur Bonsall, 'Bletchley Park and the RAF Y Service: Some Recollections', INS, 23/6, December 2008, pp. 827–41.

85 Memorandum by David Petrie, 13.2.41, KV 4/88.

86 C Ho D Alexander, 'Cryptographic History of Work on the German Naval Enigma', HW 25/1.

87 Mahon, The History of Hut Eight', p. xx, HW 25/2.

88 Memorandum by Travis, 18.2.43, HW 14/67.

89 Unsigned memorandum to 'Commander Denniston', 18.11.39, with pencil addition from uncertain date, 'Paper ? by EWT', HW 14/2. There is no possible alternative, and the paper reflects Welchman's independent account, written decades later, of his discussion with Travis at this time.

90 Memorandum by Travis, 18.2.43, HW 14/67.

91 'Report on Military Intelligence at the G.C. & C.S.', by W. E. van Cutsem, 30.1.42, WO 208/5070.

92 Sinclair to Davidson, 11.3.42, WO 208/5070.

93 Clarke, 'B.P. Reminiscences 2', HW 3/16.

94 'Meeting held at B.P. on the 27th December 1941', HW 14/25.

95 Memorandum by Travis, 18.2.43, HW 14/67.

96 Ibid.

97 American Embassy London to MILID, No. 4869, 22.5.43, American Embassy London to MILID No. 4869 25.5.43, RG 457/1009.

98 'Appreciation of the "E" Situation June to December 1942', HW 3/164.

99 'Squadron-Leader Jones' Section', n.d., or author, 1945, HW 3/164.

100 'History of Hut 3 at BP, 194–1945, Volume I', pp. 17–18, HW 3/119.

101 'Appreciation of the "E" Situation June to December 1942', HW 3/164

102 'History of Hut 3, Volume I', p. 46, HW 3/119.

103 'History of Hut 3, Volume I', p. 16, HW 3/119.

104 COS to SACSEA, Ultra 196, 'Security of Ultra Intelligence', 9.6.44, WO 203/5157.

105 Ralph Bennett, Ultra and Mediterranean Strategy, pp. 42–5.

106 'History of Hut 3, Volume II', pp. 45–46, HW 3/120.

107 Memorandum by Jones, 'The Value of Ultra – accurately handled', 897 TOPSEC U, 7.3.45, HW 3/127.

CHAPTER 6

1 F. H. Hinsley, E. E. Thomas, C. F. G. Ransom, and R. C. Knight, *British Intelligence in the Second World War, Its Influence on Strategy and Operations, Volumes 1 – 3* (HMSO, London, 1981–88), offers the best account of how Ultra affected battles and campaigns, though many accounts supersede it on special matters. Stephen Budiansky, *Battle of Wits, The Complete Story of Codebreaking in World War II* (Free Press, New York, 2000), is a useful overview.

2 Army Security Agency, *European Axis Signal Intelligence in World War* (Washington, 1946), http://www.nsa.gov/public_info/declass/european_axis_Sigint.shtml.

3 John Ferris, 'Intelligence', in John Ferris and Ewan Mawdsley (eds), *The Cambridge History of the Second World War', Volume One, Fighting the War* (CUP, 2015), pp. 637–63.

4 Alfred Price, *Targeting the Reich, Allied Photographic Reconnaissance over Europe, 1939–1945* (Greenhill Books, 2003); Peter Mead, *The Eye in the Sky, History of Air Observation and Reconnaissance, 1785–1945* (HMSO, London, 1983); Constance Babington-Smith, *Evidence in Camera. The Story of Photographic Reconnaissance in the Second World War* (London: Chatto &Windus, 1958) and Louis Brown, *A Radar History of World War Two, Technical and Military Imperatives* (Bristol, Institute of Physics Publishing, 1999).

5 R. A. Ratcliff, *Delusions of Intelligence, Enigma, Ultra and the End of Secure Ciphers* (Cambridge, CUP, 2006).

6 Cadogan to Radcliffe, 3.2.42, INF 1/380.

7 Ferris, *Intelligence and Strategy*, pp. 138–238.

8 Ibid., pp. 157–9.

9 Hinsley et al., *British Intelligence*, Vol. One, pp. 632–41.

10 Ferris, *Intelligence and Strategy*, pp. 157–9.

11 Eiji Seki, *Mrs. Ferguson's Tea-set, Japan and the Second World War: The Global Consequences Following Germany's Sinking of the SS Automeden in 1940* (Global Oriental, 2007).

12 Memorandum by Bartlett, 1946, ADM 223/184.

13 Cypher Security Committee, 23.3.44, 'Security of British Communications, Notes compiled from Conversation with COMMANDER CIANCHI, Royal Italian Navy on 13th, 15th and 16th February', ADM 223/803. CSDIC/CMF/Y 31, 'Second Detailed Interrogation Report on Two German Prisoners', undated but *c.* May–June 1945 by internal evidence, WO 208/3248.

14 Ferris, *Intelligence and Strategy*, pp. 160–70.

15 Sargent to Markham, 1.9.44, FO 1093/328.

16 CSDIC, 'Report on Interrogation of Thirteen German Intelligence Officers', July 1945, WO 204/11457.

17 David Kahn, *Hitler's Spies, German Military Intelligence in World War Two*, London: Hodder & Stoughton, 1978), is the best work in the English language on German intelligence, augmented by Hans-Otto Behrendt, *Rommel's Intelligence in the Desert Campaign, 1941–1943* (London, Kimber, 1985), United States War Dept. General Staff, *German Military Intelligence, 1939–1945* (University Press of America, 1984), Albert Praun, 'German Radio Intelligence', pp.1–128, in John Mendelsohn (ed.), *Covert Warfare: Intelligence, Counterintelligence and Military Deception in the World War II Era, Volume 6, German Radio Intelligence and the Soldatsender* (Garland Press, New York, 1989.

18 For German intelligence on the Eastern front, cf. Magnus Pahl, *Fremde Heere Ost. Hitlers militärische Feindaufklärung* (Berlin: Christoph Links Verlag 2013); David Thomas, 'Foreign Armies East and German Military Intelligence in Russia 1941–45', *The Journal of Contemporary History*, 1987, Volume 22, pp.261–301; Volker Detlef Heydorn, *Nachrichtennahaufklärung (Ost) und sowjetrussisches Heeresfunkwesen bis 1945*, Freiburg: Rombach Verlag, 1985) and DF–1123, AS–14–TICOM, Survey of Russian Military Systems, 1.4.1948. http://www.scribd.com/paspartoo/d/85583814-DF-112-Dettmann.

19 Barton Whaley, *Codeword Barbarossa* (MIT Press, 1974); John Ferris, 'The Roots of Fortitude: The Evolution of British Deception in The Second World War', in Thomas Mahnken (ed.), *The Paradox of Intelligence: Essays in Memory of Michael Handel* (Frank Cass, 2003).

20 Ferris, *Strategy and Intelligence*, pp. 163–68.

21 David Alvarez, 'Axis Sigint Collaboration: A Limited Partnership', in David Alvarez (ed.), *Allied and Axis Signals Intelligence in World War Two*, Frank Cass and Co., 1999), pp. 1–17); John Chapman, 'Axis Sigint Cooperation among the Tripartite States on the Eve of Pearl Harbor', *Japan Forum*, 3/2, 1991), pp. 231–56; Army Security Agency, *European Axis Signal Intelligence in World War* (Washington, 1946), http://www.nsa.gov/public_info/declass/european_axis_Sigint.shtml

22 Bradley Smith, *The Ultra-Magic Deals and the Most Secret Special Relationship, 1940–1946* (New York, 1993), and pp. below.

23 Bradley Smith, *Sharing Secrets with Stalin, How the Allies Exchanged Intelligence, 1941–1945* (Kansas Modern War Studies, Lawrence, KS, 1995).

24 Ferris, *Intelligence and Strategy*, pp. 164–65.

25 Ferris, 'The "Usual Source"', in Alvarez, *Allied and Axis Signals Intelligence*, pp. 84–118.

26 R. J. Overy, *Why the Allies Won* (W. W. Norton and Co, 1995), pp. 245–81; Alex Danchev, *A Very Special Relationship: Field Marshall Sir John Dill and the Anglo-American Alliance 1941–44*, (London: Brassey's Defence Publishers, 1986).

27 Helmut Heiber and David M. Glantz (eds), *Hitler and His Generals: Military Conferences 1942–1945: The First Complete Stenographic Record of the Military Situation Conferences, from Stalingrad to Berlin*, (English edition, Enigma Books, 2005); *Fuhrer Conferences on Naval Affairs, 1939–1945* (United States Naval Institute Press, 2015); David Irving, *Das Reich Hort Mit* (1989), http://www.fpp.co.uk/books/Forschungsamt/index.html

28 Memorandum by COMNAVFORGER, 21.8.51, 'Historical, Naval Radio Intelligence ("B-Dienst")', by Captain Bonatz, RG 457/604, NARA.

29 Hinsley et.al., *British Intelligence*, Vol. Three, Part 1, pp. 331–45.

30 Brad Gladman, *Intelligence and Anglo-American Air Support in World War Two: The Western Desert and Tunisia, 1940–43*, (London: Palgrave, 2009).

31 Ibid. and Ian Gooderson, *Air power at the Battlefront: Allied close air support in Europe, 1943–45* (Frank Cass, 1998).

32 Carl Boyd, *American Command of the Seas Through Carriers, Codes and the Silent Service: World War II and Beyond (*Maritime Museum, 1995); Christopher A. Ford with David Rosenberg, *The Admiral's Advantage: U.S. Navy Operational Intelligence in World War II and the Cold War* (Naval Institute Press, Annapolis, 2005).

33 John Ferris and Evan Mawdsley, 'The War in the West, 1939–40: The Battle of Britain?' in Ferris and Mawdsley, *Fighting the War*, pp. 315–30; Donald Caldwell and Richard Muller, *The Luftwaffe over Germany: The Defence of the Reich* (Greenhill Books, 2007).

34 Robert Ehlers, *Targeting the Third Reich, Air Intelligence and the Allied Bombing Campaigns* (Kansas Modern War Studies, Lawrence, KS, 2009).

35 The best account of European naval operations is Ewan Mawdsley, *The War for the Seas: A Maritime History of World War Two* (Yale University Press, 2019). Stephen Roskill, *The War at Sea, Volumes One to Three* (HMSO, 1954–61), remains valuable.

36 Hinsley et al., *British Intelligence*, Vol. One, pp. 339–46.

37 Cunningham of Hyndhope, *A Sailor's Odyssey* (London, 1951), pp. 320–37.

38 Hinsley, et al., *British Intelligence*, Vol. One, pp. 403–6; Mavis Batey, *Dilly: The Man Who Broke Enigmas* (Biteback Publishing) is illuminating, but not always reliable.

39 Christina Goulter, *A Forgotten Offensive: Royal Air Force Coastal Command's Anti-Shipping Campaign 1940–1945* (London: Frank Cass, 1995).

40 Hinsley, et.al., *British Intelligence*, Vol. Two, pp. 199–227.

41 Jurgen Rowher, *The Crucial Convoy Battles of March 1943* (Naval Institute Press, Annapolis, 1977); David Syrett, *The Defeat of the German U-Boats, The Battle of the Atlantic* (University of South Carolina Press, Columbia, SC, 1994).

42 The outstanding analysis is W. J. R. Gardner, *Decoding History, The Battle of the Atlantic and Ultra* (Naval Institute Press, Annapolis, 2002). Alan Harris Bath, *Tracking the Axis Enemy: The Triumph of Anglo-American Naval Intelligence* (Lawrence, KS: University Press of Kansas, 1998), is excellent. For B-Dienst, cf. Heinz Bonatz, *Seekrieg im Äther: Die Leistungen der Marin-Funkaufklarung, 1939–1945*, (E. S. Mittler, Herford, 1981) and Jak P. Malmann-Shovell, *German Naval Codebreakers* (Annapolis, Naval Institute Press, 2003); 'German Naval Communications Intelligence', no author cited and undated, but by Op-20-G, *c.* late, 1945, RG 457/625; Memorandum by COMNAVFORGER, 21.8.51, 'Historical, Naval Radio Intelligence ("B-Dienst")', by Captain Bonatz, RG 457/604, NARA.

43 Mark Milner, 'The Atlantic War, 1939–45', in Ferris and Mawdsley, *Fighting the War*, pp. 455–84.

44 Ibid.

45 Simon Ball, *Bitter Sea: The Struggle for mastery in the Mediterranean, 1935–1949* (HarperPress, 2009) and Douglas Porch, *The Path to Victory, The Mediterranean Mediterranean Theater in World War Two* (Farrar, Strauss and Giroux, New York, 2004) are the best modern accounts.

46 Hinsley et al., *British Intelligence*, Vol. One, pp. 210–13, 404–06.

47 Ibid., Vol. Two, pp. 323–30, 346–50.

48 Ibid., Vol. One, pp. 375–403; John Ferris, 'The British Army, Signals and Security in the Desert Campaign, 1940–42', in John Ferris, *Intelligence and Strategy, Selected Essays* (London, Routledge, 2005), pp. 181–238.

49 Hinsley et al., Vol. One, pp. 375–82; Andrew Stewart, *The First Victory, The Second World War and the Ethiopian Campaign* (I.B. Tauris, 2017).

50 Memorandum by Cunningham, 6.6.41, 'East Africa Force, Report on Operation from 1st November, 1940, to 5th April, 1941', Alan Cunningham Papers, 8303104–12-1, NAM.

51 Ferris, *Intelligence and Strategy*, pp. 181–238.

52 Jonathan Fennell, *Combat and Morale in the North African Campaign, The Eighth Army and the Path to El Alamein* (CUP, 2011); Ferris, *Intelligence and Strategy*, pp. 181–238; David French, *Raising Churchill's Army, The British Army and the War Against Germany, 1919–1945* (Oxford, Oxford University Press, 2000).

53 Perhaps the most useful English-language works on Rommel are Ian. F. Beckett, *Rommel, A Reappraisal* (Pen and Sword, 2013) and David Irving, *Rommel, The Trail of the Fox* (Weidenfield and Nicholson, 1977).

54 Otto von Behrendt, *Rommel's Intelligence in the Desert Campaign, 1941–1943* (London, Kimber, 1985).

55 Ferris, *Intelligence and Strategy*, pp. 163–68.

56 Ibid., pp. 181–239; Ferris, 'Crusader'.

57 C. J. Jenner, 'Turning the Hinge of Fate: "Good Source" and the U.S.–U.K. Intelligence Alliance, 1940–2, *Diplomatic History*, 32:2, pp. 165–205.

58 Ferris, 'Crusader', pp. 222–26; Ralph Bennett, *Ultra and Mediterranean Strategy* (William Morrow and Co., 1989).

59 Ibid.

60 Jenner, 'Hinge of Fate'.

61 The best account remains, J. A. I. Agar-Hamilton and L. C. F. Turner, *Crisis in the Desert, May–July 1942, Union War Histories* (New York, Oxford University Press, 1952).

62 Gladman, *Intelligence and Anglo-American Air Support*.

63 F. W. von Mellenthin, *Panzer Battles* (New York, Ballantine Books, 1956), p. 94.

64 'A Force War Diary', entry 2.7.42, CAB 154/1; Maunsell, 'Security Intelligence'; F. H. Hinsley and C. A. G. Simkins, *British Intelligence in the Second World War, Its Influence on Strategy and Operations, Volume IV, Security and Counter-Intelligence* (HMSO, 1990), pp. 166–67; Typescript memoir, nd, Brigadier R. J. Maunsell Papers, Imperial War Museum.

65 Bennett, *Mediterranean Strategy;* Nigel Hamilton, *British Intelligence in the Second World War, Its Influence on Strategy and Operations*

66 Bennett, *Mediterranean Strategy*.

67 Vincent P. O'Hara, *Torch, North Africa and the Allied Path to Victory* (US Naval Institute Press, 2015).

68 David Rolf, *The Bloody Road to Tunis: Destruction of the Axis Forces in North Africa, November 1942–May 1943* (Greenhill Books, Mechanicsburg PA, 2001).

69 For intelligence and operations in the Italian campaign, Carlo D'Este, *World War Two in the Mediterranean, 1942–1945* (Algonquin, Chapel Hill, New York, 1990), Bennett, *Mediterranean Strategy,* and Kevin Jones, *Intelligence and Command at the Operational Level of War: The British Eighth Army in the Italian Campaigns, 1943–1945* (Routledge, 2005).

70 David Kahn, *Hitler's Spies, German Military Intelligence in World War II*, p. 173; Irving, *Das Reich*, pp. 62–70, http://www.fpp.co.uk/books/Forschungsamt/index.html; Percy Scramm, *Kriegestagebuch des Oberkomando der Wehrmacht – 1943, Teilband II, Eine Dokumentation*, pp. 852–54. (Bernhard & Graefe, 1983).

71 Memorandum by Hugh Trevor Roper, 'The German Intelligence Service and the War', 1945, CAB 154/105

72 Katherine Barbier, *D-Day Deception: Operation Fortitude and the Normandy Invasion* (Praeger, 2007); Michael Handel, *Strategic and Operational Deception in the Second World War* (London, Frank Cass, 1987); Roger Hesketh, *Fortitude, The D-Day Deception Campaign* (Overlook Hardcover, 2000) and Thaddeus Holt, *The Deceivers, Allied Military Deception in the Second World War* (London, Weidenfeld & Nicholson, 2004).

73 Memorandum by NID 12, 20.7.45, 'German Appreciation of Allied Intentions', ADM 223/298; for copies of these reports, cf. CAB 154/76, pp. 95–96.

74 Memorandum by Nalder, 'Wireless Cover and Deception in the Italian Campaign', c.1945, CAB 154/103; Handel, *Strategic Deception*, pp. 161–62.

75 John Ferris, 'Agreed Texts: Intelligence, Military Rationality and the Planning for Operation Overlord', in John Buckley (ed.) *Overlord Sixty Years Later* (Routledge, 2006), pp. 119–56; Ralph Bennett, *Ultra in the West, The Normandy Campaign of 1944–45*, (Encore, 1980).

76 Williams to Whiteley, 2.2.44, RG 331/12/9, NARA.

77 Ferris, 'Intelligence before Overlord'.

78 JIC (44) 215 (0) 25.5.44, RG 331/3/128, NARA.

79 Nigel Hamilton, *Master of the Battlefield, Monty's War Years, 1942–1944* (New York, McGraw-Hill), pp.582–89.

80 Ferris, 'Intelligence before Overlord'.

81 Smith, *Emperor's Codes, The Thrilling Story of the of the Allied Code Breakers who Turned the Tide of World War II* (Biteback, 2011); John Ferris, '"Consistent with an Intention": The Far East Combined Bureau and the Outbreak of the Pacific War, 1940–1941', INS, 27/1, 2012, pp. 5–26.

82 Ferris, ibid.

83 Smith, *Emperor's Codes;* Alan Stripp, *Codebreaker in the Far East* (Frank Cass, 1989).

84 David Dufty, *The Secret Codebreakers of Central Bureau: how Australia's signals intelligence network helped win the Second World War* (Scribe, Melbourne, 2017); Peter Donovan and John Mack, *Codebreaking in the Pacific* (Springer, 2014).

85 Memorandum by Jones, 'Clear Decks' (832 TOPSEC U), 13.11.44, HW 3/127.

86 F. H. Hinsley, 'British Intelligence in the Second World War', in Christopher Andrew and Jeremy Noakes (eds), *Intelligence and International Relations, 1900–1945* (Exeter, 1987), pp. 217–18; Harry Hinsley, 'The Counter-Factual History of No Ultra', *Cryptologia*, XX/4, 1996, pp. 308–24.

87 Eisenhower to Menzies, 12.7.45, HW 3/168.

CHAPTER 7

1 For long-term policy, cf. David French, *The British Way in Warfare, 1688–2000* (Routledge, London, 1990); George Peden, *Arms, Economics and British Strategy: From Dreadnaughts to Hydrogen Bombs* (Cambridge. CUP, 2007) and David Reynolds, *Britannia Overruled: British policy and world power in the twentieth century* (Taylor & Francis, London, 2013). For defence policy after 1945, cf. Michael Carver, *Tightrope Walking: British Defence Policy since 1945* (London, Hutchinson, 1992); Stuart Croft, Andrew Dorman, Wyn Rees and Matthew Uttley, *Britain and Defence, 1945–2000: A policy re-evaluation* (Routledge, 2001); Michael Dockrill, *British Defence since 1945 (Making Contemporary Britain)* (Oxford: Wiley-Blackwell, 1991); Bill Jackson and Edwin Bramall, *The Chiefs: The Story of the United Kingdom Chiefs of Staff* (London: Brassey's, 1992).

2 Richard Aldrich and M. F. Hopkins, *Intelligence, defence and diplomacy: British policy in the postwar world* (Taylor & Francis, London, 2013); D. W. B. Lomas, *Intelligence, security and the Attlee governments, 1945–51, An uneasy relationship?* (Manchester University Press, Manchester, 2016); Michael Goodman, *The Official History of the Joint Intelligence Committee, Volume One: From the Approach of the Second World War to the Suez Crisis* (Taylor & Francis, London, 2015); Calder Walton, *Empire of Secrets: British Intelligence in the Cold War and the Twilight of Empire* (Outlook Press, London, 2015).

3 W. Brian Arthur, *Increasing Returns and Path Dependence in the Economy*, (Ann Arbor, Michigan: University of Michigan Press, 1994); Paul Pierson, *Politics in Time: History, Institutions, and Social Analysis* (Princeton University Press, 2004).

4 John Baylis, *Ambiguity and Deterrence: British Nuclear Strategy, 1945–1964* (Oxford, OUP, 1995), Matthew Jones, *The Official History of the British Nuclear Deterrent, Volume 1: From the V-Bomber Era to the Arrival of Polaris* (Taylor & Francis, London, 2017); Matthew Navias, *Nuclear Weapons and British Strategic Planning, 1955–1958* (Oxford, OUP, 1991).

5 *British Sigint*, Two, pp. 478–534.

6 Ibid., Four, pp. 352–370.

7 Cf. below.

8 Minute by Cadogan, 9.11.44, FO 1093/197.

9 Memorandum, unsigned and undated but *c*. June 1944, 'Re-adjustment in the Functions of M.I. 5 and M.I. 6', CAB 301/11.

10 Memorandum by Norman Brook, 12.5.43, CAB 301/11.

11 'The Intelligence Machine, Report to the Joint Intelligence Sub-Committee', by Victor Cavendish-Bentinck and Denis Capel-Dunn, 10.1.45, CAB 301/11.

12 Memorandum by Cavendish-Bentinck, 27.9.44, FO 1093/195.

13 C to Loxley, 24.4.44, FO 1093/195.

14 Until 31 March 1946, the organisation normally was called GC&CS, though many other titles as well. From 1 April 1946, it was called GCHQ, but until October 1948 also occasionally the London Sigint Centre. The text calls the organisation GC&CS until 1 September 1945, and GCHQ thereafter.

15 'The Intelligence Machine, Report to the Joint Intelligence Sub-Committee', by Victor Cavendish-Bentinck and Denis Capel-Dunn, 10.1.45, CAB 301/11, Report of Bland Committee, 12.10.44, CAB 301/48.

16 ACAS (I) Inglis to Cavendish-Bentinck, 24.4.44, MID to Cavendish-Bentinck, 15.6.44, FO 1093/195.

17 Nigel West, *The Guy Liddell Diaries, Volume Two*, entry 24 October 1944, KV 4/195, p. 236.

18 Minute by Cavendish-Bentinck, 27.9.44, FO 1093/195; 'The Intelligence Machine', 10.1.45, CAB 301/11; Report of Bland Committee, 12.10.44, CAB 301/48.

19 *British Sigint*, One, pp. 22–30.

20 Ibid., pp. 30–35.

21 Ibid., pp. 35–44.

22 Ibid., pp. 40–44.

23 Ibid., pp.76–77.

24 Loxley to C, 11.11.43, FO 1093/326.

25 Minute by Cavendish-Bentinck, 23.10.44, FO 1093/329

26 *British Sigint*, One, pp. 45–48.

27 Ibid., pp. 48–62.

28 Ibid., pp. 48–62, 534–8.

29 Ibid., pp. 537.

30 Ibid., pp. 539–41.

31 Minute by Drew, 14.2.61, DEFE 23/23; Minute by Whitehead, 11.11.74, ZCZ 1/42.

32 *British Sigint*, One, pp. 232–63.

33 Hooper to Wyatt, 17.4.61, T 296/278

34 *British Sigint*, Three, pp. 178; Field Marshal Sir Gerald Templer, 'Review of Service Intelligence', 16.12.1960, T 296/277; Interception Working Party, first meeting, 9.3.61, AIR 40/2757.

35 *British Sigint*, One, pp. 250–51.

36 Ibid., Two, pp. 84–85, 94.

37 Ibid., pp. 100–3, and Three, p. 302. Richard Aldrich, 'Counting the Cost of Intelligence: The Treasury, National Service and GCHQ', *English Historical Review,* 128/532, June 2013, pp. 602–4.

38 *British Sigint*, Two, pp. 72–5.

39 Ibid., pp. 70–92, and Three, p. 303.

40 Memorandum by Baldwin, 17.2.61, 'Service Intelligence', to Wyatt, Wyatt to Baldwin, 'Templer Report', 21.2.61, T 296/277.

41 *British Sigint*, One, pp. 539–41.

42 Memorandum by Jones, 'Summary of the Career of Mr. E. M. Jones', 12.1.52, FO 1093/96.

43 Ibid. is useful, but the constant references to his career being guided by a search for education are probably a defensive reaction to anticipated criticisms of his lack of a degree.

44 Memorandum by Reilly, 1.1.52, FO 1093/96.

45 Minute by Reilly, 'Sir William Strang', 14.3.52, minute by Strang, FO 1093/96.

46 Memorandum by Reilly, 1.1.52, FO 1093/96.

47 Memorandum by Reilly, 'Top Secret', 11.1.52, FO 1093/96.

48 *British Sigint*, Two, p. 84.

49 Memorandum by Reilly, 'Top Secret'.

50 C to Reilly, 14.1.52, 'Report by Deputy-Director G.C.H.Q.', 11.1.52, containing 11.1.52, underlining probably by Reilly, FO 1093/96.

51 Memorandum by Strang, 'Director of G.C.H.Q.', 24.1.52, Strang to Slim, 30.1.52, FO 1093/96.

52 Minutes by Eden, 25.1.52, FO 1093/96.

53 Memorandum by Menzies, n.d., 'Special Meeting to consider the appointment of Director, G.C.H.Q., 1st January 1952', FO 1093/96.

54 Helen Fulton, Sir Brian Tovey Obituary', *Guardian*, 4.1.2016.

55 *British Sigint*, Four, pp. 53–61; Memorandum by Jones, 'Summary of the Career of Mr. E. M. Jones', 12.1.52, FO 1093/96, 'Jones, Sir Eric Malcolm', DNB; 'Loehnis, Sir Clive', DNB'; 'Hooper, Sir Leonard James', DNB; 'Sir Peter Marychurch Obituary', *Guardian*, 1.6.07, *Independent*, 25.5.07.

56 *British Sigint*, Two, pp. 71–100, 90–6, and Three, p. 305.

57 Ibid., pp. 85–91.

58 Ibid., Three, pp. 123–24.

59 Ibid., p. 126.

60 Ibid., pp., 123–30.

61 Memorandum by Templer, 'Review of Service Intelligence', 16.12.60, DEFE 23/23.

62 Q/LSIB/58/62, 21.5.62, 'The Cost of Sigint–1962', LSIB 1962.

63 Aldrich, 'Counting the Cost', pp. 608–27.

64 LSIB Z1/63, 19.4.63, 'Hampshire Review of Sigint', LSIB 1963.

65 *British Sigint*, Three, pp. 131–40.

66 Memorandum by S. N. Hampshire, 'Review of Signal Intelligence', 1.2.63, LSIB 1963.

67 Ibid.

68 Ibid.

69 Ibid.

70 Memorandum by S. N. Hampshire, 'Review of Signal Intelligence', 1.2.63, LSIB 1963.

71 Ibid.

72 *British Sigint*, Three, pp. 139–50.

73 Ibid., Four, p. 63.

74 Ibid., pp. 28–29.

75 GCHQ briefing to LSIB/LSIC members, D/1401/4 pt III, 14.2.75, 21.1.75, LSIB 1975.

76 Aldrich, 'Counting the Cost'.

77 Minute by Burke Trend to Prime Minister, 13.3.67; Note for the record by Trend, 2.8.67, PREM 13/2688; J. W. Young, 'The Wilson Government's Reform of Intelligence Co-ordination, 1967–67', INS 16/2, pp. 133–151.

78 LSIB (71) 1st Meeting Minutes, 'Minutes of a Meeting held on 17 June 1971', LSIB 1971.

79 LSIB 4/74, 'Five Year Sigint Forecast (1975–1980)', 6.3.74, LSIB 1974.

80 LSIB (71), 1st Meeting Minutes, 'Minutes of a Meeting held on 17 June 1971', LSIB 1971.

81 LSIB (70), 1st Meeting Minutes, 'Minutes of a Meeting held on 11 June 1970', LSIB 1970.

82 LSIB 6/71, 3.6.71, 'Future Sigint Programmes and Costs, 1971', LSIB 1971.

83 LSIB 167/51, 6.9.51, 'List of Persons Indoctrinated in British Government Departments as of Ist July 1951', LSIB 1951; LSIB/20/63, 'Totals of U.K. Comint Indoctrinated Persons as of 1st January, 1963', LSIB 1963.

84 LSIB 1/70, 2.2.70, 'Five-Tear Sigint Programme (1971–1976), LSIB 1970; LSIB (71) 1st Meeting.

85 'Proposal for the Establishment of a Sigint Finance Committee', 19.7.63, LSIB 1963.

86 LSIB meeting, 25.5.65, LSIB (65) 1st Meeting, 25.5.65, LSIB 1065.

87 NEW JIC (66) 5th Meeting, 3.2.66, CAB 159/45.

88 LSIB 11/67, 21.8.67, 'Record of the Meeting of the PSIS (Sigint) Committee on 26th July, 1967', LSIB 1967.

89 LSIB meeting, 26.9.63, LSIB (1963) 4th Meeting (Minutes), LSIB 1963.

90 Aldrich, GCHQ.

91 LSIB meeting, 21.5.64, LSIB (64) 1st Meeting (Minutes), LSIB 1964.

92 Ibid.

93 'Attachment to LSIB/27/65, 'Extract from a letter, Burke Trend to Paul Gore-Booth, on PSIS meeting of 19.7.65', LSIB 1965.

94 LSIB (65) 3rd Meeting (Minutes), 11.11.65, LSIB/52/65, 26.10.65, LSIB/29/68, 3.12.68, 'Report of a Visit to Washington in September/October 1965 by the Director GCHQ', LSIB 1965.

95 LSIB (65) 3rd Meeting (Minutes), 11.11.65, LSIB 1965.

96 LSIB 10/65, 28.6.65, LSIB 1965.

97 LSIB 10/66, 9.8.66, 'Record of the Meeting of the PIS (Sigint) Committee on 12th July, 1966', LSIB 1966.

98 LSIB (68) 3rd and 4th Meeting (Minutes) 25.10.68, 26.1.68, LSIB/19/68, 23.7.1968, PSIS (Sigint) Commtteee meeting, 28.7.68, LSIB 1968.

99 Cost Analysis of Sigint, Annex C to LSIB/3/66, LSIB 1966.

100 LSIB (75) 1st Meeting Minutes, 28.6.75, LSIB 5/75, 'Future Sigint Programmes and Cost: Five-Year Forecast 1976–81', 6.6.75, LSIB 1975.

101 LSIB 6/77, 17.5.77, 'Implications of Cuts of 3.5 per cent and 5 per cent in the Cost of Sigint; 1977 Draft Report by LSIB to PSIS', LSIB 1977.

102 C(75)1, 25.2.75, 'Statement of the Defence Estimates 1975', CAB 129/181.

103 LSIB (71) 1st Meeting.

104 LSIB 3/76, 'Future Sigint Programmes and Cost: Five Year Forecast 1977–1982', 4.6.76, LSIB 1976; LSIB 5/77, 17.5.77, 'Future Sigint Programmes and Cost: Four Year Forecast 1978–1982', LSIB 1977.

105 LSIB (81) 2nd Meeting (Minutes), 27.5.81, 'Minutes of the Meeting held on 21 May 1981', LSIB 1981.

106 LSIB (77) 1st Meeting (Minutes), 21.6.77, 'Minutes of the Meeting held on 25 May 1977', LSIB 1977.

107 LSIB (78) 1st Meeting (Minutes), 8.6.78, 'Record of the Meeting held on 31 May 1978 to Discuss the Report to the PSIS and the Cost of Sigint Four Year Forecast 1978', LSIB 1978.

108 LSIB 5/78, 12.5.78, 'Future Sigint Programmes and Costs', LSIB 1978.

109 LSIB (81) 1st Meeting (Minutes), 'Minutes of the Meeting held on 22 January 1981', 29.1.81, LSIB 1981.

110 LSIB (79) 1st and 2nd Meetings (Minutes), 13.2.79, 'Minutes of the Meeting held on 14 January 1979', 5.6.79, 'Minutes of the Meeting held on 23 May 1979', LSIB 14/1979, 5.4.79, 'The State of Sigint, 1978', LSIB 1979.

111 LSIB (80) 1st Meeting (Minutes), 17.2.80, LSIB 1980.

112 'Ralph Benjamin: An Interview Conducted by Peter C. J. Hill', 16.9.2005, IEEE History Centre, Institute of Electrical and Electronics Engineers, Inc., ethw.org/Oral-History: Ralph_Benjamin.

113 'Visit of the Prime Minister to GCHQ', *Contact* magazine, No. 32, 2nd issue, 1980, pp. 2–3.

114 LSIB 1/81, 30.12.80, 'The State of Sigint 1981', LSIB 1981.

115 LSIB 6/82, 30.6.82, 'The State of Sigint 1982', LSIB 1982.

116 LSIB 9/82, 'Future Sigint Programmes and Costs', LSIB 1982; LSIB 13/82, 30.12.82, 'The Falklands Crisis: Review of Sigint Performance', LSIB 1982.

117 Ralph Benjamin, *Five Lives in One: An Insider's View of the Defence and Intelligence World* (Tunbridge Wells, Parapress, 1996); 'Ralph Benjamin: An Interview'.

CHAPTER 8

1 Desmond Ball and Jeffrey Richelson, *The Ties that Bind: Intelligence Cooperation between the UKUSA Countries* (Allen & Unwin, Sydney, 1985), is the pioneering work on the topic, and excellent given restrictions to the material. However, it and other subsequent works which refer to UKUSA were wrong on many issues, including whether it was a formal treaty. In 2010, British and American authorities released the basic documents on UKUSA: www.nationalarchives.gov.uk/ukusa, and /www.nsa.gov/news-features/declassified-documents/ukusa/. Any modern work must start from that basis.

2 Michael Hayden, *Playing to the Edge, American Intelligence in the Age of Terror* (Penguin, New York, 2017), pp. 41–42.

3 Sigint agencies often changed names. I follow these changes, except that I replace 'GCHQ' for 'GC&CS' from September 1945. The term 'American Sigint' includes the service Sigint elements and NSA. The term 'British Sigint' applies the same to Britain, though from 1964 the term 'GCHQ' really represents the British whole. This usage differentiates the relations between GCHQ and NSA, and of both from the American service Sigint units, matters which drive UKUSA.

4 Mark K. Wells, *Courage and Air Warfare: The Allied Aircrew Experience in the Second World War* (Frank Cass, London, 1996).

5 David Hobbs, *The British Pacific Fleet: The Royal Navy's Most Powerful Fleet Force* (Naval Institute Press, 2017).

6 John Baylis, *Ambiguity and Deterrence: British Nuclear Strategy, 1945–1964* (OUP, Oxford, 1995); Margaret Gowing, *Independence and Deterrence, Britain and Atomic Energy, 1945–52, Volume 1, Policy Making and Volume 2, Policy Execution* (London, Macmillan, 1974); Jones, *The British Nuclear Deterrent, Volume I*; Navias, *Nuclear Weapons.*

7 Bradley Smith, *The Shadow Warriors, O.S.S. and the Origins of the C.I.A.* (Basic Books, 1983).

8 John Ferris, 'Gentlemen's Agreements and Gentlemen's Mail: Communications Intelligence and the Diplomacy of Naval Disarmament, 1921–1930', *Issues in British and American Signals Intelligence, 1919–1932,* Special Series, Volume 11 (Center for Cryptologic History, Fort Meade, 2015), pp. 42–59.

9 Kennedy, *Engineers of Victory,.*

10 Thomas G. Manhken, 'U.S. Grand Strategy, 1939–1945', in Ferris and Mawdsley (eds), *Fighting the War*, pp. 189–212.

11 Smith, *The Ultra-Magic Deals* is the pioneering work in the field, and a brilliant work of intelligence history. Because he could not acquire complete documentation about the access Britain gave the United States on its work against Enigma during spring 1941, some of Smith's judgements are skewed. Later key works include Ralph Erskine, 'Churchill and the Start of the Ultra-Magic Deals', *International Journal of Intelligence and Counter-Intelligence,* 10/1, Spring 1997, pp. 57–74 and David Sherman, 'From Improvisation to Permanence: American perspectives on the U.S. signals relationship, 1940–1950', *Journal of Intelligence History,* 18/2, 2019, pp. 63–85.

12 United States Military Attaché to War Department, telegram No. 401, 5.9.40, 'Early Papers Concerning US–UK Agreement, 1940–1944', https://www.nsa.gov/news-features/declassified-documents/ukusa/.

13 Memorandum by Sherman Miles, Acting Assistant Chief of Staff, G-2, 'Codes and Ciphers', 4.10.40, 'Early Papers Concerning US–UK Agreement, 1940–1944', https://www.nsa.gov/news-features/declassified-documents/ukusa/

14 Menzies to Churchill, 31.1.41, DIR/C.
15 NSA-OH-02-79 Thru 04–79, 'Dr. Abraham Sinkov, May 1979', pp. 3–6, www.nsa.gov/Portals/70/documents/news-features/declassified-documents/oral-history-interviews/nsa-OH-02-79.sinkov.pdf
16 Sherman, 'Improvisation to Permanence'.
17 Ibid.
18 Manhken, 'U.S. Grand Strategy'.
19 *British Sigint*, One, p. 299.
20 Sherman, 'Improvisation to Permanence'.
21 CSS to 48000, 25.8.42, HW 14/50.
22 Tom Johnson, *American Cryptology during the Cold War, 1945–1989: Book One, The Struggle for Centralization, 1945–1960,* Center for Cryptologic History, National Security Agency, 1995, p. 7.
23 Memorandum by Strong, 5.12.42, 'Doctor A.M. Turing', Early Papers Concerning US–UK Agreement, 1940–1944, https://www.nsa.gov/news-features/declassified-documents/ukusa/
24 'Report by Lieut. General J. H. Tiltman on his Visit to North America during March and April 1942', HW 14/46.
25 Hastings to 'Dear John' (Tiltman), 17.8.42, HW 14/49.
26 Stevens to Denniston, 28.9.42, HW 14/53.
27 Ibid.
28 NSA-OH-01-85, Interview with Telford Taylor, 22.1.85, /www.nsa.gov/Portals/70/documents/news-features/declassified-documents/oral-history-interviews/NSA-OH-01-85-Taylor.pdf
29 Stevens to Denniston, 27.10.42, HW 14/56.
30 CSS to 48000, 25.8.42, HW 14/50.
31 Manhken, 'U.S. Grand Strategy'.
32 Dill to Marshall, 7.1.43, containing Tiltman to Strong, 7.1.43, Early Papers Concerning US–UK Agreement, 1940–1944, https://www.nsa.gov/news-features/declassified-documents/ukusa/
33 Sherman, 'Improvisation to Permanence'.
34 'Turing's Report on his Visit to NCR, December 1942', edited by Ralph Erskine, Phillip Marks and Frode Weirud, 9.2000, cryptocellar.org/US Bombe/turncr.pdf (original RG 38/Crane Library, file, CNSG 5750/441, NARA).
35 Noble to King, 19.2 44, RG 38/1038.
36 Sherman, 'Improvisation to Permanence'; Johnson, *American Cryptology: Book One*, pp. 13–15
37 Sherman, 'Improvisation to Permanence'.
38 NSA-OH-01-85. Interview with Telford Taylor, 22.1.85, www.nsa.gov/Portals/70/documents/news-features/declassified-documents/oral-history-interviews/NSA-OH-01-85-Taylor.pdf

39 Telford Taylor, 'Memorandum to Colonel Clarke', 5.4.43, Early Papers Concerning US–UK Agreement, 1940–1944, https://www.nsa.gov/news-features/declassified-documents/ukusa/

40 Ibid.

41 John Ferris, 'The British Enigma', pp. 162, 168–71.

42 Ibid.

43 Personal Minute by Churchill, 27.1.44, Bridge to Churchill, n.d., but January 1944 by internal evidence, and 31.1.44, Stewart Menzies to Bridges, 31.1.44, CAB 21/2519.

44 Ibid.

45 Ferris, 'The British Enigma', pp. 170–76; Christopher Smith, 'Bletchley Park and the Development of the Rockex Cipher Systems: Building a Technocratic Culture, 1941–1945', *War in History*, 24/2, 2017.

46 Minute by Communications Department, 3.8.44, FO 850/134

47 David Alvrez, *Secret Messages, Codebreaking and American Diplomacy, 1930–1945* (University Press of Kansas, 2000).

48 Memorandum by Safford, 15.4.47, 'Administrative History of World War II: Cryptographic Research Section', RG 38/1030/110, NARA.

49 Memorandum by Wenger 15.5.45, 000628220, 'Release of Free French Material to British', RG 38/1030/92, NARA.

50 Jebb to Loxley, 21.4.44, and minute by Bland, 18.7.44, FO 1093/195.

51 Cadogan to C 16.7.43, FO 1093/324; O'Conner to Menzies, HMOC/1486, 6.9.44, FO 1093/329.

52 Memorandum by Telford Taylor, Office of the Military Attaché, American Embassy, London. 8.6.44, FO 1093/329.

53 8th Meeting, Army–Navy Cryptanalytic Research and Development Committee, 21.2.45, RG 38/1030/91, NARA.

54 *British Sigint*, One, pp. 301–3.

55 Johnson, *American Cryptology: Book One*, p. 16.

56 Ibid.

57 Presidential Executive Order, 28.8.45, RG 38/1030/92, NARA.

58 *British Sigint*, One, pp. 299–301.

59 Ibid., pp. 301–8.

60 Ibid., pp. 306–8; Joint Meeting of Army–Navy Communication Intelligence Board, and Army–Navy Communication Intelligence Coordinating Committee, 15 October 1945, 29 October 1945, https://www.nsa.gov/Portals/70/documents/news-features/declassified-documents/ukusa/joint_mtg_15oct45.pdf., https://www.nsa.gov/Portals/70/documents/news-features/declassified-documents/ukusa/joint_mtg_29oct45.pdf

61 Ibid., One, pp. 307–8.

62 Ibid., pp.307–13; Joint Meeting of Army–Navy Communication Intelligence Board, and Army–Navy Communication Intelligence Coordinating Committee, 29 October 1945, https://www.nsa.gov/Portals/70/documents/news-features/declassified-documents/ukusa/joint_mtg_29oct45.pdf

63 Ibid., p. 309.

64 Ibid., Two, pp. 657–9; Joint Meeting of Army–Navy Communication Intelligence Board, and Army–Navy Communication Intelligence Coordinating Committee, 29 October 1945, https://www.nsa.gov/Portals/70/documents/news-features/declassified-documents/ukusa/joint_mtg_29oct45.pdf

65 Ibid., One, pp. 319–20.

66 ANCIB Memorandum for General Marshall and Admiral King, 22.8.45, https://www.nsa.gov/Portals/70/documents/news-features/declassified-documents/ukusa/ancib_22aug45.pdf

67 Memorandum by Smedberg, 19.2.46, 'U.S.–British Agreement', https://www.nsa.gov/Portals/70/documents/news-features/declassified-documents/ukusa/fbi_stancib_19feb46.pdf

68 Henry C. Clausen and Bruce Lee, *Pearl Harbor: Final Judgment* (Crown Publishers, New York, 1992).

69 *British Sigint*, One, pp. 312–19; Joint Meeting of Army–Navy Communication Intelligence Board, and Army–Navy Communication Intelligence Coordinating Committee, 1.11.45, https://www.nsa.gov/Portals/70/documents/news-features/declassified-documents/ukusa/joint_mtg_1nov45.pdf

70 Ibid., pp. 286–98; *British Sigint*, Two, pp. 656–59, 670–84;

71 *Ibid.*, pp. 76–86, 324–29.

72 1951–53, UKUSA Comint Agreement and Appendices Thereto: www.nsa.gov/news-features/declassified-documents/ukusa/

73 *British Sigint*, Two, pp. 669–70.

74 Ibid., Four, p. 857.

75 'Appendix J, Principles of UKUSA Collaboration with Commonwealth Countries Other than the UK', 13.2.61, https://www.nsa.gov/Portals/70/documents/news-features/declassified-documents/ukusa/principles_of_ukusa_collaboration_with_commonwealth_countries_other_than_the_uk_appendix_j_13_february_1961.pdf

76 *British Sigint*, Three, pp. 1107–8.

77 Ibid., Two, pp. 661–64; Three, pp. 1125–30; Four, pp. 208–20.

78 Kaplan, To Kill Nations, pp. 680–81.

79 Farquhar, Need to Know, p 36.

80 *British Sigint*, Two, pp. 680–81.

81 Cf. below.

82 Johnson, *American Cryptology: Book One,* pp.11–12, 26–30, 82–3.

83 *British Sigint*, Two, pp. 664–66; ibid., Three, pp. 399–400; ibid., Four, pp. 167–71; Johnson, *American cryptology, Book One*, pp. 93–101.

84 *British Sigint*, Three, pp. 80–91.

85 *Ibid.*

86 Johnson, *American Cryptology, Book One*, pp. 23–35; Aid, The Secret Sentry, The Untold History of the National Security Agency, pp. 8–25, 41–45.

87 *British Sigint*, Two, pp. 659–63

88 *Ibid.*, p. 661; Johnson, *American Cryptology: Book One*, p. 16.

89 General Ralph Canine USA, OH–2012–81, p. 8 /www.nsa.gov/news-features/declassified-documents/ukusa/

90 Johnson, *American Cryptology: Book One*, p. 229.

91 *British Sigint*, Three, p. 1117.

92 *Ibid.*, Two, pp. 667.

93 *Ibid.*, Three, pp. 1105–7.

94 *Ibid.*, Four, pp. 190–3.

95 *Ibid.*, Three, pp. 1113–15.

96 LSIB/102/56, 30.6.56, 'Reduction in G.C.H.Q. Establishment', 30.5.56, LSIB 1956.

97 LSIB Meeting, 8.12.56, LSIB 1956 (6th Meeting) 15.12.56, LSIB 1956.

98 LSIB (65) 3rd Meeting (Minutes), 11.11.65, LSIB/52/65, 26.10.65, LSIB/29/68, 3.12.68, 'Report of a Visit to Washington in September/October 1965 by the Director GCHQ', LSIB 1965.

99 NSA-OH-02-79, Interview with Dr. Abraham Sinkov, p. 127 /www.nsa.gov/Portals/70/documents/news-features/declassified-documents/oral-history-interviews/nsa-OH-02-79.sinkov. pdf

100 *British Sigint*, Four, pp. 236–37.

101 Richard Goette, *Sovereignty and Command in Canada–US Continental Air Defence, 1940–1957* (University of British Columbia Press, Vancouver, 2018), Joseph. T. Jockel, *Canada in NORAD, 1957–2007, A History* (McGill-Queen's University Press, Kingston, 2007).

102 *British Sigint*, Three, p. 1122.

103 *Ibid.*, Four, p. 159.

104 *Ibid.*, Two, pp. 662–63, 677–83;

105 Ibid., Three, pp. 1117, 1120.

106 Nick Hopkins and Julian Bolger, 'Exclusive: NSA pays £100 million in secret funding for GCHQ', *Guardian*, 1.8.13.

107 'UK intelligence work defends freedom, say spy chiefs', BBC News, 7.11.2013, https://www.bbc.com/news/uk-politics-24847399

108 *British Sigint*, Four, pp. 181–90.

109 Ibid., Two, pp. 666–68, 677–82.

110 Ibid., pp. 679–80.

111 Ibid., Three, pp. 1098–99.

112 Ibid., Four, pp. 49, 133, 672, 1061.

113 Ibid., Three, pp. 1099–1100; Ibid., Four, p. 239.

114 Ibid., Four, pp. 15, 190–3, 198, 237–38, 895–96.

115 Ibid., Two, p. 680.

116 Ibid., Four, p. 171.

117 Ibid., Four, pp. 162–66; Johnson, *American Cryptology: Book Three, Retrenchment and Reform, 1972–1980*, pp. 21–27.

118 *British Sigint*, Four, pp. 190–93.

119 Ibid., p. 196.

120 Joe (Hooper) to White, 3.3.69, CAB 163/119.

121 *British Sigint*, Four, pp. 134–50.

122 LSIB/2/82, 5.3.82, 'The UKUSA Sigint Balance: Fact Sheet', LSIB 1982.

123 Entry, 1.5.87, William Odom Papers, Box 25, Library of Congress.

124 LSIB/14/ 1979, 5.4.79, 'The State of Sigint, 1978', LSIB 1979.

125 SA OH 15–88, 3.10.88, General Marshall Carter, pp. 201–2, 207–8, 305, /www.nsa.gov/Portals/70/documents/news-features/declassified-documents/oral-history-interviews/NSA-OH-15-88-Carter.pdf

126 NSA OH 15–88, 3.10.88, General Marshall Carter, pp. 201–2, 207–8, 305, /www.nsa.gov/Portals/70/documents/news-features/declassified-documents/oral-history-interviews/NSA-OH-15-88-Carter.pdf

127 Johnson, *American Cryptology: Book Three*, pp. 157–59.

128 'Description of Sigint Relations between NSA and GCHQ (U)', 12.85, https://www.documentcloud.org/documents/5759138-2-Description-of-SIGINT-Relations-Between-NSA.html

129 U.S. Cryptologic Partnership with the United Kingdom, 5.97, 'An Assessment of the UKUSA Relationship: Where Do We Go From Here', undated, https://www.documentcloud.org/documents/5759141-5-an-Assessment-of-the-UKUSA-Relationship-Where.html

130 *British Sigint*, One, pp. 41–42, 334–46, 529–30.

131 Kurt Jensen, *Cautious Beginnings: Canadian Foreign Intelligence, 1939–51* (University of British Columbia Press, 2013)

132 Ibid.

133 British Delegation Washington to C.S.S./G.C.C.S., 3XC.317, 4.6.42, HW 14/47.

134 Stevens to Denniston, 2.9.42, HW 14/51.

135 Jensen, *Cautious Beginnings British Sigint*, One, pp. 332–33.

136 Joseph Straczek, 'The Empire is Listening: naval signals intelligence in the Far East to 1942', *Journal of the Australian War Memorial*, 1.12.2001.

137 *British Sigint*, One, p. 333; Edward Drea, *MacArthur's Intelligence, Codebreaking and the War Against Japan, 1942–1945* (University Press of Kansas, 1991)

138 *British Sigint*, One, pp. 321–24, 352–58.

139 Evatt and the Petrov Affair are among the most divisive issues in Australian political history. The most balanced account is John Murphy, *Evatt, A Life* (New South, 2016).

140 Johnson, *American Cryptology: Book One*, pp. 18–19; Godfrey to Kinna, 24.12.48, FO 1093/516.

141 Andrew, *Defence of the Realm*, pp.367–72.

142 David Horner, *The Spy Catchers, The Official History of ASIO, 1949–1963* (Allen & Unwin, Sydney, 2014).

143 Memorandum by Sargant, 6.7.48, 'Australian Leakages', FO 1093/ 516.

144 Horner, *Spy Catchers*.

145 Murphy, *Evatt*.

146 *British Sigint*, Four, pp. 247–69.

147 Ibid., One, pp. 358–59; Ibid., Four, pp. 262–69; Johnson, *American Cryptology: Book Three*, pp. 159–61. Two useful accounts of these issues are Jenny Hocking, *Gough Whitlam: His Time* (Updated Edition) (Melbourne University Press, 2014) and John Blaxland, *The Protest Years: The Official History of ASIO, 1963–1975* (Allen & Unwin, 2015).

148 *British Sigint*, Four, pp. 283–94.

149 Ibid., One, pp. 334, 338–39.

150 Scott Lucas, *Britain and Suez, The Lion's Last Roar* (Manchester University Press, 1996).

151 GCHQ to GCOME 8.10.56, K/517/24; 'Supplement to LSIC (56) 13th Meeting', K/517/24.

152 D/0918, 29.11.56, 'Post-Mortem on Handling of Suez Crisis and Lessons for the Future', J/188/1

153 Palmer to Hooper, 7.1.57, D/353/4.

154 SUKLO to GCHQ, 9.1.57, I/09557, V. S, Palmer to Hooper, 17.1.57, D/353/4.

155 D/0918, 29.11.56, 'Post-Mortem' 'NSA Comments on GCHQ "Post-Mortem on Handling of Suez Crisis and Lessons for the Future", n.d., *c*.4.57, D/353/4.

156 *British Sigint*, Four, pp. 1160–63.

157 Memorandum by F. C. W. Figgs, 'Top Secret & Dinar', 24.5.64, ZW 83.

158 Bonsall to Figgs, 28.5.64, ZW 83.

159 Aldrich, 'GCHQ', pp. 277–99; *British Sigint*, Four, pp. 240–44.

160 Falklands Sigint History, pp. 16–21.

161 Entry 11 June 1985, William Odom Papers, Library of Congress, Box 25.

162 Cf. below.

163 *British Sigint*, Four, pp. 232–34.

164 Millward, 'Service of Middle East Reports to Australia', 19.12.56, Z/239/321/2, 'Extract from SUKO DSB's Letter dated 10th December 1956', K/517/24.

165 *British Sigint*, Two, pp. 683, 535–41,

166 Johnson, *American Cryptology: Book Three*, pp. 26–27

167 *British Sigint*, Two, pp. 581–83.

168 Ibid., pp. 539–41.

169 Ibid., pp. 18–609.

170 Ibid., pp. 599–600; Ibid., Three, pp. 997–1029;

171 Ibid., Two, p. 602.

172 Ibid., Four, pp. 395–98.

173 Ibid., Two, pp. 590–94, 600–4.

174 Ibid., Four, pp. 385–404.

175 Ibid., Three, pp. 997, 1012–13.

176 Cees Wiebes, 'Dutch Sigint during the Cold War, 1945–1994', pp. 243–84, in Cee Wiebes and Matthew Aid (eds), *Secrets of Sigint during the Cold War and Beyond* (Frank Cass and Co., London, 2001).

CHAPTER 9

1 *British Sigint*, One, pp.72–74.

2 Field Marshal Sir Gerald Templer, 'Review of Service Intelligence', 16.12.1960, T 296/277.

3 *Gloucestershire Echo*, 1 June 1953.

4 Hooper to Stephenson, 16.5.61, including undated memorandum by GCHQ, 'Summary of Evidence Available Outside UK Official Circles That the Government of the UK Indulges in Sigint Activities and That GCHQ is the UK Sigint Centre', T 296/278.

5 Personal Memoirs in GCHQ Archives.

6 Personal Memoirs in GCHQ Archives.

7 Personal Memoirs in GCHQ Archives.

8 Personal Memoirs in GCHQ Archives.

9 Memorandum by Denniston, 14.11.44, HW 62/21

10 Cooper to Rendle, 6.3.67 D/1102/1 pt II.

11 *British Sigint*, Two, pp. 126–47.

12 Personal Memoirs in GCHQ Archives.

13 CAB 301/11, Report of Bland Committee, 12.10.44, CAB 301/48.

14 Information from Tony Comer.

15 *British Sigint*, One, pp. 245–46.

16 Ibid., One, pp. 245–50.

17 CSC 2.9.49,'Recruitment under Normal Regulations to the Government Communication Headquarters (A Department of the Foreign Office)', Open Competition, 1950, CSC 6/55.

18 CSC, 9/65, 'Recruitment to the "A" Class and to the Departmental Specialist Class in Government Communication Headquarters (A Department of the Foreign Office)', CSC 6/70.

19 Rendle to Gedd, 5.6.63, CSC 5/1843.

20 Memorandum, 29.1.80, 'Selection of GCT 2s, Part 2, Review of Advertising and Selection Procedures', E/1100/28 pt II.

21 *British Sigint*, Three, p. 278 passim.

22 *Ibid.*, pp. 278–90.

23 *Ibid.*, p. 281.

24 Memorandum, 25.10.79, 'GCT Scheme: A Paper for Discussion with Staff Side', E/1100/28 pt II.

25 Ibid.

26 Minute by H, 4.1.80, E/1100/28 pt II.

27 Memorandum, 25.10.79, 'GCT'.

28 Minute by K1, 'Recruitment of Cadets', n.d., *c.* June 1982, E/1100/28 pt II.

29 Ibid.

30 Memorandum by S, 6.2.80, Minute by K1,, 'Recruitment of Cadets'.

31 Memorandum, 18.7.80, 'GCT Profile', E/1100/28 pt II.

32 GCHQ and the JTLS Cheltenham, 'Careers for Graduates', 1983, recruitment brochure in GCHQ Archives.

33 *British Sigint*, One, pp. 245, 248, 252.

34 Minute by K1, 'Recruitment of Cadets'.

35 Minutes of the Meeting of the Apprentices' Committee, 13.10.65, E/1000/12.

36 CSC 1964, GCHQ, 'Government Communication Headquarters, AIV and Assistant Departmental Specialist Posts Limited Competition, 1965', CSC 6/70; 12.68, 'Government Communication Headquarters Departmental Specialist Class: Technical Signals Officers', CSC 6/73.

37 'Professor Robert Churchhouse: 1927–2018 (1949, Mathematics)'. https://www.trinhall.cam.ac.uk/alumni/keep-in-touch/obituaries/robert-churchhouse/

38 Interview with David Pepper, 25.6.2018.

39 'Ralph Benjamin: An Interview'.

40 Tom Espiner, 26.10.2010, 'GCHQ pioneers on birth of public-key cryptography', ZDNet, https://www.zdnet.com/article/gchq-pioneers-on-birth-of-public-key-crypto/

41 Interview with John Adye, 20.6.2018.

42 Personal Memoirs in GCHQ Archives.

43 Simon Singh. 'Unsung Heroes of Cryptography', https://simonsingh.net/media/articles/maths-and-science/unsung-heroes-of-cryptography/ cf. Steven Levy, 'The Open Secret', *Wired*, 1/1999, 04.1.1999.

44 Ibid. The citation comes from a 1997 release by GCHQ which is no longer accessible on the internet, but is reproduced in James Ellis, 'The Story of Non-Secret Encryption', 1987, https://cryptome.org/jya/ellisdoc.htm

45 W. T. Gowers, 'The Two Cultures of Mathematics', in V. Arnold et al. (eds), *Mathematics, Frontiers and Perspectives* (American Mathematical Society, Providence, 2000).

46 *British Sigint*, Three, pp. 60, 64.

47 Smith, 'Bletchley Park and the Development of the Rockex.

48 Templer, 'Review of Service Intelligence'.

49 2.72, GCHQ, 'Graduate Electrical Engineers, CSC 6/77.

50 GCHQ and the JTLS Cheltenham, 'Careers for Graduates'.

51 Report of 'Inter-Departmental Languages Requirement Committee', 4.67, D/1102/1 pt II.

52 S.L.P. /P (59)11, 16.11.59, DEFE 10/343; Minute by K 31, 'Russian Language Training: Conference of Chief Instructors', 10.12.70, E/1105/6 pt I.

53 *British Sigint*, Young to Hooper, 7.2.67, FCO 79/2-; ML (67) Ist meeting, Appendix, 'Inter-Universities Chinese Language School', 28.2.67, ED 181/110.

54 Minute, 6.3.72, D/1104/5 pt II Annexe.

55 Memorandum by Templer, 16.12.1960, DEFE 23/23.

56 Minute in DK, 5.10.65, 'Interpretership Examinations', E/1105/6 pt I.

57 CSC, 5.68, 'Government Communications Headquarters (A Department of the Foreign Office). Language Specialist Class', CSC 6/73.

58 GCHQ and the JTLS Cheltenham, 'Careers for Graduates'.

59 Memorandum by Nicholl, 9.4.68, D/1102/1 pt II.

60 S.L.P. /P. (59) 9, 5.8.39, DEFE 10/343.

61 Memorandum 'Linguist Specialist Open Competition, 1967', 29.6.67, D/1102/1 pt II.

62 *British Sigint*, Four, p. 448.

63 'Language Incentives, Record of a Meeting held in A/0610 on 28 February 1972', 22.3.72, E/1105/6 pt I.

64 'Language Allowances in the Administration Group and the LS Class', 9.6.82, E/1105/6 pt II.

65 'Note of a Meeting held on 25th January 1956, at the Civil Service Commission', Minute by E. J. D. Warne, CSC, to Mayes, 6/2/56, CSC 5/1105.

66 Memorandum 9.12.69, 'Supply of LS Class for J30', D/1102/1 pt II.

67 Memorandum J21T, 'Language Incentives', 17.4.72, E/1105/6 pt I.

68 Personal Memoirs in GCHQ Archives. This particular source mentions an 'ICL 1604' computer, which did not exist. Obviously, it referred to the 'ICT 1904' model, the best British computer of the day, and good by international standards, which were just being introduced in 1965.

69 GCHQ, 'General Interim Report No. 2, Electronic Computers, An account of early computers based on based on six lectures delivered at GCHQ between July and November 1949', HW 76/1.

70 *British Sigint*, Two, pp. 137–38.

71 Ibid., Three, pp. 202–5, 630–32.

72 Johnson, *American Cryptology: Book One*, pp. 195– 205; 'NSA Early Computer History', especially 'History of NSA General-Purpose Electronic Digital Computers' (1964) and 'NSA's Key Role in Major Developments in Computer Science, Parts One and Two' (2006), https://www.nsa.gov/news-features/declassified-documents/nsa-early-computer-history/

73 'Notes of Discussion at Cheltenham on 11 March, 1957, with Dr. J. Morgan and Staff', by Milner Barry, T 222/1304.

74 *British Sigint*, Three, pp. 646–69.

75 Ibid., p. 649.

76 Ibid., Three, p. 654.

77 Ibid., p. 651.

78 Ibid., pp. 865–66.

79 Poulden to Carey, 12.11.71, CAB 184/15.

80 'Notes of Discussion at Cheltenham on 11 March, 1957, with Dr. J. Morgan and Staff', by Milner Barry, T 222/1304.

81 Poulden to Carey, 19.9.71, CAB 184/14; Richard Aldrich, 'GCHQ and UK Computer Policy, Teddy Poulden, ICL and IBM', pp. 240–61, in Malcolm Murfett (ed.), *Shaping British Foreign and Defence Policy in the Twentieth Century, a Tough Ask in Turbulent Times* (Palgrave Macmillan, 2014); Martin Campbell-Kelly, *ICL: A business and Technical History* (OUP, 1989); John Hendry, *Innovating for Failure: government policy and the early British computer industry* (MIT Press, 1990.

82 Foreign Office, 'Working Party on Computers', Third Meeting, 14.12.67, CAB 163/119.

83 'Something More about Computers', *Contact*, No. 24, 3rd Issue 1977, pp. 10–14; 'T Division GCHQ', *Contact*, No. 39, 3rd Issue, 1982, p. 15.

84 'CSOS Bude Part 1', *Contact*, No. 27, 3rd Issue, 1978, pp. 10–11.

85 'The Hewlett Packard 9845T Microcomputers for Local Aids on Stations', *Contact*, No. 36, 3rd Issue, 1981.

86 Personal Memoirs in GCHQ Archives.

87 'GCHQ Organisation -4, K Division', *Contact*, No. 33, 3rd Issue, 1980, p. 20.

88 'The Falklands Crisis: Review of Sigint Performance and Lessons'. P/8210/7/1 Part 1.

89 Memorandum by Poulden, 'Central Policy Review of the British Computing Industry, 29.6.71, CAB 184/12.

90 'The Hewlett Packard 9845T', *Contact*.

CHAPTER 10

1 FCO Historians, *Women and the Foreign Office, A History, History Notes: Issue 20* (FC); Helen McCarthy, *Women of the World, The Rise of the Female Diplomat* (London, Bloomsbury, 2014).

2 Knox to Denniston, 10.8.40, HW 14/8.

3 Marion Hill, *Bletchley Park People* (The History Press, Stroud, 2008); Hill, p. 79.

4 Michie to Good, 13.7.97, 1.9.98, Donald Michie papers, ADD MS 89072/1/1, British Library.

5 I. J. Good, 'Early Work on Computers at Bletchley', *Annals of the History of Computing* 1/1, July 1979, p. 41.

6 Memorandum by Clarke, 'Naval Cryptography in War Time', *c.* 2.37, HW 3/1; Squadron-Leader Jones's Section, no date or author, HW 3/164.

7 LDO to A.D. (A), 25.2.44, HW 3/166; Squadron-Leader Jones's Section, no date or author, HW 3/164.

8 'History of C.M.Y. Section and The Development of Civil (International) W/T Interception during the War, 1939–1945', HW 3/162.

9 'History of Hut 3, Volume 1, HW 3/119, pp. 45–46, 122.

10 Nigel de Grey, 'Summary of Sigint Operations 1939–1945', HW 14/145.

11 Margaret Porter, 'Memories of a WW 2 WAAF W/Op', 10.8.03, Intelligence Corps Museum (ICM), Chicksands.

12 BPTA, *Other peoples' stories book three* (2001), transcript of interview with Joan Allen.

13 Yvonne Jones, n.d., 'R.A.F. Chicksands Priory', ICM, Chicksands.

14 Marjorie Arbury, 'Memories of a Y Operator', 9.7.2002, ICM, Chicksands.

15 Aileen Clayton, *The Enemy is Listening, The Story of the Y Service* (1982).

16 E. M. Kemp-Jones et al., *Civil Service Department, Management Studies 3, The Employment of Women in the Civil Service*, 14.6.71.

17 GCHQ, 'Careers for Graduates', 1970, GCHQ Archives.

18 Memorandum by K, 'Falklands Crisis Review', 20.7.82, P/8210/7/1 pt I.

19 *Contact*, No. 2, Second Quarter 1971, 'Hawklaw', p. 13; *Contact*, No. 25, Ist Issue, 1978, 'Station Closures, CSOS Gilnahirk', p. 18–19; *Contact*, No. 12, 4th Quarter 1973, CSOS Cheadle', pp. 12–13.

20 *British Sigint*, Two, p. 81.

21 David French, *Military Identities: The Regimental System, the British Army and the British People, c. 1870–2000* (OUP, 2008).

22 Marie Hicks, *Programmed Inequality: How Britain Discarded Women Technologists and Lost its Edge in Computing* (Boston, MIT Press, 2018).

23 Joe Devanney and Catherine Haddon, *Women and Whitehall, Gender and the Civil Service since 1979,* Institute for Government, King's College, London, September 2015, pp. 12–13.

24 'Speech to 'Ladies of CIA'', 31.10.91, by Anne Z. Caracristi, Caracristi Papers, National Cryptologic Museum Library.

25 Ibid., p. 57–8.

26 History of Postal Censorship, pp. 409–10.

27 Lycett to Rozer, 2.5.48, HW 3/88. TNA WO 374/32200.

28 Elsdale to Harris, 25.5.28, HW 62/19; *London Gazette,* issues 33121, 5.1.26, 39080, 1.12.50.

29 Foreign Office to Civil Service Commission, 16.12.24, FO 366/815.

30 'Summary of Documents relating to Staff of G.C.& C.S.', Chief Clerk, 7.7.22, HW 3/35.

31 Martin Sugarman, 'Breaking the Codes: Jewish personnel at Bletchley Park', and 'A supplement to 'Breaking the Codes: Jewish personnel at Bletchley Park', *Jewish Historical Studies*, Vols 40 (2005) and 43 (2011), pp. 197–246, 213–222.

32 Cf. p. 559.

33 'Wybrow Case', no date or author, but 1950 by internal evidence, KV 2/3293; minute by Hayter, 8/3/49, FO 1093/390; Andrew, *Defence of the Realm*, pp. 365–6. For the Lavon affair, cf. Uri Bar Joseph, *Intelligence Intervention in the Politics of Democratic States, The United States, Israel and Britain*, Pennsylvania State University Press, 1995, pp. 149–254.

34 Minute by Burrows, 2.3.49, FO 1093/390. Michael Ettinghausen to John Ferris, email of 25.5.2021.

35 Somerville to Hayes, 27.2.56, CSC 5/1139.

36 'Nationality Rules for Staff Employed on Special Signals Duties – Note by the Air Ministry', 1962, CAB 21/4744.

37 'Civil Servants as security risks on other than Communist or Fascist Grounds', 26.4.57, CAB 21/4530.

38 For introductions to the lengthy literature on positive vetting, cf. Lomas, *Attlee Governments,* Chapter Six, and Andrew, *Defence of the Realm,* pp. 389–99.

39 Security Conference of Privy Councilors, SCPC (55) 3rd meeting, 12.12.55, CAB 134/1325.

40 Security Conference of Privy Councilors, SCPC (55) 5th meeting, 22.12.55, CAB 134/1325.

41 James Southern, 'Homosexuality in the Foreign Office, 1967–1991', *FCO History Notes: Issue 19* (London, FCO).

42 Ibid.

43 https://www.gchq.gov.uk/speech/director-gchq-s-speech-at-stonewall-workplace-conference-as-delivered

44 Report of the Security Commission, D 16.12.81, PREM 19/1634; Daniel W. B. Lomas, 'Research Note: Security, Scandal, and the Security Commission report, 1981', INS, 2020.

45 Southern, 'Homosexuality'.

46 'Langeleben in the Beginning-1951', Draft History Project, Langeleben and the Intercept Business, Chapter One, www.langeleben.co.uk/draftproject/draft_004.htm

47 *Contact,* No. 4, 4th Quarter 1971, 'CSOS Flowerdown', pp. 11–12.

48 Ibid., No. 12, 4th Quarter 1973, CSOS Cheadle', pp. 4–22.

49 Ibid., No. 8, 4th Quarter 1972, 'CSOS Scarborough', pp. 14–31; ibid. No. 37, 4th Issue, 1981, 'CSOS Scarborough (UKC 117)–Part 2'.

50 Ibid., No. 23, 2nd Edition, 1977, 'UKC 100 Part Two', pp. 18–22; Contact, No. 24, 3rd Issue, 1977, 'UKC 100–Part 3', pp. 14–22.

51 David Thorp, *The Silent Listener* (History Press, 2012), pp. 10–23.

52 Draft History Project, Langeleben and the Intercept Business, Chapter Four, 'Langeleben 1958–59, As Recalled by Chris Rundle', op.cit.

53 Tony Cash, *The Coder Special Archive* (Hodgson, Kingston upon Thames, September 2012), Chapter Nine, pp. 9–16.

54 Ibid., Chapter Five.

55 *Contact*, No. 24, 3rd Issue, 1977, 'UKC 100 – Part 3', p. 16.

56 Ibid., No. 25, 1st Issue, 1978, 'Station Closures, CSOS Gilnahirk', p. 16.

57 Ibid., No. 6, Second Quarter 1972, 'Malta', p. 2.

58 Ibid., No. 3, 3rd Quarter, 1971, 'Singapore', p. 17.

59 Ibid., No. 1, First Quarter 1971, 'Ascension Island', pp. 10–20.

60 *British Sigint*, Two, p. 463.

61 Ibid., p. 461.

62 *Contact*, No. 10, 2nd Quarter 1973, Letter to the Editor, pp. 2–3.

63 *Contact*, No. 24, 3rd Issue 1977, 'Grouper II Training and Trials 1977/78', pp. 24–26.

64 *Contact*, No. 8th Quarter 1972, 'CSOS Scarborough', p. 23.

65 *Conflict*, p 40.

66 *British Sigint*, Three, pp. 269–77.

67 Ibid., p. 277.

68 Minute by Winnifrith, 11.11.59, T 215/391.

69 *British Sigint*, Three, p. 458.

70 Ibid., p. 459.

71 Ibid., p. 459.

72 Ibid., p. 456.

73 Michael Herman, *Intelligence Services in the Information Age, Theory and Practice* (Taylor & Francis, London, 2001), pp. 180–91.

74 *British Sigint*, Three, pp. 454–64; Ibid., Four, pp. 453–75.

75 *Contact*, No.1, First Quarter 1971, 'From the Director', p. 3.

76 *Conflict*, pp. 39, 42.

77 *Contact*, No. 6, Second Quarter 1972, 'CSOS Wincombe', p. 11.

78 'Language Allowances in the Administration Group and the LS Class', 9.6.82, E/1105/6 pt II.

79 Minutes of Evidence Taken Before the Eployment Committee of the House of Commons, 8.2.1984, pp. 50–70.

80 *British Sigint*, Five.

81 'Memories of the Cryptologic Business'.

82 *Conflict*, pp.35–6.

83 'Note for the Record', by Badham, 31.10.79, memorandum by Herbecq, 22.10.79, to PS/Minister of State, 'No Strike Agreements in the Civil Service', BA 19/721; Armstrong Affadavit.

84 *Conflict*, p 33.

85 *British Sigint*, Five.

86 'Secret War', *Sunday Times*, 5.2.84.

87 Ian Beesley, *The Official History of the Cabinet Secretaries*.

88 Ibid., pp. 442–9.

89 The best account of the union ban is Aldrich, 'GCHQ', though key evidence was published later, augmented by Charles Moore, *Margaret Thatcher: The Authorised Biography, Volume Two: Everything She Wants* (Penguin, 2016) and Beesley, *Cabinet Secretaries*. Susan Corby, 'The GCHQ Union Ban: 1984–1997: the unions' strategy and the outcome', *Labour History Review*, 65/3, Winter 2000, pp. 317–32, is a sound study. H. Lanning and Richard Norton-Taylor, *A Conflict of Loyalties: GCHQ, 1984–1991* (Cheltenham: New Clarion Press, 1991) contains useful material, but its comments on GCHQ leadership and the government, and union actions, are partial.

90 *Conflict*, pp.109–12.

91 Moore, *Thatcher*, pp. 138–42, 142–150.

CHAPTER II

1 Memo 25.10.79, 'GCT Scheme: A Paper for Discussion with Staff Side', E/1100/28 pt II.

2 *Contact*, No. 12, 4th Quarter 1973, 'CSOS Cheadle', pp. 4–22; ibid., No. 20, 2nd Edition, 1976, 'No. 399 Signals Unit Royal Air Force Digby', pp. 7–12; ibid., No. 23, 2nd Edition, 1977, 'UKC 100 Part 2', pp. 18–22; ibid., No. 24. 3rd Issue, 1977, 'UKC 100 – Part 3', pp. 14–22; ibid., No. 36, 3rd Issue, 1981, 'CSOS Scarborough (UKC 117) – Part 1', p. 13. ibid., No. 37, 4th Issue, 1981, 'CSOS Scarborough (UKC 117) – Part 2'.

3 Ibid., No 27/3, 1978, 'CSOS Bude', pp. 2–14.

4 Alfred Price, *The History of US Electronic Warfare*, Volumes One (Association of Old Crows, Westford MA, 1984), Two (*The Renaissance Years, 1946 to 1968*) (1989) and Three, *Rolling Thunder Through the Allied Forces, 1964 to 2000* (2000).

5 *British Sigint*, Two, pp. 32–44.

6 Ibid., Four, p. 23.

7 Ibid., Three, p. 64

8 Personal Memoirs in GCHQ Archives.

9 Ibid.

10 Ibid.

11 'FOLKLORE: An Innovative Approach Toward a User Interface', *Cryptolog, The Journal of Technical Health*, 22/4, 1996, pp. 11–16, https://www.nsa.gov/Portals/70/documents/news-features/declassified-documents/cryptologs/cryptolog_134.pdf

12 'FALKLANDS: Notes of Meeting Held on 18 May 1982', 18.5.82, D/2304/14 pt IV.

13 'The Falklands Crisis: Review of SIGINT Performance and Lessons', n.d., *c.* August 1982, P/8210/7/1.

14 Ibid.

15 Personal Memoirs in GCHQ Archives.

16 Ibid.

17 Interview with unnamed official.

18 Kit Braunholtz, email 14.8.2016, on Robert Churchhouse, 'A GCHQ memoir', 15.1.2010, https://18thcenturydiary.org.uk/a-gchq-memoir/

19 Interview with unnamed official.

20 Cavendish-Bentinct and Capel-Dunn, 'The Intelligence Machine'.

21 Minute 'Language Money for GCHQ's Executive and Clerical Classes', E/1105/6.

22 *British Sigint*, Two, p. 162.

23 LSIB/14/ 1979, 5.4.79, 'The State of Sigint, 1978', LSIB 1979.

24 Leonard Hooper, A 2, 'Suez Telegrams', 4.9.56, K/517/24.

25 Selwyn Lloyd to Jones, 20.9.56, K/517/24.

26 Le Bailly to Hooper, 16.4.78, ZIC /4/21.

27 Draft memorandum by Hooper, 'What Intelligence can and cannot do', n.d. but *c.* July 1974, ZIC /4/21.

28 Ibid.

CHAPTER 12

1 Johnson, *American Cryptology, Book One*, p. 118. For the best exposition of the conventional version of Berlin and espionage, cf. David. E. Murphy, Sergei A. Kondrashev, George Bailey, *Battleground Berlin, CIA vs. KGB in the Cold War* (Yale University Press, 1997).

2 Robert Louis Benson and Michael Warner, *Venona: Soviet Espionage and the American Response, 1939–1957* (NSA/CIA, Washington, 1996); Johnson, *American Cryptology, Book One*. pp. 277–78.

3 Carol B. Davis, *Candle in the Dark: COMINT and Soviet Industrial Secrets, 1946–1956* (CCH, 2017), quoting Robert Benson and John Schindler, 'LINK: The Greatest Intelligence Disaster in U.S. History', paper presented to 2003 Cryptologic History Symposium.

4 Peterson, *Bourbon*, pp. 29–297.

5 S/ARU/T3368, 14.10.49, *passim*, HW 75/482.

6 *Sigint History*, Two, pp. 802–10.

7   HW 75/24, HW 75/47–8, HW 75/73, HW 75/78.

8   Davis, *Candle*, pp. 12–15, 19, 47; *British Sigint*, Two, pp. 20–22.

9   See pp. 522–4.

10 Davis, *Candle*, p. 5.

11 Halford to C, 26.1.49, FO 1093/490.

12 Ibid.

13 COS Confidential Annex to COS (48) 155th Meeting, 3.11.48, 'Intelligence Requirements for "Cold War" Planning', FO 1093/370.

14 Ibid.

15 JIC (48) 19 (o) (2nd Revised Draft, 11.5.48, 'Sigint Intelligence Requirements – 1948', L/WS/1/1196).

16 Minutes, JIC Meeting, 24.3.55, JIC (55) 25th Meeting, CAB 159/18; 'Confidential Annex' to JIC (55) 34th Meeting, 28.4.55, CAB 159/19.

17 JIC (51) 126, 'Present State of our Intelligence on the Soviet Union, The European Satellites and China and Measures to Improve It', 7.1.52, CAB 158/13.

18 *British Sigint*, Three, pp. 44–60, 1143–8, 1176–83; Goodman, JIC, Volume One, XXX.

19 USAREUR Intelligence Estimate 1961 (U), Headquarters, United States Army, Europe, Office of the Deputy Chief of Staff, Intelligence, 1.1.61; William Burr and Robert A. Wampler (eds), *Lifting the Veil on Cosmic: Declassified US and British Documents on NATO Military Planning and Threat Assessments on the Warsaw Pact,* Parallel History Project on Cooperative Security, 2002.

20 LSIB(80) 3rd Meeting, Minutes, 5.11.80, LSIB 7/80, 17.10.80, 'The Concept of Sigint Support to Military Operations in Tension and War', LSIB 1980.

21 *Contact*, No. 37, 1/1982, 'WINTEX 81', pp. 9–11; *Contact*, 3/38, 'WINTEX 81 Part 2', pp. 20–23.

22 COS (57) 174, 29.7.57, 'Period of Planning for Global War', DEFE 5/77.

23 COS (61), 3rd Meeting, 10.1.61, DEFE 4/133.

24 Strong to Dickson, 24.1.58, JIC (58) 4 (Final), CAB 158/31. William Burr and Svetlana Savranskaya, 'Previously Classified Interviews with Former Soviet Authorities Reveal U.S. Strategic Intelligence Failure over Decades' National Security Archive, 11.9.09, https://nsarchive2.gwu.edu/nukevault/ebb285/), reprints a 1995 study by the Office of Net Assessment at the Pentagon, which offers useful material on Soviet attitudes on these issues during the middle and late Cold War.

25 JP (58) 34 Final, 26.3.58, DEFE 6/49; JIC (55) 7 (Final), 'The Soviet Strategic Air Plan in the Early Stages of a General War in the period up to 1959', 16.2.55, CAB 158/19.

26 USAREUR Intelligence Estimate–1961; Burr and Wampler (eds), *Lifting the Veil*.

27 JIC (59) 33, 'Warning of an Attack on the West in Global War up to the end of 1960, 1.4.59, CAB 158/36; JIC (6), 33 (Final) 'Warning and Timing of a Soviet Attack on the West in Global War', 21.10.60, CAB 158/40.

28 Ehlers, *Targeting the Third Reich*.

29 Kaplan, To Kill Nations; Len Scott and Stephen Twigge, *Planning Armageddon, Britain, The United States, and the Command of Western Nuclear Forces, 1945–1964* (Routledge, London, 2013).

30 Michael Warner, 'The Collapse of Intelligence Support for Air Power, 1944–52', *Studies in Intelligence*, 49/3, https://www.cia.gov/library/center-for-the-study-of-intelligence/csi-publications/csi-studies/studies/vol49no3/html_files/Intel_Air_Power_4.htm

31 Kevin O'Daly, 'Living in the shadow: Britain and the USSR's nuclear weapon delivery systems 1949–62', PhD diss., University of Westminster, 2016, pp. 115–47.

32 Donald E. Welzenbach and Gregory W. Pedlow, *The CIA and Overhead Reconnaissance: The U2 and Oxcart Programs, 1954–74* (Simon & Schuster, 2016; original, CIA, Washington, 1992); CIA history of the office of special activities to 1969, https://archive.org/details/HistoryOfTheOfficeOfSpecialActivitiesFromInceptionTo1969/page/n8

33 Stanley G. Zabetakis and John F. Peterson, 'The Diyarbikir Radar', 2.7.96. CIA Library, https://www.cia.gov/library/center-for-the-study-of-intelligence/kent-csi/vol8no4/html/v08i4a05p_0001.htm.

34 O'Daly, 'Living in the shadow', pp. 72–74, Aldrich, 'GCHQ', pp. 320–5.

35 'Soviet Research and Development 1957', 14.4.58, JIC (58) 42, CAB 158/32.

36 Joint Technical Committee Meeting, 7.9.54, DEFE 10/497; JIC to ACAS (I) 9.9.60, AIR 8/1953; Memorandum by JIB 18.8.60, 'Definition of Responsibilities for the Assessment of Intelligence in the Sphere of National Defence: Comment of JIB on an Undated Air Ministry Note', AIR 8/1953.

37 Templer, 'Review of Service'.

38 *Aviation News*, 21.20.57, 'How U.S. Taps Soviet Missile Secrets'.

39 Sigint Production Review, 1977, 4.4.78,

40 *British Sigint*, Three, pp. 44–60, 1143–48, 1176–83

41 Ibid., pp. 53; Johnson, *American Cryptology, Book One*, pp. 253–56.

42 Minute by Tovey, 9.8.68, 'DGI/DIS Colonel Discussion with Mr. Healey on Czech Crisis Intelligence', J/2300/18 Part 1.

43 Peter Davies, *The Authorised History of British Defence Economic Intelligence, A Cold War in Whitehall, 1925–1990* (Routledge, London, 2018); Huw Dylan, Defence Intelligence and the Cold War, Britain's Joint Intelligence Bureau, 1945–1964 (OUP, Oxford, 2014).

44 S/ARU-E/C125, 12.2.48, HW 75/127.

45 CREAM/ZIP/RUE/C91, 28.1.47, HW 75/105; S/ARU-E/C490, 19.1.1950, HW 75/160.

46 Minute, 'Czech Crisis and J Division', 22.11.68, J/2300/18 Annexe.

47 Production Review Meeting, 10.4.81, Memorandum by Johnson, 'Production Review 1984', 13.5.84; LSIB/1/81, 30/12/80, 'The State of Sigint 1981', LSIB 1981.

48 *Contact*, No. 12, 4th Quarter 1973, 'CSOS Cheadle', pp. 4–22.

49 Ibid., No. 8, 4th Quarter 1972, 'CSOS Scarborough', pp. 14–31; ibid., No. 36, 3rd Issue, 1981, 'CSOS Scarborough – Part 1', p. 13, ibid., No. 37, 4th Issue, 1981, 'CSOS Scarborough – Part 2'.

50 Ibid., No. 23, 2nd Edition, 1977, 'Part Two', pp. 18– 22, ibid., No. 24. 3rd Issue, 1977, ' Part 3', pp. 14–22.

51 Peter Hennessy, *Silent Deep, The Royal Navy Submarine Service since 1945* (Penguin, 2016).

52 Johnson, *American Cryptology*, Book One, p. 118

53 'Berlin Crisis, Record of a Meeting Held on 26th May, 1959', 26.5.59, D/2303/3 pt II.

54 Roy Marsden, 'Operation 'Schooner/Nylon/: RAF Flying in the Berlin Control Zone', INS, 13/4 ((1998), pp. 178–93; Kevin Paul Wright, 'Cold War Reconnaissance Flights along the Berlin Corridors and in the Berlin Control Zone 1960–90: Risk, Coordination and Sharing', INS, 30/5, 2014, pp. 615–36.

55 Tony Geraghty, *BRIXMIS: the untold exploits of Britain's most daring Cold War spy mission* (London: HarperCollins, 1997); Major General Peter Williams, 'BRIXMIS in the 1980s: The Cold War's "Great Game"', in British Commanders'-in-Chief Mission to the Soviet Force in Germany (BRIXMIS): Photographs and Documents, Parallel History Project on Cooperative Security, http://www.php.isn.ethz.ch/kms2.isn. ethz.ch/serviceengine/Files/PHP/29544/ipublicationdocument_ singledocument/ cfc33b48-d4eb-4ad4-a253-fb9dec50d345/en/BRIXMIS_ 1980s.pdf .

56 Tony Cunnane, *A Yorkshire Aviator's Autobiography*, 'No. 26 Signals Unit'.

57 'Post-Mortem of Handling of Suez Crisis and Lessons for the Future', 29.11.56, K/517/24/Middle East Crisis.

58 Lucas, *Britain and Suez*.

59 'Post-Mortem of Handling of Suez Crisis and Lessons for the Future', 29.11.56, K/517/24/Middle East Crisis.

60 Action at 1700 Meeting on 1st November, 1956, XII/I/48, Policy Suez Crisis 1956.

61 SUKLO to GCHQ, 22.11.56, 961/11, XII/1/48.

62 NSA Comments on GCHQ 'Post-Mortem on Handling of Suez Crisis and Lessons for the Future', no author or date, *c.* May 1957, J/188/I, Crisis Planning.

63 Memorandum by K1H, 14.12.56, '1 WRLS. REGT. – A point arising from the crisis', J/188/1.

64 SUKLO to GCHQ, 15.11.56, D/12/1/48, Policy Suez Crisis 1956.

65 GCHQ London to GCHQ, 9.22.56, D/12/1/48, Policy Suez Crisis 1956.

66 AD2 to Director, 8.11.56, D/12/1/48, Policy Suez Crisis 1956.

67 3/ARU/C9088, 9.6.57, 'Summary of Activities of Soviet Army Divisions in Hungary 24th October, 1956–31st April 1957', *passim*, ARU/C Reporting 1957.

68 'Report on 1615 Meeting on 7th November, 1956', D/12/1/48, Policy Suez Crisis 1956.

69 *British Sigint*, Three, pp. 1159– 62.

70 'Report on 1615 Meeting on 7 th November, 1956', D/12/1/48, Policy Suez Crisis 1956.

71 *British Sigint*, Three, pp. 1159–62.

72 James H. Hansen, 'Soviet Deception in the Cuban Missile Crisis', Center for the Study of Intelligence, CIA, 46/1, is the best account of Soviet *maskirovka*, as Dino Brugioni, *Eyeball to Eyeball, The Inside Story of the Cuban Missile Crisis* (New York, Random House, 1991) is of American intelligence during the crisis. Neither author had access to the Sigint record, and Brugioni's account rests largely on personal experience and interviews, and largely is unsourced. 'NSA and the Cuban Missile Crisis' (Ft. Meade, Maryland, Center for Cryptologic History, 1998), and Johnson, *American Cryptology: Book II, Centralization Wins*, pp. 317–30 are the best accounts of US Sigint.

73 Minute, 26.11.56, J/188/1 – Crisis Planning.

74 UKN 125 to SCA 2078 et al., 20.7.62, 2X-AR3U-S-C2338/620720//SE, Cuba/1962.

75 UKN 125 to SCA 2078. et al., 31.7.62, 2X-AR3U-S-C2366/620731//SE, 13.9.62, 2X-AR3U-C/2524/620923//SE, 4.10.62, 2X-AR3U-C/2597/621004//SE, Cuba/1962.

76 UKN 125 to SCA 2078. et al., 27.10.62, 2X-AR3U-S-C2682/621026//SE, Cuba/1962.

77 Kaplan, *Kill Nations*.

78 Petit to Tovey, 16.1.69, DIS, First Draft, 'Warning of Warsaw Pact Attack Against NATO in the Central Area of ACE', J/2300/18 Part 1.

79 Memorandum 25.5.68, 'J Division Post Mortem of the Czechoslovak Crisis (5th to 21st May)', J/2300/18 Part 1.

80 David Glantz, *Soviet Military Deception in the Second World War* (Frank Cass, 1988).

81 Anatoly Golitzyn, *New Lies for Old* (New York, Dodd, Mean and Co., 1984)

82 James H. Hansen, 'Soviet Deception in the Cuban Missile Crisis', CIA.

83 Memorandum by Tovey, 21.7.69, 'Service to BAOR and RAF Germany: Proposed Presentation of the Czech Crisis', J/2300/18, Pt. 2.

84 Memorandum by Tovey, 15.12.69, 'Czech Crisis Presentation: Secretary JIC's request for a 'Record'', J/2300/18 Pt. 2.

85 J 276/1, 1.12.69, J/2300/18, Pt. 2.

86 Memoranda by Tovey, 21.7.69, 'Service to BAOR and RAF Germany: Proposed Presentation of the Czech Crisis', 15.12.69, 'Czech Crisis Presentation: Secretary JIC's request for a 'Record', and 26.1.70, 'The CPX of August 1968', J/2300/18, Pt. 2.

87   MOD Secretary to GCHQ, 2.8.68, P 021100Z, Tovey to Murray, 21.1.69, J/4578/2300/18, J/2300/18 Part 1.

88   Memorandum by Tovey, 20.10.68, 'Post-Mortem on the Czech Crisis', J/2300/18 Part 1, Annexe.

89   Memorandum by Tovey, 11.9.68, 'Czech Crisis: Sigint Contribution', J/2300/18 Part 1.

90   Memorandum by Tovey, 20.10.68, 'Post-Mortem on the Czech Crisis'; J/2300/18 Part 1, Annexe.

91   Memorandum by Hooper, 5.8.68, J/2300/18 Part 1.

92   This paragraph is based on Memorandum 25.5.68, 'J Division Post Mortem of the Czechoslovak Crisis, and Memorandum by Tovey, 20.10.68, 'Post-Mortem on the Czech Crisis', J/2300/18 Part 1, Annexe.

93   Memorandum by Tovey, 20.10.68, 'Post-Mortem on the Czech Crisis'; J/2300/18 Part 1, Annexe; 3/A/CMJ/C33-69, 21.10.69, 'The Czechoslovakia Crisis, Part II. Activity by Warsaw Pact Forces Associated with Exercise Sumava', C33-69, Czech Summaries; 3/A/CMJ/C43-70, 8.6.70, 'The Czechoslovakia Crisis Part V. The Invasion of Czechoslovakia', CS43-70, Czech Summaries.

94   Documents No. 53–54, Vojtech Masty, Malcolm Byrne, Anna Locher and Christian Neunlist, 'An Inside History of the Warsaw Pact, 1955–1991: Documentary Companion to A Cardboard Castle?', Parallel History Project on Cooperative Security, https://www.fi les.ethz.ch/isn/108638/10_ACardboardCastle.pdf

95   Memorandum by Tovey, 20.10.68, 'Post-Mortem on the Czech Crisis'; J/2300/18 Part 1, Annexe.

96   Memorandum by Tovey, 9.8.68, 'DGI/DSI Colonel Discussions with Mr. Healey in Czech Crisis Intelligence', J/2300/18 Part 1.

97   Tovey to Rendle, 13.9.68, J/2300/18 Part 1.

98   Petit to Tovey, 12.8.68, DIS 9.8.68, 1500/DIS/26/5, 9.8.68, 'Military Intelligence Gathered on Czechoslovak/Soviet Military Confrontation and the Relevance to any Future Soviet Bloc Troop and Aircraft Movements Threatening NATO', J/2300/18 Part 1.

99   Petit to Tovey, 16.1.69, DIS, First Draft, 'Warning of Warsaw Pact Attack Against NATO in the Central Area of ACE', J/2300/18 Part 1.

100 Tovey to Rendle, 13.9.68, J/2300/18 Part 1. The Cierna-Bratislava discussions were between the Czechoslovak government and those of other Warsaw Pact nations.

101 Tovey to Petit, 17.12.68, J/4371/2300/18, J/2300/18 Part 1.

102 Minute by Tovey, 18.11.68, J/2300/18 Part 1.

103 Memorandum by Tovey, 20.10.68, 'Post-Mortem on the Czech Crisis'; J/2300/18 Part 1, Annexe.

104 Memorandum, 25.5.68, 'J Division Post Mortem'.

105 Memo, 6.11.68, 'Sigint and the Czech Crisis, 'A Strategy for J Division', J/2300/18 Part 1, Annexe.

106 Technical Supplement to 2/AA/24068-79 (RUA), Minsk ADD: 'Status of Fighter Direction Posts in the Riga ADZ as at 1 March 1979', 31.7.79.

107 2/AA/APP/J26K2-81 (RUJ), 'GSFG: 47 GTD, 3SA, Field Training Exercise, 4–9 August 1980', 13.5.81,.

108 2/AA/27092-81, 5.6.81, 'Soviet Baltic Fleet and Baltic Fleet Air Force Development Report, 1– 81'.

109 2/AA/24043-79 (RUA), 10.5.79, 'Soviet Long Range Air Force Order of Battle', 3/AA/26168-79 (RUM), 13.12.79, 'GSFG: Ground Forces Order of Battle from Sigint 31 August 1979'; 2/AA/29102-81, 15.11.81, 'EGAF: Locations, Equipments and Pilot Strengths as at 31 Oct 1981', 2/AA/29074-81, 'GDR: Ground Forces Sigint Order of Battle as at 30 June 1981', 7.10.81.

110 2/AA/23512 79 (CMJ), 2.5.79, 2/AA/24070-79 (RUA), 'Operations by PX090 TU-126 Airborne Warning and Control (AWAC) Aircraft over the Western USSR sic, 1978', 13.6.79.

111 Douglas MacEachin, 'Predicting the Soviet Invasion of Afghanistan: The Intelligence Community's Record' (CIA, 2000); Interagency Intelligence Memorandum, October 1980, 'The Soviet Invasion of Afghanistan: Implications for Warning', https://www.cia.gov/library/readingroom/docs/DOC_0000278538.pdf

112 2/AA/22038-79 (RUJ), 6.8.79, 'Increased Soviet General Staff Communications with Kabul since 3 Aug 1979', 2/AA/23003-79 (RUH), 17.9.79, 'Soviet Reaction to Unrest in Afghanistan, 13–17 September 1979', 2/AA/22046-79, 28.9.79, 'Codeword Messages and increased Messages Affecting sic VTA and VDV', 2/AA/22058-79 28.11.79, 'Slightly Increased General Staff Communications to the Turkistan Central Asian and Transbajkal MDs, 25–28 Nov'.

113 3/AA/23137-79 (CMH), 13.12.79, 'Soviet Bloc Political and Military Activity Abroad, Number No. 48–79: 6–12 Dec 1979, 3/AA/23138-79 (CMH), 15.12.79, 'Soviet Activity in Afghanistan and the Southern USSR, 15/12/79', 3/AA/23140-79 (CMH), Soviet Military Activity in' Afghanistan and the Southern USSR, 17/12/79, 17.12.79, 3/AA/23148-79 (RUH) Soviet Military Activity in the Southern USSR and Afghanistan 23/12/79'.

114 LSIB (80) 1st Meeting, 11.2.80, LSIB 1980, LSIB/6/84, 'The State of Sigint 1984', 20.7.84, LSIB 1984.

115 3/AA/23078-80 (RUH), 14.8.80, 'Exercise Activity in Transcaucasia and Turkestan MDs, August 1980'.

116 Ibid.

117 3/AA/22037-80 (RUJ) 12.9.80, 'Unusual Communications Involving Poland and Adjacent Areas'.

118 3/AA/29148, 4.11.80, 'Review of Eurcom Activity 26 October–1 November 1980'.

119 3/AA/29028-81 (CMY), 'Review of Eurcom Activity 8–14 February 81 sic',
     17.2.81, 3/AA/29054-81, 'Review of Eurcom Activity 29 March–4 April 1981',
     7.4.81; 2/AA/29071-81 (PLJ). 28.7.81, 'Polish Contingency Communications
     Close Down'.
120 Andrew, *Defence of the Realm*, pp. 836–45.
121 R. L. Garthoff, 'The KGB Reports to Gorbachev', INS, 11/2, April 1996,
     pp. 224–44; David Kahn, 'Soviet Comint in the Cold War', *Cryptologia*, 22/1,
     January 1998, pp. 1–24.

CHAPTER 13

 1 C.C. 65 (33), 19.9.63, CAB 195/23/7; Minute by Healey to Commonwealth
    Secretary, 3.2.65, FO 371/181454.
 2 The best account of Anglo-Zionist politics are Bernard Wasserstein, *The British
    in Palestine: The Mandatory Government and the Arab–Jewish Conflict, 1917–1929*
    (Royal Historical Society Studies in History Series, Number 10, RHS, London,
    1978) and Michael J. Cohen, *Palestine and the Great Powers* (Princeton University
    Press, 1982).
 3 'Visit to the Middle East by Mr. A. J. Kellar', 19.2.45, KV 4/384.
 4 C. M. (47), 6th Conclusions, Minute 3, Confidential Annexe, 15.1.47, *passim*,
    CAB 128/11.
 5 'Report on Visit to Middle East by Mr. A. J. Kellar', 7.46, KV 3/384.
 6 High Commissioner to Secretary of State, telegram No. 1111, 3.10.46, Alan
    Cunningham Papers, MECA.
 7 High Commissioner to Secretary of State, telegram No. 1119, 12.10.46, Alan
    Cunningham Papers, MECA.
 8 'Visit to the Middle East by Mr. A. J. Kellar'.
 9 Charles Tegart papers. 4/6. Diary Entry 30.12.1937, MECA.
10 SLU Clover to LSIC, BRAN/YD 300, 13.3.47, SLU Clover to SLU Fayid,
    BRAN/YD 945, 19.11.47, SLU Clover to SLU Cairo, BRAN/YD 966, 27.11.47,
    PALESTINE BRAN/YD 1947.
11 Minute by Stiebel, B.5.a., 18.7.47, KV 2/1435.
12 'Appendix to Part II, Messages Referred to in the Text', n.d. but *c.* July 1946 by
    internal evidence, CO 537/1715.
13 C to Loxley, 7.3.44, FO 1094/328.
14 West, *Liddell Diaries*, p. 235.
15 GC&CS to SLU Clover, G 6041, 17.10.45, PALESTINE PROC 1945.
16 D.D. 3 to D.D. C, 27.9.44, HW 14/112.

17 CO to GCCS, BRAN/CO 18, 20.10.45, BRAN/CO 1945.

18 Barber to DD 1, 5,8.45, HW 14/133.

19 Report of the Bland Committee, 12.10.44, CAB 301/48.

20 GC&CS to Clover, 10.10.45, No. 6150, 16.11.45, PALESTINE PROC 1945; Trafford Smith to Chadwick, 7.9.46, minute by Trafford Smith, 4.7.46, *passim*, CO 537/1735.

21 SLU Clover to SLU Cairo, BRAN/YD 578 5.7.46, PALESTINE BRAN/YD 1946.

22 SLU Clover to LSIC, 5.7.46, CO 537/1735.

23 BRAN/CO 31, 28.11.45, BRAN/CO 1945.

24 'Report on Visit to Middle East by Mr. A. J. Kellar'.

25 SLU Clover to LSIC BRAN/YD 375, 12.4.47, PALESTINE BRAN/YD 1947.

26 SLU Clover to SLU Cairo, BRAN/YD 804, 19.9.47, PALESTINE BRAN/YD 1947.

27 'Report on Visit to the Middle East by Mr. J. C. Robertson, 14th April–14th June 1947', KV 4/438. In the TNA version of this paragraph, all references to 'FOG' and 'CREAM' are redacted; I have replaced them.

28 GL Diary, pp. 156, 172, 174, 177.

29 SLU Clover to LSIC BRAN/YD 375, 12.4.47, PALESTINE BRAN/YD 1947.

30 SLU Clover to LSIC, BRAN/YD 162, 15.1.48, BRAN/YD 226, 29.1.48, SLU Clover to SLU Fayid, BRAN/YD 230, 29.1.48, BRAN/YD 1948.

31 'Report on Visit to the Middle East by Mr. J. C. Robertson.

32 SLU Clover to LSIC, BRAN/YD 561, 14.6.47, PALESTINE BRAN/YD 1947.

33 SLU Clover to LSIC, BRAN/YD 903, 3.11.47 (two telegrams) PALESTINE BRAN/YD 1947.

34 SSLU Cairo to GC&CS, BRAN/CO 37, 22.12.45, BRAN/CO 1945.

35 GL Diary, p. 247.

36 High Commissioner to Secretary of State, 1.8.46, telegram No. 1258, Alan Cunningham Papers, MECA.

37 'Visit to the Middle East by Mr. A. J. Kellar'.

38 SLU Clover to LSIC, BRAN/YD 440, 25.4.47, PALESTINE BRAN/YD 1947; 'Report on Visit to the Middle East by Mr. J. C. Robertson.

39 SLU Clover to LSIC, 3.7.46, BRAN/YD 560, PALESTINE BRAN/YD 1946.

40 'Illegal Zionist Armed Forces in Palestine and the Complicity of the Jewish Agency', n.d., *c.* July 1946, CO 537/1735.

41 SLU Cairo to LSIC, BRAN/CO 114, 19.6.46, BRAN/CO 117, 19.6.46, BRAN/CO 118, 20.6.46, *passim*, BRAN/CO 1946.

42 'Notes on the White Paper of Evidence (CMD. 6863)', n.d. or author, but by MI5 and *c.*31.7.46, by internal evidence, CO 537/1735.

43 'Illegal Zionist Armed Forces in Palestine and the Complicity of the Jewish Agency', n.d., *c.* July 1946, CO 537/1735.

44 Unsigned and undated, 'Implication of Ben-Gurion and Shertok in Hagana Activities', CO 537/1735.

45 Aaron Edwards, *Defending the Realm? The Politics of Small Wars in Britain since 1945* (OUP, 2013), pp. 25–40.

46 SLU Clover to LSIC, 28.6.46, BRAN/YD 543, PALESTINE BRAN/YD 1946.

47 SLU Clover to LSIC, BRAN/YD 556, 1.7.46, PALESTINE BRAN/YD 1946.

48 Hall to Attlee, 12.7.46, CO 537/1735.

49 Menachem Begin, *The Revolt, Story of the Irgun* (WF Allen, 1951).

50 'Illegal Zionist Armed Forces in Palestine and the Complicity of the Jewish Agency', n.d., *c.* July 1946, CO 537/1735.'Hayyim' was Weizmann and Sir John Shaw was the British Political Secretary in Jerusalem. The 'Executive' of the Jewish Agency meant power there. Rcksch perhaps was Yisrael Rokach, the mayor of Tel Aviv. 'Yemin' might be 'Yellin', for whom many candidates are possible.

51 SLU Clover to LSIC, BRAN/YD 585, 9.7.46, PALESTINE BRAN/YD 1946.

52 SLU Clover to LSIC, BRAN/YD 603, 15.7.46, PALESTINE BRAN/YD 1946.

53 SLU Cairo to LSIC, BRAN/CO 133, 15.7.46, BRAN/CO 1946.

54 SLU Clover to LSIC, BRAN/YD 564, 3.7.46, PALESTINE BRAN/YD 1946.

55 SLU Clover to LSIC, BRAN/YD 561, 3.7.46, PALESTINE BRAN/YD 1946.

56 SLU Clover to SLU Cairo, BRAN/YD 580, 8.7.46, PALESTINE BRAN/YD 1946.

57 Cabinet meeting, 11.7.46, CAB 67 (46), CAB 128/6/5.

58 SLU Clover to LSIC, BRAN/YD 627 23.7.46, PALESTINE BRAN/YD 1946.

59 Calder Walton, 'British Intelligence and Threats to British National Security after the Second World War', p. 158–60, in Matthew Grant (ed.), *The British Way in Cold Warfare: Intelligence, Diplomacy and the Bomb, 1945–1975* (Continuum, 2009)

60 'Summary of Letter from D.S.O. Palestine ref. DSO/S/P1 dated 26 July 1946', Robertson to Trafford Smith, 29.7.46, KV 2/1389.

61 SLU Clover to SLU Cairo, BRAN/YD 715, 14.8.46, PALESTINE BRAN/YD 1946.

62 SLU Clover to LSIC, BRAN/YD 800, 2.9.46, PALESTINE BRAN/YD 1946.

63 'Extract from CIRCUS report on Jewish Affairs dated 12.9.46 forwarded by D.S.O. Palestine', KV 2/1389.

64 SLU Clover to SLE Cairo, BRAN/YD 987, 30.10.46, PALESTINE BRAN/YD 1946.

65 Stephen Wagner, *Statecraft by Stealth: Secret Intelligence and British Rule in Palestine* (Ithaca, Cornell University Press, 2019).

66 'Notes on the White Paper of Evidence (CMD. 6863)', n.d. or author, but by MI5 and *c.* 31.7.46, by internal evidence, CO 537/1735.

67 Chief Secretary, Palestine, to Secretary of State, No. 1061, 12.7.46, CO 537/1735.

68 SLU Clover to LSIC, BRAN/YD 562, 3/7/46, PALESTINE BRAN/YD 1946.

69 Secretary of State to High Commissioner, telegram No. 1158, 8.7.46, CO 537/1735.

70 Hall to Attlee, 8.7.46, CO 537/1735.

71 High Commissioner to Secretary of State, No. 1156, 14.7.46, Jowitt to Hall, 15.7.46, CO 537/1735.

72 SLU Clover to PSIC, BRAN/YD 596, 11.7.46, PALESTINE BRAN/YD 1946.

73 Kellar to Trafford Smith, 30.7.46, High Commissioner to Secretary of State, telegram No. 1061, 12.7.46, CO 537/1735.

74 'Operations in Palestine, Illegal Zionist Armed Forces in Palestine and the Complicity of the Jewish Agency', minutes of ministerial meeting, 11.7.46, CO 537/1735.

75 'Illegal Zionist Armed Forces in Palestine and the Complicity of the Jewish Agency', n.d., c. July 1946, CO 537/1735.

76 Gutch to Trafford Smith, 19.8.46, CO 537/1735.

77 SLU Clover to LSIC, BRAN/YD 440, 25.4.47, PALESTINE BRAN/YD 1947.

78 Minute by Stiebel, B.5.a., 18.7.47, KV 2/1435.

79 SLU Clover to SLU Cairo, BRAN/YD 873, 23.9.46, PALESTINE BRAN/YD 1946.

80 For examples, cf. KV 2/1389–90.

81 SLU Clover to LSIC, BRAN/YD 181, 13.2.47, PALESTINE BRAN/YD 1947.

82 SLU Clover to SLU Cairo, BRAN/YD 165, 10.2.47, SLU Clover to LSIC, BRAN/YD 367, 380, 441, 31.4.47 (probably misdated for 31.3.47), 3.4.47, 25.4.47, PALESTINE BRAN/YD, 1947.

83 SLU Clover to LSIC, BRAN/YD 566, 598, 14.6.47, 28.6.47, PALESTINE BRAN /YD 1947.

84 SLU Clover to SLU Cairo, BRAN/YD 518, 24.5.47, PALESTINE BRAN/YD 1947.

85 SLU Clover to LSIC, BRAN/YD 362, 31.3.47, PALESTINE BRAN/YD 1947.

86 SLU Clover to LSIC, BRAN/YD 870, 17.10.47, PALESTINE BRAN/YD 1947.

87 Minutes by FitzGerald, 27.1.47, passim, CO 537/2405.

88 SLU Cairo to SLU Clover, BRAN/CO 180, 27.8.46, BRAN/CO 1946.

89 SLU Clover to SLU Cairo, BRAN/YD 408, 15.4.47, PALESTINE BRAN/YD 1947.

90 SLU Clover to SLU Cyprus, BRAN/YD 499, 20.5.47, PALESTINE BRAN/YD 1947.

91 For an analysis by the DSO and NLO of the role of intelligence in these operations, cf. SLU Clover to LSIC, BRAN/YD 152, 12.1.48, BRAN/YD 01/48.

92 SLU Clover to SLU Fayid, BRAN/YD 221, 27.1.48, BRAN/YD 01/48.

93 SLU CAIRO to SLU CLOVER, BRAN/CO 99, 16.5.46, BRAN/CO 1946.

94 CO to CRACKER, BRAN/CO 15, 9.10.45, BRAN/CO 1945.

95   High Commissioner to Secretary of State, No. 1255, 1.8.46, Cunningham Papers. MECA.

96   'Military Implications of Establishing Malaysia Without Singapore and Possibly without Brunei, Note by the Secretary', 27.6.63, DEFE 5/140; Saki Dockrill, *Britain's Retreat from East of Suez: The Choice Between Europe and the World* (Palgrave Macmillan, London, 2002).

97   David Easter, *Britain and the Confrontation with Indonesia, 1960–1966*.

98   Australian report.

99   Cf. pp. 595–601.

100 C.P. 64 (5), Minute by Butler, 6.1.64, 'Policy Towards Indonesia', CAB 129/11/6/5.

101 COS/58th Meeting/64, 29.9.64, DEFE 4/175; 'Measures to Control Indonesian Confrontation, Report by the Defence Planning Staff ', DP 70 (65) Final, 15.10.65, DEFE 25/170.

102 Easter, *Confrontation*; Alexander Nicholas Shaw, 'British counterinsurgency in Brunei and Sarawak, 1962–63: developing best practices in the shadow of Malaya', *Small wars & Insurgencies*, 27/4, 2016, pp. 702–25.

103 H. A. Majid, *Rebellion in Brunei: The 1962 Revolt, imperialism, confrontation and oil* (IB Tauris, London, 2007).

104 GSO (S) to D.D. GCHQ, 3.1.63, D/2201/20 pt I.

105 GSO (S) to D.D. GCHQ, 18.12.62, *passim*, D/2201/30 pt I.

106 GCO (S) to GCHQ, 14.12.62, *passim*, D/2201/30 pt I.

107 10.9.63, D/2201/30 pt II.

108 DSB to UKF 200, 26.12.62, D/2201/30 pt I.

109 GCHQ (London) to GCHQ, 10.12.62, DZ/B/32, /D/2201/30 pt I.

110 DSB to GCO (S), 26.12.62, D/2201/30 pt I.

111 DSB to GCHQ, 8.2.63, D/2201/30 pt I.

112 DSB to GCO (S), 19.2.63, D/2201/30 pt I.

113 29.11.63, D/2201/30 pt II.

114 GCO (S) to SLO (M), 2.9.66, D/2201/30 pt VII.

115 DSD to GCHQ, 1.5.67, D/2304/5 pt II.

116 Ibid.

117 22.8.63, D/2201/30 pt I.

118 5.12.63, D/2201/30 pt II.

119 DSB to GCO (S), PR 300514Z/1/63, 30.1.63, D/2201/30 pt I.

120 GCHQ to MI8, and DSD (9), 22.11.63, D/2201/30 pt II.

121 Memorandum by Hooper, 'Borneo', 13.2.63, D/2201/30 pt I.

122 GCO (S) 2.4.65, 'Visit to Borneo by GCO, O.C. 7 Sigs Regt (Aust) and OC 121 Sig Sq, 29 March–1 April, Matters Arising', GCO (S) to SIN/901 PLUS, 29.4.65, D/2201/30 pt V.

123 Nicholl to Director, 11.2.63, D/2201/30 pt I.

124 *Contact*, No. 3, 3rd Quarter 1971, 'Singapore', pp. 14–15.

125 Australian report, June 1964.

126 Ibid.

127 DSD to GCHQ, 10.1.64, D/2201/30 pt II.

128 DSD to GCHQ, 3.7.64, D/2201/30 pt IV.

129 DSD to GCHQ, 1.5.67, D/2304/5 pt II.

130 Australian report, June 1964.

131 DSD to UKC 200 and other recipients, 30.6.64, passim, D/2201/30 pt IV.

132 C-in-C FE to MOD Sec, 9.7.64, D/2201/30 pt IV.

133 8.1.65, 'Sigint Implications of the Current Indonesian Reinforcement of Kalimantan', D/2201/30 pt V.

134 'Record of a Meeting Held on 9th June to Discuss the Borneo Operation', D/2201/30 pt V.

135 LSIB (64) 2nd meeting, LSIB 1964.

136 GCO (S) to GCHQ, 1.2.65, D/2201/30 pt V.

137 15.11.63, 'Note for the File' by Hooper, 26.11.63, D/2201/30 pt II.

138 DSO (S) to GCHQ, 13.8.63, ZCZCRZA051, D/2201/30 pt IV.

139 GCO (S) to GCHQ 9.3.65, GCO (S) 2.4.65, 'Visit to Borneo by GCO, O.C. 7 Sigs Regt (Aust)'.

140 GCO (S) to GCHQ, 24.5.65, D/2201/30 pt V.

141 GCO (S) to DSD, 12.8.65, ZCZCHSA011, D/2201/30 pt V.

142 GCO (S) 2.4.65, 'Visit to Borneo by GCO, O.C. 7 Sigs Regt (Aust) and OC 121 Sig Sq, 29 March–1 April, Matters Arising', D/2201/30 pt V.

143 DSD to GCHQ, 1.5.67, D/2304/5 pt II.

144 David Easter, 'British Intelligence and Propaganda during the "Confrontation", 1963– 66', INS, 16.2.2001, pp. 83–102.

145 Australian report, March 1964.

146 Ibid., August 1964.

147 Ibid.

148 Ibid., September 1964.

149 Ibid.

150 Ibid., October 1964.

151 Ibid., September and December 1964.

152 DSD to GCHQ, 1.5.67, D/2304/5 pt II.

153 Australian report, October 1964.

154 Ibid., January 1965.

155 Ibid., March 1964.

156 Ibid., June 1964.

157 Ibid., September 1964.

158 Ibid.

159 Ibid.; DSD to GCHQ, 1.5.67, D/2304/5 pt II.

160 Van der Bijl, *Confrontation*, pp. 133–35.

161 COS/58th Meeting/64, 29.9.64, COS 61st Meeting/64, 15.10.64, DEFE 4/175.

162 JIC meeting, JIC (64) 49th Meeting, 1.10.64, CAB 159/42.

163 Australian report, June 1964.

164 Ibid., October and November 1964.

165 DSD to GCHQ, 8.1.65, D/2201/30 pt V.

166 8.1.65, 'Sigint Implications of the Current Indonesian Reinforcement of Kalimantan', D/2201/30 pt V.

167 Van der Bijl, *Confrontation*, p. 159.

168 GCO (S) to GCHQ 24.3.65, D/2201/30 pt V.

169 Ibid.

170 8.1.65, 'Sigint Implications of the Current Indonesian Reinforcement of Kalimantan', D/2201/30 pt V.

171 GCHQ to DSD, 9.3.65, GCO (S) to DSD, 10.3.65, D/2201/30 pt V.

172 Foreign Office to Djakarta Embassy, No. 1920, 16.10.65, DEFE 25/214.

173 DSO (S) to GCHQ/DSD, 2.6.66, D/2201/30 pt VI.

174 Memorandum n.d., *c.* July 1966, 'The Bau Incursions – June 1966', D/2201/30 pt VI.

175 GCO (S) to DSD, 13.9.66, JIC 66/72, 'Preliminary Draft', 'Intelligence Requirements Concerning East Malaysia and Brunei', 30.9.66, and 'Revised Draft', 8.10.66, D/2201/30 pt VII.

176 DSO (S) to DSD, 19.2.66, D/2201/30 pt VI.

177 Memorandum n.d., *c.* July 1966, 'The Bau Incursions'.

178 DSD to GCHQ, 1.5.67, D/2304/5 pt II.

179 GCO (S) to DSD, 13.9.66, ZCZCRVA026, D/2201/30 pt VII.

180 Van der Bijl, *Confrontation*, p. x.

181 Minutes by Grandy, 17.1.69, and Healey, 'Confrontation Operations', 20.1.69, AIR 8/2441.

182 Van der Bijl, *Confrontation*, p. x.

183 Robert J. Hanyok, *Spartans in Darkness, American SIGINT and the Vietnam War, 1945–1975* (CCH, 2002).

184 John Roosa, *Pretext for Mass Murder, The September 30th Movement and Suharto's Coup D'Etat in Indonesia* (University of Wisconsin Press, 2006), pp. 198–201, 208.

185 UKMIS New York to FCO, Telegram No. 909, 23.9.81, *passim*, PREM 19/643.

186 The best account of the war, using Argentine and British sources well, is Freedman, *Falklands*. Antony H. Cordesman, *The Lessons of Modern Wars, III, The Afghan and Falklands Confl icts* (Westview Press, 1991) and Norman Friedman, *Fighters over the Fleet, Naval Air Defence from Biplanes to the Cold War* (Seaforth, 2016), Chapter Twelve, are useful operational analyses of key issues. A useful English-language account of the Argentine navy is Mariano Sciaroni,

A Carrier at Risk: Argentinian Aircraft Carrier and Anti-Submarine Operations against Royal Navy's Attack Submarines during the Falklands/Malvinas War 1982 (Helion and Co., 2019).

187 COS (Misc) 105/742/1, 10.4.82, Navy Department, 'Operational and Support Planning – Operation Corporate', FCO 7/4472; Operation Corporate – Long Term Measures, 2.5.82, DEFE 25/466.

188 Friedman, *Fighters over the Fleet*.

189 GCHQ London to GCHQ, 29.4.82, D/2403/14 pt III.

190 'The Argentine Air Force', *Secret Air Intelligence Quarterly Review*, Summer 1970, pp. 24–25.

191 'An Examination of Argentine Air Effort during the Falklands Campaign'. Operational Research Branch, Strike Command, 9.83, DEFE 58/212.

192 COS 9/82, Operation Sutton, Directive to the Commander-in-Chief Fleet, 15.4.82, DEFE 24/2504.

193 Memorandum by Controller of the Navy, 27.4.82, 'Operation Corporate –HMS *Illustrious*', Evans to PSO/CDS, 'Operation Corporate– HMS Illustrious', 4.5.82, DEFE 24/2504.

194 Presentation to OD (SA) – 22 April 1982, DEFE 25/479.

195 'Naval Staff Assessment of the Balance of Fighting Capability between TGs 317.8/324.3 and the ARA', DEFE 25/564

196 Minute by Whitmore, 'Landing on the Falkland Islands', 14.5.82, PREM 19/647.

197 Presentation to OD (SA) – 22 April 1982, DEFE 25/479.

198 'Falklands: Record of Meeting Held on 29 April 1982', 29.4.82, D/2304/14 pt III.

199 'Falklands: Minutes of Meeting 26 April 1982', D/2304/14 pt III; GCHQ London to GCHQ 24.5.82, D/2304/14 pt V.

200 'Falklands: Record of Meeting Held on 20 April 1982', 21.4.82, D/2304/14 pt II; Flower, PUSD to Johnson, 20.5.82, D/2304/14 pt IV.

201 GCHQ London to GCHQ 4.5.82, D/2304/14 pt III; 'Falklands: Notes of Meeting held on 14 May 1982', 17.5.82, D/2304/14 pt IV; 'Falklands: Notes of Meeting held on 21 May 1982', 24.5.82, D/2304/14 pt V.

202 *Contact*, No. 39, 3rd Issue, 1982, 'The Falklands Crisis 1982', p. 20.

203 'Record of a Meeting Held at 10 Downing Street on Tuesday 13 April 1982 At 0915 Hours PREM 19/617.

204 'Record of Meeting Held in 12 Downing Street on 12 April 1982, at 0930', PREM 19/617.

205 Duff to Carrick, 16.4.82, D/2304/14 pt III.

206 'Telephone call between the Prime Minister and Sir Antony Parsons on Saturday 8 May 1982', PREM 19/626.

207 Armstrong to Thatcher, 11.5.82, AO8378, 'The Falkland Islands', PREM 19/647; COSC, Confidential Annexe to COS/24th Meeting/82 held on Monday 19 April 1982 at 9.30 a.m.', Confidential Annexe to COS/25th Meeting/82 held

on Tuesday 20 April 1982 at 10.00 a.m.', Confidential Annexe to COS/34th Meeting/82 held on Wednesday 28 April 1982 at 2.00 p.m.', FCO 7/4472.

208 Antony Duff to Johnson/Palliser, 16.4.82, D/2304/14 pt II. Eighty words of detail about GCHQ material are redacted in this letter.

209 22.6.82, D/2304/14 pt VI; 'The Falklands: Operation Royce', *Contact*, No. 39, 3rd Issue, 1982, pp. 26– 27.

210 Memorandum by DCDS (1), 'Operation Corporate – The Intelligence Lessons', 21.12.82, P/8210/7/1 pt I.

211 Memorandum, 'Falkland Islands: The Nicholl Report', 13.5.82, D/2304/14 pt IV.

212 Nick Barker, *Beyond Endurance: An Epic of Whitehall and the South Atlantic Conflict* (Leo Cooper, 2002), pp.30–31

213 GCHQ LDN to GCHQ, 061700Z, 6.4.82, D/2304/14 pt I.

214 GCHQ to Northwood, 9.6.82, D/2304/14 pt V; *History*; *Contact*, No. 39, 3rd Issue 1982, 'The Falklands Crisis 1982', pp. 21–22.

215 'Falkland Island Review Committee, Note of an oral evidence session', 25.10.82, CAB 292/47.

216 Michael S. Goodman, 'The Dog that Didn't Bark: The Joint Intelligence Committee and Warning of Aggression', *Cold War History*, 7/4, pp. 529– 51.

217 During the war, MOD said that DIS had assigned one officer to Latin America before the crisis, but after the war listed this number as two. MOD to GCHQ, 9.5.82, D/2304/14 pt III.

218 Y-3/AA/73087-82, 25.3.82.

219 'Falkland Island Review Committee, Note of an oral evidence session', 15.10.82, CAB 292/47.

220 Carrington to Thatcher, 24.3.82, PREM 19/656; sentence redacted under Section 3 (4).

221 'Defence Implications of Argentine Action Against the Falkland Islands by MOD)', n.d., *c.* 26.3.82, PREM 19/656.

222 Minute by Foreign Secretary and Minister of State (Armed Forces), undated but 30 March by internal evidence, PREM 19/656.

223 GCHQ incoming telegram No. 36, 30.3.82, GCHQ outgoing telegram 31.3.82, D/2304/14 pt I.

224 3/AA/73089-82, 30.3.82, D/2304/14/1 pt I.

225 Interview with Omand, 21 June 2018; *Sigint History*, pp.2–8; 'Illegal Landings on South Georgia: Chronology of Events', minute by Weyland, 21.4.2012, PREM 19/614.

226 'Falkland Island Review Committee, Note of an oral evidence session', 25.10.82, CAB 292/47.

227 Ibid.

228 D/Ops/Staff, 7.10,42, Operation Corporate – First Impressions', D. W. Brown, ACDS (ops), DEFE 25/477; Interview with Sir Michael Beetham – 1 Nov 83', AIR 20/13044.

229 *Sigint History*, pp. 2–3.

230 *Sigint History*, p. 33.

231 'Falkland Crisis, Meeting held on 14 April 1982', 16.4.82, D/2304/14 pt II.

232 Memorandum, 'Sigint Alert Margay: Requirements of 22 SAS, Hereford', 5.5.82, D/2304/14 pt III; ibid., 17.5.82, D/2304/14 pt IV; MOD to GCHQ, 6.6.82, D/2304/14 pt V.

233 GCHQ London to GCHQ, 4.4.82, D/2304/14 pt I.

234 Minute by Z, 3/4/82, 'Priority of Requirement for Intelligence on Argentine and the Falklands', D/2304/14 pt I.

235 GCHQ LDN to GCHQ, 6.4.84, D/2304/14 pt I.

236 GCHQ London to GCHQ, 29.4.82, D/2304/14 pt III; *Contact*, No. 39, 3rd Issue 1982, 'The Falklands Crisis 1982', pp. 20–21.

237 Ibid.

238 Fieldhouse to Tovey, 27.4.82, D/2304/14 pt III; Office of the Commander Task Force 317, 22. 10. 82, 'Report by CTF 317 on Intelligence Aspects of Operation Corporate', P/8210/7/1 pt I.

239 Memorandum 1.6.82, 'Alert Margay –Financial Consequentials', D/2304/14 pt V.

240 Memorandum, 5.4.82, 'Falkland Islands – Cover and Reporting', D/2304/14 pt I.

241 Sigint *History*, p. 63.

242 'The Falklands Crisis: Review of Sigint Performance and Lessons'. P/8210/7/1 pt I.

243 Memorandum by K, 'Falklands Crisis Review', 20.7.82, P/8210/7/1 pt I.

244 Ibid.

245 Memorandum 'Alert Margay: Comms Status 19 April', 19.4.82, D/2304/14 pt II; memorandum, 26.4.82, 'Alert Margay: Communications Minimize', D/2304/14 pt III; cf. *Contact*, No. 37, 1st Issue 1982, 'The Duty Signal Officer GCHQ', pp. 5–8.

246 *Sigint History*, p. 11.

247 *Sigint History*, p. 18.

248 Minute 'The Elint Effort on Alert Margay', 20.5.82, D/2304/14 pt IV.

249 Interview with Herman, 22 June 2018.

250 Ibid.

251 *Sigint History*, p. 22.

252 'Falklands: Minutes of Meeting 26 April 1982', D/2304/14 pt III.

253 CTG 317.9 to MODUK/Navy, 26.4.82, D/2403/14 pt III; History, p. 24.

254 Memorandum by Fear, 'Alert Margay: Fort Grange Sigint Fit', 12.5.82, D/2304/14 pt IV.

255 *Contact*, No. 39, 3rd Issue 1982, 'Operation Corporate/Sigint Alert Margay', p. 23.

256 Memorandum by, 'Falklands Contingency Plans', 8.6.82, D/2304/14 pt V.

257 C-in-C Fleet to GCHQ, XXX, D/2304/14 pt I.

258 Memorandum by K, 'Crisis Handling at Northwood and GCHQ', 15.4.82, D/2304/14 pt II; Memorandum 14.5.82, 'New Moon: Alert Margay', D/2304/14 pt IV.

259 *Sigint History*, p. 19, 43–44.

260 *Sigint History*, p. 8.

261 Memorandum by 7.4.82, 'Sigint Support to the Task Force', D/2304/14 pt I; *History* pp. 12, 27.

262 Hansard, House of Commons, 3.4.82, Volume 21, column 648.

263 'Falkland Island Review Committee, Note of an oral evidence session', 18. 10. 82, CAB 292/36.

264 Memorandum by Cooper, 'The Falklands: Sunday Times Insight Articles, 23 May 1982', D/2304/14 pt V.

265 BDS Washington to FCO, 5.5.82, D/2304/14 pt III.

266 Memorandum by Armstrong, 22.4.82, PREM 19/621.

267 A1 to PSO/CDS, 24.4.82, DEFE 25/492.

268 Interview with Sir David Omand, 21 June 2018.

269 S. Webb, 6.5.82, 'Note for the Record, Third Meeting with Editors on Falklands Emergency', SW/82/666, 9/31/F, PREM 19/626.

270 SUKLO to GCHQ, 101403Z, 10.4.82, D/2304/14 pt I; UKLO to GCHQ, 171800z, 17.4.82, D/2304/14 pt II.

271 Ibid.

272 Memorandum by K, 'Falklands Crisis Review', 23.8.82, P/8210/7/1 pt I.

273 'Falklands: Notes of Meeting Held on 17 May 1982', 18.5.82, D/2304/14 pt IV.

274 DCDS (I) to Tovey, 5.8.82, P/8210/7/1 pt I.

275 Office of the Commander Task Force 317, 22. 10. 82, 'Report by CTF 317 on Intelligence Aspects of Operation Corporate', P/8210/7/1 pt I.

276 Minute 'The Elint Effort on Alert Margay', 20.5.82, D/2304/14 pt IV.

277 COSC, Confidential Annexe to COS/9thMeeting/82 held on Thursday 8 April 1982 at 930 a.m.', FCO 7/4472.

278 Presentation to OD (SA) – 22 April 1982, DEFE 25/479.

279 3/AA/97174-82, 23.4.82, 3/AA/97423-82, 23.4.83, 3/AA/97514-82, 26.4.82.

280 'Falklands: Notes of Meeting on 22 April 1982', 23.4.82, D/2304/14 pt II.

281 3/AA/97246-82, 18.4.82, 3/AA/97543-82, 26.4.82.

282 3/AA/97487-82, 24.4.82.

283 3/AA/90057-82, 30.4.82; *Sigint History*, pp. 99–108, reproduces all of the relevant messages.

284 Presentation to OD (SA) – 22 April 1982, DEFE 25/479.

285 'Operation Corporate – Threat from Argentine Carrier', COS (Misc). 163/742/1, 26.4.82, DEFE 25/465; COSC, Confidential Annexe to COS/32nd Meeting/82 held on Tuesday 27 April 1982 at 10.30 a.m.', COSC, Confidential Annexe to COS/33rd Meeting/82 held on Wednesday 28 April 1982 at 10.45 a.m.' FCO 7/4472.

286 Pym to Thatcher, 1.5.82, DEFE 25/466.

287 Interview with Omand, 21 June 2018.

288 Telegram No. 1574, British Embassy Washington to FCO, 3.5.82, PREM 19/624.

289 GCHQ London to GCHQ, 13.5.82, D/2304/14 pt IV.

290 CDS Brief as of 0600 11 May 1982, DEFE 25/467.

291 Office of the Commander Task Force 317, 22.10.82, 'Report by CTF 317 on Intelligence Aspects of Operation Corporate', P/8210/7/1 pt I.

292 *Sigint History*, p. 62.

293 GCU Northwood to GCHQ, 14.5.82, 27.5.82, D/2304/14 Annex 1.

294 'Falklands: Notes of Meeting Held on 25 May 1982', 26.5.82, D/2304/14 pt V.

295 CDS to S of S, 21.4.82, DEFE 69/1098.

296 Presentation to OD (SA) – 22 April 1982, DEFE 25/479.

297 3/AA/098229-82, 9.5.82.

298 3/AA/099471-82, 13.6.82.

299 3/AA/098388-82, 13.5.82.

300 Memorandum by Sneyd, 'SPG 007-Deception Proposals-Liaison with CinCFleet HQ Northwood', 4.82, DEFE 24/2504.

301 GCU Northwood to GCHQ 16.5.82, D/2304/14 Annex 2.

302 British Embassy Santiago to FCO, telegram No. 94, 12.4.82, PREM 19/616.

303 GCU Northwood to GCHQ, 20.5.82, D/2304/14 Annex 1.

304 GCHQ to DIRNSA, No. 3244, 4.5.82, D/2304/14 pt III.

305 DCDS (I) to Tovey, 5.8.82, P/8210/7/1 pt I.

306 *Sigint History*, pp. 108–10.

307 GCHQ to TF 317, P/8210/7/1 pt I.

308 *Sigint History*, pp. 14, 48.

309 CTG 317.0 to CTF 317, 25.5.82, DEFE 68/630.

310 CTF 317 TO CTG 310.0, 27.5.82, DEfE 68/630.

311 GCU Northwood to GCHQ, 23.5.82, D/2304/14 Annex 1.

312 'Falklands: Notes of Meeting on 1 June 1982', 2.6.82, D/2304/14 pt V.

313 3/AA/099127-82, 3.6.82,.

314 3/AA/098965-82, 30.5.82, 2/AA/090090-82, 4.6.82,

315 GCHQ London to GCHQ, 24.5.82, Flower to Duff, 27.5.82, D/2304/14 pt V.

316 GCHQ to SUKLO, 15.4.82, D/2304/14 pt II.

317 For a description of the system cf. MOD to GCHQ, 9.5.82, D/2304/14 pt III.

318 SCDS (A) 1 to PS/CDS, 11.4.82, 'Operation Corporate – CDS and the New MOD Organisation', DEFE 25/461.

319 JIC meeting 27.4.82, JIC (82) 20, CAB 185/33.

320 Interview with senior official.

321 DCDS (I) to Tovey, 5.8.82, P/8210/7/1 pt I.

322 Memorandum by Cumming, 18.5.82, 'Falklands Crisis: Letter of Appreciation from COS UKLF', D/2304/14 pt IV.

323 Group Captain Edwards to Gp Capt Ops, 18.8.82, DEFE 58/274.

324 'The Falklands Crisis: Review of Sigint Performance and Lessons', P/8210/7/1 pt I.

325 'The Falklands Conflict: Sigint Post-Mortem (First R Division Contribution)', 12.7.82, P/8210/7/1 pt I.

326 UKN 292L to GCHQ, 28.5.82, D/2304/14/5.

327 CTF 317 to CTG 317.8, 24.5.82, DEFE 68/630.

328 CTF 317 to CTG 317.1, 24.5.82, DEFE 68/630.

329 CTF 317 to CTU 317.1.1, 12.5.82, DEFE 68/630.

330 CTG 317.1 to CTU 317, 25.5.82, DEFE 68/630.

331 CTG 317 to CTU 317.1.1., 25.5.82, DEFE 68.630.

332 CTF 317 to CTG 317.1, 26.5.82, DEFE 68/630.

333 CTG 317.1 to CTF 317. 30.5.82, DEFE 68/630.

334 CTG 317.1 to CTF 317, 31.5.82, DEFE 68/630.

335 *Sigint History*, pp. 78–79; D. J. Thorp, *The Silent Listener: British Electronic Surveillance Falklands 1982* (Spellmount, Stroud, 2011), pp. 115–18.

336 Aldrich, 'GCHQ', pp. 407–16.

337 2/AA/090106-82, 13.6. 82, 2/AA/190108-82, 14.06.82.

338 GCHQ LDN to GCHQ, 6.4.82, D/2304/14 pt I.

339 3/AA/099242-82, 7.6.82,.

340 Group Captain Clerk to Air Cdre Ops, 13.7.82, DEFE 58/274.

341 *Sigint History*, pp. 47–48.

342 'Falklands: Record of Meeting Held on 19 April 1982', 19.4.82, D/2304/14 pt II.

343 GCHQ to SUKLO, 17.4.82, D/2304/14 pt II.

344 GCHQ to MOD, 17.4.82, D/2304/14 pt II.

345 3/AA/97367-82, 22.4.82.

346 'Falklands: Notes of Meeting 26 April 1982', 27.4.82, D/2304/14 pt III, *Sigint History*, pp. 76–8.

347 Ibid.

348 GCHQ to C-in-C Fleet, 29.4.82, D/2304/14 pt III.

CHAPTER 14

1 Cf. pp. 275–8.

2 Ferris, *Intelligence and Strategy*, pp. 165–80.

3 AVIA 65/977 contains material on the development of Typex Mercury and 5 U.C.O.; cf. Ferris, 'British Enigma', for that of Typex and Rockex II.

4 Colonel H. C. B. Rogers, *The History of the Communications-Electronics Security Department and its Predecessors, c. 1970*, pp. 93–120.

5 Ibid., pp. 259, 267–8.

6 'Report of the Working Party on The Future of the Communications-Electronic Security Department', 13.5.69, CAB 163/125.

7 Allinson to Burroughs, 9.5.69, including 'Report of the CESD Working Party, Summary and Conclusions', CAB 163/125.

8 Rogers, *History of the Communications-Electronics Security Department*, p. 344.

9 Ibid., pp. 121–37, 321–34,

10 J. V. Boone and R. R. Peterson, *The Start of the Digital Revolution: SIGSALY Secure Digital Voice Communications in World War Two* (CCH, Fort Meade, MD, 2000).

11 Rogers, *History of the Communications-Electronics Security Department*, pp.471–73.

12 Bill Cunningham, 'From Telegrams ... to eGrams, A Potted History of FCO Communications', FCO, 16.8.2004, pp. 20–21.

13 Ibid., pp. 16–20.

14 Rogers, *History of the Communications-Electronics Security Department*, pp. 335–75.

15 Ibid., p. 534.

16 Ibid. pp. 165–84, 451–69.

17 M. Savage, 'Houseman Part I: BRENT, Autumn 1988 to Autumn 1995', CESG Case Studies No. 3, November 1997; Peter Osborn, 'Pippa, Project Case History No. 4, n.d.

18 John Tiltman, 'Winterbotham's "The Ultra Secret", A Personal Comment', *Cryptologia*, December 1975, pp. 1–5, https://www.nsa.gov/Portals/70/documents/news-features/declassified-documents/cryptologs/cryptolog_15.pdf; Malcolm Kennedy Diary, 10.1.46.

19 Hansard, Commons, Fifth Series, Vol. CLXXIV, col. 674, 15.12.24.

20 Report on Postal Censorship, 1914–1919, DEFE 1/131, p. 77.

21 Basil Thomson, Director of Intelligence, No. E.A.S., 5.7.19, to Secretary for War, Churchill, WO 32/4899

22 Section Four, Official Secrets Act, 1920.

23 Blackwell (Home Office) to Grant (Eastern Telegraph Company), 11.5.26, 493263, Telegraph Museum, Porthcurno,

24 *British Sigint*, Four, pp. 88.

25 Nicholas Wilkinson, *Secrecy and the Media: the Official History of the United Kingdom's D-Notice System* (Routledge, 2009); Pauline Sadler, *National Security and the D-Notice System* (Routledge, 2018). Sadler correctly detected GCHQ's involvement in handling this issue.

26 *British Sigint*, Four, pp. 89–90.

27 Cmnd. 283, October 1957, 'Report of the Committee of Privy Counsellors appointed to inquire into the interception of communications', paras. 64–70, 141–2/

28 Cmnd, 3309, 19.5.67.

29 *British Sigint*, Four, pp. 87–99.

30 Section 11, Post Offi ce Bill, July 1969.

31 Ferris, 'Whitehall's Black Chamber'.

32 DNI to Managing Director, Marconi Company, 17.6.20, *passim*, HIS 185, Marconi Archive, Bodleian Library.

33 Round to James, 8.5.18, Round to Buxton, 30.10.19, ADM 137/4692.

34 LSIB 57/57, 6.5.57, 'GCHQ Cover Story', LSIB 1957.

35 *British Sigint*, Four, p. 495.

36 Goodall, GCHQ, to Morrison, Cabinet Office, 6.6.74, 'Co-Ordinator's Working Party on World War II Intelligence Matters', CAB 190/74.

37 Duncan Campbell, 'My Life Unmasking British Eavesdroppers', 3.8.15, *The Intercept*, https://theintercept.com/2015/08/03/life-unmasking-british-eavesdroppers/

38 Aldrich, 'GCHQ', pp. 367–86; Report of the Security Commission, May 1983, CMND, 8876.

CHAPTER 15

1 Memorandum by Clark, 22.6.89, 'Royal Air Force and United States Radio Proving Flights', AHB 16-4-3.

2 LSIB/3/89, 19.4.89, 'The State of Sigint 1989', LSIB 1989.

3 LSIB/2/89, 18.4.89, 'Sigint Support to Military Operations 1989', LSIB 1989; LSIB/4/1991, 27.3.91, 'Future of the Services Component of the National Sigint Organisation', LSIB 1991.

4 Roger Hurn, 24.3.95, '"Accelerating Change", Special Study of GCHQ, Part 1: Main Report'.

5 'Review of Defence Requirements and Resources, Conducted by Sir Michael Quinlan 1994, GCHQ Precis'.

6 Roger Hurn, 24.3.95, '"Accelerating Change", Special Study of GCHQ, Part 1: Main Report'.

7 HC 65, 15.6.04, House of Commons Committee of Public Accounts, 'Government Communications Headquarters (GCHQ): New Accommodation Programme', Twenty-third Report of Session 2003–04, pp. 453, 469–70, *passim*.

8 Ibid.

9 Interview with Sir John Adye, 20.6.2018.

10 LSIB/6/91, 11.6.91, 'Minutes of Meeting Held on 11 April 1991', LSIB 1991.

11 Ibid.

12 John Perry Barlow, 'The Declaration of Independence of the Internet'.

13 Intelligence and Security Committee of Parliament, 'Uncorrected Transcript of Evidence', 7.11.13, http://isc.independent.gov.uk/publicevidence/7november2013

14 David Anderson, Q.C., 'Report of the Bulk Powers Review', CM 9326, 8.2016, pp. 152–56, 159–62, https://terrorismlegislationreviewer. independent.gov.uk/wp-content/uploads/2016/08/Bulk-Powers-Reviewfinal-report.pdf

15 Ibid.

16 Draft memoirs of Admiral Hall, Chapter on 1914–15, Hall 3/2, Reginald Hall Papers, Churchill College, Cambridge.

17 Andrew, *Defence of the Realm*, p. 147.

18 Viceroy to Secretary of State, telegram No. 17-U, 30.9.36, L/PO/10/31 i.

19 Minute by unknown Treasury official, 23.6.25, T 161/252, S. 27259.

20 Blackwell (Home Office) to Grant (Eastern Telegraph Company), 11.5.26, 493263, Telegraph Museum, Porthcurno.

21 'UK Debate Grows over "Orwellian" NSA and GCHQ Surveillance', *Guardian*, 9.10.2013.

22 Ibid.

23 David Anderson Q.C., 'A Question of Trust, Report of the Investigatory Powers Review', June 2015, pp. 4, 8, 268, https://www.daqc.co.uk/2015/06/11/a-question-of-trust-report-of-the-investigatory-powers-review/; David Anderson, 'A Democratic Licence to Operate, Report of the Independent Surveillance Review', to RUSI, July 2015, https://rusi.org/sites/default/files/20150714_whr_2-15_a_democratic_licence_to_operate.pdf

24 Ewan MacAskill, '"Extreme Surveillance" Becomes UK Law with Barely a Whimper', *Guardian*, 19.11.2016; 'Liberty's Briefing on the Investigatory Powers Act for Report Stage in the House of Commons', August 2016, https://www.libertyhumanrights.org.uk/sites/default/files/campaigns/resources/Liberty

25 'A Democratic License to Operate: Report of the Independent Surveillance Review', RUSI, July 2015, https://rusi.org/sites/default/files/20150714_whr_2-15_a_democratic_licence_to_operate.pdf

26 Intelligence and Security Committee of Parliament, 'Uncorrected Transcript of Evidence', 7.11.13, http://isc.independent.gov.uk/publicevidence/7november2013.

27 Cabinet Office, 'Cyber Security Strategy of the United Kingdom, safety, security and resilience in cyber space', CM 7642, 25.6.2009.

28 Robert Hannigan, 'Organising a Government for Cyber, The Creation of the UK's National Cyber Security Centre', RUSI Occasional Paper, February 2019, pp. 7–10.

29 'Securing Britain in an Age of Uncertainty, The Strategic Defence and Security Review, CM 7948, 10.2010, pp.47–49.

30 Cabinet Office, 'The UK Cyber Security Strategy, Protecting and promoting the UK in a digital world', November 2011.

31 Hannigan, 'Organising a Government', p. 14.

32 Ibid.

33 Hannigan, 'Organising a Government', pp. 10, 39.

34 Ibid., p. 14.

35 'Dr. Ian Levy', Enigma 2017, https://www.usenix. org/conference/enigma2017/speaker-or-organizer/dr-ian-levy-national-cyber-security-centre-uk

36 'A new Approach for cyber security in the UK', 13.9.2016, https://www.ncsc.gov.uk/news/new-approach-cyber-security-uk

37 Hannigan, 'Organising a Government', pp. 40–42.

38 Ibid.

39 Iain Thompson, 3.2.17, 'GCHQ cyber-chief slams security outfits peddling 'medieval witchcraft', The Register, https://www.theregister.co.uk/2017/02/03/security_ threat_ solutions/

40 Ian Levy, blog post, 1.11.16, 'Active Cyber Defence – tackling cyber attacks on the UK, https://www.ncsc.gov.uk/blog-post/active-cyber-defence-tackling-cyber-attacks-uk

41 NCSC Annual Report 2018, p. 10.

42 Ibid.

43 NCSC Annual Report 2018, pp.42–46; NCSC, 'Education and Skills, 11 to 19 year olds (CyberFirst)', https://www.ncsc.gov.uk/section/educationskills/11-19-year-olds; 'GCHQ CyberFirst', https://www.gchq-careers. co.uk/early-careers/cyberfi rst.html.

CONCLUSION

1 'Director GCHQ's Speech at CYBERUK 2019', 2.5.2019, https://www.gchq.gov.uk/speech/director-s-speech-at-cyberuk-2019

2 HM Treasury, 'Policy Paper 2018', Table 1.6, 'Departmental Resource Budgets', 29.10.18.

Glossary

A/C – aircraft

ACAS(I) – Assistant Chief of Air Staff (Intelligence)

ACP – Anti-Comintern Pact

AFSA – Armed Forces Security Agency

AFSS – Air Force Security Service

AGSRO – Association of Government Supervisors and Radio Operators

ANCIB – Army–Navy Communications Intelligence Board

ASA – Army Security Agency

ASIO – Australian Security Intelligence Organisation

ATS – Auxiliary Territorial Service

B-Dienst – Beobachtungsdienst, Observation Service

BAOR – British Army of the Rhine

BEF – British Expeditionary Force

BND – Bundesnachrichtendienst, German Federal Intelligence Service

BRIXMIS – British Commanders'-in-Chief Mission to the Soviet Forces in Germany

BRUSA – British–US Communication Intelligence Agreement

BTM – British Tabulating Machines

C – Head of MI6

C&W – Cable and Wireless Company

C3I – Command, Control, Communications and Intelligence

C3ISR – Command, Control, Communications, Intelligence Surveillance and Reconnaissance

C4ISR – Command, Control, Communications, Computers, Intelligence Surveillance and Reconnaissance

CBNRC – Communications Branch, National Research Council, Canada

CDS – Chief of Defence Staff

CESD – Communications-Electronics Security Department

CESG – Communications-Electronics Security Group

CIA – Central Intelligence Agency

CNA – Computer Network Attack

CND – Computer Network Defence

CNE – Computer Network Exploitation

CNO – Computer Network Operations

CNOs – Computer Network Operators

Comint – Communications Intelligence

Comintern – Communist International

Comsat – Communication Satellite

Comsec – Communications Security

COS – Chiefs of Staff

COSIG – Cost of Sigint

'Cryppies' – Cryptanalysts

CSC – Civil Service Commission

CSD – Civil Service Department

CSE – Communications Security Establishment

CSS – Chief of the Secret Service, Head of MI6 and Director of GC&CS

CSU – Civil Service Union

D&R – Distribution and Reference section

DCDS(I) – Deputy Chief of Defence Staff (Intelligence)

DCDS(O) – Deputy Chief of Defence Staff (Operations)

DGI – Director General Intelligence

DGSE – Direction générale de la sécurité extérieure, Directorate-General for External Security

DID – Director, Intelligence Division (Naval)

DIRNSA – Director, National Security Agency

DIS – Defence Intelligence Service

DNI – Director of Naval Intelligence

DOBOPS – Director of Borneo Operations

DS – Departmental Specialists

DSB – Defence Signals Bureau, or Defence Signals Branch

DSD – Defence Signals Department, or Defence Signals Directorate

DSO – Defence Security Officer

DTN – Defence Teleprinter Network

E Division – Establishments/Human Resources in GCHQ

ECM – Electronic Countermeasures

Elint – Electronic Intelligence

EO – Executive Officer

EW – Electronic Warfare

FCO – Foreign and Commonwealth Office

FECB – Far East Combined Bureau

GC&CS – Government Code & Cypher School

GCB – Government Communication Bureau

GCHQ – Government Communications Headquarters

GCO(N) – Government Communications Officer (Northwood)

GCO(S) – Government Communications Officer (Singapore)

GCRB – Government Communications Radio Branch, or Government Communications Radio Bureau

GCSB – New Zealand Government Communications Security Bureau

GCT – Government Communication Trainee

GCU – Government Communications Unit

GHQ – General Headquarters

GOC – General Officer Commanding

GPO – General Post Office

GSFG – Group of Soviet Forces Germany

H Division – Codebreaking Division in GCHQ

Hectra – Handling and Editing of Cipher Traffic Automatically

HFDF – High-Frequency Direction Finding

Humint – Human Intelligence

I(e) – Intelligence (e), Signals Intelligence

I&W – Indicators and Warnings

IBM – International Business Machines

ICL – International Computers Limited

ID – Intelligence Division

ILC – International Leased Carrier

Imint – Imagery Intelligence

IRSIG – Instructions and Regulations Concerning the Security of Signal Intelligence

ISPAL – Illicit Signals Palestine

IT – I-Toc, Intelligence Telephones

J Division – Warsaw Pact Sigint in GCHQ

JCOS – Joint Chiefs of Staff

JFHQ – Joint Force Headquarters, Malaysia

JIB – Joint Intelligence Bureau

JIC – Joint Intelligence Committee

JICFE – Joint Intelligence Committee Far East

JOC – Joint Operations Centre

JTLS – Joint Technical Languages School

K Division – Rest of the World Sigint in GCHQ

L Division – Comsec in GCHQ

LRAF – Soviet Long Range Air Force

LS – Language Specialist

LSIB – London Signals Intelligence Board

LSIC – London Signals Intelligence Committee

M Division – Engineering Division in GCHQ

MI1(b) – Military Intelligence 1(b), Codebreaking

MI5 – Military Intelligence 5, Security Service

MI6 – Military Intelligence 6, Secret Intelligence Service

MI8 – Military Intelligence 8, Signals Intelligence Management, War Office

MID – Military Intelligence Department

Moritz – Intelligence Telephones

MWDP – Mutual Weapons Development Program

Narkomindel – Soviet Ministry of Foreign Affairs

NATO – North Atlantic Treaty Organisation

NCML – Naval Computing Machine Laboratory, US Navy

NCSC – National Cyber Security Centre

NID – Naval Intelligence Division

NKVD – People's Commissariat for Internal Affairs

NSOC – National Security Operations Center

Op-20-G – US Navy's Office of Chief of Naval Operations (OpNav), 20th Division of the Office of Naval Communications, G Section / Communications Security (Op-20-G)

OPs – Observation Posts

OTP – One-Time Pad

PKI – Partai Komunis Indonesia

PSIS – Permanent Secretaries' Subcommittee on the Intelligence Services

PUS – Permanent Under Secretary

PVO – Soviet Air Defence Forces

RAF – Royal Air Force

RIPA – Regulation of Investigatory Powers Act of 2000

RN – Royal Navy

Room 40 – Admiralty Sigint Bureau, First World War

RSS – Radio Security Service

SAC – Strategic Air Command

SAS – Special Air Service

SBS – Special Boat Squadron

SCIs – Special Compartmented Intelligence

SCS – Senior Civil Servant

SCUs – Special Communications Units

SEO – Senior Executive Officer

SHAEF – Supreme Headquarters Allied Expeditionary Forces

SHDs – Special Handling Detachments

SIFE – Security Intelligence Far East

Sigint – Signals Intelligence

SIME – Security Intelligence Middle East

SIS – Secret Intelligence Service

SIS(US) – Signals Intelligence Service (United States)

SLUs – Special Liaison Units

SNF – Soviet Strategic Nuclear Forces

SSA – Special Support Activity

SSN – Strategic Nuclear Attack Submarine

STANCIB – State–Army–Navy Communications Intelligence Board

SUKLO – Senior United Kingdom Liaison Officer, in the United States

SUSLO – Special United States Liaison Officer, in Britain

T/A – Traffic Analysis

Theta – Telecipher Handling and Editing of Traffic Automatically

UABs – University Appointments Boards

UKUSA – Sigint Agreement between Australia, Britain, Canada, New Zealand and the United States

USCIB – United States Communications Intelligence Board

USN – United States Navy

V Division – Elint in GCHQ

VRK – Very Restricted Knowledge

W Division – Communications in GCHQ

W/T – Wireless

WAAF – Women's Auxiliary Air Force

WRNS/Wrens – Women's Reserve Naval Service

WT/I – Wireless Intelligence

WTID – War Trade Intelligence Department

X Division – Computers in GCHQ

Y – Wireless Interception and Traffic Analysis

Z – Intelligence Policy, Distribution and Action-On Section in GCHQ

Acknowledgements

I have incurred many debts in writing this book. I owe much to friends now passed – Mike Dockrill, Peter Freeman, Michael Handel, Keith Neilson, Brad Smith and Zara Steiner – and also to those still among us: Richard Aldrich, Chris Andrew, David Alvarez, Jim Beach, Liz Bruton, Ralph Erskine, Markus Faulkner, David French, Michael Herman, Peter Jackson, David Kahn, Andrew Lambert, Richard Poppelwell and Dave Sherman. I owe particular thanks to several friends and scholars who helped me to understand issues and to find evidence, particularly Seb Cox, Ed Kaplan, Dan Lomas and Steve Wagner. I have gained much from members of the Cryptologic History Center at the National Security Agency, especially David Hatch, Betsy Smoot and Bill Williams. I owe much to my friends in the Department of History, and the Centre for Military, Security and Strategic Studies at the University of Calgary. I received help from many people whom I do not know at GCHQ, which is characteristic of how that institution works. At GCHQ, however, Peter Freeman, Tony Comer and James Bruce provided advice, debate and help, as did many others, including Stu R., Annette E. and Tim N.. James Bruce, Annette E. and Stu R. were invaluable in finding and selecting the images which are fundamental to this work. Other members of GCHQ staff contributed to the production of this book: Daniel, Abby, James, Doug, Greg, Neil, Emma, Jenny, Phillip, Steve, and staff in the UKKPA and the NCSC, as did members of Five Eyes Sigint Agencies and UK government departments. I am grateful to my literary agent, Bill Hamilton, and to members of Bloomsbury's editorial team, especially Michael Fishwick, Kate Johnson and Sarah

Ruddick, for seeing this work through to completion, which sometimes did not seem easy to envisage. Nuffield College, Oxford, kindly gave me a place to work for several months while in Britain. Without the love and support of Elizabeth, Morgan, Owen and Edmund, this work could not have been written. I dedicate it to them.

Index

A Note on the Type

The text of this book is set in Adobe Garamond. It is one of several versions of Garamond based on the designs of Claude Garamond. It is thought that Garamond based his font on Bembo, cut in 1495 by Francesco Griffo in collaboration with the Italian printer Aldus Manutius. Garamond types were first used in books printed in Paris around 1532. Many of the present-day versions of this type are based on the Typi Academiae of Jean Jannon cut in Sedan in 1615.

Claude Garamond was born in Paris in 1480. He learned how to cut type from his father and by the age of fifteen he was able to fashion steel punches the size of a pica with great precision. At the age of sixty he was commissioned by King Francis I to design a Greek alphabet, and for this he was given the honourable title of royal type founder. He died in 1561.